Contents

Preface

Business Studies does not provide a step-by-step guide to how to be 'good at business'. There is no simple set of rules that can be applied at all times which will always be successful. However, by being analytical, rigorous and critical it may be possible to develop skills and approaches which can be useful, at certain times and in certain situations, when making business decisions. It is possible that different approaches will be used by different people in business and there may be disagreement as to which approach to take.

Business Studies is integrated and different areas of business are interdependent. There are links, for example, between:

- what is being produced and the funds available to pay for it (production and finance);
- the selling of the product and ethical considerations (marketing and ethics);
- the type of business and many aspects of its operation.

Being aware of these aspects of business will help us to understand how and why business decisions are made, and how they affect a variety of people, both within and outside the business. The aim of **Business Studies A level AQA (Fourth Edition)** is to help those studying Business to understand business decisions and to be analytical, rigorous and critical in their business thinking. A number of features are included in the book which we believe will help this task.

Comprehensive course coverage The book contains material that covers the AQA A level Business Studies specification. It is organised into short units, based on the A level course:

- AS level 3.1 Unit 1 Planning and financing a business
- AS level 3.2 Unit 2 Managing a business
- A2 level 3.3 Unit 3 Strategies for success
- A2 level 3.4 Unit 4 The business environment and managing change

There is a development in the units contained in each section which reflects progress throughout the course. In addition, there are three units on analysing business data, study skills and assessment at the end.

Flexible unit structure The units in the book follow the AQA A level specification (both AS level and A2 level). However, Business Studies teachers and lecturers often teach different aspects of the course in different orders. So, whilst there is a logical order to the book, following the specification, it has been written on the assumption that teachers or lecturers and students may also piece the units together to suit their own teaching and learning needs and the requirements. **Business Studies AS level AQA (Fourth Edition)** is also available. It provides the AS level units in separate book for students talking the AS level course.

Accessibility The book has been written in a clear and logical style which should make it accessible to all readers. Each unit is divided into short, easily manageable sections.

A workbook The text is interspersed with questions. The questions which appear as part of the units mostly refer to preceding information. Answers in most cases are expected to be relatively short. Questions are based on a variety of case studies, data, articles, photographs, etc. They should allow the student and teacher/lecturer to assess whether the information has been understood. Shorter 'knowledge' questions provide a means of revising each unit. A longer case study appears at the end of each unit. It draws on information contained in the whole unit and answers are expected to reflect this. The questions asked reflect the type which are set in examinations. They help students to develop knowledge, application, analysis and evaluation - the criteria used in examinations to assess responses.

Business Studies A level AQA Teachers' Guide (Fourth Edition) provides suggested answers and mark schemes for the activities and questions that appear in this book. Further case study materials can be downloaded free at www.alevelbus.co.uk

Use of business examples, case studies and data Modern technology has allowed much of the book to proceed from manuscript to book form in a very short period. This has meant that we have been able to use the latest statistics and business examples available. The materials used have been chosen to demonstrate appropriate arguments and theories. They should, therefore, allow students to answer questions which require knowledge of what has happened 'in recent years' or 'over the past decade', as well as questions which deal with current debates.

Skills At the end of the book there is a skills section. The unit on 'Analysing Business Data' allows students to learn and practice the presentation and analysis of business data. The last two units in the book provide guidance on how to study and the methods of assessment used in Business Studies. They are presented in the form of a manual and are designed to be used at various stages throughout the course.

Key terms Many units contain a key terms section. Each section defines new concepts, which appear in capitals in the text of the unit. Taken together, they provide a comprehensive dictionary of business terms.

Presentation Great care has been taken with how the book has been presented. It is hoped that the layout of the book, the use of colour and the use of diagrams will help learning.

Critque At appropriate points in the book there are sections which highlight that the mainstream views and theories in an area of Business Studies are not without their critics. Students are encouraged to be aware that there are sometimes alternative opinions and to consider and evaluate alternatives.

Support MyBusSpace.co.uk is an online support resource for use by teachers and students using the book. It includes an online student book, an accurate graphing tool, questions from the student book that can be answered and marked online, links to key websites providing access to latest economic data and a regular updated news section.

We would like to thank the following for their efforts in the preparation of the three editions of this book: Richard Dunill, for keeping the debate sharp and yet accessible; Ingrid Hamer and Annette Birchall for their long hours of typing; Nigel Lewis; Michael J. Forshaw and Chris Sawyer for bringing a 'real' accountant's view to the book; all staff and students at Bolton Sixth Form College, King George V College, Loreto College, and Manchester University School of Education; Diane Wallace and Steve Robertson for working on the early development of the book; everyone who has proof read earlier editions.

Dave Hall   Rob Jones   Carlo Raffo   Alain Anderton
Ian Chambers   Dave Gray

BUSINESS STUDIES

Fourth Edition

A Level

AQA

Dave Hall-Rob Jones-Carlo Raffo-Alain Anderton

Edited by Ian ave Gray

Acknowledgements

Dedication
To Elaine, Holly, Caitlin, Amanda Jane, Mandy, Sandra, Georgina, Rebecca, Jan, Natalie, Holly and Nicole for all their love and support in the writing of this book.

Cover design by Tim Button, illustration provided by Shutterstock.
Graphics by Caroline Waring-Collins, Kevin O'Brien and Anneli Jameson.
Photography by Andrew Allen and Dave Gray.
Typing by Annette Birchall
Proof reading by Sheila Evans-Pritchard, Sue Oliver and Heather Doyle.

The publishers would like to thank the following for the use of photographs and copyright material. Other copyright material is acknowledged at source.

Alvey & Towers p 152(c), Corel p 77, DigitalVision pp 149, 152(b), 423, 427, 435, 438, 473, John Menzies plc p 526, John Powell/Rex Features p 496, Manganese Bronze Holdings p 222, Paula Sollaway/Photofusion p 321, PhotoDisc p 281, 373, 379, 384, 389, 490, 498, 504, Philippe Hays/Rex Features p 117, Rex Features p 466, Richard Burns/Reuters/Popperfoto p 209, Shutterstock pp 2, 3, 5, 7, 8, 10, 12, 16, 20, 22, 23, 24, 26, 29, 31, 36, 39, 56, 59, 63, 66, 68, 73, 84, 89, 92, 93, 98, 103, 107, 113, 116, 135, 139, 141, 143, 146, 151, 156, 159, 160, 162, 176, 206, 218, 225, 227, 231, 236, 239, 246, 254, 257, 260, 275, 278, 286, 389, 302, 319, 33, 324, 330, 336, 341, 353, 360, 374, 381, 390, 415, 420, 422, 437, 441, 445, 447, 454, 460, 463, 470, 481, 501, 514, 517, 522, 525, Sam Morgan/Rex Features p 397, Stockbyte pp 61, 87, 101, 123, 129, 142, 152(t), 213, 371, 363, 424, 426, 428, 433, 457, 491, 509, 528, Suma p 391.

Office for National Statistics material is Crown Copyright, reproduced here with the permission of Her Majesty's Stationery Office.

Every effort has been made to locate the copyright owners of material used in this book. Any errors and omissions brought to the notice of the publisher are regretted and will be credited in subsequent printings.

British Library Cataloguing in Publication Data
A catalogue record for this book is available from the British Library.

ISBN 978 1 4058 9221 6

Pearson Education
Edinburgh Gate, Harlow, Essex CM20 2JE
Contribution © Dave Hall, Rob Jones, Carlo Raffo, Alain Anderton, Ian Chambers, Dave Gray
1st edition 1993
2nd edition 1999
3rd edition 2004
4th edition 2008.

Typesetting by Caroline Waring-Collins, Waring Collins Ltd. www.waringcollins.com
Printed and bound in Great Britain at Scotprint, Haddington.

1 Enterprise

Small businesses

There are over 60 million people living in the UK today. In 2006, according to official government statistics, there were 4.5 million private business enterprises. This means there was approximately one business for every 13 people in the country. Here are three more statistics about UK business.

- Three quarters of these businesses were small businesses where there was only one person working in the business.
- Almost all other businesses were also small businesses where there were between 2 and 49 people working in the business.
- There were only 33,000 businesses in the UK which were classified as medium or large where there were 50 or more people employed. This can be compared to the 4.27 million small businesses that existed.

A BUSINESS or ENTERPRISE is an organisation whose purpose is to produce goods and services. Of the 4.5 million UK businesses, some extract oil from the North Sea and some produce the carrots you eat on your plate. Others manufacture cars, provide taxi services or are local shops. The word 'business' comes from the word 'busy'. 'Enterprise' also comes from the idea that the organisation has a purpose, providing comes what they want to buy.

Entrepreneurs

Small businesses are run by ENTREPRENEURS. An entrepreneur is someone who:

- **owns** the business and has provided the money to start it up and possibly to expand it;
- **organises** the business, from hiring and buying inputs like raw materials and workers to producing the finished product for sale;
- has to be a **risk taker** because the business could perform poorly or even fail; the entrepreneur can lose money in a business as well as make it.

So the **role** of the entrepreneur is to provide at least some of the finance for the start up, run the business but take the risk of success or failure.

There are some famous entrepreneurs. Richard Branson, for example, has built a business empire from small beginnings publishing a magazine called 'Student' at the age of 15. Today he owns a string of companies from airlines to mobile phone companies to record companies. However, Richard Branson is exceptional. The more typical entrepreneur running one of the 4.27 million small businesses in 2006 is someone who is self employed.

- They are painters and decorators, plumbers or owners of a corner shop. They are farmers, architects or doctors.
- They may run their business full time. Or they may have an ordinary job working for someone else and run their business on the side, part time.
- They are likely to have started the business themselves but in some industries like farming it is common for the entrepreneur to have inherited the business from parents. Also some entrepreneurs may buy existing mature businesses.
- They may take on a lot of risk in their business or the business may have little risk attached.
- Entrepreneurs may be at the cutting edge of innovation. Or they may be providing traditional services like decorators cutting wallpaper or owners of a hairdressing salon cutting hair.

Risks, rewards and opportunity cost

According to the CBI, approximately 200 000 new businesses are started each year. But 10 per cent of these have ceased trading within 12 months. One third have been closed within three years of starting to trade. Less than half are still trading after five years. Starting up a new business offers the potential for high rewards. Some entrepreneurs, like Richard Branson, have become rich through developing their own businesses. Starting a new business also offers a chance for many people to do something different. If nothing else, it means working for yourself rather than for someone else.

However, being an entrepreneur is risky. The downside of success is business failure. If the business fails, it may leave debts to be paid off. The entrepreneur might have borrowed money to start the business or to finance growth. Getting back into a normal job may also be difficult, especially if the entrepreneur left a well paid job in the first place. The risk of failure is a major motivator for entrepreneurs to carry on and made a success of their enterprise even when the going is tough.

Success and failure have an OPPORTUNITY COST. The opportunity cost of an activity is the benefits lost from the next best alternative. For example, an entrepreneur who has just started up a business might have left a job earning £40,000 a year. Part of the opportunity cost of setting up the business would then be the benefits gained from earning £40,000 a year. They would only be part of the opportunity cost because the job would probably have had other benefits too, including the satisfaction from doing the job. For a successful entrepreneur, the opportunity cost of being an entrepreneur is likely to be lower than the benefits of owning a business. For an unsuccessful entrepreneur, the opportunity cost is likely to be higher. This is why the unsuccessful entrepreneur is likely to close the business and move on to something else.

Characteristics of entrepreneurs

Starting your own business is very common. Hundreds of

Question 1.

John Baker set up his business after working for an airline. As security manager, he was given an office with a box full of foreign coins collected from the on-board duty free sales of products like whisky and cigarettes. He thought that his airline might not be the only organisation which had boxes full of assorted foreign coins. When he left the airline, he set up his own business, Coin Co International, to collect, sort and cash coins.

His most lucrative years were when the euro was introduced and replaced the currencies of 12 different countries. There were a lot of old currency coins which needed to be exchanged for new euros. In 2001, he collected and exchanged more than 3,500 tonnes of cash and employed 110 people with offices in Germany, Canada and Australia. But this bonanza didn't last and within a couple of years, he had cut his workforce in half and sales were tumbling.

Today he is exploring new lines of business. He has already won contracts to collect the drivers' cash boxes on London buses, sort the coins and then bank them. He would like to win contracts to empty parking meters.

Source: adapted from the *Financial Times*, 7.7.2007.

(a) An entrepreneur is someone who owns a business, runs it and takes risks. Explain why John Baker is an entrepreneur.

(b) Suggest what might have been the opportunity cost for John Baker of setting up his own business.

(c) John Baker is thinking of retiring and would like to pass the business on to his two children who already work in the business. (i) Think of ONE possible problem that could occur for the business if he did this. (ii) Compare TWO possible ways round this problem and suggest which would be the best solution to the problem.

which encourages business start ups, identifies seven characteristics of successful entrepreneurs.

Self-confidence Successful entrepreneurs are people who believe that they are going to succeed. They think they have a winning formula for their business. They can persuade other people, for example, to buy the product or help finance the business.

Self-determination Successful entrepreneurs are ones who think they can take control of events going on around them. They can influence those events and turn them into something which will benefit their business.

Being a self-starter Many people work best when being told what to do. But to be a successful entrepreneur, you have to be a self-starter. Entrepreneurs are able to work independently and can take decisions. They have their own ideas about how things should be done and they are able to develop those ideas.

Judgment The business environment is changing all the time. A successful entrepreneur is one who is taking in information and listening to advice. At the same time, they are able to see where the business might go in the future and what they want out of the business. This helps them to make judgements and decisions.

Commitment Many people think when starting up a business that it is going to be easier than working for someone else. All the evidence shows that entrepreneurs work longer hours than those with a normal job. Running your own business can sometimes be more stressful because of the risks that are always present. So successful entrepreneurs are ones who are committed to what they do.

Perseverance All businesses have successes and failures. There is always an element of risk that their business could perform poorly or even fail. Therefore, successful entrepreneurs have to show perseverance. They have to be able to get through the bad times and the setbacks.

Initiative Successful entrepreneurs are able to take the initiative in situations. They don't allow events to overwhelm them by doing nothing. They are able to change and be proactive.

Not every successful entrepreneur has all of these characteristics. Few entrepreneurs are strong in every area. But people who run their own businesses tend to show different characteristics from people who work for someone else.

Motives for becoming an entrepreneur

People start their own business for a variety of different reasons.

Financial reward When people work for someone else, there is

thousands of small businesses are started each year. People give up their jobs to work for themselves or they start a new business alongside a normal full-time job. Not everyone is suited to becoming an entrepreneur either because they lack the skills needed or because they don't want to cope with the risk involved in setting up a business. Business Link, the government agency a limit to what they can expect to get paid. But owning a business gives someone the opportunity to earn much more. In practice, entrepreneurs tend, if anything, to earn less per hour than those in a paid job. Entrepreneurs have to work longer hours to earn their money. But there is always the possibility that you will become the next Richard Branson.

Independence Entrepreneurs tend to enjoy being independent

and in control. They prefer to be in charge of their day to day work affairs rather than having an employer telling them what to do. In practice, this independence is limited. Work has to be done. Taxes have to be paid. Those financing the business, like a bank giving a loan, have to kept satisfied that the business is doing well. But those who own their own business, in general, do have more independence than employees working for someone else.

Building a business Entrepreneurs get satisfaction from having built their own business. Creating a successful business is a deeply satisfying experience and can help people to meet higher level goals in life.

Job satisfaction Many entrepreneurs start a business because they think they will get greater job satisfaction by working for themselves. It could be that they prefer working on their own. Or they might be able to change the sort of work they do compared to a normal job.

The product Many entrepreneurs have an interest in what they sell. They are passionate about brewing beer or selling goth clothes or providing high quality care for the elderly.

Different entrepreneurs are motivated by different factors. Some are highly motivated by financial rewards. Others are highly motivated by the job satisfaction they get from running their own business. Equally for some, also, running a business is little different from working for someone else.

Government support for enterprise and entrepreneurs

The government promotes the creation of small businesses. It knows that small businesses are vital to the success of the economy. Nearly half of all jobs in the private sector are in small businesses and they produce one third of private sector output. Small businesses are essential for the future success of the economy because many of tomorrow's large businesses will come from today's small businesses. They are also linked to new ideas and new products. They provide an essential competitive dynamism in the economy.

To help new small businesses, the government has set up **Business Link**. Controlled by Regional Development Agencies, different areas of the country have their own Business Link organisation. They provide advice and support to business start-ups and to existing small businesses. They aim to provide a single point of contact on a wide variety of issues from finance and sales to tax and employment.

More generally, the government offers grants and subsidised services through a variety of schemes. For example, new start-ups might be eligible for grants if the entrepreneur is unemployed, or setting up in a rural area. More support is likely to be available in areas where unemployment is relatively high or incomes below the national average.

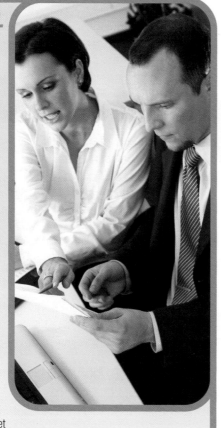

Question 2.

Joshua Roberts has worked for three years as the sales representative for a small print company. It employs ten people and serves the needs of local businesses in a market town and the surrounding rural areas. It prints everything from brochures and posters to invitations, specifications and flyers.

Joshua is ambitious and would like to set up his own business so that he can earn substantially more money. Over the past three years, he has been disappointed with his earnings. He has consistently failed to meet sales targets set for him by the company and so his bonuses have been negligible. In the next market town, there is no print company. By setting up there, he hopes to be able to carve out a profitable market niche.

Joshua's boss couldn't deny that he has enormous self-confidence. He is always talking about what sales he will achieve over the next few weeks and months. When he doesn't win sales contracts, he always picks himself up and gets on with the next job. In his appraisals, however, his boss is constantly pointing out that his timekeeping could improve. He can be late into the office and almost never in the office at closing time. Joshua always says he is seeing a client at that time. A quick check in his diary shows he never makes appointments to see clients outside of office hours. Joshua's boss, Natalie, thinks he tends to only see those clients who he is fairly certain will give him work. Once or twice, she has pointed out that Joshua is not pursuing sufficiently large contracts. He doesn't seem to listen, though, to this constructive criticism.

(a) Do you think Joshua would be successful if he set up his own business? In your answer, consider whether Joshua has the right characteristics to be an entrepreneur.

KEY TERMS

Business or enterprise – an organisation whose principal economic purpose is to produce goods and services.
Entrepreneur – an individual who, typically, sets up and runs a business and takes the risks associated with this.
Opportunity cost – the cost of a decision as measured by the benefits foregone of the next best alternative.

KNOWLEDGE

1. How many businesses are there in the UK?
2. What is the role of an entrepreneur?
3. Why is profit and risk important for a business?
4. What might be the opportunity cost for you of studying Business Studies?
5. Outline two characteristics of successful entrepreneurs.
6. What might motivate someone thinking of starting up their own business?
7. What support does government give to entrepreneurs?

Case Study:
Annabel Karmel Group

Annabel Karmel is a highly successful entrepreneur. She started her working life as a professional harpist, performing in concerts, appearing on television and recording CDs. She wrote her first book after the death of her first child from a viral infection. Her second child was not eating well and she decided to write a cookery book for feeding children. 'I didn't know anything about it,' said Annabel Karmel.' I didn't even know how to type. But I thought it would be good therapy.' Two and half years later, the book was finished and she sent it to 15 publishers who all turned it down. Then a friend took it to Europe's biggest book fair in Frankfurt and she finally found a publisher to take it on. The book, The Complete Baby and Toddler Meal Planner, has since sold more than 2 million copies. 'You do need luck', she said. 'But you should never give up.' Since then, she has written another 14 books about feeding children.

After her success, she was approached by Boots, the high street chemist chain, to design a range of cookery equipment which could be used to prepare food for children. When the range was a commercial success, this set her thinking about developing a range of ready-prepared meals. 'I was approached by a lot of very large companies to work with them and I think I lost time by talking to them. Eventually I realised that, to begin with, it would be better to do it by myself because I wanted to be in control of what I was doing.'

In 2007, her new range was launched after an investment of £350,000. It is now stocked by J Sainsbury and Ocado. Total sales from her books, meals and cooking equipment are expected to be £14 million in 2008.

'If you have a vision, you have to trust yourself. Don't let other people put you off. And don't be worried about doing something by yourself', said Annabel. 'I was worried about doing a food range by myself. I though I had to have a big company behind me, but actually it has been okay doing it by myself and very rewarding. Sometimes you

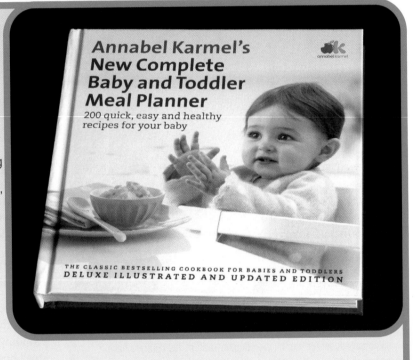

think that everyone else is an expert and you are not, but if you have a passion, then go with it.' Success has come partly by working long hours. 'I regularly stay up until 3 a.m. just to finish something off. I don't sleep much and I usually work the whole weekend. I gave up my social life for several years.'

Source: adapted from *The Sunday Times*, 20.5.2007.

(a) 'Annabel Karmel is a highly successful entrepreneur.' Explain, using Annabel Karmel as an example, what is meant by an 'entrepreneur'. (15 marks)
(b) What might have been the opportunity cost for Annabel Karmel of writing her first book? (5 marks)
(b) Analyse what characteristics are likely to be make an entrepreneur successful. In your answer, use Annabel Karmel as an example. (15 marks)
(c) To what extent do you think Annabel Karmel has been motivated by the financial rewards of running her own business? (15 marks)

2 Business ideas

Finding an initial idea

Each year, hundreds of thousands of people set themselves up in business. Instead of working for someone else, they become the owner. Or, they move from owning one business to owning another business. If they are successful, they may start to own and set up a string of businesses. But how do most would-be **entrepreneurs**, (those who risk their own capital in setting up and running a business) find a business idea? There are a number of ways.

Business experience For most people starting a small business, the business idea comes from their existing job. A plumber might work for a plumbing company and decides to set up on her own. A marketing consultant working for an advertising agency sets up his own marketing agency. This is likely to be the most risk free way of setting up a business because the would-be entrepreneur already has knowledge of the market.

Personal experience Some people draw on their personal experience outside of work to find a business idea. Some turn a hobby into a job. An amateur cyclist might buy a cycle shop. A keen gardener might set up a nursery. Some use their customer experience to spot a gap in the market. A mother might find it difficult to find a baby product and so sets up up a business to provide it.

Skills Some entrepreneurs draw on their broad skills base to start a business. A person with an administration job might judge that they have good 'people skills' and decide to set up a business in selling. A plumber might judge that in his area electricians can charge more for their work. So he gets training as an electrician and set himself up as a self employed electrician.

Lifestyle choices Some business areas attract people who want to make a lifestyle change. They might want to move to the country and invest in a small holding. They might always have wanted to run a pub and so buy a pub. Or they might be retiring from a full-time job but still want to carry on working on their own. So they invest in a seasonal Bed and Breakfast (B&B) business.

Identifying a product or market niche

For most entrepreneurs, identifying a broad business idea is relatively easy. But it becomes much more difficult to turn a vague idea into a practical reality. What will be the exact product to be made? What will be the market niche to be occupied?

For example, a painter and decorator setting up on his own may have to decide whether to go mainly for domestic work or for contract work with companies. Will he specialise in indoor

work or outdoor work? Someone setting up in the B&B business has to decide whether to go upmarket or downmarket. Do they want to convert their own home into a B&B or will they buy new premises? Will the B&B be aimed mainly at holiday makers or people on business?

The process of identifying an exact product or market niche can take a long time. A process might be used where a lot of different ideas are discussed. Then ones which are worth exploring can be selected and worked on further. Sometimes, would-be entrepreneurs start out with an initial idea. As they explore it further, they realise it won't work but something very similar might be better. A whole range of options might be explored as each idea is considered, rejected but opens up a further idea.

Question 1.

Claire Brynteson is an entrepreneur who found the right idea. She was working in a high powered job in the City of London. She noticed that there were plenty of people around her earning very large salaries but worked such long hours that they didn't have the time to organise the ordinary, everyday things in life. So she founded Buy Time, a lifestyle management service for businesses and individuals.

The business gives clients access to a personal assistant. The personal assistant will do everything from organising a parking permit, to getting broadband connected, to buying flowers for a partner, to getting a leaking tap fixed to organising a foreign holiday. The current 300 customers of Buy Time are either individuals or businesses which buy the service on behalf of their top employees. It employs 12 staff.

Claire Brynteson said: 'I could see that people round me were suffering from a lack of time and really needed this service. With women increasingly working the same hours as men, there was nobody at home to take care of anything.'

Source: adapted from *The Sunday Times*, 20.7.2007.

(a) How did Claire Brynteson get the idea for her business?

(b) Business Link sets out a number of criteria for checking against a possible business idea (see top of page 6). How well does Claire Brynteson's idea do when compared to this list of criteria?

Business Link, the government organisation set up to help small businesses, suggests that each business idea needs to be checked out against a number of criteria.

- What can the would-be entrepreneur bring to the business in terms of relevant experience and expertise?
- Is there a market for the product? Does it serve a need and will customers will pay for it?
- How big is the market and how can it be reached?
- What will be the main competitors in the market?
- Is there something special about the idea? Or will it be a similar product to what is already in the market place?
- How will the business be funded?
- What are the risks involved and what can go wrong?

Franchises

Starting up your own business carries a lot of risk. Most new start-ups have ceased to exist after five years of trading. One way of possibly reducing this risk is to buy a FRANCHISE. The **franchisor** is a company which owns the franchise. It has a track record of running a successful business operation. It allows another business, the **franchisee**, to use its business ideas and methods in return for a variety of fees. In the UK, there are a large number of franchise operations including Dairy Crest, Domino's Pizza, Dyno-Rod, McDonald's, Subway and Tumble Tots.

The franchisor provides a variety of services to its franchisees.

- Its gives the franchisee a licence to make a product which is already tried and tested in the market place. This could be a physical product but is far more likely to be a service.
- The franchisor provides a recognised brand name which customers should recognise and trust. This helps generate sales from the moment the franchise starts trading.
- The franchisor will provide a start-up package. This will include help and advice about setting up the business. The franchisor might provide the equipment to start the business. It might help find a bank which will lend money. It will provide training for the new franchisee.
- Many franchises provide materials to use to make the product. A company like McDonald's, for examples, sells food ingredients to its franchisees. If the franchisor doesn't directly sell to the franchisee, it might organise bulk-buy deals with suppliers to cut costs for all its franchise operation.
- It is likely to provide marketing support. For example, it might have national advertising campaigns. It may provide marketing materials like posters to place in business premises or leaflets to circulate to customers.
- There should be ongoing training. This will be linked to issues such as maintaining standards, sales and new products.
- There is likely to be a range of business services available at competitive prices. For example, the franchisor might negotiate good deals on business insurance or vehicle leasing with suppliers.
- Many franchises operate exclusive area contracts. This is where one franchisee is guaranteed that no franchise deal will be signed with another franchisee to operate in a particular geographical area. This prevents competition between franchisees and so helps sales.
- Over time, the brand should be developed by the franchisor. For example, new products should be developed to appeal to customers.

In return for these services, the franchisee has to pay a variety of fees.

- There will be an initial start-up fee. Part of this will cover the costs of the franchisor in giving advice or perhaps providing equipment. Part of it will be a payment to use the franchise name.
- Most franchisors charge a percentage of sales for ongoing management services and the ongoing right to use the brand name.
- Franchisors will also make profit on the supplies they sell directly to their franchisors.
- There may also be one-off fees charged for management services such as training.

The benefits and costs for franchisors and franchisees

There are a variety of benefits and costs to both franchisors and franchisees of the franchise model.

Benefits to franchisees For the franchisee, franchising could be a relatively safe way to start a business. Partly this is because the franchisor has vetted potential franchisees and rejected applications from individuals it thinks will fail. Partly this is because the franchise already has a successful business formula which has succeeded in the past. So the new franchisee only has to copy the performance of others. The cost of setting up the franchise is predictable. Too many start-ups have grossly over-optimistic forecasts of how little they can spend to get the business up and running on a sound financial footing. The franchisor also provides ongoing support and will provide help to franchisees which are underperforming.

Costs to franchisees Franchisees have to pay a variety of fees to the franchisor. These costs vary from franchise to franchise but franchisees are likely to lose at least 10 per cent of their revenues. This can have a significant impact on profit margins. Franchisees are locked into contracts. If they fail to keep to the contract, they can lose the franchise and as a result lose most, if not all, of their investment in the business. In some cases, contracts allow franchisors to take away a franchise without any compensation simply because it is in their commercial interests to do so.

Benefits to franchisors Many businesses are highly successful. But they find it difficult to expand because of finance and control. Finance is a problem because banks are not always prepared to lend for growth. Even if they do, it might be too little money to take the business in the right direction. Control is a problem because employees don't necessarily have the same motivation for success as the entrepreneur who founded the business. A franchise model is one way of getting round these problems. Finance for growth comes from franchisees who pay most of the cost of expanding the business. Franchisees also have the motivation to succeed. The franchisor is harnessing the skills and enthusiasm of another entrepreneur, the franchisee. Another benefit to the franchisor is that it reduces risks from failure. If the franchise proves a failure, much of the cost is borne by the franchisee rather than the franchisor.

Costs to franchisors In successful franchises, some of the profit goes to the franchisee. The franchisor, therefore, might have been better off with a traditional business expansion model rather than turning the business into a franchise operation. Running a franchise can increase costs because franchisees have to be supported in various ways. Franchisees can also be a problem. Some franchisees will fail to work hard enough or show sufficient business skills. Their franchises will underperform or fail and this will hit the profits of the franchisor. Other franchisees will not operate according to the franchise formula. For example, if it is a fast food franchise, some franchisees might cut costs by not cleaning the premises sufficiently and not keep the furniture and decor in good condition. This could tarnish the brand image of the whole chain of franchises.

Franchising associations claim that franchising is a much safer business model for an entrepreneur than opening their own business. They claim the failure rate for franchisees is much lower than for other business start-ups. Some academic research, however, suggests that franchisees, if anything, are more likely to fail than if they set up independently. This is mainly because the cost base of franchisees is higher since they have to pay a percentage of their sales to the franchisor. Successful franchises are ones where being a franchisee generates substantially more sales than if the business were independent.

Trademarks, copyright and patents

Every business has a name which is crucial to its business success. If another business starts using your business name to sell the same goods or services in the same markets, then you may be able to sue them and stop them using your business name. Businesses can further protect their name, or the names of their products, by registering them as a TRADE MARK. In the UK, this is done by registering them with the Intellectual Property Office (UK-IPO). Other businesses are then not allowed in law to use that trademark name. Trade mark protection can also be applied to signs, symbols, logos, words, sounds or music.

Business start-ups should also think about whether they want an Internet domain name (i.e. a web address). Unique domain names can be registered so that no one else can use that address.

Question 2.

Domino's Pizza is a highly successful worldwide franchise operation. It provides a pizza delivery service, taking pizzas to your door. In the UK, in 2008 it had over 500 outlets owned by franchisees.

According to www.whichfranchise.com, franchisees pay a royalty to the franchisor of 5.5 per cent on sales plus 5 per cent of sales to pay into a national advertising fund. The minimum initial investment to open a single store for a franchisee is £240,000 + VAT. However, for this initial investment, Domino's Pizza provides all the equipment needed and finds premises. New franchisees are given three weeks initial training (the Franchise Development Programme) and further training on an ongoing basis. The brand is supported by national advertising campaigns. In recent years, this has included sponsoring The Simpsons on television. Franchisees are monitored for quality of service by the franchisor.

Antony Tagliamonti is a franchisee who now owns three outlets. He says: 'I never get bored and, even after ten years, I am still finding new ways of operating, recruiting team members, increasing sales and pushing the business forward.'

With information from www.franchise.com; www.thebfa.org.

(a) What is the difference between a franchisor and a franchisee?
(b) What might be the advantages and disadvantages to an entrepreneur of buying a Domino's Pizza franchise rather than setting up their own pizza delivery service?
(c) What might be the advantages to the American company which owns the Domino's Pizza franchise of using a business franchise model?

For example, no one can use www.tesco.com because it has already been registered by Tesco, the supermarket chain. Common popular names are likely to have been taken already. So a start-up business might have to use a less obvious name for their web address.

A small number of business start-ups are linked to selling a new, innovative product which can be protected through copyright and patents. COPYRIGHT is given for original artistic works such as music, films, photographs, plays and books. PATENTS are given for inventions. Both copyrights and patents have to be registered with the Intellectual Property Office.

Trademarks, copyrights and patents aren't just there to

KEYTERMS

Copyright – legal ownership of material such as books, music and films which prevents these being copied by others.
Franchise – an agreement where a business (the franchisor) sells the rights to other businesses (the francisees) allowing them to sell their products or use the company name.
Patents – right of ownership of an invention or process granted by government for a fixed period of time to the individual or business which registers the original invention or process.
Trade mark – signs, symbols, logos, words, sounds or music that distinguish the products and services of one business from those of competitors.

KNOWLEDGE

1. How might would-be entrepreneurs find a business idea?
2. What criteria might an entrepreneur use to judge whether an idea can be turned into a successful business?
3. Explain what a franchisee and a franchisor might gain from a franchising arrangement.
4. Explain what a franchisee and a franchisor might lose from a franchising arrangement.
5. What is the difference between a trade mark, copyright and a patent?

protect a business from others copying their ideas. They can be used to generate income by **licensing** them to other businesses.

These other businesses then pay **royalties** to copy the idea legally. Businesses can also generate income from their intellectual property by selling it. So the rights to a song, for example, can be sold by one record company to another record company. The patent on a new drug can be sold by one pharmaceutical company to another pharmaceutical company.

Case Study: Business ideas

The Rolla Washa

A Wolverhampton firm, Washa Ltd, has developed a revolutionary new device for cleaning paint rollers. The Rolla Washa is 'designed to save users time, effort and water' according to Brett Smart, Wash's managing director. Rollers, rather than paint brushes, are used by painters and decorators for walls and ceilings. But rollers take time to clean properly and normal cleaning takes a lot of water. The Rolla Washa is a plastic container into which rollers are put for cleaning. Water mains pressure cleans dirty rollers quickly and easily. Far less water is used making it environmentally friendly.

The Rolla Wash is a now it its final stage of development and a patent has been applied for. It is currently on trial with two of Europe's leading paint manufacturers for their endorsement.

Business advisors have put a potential value on Washa Ltd of £2.5 million assuming the invention takes off.

Source: adapted from the *Express & Star*, 18.6.2007.

Red Star Natural Liquid Soaps

A Staffordshire couple, who started their business in their kitchen, are looking to sell their products globally. After two years of formulating and selling handmade soap in their spare time, Tim and Elaine Woodley launched their business product in 2004. Red Star soaps are made using cruelty and animal product free soaps. 'We're determined to make soaps from scratch using the original, constituent natural ingredients that contain no animal products and involve no animal testing,' said Tim.

The Red Star range includes liquid soap products for people, dogs and most recently, horses. 'The jewel in our crown is the new Red Star Pony Polish,' said Tim. 'It's the only horse shampoo on the market that's both natural and free from animal products and we worked with horse owners around the country to make sure it's right.'

The soaps are mainly sold online direct to customers, but the business is steadily building a distributor network both in the UK and overseas with products regularly exported to Europe and the Americas. They are even talking to the camel racing community in Arabic countries to develop a specialist shampoo for camels.

Business Link West Midlands, the government agency, have helped Tim and Elaine to develop their business model. It has ensured that steps were taken to protect intellectual property, including the business name and logo.

Source: adapted from the *Express & Star*, 18.6.2007.

(a) What is distinctive about the products described in the data which might make them stand out against competing products? (5 marks)
(b) Explain how the developers of each idea might have checked that their innovate product could be turned into a successful business. (10 marks)
(c) What is meant by 'intellectual property'? (10 marks)
(d) To what extent was it important for both businesses to protect their intellectual property? (15 marks)

3 Transforming resources

Inputs

From an economic viewpoint, the function of a business is to transform inputs into outputs. There are a variety of inputs to the production process which a business might use.

- There are raw materials such as oil and gas.
- They might use semi-manufactured and finished manufactured goods. For example, a car manufacturer might use steel, a semi-manufactured product, to make body panels. It might use pencils and pens, a manufactured good, in its offices.
- Capital equipment such as machines and buildings are likely to be part of the production process.
- Workers are an essential input.

Sometimes, inputs are classified into four different FACTORS OF PRODUCTION. These are **land** (all raw materials including land itself), **labour** (workers), **capital** (capital equipment) and **entrepreneurship**. Entrepreneurs are individuals who combine the other factors of production to create outputs.

Outputs

Outputs are what is produced by a business. Outputs might be **goods**, such as coal or cars, or **services** such as haircuts, holidays or management consultancy. In the private sector of the economy, outputs are sold by businesses either to other businesses or to consumers. For example, a gas company might sell gas to a hotel chain. It might also sell gas to a domestic consumer. A machine manufacturer might sell lathes to a car manufacturer. A car manufacturer might sell cars to consumers.

Sometimes the economy is split up into three sectors to show what types of good or service is produced.

The primary sector In the primary sector, raw materials are produced, grown or extracted. These include fuels such as coal or crude oil, and forestry, agriculture and fishing.

The secondary or manufacturing sector Manufactured goods are produced in the secondary sector of the economy. This includes all goods such as processed food, steel, car components, textiles and aeroplanes.

The tertiary or service sector The tertiary sector is where services are produced.

In an advanced economy like the UK, the primary sector is relatively small. It accounts for only a few per cent both of total output and total employment. The secondary sector accounts for less than 20 per cent of output and employment. Around 80 per cent of output and employment is accounted for by the tertiary or service sector. So most businesses make services rather than goods and most workers are employed in the tertiary sector.

In less advanced economies, the primary and secondary sectors are more important. In very poor countries, up to 50 per cent of the workforce can still be employed in agriculture. In rapidly developing countries like China, the manufacturing sector is growing fast at the expense of agriculture. But over time, it will start to shrink again as a percentage of the total as

Figure 1: Transforming resources into output and adding value

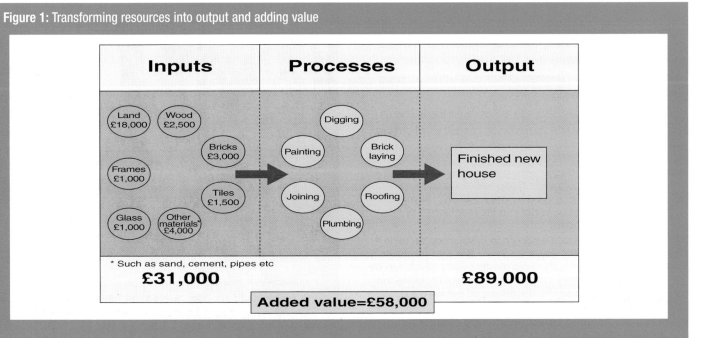

services become more important.

Adding value

Businesses **add value** as goods and services pass down the **chain of production**. Take the example of a haircut.

The chain of production for a haircut can stretch right back to a gas field in the North Sea where natural gas is being extracted by a company. It is then sold to a gas distributor company. This pays for the gas to pass through the pipelines owned by another company to arrive at the hairdressing salon. Here it is used to heat the premises.

The haidressing salon adds value by selling its services for more than the combined total of the inputs its pays from other businesses. If it sold £10,000 worth of hair cuts and heating bills of £1,000 were its only paid input, then the added value of the salon would be £9,000. This £9,000 will have been used mainly to pay wages and salaries for staff but it will also include the taxes the business has to pay as well as profit for the owners.

Sales and value added can be very different. The value of sales of the supermarket chain, Tesco, in 2007, was over

£50 billion. But its value added was only a fraction of this because most of the £50 billion was used to pay other businesses for all the items sold on Tesco shelves.

Case Study: Recycling

The two friends who set up Recycled UK, Paul Green and Paul Cotton, have seen it expand beyond their wildest dreams in just 12 months. First year turnover rocketed past £250,000, which was 20 per cent up on expectations.

The company specialises in waste management and the recycling of plastic. With the cost of taking waste to landfill sites going up and new government regulations and targets coming in, recycling is big business today. The company collects plastic waste from companies and local authorities in its own collection vehicles. It brings them back to its large storage yard in Cosely in the Black Country. The plastic is processed using a state-of-the-art granulating system which cost the company £100,000. 'All plastics are recyclable and we can handle scrap mouldings, scrap packing, post industrial rejects, components, video cassettes, bottles, shrink wrap and even crisp wrappers,' said Paul Green. 'We are collecting from all sorts of industries, including automotive, aerospace and food processing.'

The company currently employs six workers but plans to take on four more staff within the next six months as demand for its services increases.

Source: adapted from the *Express & Star*, 14.5.2007.

(a) What inputs are being used by Recycled UK? In your answer, classify these inputs into the four factors of production. (10 marks)
(b) 'Recycled UK provides a service to businesses because it removes their plastic waste for them. It is also produces a good because it manufactures plastic pellets which can be reused to make new plastic products.' Explain, using the example of Recycled UK, the difference between a good and a service. (8 marks)
(c) How does Recycled UK add value in the chain of production? (7 marks)

(d) Recycled UK has expanded fast in its first twelve months of operation. Evaluate the factors which will determine whether it continues to grow and be successful in the future.

4 Business plans

Why write a business plan?

Research shows that start-up businesses which have prepared a BUSINESS PLAN are more likely to survive than ones which have not. The business plan is a plan of how the business will develop over a period of time, like one or two years. Writing a business plan is important for a potential start-up business for three main reasons.

- Writing the plan forces the would-be entrepreneur to look at every key aspect of the future business. It is easy to concentrate on some aspects of running a business, like the product to be sold or its location. Most start-ups have some idea about what might give the business a **competitive advantage** against other businesses But other aspects are often not thought out well, such as finance or tax. The business plan forces the entrepreneur to consider every aspect equally.
- If the business is to borrow money from a bank, it will expect there to be a business plan. It uses the business plan to judge whether the business is likely to be creditworthy.
- The plan is useful once the business has started to trade. The actual operation of the business can be compared to the forecasts contained in the plans. This will highlight problems that are occurring. The business owner can then take steps to overcome the problem.

The contents of a business plan

The outline of a business plan can be obtained from any of the major banks in leaflets they produce on starting up a business. They give a very detailed list of points which must be addressed in the plan. These include the following.

An executive summary – this is an overview of the business start-up. It describes briefly the business opportunity to be exploited, the marketing and sales strategy, operations and then finance. According to the government organisation, Business Link, many lenders and investors make judgements about the business on this section alone.

The business and its objectives – the name of the business, its address, its legal structure and is aims and objectives.

The business opportunity – a description of the product or range of products to be made, the quantity to be sold and the estimated price;

The market – the size of the potential market and a description of the potential customers, the nature of the competition, marketing priorities, all backed up with evidence from market research.

Question 1.

Robert Crampton is a journalist who had a great idea for a business. He called it the Bobstacle: a soft play area, a cross between an obstacle course and an assault course with slides, trapezes and nets. It would aimed not just at children but at teenagers and adults too.

He took his idea to the television cult show, Dragons' Den. On this show, five multimillionaires who have already successfully run their own businesses, act as a panel. Would-be entrepreneurs have to 'pitch' their ideas. If any one of the multimillionaires likes the idea, then they say they are prepared to put their own money into the start-up and help it become established.

The panel of multimillionaires quickly punched huge holes in Robert Crampton's business plan. Robert hadn't thought through his future sales or costs. He found it difficult to state accurately how any money put into the business at the start would be spent. He hadn't thought through how many staff he would need, let alone what qualities he would be looked for in them. He also hadn't thought through what would be his competitive advantage.

By the end of the interview, Robert was thinking to himself that he still liked the idea of the Bobstacle. The adventure and the risk were attractive as would be the profits. But he wouldn't want to work there himself. At that point, he gave up on any dream of becoming an entrepreneur. Perhaps a career in journalism was attractive after all.

Source: with information from *The Times*, 3.2.2007.

(a) What is the advantage for a would-be entrepreneur, like Robert Crampton, to write a business plan? Use the passage to help you write your answer.

(b) Is it a waste of time of time to write a business plan when afterwards you decide not to go ahead with the business idea?

Personnel – who will run the business, how many employees if any there will be, the skills, qualifications and experience of those in the business.

Buying and production – where the business will buy its supplies, production methods to be used, the cost of production.

Premises and equipment – the premises to be used, equipment which needs to be obtained and financed.

Financial forecasts – a variety of financial forecasts need to be included. They include a **sales forecast** showing how the value of sales will change over time; a **cash flow forecast** which shows how money will move into and out of the business on a week to week or month to month basis; a **profit and loss forecast**, showing when the business might move from making a loss to making a profit and how big a profit; and a **break-even analysis**, showing at what level of sales the business will make

Question 2.

Tahira Hussein wants to open her own beauty salon which would offer a range of beauty treatments. She is in the process of drawing up a business plan and has just written down her objectives. These are as follows.

Objectives

1. By the third month of opening, to have sales of £25 000 per month offering 20 treatments per day.
2. By the sixth month of opening, to have sales of £40 000 per month offering 32 treatments per day.
3. By the end of 12 months, to have sales of £50 000 per month offering 40 treatments per day.
4. At the end of 12 months, to have 80 per cent of clients as repeat clients and 20 per cent as new clients.
5. By the end of 12 months, to be making a profit before tax of £1 000 per month.
6. By the end of 3 years to be in a position to open a second beauty salon.

(a) List six other items that might be found in a business plan apart from objectives.

(b) Suggest why it might be important to list business objectives in a business plan for a start-up company.

zero profits or losses.

Finance – where the finance to start-up and run the business will come from, including savings of owners and borrowing.

Sources of information and guidance

Entrepreneurs setting up a business can turn to a wide variety of sources of help.

Friends, family and work colleagues Initially, would-be entrepreneurs are likely to talk about their ideas to friends, family and work colleagues. They may just provide common sense advice. But some could have specialist business knowledge. They might have started up a business themselves in the past. They might be running a successful business now. Networking, talking to a wide variety of individuals or organisations, will generate ideas and identify obstacles to be overcome.

Bank managers All the major banks offer banking services to start-up businesses including loans. They have specialist teams of advisors who assess applications for loans from those wanting to start a new business. They will give advice about preparing a business plan and identify strengths and weaknesses in the plan. Their aim is to lend to a start-up which will be strong enough financially to repay any loans taken out.

Accountants There are many accountancy firms which specialise in preparing the accounts for small and medium sized businesses. They will sell advice to start-up businesses. They will be particularly good at providing advice on the finance side of the business.

Small business advisors Would-be entrepreneurs can buy advice from a wide range of small business advisors. They will help with everything from writing a business plan, to market research to recruiting workers.

Business Link The government provides help and advice to small businesses through Business Link. Each region in the UK has its own Business Link organisation. They provide a wide range of written resources, including a website. They also have business advisors who will provide help on a one-to-one basis. They run seminars and courses for would-be entrepreneurs. They also provide advice as the business grows. For the most part, these services are free.

Local Enterprise Agencies These are non-for-profit companies whose primary objective is to help new and growing businesses. Like Business Link, they provide a wide variety of resources and help to business start-ups including consultancy and training. Their funds come mainly from local authorities and other bodies.

The Prince's Trust and Shell LiveWIRE The Prince's Trust and Shell LiveWIRE are two organisations which provide help to young people starting up in business. They will not only provide advice, but they will also give limited financial support for new businesses.

KEY TERMS

Business plan – a plan for the development of a business, giving details such as the products to be made and sold and forecasts such as costs and cash flow.

KNOWLEDGE

1. 'Writing a business plan helps identify the problems with a business idea.' Explain what this means.
2. What might be contained in the part of a business plan which deals with personnel for a start-up (a) restaurant; (b) local grocery store; (c) biological research company?
3. Where could a would-be entrepreneur find advice in writing a business plan which (a) would be free of charge; (b) would have to be paid for.

Case Study: AKC Home Support

Darren Jones launched his care business, AKC Home Support Services, in 1991 with his wife Sharron. One of the first things they did was to write a business plan. But they saw it more as just one more form to fill in. 'When we started the firm, I knew we needed a business plan but saw it more as a document for everyone else than something to help us.'

They got help to write the business plan from their local enterprise centre. 'We looked at examples from other businesses and a template from the bank. We mixed and matched bits from these sources because not everything applied to us. For example, because we were going into a new market, we couldn't write about our competitors but needed a lot of information about the market for care services.'

The business plan contained their financial and strategic goals - what they wanted to achieve with the business. This helped them early on when they were offered work in another county. Looking at their business plan, they realised that they could get into short-term financial difficulties if they took on too much work. This was because they would have to pay out costs like wages months before they themselves might get paid by the client.

They regularly update their business plan. This helped them four years ago when they wanted a loan from the bank to buy a residential unit care home. Carefully working out how the loan could be repaid from the extra revenues coming into the business impressed the bank.

Their business plans also helped them get support from Shell LiveWIRE. They were awarded prizes twice which brought into both publicity for the business and extra money. Their business plan essential because you have to have a business plan to enter the competition.

Their advice when drawing up a business plan is to get as much help and advice as possible. 'Show the plan to an independent third party - such as friends or family who have run their own businesses - who will be able to point out if anything is missing. It's much better to make mistakes on a practice run than when it really matters.'

Source: adapted from www.businesslink.gov.uk.

(a) Explain, using AKC Home Support Services as an example, what might be contained in a business plan. (15 marks)
(b) How might outside organisations help a would-be entrepreneur write a business plan? (10 marks)
(c) 'Writing a business plan is a waste of time. You are better off starting your business as quickly as possible.' To what extent do you think this is correct? Use AKC Home Support Services as an example in your discussion. (15 marks)

5 Market research

What is market research?

Business activity will only be successful if the output produced can satisfy people's wants and needs. Information about the things people want and need will help businesses to decide what to produce. This information is often found through MARKET RESEARCH.

Market research can be defined as the collection, collation and analysis of data relating to the marketing and consumption of goods and services. For example, a business might gather information about the likely consumers of a new product and use the data to help in its decision-making process. The data gathered by this research might include:

* whether or not consumers would want such a product;
* what type of promotion will be effective;
* the functions or facilities it should have;
* what style, shape, colour or form it should take;
* the price people would be prepared to pay for it;
* where people would wish to purchase it;
* information about consumers themselves - their ages, their likes, attitudes, interests and lifestyles;
* what consumers buy at present.

Some, mainly smaller or local, businesses have just a few customers who are well known to them. For these businesses, information about their markets can be relatively easy to find. This may be through personal and social contact with their customers. Such businesses, however, must be careful that they do not misread their customers' views and actions. Other businesses, both small and large, have a more distant relationship with their customers. This may be because they have a large number of customers, operate in a range of different markets or market their products in international as well as national markets. For these businesses, market information may be less easy to come by. Such businesses often find that in order to gather marketing information they need to use sophisticated marketing research methods.

The terms **market research** and **marketing research** are usually used interchangeably in business books and in the media. This is the approach taken in this book. Some have suggested a distinction between the two terms. Market research, they argue, is about researching consumers' preferences and tastes. Marketing research is a wider term, which also includes the analysis of marketing strategies, for example the effect of promotions such as advertising.

The uses of market research

A market is anywhere that buyers and sellers come together to exchange goods and services. Markets are in a constant state of change. As a result, a business is likely to use market research on a regular basis for a number of reasons.

Descriptive reasons A business may wish to identify what is happening in its market. For example, a brewery may want to find trends in its sales of various types of beer over a certain period, or to find out which types of customer are buying a particular beer.

Predictive reasons A business may wish to predict what is likely to happen in the future. For example, a travel company will want to discover possible changes in the types of holiday that people might want to take over the next two to five years. This will place it in a better position to design new holiday packages that will sell.

Explanatory reasons A business may want to explain a variety of matters related to its marketing. This may include sales in a particular part of the country. A bus company, for example, might wish to research why there has been a fall in the number of passengers on a specific route.

Table 1: The scope of market research

Area of research	Possible elements to be considered
The market	Identifying market trends Discovering the potential size of the market Identifying market segments Building up a profile of potential/actual consumers Forecasting sales levels
Competition	Analysing the strengths and weaknesses of competitors Identifying relative market shares Identifying trends in competitors' sales Finding information on competitors' prices
Promotion	Analysing the effectiveness of promotional materials Deciding upon choice of media for promotions
The product	Testing different product alternatives Identifying consumer wants Developing new product ideas Assessing consumer reaction to a newly launched product
Distributing the product	Identifying suitable retail outlets Exploring attitudes of distributors towards products
Pricing the product	Discovering the value consumers place on the product Identifying the sensitivity of the demand for the product to changes in its price

Exploratory reasons These are concerned with a business investigating new possibilities in a market. For example, a soft drinks manufacturer could trial a new canned drink in a small geographical area to test customer reaction before committing itself to marketing the product nationally.

Once a business has decided how it wishes to use market research data, the next stage is to identify the aspects or areas that it wants to concentrate on. Table 1 shows the different areas that could be researched and some possible elements that might be considered in each.

Secondary research

SECONDARY or DESK RESEARCH involves the collection of SECONDARY DATA. This is information which **already exists** in some form. It can be internal data, from records within the business or external data, from sources outside the business.

Internal data This may be collected from existing business documents or other publications, including the following.

- Existing market research reports.
- Sales figures. The more sophisticated these are the better. For example, sales figures which have been broken down according to market segments can be particularly useful.
- Reports from members of the sales force resulting from direct contact with customers.
- Annual Report and Accounts published by businesses.
- Businesses increasingly make use of company intranets to provide up-to-date information. These are restricted to company employees. But some information may be available on the Internet on company websites.
- Stock movements. These can often provide the most up-to-date information on patterns of demand in the market. This is because they are often recorded instantly, as opposed to sales figures, which tend to be collected at a later date.

External data Secondary data will also be available from sources outside the business. Individuals or other organisations will have collected data for their own reasons. A business might be able to use this for its own market research. Examples are given below.

- Information from competitors. This may be, for example, in the form of promotional materials, product specifications or price lists.
- Government publications. There are many government publications that businesses can use. These include general statistical publications such as *Social Trends*, the *Census of Population* and the *Annual Abstract of Statistics*. Many are now online.
- Data from customer services on complaints which have been received about a product.
- The European Union. The EU now provides a wide range of secondary data which can be highly valuable to businesses operating within EU countries. Such publications include *Eurostatistics*, which is published by

Eurostat (the Statistical Office of the European Union).

- International publications. There is a huge amount of information about overseas marketing published each year by organisations such as the World Bank and the International Monetary Fund.
- Commercial publications. A number of organisations exist to gather data about particular markets. This information is often highly detailed and specialised. Mintel, Dun & Bradstreet and Verdict are examples of such organisations.
- Retail audits. The widespread use of Epos (electronic point of sale) has meant that it is now much easier to collect detailed and up-to-the-minute data on sales in retail outlets such as supermarkets and other retail chains. Retail audits provide manageable data by monitoring and recording sales in a sample of retail outlets. Businesses find these audits especially helpful because of the way in which they provide a continuous monitoring of their performance in the market. A well known example is data on the best selling records or CDs which make up weekly music charts. This information is collected from retail outlets in the UK.

Table 2: Advantages and disadvantages of secondary or desk research

Advantages

- It is relatively easy, quick and cheap to collect, especially if the sources that exist are known. This makes it very useful for smaller businesses.
- Several sources may be used. This allows the data to be checked and verified.
- Historical data may be used which can show a trend over time.
- It can be used before carrying out secondary research, which helps to establish the most useful questions to be asked in questionnaires.

Disadvantages

- Data is not always in a form that a particular business would want because it has been collected for another purpose. Adapting it may take time and become expensive.
- Data may be out of date and not relevant, especially in fast changing markets.
- Researchers must be aware of bias. For example, company reports and accounts may show figures in the best possible light to satisfy shareholders.
- There may have been problems with the research. For example, the footnotes to research may state that the sample used was too small and that the results may be inaccurate as a result.

- General publications. A business may use a range of publications widely available to members of the public for its market research. These include newspaper and magazine articles and publications such as the *Yellow Pages*.
- Internet website pages. Increasingly businesses make use of the Internet to search for secondary data outside of their own organisations. Many of the sources of secondary information above (including, for example, government publications) can now be found on the Internet.

Primary research

PRIMARY or FIELD RESEARCH involves collecting PRIMARY DATA. This is information which did not exist before the research began. In other words, it has to be collected by the researcher. It can either be carried out by a business itself or by a **market research agency**. Because of the high costs of using the services of a market research agency many small businesses choose to conduct market research themselves.

Most primary information is gathered by asking consumers questions or by monitoring their behaviour. The most accurate way to do this would be to question or observe all consumers of a particular product (known as the population). However, in all but a few instances this would be either impractical to carry out or expensive. It is usual to carry out a SURVEY of a SAMPLE of people who are thought to be representative of the total market. Methods of choosing samples are dealt with in the next unit.

Methods of primary research

There is a number of different field research methods a business can use. Many of these methods make use of QUESTIONNAIRES. A questionnaire is a series of questions designed to find out the views and opinions of a respondent. It must be designed to meet the needs of the business carrying out the survey. A poorly designed questionnaire may not obtain the results the business is looking for. There are certain features of questionnaires which are important in their design.

- The balance between **closed** and **open** questions. Closed questions, such as 'How many products have you bought in the last month?', only allow the interviewee a limited range of responses. Open questions, however, allow interviewees considerable scope in the responses which they are able to offer. Open questions allow certain issues to be investigated in great detail, but they do require a high degree of expertise from the interviewer. For example, an open question might be 'Suggest how the product could be improved'.
- The clarity of questions. The questions used must be clear and unambiguous so that they do not confuse or mislead the interviewee. 'Technical' language should be avoided if possible.
- The use of leading questions. Leading questions are those which encourage a particular answer. For example, a small shop wanting to find out about its consumer preferences for Coke and Pepsi should avoid the question: 'Do you

Question 1.

The local gym could be the new place for match making. A survey by Mintel found that around 19 per cent (1 in 5) of members have met good friends or partners there. Around 25 per cent (1 in 4) see it as a place to meet people with similar interests. 'Health and fitness clubs are now so much more than just somewhere to exercise and get fit... . Clubs could look to organise more networking and evening socials for their members, while major dating agencies might like to consider acquiring a strategic stake in health and fitness clubs as a base for their activities,' said Mark Brechin, senior leisure analyst at MINTEL.

After a number of years of facing rising costs and competition MINTEL predicted a 9 per cent rise in revenue in 2006, compared with around 5 per cent in the recent past. The size of the market for leisure services was predicted to reach £2.5 billion, with more than 5 million visitors, and one in ten as club members. Most revenue (76 per cent) was from membership fees, but a growing amount comes from bars and personal treatments. This grew 32 per cent between 2002 and 2006. MINTEL's research also showed that among those adults who have never been to a health and fitness club, 8 per cent would be interested in using one. MINTEL also forecast impressive growth. The market value was predicted to reach £3.4 billion by 2012, increasing almost 40 per cent over the next five years, with the number of members set to reach 7.6 million. ' Competitive pressures and energy prices have eased off from their peak at the end of 2005 and the start of 2006. Meanwhile, consolidation within the industry has removed a lot of the discounting on membership and joining fees among the leading club chains,' explained Mark Brechin.

Source: adapted from www.mintel.com.

(a) If a health club seeking to research its market found the above report on the Internet would this be an example of primary or secondary research? Explain your answer.

(b) Explain, using examples from the article, how a health and fitness club might use the research conducted by Mintel for: (i) descriptive reasons; (ii) predictive reasons; (iii) explanatory reasons.

think that Diet Pepsi is better than Diet Coke?' A better question would be: 'Which brand of diet cola do you prefer - Pepsi or Coke?'

- The questionnaire can provide **quantifiable** information. For example, it might tell a business that 75 per cent of its sales are to people below the age of 25 and only 25 per cent are to over-25s. It may be able to use this information to make decisions.
- Whether it is to be completed by the person carrying out the survey or completed by the respondent.

Personal interviews These involve an interviewer obtaining information from one person face-to-face. The interviewer rather than the interviewee fills out the responses to questions on a questionnaire, which contains mainly 'open' questions. The main advantage of interviews is that they allow the chance for interviewees to give detailed responses to questions that concern them. Long or difficult questions can also be explained by the interviewer and the percentage of responses that can be used is likely to be high. If needed, there is time and scope for answers to be followed up in more detail. Interviews, however, can be time consuming and tend to rely on the skill of the interviewer. For example, a poorly trained interviewer asking questions on a product she did not like may influence the responses of the interviewees by appearing negative.

IT-based research Advances in IT have led to the development of new ways in which businesses can carry out field research.

- Businesses are increasingly making use of Internet and email surveys, where customers can provide data on a business website or email directly to businesses' email addresses.
- Retail audits consist of information collected by retailers about consumers, usually at the point at which a purchase is made. Epos (electronic point of sale) data can be used, for example, to analyse patterns and trends in sales. Data gathered from retail audits is also valuable for identifying the types of consumers purchasing particular products.
- In the UK many shopping centres have devices installed which record where customers shop. Recorders have been developed which 'count' the number of customers entering a shop and some even differentiate between adults, children and pushchairs. The technology provides information which allows shops to see which areas of the centre attract most shoppers. It can also be used to compare shopping centres.
- Interactive methods can also be used to gather information. Consumers may be able to express their views via Internet websites or digital television. Information can be collected when orders are placed directly via the Internet or a digital television link.
- Spending patterns may be analysed from the use of credit cards and store loyalty cards. Loyalty cards allow customers to obtain a certain amount of benefits and discounts with each purchase they make within a shop or supermarket.

Question 2.

Vegran is a company that has developed a healthy lunch bar made from carob and oats. Initially, it has decided to sell the bar in the South West for a trial period, before launching the product throughout the country. Before this, however, it wants to collect views of consumers on the taste and appearance of the bar. It is particularly interested to find out whether consumers would notice a difference in taste between chocolate and carob and their views on the bar's size and packaging. Vegran is only a small company with a limited budget for its marketing projects.

(a) What potential advantages might test marketing have for Vegran?
(b) How useful might:
(i) postal surveys; (ii) consumer panels;
(iii) personal interviews; (iv) Internet surveys;
be to the business?

Telephone interviews This method allows the interview to be held over the telephone. It has the advantage of being cheaper than personal interviewing and allows a wide geographical area to be covered. However, it is often distrusted by the public and it is only possible to ask short questions.

Postal surveys These involve the use of questionnaires sent to consumers through the post. It is a relatively cheap method of conducting field research. It also has the advantage that there is no interviewer bias and a wide geographical area can easily be covered. Unfortunately, the response rate to postal questionnaires can be poor and responses can take as long as six weeks. In addition, questions must be short, so detailed questioning may not be possible. Questionnaires must also be well designed and easy to understand if they are to work.

Observation Observation is often used by retail firms 'watching' consumers in their stores. Observers look out for the amount of time consumers spend making decisions and how readily they notice a particular display. Its advantage is that a tremendous number of consumers can be surveyed in a relatively short space of time. However, observation alone can leave many questions unanswered. For example, it may reveal that a particular display at a supermarket is unpopular, but provide no clues as to why this is the case.

Focus groups These involve a group of customers being brought together on one or a number of occasions. They are asked to answer and discuss questions prepared by market researchers. The groups contain a range of individuals who are thought to be representative of the customers of the business or of a particular segment of customers. Because they only involve a small number of customers, focus groups are a relatively cheap and easy way of gathering marketing research information. A problem is that the views of a fairly small number of customers may not reflect the views of the market or the market segment in which the business is interested.

Consumer panels These involve a group of consumers being consulted on their reactions to a product over a period of time. Consumer panels are widely used by TV companies to judge the reactions of viewers to new and existing programmes. Their main advantage is that they can be used to consider how consumer reaction changes over time. Firms can then build up a picture of consumer trends. Their disadvantage is that it is both difficult and expensive to choose and keep a panel available for research over a long period.

Test marketing Test marketing involves selling a product in a restricted section of the market in order to assess consumer reaction to it. Test marketing usually takes place by making a product available within a particular geographical area. For example, before the Wispa chocolate bar was marketed nationally, it was test marketed in the North East of England.

The benefits of market research

A business may benefit in a number of ways from carrying out market research.

An aid to decision making Perhaps the main benefit of market research is that it allows a business to make more informed decisions. This is especially important in fast-changing markets. Businesses operating in such markets constantly need to adjust

their marketing activities.

Reducing risk While the reliability of market research information cannot be guaranteed, it does reduce risk for a business. Without market research, a business might spend large sums developing and launching a new product, which could prove to be unsuccessful. Businesses are less likely to waste resources on failed activities if careful marketing research is carried out.

Providing a link with the outside world Without market research might businesses operate in a vacuum. They would have little or no way of finding out the views of their actual and potential customers. They would also find it difficult to identify future trends in their existing markets and the markets in which they plan to operate in future.

Estimating the size of markets As markets become ever larger and as new markets open up, market research becomes ever more important. As markets get larger it becomes more difficult for businesses to operate without detailed information about the needs of their customers. This is because of differences in their tastes.

Public relations Carrying out market research may be good for the image of a business. Consumers may feel that their views are being considered. They may also think that the business is concerned that its customers are happy. This may lead to 'corporate' brand loyalty.

The problems of market research

If market research was totally dependable, businesses could use it when introducing or changing products and be completely confident about how consumers would respond to them. This would mean that all new products launched onto the market, which had been researched in advance, would be a success. Similarly, no products would flop because businesses would receive advance warning from their research and take any necessary measures.

In reality, things can be different. It has been estimated that 90 per cent of all products fail after they have been initially launched. Some of this may be put down to a lack of, or inadequate, market research. However, a number of businesses that have conducted extensive research among consumers before committing a product to the market place have launched products which have failed. Given estimates which suggest that the minimum cost of launching a new product nationally is £1 million, this is a risky business. Famous examples of thoroughly researched products which have turned out to be flops include the Sinclair C5, a cheap vehicle with more stability than a moped and lower costs than a car. In research, consumers enthused over this vehicle. In reality, it was almost impossible to sell. Similarly, when Coca-Cola launched 'New Coke' with a new formula flavour onto the market, research suggested it would be a huge success. In practice, 'New Coke' was quickly withdrawn from the shops.

Table 3: Advantages and disadvantages of primary or field research

Advantages

- Data can be collected that directly applies to the issue being researched. Secondary data will be data collected for another purpose.
- The business which initially collects the data will be the only organization with access to it. It can be used to gain marketing advantages over rival firms.
- Secondary data may be unavailable in a certain area.

Disadvantages

- It can be expensive to collect and may take longer than desk research
- The sample taken may not represent the views of all the population.
- If the research method is flawed, the findings will also be flawed. For example, a badly worded questionnaire may not provide the data a business requires.

Businesses want to be sure that the data they collect is reliable. One way of checking the reliability of data is to pose the question, 'If this information was collected again would the same or broadly similar results be obtained?' Businesses acting upon research data need to be sure that they can depend upon it. There is a great deal of debate among researchers about the reliability of different research methods. There is a number of reasons why **primary research** does not always provide reliable information for businesses.

- **Human behaviour.** Much marketing research depends upon the responses of consumers who participate in the collection of primary data. While the responses of consumers may be honest and truthful at the time, it does not mean that they will necessarily respond in the same manner in future. This is because all human behaviour, including the act of consuming and purchasing goods, is to some extent unpredictable.
- **Sampling and bias.** When carrying out market research, it is usual to base the research upon a sample of the total population. This is because it would be impossible and costly to include every person when dealing with a large population. It is possible, however, that results from the sample may be different from those that would have been obtained if the whole population had been questioned. This is known as a sampling discrepancy. The greater the sampling discrepancy, the less reliable will be the data obtained.
- As mentioned earlier, questionnaires need to be carefully constructed to avoid the problem of encouraging particular responses from consumers through the use of leading questions. Similarly, the behaviour of interviewers can affect the outcome of interviews.

Businesses must also be careful when using **secondary data**. For example, businesses may use a government publication to estimate the size of markets in which they might wish to operate. However, these market sizes may not always accurately match the product market being researched.

Quantitative and qualitative research

Data collected through desk and field research can be either quantitative or qualitative in nature. QUALITATIVE RESEARCH involves the collection of data about attitudes, beliefs and intentions. Focus groups and interviews are common methods used to collect qualitative data. An example of qualitative research could be face-to-face interviews with 100 purchasers of new Land Rover Discoveries to find out why they prefer this product to similar four wheel drives sold by other car manufacturers. The information collected through qualitative research is usually regarded as being open to a high degree of interpretation. This means that there are often disagreements within businesses about the significance and importance of qualitative research data.

QUANTITATIVE RESEARCH involves the collection of data that can be measured. In practice this usually means the collection of statistical data such as sales figures and market share. Surveys and the use of government publications are common methods of collecting quantitative research data. An example of quantitative research would be a survey of four wheel drive owners in West Derbyshire to establish their places of residence, ages, occupations, incomes and gender. The information collected through quantitative research is usually regarded as being open to less interpretation than that collected through qualitative research.

KEY TERMS

Confidence level – a statistical calculation which allows a business to gauge the extent of its confidence in the results of research.
Market or marketing research – the collection, collation and analysis of data relating to the marketing and consumption of goods and services.
Primary data – information which does not already exist and is collected through the use of field research.
Primary or field research – the gathering of 'new' data which has not been collected before.
Qualitative research – the collection of data about attitudes, beliefs and intentions.
Quantitative research – the collection of data that can be quantified.
Questionnaire – a series of questions designed to find out the views and opinions of a respondent.
Sample – a selection of part of the population, which must be representative of the population to be effective.
Secondary data – data which is already in existence. It is normally used for a purpose other than that for which it was collected.
Secondary or desk research – the collection of data that has already been collected for another purpose.
Survey – where respondents provide information to researchers about their actions, habits, attitudes and perceptions.

KNOWLEDGE

1. Why is market research important to businesses?
2. Explain the difference between:
   (a) descriptive research;
   (b) predictive research;
   (c) explanatory research.
3. State five areas that market research could concentrate on.
4. What is meant by desk research?
5. What is meant by field research?
6. Why might field research be of benefit to a business?
7. In what circumstances might:
   (a) postal surveys;
   (b) questionnaires;
   (c) observation;
      be useful?
8. Suggest three benefits of market research to a business
9. What is the difference between qualitative and quantitative market research?

Case Study: Beer sales plunge as Britons stay at home

Sales of beer dropped to their lowest level since the 1930s, according to figures released today. The British Beer and Pub Association (BBPA), which represents the brewing and pub industry, revealed that 14 million fewer pints are being sold daily in pubs today - a slump of 49 per cent since the peak in 1979. Part of the long-term trend has been the move towards drinking at home. In the late 70s, 90 per cent of beer was drunk in pubs, but the figure now stands at 58 per cent. While the biggest casualties of Britain's increasing preference for wine and spirits have been the pubs, they are, however, not alone: overall beer sales have plunged by 22 per cent from the peak 1979 level.

The BBPA says the situation is exacerbated by rising production costs as the prices of barley, malt, glass, aluminium and energy increase. It also feels that taxes on beer in the form of a duty imposed by the Treasury is making matters worse. Since 1997, beer duty has risen by 27 per cent while consumption has fallen by 11 per cent. Wine duty, meanwhile, has increased by just 16 per cent, while wine-drinking has gone up by 46 per cent. It's a similar story with spirits. Although consumption has risen by 20 per cent over the last decade, duty has increased by only 3 per cent.

Major British brewers saw their profits tumble by 78 per cent between 2004 and 2006. Last week, two major brewers - Scottish & Newcastle UK and Carlsberg UK - warned pubs that rising costs and a poor summer meant that big rises in wholesale beer prices were likely.

A senior executive at S&NUK told the pub trade paper *The Morning Advertiser* that prices would probably increase 'way above the rate of inflation' during the first part of next year. He said that rising cereal, crude oil and aluminium prices meant that brewers would be forced to charge more to recoup their losses.

Beer is not only falling victim to the growing fondness for wine among Britons. Its popularity is also suffering because of a cultural shift to drinking at home. In 2005, 60 per cent of all the wine sold in the UK was bought in supermarkets. And the wine and champagne market, which is now worth more than £10.2 billion, increased by 26 per cent between 2002 and 2006. Over the same period, sales of spirits and liqueurs went up by 16 per cent. However, some sections of the brewing industry are performing well, and real ale has enjoyed a quiet revival over recent years as consumers develop a taste for more authentic, natural and traditional products.

'This comes against a backdrop of a slump across the whole beer market,' said Owen Morris, a spokesman for the Campaign for Real Ale, a pressure group seeking to promote sales of traditionally brewed beers. 'But we've seen a 7.5 per cent year-on-year growth in sales of regional beers. People are enjoying regional beer more, even though the large breweries are forgetting about traditional beers and pushing lagers.' Mr Morris also referred to the threat posed by the supermarkets, which use cheap beer as a loss leader.

Table 4: The UK beer market

1930s The last time the volume of beer sold through pubs was this low
22 per cent The amount by which the total beer market has fallen since its peak in 1979
49 per cent The amount by which pub beer sales have fallen since 1979, equivalent to 14 million fewer pints every day
78 per cent The fall between 2004 and last year in the profits enjoyed by the major British brewers

Source: adapted from the *Guardian*, 20.11. 2007.

Consider the research above from the perspective of the owner of an independent pub.

(a) Is the research referred to in the article primary or secondary research? Explain your answer. (4 marks)

(b) Outline the reasons why a pub owner may find the research in the above article useful. (6 marks)

(c) Explain the various ways in which a pub owner might seek to collect primary data to complement the data provided in the article above. (10 marks)

(d) Analyse the potential usefulness of the data provided in the article for a pub owner. (10 marks)

6 | Sampling

What is a sample?

Sometimes a business or market research organisation may be able to carry out market research by means of a **survey** of all its target POPULATION. The **target population** is those people whose views it wants to find out. For example, a business making components might only supply five companies with parts. So it should be fairly easy to survey all of its customers. But in most cases it is impractical to survey the whole population. It would take too long and would be too costly to gather and process the information.

Instead, researchers take a sample of the population. Samples should be REPRESENTATIVE. They should have the same characteristics as the whole population. If they don't, results from the sample which are generalised to the whole population may be inaccurate. For example, a survey may be carried out by

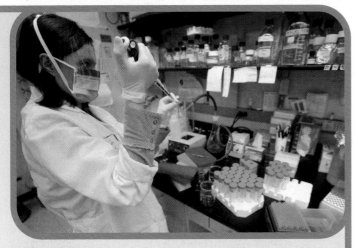

Question 1.

A pharmaceutical (drugs) company wanted to commission a study on male health worldwide. The results would be used to make major marketing decisions. A market research agency was commissioned to carry out the study. It set about conducting a two phase research project using survey techniques. In the first phase, 20,000 interviews were completed with target respondents in eight countries. A combination of phone and web interviewing was used. In the second phase, a random selection of about 5 per cent of the initial respondents for participation in a second interview were identified. These interviews were conducted on the Internet for those with access or through the use of a paper questionnaire.

The research methods used meant that the same questions were put to all respondents and answers collated in the same manner.

(a) Explain the type of sampling method used by the business.
(b) The market research agency interviewed 20,000 males in eight countries. Suggest why it interviewed (i) males only; (ii) respondents in eight countries rather than one country only and (iii) 20,000 people rather than 1,000 or 500,000.
(c) How much statistical bias would you expect to see in the findings from this research?

a food company to find out how many people would buy a new, up-market product. If it only asked pensioners on low incomes, it would almost certainly find that the survey predicted fewer sales than would actually be the case. This is because the sample chosen did not accurately reflect the whole population. In this case SAMPLING BIAS is present. **Questionnaires** are often used to gather data from a sample.

Size of sample

The SAMPLE SIZE will influence how representative the sample is of the population. Larger samples tend to be more representative. For example, say that the target population is 10,000 customers. If the sample were the same size as the target population, 10,000, it would be totally representative. A sample of 9,000 people is more likely to reflect the characteristics of the target population than 10 people surveyed on the street. So decisions based on the results of the larger sample are more likely to be accurate. There is a number of ways in which a sample can be chosen.

Type of sample

There are different types of sample and sampling methods that can be used by a business carrying out primary research.

Random sampling RANDOM SAMPLING gives each member of a group an equal chance of being chosen. In other words, the sample is selected at random, rather like picking numbers out of a hat. Today computers can be used to produce a random list of numbers, which are then used as the basis for selecting a sample. The main advantage of random sampling is that bias cannot be introduced when choosing the sample. However, it assumes that all members of the group are the same (homogeneous), which is not always the case. A small sample chosen in this way may not have the characteristics of the population, so a very large sample would have to be taken to make sure it was representative. It would be very costly and time consuming for firms to draw up a list of the whole population and then contact and interview them.

Systematic sampling One method sometimes used to reduce the time taken to locate a random sample is to choose every tenth or twentieth name on a list. This is known as SYSTEMATIC SAMPLING. It is, however, less random.

Stratified random sampling This method of sampling is also random. However, unlike the types of random sampling described above, STRATFIED RANDOM SAMPLING is where the sample is divided into **segments** or **strata** based on previous knowledge about how the population is divided up. For example, a business may be interested in how employment status affected the demand for a food product. It might divide the population up into different income groups, such as higher managerial and professional occupations, small employers and 'own account' workers etc. A random sample could then be chosen from each of these groups, making sure that there were the same proportions of the sample in each category as in the population as a whole. Therefore, if the population had 10 per cent upper class males, so would the sample. Stratified sampling is often preferred by researchers as it makes the sample more representative of the whole group and is less likely to privilege particular sub-groups than random sampling.

Quota sampling QUOTA SAMPLING involves the population being segmented into a number of groups which share specific characteristics. These may be based on the age and sex of the population. Interviewers are then given targets for the number of people out of each segment who they must interview. For example, an interviewer may be asked to interview 10 males between the ages of 18 and 25, or 15 females between the ages of 45 and 60. Once the target is reached, no more people are interviewed from that group. The advantage of this sampling method is that it can be cheaper to operate than many of the others. It is also useful where the proportions of different groups within the population are known. However, results from quota sampling are not statistically representative of the population and are not randomly chosen.

Snowballing SNOWBALLING is a highly specialised method of sampling. It involves starting the process of sampling with one individual or group and then using these contacts to develop more, hence the 'snowball' effect. This is only used when other sampling methods are not possible, due to the fact that samples built up by snowballing cannot be representative. Businesses operating in highly secretive markets, such as the arms trade, may use this method of sampling. Similarly, firms engaged in producing highly specialised and expensive one-off products for a very limited range of customers may need to rely upon snowballing when engaged in marketing research. Examples might include firms engaged in the nuclear and power generating industries.

Cluster sampling CLUSTER SAMPLING involves separating the population into 'clusters', usually in different geographical areas. A random sample is then taken from the clusters, which are assumed to be representative of the population. This method is often used when survey results need to be found quickly, such as in opinion polls.

Multi-stage sampling This involves selecting one sample from another sample. So, for example, a market researcher might choose a county at random and then a district of that county may be selected. Similarly, a street within a city may be chosen and then a particular household within a street.

Factors affecting the sampling method and size of sample

Businesses will take account of a number of key factors when making their choice as to which sampling method to deploy:

Finance available For some small businesses this means that random sampling can be beyond their means. Larger businesses, however, may have the resources to undertake market research methods that give more random results and use larger sample sizes.

The nature of the product The nature of a product produced by a business can affect the sampling method chosen during market research. This relates, in particular, to whether a product is the same for all consumers (uniform) or carefully adapted to meet the needs of individual consumers or very small groups of consumers (bespoke). For products that are uniform, a business will need to ensure that all of the population are properly represented in a sample and will need to ensure that little or no statistical bias is introduced in the sample. This is likely to mean a relatively large sample size. For products that are 'one-offs', bespoke or made to order, the population is likely to be very small or confined to just one person or business. In this case sampling is likely to be very straightforward and rely upon a relatively small sample, without the accompanying need for

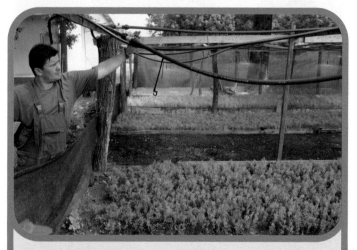

Question 2.

Graham Hunter is a farmer in Cambridgeshire, producing a range of vegetables. All of his supplies go to three large supermarket chains and he and his farm have been featured on the packaging at one of these supermarkets. In making decisions about what vegetables to grow in the forthcoming year, Graham has decided to undertake some market research. His research will be based upon speaking to the Head Buyer at each of these supermarkets and asking their opinions.

(a) Explain why Graham Hunter can be said to have used a sample.
(b) Explain TWO factors that may have influence Graham's choice of sample.
(c) How reliable do you think the results of his research might be?

Question 3.

DPX is a market research company. In 2003, it completed a report for a manufacturer of building materials and fittings which had seen an unexpected fall in sales over the previous 12 months. The manufacturer wanted to find out how its immediate customers, DIY chains such as B&Q and Wickes, and the larger number of builders' and plumbers' merchants, viewed its products. For example, it wanted to find out whether customers saw its products as giving value for money compared to those of competitors, whether the fittings were reliable and whether the range of products was large enough. It also wanted information about sales and profits of rival businesses to see if they had experienced a similar downturn.

DPX devised a telephone questionnaire for customers. In its sample, it interviewed all the large DIY chains. But it only conducted 30 interviews with smaller builders' and plumbers' merchants. The sample of 30 was judged to be representative of all smaller builders' and plumbers' merchants and a 95 per cent confidence level was given for the responses.

The research showed that a major rival company had completely updated its range over the previous 24 months. The products of the manufacturing company commissioning the research had lost competitiveness as a result. For example, they were said by respondents to be giving less good value for money than before.

(a) Explain what is meant by 'a 95 per cent confidence level was given for the responses' from the smaller plumbers' and builders' merchants.

(b) How might the business reduce the chance that its results did not reflect the views of all small builders and plumbers' merchants?

(c) Discuss ONE strategy the manufacturing company might develop to reverse the decline in its sales.

---

sophisticated sampling techniques such as those described above.

The risk involved The greater a risk a business is taking, the more reliable it would like its results to be. Thus a business taking a large risks for example financially, or in terms of the business's future survival, would want to use the most reliable and sophisticated sampling method available to it. This would for many businesses mean a relatively larger sample size. It would reduce the risk of statistical bias and increase the reliability of the findings from the sample. By way of contrast, a business taking a small risk might be prepared to go ahead with less reliable and, possibly, informal sampling methods such as talking to a few customers. A small ice cream business that has one shop, for example, might introduce a new flavour of ice cream after asking the views of, or in response to requests from, just a few customers. If the new flavour doesn't prove popular with customers, it could be rapidly withdrawn and replaced by another. Little would be lost by the business. A large ice cream manufacturer, on the other hand, selling products to millions of customers, would be unlikely to change its production processes on the basis of such a small sample. This is because the risk associated with a wrong decision would be so great.

The target market The nature of a product's target market will influence the sampling undertaken as part of market research. For example, if there is a small target market for a product, then the sample chosen will be smaller. Similarly, if the characteristics of a products' target market are similar or the same and they are in a particular market segment, then this will influence the sampling method. In such cases businesses may use cluster or quota sampling. For products aimed at mass markets with a range of consumers, the sampling methods chosen will need to reflect this diversity and this is likely to mean a larger sample size.

Sample results and statistical significance

The only way to get an accurate picture of a population is to have all relevant data about that population. But this takes time and is expensive. So researchers take a sample and the results obtained from the sample are then applied to the whole population. But how confident can a business be about the results of such a survey? When analysing data from a sample, researchers are interested in certain statistics.

* The mean. This is the average result For example, the average amount spent on a Monday by a shopper may be £10. On Saturday it may be £20.
* The STANDARD DEVIATION. This tells researchers about the spread of results. Standard deviation measures the average difference (deviation) of each item of data from the mean. For example, the standard deviation from the average amount spent may be £2 on Monday and £5 on Saturday. Comparing the means shows that shoppers spent

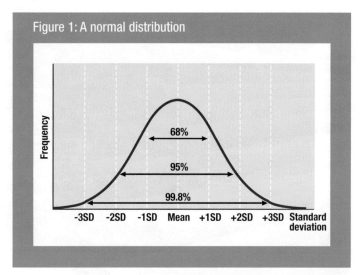

Figure 1: A normal distribution

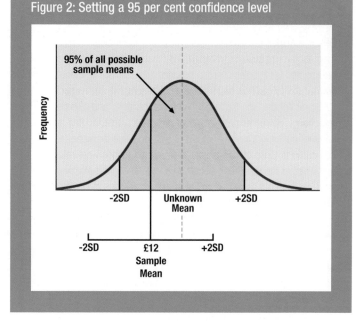

Figure 2: Setting a 95 per cent confidence level

twice as much on Saturday than on Monday. The standard deviations show that the spread of amounts spent was greater on Saturday than on Monday. So, on Monday, the amounts spent by shoppers varied less and were generally closer to the mean.

- Researchers also make use of a NORMAL DISTRIBUTION curve. This is a 'bell shaped' frequency distribution. It shows the results that can be usually be expected when the whole population is surveyed.

There is a relationship between the normal distribution, the mean and the standard deviation. The mean is in the centre. Most results cluster around the mean, with a few high and low values away from the mean. The data is symmetrically distributed around the mean, so that 50 per cent of results lie either side of the mean, as in Figure 1. In a normal distribution:

- about 68 per cent of values lie within 1 standard deviation of the mean on either side;

- about 95 per cent of values lie within 2 standard deviations of the mean on either side;
- about 99.8 per cent of values lie within 3 standard deviations of the mean on either side.

Look at Figure 2. What if a business did not know the mean (average) spending, but a sample found that it was £12? How would it know whether this was an accurate reflection of the population? To do this a range of values must be taken either side of £12, which will hopefully include the unknown mean spending. A 95 per cent CONFIDENCE LEVEL could be set, where values of 2 standards deviations either side of the mean are included. The business would then know that in 95 out of

KEYTERMS

Cluster sampling – where respondents are chosen for interview in a few locations, to reduce the cost of research, rather than being spread evenly across the population.

Confidence level – expresses as percentages an indication of how likely results obtained from a sample can be applied to the population. A 95 per cent confidence level, for example, indicates that the results will be representative 95 times out of 100.

Normal distribution – a naturally occurring frequency distribution where many of the values cluster around the mean, and where there are few high and low values away from the mean.

Population – the total number of consumers in a given group.

Questionnaire – a list of questions, given to a number of respondents to answer, which provide data.

Quota sampling – where respondents are selected for interview in a non-random manner in the same proportion as they exist in the whole population.

Random sampling – where respondents are selected for interview at random.

Representative (sample) – a sample which has the same characteristics as the population.

Sampling bias – where the sample chosen is not representative of the population studied.

Sample size – the number of people chosen for the sample from the whole population.

Snowballing – a non-random method of market research, where a small number of selected respondents are asked to nominate further potential respondents for interview and so on.

Standard deviation – a measure of the average difference (deviation) of each result from the mean.

Stratified random sampling – a method of quota sampling where respondents are chosen at random.

Systematic sampling – a non-random method of sampling, where a researcher chooses respondents by taking every nth name on a list.

100 (19÷20) cases the unknown mean would fall within the range either side of the £12 sample mean. If it wanted to reduce the margin of error, it could set a confidence level of 99 per cent. This would involve a larger range of results. So the business could be more certain that the sample reflected the population.

Researchers often use 95 per cent and 99 per cent confidence levels. For a normal distribution, a 95 per cent confidence level spans 2 standard deviations either side of the population mean. A 99 per cent confidence level spans just under 3 standard deviations either side of the mean.

What about sample size? In terms of time and cost, the smaller the sample, the better. But to give meaningful results from random or stratified samples, researchers argue that the size of the sample should be over 30. As the sample gets larger, the variance of results decreases. So there is less chance that

there would be a 'distorted sample', which would give an inaccurate picture of the population.

KNOWLEDGE

1 Why do most surveys involve a sample of a population rather than all the population?
2 What is the difference between a random sample and a systematic sample?
3 What is the difference between stratified random sampling and cluster sampling?
4 What does standard deviation show?
5 Explain the meaning of 'confidence levels'.

Case Study: Public transport in South West England

In 2006 Synovate Ltd, a market research company, published a report that it carried out on behalf of the Competition Commission. The report was based upon an investigation into the attitudes of the public towards transport links in the South West of England. They focused upon rail and bus services and the customers of the two main companies operating in the area at the time of the research: Wessex Rail and First Group buses. They wanted to know why people chose particular transport services and to establish whether they considered other possible services as realistic transport alternatives.

The research was based upon questionnaires. The questionnaires were conducted by researchers who boarded trains and buses between 7.00 a.m. and 7.45 p.m. Reply paid envelopes were provided where passengers did not have sufficient time to complete the survey during their journey. The sample size was 10,111 with 482 FirstGroup passengers and 529 Wessex passengers.

Some of the key findings of the research were as follows.

- Over a third of Wessex passengers are heading to work (36%) compared to just 17% of FirstGroup passengers.
- 31% of FirstGroup passengers travel on the bus route three or more times a week compared to 41% of Wessex Trains passengers.
- The factors of most importance to passengers of FirstGroup are 'stops at convenient station/stop', 'frequency of service' and 'cost of ticket', which are identified as the top three factors of importance.
- Wessex Trains passengers identify the 'short journey time', 'departure time' and 'stops at convenient station/stop' as most important.
- 'Space for luggage' is of least importance to passengers on both FirstGroup buses and Wessex Trains. In terms of how easy it would be to permanently change their mode of transport, no more than half of the FirstGroup or Wessex passengers identify any alternatives as quite or very easy to change to.
- FirstGroup passengers would find it easiest to change to 'train' (48% saying it would be quite or very easy) and Wessex Trains passengers would find it easiest to change to using a 'car as a driver' (48% saying quite or very easy).

Source: adapted from www.competition-commission.org.uk.

Table 1: Respondent Profile

		FirstGroup	Wessex Trains
		Base: 482	Base: 529
Age (Q26)	16-34	48%	50%
Excludes 'not answered'	35-54	23%	35%
	55-64	13%	9%
	65+	14%	4%
Gender (Q25)	Male	33%	49%
Excludes 'not answered'	Female	65%	50%
Employment (Q28)	Employed (FT/PT/self)	58%	78%
Excludes 'not answered'	Retired	17%	5%
	Other	24%	16%
Number of Adults in Group (Q27)	One	72%	75%
	Two	15%	14%
Excludes 'not answered'	Three +	6%	4%

1 Explain what is meant by the terms:
   (a) 'sample size'; (3 marks)
   (b) 'questionnaire'. (3 marks).
2 Explain TWO reasons why the research was commissioned. (6 marks)
3 Explain the sampling method used by Synovate Ltd. (8 marks)
4 How useful might the owner of a taxi business in the South West of England find the research? (10 marks)

7 Markets and demand

The nature of markets

A MARKET is anywhere that buyers and sellers communicate to exchange goods or services. They can range from street markets, to markets for cars in many countries around the world, to goods and services bought over the Internet. Sometimes markets are actual places, such as the fruit and vegetable markets or the shopping centres and high streets found in towns and cities. At other times markets are virtual and cannot be seen. For example, the market for many second-hand goods operates through the Internet on websites such as eBay and through newspapers such as *Loot*.

Types of market

Markets might be classified in a number of ways.

Geographical Markets might be **local**, **national** or **international**. A market held every Saturday in a small town is an example of a local market, as products are sold in the local area. National markets in the UK might be newspapers sold around the UK, such as *The Guardian* or the *Financial Times*. Some products are sold in many countries, in international markets, such as Coca-Cola and Pepsi, whereas some are sold only in areas such as Europe or Asia.

Electronic and physical Markets that are **electronic** are those where the buyer and seller do not come into contact. In electronic markets business is mainly conducted over the Internet or through other computer-based networks. Electronic markets are also sometimes referred to as virtual markets. For example, a consumer buying a book from amazon.com never meets an actual bookseller in the transaction. Instead, the transaction is conducted entirely electronically. On the other hand, a consumer buying a book from a bookshop will **physically** enter the bookshop and make a transaction. Thus physical markets are those where the buyer and seller physically come into contact.

Buyer Here markets are classified according to who the buyer is. Goods such as ice cream and services such as DVD rental are bought by consumers in **consumer markets**. But sometimes products, such as machinery, are bought from a business by another business in **industrial** or **producer markets**.

Industry Markets might be classified according to whether they involve PRIMARY INDUSTRY, such as oil extraction or fishing, SECONDARY INDUSTRY involving manufacturing, or TERTIARY INDUSTRY involving services. Sometimes markets are classified according to individual industries or products. So, for example, the motor car industry and the computer industry

Question 1.

(a) Using different market classifications, describe each of the markets shown in the photographs.

make up different markets within the manufacturing sector.

Size Markets might be **mass markets**, where products are sold to many people in many countries who have similar needs, such as market for washing up liquid. Or they might be **niche markets** for specialist products sold to consumers with particular tastes and needs, such as the market for vegan food products.

Products are likely to fit into different categories. For example, a computer business such as Apple is a manufacturer in secondary industry, selling computer products in international markets, to both businesses and consumers. A hair salon might sell niche market hair products and beautician tertiary services to consumers in local markets.

The importance of demand

Businesses operate in markets where they produce and sell, or supply, products that consumers want and are able to buy, or demand. There is a number of factors that can affect the demand for an individual business's products.

The price of the product For most products:
- as the price goes up, the quantity demanded goes down;
- as the price goes down, the quantity demanded goes up.

For example, a bicycle shop selling a particular brand of bike at £175 each might sell on average ten of these bikes per week. If this bicycle shop lowered the price to £99 it might sell 25 in a week. On the other hand, if the bicycle shop raised the price of this bike to £240 it might sell as few as two or three bikes per week on average. This illustrates the inverse relationship between the price of a business' products and the demand for the product.

However, there are some products where this relationship is different over particular price ranges. 'Prestige' products such as luxury perfumes are designed to appeal to consumers' sense of exclusivity and feeling special. A low price might put off consumers of such a product, as there is an association made between a higher price and high quality. This means that the quantity demanded over lower price ranges may increase as the price rises for such a product. Speculative goods can also act in this way. As prices rise people buy more of them, hoping to sell them for a profit at a later date. For example, as the prices of houses rose in the UK between 2000-2005 the demand for houses also rose as house buyers anticipated prices rising even further.

Consumer incomes The incomes of the consumers of a product will affect demand. The consumers at whom a product is aimed may experience an increase in income. If this happens a business may be able to sell more of the product at a given price or charge a higher price. So, the bicycle shop owner is likely to experience an increase in demand from target customers if their incomes rise. On the other hand, if consumer incomes fall, the demand for products is also likely to fall on average. So, the bicycle shop owner may experience a fall in demand for bicycles if the target customers' incomes fall.

Competitor actions There are two main ways in which the action of a competitor may affect the demand for a business' products. First, the price of a rival's goods may change. If a rival's price goes up, customers may be more willing to buy more of this product. If a rival's prices fall, customers may reduce demand for this product. For example, the bicycle shop described above may be competing with a larger retailer of bicycles such as Decathlon. If Decathlon lowers the prices of its equivalent bicycles, then the bicycle shop may find that the demand for its bikes falls. Second, a competitor business may have a successful marketing campaign. For example, were Decathlon to run a popular and successful marketing campaign that was successful in attracting large numbers of new customers, then this would be likely to have a negative effect upon the demand for the bicycle shop's products.

Success of a business' marketing A business may run a successful marketing campaign that attracts new customers and increases demand. So, for example, the bicycle shop may sponsor a series of popular local bike races. This may lead to an increase in the number of customers visiting the shop.

Changes in tastes and fashion Changes in consumer tastes and fashions can have major effects upon the demand for particular products. For example, there have been many changes in the type of bicycles favoured by consumers over the past 30 years. These have ranged from 'choppers' in the 1970s through to BMX bikes and mountain bikes in the 1990s. These changes in tastes have had an effect upon the demand for particular types of bikes.

Changes in population Demographic changes can affect the demand for a product. For example, the increase in the number of specialist 'Polish shops' in UK towns and cities reflects the increase in the number of Polish people who have moved to the UK. Similarly, the increase in the number of up-market furniture stores in regional cities such as Manchester, Birmingham and Leeds reflects the movement into these cities of large numbers of young, affluent consumers.

Seasonal factors Many businesses experience large changes in the demand for their products between different seasons. For example, many isolated Cornish beaches have cafes that are very busy in the summer season due to a high demand for consumers. Yet these same cafes may close or offer only a limited service during other seasons due to a lack of consumer demand.

Government legislation and regulation Government legislation and regulation can affect demand. Pubs, for example, may experience a fall in demand as a result of an increase in the legal age of people buying alcohol or as a result of the ban on smoking indoors.

Case Study: *Marple Road Garage*

Marple Road Garage is a thriving Cheshire based family business that offers a range of garage-based services, such as repairs and MOTs to local car drivers. As well as providing these more general garage services, it also sells second hand vehicles with a particular specialism in Land Rover Defenders.

Tim Hill, one of the partners in the business, has been responsible for Land Rover sales and has overseen the expansion of this part of the business over recent years. Tim described the success of his business in the following terms: 'One of the key factors in driving our business has been an increase in the general popularity of four wheel drive vehicles. The Land Rover Defender has remained popular among consumers such as land owners and farmers wanting a sturdy, practical and 'down to earth' vehicle, but it has also attracted new customers, particularly well off business people and professionals, who use their Defenders mainly at weekends'. One of Tim's principal marketing innovations was the establishment of a website (www.marpleroadgarage.co.uk) that enabled him to trade in Land Rovers to customers nationally and, in some cases, throughout the world. Reflecting upon this Tim reported: 'Before we created our website we mainly sold to local customers in Cheshire and Greater Manchester. In those days our business used to be much more regionally based, with very few sales outside of our immediate region. Now we have customers all over the UK and 90 per cent of our Land Rover sales are internet led. Recently we sold four Defenders to a game park in Africa and we now have Reuters, the international news agency, as an established customer'. Looking to the future, Tim expects demand for second-hand Defenders to remain strong, but he does have some concerns about the state of the economy and is worried that a fall in income among consumers in his target groups will reduce demand.

Source: adapted from www.marpleroadgarage.co.uk.

(a) Identify THREE different markets in which Marple Road Garage operates. (3 marks)
(b) Using evidence from the article, outline factors influencing the demand for second-hand Land Rover Defenders (6 marks)
(c) Explain how the creation of a website has enabled Marple Road Garage to increase sales of second-hand vehicles. (8 marks)
(d) Analyse the possible threats to Marple Road Garage's future sales of second-hand Defenders. (8 marks)

8 Market segmentation

Market segments

Market research provides a variety of information about the people who may be interested in buying a business's products. For example, it might tell a business that a new car will mainly be bought by women aged 18-35. It might indicate that older people have bought more copies of a magazine than younger people in the last year. Producers may use this information to identify people with similar needs. Breaking down a market into sub-groups with similar characteristics is known as MARKET SEGMENTATION. A business can then target these groups and develop products and services for each of them.

Health clubs in the UK make use of segmentation. For example, daytime users tend to be younger mothers with children and older retired people. Clubs often provide facilities such as crèches for such members. Members who visit in the evening tend to be people who work in the day and want to exercise at night.

The benefits of market segmentation

There is a number of benefits of market segmentation that lead businesses to attempt to identify different market segments.
- Successful market segmentation should allow a business to sell more products overall and perhaps increase its profit.
- By identifying different MARKET SEGMENTS, a business should understand its consumers better. Greater knowledge about its customers will allow a business to vary its products to suit their needs better.
- It might enable a business to target particular groups with particular products.
- It can help to prevent products being promoted to the wrong people. This would be wasteful of resources and might possibly lead to losses.
- It might allow a business to market a wider range of differentiated products.
- Customers may feel that their needs are being better targeted and develop loyalty to the business.

Types of market segmentation

There are four main ways in which consumers tend to be segmented:
- geographically – by where they live;
- demographically – by their gender, social class, age, income, ethnicity or religion;
- psychographically – by their lifestyle and personality;
- behaviourally – by how they act, for example whether they make repeat purchases, buy on impulse or want high quality products.

Question 1.

One of the most commonly targeted groups for advertisers are ABC1s. In the past commercial radio was not seen as a useful way of reaching such audiences. However, recently there has been a growth in the number of 'medium' ABC1s which are part of the listenership. During a typical week, 65 per cent of ABC1s tune in or listen to commercial radio. Over a month its reach rises to 83 per cent. ABC1s tend to listen for extended periods of time, around 12 hours a week. They also have high loyalty levels to their favourite stations. On average they tune in to 2.6 different stations a week. Even younger ABC1s, who might be more experimental, tend to stay loyal to one or two stations. This information is particularly useful for advertisers using a mixed media to promote products. ABC1s often avoid TV advertising.

Main listening periods tend to take place in the morning. In a typical week 61 per cent of ABC1 adults tune in to commercial radio. nineteen per cent listen on Saturdays and 15 per cent on Sundays. Around a fifth of time spent listening to commercial radio by ABC1s is in the car. Most is done at breakfast and when going home.

Source: adapted from www.rab.co.uk.

Figure 1: ABC1 profiles

	Population	All commercial radio	Commercial radio listeners who are light commercial TV viewers
C2DE	52%	51%	35%
ABC1	48%	49%	65%

ABC1   C2DE

(a) Examine the reasons why commercial radio might be a useful promotional medium for small and medium sized businesses aiming at ABC1s.

(b) Suggest how a small to medium sized business might appeal to ABC1s most effectively using this medium.

Geographic segmentation

This might include considering the region of a country where consumers live and the nature of the region, e.g. rural, urban, semi-rural or suburban. It may also consider the type of house, road or area of a city that people live in. This method can be especially useful in large or highly culturally diverse markets, where buying patterns are influenced by region. Businesses selling into the EU are likely to break this area down into more manageable segments. Many large businesses selling into global markets have different products for different countries or areas. For example, Nestlé has sold refrigerated profiteroles in France and a fortified drink called Milo with a malted taste in Japan. The Maggi and Crosse & Blackwell soups are adapted to suit different tastes, by varying the ingredients from one country to another. It may also be possible for a company to price goods differently in different markets. For example, car manufacturers sell the same cars at different prices in different countries in the European Union. The prices will depend, in part, on what they think customers are prepared to pay.

A drawback of geographic segmentation is the evidence that consumer tastes are becoming more uniform across geographic boundaries. This can mean that regional boundaries and national boundaries become less important in determining tastes. For example, 30 years ago the vast majority of supporters of Manchester United or Liverpool FC could be found within a 30 mile radius of the clubs. Today supporters of these clubs and consumers of their products can be found in large numbers in other locations such as the South East of England, Asia or Southern Africa.

Demographic segmentation

DEMOGRAPHY is the study of population. Demographic segmentation splits people up into different groups according to different characteristics.

Age Many businesses pay attention to the age of their customers. For example, the over-65s could be seen as one segment, while teenagers aged 14-18 could be seen as another. R&B CDs might be marketed to teenagers, whilst a 'Hits of the 1960s' CD may be more likely to be attractive to older buyers. The over-60s are of particular interest to business as this segment is

Table 1: Socio-economic groups – IPA classification

Social grade	Social status	Head of household's occupation
A	Upper middle class	Higher managerial, administrative or professional such as doctors, lawyers and company directors
B	Middle class	Intermediate managerial, administrative or professional such as teachers, nurses and managers
C1	Lower middle class	Supervisory or clerical and junior managerial, administrative or professional such as shop assistants, clerks and police constables
C2	Skilled working class	Skilled manual workers such as carpenters, cooks and train drivers
D	Working class	Semi-skilled and unskilled manual workers such as fitters and store keepers
E	The poorest in society	State pensioners or widows, casual or lower grade workers, or long-term unemployed

Table 2: Socio-economic groups – Registrar General's classification

Class 1	Higher managerial and professional occupations
	1.1 Employers in large organisations (eg corporate manager)
	1.2 Higher professionals (eg doctor or barrister)
Class 2	Lower managerial and professional occupations (eg journalist, actor, nurse)
Class 3	Intermediate occupations (eg secretary, driving instructor)
Class 4	Small employers and own account workers (eg publican, taxi driver)
Class 5	Lower supervisory, craft and related occupations (eg plumber, butcher, train driver)
Class 6	Semi routine occupations (eg shop assistant, traffic warden)
Class 7	Routine occupations (eg waiter, road sweeper)
Class 8	Never worked/long-term unemployed

Table 3: Financial Services and ABC1s

- More than one-third of ABs and more than three in ten C1s borrow more than they save. Those with children are nearly twice as likely as those without to owe more than they have saved.
- ABs and C2s find saving easier than C1s, Ds and Es.
- Just over two-thirds of ABs, and almost two-thirds of C1s, expect to fund their children out of savings and investments.
- Around one-third of ABs and one-fifth of C1s have bought savings plans, investments or insurance over the telephone. Only three ABs and two C1s in 100 have bought them over the Internet.
- Only one AB in eight, and one C1 in 16, sets aside more than £200 a month to save for a retirement pension, in addition to National Insurance contributions.
- Almost one in five ABs, and nearly one in four C1s, puts less than £50 a month into a pension.
- ABs are less worried than other social groups about the accessibility of bank or building society branches, and so are less worried about branch closures.

Source: adapted from www.researchmarkets.com.

growing as a proportion of the total population. The marketing of financial services for older people has become popular in recent years. So has a number of other products and service areas, ranging from specialist holidays to the development of retirement housing.

Gender Businesses may target either males or females. This is because men and women often have different spending patterns. Some car producers, for example, have targeted women in their promotional campaigns for smaller hatchbacks. Manufacturers of perfumes and related products have realised the growing market for personal care products among men. Major brand names such as Armani and Yves Saint Laurent, as well as sports companies, have produced a range of products geared towards

males. Mobile phone manufacturers target a growing number of females buying the latest 'technological gadgets', by designing accessories to suit their requirements.

Social class Markets are often divided by social class. Tables 1 and 2 show two measures of social class used in the UK. For the 2001 population census, the Registrar General divided social class into eight areas. Classes are based on employment status and conditions. This division is usually used in government reports and surveys. The Institute of Practitioners in Advertising (IPA) divides social class into six categories. These are used to decide which group to target for promoting a product. Because of regular changes in the pay and status of different occupations, these categories are revised from time to time. For example, the

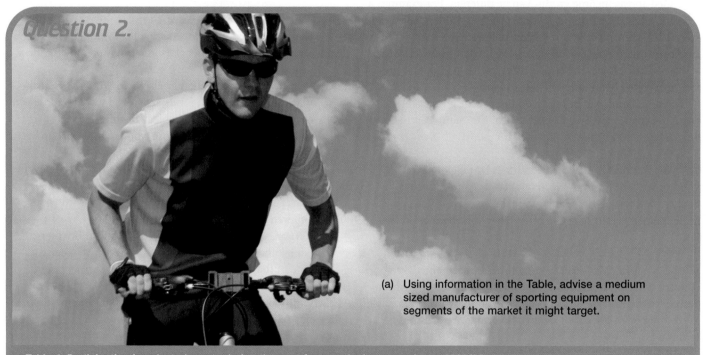

Question 2.

(a) Using information in the Table, advise a medium sized manufacturer of sporting equipment on segments of the market it might target.

Table 4: Participation in selected sports during the past four weeks by sex and age, 2005/06

England										Percentages
	Men					Women				
	16-24	25-44	45-64	65 and over	All aged 16 and over	16-24	25-44	45-64	65 and over	All aged 16 and over
Indoor swimming or diving	16	18	10	5	13	23	24	16	6	18
Health, fitness, gym or conditioning activities	22	18	9	4	13	19	16	13	3	13
Recreational cycling	16	16	11	4	12	8	9	6	1	6
Snooker, pool, billiards	34	13	7	4	13	12	3	1	-	3
Keep fit, aerobics, dance exercise	4	4	4	3	4	13	12	10	5	10
Outdoor football	43	14	3	-	12	5	1	1	-	1
Golf, pitch and putt, putting	10	9	9	9	9	1	1	2	1	1
Jogging, cross-country, road running	11	10	4	-	7	6	5	2	-	3
Tenpin bowling	9	4	3	1	4	8	4	2	-	3
Darts	16	6	3	1	6	4	2	1	1	2

Source: *Taking Part: The National Survey of Culture, Leisure and Sport*, Department for Culture, Media and Sports.

Registrar General's classification previously had only five classes.

Research often breaks these categories down even further. For example, AB, C1, C2, D and E are sometimes used to highlight the differences between levels of management, and skilled and unskilled manual workers. The media often refers to ABC1s. It is suggested that some businesses are particularly interested in people who might fall into this category as they tend to have higher incomes and levels of spending. Table 3 shows information from a study about the attitudes of people in the ABC1 group to financial services. This could be used by banks, insurance or pension companies to decide which customers to target.

Income Although linked to some extent to the 'social classes' described above, income groups can be different. For example, a self-employed skilled manual worker, such as an electrician, may receive the same income as a middle manager. Similarly, a self-employed builder may receive the same income as or more than a professional. However, because of his or her occupation the two people will be in different social classes.

The population can be split up into income groups and targeted accordingly. So a Cartier watch, for example, is likely to be marketed at the highest income groups.

Religion Businesses may divide markets by religious groups. Food producers, for example, may specialise in producing Kosher food for Jewish people. Digital television has seen the growth of American style Christian television channels in the UK.

Ethnic grouping Markets can sometimes be segmented by country of origin or ethnic grouping. Radio stations have been geared towards African-Caribbean groups. Some products, such as clothing or hair accessories, are also geared towards this grouping.

A drawback of demographic segmentation is that consumers try to defy consumption patterns associated with their demographic groups. For example, young people from lower income groups may seek out expensive high status products, such as certain brands of designer clothes, that were initially marketed at high income groups.

Psychographic segmentation

Geographic and demographic segmentation have limitations. For example, there is a wide variety of spending patterns among females aged 16-18 living in Manchester. Yet people in this consumer group share the same gender, age and location. An alternative way of grouping customers is through psychographic segmentation. This groups customers according to their attitudes, opinions and lifestyles.
- Sports products may be aimed at those who are interested in 'extreme' sports such as skiboarding.
- Chocolate manufacturers have identified two categories of

chocolate eaters. 'Depressive' chocolate lovers eat chocolate to unwind predominantly during the evening. 'Energetic' chocolate eaters eat chocolate as a fast food and live life at a fast pace.
- People's attitudes to life may also be used to segment the market. Some pension funds are geared towards those who only want investments in 'ethical' businesses.
- Clothes may be geared at those who are interested in 'retro' fashions from earlier decades.
- Mobile phones provide services such as Internet access for business travellers.
- Travel companies target holidays at families with younger children.
- Certain newspapers are geared towards Labour voters, while others are geared towards Conservative voters.

One of the drawbacks of psychographic segmentation is that it can be difficult for businesses to collect data about the beliefs, attitudes and lifestyles of consumers. In order to do this they may require the help of specialist businesses.

Behavioural segmentation

Behavioural segmentation attempts to segment markets according to how consumers relate to a product. There is a number of different methods of behavioural segmentation:

Usage rate This is when consumers are categorised according to the quantity and frequency of their purchases. One example of this is British Airways, which established an 'Executive Club' to encourage and develop the custom of regular business travellers.

Loyalty Consumers can be categorized according to their product loyalty. The Tesco Clubcard, for example, which offers discounts to regular customers of Tesco supermarkets seeks to reward and encourage loyalty to Tesco and its products.

Time and date of consumption Consumers often consume particular products at particular times and dates. Businesses can take advantage of this in order to improve their marketing. So, for example, manufacturers of breakfast cereals, while recognising that their product will be primarily consumed in the morning, encourage consumers also to consume their products in the evening. Similarly, many bars and clubs seek to encourage different groups of consumers according to the night of the week. For example, Thursday nights are often for older singles and Friday nights for younger consumers in many such establishments.

Like other segmentation methods, a drawback of behavioural segmentation is that on its own it may fail to adequately capture a target market for a business. For this reason, in many cases a business might employ a **variety** of the segmentation methods explained above. So, for example, a manufacturer of luxury apartments may be interested in segments that included single men or women with no children, in the 30-40 age range, with high incomes that fall into social class AB. Because of the likely one-off nature of such a purchase, behavioural segmentation would be less important in this instance.

KEYTERMS

Demography – the study of population, its composition and how it is changing over time.
Market segment – part of a whole segment which contains a group of buyers with similar characteristics, such as age, income, social class or attitudes.
Market segmentation – breaking down a market into sub-groups which share similar characteristics.

KNOWLEDGE

1. How can a market be segmented geographically?
2. Explain three ways in which the spending patterns of females aged 25-35 with children who are in paid employment might differ from those of males aged 55-65 who have taken early retirement and whose children have left home.
3. (a) What is meant by 'social class'?
   (b) Give two ways in which the spending of social class A households might differ from that of social class D.
4. How might understanding the personalities of different groups of consumers help in the marketing of a product?
5. Briefly explain five ways in which consumers might be segmented on a behavioural basis.

Case Study: The power of the Muslim pound

Marian Salzman is one of the world's foremost trend-spotters. She can see something coming before others have even raised their heads to look and the next big thing in marketing she argues is the 'Muslim pound'. According to Mintel, a market research company, the estimated spending power of Muslim people in the UK is £20.5 billion. There are more than 5,000 Muslim millionaires in the UK, with combined assets worth more than £3.6 billion.

'It's a unique market with a unique set of needs, for example in the banking area,' says Salzman, the executive vice president and chief marketing officer of consultancy JWT. 'Under sharia law (which governs how Muslims can borrow money), different kinds of mortgages need to be written in order for someone who is Muslim to acquire a home. And there's halal law (which is concerned with the way in which animal are slaughtered) which affects consumption of food, beauty and healthcare products.'

This trend may provide demographic segmentation opportunities for business. There has been a huge surge in marketing to Muslims this year, according to Salzman. 'I think it is a recognition of the size of the market,' she says. 'Another thing I believe has been driving it is all the coverage of whether Turkey will be part of the EU, which has also raised the visibility of the question about the sheer percentage of the European population that is Muslim.' Muslims are also more sensitive about the moral attributes of brands and the way in which they are marketed according to research. Fifty-nine per cent agreed that there was too much suggestiveness or immodesty in most advertising compared to 28 per cent of the general sample.

Their buying behaviour is also heavily influenced by expert endorsement and opinion. In the survey, almost two-thirds agreed with the statement, 'I feel reassured if a product has been endorsed by an expert' – almost twice as many as the general sample. Muslims also have a higher level of trust in expert opinions and reviews than non-Muslims: 75 per cent compared to 56 per cent.

Source: adapted from *The Independent*, 9.7. 2007.

(a) What is meant by (i) market segmentation (3 marks) and (ii) demographic segmentation in the article? (3 marks)
(b) Explain why a small business offering financial services might benefit from market segmentation. (8 marks)
(c) Examine how targeting Muslim customers might affect a business marketing financial services. (6 marks)
(d) Discuss the extent to which selling to one market segment, such as people of a particular religion, is likely to be a successful marketing strategy for a small business offering financial services. (10 marks)

Market size

The size of a market can be estimated or calculated by the total sales of all businesses in the market. Market size is usually estimated in a number of ways.

Value This is the total amount spent by customers buying products. For example, it was estimated that fast food products in the UK accounted for sales worth £8.38 billion in 2004. This included branded fast food chains and independent outlets selling hot or cold eat-in food without table service, or takeaway food.

Volume This is the physical quantity of products which are produced and sold. For example, global crude steel production was over 1.1 billion tonnes in 2005, the highest ever. The UK produced around 12 million tonnes. Some estimates of volume are based on the number or percentage of users, subscribers or viewers. This is often the case in markets for services, such as the number of mobile phone users, the number of television viewers or the percentage of households with digital television.

Different markets are likely to differ in size. For example, sales of chilled desserts like cream cakes, cheesecakes and trifles were £390 million in 2006. On the other hand over £1.9 billion was spent by British consumers on increasingly popular holiday cruises.

Market growth

Markets can grow either rapidly or slowly, or they might contract and get smaller. Take the example of the market for sandwiches in the UK. Between 2002 and 2006 average year on year growth in sandwich sales was 3.5 per cent, but from 2006-2007 growth was 9 per cent, almost three times that of previous years. Similarly, the value of the UK budget hotel market increased by 38 per cent between 2002 and 2006, to reach £1 billion. This growth was three times that of the overall UK hotel market (worth £11.2 billion), which increased by just 12 per cent over the same four year period. On the other hand the market for sales of ties fell from £158 million in 1999 to just £154 million by 2004. It was suggested that the fall was due to the growing trend amongst men for dressing down at work.

What factors are likely to influence whether a market gets bigger or becomes smaller and the rate of growth or decline?

- **Economic changes.** An increase in income, for example, can affect different markets. Rising incomes might help the growth of the market for high class restaurants or specialist furniture makers.
- **Social changes.** Changes in society can lead to a growth or a decline in markets. The decline in the number of marriages, an increase in the proportion of working

Question 1.

Ormskirk is a town in Lancashire. It has a market on Thursdays and Saturdays every week which attracts customers from both the town and local counties. Traditionally it has had local teashops and a few restaurants. But over the period 2000-2007 the market for shops providing food has increased. There are now retailers selling ready made sandwiches and meals. There are takeaways. There are Chinese, Indian, Italian, French and Tapas restaurants. There are wine bars selling food in the daytime as well as the traditional teashops. There are regular rail and bus Links to Liverpool and Preston. In 2005 after 120 years of providing education, Edge Hill was granted university status. In 2007, the university had 17,000 students. It planned to spend £220 million from its own coffers to provide extra student accommodation, new teaching buildings and facilities. A study to assess its impact on the area found that it contributed £77 million a year to the North West of England's economy. This figure was predicted to rise to £172 million by 2022. The study also showed that the number of jobs supported by the university is anticipated to rise from its current level of 2,650 to 4,850. In 2007 a planned bypass was being proposed, linking the M58 to the Ormskirk to Southport main road.

Source: adapted in part from http://info.edgehill.ac.uk, http://news.bbc.co.uk.

(a) Suggest factors that might affect the size and growth of the market in which an Ormskirk restaurant operates.

(b) Discuss whether this market will grow in future.

Question 2.

Commercial radio stations have found it difficult to match the listener numbers of BBC. In 2007 the BBC attracted 54.5 per cent of listening, up 0.3 percentage points on 2006 Commercial radio was 0.3 percentage points down to 43.3 per cent. Radio 1 gained listeners, partly due to the stability of the weekday DJ line-up and the extension of Chris Moyles' breakfast show to start half an hour earlier at 6.30a.m. Radio 2's audience was up by a quarter of a million people and market share was up from 15.5 per rcent to 15.8 per cent, attracted by long-standing, popular programmes such as Terry Wogan's breakfast show.

Johnny Vaughan, at Capital Radio, made a strong gain in number of listeners, adding 246,000 with market share holding steady. The worry for Capital is that its new listeners can easily change to other stations. Capital must build on its gains if the station is to catch up with Heart and Magic. Both have opened up and sustained a sizeable lead in London. Radio 1 and Radio 2 have also both increased their listener base in the capital in the past 12 months.

The decline in total listening to local commercial stations has been the trend for two years. This continues, with a drop in the past year from 32.6 per cent to 31.7 per cent of total listening. Stations such as Radio City in Liverpool, Clyde 2 in Glasgow and Smooth Radio in North-West England were among those to lose audience. But not all stations lost out. Choice FM in London gained 111,000 new listeners, taking the station to a new record of 611,000 listeners. Xfm Manchester increased its weekly audience by 33 per cent, lifting its market share by a third.

Source: adapted from the *Guardian*, 29.10.2007.

(a) Outline the changes in the share of the market of (i) Radio 2, (ii) national commercial and non-commercial radio stations and (iii) local commercial radio stations.

(b) Explain two factors that may influence the share of the market of radio stations.

women and the growth in the number of one parent families is linked to a growth in the market for child care and other child support services, and for housing.

- **Technological changes.** Changes in technology can cause a rapid growth in certain markets and a decline in others. The DVD market has expanded rapidly in recent years at the expense of the video market. The growth in iPods and other MP3 players and the downloading of music from the Internet are associated with a decline in CD sales.

- **Demographic changes.** Changes in the age structure of the population can affect markets. The ageing of the UK population has led to a growth in products aimed at people aged over 50, such as specialist holidays, mobility aids and insurance products.

- **Changes in legislation.** Changes in the law governing the use of radio frequencies has enabled a large growth in the number of commercial radio stations.

Market share

MARKET SHARE or MARKET PENETRATION is the term used to describe the proportion of a particular market that is held by a business, a product, a brand or a number of businesses or products. Market share is shown as a percentage. The market share of a business can be calculated as:

$$\frac{\text{Sales of a business}}{\text{Total sales in the market}} \times 100\%$$

Why might the measurement of market share be important? It might indicate a business that is a market leader. This could influence other companies to follow the leader or influence the leader to maintain its position. It might influence the **strategy** or **objectives** of a business. A business that has a small market share may set a target of increasing its share by 5 per cent over a period of time. It may also be an indication of the success or failure of a business or its strategy.

Figure 1 shows the market shares of supermarkets in the UK in June 2007. It shows, for example, that the market leader was Tesco and that three quarters of the market sales were accounted for by the 'big five' supermarket chains. However, care must be taken when interpreting the market share of businesses.

- The share of the market can be measured in different ways. Market share is calculated as the sales of a business as a percentage of total market sales. Sales can be calculated in a number of ways. They might be the value of sales, such as £100 million a year. Or they might be calculated by the number or volume of sales, for example, 6 million products sold each year or 10 million visitors to attractions owned by a theme park company.

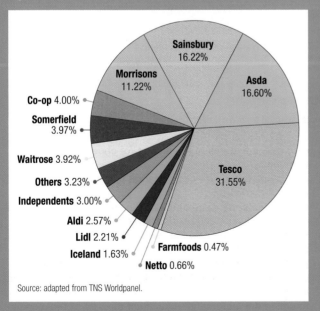

Figure 1: UK market share, supermarkets, %, 17 June 2007

Sainsbury 16.22%
Morrisons 11.22%
Asda 16.60%
Co-op 4.00%
Somerfield 3.97%
Waitrose 3.92%
Others 3.23%
Tesco 31.55%
Independents 3.00%
Aldi 2.57%
Lidl 2.21%
Farmfoods 0.47%
Iceland 1.63%
Netto 0.66%

Source: adapted from TNS Worldpanel.

- The market and the time period chosen can affect the results. For example, in 2004 Safeway was taken over by Morrisons. This significantly increased Morrison's market share from below 10% to over 11% as shown in Figure 1.
- The type of product and business included might also affect the results. For example, in 2007 it was reported that Scottish and Newcastle plc had 26 per cent of the beer market. However, in the UK drinks market, beer made up only 35 per cent of drinks spending. So the market share of the UK drinks market of Scottish and Newcastle plc would be less than 26 per cent because the drinks market would include the sales of other drinks manufacturers such as Coca-Cola (carbonated soft drinks) and Tetley GB Ltd (tea).

KEYTERMS

Market share or market penetration – the proportion of total sales in a particular market for which one or more businesses or brands are responsible. It is expressed as a percentage and can be calculated by value or volume.

KNOWLEDGE

1. Explain two ways in which the size of a market can be calculated.
2. What is meant by a market that is (a) growing and (b) declining?
3. Give four factors that might influence market growth.
4. What is the formula used to calculate market share?
5. Give three examples of the problems of measuring market share.

Case Study: British cheese

When it comes to cheese, continental varieties such as Brie and Emmental were once the height of sophistication. Research from Mintel has found that cheese buyers are increasingly opting for British regional cheeses, such as Lancashire, Cheshire and Red Leicester. Sales of specialist British cheese increased by as much as 16 per cent between 2004 and 2006, to reach £220 million. Growth has outpaced the likes of soft and continental cheese.

'With growing interest in environmental and ethical concerns we are becoming increasingly interested in the origin of our food. As a result we are seeing a growing trend towards "buying British", which has provided a huge boost for sales of British regional cheese,' comments David Bird, Senior Consumer Analyst. 'Many varieties of regional British cheese have extended their ranges by adding fruits, liqueurs and even curry. This has really caught the imagination of cheese customers and has lead to the rise in sales of locally produced cheese,' he adds.

Although sales by volume of continental cheese have continued to rise, the value of sales has not. Market value fell 7 per cent between 2004 and 2006 to £340 million. 'Continental cheese such as Brie used to be seen as a luxury for special occasions. But today many continental varieties are now more an everyday staple than an occasional treat. This has inevitably brought prices down and as a result market value has declined, despite rising volume sales,' explains David Bird.

Specialist British regional cheese has seen the greatest growth. But cheddars, which are not classified as specialist cheeses, from the UK and abroad accounted for over half (52 per cent) of all cheese sales in the UK last year, having grown 7 per cent between 2004 and 2006 to reach £985 million. What is more, this year sales of the humble block of cheddar will hit the £1 billion mark for the first time ever. 'Cheddars have clearly stood the test of time and are now still very much a British staple. The market has done well to see growth despite heavy

discounting and many buy-one-get-one-free offers in the supermarkets,' comments David Bird.

The British cheese market was worth £1.9 billion in 2006, having increased 4 per cent between 2004 and 2006. Sales are set to rise to £1.93 billion this year. This is no mean feat considering the trend towards healthy eating.

Source: adapted from www.mintel.com.

(a) Outline the features of the market for cheeses in the UK. (4 marks)
(b) (i) Calculate the size of the market for British cheese in 2004. (4 marks)
    (ii) Calculate the value of the decline in sales of continental cheeses between 2004 and 2006. (4 marks)
(c) How would you explain the increase in sales volume of specialist and regional British cheeses? (8 marks)
(d) How would you explain why the value of the sales of continental cheeses has fallen while the volume of sales has increased over the period 2004-2006? (8 marks)
(e) Examine the factors that may affect the size of the market for Cheddar cheeses in the UK in future. (8 marks)

What is a business organisation?

Businesses are often referred to as organisations. An ORGANISATION is a body that is set up to meet needs. For example, the St. John's Ambulance organisation was originally set up by volunteers to train the public in life saving measures.

Business organisations satisfy needs by providing people with goods and services. All organisations will:

* try to achieve objectives;
* use resources;
* need to be directed;
* have to be accountable;
* have to meet legal requirements;
* have a formal structure.

Private sector business organisations

One method of classifying businesses is by **sector**. The PRIVATE SECTOR includes all those businesses which are set up by individuals or groups of individuals. Most business activity is undertaken in the private sector. The types of business in the private sector can vary considerably. Some are small retailers with a single owner. Others are large multinational companies such as Cadbury Schweppes. Businesses will vary according to the legal form they take and their ownership.

* **Unincorporated businesses.** These are businesses where there is no legal difference between the owners and the business. Everything is carried out in the name of the owner or owners. These firms tend to be small, owned by either one person or a few partners.
* **Incorporated businesses.** An incorporated body is one which has a separate legal identity from its owners. In other words, the business can be sued, can be taken over

and can be liquidated.

Figure 1 shows the different types of business organisation in the private sector, their legal status and their ownership. These are examined in the rest of this unit.

Sole traders

The simplest and most common form of private sector business is a SOLE TRADER or SOLE PROPRIETOR. This type of business is owned by just one person. The owner runs the business and may employ any number of people to help.

Sole traders can be found in different types of production. In the primary sector many farmers and fishermen operate like this. In the secondary sector there are small scale manufacturers, builders and construction firms. The tertiary sector has large numbers of sole traders. They supply a wide range of services, such as hairdressing, retailing, restaurants, gardening and other household services. Many sole traders exist in retailing and construction, where a very large number of shops and small construction companies are each owned by one person. Although there are many more sole traders than any other type of business, the amount they contribute to total output in the UK is relatively small.

Setting up as a sole trader is straightforward. There are no legal formalities needed.

However, sole traders or self-employed entrepreneurs do have some legal responsibilities once they become established. In addition, some types of business need to obtain special permission before trading.

* Once turnover reaches a certain level sole traders must register for VAT.
* They must pay income tax and National Insurance contributions.

Figure 1: Business organisations in the private sector

Private sector business organisations

Unincorporated businesses → Sole trader. (One owner) / Partnership. (Owned by partners)

Incorporated businesses → Private limited company. (Owned by a few shareholders) / Public limited company. (Owned by many shareholders)

Question 1.

Joanna Carter owns Joanna Carter Contemporary Flowers in Wallingford. She attracts customers in three areas - weddings, corporate work for local business and flowers for private homes. Despite only setting up in July last year, demand has soared thanks to Joanna's growing reputation for creative arrangements. She set up as a sole trader after leaving her job to raise a family. 'After leaving my personnel job to have my children, now aged nine and six, I had time to think about where I really wanted to go in my career. I was keen to develop my passion for flowers with proper training and so I took a two-year part-time course at Abingdon and Witney College'. She also gained work experience working one day a week in a florists' shop in Wallingford. When she graduated, she had already received a number of offers from people wanting her to do private arrangements for them. So she left the shop to run her own business from home.

Joanna approached the local Business Link, a free and impartial guide to business advice, resources and information shortly after setting up the business. 'I've been able to book a place on an advanced bridal skills course with highly respected London florist Jane Packer in May. The course costs £900 and half of the cost will be paid for through the Skills Development Team at Business Link. I am also looking into a broadband grant so I can provide a slide show of my work for potential corporate customers and wedding bookings.   I'm in the process of applying for an Enterprising Woman grant run by Surrey University which will give me £350-worth of funding'.

Source: adapted from www.businesslink.gov.uk.

(a)   As a sole trader Joanna Carter has unlimited liability. What does this mean?

(b)   Explain two advantages to Joanna Carter of operating as a sole trader.

(c)   How did Business Link help Joanna Carter in running her small business?

- Some types of business activity need a licence, such as the sale of alcohol or supplying a taxi service or public transport.
- Sometimes planning permission is needed in certain locations. For example, a person may have to apply to the local authority for planning permission to run a fish and chip shop in premises which had not been used for this activity before.
- Sole traders must comply with legislation aimed at business practice. For example, legally they must provide healthy and safe working conditions for their employees.

Advantages of sole traders

Sole traders have a number of advantages.
- The lack of legal restrictions. The sole trader will not face a lengthy setting up period or incur expensive administration costs.
- Sole proprietorships can be set up with little or no money in the business. They don't cost anything to set up. So the capital cost of creating a sole proprietorship can be minimal.
- Any profit made after tax is kept by the owner.

- The owner is in complete control and is free to make decisions without interference. For many sole traders independence is one of the main reasons why they choose to set up in business.
- The owner has flexibility to choose the hours of work he or she wants and to take holidays. Customers may also benefit. Sole traders can take individual customers' needs into account, stocking a particular brand of a good or making changes to a standard design, for example.
- Because of their small size, sole traders can offer a personal service to their customers. Some people prefer to deal directly with the owner and are prepared to pay a higher price for doing so.
- Such businesses may be entitled to government support.

Disadvantages of sole traders

However, there are also disadvantages of sole traders.
- Sole traders have UNLIMITED LIABILITY. This means that if the business has debts, the owner is personally liable. A sole trader may be forced to sell personal possessions or use personal savings to meet these debts.
- Sole proprietorships can be risky for their owners. If the business is unsuccessful, sole traders can end up working for nothing or even subsidising the business out of their own private resources. Also, because the business is the sole trader, long term illness can have a devastating effect on it. Becoming an employee is less risky and is one reason why workers may not want to work for themselves.
- Sole proprietorships face continuity problems. Will the business survive if the sole trader dies, takes retirement or decides to do something different? Some sole traders run family businesses where parents tend to pass on their business to their children. Farming is an example. However, many sole traders will not pass their businesses on to family members. So these businesses will disappear.
- The money used to set up the business is often the owner's savings. It may also come from a bank loan. Sole traders may find it difficult to raise money. They tend to be small and lack sufficient **collateral**, such as property or land, on which to raise finance. This means money for expansion must come from profits or savings.
- Independence is an advantage, but it can also be a disadvantage. A sole trader might prefer to share decision making, for example. Many sole traders work very long hours, without holidays, and may have to learn new skills.
- In cases where the owner is the only person in the business, illness can stop business activity taking place. For example, if a sole trader is a mobile hairdresser, illness will lead to a loss of income in the short term, and even a loss of customers in the long term.
- Because sole traders are unincorporated businesses, the owner can be sued by customers in the event of a dispute.
- Large businesses can employ specialist workers. A sole trader often has to be purchaser, driver, accountant, lawyer and

labourer to run the business. Allowing workers to specialise can lead to lower costs of production per unit. So sole traders can be at a disadvantage competitively which they are forced to make up for by paying themselves lower wages.

- Sole proprietorships are usually small businesses. So they are unable to gain reductions in unit costs of production as the volume of output rises, known as **economies of scale**. Sole traders tend to be concentrated in industries such as farming, where economies of scale are limited.

Partnerships

A PARTNERSHIP is defined in **The Partnership Act, 1890** as the 'relation which subsists between persons carrying on business with common view to profit'. Put simply, a partnership has more than one owner. The 'joint' owners will share responsibility for running the business and also share the profits. Partnerships are often found in professions such as accountants, doctors, estate agents, solicitors and veterinary surgeons. After sole traders, partnerships are the most common type of business organisation. It is usual for partners to specialise. A firm of chartered accountants with five partners might be organised so that each partner specialises in one aspect of finance, such as tax

Question 2.

Sarah Otaka, Gillian Peters and Maria Ampat run a dental practice in Scunthorpe. They operate as a partnership. They undertake work for the NHS, but an increasing amount of their income comes from private work. The partnership was established in 2003. The three dentists each contributed £20,000 to provide start-up capital. A further £20,000 was borrowed from a bank. The money was used to convert a property into dental surgeries and buy equipment. The business employs four other staff – three dental assistants and a receptionist.

   After three successful years in business together a problem arose. Gillian wanted to attract more private clients, particularly those requiring cosmetic work which is usually very lucrative. Sarah and Maria were more committed to NHS work. They were not in it just for the money. After a period of disagreement, where communications deteriorated, a partners' meeting was held to find a solution. Gillian, however, felt that the only way forward was for her to break away from the partnership.

(a) At the end of the third year a profit of £180,000 was made by the practice. How much is each partner likely to get if there is no deed of partnership?

(b) Explain two advantages to the dentists of operating as a partnership.

(c) How does this case illustrate one of the main disadvantages of partnerships?

law, investments or VAT returns.

There are no legal formalities to complete when a partnership is formed. However, partners may draw up a DEED OF PARTNERSHIP. This is a legal document which states partners' rights in the event of a dispute. It covers issues such as:

- how much capital each partner will contribute;
- how profits (and losses) will be shared amongst the partners;
- the procedure for ending the partnership;
- how much control each partner has;
- rules for taking on new partners.

If no deed of partnership is drawn up the arrangements between partners will be subject to the Partnership Act. For example, if there is a dispute regarding the share of profits, the Act states that profits are shared equally among the partners.

Advantages of partnerships

Partnerships have a number of advantages.

- There are no legal formalities to complete when setting up the business.
- Like a sole proprietorship, an ordinary partnership does not need to publish any accounts which may be seen by the public. Only the tax authorities must have access to the accounts of a partnership. In contrast, the accounts of a company are available to anyone who asks to see them via Companies House. The accounts of a limited liability partnership are open to inspection by the public, but in a less detailed format than those of a company.
- Each partner can specialise. This may improve the running of the business, as partners can carry out the tasks they do best.
- Since there is more than one owner, more finance can be raised than if the firm was a sole trader.
- Partners can share the work. They will be able to cover each other for holidays and illness. They can exchange ideas when making key decisions. Also, the success of the business will not depend upon the ability of one person, as is the case with a sole trader.
- Since this type of business tends to be larger than the sole trader, it is in a stronger position to raise more money from outside the business.

Disadvantages of partnerships

- The individual partners have unlimited liability. Under the Partnership Act, each partner is equally liable for debts.
- Profits have to be shared among more owners.
- Partners may disagree. For example, they might differ in their views on whether to hire a new employee or about the amount of profit to retain for investment.
- The size of a partnership is limited to a maximum of 20 partners. This limits the amount of money that can be introduced from owners.
- The partnership ends when one of the partners dies.
- The partnership must be wound up so that the partner's family can retrieve money invested in the business. It is

normal for the remaining partners to form a new partnership quickly afterwards.

- Any decision made by one partner on behalf of the company is legally binding on all other partners. For example, if one partner agreed to buy four new company cars for the business, all partners must honour this.
- Partnerships have unincorporated status, so partners can be sued by customers.

Limited partnerships

The Limited Partnerships Act 1907 allows a business to become a LIMITED PARTNERSHIP, although this is rare. This is where some partners provide capital but take no part in the management of the business. Such a partner will have LIMITED LIABILITY - the partner can only lose the original amount of money invested. A partner with limited liabillity cannot be made to sell personal possessions to meet any other business debts. This type of partner is called a **sleeping partner**. Even with a

limited partnership there must always be at least one partner with **unlimited liability**. The Act also allows this type of partnership to have more than 20 partners.

The Limited Liability Partnership Act, 2000 allows the setting up of a LIMITED LIABILITY PARTNERSHIP. All partners in this type of partnership have limited liability. To set up as a limited liability partnership, the business has to agree to comply with a number of regulations, such as filing annual reports with the Registrar of Companies.

KNOWLEDGE

1. What is the difference between a corporate body and an unincorporated body?
2. State three advantages and three disadvantages of being a sole trader.
3. What is the advantage of a deed of partnership?
4. State three advantages and three disadvantages of partnerships.
5. What is meant by a sleeping partner?

KEYTERMS

Deed of Partnership – a binding legal document which states the formal rights of partners.
Limited liability – where a business owner is only liable for the original amount of money invested in the business.
Limited Liability partnership – a partnership where all partners have limited liability.
Limited partnership – a partnership where some members contribute capital and enjoy a share of profit, but do not participate in the running of the business. At least one partner must have unlimited liability.
Organisation – a body set up to meet a need.
Partnership – a business organisation which is usually owned by between 2-20 people.
Private sector – businesses that are owned by individuals or groups of individuals.
Sole trader or sole proprietor – a business organisation which has a single owner.
Unlimited liability - where the owner of a business is personally liable for all business debts.

Case Study: Oxford Vintage cars

Hristo Petrov runs a small business buying and selling vintage cars. He buys cars at auctions and from dealers and currently sells them on Ebay. At the moment Hristo does not undertake any renovation work on the cars. He just buys them and sells them on. Last year he made a profit of £37,000. However, Hristo is ambitious.and wants to set up his own website and operate from a car showroom in Oxford. A lot of the cars he sells are MGBs and MGAs. These cars were originally made in Oxford and Hristo likes the idea of locating a showroom in their home city. He also wants to employ a team of mechanics to renovate them. He knows that premium prices are paid for well restored vintage cars.

Unfortunately Hristo can only raise £50,000 of the £100,000 needed to develop the business. He has approached several banks but has not been able to secure funding as he has a poor credit rating after having his house repossessed. A friend of his, however, is keen to get involved in the business. Mark Watkins bought a car from Hristo three years ago and the two have remained in touch ever since. Mark is happy to provide the other £50,000 if he can become an equal partner.

Hristo has eventually accepted Mark's offer and the new showroom is due to open very shortly. The partnership, called Oxford Vintage Cars,

has a smart website which contains details of all the cars in stock and other useful information for enthusiasts.

After a deed of partnership was drawn up Hristo said 'At first I did not want to go into partnership, but now I think it will work. Mark is as committed as me and has come up with some good ideas. For example, he reckons we can rent out some of the cars in stock for special occasions such as weddings. I hadn't even though of that. He will also be good on the restoration side and he will be able to supervise the mechanics more effectively than me. I will concentrate on the buying and selling, that's what I'm good at'.

(a) Using this case as an example, explain what is meant by a partnership. (4 marks)
(b) Oxford Vintage Cars is an unincorporated business. What does this mean? (6 marks)
(c) How does this case highlight one of the problems of operating as a sole trader? (6 marks)
(d) Why do you think Hristo did not want to enter a business partnership? (8 marks)
(e) To what extent will the partners be able to specialise in the business? (12 marks)

Companies

There are many examples of LIMITED COMPANIES in the UK. They range from Garrick Engineering, a small family business, to British Airways which has many thousands of shareholders. One feature is that they all have a separate legal identity from their owners. This means that they can own assets, form contracts, employ people, sue and be sued in their own right. Another feature is that the owners all have **limited liability**. If a limited company has debts, the owners can only lose the money they have invested in the firm. They cannot be forced to use their own money, like sole traders and partners, to pay business debts.

The **capital** of a limited company is divided into **shares**. Each member or **shareholder** owns a number of these shares. They are the joint owners of the company and can vote and take a share of the profit. Those with more shares will have more control and can take more profit.

Limited companies are run by **directors** who are appointed by the shareholders. The board of directors, headed by a **chairperson**, is accountable to shareholders and should run the company as the shareholders wish. If the company's performance does not live up to shareholders' expectations, directors can be 'voted out' at an **Annual General Meeting** (AGM).

Whereas sole traders and partnerships pay income tax on profits, companies pay corporation tax.

Forming a limited company

How do shareholders set up a limited company? Limited companies must submit some important information to the Registrar of Companies.

Memorandum of Association The Memorandum sets out the constitution and gives details about the company. The Companies Act 1985 states that the following details must be included.
*   The name of the company.
*   The name and address of the company's registered office.
*   The objectives of the company, and the scope of its activities.
*   The liability of its members.
*   The amount of capital to be raised and the number of shares to be issued.

A limited company must have a minimum of two members, but there is no upper limit.

Articles of Association The Articles of Association deal with the internal running of the company. They include details such as:
*   the rights of shareholders depending on the type of share they hold;

*   the procedures for appointing directors and the scope of their powers;
*   the length of time directors should serve before re-election;
*   the timing and frequency of company meetings;
*   the arrangements for auditing company accounts.

Form 10 This form gives details of the first directors, secretary and the address of the registered office. Directors must give their names and addresses, dates of birth, occupations and details of other directorships they have held within the last five years.

Form 12 This form is a statutory declaration of compliance with all the legal requirements relating to the incorporation of the company. It must be signed by a solicitor who is forming the company, a director or the company secretary.

These documents will be sent to the **Registrar** at **Companies House**. If they are acceptable, the company's application will be successful. It will be awarded a **Certificate of Incorporation** which allows it to trade. The Registrar keeps these documents on file and they can be inspected at any time by the general public for a fee. A limited company must also submit a copy of its **Annual Report and Accounts** to the Registrar each year. The accounts will include information such as the balance sheet and income statement or profit and loss accounts of the business. Finally, the shareholders have a legal right to attend the AGM and should be told of the date and venue in writing well in advance.

Question 1.

MD Chris Lay re-mortgaged his house to launch Gigasat Limited in 2000. The business was incorporated on 16.10.2000 and the registered address is 12 Rylands Mews, Lake Street, Leighton Buzzard, Bedfordshire. The company's registration number is 04090608. The company develops satellite communications equipment, such as lightweight, carbon-fibre antennas, and vehicles installed with satellite systems. Clients include the news channels CNN and Al Jazeera. They use Gigasat technology for live television coverage. The equipment has also been adopted by the government and the military for secure satellite transmissions. For example, its equipment allows troops posted abroad to access the Internet and talk to loved ones. Sales have grown 67 per cent a year from £2 million in 2003 to £5.7 million in 2005.

Source: adapted from Tech Track 100 and information from Companies House.

(a)   What evidence is there in the case to suggest that Gigasat is a private limited company?
(b)   What legal obligations will Gigasat Limited have to: (i) shareholders and (ii) the Registrar of Companies each year?
(c)   Discuss two advantages to the owners of Gigasat Limited of operating as a private limited company.

Private limited companies

Private limited companies are one type of limited company. They tend to be relatively smaller businesses, although certain well known companies, such as Reebok and Littlewoods, are private limited companies. Their business name ends in **Limited** or **Ltd**. Shares can only be transferred 'privately' and all shareholders must agree on the transfer. They cannot be advertised for general sale. Private limited companies are often family businesses owned by members of the family or close friends. The directors of these firms tend to be shareholders and are involved in the running of the business. Many manufacturing firms are private limited companies rather than sole traders or partnerships.

Advantages of private limited companies

There are certain advantages in setting up a business as a private limited company.

- Shareholders have limited liability. As a result more people are prepared to risk their money than in, say, a partnership.
- More capital can be raised as there is no limit on the number of shareholders.
- Control of the company cannot be lost to outsiders. Shares can only be sold to new members if all shareholders agree.
- The business will continue even if one of the owners dies. In this case shares will be transferred to another owner.
- There may be tax advantages for the owners, particularly if owners are currently paying the higher rate of income tax. Profits can be retained by the company and distributed to the owners at a later date, for example when they retire.
- Some businesses may not deal with unlimited businesses or businesses that are not registered for VAT. This is because they think that limited companies registered for VAT are more likely to be run well, since, they have to keep proper accounts and tend to use the professional advice of accountants and solicitors.

Disadvantages of private limited companies

There are some disadvantages in setting up a business as a private limited company.

- Profits have to be shared out among a much larger number of members.
- There is a legal procedure in setting up the business. This takes time and also costs money.
- Firms are not allowed to sell shares to the public. This restricts the amount of capital that can be raised.
- Financial information filed with the Registrar can be inspected by any member of the public. Competitors could use this to their advantage.
- If one shareholder decides to sell shares it may take time to find a buyer.

Public limited companies

The second type of limited company tends to be larger and is

Question 2.

Burton's Foods, famous for its Wagon Wheels and Jammie Dogders biscuits, was bought by the private equity company, Duke Street Capital in 2007. Burton's, the UK's second largest biscuit producer, employs 3,000 people on five sites in the UK. Founded in the 1930s it became part of Associated British Foods in 1949 before being sold to Hicks, Muse, Tate & Furst seven years ago. The deal was said to be worth around £200 million. However, just two months later the new owners announced that biscuit production would cease at its factory in the Wirral, with the loss of 660 jobs. The announcement of the job cuts sparked an angry reaction from unions.

Tony Woodley, joint general secretary of the newly-created Unite union, said: 'We are not going to just roll over and accept this. We will be urgently consulting with our members about a strategy to keep the factory open and will meet management on Monday to hear their rationale for this body-blow to Merseyside manufacturing'.

The factory in Moreton is the biggest employer in the Wirral after Vauxhall cars. Mr Woodley said the job losses would 'devastate the community'. The company is to stop making biscuits, at the site but will continue to manufacture chocolate and assemble seasonal assortments at the factory. It is thought 330 jobs will remain on the site. Paul Kitchener, chief executive of Burton's Foods, said that while the company 'sincerely' regretted the loss of jobs, the changes were needed because of overcapacity in the biscuit market.

Source: adapted from *The Guardian*, 19.3.2007.

(a) **Using this case as an example, explain what is meant by a private equity company.**
(b) **What evidence is there in the case to suggest that the private equity company is pursuing ruthless efficiency gains?**

called a **public limited company**. This company name ends in plc. There were around 1.85 million registered limited companies in the UK in 2006. Only around 1 per cent were public limited companies. However, they contributed far more to national output and employed far more people than private limited companies. The shares of these companies can be bought and sold by the public on the stock exchange.

When 'going public' a company is likely to publish a **Prospectus**. This is a document which advertises the company to potential investors and invites them to buy shares before a FLOTATION. An example of a company floated on the stock exchange in 2006 is Styles & Wood. It supplies property services to retailers such as Waitrose and B&Q. 'Going public' can be expensive because:

- the company needs lawyers to ensure that the prospectus is 'legally' correct;
- a large number of 'glossy' publications have to be made available;
- the company may use a financial institution to process share applications;
- the share issue has to be underwritten (which means that the company must insure against the possibility of some shares remaining unsold) and a fee is paid to an underwriter who must buy any unsold shares;
- the company will have advertising and administrative expenses;
- it must have a minimum of £50,000 share capital.

A public limited company cannot begin trading until it has completed these tasks and has received at least a 25 per cent payment for the value of shares. It will then receive a **trading certificate** and can begin operating, and the shares will be quoted on the **Stock Exchange** or the **Alternative Investment Market** (AIM).

A stock exchange is a market where second hand shares are bought and sold. A full stock exchange listing means that the company must comply with the rules and regulations laid down by the stock exchange. Many of these rules are to protect shareholders from fraud. The AIM is designed for companies which want to avoid some of the high costs of a full listing. However, shareholders with shares quoted on the AIM do not have the same protection as those with 'fully' quoted shares.

Advantages of public limited companies

Some of the advantages are the same as those of private limited companies. For example, all members have limited liability, the firm continues to trade if one of the owners dies and more power is enjoyed due to their larger size. Others are as follows.

- Huge amounts of money can be raised from the sale of shares to the public.
- Production costs may be lower as firms may gain economies of scale.
- Because of their size, plcs can often dominate the market.
- It becomes easier to raise finance as financial institutions are more willing to lend to plcs.

- Pressures from the financial media and financial analysts, as well as the danger that the plc might be taken over by another company, encourage executives and managers to perform well and make profits. These pressures do not exist for private limited companies.

Disadvantages of public limited companies

There are also disadvantages in setting up a public limited company.

- The setting up costs can be very expensive - running into millions of pounds in some cases.
- Since anyone can buy their shares, it is possible for an outside interest to take control of the company.
- All of the company's accounts can be inspected by members of the public. Competitors may be able to use some of this information to their advantage. They have to publish more information than private limited companies.
- Because of their size they are less able to deal with their customers at a personal level.
- The way they operate is controlled by various Company Acts which aim to protect shareholders.
- There may be a divorce of ownership and control which might lead to the interests of the owners being ignored to some extent.
- It is argued that many of these companies are inflexible due to their size. For example, they can find change difficult to cope with.

Some public limited companies are large and have millions of shareholders and a wide variety of business interests all over the world. They are known as **multinationals**, which means that they have operations in a number of different countries. For example, Kellogg's is an American based multinational company with a production plant and head office situated in Battle Creek, USA. It has also had factories in Manchester, Wrexham, Bremen, Barcelona and Brescia.

Exiting the stock market

Sometimes a business operating as a public limited company is taken back into private ownership. This may be called 'exiting the stock market'. Why does it happen?

- The people responsible for running the business might no longer be willing to tolerate interference from the external shareholders. For example, shareholders such as financial institutions may demand higher dividends when the senior managers would prefer to reinvest profits to generate more growth.
- Sometimes businesses lose favour with the stock market. This may happen when city analysts publish unhelpful or negative reports about companies failing to reach profit targets for example. Such publicity often has the effect of lowering the share price very sharply.
- A business currently operating as a plc may be bought

CRITIQUE

Private equity companies have been criticised for a number of reasons. It is argued that they are often too ruthless when pursuing efficiency gains and that job losses nearly always follow an acquisition by a private equity company. Private equity investors pay very little tax on the profits of their sales. Businesses bought by private equity companies are often saddled with huge debts and some private equity companies have been accused of asset stripping. However, many of the businesses bought by private equity companies are badly managed and in need of change. Some are also undervalued by the stock market and it is suggested that the owners are not getting value for their investment. It is also argued that being taken into private ownership removes unnecessary costs such as compliance and accountancy. Finally, under private ownership the business can focus on the longer term.

outright by a private individual. For example, Philip Green, bought Bhs, the high street clothes retailer, from Storehouse in 2000. He also bought Arcadia in 2002 for a reported £770 million. Both of these companies were part of a plc organisation until purchased.

Private equity companies

An increasing number of businesses are owned by PRIVATE EQUITY COMPANIES. These are organisations that borrow money from banks, add a little of their own, and then use the cash to buy a business. Usually, the businesses they buy are public limited companies, although not always. This often means that public limited companies are taken into private ownership. Three key features of the way in which private equity companies operate are:

- they tend to put the debt used to buy the business into the company. This usually means the company will now have more debt than before it was purchased;
- since they stand to gain all of the profit made by the business, they aim to make ruthless efficiency gains;
- they tend to sell the business after about three years.

How does a private equity deal work? Assume a private equity company borrows £90 million to buy a company worth £100 million, and puts up £10 million of its own money. Its investment is heavily geared. If it can create a 5 per cent increase in the value of the company, it adds £5 million to it. But, because it keeps the whole increase in value for itself, the initial £10 million investment has not risen by 5 per cent, but by 50 per cent - a fantastic return. Some examples of private equity companies include Bain Capital, Apollo Management, Terra Firma, Blackstone Group and Apax Partners. One example of a deal involving a private equity company was the purchase of Alliance Boots, the owner of the 158-year-old high street chemists chain. Boots was bought by Stefano Pessina and his backers, Kohlberg Kravis Roberts (KKR), for £11 billion.

Holding companies

Some public limited companies operate as HOLDING COMPANIES. This means that they are not only companies in their own right, but also have enough shares in numerous other public limited companies to exert control. This type of company tends to have a very diversified range of business activities. For example, in the UK the TTP Group plc is a holding company for a number of technology businesses. These include TTP LabTech, which supplies products to the healthcare and pharmaceutical sectors, and Acumen Bioscience, which develops and provides screening instruments for the drug discovery industry.

The main advantage of this type of company is that it tends to have a diverse range of business activities. This helps protect it when one of its markets fails. Also, because it is so large, it can often gain financial economies of scale. The main disadvantage is that the holding company may see the businesses it owns only as a financial asset. It may have no long-term interest in the businesses or its development.

KNOWLEDGE

1. What is the role of directors in limited companies?
2. What is the difference between the Memorandum of Association and the Articles of Association?
3. What is a Certificate of Incorporation?
4. Describe the advantages and disadvantages of private limited companies.
5. What are the main legal differences between private and public limited companies?
6. State four financial costs incurred when forming a public limited company
7. What is meant by a statutory declaration?
8. Describe the advantages and disadvantages of plcs.
9. How is a company prospectus used?
10. State one advantage and one disadvantage of a holding company.

KEYTERMS

Flotation – the process of a company 'going public'.
Holding companies – public limited companies which owns enough shares in a number of other companies to exert control over them.
Limited company – a business organisation which has a separate legal entity from that of of its owners.
Private equity company – a business usually owned by private individuals backed by financial institutions.

Case Study: *ImmuPharma plc*

ImmuPharma plc, a drug discovery and development company, floated on the Alternative Investment Market (AIM) at the beginning of 2006. The main purpose of the float was to raise money to finance initial clinical trials on ImmuPharma's drugs for severe pain and MRSA-related infections. At the forefront of ImmuPharma's drug pipeline is a product that targets Lupus, a disease for which there is currently no cure or specific treatment. By 2010 there will be an estimated 1.4 million patients diagnosed with Lupus in the seven key markets. The proceeds of the flotation, together with certain grants, are expected to fund the Phase I trial and a Phase II study for the Lupus product. The flotation involved placing 67.8 million shares with institutional and private investors at the price of 42.5p a share.

Lupus is a chronic, potentially life-threatening autoimmune disease. An estimated one million people worldwide have been diagnosed with this inflammatory disease, which attacks multiple organs such as the skin, joints, kidneys, blood cells, heart and lungs. There is currently no cure or specific treatment and Immupharma's drug, IPP-201101, has a mechanism of action aimed at modulating the body's immune system so it does not attack healthy cells without causing adverse side effects. It has the potential to halt the progression of the disease in a substantial proportion of patients.

According to a Datamonitor report, the currently unique ImmuPharma drug, IPP-201101, has an 'achievable' peak market share of 50 per cent. The report also suggests that the drug could sell at a similar cost to interferon, the multiple sclerosis treatment - around $10,000 a year per patient. Immupharma have stated that due to the nature of the disease and lack of treatments, the US Food and Drug Administration may permit a fast track development and approval process for Phase III once the Phase II study is finished in the first quarter of 2007. If approved, the drug could be available on the market as early as 2010.

Source: adapted from www.drugresearcher.com and ImmuPharma, *Annual Report and Accounts 2006.*

Table 1: Financial Information for ImmuPharma

	2006*	2005**
Turnover	£44,818	£25,409
Loss	(£1,860,038)	(£2,482,778)

*1/4/06 – 31/12/06.
**13/1/05 – 31/3/06.

(a) Why do you think ImmuPharma has decided to become a public limited company? (6 marks)

(b) What is the main advantage of floating on the Alternative Investment Market? (4 marks)

(c) Calculate how much money the flotation will raise for ImmuPharma. (6 marks)

(d) What might be the disadvantages to ImmuPharma of operating as a public limited company? (10 marks)

(e) Evaluate the potential for the success of ImmuPharma in the future. (14 marks)

12 | Legal structure - not-for-profit organisations

Not-for-profit organisations

A number of organisations are run according to business principles, but do not aim to make a profit. They are known as NOT-FOR-PROFIT ORGANISATIONS. Their proceeds or surpluses from trading may be shared with employees and customers or passed on to a third party. Such organisations may be involved in a range of business activities. They may also employ staff, raise finance, buy resources, sell goods or services, market themselves, have a formal structure and be required to meet the needs of different stakeholders. They have to operate within the law and may also be faced with competition. Not-for-profit organisations include the following:

- public sector organisations;
- co-operatives;
- mutual organisations;
- charities;
- pressure groups.

Public sector organisations

The PUBLIC SECTOR is made up of organisations which are owned or controlled by central or local government. They may be funded from taxation or generate their own revenue by selling services and in some cases both. Some have unique financing arrangements. For example, the BBC raises money from the sale of television licences. Public sector organisations often exist because the private sector does not make adequate provision for certain services, like health care and education, or because the government wants to keep control of certain services, to protect the public's interest.

The nature of public sector organisations can vary significantly depending on their roles and the types of services they supply. For example, some, like the Post Office, resemble private sector businesses in the way they operate. Others, like The Treasury, are large government departments. Some cater for local needs. For example, libraries, sports halls and parks are provided by local authority organisations. Finally, organisations called executive agencies now provide some services that were previously the responsibility of government departments. For example, Jobcentre Plus, which employs around 100,000 people, is an executive agency responsible for supporting people of working age from welfare into work and for helping employers to fill their vacancies.

Co-operatives

The origins of Co-operatives The UK Co-operative Movement grew from the activities of 28 workers in Rochdale, Lancashire. In 1844 they set up a retail co-operative society - The Rochdale Equitable Pioneers Society. With capital of just £28 they bought

---

Figure 1: The Co-operative's business activities

Food The largest community food retailer in the UK with more than 2,200 stores, over 52,000 employees.

Healthcare Has more than 700 outlets and 5,000 employees. It is the third largest pharmacy business in the UK.

Travel The UK's most diverse retail travel business, with more than 450 high street branches, strong internet, call centre and home working businesses as well as significant cruise, franchise and business travel operations.

Funeralcare The UK's largest funeral business with over 800 funeral branches and in excess of 3,500 employees.

End of Life Planning A newly established End of Life Planning business which aims to grow its stake in the funeral planning market.

Sunwin Motors One of the top 25 motor businesses in the UK, with a turnover of £250million and 22 dealerships in Yorkshire, Lancashire and the East Midlands.

Cash in Transit Provides services for over half of The Co-operative Bank's ATM estate.

E-Store Operates several e-commerce sites and provides electrical buying, warehousing and distribution services for the Co-operative Movement.

The Co-operative Legal Services Offers free advice and legal help for members of The Co-operative Group on everything from buying or selling a property to will writing.

Property Responsible for property assets including an investment portfolio which is largely invested in the retail and commercial property sectors.

The Co-operative Farms The largest farmer in the UK with over 70,000 acres of farmland in England and Scotland. They supply products such as soft fruit, cider, potatoes and packet flour to The Co-operative food stores.

Shoefayre A leading footwear and accessories retailer with over 1,700 employees and 240 stores throughout the UK.

Mandate A leading designer, manufacturer and distributor of corporate clothing.

Co-operative Financial Services (CFS) An Industrial and Provident Society, which brings together Co-operative Insurance (CIS), The Co-operative Bank and the internet bank Smile under common leadership.

The Co-operative Bank A bank famous for its ethical stance and high standards of customer service.

CIS/Co-operative Insurance A major life assurance and general insurance business with over four and a half million customers.

Smile An award-winning full-service internet bank.

Source: adapted from www.co-operative.co.uk.

---

food from wholesalers and opened a shop, selling 'wholesome food at reasonable prices'. The surplus (or profit) made was returned to members of the society in the form of a 'dividend'. The dividend was in proportion to how much each member had spent. The principles of the society were:

- voluntary and open membership;
- democratic ownership - one member, one vote;
- the surplus allocated according to spending (the dividend);
- educational facilities for members and workers.

Modern co-operatives Most modern co-operatives operate as CONSUMER or RETAIL CO-OPERATIVES. They are owned and controlled by their members. Members can purchase shares which entitles them to a vote at Annual General Meetings. The members elect a board of directors to make overall business decisions and appoint managers to run day to day business. Co-operatives are run in the interests of their members. Any surplus made by the co-operative is distributed to members as a dividend according to levels of spending. Shares are not sold on a stock exchange, which limits the amount of money that can be raised.

On Sunday 29 July 2007, the two main arms of the Co-op, The Co-operative Group and United Co-operatives, merged The new society, called 'The Co-operative', is the world's largest consumer co-operative with a turnover of more than £9 billion, 4.5 million members and 87,500 employees. The new organisation operates over 4,500 trading outlets throughout the UK. Figure 1 gives a summary of The Co-operatives' business activities.

Worker co-operatives

Another form of co-operation in the UK with common ownership is a WORKER CO-OPERATIVE. This is where a business is jointly owned by its employees. A worker co-operative is an example of a producer co-operative where people work together to produce a good or service. Examples might be a wine growing co-operative or a co-operative of farmers producing milk.

In a worker co-operative employees are likely to:
- contribute to production;
- be involved in decision making;
- share in the profit (usually on an equal basis);
- provide some capital when buying a share in the business.

In 2006 there were less than 400 worker owned and controlled co-operatives in the UK according to Co-operatives UK. One example is the Edinburgh Bicycle Co-operative, a cycle retailer. One advantage of a worker co-operative is that all employees, as owners of the business, are likely to be motivated. Conflict will also tend to be reduced as the objectives of shareholders and employees will be the same. Worker co-operatives can involve the local community, either by giving donations to local bodies or even having them as members of the co-operative. However, there may be problems when operating as a worker co-operative.
- It is often difficult to persuade other workers to join a worker co-operative because it is much easier to set up a partnership.
- Some workers, new ones for example, may not want to join. They may not be able to afford the share.

Question 1.

Suma is an independent wholefood wholesaler-distributor. It specialises in vegetarian, fairly traded, organic, ethical and natural products and also has its own successful brand of food and non-food products. Suma operates as a workers' co-operative and has a truly democratic system of management that isn't bound by the conventional notions of hierarchy that often hinder progress and stand in the way of fairness. It uses an elected Management Committee to implement decisions and business plans but the decisions themselves are made at regular General Meetings with the consent of every co-operative member. There's no chief executive, no managing director and no company chairman. In practice, this means that their day-to-day work is carried out by self-managing teams of employees who are all paid the same wage, and who all enjoy an equal voice and an equal stake in the success of the business.

Source: adapted from www.suma.co.uk.

(a) Using this case as an example, explain what is meant by a workers co-operative.
(b) Explain the likely effect on worker motivation at Suma of operating as a workers co-operative.

- Successful worker co-operatives often get sold to companies and the workers are happy to 'sell out' due to the lucrative offers made.
- Fresh capital cannot be raised by recruiting new shareholders. This often limits growth.
- Difficulties might be encountered when trying to recruit highly skilled and qualified staff. They may want more money then the equal wages being paid to existing members.

Building and friendly societies

Most building societies and friendly societies in the UK are MUTUAL ORGANISATIONS. They are owned by their customers, or members as they are known, rather than shareholders. Profits go straight back to members in the form of better and cheaper products. Friendly societies began in the 18th and 19th centuries to support the working classes. Today friendly societies offer a wide range of 'affordable' financial services. These include savings schemes, insurance plans and protection against the loss of income or death. They also provide benefits such as free legal aid, sheltered housing or educational grants to help young people through university. These extra benefits are distributed free of charge, paid for by trading surpluses. The government gives friendly societies special tax treatment, which reduces the amount of tax that members pay.

Building societies used to specialise in mortgages and savings accounts. Savers and borrowers got better interest rates than those offered by banks. This was possible because building societies were non-profit making. In the 1980s building societies began to diversify and compete with banks. In the late 1990s a number of building societies, such as Halifax, Alliance and Leicester, and Northern Rock, became public limited companies.

The main reason for this was that mutual organisations are restricted by law from raising large amounts of capital which might be used to invest in new business ventures. This demutualisation process involved societies giving members 'windfall' payments, usually in the form of shares, to compensate them for their loss of membership.

Charities

Charities are organisations with very specialised aims. They exist to raise money for 'good' causes and draw attention to the needs of disadvantaged groups in society. For example, Age Concern is a charity which raises money on behalf of senior citizens. They also raise awareness and pass comment on issues, such as cold weather payments, which relate to the elderly. Other examples of national charities include Cancer Research Campaign, British Red Cross, Save the Children Fund and Mencap.

Charities rely on donations for their revenue. They also organise fund raising events such as fetes, jumble sales, sponsored activities and raffles. A number of charities run business ventures. For example, Oxfam has a chain of charity shops which sells second hand goods donated by the public.

Charities are generally run according to business principles. They aim to minimise costs, market themselves and employ staff. Most staff are volunteers, but some of the larger charities employ professionals. In the larger charities a lot of administration is necessary to deal with huge quantities of correspondence and to handle charity funds. Provided charities are registered, they are not required to pay tax. In addition, businesses can offset any charitable donations they make against tax. This helps charities when raising funds.

Pressure groups

PRESSURE GROUPS are groups of people that attempt to influence decision makers in politics, business and society. There is a wide variety of pressure groups since they can differ significantly in their aims, objectives and size. For example, a very small pressure group might be made up of residents in a small locality that are campaigning for traffic-calming measures in a particular street to be taken by the council. Such a group would then disband if the council did take acceptable measures. Some groups are quite large and operate as registered charities. Examples include Greenpeace and Friends of the Earth – big environmental pressure groups. Such groups may have formal structures, operate from central offices, employ staff, use large quantities of resources (for example, Greenpeace own a large boat) and promote themselves actively. Some generate large amounts of revenue through donations, fund-raising activities and other sources. Some pressure groups even represent businesses. For example, The Confederation of British Industry (CBI) represents the interests of a wide variety of British companies.

Factors affecting the choice of organisation

Age Many businesses change their legal status as they become older. Most businesses when they start out are relatively small and operate as sole traders. Over time, as needs change, a sole trader may take on a partner and form a partnership. Alternatively, a sole trader may invite new owners to participate in the business, issue shares and form a private limited company. Public limited companies are often formed from established private limited companies that have been trading for many years.

The need for finance A change in legal status may be forced on a business. Often, small businesses want to grow but do not have the funds. Additional finance can only be raised if the business changes status. Furthermore, many private limited companies 'go public' because they need to raise large amounts for expansion.

Size The size of a business operation is likely to affect its legal status. A great number of small businesses are usually sole traders or partnerships. Public limited companies tend to be large organisations with thousands of employees and a turnover of millions or billions of pounds. It could be argued that a very large business could only be run if it were a limited company. For example, certain types of business activity, such as oil processing and chemical manufacturing, require large scale production methods and could not be managed effectively as sole traders or partnerships.

Limited liability Owners can protect their own personal financial position if the business is a limited company. Sole traders and partners have unlimited liability. They may, therefore, be placed in a position where they have to use their own money to meet business debts. Some partnerships dealing with customers' money, such as solicitors, have to have unlimited liability in order to retain the confidence of their clients.

Degree of control Owners may consider retaining control of their business to be important. This is why many owners choose to remain as sole traders. Once new partners or shareholders become a part of the business, the degree of control starts to diminish because it is shared with the new owners. It is possible to keep some control of a limited company by holding the majority of shares. However, even if one person holds 51 per cent of shares in a limited company, the wishes of the other 49 per cent cannot be ignored.

The nature of the business The type of business activity may influence the choice of legal status. For example, household services such as plumbing, decorating and gardening tend to be provided by sole traders. Professional services such as accountancy, legal advice and surveying are usually offered by partnerships. Relatively small manufacturing and family businesses tend to be private limited companies. Large manufacturers and producers of consumer durables, such as cookers, computers and cars, are usually plcs. The reason that these activities choose a particular type of legal status is because of the benefits they gain as a result. However, there are many exceptions to these general examples.

KNOWLEDGE

1. What is meant by a not-for-profit organisation?
2. How might a trading 'surplus' be used by a not-for-profit organisation?
3. State three features of a consumer co-operative.
4. Why do charities promote themselves?
5. Who are the owners of a mutual organisation?

Case Study: Claire House

Claire House is a registered charity. It cares for children aged between 0-18 years with life threatening or life limiting conditions and their families from Merseyside, Cheshire, North Wales and the Isle of Man. Claire House runs a children's hospice on the Wirral which is dedicated to enhancing the quality of life, providing specialist respite, palliative, terminal and bereavement care. The hospice facilities include a multi-sensory room, jacuzzi, hydrotherapy pool, teenage room, art and craft area and physiotherapy/complementary therapy. There is also a multi purpose room where they provide music therapy, group activities or quiet reflection.

The charity has demanding financial needs. Claire House has to raise £120,000 every month to keep the doors of the hospice open. For example, £2,500 is needed each month to pay for a nurse, £1,750 for physiotherapy, £1,500 for medical cover, £550 for family and bereavement support, £400 for pharmacy and sundry expenses and so on. A further £2 million is also needed to build, equip and run the new teenager wing for 12 months.

Claire House has a number of income sources. It relies heavily on donations from the public. For example, it has a web site where donations can be made online. A proportion of income is generated by organising special fundraising events. Examples for 2007 include a beer festival, a golf tournament, a sponsored parachute jump, a comedy night, a garden party, a charity ball and sponsored treks to Brazil and Nepal. It also runs around 20 charity shops in the region. It sells a range of second-hand items, such as unwanted clothes, books, toys, DVDs/videos and ornaments, that have been donated by the general public. It can also take suitable items of furniture for resale at a shop in Mold. Finally, like many charities, Claire House enjoys the support of a number of celebrities. The comedian and actor Norman Wisdom, the actress Patricia Routledge, the Tranmere Rovers goalkeeper Eric Nixon, 60s pop legend Gerry Marsden and the entertainer Claire Sweeney are just a few of the region's celebrities that support Claire House.

Source: adapted from www.claire-house.org.uk.

(a) 'Charities have specialised aims'. Explain what this means using the case as an example. (6 marks)
(b) Describe how Claire House finances its activities. (6 marks)
(c) Examine the role that the celebrities mentioned in the case play in the running of Claire House. (8 marks)
(d) Explain how Claire House faces competition. (8 marks)
(e) Analyse the ways in which Claire House resembles a profit-making organisation. (12 marks)

13 Raising finance

The need for funds

Firms need money to get started, i.e. to buy equipment, raw materials and obtain premises. Once this initial expenditure has been met, the business can get under way. If successful, it will earn money from sales. However, business is a continuous activity and money flowing in will be used to buy more raw materials and settle other trading debts.

If the owner wants to expand, extra money will be needed over and above that from sales. Expansion may mean larger premises, more equipment and extra workers. Throughout the life of a business there will almost certainly be times when money has to be raised from outside.

The items of expenditure above fall into two categories – CAPITAL EXPENDITURE or REVENUE EXPENDITURE. Capital expenditure is spending on items which may be used over and over again. A company vehicle, a cutting machine and a new factory all fall into this category. Capital expenditure will be shown in a firm's balance sheet because it includes the purchase of fixed assets. It also includes the maintenance and repair of buildings and machines.

Revenue expenditure refers to payments for goods and services which have either already been consumed or will be very soon. Wages, raw materials and fuel are all examples. It also includes the maintenance and repair of buildings and machines. Revenue expenditure will be shown in a firm's profit and loss account or income statement because it represents business costs or expenses.

Internal sources of finance

Figure 1 shows how sources of finance are either internal or external. Internal sources can only be used when a business is established because money cannot be taken out of a business until revenue has been generated by trading activities. Although most of this unit focuses on external sources of finance, internal sources are very important. This is because internal sources are cheap. A business does not have to pay interest, for example, if it uses its own money to fund activities.

There are three important internal sources of finance.

Profit Retained profit is profit after tax that has not been returned to the owners. It is the single most important source of finance for a business. Around 65 per cent of all business funding comes from retained profit. It is the cheapest source of finance, with no financial charges such as interest, dividends and administration. However, there is an opportunity cost. If retained profit is used by the business it cannot be returned to the owners. This may lead to conflict if the shareholders of a public limited company, for example, see that dividend payments have been frozen because the directors have used the profit in the business.

Working capital It may be possible to 'squeeze' working capital to provide extra finance for the business. One way of doing this is to operate a 'tighter' credit policy. For example, a business might reduce the trade credit period, so that money is received

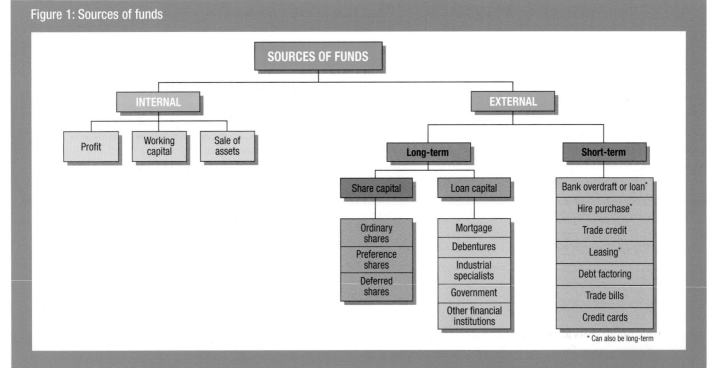

Figure 1: Sources of funds

SOURCES OF FUNDS
- INTERNAL
  - Profit
  - Working capital
  - Sale of assets
- EXTERNAL
  - Long-term
    - Share capital
      - Ordinary shares
      - Preference shares
      - Deferred shares
    - Loan capital
      - Mortgage
      - Debentures
      - Industrial specialists
      - Government
      - Other financial institutions
  - Short-term
    - Bank overdraft or loan*
    - Hire purchase*
    - Trade credit
    - Leasing*
    - Debt factoring
    - Trade bills
    - Credit cards

* Can also be long-term

Question 1.

Godwin's Ice Cream is located in Weston-on-the-Green, Oxfordshire. The business has an ice cream factory and shop attached to a working farm. The business's activities include ice cream manufacture from the farm's own milk, sale of ice cream on-site and sale through a limited number of shops and restaurants. The aim of the business was to replace lost income from falling product prices, through adding value to the existing product. Before setting up the owners wrote a business plan and made an application for a Rural Enterprise Scheme (RES) grant. There were initial problems with the grant due to different interpretations by DEFRA staff of which aspects of the business were eligible for the RES grant. However, it was felt this was probably a teething problem with the scheme as they were one of the first applicants and the forms and guidance are now clearer. The grant was eventually awarded to Godwin's. The other main source of finance for the business is a bank overdraft.

Source: adapted from www.southeast-ra.gov.uk.

(a) What is the advantage to Godwin's Ice Cream of obtaining a grant to help fund the business?
(b) Why do you think it is important to write a business plan when applying for funds?
(c) One of Godwin's main sources of finance is a bank overdraft. Explain (i) why this is an external source of finance and (ii) why this will be a flexible source of finance to Godwin's.

from customers more quickly. Or a business might collect long-standing debts by applying more pressure to customers. Both these options might result in a loss of orders and damage customer relations. Another approach is to reduce stock holding. Money tied up in stocks is unproductive. If a business can reduce stock, money is released and can be used for more productive activities. But having too little stock can be a problem. For example, a business might find it difficult to cope with a surge in demand if stocks are too low.

Sale of assets An established business may be able to sell some unwanted assets to raise finance. For example, machinery, land and buildings that are no longer required could be sold off. Large companies can sell parts of their organisation to raise finance. Another option is to raise money through a SALE AND LEASEBACK. This involves selling an asset, such as property or machinery, that the business still wants to use. The sale is made to a specialist company that leases the asset back to the seller. This is an increasingly popular source of finance. For example, in 2007, HSBC agreed the sale and leaseback of its head office building in Canary Wharf, London for £1.09 billion. A wholly-owned subsidiary of Metrovacesa, S.A., one of Europe's most respected property companies, and HSBC exchanged contracts on the deal which sees the bank retain full control of occupancy while Metrovacesa takes a 998-year lease. HSBC has leased the building back for 20 years at an annual rent of £43.5 million with an option to extend for a further five years.

External long-term sources of finance

External long-term capital can be in the form of share capital or loan capital.

Share capital For a limited company SHARE CAPITAL is likely to be the most important source of finance. The sale of shares can raise very large amounts of money. ISSUED SHARE CAPITAL is the money raised from the sale of shares. AUTHORISED SHARE CAPITAL is the maximum amount shareholders want to raise. Share capital is often referred to as PERMANENT CAPITAL. This is because it is not normally redeemed, i.e. it is not repaid by the business. Once the share has been sold, the buyer is entitled to a share in the profit of the

Table 1: Summary and explanation of the ways in which new shares can be made available to investors on the stock exchange

INITIAL PUBLIC OFFERING (IPO)	
Public issue	Potential investors might apply to an ISSUING HOUSE, such as a merchant bank, after reading the company prospectus. This is an expensive method, but suits big issues.
Offer for sale	Shares are issued to an issuing house, which then sells them at a fixed price. This is also expensive but suits small issues.
Sale by tender	The company states a minimum price which it will accept from investors and then allocates shares to the highest bidders.
PLACING	
Private placing	Unquoted companies (who do not sell on the Stock Exchange) or those with small share sales approach issuing houses to place the shares privately with investors.
Stock exchange placing	Less popular issues can be placed by the stock exchange with institutional investors, for example. This is relatively inexpensive.
AN INTRODUCTION	Existing shareholders get permission from the Stock Exchange to sell shares by attracting new shareholders to the firm. No new capital is raised.
RIGHTS ISSUE	Existing shareholders are given the 'right' to buy new shares at a discounted price. This is cheap and simple, and creates free publicity. Issues can be based on current holdings. A one for five issue means that 1 new share is issued for every five currently held.
BONUS ISSUE	New shares are issued to existing shareholders to capitalise on reserves which have built up over the years. No new capital is raised and shareholders end up with more shares, but at lower prices.

company, i.e. a dividend. Dividends are not always declared. Sometimes a business makes a loss or needs to retain profit to help fund future business activities. A shareholder can make a CAPITAL GAIN by selling the share at a higher price than it was originally bought for. Shares are not normally sold back to the business. The shares of public limited companies are sold in a special share market called the STOCK MARKET or STOCK EXCHANGE, dealt with later in this unit. Shares in private limited companies are transferred privately. Shareholders, because they are part owners of the business, are entitled to a vote. One vote is allowed for each share owned. Voting takes place annually and shareholders vote either to re-elect the existing board of directors or replace them. Different types of shares can be issued.

- **Ordinary shares.** These are also called EQUITIES and are the most common type of share issued. They are also the riskiest type of share since there is no guaranteed dividend. The size of the dividend depends on how much profit is made and how much the directors decide to retain in the business. All ordinary shareholders have voting rights. When a share is first sold it has a nominal value shown on it - its original value. Share prices will change as they are bought and sold again and again.
- **Preference shares.** The owners of these shares receive a fixed rate of return when a dividend is declared. They carry less risk because shareholders are entitled to their dividend before the holders of ordinary shares. Preference shareholders are not strictly owners of the company. If the company is sold, their rights to dividends and capital repayments are limited to fixed amounts. Some preference shares are cumulative, entitling the holder to dividend arrears from years when dividends were not declared. Some are also redeemable, which means that they can be bought back by the company.
- **Deferred shares.** These are not used often. They are usually held by the founders of the company. Deferred shareholders only receive a dividend after the ordinary shareholders have been paid a minimum amount.

When a company issues shares there is a variety of ways in which they can be made available to potential investors as shown in Table 1.

Loan capital Loan capital may come from a number of sources.
- **Debentures.** The holder of a debenture is a creditor of the company, not an owner. This means that holders are entitled to an agreed fixed rate of return, but have no voting rights. The amount borrowed must be repaid by the expiry date.
- **Mortgages.** Only limited companies can raise money from the sale of shares and debentures. Smaller enterprises often need long-term funding, to buy premises for example. They may choose to take out a mortgage. A mortgage is usually a long-term loan, from, say, a bank or other financial institution. The lender must use land or property as security on the loan.

Figure 2: A hire purchase agreement and the parties involved in the three way transaction

- **Industrial loan specialists.** A number of organisations provide funds especially for business and commercial uses. These specialists tend to cater for businesses which have difficulty in raising funds from conventional sources. In recent years there has been a significant growth in the number of VENTURE CAPITALISTS. These provide funds for small and medium sized companies that appear to have some potential, but are considered too risky by other investors. Venture capitalists often use their own funds, but also attract money from financial institutions and 'Business Angels'. Business Angels are individuals who invest between £10,000 and £100,000, often in exchange for an equity stake. A typical Angel might make one or two investments in a three year period, either individually or together with a small group of friends, relatives or business associates. Most investments are in start-ups or early stage expansions. There are several reasons why people become Business Angels. Many like the excitement of the gamble involved, or being part of a new or developing business. Others are attracted by the tax relief offered by the government. Some are looking for investment opportunities for their unused income, such as retired business people.
- **Government assistance.** Both central and local government have been involved in providing finance for business. Business start up schemes can provide a small amount of income for those starting new businesses for a limited period of time, providing they meet certain criteria. Financial help is usually selective. Smaller businesses tend to benefit, as do those setting up in regions which suffer from heavy unemployment.
- **Other financial institutions.** Banks, for example might under certain conditions give a business a long-term loan

which will be repaid over a number of years. The bank may require some form of collateral on the loan, and a business may need to present a business plan to secure the loan.

External short-term sources of finance

Bank overdraft This is probably the most important source of finance for a very large number of businesses. Bank overdrafts are flexible. The amount by which a business goes overdrawn depends on its needs at the time. Interest is only paid by the business when its account is overdrawn.

Bank loan A loan requires a rigid agreement between the borrower and the bank. The amount borrowed must be repaid over a clearly stated time period, in regular instalments. Most bank loans are short or medium term. Banks dislike long term lending because of their need for security and liquidity. Sometimes, banks change persistent overdrafts into loans, so that firms are forced to repay at regular intervals.

Hire purchase This is often used by small businesses to buy plant and machinery. Sometimes, a hire purchase agreement requires a down payment by the borrower, who agrees to repay the remainder in instalments over a period of time. FINANCE HOUSES specialise in providing funds for such agreements. Figure 2 illustrates the working of an agreement and the parties involved. The buyer may place a down payment on a machine with the supplier and receives delivery. The finance house pays the supplier the amount outstanding and collects instalments (including interest) from the buyer. The goods bought do not legally belong to the buyer until the very last instalment has been paid to the finance house. If the buyer falls behind with the repayments the finance house can legally repossess the item. Finance houses are less selective than banks when granting loans. Hence their interest rates are higher. They add a servicing charge for paying in instalments which also leads to higher rates. Hire purchase agreements can sometimes be for longer periods.

Trade credit It is common for businesses to buy raw materials, components and fuel and pay for them at a later date, usually within 30-90 days. Paying for goods and services using trade credit seems to be an interest free way of raising finance. It is particularly profitable during periods of inflation. However, many companies encourage early payment by offering discounts. The cost of goods is often higher if the firm does not pay early. Delaying the payment of bills can also result in poor business relations with suppliers.

Leasing A LEASE is a contract in which a business acquires the use of resources such as, property, machinery or equipment, in return for regular payments. In this type of finance, the ownership never passes to the business that is using the resource. With a finance lease, the arrangement is often for three years or longer and, at the end of the period, the business is

given the option of then buying the resource. In accounting, the payments are treated as capital expenditure. With an operating lease, the arrangement is generally for a shorter period of time, and the payments are treated as revenue expenditure.

There are some advantages of leasing.
- No large sums of money are needed to buy the use of equipment.
- Maintenance and repair costs are not the responsibility of the user.
- Hire companies can offer the most up to date equipment.
- Leasing is useful when equipment is only required occasionally.
- A leasing agreement is generally easier for a new company to obtain than other forms of loan finance. This is because the assets remain the property of the leasing company.

However:
- over a long period of time leasing is more expensive than the outright purchase of plant and machinery;
- loans cannot be secured on assets which are leased.

Factoring When companies sell their products they send invoices stating the amount due. The invoice provides evidence

---

Question 2.

A mobile phone-based information service, 82Ask, launched by one of Britain's top rising female entrepreneurs, is aiming to float on the stock market early next year after raising £1.3 million in funds. The company, which is changing its name to Texperts, is led by Sarah McVittie, a former UBS investment banker. Texperts allows users to text a question to a team of research experts who promise to provide an answer within five minutes. Users are charged £1 per question only if the inquiry is fully completed. The service, which has close to 400,000 users, has a network of 220 experts answering questions on anything from trivia and entertainment to recommending restaurants, providing travel information and sending maps to people's mobile phones.

Odey Asset Management (an industrial loan specialist), is understood to have provided most of the new funding and now has a stake of around 14 per cent in Texperts. McVittie and co-founder Thomas Roberts, each have about a 15 per cent stake. Over the past four years, Texperts has raised £2.5 million, mainly from wealthy individuals in three fundraising rounds. About £1 million of the £1.3 million from the latest round of fund raising is earmarked for advertising and marketing. This is well above the £200,000 spent to date.

Source: adapted from the *Sunday Times*, 19.8.2007.

(a) Why is Texperts raising finance?
(b) How much of the business is owned by the original founders?
(c) Describe the two key sources of finance used by Texperts?
(d) Discuss the drawback to the founders of Texperts of using this type of finance.

Table 2: Advantages and disadvantages of being high geared and low geared

	Advantages	Disadvantages
Low geared	The burden of loan repayments is reduced. The need for regular interest payments is reduced. Volatile interest rates are less of a threat.	Dividend payments have to be met indefinitely. Ownership of the company will be diluted. Dividends are paid after tax.
High geared	The interest on loans can be offset against tax. Ownership is not diluted. Once loans have been repaid the company's debt is much reduced.	Interest payments must be met. Interest rates can change, which causes uncertainty. Loans must be repaid and may be a burden, increasing the risk of insolvency.

administration costs while the interest payments on bank overdrafts tend to be relatively low.

Use of funds When a company undertakes heavy capital expenditure, it is usually funded by a long-term source of finance. For example, the building of a new plant may be financed by a share issue or a mortgage. Revenue expenditure tends to be financed by short-term sources. For example, the purchase of a large amount of raw materials may be funded by trade credit or a bank overdraft.

of the sale and the money owed to the company. Debt factoring involves a specialist company (the factor) providing finance against these unpaid invoices. A common arrangement is for a factor to pay 80 per cent of the value of invoices when they are issued. The balance of 20 per cent is paid by the 'factor' when the customer settles the bill. An administrative and service fee will be charged.

Trade bills This is not a common source of finance, but can play an important role, particularly in overseas trade and commodity markets. The purchaser of traded goods may sign a **bill of exchange** agreeing to pay for the goods at a specified later date. Ninety days is a common period. The seller of the goods will hold the bill until payment is due. However, the holder can sell it at a discount before the maturity date to a specialist financial institution. There is a well developed market for these bills and all holders will receive payment at the end of the period from the debtor.

Credit cards Businesses of all sizes have uses for credit cards. They can be used by executives to meet expenses such as hotel bills, petrol and meals when travelling on company business. They might also be used to purchase materials from suppliers who accept credit cards. Credit cards are popular because they are convenient, flexible, secure and avoid interest charges if monthly accounts are settled within the credit period. However, they tend to have a credit limit. This may make them unsuitable for certain purchases.

The choice of the source of finance

A number of factors are important when choosing between alternative sources of finance.

Cost Businesses obviously prefer sources which are less expensive, both in terms of interest payments and administration costs. For example, share issues can carry high

Status and size Sole traders, which tend to be small, are limited in their choices of finance. For example, long-term sources may be mortgages and perhaps the introduction of some personal capital. Public and private limited companies can usually obtain finance from many different sources. In addition, due to their size and added security, they can often demand lower interest rates from lenders. There are significant economies of scale in raising finance.

Financial situation The financial situation of businesses is constantly changing. When a business is in a poor financial situation, it finds that lenders are more reluctant to offer finance. At the same time, the cost of borrowing rises. Financial institutions are more willing to lend to secure businesses which have **collateral** (assets which provide security for loans). Third World countries which are desperate to borrow money to fund development are often forced to pay very high rates indeed.

Gearing GEARING is the relationship between the loan capital and share capital of a business. A company is said to be **high geared** if it has a large proportion of loan capital to share capital. A **low geared** company has a relatively small amount of loan capital. For example, two companies may each have total capital of £45 million. If the first has loan capital of £40 million and share capital of only £5 million it is high geared. The other company may have share capital of £30 million and loan capital of £15 million. It is relatively low geared.

The gearing of a company might influence its finance. If a business is high geared, it may be reluctant to raise even more finance by borrowing. It may choose to issue more shares instead, rather than increasing the interest to be paid on loans.

Table 2 shows the advantages and disadvantages of being low or high geared.

KEYTERMS

Authorised share capital – the maximum amount which can be legally raised.

Capital expenditure – spending on business resources which can be used repeatedly over a period of time.

Capital gain – the profit made from selling a share for more than it was bought.

Equities – another name for an ordinary share.

Finance houses - specialist institutions which provide funds for hire purchase agreements.

Gearing – the relationship between funds raised from loans and from issuing shares.

Issuing house – any institution that deals with the sale of new shares.

Issued share capital – amount of current share capital arising from the sale of shares.

Lease – a contract to acquire the use of resources such as property or equipment.

Permanent capital – share capital which is never repaid by the company.

Revenue expenditure – spending on business resources that have already been consumed or will be very shortly.

Sale and leaseback – the practice of selling assets, such as property or machinery, and leasing them back from the buyer.

Share capital – money introduced into the business through the sale of shares.

Stock market or stock exchange - a market where second-hand shares are bought and sold.

Venture capitalists – providers of funds for small or medium sized companies that may be considered too risky for other investors.

KNOWLEDGE

1. Why do businesses need to raise finance?
2. State the internal sources of finance.
3. State the main advantage of using internal finance.
4. What is the difference between ordinary, preference and deferred shares?
5. Why would someone want to become an Business Angel?
6. State the advantages to a business of a bank overdraft compared with a bank loan.
7. What is trade credit likely to be used for?
8. Which is likely to be more expensive, a bank loan or HP?
9. What is the difference between a finance lease and an operating lease?
10. What factors affect the choice of source of finance?

Case Study: Gamingking

Gamingking plc was established in 1993 and floated on the Alternative Investment Market (a market for shares) in 1996. In May 2005 Gamingking acquired its largest competitor, Kelly's Eye (No. 1) Ltd. In doing so the Group became the leader in the provision of lotteries and game play products and services to the registered members' club marketplace. The Group now has a client base of around 5,000 clubs in the UK. The Group comprises three main wholly-owned trading subsidiaries:

Kelly's Eye No. (1) Kelly's Eye, based in Hemel Hempstead, is responsible for all sales and marketing activities related to lottery and game play products. The Kelly's Eye salesforce operates nationwide and is able to supply the wide-ranging product portfolio into clubs quickly and efficiently.

Lotteryking Ltd. Lotteryking was the original business providing vending machines; pull-tab lottery tickets and online lottery solutions to the private members' clubs.

Following the acquisition of Kelly's Eye, Lotteryking is now focused on the provision of technical support services, manufacturing, R&D, and purchasing.

Logoking Ltd. This division supplies logo-embroidered leisure and workwear to a wide market including the substantial staff and sports needs of the private members' clubs.

In 2006, Gamingking made a profit of £51,000 and retained the entire sum. It did the same in 2005 when profit was £38,000. At 30 April Gamingking had a loan facility of £800,000 from Barclays Bank much of which was used to buy Kelly's Eye (No.1) Ltd. This loan was due to mature on 15th April 2010. Also, at 30th April 2006, Gamingking had authorised share capital of £5 million and issued share capital of £2.907 million. Other sources of finance used by Gamingking include trade credit and hire purchase.

Source: adapted from www.gamingking.co.uk.

(a) Explain the difference between authorised and issued share capital. (6 marks)

(b) How will floating on the Alternative Investment Market (a stock market) affect GamingKing's ability to raise finance? (8 marks)

(c) (i) Why did Gamingking borrow £800,000 from Barclay's Bank? (4 marks)

(ii) How will this loan affect the gearing of the company? (8 marks)

(d) Discuss the advantages and disadvantages to Gamingking of retaining all of its profit in 2005 and 2006. (14 marks)

Making location decisions

Choosing a suitable place to locate a business is an important decision for a business when setting up. This is because it is a long-term decision. Once a business has been set up in a particular location, it is likely to stay there for a period of time. Relocation can be expensive. So a business must find the best possible location when setting up. Business owners may, however, review their location decision from time to time to see if relocation is needed.

Business owners may choose a location near to where they live. But other factors have to be taken into account. Location decisions are likely to be based on the costs and benefits of specific locations. For example, an owner looking to open a restaurant will consider the cost of rent and refurbishment, as well as the proximity to customers and the image a particular location might present. The costs and benefits affecting a location decision may be **quantitative**. This means that they can be measured in monetary terms. An example would be the cost of transporting goods to customers. Other costs and benefits may be **qualitative**. This means that they cannot be measured in monetary terms. An example would be the distance staff have to travel to work.

An increasing number of businesses are being set up at home. This may be because it is cheap and convenient for the owners. Many new businesses are also web-based and can be located anywhere. For example, a business offering educational services over the Internet could be based anywhere in the world.

Technology

Developments in technology have had an impact on business location in recent years. Most businesses now require fast telecommunication links that have the capacity to send and receive voices, text, documents and other images instantly. This usually means that they require access to broadband connections. Developments in technology mean that such links are available almost anywhere and therefore businesses have a wider choice of locations when setting up. Red Gate is a software designer in Cambridgeshire that helps users to run, update and compare databases more efficiently. It delivers its software from its website. Its 200,000 users can download its software and so avoid packaging and shipping costs. Modern telecommunication links might also mean that businesses can set up with less space, as an increasing number of people can work from home.

Many new businesses set up in recent years have produced technological products or offered technology services. Yorkshire-based Sarian Systems, for example, designs and manufactures routers used to process and send data from lottery terminals and cash machines. These companies may operate from **Science Parks**. A Science Park is a business support and technology transfer initiative that:

- encourages and supports the start-up, incubation and growth of innovation-led, high-growth, knowledge-based businesses;
- provides an environment where larger international businesses can develop relations with a particular centre of knowledge creation for their mutual benefit;
- has links with centres of knowledge creation such as universities, higher education institutes and research organisations.

An example of a science park is Aston Science Park based in Aston, Birmingham. Some of the companies located there operate in fields such as software, pharmaceuticals, IT Solutions, E-commerce, multimedia, environmental services and computer hardware.

Location costs

When choosing a suitable location to start a new business, the most important factor is likely to be cost. This is because new businesses are often short of cash and need to minimise location costs. Location costs fall into two categories.

Fixed location costs When setting up a business some 'one-off' costs will be incurred in relation to location. These are fixed costs because they do not vary with output. They might include

Question 1.

Clevon Guillaume is starting up a business to supply high quality desserts to restaurants and hotels. He was encouraged to do so after winning first prize in a local cooking competition. The awards ceremony was covered in the local press and afterwards Clevon was overwhelmed by the enquiries he got from a range of businesses in the catering industry. One of the tasks he is currently faced with is finding a suitable location. Ideally, he wants to rent a factory unit which can be converted into a working kitchen. He has spoke to a number of estate agents and been in touch with the local Chamber of Commerce.

(a) Identify two (i) qualitative and (ii) quantitative factors that Clevon might take into account when choosing a location.
(b) Which of the above factors do you think might be the most important to Clevon?

the following.

- **Search costs.** Finding a suitable location may take time and cost money. These are search costs. They might include the cost of travelling to different sites, fees paid to surveyors for advice or legal searches carried out by solicitors.

- **Planning permission.** It may be necessary to get planning permission when converting premises for business use. This is particularly the case when a property is used for business purposes for the very first time. Obtaining planning permission may incur legal and administration costs.

- **Refurbishment.** Unless new business premises are purpose-built, it will be necessary to pay refurbishment costs. Examples might include painting and decorating, refitting, renovation or wholesale conversion.

- **Purchase cost.** In a minority of cases an entrepreneur might buy a shop, factory, office or other form of premises. This would be a very high cost and because of this many new business owners prefer to start by renting or leasing premises.

- **Government help.** In some cases a new business may choose a location because the government offers to meet some of the costs. The government may offer grants if businesses locate on specific sites – where unemployment is high for example. Grants help to reduce the fixed cost of location.

Other fixed costs relating to location might be ongoing. They do not vary with output but have to be incurred on a regular basis, such as monthly or yearly.

- **Rent or leasing charges.** Rent or leasing charges have to be paid every month and businesses are often tied to long-term agreements that can last five years, for example. Rents can vary significantly. For example, office space in London is more expensive than office space in Glasgow. The rent for a high street shop will be higher than for a side street shop. Business owners will tend to search for premises with lower rents or leasing charges, but the position of premises will also have to be taken into account.

- **Business rates.** Businesses have to pay rates to the local council to pay for amenities such as refuse collection, policing and the fire service. These may vary in different parts of the country. Business rates are usually paid in instalments.

- **Labour.** Some labour costs may be fixed. A certain number and type of staff have to be employed whatever the level of output. Wage rates do vary around the country. For example, wages tend to be higher in London and other parts of the south east.

Variable location costs Variable location costs are those that increase as output rises. Only a minority of location costs are variable.

- **Labour costs.** When businesses expand and sell more, they are likely to need more labour. Businesses that need a large and increasing number of workers might have to consider labour costs carefully. They may decide to locate in regions

Question 2.

Founded by managing director Anthony Cook when he was only 21, Mobile Fun has capitalised on the mobile-phone craze by selling accessories and ringtones online. Launched in 2000 with virtually no set-up costs, it now offers 5,000 accessories and 100,000 mobile downloads from its headquarters in Birmingham. Goods are despatched to customers using the services outlined below.

- Royal Mail First Class Delivery (UK) - £2.50 per order. Safe & secure shipping. Usually next working day. Please allow up to 5 working days.
- Royal Mail Special Delivery (UK) - £5.95 per order. Guaranteed next working day by 1pm for orders received before 6pm. *(Except Scottish Highlands).
- Royal Mail Saturday Special Delivery (UK) - £7.50 per order. Guaranteed Saturday delivery for 'In stock' items ordered on Thursday evenings & Fridays until 6pm. *(Except Scottish Highlands).
- First Class International Recorded Post (EU) - £10.00 per order. Usually takes 2-5 working days, although varies on customer's local postal service.

Source: adapted from www.fasttrack.co.uk and www.mobilefun.co.uk.

(a) Mobile Fun could be described as footloose. Explain what this means.

(b) (i) Explain why transport is a variable location cost.
(ii) To what extent is Mobile Fun's location influenced by transport costs?

where labour costs are lower. Some businesses have decided to locate overseas for this reason.

- **Transport costs.** Businesses that use bulky or heavy raw materials may need to locate near to their suppliers. This will help to minimise transport costs. For example, oil refineries are usually located on the coast to avoid the high cost of transport crude oil across land. Businesses that produce bulky or heavy products may need to locate near to their customers. Today this is true, for example, for suppliers to just-in-time manufacturers. In the car industry, some suppliers have chosen to locate close to assembly plants in order to reduce transport costs. The main reason for this is because just-in-time manufacturers require multiple deliveries of small quantities. Transport costs would be considerably higher if suppliers were located some distance away.

Infrastructure

When setting up a business will need the support of a sound infrastructure. The quality and proximity of roads, railways, airports, hospitals and schools, for example, can play an important part in the success of a business. Consequently the quality of the infrastructure in different locations will affect the location decision. The following examples help to illustrate the role played by the infrastructure.

- A business that needs to distribute goods quickly to customers on a frequent basis will require access to the motorway network – a business selling goods from the Internet for example.

- A business which plans to export to France might choose to locate near to the Channel Tunnel.
- A business setting up in London might choose to locate near to a Tube station to make it easier for staff to get to work.
- A business trying to attract experienced executives might need to be located close to a good school and an attractive living environment with lots of modern facilities.

A business location that is not supported by a sound infrastructure is likely to incur higher costs and suffer a degree of inconvenience. The image of the business might also suffer.

The market

With some types of business, location near to customers is very important. New businesses are set up to provide financial, domestic, personal, leisure and health services for example. In many cases it is essential that these types of businesses are close to heavily populated areas. People will generally not wish to travel more than a few miles to visit a restaurant or health centre. Also, businesses that offer services in people's homes will not wish to travel long distances when serving a number of customers in the same day.

For some products the market may not be important. An increasing amount of business is done using the Internet. For example, retailers are finding that more and more people are not bothering to go to shops but purchase products online. Enterprises that are set up to provide business services such as advertising, PR and software design do not need to be located near to their customers. Such services can be delivered electronically and effective communications with customers can be maintained in the same way.

Qualitative factors

Qualitative factors are factors which cannot be measured using numbers. There is a variety of qualitative factors which a business might take into consideration when deciding where to set up.

Laws and regulations Any location decision will have legal and regulatory aspects. In many cases, laws and regulations will determine what type of business can occupy what type of premises in what areas. Getting planning permission will be necessary if a business is building new premises. Also, when setting up a new business it may be prudent to get professional advice when in doubt about laws relating to location.

Social, environmental and ethical considerations Many new businesses take social, environmental and ethical considerations into account. For example, a business setting up a market garden to produce organic food may need a plot of land that has been free from pesticides and fertilizers for a period of time. A business setting up a new manufacturing venture may decide to locate a factory in an area where there is high unemployment. It could be argued that the new, younger generation of

entrepreneurs, is more likely to take social, environmental and ethical considerations into account because they are more aware of such issues.

Quality of life Evidence suggests that the interests of those making a location decision are very important. Many new businesses, for example, tend to be located where their owner managers live. Small to medium sized businesses, when considering relocating, will typically relocate within a few miles of the present location. Owner managers don't want to move house or locality even if cheaper premises could be found just 50 miles away. The quality of people's living environments is considered to be very important.

Quality of the workforce The quality of the local workforce is important. A business is unlikely to locate to a place where it is unable to recruit the right quality of local labour. In the UK, London and the South East continue to attract new companies because, despite relatively high wages, there is a large pool of highly educated workers from which to draw.

The importance of location

When setting up a business the importance of location is likely to vary. For some businesses location is not a crucial issue. Businesses that are run from home, web-based businesses and businesses that supply national markets, for example, are FOOTLOOSE. This means that they can locate anywhere. They are not tied by any particular location factor.

However, in other cases, finding the right location is vital. A business that needs large areas of land, such as a new golf course, may have to choose a site where land is cheap. A new guest house hoping to attract visitors to an historic city would clearly benefit from a central location in the city. Businesses that export goods would prefer to be located near to ports. A new fast food outlet hoping to attract shoppers and workers would benefit from a prominent position on the high street. These examples show that the importance of location, and the relative importance of different location factors, all depend on the type of business that is being set up.

KEYTERMS

Footloose businesses – businesses that are not tied to a particular location.

KNOWLEDGE

1. Explain the difference between qualitative and quantitative location factors.
2. State two fixed costs of location.
3. Why is transport a variable cost in relation to location?
4. Why are restaurants likely to be located close to their market?
5. How important is location to a taxi driver?

Case Study: *Locating a campsite*

Gordon Powell left his job at the age of 55 but was not ready for retirement. He wanted to run a business. Gordon enjoyed camping, particularly in the Scottish Highlands and Islands. He planned to move from his home in Doncaster and set up a camp site on the Isle of Skye. Gordon spent eight months planning his business venture. One important issue was the location of the site. He spent four weeks in Skye searching for 'the perfect location'. He thought location would be important because people are more likely to return to the site if the location is attractive. He wanted a site with scenic views close to the sea or a loch. At the end of his four week search Gordon had identified two suitable locations.

- **Dunvegan**. The pretty village of Dunvegan lies on the east side of the head of Loch Dunvegan, which bites deeply into the Isle of Skye from the north west. It is the largest village on Skye that doesn't stand on the island's east coast. On the village main street is the Giant Angus MacAskill Museum, dedicated to the tallest Scotsman that ever lived. There is also a castle, coral beaches nearby and the views from the village are dominated by the loch and Healabhal Mhòr, a table mountain. The site found by Gordon is about one acre in size, enough for 25 tents and 15 caravans. It also has a derelict farm building which would be suitable for conversion into a toilet block and wash room. However, it would need to be connected to a water supply and the mains electricity.

- **Portree**. Gordon's second site is three miles from Portree, the largest town on the island. Portree has a harbour, fringed by cliffs, with a pier. Attractions in the town include the Aros Centre and the An Tuireann Arts Centre, both of which celebrate the island's Gaelic heritage. The site is on a cliff top with views across the sea to the island of Raasay. There is a derelict croft which has a water supply and could be converted into a toilet block and washroom. There would also be enough room for a small café. The site is over an acre and could accommodate 34 tents and 20 caravans. However, one problem with this site is the prevalence of the Highland Midge, a biting insect. Midges are particularly bad on Skye and on this side of the island.

Some cost information relating to the proposed locations for the

Map of Skye identifying the two locations

camp site is shown in Table 1.

(a) Explain why location is likely to be an important issue for the business in this case. (4 marks)

(b) Do you think Gordon will need to obtain planning permission at all? Explain your answer. (4 marks)

(c) Describe three search costs that Gordon may have incurred when choosing a suitable location for his camp site. (6 marks)

(d) Using this case as an example, explain the difference between 'one-off' fixed costs and 'ongoing' fixed costs, in relation to location. (10 marks)

(e) After a discussion with his accountant, Gordon decided to set up his camp site at Portree. Evaluate whether Gordon should have chosen the Dunvegan site instead. (16 marks)

Table 1: Cost information for the proposed camp site locations

	Dunvegan	Portree
Rent per month	£1,000	£1,200
Toilet block conversion costs	£13,000	£8,000
Other 'one-off' location costs	£2,500	£1,000
Business rates pa*	£2,000	£2,200

* Estimated

15 Employing people

Types of people needed by small businesses

Whatever businesses entrepreneurs set up, they need to think about the type of employees that are required. In small businesses, a large amount of work may be done by the entrepreneur, such as in a window cleaning business. But many entrepreneurs will need help and employ other people. Entrepreneurs need to think about the reasons, drawbacks and difficulties of employing staff. They also need to consider when it might be more beneficial to use consultants and advisors or contract out work, instead of recruiting employees.

Employees and self-employment

If a business provides and controls work, supplies equipment and pays tax and National Insurance contributions for a worker, then the worker is an EMPLOYEE. An employee will work under the conditions of the contract of employment agreed with the business.

However, if workers make their own decisions about accepting work and conditions of work, and pay their own tax and National Insurance contributions, they are likely to be SELF-EMPLOYED. Working at home does not necessarily mean a worker is self-employed. To be self-employed, a worker must be in business on his or her own account. Businesses sometimes 'contract out' work to self-employed people to save on the costs of extra employees. For example, businesses may employ cleaning contractors rather than employing staff, even though regular cleaning may be needed.

Permanent and temporary employment

PERMANENT workers are employed by a business for an indefinite period of time. For example, an alternative therapy clinic may employ a full-time reflexologist to cover that particular type of treatment in the clinic. He will work for the business until he leaves, either by choice, because he is forced to by the business or when he retires. Employing a worker permanently might help to motivate the employee. It might also help the business to plan in future, knowing it has staff with skills to carry out work.

TEMPORARY workers are employed for a limited period. The clinic may employ a temporary reflexologist for short periods to cover busy periods, for example. Small businesses needing casual work at busy times employ temporary workers. A shop might need to employ retail assistants at Christmas for a fixed period. One advantage of temporary workers is that they no longer have to be employed once demand falls off. They can also be hired when required, to cover staff on maternity leave or for 'one-off' tasks. Costs may be lower because temporary workers do not receive the benefits of permanent workers. Some businesses use temporary jobs to try out workers who may later become permanent. One problem with temporary workers, businesses argue, is that they are less reliable than permanent staff.

Full-time and part-time employment

Workers may be employed full-time or part-time by a business. The Central Office of Information, which communicates government information, says that a part-time worker is someone who works less hours than a full-time worker. It suggests that there is no specific number of hours that makes someone full-time or part-time, but a full-time worker will usually work 35 hours or more a week.

Full-time workers may be taken on by businesses when orders or work are guaranteed on a regular basis. If this is not the case then there may be times when employees are being paid and there is no work for them. A business may also employ a skilled full-time worker to motivate them and retain their services. An advantage of part-time workers is the flexibility they provide. For example, part-time workers may be employed at times of peak trade, such as in public houses at the weekend. They may be employed to allow supermarkets to stay open later in the evening.

Homeworkers and teleworkers

For some businesses setting up, homeworkers may be an ideal solution. Homeworkers can include telesales and computer operators. They may be employed by a business to work at home or they may be self-employed. They may be full-time or part-time. Teleworker homeworkers are people who work from their own home, or use it as base, and who could not do so without a telephone or computer.

For a small business, the use of homeworkers has a number of advantages. As these workers are not based at the place of employment, the cost of equipment is reduced and less space is needed. There are also fewer problems with absenteeism and transport delays, such as people arriving late to work or who are unable to get to work because of bad weather. People with children are able to work more easily, at times when they want. However, there may be communication problems if staff cannot be contacted. Also, it is far more difficult to monitor and control the work of employees.

Using flexible working arrangements

Businesses may decide that they want to organise staff as flexibly as possible and have flexible working arrangements. There are many different types of flexibility open to businesses. Employees may have flexible working hours, working a number of hours in the day or week, but able to choose what hours to work. Or they might work a reduced number of days but longer hours each day.

Job sharing is becoming more popular as people seek part-time work. This is where the tasks involved in a job description are divided between two people, for example. They often work at different times. Examples could be a legal secretary's job, part of which is carried out by one person from 9 a.m. to 12 a.m. and another person from 12 a.m. to 5 p.m. A growing number of businesses are taking advantage of the use of flexible arrangements. It provides them with the chance to change work patterns to fit in with production and demand.

Consultants and advisors

One way a business can take advantage of extra skills and labour without taking on many of the responsibilities of an employer is to use advisors or outside consultants. These are workers who are self-employed or belong to separate outside companies. For example, a business might use an outside IT contractor to build a business's web pages, or hire a freelance PR consultant when it wants a promotional push. An advantage of using consultants or advisors is that in many cases they look after all their own income tax affairs and National Insurance contributions. People who are genuinely self-employed may not be entitled to the same rights afforded to employees. However, depending on the contract under which they are providing services, they may qualify as workers. Under these circumstances they would be entitled to workers' rights such as holiday pay. Quite often independent consultants can be expensive and a business will need to ensure that the services it receives from consultants are deemed to be value for money.

Drawbacks of employing staff

In setting up a business, entrepreneurs must be aware of legal rights that protect employees and that may act as drawbacks and difficulties in employing staff. These rights may lead to constraints on how people are used in the business.

The contract of employment Once a business appoints an employee that employee is entitled to a CONTRACT OF EMPLOYMENT. This is an agreement between the employer and the employee under which each has certain obligations. It is 'binding' to both parties in the agreement, the employer and the employee. This means that it is unlawful to break the terms and conditions in the contract without the other party agreeing. As soon as an employee starts work, and therefore demonstrates that she accepts the terms offered by the employer, the contract comes into existence. It is sometimes a written contract, although a verbal agreement or an 'implied' agreement are also contracts of employment. Employees taken on for one month or more receive a written statement within two months of appointment. This written statement sets out the terms and conditions in the contract.

Employment law Employees that are appointed by a business are covered by certain employment protection rights. Government legislation makes it a duty of employers to

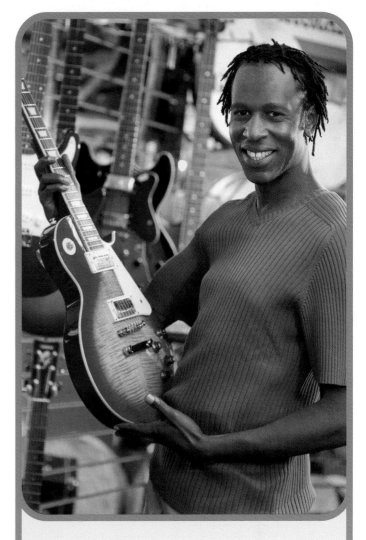

Question 1.

Micah Lampkin recently set up Picks, a guitar and musical instrument workshop in Glasgow. The business wants to offer a variety of services to its customers, including cleaning, setting up and refretting. It also offers more specialist services, including bodywork repair. Micah currently employs one full-time worker, Carla. She deals with most of the professional clients of the business, including regular work on guitars for touring bands that often need work done immediately which requires technical expertise. His other worker is part time. Kevin works in the afternoons. He helps Micah to set up guitars and takes orders that come in.

Recently more orders have come in that need to be worked on during the mornings. Micah is considering employing Ged a young school leaver who wants to learn more about the business. He will work at different times of the day to Kevin. Micah is wondering whether to employ him on a temporary contract or as a permanent part-time employee.

(a) Explain the difference between a full-time and part-time employee.
(b) Why does Micah employ Carla full-time?
(c) Explain TWO factors that might affect Micah's decision about whether to employ Ged as a temporary or permanent part-time worker.

safeguard the rights of individuals at work. These are individual labour laws, as opposed to collective labour laws which affect all employees). They fall into a number of areas.

- **Discrimination.** Employees cannot be discriminated against on grounds of gender, race or disability. So, for example, a business cannot refuse to appoint a candidate for a job only because that person is female.

- **Equality of treatment and pay.** Employees must be paid the same rate as other employees doing the same job, a similar job or a job with equal demands. They also have the right to itemised pay statements and not to have pay deducted for unlawful reasons. Temporary and part-time employees cannot be treated less favourably than similar permanent staff in most cases. Equal treatment also applies to redundancies, training and access to pensions schemes.

- **Absences.** Employees have a right to maternity leave, paternity leave, time off for union or public duties and time off to look for training or work at times of redundancy. They also have a right to guaranteed payments during a period of lay-off or medical suspension. Employees have a right to return to work after maternity leave.

- **Dismissal.** Employees have the right not to be dismissed or face disciplinary action for trade union activity or on health and safety grounds. They also have a right to notice of dismissal. Employers have the right to terminate contracts of employment under certain circumstances, such as misconduct.

- **Health and safety.** Businesses have duties to provide a safe and healthy environment in which employees can work. Many UK and EU regulations exist and are being constantly introduced to raise standards of safety at work.

- **Vicarious liability.** In certain circumstance legislation forces business to have VICARIOUS LIABILITY. This is where a business must accept responsibility for the actions of its employees. Employers are liable for the wrongful acts of employees providing these happen during the course of their employment and are connected with it. So, for example, a construction business may be liable if its workers cause damage to an adjoining building while carrying out repairs to a client's building. Businesses found to be vicariously liable might incur fines or other penalties.

- **Conditions of work and service.** The written statement of the contract of employment will contain information about the conditions of work and service agreed by the employer and employee.

- **The number of hours worked.** A contract of employment will show the hours to be worked per week or over a period such as a year. The number of hours must conform to legislation. Details of the start and finish times may also be included, along with any meal or rest breaks. If an employee is expected to work 'shifts', this should be stated. Shift work is where an employee may work, for example, from 9 a.m.-5 p.m. in the day for a week and then from 9 p.m.-5 a.m. at night the following week. Employees can request flexible working.

KNOWLEDGE

1. Explain three differences between an employee and a person who is self-employed.
2. Why might a business employ temporary workers?
3. What is meant by job sharing?
4. What is meant by a homeworker?
5. Suggest three advantages of homeworkers for a business.
6. What are the advantages and disadvantages of hiring consultants or advisors?
7. Suggest four obligations that businesses have to employees that may be viewed as drawbacks.

KEYTERMS

Contract of employment – an agreement between an employer and an employee in which each has certain obligations.

Employee – a worker for whom an employer provides and controls work, supplies equipment and pays tax and National Insurance contributions.

Permanent employment – employment for an indefinite period of time.

Self-employed – a worker who makes his or her own decisions about accepting work and conditions of work, and pays his or her own tax and National Insurance contributions.

Temporary employment – employment for a limited or finite period of time.

Vicarious liability – when employers are liable for the wrongful actions of their employees.

Case Study: Benefits of a virtual workforce

Small business owners may find it tough to find a balance between giving enough time to ensure success and not running themselves into the ground. They often say that the first few years are the hardest, putting a strain on life outside work. They often find it necessary to get help. But employing additional, permanent staff brings with it extra headaches. Permanent recruitment can be time-consuming. There are costs in advertising the position and time taken on interviews. A small start-up business doing this may lose valuable time making sales or winning new business. There are also training costs and time and effort spent to stay in line with employment legislation. Also there are other fixed costs like tax and National Insurance contributions.

To ease this, many businesses are outsourcing support functions, freeing up time. Virtual personal assistants (PAs), off-site staff who can work on small or large projects for a fixed fee, are an example. Xenios Thrasyvoulou, founder and chief executive of Peopleperhour.com says, 'Small companies are increasingly looking for flexible labour and need a platform on which to do that. Forums, like Peopleperhour.com, help people find skilled freelance professionals to undertake support tasks or functions on a 'per project' basis ... It functions like an online marketplace where professionals can put up their profile and companies or 'buyers' can list their requirements. Buyers then receive bids from professionals willing to carry out the work and can choose the most suitable one. We take a 10 per cent commission from the freelancers, which works out less than you'd see from an agency and it remains completely free for the buyers ... Remote support can really help small businesses and busy individuals to get projects done in an easy, cost-effective and transparent way, without the hassle and costs associated with employing someone full-time to carry out these tasks.'

A forum, he argues, cuts out intermediaries in the recruitment process. Some employees, like freelancers, are hard to find. So small businesses use a recruitment agency. But recruitment agencies often want to place people in a permanent position because they get better commission. This means they can be quite pricey.

Outsourcing is not new, but until recently it was seen as the privilege of larger companies. Small businesses didn't have the resources to outsource on the large scale needed for it to be worthwhile. Through forums, off-site staff or freelance workers could offer small companies a viable alternative to permanent recruitment.

Source: adapted from http://www.smallbusiness.co.uk/5.6/human-resources/guides/256602/the-benefits-of-a-virtual-workforce.thtml.

(a) Identify the problems of employing permanent staff. (4 marks)

(b) What does outsourcing mean? Give two examples. (4 marks)

(c) Explain how the various services of Peopleperhour.com might help a small business. (8 marks)

(d) Evaluate the potential effectiveness of using outsourcing services such as Peopleperhour.com. (12 marks)

16 Costs, revenue and profit

The costs of production

A business needs accurate and reliable cost information to make decisions. A firm that is aiming to expand production to meet rising demand must know how much that extra production will cost. Without this information it will have no way of knowing whether or not it will make a profit. You will be familiar with your own costs. These are the expenses you have, such as travel costs to school or college. Similarly, businesses have expenses. These might include wages, raw materials, insurance and rent.

Economists usually think of costs as opportunity costs. The **opportunity cost** is the value that could have been earned if a resource was employed in its next best use. For example, if a business spends £40,000 on an advertising campaign, the opportunity cost might be the interest earned from depositing the money in a bank account. A business is also concerned, however, with ACCOUNTING COSTS. An accounting cost is the value of a resource used up in production. This is shown in the business accounts as an asset or an expense. For example, if a firm buys some fuel costing £5,500, this is shown as an expense in the accounts.

It is also important to understand how a firm's costs change in the SHORT RUN and the LONG RUN.

- The short run is the period of time when at least one factor of production is **fixed**. For example, in the short run, a firm might want to expand production in its factory. It can acquire more labour and buy more raw materials, but it has a fixed amount of space in the factory and a limited number of machines.
- In the long run, all factors can vary. The firm can buy another factory and add to the number of machines. This will increase **capacity** (the maximum amount that can be produced and begin another short run period.

Fixed costs

Costs which stay the same at all levels of output in the short run are called FIXED COSTS. Examples might be rent, insurance, heating bills, depreciation and business rates, as well as **capital costs** such as factories and machinery. These costs remain the same whether a business produces nothing or is working at full capacity. For example, rent must still be paid even if a factory is shut for a two week holiday when nothing is produced. Importantly, 'fixed' here means costs do not change as a result of a change in **output** in the short run. But they may increase due to, say, inflation. Figure 1 shows what happens to fixed costs as a firm increases production. The line on the graph is horizontal which shows that fixed costs are £400,000 no matter how much is produced.

What happens over a longer period? Figure 2 illustrates

Figure 1: Fixed costs

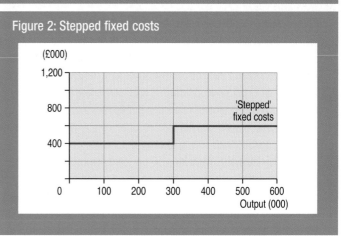

Figure 2: Stepped fixed costs

'stepped' fixed costs. If a firm is at full capacity, but needs to raise production, it might decide to invest in more equipment. The new machines raise overall fixed costs as well as capacity. The rise in fixed costs is shown by a 'step' in the graph. This illustrates how fixed costs can change in the long run.

Variable and semi-variable costs

Costs of production which increase directly as output rises are called VARIABLE COSTS. For example, a baker will require more flour if more loaves are to be produced. Raw materials are just one example of variable costs. Others might include fuel, packaging and wages. If the firm does not produce anything then variable costs will be zero.

Figure 3 shows a firm's variable costs. Assume that the firm buying new machinery in Figure 1 produces dolls and that variable costs are £2 per doll. If the firm produces 100,000 dolls it will have variable costs of £200,000 (£2 x 100,000). Producing 600,000 dolls it will incur variable costs of £1,200,000 (£2 x 600,000). Joining these points together shows the firm's variable costs at any level of output. As output increases, so do variable costs. Notice that the graph is **linear**. This means that it is a straight line.

Figure 3: Variable costs of a doll manufacturer

Some production costs do not fit neatly into our definitions of fixed and variable costs. This is because they are not entirely fixed or variable costs. Labour is a good example. If a firm employs a member of staff on a permanent basis, no matter what level of output, then this is a fixed cost. If this member of staff is asked to work overtime at nights and weekends to cope with extra production levels, then the extra cost is variable. Such labour costs are said to be SEMI-VARIABLE COSTS. Another example could be the cost of telephone charges. This often consists of a fixed or 'standing charge' plus an extra rate which varies according to the number of calls made.

Total costs

If fixed and variable costs are added together they show the TOTAL COST of a business. The total cost of production is the cost of producing any given level of output. As output increases total costs will rise. This is shown in Figure 4, which again shows the production of dolls. We can say:

Total cost (TC) = fixed cost (FC) + variable cost (VC)

The business has fixed costs of £400,000 and variable costs of £2 per doll. When output is 0 total costs are £400,000. When output has risen to 300,000 dolls, total costs are £1,000,000, made up of fixed costs of £400,000 and variable costs of £600,000 (£2 x 300,000). When output is 600,000, total costs are

Figure 4: Total costs of a doll manufacturer

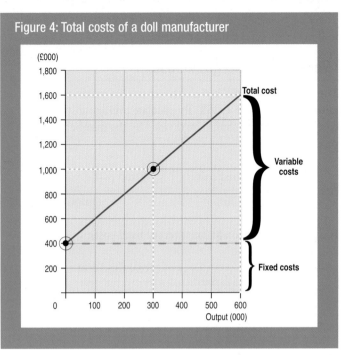

£1,600,00 made up of fixed costs of £400,000 and variable costs of £1,200,000 (£2 x 600,000). This information is summarised in Table 1. Figure 4 shows the way that total costs increase as output increases. Notice that as output increases fixed costs become a smaller proportion of total costs.

Direct and indirect costs

Costs can also be divided into direct and indirect costs. DIRECT COSTS are costs which can be identified with a particular product or process. Examples of direct costs are raw materials, packaging, and direct labour. INDIRECT COSTS or OVERHEADS result from the whole business. It is not possible to associate these costs directly with particular products or processes. Examples are rent, insurance, the salaries of office staff and audit fees. Indirect costs are usually fixed costs and

Table 1: Summary of cost information for the doll manufacturer

000			£000
Output	Fixed cost	Variable cost	Total cost
0	400	0	400
300	400	600	1,000
600	400	1,200	1,600

Question 1.

Dale Roberts runs EdMedia, an education and training services company based in Stevenage, Hertfordshire. EdMedia produces online and video information films about workplace issues, from disability discrimination to bullying and harassment. Orders have soared as new employment laws create demand for staff training. Large contracts with high profile clients have helped to boost sales from £1.1 million in 2005 to £3.9 million in 2007. In 2006, Dale had to hire a new photocopier. The monthly hire rate was £100. Other costs associated with the photocopier were toner, paper and electricity. These costs amounted to £1 per 100 copies.

(a) Using the photocopier as an example, explain the difference between fixed and variable costs.

(b) Calculate the total annual cost of the photocopier if 68,000 copies were made during the year.

(c) Explain why the total cost of the photocopier is an indirect cost for EdMedia.

direct costs variable costs, although in theory both direct and indirect costs can be fixed or variable.

Average and marginal costs

The AVERAGE COST is the cost per unit of production, also known as the UNIT COST. To calculate average cost the total cost of production should be divided by the number of units produced.

$$\text{Average cost} = \frac{\text{Total cost}}{\text{Output}} \quad \text{or} \quad \frac{\text{Fixed cost + variable cost}}{\text{Output}}$$

It is also possible to calculate average fixed costs:

$$\text{Average fixed cost} = \frac{\text{Total fixed cost}}{\text{Output}}$$

and average variable costs:

$$\text{Average variable cost} = \frac{\text{Total variable cost}}{\text{Output}}$$

Take the earlier example of the doll manufacturer with fixed costs of £400,000 and variable costs of £2 per unit. If output was 100,000 units:

$$\text{Average fixed cost} = \frac{£400,000}{100,000} = £4$$

$$\text{Average variable cost} = \frac{£2 \times 100,000}{100,000} = £2$$

$$\text{Average total cost} = \frac{£400,000 + (£2 \times 100,000)}{100,000}$$
$$= \frac{£600,000}{100,000} = £6$$

MARGINAL COST is the cost of increasing total output by one more unit. It can be calculated by:

$$\text{Marginal cost} = \frac{\text{change in total cost}}{\text{change in output}}$$

For example, if the total cost of manufacturing 100,000 dolls is £600,000 and the total cost of producing 100,001 dolls is £600,002, then the marginal cost of producing the last unit is:

$$\text{Marginal cost} = \frac{£600,002 - £600,000}{100,001 - 100,000} = \frac{£2}{1} = £2$$

Question 2.

Carefabric is a home-based business run by Margaret Parry. She makes a small range of towelling and other products for children. The products are advertised on her website and she distributes about 50 per cent of output to retailers in the southwest on a sale or return basis. Recently she has concentrated more on design and has employed someone full time to do most of the manufacturing - although Margaret still helps out when the orders pile up. One of the new products Margaret has recently added to her line is a skin-friendly suit for small children. Made from natural materials, the costs for each suit are given below.

Fabric	£5.60 per unit
Other materials	£2.40 per unit
Packaging	£1.00 per unit
Machining	£11.00 per unit
Fixed overheads	£50 per month

When setting the price for her products Margaret just adds on 50% of costs. This method has generated good sales and profits in the past and she has no reason to change a successful strategy. Margaret plans to produce 400 suits in the next trading year.

(a) Calculate: (i) total fixed cost; (ii) total variable cost; (iii) total costs (iv) average cost; (v) price.
(b) During the year Margaret managed to sell just 250 suits. Calculate the total revenue.

The problems of classifying costs

There is a number of possible ways in which costs can be classified.
- By type. This involves analysing business costs and deciding whether they are **direct** or **indirect**.
- By behaviour. Economists favour this method. They classify costs according to the effect that a change in the level of output has on a particular cost. **Fixed**, **variable**, **semi-variable**, **average and marginal costs** all fall into this category.
- By function. It is possible to classify costs according to the business function they are associated with. For example, costs could be listed as **production**, **selling**, **administrative** or **personnel**.
- By nature of resource. This involves classifying costs according to the resources which were acquired by a business, for example, **materials**, **labour** or **expenses**.
- By **product**, **job**, **customer** or **contract**. A multi-product manufacturer, such as Heinz for example, might classify costs according to the product line (beans, soups,

Figure 5: Total revenue

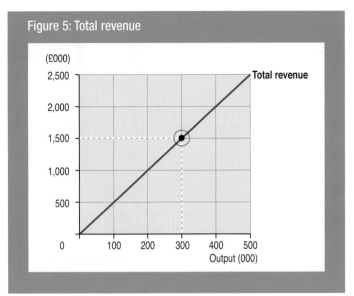

puddings) they are associated with. Solicitors might classify costs by identifying them with particular clients.

The classification of costs is not always straightforward. In some cases the same business cost can be classified in several ways. For example, the earnings of a full-time administrative assistant may be classified as a fixed cost, if they do not vary with output, and an indirect cost, if they are not associated with a particular product. The costs of a worker earning piece rates might be a direct cost if they can be associated with a particular product and a variable cost if they rise as the output of the worker increases.

Another problem relating to costs concerns the allocation of indirect costs. When calculating the cost of producing particular products it is necessary to allocate indirect costs to each of the different products a business manufactures. In practice this may be difficult.

The way in which costs are classified will depend on the purposes for which the classification is being undertaken and the views of the management team.

Long-run costs

Most of the costs discussed so far in this unit have been short-run costs, ie the time period where at least one factor of

production is fixed. In the long run, all factors of production are likely to be variable.

Total revenue

The amount of money which a firm receives from selling its product can be referred to as TOTAL REVENUE. Total revenue is calculated by multiplying the number of units sold by the price of each unit:

Total revenue = quantity sold x price

For example, if the doll producer mentioned earlier sells 300,000 dolls at a price of £5 each:

Total revenue = 300,000 x £5 = £1,500,000

Figure 5 shows what happens to total revenue as output rises. Notice that the graph is linear.

Profit and loss

One of the main reasons why firms calculate their costs and revenue is to enable them to work out their **profit** or **loss**. Profit is the difference between revenue and costs.

Profit = total revenue - total costs

For example, if the doll manufacturer in the earlier example produces and sells 300,000 dolls, they sell for £5, fixed costs are £400,000 and variable costs are £2 per unit, then:

Profit   = £5 x 300,000 - (£400,000 + [£2 x 300,000])

= £1,500,000 - (£400,000 + [£600,000])

= £1,500,000 - £1,000,000

= £500,000

It is possible to calculate the profit for a business at any level of output using this method.

KEYTERMS

Accounting cost – the value of an economic resource used up in production.
Average cost or unit cost – the cost of producing one unit, calculated by dividing the total cost by output.
Direct cost – a cost which can be clearly identified with a particular unit of output.
Fixed cost – a cost which does not change as a result of a change in output in the short run.
Indirect cost or overhead – a cost which cannot be identified with a particular unit of output. It is incurred by the whole organisation or department.
Long run – the time period where all factors of production

are variable.
Marginal cost – the cost of increasing output by one more unit.
Semi-variable cost – a cost which consists of both fixed and variable elements.
Short run – the time period where at least one factor of production is fixed.
Total cost – the entire cost of producing a given level of output.
Total revenue – the amount of money the business receives from selling output.
Variable cost – a cost which rises as output rises.

But if the variable costs were £4 per unit, the business would make a loss.

Loss = £5 x 300,000 - (£400,000 + [£4 x 300,000])

= £1,500,000 – (£400,000 + £1,200,000)

= £1,500,000 – £1,600,000

= - £100,000

Case Study: Wilkins

Wilkins manufactures and supplies a range of PVC products such as windows, doors, door canopies, conservatories, garage doors and porches. It is a north eastern company and operate from a factory in Gateshead. The company is committed to high quality standards and as a result gets regular work from large building contractors. Wilkins uses a number of control procedures which are outlined briefly below.

- **The Environmental Test Chamber** uses computer technology to reproduce the conditions of a warm living room and more extreme weather conditions.
- **Weather Cycle Tests** are carried out using data from studies undertaken with the Met Office over the last 30 years, and subjecting our samples to similar patterns.
- **Weld Testing Equipment** is used to check the quality of welds, and a Salt Spray Cabinet ensures that the metal fittings are of the highest quality.
- **Security Test Rig** simulates the damage that a burglar might inflict and the results are assessed to ensure high standards of security in our products.

Wilkins' management system is registered to BS EN ISO 9001-2000 and all products are covered by British and European Standards.

Wilkins is about to start work on a large contract in Newcastle. The contract is to supply 100 standard conservatories on a new housing development. The variable costs for manufacturing and supplying the conservatories are £4,000 each. The fixed costs for the contract are £20,000. An incomplete cost schedule is shown in Figure 6. Wilkins will receive £6,000 for each conservatory.

(a) Give two examples of variable costs that Wilkins is likely to incur when manufacturing and supplying the conservatories. (4 marks)
(b) Complete the cost schedule in Figure 6. (10 marks)
(c) Plot the: (i) fixed cost; (ii) variable cost; (iii) total cost functions on a graph. (12 marks)
(d) Calculate the profit that Wilkins will make on the contract. (8 marks)
(e) How will this profit be affected if fixed costs rise to £35,000? (6 marks)

Figure 6: Cost information for Wilkins

	0	10	20	30	40	50	60	70	80	90	100
Fixed cost	£20,000										
Variable cost											
Total cost											

17 Contribution

What is contribution?

Craig Eckert sells second-hand cars. His last sale was £990 for a Golf GTI. He bought the Golf at a car auction for £890. The difference between what he paid for the car and the price he sold it for is £100 (£990 - £890). This difference is called the CONTRIBUTION. It is not profit because Craig has fixed costs to pay such as rent, insurance and administration expenses. Contribution is the difference between selling price and variable costs. In this case the selling price was £990 and the variable cost was £890. The £100 will **contribute** to the **total fixed costs** of the business and the profit.

Contribution per unit and total contribution

A business might calculate the contribution on the sale of a single unit, or the sale of a larger quantity, such as a whole year's output.

Unit contribution In the above example the unit contribution was calculated. It was the contribution on the sale of one unit, a single car. The formula for calculating the unit contribution is:

$$\begin{aligned} \text{Contribution per unit} &= \text{selling price - variable cost} \\ &= £990 - £890 \\ &= £100 \end{aligned}$$

Total contribution When more than one unit is sold the total contribution can be calculated. For example, a textile company receives an order for 1,000 pairs of trousers. The variable costs are £7.50 a pair and they will be sold for £9.00 a pair. The total contribution made by the order is:

$$\begin{aligned} \text{Total contribution} &= \text{total revenue - total variable cost} \\ &= (£9.00 \times 1,000) - (£7.50 \times 1,000) \\ &= £9,000 - £7,500 \\ &= £1,500 \end{aligned}$$

The £1,500 in this example will contribute to the textile company's fixed costs and profit. The total contribution can also be calculated by multiplying the unit contribution by the number of units sold.

$$\begin{aligned} \text{Total contribution} &= \text{unit contribution x number of units sold} \\ &= (£9.00 - £7.50) \times 1,000 \\ &= £1.50 \times 1,000 \\ &= £1,500 \end{aligned}$$

Contribution and profit

Contribution can be used to calculate profit. Take the example again of Craig Eckert the car salesperson. He wants to calculate the profit his business makes in January. Table 1 shows the variable cost and selling price of cars in January.

The fixed costs of the business in the same month are also shown in Table 2.

The total contribution from car sales in January was £3,160. This is calculated by subtracting the total variable costs, ie the cost of purchasing the cars, from the total revenue (£21,760 - £18,600). Total revenue is the amount of money received from the sale of the 10 cars during January. The profit for January 2007 is:

$$\begin{aligned} \text{Profit} &= \text{total contribution - fixed costs} \\ &= £3,160 - £1,160 \\ &= £2,000 \end{aligned}$$

So the business made £2,000 profit in January.

Profit can be calculated by subtracting total costs from total revenue. If this method is used here, the profit made by Craig Eckert's business in January is:

$$\begin{aligned} \text{Profit} &= \text{total revenue - total cost} \\ &= \text{total revenue - (fixed cost + variable cost)} \\ &= £21,760 - (£1,160 + £18,600) \\ &= £21,760 - £19,760 \\ &= £2,000 \end{aligned}$$

Table 1: Variable cost and selling price of cars in January

Description	Variable cost	Selling price	(£) Contribution
Nissan Micra	900	1,100	200
VW Polo	1,100	1,450	350
Fiat Tipo	780	900	120
Volvo 740 SE	1,400	1,700	300
Seat Ibiza	670	700	30
Astra Auto	2,300	2,700	400
Nissan Primera	3,100	3,600	500
BMW 318i	6,900	8,000	1,100
Escort estate	560	620	60
Golf GTI	890	990	100
Total	**18,600**	**21,760**	**3,160**

Table 2: Monthly fixed costs for Craig Eckert

Description	(£)
Office rent	700
Insurance	60
Telephone	100
Administrative expenses	300
	1,160

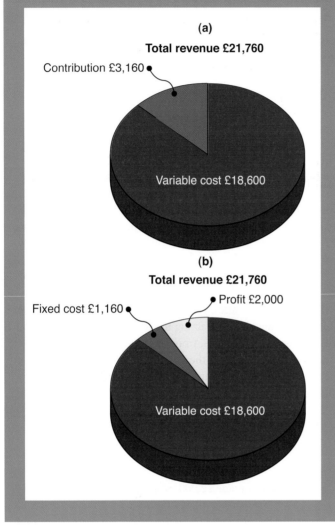

Figure 1: The relationship between fixed costs, variable costs, profit and contribution for Craig Eckert's business in January

(a)
Total revenue £21,760
Contribution £3,160
Variable cost £18,600

(b)
Total revenue £21,760
Fixed cost £1,160   Profit £2,000
Variable cost £18,600

The answer is the same as before, £2,000. However, the contribution method can often be quicker than this method because there is slightly less calculation.

Fixed costs, variable costs, contribution and profit

The relationship between fixed costs, variable costs, profit and contribution is shown in Figure 1. The pie charts show information from Craig Eckert's business in January.

Figure 1(a) shows how the total revenue of £21,760 is divided between the variable cost (£18,600) and contribution (£3,160). Figure 1(b) shows how total revenue of £21,760 is divided between variable cost (£18,600), fixed costs (£1,160) and profit (£2,000). Note that the value of contribution (£3,160) is equal to the value of fixed cost (£1,160) and profit (£2,000) added together.

Contribution costing

How can a business make use of contribution calculations? Calculating the contribution to fixed costs and profit that a

product makes might help a business in decision making. This is known as contribution costing. For example, say that a design business has limited time and resources. It has been approached by two clients who want a new corporate logo and image designing this week. The prices and variable costs and contribution are shown below.

- Design 1 - Price £3,000, variable costs £2,500, contribution per unit £500 (£3,000 - £2,500)
- Design 2 - Price £3,000, variable costs £800, contribution per unit £2,200 (£3,000 - £800)

So the business might choose the second design as it contributes more to fixed costs and profit.

Contribution pricing

Some businesses use contribution when setting their price. This approach involves setting a price for orders or individual products which exceeds the variable cost. This means that a particular order or product will always make a contribution when sold. This approach ignores fixed costs since a single order or product may not generate enough contribution to cover fixed cost. This approach needs to be used with caution. Obviously, to make a profit fixed costs have to be covered. Contribution pricing is most likely to be used when fixed costs are low or when a business knows through experience that fixed costs will be covered.

Table 4 shows some financial information for R G Edwards, an engineering company, that receives four big orders in a particular month. The table shows the price charged, the variable cost and contribution for each order. The total contribution is £35,500. Through experience R G Edwards knows that these prices will cover fixed costs. Fixed costs are £10,000 per month. Therefore the profit for the month is £25,500 (£35,500 - £10,000).

Contribution can also be used to calculate the break-even output of a business. This is covered in the next unit.

Question 1.

AblePrint Ltd is a medium-sized printing company based in Worcester. It offers professional quality-controlled printing with a clear and competitive pricing policy. Examples of its servcies include the printing of business cards, compliment slips, brochures and price lists. AblePrint Ltd has received an order from a local tour operator. It wants 1,000 brochures printed to supply travel agents. The business has agreed a price of £540 for the job.

(a) Calculate the total contribution for the job.
(b) Calculate the profit from the job.

Table 3: Print costs

Fixed costs	£100
Variable costs	
Paper	15p per brochure
Ink	10p per brochure
Other variable costs	10p per brochure

Table 4: Financial information for R G Edwards

	Price	Variable cost	Contribution (£)
Order 1	45,000	32,000	13,000
Order 2	23,000	21,000	2,000
Order 3	49,000	39,500	9,500
Order 4	58,000	47,000	11,000
Total	175,000	139,500	35,500

KEY TERMS

Contribution – the amount of money left over after variable costs have been subtracted from revenue. The money contributes towards fixed costs and profit.

KNOWLEDGE

1. A product sells for £10 and the variable costs are £8.50. What is the contribution per unit?
2. A clothes retailer buys 240 jumpers for £27. The jumpers are sold for £39 each. What is the total contribution made by the jumpers?
3. What is the formula for calculating profit using contribution?
4. If the total contribution is £120,000 and fixed costs are £96,000, what is the profit?
5. If the total variable costs are £450,000 and contribution is £225,000, what is the total revenue?
6. State three ways in which contribution can be used by a business to help make decisions.

Question 2.

Laura Wooding runs a catering company. She provides dinner parties for people in their own homes. Laura has built up an excellent reputation in her local town and only has to work four nights a week to make a very comfortable living. Most of her costs are variable. These include the cost of food, wine, dining accessories such as table decorations and napkins and the hire of glassware and eating utensils if necessary. Laura uses her client's kitchen and cooking utensils when working. The fixed costs of the company are only £100 per week. Laura uses contribution pricing. The price is influenced by the number of diners and the choice of food. Table 5 shows some financial information for a typical week.

(a) What is meant by contribution pricing?
(b) Calculate the week's profit made by Laura's company using the information in Table 5.
(c) Why should contribution pricing be used with caution?

Table 5: Financial information for Laura's company

	Price	Variable cost	Contribution (£)
Party 1	240	155	85
Party 2	140	70	70
Party 2	320	180	140
Party 3	200	60	140

Case Study: Timmings Ltd

Timmings Ltd is a family business set up in 2001 when Frank Timmings, a plastics factory manager, decided that he no longer wanted to work for someone else. Frank set up a small production facility to manufacture transparent plastic containers for storage of documents. He was surprised by the demand because he thought that most documents were stored electronically now. His main customers are office suppliers and large businesses.

Sales have grown from £1.1 million in 2003 to £3.64 million in 2006. Timmings Ltd is operating at almost full capacity. At the moment Frank has no plans to expand and is content with current profit levels. But Frank does have to turn work down. When faced with a choice of orders he only accepts those which make the largest contribution. One week in February 2007 he received the four orders outlined in Table 6. The factory can only meet the demands of two.

(a) State three possible fixed costs for Timmings Ltd. (3 marks)
(b) Using the Butlers order as an example, explain the difference between unit contribution and total contribution. (6 marks)
(c) Calculate the total contribution made by each of the four orders. (8 marks)
(d) (i) Which two orders should Timmings accept? (2 marks)
    (ii) Calculate the profit made by the two orders. (6 marks)
(e) What might be the long-term effect on Timmings Ltd of selecting orders in this way? (8 marks)

Table 6: Details of four orders for Timmings Ltd

	Butlers	A & P Ltd	VC Singh	VWD plc (£)
Number of units	20,000	30,000	25,000	20,000
Contract price per unit	£8.00	£8.50	£7.00	£10.50
Material costs per unit	£2.20	£2.00	£2.40	£3.00
Labour costs per unit	£3.40	£4.20	£2.10	£3.80
Other variable costs per unit	£1.00	£1.40	£1.20	£1.30
Fixed costs	£5,000	£5,000	£5,000	£5,000

18 Break-even analysis

The break-even output

Businesses, particularly those that are just starting up, often like to know how much they need to produce or sell to BREAK-EVEN. If a business has information about fixed costs and variable costs and knows what price it is going to charge, it can calculate how many units it needs to sell to cover all of its costs. The point where **total costs** are exactly the same as **total revenue** is called the BREAK-EVEN POINT. The level of output a business needs to produce so that **total costs** are exactly the same as **total revenue** is called the BREAK-EVEN OUTPUT.

For example, if a business produces 100 units at a total cost of £5,000, and sells them for £50 each, total revenue will also be £5,000 (£50 x 100). The business will break-even at this level of output. So the break-even output is 100 units. It makes neither a profit nor a loss.

Calculating break-even using contribution

It is possible to calculate the break-even output if a firm knows the value of its fixed costs, variable costs and the price it will charge. Take an example of a small producer, Jack Cadwallader, who has just set up a business making wrought iron park benches. His fixed costs (FC) are £60,000 and variable costs (VC) £40 per bench. He sells the benches to local authorities across the country for £100 each.

The simplest way to calculate the break-even output is to use **contribution**. Contribution is the amount of money left over after the variable cost per unit is taken away from the selling price. For Jack's park benches, the contribution is:

Contribution	=	selling price - variable cost
Contribution	=	£100 - £40
Contribution	=	£60

To calculate the number of benches Jack needs to sell to break-even, the following formula can be used:

$$\text{Break-even output} = \frac{\text{Fixed costs}}{\text{Contribution}}$$

$$= \frac{£60,000}{£60}$$

$$= 1,000 \text{ benches}$$

Jack Cadwallader's business will break-even when 1,000 park benches are sold.

Calculating break-even using revenue and costs

Another way of calculating the break-even output is to use the total cost and total revenue figures. In the case of Jack Cadwallader:

Total cost	=	fixed cost + variable cost
or TC	=	£60,000 + £40Q
and Total revenue	=	price x quantity sold
or TR	=	£100Q

where Q is the quantity produced and sold, ie the number of park benches. A firm will break-even where total cost is equal to total revenue. Therefore we can write:

TC	=	TR
£60,000 + £40Q	=	£100Q

To find Q we can calculate:

60,000	=	100Q - 40Q
60,000	=	60Q
$\dfrac{60,000}{60}$	=	Q
1,000	=	Q

It is possible to check if this answer is correct by calculating total cost and total revenue when 1,000 benches are produced. If the answers are the same, the break-even output is correct.

TC = £60,000 + (£40 x 1,000) = £60,000 + £40,000 = £100,000
TR = £100 x 1,000 = £100,000

Both TC and TR are equal to £100,000, so the break-even output is 1,000 benches. This also confirms that the answer using the contribution method was correct.

Total cost and total revenue figures can be used to calculate the amount of profit or loss the firm will make at particular levels of output.

- At any level of output below the break-even output the firm will make a **loss**.
- Output produced above the break-even level will make a **profit**. If the bench manufacturer were to produce 1,200 benches, profit would be:

Profit	=	TR - TC
	=	(£100 x 1,200) - (£60,000 + [£40 x 1,200])
	=	£120,000 - (£60,000 + £48,000)
	=	£120,000 - £108,000
Profit	=	£12,000

Figure 1: Break-even chart for Jack Cadwallader

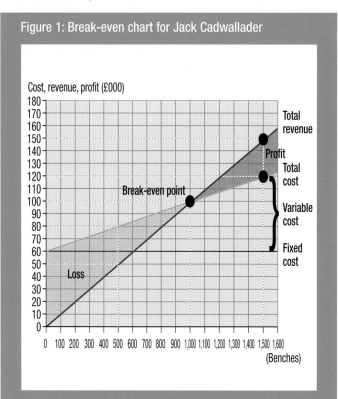

Calculating break-even using break-even charts

The use of graphs is often helpful in break-even analysis. It is possible to identify the break-even point and break-even output by plotting the total cost and total revenue equations on a graph. This graph is called a BREAK-EVEN CHART. Figure 1 shows the break-even chart for Jack Cadwallader's business.

Output is measured on the horizontal axis and revenue, costs and profit are measured on the vertical axis. What does the break-even chart show?

- The value of total cost over a range of output. For example, when Jack produces 1,500 benches total costs are £120,000.
- The value of total revenue over a range of output. For example, when Jack produces 1,500 benches total revenue is £150,000.
- Break-even charts can show the level of fixed costs over a range of output. For example, the fixed costs for Jack's business are £60,000.
- The level of output needed to break-even. The break-even point is where total costs equal total revenue of £100,000. This is when 1,000 benches are produced. So the break-even output is 1,000 benches.
- At levels of output below the break-even output, losses are made. This is because total costs exceed total revenue. At an output of 500 a £30,000 loss is made.
- At levels of output above the break-even output, a profit is made. This profit gets larger as output rises. At an output of 1,500 a profit of £30,000 is made.
- The relationship between fixed costs and variable costs as output rises. At low levels of output fixed costs represent a large proportion of total costs. As output rises, fixed costs become a smaller proportion of total costs.
- The profit at a particular level of output. If Jack produces 1,500 benches, profit is shown by the vertical gap between the total cost and total revenue equations. It is £30,000.

The margin of safety

What if a business is producing more than the break-even output? It might be useful to know by how much sales could fall before a loss is made. This is called the MARGIN OF SAFETY. It refers to the range of output over which a profit can be made. The margin of safety can be identified on the break-even chart by measuring the distance between the break-even level of output and the current (profitable) level output. For example, Figure 2 shows the break-even chart for Jack Cadwallader. If Jack produces 1,200 benches the margin of safety is 200 benches. This means that output can fall by 200 before a loss is made. If Jack sells 1,200 benches the chart shows that total revenue is £120,000, total cost is £108,000 and profit is £12,000.

Businesses prefer to operate with a large margin of safety. This means that if sales drop they still might make some profit. With a small margin of safety there is a risk that the business is more likely to make losses if sales fall.

Question 1.

Jun Shan produces Chinese rugs using traditional techniques and sells them online. The rugs are high in quality and made from natural materials. The rugs sell for £105 and variable costs are £65 per rug. Jun Shan's fixed costs are £2,000 pa.

(a) Calculate how many rugs Jun Shan needs to produce and sell to break-even.
(b) How much profit will Jun Shan make if 500 rugs are sold during a year?
(c) How many rugs will Jun Shan need to sell to break-even if the price is increased to £115?

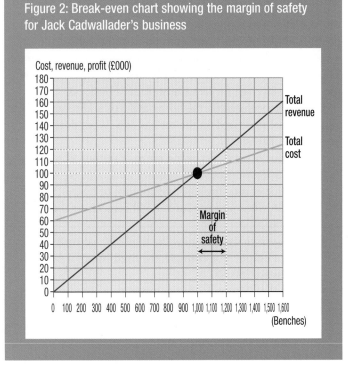

Figure 2: Break-even chart showing the margin of safety for Jack Cadwallader's business

Using break-even analysis

Break-even analysis is used in business as a tool to make decisions about the future. It helps answer 'what if' questions. For instance:

- if price went up, what would happen to the break-even point?
- if the business introduced a new product line, how many would the new product have to sell to at least break-even?
- if the business is just starting up, what has to be the level of output to prevent a loss being incurred?
- what will happen to the break-even point if costs are forecast to rise?
- would the break-even point be lower if components were bought in from outside suppliers rather than being made

KEYTERMS

Break-even – where a business sells just enough to cover its costs.
Break-even chart – a graph containing the total cost and total revenue lines, illustrating the break-even output.
Break-even output – the output a business needs to produce so that its total revenue and total costs are the same.
Break-even point – where total revenue and total costs are the same.
Margin of safety – the range of output between the break-even level and the current level of output, over which a profit is made.

in-house?

Break-even analysis is also found in business plans. Banks often ask for business plans when deciding whether or not to give a loan. So break-even analysis can be vital in gaining finance, especially when starting up a business.

Weaknesses of break-even analysis

Break-even analysis does have some limitations. It is often regarded as too simplistic and some of its assumptions are unrealistic.

Output and stocks It assumes that all output is sold, so that output equals sales, and no stocks are held. Many businesses hold stocks of finished goods to cope with changes in demand. There are also times when firms cannot sell what they produce and choose to stockpile their output to avoid laying off staff.

Unchanging conditions The break-even chart is drawn for a given set of conditions. It cannot cope with a sudden increase in wages and prices or changes in technology.

Accuracy of data The effectiveness of break-even analysis depends on the quality and accuracy of the data used to construct cost and revenue functions. If the data is poor and inaccurate, the conclusions drawn on the basis of the data are flawed. For example, if fixed costs are underestimated, the level of output required to break-even will be higher than suggested by the break-even chart.

Non-linear relationships It is assumed that the total revenue and total cost lines are linear or straight. This may not always be the case. For example, a business may have to offer discounts on large orders, so total revenues fall at high outputs. In this case the total revenue line would rise and then fall, and be curved. A business can lower costs by buying in bulk. So costs may fall at high outputs and the costs function will be curved.

Multi-product businesses Many businesses produce more than one single product. It is likely that each product will have different variable costs and different prices. The problem is how to allocate the fixed costs of the multi-product business to each individual product. There is a number of ways, but none is perfect. Therefore, if the fixed costs incurred by each product is inaccurate, break-even analysis is less useful.

Stepped fixed costs Some fixed costs are stepped. For example, a manufacturer, in order to increase output, may need to acquire more capacity. This may result in rent increases and thus fixed costs will rise sharply. Under these circumstances it is difficult to use break-even analysis.

KNOWLEDGE

1. How can the contribution be used to calculate the break-even level of output?
2. How can the break-even level of output calculation be checked?
3. State five things which a break-even chart can show.
4. What effect will a price increase have on the margin of safety?
5. What effect will a fall in fixed costs have on the margin of safety?
6. State three uses of break-even analysis.
7. State three weaknesses of break-even analysis.

Question 2.

Paul Roberts makes Spanish guitars from a rented room in a rural business park. Figure 3 shows a break-even chart for his business.

(a) What is the total revenue of the business at an output and sales level of (i) 0 (ii) 20 guitars?
(b) What are the fixed costs of the business?
(c) (i) What is the break-even level of output? (ii) What are the revenue and costs at this level?
(d) What is the margin of safety if the business sells (i) 12 guitars; (ii) 20 guitars?
(e) If the business produces and sells 15 guitars, what would be the: (i) total revenue; (ii) total costs; (iii) profit or loss (iiii) total variable costs; (v) variable cost of each guitar?

Figure 3: A break-even chart for Paul Roberts' business

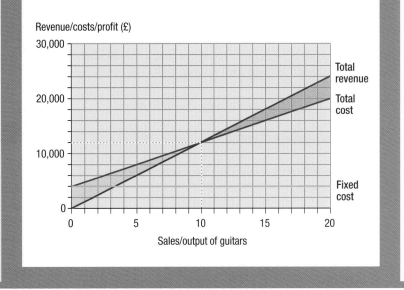

Case Study: Carl Hurst Balti Pies

After following his football team to an away fixture at Villa Park last year, Carl Hurst discovered Balti pies on sale at half-time at the ground. These are pies, filled with chicken balti, a curry dish for which Birmingham is famous. Carl decided that Balti pies could provide him with a new and successful opportunity. He thought he could make the pies himself and sell them in the north-west.

Carl did some research and found that there were few outlets in the north-west where Balti pies were sold. He made some pies at home and took them to various retailers, pubs and clubs to see whether they would be interested. People who liked curry (an overwhelming majority) loved them. Those that had no taste for curry were uninterested.

But Carl was sure he had a winner. He found a disused kitchen unit in Wigan, previously used for pie-making. A week before he signed a 12 month lease for the unit, Carl put some figures together to help him assess the possible profitability of the venture. Carl planned to produce pies in batches of 100 and sell pies for 50p each. He also prepared a business plan to help in the setting-up process. Some financial information is shown below.

Fixed costs

Lease	£2,500 per year
Other fixed costs	£500 per year

Variable costs

Food ingredients	£14 per batch
Fuel	£2 per batch
Other variable costs	£4 per batch

(a) Calculate the contribution per batch of pies. (4 marks)
(b) How many batches would Carl need to produce in his first year of trading to break-even? (6 marks)
(c) How much profit would Carl make if he sold 55,000 pies in his first year? (6 marks)
(d) In the second year of trading the landlord raised the lease for the kitchen unit to £4,500 per year. Carl responded to this by raising the price of his pies to 70p each. What effect would this have on the break-even level of output? (6 marks)
(e) To what extent will break-even analysis be useful to Carl Hurst? (18 marks)

Constructing break-even charts

A break-even chart can be constructed by plotting the total cost and total revenue lines on a graph. The graph should measure output on the horizontal axis and costs, revenue and profit on the vertical axis. Consider Reidle Bros, a small canoe manufacturer. It incurs fixed costs of £20,000 per annum and variable costs of £75 per canoe. The canoes are sold for £125 to agents and wholesalers. The following steps can be used to construct a break-even chart.

Calculating the break-even output It is helpful to calculate the break-even output before constructing the graph. For Reidle Bros the total costs (TC) and total revenue (TR) equations are:

TC = £20,000 + £75Q (fixed costs + variable costs)

TR = £125Q (price x quantity)

Reidle Bros will break-even when total revenue equals total costs. This is where:

$$£20,000 + £75Q = £125Q$$
$$£20,000 = £125Q - £75Q$$
$$£20,000 = £50Q$$
$$\frac{£20,000}{£50} = Q$$
$$400 = Q$$

Therefore, Reidle Bros will break-even when it manufactures 400 canoes.

Calculating revenue and total cost Both the total cost and total revenue lines are linear or straight. Therefore the lines can be drawn by joining two points which lie on each function. To plot total revenue choose two levels of output and calculate the total revenue at each level. Any two levels of output could be chosen but 0 is often chosen as one of the points. Chose a second value which is twice that of the break-even point, such as 800 (2 x 400) in the case of the canoe manufacturers. This will ensure that the break-even point is in the centre of the chart, improving

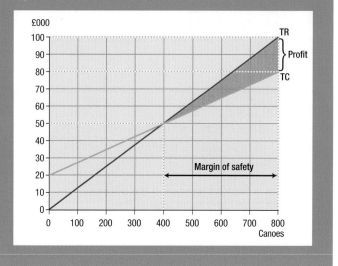

Figure 1: Break-even chart for Reidle Bros

presentation. The value of total revenue at each of these output levels is shown in Table1. This is based on fixed costs of £20,000, variable costs of £75 per canoe and a sale price of £125.

Plotting total revenue Total revenue (TR) can now be plotted on the graph. The output axis should run from 0 to 800 canoes and the other axis from 0 to £100,000. Using the information in Table 1, the two points, or coordinates, on the total revenue line are (0, 0) and (800, £100,000). If these are plotted on the graph and joined up the total revenue will appear as shown in Figure 1.

Plotting total costs To plot total costs, calculate the total cost at two levels of output. It is useful to use the same values as those used for total revenue, ie 0 and 800. From Table1 the two points which lie on the total cost line are (0, £20,000) and (800, £80,000). If these are plotted on the graph and joined up the total cost line will appear as shown in Figure 3. Total costs do not start at coordinates 0,0. At an output of zero, the business still has fixed costs of £20,000.

Analysis from the diagram The break-even chart is now complete. An analysis of certain points on the diagram can be made.

The break-even output can be identified and plotted. It is usual to draw lines to show the number of canoes Reidle Bros

Output (£)	Fixed costs (£)	Variable costs (£)	Total costs (£)	Total revenue (£)	Profit /loss (£)
0	20,000	0	20,000	0	-20,000
800	20,000	60,000 (800 x £75)	80,000	100,000 (800 x £125)	+20,000

Table 1: Values of TR and TC at two levels of output for Reidle Bros

Figure 2: Break-even chart – an increase in price

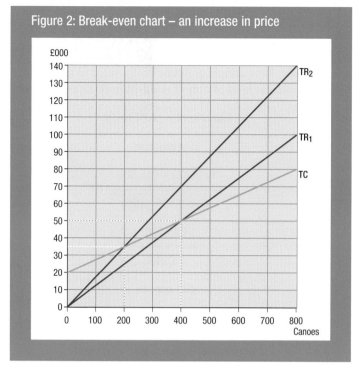

must sell to break-even (400), and the value of TR and TC at this level of output (£50,000). The break-even output should coincide with the calculation made in the first step, ie 400 canoes.

- The profit at certain levels of output may be indicated. For example, at an output of 800 canoes, the profit is £100,000 - £80,000 = £20,000.
- The margin of safety can be indicated. This is the difference between the current output of the business and the break-even point. At an output of 800 canoes it is 800 - 400 = 400 canoes.

Figure 3: Break-even chart – an increase in fixed costs

Question 1.

Ryestairs is a Benedictine monastery which earns part of its living by running The Haven, a guest house and retreat centre. It charges £80 per day for full board and overnight stay per person. The variable costs of items such as food and laundry cleaning come to £30 per day per visitor. The fixed costs of running the business venture are £50 000 per year.

(a) Draw a break-even diagram for The Haven. The horizontal axis will be the 'number of overnight stays per year'. Label the axis up to 1,500 overnight stays per year. Mark on it the break-even level of output.

(b) The management of The Haven decide to raise the price to £110 per day. (a) Draw a new total revenue function on your diagram for question 1. (b) Show on the diagram what has happened to the break-even level of output.

(c) If prices remained at £80 per day and variable costs are still £30, but The Haven cut its fixed costs to £40,000 per year, what would happen to the break-even level of output? Illustrate your answer by drawing a new diagram.

(d) Prices remain at £80 per day and fixed costs remain at £50,000, but The Haven manages to reduce its variable costs to £20. Explain, using a diagram, the effects of this on: (a) the break-even point, (b) the margin of safety assuming the number of overnight stays is 1,200 a year.

Changes in variables

Break-even charts provide a visual means of analysing the effect of changes in output on total cost, total revenue, profit and the margin of safety. The effects of changes in fixed costs, variable cost and price on profit and the margin of safety can also be shown. These will help a new or existing business to make decisions.

Changes in price Figure 2 shows the effect of an increase in price from £125 to £175 for Reidle Bros. This causes the total revenue line to become steeper, shifting from TR_1 to TR_2. This shows that total sales revenue has increased at all levels of

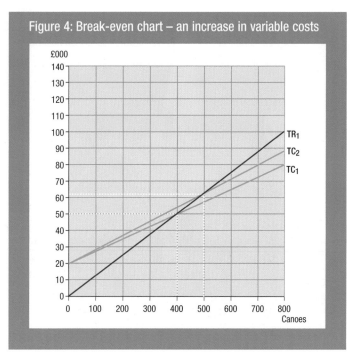

Figure 4: Break-even chart – an increase in variable costs

Other uses of break-even charts

Target rate of profit Break-even analysis can be used to calculate the amount of output needed to generate a certain level of profit. For example, if Reidle Bros wanted to make £15,000 profit, the level of output required to do this would be:

$$\frac{\text{Fixed cost} + \text{profit target}}{\text{Contribution}}$$

$$= \frac{£20,000 + £15,000}{£50 (£125 - £75)}$$

$$= \frac{£35,000}{£50}$$

$$= 700 \text{ canoes}$$

Thus, when Reidle Bros produces and sells 700 canoes profit is:

Profit	=	total revenue - total costs
	=	£125 x 700 - (£20,000 + [£75 x 700])
	=	£87,500 - (£20,000 + £52,500)
	=	£87,500 - £72,500
	=	£15,000

Break-even price Sometimes a business may want to know how much to charge for its product to break-even. In these circumstances a business must know how much it is going to produce and sell. For example, assume Reidle Bros aimed to sell 500 canoes and its objective was to break-even at that level of output. The price it should charge to break-even would be:

output. The higher price means that the business will break-even at a lower level of output. This is 200 canoes. It will also mean higher levels of profit (or lower losses) at every level of output. The margin of safety will also increase assuming an output of 800 canoes is produced. This is not shown in Figure 2.

For a price reduction, the total revenue line would become flatter. This would raise the break-even level of output and reduce the margin of safety. At a lower price more canoes would have to be sold to break-even.

Changes in fixed costs Figure 3 shows the effect of an increase in fixed costs from £20,000 to £30,000 for Reidle Bros. The total cost function makes a parallel shift upwards from TC_1 to TC_2. This occurs because a rise in fixed costs causes total cost to increase by the same amount at every level of output. As a result the break-even level of output rises to 600 canoes. At all levels of output profit falls (or losses rise). The margin of safety has also fallen assuming production remains at 800 canoes. This is not shown in Figure 3.

If fixed costs fell, the total cost function would make a parallel shift downwards. This would lower the break-even level of output and raise the margin of safety. Fewer canoes would need to be sold to break-even.

Changes in variable costs An increase in variable costs will increase the gradient of the total cost function. This is illustrated in Figure 4 by a shift from TC_1 to TC_2 when variable costs rise from £75 to £85 per canoe. The break-even level of output for Reidle Bros rises to 500 canoes. Assuming that production remains at 800 canoes, the margin of safety will fall.

If variable costs fell the total cost function would become flatter. This would lower the break-even level of output and raise the margin of safety. With lower variable costs, fewer canoes need to be sold to break-even.

> ## Question 2.
>
> Julia Robinson owns a large farm and supplies apples to cider producers. Apple production is only part of the farm's output. Most of the profit is generated from milk production. Julia is happy if apple production breaks-even each year. The orchard was inherited from her grandfather and Julia does not wish to cease apple production for sentimental reasons, even though it is generally unprofitable. Whether she achieves her aim depends on how many apples she harvests and the going market price. At the end of the season Julia had picked 60,000 kilos. The fixed costs associated with apple production were £6,000 for the year. Variable costs were 40p per kilo.
>
> (a) Calculate the price per kilo Julia would need to receive in order for apple production to break-even.
> (b) Calculate the profit Julia would make from apple production if the market price was: (i) 48p per kilo; (ii) 51p per kilo.

$$\text{Break-even price} = \frac{\text{Total cost}}{\text{Output}}$$

$$= \frac{£20,000 + (500 \times £75)}{500}$$

$$= \frac{£20,000 + £37,500}{500}$$

$$= \frac{£57,500}{500}$$

$$= £115$$

Thus, if output was 500, Reidle Bros must charge £115 per canoe to break-even.

Price needed to reach a target rate of profit A business may want to determine the price it needs to charge in order to reach a target rate of profit. For example, if Reidle Bros wanted to make a profit of £40,000, and its production capacity was 1,000 canoes, the price it would need to charge to reach this target rate of profit would be:

$$\text{Price} = \frac{\text{Profit target} + \text{total cost}}{\text{Output}}$$

$$= \frac{£40,000 + (£20,000 + 1,000 \times £75)}{1,000}$$

$$= \frac{£40,000 + £95,000}{1,000}$$

$$= \frac{£135,000}{1,000}$$

$$= £135$$

Thus, Reidle Bros would have to charge £135 for each canoe in order to make £40,000 profit if it produced and sold 1,000.

KNOWLEDGE

1. When constructing a break-even chart, why is zero always used as one of the levels of output?
2. What does the vertical distance show between TC and TR on a break-even chart?
3. What happens to the break-even level of output if price is increased?
4. What effect will a fall in variable costs have on the break-even level of output?
5. What happens to the margin of safety if fixed costs fall?
6. What happens to the margin of safety if price is cut?
7. How is break-even price calculated?

Case Study: Organic Hampers

Amelia Hume and Julia Nuttall worked in a food factory, but wanted to start their own business. They had seen adverts for organic hampers. Having bought one, they found it was 'all show and presentation' as Amelia put it. The food was unimaginative and inadequate for a large family. The hamper was also expensive at £120. Amelia and Julia both felt they could improve easily on this and exploit the current trend in organic food. They decided to set up a business selling organic picnic hampers from a website.

After estimating demand and finding suppliers to use they were able to come up with some costs. These are outlined below. The fixed costs included items like website design, advertising, insurance and a variety of setting-up costs. These fixed costs were for the first year of trading. They were expected to fall in future years. Examples of the food they planned to include in the hampers were French cheese, antipasta, pickles, pasta salad, rice salad, pitta breads, olives, fresh fruit salad, a bottle of organic wine and fruit juice.

Amelia and Julia decided they would sell the hampers for £80. This was lower than many of their competitors. At this price it was felt that 400 hampers could be sold in the first year of trading. Before making the final decision to launch the business, Amelia insisted that they work out how many hampers they would need to sell to break-even. Amelia and Julia also agreed that they should not give up their jobs at the factory until the business was established.

Fixed costs = £4,000	
Wicker hamper	£12
Food	£39
Utensils	£2
Delivery	£3
Other variable costs	£4

(a) Using this case as an example, explain what is meant by break-even. (4 marks)

(b) (i) Construct a break-even chart for Organic Hampers. (10 marks)
(ii) How many hampers need to be sold to break-even in the first year? (2 marks)

(c) (i) Show the margin of safety if annual sales meet the 400 sales target. (2 marks)
(ii) How much profit is made at this level of sales? (2 marks)

(d) In the second year, it was expected that fixed costs would only be £2,000.
(i) Why are fixed costs likely to fall in the second year of trading? (4 marks)
(ii) Show the new break-even output on the chart. (2 marks)
(iii) If 500 hampers were sold in the second year, could Amelia and Julia leave their factory jobs? (Show any necessary calculations). (6 marks)

(e) What measures could be taken to lower the break-even output in this case? (8 marks)

The importance of cash

Cash is the most LIQUID of all business assets. A business's cash is the notes and coins it keeps on the premises and any money it has in the bank, for example. Cash is part of, but not the same as, working capital. Working capital contains other assets, such as money owed by debtors, which are not immediately available if a business needs to pay bills, for example.

Why is cash so important to a business? Without cash, it would cease to exist. There is a number of reasons why firms fail. The most common tend to be:

- lack of sales;
- inadequate profit margins;
- poor choice of location;
- reliance on too small a customer base;
- poor management of working capital;
- poor cash flow.

According to a Confederation of British Industry (CBI) survey, 21 per cent of business failures are due to poor cash flow or a lack of working capital. Even when trading conditions are good, businesses can fail. Many of these businesses may offer good products for which there was some demand. They have the potential to be profitable and yet still went into RECEIVERSHIP. Probably the most likely cause of this is that they ran out of cash.

The role of cash in a business is shown in Figure 1. It shows a

Figure 1: Continuous cash flow into and out of a business

simple CASH FLOW cycle. Cash flow is the continuous movement of cash into and out of a business. Initially, cash is used to buy or hire resources. These resources are converted into goods or services which are then sold to customers in exchange for cash. Some of the money from sales will be used to finance further production. In a successful business, this flow of cash is endless. If this flow of cash ceases at some stage then the business will be unlikely to continue.

Table 1: Cash flow forecast for Fishan's Ltd

												(£000s)
	Jan	Feb	Mar	Apr	May	Jun	Jul	Aug	Sep	Oct	Nov	Dec
Receipts												
Cash sales	451	360	399	410	490	464	452	340	450	390	480	680
Capital introduced									300			
Total receipts	451	360	399	410	490	464	452	340	750	390	480	680
Payments												
Goods for resale	150	180	150	180	150	180	150	180	150	180	220	250
Leasing charges	20	20	20	20	20	20	20	20	20	20	20	20
Motor expenses	40	40	40	40	40	40	40	40	40	40	40	40
Wages	100	100	100	100	100	100	100	105	105	105	125	125
VAT			126			189			187			198
Loan repayments	35	35	35	35	35	35	35	35	35	35	35	35
Telephone		11				12			12			14
Miscellaneous	20	20	20	20	20	20	20	20	20	20	20	20
Total payments	365	406	491	395	377	584	365	412	557	400	474	688
Net cash flow	86	(46)	(92)	15	113	(120)	87	(72)	193	(10)	6	(8)
Opening balance	11	97	51	(41)	(26)	87	(33)	54	(18)	175	165	171
Closing balance	97	51	(41)	(26)	87	(33)	54	(18)	175	165	171	163

Brackets show minus figures.

Controlling cash flow

It is important that a business continually monitors and controls its cash flow. It must ensure that it has enough cash for its immediate spending. However, it should avoid holding too much cash because cash is an unproductive asset. Holding cash means that the business might lose out on the profit from investing the cash. A business will have more effective control over its cash flow if it:

- keeps up to date business records;
- always plans ahead, for example by producing accurate cash flow forecasts;
- operates an efficient credit control system which prevents slow or late payment.

The need to keep up to date records of business transactions is very important. The quality of decision making is better if accurate information is available when choosing between different courses of action. Problems can arise if decisions are based on inadequate or inaccurate information. For example, say a business fails to record that a £20,000 payment has been made to a supplier. A manager may go ahead with the purchase of a new machine costing £30,000 believing that the firm's cash position is better than it actually is. The business may not have enough money in the bank to cover a cheque given in payment.

Advances in information technology have enabled businesses to keep more up to date records and access information very quickly. However, mistakes can still occur if computer operators fail to input information correctly.

Cash flow forecasts

Most businesses produce a regular CASH FLOW FORECAST. This lists all the likely receipts (**cash inflows**) and payments (**cash outflows**) over a future period of time. All the entries in the forecast are estimated because they have not occurred yet. The forecast shows the planned cash flow of the business month by month. Table 1 shows a twelve month cash flow forecast statement for Fishan's Ltd, a grocery wholesaler located in Ipswich.

What is predicted to happen to cash flow at Fishan's over the twelve month period?

January The company will have an opening cash balance of £11,000 in January. In January receipts are expected to be £451,000 and payments £365,000. This means that an extra £86,000 (£451,000 - £365,000) will be added in this month - a positive NET CASH FLOW. The closing balance should be £97,000 (£11,000 +£86,000).

February In February expected payments (£406,000) are greater than expected receipts (£360,000). This means that there will be a negative net cash flow of £46,000 in February. However, the opening balance of £97,000 will cover this and the business will not have a cash flow problem. It ends the month with a positive closing balance of £51,000 (£97,000 - £46,000).

March In March payments again will be greater than receipts,

The **receipts** of the business are the monthly inflows of cash. For Fishan's, cash sales result from the sale of groceries to local retailers and other customers. The sales figures are probably based on the previous year's. In September the owners have introduced £300,000 of fresh capital to the business. The total amount of cash a business expects to receive each month is shown as total receipts. Some businesses sell goods on credit. If this is the case, the figures in the statement should show cash actually received in that month and not the value of goods sold.

Payments are the outflows from the business. Some payments are for the same regular amounts, such as leasing charges (£20,000) and loan repayments (£35,000). Other payments vary, such as purchases of goods for resale. Some payments such as telephone charges are made on a quarterly basis. It is also possible for payments to be annual such as accountancy fees. These do not appear for Fishan's, perhaps because they employ their own accountant. The total amount of cash a business expects to pay out each month is shown as total payments. If a business buys goods on credit, cash payments made to suppliers are included when they occur and not the value of goods received in a particular month.

Net cash flow for a month is found by subtracting total payments from total receipts. If receipts are greater than payments, net cash flow is positive. If payments are greater than receipts, net cash flow is negative - shown by brackets around a figure.

- The **opening balance** in January will be the value of December's closing balance in the previous year.
- The **closing balance** for a month is found by adding or subtracting the net cash flow for the month from the opening balance.
- The closing balance of one month becomes the opening balance of the next month. It can be a positive or negative figure.

giving a negative net cash flow of £92,000. However, this is now greater than the opening balance of £51,000. This means that the business faces a negative closing balance of £41,000 and will have a cash flow problem. It would have to find some way to finance this, perhaps by borrowing from a bank.

March to May The business will have cash flow problems in March and April, when it faces negative closing balances, even though in April receipts are greater than payments (a positive net cash flow). In May, however, the negative opening balance of £26,000 is outweighed by the positive net cash flow of £113,000. The business will have a positive closing balance of £87,000 and no cash flow problem.

June to December In June and August, but not July, the business would have cash flow problems. From September onwards, when there will be positive closing balances every month, there appear to be no cash flow problems. This is because the owners plan to introduce £300,000 into the business in September.

Why do businesses prepare cash flow forecasts?

Businesses draw up cash flow forecast statements to help control and monitor cash flow in the business. There are certain advantages in using statements to control cash flow.

Identifying the timing of cash shortages and surpluses A forecast can help to identify in advance when a business might wish to borrow cash. At the bottom of the statement the monthly closing balances are shown clearly. This will help the reader to identify when a bank overdraft will be needed. For example, Table 2 showed that Fishan's would need to borrow money in March, April, June and August. In addition, if a large cash surplus is identified in a particular month, this might provide an opportunity to buy some new equipment, for example. A business should try to avoid being overdrawn at the bank because interest is charged. If certain payments can be delayed until cash is available, this will avoid unnecessary borrowing.

Supporting applications for funding When trying to raise finance, lenders often insist that businesses support their applications with documents showing business performance, outlook and solvency. A cash flow forecast will help to indicate the future outlook for the business. It is also common practice to produce a cash flow forecast statement in the planning stages of setting up a business.

Enhancing the planning process Careful planning in business is vital. It helps to clarify aims and improve performance. Producing a cash flow forecast is a key part of the planning process because it is a document concerned with the future.

Monitoring cash flow During and at the end of the financial year a business should make comparisons between the predicted figures in the cash flow forecast and those which actually occur. By doing this it can find out where problems have occurred. It

Question 1.

Norfolk-based Longacre Farm is owned by the Durrant family. The farm has a shop and one weekend a number of customers asked Janet Durrant if they sold homemade soup. This set Janet thinking. She approached her father with the idea of a new business activity - making soup and selling it in the farm shop. She explained that vegetables produced on the farm could be used. Janet produced a business plan with a cash flow forecast. Her father said he would lend Janet £1,000 if she could match the amount to provide start-up capital for Janet's new business venture, Longacre Farm Homemade Soups. A copy of the nine month forecast is shown in Table 2.

Table 2: Cash flow forecast for Longacre Farm Homemade Soups

	May	Jun	Jul	Aug	Sep	Oct	Nov	Dec	(£) Jan
Receipts									
Loan from Mr Durrant	1,000								
Own capital	1,000								
Cash	200	400	500	400	500	600	900	800	1,200
Total receipts	2,200	400	500	400	500	600	900	800	1,200
Payments									
Cooking equipment	900								
Other setting up costs	700								
Vegetables	50	100	125	100	125	150	225	200	300
Other food ingredients	60	80	90	80	90	100	150	130	180
Packaging	50	100	125	100	125	150	225	200	300
Overheads	100	100	100	100	100	100	100	100	100
Total payments	1,860	380	440	380	440	500	700	630	880
Net cash flow	140	20	60	20	60	100	200	170	320
Opening balance	0	140	160	220	240	300	400	600	770
Closing balance	140	160	220	240	300	400	600	770	1,090

(a) Using examples from the month of June, explain how Janet would calculate:
   (i) total payments;
   (ii) net cash flow;
   (iii) closing balance.

(b) Why is the opening balance in May zero?
(c) Explain what is happening to the cash balance resulting from Janet's soup venture.

Question 2.

Kieran Venkat runs an off-licence in the Manchester suburb of Rusholme. He has recently extended his premises into the property next door and is looking to acquire a wider range of stock. The cost of the extension has completely exhausted the business of its cash reserves and Kieran needs to borrow some money to buy stock. He needs to borrow £5,000 for nine months. In order to support his application for a bank loan he drew up the nine month cash flow forecast shown in Table 3. The forecast assumes that the loan has been granted and repayments are included.

(a) Calculate the following figures for Kieran's cash flow forecast.
   (i)   Cash sales and total receipts for October.
   (ii) Total payments for August.
   (iii) Closing balance for November.
   (iv) Opening balance for January.

Table 3: Cash flow forecast statement for Kieran Venkat

	Jul	Aug	Sep	Oct	Nov	Dec	Jan	Feb	Mar
									(£)
Receipts									
Cash sales	3,800	4,000	5,000	?	6,000	9,000	7,000	3,000	3,500
Bank loan	5,000								
Total receipts	8,800	4,000	5,000	?	6,000	9,000	7,000	3,000	3,500
Payments									
Stock	7,000	3,000	3,400	3,400	4,000	6,100	4,800	2,000	2,400
Loan repayments	620	620	620	620	620	620	620	620	620
Casual labour	200	200	200	200	200	400	200	200	200
Miscellaneous costs	100	100	100	100	100	100	100	100	100
Drawings	500	500	500	500	500	500	500	500	500
Insurance				450					
Advertising	370								
Telephone			170			200			210
Total payments	8,790	?	4,990	5,270	5,420	7,920	6,220	3,420	4,030
Net cash flow	10	(420)	10	(270)	580	1,080	780	(420)	(530)
Opening balance	(90)	(80)	(500)	(490)	(760)	(180)	?	1,680	1,260
Closing balance	(80)	(500)	(490)	(760)	?	900	1,680	1,260	730

(b) As well as supporting his application for a bank loan, how else might this cash flow forecast help Kieran in running his business?

(c) On the basis of this cash flow forecast alone, discuss whether a bank would grant Kieran a loan.

---

could then try to identify possible reasons for any significant differences between the two sets of figures. For example, it might be that an overpayment was made. Constant monitoring in this way should allow a business to control its cash flow effectively.

Improving forecasts

Cash flow forecasts may not be helpful if they are inaccurate. Very inaccurate forecasts could lead to businesses getting into trouble and running out of cash. How can a business improve the accuracy of its cash flow forecasts?

Accurate data A cash flow forecast is based on anticipated flows of cash into and out of the business. Some of these flows will be known for certain. For example, a business usually knows what some of its overheads will be next year, such as rent, rates and insurance. Other costs such as wages may have been negotiated for the next year. Variable costs such as raw materials are may be more difficult to predict. This is because output might fluctuate unexpectedly or suppliers may change their prices.

Generally, cash outflows are easier to predict than cash inflows. Most of the cash coming into the business is from sales. It can sometimes be difficult to estimate what sales will be exactly in future. Some businesses have advanced orders, such as firms in the holiday industry, which will help to improve accuracy. Others do market research, while many rely on projections based on the previous year's figures. When cash

inflows and outflows are unknown it is better to overestimate costs and underestimate revenues. New businesses have particular problems when producing forecasts. This is because they have no past data on which to base projections. They also tend to underestimate costs and over-estimate revenues.

Biased forecasts Businesses sometimes manipulate cash flow forecasts. For example, a business may overestimate cash inflows to improve the strength of the business on paper. It might do this if it was borrowing money from a bank. A manager may overestimate costs and underestimate sales so that credit can be taken when the real figures are better. If forecasts are biased they are not likely to be accurate.

Coping with external factors Cash flow forecasts could be improved if business managers could predict future events such as changes in interest rates, the weather and the behaviour of competitors. One way to allow for unforeseen events is to have **contingency funds** built into the cash flow forecast. For example, a business may make a monthly allowance for unexpected costs, including it as a cash outflow. Another approach could be to make regular adjustments to cash flow forecasts during the trading period. If forecasts are updated regularly, predictions may be more accurate. It is also possible to produce a series of forecasts. For example, a business might produce three, a 'worst case', a 'best case' and one in the 'middle'. This could show the business what is likely to happen to its cash position in different situations.

KNOWLEDGE

1. Explain the operation of the cash flow cycle.
2. Why is it important that a business: (i) does not hold too much cash; (ii) holds sufficient cash?
3. Briefly explain what a cash flow forecast includes.
4. How does a cash flow forecast indicate whether a business faces cash flow problems in future?
5. Explain why a business prepares a cash flow forecast.
6. What are the advantages of businesses preparing cash flow statements?
7. How is it possible for a profitable business to collapse?

KEYTERMS

Cash flow – the continuous movement of cash in and out of the business.
Cash flow forecast – the prediction of all expected receipts and expenses of a business over a future time period which shows the expected cash balance at the end of each month.
Liquid asset – an asset which is easily changed into cash.
Net cash flow – cash inflows minus cash onflows over a period of time.
Receivership – the liquidation (selling) of a firm's assets by an independent body following its collapse.

Case Study: Kay Jones Garden Designs

Having completed a HND in Landscape Construction and Garden Design, Kay Jones wanted to run her own garden design business. The design process would involve Kay meeting with a client to discuss their needs and carrying out a survey. A second meeting would establish a more precise brief and a budget. Kay would then put together a 3D masterplan, showing drawings and materials. In addition to design, Kay also planned to do all the construction work. She felt that people might spend between £500 and £5,000 on a new garden design in her local area.

Kay did not have very much capital of her own, so she needed a bank loan. To obtain a loan she would have to draw up a business plan, including an accurate and realistic cash flow forecast. Kay knew that she would stand a better chance of a loan if she had some orders. She decided to get a job and save, develop some orders in her spare time and then launch the business in April. She lived at home and thought she could save £2,000 before the launch.

By February Kay had 5 definite orders for garden designs. She was sure that once she got started people would see her work and orders would follow. However, she did plan to market the business and applied for a listing in *Yellow Pages*. Table 4 shows the predicted revenue for the first nine months of her business. The following financial information was also gathered.

- A bank loan of £3,000 would be needed.
- Kay would contribute £2,000 of her own savings as capital in April.
- A van for £2,000 would be purchased in April.
- Tools and equipment for £3,400 would be purchased in April.
- A laptop computer with specialist design software for £600 would be purchased in April.
- A *Yellow Pages* listing will cost £100 in May.

- General overheads would be £400 per month.
- Advertising will be £100 in alternate months starting in May.
- Kay would take out £800 per month starting in June.
- Loan repayments will be £200 per month.

(a) Explain the meaning of the term 'cash flow forecast'. (4 marks)
(b) Draw up a nine month cash flow forecast for Kay Jones Garden Designs. (12 marks)
(c) (i) Comment on the cash position of the business during the nine month period. (4 marks)
(ii) What would you expect to happen to the cash position of the business in early 2008? Explain your answer. (4 marks)
(d) Once Kay was 'up and running' she had some bad news at the end of April. The van she bought needed some urgent repairs to the value of £1,200. A client with a firm £1,300 order in June cancelled. Produce an amended cash flow forecast. (6 marks)
(e) Do you think the bank would grant a loan based on the amended forecast? (10 marks)

Table 4: Predicted revenue for Kay Jones Garden Designs (first nine months)

	Apr	May	Jun	Jul	Aug	Sep	Oct	Nov	(£) Dec
Predicted revenue	2,000	2,100	2,000	2,500	2,500	2,000	1,000	500	0

NB The predicted revenue is net of the cost of plants and other materials used in the construction of the gardens.

21 Setting budgets

What is a budget?

The control of a business becomes more difficult the larger it is. A new, small business setting up may be run informally. The owner is the manager, who will know everyone, be aware of what is going on and will make all decisions. In medium sized and larger firms, work and responsibility are delegated, which makes informal control impractical. To improve control, budgeting has been developed. This forces others to be accountable for their decisions.

A BUDGET is a plan which is agreed in advance. It must be a plan and not a forecast. A forecast is a prediction of what might happen in the future, whereas a budget is a planned outcome which the firm hopes to achieve. A budget will show the money needed for spending and how this might be financed. Budgets are based on the objectives of businesses. They force managers to think ahead and improve co-ordination. Most budgets are set for twelve months to coincide with the accounting period, but there are exceptions. Research and Development budgets, for example, may cover several years.

Information contained in a budget may include revenue, sales, expenses, profit, personnel, cash and capital expenditure. In fact, budgets can include any business variable (known as a budget factor) which can be given a value. One well known budget is 'The Budget'. The Chancellor of the Exchequer prepares a budget for a particular period. It will take into account the government's spending plans and how these plans will be financed by taxes and other sources of funds.

The reasons for setting budgets

There is a number of reasons why a business sets budgets.

Control and monitoring Budgeting helps control a business. It does this by setting objectives and targets. These are then translated into budgets for, say, the coming year. Success by the business and the workforce in achieving those targets can be found by comparing the actual results with the budget. The reasons for failing to achieve the budget can then be analysed and appropriate action taken.

Planning Budgeting forces businesses to think ahead. Without budgeting, people might work on a day-to-day basis, only dealing with opportunities and problems as they arise. Budgeting, however, plans for the future. It anticipates problems and their solutions.

Co-ordination As a business grows in size its organisation becomes more complicated. There may be different departments or different production and administrative sites. A multinational company will have workers spread across the world. Budgeting is one way of co-ordinating the activities of areas of the business.

Communication Planning allows the objectives of the business to be communicated to its employees. By keeping to a budget, employees have a clear framework within which to operate. So budgeting removes an element of uncertainty within decision making throughout the business.

Efficiency In medium sized or larger businesses it may be difficult for one person to make every decision. Budgeting gives financial control to those workers who are best able to make decisions in the business.

Motivation Budgeting should act as a motivator to employees. It provides workers with targets and standards. Improving on the budget position is an indication of success. Fear of failing to reach budgeted targets may make workers work harder.

The preparation of budgets

The way in which a budget might be prepared is shown in Figure 1. It is a step-by-step process.

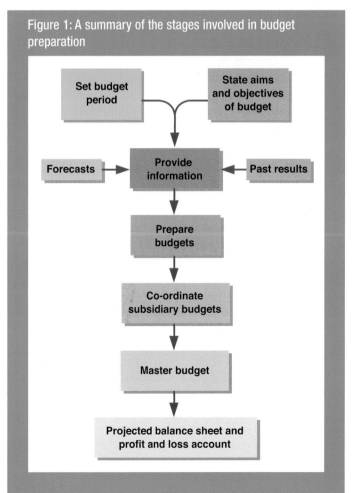

Figure 1: A summary of the stages involved in budget preparation

85

Table 1: Planned sales figures for Emerald Artwork

	Feb	Mar	Apr	May
AD23	100	100	100	100
AD24	50	80	80	100
AE12	40	50	40	50
AE13	30	30	50	50

Table 2: A sales revenue (income) budget for Emerald Artwork

				(£)
	Feb	**Mar**	**Apr**	**May**
AD23	1,200	1,200	1,200	1,200
	(12 x 100)	(12 x 100)	(12 x 100)	(12 x 100)
AD24	1,000	1,600	1,600	2,000
	(20 x 50)	(20 x 80)	(20 x 80)	(20 x 100)
AE12	1,000	1,250	1,000	1,250
	(25 x 40)	(25 x 50)	(25 x 40)	(25 x 50)
AE13	900	900	1,500	1,500
	(30 x 30)	(30 x 30)	(30 x 50)	(30 x 50)
Total	4,100	4,950	5,300	5,950

- Decide on a budget period and state the objectives and targets which are to be achieved. The budget period may vary according to the type of budget. One month or one year is usual. Targets for performance, market share, quality (provided it can be quantified) and productivity are all examples.
- Obtain information upon which to base the budget. A new business setting up will not be able to base its budgets on its own historical information. So it will need to estimate future figures. It may do this from market research. Some business variables are easier to estimate than others. It may be easier to quantify future costs than future sales, for example. This is because sales levels are subject to so many external factors. Once the business has traded for a period, budgets can be based on past figures.
- Prepare budgets. Two important budgets are the sales budget and the production budget. These budgets are related and affect all other budgets. For example, sales targets can only be met if there is productive capacity. Also, a firm would be unlikely to continue production if it could not sell its products. The sales budget will contain monthly sales estimates, expressed in terms of quantities per product, perhaps, and the price charged. From the sales budget, and with knowledge of stock levels, the production budget can be determined. This will show the required raw materials, labour hours and machine hours. At this stage the business should know whether or not it has the capacity to meet the sales targets. If it is not possible, then it may be necessary to adjust the sales budget.
- Draw up subsidiary operating budgets. These are detailed budgets usually prepared by medium sized and larger businesses. Budgets can be broken down, so that each person in the hierarchy can be given some responsibility for a section of the budget.
- The MASTER BUDGET is a summary statement of all budgets. For example, it shows the estimated income, anticipated expenditure, and, thus, the budgeted profit for the period. The cash budget can be prepared when all other budgets are complete. This budget is particularly useful since it shows the monthly flows of cash into and out of the business. It will help to show

whether future cash flow problems might occur.
- Prepare the projected balance sheet and profit and loss of the business. These show the financial position that will result from the firm's budgets.

Income or sales revenue budget

An INCOME or SALES REVENUE BUDGET shows the planned income or revenue for a period of time. Emerald Artwork produces four products, AD23, AD24, AE12 and AE13. They sell for £12, £20, £25 and £30 respectively. The planned sales levels for a four month period are shown in Table 1.

The budget is prepared by showing the planned income or sales revenue in each month. This is calculated by multiplying the predicted sales levels by the prices. The sales revenue budget is shown in Table 2.

Table 3: A production budget for Emerald Artwork covering production of all 4 products

	FEB	MAR	APR	MAY (£)
Cost of materials	660	780	810	900
(£3 per unit)	(3 x 220)	(3 x 260)	(3 x 270)	(3 x 300)
Direct labour costs	880	1,040	1,080	1,200
(£4 per unit)	(4 x 220)	(4 x 260)	(4 x 270)	(4 x 300)
Indirect labour costs	440	520	540	600
(£2 per unit)	(2 x 220)	(2 x 260)	(2 x 270)	(2 x 300)
Production Overheads				
(10% of direct &	1,320 x 10%	1,560 x 10%	1,620 x 10%	1,800 x 10%
indirect costs)	= 132	= 156	= 162	= 180
Total	2,112	2,496	2,592	2,880

Table 4: An expenditure budget for Emerald Artwork

	Feb	Mar	Apr	May (£)
Materials	660	780	810	900
Direct labour	880	1,040	1,080	1,200
Indirect labour	440	520	540	600
Production overheads	132	156	162	180
General overheads	300	600	200	700
Capital expenditure	2,000	0	200	1,700
Total expenditure	4,412	3,096	2,992	5,280

Table 5: Profit budget for Emerald Artwork

	Feb	Mar	Apr	May (£)
Income (sales revenue)	4,100	4,950	5,300	5,950
Expenditure	2,412	3,096	2,792	3,580
Profit	1,688	1,854	2,508	2,370

Production budget

Once Emerald Artwork has produced a sales budget, it is possible to calculate its production budget. The example in Table 3

assumes stock levels stay the same throughout the four month period. The figures are based on expected sales in Table 1.

Expenditure budget

An EXPENDITURE or TOTAL COST BUDGET shows how much money a business is expected to spend for a period of time. It is based on the production budget. Expenditure might include raw materials, labour, production overheads, general overheads and capital expenditure such as new machinery. An expenditure budget is shown for Emerald Artwork in Table 4. It is based on the production budget but includes all other business expenditure for the four month period.

Profit budget

A PROFIT BUDGET shows the amount of profit a business is expected to make over a period. It contains information on all income generated by the business and all expenditure. However, the profit budget would not include capital expenditure. A profit budget for Emerald Artwork is shown in Table 5. Note that capital expenditure has been excluded. In the profit budget, expenditure is subtracted from income to get the monthly profit.

Problems of setting budgets

Businesses may sometimes find that there are problems when setting budgets.

Question 1.

Hannah Ngilo and David Saunders run Penzance Motor Services. The business generates revenue in a number of ways. It sells petrol, a limited range of grocery and confectionery items, car accessories and a few second-hand cars. The garage also carries out servicing, motor repairs and MOT testing. An income budget for a six month period is shown in Table 6.

(a) Complete the income budget for Penzance Motor Services by calculating the total monthly income.
(b) Hannah and David set sales targets for each source of income. What role will setting budgets play when setting such targets?
(c) Explain how the information in this budget might be used in a profit budget.

Table 6: Income budget for Penzance Motor Services

	Jan	Feb	Mar	Apr	May	Jun (£)
Petrol sales	3,400	3,500	3,400	3,600	4,000	4,500
Grocery sales	650	650	700	700	750	800
Car accessories	450	500	500	550	550	600
Car sales	1,000	1,500	2,000	4,000	5,000	6,000
Servicing and repairs	4,300	4,800	5,000	4,500	4,000	3,500
MOTs	400	500	450	550	600	500
Total income						

Question 2.

Melanie Croft runs the Motherwell Leisure Centre, a private leisure facility for residents in the Motherwell and Hamilton areas of Scotland. The centre has about 900 members and offers a range of facilities. In order to keep control of costs Melanie sets expenditure budgets every six months for the various departments within the complex. An expenditure budget for the first six months of 2007 is shown in Table 7.

(a) Complete the expenditure budget shown in Table 7 and calculate the total expenditure for the sixth month period.
(b) What might account for the pattern of expenditure for the café bar over the time period?
(c) Explain how using an expenditure budget could help Melanie control costs in the business.

Table 7: Expenditure budget for the Motherwell Leisure Centre – January to June 2007

						(£)
	Jan	**Feb**	**Mar**	**Apr**	**May**	**Jun**
Sports Hall	1,400	1,600	1,700	1,700	1,500	1,300
Swimming pool	2,300	2,400	2,400	2,500	3,000	3,500
Games room	600	700	600	500	400	200
Fitness centre	3,200	3,500	3,600	3,600	3,400	3,200
Outdoor activities	500	400	500	600	800	1,000
Massage & beauty treatments	5,300	5,300	6,000	6,000	7,000	7,000
Administration	2,000	2,000	2,000	2,000	2,000	2,000
Café bar	3,200	3,500	3,700	4,000	5,000	7,000
Total expenditure						

Using planned figures Problems tend to arise because figures in budgets are not actual figures. Planned figures may be inaccurate. The most important data in the preparation of nearly all budgets is sales data. If sales data are inaccurate, many of the firm's budgets will be inexact. The accuracy of sales data might be improved if market research is used However, it may be difficult to estimate sales of new products for a future period.

Collecting information The setting of budgets in some businesses may require a great deal of co-ordination. This is because different parts of the business may provide information for budgets. Some medium sized and larger businesses appoint a budget officer. This person is responsible for collecting data and opinions, keeping managers to the budget timetable and carrying out budgetary administration.

Conflict The setting of budgets may lead to conflict between staff. For example, a business may only have limited funds. One person may want to spend this on marketing, but another may feel that new machinery is needed.

Cost The time spent setting budgets could have been spent on other tasks. This is very important for a small, new business with limited resources.

Over-ambitious objectives Sometimes businesses set over-ambitious objectives. When this happens, the budgeting process is pointless because budgets are being drawn up for targets which are unachievable. The budget then ceases to become a benchmark with which to compare the outcome.

External influences In some industries, it is difficult to plan ahead because of large and unpredictable changes in the external environment. In farming, for instance, there can be variations in price from year to year and the weather can have large effects on output. This doesn't mean that businesses in such industries should not draw up budgets. However, it can be difficult to analyse outcomes against the budget. It may be unclear if external influences or the way in which a business is run have affected whether a budget is achieved or not.

KNOWLEDGE

1. How might a budget improve employee accountability?
2. Why is the sales budget such an important budget?
3. How might budgets motivate staff?
4. State examples of three types of budget.
5. Why might a business manipulate a budget?
6. What costs are incurred when setting budgets?

KEY TERMS

Budget – a quantitative economic plan prepared and agreed in advance.
Income or sales revenue budget – shows the planned income or revenue for a period of time.
Expenditure or total cost budget – shows how much money a business is expected to spend for a period of time
Profit budget – shows the amount of profit a business is expected to make over a period.
Master budget – a summary statement which brings together information from budgets.

Case Study: Agarka Mini Market

Agarka Mini Market is a small supermarket serving residents in the Poole area of Dorset. The store is divided into a number of sections.

- Dairy – maintains refrigerated products such as milk, cheese, other dairy products, smoothies and fruit juices.
- Delicatessen – serves cold meats, olives, fresh pickles, dips and other delicatessen products.
- Fresh produce – is responsible for all fruit and vegetables.
- Grocery – is the largest department and is responsible for all food products in cans and packets, household goods such as cleaning materials, drinks, confectionery and products which do not fall neatly into other departments.
- Meat – stocks pre-packaged refrigerated meat products for customers and prepares many of these packages for sale. Also cuts meat to order for customers.
- Liquor – this is a new department since a liquor licence was only granted in 2006. However, it is expected to grow rapidly. A wide range of wines, beers and spirits are offered.

Six members of the Agarka family work in the store and a further nine people are employed part-time. In order to monitor the progress of different parts of the business profit budgets are set for every department. The head of each department is paid a six month bonus of 5 per cent of profit if the profit targets are reached. The income and expenditure budgets are shown in Tables 8 and 9.

(a) Explain what is meant by the term budget. (2 marks)

(b) Produce separate profit budgets for each of the sections at the Agarka Mini Market. (18 marks)

(c) (i) Which section has the poorest profit record over the time period? (4 marks)
(ii) How might you account for the poor profit record of the section identified in (i)? (4 marks)

(d) (i) How will profit budgets serve to motivate staff in the store? (6 marks)
(ii) Calculate the six month bonus due to the person responsible for the Grocery department. (4 marks)

(e) Discuss three problems which might be encountered by the Agarka family when setting budgets for their Mini Market. (12 marks)

Table 8: Income budget for Agarka Mini Market

						(£)
	Jul	Aug	Sep	Oct	Nov	Dec
Dairy	7,500	7,500	8,000	8,000	8,000	9,000
Delicatessen	9,000	9,000	9,500	9,500	9,500	12,000
Fresh produce	5,700	6,000	6,000	6,500	6,000	8,000
Grocery	27,000	28,000	29,000	29,000	30,000	34,000
Meat	8,000	8,000	8,500	8,500	9,000	12,000
Liquor	3,000	4,000	5,000	6,000	8,000	17,000

Table 9: Expenditure budget for Agarka Mini Market

						(£)
	Jul	Aug	Sep	Oct	Nov	Dec
Dairy						
Goods for resale	5,000	5,000	5,200	5,300	5,300	6,100
Wages and other costs	1,300	1,200	1,600	1,600	1,500	1,700
Delicatessen						
Goods for resale	6,000	6,000	6,100	6,200	6,000	7,500
Wages and other costs	2,000	2,000	2,100	2,100	2,200	3,000
Fresh produce						
Goods for resale	4,300	4,400	4,700	5,300	5,200	6,300
Wages and other costs	1,000	1,000	1,000	1,000	1,000	1,300
Grocery						
Goods for resale	19,000	19,500	20,000	20,500	20,600	21,200
Wages and other costs	4,200	4,200	4,300	4,300	4,500	6,000
Meat						
Goods for resale	5,100	5,000	5,100	5,300	5,400	7,100
Wages and other costs	1,400	1,400	1,400	1,600	1,600	2,100
Liquor						
Goods for resale	1,800	2,200	3,000	3,500	5,200	10,000
Wages and other costs	500	500	700	700	900	1,200

Assessing start-ups

Business start-ups may succeed or they may fail. Most new businesses have ceased to operate within five years of their starting. So how is it possible to judge the strengths and weaknesses of a business start-up? The place to start is to consider the **objectives** of the start-up and assess the risks involved in the business activity. The business plan should give an indication about whether the objectives are realistic and whether **risks** have been assessed. If the business plan has been poorly thought through, or there is no business plan at all, the chance of failure is much higher.

Objectives of business start-ups

The business plan for a start-up should contain a number of financial objectives. These are likely to include the following.

Sales objectives The plan will almost certainly contain sales objectives. Monthly projections of sales revenue will be given in the cash flow forecast. But there may 'headline' objectives elsewhere in the business plan. For example, the plan may set out objectives for sales in the first month, the sixth month and the twelfth month of operation. There are likely to be two sales figures given. One is the volume of sales. For example, the objective is to sell 20 beds a week, or service 1000 customers a week. The other is the value of sales, the sales revenue or turnover. This is the money generated from sales and is equal to the volume of sales times the average selling price.

Sales objectives might also contain a breakdown of sales. A business plan for a car dealership, for example, might state that first year sales volume will be made up of 40 per cent new cars and 60 per cent second-hand cars. Or a plumber starting up on his own might state that 70 per cent of the work in the first year would be as a contractor for building companies and 30 per cent would be working for private clients.

Profit objectives The plan will almost certainly have profit objectives. One set of profit objectives is likely to relate to the break-even point: at what point in time will the business move from making a loss to making a profit? This may be linked in as well to cash flow forecasting, although profit and cash flow are different. Another set of profit objectives will concern the level of expected profitability on an ongoing basis. For example, the business plan may state that the business will make a profit of £5 000 in its first year and £30,000 in its second year of operation. The plan may also sometimes contain objectives about profit margins: the ratio of profit to sales.

Market share objective Some business plans have market share objectives. For these to be meaningful, the business plan must also contain some research about the size of the market. Market share objectives are helpful to identify what is needed to be competitive against other businesses in the market.

Drawings from the business Some business plans will have objectives about how much the owner will draw from the business over a period of time. Drawings from the business for a start-up one-person business are the equivalent of a wage paid to the owner of the business. It can be different from profit. For example, a person may aim to draw £10,000 from the business in its first year, but another objective might be to make £8,000 operating profit in the first year. The implication is that the owner would have to borrow an extra £2,000 in the first year to finance the drawings. On the other hand, the second year objective might be to draw £20,000 from the business but operating profit will be £30,000. There will then be £10,000 left in the business perhaps to repay loans or to finance expansion of the business.

Cost objectives Most business plans are unlikely to have explicit cost objectives. Sometimes, there is one relating to the start-up costs of the business. For example, for a new restaurant, an objective might be to refurbish premises at a cost £50,000. However, there are always implicit cost objectives if the plan has both profit and sales revenue objectives. This is because cost is equal to profit minus sales revenue.

Question 1.

Expresso Maestro is the name that has been chosen by Retta Feyissa and Emma Hartley for a new coffee and cake shop in Leeds. Their objective is to take £150,000 in sales in the first year. They each need to take £15,000 from the business to live off. With these sales and drawings from the business, they will be breaking even. By the end of the second year, their objective is to take £200,000 in sales andbe able to draw £25,000 each from the business which again would see the business break-even. In their business plan, they have stated no further financial objectives.

John Miles is setting up his own recruitment agency. In his business plan, he expects to take on ten staff within the first year and have a sales turnover of £700,000. He has set himself the objective of taking a 10 per cent share of the market in his local area within 12 months, rising to 20 per cent by the end of his third year of operation. At this stage, three years into operation, his objective is to have a business which could be sold to a buyer for £1 million. He needs to raise £150,000 in capital to start the business.

(a) State two differences in the objectives of the two businesses.
(b) Explain which business has the more ambitious objectives.
(c) Evaluate whether these business objectives are in any way linked to the risk of failure of the business start-up.

Raising capital Many business plans for start-ups will contain objectives about the amount of financial capital that needs to be raised. So, for example, an objective may be to raise £70,000 of capital before starting operations and then a further £50,000 in the following 12 months. Raising capital is an important objective in itself because without start-up capital, the business won't be able to start trading. However, it is also placed as an objective because the business plan will be read by anyone thinking of investing in or lending to the business.

The financial objectives of a start-up will differ according to the size of the start-up and the audience for the business plan. The objectives above would be typical for a small business start-up. However, if the business start-up were a multi million pound company with a number of shareholders as owners, then there would be likely to be a more complex mix of financial objectives. For example, there might be an objective about the value of the company in three years' time. Or there might be an objective about when the first dividend, a share of the profit made, would be paid to shareholders.

Financial objectives also cannot be completely separated from other objectives. For an ordinary start-up, the overall aim will be to get the business up-and-running and profitable as quickly as possible. Then growth of the business should see a growth of profits and an increase in the value of the business. However, the main aim of some start-ups is not financial. Some start-ups are **social enterprises**, where providing a service to disadvantage groups is the main aim. These start-ups have to break-even to survive. But other objectives are more important.

Risk

All economic activity has an element of risk. If you get a job today with a company, there is a possibility that tomorrow the company will fail and everyone will lose their jobs. You buy a new car and may be involved in an accident within minutes of driving it off the garage forecourt.

Starting up a business, however, is likely to carry greater risks than working for someone else. There is so much more that could go wrong: sales might be disappointing, costs higher than predicted, the entrepreneur might fall ill at a crucial moment or the bank may refuse to lend more money.

Risks differ from start-up to start-up. For example, a painter and decorator may be working for a company. He works on a lot of jobs where the company is taking on self-employed painters and decorators. He finds out that it is easy to get contracts and gets information about how to do this. Then he quits his job and sets up on his own. He has no problems about getting work from day one. But he also knows that it would be relatively easy to go back to getting a job working for someone else. His costs of setting up on his own are very low whilst his revenues are reasonably assured. The risk of the start-up here is very low.

At the other extreme might be a new biological research company. Its objective is to find a cutting edge new process or product that can be developed into something that can be sold to customers. There is no guarantee at the start that it will find anything that will be marketable. Millions of pounds could be spent and no revenues generated. Eventually it will run out of start-up money and be forced to close. Science research companies like this are very high risk because there is no assured source of revenues.

Most business start-ups fall between these two extremes. However, the greater the uncertainty about future costs and revenues, the riskier the start-up. To understand more about risk, it is important to consider what can cause a business to fail.

Why businesses fail

Businesses fail from a financial viewpoint for a number of reasons.

Lower than expected revenues Many start-ups don't generate enough sales revenues. Either they don't sell enough or the price they get for what they sell is too low. For example, in its business plan, a hairdressing salon might have predicted that it would have 150 customers a week each paying on average £20. Its sales revenue was therefore predicted at £3,000 per week. By the end of its first year, the salon is only attracting 100 customers a week each paying on average £15. Sales revenue is therefore only £1,500, half of what was predicted. If revenues are too low, the business could make a loss which would lead to its failure. Or it may make insufficient profit for the entrepreneur to want to carry on in business. For example, the owner of the hairdressing salon might make £10,000 a year from the business. But if she could make £20,000 a year working for someone else, there would be a strong financial incentive for her to close her business and go back to an ordinary paid job.

Higher than expected start-up costs The majority of start-ups underestimate the cost of the start-up. For example, for a new restaurant, the cost of fitting out a building is likely to be higher than expected. Or an entrepreneur setting up a recruitment agency might underestimate the amount of time needed to comply with regulations. Some entrepreneurs simply run out of money at this stage and the start-up fails to get off the ground. Most will find extra money often by borrowing more from the bank. But then they have higher than expected loan repayments to make. If their revenues aren't high enough to cover these, the business will fail.

Higher than expected operating costs Many business plans underestimate the day-to-day running costs of the business. Sometimes this is because costs are simply not included in the business plan. More often, it is because actual costs are higher than predicted costs. If costs are too high, profits will be too low or the business might make a loss. In the long term, this is likely to lead to the closure of the business.

Unexpected shocks Some businesses fail because of unexpected shocks. In 1988, for example, the UK was experiencing an economic boom. The government was encouraging people to set up their own businesses. Within two years, the economy was in recession. Unemployment doubled, interest rates doubled and house prices fell. Not surprisingly, many new

Question 2.

Drawing up a business plan is no guarantee of success as Chris Watkins found out. Chris Watkins was the production manager for a firm which produced mainly own label toiletries for some of the big supermarket groups. It was in a competitve market and profit margins were wafer thin. Chris was continually being asked to cut costs at the factory or risk facing redundancy along with the rest of the production staff. He decided that he had had enough and would start his own business manufacturing toiletries. His business idea was that he would go up-market to avoid price competition. He would sell mainly to smaller stores and avoid dealing with the major supermarket chains.

He did some market research, contacting a number of small local stores, and they all said that they would definitely be interested in buying his products. He produced samples and did some costings based on buying some second-hand equipment and renting a unit on an industrial estate. The financial figures looked good and there was a substantial margin between revenues and costs, even in the first year of operation. But he had trouble borrowing the £100,000 he needed as start-up capital. Three banks refused him an ordinary business loan saying that his business plan was weak. In the end, he remortgaged his house for the £100,000 he needed.

He was full of hope when he started operations. He had some small orders for his products but he intended to launch his real marketing campaign once he had sorted out production. The problem was that the marketing campaign was a disaster. He ended up with four weeks of unsold stock and no cash left to continue. He was forced to close the business.

(a) Explain three reasons for the failure of Chris Watkins' business.
(b) 'The most important reason why the business failed was the weak business plan.' To what extent to do you agree with this?

start-ups failed too because they couldn't generate enough sales to survive. Also their cost of borrowing was substantially more than they had expected. Another example of an unexpected shock is flooding. In recent years, a number of areas of the UK have experienced unexpected flooding. Some businesses have failed as a result. They have lost orders and equipment. Some have been uninsured and haven't had the financial capital to be able to restart.

Reliance on a few large customers Small businesses are vulnerable if they rely on just a few customers for most of their orders. For example, a new start-up business may have landed a contract which accounts for 40 per cent of its orders. It borrows a substantial amount of money to buy equipment to fulfill the contract. Then, suddenly, the customers cancels the contract. Forty per cent of sales immediately have gone. But the repayments on the loans for the equipment have to be kept up. In these circumstances, a new business start-up can go from being profitable to being loss making and subsequently fail.

Operational problems Some start-ups fail because of operational problems. For example, a business may suddenly find it very difficult to find supplies. Perhaps an existing supplier discontinues a product and the start-up business then can't find an alternative supplier. Or it takes much longer to do a job than expected.

Cash flow problems Cash flow through a business is the difference between the money coming in and the money going out on a day-to-day, month to month basis. Start-ups can be profitable but fail because of cash flow problems. One reason for this is the system of credit operated by businesses. When a business sells to another business, it typically has to give at least 30 days' credit. So it won't get paid for 30 days after the work has been completed. Even then, many businesses pay late. So it could be 60 days or 90 days before the start-up business is paid. On the other hand, many costs have to be paid now. Rents, loan repayments, cost of supplies and wages have to be paid on a regular basis. A start-up can simply run out of cash and then fail.

Lack of profitability Some start-ups fail because they are loss making. They make a loss on their day-to-day operations and on top of that the entrepreneur will have spent money on starting up the business. Entrepreneurs can lose tens of thousands of pounds if not more on a new business venture. Some have mortgaged their houses to raise the money to start the business and are forced to sell the house to repay the debts. Most start-ups, however, cease trading because they are not sufficiently profitable. Running your own business has many advantages. But most entrepreneurs work much longer hours running their own business than they would if they were in a normal paid job. If then they are getting much less financially from their business than they would as a wage, they are likely to give up their business. Entrepreneurs have to weigh up the **opportunity cost**, the benefits from their next best activity, of running their own business. If the opportunity cost is too high, because they could be earning £30,000 a year in a job but the profits on their business are only £3,000 a year, then they are likely to close down their business.

Strengths and weaknesses of a business plan

Research evidence shows that business planning is crucial to the success or failure of a start-up business. A good business plan is one which has three characteristics.

- It is comprehensive and has been well researched. It covers all aspects of the business and each aspect has been explored thoroughly.
- It is realistic. The objectives of the business must be

realistic. So too must the assumptions built into the plan. One key reason why business start-ups fail is because the would-be entrepreneur is far too optimistic about sales, costs and profits. It is very easy to get carried away with an idea and overestimate sales or underestimate costs.

- It is coherent. So one part of the business plan must fit with another part of the plan. For example, a would-be entrepreneur might develop a business plan for football coaching for 5-11 year olds. If one part of the business plan says that there will be 40 children attending between 10 and 11 o'clock on a Saturday morning, but another part of the business plan states that he will not be employing anyone to help him, then the business plan is not coherent. One person legally cannot look after 40 children.

Weak business plans are over-optimistic, poorly researched and not properly thought through. Many start-ups, particularly when the business is small and is operated on a part-time basis, have never had a business plan. Where the business is very

simple, and there are few costs and revenues, this probably won't matter. But effective business planning helps sort out complex issues. It allows the owner to align the goals of the business with its operations. It considerably reduces the risk of failure because potential problems and opportunities have been identified.

KNOWLEDGE

1. Explain the differences between a sales objective, profit objective and market share objective for a business start-up.
2. Why might raising capital be an important objective for a business start-up?
3. Explain two sources of risk for a start-up business.
4. A business can fail because sales are lower than expected or costs are higher than expected. Explain why.
5. Business failure can sometimes occur because of unexpected events. Give two examples of such events and explain why they might force a business to cease trading.

Case Study: RD Servicing and Repairs

Rosie and Dean Spencer have just finished their first year of trading and it has been an unimaginable success. Dean worked for 20 years as a driver and then a mechanic of HGVs (heavy goods vehicles). Rosie had worked in the same garage as a car mechanic. For a long time, they felt that the business they worked for was inefficient. It didn't seem to care about its customers. Prices were high and the quality of workmanship was not always very good. Two years ago, they decided they wanted to set up on their own. Their business idea was to offer a better quality of service at lower prices than other firms in the area.

They spent a year drawing up their business plan. Two of their financial objectives were for sales revenue to be £200,000 in their first year and for the business to break even after Rosie and Dean had been paid a salary of £20,000 each. A third objective was to get an overdraft facility of £10,000 and a bank loan of £50,000 to cover start-up costs.

Having resigned from their jobs where between them they were earning £50 a year, they started operations. The first year of operation was hectic. The first month, Rosie and Dean spent a great deal of time marketing their new HGV maintenance and repairs service to local customers. Then, as the work built up, over the next couple of months, Dean was forced to spend all his time as the mechanic. The business plan anticipated that the company would have to take on two more mechanics at the end of the sixth month of operation. In fact, he had to take on three mechanics. By the end of the twelfth month they were employing thirteen staff, including seven mechanics. By that stage, the first year's sales turnover was £370,000.

However, this growth had not been without its problems. Half way through the year, it became apparent that they were running out of cash. Bills were having to be paid faster than customers were paying their invoices. The £10,000 overdraft was going to be breached. What's more, customers were asking for services which needed equipment the business didn't have. They went back to the bank to ask for £30,000 in loans, but the bank refused them saying they were too risky at this stage. They then

turned to a local government funded business development agency which stepped in with the £30,000 loan. The crisis was averted, but only just.

Another major problem occurred when they had to move premises after six months. Because of their unexpected expansion, they found their initial premises on an industrial estate were too small. They arranged to move to larger premises on the same industrial estate. On the Friday night before they were due to move on the Saturday, vandals burnt down the industrial unit they were to occupy. Equipment had been packed and three working days cleared of all appointments. The move had to be put back by two months until another industrial unit became available. Not only was time lost, but customers had to wait longer for an available appointment and it took more time to do the work because of the lack of space.

(a) Briefly explain why drawing up a business plan is important for a business start-up. (10 marks)

(b) Evaluate the risks that Rosie and Dean Spencer took in starting their business. (15 marks)

(c) 'Rosie and Dean's business plan was poor because it failed to identify how quickly the business would grow and the risks that it might face.' To what extent do you agree with this statement? (15 marks)

Managing finance

Once a business is established the owners will generally want to improve its performance. In the early stages of business development the emphasis is often on survival. But once the business is through this stage, other issues become important. Owners will probably want to grow their businesses and improve their effectiveness. One aspect of improving the effectiveness of a business is financial management. This involves managing the financial resources of the business. In most businesses this means:

* making sure that costs are kept down;
* ensuring that there is enough money to buy resources;
* ensuring that customers pay for what they have bought;
* measuring and monitoring financial performance indicators, such as profit and returns on capital.

Businesses have developed a number of systems to help manage financial resources and one of these is budgeting.

Using budgets

BUDGETARY CONTROL or BUDGETING involves a business using budgets to look into the future, stating what it wants to happen, and then deciding how to achieve these aims. The control process is shown in Figure 1.

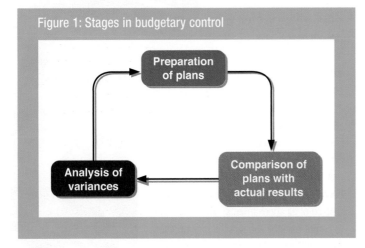

Figure 1: Stages in budgetary control

Preparation of plans

Comparison of plans with actual results

Analysis of variances

Preparation of plans All businesses have objectives. If the sales department increases sales by 10 per cent, how does it know whether or not this is satisfactory? Targets are usually set which allow a business to determine whether its objectives have been met. The results it achieves can then be compared with the targets it sets.

Comparisons of plans with actual results Control will be effective if information is available as quickly as possible. Managers need budgetary data as soon as it is available. Recent developments in information technology have helped to speed

up the supply of data. For budgeting purposes the financial year has been divided up into smaller control periods - usually four weeks or one calendar month. It is common to prepare a budget for each control period. At the end of the period the actual results can then be compared with targets set in the budget.

Analysis of variances This is the most important stage in the control process. VARIANCE ANALYSIS involves trying to find reasons for the differences between actual and expected financial outcomes. Variances are explained in the next section. A variance might be the result of some external factor influencing the business. In this case the business may need to change its business plans and adjust the next budget.

Variances

A VARIANCE in budgeting is the difference between the figure that the business has budgeted for and the actual figure. Variances are usually calculated at the end of the budget period, as that is when the actual figure will be known.

Variances can be **favourable** (F) or **adverse** (A). Favourable variances occur when the actual figures are 'better' than the budgeted figures.

* If the sales revenue for a month was budgeted at £25,000, but turned out to be £29,000, there would be a £4,000 favourable variance (£29,000-£25,000) as sales revenue was higher than planned.
* If costs were planned to be £20,000 and turned out to be £18,000, this would also be a favourable variance of £2,000, as actual costs were lower than planned.

Adverse variances are when the actual figures are worse than the budgeted figures. Actual sales revenues may be lower than planned, or actual costs may be higher than planned. Managers will examine variances and try to identify reasons why they have occurred. By doing this they might be able to improve the performance of the business in the future.

Types of variance

Variances can be calculated for a wide range of financial outcomes. Most budgets are set for expenditure (costs) and income (sales revenue). Consequently, variances will also focus on a firm's expenditures and income. This suggests that variance analysis provides a very good way of monitoring business costs. Examples of variances could be wages, materials, overheads and sales revenue. Variances can also be calculated for volumes. For example it is possible to calculate a sales variance or a labour hours variance. One of the most important variances of all is the profit variance. The profit variance is influenced by all other variances. A change in any variance will affect profit. This is because all variances relate to either the costs or the revenue of a business, both of which affect profit levels. The number of

Table 1: Income budget, actual income and income variances for Wishart Ltd

	Jan	Feb	Mar	Apr	May	Jun	(£) Total
Budgeted income	16,500	17,000	17,500	18,000	19,000	20,000	108,000
Actual income	16,600	17,400	17,900	17,700	18,500	20,800	108,900
Variance	**100F**	**400F**	**400F**	**300A**	**500A**	**800F**	**900F**

Table 2: Budgeted expenditure, actual expenditure and expenditure variances for Wishart Ltd

	Jan	Feb	Mar	Apr	May	Jun	(£) Total
Budgeted expenditure	11,400	11,900	12,500	13,000	14,000	15,000	77,800
Actual expenditure	11,500	11,600	12,700	13,500	14,200	15,600	79,100
Expenditure variances	**100A**	**300F**	**200A**	**500A**	**200A**	**600A**	**1,300A**

Table 3: Budgeted profit, actual profit and profit variance for Wishart Ltd

	Jan	Feb	Mar	Apr	May	Jun	(£) Total
Budgeted profit	5,100	5,100	5,000	5,000	5,000	5,000	30,200
Actual profit	5,100	5,800	5,200	4,200	4,300	5,200	29,800
Profit variances	**0**	**700F**	**200F**	**800A**	**700A**	**200F**	**400A**

monthly expenditure variances are adverse over the time period. For example, in April the variance was £500A. This means that costs were £500 higher than planned. Over the whole six month period the expenditure variance was adverse at £1,300. There is a number of possible reasons for such adverse variances.

- Costs might be higher because production was higher.
- Suppliers may have raised prices.
- There may be some inefficiencies in production.
- Wages may have been higher due to wage demands by workers.

Profit variances The most important of all variances is the profit variance. Differences between actual profit and planned profit will be of particular interest to business owners, managers and other stakeholders. The performance of most businesses is often measured by profit. Table 3 shows the budgeted profit, actual profit and profit variance for Wishart Ltd. Some of the monthly variances are favorable while others are unfavourable. In January there was no variance at all. This is because budgeted profit was exactly the same as actual profit. Over the six month period the profit variance was adverse at £400. This means that profit was £400 lower than planned.

The main reason for Wishart's adverse profit variances over the six month period is the adverse cost variance of £1,300. Costs have been higher than planned. Higher costs may have been caused by a number of factors, such as those listed in the examples above.

Using variances for decision making

The final stage in budgetary control is the analysis of variances. It is important to identify the reasons why variances have occurred. If variances are adverse it will be necessary to take action to ensure that adverse variances are avoided in future. If variances are favourable the business can learn from understanding the reasons why this has occurred and can introduce strategies and systems to help sustain performance improvements in the future.

When making decisions about how the business should be run, information about the causes of variances will be very helpful. For example, if a business has an adverse cost variance, it might discover that the cause was higher prices charged by suppliers. The business might then decide to look for new suppliers. A favourable sales revenue variance might be the result of an effective advertising campaign. The business might

possible variances is equal to the number of factors which can influence business costs and revenue.

Income or sales revenue variances Table 1 shows the budgeted income, actual income and income variances for Wishart Ltd, a bamboo and wicker furniture manufacturer. Four of the monthly variances are favourable while two are adverse. The biggest variance occurred in June. In this month actual income was £800 greater than the budgeted income. The variance for the whole six month period is also shown. Over the period the total income variance was £900. Wishart Ltd's shareholders are likely to be pleased with this.

Possible causes of the favourable income variance over the six months in this case might be the result of:

- the ability to charge higher prices;
- an increase in demand due to a marketing campaign;
- improvements in the quality of the product;
- an increase in consumer incomes;
- a change in consumer's tastes in favour of bamboo and wicker furniture.

Expenditure or cost variances Table 2 shows the budgeted expenditure, actual expenditure and expenditure or total cost variances for Wishart Ltd over the six month period. Most of the

Question 1.

FT Office Supplies sells office equipment and computer accessories such as printers, toners, computer cables, port hubs and laptop bags. It used to operate three stores in the south of England, but it recently closed the stores and now conducts all business online. To monitor sales the business sets budgets every six months. Table 4 shows an income (sales revenue) budget for the first six months of 2007. Actual income figures are also shown.

Table 4: Income budget and actual income for FT Office Supplies

	Jan	Feb	Mar	Apr	May	Jun	(£000) Total
Budgeted income	1,200	1,300	1,400	1,400	1,500	1,600	8,400
Actual income	1,140	1,190	1,430	1,400	1,390	1,450	8,000

(a) Calculate the sales revenue variances for each month and the total sales revenue variance for the whole budget period.

(b) Explain the variance in April.

(c) Analyse two possible reasons for the pattern of variances for FT Office Supplies over the six month time period.

decide to make more use of the same or similar campaigns in the future. Variance analysis can help business decision-makers because of the information they provide about financial outcomes and their causes.

Zero-based budgeting

The financial information used in most budgets is based on **historical** data. For example, the cost of materials in this year's production budget may be based on last year's figure, with perhaps an allowance for inflation. Production and manufacturing costs, such as labour, raw materials and overheads, are relatively easy to value and tend to be controlled using methods such as standard costing.

However, in some areas of business it is not so easy to quantify costs. Examples might be certain marketing, administration or computer services costs. Where costs cannot be justified then no money is allocated in the budget for those costs. This is known as ZERO-BASED BUDGETING (ZBB) or ZERO BUDGETING. A manager must show that a particular item of spending generates an adequate amount of benefit in relation to the general objectives of the business in order for money to be allocated in a budget.

This approach is different to the common practice of extrapolating from past costs. It encourages the regular evaluation of costs and helps to minimise unnecessary purchases. The concept of **opportunity cost** is linked to ZBB. Opportunity cost is the cost of the next best alternative. When choices are made, businesses try to minimise the opportunity cost. ZBB also involves a cautious approach to spending, so that costs are minimised. Both approaches include an element of 'value for money'.

The main advantages of ZBB are that:
- the allocation of resources should be improved;

- a questioning attitude is developed which will help to reduce unnecessary costs and eliminate inefficient practices;
- staff motivation might improve because evaluation skills are practised and a greater knowledge of the firm's operations might develop;
- it encourages managers to look for alternatives.

ZBB also has some disadvantages.
- It is time consuming because the budgeting process involves the collection and analysis of quite detailed information so that spending decisions can be made.
- Skilful decision making is required. Such skills may not be available in the organisation. In addition, decisions may be influenced by subjective opinions.
- It threatens the status quo. This might adversely affect motivation.
- Managers may not be prepared to justify spending on certain costs. Money, therefore, may not be allocated to spending which could benefit the business.

To deal with these possible problems, a business might give each department a 'base' budget of, say, 50 per cent. Departments could then be invited to bid for increased expenditure on a ZBB basis.

Benefits of using budgets

Monitoring performance Budgets allow managers to monitor the performance of a business as a whole, as well as different sections. For example, analysing departmental cost variances may allow a business to find out why certain departments are incurring high costs. Alternatively, it allows businesses to identify good practice and discover why some costs are lower.

Identifying factors affecting performance Prompt variance analysis allows managers to assess whether variances are caused by internal or external factors. Once causes have been traced, they can be corrected.

Improved plans in future By identifying variances and their causes managers may be able to produce more accurate budgets in future. This will aid planning and perhaps improve the performance of the business.

Improved accountability Budgetary control in general helps to improve accountability in businesses. It can also be linked to performance-related pay. For example, budget holders may receive a bonus payment at the end of the budget period if they can show favourable variances. Consequently motivation in a business can be improved.

Question 2.

Armstrong Ltd makes components for games machines in arcades. The company operates from an industrial estate in Slough. It has experienced some problems in recent months due to worn out machinery. An expenditure budget and actual expenditure are shown in Table 5.

Table 5: Budgeted costs and actual costs for Armstrong Ltd

							(£000)
	Jan	**Feb**	**Mar**	**Apr**	**May**	**Jun**	**Total**
Budgeted direct costs	2,300	2,500	2,500	2,600	2,600	2,700	15,200
Budgeted overheads	200	200	200	300	300	300	1,500
Budgeted total cost	2,500	2,700	2,700	2,900	2,900	3,000	16,700
Actual direct costs	2,200	2,450	2,400	2,550	2,600	2,600	14,800
Actual overheads	210	220	190	890	750	320	2,580
Actual total cost	2,410	2,670	2,590	3,440	3,350	2,920	17,380

(a) Calculate the following variances: (i) direct cost (ii) overheads and (iii) total cost.
(b) Analyse the variances calculated in (a).

Drawbacks of using budgets

Motivation In some businesses, workers are left out of the planning process. If workers are not consulted about the budget, it will be more difficult to use that budget to motivate them. Budgets which are unrealistic can also fail to motivate staff.

Manipulation Budgets can be manipulated by managers. For example, a departmental manager might have great influence over those people co-ordinating and setting budgets. The manager may be able to arrange a budget which is easy to achieve and makes the department look successful. But the budget may not help the business achieve its objectives.

Rigidity Budgets can sometimes constrain business activities. For instance, departments within a business may have different views about when it is best to replace vehicles. The more often vehicles are replaced, the higher the cost. However, the newer the vehicle, the lower the maintenance cost and the less likely it is to be off the road for repairs. The budget may be set so that older vehicles have to be kept rather than replaced. But this may lead to customer dissatisfaction and lost orders because deliveries are unreliable.

Short-termism Some managers might be too focused on the current budget. They might take actions that undermine the future performance of the business just to meet current budget targets. For example, to keep labour costs down in the current budget period, the manager of a supermarket might reduce staffing on customer service. This might save costs now, but it could lead to customers drifting away over time due to poor service. Consequently the long-term performance of the business would suffer.

KEYTERMS

Budgetary control or Budgeting – a business system which involves making future plans, comparing the actual results with the planned results and then investigating causes of any differences.
Variance – the difference between actual financial outcomes and those which were budgeted.
Variance analysis – the process of calculating variances and attempting to identify their causes.
Zero-based budgeting or zero budgeting – a system of budgeting where no money is allocated for costs or spending unless they can be justified by the fundholder (they are given a zero value).

KNOWLEDGE

1. What is meant by financial management?
2. Describe the three steps in budgetary control.
3. Explain how a variance is calculated.
4. What is meant by an adverse variance?
5. State two possible causes of a favourable sales revenue variance.
6. State two possible causes of an adverse cost variance.
7. State four benefits of using budgets.

Case Study: *Cynplex.com*

Cynplex.com, founded and owned by Josh Howarth, develops software for e-transactions including payments, document distribution and account verification. Cynplex.com, based in Glasgow, has a good proportion of the UK market for electronic funds transfer with over 10,000 business customers. Cynplex.com's software provides a range of integrated e-business solutions for businesses of any type and size. The software is designed to improve efficiency by reducing the time and expense of manual day-to-day business processes. The products include:

- payment solutions – for processing transactions such as payroll and supplier payments;
- electronic data interchange – for streamlined communications between trading partners;
- collections management – for managing multiple Direct Debit and credit card transactions;
- e-document distribution – for fast, efficient distribution of financial documents such as purchase orders and invoices.

Josh has grown the business successfully since it was setup five years ago. He employs an accountant who is responsible for the financial management of the business. He uses variance analysis to monitor income, expenditure and profit. Some financial information is shown in Table 6 for Cynplex.com.

Table 6: Financial information for Cynplex.com

			(£000)
	2007	2006	2005
Budgeted income	4,500	3,800	3,200
Budgeted expenditure	3,900	3,350	2,800
Budgeted profit	600	450	400
	2007	**2006**	**2005**
Actual income	4,890	4,010	3,600
Actual expenditure	4,050	3,400	3,100
Actual profit	840	610	500

(a) Using this case as an example, explain what is meant by a favourable variance. (3 marks)

(b) Calculate the income, expenditure and profit variances for Cynplex.com for each year. (9 marks)

(c) Why is the profit variance probably the most important of all? (4 marks)

(d) Analyse the variances calculated in (c). (10 marks)

(e) Josh is hoping to float the company on the stock market in order to raise finance to break into overseas markets. How might the profit variances influence this decision? (10 marks)

(f) Evaluate the drawbacks to Cynplex.com of using budgets as a means of financial management. (14 marks).

24 | Improving cash flow

Cash flow and financial management

One crucial aspect of financial management is making sure that the business has enough cash when it is needed. If a business runs out of cash it will find it difficult, if not impossible, to trade. It will probably have to close down. In 2007, music retailer Fopp closed down after an 'extraordinary stock take'. It revealed that it had run out of cash after the company overreached itself through the purchase of the ailing Music Zone group in February. In July receivers were called in and it was announced that all 105 of its stores would be closed at the expense of 700 jobs.

This example illustrates the importance of careful financial management. Prudent owners and managers may use budgets, cash flow forecasts and credit control systems to manage financial resources effectively. Effective financial management will ensure that the business has enough cash when it is needed.

Causes of cash flow problems

Shortages of cash in a business often result from a number of errors in the control of financial resources.

Overtrading Young and rapidly growing businesses are particularly prone to OVERTRADING. Overtrading occurs when a business is attempting to fund a large volume of production with inadequate cash. Established companies trying to expand can also face this problem.

Investing too much in fixed assets In the initial stages of a business, funds are limited. Spending large amounts quickly on equipment, vehicles and other capital items drains resources. It may be better to lease some of these fixed assets, leaving sufficient cash funds.

Stockpiling Holding stocks of raw materials and finished goods is expensive. Money tied up in stocks is unproductive. Stocks may become obsolete. In addition, stocks of raw materials in particular cannot easily be changed into cash without making a loss. Stock control is an important feature of managing liquid resources. Firms should not buy in bulk if discounts are not enough to compensate for the extra cost of holding stocks.

Allowing too much credit A great deal of business is done on credit. One of the dangers is that businesses allow their customers too long to pay their bills. This means that they are waiting for money and may actually be forced to borrow during this period. Failure to control debtors may also lead to bad debts. Taking early action is the key to the effective control of debtors. At the same time businesses must maintain good relations with customers. Small firms are particularly vulnerable

if they are owed money by much larger companies. Powerful businesses are often accused of endangering smaller companies by delaying payments to them.

Taking too much credit Taking more credit might appear to help a firm's cash position since payments are delayed. However, there are some drawbacks. Taking too much credit might result in higher prices, lost discounts, difficulties in obtaining future supplies and a bad name in the trade. At worst, credit might be withdrawn.

Overborrowing Businesses may borrow to finance growth. As more loans are taken out, interest costs rise. Overborrowing not only threatens a firm's cash position, but also the overall control of the business. It is important to fund growth in a balanced way, for example by raising some capital from share issues. Examples of overborrowing are not uncommon in the mortgage market. Sometimes people 'overstretch' themselves. They take out mortgages to buy houses that they can't really afford. In the worse cases, people are not able to meet interest payments and their houses are repossessed. The same could happen to businesses if they borrow too much. If they are not able to meet interest payments, their businesses could be wound up.

Underestimating inflation Businesses often fail to take inflation into account. Inflation raises costs, which can cause cash shortages. This is often the case if higher costs, such as wages or raw materials, cannot be passed on in higher prices. Inflationary periods are often accompanied by higher interest rates which place further pressure on liquid resources. Inflation is also a problem because it is difficult to predict future rates. Although it can be built into plans, firms often underestimate it. In the last ten years inflation has not been a real problem. However, sharp increase in the price of certain raw materials, such as oil, has put pressure on some businesses, particularly those that rely heavily on oil.

Unforeseen expenditure Businesses are subject to unpredictable external forces. They must make financial provision for any unforeseen expenditure. Equipment breakdowns, tax demands, strikes and bad debts are common examples of this type of emergency expense. In the early stages of business development, owners are often hit by unforeseen expenditure. This might be because they lack experience or have not undertaken sufficient planning.

Unexpected changes in demand Although most businesses try to sustain demand for their products, there may be times when it falls unexpectedly. Unpredicted changes in fashion could lead to a fall in demand. This could lead to a lack of sales and cash

Question 1.

In July 2007, Kwik Save the supermarket chain, collapsed after it ran out of cash. Most of its workers had not been paid for up to six weeks. Kwik Save was founded in 1959 as one shop in Rhyl, north Wales, and floated on the stock exchange in 1970. By the 1990s it had more than 1,000 stores and recently became part of Somerfield. However, it was sold on to a new firm, BTTF, headed by Mr Niklas, in February 2007. Some new cash was injected into the business but it was not enough to save the chain.

The firm collapsed due to a combination of tough competition from the big supermarkets which have slashed prices, foreign low-cost rivals such as Aldi and Lidl, and bad management. In May suppliers halted bread and milk deliveries saying that there were considerable difficulties getting paid by Kwik Save. Just before the company collapsed 81 stores were closed and 700 people lost their jobs. A further 90 stores were closed on the day it collapsed with around 1,100 people being laid off. However, it was hoped that some of the stores would be bought by other retailers and that some people would be kept on. Amanda Higgins, the former deputy manager of a store in Ellesmere Port that has been closed down, heard the news on television, while the company remained silent. 'It's diabolical,' she said. 'I just don't know what to do.'

She phoned the Little Sutton store near her home and was told by staff there that the shop had been shut down. Staff were also told that if they came in and handed over the store in a rational manner they would be paid a week's wages, but Ms Higgins could not believe it.

Source: adapted from *The Guardian*, 6.7.2007 and www.a2mediagroup.com

(a) Using this case as an example, explain the importance of cash when running a business.
(b) Explain how: (i) employees and (ii) the owner will be affected by the collapse of Kwik Save.
(c) Analyse the possible causes of the collapse of Kwik Save.

---

flowing into a company. Travel companies in the UK have faced this problem in the past. Companies have to 'buy' holidays before they are sold. External factors, including a recession, may have led to many of these holidays remaining unsold as consumers changed their holiday buying patterns. Firms may also have lost revenue if holidays were discounted in an attempt to sell them.

Seasonal factors Sometimes trade fluctuates for seasonal reasons. In the agriculture industry, cereal farmers have a large cash inflow when their harvest is sold. For much of the year,

---

though, they have to pay expenses without any cash flowing in. This situation requires careful management, although it is possible to predict these changes.

Poor financial management Inexperience in managing cash or a poor understanding of the way cash flows into and out of a business may lead to cash flow problems. For example, if a business plans to spend heavily just before it receives large amounts of cash from customers who have bought on credit, it is likely to face problems. It is not prudent to spend cash when it is not definitely there.

Methods of improving cash flow

Cash flow problems can be prevented by keeping a tight control on financial resources. The use of budgets and cash flow forecasts will improve the financial management of the business. Inevitably, though, there will be occasions when firms run short of cash. When this does happen the firm's main aim will be survival rather than profit. The following measures might be used to either generate cash or save it.

Use of overdraft facilities If a business is not able, or does not wish, to use the options listed above, an obvious option is to borrow money. Most businesses have an overdraft facility with their banks. An overdraft is a type of flexible loan. The borrower can choose to borrow up to a certain sum of money agreed with the bank, called the overdraft limit. But they are free to pay back part of the money borrowed at any time and do not have to be borrowing money to have an overdraft facility. A business can increase its cash by borrowing more money on its overdraft. For example, it might have an overdraft limit of £5,000. It is currently borrowing £3,000. So it could borrow up to £2,000 extra.

There is more of a problem if a business is already borrowing up to its overdraft limit. Then it has to negotiate with its bank to that limit. There is no guarantee that the bank will do this. A business experiencing cash flow problems could well be a business in difficulties. The bank will not want to increase lending to a business which could cease trading in the immediate future. The bank is likely to want to see a cash flow forecast to judge whether or not the business will be able to pay the interest on the overdraft and the overdraft itself in the future.

Negotiate additional short-term or long-term loans A business may be able obtain a short-term loan from a bank to inject some extra cash. If a business feels that extra money will be needed for a longer period of time a long-term loan might be considered. A business could pay back smaller installments over a longer period of time to help cash flow. However, once it is known that a business is short of cash, banks and other money lenders may be reluctant to provide cash for fear of the business collapsing.

Sell off or reduce stocks Sometimes it may be possible to sell stocks of raw materials, components or semi-finished goods for cash. To generate cash quickly they can be sold cheaply in a sale or below cost if necessary. Some stocks may be quite specialised and prove difficult to sell quickly.

A business might simply reduce the amount of stocks it holds. A machine manufacturer may buy in fewer stocks of components to make machines. Stocks cost money to hold. So fewer stocks can increase cash in the business. The danger is that stocks will not be available to make products that are required for sale.

Use a factoring company An alternative to pressurising customers for money is to sell the debts to a specialist **debt factor**. A factor is a business that will provide finance to another business against its debts for a fee. It often pays a certain amount to the business 'up front' and the remainder once debts are collected. Debt factors give businesses cash immediately and take the responsibility for collecting the debt. However, they make a charge for this and the debts must be good.

Sell off unwanted or non-vital fixed assets A business may be able to sell off unwanted or non-vital fixed assets like vehicles, machines and property. Unfortunately, to sell assets like these quickly they are likely to be sold at auctions and they may be sold below their true value.

Use of sale and leaseback Businesses are increasingly using sale and leaseback to raise cash. Assets like property and machinery can be sold to specialists in the market, such as Arnold Clark and Lease Direct. The assets are then leased back to the seller. This means that cash can be raised and the business can

continue to use the assets. However, it may take a while to set up such agreements and can be an expensive way to fund assets in the long term.

Stimulate sales for cash Many businesses, retailers for example, can generate cash by offering large discounts for customers who pay in cash. In the example at the beginning of this unit, Fopp tried to generate cash in this way by selling records, CDs and other stock for cash only. Unfortunately, the measure was not enough to save the business.

Mount a rigorous drive on overdue accounts This involves a business putting pressure on its customers to pay back what they owe more quickly. Allowing customers to receive products and pay for them at a later date is called TRADE CREDIT. The DEBTORS of a business are those customers (individuals or businesses) that owe a business money. However, pressurising customers in this way may mean that they find other suppliers.

Only make essential purchases It obviously makes sense during a cash crisis to postpone or cancel all unnecessary spending. A business should only buy resources for cash when it absolutely has to.

Delaying payments A business may simply delay payments. It then keeps this cash in the business for a longer period of time. It will only make payments when it is put under pressure to do so by CREDITORS – businesses that are owed money.

Extend credit with selected suppliers It will help a business to save cash if it can delay paying suppliers for goods and services that have already been bought. It may be able to extend its credit payment period from 30 to 60 days, for example. However, delaying for too long could mean that suppliers withdraw their credit facilities or refuse to deliver goods in the future.

Reduce personal drawings from the business Owners who regularly take cash from the business for their own personal use could attempt to take less. Obviously some cash might be needed for living expenses, but making a reduction in drawings is a quick way to stop cash leaving the business.

Introduce fresh capital Owners may be able to provide some new capital to improve cash flow. For example, small businesses may be able to use savings or take out loans using personal possessions as security. A small business may be able to persuade friends or relatives to invest in it – new partners might be taken on for example. Larger companies may be able to sell shares to raise fresh capital. However, attracting fresh capital might be very difficult if the business is struggling. It is likely to be up to the current owners to provide more capital.

In all the above cases, action must be taken quickly. If the business survives the cash crisis, it is important to identify the causes and to make sure it does not happen again. It is also

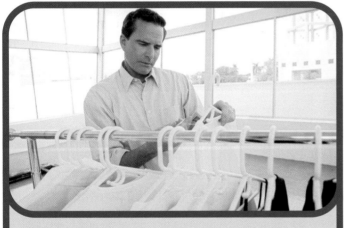

Question 2.

Adrian Talbot owns and runs a small garment manufacturing business. He employs 12 workers, using rented premises in London. Cash flow is always a problem for him. The businesses that buy from him often pay late while the profit margins he earns are wafer thin in an industry notorious for cut throat competition. At least finished stock is never a problem. He makes a sample and wins orders based on that. As soon as an order is complete, it is sent out to the purchaser.

(a) **Suggest and explain THREE ways in which Adrian Talbot could possibly improve his cash flow situation.**

Figure 1: Summary of a typical credit control procedure

- Check creditworthiness
- Establish credit limit
- Stop all orders that exceed the limit
- Continuously update sales ledger
- 'Age' outstanding invoices
- Revise credit limits
- Act on longstanding debts
- Evaluate department's performance

they set targets for the credit control department, such as the maximum value of bad debts or the length of time it takes to collect debts.

Firms have procedures to help credit control. Figure 1 shows an example.

- Many firms will not do business with new customers until their creditworthiness has been checked. This can be done by asking for references from a supplier, a banker's reference or a credit-rating agency's report. From this information the credit controller can set a credit limit based on the risk involved.
- When an order exceeds the credit limit, the credit controller should investigate. This may result in a stop being placed on the order, requesting the customer to pay any outstanding debt or simply allowing the order to go ahead.
- Credit control records, which show customer orders and payments, must be up to date. Every month, outstanding invoices must be 'aged' to identify customers who owe money over 30, 60 and 90 days.
- If there are persistent debts, the credit controller must take action. A statement of the account should be sent, followed by a second one with a letter. Next, a telephone call to the debtor should be followed by a personal visit. Finally, as a last resort, it may be necessary to take legal action to recover the debt.
- Some firms use an independent **debt factor** to assist in credit control. There has been quite a growth in this type of business in recent years. A factor is a business that will provide finance to a business against its debts for a fee. It often pays a certain amount to a business' up front' and the remainder as debts are collected.

evident that measures taken to alleviate a cash crisis are likely to reduce profits. For example, selling goods at a discount to raise cash will reduce profit margins; selling off assets and leasing them back can reduce profit in the long term; borrowing money from banks will incur interest charges; inviting new members to provide capital will dilute ownership.

Credit control

Most businesses have some sort of CREDIT CONTROL system, so that cash that is owed can be collected quickly and easily. A 'tight' or 'easy' credit policy may be adopted. Tight credit terms may be used to improve liquidity, reduce the risk of bad debts, exploit a seller's market or maintain slender profit margins. Easy credit terms may be designed to clear old stocks, enter a new market or perhaps help a regular customer with financial difficulties.

The company accountant and the sales manager often work closely with the credit controller, since credit policy will affect the financial position of the firm and its sales. Between them

KEYTERMS

Creditors – those to whom a business owes money for goods or services delivered but not yet paid for.
Credit control – the process of monitoring and collecting the money owed to a business.
Debtors – those who owe a business money for goods or services delivered but for which they have not yet paid.
Overtrading – a situation where a business does not have enough cash and other liquid resources to support its production and sales.
Trade credit – given when a supplier allows a customer to receive goods or services but pay for them at a later point in time. Typically, trade credit is given for 30 days.

KNOWLEDGE

1. What might happen if a business runs out of cash?
2. What methods might a business use to manage its financial resources effectively?
3. Explain why young and rapidly growing businesses are prone to overtrading.
4. Explain how: (i) stock piling (ii) overborrowing and

(iii) underestimating inflation can cause cash-flow problems.
5. State four ways in which a business can improve cash flow.
6. Why might it be difficult to extend a bank overdraft to generate more cash?
7. What is meant by 'credit control'?

Case Study: *Hotel Condor*

Hotel Condor is a 45 room hotel, with conference facilities, a restaurant and a bar. It is located in north London, about 35 minutes drive from Heathrow Airport. The hotel business, which includes the property, is owned by Asif and Ashraf Hussain. The hotel uses a booking agent in the USA and about 80 per cent of the hotel's guests are American business travellers and tourists. The hotel has many facilities, including coffee makers in the room, room service, safe deposit boxes, televisions with cable and high-speed Internet connection.

The hotel has not performed particularly well in the last couple of years. The flow of American guests has dwindled due to the strength of the pound against the dollar. Occupancy rates have fallen from 82 per cent in 2005 to less than 50 per cent in 2006. To keep the business going, the owners put in £20,000 cash, in the hope that the exchange rate would eventually reverse. £4,000 of the money was spent on obtaining some listings in hotel directories. Although this did generate some more business, it was nowhere near as much as promised. £4,000 was spent relaunching the restaurant, but unfortunately the appointment of a new head chef, and a change in the menu, did not attract many more customers. By the end of 2006, the hotel had £5,600 in the bank and cash flow forecasts showed that more cash would need to be injected in June 2007 unless business picked up significantly.

The hotel was contacted by a British company that was undertaking some work in the north London area. The company wanted to book 25 rooms for three months (May to July) to accommodate their employees. They also wanted to make regular use of the conferencing facilities. A price was agreed, a deposit was received, and it looked as though the hotel was about to get back on an even keel. However, as luck would

have it, the hotel was forced to close for two weeks in April after a visit from health and safety inspectors. Hygiene conditions in the large kitchen, which served both the hotel and the restaurant, were not up to standard. About £15,000 of work needed to be done before it could reopen. There was £9,200 in the bank.

(a) Using this case as an example, explain what is meant by a cash flow problem. (4 marks)
(b) Explain how external factors have contributed to cash flow problems in this case. (12 marks)
(c) Ashraf and Asif have invited a relative of theirs to become a sleeping partner in the business and contribute £50,000 capital. Do you think the relative should accept the invitation? (14 marks)
(d) Evaluate the measures the Hotel Condor might take to resolve its cash crisis. (20 marks)

Measuring profit

Business owners and financial managers will monitor the profitability of a business very carefully. Profit is perhaps the most important performance indicator. This is because, for most businesses, making profit is the main aim.

The actual size of profit is not always a true indicator of performance. In 2007, Next, the high street clothes retailer, made a profit of £478 million and BA, the airline, made a profit of £611 million. In contrast, Wetherspoons, the pub chain, made a profit of just £62 million.

Does this mean that BA was the best performing business out of the three? It may do but not necessarily. A number of other factors have to be taken into account. For example, how much money was invested in the business and how much profit was made in relation to turnover? A closer examination of more financial information would be required before a conclusion could be drawn about which company had performed the best.

Profit margins

One way of measuring profit is to calculate a PROFIT MARGIN. A profit margin expresses profit as a proportion of turnover, usually as a percentage. A profit margin can be used to compare the performance of a business in different periods when turnover changes. It can also be used to compare the performance of different sized businesses. There are two common profit margins.

Gross profit margin GROSS PROFIT is the amount of profit a business makes after direct costs have been subtracted from turnover. It can be calculated using the formula:

$$\text{Gross profit} = \text{turnover} - \text{cost of sales}$$

It is the profit before overheads (indirect costs) are subtracted. For a retailer gross profit would be turnover minus the cost of buying goods for resale. For a manufacturer it would be turnover minus the costs of raw materials, components and direct labour.

The GROSS PROFIT MARGIN or MARK-UP is the gross profit expressed as a percentage of turnover. It is calculated using the formula:

$$\text{Gross profit margin} = \frac{\text{Gross profit}}{\text{Turnover}} \times 100$$

Table 1 shows some financial information for Prior's, a large independent electrical goods store. Figures are shown for 2006 and 2007. The gross profit margins for the two years are calculated as follows.

$$\text{For 2007 Gross profit margin} = \frac{£550,000}{£1,230,000} \times 100 = 44.7\%$$

$$\text{For 2006 Gross profit margin} = \frac{£450,000}{£1,100,000} \times 100 = 40.9\%$$

Higher gross profit margins are preferable to lower ones. However, it is difficult to say what a 'good' margin is likely to be. Gross profit margins will vary in different industries. For example supermarkets, which generally have a fast stock turnover, will have lower gross profit margins than, say, a car dealer, which will operate with a much slower stock turnover. The gross profit margins for Prior's have increased over the two years from 40.9 per cent to 44.7 per cent. This shows that performance has improved. Margins of around 40 per cent for

Table 1: Financial information for Prior's

	2007	**(£) 2006**
Turnover	1,230,000	1,100,000
Cost of sales	780,000	650,000
Gross profit	550,000	450,000
Overheads	340,000	280,000
Net profit	210,000	170,000

Question 1.

Goodalls is a small chain of butchers operating in Kent. It has a shop in Dover, Ashford and Canterbury. Table 2 shows some financial information for Goodalls for 2007.

Table 2: Financial information for Goodalls

	Dover	**Ashford**	**(£) Canterbury**
Turnover	158,000	142,000	197,000
Cost of sales	102,000	101,000	146,000
Gross profit			
Overheads	31,000	29,000	33,000
Net profit			

(a) Complete the table by calculating gross profit and net profit.
(b) Calculate the net profit margins for the three shops.
(c) (i) Which shop has performed the best in 2007?
(ii) How will these figures assist Goodalls in the financial management of the business?

an electrical goods retailer are probably acceptable.

Net profit margin NET PROFIT is the amount of profit after all costs have been subtracted from turnover. It is calculated as:

Net profit = gross profit - overheads

Or

Net profit = turnover – cost of sales - overheads

The NET PROFIT MARGIN is net profit expressed as a percentage of turnover. The net profit margin shows how effectively a business has controlled its overheads and its cost of sales. The net profit margin is calculated by:

$$\text{Net profit margin} = \frac{\text{Net profit}}{\text{Turnover}} \times 100$$

When calculating the net profit margin it is important to use net profit before tax and interest. The net profit margins for Prior's in 2006 and 2007 are calculated as follows.

$$\text{For 2007 Net profit margin} = \frac{£210,000}{£1,230,000} \times 100 = 17.1\%$$

$$\text{For 2006 Net profit margin} = \frac{£170,000}{£1,100,000} \times 100 = 15.5\%$$

Again, higher margins are better than lower ones. The net profit margin for Prior's has improved over the two years from 15.5% to 17.1%. This suggests that the business has been able to control its overheads slightly more effectively in 2007.

Return on capital

Another way to measure the profitability of a business is to calculate the RETURN ON CAPITAL. Capital is the money invested in a business by the owners. The return on capital is the amount of profit expressed as a percentage of the capital invested in a business. Owners can use this measure to see how well their investment in the business is doing. The return on capital is:

$$\text{Return on capital} = \frac{\text{Net profit}}{\text{Capital}} \times 100$$

In 2007, the amount of capital invested in Prior's, the electrical goods retailer in the example above, was £1 million. The same amount was invested in 2006. The return on capital for 2007 and 2006 is shown below.

$$\text{For 2007 Return on capital} = \frac{£210,000}{£1,000,000} \times 100 = 21\%$$

$$\text{For 2006 Return on capital} = \frac{£170,000}{£1,000,000} \times 100 = 17\%$$

Clearly, the return on capital increased over the two-year period. In 2006 the owners of Prior's got a 17 per cent return on their £1,000,000 investment. This rose to 21 per cent in 2007. One way to determine whether 21 per cent is a good return or not, is to make a comparison with another electrical goods retailer. However, it may not be possible to obtain the information required to do this. A 21 per cent return does look good when compared with the return the owner might get if the £1,000,000 was deposited in a bank. This would have been about 6 per cent in 2007 (£60,000). Clearly, the money is generating a much bigger return when it is invested in the business. However, the £1,000,000 invested in the business is at risk and investors would expect a bigger return to compensate for this risk.

Finally, when comparing profit measures between businesses, it is important to compare 'like with like'. The profit margins and returns on capital may vary from industry to industry and from business to business. Fair comparisons can only be made between businesses if they operate in the same industry and have the same characteristics. For example, comparing the rate of return of a shoe manufacturer with that of a bank may not be appropriate.

Question 2.

Leonard & Co manufactures glassware in Hereford. It employs 45 staff and has a reputation for high-quality wine glasses, vases and crystalware. The company has won awards for innovation in recent years but is facing pressure from overseas competitors.

Simpsons plc is a sheet glass retailer. It operates from a huge site in Bradford and mainly serves traders such as builders and glaziers. In the last year it has taken over a local rival and the integration of the two businesses raised costs for the year.

Argo Ltd makes a range of glass products such as glass tables, show cases and cabinets. It employs seven staff and operates from an industrial unit in Sunderland. The company was bought from the previous owner by the present manager two years ago. Some financial information for the three companies is shown in Table 3.

Table 3: Financial information for Leonard & Co, Simpsons plc and Argo Ltd

	Leonard & Co	Simpsons plc	Argo Ltd (£)
Capital invested	2,340,000	7,800,000	1,400,000
Net profit	245,000	466,000	156,000

(a) Explain what is meant by return on capital.
(b) Calculate the return on capital for the three businesses in the case.
(c) Comment on and compare the returns calculated in (b).
(d) How useful are the comparisons made in (c)?

Methods of improving profitability

All businesses will want to improve their performance. An improved performance is likely to benefit all stakeholders. The returns on capital can be increased by making more profit with the same level of investment. This might be achieved by growth funded externally. This means the business increases sales using fresh capital.

Increasing profit margins will also improve performance. If profit margins can be raised, the business will make more profit at the existing level of sales. The profit margins can be improved in two ways.

Raising prices If a business raises its price it will get more revenue for every unit sold. If costs remain the same then profitability should improve. However, raising price might have an impact on the level of sales. Generally, when price is raised demand will fall. However, if demand is not too responsive to changes in price, the increase in price will generate more revenue even though fewer units are sold. Raising price is always risky because it is never certain how competitors will react.

Lowering costs A business can also raise profit margins by lowering its costs. It can do this by buying cheaper resources or using the existing resources more effectively.

- **Using existing resources more efficiently.** It might be possible to buy raw materials and components from new suppliers that offer better prices. It may also be possible to find new providers of essential services such as telecommunications, electricity, insurance and IT support. For example, there has been increased competition recently in the supply of gas, electricity and telecommunications. Another option might be to find ways of using cheaper labour. For example, some businesses have moved overseas to take advantage of cheap labour in places like China and eastern Europe. However, these measures may have drawbacks. When taking on new suppliers the possibility that they are cheaper because they are not as good should be considered. The quality of raw materials might be inferior, they may be unreliable and supply might not be guaranteed. For example, a number of new, and cheaper, broadband providers have not been able to guarantee supply. Moving abroad to take advantage of cheap labour may be disruptive. It may also damage the image of the company if it lays off large numbers of staff in the UK. Consequently, when looking to acquire cheaper resources, a business must be cautious and understand the pitfalls.
- **Buying cheaper resources.** Making better use of current resources will improve efficiency and lower costs. A business might do this by introducing new working practices or training staff. This would help to raise labour productivity. It could upgrade its machinery by acquiring newer, more efficient models. This would raise capital productivity. A business might be able to reduce waste by recycling materials, for example. Some of these measures

might also have drawbacks. For example, the workers might resist new working practices and new technology often has teething problems. This could disrupt the business.

The difference between cash and profit

It is important for businesses to recognise the difference between cash and profit. At the end of a trading year it is unlikely that the value of profit will be the same as the cash balance. Differences between cash and profit can arise for a number of reasons.

- During the trading year a business might sell £200,000 worth of goods with total costs of £160,000. Its profit would be £40,000. However, if some goods had been sold on credit, payment by certain customers may not yet have been received. If £12,000 was still owing, the amount of cash the business had would be £28,000 (£40,000-£12,000). Thus, profit is greater than cash.
- A business may receive cash at the beginning of the trading year from sales made in the previous year. This would increase the cash balance, but would not affect profit. In addition, the business may buy resources from suppliers and not pay for them until the next trading year. As a result its trading costs will not be the same as cash paid out.
- Sometimes the owners might introduce more cash into the business. This will increase the cash balance, but will have no effect on the profit made. This is because the introduction of capital is not treated as business revenue in the profit and loss account. The effect will be the same if a business borrows money from a bank.
- Purchases of fixed assets will reduce cash balances, but will have no effect on the profit a company makes. This is because the purchase of assets is not treated as a business cost in the profit and loss account.
- Sales of fixed assets will increase cash balances but will have no effect on profit unless a profit or loss is made on disposal of the asset. This is because the cash from the sale of a fixed asset is not included in business turnover.
- The amount of cash at the end of the year will be different from profit because at the beginning of the year the cash balance is unlikely to be zero. If, at the beginning of the year, the cash balance for a business is £23,000, then the amount of cash a business has at the end of the year will exceed profit by £23,000.

It is possible for a business to trade for many years without making a profit. For example, Oxford Biomedica, a biopharmaceuticals company, began trading in 1995 and has never made a profit. The company survives because it has been able to generate cash. Extra cash has been introduced by shareholders on several occasions (a total of £117 million over the life of the company). In 2006 the company lost £17.62 million. However, the company had £33 million in liquid assets – including about £8 million in cash.

On the other hand it is possible for a profitable business to collapse if it runs out of cash. This is likely to happen if a business has to meet some substantial unexpected expenditure or if a bad debt occurs.

KEYTERMS

Gross profit – total sales revenue or turnover minus cost of sales, the direct costs of production.

Gross profit margin or mark-up – gross profit expressed as a percentage of turnover.

Net profit – total sales revenue or turnover minus cost of sales and overheads.

Net profit margin – net profit expressed as a percentage of turnover.

Profit margins – profit expressed as a percentage of turnover.

Return on capital – the amount of profit expressed as a percentage of the capital invested in a business.

KNOWLEDGE

1. How reliable is the size of profit as a performance indicator?
2. Explain the difference between net profit and gross profit.
3. What does an increase in the net profit margin tell a business?
4. Why would an investor expect a greater return on capital when investing in a business compared with depositing money in a bank?
5. What might be a negative impact of raising price to improve the net profit margin?
6. State two ways in which a business can lower costs.
7. State two reasons why profit and cash may not be the same in a business.

Case Study: *Compton Foods*

Compton Foods is a food-processing company. It buys fresh fruit and vegetables from farmers and produces a wide range of packaged products, including mangetout, beans, baby carrots, mushrooms and bean sprouts. It adds value to some products by slicing and dicing fruit and vegetables before packing. It also produces variety packs where several vegetables or mixed vegetables are combined in the same pack. All of Compton Foods' products are sold to supermarkets in the south of England.

The processing plant is located in Reading. Around 50 people are employed in the plant, most of whom are unskilled. In 2006, the company's shareholders provided an injection of fresh capital. £300,000 was raised to pay for a computerised packing machine and the introduction of new shift patterns. Unfortunately, this resulted in seven staff being laid off, affecting the relationship between the owners and the workers. The workers benefited financially from the new shift patterns, but they resented their colleagues being laid off. This was the first time in the history of the company that staff had been made redundant. A worker representative said 'Working here will never be the same. There used to be an atmosphere of a family company, but that's all changed now. The company is dominated by the accountants.'

Table 4: Financial information for Compton Foods

	2004	2005	2006	(£) 2007
Turnover	2,440,000	2,820,000	3,190,000	3,210,000
Net profit	235,000	242,000	246,000	331,000
Capital invested	1,500,000	1,500,000	1,500,000	1,800,000

(a) Calculate the net profit margins for the four years. (8 marks)

(b) Using this case an example, explain why the size of profit might be misleading when measuring the performance of a business. (6 marks)

(c) How might you account for the changes in the net profit margin between 2006 and 2007? (8 marks)

(d) At the end of the trading year in 2007, Compton Foods had £378,000 in the bank. Explain the difference between cash and profit for the year. (8 marks)

(e) Calculate the returns on capital between 2006 and 2007. (8 marks)

(f) Do you think the measures taken to improve the performance of the company were worthwhile? (12 marks)

26 | Improving organisational structures

Organisational structures

Each business has its own ORGANISATIONAL STRUCTURE or BUSINESS STRUCTURE. The structure is the way in which positions within the business are arranged. It is often know as the **internal structure** or FORMAL ORGANISATION of the business.

The organisational structure of the business defines:
- the workforce roles of employees and their job titles;
- the route through which decisions are made;
- who is responsible and who is accountable to whom, and for what activities;
- the relationship between positions in a business;
- how employees communicate with each other and how information is passed on.

Different businesses tend to have different objectives, relationships and ways in which decisions are made. So they may have different structures. But there may also be some similarities. For example, small businesses are likely to have simple structures. Larger businesses are often divided into departments with managers.

Structure is important to all businesses. It helps them to divide work and co-ordinate activities to achieve objectives. But it may be more important for larger businesses. For example, a two person plumbing business is likely to have fewer problems deciding 'who does what' than a business operating in many countries.

One method of organising a business is where managers put people together to work effectively based on their skills and abilities. The structure is 'built up' or it 'develops' as a result of the employees of the business. In contrast a structure could be created first, with all appropriate workforce roles outlined, and then people employed to fill them. It has been suggested that the entrepreneur Richard Branson worked out a complete organisation structure for his Virgin Atlantic airline before setting up the company and then recruited the 102 people needed to fill all the positions.

Workforce roles

The positions in an organisation will have particular workloads and jobs allocated to them.

Directors Directors are appointed to run the business in the interest of its owners. In smaller businesses, owners may also be directors. But in larger businesses owned by shareholders, for example, they may be different. Directors are in overall charge of activities in an organisation. They meet, as the **Board of Directors**, to make major decisions that will affect the owners. Some directors, known as executive directors, will be involved in the running of a business. Non-executive directors may play little part in its running. The **managing director** (MD) will have overall responsibility for the organisation and have AUTHORITY over specific directors, such as the **finance** or **marketing director**.

Managers Managers are responsible for controlling or organising within the business. They often make day-to-day decisions about the running of the business. The sales manager, for example, would have responsibility for sales in the business and be responsible to the marketing director. Businesses often have **departmental** managers, such as the marketing, human

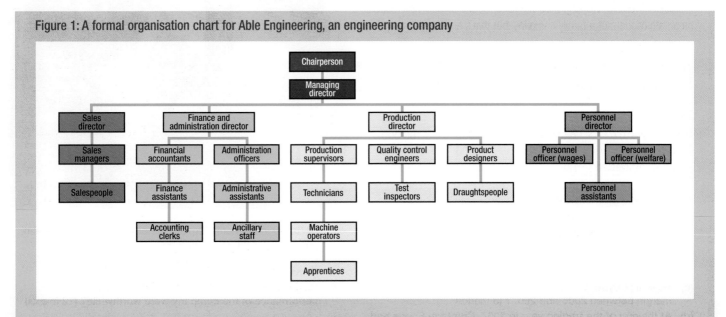

Figure 1: A formal organisation chart for Able Engineering, an engineering company

resources, finance and production manager. There may also be **regional** managers, organising the business in areas of a country or **branch** managers, organising particular branches or stores.

Team leaders Team leaders are members of a team whose role is to resolve issues between team members and co-ordinate team efforts so that the team works effectively. A team leader may be part of a permanent cell production team or a team set up for a particular job, such as investigating staff morale. A team leader may also take responsibility for representing the views of a team to the next higher reporting level, for example to report the findings of a market research team.

Supervisors Supervisors monitor and regulate the work in their assigned or delegated area, for example stock supervisor or payroll supervisor. Supervisors may be given some of the roles of managers, but at a lower level. Their roles in this case may be to hire, discipline, promote, punish or reward.

Professionals These are positions for staff with high levels of qualifications and experience. The job roles are likely to involve a degree of decision making and responsibility for ensuring that task are carried out effectively to a high standard. Examples might include doctors, architects, stockbrokers, product designers, chefs and accountants.

Operatives These are positions for skilled workers who are involved in the production process or service provision. They carry out the instructions of managers or supervisors. In their own area of activity they may have to ensure targets are met and tasks are carried out effectively. Examples of operatives in business might include staff in:

- production, for example assembling a car or manufacturing furniture;
- warehousing, for example checking invoices against goods and ensuring effective deliveries;
- IT, for example giving technical support for machinery.

General staff There is a variety of positions in business which are carried out by staff with non-specific skills. They follow instructions given by superiors to carry out particular tasks and are an essential part of the production process or service provision. Examples might include checkout staff and shelf stackers in supermarkets, cleaners and receptionists in offices. They might also include general jobs on a farm or building site, such as cleaning out.

Although there may be similar generic job roles, there will be differences between organisations in the precise nature of these roles, relationships between various job roles, how they are managed and how decisions are made.

Organisation charts

Businesses often produce ORGANISATION CHARTS. These

Figure 2: Different chains of command and spans of control

(a) A long chain of command and a narrow span of control. A production department may look like this. One manager is helped by a few assistant managers, each responsible for supervisors. These supervisors are responsible for skilled workers, who are in charge of a group of semi-skilled workers. Close supervision is needed to make sure quality is maintained. This is sometimes referred to as a tall organisational structure.

(b) A short chain of command and a wide span of control. A higher or further education department may look like this, with a 'head' of department, a few senior staff and many lecturing staff. Staff will want a degree of independence. This is sometimes referred to as a flat organisational structure.

illustrate the structure of the business and the workforce roles of people employed with the business. Figure 1 shows a 'traditional' type of chart. It is a chart for an engineering firm, Able Engineering. It illustrates the formal relationship between different workforce roles and people in the business. Why do businesses draw such charts?

- To spot communication flow problems. An organisation chart indicates how employees are linked to other employees in the business. If information is not received, the business can find where the communication breakdown has occurred by tracing the communication chain along the chart.
- Organisation charts help individuals see their position in a business. This can help them appreciate the responsibilities that have been delegated to them, who has authority over them and who they are accountable to.
- Organisation charts allow firms to pinpoint areas where specialists are needed. For example, in Figure 1 Able Engineering recognises it needs designers and draughtspeople as part of the production 'team'.
- Organisation charts show how different sections of the firm relate to each other. For example, the chart for Able

Engineering shows the relationship between salespeople and technicians. They are both at the same level in the hierarchy, but work in different departments and are responsible to different managers.

Simply producing an organisation chart is of limited use to a business. The business will only achieve its objectives if it understands the relationships between employees and other parts of the business.

Key elements of organisational structures

Chain of command The HIERARCHY in a business is the levels of management in a business, from the lowest to the highest rank. It shows the CHAIN OF COMMAND within the organisation - the way authority is organised. Orders pass down the levels and information passes up. Businesses must also consider the number of links or levels in the chain of command. R. Townsend, in his book *Up the Organisation*, estimated that each extra level of management in the hierarchy reduced the effectiveness of communication by about 25 per cent. No rules are laid down on the most effective number of links in the chain. However, businesses generally try to keep chains as short as possible.

Span of control The SPAN OF CONTROL refers to the number of subordinates working under a superior or manager. In other words, if one production manager has ten subordinates his span of control is ten. Henri Fayol argued that the span of control should be between three and six because:
- there should be tight managerial control from the top of the business;
- there are physical and mental limitations to any single manager's ability to control people and activities.

A narrow span of control has the advantage for a firm of tight control and close supervision. It also allows better co-ordination of subordinates' activities. In addition, it gives managers time to think and plan without having to be burdened with too many day-to-day problems. A narrow span also ensures better communication with subordinates, who are sufficiently small in number to allow this to occur.

A wide span of control, however, offers greater decision-making authority for subordinates and may improve job satisfaction In addition, there are likely to be lower costs involved in supervision. Figure 2 shows two organisation charts. In the first (a), there is a long chain of command, but a narrow span of control. The second (b) shows a wide span, but a short chain.

Authority and responsibility Employees in the hierarchy will have RESPONSIBILITY and authority. However, these terms do not mean the same thing. Responsibility involves being accountable or being required to justify an action. So, for example, managers who are responsible for a department may be asked to justify poor performance to the board of directors. The personnel department may be responsible for employing workers. If a new worker was unable to do a particular job, they would be asked to explain why.

Authority, on the other hand, is the ability to carry out the task. For example, it would make no sense asking an office worker to pay company debts if she did not have the authority to sign cheques. Employees at lower levels of the hierarchy have less responsibility and authority than those further up. However, it may be possible for a superior to delegate (pass down) authority to a subordinate, eg a manager to an office worker, but retain responsibility. Increasingly, businesses are realising the benefits of delegating both authority and responsibility.

Line, staff and functional authority Line, staff and functional authority are terms used to describe the type of relationship that managers may have with others in the hierarchy.

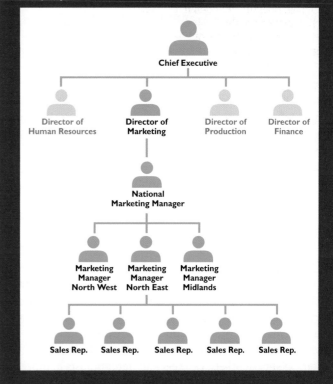

Question 1.

Figure 3 shows part of an organisation chart for a UK engineering company.

Figure 3: Part of an organisation chart of a UK engineering company

(a) The company sells into regional markets. How can this be seen from the chart?
(b) Describe the chain of command from Chief Executive to UK sales representative.
(c) How large is the span of control of the Marketing Manager?
(d) Who is immediately subordinate to the Director of Marketing?
(e) The Chief Executive is considering reducing the number of sales reps from five to three. How might this affect the Marketing Managers?

Question 2.

During 2007 BP aimed to cut overheads and re-energise the oil and gas company. Tony Hayward, the chief executive, insisted the overall strategy was not about 'cost reduction and cull', but about a radical change in culture. There were no specific numbers for how many staff would be cut, but Mr Hayward said it 'could be thousands over several years'.

The BP boss sent a message to his 100,000 staff outlining other plans to streamline the business into two basic units. This would be exploration and production on one side and refining and marketing on the other, similar to the type of structure at Exxon. The third segment, gas, power and renewables, is to be incorporated mainly into the other two.

A city analysts said, 'I think it is really good. This is copying the Exxon model of keeping things simple and ensuring unit managers are given responsibility but held accountable too.'

Mr Hayward promised that in future, corporate infrastructure would be 'rigorously' reviewed and up to four layers of management would be shed. 'Managers will be listening more acutely, particularly to frontline staff. We will make sure individuals are fully accountable for things they control,' he said.

Source: adapted from www.guardian.co.uk, 12.10.2007.

(a) Explain how the changes might affect:
(i) employees at the businesses; (ii) management at the businesses; (iii) clients of the business.
(b) Discuss to what extent BP might experience resistance from managers and employees.

- **Line authority** is usual in a hierarchy. It shows the authority that a manager has over a subordinate. In Figure 1, the production director would have line authority over the designers. Communication will flow down from the superior to the subordinate in the chain of command. The advantage of this is that a manager can allocate work and control subordinates, who have a clear understanding of who is giving them instructions. The manager can also delegate authority to others if they feel this will make decision making more effective. In large organisations, the chain of command can be very long. This means that instructions given by those at the top of the chain of command may take time before they are carried out at a lower level.
- **Staff authority** might be when a manager or department in a business has a function within another department, for example, giving specialist advice. A marketing manager may give advice to the production department based on market research into a new product. Personnel managers have responsibilities for personnel matters in all departments. Although the specialist can give advice, they have no authority to make decisions in the other department.
- **Functional authority** is when a specialist has the authority to make a line manager accept his or her advice. It is different from staff authority, where the specialist can only advise. For example, the finance manager may have overall authority over the budget holder in the marketing department.

Problems may occur in a business if people do not understand where authority and responsibility rest. This means that managers must know whether their authority is line, staff or functional. Unfortunately, this can lead to friction. Line managers are sometimes thought of as 'first class citizens' and staff managers are thought of as costly 'overheads' who are not contributing anything of worth to the organisation. Also, the authority of functional managers is not accepted by line managers at times.

Delegation Managers are increasingly being asked to carry out strategic activities that affect the whole business. This has resulted in the need to DELEGATE activities for certain tasks to employees further down the hierarchy. Delegation can provide benefits to a business, as explained in the next section. When is delegation likely to be effective?

- Researchers such as Spetzer (1992) have suggested that employees need to be empowered in order to make effective decisions. They need to be given self-confidence and control of what they do.
- If managers only delegate when they are overloaded, subordinates may be resentful.
- Delegation requires planning. Managers must be clear about what needs to be done. Instead of freeing time, poor delegation may take up managers' time as they try to correct problems.
- Managers must take time to explain delegated tasks clearly. Employees may waste time or make mistakes because of lack of information. Telling subordinates why the work is important helps to create shared values.
- Allow participation. It is useful to discuss the task with those to whom it has been delegated. Subordinates will then know from the start what the task will include. It also helps managers to decide if delegation is appropriate. A person may feel they do not have the skills to carry out the task.
- The employee given a delegated task should also be given the authority and responsibility to carry it out. Managers must tell others in the business that the delegated person is acting on his or her behalf. This will avoid difficulties, such as the questioning of authority.
- Managers must avoid interfering with delegated tasks.
- Delegated tasks should be given to suitable employees. It would be inappropriate to delegate a marketing task to an employee in personnel. Employees must also have the training to carry out the task.
- Provide support and resources. If an employee is delegated a task without suitable support and resources this could lead to anxiety, frustration and the task being badly done.

Research has shown that when factors like these are taken into account, delegation was four times as likely to be successful.

Different forms of business structure

Despite the variety of formal business organisation that exists, there are four main types of structure most often found.

The entrepreneurial structure In this type of business structure, all decisions are made centrally. There are few collective decisions and a great reliance on 'key' workers. It is often found in businesses where decisions have to be made quickly, such as newspaper editing. Most small businesses also have this type of structure, as illustrated in Figure 4(a). These businesses rely on the expertise of one or two people to make decisions. Decision making is efficient up to a point because:

- decisions can be made quickly;
- subordinates understand to whom they are accountable;
- little consultation is required.

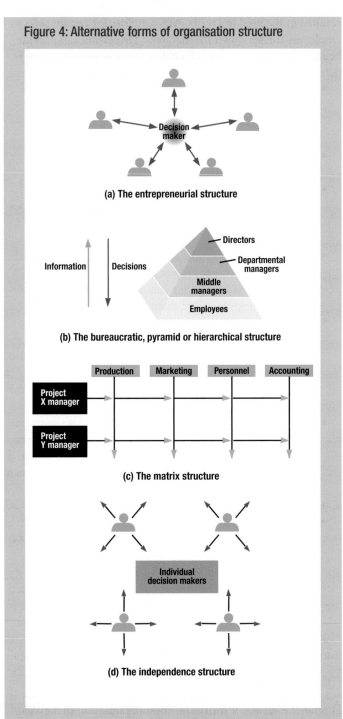

Figure 4: Alternative forms of organisation structure

(a) The entrepreneurial structure

(b) The bureaucratic, pyramid or hierarchical structure

(c) The matrix structure

(d) The independence structure

However, as the business grows, this structure can cause inefficiency as too much of a load is placed on those making decisions.

The bureaucratic, pyramid or hierachical structure This is the traditional hierachical structure for most medium-sized and large businesses and perhaps the most well known. It is illustrated in Figure 4(b). Decision making is shared throughout the business. Employees are each given a role and procedures are laid down which determine their behaviour at work. Specialisation of tasks is possible. This means that a departmental structure, with finance, personnel, production and marketing employees, can be set up. Specialisation may allow the business to enjoy economies of scale. Recently, this type of structure has been criticised for its inability to change and meet new demands.

The matrix structure This emphasises getting people with particular specialist skills together into project teams, as illustrated in Figure 4(c). Individuals within the team have their own responsibility. The matrix structure was developed to overcome some of the problems with the entrepreneurial and bureaucratic structures. Matrix management involves the co-ordinating and support of specialist teams within a matrix structure.

Managers often argue that this is the best way of organising people, because it is based on the expertise and skills of employees and gives scope for people lower down the organisation to use their talents effectively. For example, a project manager looking into the possibility of developing a new product may draw on the expertise of employees with skills in design, research and development, marketing, costing etc. A college running a course for unemployed people may draw on the skills of a number of lecturers in different departments. In this way, a matrix structure can also operate within a business that has a bureaucratic structure. The matrix model fits in with managers who have a Theory Y view of employees It is suggested that this structure improves flexibility and motivation of employees. It has recently lost favour because it often needs expensive support systems, such as extra secretarial and office staff. There may also be problems with co-ordinating a team drawn from different departments and the speed of decision making.

The independence structure This emphasises the individual and is almost a 'non-organisation'. The other three methods put together the contributions of a number of people so that the sum of their efforts is greater than the parts. All efforts are co-ordinated so that the business benefits. The independence structure is a method of providing a support system. Barristers' chambers and doctors' clinics have worked in this way. It is attractive to independent people who are confident of their ability to be successful. This form of organisation tends to be unsuitable for most types of business because of the lack of control and co-ordination.

Question 3.

The Manchester Film Association is an SME in the centre of the city's 'cultural quarter'. Its main activities are video, film and multimedia production. It employs nine full-time staff. Mike joined the company six months ago. He recently graduated, but has little work experience. However, he has proven so far in the work that he has done for clients to be innovative. He often has ideas that no-one else has considered. Shoaib has worked for the business for 15 years. He has built up considerable production and post-production skills. Lisa had previously set up her own website design and consultancy operation. She has experience in managing projects, working to deadlines and taking responsibility for clients' requests. The managing director of the business, Paula, has been approached by a fast growing leisure company to produce an innovative multimedia training programme on CD Rom for newly recruited employees. The company wants the programme to be interactive, but it must be ready within two months. Paula decided to ask Mike to look after the project.

Source: adapted from company information.

(a) Explain what type of organisational structure do you think might best reflect the business needs of Manchester Film Association.

Informal business structure

Organisation charts show the formal organisation of a business. However many relationships between employees in business are informal. The INFORMAL BUSINESS STRUCTURE is the network of relationships that develops between members on the basis of their common interests and friendships. These relationships can affect the way a business operates. A study of informal networks in the banking industry, for example, found three types of relationship.

- Advice networks – who depends on who to solve problems and provide information.
- Trust networks – which employees share potential information and back each other up in times of crisis.

- Communication networks – which employees regularly talk to each other on work related matters.

They recommended that businesses use informal structures to solve problems. For example, a study showed that a bank's task force group was unable to find ways of improving the bank's performance. The leader of the task force held a central position in the 'advice network'. Employees relied on her for technical advice. However, she only had one 'trust link' with a colleague. Management did not want to label the group as a failure or embarrass a valued employee by dismissing her as team leader. Instead, it redesigned the task force in line with the informal organisation of the business by adding a person in the trust network to share responsibility for group leadership.

KEYTERMS

Authority – the right to command a situation, a task or an activity.
Chain of command – the way authority and power are passed down in a business.
Delegation – authority (and sometimes responsibility) to pass down from superior to subordinate.
Formal organisation – the relationships between employees and the organisational structure determined by the business, as shown in an organisation chart.
Hierarchy – the order or levels of management of a business, from the lowest to the highest.
Informal business structure – the relationships between employees that are based on the common interests of employees.
Organisation chart – a diagram which illustrates the structure of an organisation.
Organisational or business structure – the way in which a business is organised.
Span of control – the number of subordinates working under a superior.

KNOWLEDGE

1. What are the features of the internal structure of a business?
2. How might an organisation chart be used in a firm's induction programme?
3. Draw a simple organisation chart showing:
   (a) a partnership with two partners and six employees;
   (b) a large company with a board of directors, six departments, and two more levels in the hierarchy.
4. What is meant by a 'wide span of control'?
5. What problems might a 'wide span of control' have for a business?
6. Explain the difference between line, staff and functional authority.
7. What factors influence effective delegation?
8. Why is empowerment important when tasks are delegated?
9. What problems might a matrix structure cause for a business?
10. What type of business might be organised with:
    (a) an entrepreneurial structure;
    (b) an independence structure?
11. Why is it important for businesses to understand their informal business structures?

Case Study: *Avalanche*

Avalanche control operations at the Lake Louise Ski Area have a history spanning nearly 30 years. Lake Louise is in the Banff National Park in Canada. The area currently receives half a million guests per year for skiing, snowboarding and related activities. Safety is a key aspect and part of that relates to the danger of avalanches of snow burying skiers in their wake. The ski resort covers over 17 square kilometres and there are over 100 places where avalanches can occur. In addition, some skiers deliberately go outside the resort area for the thrill of skiing in uncrowded, uncontrolled areas. But this increases the number of potential avalanche areas.

In the 1980s, there were effectively three separate departments working on the mountain. The main responsibility of the Ski Patrol was pre-hospital care for skiers who had accidents. For the Warden/Ski Patrol Avalanche Crew, it was monitoring and controlling avalanches. For the Trail Crew, it was managing the slopes, including putting up fencing. However, there was overlap between the three departments. Members of the Trail Crew, for example, would organise help if they were first on the scene at an accident.

These three departments were then reorganised into one Snow Safety Department. This was partly prompted by budget costs. The previous three departments had over 40 staff in total. The new single department now consisted of just 25 staff. Efficiency gains were possible because staff were used more intensively. In particular, on the mountain, patrollers were expected to perform any of the functions which before had been the main responsibility of just one of the departments.

Under the new structure, shown in Figure 5, a Snow Safety Manager was put in charge of the whole department, answerable to the Area Manager for the ski resort. Beneath the Snow Safety Manager in the hierarchy are three Snow Safety Supervisors. Two of these are Avalanche Forecasters and one is a Patrol Leader. Working under the the Snow Safety Supervisors are four Senior Avalanche Patrollers. Their main duties are as Team Leaders in snow research and avalanche control. In addition, they have become involved in other facets of the department, such as training and acting as roving 'troubleshooters'. They are not scheduled into the daily routine of run checks and accident coverage or to patrol specific areas. In addition, there are five Senior Patrollers and 13 Patrollers who have as their primary responsibilities pre-hospital care and risk management (in the form of run checks and trail work). These 18 people also act as Avalanche Team Members on a rotating basis wherever needed. Generally, between two and five teams are used daily for research and control, depending on conditions.

Adapted from a paper by Mark Klassen, Skiing Louise Ltd, Alberta, Canada.

(a) Explain what is meant by the terms: (i) 'hierarchy'and (3 marks)
    (ii) 'department' (3 marks).
(b) (i) Explain what is the span of control of the Snow Safety Manager shown in Figure 5. (3 marks). (ii) Explain to whom the Patrol Leader, who is one of the three Snow Safety Supervisors, might delegate a task. (3 marks)
(c) Analyse how the change in structure between the 1980s and the 1990s described in the data has affected job roles, responsibilities and communication. (8 marks)
(d) Discuss the possible costs and benefits of delegating greater authority and responsibility further down the hierarchy. (10 marks)

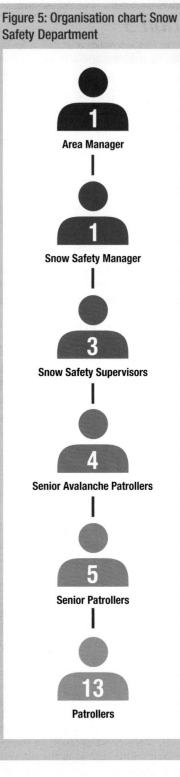

Figure 5: Organisation chart: Snow Safety Department

1 Area Manager

1 Snow Safety Manager

3 Snow Safety Supervisors

4 Senior Avalanche Patrollers

5 Senior Patrollers

13 Patrollers

Measuring personnel effectiveness

Advocates of human resource management (HRM) claim that the performance of the workforce is enhanced through adopting appropriate personnel policies. In many other areas of business, such as finance or production, there is a large number of possible measures of performance, from sales revenue to profit after tax to output per day. In personnel, there are fewer key measures. Some of these only point indirectly at key variables. For example, it is not possible to measure directly:

- the motivation of a workforce;
- the ability of a workforce to accept and implement change;
- the teamworking capabilities of workers;
- the commitment of workers to the business;
- the contribution of £1 spent on personnel such as higher pay or spending on training to profit.

However, there are a few measures which can be used, including labour productivity, absenteeism rates, labour turnover, working days lost for health and safety reasons and wastage rates.

Labour productivity

Labour productivity is defined as output per worker. As a formula:

$$\text{Labour productivity} = \frac{\text{Total output (per period of time)}}{\text{Average number of employees (per period of time)}}$$

Labour productivity is an important measure of the efficiency of a workforce. For example, if there are two teams of workers in a factory, each with identical equipment and the same number of workers, then the team with the highest productivity could be identified as the most effective team.

Figures for labour productivity need to be used with caution. For example, differences in labour productivity between factories or plants may be accounted for by differences in equipment used rather than the efficiency of the workforce. A plant with newer equipment is likely to have higher labour productivity than one with old equipment. Equally, productivity differs widely between processes within a business and between businesses in different industries. A highly automated section of a factory is likely to have much higher labour productivity than a labour-intensive packing section in the same factory using little capital equipment. Manufacturing industry may have a higher average labour productivity than service industries simply because more capital is used per employee in manufacturing.

A business wishing to improve the labour productivity of groups of workers can adopt a number of strategies.

- Improving the capital equipment with which they work.
- Changing the way in which workers are employed, for example, moving from an assembly line production system to a cell production system.
- Disappointing labour productivity may be due to a lack of training on the part of workers. Increased training may therefore raise productivity.
- Changing the reward system may increase motivation and commitment and so improve productivity. There are many other ways that motivation may be increased. These include changing the structure of the business and devolving decision making power down the chain of command.

Increasing labour productivity is generally assumed to increase the competitiveness of a business. Higher labour productivity should drive down costs, allowing a business either to lower its prices and so gain higher sales, or to keep its prices the same but increase its profit margins.

However, businesses sometimes find that they become less competitive despite increasing their labour productivity. This may occur for a number of reasons.

- Rival businesses may increase their productivity at an even faster rate.
- New rival businesses may set up which pay considerably lower wages. Many UK manufacturing businesses have become less competitive over the past ten years due to the emergence of competition from low wage, low cost businesses in the Far East and eastern Europe.
- Other factors apart from cost may change adversely for a business. For example, a rival business may bring out a far better new product. However, productive the workforce and however low the cost, customers may prefer to buy the new product rather than a cheaper old product.

Absenteeism

Absenteeism is a problem for all businesses for a number of reasons.

- Staff who are absent often claim to be ill. The business then, in most cases, has to pay sick pay.
- If temporary staff are brought in to cover for absent staff, this leads to increased costs. Equally, costs will increase if permanent staff have to work overtime and are paid at higher rates than their basic rate of pay.
- Output may suffer if workers are expected to cover for sick colleagues or if temporary staff are not as productive as the absent workers.
- Prolonged absences can lead to major disruption if the worker is key to a particular area of work or a new project.
- If production is delayed or there are problems with quality, customers can be lost.

Question 1.

The NHS Executive has introduced the labour productivity index for all NHS trusts in England. The index is a measure of the value of the output per trust employee. It is calculated by multiplying each type of activity, eg inpatients, outpatients, health visitor contacts, by its average cost, adding all these costs together and dividing the total by the number of employees in the trust. The index allows trusts to compare their labour productivity with others. It may also be a useful tool in contract negotiations. Theoretically, a trust with a labour productivity index of 6000 can be interpreted not only as being more productive than a trust with an index of 3000, but of being twice as productive.

This simple interpretation however, is not without difficulties. Major areas of activity, such as research and diagnostic services, are excluded, distorting the index. It is also assumed that those activities included are the same in each trust. This does not take into account variations in the quality or effectiveness of different contacts. Another problem is that the effort (cost, labour, etc) to produce one 'unit' of activity will vary across trusts and will depend on patient characteristics such as age or complexity. Further, only full-time staff are included but many trusts subcontract work.

Source: adapted from *British Medical Journal*, 2006.

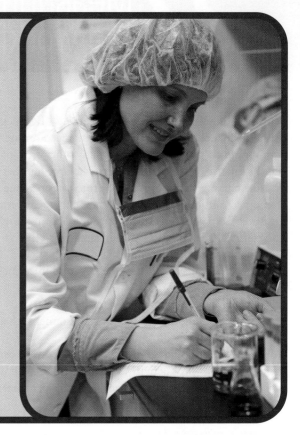

(a) How is the productivity of employees in the NHS being measured?
(b) Explain how the measurement of employees' productivity can benefit NHS trusts.
(c) Discuss how useful the labour productivity index will be in measuring NHS employees' productivity.

- Absenteeism can be demotivating to staff left to cope with the problems.
- The higher the rate of absenteeism, the more likely it is that workers will report ill. This is because a culture of absenteeism will develop where it becomes acceptable for workers to take extra days holiday by reporting in sick.

The RATE OF ABSENTEEISM or ABSENTEEISM RATE or ABSENTEE RATE can be calculated by dividing the number of staff absent by the total number of staff employed. The rate is expressed as a percentage. It can be calculated as a daily rate using the formula:

$$\frac{\text{Number of staff absent on a day}}{\text{Total number of staff employed}} \times 100\%$$

For example, if 1,000 staff are employed, and 30 are absent on a particular day, then the rate of absenteeism for that day is 3 per cent (100% x 30 ÷ 1,000). If the rate of absenteeism for a year is calculated, the total number of staff days lost through absenteeism must by divided by the number of staff days that should have been worked over the year. This is calculated using the formula:

$$\frac{\text{Total number of staff absence days over the year}}{\text{Total number of staff days that should have been worked}} \times 100\%$$

For example, assume 6,000 staff days were lost through absence. There were 500 staff, each of whom should have worked 240 days during the year. So the total number of staff days that should have been worked was 120,000 (500 x 240). The rate of absenteeism was therefore 5 per cent (100% x 6,000 ÷ 120,000).

Rates of absenteeism can be calculated for a business as a whole and compared to industry averages or national averages. They can also be compared between one part of a business and another or compared over time. Differences in rates of absenteeism occur for a number of reasons.

- Small businesses tend to have lower rates of absenteeism than larger businesses. Arguably this is because there is much more commitment and feeling of teamwork in a small business than in a large business. Workers in large businesses can feel that no-one will suffer if they take a day off work and so absenteeism is acceptable.
- Health and safety is a factor. Businesses which have good health and safety procedures will tend to suffer less illness-related absenteeism than those with poor procedures. Equally, some jobs are inherently more dangerous to health than others and so absenteeism is more likely.
- The nature of the tasks given to workers is another factor. Tasks which are fragmented and repetitive lead to low job satisfaction and demotivation. This encourages workers to report sick. Workers in jobs which are interesting and rewarding tend to have lower absentee rates.
- The culture of a workplace can cause absenteeism. Where workers are overworked, where there is a climate of

intimidation and bullying by superiors of subordinates, and where the needs of workers are ignored, work-related stress becomes much more common. Workers off through stress are a particular problem because they often take months off work at a time.

- Stress-related illness is also more common where workers are oversupervised and feel that they are not trusted by their superiors to accomplish tasks.
- Workers who feel that they are grossly underpaid are more likely to take time off work. They see it as compensation for the lack of monetary reward they receive. Low pay is also a demotivator and so contributes to absenteeism.

Businesses can adopt a variety of methods to reduce absenteeism. Some assume that absenteeism is mainly caused by inappropriate or a lack of human resource management policies. Problems such as lack of commitment, low motivation, bullying, oversupervision and perceptions of low pay can be tackled through methods such as more teamwork, devolving power down the chain of command, more democratic leadership, better reward systems and policies which make bullying and harassment at work a major disciplinary offence. Health and safety issues can be addressed through the rigorous application of a well thought out health and safety policy. Adoption of lean production techniques are also likely to improve absenteeism rates.

The UK government in the early 2000s stressed the importance of a WORK LIFE BALANCE in dealing with a number of HR issues including absenteeism. Absenteeism can be caused by conflicts between work and family commitments, or work and leisure goals. A parent may phone in sick when in fact he or she is having to stay at home to look after his or her ill eight year old. Or a worker may phone in sick on a Monday morning because he can't face work after a weekend's activities. The solution is for more flexible working patterns. For example, workers may be able to take a few hours off work if they work them at some other time in the week or the month. Or workers may have a number of individual days holiday a year which can be taken without giving notice. Or a worker may have the right permanently to the number of hours worked per week, changing for example from full time to three days a week.

On the other hand, a scientific management approach would tend towards the introduction of systems of rewards and punishments. Cutting down the number of days when staff can claim sick pay is one measure. Another is for superiors to monitor closely staff who are absent. Telephoning them or even visiting them in their homes when they are off sick can be effective in deterring absenteeism. Being prepared to sack staff who abuse the system can also be an important deterrent to the rest of the workforce. Some employers offer bonuses to workers who have not had time off work due to illness. A few even offer all their staff a number of paid days off work each year which can be taken when staff don't feel like going into work or have problems with childcare arrangements.

Another policy which is frequently advocated is 'back to work' interviews. Any member of staff who has been absent has to be interviewed by a superior about why they were absent. This can be seen from a human relations school perspective as supportive of the worker. Their superior cares for them enough to want to know why they were away. Equally it can be judged from a scientific management school perspective. The superior

Question 2.

Royal Mail's cure for Britain's £1.75bn problem of absenteeism is simple - a Ford car and holiday vouchers. Its incentive scheme has improved attendance levels by more than 10 per cent in six months, equivalent to 1,000 extra staff. It is so pleased that it is extending the scheme for 12 months. Under the initial scheme staff who worked for six months without a day off work sick were entered for a prize draw. More than half of the 170,000 employees at Royal Mail and Parcelforce Worldwide qualified. Thirty-seven won a new Ford Focus car, worth £12,000 each and 75 won the £2,000 holiday vouchers. Even the 90,000 who qualified for the draw but missed out got a £150 holiday voucher.

Royal Mail will not say how much the scheme cost, but insists it makes financial and commercial sense. 'The employees like it, as a company we like it – we have 1,000 more people every day than we would otherwise have had if nothing had changed. It benefits the customers too because good attendance goes hand in glove with good quality of service', said a Royal Mail spokesperson. Some have estimated the costs at £1.9m before allowing for any discounts.

The company denies it is putting pressure on genuinely ill workers to turn up for work. Its people and operational development director, said 'We must support and reward postmen and women. They deserve it. They do a demanding job to a high standard, day in and day out, in all weathers.'

The Communication Workers Union had a more old-fashioned explanation for the fall in absenteeism - better pay and conditions. The union's deputy general secretary said: 'Giveaways are not the reason why attendance levels have improved and they are certainly not a substitute for continuing to invest in our members' overall employment package.'

Source: adapted from *The Guardian*, 26.4.2005.

(a) Why is it important for the Royal Mail to measure absenteeism rates?
(b) Examine the advantages and disadvantages of the scheme to reduce absenteeism at Royal Mail for (i) the business and (ii) its employees.
(c) Discuss whether the scheme is likely to be more effective than 'better pay and conditions'.

is checking up on the worker to see whether the absence was genuine.

Labour turnover

Labour or staff turnover is another measure of personnel effectiveness. **Labour turnover** is the proportion of staff leaving a business over a period of time. It is measured by the formula:

$$\text{Labour turnover} = \frac{\text{Number of staff leaving over a period of time}}{\text{Average number of staff in post during the period}} \times 100\%$$

For example, if 20 staff left over a year and there were on average 40 on the staff, then the staff turnover would be 50 per cent ($100\% \times 20 \div 40$).

As with other measures of personnel performance, labour turnover differs from department to department within a business, from business to business within an industry and from industry to industry within an economy. Relatively high labour turnover is caused by a number of factors.

- Relatively low pay leads to higher labour turnover as workers leave to get better paid jobs.
- Relatively few training and promotion opportunities will encourage workers to leave their current jobs.
- Poor working conditions, low job satisfaction, bullying and harassment in the workplace are other factors.
- Some businesses are relatively poor at selecting and recruiting the right candidates for posts. Where workers are ill suited to their jobs, there is more chance that they will leave relatively quickly.
- In a recession, labour turnover tends to fall as the number of vacancies falls and workers become worried that if they leave their job without having got another one to go to, they will become part of the long-term unemployed. In a boom, when there might be labour shortages, there are far more vacancies and so labour turnover tends to rise.

Relatively high labour turnover is usually seen as a problem for businesses for a number of reasons.

- Recruiting new staff can be costly.
- It takes time for new staff to become familiar with their roles and the way in which the business operates. High labour turnover is likely to reduce the human process advantage of a business.
- Larger companies may put on induction programmes which further adds to costs.
- If the post is filled internally, there may be training needs for the worker who gets the job.

However, some labour turnover is usually beneficial to a business.

- New staff can bring in fresh ideas and experience from their work with other businesses.
- Some workers may be ineffective and need to be encouraged to leave. Getting rid of ineffective staff leads to

labour turnover.

- If a business is shrinking in size, reducing the size of the workforce will lead to higher labour turnover.
- Where a business pays low wages, or where conditions of work are poor, it may be more profitable to have a constant turnover of staff rather than raise wages or improve conditions of work.

Businesses can attempt to reduce their labour turnover if they see it as a problem. Higher pay and better working conditions might be one strategy. Another might be offering better internal promotion prospects to workers. Better selection procedures would be appropriate if the problem is poor recruiting. Effective procedures against bullying and harassment could help too. For senior workers, a business might offer bonuses in the future (often in the form of share option schemes) which can only be claimed if they are still employed by the business at the point in time.

Health and safety

The safety of the working environment can be measured in a number of different ways. For example, health and safety could be measured by the number of working days lost through accidents or injuries per thousand employees over a time period.

$$\frac{\text{Number of working days lost for health and safety reasons per time period}}{\text{Total number of workers}} \times 100\%$$

For example, if there were 300 days lost through accidents or injury over a year and the workforce were 6,000, then the number of working days lost per thousand employees would be ($300 \div 6,000$) x 1,000, which is 50.

Another measure relates working days lost to the total number of working days that could have been worked over the period, expressed as a percentage.

$$\frac{\text{Number of working days lost for health and safety reasons per time period}}{\text{Total number of possible working days during the period}} \times 100\%$$

For example, if 2,000 days are lost due to health and safety reasons over a year, and the number of possible working days for the workforce over the period was 100,000, then the health and safety ratio is 2 per cent ($100\% \times 2,000 \div 100,000$).

A poor health and safety record may occur for a number of reasons.

- Equipment used may be dangerous. For example, it might be poorly maintained or be too old.
- The working environment itself may be dangerous. For example, unsafe levels of dangerous gases or chemicals may be found in the atmosphere in a factory building.
- There may be a lack of safety equipment. For example, workers should perhaps be wearing safety hats, but these

are not provided by the employer.

- Workers may not receive sufficient health and safety training.
- The business may not enforce its own health and safety procedures. It may turn a 'blind eye' to abuses because otherwise production would be slowed down.
- Work may be contracted out to self-employed workers who prefer to disregard time-consuming health and safety procedures in order to earn more money. In the building industry, the widespread use of subcontractors is sometimes given as a reason for a poor health and safety record.

Improving a poor health and safety record may be achieved by:

- increasing expenditure on buildings and equipment to bring them up to health and safety standards;
- drawing up an appropriate set of health and safety policies and procedures;
- training all staff to ensure that they understand these policies and procedures and can carry them out;
- strictly enforcing health and safety policies, putting safety above profit and output.

Businesses which have poor health and safety records are either poorly organised and managed, or deliberately exploiting the situation to cut their costs. Lower health and safety standards is one way in which some businesses can gain a competitive advantage. One of the criticisms of globalisation is that producers in Third World countries operate under much less stringent health and safety standards than in the UK. Hence, it could be argued that they have an 'unfair' competitive advantage.

A poor health and safety record can be a disadvantage to a business.

- Poor health and safety standards are likely to lead to the demotivation of staff. Their basic needs are being threatened.
- Such businesses are liable to have their operations closed down or be open to prosecution by health and safety inspectors. Equally, they are open to being sued by workers involved in accidents or by customers if products are put at risk. At worst, such a business could be forced to close because of this issue.
- Staff absences due to accidents may have the same costs as absences due to illness, as explained in the last section. Businesses may also be fined or sued as a result of accidents.
- A poor health and safety record could contribute towards

giving a business a poor reputation with customers and so it could affect sales. In the Third World, suppliers to some Western multinationals have to conform to basic standards to win and retain orders. This is because the reputation of the multinationals in their First World markets can be at stake.

KEYTERMS

Rate of absenteeism or absenteeism rate or absentee rate – the number of staff absent as a percentage of the total number of staff employed. It can be calculated for different periods of time, ie daily rates or annual rates.
Work life balance – the relationship between time spent at work and time spent away from work or the time spent at work as a proportion of total time.

KNOWLEDGE

1. How is labour productivity calculated?
2. A component manufacturer makes 10,000 metal washers with ten workers. After employing five extra workers it makes 20,000. Calculate the effect on labour productivity.
3. List four ways in which a business may improve labour productivity.
4. How can a business calculate its rate of absenteeism?
5. List five reasons why rates of absenteeism are different in different industries.
6. State three ways in which a business might reduce rates of absenteeism.
7. What is the relationship between absenteeism and a work life balance?
8. A business finds that its labour turnover falls from 20% to 15%. Should it be concerned?
9. List four factors that might lead to high labour turnover.
10. State five problems of high labour turnover for a business.
11. State two formulae that a business might use to measure its health and safety record.
12. List five factors that may cause a business to have a poor health and safety record.
13. State five possible problems for a business with a poor record of health and safety.

Case Study: *Supermarkets' labour turnover and absenteeism*

First there were duvet days for staff temporarily 'sick' of work - offered by companies trying to reduce absenteeism by gentle persuasion. Then there was time off for everything from a religious festival to a child's first day at school. In 2004 Tesco, opted for the stick approach, cutting sick pay in some of its stores and tested other schemes in an attempt to cut rates of absenteeism. Tesco spokesperson Jonathan Church said that absenteeism '...impacts on our business as well as creating more work for people in the store. These trials are about encouraging people to use planned absence whenever they can. If they need to take little Johnnie to the dentist, then we will bend over backwards to make that possible.'

One scheme, introduced in two stores in the south, meant workers got no pay for the first three days off sick, but after the fourth day would get paid again with compensation for the first three days. That could encourage people to go sick for a whole week. Other options are to offer staff more holiday allowance up front, but reduce it every time they take a day off sick. Tesco said there are fewer absences in stores testing the schemes. 'Our intention is not to penalise people who are genuinely ill. It is to discourage people from taking those odd days.'

Asda offers incentives such as prizes to reward low absenteeism. 'It might be a week's extra holiday or a weekend break or vouchers. It has really helped bring absenteeism down because people think hard about

whether they really need to be off.' The company already has 'carers leave' and 'first day/half day' leave for parents taking children to school.

Sick leave costs British companies around £11 billion every year through 166 million lost working days. Stress-related absence is rising, according to the Health and Safety Executive. This has prompted organisations like The Work Foundation for businesses to look more carefully at how they treat staff and the work environment.

In 2003, seasonal workers at Asda at Christmas were entitled to benefits and job security equivalent to those enjoyed by their full-time colleagues, after the supermarket created 10 000 new permanent positions for contract workers. The new 'seasonal squad' would have the same status as permanent staff but with a contract to work an annual, rather than weekly, number of hours. They could work for as little as ten weeks of the year. The contracts would cover Christmas, Easter and the school summer holidays and cover jobs such as greeters, porters, checkout operatives and warehouse workers. 'We recognise that people are looking for flexibility across the working year, not just the working week' said Caroline Massingham, Asda retail people director. 'If you're one of the many people that want to balance long periods of leave with a fulfilling job, the options are limited'. Asda hopes the initiative would encourage more over 50s to join. The supermarket said that since actively recruiting older workers, it has seen absence levels drop, customer service levels rise and labour turnover fall. The flexible working package includes one week's leave for new grandparents, five days leave for IVF treatment and up to two years for a career break. Asda is hoping to make huge savings from the initiative by reducing turnover, as it has spent around £3,500 per person in recruitment costs.

Source: adapted from *The Observer*, 16.5.2004.

(a) (i) Explain why supermarkets may want to reduce rates of absenteeism and labour turnover. (8 marks)

(ii) Examine the factors that might affect rates of absenteeism and labour turnover at supermarkets. (12 marks)

(b) Evaluate the methods used by supermarkets in the article to reduce rates of absenteeism and labour turnover. (20 marks)

Stages of recruitment

Successful businesses are able to develop an effective workforce. The first stage in this process is **recruitment** and **selection**. In a small business, it may seem obvious to the employer what will be required of a new recruit. The employer may put in an advertisement for, say, an 'administrative assistant' and explain at the interview what the job entails. However, where the business is larger, and if there is a personnel department, more formal procedures are likely to be used.

Job description

First, a JOB DESCRIPTION will be drawn up. This gives the title of the job. It is a statement of the tasks to be undertaken and responsibilities of the employee holding that job. The job description may describe the employee's place in the hierarchy of the business. Working conditions may also be specified, such as rates of pay or holiday entitlements. An example of a job description is shown in Figure 1. In many cases, the job description for the new recruit will simply be the job description of the person leaving the job. Large businesses, where many employees do the same job, such as a sales assistant or production line worker, might have a common job description for a particular job.

Job descriptions tell the new employee what is expected of them. It can be used when appraising the performance of a worker. If the worker fails to perform satisfactorily and is threatened with dismissal, it can also be used by the employer as evidence to support the dismissal.

The details about the job included in job description can be found by JOB ANALYSIS. This is a study of what the job entails. It will include the skills needed to do the job, the tasks that are needed to carry out the job, the activities that enable these tasks to be done, the roles and duties of the job holder and the criteria used to measure performance. It is important for a business to gather views of all people associated with the job including the job holders, their superiors and subordinates and other advisors such as work analysts.

Person specification

A job description can be used to draw up a PERSON SPECIFICATION. This is a description (or profile) of the personal qualities that match the requirements of the job specification. The person specification might include the educational and professional qualifications needed for the post. Previous experience required might be outlined. General skills and character traits could also be described.

The person specification can be used to 'screen' applicants. If there are many applicants, selectors will be able to discard those

---

Figure 1: A job description for a cabin crew assistant with an airline

Job title
Cabin crew member.

Function
Perform ground and air duties that the company may reasonably require. Ground duties apply to any area of work connected to aircraft operational requirements.
Other duties, including boardroom functions and publicity, are voluntary.

Cabin crew must also:
- be familiar and comply with company policy and procedures;
- provide a high standard of cabin service and perform their duties conscientiously at all times;
- not behave in any way that reflects badly upon the company or harms its reputation.

Pay and expenses
Salary will be £13,000 per annum.
Payment will be one month in arrears, paid directly into the employee's bank account.
Expenses will be paid as set out in the current contract.
If flights are cancelled, you will be entitled to a reporting allowance as set out in the current contract.

Work time
You are required to work 20 days in every 28 day roster period.
Days and hours will vary according to the company's requirements.
Details of rest periods and flight time limitations are set out in the staff manual.

Figure 2: Person specification for an administrative assistant in an engineering plant

	Essential/Desirable
Aptitudes/skills/abilities	
Able to take a flexible approach to working conditions and a changing working environment	E
Self-motivated and enthusiastic	E
Ability to work on own initiative	D
Work effectively as part of a team	D
Qualifications/knowledge and experience	
4 GCSE level C or above	E
Computer literate in Word and Excel	E
Good written and verbal communication skills	E
Able to solve problems effectively	E
Planning and organisational skills	D
Experience of working in a manufacturing environment	D

Question 1.

Job Designation: Broadcast Journalist

Grade: Towers Perrin Level 5/7

Ref: 59858

JOB PURPOSE

To initiate and produce, as part of a team, a wide variety of news and current affairs material for Radio and/or Television.

KEY BEHAVIOURS

1. To carry out in-depth research to a broad brief, with minimal supervision across the whole range of Regional Broadcasting news and current affairs output.

2. To write material for programme scripts, bulletins and links, exercising editorial judgment, maintaining professional journalistic standards and adhering to BBC policy and legal and contractual guidelines.

3. To undertake interviewing and reporting duties, under broad direction in both recorded and live situations, in studio or on location, for both Radio and Television.

4. To prepare and present bulletins, including assessing incoming copy, sub-editing news copy and deploying the necessary resources.

(a) Explain what is meant by a 'job description', illustrating your answer with examples from the data.

(b) The job being advertised was for the presenter of the Good Afternoon Show on BBC Radio Leeds. Discuss whether the BBC was likely to recruit internally or externally for the post.

which don't match the person specification. If there are only a few applicants, and none match the specification exactly, the employer may have to compromise and decide which aspects of the person specification are most important. Alternatively, the employer might decide to readvertise the post. An example of a person specification is shown in Figure 2.

Internal recruitment

INTERNAL RECRUITMENT is recruitment from within the business. An employee may be chosen to be offered a post. Or the business may advertise internally, asking employees to apply for the vacancy. The advertisement may be sent round via email or posted on a noticeboard. Larger organisations may have regular newsletters devoted to internal vacancies or notices may be put in the company magazine or on the company website. Internal recruitment has a number of advantages compared to external recruitment.

*   It is often cheaper because no adverts have to be placed

and paid for at commercial rates.

*   Internal recruits might already be familiar with the procedures and working environment of the business. They may, therefore, need less induction training and be more productive in their first year of employment.

*   The qualities, abilities and potential of the candidates should be better known to the employer. It is often difficult to foresee exactly how an external recruit will perform in a particular work environment.

*   Regular internal recruiting can motivate staff. They might see a career progression with their employer. Even for those who aren't seeking promotion, internal recruitment suggests that the employer is looking after existing staff.

External recruitment

EXTERNAL RECRUITMENT is when someone is appointed from outside the business. External recruitment has two main advantages over internal recruitment.

*   The employer may want someone with new and different ideas to those already working in the business. Bringing in experience of working in different organisations can often be helpful in keeping a business competitive.

*   External recruitment might attract a larger number of applicants than internal recruitment. The employer then has more choice of whom to appoint.

External recruitment requires the employer to communicate with potential employees. Ideally, every person who is suitable and who might consider the job should apply. That way, the employer will have the maximum number of candidates from which to choose. There is a number of ways in which an employer can do this.

Word of mouth A common method of hearing about a job is through word of mouth. This means a person hearing about a job from someone else, often someone who works in the place of employment. For example, a person might hear about a vacancy for a hospital porter from their next door neighbour who works as a nurse in a local hospital.

Direct application Many jobseekers send their details to employers for whom they would like to work on the off-chance that they would have a vacancy. An employer might then use these to recruit if a vacancy arises.

Advertising The employer may place advertisements in local or national newspapers and specialist magazines and journals. The Internet is another medium for job advertisements. Advertisements may appear on a company website. The largest sector covered by Internet advertising is jobs in IT. Advertisements on a board or window on the employer's premises can also be successful. Advertisements are sometimes costly. But they can reach a wide number of potential applicants. People wanting to change their job are likely to seek out advertisements.

Private employment agencies The business may employ a private employment agency to find candidates. Private employment agencies are probably best known for finding temporary workers (temps). However, many also specialise in finding permanent staff. At the top end of the range, private employment agencies tend to call themselves executive agencies. They specialise in recruiting company executives and finding jobs for executives seeking a change or who have been made redundant. Using an employment agency should take much of the work out of the recruitment process for the employer. But it can be costly because the employment agency charges a fee. Private employment agencies sometimes have a website where specialist workers can look for jobs or advertise their services.

Headhunting For some posts, such as chief executive of a company, it may be possible to headhunt a candidate. This is where the agency draws up a list of people they think would be

Question 2.

Pete Roghey owns and runs a small building company with 20 employees. Turnover of staff is relatively high. Skilled workers are constantly in demand and he can find that they have been poached by another company, often on short-term contracts, to work at higher rates of pay.

This week, Pete needs to hire three workers. There is a part time office cleaner's job, working in the evening from 5-7, five nights a week. He is looking for a skilled full time bricklayer. Then there is a general labourer's job, which could suit a young person just starting.

There never seems to be a right way to get hold of new staff. Sometimes, Pete advertises in the local newspaper and gets no replies. Other times, he can be spoilt for choice. More often than not, he gets approached by someone who has heard about the job vacancy from one of his workers. But there is never any guarantee that anyone will turn up this way.

(a) Discuss the advantages and disadvantages for Pete Roghey of using word of mouth to fill job vacancies compared to placing adverts in local newspapers.

(b) What might be the advantages of placing an advert in a local newsagent for the cleaner's job?

suitable for a job. Having cleared the list with the organisation making the appointment, the agency will approach those on the list and discuss the possibility of them taking the job. Some will say no. Others will indicate that, if the terms were right, they might take the job. A final selection is then made and one person is offered the job. Nobody has formally applied or been interviewed. Headhunting works best where there is only a limited number of people who potentially could take on the post and where the agency knows about most of those people.

Jobcentres Businesses can advertise vacancies through Jobcentres run by the government. Jobcentres are often used by the unemployed and vacancies tend to pay less than the average wage. So a cleaner's post is more likely to be advertised in a Jobcentre than a chief executive's post. For a business, this is a relatively cheap way of advertising, but it is not suitable for many vacancies.

Government funded training schemes Some businesses take on trainees from government funded training schemes. The current main scheme is called the New Deal. The schemes are designed to give the unemployed a chance to work for six or 12 months with some element of training. Businesses may choose then to offer these workers a permanent job if there is a vacancy and they have proved satisfactory.

Selection

Having advertised the post or gone through an employment agency, a business needs to select the right candidate. Those expressing an interest may be sent details about the post and how to apply or the details may be included on an advertisement. A number of stages will the take place.

Application forms, letters of application or curriculum vitae Sometimes, a business has an application form that it wants to be filled in giving details of the applicant. Or a business may ask candidates to send in a CURRICULUM VITAE (CV), possibly with a letter explaining why they want the post. A CV is a short document which gives the main details about a candidate. Like an application form, it should show information such as their name, address, age, gender, qualifications and job experience.

Long and short lists If a business receives many applications, it is likely to shortlist or longlist candidates. This involves selecting a small or large number of candidates who appear most suitable from their applications.

Interviews Some or all of these candidates might then be asked to an INTERVIEW. Short- and long-listings might reduce the cost of selection for a business as it would be time consuming and costly to interview, say, 200 applicants. At an interview, applicants will be asked questions about themselves and about issues related to the job. Applicants may have the chance to ask their own questions about the job. Almost every selection process involves some sort of interview. Applicants may even be

123

put through several interviews with different interviewers or panels of selectors. Interviews may be conducted by the personnel department or by department heads.

Some research has shown that interviews are poor at selecting the best candidate for the job. Some candidates are very good at interviews, but poor at their job. Others are bad at interviews, but are excellent employees. Interviewers tend to look for someone with qualities similar to their own rather than qualities required by the job and person specification. Judgments are often formed within the first few minutes of most interviews.

Because interviews are so unreliable, some businesses choose to use additional selection techniques.

- Candidates may be asked to role play or take part in a simulation relating to the job. This involves interviewees acting out a situation. It gives assessors a better insight into how a candidate might perform in a post.
- Tests may also be used. These could be simple numerical or literacy tests to see whether candidates can perform calculations and write effectively. There could be complicated tests, such as IQ tests. PSYCHOMETRIC TESTS aim to uncover the personality of the candidates. This helps selectors gain insights, for example, into whether a candidate would be good with customers, a useful part of a team, or could cope with stress.
- A number of large organisations today use assessment centres for some of their appointments. These are specialist organisations that deal only with making appointments. They use a variety of selection techniques to gain as wide a picture of candidates as possible. Even so, they can recommend unsuitable appointments, showing that selection procedures are not 100 per cent accurate.

Appointment

The successful candidate for a job will be appointed by the business. Candidates might be offered a job conditionally. For example, if, after the interview, they fail medical tests or police checks the offer of the job may be withdrawn. Employers also usually take up references from previous employers. A current or previous employer may give unflattering references because they don't want to lose the employee or simply out of spite. This is one reason why most employers don't ask for references before the interviews. However, a reference may turn up something like a police conviction which would again mean the offer of the job being withdrawn.

Legal constraints

Businesses recruiting and selecting new staff are bound by various employment laws.

- The Sex Discrimination Act 1975 and the Race Relations Act 1976 state that there must be no discrimination against applicants, whether male or female, or whatever ethnic origin. Discrimination can occur at any stage of the recruitment process. For example, an advertisement saying 'Males only need apply' might be a case of discrimination.

Cases are also brought against employers through employment tribunals (courts which deal with employment law) mainly by women or those from ethnic minorities arguing that jobs were given not to the best applicant, but on gender or race grounds.

- The Disability Discrimination Act 1995 states that it is unlawful for businesses to discriminate against an applicant with a disability, unless there is justification. Justification might be shown if the employer had to take unreasonable measures to allow the person with the disability to work successfully. For example, an employer might not be able to reject a candidate in a wheelchair if there were a few steps at the entrance to the place of work because a ramp could easily and cheaply be installed. However, it might be unreasonable to expect an employer to move premises just to employ the disabled worker.
- The Age Discrimination Act 2006 gives protection against age discrimination, unless it can be justified, for example if there are saftey issues. The laws protect employees of any age against age discrnimation over recruitment, terms and conditions, promotions, transfers, dismissals and training.
- After appointment, employees must be given a contract of employment detailing their duties and their rate of pay, for example.

How recruitment and selection can improve the workforce

Good recruitment and selection procedures can help to improve the workforce of a business and ensure it works effectively. They will identify the type of person required for the a job. This means that a suitable person can be appointed. They will have the skills to do the job and labour productivity may be high. They are likely to make fewer mistakes, which can be costly and time consuming.

Effective procedures may also be able to identify ways in which employees can improve. For example, if training needs are highlighted at an early stage then employees' skills may improve as they are employed for a period and receive training.

If the wrong person is recruited, this can cause problems for a business. The person appointed may find the job boring or too difficult, which could lead to a lack of motivation and poor productivity. If the person leaves, there will be administration costs for the human resource department. The business will face the extra costs of advertising and interviewing. There will also be a settling in period until the new employee has learned the job. Good recruitment and selection procedures can prevent this.

Identifying the most suitable employees may give a business a competitive edge over rivals. Productive and motivated employees will help a business to operate effectively. Business may also develop a good reputation, which can help attract customers. For example, a restaurant that has attentive staff and chefs that cook to a high standard may encourage customers to return.

KEYTERMS

Curriculum vitae – a brief description of an individual's personal details, experience and qualifications.

External recruitment – when an employee looks for applicants for a job from outside the organisation.

Internal recruitment – when an employee seeks to find applicants for a job from inside the organisation.

Interview – a meeting where an applicant answers questions from and asks questions of selectors for a job.

Job analysis – a study of what the job entails, such as skills, tasks and performance expected.

Job description – a statement of the tasks to be undertaken and responsibilities of the employee holding the job.

Person specification – a description (or profile) of the personal qualities that match the requirements of the job specification.

Psychometric tests – tests which aim to uncover the personality of individuals.

KNOWLEDGE

1. What is the difference between a job description and a person specification?
2. Compare the advantages of recruiting internally with recruiting externally.
3. Briefly explain the different ways in which a business might recruit externally.
4. Explain the difference between a short-list and a long-list.
5. What techniques may a business use to select candidates for a post?
6. Briefly explain the legal constraints on employment.

Case Study: *Using online information in recruitment and selection*

The recruitment activities of a business has shortlisted a number of candidates for the job. There appears to be the perfect person for the job at an interview with a perfect CV. An hour before the interview you look on Facebook and find a photo of the candidate looking drunk. What do you do?

CVs, interviews, references and psychometric testing used to be the main tools for selecting candidates. But more and more employers are using web browsers to check out potential staff. According to one recruitment consultancy survey, one in five employers are using information from network sites such as Facebook and MySpace as an aid to recruitment and selection. Employees used to be able to predict how prospective employers would research them, but social networking sites have changed this. Candidates may not realise the effect their websites are having on their job prospects and may not have full control over the details being posted. Employer surveys indicate the key recruitment 'turn-offs' are:

- disparaging a previous employer or disclosing confidential work information;
- disparity between the website and the CV/application form, for example, qualifications;
- intolerance of others that could cause disruption in the workplace;
- criminal activity.

It can be to employers' advantage to use online information. But there are employment law risks. For example, employers could be guilty of not processing personal data fairly under the Data Protection Act 1998 Or they might breach guidelines in the Information Commissioner's Employment Practices Code (DPA Code). Employers also face potential discrimination claims. For example, employers could may discrminate against people using Facebook on the grounds of age, since most users are aged between 18 and 24. Checking existing employees without good reason could breach the implied contract term of trust and confidence.

How can employers reduce the risk? The DPA Code recommends candidates are told that web-checking may be part of the selection process. Employers could also nominate someone removed from the decision making to research and document information. This reduces the scope for unlawful bias. Employers could also give applicants a chance to explain discrepancies in qualifications, for example. Employers could limit checking in this way to those they intend to offer a job to rather than shortlist candidates. And they should consider carefully the information they find. They may be put off by images of drunkenness, but having too many drinks at the weekend does not necessarily mean that a person can not do their job, nor are they an alcoholic.

Employers need to weigh up what message 'web-vetting' sends out about the business. Some will see it as intrusive. Others as a legitimate way of getting a feel for how a person behaves when not in a formal interview.

Source: adapted from *People Management*, 18.10. 2007.

A footwear retailer with a number of branches in the South West is opening three new shops.

(a) Explain the meaning of the terms:
   (i) 'shortlist'; (3 marks) (ii) 'recruitment'. (3 marks)

(b) Describe two different methods of selecting candidates that the business can use. (6 marks)

(c) Explain why the business may want to use network sites such as Facebook and MySpace in the recruitment and selection process. (8 marks)

(d) Evaluate the extent to which using such networks might help the business recruit and select effectively. (10 marks)

29 | Developing an effective workforce - training

Why business train their workforce

TRAINING is the process of increasing the knowledge and skills of workers so that they are better able to perform their jobs. The objectives of training differ from business to business but they include:

- making workers more productive by teaching them more effective ways of working;
- familiarising workers with new equipment or technology being introduced;
- educating workers in new methods of working, such as shifting from production line methods to cell methods;
- making workers more flexible so that they are able to do more than one job;
- preparing workers to move into a different job within the business, which could be a new job at a similar level or a promotion;
- improving standards of work in order to improve quality;
- implementing health and safety at work policies;
- increasing job satisfaction and motivation, because training should help workers feel more confident in what they are doing and they should gain self-esteem;
- assisting in recruiting and retaining high quality staff, attracted by the quality of training offered.

Sometimes, individual employees request training or undertake training without the financial or time support of their employers. For example, a manager may take an MBA university course in her own time. More frequently, training is provided by the employer. The need for training is sometimes identified in the appraisal process.

Induction training

Many businesses put on training for people starting a job. This is known as INDUCTION TRAINING. It is designed to help new employees settle quickly into the business and their jobs. Exactly what is offered differs from business to business and job to job. For example, a small business might simply allocate another worker to look after the new employee for a day to 'show them the ropes'. A young person just out of university might have a year long induction programme to a large company. They might spend time in a number of departments, as well as being given more general training about the business. But most induction training attempts to introduce workers to the nature of the business and work practices, including health and safety issues.

On-the-job training

ON-THE-JOB TRAINING is training given in the workplace by the employer. There are many ways in which this could happen.

Learning from other workers An employee might simply work next to another worker, watch that worker do a task and with their help repeat it.

Mentoring This is where a more experienced employee is asked to provide advice and help to a less experienced worker. The less experienced worker can turn for help and advice to another more experienced worker at any time.

Job rotation This is where a worker spends a period of time doing one job, then another period of time doing another job and so on. Eventually they have received the broad experience needed to do a more specialist job.

Question 1.

Michelle Hallett went from sales assistant to store manager with the help of two training courses available through Modern Apprenticeships. A basic retail training programme led to a National Vocational Qualification level 2 achievement followed by a management course tied to level 3 saw her climb the ladder with Chockers, a small Essex-based shoe retailer. Michelle, said: 'I feel I've benefited in a number of ways. I'm more confident with customers and am better at handling staff. It's all been worthwhile.' Chockers, an eight-store chain with a flagship shop in The Strand in London, is a classic example of a business faced with a training problem in a sector with a high staff turnover.

Rosanne Lewis, area manager co-ordinator, said: 'We couldn't afford to operate a training scheme of our own but now we're able to put more of our sales staff through the apprenticeship programmes.' John Gill, the founder, trained the hard way, on a market stall, before launching the business, but is now committed to using the framework to provide a comprehensive training to add some extra staff polish and performance.

There was some apprehension among young sales assistants at the start.

'Some felt it would be like going back to school but I quickly reassured them on that score. We have a staff of 50 and I want all of them to take up the training programme,' says Ms Lewis.

Michelle did on-the-job training with a supervisor monitoring progress and discussing the finer points of customer relations at the end of a day's work. Her deputy, Hayley Clarke, has followed a similar programme. She said: 'I found it a bit hard at first to fit into the routine but the others in the shop have been really helpful. Being assistant manager now means I have more responsibility.'

Source: adapted from *The Telegraph*, 18.3.2004.

(a) Using examples from the article explain what is meant by on-the-job training?

(b) Explain why there might be potential problems with training staff at Chockers.

(c) Discuss whether Chockers might offer its own training scheme in future.

Traditional apprenticeships In the past, workers in traditional skilled trades, such as carpentry or engineering, would undertake training over, say, three-five years in an apprenticeship. This would involve a mix of training methods. When the business decided they had 'qualified' they would be employed as a full-time worker. Many of these schemes died out due to the cost for the business, the decline in traditional trades, mechanisation and the need for more flexible work practices.

Graduate training Medium- to large-sized businesses may offer graduate training programmes. They are typically designed to offer those with university degrees either professional training, such as in accountancy or the law, or managerial training.

Off-the-job training

OFF-THE-JOB TRAINING is training which takes place outside the business by an external training provider like a local college or university. For example, 16-25 year olds might go to college one day a week to do a catering course or an engineering course. A trainee accountant might have an intensive course at an accountancy college or attend night classes before taking professional exams. A graduate manager might do an MBA (Masters in Business Administration) course at a Business School in the evening and at weekends.

Off-the-job training can provide courses which a business internally would be unable to provide. But it can be expensive, particularly if the business is paying not just for the course but also a salary for the time the employee is attending the course.

Training initiatives

The government promotes training through a variety of initiatives and schemes.

Learning and Skills Councils These are bodies which have been set up by government to cover the whole of the UK. Each area of the UK has its own regional Learning and Skills Council. They are responsible for promoting training and manage funding for a wide range of schemes such as modern apprenticeships (see below). They are funded by the government from taxes. But businesses taking part in training may also be required to contribute towards the cost of training which directly benefits them.

Modern Apprenticeships In the past, apprenticeships were the most common way for a school leaver to become a skilled manual worker with a qualification. In the 1970s, with a sharp decline in employment in manufacturing industry, most businesses scrapped their apprenticeship schemes. Today, the government sponsors Modern Apprenticeships. This scheme aims to give young people an apprenticeship training which will equip them for a specific job in an industry. Businesses run Modern Apprenticeships and then receive a subsidy from the government for each apprentice on the scheme. Typically the Modern Apprenticeship training runs for three years.

Question 2.

Asda operates one of the most rigorous retail training programmes in the UK. New employees spend the equivalent of 25 weeks, mainly in-house, learning how to do their job. In 2004 Asda linked its own programme with National Vocational Qualifications in retailing and Modern Apprenticeships. It hoped this would will help increase productivity, encourage a higher level of internal promotion and reduce a staff turnover rate currently running at 26 per cent. The Learning and Skills Council provided more than £500,000 to the project. Asda, rather than a training provider, would control the money which will be used to cover the cost of outside assessors ensuring that its training is in line with the NVQ programme.

Mrs Sam Smith, people development manager, said: 'We're not doing this for profit but to raise the standard of our training and provide the staff with extra qualifications which will benefit them and the company.' There was extensive discussions between the company, the Learning and Skills Council and City & Guilds to validate the Asda in-house training set-up as a retail NVQ.

Source: adapted from *The Telegraph*, 18.3.2004.

(a) What is meant by (i) a Modern Apprenticeship and (ii) in-house training?
(b) Why is training likely to be so important for a business like Asda?
(c) Discuss whether Asda rather than a training provider should provide training.

The New Deal Since the late 1970s, governments have run a variety of schemes aimed at getting unemployed workers, particularly young workers, into a job. The New Deal, for example, promises to give any young unemployed person under the age of 25 either full-time training or work experience. The New Deal also offers older long-term unemployed workers a similar package.

Investors in People (IiP) IiP is a national standard developed by industry bodies such as the CBI and TUC with the support of the Employment Department, which businesses have to meet if they wish to gain IiP accreditation. To get accreditation, they have to show that the need for training is considered at every level and in every major decision made by the business. Businesses which go through the process of gaining IiP accreditation typically find that there are inefficiencies in the way the business operates because staff have not been trained properly. These training needs then have to be addressed. Gaining IiP is a useful marketing tool for a business. This is because customers perceive that, by gaining IiP accreditation, the business is a modern, forward-thinking business where staff are properly trained to deal with their work.

Labour market failure

It can be argued that, if left to free market forces, too little training would take place. This is an example of MARKET FAILURE. In the labour market, it occurs for two reasons.

- Businesses spend too little money on training because it is often cheaper for them to recruit new workers who have already been trained by another business or on a government training scheme.
- Individual workers don't spend enough on training themselves because they don't want to get into short-term debt. They also fail to realise how much more they could earn if they had better training.

In the past, traditional apprentices might have signed an agreement to stay with their employer a number of years after they became qualified. This meant they could not be 'poached' by a rival business. Today, linking training with staying on in the business is rare. There is nothing to stop a newly trained worker from leaving one business to take up a post at a higher salary elsewhere.

Generally, when there is market failure, it is argued that the government should step in to correct that market failure. Governments have two broad ways of doing this.

- They can provide training themselves and pay for it from tax revenues. Currently, the UK government provides training for the unemployed through its New Deal programme for example. Training is also provided through free college or further education courses.
- The government can pay grants to industry bodies or individual businesses to undertake training. This can be funded from general taxation or by a levy on all businesses in the industry. For example, in the UK construction industry, businesses have to pay a levy (effectively a tax) to pay for the work of the Construction Industry Training Board. This provides training for construction workers.

KEYTERMS

Induction training – training which occurs when a worker starts a job with a business.

Market failure – when the operation of free market forces fails to provide an optimal level of output.

Off-the-job training – training which takes place outside the business through an external training provider like a local college or university.

On-the-job training – training given in the workplace by the employer.

Training – the process of increasing the knowledge and skills of workers so that they are better able to perform their jobs.

KNOWLEDGE

1 List the reasons why a business might train its employees.
2 Why might a business offer induction training?
3 Explain the difference between mentoring and job rotation.
4 What is graduate training?
5 Who benefits from training through the New Deal programme?
6 What is Investors in People?
7 What is the role of Learning and Skills Councils in training?
8 Explain why businesses might spend less on training than is desirable.

Case Study: *Training in social housing*

Kiran Singh argues that his job as a housing officer for a housing association is more than just sorting out anti-social tenants and chasing rent. When he says he works in social housing, his friends think he works with awkward tenants and council homes – a stereotypical view. However there are now many more jobs out in housing than there were 20 years ago, particularly in regeneration. Kiran is responsible for 300 homes managed by the social landlord, East Midlands Housing. Earning £20,000 a year just months after graduating with a housing degree. He hopes to carve himself a successful career in the sector. It is now common for experienced housing managers to earn a minimum £40,000, and it is not unusual for top chief executives or directors to command salaries of up to £100,000.

Unlike other public services, such as the NHS, there are few graduate training programmes in this area, although they are starting to appear in some of the larger organisations. It is not essential to have a housing degree to work in housing. But it does attract graduates from different disciplines such as social sciences, human geography, economics and politics. A Modern Apprenticeship offers another route into the sector. Apprentices are given on-the-job training, but also learn about the historical context of social housing, its management and Housing law. Roger Keller, head of education at the Chartered Institute of Housing, the professional organisation for housing, says: 'An apprenticeship offers a proper understanding of why social housing is important in a country which doesn't have enough housing and how people can get access to housing when prices are rising.' Keller says that the uptake of Modern Apprenticeships in housing is low. 'They aren't widely taken up and you could argue that the sector ought to be recommending more young people take them on.' Once in the sector, it is possible to study for a range of professional qualifications offered by the Institute. Keller estimates that around 90 per cent of people studying for a professional qualification are sponsored by their employer.

The job opportunities within social housing sector have increased over the last 30 years as it has made a greater contribution it makes to public services. In the 1980s social housing was limited, geared towards rent collection and bad neighbours and there was little money available for development. Training may have simply meant learning from a colleague. New job titles today include regeneration officers, tenant participation officers, urban designers, antisocial behaviour managers and financial inclusion officers. These jobs require people to work with agencies like health, education, the police force and the army. There is a need for appropriate people skills and an understanding of different professional perspectives, requiring training and development of staff. With 50,000 people working in social housing sector due to retire by 2014, it may be just the right time to consider a career move into the sector.

Source: adapted from *The Guardian*, 8.11.2007.

(a) What us meant by (i) Apprentices (3 marks) and (ii) a graduate training programme? (3 marks)

(b) Outline one of example of 'on-the-job training' and one example of 'off-the-job training' mentioned in the article. (6 marks)

(c) Examine the advantages to an 18 year old of accepting a Modern Apprenticeship in housing rather than doing a university degree. (8 marks)

(d) Evaluate the type of training that might be needed in the future for individuals working in housing. (10 marks)

The satisfaction of needs

If asked, most people who work would probably say they do so to earn money to buy goods and services. However, this is not the only need that is satisfied by working. A list of people's needs that may be satisfied from work might be very long indeed. It could include, for example, the need for variety in the workplace, which may be satisfied by an interesting job. Employees may also need to feel appreciated for the work they do, which could be reflected in the prestige attached to their job.

Individuals are not the same. Therefore, it is likely that lists made by any two people of their needs and how they can be satisfied will be very different. There are some reasons for working that could apply to everyone, such as the need to earn money. However, some reasons have more importance for particular individuals than others. One employee may need to work with friendly colleagues, whereas another might be happy working on his own.

The importance of motivation

Why is it important for a business to find out what satisfies the needs of its employees? It is argued that if an individual's needs are not satisfied, then that worker will not be MOTIVATED to work. Businesses have found that even if employees are satisfied with pay and conditions at work, they also complain that their employer does not do a good job in motivating them. This applies to all levels, from the shop floor to the boardroom. It appears in many companies that employers are not getting the full potential from their employees because they are not satisfying all of their employees' needs. Figure 1 shows one example of how a business might make decisions, having first identified an employee's needs.

It is important for a business to motivate its employees. In the short run a lack of motivation may lead to reduced effort and lack of commitment. If employees are watched closely, fear of wage cuts or redundancy may force them to maintain their effort even though they are not motivated. This is negative motivation. In the long term, a lack of motivation may result in high levels of absenteeism, industrial disputes and falling productivity and profit for a business. So it is argued that well motivated employees will be productive which should lead to greater efficiency and profits for a business.

Maslow's hierarchy of needs

The first comprehensive attempt to classify needs was by Abraham Maslow in 1954. Maslow's theory consisted of two parts. The first concerned classification of needs. The second concerned how these classes are related to each other. Maslow suggested that 'classes' of needs could be placed into a hierarchy. The hierarchy is normally presented as a 'pyramid', with each level consisting of a certain class of needs. This is shown in Figure 2. The classes of needs were:

- physiological needs, e.g. wages high enough to meet weekly bills, good working conditions;
- safety needs, e.g. job security, safe working conditions;
- love and belonging, eg working with colleagues that support you at work, teamwork, communicating;
- esteem needs, e.g. being given recognition for doing a job well;
- self-actualisation, e.g. being promoted and given more responsibility, scope to develop and introduce new ideas and take on challenging new job assignments.

Figure 2 can also be used to show the relationship between the different classes. Maslow argued that needs at the bottom of the pyramid are basic needs. They are concerned with survival. These needs must be satisfied before a person can move to the next level. For example, people are likely to be more concerned with basic needs, such as food, than anything else. At work an

Figure 1: Satisfying an individual's needs

REVISE — If need is not satisfied

IDENTIFY THE NEED/MOTIVATION → INCENTIVE → SATISFACTION → RESULT/OUTCOME

The employee may need to be involved in decisions to feel wanted and recognised as important to the company.

Set up discussions with management about goals and working practices.

The employee feels as if their opinion and contribution is valuable.

The employee may be willing to work longer hours or take more responsibility.

employee is unlikely to be concerned about acceptance from colleagues if he has not eaten for six hours. Once each level is satisfied, the needs at this level become less important. The exception is the top level of SELF-ACTUALISATION. This is the need to fulfil your potential. Maslow argued that although everyone is capable of this, in practice very few reach this level.

Each level of needs is dependent on the levels below. Say an employee has been motivated at work by the opportunity to take responsibility, but finds he may lose his job. The whole system collapses, as the need to feed and provide for himself and his dependants again becomes the most important need.

Maslow's ideas have great appeal for business. The message is clear – find out which level each individual is at and decide on suitable rewards. Unfortunately the theory has problems when used in practice. Some levels do not appear to exist for certain individuals, while some rewards appear to fit into more than one class. Money, for example, needs to be used to purchase 'essentials' such as food, but it can also be seen as a status symbol or an indicator of personal worth. There is also a problem in deciding when a level has actually been 'satisfied'. There will always be exceptions to the rules Maslow outlined. A well motivated designer may spend many hours on a creative design despite lack of sleep or food.

Taylor's Scientific Management

Research into the factors that motivate individuals had been carried out long before Maslow's 'hierarchy' of needs. Frederick W. Taylor set out a theory of SCIENTIFIC MANAGEMENT in his book *The Principles of Scientific Management* in 1911. Many of the ideas of today's 'scientific management school' come from the work of Taylor.

The turn of the 20th century in the USA was a time of rapid expansion. Compared to today, the organisation of work on the

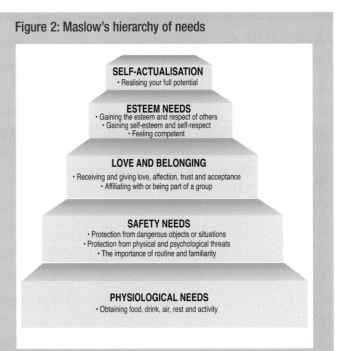

Figure 2: Maslow's hierarchy of needs

SELF-ACTUALISATION
· Realising your full potential

ESTEEM NEEDS
· Gaining the esteem and respect of others
· Gaining self-esteem and self-respect
· Feeling competent

LOVE AND BELONGING
· Receiving and giving love, affection, trust and acceptance
· Affiliating with or being part of a group

SAFETY NEEDS
· Protection from dangerous objects or situations
· Protection from physical and psychological threats
· The importance of routine and familiarity

PHYSIOLOGICAL NEEDS
· Obtaining food, drink, air, rest and activity

shop floor was left much more in the hands of workers and foremen. Workers often brought their own tools and decisions about the speed of machines were left to operators. There were few training programmes to teach workers their jobs and skills were gained simply by watching more experienced colleagues. Decisions about selection, rest periods and layoffs were frequently made by foremen.

Taylor suggested that such arrangements were haphazard and inefficient. Management did not understand the shop floor and allowed wasteful work practices to continue. Workers, on the other hand, left to their own devices, would do as little as possible. 'Soldiering' would also take place (working more slowly together so that management did not realise workers' potential) and workers would carry out tasks in ways they were used to rather than the most efficient way.

Taylor's scientific principles were designed to reduce inefficiency of workers and managers. This was to be achieved by 'objective laws' that management and workers could agree on, reducing conflict between them. Neither party could argue against a system of work that was based on 'science'. Taylor believed his principles would create a partnership between manager and worker, based on an understanding of how jobs should be done and how workers are motivated.

Taylor's approach How did Taylor discover what the 'best way' was of carrying out a task? Table 1 shows an illustration of Taylor's method. Taylor had a very simple view of what motivated people at work – money. He felt that workers should receive a 'fair day's pay for a fair day's work', and pay should be linked to output through piece rates. A worker who did not produce a 'fair day's work' would face a loss of earnings; exceeding the target would lead to a bonus. In 1899 Taylor's

---

Question 1.

Anmac Ltd is a small expanding high-tech company. It employs approximately 25 workers in two factories, one at Chester and one at Stafford. The employers organise work on a fairly informal basis. Workers work at their own pace, which often results in a variable level of output. Recently orders for their advanced micro-electronic circuit boards have increased rapidly. The firm has decided that, to cope with the orders, increased production is needed. Two suggestions have been put forward.

- Encourage the workers to work overtime at the Chester plant.
- Redeploy some of the workers from Chester to Stafford where there is a shortfall of workers.

The workers at the Chester plant are mainly married women in their twenties, many with young, school-aged children and husbands who also work.

(a) Explain how Taylor's scientific management principles might be used to solve the problems faced by Anmac Ltd.

(b) What problems might Anmac Ltd find in using such principles?

Question 2.

Table 2 shows the results of a survey carried out in Bryant and Gillie, a SME that manufactures children's clothing. The company introduced a piece rate system of work - a system where employees are paid according to the number or quantity of items they produce. Five groups were involved in the new system. Different actions were taken to introduce the system to each group. The table shows the effect on labour turnover and output of these actions.

Table 2: The effect of introducing a piece rate system into a clothes manufacturing business				
Group	Number in group	Action taken to introduce system	Resignations within 40 days of introduction	Change in output
A	100	Group told the changes will take place next week	17%	-2%
B	150	Management introduces changes with the help of group to suit their needs	0%	+10%
C	200	Group told the changes will take place next week	7%	0%
D	50	Management explains the need for change to group	2%	+2%
E	100	Management explains the need for change and discusses this with the group	0%	+5%

(a) To what extent do the results support the human relations explanation of workers' motivation?

(b) Using the results of the survey in Table 2, advise the management on the likely action needed to motivate workers when changing work practices.

methods were used at the Bethlehem Steel Works in the USA, where they were responsible for raising pig iron production by almost 400 per cent per man per day. Taylor found the 'best way to do each job' and designed incentives to motivate workers.

Taylor's message for business is simple - allow workers to work and managers to manage based on scientific principles of work study. Many firms today still attempt to use Taylor's principles. In the 1990s for example some businesses introduced **Business process reengineering (BPR)**. This is a management approach where organisations look at their business processes from a 'clean slate' perspective and determine how they can best construct these processes to improve how they conduct business. Taylor's approach is similar in that it advocates businesses finding the best way of doing something to add value to the business.

Problems with Taylor's approach There is a number of problems with Taylor's ideas. The notion of a 'quickest and best way' for all workers does not take into account individual differences. There is no guarantee that the 'best way' will suit everyone.

Taylor also viewed people at work more as machines, with financial needs, than as humans in a social setting. There is no doubt that money is an important motivator. Taylor overlooked that people also work for reasons other than money. A survey in America by the Robb and Myatt in 2004, for example, found that of the top ten factors motivating workers, the first three categories were a sense of achievement, having that achievement recognised, and positive working relationships. This suggests there may be needs that must be met at work, which Taylor ignored, but were recognised in Maslow's ideas which came later.

Human relations

Taylor's scientific management ideas may have seemed appealing at first glance to business. Some tried to introduce his ideas in the 1920s and 1930s, which led to industrial unrest. Others found that financial incentives did motivate workers, and still do today. However, what was becoming clear was that there were other factors which may affect workers' motivation.

The Hawthorne studies Many of the ideas which are today known as the 'human relations school' grew out of experiments between 1927 and 1932 at the Hawthorne Plant of the Western Electric company in Chicago. Initially these were based on 'scientific management' - the belief that workers' productivity was affected by work conditions, the skills of workers and

---

Table 1: Taylor's method, designed to find the 'best way' to carry out a task at work

- Pick a dozen skilled workers.
- Observe them at work and note down the elements and sequences adopted in their tasks.
- Time each element with a stop watch.
- Eliminate any factors which appear to add nothing to the completion of the task.
- Choose the quickest method discovered and fit them in their sequence.
- Teach the worker this sequence; do not allow any change from the set procedure.
- Include time for rest and the result will be the 'quickest and best' method for the task. Because it is the best way, all workers selected to perform the task must adopt it and meet the time allowed.
- Supervise workers to ensure that these methods are carried out during the working day.

financial incentives. Over the five year period, changes were made in incentive schemes, rest periods, hours of work, lighting and heating and the effect on workers' productivity was measured. One example was a group of six women assembling telephone relays. It was found that whatever changes were made, including a return to the original conditions, output rose. This came to be known as the HAWTHORNE EFFECT.

The study concluded that changes in conditions and financial rewards had little or no effect on productivity. Increases in output were mainly due to the greater cohesion and communication which workers in groups developed as they interacted and were motivated to work together. Workers were also motivated by the interest shown in their work by the researchers. This result was confirmed by further investigations in the Bank Wiring Observation where 14 men with different tasks were studied.

The work of **Elton Mayo** (and Roethlisberger and Dickson) in the 1930s, who reported on the Hawthorne Studies, has led to what is known today as the human relations school. A business aiming to maximise productivity must make sure that the 'personal satisfactions' of workers are met for workers to be motivated. Management must also work and communicate with informal work groups, making sure that their goals fit in with the goals of the business. One way to do this is to allow such groups to be part of decision making. Workers are likely to be more committed to tasks that they have had some say in.

CRITIQUE

Motivation theories may not work in practise for a number of reasons.

Different circumstances If the business is geared towards hierarchy and authority, and work is routine, people may choose to do such work in return for financial rewards, for example to enjoy themselves away from work. At other times, job interest and involvement may outweigh financial rewards. This may be true, for instance, in worker buyouts, when employees are prepared to accept lower financial rewards to maintain job security and have a say in the running of the business.

Different types of operation It is also argued that many motivation theories were developed in earlier times, when work conditions were different. Work methods did not need the advanced levels of technological knowledge and problem-solving skills that they do today. These skills change the relationship between management and the shop floor, for example by empowering workers.

Capitalism Theories of motivation based on the ideas of Marx suggest that getting people motivated will always be a problem under capitalism. This is because, although we depend on each other to produce wealth, private ownership of business allows owners to exploit those employees who must sell their labour in order to live. Though profits are only made through labour, the interests of owners and workers, diverge since labour is a cost to be minimised if profits are to be maximised.

There are examples of these ideas being used in business. The Volvo plant in Uddevalla, opened in 1989, was designed to allow workers to work in teams of eight to ten. Each team built a complete car and made decisions about production. Volvo found that absenteeism rates at Uddevalla averaged 8 per cent, compared to 25 per cent in their Gothenburg plant which used a production line system. Other examples have been:

- Honda's plant in Swindon where 'teamwork' has been emphasised - there were no workers or directors, only 'associates';
- McDonald's picnics, parties and McBingo for their employees where they were made to feel part of the company;
- Mary Kay's seminars in the USA, which were presented like the American Academy awards for company employees.

Problems There is a number of criticisms of the human relations school.

- It assumes workers and management share the same goals. This idea of workplace 'consensus' may not always exist. For example, in the 1980s Rover tried to introduce a programme called 'Working with Pride'. It was an attempt to raise quality by gaining employee commitment. This would be achieved by greater communication with employees. The programme was not accepted throughout the company. As one manager stated: 'We've tried the face-to-face communications approach. It works to a degree, but we are not too good at the supervisory level ... enthusiasm for the Working with Pride programme is proportionate to the level in the hierarchy. For supervisors

Question 3.

Larry Page and Sergey Brin graduated from America's Stanford University in computer science in 1995. They found common ground in a unique approach to solving one of computing's biggest challenges – retrieving relevant information from a massive set of data. They spent 18 months perfecting their technology, following a path that would ultimately become Google Inc. At Mountain view, California, where Google is based, there is a beach volleyball court, a dinosaur skeleton and gaudy parasols aplenty. There is an abundance of open space, courtyards, quadrangles and forums. The buildings are uncluttered, mixing functionality and hi-tech feng shui. Staff travel between buildings on electric mini-scooters. Whiteboards are dotted throughout and the famous 'help yourself' juice counters are also in evidence. Lunch is free for employees and there's more choice than one would find in a small town. Open a laptop in Mountain View anywhere and you are invited to join the free Google wi-fi network. Everywhere there are examples of the legendary 20 per cent scheme that Google operates – letting engineers spend a fifth of their time pursuing personal projects. On one plasma screen a spinning globe shows search engine queries to Google made in real time. It was created by one of the engineers in his 20 per cent time. Google also has its on-site gym, on-site dentist and on-site celebrity chef who previously served the Grateful Dead.

Source: adapted from www.matr.net, www.bbc.co.uk.

(a) Outline the various ways that Google uses to motivate its staff.
(b) Using a motivation theory, examine why Google is successful at motivating its employees.

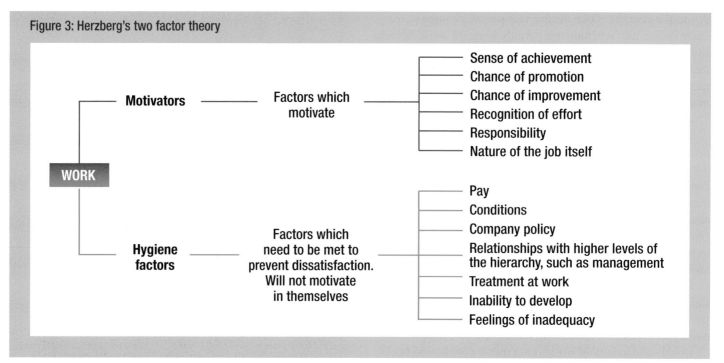

Figure 3: Herzberg's two factor theory

it's often just seen as a gimmick ...'
- It is assumed that communication between workers and management will break down 'barriers'. It could be argued, however, that the knowledge of directors' salaries or redundancies may lead to even more 'barriers' and unrest.
- It is biased towards management. Workers are manipulated into being productive by managers. It may also be seen as a way of reducing trade union power.

Herzberg's two-factor theory

In 1966 Fredrick Herzberg attempted to find out what motivated people at work. He asked a group of professional engineers and accountants to describe incidents in their jobs which gave them strong feelings of satisfaction or dissatisfaction. He then asked them to describe the causes in each case.

Results Herzberg divided the causes into two categories or factors. These are shown in Figure 3.
- **MOTIVATORS.** These are the factors which give workers **job satisfaction**, such as recognition for their effort. Increasing these motivators is needed to give job satisfaction. This, it could be argued, will make workers more productive. A business that rewards its workforce for, say, achieving a target is likely to motivate them to be more productive. However, this is not guaranteed, as other factors can also affect productivity.
- **HYGIENE or MAINTENANCE FACTORS.** These are factors that can lead to workers being **dissatisfied**, such as pay or conditions. Improving hygiene factors should remove dissatisfaction. For example, better canteen facilities may make workers less dissatisfied about their environment. An improvement in hygiene factors alone is not likely to motivate an individual. But if they are not

met, there could be a fall in productivity.

There is some similarity between Herzberg's and Maslow's ideas. They both point to needs that have to be satisfied for the employee to be motivated. Herzberg argues that only the higher levels of Maslow's hierarchy motivate workers.

Herzberg's ideas are often linked with **job enrichment**. This is where workers have their jobs 'expanded', so that they can experience more of the production process. This allows the workers to be more involved and motivated, and have a greater sense of achievement. Herzberg used his ideas in the development of clerical work. He selected a group of workers in a large corporation. Performance and job attitudes were low. Herzberg redesigned these jobs so that they were given more responsibility and recognition.

Problems Herzberg's theory does seem to have some merits. Improving pay or conditions, for example, may remove dissatisfaction at first. Often, however, these things become taken for granted. It is likely that better conditions will be asked for in following years. Evidence of this can be seen in wage claims which aim to be above the rate of inflation in some businesses every year. Job enrichment may also be expensive for many firms. In addition, it is likely that any benefits from job improvements will not be seen for a long time and that businesses will not be able to continue with such a policy in periods of recession.

Surveys that have tried to reproduce Herzberg's results have often failed. This may have been because different groups of workers have been examined and different techniques used. Also, there is a problem in relying too much on what people say they find satisfying or dissatisfying at work as this is subjective. For example, if things go wrong at work individuals have a tendency to blame it on others or factors outside of their control. On the other hand if individuals feel happy and satisfied when they are at work then they tend to see it as their own doing.

KEYTERMS

Hawthorne effect – the idea that workers are motivated by recognition given to them as a group.
Hygiene or maintenance factors – those things that can lead to workers being dissatisfied.
Motivated – being encouraged to do something.
Motivators – those things that can lead to workers being satisfied.
Self-actualisation – a level on Maslow's hierarchy where an employee realises his or her full potential.
Scientific management – a theory that suggests that there is a 'best' way to perform work tasks.

KNOWLEDGE

1. Why is it important for business to satisfy workers?
2. Name five needs in Maslow's hierarchy that an individual might have at work.
3. What are the aims of Taylor's scientific management theory?
4. According to Taylor, how are people motivated?
5. What is meant by the human relations school of thought?
6. What, according to the human relations school, is the main motivator at work?
7. Explain the difference between Theory X and Theory Y.
8. How is Theory X like Taylor's view of scientific management?
9. According to Herzberg's theory, what factors are likely to: (a) increase job satisfaction; (b) reduce dissatisfaction at work?
10. What general conclusions can a business draw from the criticisms of motivation theory?

Case Study: *Mendelsons*

Lee Worsnip has worked as an assistant in the financial analysis department of Mendelsons Insurance for two years. He is 24 years of age and joined Mendelsons from college with good exam results. Lee also obtained some extra qualifications by taking night school courses. He started as junior clerk, and quickly moved to a more senior post, which paid a better salary. However, he has been in this post for a while now.

Lee's aim was to use the job as a stepping stone to one of the sales teams. The business was pleased that Lee looked on the job in this way, as it is in favour of encouraging people to get on. However, it is difficult to get onto one of the sales teams, particularly when the company has placed so much emphasis on its graduate recruitment. This may be one of the things that seems to be bothering Lee. Recently the Unit Trust team hired a graduate trainee instead of Lee, although he did accept that the new recruit had an advantage as she was a qualified actuary.

Until a few months ago, Lee had been an above average employee. He was always cheerful, enthusiastic and willing, and picked things up quickly. Lee used to make an excellent contribution to regular weekly meetings. And he was prepared to do one-off projects, always seeming to be able to squeeze in the extra work. He was also quite prepared to work late.

Lately, however, he seems to lack motivation. He has missed some meetings and taken days off. He complained that other members of the meetings had more senior posts and felt they did not listen to his views. He said, 'I shouldn't be treated as a worker who is satisfied just by basic physiological needs.'

The other day, Lee refused to take on a low level task. He suggested that he was fed up doing routine work and not leaving the office every day until 8 o'clock. Lee also argued that he was never allowed to make decisions and his work was always checked, as if he wasn't trusted. In the end some of these tasks had to be given to other members of staff, increasing their workload. Lee's absences have put additional pressure on the team.

Lee has also started being offhand. He was overheard several times being rude to people who asked him for information or help. Last week, at a team meeting about new procedures, Lee suggested that they had been drawn up in secret behind his back.

(a) What is meat by the terms:
    (i) lack of motivation (3 marks) and
    (ii) physiological needs. (3 marks)
(b) Explain the problems that (i) Lee and (ii) the business might have as a result of a lack of motivation. (10 marks)
(c) Using a motivation theory, examine reasons why Lee may lack motivation. (12 marks)
(d) Suggest ways in which the business might improve Lee's motivation. (12 marks)

Financial and non-financial rewards

A number of theories have tried to explain the factors that motivate people at work. Some of these theories stress that money is the most important factor. The scientific approach, in particular, argues that workers respond to financial rewards. It is argued that such rewards are necessary to motivate a reluctant workforce. Employees see work as a means to an end. As a result they are far more likely to be interested in **financial rewards.** In contrast, the human relations view argues that workers are motivated by a variety of factors. An employee working in a car assembly plant, for example, may be highly motivated by working as part of a team. Poor pay may lead to employees being dissatisfied, which can make other **non-financial rewards** less effective in motivating them. The next two units examine how financial and non-financial rewards can be used.

Salaries and wages

For nearly all workers, the main reason for going to work is to earn money to buy goods and services. Most workers in the UK are either paid a wage or a salary.

Wages WAGES tend to be associated with lower paid workers and BLUE COLLAR WORKERS (i.e. MANUAL WORKERS). Wages are typically expressed as hourly TIME RATES of pay, such as £5.50 an hour or £12.75 an hour. This then forms weekly rates of pay, such as £250 a week, for a fixed number of hours work, such as 38 hours. The 38 hours would then be the basic working week. Time rates are useful when a business wants to employ workers to do specialist or difficult tasks that should not be rushed. Employees can ensure that work is of a high quality without worrying about the time they take.

Waged employees often have the opportunity to work OVERTIME. These are hours worked over and above the basic working week. To motivate workers to accept overtime, employers often pay higher rates of pay. If the basic wage is £10 an hour, overtime might be paid at time and a quarter (£12.50 an hour) or time and a half (£15 an hour). Saturday or Sunday overtime working might be paid at higher rates than weekday overtime, to encourage people to work at weekends.

Salaries SALARIES tend to be associated with better paid workers, particularly WHITE COLLAR WORKERS (i.e. NON-MANUAL WORKERS). Salaried staff are typically paid each month. Some salaried staff might earn overtime because they are only expected to work a fixed number of hours per week. However, most salaried staff are paid to do a particular job. There might be a recommended number of hours work per week, like 38 hours. But they are often expected to work as many hours as it takes to complete the job. A yearly salary is usually higher than that which could be earned by workers if they were in a less senior job and paid a wage.

The main long-term factors which determine the level of wages and salaries are the forces of demand and supply. Businesses have to pay the 'market rate' for the job if they want to retain existing staff and recruit new staff. Paying below the market rate can also demotivate staff. They might feel that they are not valued by their employer. Paying above the market rate can be motivating. Workers might feel that their contribution is being rewarded by higher pay.

Workers are sometimes paid a basic wage or salary and a BONUS at the end of the year or other period if **targets** are reached, or for attendance or punctuality. Sometimes the 'best employee' over a period may be rewarded with a bonus. This is usually a money payment, although Richer sounds, the electronics retailer, has rewarded the retail outlet that performed bets over a period with the use of a classic car such as a Rolls Royce. A problem with regular bonuses is that they are often seen as part of the employee's basic pay. As a result, they may no longer act as a motivator.

Many employers have found that payment based on a fixed working week can be inflexible. For example, half the year employees may be idle after 3 p.m. every day, but are still paid for a 'full day's' work. The other half of the year they may work into the evening and be paid overtime. To cater for fluctuations in demand some employers pay staff on the basis of a certain number of hours to be worked in a year. These are known as ANNUALISED HOURS CONTRACTS. For annualised hours contracts, the number of hours to be worked each year is fixed. However, the daily, weekly or monthly hours are flexible. So employees may have a longer working day at peak times and work less when demand is slack. An employee's pay is calculated on the basis of an average working week, for example 35 hours, which is paid regardless of the actual number of hours the employee works. There are certain advantages of annualised hours. An employee has a guaranteed income each week. Employers often see this as a way of avoiding overtime, reducing costs, increasing flexibility and improving efficiency.

Piece rates, commission and fees

Not all workers are paid wages or salaries. Some are paid piece rates, commission or fees.

Piece rates Piece rates are payments for each unit produced. They are an example of PAYMENT BY RESULTS. For example, a worker might be paid £0.50 per parcel delivered or £1.00 per kilo of strawberries picked. PIECE RATES were recommended by Frederick Taylor, founder of the scientific management school. He thought they were an ideal way to motivate workers. Workers who produced more were more highly paid. However,

Question 1.

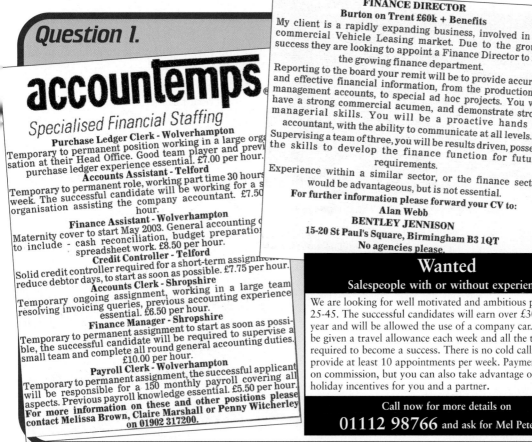

accountemps
Specialised Financial Staffing

Purchase Ledger Clerk - Wolverhampton
Temporary to permanent position working in a large organisation at their Head Office. Good team player and previous purchase ledger experience essential. £7.00 per hour.

Accounts Assistant - Telford
Temporary to permanent role, working part time 30 hours week. The successful candidate will be working for a small organisation assisting the company accountant. £7.50 hour.

Finance Assistant - Wolverhampton
Maternity cover to start May 2003. General accounting to include - cash reconciliation, budget preparation spreadsheet work. £8.50 per hour.

Credit Controller - Telford
Solid credit controller required for a short-term assignment reduce debtor days, to start as soon as possible. £7.75 per hour.

Accounts Clerk - Shropshire
Temporary ongoing assignment, working in a large team resolving invoicing queries, previous accounting experience essential. £6.50 per hour.

Finance Manager - Shropshire
Temporary to permanent assignment to start as soon as possible, the successful candidate will be required to supervise a small team and complete all round general accounting duties. £10.00 per hour.

Payroll Clerk - Wolverhampton
Temporary to permanent assignment, the successful applicant will be responsible for a 150 monthly payroll covering all aspects. Previous payroll knowledge essential. £5.50 per hour. For more information on these and other positions please contact Melissa Brown, Claire Marshall or Penny Witcherley on 01902 317200.

FINANCE DIRECTOR
Burton on Trent £60k + Benefits
My client is a rapidly expanding business, involved in the commercial Vehicle Leasing market. Due to the group's success they are looking to appoint a Finance Director to run the growing finance department.
Reporting to the board your remit will be to provide accurate and effective financial information, from the production of management accounts, to special ad hoc projects. You will have a strong commercial acumen, and demonstrate strong managerial skills. You will be a proactive hands on accountant, with the ability to communicate at all levels. Supervising a team of three, you will be results driven, possess the skills to develop the finance function for future requirements.
Experience within a similar sector, or the finance sector would be advantageous, but is not essential.
For further information please forward your CV to:
Alan Webb
BENTLEY JENNISON
15-20 St Paul's Square, Birmingham B3 1QT
No agencies please.

Wanted
Salespeople with or without experience
We are looking for well motivated and ambitious people aged 25-45. The successful candidates will earn over £30,000 a year and will be allowed the use of a company car. You will be given a travel allowance each week and all the training required to become a success. There is no cold calling. We provide at least 10 appointments per week. Payment is based on commission, but you can also take advantage of the great holiday incentives for you and a partner.
Call now for more details on
01112 98766 and ask for Mel Peterson

(a) Compare the different payment systems shown in the advertisements.

(b) What fringe benefits were being offered?

(c) Discuss what might happen if any of the employers advertising were offering a remuneration package which was below the market rate for the job.

---

piece rates are only suitable for jobs where it is easy to identify the contribution of an individual worker. It would be difficult to devise a piece rate system for, say, secretaries or managers. Piece rates have been criticised on health and safety grounds. They might encourage workers to take dangerous short cuts in a bid to reduce the amount of time taken for each item. Rushing production might also affect the quality of the product.

Commission COMMISSION is a payment system mainly used with white collar workers. Commission, like piece rates, is a payment for achieving a target. For example, car salespeople may get a commission of £100 for each car they sell. Some white collar workers are paid entirely on commission. A salesperson, for example, may be paid entirely on the basis of their sales record. Alternatively, a worker may be paid a basic salary and then receive commission on top. Commission based pay systems are intended to 'incentivise' workers by tying in pay with output.

Fees Fees are payments made to people for 'one-off' tasks. Tasks tend to be geared towards the needs of the client, rather than a standard service or product. The amount paid will depend on a variety of factors. These might include the time taken to finish the task or the difficulty of the task. Often fees are paid to people providing services, such as solicitors, performers etc.

Fringe benefits

FRINGE BENEFITS are benefits received over and above that received from wages or salaries. Fringe benefits are payments 'in kind' rather than in cash. Typical examples of fringe benefits include contributions to pensions, a company car, private health insurance, subsidised meals including luncheon vouchers, and subsidised loans or mortgages.

One reason why fringe benefits are given is because they are a tax-efficient way of rewarding employees. It may cost a business less to give the fringe benefit than the equivalent sum of money needed to buy it by the employee. Some fringe benefits help the running of the business. For example, private health care might reduce the number of days off sick by employees and give the business greater control about when an employee has an operation.

Businesses also give fringe benefits as a way of motivating staff. They can act as a motivator in two ways.

- Many satisfy the basic physiological and safety needs of workers, as outlined by Maslow. They also meet the hygiene factors as outlined in Herzberg's two-factor theory.
- The awarding of fringe benefits can be linked to achievement and promotion. Free private medical health care insurance, for example, is sometimes only available to more senior members of staff within an organisation.

Performance related pay

PERFORMANCE RELATED PAY (PRP) is a pay system designed specifically to motivate staff. Introduced in the 1980s and 1990s, it is now used widely in the UK among white collar workers,

Table 1 Examples of fringe benefits that have been used by businesses

Company	Function	Fringe benefit
Dyson Appliances	Vacuum cleaner manufacturer	Dyson cleaner at reduced rate for new employees
Text 100	PR Agency	2 'Duvet days' (unscheduled holidays) a year
Air Products	Industrial gas supplier	Free exercise classes and subsidised gym and yoga classes, free annual medical checks
Saatchi & Saatchi	Advertising agency	Company pub – 'The Pregnant Man'
Virgin Group	Travel, entertainment, media, retail and financial services	24 hour parties
Body Shop	Cosmetics manufacturer and retailer	£100 a year to 'buy' a training course in new skill of their choice
Tesco	Food retailer	SAYE tax-free share option scheme
Google	Internet search engine provider	Free meals for staff

especially in the financial services industry, such as banking, and in the public sector.

PRP gives workers extra pay for achieving targets. The extra pay may be a lump sum such as £1,000 or it could be a percentage of salary. Some PRP systems make distinctions between levels of achievement. For example, one worker may be rated 'excellent' and receive a 10 per cent bonus, another 'good' and receive a 5 per cent bonus, another 'satisfactory' and receive no bonus.

The targets are likely to be set through a system of APPRAISAL. This is where the performance of individual staff is reviewed against a set of criteria. These criteria could include factors such as arriving for work on time, ability to get on with other workers, improving skills through training or achieving a particular task within the job. Staff are likely to have a performance appraisal interview where someone more senior, such as their line manager, conducts the appraisal.

PRP is widely used because it directly links performance with pay. According to the scientific management school, it should motivate workers to achieve the goals set for them by the organisation.

However, PRP and performance appraisal have been widely criticised for a number of reasons.

- The bonus may be too low to give workers an incentive to achieve their targets.
- Achieving the targets may have far more to do with the smooth running of machinery or technological systems, or how a group of workers perform than the performance of an individual. For example, a worker may set a goal of increasing forms processed by 5 per cent. But the number of forms she receives may depend on how many are processed by other members of her team or whether the printing machines are working smoothly. Where

teamworking is an important management tool, it is likely to be better to give bonuses based on the output of a team rather than an individual.

- Targets may be difficult or even impossible to achieve in the eyes of workers. If this is the case, then they are unlikely to make any effort to achieve them.
- Few staff see appraisal as an independent objective procedure. Staff are quite likely to put their failure to achieve a grade in an appraisal interview down to the unfairness of the interviewer. This is particularly true when there are already problems in the relationship between, say, a worker and his or her boss. Staff who do achieve highly in appraisal interviews may be seen by others as 'favourites' of the interviewer.

Failure to receive a high enough grade in the appraisal process may act as a demotivator of staff. Instead of staff wanting to improve their performance, they may simply give up attempting to change their behaviour and attitudes. Failure to receive a PRP bonus could challenge the physiological needs of staff in Maslow's hierarchy of needs because it deprives them of money. It could also make them feel less 'loved' by the organisation, challenging their need for love and belonging. It will almost certainly knock their self-esteem.

Profit sharing

Some businesses have PROFIT SHARING schemes. In a company, profits would normally be distributed to shareholders. Profit sharing occurs when some of the profits made are distributed to workers as well as shareholders.

Profit sharing can motivate workers to achieve the objectives of the business. Shareholders want higher profits. So too do workers if they are to receive a share of them. Profit sharing therefore unites the goals of both owners and workers for extra money. Profit sharing can also be a way of showing staff that they are appreciated. In Maslow's hierarchy of needs, it may help satisfy the need for love and belonging.

However, most individual workers will have little or no control over how much profit their company makes. If they make extra effort to raise sales or reduce costs, the benefit of that extra effort will be shared between all the other workers. There is no link between individual effort and individual reward in profit sharing. Profit sharing is also unlikely to motivate financially if the amount received is fairly small.

A UK business which uses profit sharing is the John Lewis Partnership, which owns the John Lewis department stores and the supermarket chain Waitrose. The John Lewis Partnership is owned in trust for its workers. So all the profits after tax and retentions are distributed to its workers. The amount given varies according to the salary of the worker. In a good year,

Question 2.

Nick Barnes runs a small printing company in Norwich. It prints cards, leaflets and catalogues for local businesses. It has three design staff and two staff who work as printers. The business pays all its staff the same salary, although at peaks times it might ask employees to work overtime. The business is a limited company and all the shares are owned by Paul and his brother, Wes, who is the company secretary and handles the marketing.

Recently the business has expanded into printing larger posters and designs for exhibitions. Nick has asked Natalie, his longest serving employee, if she will take responsibility for this. He knows that it will be a very profitable venture and wants someone who is experienced and motivated. He is concerned, however, that if he pays her more for the work than other staff they could become demotivated.

Paul has suggested that if this area of the business expands, Natalie could be given a small part-ownership of the business. She would be allowed to buy shares and benefit in future. Nick is still concerned that others in the business may feel that they also deserve shares, as they have all worked for a number of years, although not as long, currently, as Natalie. Nick wonders whether he should involve others in exhibition design and hopes that the revenue gained will generate enough so that he can raise all wages.

(a) Outline ONE advantage and ONE disadvantage of Nick paying his staff overtime.

(b) Explain why a financial rewards system at the business can be a problem.

(c) Discuss whether Nick should use share ownership as a means of financial incentive.

Waitrose workers will receive a profit share handout of more than 20 per cent of their salary. This is a substantial sum. Whether it motivates John Lewis Partnership workers to work harder is debatable.

Share ownership

Some have argued that workers would be motivated by owning a share of their business. They would then have an incentive to work hard because their efforts would contribute to profit. They would benefit from high profits because they would get part of those profits. The value of their shares in the business would also rise if the business were successful.

There are many ways in which employees might acquire shares. One is through **save-as-you-earn schemes**. Here, employees are able to save a regular amount of money from their pay over five years. At the end of five years, they are able to buy shares in the company at the price that they were five years previously. If the share price has gone up over the five years, the saver will make a capital gain.

The granting of **share options** has become a common way of rewarding senior managers and chief executives of large companies. A member of staff is given the option to buy shares in the company at a fixed point in the future, say three years, at a price agreed today. This price may be below, above or at the same level as today's share price. Share options are supposed to be an incentive to senior management to act in a way which will raise the share price significantly. This means that senior management have the same objective as shareholders.

Share options have been controversial. Some chief executives have been able to earn millions of pounds from **exercising** their share options (i.e. buying the shares at the end of the period and then, usually, selling them immediately, make a large capital gain). But when the stock market is rising, the performance of a company can be average and still its share price will rise. So chief executives can earn large amounts even though their company has not done particularly well.

Problems with financial rewards

There is a number of problems that financial incentives schemes have.

Operating problems For financial incentives to work, production needs to have a smooth flow of raw materials, equipment and storage space, and consumer demand must also be fairly stable. These conditions cannot be guaranteed for long. If raw materials did not arrive or ran out, for example, the worker may not achieve a target and receive no bonus for reasons beyond his control. If this happens the employee is unlikely to be motivated by the scheme, and may negotiate for a larger proportion of earnings to be paid as guaranteed 'basic' pay.

Fluctuating earnings A scheme that is linked to output must result in fluctuating earnings. This might be due to changes in demand, the output of the worker or machinery problems. As in the case above, the worker is likely to press for the guaranteed part of pay to be increased, or store output in the 'good times' to prevent problems in the 'bad'. Alternatively, workers may try to 'slow down' productive workers so that benefits are shared out as equally as possible.

Quality The need to increase output to gain rewards can affect quality. There is an incentive for workers to do things as quickly as possible and this can lead to mistakes. Workers filling jars with marmalade may break the jars if they work too quickly. This means the jar is lost and the marmalade as well, for fear of splinters. For some businesses, such as food processing, chemicals or drug production, errors could be disastrous.

Changes in payment Because of the difficulties above, employers constantly modify their incentive schemes. Improved financial reward schemes should stop workers manipulating the system and may give renewed motivation to some workers. However, constant changes mean that employees do not always understand exactly how to gain rewards.

Quality of working life Financial rewards based upon payment by results require a certain type of job design. This often means tight control by management, routine and repetition. The scientific management school argues that production will only be efficient if workers know exactly what to do in any situation and their activities are tightly controlled by management. The result of this is that boredom and staleness may set in and the worker's 'standard of life' at work may be low.

Jealousy Individual workers may be jealous of the rewards earned by their colleagues. This can lead to problems in relationships and a possible lack of motivation. Increasingly, businesses are using group or plant-wide incentives to solve this.

Measuring performance For incentives to work effectively it must be possible to measure performance. For example, a business must be able to measure the number of components made by a worker if she is paid a bonus after 20,000 are made a month.

Team-based rewards Problems may take place if rewards are based on the performance of a team, but some workers are more productive then others in the team.

Given these problems, why are financial incentive schemes still used by many firms? Managers may find a use for a certain scheme. For example, financial rewards may be used to overcome resistance to change. A business introducing new technology, such as computers, may offer an incentive for staff to retrain or spend extra time becoming familiar with the new system. Employees often see benefits in such systems of payment. They may feel that they are gaining some control over their own actions in the workplace, being able to work at their own pace if they so wish. Furthermore, many businesses believe that financial rewards ought to work as it is logical to assume that employees work harder if they are offered more money.

KEYTERMS

Annualised hours contracts – a payment system based on a fixed number of hours to be worked each year, but a flexible number of hours each day, week or month.

Appraisal – where the performance of an individual worker is reviewed against a set of criteria.

Blue collar (or manual) workers – workers who do mainly physical work, like assembly line workers.

Bonus – an extra payment made in recognition of the contribution a worker has made to the company.

Commission – payment made, typically for achieving a target such as a sales target.

Fringe benefits – payment in kind over and above the wage or salary paid, such as a company car or luncheon vouchers.

Overtime – time worked over and above the basic working week.

Payment by results – payment methods that reward workers for the quantity and quality of work they produce.

Performance related pay (PRP) – a payment system, typically where workers are paid a higher amount if they achieve certain targets set for them by their employer.

Piece rates – a payment system where employees are paid an agreed rate for every item produced.

Profit sharing – where workers are given a share of the profits made by the company which employs them.

Salary – pay, usually of non-manual workers, expressed as a yearly figure but paid monthly.

Time rates – rates of pay based on an amount of time, usually per hour.

Wages – payments made to employees for work done, usually given weekly to manual workers.

While collar (or non-manual) workers – workers who do non-physical work like office workers or teachers.

KNOWLEDGE

1. Explain the difference between payment systems frequently found for blue collar workers and white collar workers.
2. Explain the difference between piece rates and commission.
3. Why might fringe benefits motivate workers?
4. Explain the role of targets in performance related pay systems.
5. How might profit sharing schemes motivate workers?
6. Explain the difference between a save-as-you-earn scheme for buying shares and share option schemes.
7. Identify five problems of financial reward schemes.

Case Study: *Incentives for Value Added Resellers*

Value Added Resellers (VARs) are businesses which take a manufacturer's product and add their own value before selling it. For example, a VAR might take an operating system, add its own specialist software for, say, architects, and then sell the bundle to architect businesses. Manufacturers offer VARs a number of incentives to sell their products.

'The best incentive is money in the pocket' said one VAR. Most incentive schemes are based on money and commissions. Other means are used, but do they work? 'Freebies' such as day trips and air miles are commonly on offer. But in the day-to-day slog of running a business, motivation to take advantage of such benefits can be hard to muster. 'We don't really bother with these schemes' said one VAR. 'They create more administration than they're worth. 'Luxury rewards are still available as part of wider packages. For example, the top performing VAR for SolidWorks, was invited to Hawaii.

Opinions on whether rewards for individuals are effective will depend on to whom you speak. There will always be salespeople who thrive on beating the competition and who want to gain recognition for doing so. Peter Dickin, marketing manager at Delcam, feels that a more inclusive approach is required. 'Incentives targeted just at salespeople neglect the contribution of others, which can be demotivating. We tend to favour schemes that foster team building.'

Incentive schemes that reward a group of high-performing VARs have to be carefully structured to create a level playing field to give companies of different sizes and locations a chance. Clearly this is not always being achieved. One disgruntled VAR said 'I have never, ever been incentivised by any scheme I have worked with in the past. Overpaid VAR managers justify their own existence, even so far as coming up with jollies that they had no prior interest in, such as driving racing cars and sailing around the Leeward Isles.'

Schemes based mainly on the volume of sales can have negative implications for all parties. 'The aims of the incentives that we work to are not those that suit our long-term business goals, nor the needs of our customers,' said one VAR. 'They are generally incentives to motivate short-term business.'

The opportunity to gain marketing funds is another regular element of incentive schemes, particularly where a business wants to make inroads into a particular market. IBM, for example, offers a special marketing fund to companies who join its Top Contributor Programme and commit themselves to selling $100,000 of software to the SME (small and medium-sized business) market.

As free trips and luxury gifts are used less, terms such as 'active business management' have crept into the language of incentives. 'We don't incentivise on volume' explains John Mitchell, Manager of Indirect Channels, Europe, PLM Solutions. 'We incentivise VARs to invest in their business and improve the quality of their service to our customers.'

Many VARs are dubious about whether the incentives on offer actually made them do anything differently. Not offering incentives doesn't go down well either. One VAR said "Our own main vendor doesn't offer any incentive schemes (or even buy drinks at the bar at sales events). So we will have to do our best focusing upon making money for ourselves.'

Source: adapted from retailsystemseller.com.

(a) What is meant by the terms:
   (i) luxury rewards (3 marks);
   (ii) incentivise on volume? (3 marks)
(b) Describe the different financial rewards in the article. (10 marks)
(c) Examine the advantages and disadvantages of each financial reward scheme for VARs. (12 marks)
(d) Assess which financial rewards are likely to be most motivating to VARs selling products such as computers for manufacturers to small businesses. (12 marks)

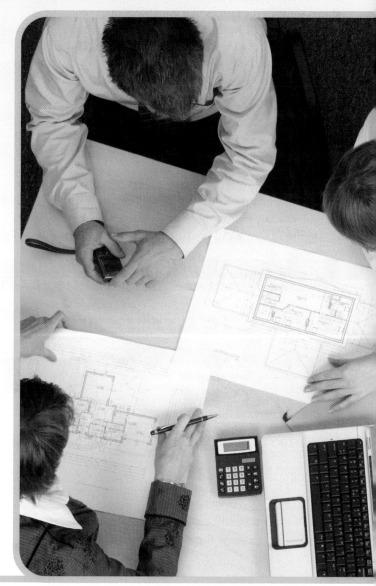

The need for non-financial rewards

Financial rewards have often been used in the past by firms in an attempt to motivate employees to improve productivity. However, increasingly businesses have realised that:

- the chance to earn more money may not be an effective motivator;
- financial incentive schemes are difficult to operate;
- individual reward schemes may no longer be effective as production has become organised into group tasks;
- other factors may be more important in motivating employees.

If other factors are more important than pay in motivating workers, it is important for firms to identify them. Only then can a business make sure its workforce is motivated. Figure 1 shows some of the factors that employees might consider important in their work environment. Many of these have been identified by the **human relations approach**. A business may consider introducing non-financial incentives to help employees satisfy these needs.

Job design and job redesign

The dissatisfaction with financial incentive schemes reached its peak in the 1960s and 1970s. In response the 'Quality of Working Life Movement' began to develop ideas which were based around the **human relations school**, as first outlined by the Hawthorne studies. It was argued that workers were likely to be motivated by non-monetary factors and that jobs needed to be DESIGNED or REDESIGNED to take these factors into

account. Five principles were put forward which any incentive scheme needed to consider.

- The principle of closure. A job must include all tasks necessary to complete a product or process. This should ensure that work is meaningful for employees and that workers feel a sense of achievement.
- Control and monitoring of tasks. Jobs should be designed so that an army of inspectors is not needed. The worker, or the team, should take responsibility for quality.
- Task variety. There should be an increase in the range of tasks that a worker carries out. This should allow job rotation to occur and keep the workers interested in their work.
- Self-regulation. Employees should have control of the speed at which they work and some choice over work methods and sequence.
- Interaction and co-operation. The job structure should allow some social interaction and the chance for an employee to work in a group.

Various methods were devised to try and put these principles into practice. They included job enrichment, job enlargement, job rotation, quality control circles and employee participation in groups. These are examined in this unit.

Poor job design may mean that employees do not achieve their full potential. This means that the firm's output may suffer as a result. For example, an architect who is constantly having her work checked for accuracy is unlikely to be as productive as possible, due to constant interruptions. Also, jobs that do not meet workers' needs are likely to lead to poor motivation,

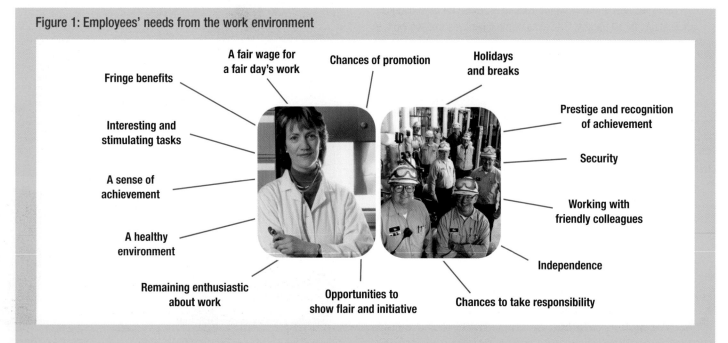

Figure 1: Employees' needs from the work environment

Fringe benefits

A fair wage for a fair day's work

Chances of promotion

Holidays and breaks

Interesting and stimulating tasks

Prestige and recognition of achievement

Security

A sense of achievement

Working with friendly colleagues

A healthy environment

Independence

Remaining enthusiastic about work

Opportunities to show flair and initiative

Chances to take responsibility

Table 1: Problems of job redesign

- Employees may be familiar with the old approach to doing a job and may resent new changes. They might not want the extra duties that result from job redesign.

- Job redesign may be expensive. New methods often require extra training. In addition, redesigned jobs might lead employees to claim extra pay for new responsibilities. There is no guarantee that the redesign of jobs will increase productivity in the long term.

- The introduction of new machinery can make job redesign more difficult. Certain jobs have had to be redesigned almost totally as new technology has changed production processes. In some cases employees have had to learn totally new skills, such as when newspaper page design on computer screens replaced old methods of cutting and pasting type onto pages. At other times skills may be made redundant.

- Effects on output and productivity. Redesigned jobs need to be evaluated to gauge whether they have actually motivated the workforce to increase output.

absenteeism and a lack of quality in work. The process of redesigning existing jobs is often difficult to carry out in practice for a number of reasons, as shown in Table 1.

Job enlargement

JOB ENLARGEMENT involves giving an employee more work to do of a similar nature. For example, instead of an employee putting wheels onto a bicycle he could be allowed to put the entire product together. It is argued that this variety prevents boredom with one repetitive task and encourages employees' satisfaction in their work, as they are completing the entire process. Job enlargement is more efficient if workers are organised in groups. Each worker can be trained to do all jobs in the group and job rotation can take place. Other forms of job enlargement include job rotation and job loading.

Critics of this method argue that it is simply giving a worker 'more of the same'. It is often called the problem of **horizontal loading** - instead of turning five screws the worker turns ten. In many businesses today such tasks are carried out more effectively by machines, where repetitive tasks can be completed quickly and efficiently without strain, boredom or dissatisfaction. It could even be argued that allowing employees to complete the entire process will reduce efficiency. This is because the fall in productivity from carrying out many tasks more than offsets any productivity gains from increased worker satisfaction.

Job rotation

JOB ROTATION involves an employee changing jobs or tasks from time to time. This could mean, for example, a move to a different part of the production line to carry out a different task. Alternatively, an employee may be moved from the personnel to the marketing department where they have skills which are common to both. From an employee's point of view this should reduce boredom and enable a variety of skills and experience to be gained. An employer might also benefit from a more widely trained workforce.

Although job rotation may motivate a worker, it is possible that any gains in productivity may be offset by a fall in output as workers learn new jobs and take time to 'settle in'. Worker motivation is not guaranteed if the employee is simply switched from one boring job to another. In fact some workers do not like the uncertainty that job changes lead to and may become dissatisfied. Although used by firms such as Volkswagen in the past, where employees carried out a variety of production tasks, job rotation has been less popular in the last decade.

Job enrichment and job loading

The idea of JOB ENRICHMENT came from Herzberg's two factor theory. Whereas job enlargement expands the job 'horizontally', job enrichment attempts to give employees greater responsibility by 'vertically' extending their role in the production process. An employee, for example, may be given responsibility for planning a task, quality control, work supervision, ordering materials and maintenance.

Job enrichment gives employees a 'challenge', which will develop their 'unused' skills and encourage them to be more

Question 1.

Instyle is a fashion design company. It has placed an advertisement on a recruitment website. Part of the advertisement included the following.

Instyle is a modern fashion design company. We want a tailor with at least one year's experience to help with making up our bespoke fashion designs. The main duties will include making up clothing such as suits, shirts, dresses and trousers, including sewing parts together, adding buttons and pressing. You will also work as part of a small team dealing directly with customers. This will involve measuring clients, making a draft of a master pattern and altering patterns to fit customers.

(a) Explain the term 'job design' using an example from the advertisement.

(b) How might the business be making use of job enlargement?

(c) Discuss how the business might make use of job enrichment techniques.

productive. The aim is to make workers feel they have been rewarded for their contribution to the company. Employees will also be provided with varied tasks, which may possibly lead to future promotion. It is not, however, without problems. Workers who feel that they are unable to carry out the 'extra work', or who consider that they are forced into it, may not respond to incentives. In addition, it is unlikely that all workers will react the same to job enrichment. Trade unions sometimes argue that such practices are an attempt to reduce the labour force, and disputes about the payment for extra responsibilities may arise. In practice, job enrichment has been found to be most successful in administrative and technical positions.

Job loading is where workers are given extra tasks when colleagues are off sick or if they have left and not been replaced. It can be particularly important in manufacturing, where absence can disrupt an assembly line for example.

Empowerment

Delegated decision making can be more successful if employees were empowered. EMPOWERMENT of employees involves a number of aspects.

- Recognising that employees are capable of doing more than they have in the past.
- Making employees feel trusted, so that they can carry out their jobs without constant checking.
- Giving employees control of decision making.
- Giving employees self confidence.
- Recognising employees' achievements.
- Developing a work environment where employees are motivated and interested in their work.

Many businesses now recognise the need to empower employees. There is a number of advantages of this for a business and for employees.

- Employees may feel more motivated. They feel trusted and feel that businesses recognise their talents. This should improve productivity and benefit the business in the long term, for example by reducing absenteeism.
- Employees may find less stress in their work as they have greater control over their working lives. This could reduce illness and absenteeism.
- Decisions may be made by those most suited to make them. Also, employees may feel less frustrated that senior staff who are less equipped to make decisions are making them.
- There may be greater employee skills and personal development.
- Businesses may be able to streamline their organisations and delegate decision making.
- Workers may feel less frustrated by more senior staff making decisions which they feel may be incorrect.

However, empowerment is sometimes criticised as simply a means of cutting costs and removing layers from the business. Passing decision making down the hierarchy might allow a company to make managers redundant. Employees are given more work to do, but for the same pay. Some businesses argue that they want to empower workers, but in practice they are unable or

144

Question 2.

St Luke's Communications is a London Advertising Agency owned by its staff. It was formed on St. Luke's day 1995 and has expanded from 35 to 75 staff. It is renowned for its innovative approach to stimulating staff. Teams are a core part of what the advertising agency does. People can sit anywhere and work anytime, but it is their personal responsibility to see that their behaviour doesn't damage the team. In a more traditional structure, empowerment means the handing down of power. If the organisation is owned by everyone, then everyone can 'rise to true freedom from the concepts of authority and power'. Asserting power would seriously damage this concept, so that discipline is through peers, not from above.

Staff are encouraged to contribute to projects other than those to which they have been specifically assigned. Everyone has the right to stumble into meetings. At meetings staff can mention incomplete ideas. It is argued that such thoughts may inspire others. There is also no owned space. Computers are available to all, and if there are not enough to go around, staff may bring in their own. It has been suggested that business has a turnover rate of around 10 per cent, although only around 1 per cent go to competitors. A turnover rate of 25 per cent is typical for advertising agencies.

Source: adapted from www.flexibility.co.uk, harvardbusinessonline, www.fastcompany.com, *The Sunday Times*.

(a) **Using examples from the article, explain how the business motivates employees.**
(b) **Explain how this will benefit (i) employees and (ii) the business.**

---

unwilling to do this. For example, a manager may feel insecure about subordinates making decisions that might affect his position in the business. Feeling that they may 'make the wrong decision' might lead to constant interruptions which are counter-productive. A further problem is the cost involved to the business, such as the cost of training employees or changing the workplace.

Team working

The Swedish car firm Volvo is a well quoted example of a company that has effectively introduced 'teamwork'. In both its plants at Kalmar and Uddevalla, it set up production in teams of eight to ten highly skilled workers. The teams decided between themselves how work was to be distributed and how to solve problems that arise. It is arguable whether these practices led to an increase in productivity, but the company firmly believed that this method of organisation was better than an assembly line system. A similar system has been used at Honda UK. Team working has a number of benefits.

- Productivity may be greater because of pooled talents.
- People can specialise and draw on the skills and knowledge of others in the team.
- Increasingly businesses are finding that the abilities of teams are needed to solve difficult business problems.
- Responsibility is shared. People may be more prepared to take risks.
- Ideas may be created by brainstorming.
- It allows flexible working.

However, in practice team work does not always produce the desired results. Part of the problem may lie in the way teams are organised. Members may fail to work well together for several reasons, from lack of a sense of humour to clashing goals. Studies of teams in the US have shown a number of problems with team work.

- Too much emphasis on harmony. Teams probably work best when there is room for disagreement. Papering over differences sometimes leads to vague or bland recommendations.
- Too much discord. Tension can destroy team effectiveness.
- Poor preparation. It is important that team members prepare for meetings by focusing on the facts. Members should have a detailed knowledge of the issues at hand and all work with the same information.
- Too much emphasis on individualism. For example, teams may fail to deliver results if the emphasis of the company is placed on individualism.
- A feeling of powerlessness. To work well, teams must be able to influence decisions.
- The failure of senior management to work well together. This creates problems because team members may walk into meetings with different priorities.
- Meeting-itis. Teams should not try to do everything together. Too many meetings waste the team's time.
- Seeing teams as the solution for all problems. Some tasks are better accomplished by individuals, rather than groups.

Quality control circles

QUALITY CONTROL CIRCLES or QUALITY CIRCLES are small groups of workers (about 5-20) in the same area of production who meet regularly to study and solve production problems. In addition, such groups are intended to motivate and involve workers on the shopfloor. Unlike job enlargement and job enrichment, they allow the workforce directly to improve the nature of the work they are doing.

Quality control circles started in America, where it was felt workers could be motivated by being involved in decision making. The idea gained in popularity in Japan and was taken up by Western businesses. Examples of their use can be found in Japanese companies setting up plants in the UK in the 1990s. Honda at Swindon has had 52 teams of six people looking at improvements that can be made in areas allocated to the groups, for example, safety.

Quality control circles are only likely to work if they have the support of both management and employees. Businesses have to want worker participation and involvement in decision making, and set up a structure that supports this. Workers and their representatives also need to support the scheme. Employees must feel that their views within the circle are valued and must make a contribution to decisions.

Multiskilling

MULTISKILLING is a term used to describe the process of enhancing the skills of employees. It is argued that giving individuals the skills and responsibilities to deal with a greater variety of issues will allow a business to respond more quickly and effectively to problems. So for example, a receptionist might have been trained to pass on calls to other people in a business. Multiskilling this job could mean that the receptionist now deals with more straightforward enquiries himself. This would result in a quicker response to the customer's enquiry. It would also free up time for other people to work on more demanding activities.

Certain motivation theories suggest that giving individuals more skills and responsibilities can improve their work performance. A criticism of multiskilling is that individuals are only given more skills so that they are expected to work harder without any extra pay. Problems may also result if workers are not trained adequately for their new roles.

Achieving a work-life balance

Recently there has been a stress on the need for employers to deal with the work-life balance of employees. Life is becoming faster and more complex, but without the support of communities or extended families. It is suggested that unless employers are sympathetic and supportive of employees' external needs, there could be an increase in health related absences such as stress. This could affect the operation and efficiency of the business.

Organisational structure, financial and non-financial rewards

There is a link between the motivational techniques used by managers in business and the organisational structure of a business. For example, a business with a traditional and rigid hierarchy will often make use of financial rewards. Each level of the hierarchy will have an associated level of financial reward, which is clear to employees in the organisation. Employees can see this and be motivated into working to achieve promotion or move through the levels of the business.

In a hierarchy non-financial rewards may also be motivating in certain circumstances. As workers achieve a certain living standard with which they are comfortable, they may find that other factors are more motivating, such as the ability to make their own decisions or to have flexibility in their work. These factors can be motivating for higher level posts. Job enrichment and empowerment further down the hierarchy may also be motivating to employees, especially if their jobs are repetitive and boring. However, a manger must take care when empowering workers as not all employees want to or feel able to take extra responsibility.

In other forms of organisational structure non-financial rewards may be particularly motivating. For example, in a matrix structure workers are working in teams. The support of other members of the team or respect from colleagues may be important as a motivation factor. Managers may have to generate a sense of team belonging to motivate staff. In an independent structure the ability to make decisions is likely to be very motivating to employees.

KEY TERMS

Empowerment – to give official authority to employees to make decisions and control their own activities.

Job design – the process of organising the tasks and activities required to perform a job.

Job redesign – changing the tasks and activities of a job, perhaps in an attempt to motivate workers.

Job enlargement – giving an employee more work to do of a similar nature.

Job enrichment – an attempt to give employees greater responsibility and recognition by 'vertically' extending their role in the production process.

Job rotation – the changing of jobs or tasks from time to time.

Multiskilling – the processes of enhancing the skills of employees.

Teamworking – Employees working in small groups with a common aim.

Quality control circles or Quality Circles – small groups of workers in the same area of production which meet regularly to study and solve all types of production problems.

KNOWLEDGE

1. State five possible non-financial rewards that may be an incentive for individuals.
2. What principles would a 'good' job have according to the 'Quality of Working Life Movement'?
3. State four methods of job redesign.
4. 'Job enlargement is simply a method of horizontal loading.' Explain this statement.
5. Under what circumstances might job rotation not lead to an increase in productivity?
6. Suggest four problems of working in teams.
7. Why is job enrichment said to extend an employee's role in the firm vertically?
8. What are the advantages to an employee of quality control circles?
9. State three features of empowerment.
10. What is meant by achieving a work-life balance?

Case Study: *Zinx*

Zinx is an independent boutique hotel and restaurant in the South East of England. It employs 60 staff. It has always had a very traditional organisation with senior managers, departmental managers, supervisors, head waiters, bar staff, cleaners and administrators. It has read the following article about staff in independent hotels and is considering changing its operations to increase staff motivation.

'Empowerment is a frequently used buzzword, not just in the hospitality industry. Empowerment means staff can make decisions. If hotels want to remain successful, they need to be driven by their staff on customer service. Independent hotels have to go "above and beyond" and work harder in a competitive environment. This helps to ensure survival through a high percentage of repeat business, while fostering growth of new clients.

Guests appreciate dealing with people who are empowered. The last thing an arriving guest needs is to be given the runaround, going through "layers" of management to get what they need. Empowerment means, rather than becoming defensive, staff assume accountability mistakes and put them right.

Essential to empowerment is the practice of "trust, but verify". A balance is necessary because empowerment can backfire especially in the wrong application or misguided interpretation. Owners and managers cannot give responsibility to staff without empowering them. But attention should be given to training staff to be ensure empowerment works. Empowerment can work against you if you have a staff member too empowered without direction.

In the hotel industry employees should be seen as part of a team. The terms employee and management create divisions. Such a divide in organisational structure does not foster a sense of teamwork. It's a

"them and me" situation rather than a "we or us". Terms such as staff member illustrate better and reinforce working together. This creates a culture of "leadership teamwork" for the staff working with guests. Having fluid organisational structures reduce levels of management, separating President/CEO/General Manager from guests. The more layers you have, the more distant you remain from the guest and from the pulse of the staff.'

Source: adapted in part from www.hotelinteractive.com.

(a) Explain the meaning of the terms (i) empowerment (3 marks) and (ii) teamwork (3 marks).

(b) Explain TWO ways in which the organisation at Zinx might change to help motivate employees. (6 marks)

(c) Explain how greater empowerment at Zinx can affect (i) employees, (ii) clients and (ii) the business. (8 marks)

(d) Discuss whether Zinx should increase empowerment at the business. (10 marks)

33 Operational decisions and capacity utilisation

Operational decisions and targets

OPERATIONS MANAGEMENT is the organisation and control of the process by which inputs, such as labour, materials and machinery, are transformed into final products or by which services are provided to customers. Production managers, for example, are responsible for making decisions about:

- what production methods are to be used;
- what levels of input of labour, machinery and materials are needed to produce a given quantity of output;
- how best to utilise the firm's capacity;
- what stock levels are required to support production;
- how to ensure that work is completed on time;
- how best to ensure quality.

Decisions about the entire business that affect production also need to be made. For example:

- What is the optimal size for a business? Should there be five employees, 500 or 500,000?
- Where should production take place? On one or two sites? In the UK or the Far East?

Good operations management can help a business to be more effective. One approach which operations managers are likely to use is to set OPERATIONAL TARGETS. Setting targets can help managers monitor the performance of the production department. A number of key targets might be used, as shown in Figure 1.

Unit costs

Unit cost is the cost of producing a single unit of output. It is the same as average cost. It can be calculated as:

$$\text{Unit cost} = \frac{\text{Total cost}}{\text{Output}}$$

So, for example, if a computer manufacturer produced 12,000 laptop computers in a year at a total cost of £3,480,000, the unit cost would be given by:

$$\text{Unit cost} = \frac{£3,480,000}{12,000} = £290$$

This means that each single laptop computer cost £290 to make.

Production managers may set operational targets for unit costs. These costs can be measured at the end of a production run and compared with the targets. If actual unit costs are higher than the targets, the production manager is likely to search for reasons why so that appropriate action can be taken. Generally, businesses are always looking for ways to *control* or reduce unit costs.

Figure 1: Operational targets

Unit costs — Productivity — Capacity utilisation — **Operational targets** — Quality — Stock levels

Capacity utilisation

CAPACITY UTILISATION is about the use that a business makes from its resources. If a business is not able to increase output, it is said to be running at full capacity. Its capacity utilisation is 100 per cent. So if a 52 seater coach from London to Edinburgh has 52 passengers, it is operating at full capacity. If it had 32 passengers it would be operating at less than full capacity and so it would have EXCESS, SURPLUS, SPARE or UNUSED CAPACITY.

Businesses do not always operate at full capacity. It may not be possible to keep all resources and machinery fully employed all the time. However, most businesses would wish to be operating at close to full capacity, such as 90 per cent.

In some cases businesses even choose to operate at less than full capacity in order to be flexible. For example, they might want to have capacity to cope with increased orders from regular customers. Without this, a business might let down its customers and risk losing them.

Capacity utilisation can be measured by comparing actual or current output with the potential output at full capacity using the formula:

$$\text{Capacity utilisation} = \frac{\text{Current output}}{\text{Maximum possible output}} \times 100$$

A printing operation might be able to operate for ten hours, six days a week using shifts. If it only had enough work to operate for 48 hours last week, the capacity utilisation would be:

$$\text{Capacity utilisation} = \frac{48}{(10 \times 6)} \times 100 = 80\%$$

Another example might be a printing machine that is capable of printing 10,000 leaflets in a time period but only prints 9,000. It has a capacity utilisation of (9,000 ÷ 10,000) x 100 = 90 per cent. In this case the machine has unused, excess, surplus or spare capacity of 10 per cent.

Costs and capacity utilisation

A business can lower its unit or average costs if it can increase its capacity utilisation. This is because some of its costs are fixed. Higher levels of capacity utilisation and higher levels of output, will make a business more efficient. Table 1 shows capacity utilisation output, variable cost, fixed cost, total cost and average cost (unit cost) for a component manufacturer. When capacity utilisation is raised from 60 per cent to 80 per cent, for example, average cost falls from £2.42 to £2.31. This is because the fixed costs of £50,000 are spread over more units of output. This explains why firms will always be keen to raise capacity utilisation.

Table 1: Capacity utilisation, output, variable cost, fixed cost, total cost, unit cost for a component manufacturer

Actual output (units)	120,000	160,000
Maximum possible output (units)	200,000	200,000
Capacity utilisation	60%	80%
Variable costs (£2 per unit)	£240,000	£320,000
Fixed costs	£50,000	£50,000
Total cost	£290,000	£370,000
Unit cost	£2.42	£2.31

Improving capacity utilisation

A business will make better use of its resources if it increases its capacity utilisation. Its unit costs will be lower and profits will be higher. How can firms increase capacity utilisation?

Reduced capacity A business might decide to cut capacity. It might do this by RATIONALISING, for example. This involves reducing excess capacity by getting rid of resources that the business can do without. There is a number of measures a business might take.
- Reducing staff by making people redundant, employing more part-time and temporary staff and offering early retirement.
- Selling off unused fixed assets such as machinery, vehicles, office space, warehouses and factory space.
- Leasing capacity. Debenhams has leased unused floor space in its stores to other retailers, for example. Parts of a factory could also be leased to another manufacturer. The advantage of this is that the space may be reclaimed if demand picks up again.
- Moving to smaller premises where costs are lower.
- MOTHBALLING some resources. This means that fixed assets, such as machinery, are left unused but are

Question 1.

Oliver Handy make mattresses. It is an established business and operates from a small factory in Swindon. It employs twelve staff and has recently appointed a new production manager. In 2006, the then manager retired after 25 years of service to the company. He was replaced by the current manager. Within two months of the new manager arriving some sweeping changes were made to production methods and working practices. The new manager emphasised the importance of production targets, unit costs, staff rewards and operations management. Table 2 shows some financial information for Oliver Handy.

Table 2: Financial information for Oliver Handy

				(£)
	2004	**2005**	**2006**	**2007**
Total output	12,000	13,500	14,000	17,000
Total cost	252,000	297,000	305,200	297,500

(a) What is meant by operations management?
(b) (i) Calculate the unit costs for the four years.
   (ii) What impact has the new production manager had on unit costs?
(c) How can setting operational targets help a business like Oliver Handy?

maintained, so that they can be brought back into use if necessary.

Increased sales If a business sells more of its output, it will have to produce more. Therefore capacity utilisation will rise. A business might need to spend money on promotion to increase sales, for example. If these costs are not covered by the extra revenue generated, raising capacity utilisation in this way may not be viable.

Increased usage A problem that many businesses face is dealing with peak demand. Train operators can find that capacity utilisation is close to 100 per cent during the 'rush hour', but perhaps as low as 10 per cent late at night. Such businesses would like to increase capacity utilisation during 'off-peak' hours. This might explain why discounts are offered for 'off-peak' travel.

Subcontracting Capacity utilisation can vary considerably within a business. Where capital equipment has low utilisation rates, it might be more efficient for the business to SUBCONTRACT or OUTSOURCE the work. This means hiring or contracting another business to do work which was previously done in-house.

For instance, a business might run a small fleet of delivery vans which on average are on the road for four hours per day. It is likely that it would be cheaper for the business to sell the vans and employ a company to make the deliveries. The delivery company would be more efficient because it would be running its vans for much longer during the day. There may also be cost savings in terms of staff. If the business employed full-time drivers for the vans, they would have been under-utilised if they only worked four hours per day.

Subcontracting can also lead to other cost advantages. The delivery business will be a specialist business. It should operate its delivery service more efficiently than a business with a few vans and little knowledge of the industry. If nothing else, it should have greater buying power. It might be able, for instance, to negotiate lower prices for its vans because it is buying more vans. If it is a very small business, its hourly wages may be less than, say, a union-negotiated rate at the larger business.

An alternative outsourcing strategy is to take on outsourcing contracts for other businesses. For example, a major manufacturer of soap could accept contracts from rival soap manufacturers to improve its capacity utilisation. Outsourcing then becomes a strategy for increasing demand for the business.

Redeployment If a business has too many resources in one

part, it may be possible to deploy them in another part. For example, a bank may ask some of its employees to work in another branch for a short period.

Advantages and disadvantages of working at full capacity

Advantages Working at full capacity has some benefits.
- Average costs will be minimised because fixed costs will be spread across as many units of output as possible. This will help to raise profits.
- Staff motivation might be good if workers feel secure in their jobs.
- A busy operation can improve the company's image. As a result, customers might be more confident when placing orders.

Problems However, there may be some drawbacks when a firm is unable to increase output any more.
- The pressure of working at full capacity all the time might put a strain on some of the resources. For example, workers might be doing too much overtime, resulting in tiredness and stress. This might cause accidents or absence.

Question 2.

Zaman & Nazran is a business which specialises in the manufacture of diecast zinc and aluminium products. It produces components for a variety of industries. Since being founded in the mid-1990s, it has grown to today's workforce of 14 employees. Sales were up 7 per cent last year and 50 per cent up from five years ago. It is confident that in the next five years, it can increase its sales by another 50 per cent.

Table 3 shows the number of hours that machinery and equipment were used during each week between July and August 2008. Management works on the assumption that 60 hours per week represents full capacity for the business. This reflects the maximum number of hours that the existing labour force would be prepared to work, including overtime.

Currently, equipment in a typical week is used to 75 per cent capacity. Working to 100 per cent capacity in any week, such as in the second week of July 2008, is unusual and difficult to maintain because machines break down or employees are off work sick. In fact, in the second week of July, the business was forced to sub-contract some of the work to rival companies because it couldn't cope with delivery deadlines set by customers. Seasonal factors affect demand. Orders often fall in late July and early August because customers tend to produce less due to their workers taking summer holidays.

Management has considered rationalisation to reduce costs. Equally the business is committed to an investment programme to buy the latest equipment, which will increase productive efficiency and allow for expansion of sales in the future.

(a) Explain what is meant by:
    (i) 'capacity utilisation';
    (ii) 'rationalisation'.
(b) Calculate capacity utilisation for weeks 3–4 in July and weeks 1–4 in August.
(c) Analyse two ways in which the business could increase capacity utilisation.
(d) Discuss whether the business would perform better in the long term if it sold off half its plant and equipment, moved to smaller premises, sacked half the workforce and used subcontractors to complete work which it could not manufacture to meet delivery deadlines from customers.

Table 3

		July				August			
Week		1	2	3	4	1	2	3	4
Hours worked		44	60	47	31	41	45	45	47
Capacity utilisation (%)		73	100	?	?	?	?	?	?

Machines may also be overworked to breaking point.
- The business might lose lucrative orders from new customers.
- There may be insufficient time for staff training and important maintenance work.

Matching production to demand

A production manager has to make sure that production levels tie in with the level of demand. If production levels exceed demand there will be a build up of stocks. This may be expensive because stock holding costs can be very high indeed. Also, if the stocks are not being sold, there will be a drain on resources. However, if production levels are too low, the business may not be able to satisfy demand. This could lead to a loss of trade if customers are kept waiting and decide to buy from a rival. Matching production with demand often means that operational methods should have some flexibility built in. This can be achieved in a number of ways.

Offering overtime Production managers could ask staff to work overtime if orders increase. Overtime is often popular with workers because overtime rates are usually higher than basic wage rates. They may be time and half or double time. However, not all workers will want to work overtime because they have other commitments.

Hiring part-time or temporary staff A business might use temporary or part-time staff to deal with surges in demand. Temporary staff can be 'hired and fired' according to demand levels. They will be employed on very short-term contracts. However, temporary staff will have to be trained and may not be as reliable as permanent staff. Part-time staff are generally more flexible than full-time staff. They can often adapt to changes in the hours they work.

Making flexible use of capital Fluctuations in demand may also mean that capital needs to be flexible. This might be achieved by leasing machinery and equipment in the short-term. For example, vehicles, tools and machinery can be leased to cope with increases in demand.

Using suppliers Businesses will need flexible suppliers. When orders increase a business might need to call on suppliers to make emergency deliveries. Suppliers that cannot offer flexibility and reliability might be avoided.

Adjusting production Production levels can also adjusted to match demand through rationalisation and subcontracting. This is discussed above.

Holding finished stocks A common way of matching production and demand is to hold stocks of finished goods. If demand increases, orders can be satisfied from stocks. If demand falls, then stocks can be accumulated. However, stock holding costs need to be taken into account when using this approach.

Some businesses have to cope with **seasonal demand**. These could be businesses operating farms, hotels and other leisure activities, for example. They have to organise their operations to deal with 'peak' demand in the high season and very low demand out of season. The methods discussed above are likely to be even more important to such businesses.

Non-standard orders

It is not unusual for businesses to receive **non-standard orders**. These are orders for goods that the business does not normally produce. For example, a publisher may be asked for a particular book to be available in the Welsh language. To meet such an order businesses may need to reset machines, use different labour skills, different raw materials and possibly different tools. In the example above the publisher would need to employ someone to translate the text, typeset the whole book again and organise a small production run. To meet non-standard orders extra costs will be incurred and a business may charge a premium price. Non-standard orders might be irritating but refusing such orders might lead to a loss of custom. However, accepting non-standard orders might gain new long-term customers.

KEYTERMS

Capacity utilisation – the use that a business makes of its resources.

Excess or surplus capacity – when a business has too many resources, such as labour and capital, to produce its desired level of output.

Mothballing – when machines, equipment or building space are left unused but maintained so they could be brought back into use if necessary.

Operations management – the organisation and control of the process by which inputs, such as labour, materials and machinery, are transformed into final products or by which services are provided to customers.

Operational targets – the goals set by a business that must be achieved in the production of a product or provision of a service.

Rationalising – reducing the number of resources, particularly labour and capital, put into the production process, usually undertaken because a business has excess capacity.

Subcontracting or outsourcing – hiring or contracting another business to do work which could be done in-house by a business.

KNOWLEDGE

1. State four decisions a production manager might have to make.
2. State four operational targets that might be set by a business.
3. Explain what is meant by unit cost.
4. Why will unit costs fall if capacity is better utilised?
5. State three ways in which a business might reduce capacity.
6. What is meant by redeployment?
7. What are non-standard orders?
8. State four measures that a business might take to help match production with orders.

Case Study: Gibson's Golf Buggies Ltd

Gibson's has manufactured golf buggies for 27 years. The company employs 48 staff and has a factory in Manchester. Its standard product has the following features.

- Double-seated, four-wheeled electric powered
- Twist grip stepless speed control for smooth operation
- Forward/reverse switch conveniently located
- Safe operator controlled speed governor
- Maximum speed restricted to 8mph in consideration of other golfers
- Hill climbing ability: 1:3 gradient
- Battery charging unit simply plugged into rear of buggy
- Two heavy duty batteries – 12V 75 amp/hour coupled in series.

In 2004, the company started to experience some problems. Intense competition from overseas manufacturers, China in particular, resulted in a decline in sales. The company responded by making cost savings and investing in a new marketing campaign. This appeared to halt the decline in sales and boost profit margins. However, the factory was left with a great deal of unused capacity, particularly in the winter when demand always fell. Table 4 shows some production information for Gibson's Golf Buggies Ltd.

(a) Explain what is meant by 'capacity utilisation'. (3 marks)
(b) (i) Calculate the capacity utilisation for Gibson's over the five year time period. (5 marks)
(ii) Comment on the capacity utilisation of Gibson's over this time period. (5 marks)
(c) Why is the capacity utilisation at Gibson's a problem? (6 marks)
(d) How might Gibson's deal with the problem of seasonal demand in the factory? (10 marks)
(e) Evaluate the measures that might be used by Gibson's Golf Buggies Ltd to improve capacity utilisation. (20 marks)

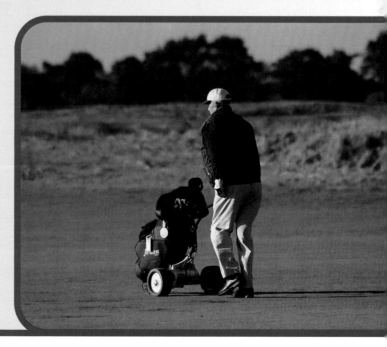

Table 4: Gibson's Golf Buggies Ltd

	2003	2004	2005	2006	2007
Output	14,000	12,000	11,000	10,500	10,900
Total capacity	18,000	18,000	18,000	18,000	18,000

Operational decisions and stocks

Businesses purchase raw materials, semi-finished goods and components. A washing machine manufacturer, for example, may buy electric motors, circuit boards, rubber drive belts, nuts, bolts, sheet metal and a variety of metal and plastic components. These stocks of materials and components are used to produce products which are then sold to consumers and other businesses. Managing these materials is the responsibility of the production or operations manager. Materials management involves:

- the purchasing of stocks and their delivery;
- the storing and control of stocks;
- the issue and handling of stocks;
- the disposal of surpluses;
- the provision of information about stocks.

The nature of stocks

Businesses prefer to minimise stock holding because it is costly. In practice a variety of stocks are held, for different reasons.

Raw materials and components These are purchased from suppliers before production. They are stored by firms to cope with changes in production levels. Delays in production can be avoided if materials and components can be supplied from stores rather than waiting for a new delivery to arrive. Also, if a company is let down by suppliers it can use stocks to carry on production.

Work-in-progress These are partly finished goods. In a television assembly plant, WORK IN PROGRESS would be televisions on the assembly line, which are only partly built.

Finished goods The main reason for keeping finished goods is to cope with changes in demand and stock. If there is a sudden rise in demand, a firm can meet urgent orders by supplying customers from stock holdings. This avoids the need to step up production rates quickly.

Normally, at least once every year, a business will perform a STOCK TAKE. This involves recording the amount and value of stocks which the firm is holding. A stock take is also required for security reasons – to check that the items actually in stock match the stock records kept by the business. The stock take is also necessary to help determine the value of total purchases during the year for a firm's accounts. A physical stock take can be done manually by identifying every item of stock on the premises. Many firms have details of stock levels recorded on computer.

The cost of holding stocks

In recent years stock management has become more important

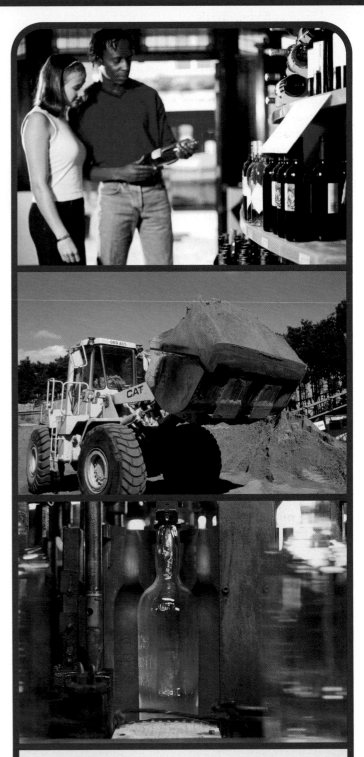

Question 1.

(a) Look at the photographs. Explain which of them shows: (i) stocks of raw materials; (ii) work-in-progress; (iii) stocks of finished goods.
(b) Explain why businesses hold stocks of finished goods.

for many firms. Careful control of stock levels can improve business performance. Having too much stock may mean that money is tied up unproductively, but inadequate stock can lead to delays in production and late deliveries. Efficient stock control involves finding the right balance. One of the reasons why control is so important is because the costs of holding stocks can be very high.

- There may be an **opportunity cost** in holding stocks. Capital tied up in stocks earns no rewards. The money used to purchase stocks could have been put to other uses, such as buyingnew machinery. This might have earned the business money.
- Storage can also prove costly. Stocks of raw materials, components and finished goods occupy space in buildings. A firm may also have to pay heating, lighting and labour costs if, for example, a night watchman is employed to safeguard stores when the business is closed. Some products require very special storage conditions. Food items may need expensive refrigerated storage facilities.   A firm may have to insure against fire, theft and other damages.
- Spoilage costs. The quality of some stock, for example perishable goods may deteriorate over time. In addition, if some finished goods are held too long they may become outdated and difficult to sell.
- Administrative and financial costs. These include the cost of placing and processing orders, handling costs and the costs of failing to anticipate price increases.
- Out-of-stock costs. These are the costs of lost revenue, when sales are lost because customers cannot be supplied from stocks. There may also be a loss of goodwill if customers are let down.

Stock levels

One of the most important tasks in stock control is to maintain the right level of stocks. This involves keeping stock levels as low as possible, so that the costs of holding stocks are minimised. At the same time stocks must not be allowed to run out, so that production is halted and customers are let down. A number of factors influence stock levels.

- Demand. Sufficient stocks need to be kept to satisfy normal demand. Firms must also carry enough stock to cover growth in sales and unexpected demand. The term BUFFER STOCK is used to describe stock held for unforeseen rises in demand or breaks in supply.
- Some firms stockpile goods. For example, toy manufacturers build up stocks in the few months leading up to December ready for the Christmas period. Electricity generating stations build up stocks of coal in the summer. During the summer, demand for electricity is low so less coal is needed. At the same time, prices of coal during the summer months are lower, so savings can be made.
- The costs of stock holding. The costs of holding stock were described earlier. If stock is expensive to hold then only a

small quantity will be held. Furniture retailers may keep low stock levels because the cost of stock is high and sales levels are uncertain.

- The amount of working capital available. A business that is short of working capital will not be able to purchase more stock, even if it is needed.
- The type of stock. Businesses can only hold small stocks of perishable products. The stock levels of cakes or bread will be very small. Almost the entire stock of finished goods will be sold in one day. The 'life' of stock, however, does not solely depend on its 'perishability'. Stocks can become out of date when they are replaced by new models, for example.
- LEAD TIME. This is the amount of time it takes for a stock purchase to be placed, received, inspected and made ready for use. The longer the lead time, the higher the minimum level of stock needed.
- External factors. Fear of future shortages may prompt firms to hold higher levels of raw materials in stock as a precaution.

Stock control

It is necessary to control the flow of stocks in the business. This ensures that firms hold the right amount. Several methods of stock control exist. They focus on the RE-ORDER QUANTITY (how much stock is ordered when a new order is placed) and the RE-ORDER LEVEL (the level of stock when an order is placed).

- **Economic order quantity (EOQ)**. It is possible to calculate the level of stocks which minimises costs. This is called the economic order quantity. It takes into account the costs of holding stock, which rise with the amount of stock held, and the average costs of ordering stock, which fall as the size of the order is increased. A business must calculate the EOQ to balance these costs.
- **Fixed re-order interval**. Orders of various sizes are placed at fixed time intervals. This method ignores the economic

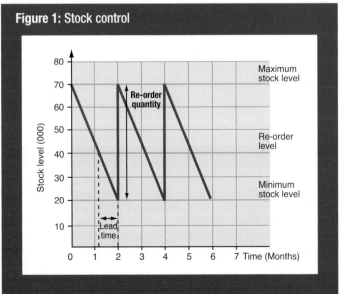

Figure 1: Stock control

order quantity, but ensures that stocks are 'topped up' on a regular basis. This method may result in fluctuating stock levels.
- **Fixed re-order level**. This method involves setting a fixed order level, perhaps using the EOQ. The order is then repeated at varying time intervals.
- **Two bin system**. This simple method involves dividing stock into two bins. When one bin is empty a new order is placed. When the order arrives it is placed into the first bin and stocks are used from the second bin. When the second bin is empty stocks are re-ordered again.

A stock control system is shown in Figure 1. It is assumed that:
- 50,000 units are used every two months (25,000 each month);
- the **maximum stock level**, above which stocks never rise, is 70,000 units;

- the **minimum stock level**, below which stocks should never fall, is 20,000 units, so there is a buffer against delays in delivery;
- stock is re-ordered when it reaches a level of 40,000 units (the **re-order level**);
- the **re-order quantity** is 50,000 units - the same quantity is used up every two months;
- the **lead time** is just under one month. This is the time between the order being placed and the date it arrives in stock.

This is a hypothetical model which would be the ideal for a business. In practice deliveries are sometimes late, so there is a delay in stocks arriving. Firms may also need to use their buffer stocks in this case. It is likely that re-order quantities will need to be reviewed from time to time. Suppliers might offer discounts for ordering larger quantities. The quantities of stocks used in each time period are unlikely to be constant. This might be because production levels fluctuate according to demand.

Too much or too little stock

Why might having too much or too little stock be bad business practice?

Too much stock
- Storage, insurance, lighting and handling costs will all be high if too much stock is held.
- Large stock levels will occupy space in the premises. There may be more productive ways of using this space, such as improving the layout of the factory.
- The opportunity cost will be high. Money tied up in stocks could be used to buy fixed assets, for example.
- Large stock levels might result in unsold stock. If there is an unexpected change in demand, the firm may be left with stocks that it cannot sell.
- Very large stocks might result in an increase in theft by employees. They may feel the business would not miss a small amount of stock relative to the total stock.

Too little stock
- The business may not be able to cope with unexpected increases in demand if its stocks are too low. This might result in lost customers if they are let down too often.
- If deliveries are delayed the firm may run out of stock and have to halt production. This might lead to idle labour and machinery while the firm waits for delivery.
- The firm is less able to cope with unexpected shortages of materials. Again, this could result in lost production.
- A firm which holds very low stocks may have to place more orders. This will raise total ordering costs. Also, it may be unable to take advantage of discounts for bulk buying.

Question 2.

Hahmid & Odusanya is a machine fabrications specialist. It makes large parts for machine tools and special parts machines such as those be found on production lines. It holds stocks of steel. The pattern of its stockholding is shown in Figure 2.

Figure 2:

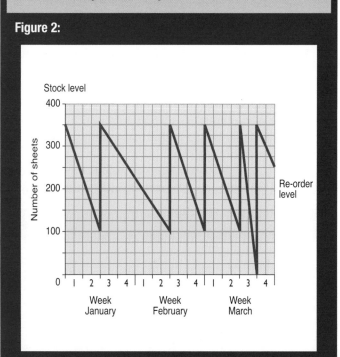

(a) Measured in numbers of sheets of steel, what is
(i) the maximum stock level; (ii) the buffer stock level;
(iii) the re-order level?
(b) Explaining your reasoning, suggest in which weeks there was (i) an unexpected large rush order; (ii) very disappointing sales.
(c) Explain what might happen to maximum stock levels if the business began to experience cash flow problems.

Computerised stock control

Stock control has been improved by the use of computers. Many businesses hold details of their entire stock on computer databases. All additions to and issues from stocks are recorded and up to date stock levels can be found instantly. Actual levels of stock should be the same as shown on the computer printout. A prudent firm will carry out regular stock checks to identify differences.

Some systems are programmed to automatically order stock when the re-order level is reached. In some supermarkets, computerised checkout systems record every item of stock purchased by customers and automatically subtract items from total stock levels. The packaging on each item contains a bar code. When this is passed over a laser at the checkout, the sale is recorded by the system. This allows a store manager to check stock levels, total stock values and the store's takings at any time of the day. Again, the system can indicate when the re-order level is reached for any particular item of stock.

Access to stock levels is useful when manufacturers are dealing with large orders. The firm might need to find out whether there are enough materials in stock to complete the order. If this information is available, then the firm can give a more accurate delivery date.

JIT and stock rotation

In recent years many businesses have changed their approach to stock management. To reduce costs, firms have held low levels of stocks. In some cases holdings of both finished goods and raw materials have been reduced to zero. This approach to stock control is the key feature of just-in-time manufacturing (JIT). It is explained fully in the unit on lean production.

Businesses often use systems to control the flow of stocks in and out of their store areas. This flow of stock is sometimes called STOCK ROTATION. One system used to rotate stock is called First In First Out (FIFO). This means that those stocks which are delivered first are the first ones to be issued. This method is useful if stocks are perishable or if they are likely to become obsolete in the near future. A second method of stock rotation is called Last-In-First-Out (LIFO). This system involves issuing stock from the latest rather than the earliest deliveries. This method might be used if the stocks are difficult to handle and it is physically easier to issue the more recent deliveries. However, when using this method it is important that stocks are not perishable. 'Old' stock could remain in store for long periods before it is finally used.

KEY TERMS

Buffer stocks – stocks held as a precaution to cope with unforeseen demand.

Lead time – the time between the placing of the order and the delivery of goods.

Re-order level – the level of stock when new orders are placed.

Re-order quantity – the amount of stock ordered when an order is placed.

Stock rotation – the flow of stock into and out of stores.

Stock take – the process of counting the amount of stock held at a point in time in order to calculate the total stock level held.

Work-in-progress – partly finished goods.

KNOWLEDGE

1. What are the activities involved in materials management?
2. Why do businesses prefer to minimise stock holdings?
3. What is meant by: (a) components; (b) finished goods?
4. What are the costs of holding stocks?
5. Why are buffer stocks held by firms?
6. Why do some firms stockpile?
7. What is meant by LIFO and FIFO?

Case Study: *Regal Jewels*

Regal Jewels is a small chain of jewellers. It has nine outlets in the south east. Each shop has a manager and employs one or two other full-time staff with some part-time staff who help out at busy times, such as Christmas. The shops stock a wide range of rings, earrings, bracelets, necklaces, gemstones and watches. They also produce specialist, tailor made pieces for wealthy customers. The business has flourished by focusing on the old fashioned virtues of personal service and value for money. All managers are members of the HRD Institute of Gemology, Antwerp (Europe's diamond capital). This is a highly regarded professional qualification and gives the business a great deal of credibility. The shop operates at the top end of the market and most of their pieces sell for over £100 – with many pieces going for £1,000s.

Stock is the most valuable asset for the business. After the last stock take, the total value of stocks held by Regal Jewels was £3,560,000. The stock is purchased centrally by the owner of the business. Regal Jewels uses a number of different suppliers, some of them from overseas. However, there have been one or two problems relating to stock management at the business.

One problem is maintaining the supply the supplier of customised carrier backs. All customers leave the shops with their purchases packaged in a specially designed Regal Jewels bag, adorned with gold ribbon and the business logo. Regular purchases of these carrier bags are made every month. The diagram in Figure 2 shows stocks of the carrier bags for a nine month period.

Another problem faced by the business owner is keeping right up to date with the stocks held in each shop. At the moment a manual, paper-based stock system is used. This is proving to be increasingly cumbersome and inefficient as the business grows. She is thinking of setting up an online stock control system. A new online system has been developed which allows small businesses, such as Regal Jewels, to login and manage their stock levels. It is perfect for a business with more than one location. It is possible to monitor stock movements and react to information delivered to a computer from anywhere in the world. The system has a number of benefits.

- Cost effective (no software to purchase/upgrade).
- No new hardware needed.
- Available from multiple locations.
- Easy to use system/set-up system.
- Free support available (unlike all other systems).
- Time saving (no need to produce your own reports or fill in endless paperwork).
- Up/downsizeable for when your business grows or shrinks.

- Easy to train other members of staff.
- 30 day free trials available.

(a) Regal Jewels have monthly stock takes.
(i) What is meant by a stock take? (3 marks)
(ii) Why do you think a stock take is so important for Regal Jewels? (6 marks)

(b) Discuss two stock holding costs that Regal Jewels will incur. (6 marks)

(c) Look at Figure 3. Identify the (i) lead time; (ii) the re-order quantity; (iii) re-order level; (iv) minimum stock level for the carrier bags. (8 marks)

(d) In September 2007, Regal Jewels found a new supplier of carrier bags. Why do you think it took this action? (6 marks)

(e) Do you think Regal Jewels should introduce the online stock system? (10 marks)

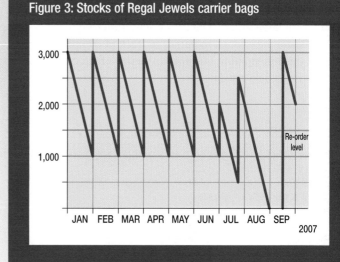

Figure 3: Stocks of Regal Jewels carrier bags

35 | Types of production

Deciding how to produce

A business must decide on the most suitable method to manufacture its goods or to provide services. It is likely that products which are different will be produced differently. For example, a plastic drinks bottle may be produced using automated machinery, but a wrist watch may be assembled by hand. Products that are similar can also be produced in different ways. The Ford Motor Company and Morgan Cars both produce cars, but different processes are used. Ford builds cars using a production line and semi-skilled labour, but Morgan cars are hand built by skilled workers. There are three important decisions that businesses must make when choosing how to produce. These are shown in Figure 1, along with the factors which influence these decisions. In the diagram it is assumed that the firm has already decided 'what' to produce. When deciding how to produce, the objective of the firm will be to minimise the cost per unit of output, i.e. PRODUCTIVE EFFICIENCY.

What production method will be used? Production is sometimes divided into one of three methods. JOB PRODUCTION is where one job is completed at a time before moving on to another. An example might be a costume made

for a television play set in the nineteenth century. BATCH PRODUCTION involves dividing the work into a number of different operations. An example would be bread production, where each batch goes through several different baking stages before it is completed. FLOW PRODUCTION involves work being completed continuously without stopping. The production of cars on a production line might be one example.

Some industries may combine different methods of production. For example, a large brewery may produce 'batches' of beer, but then send them to a bottling line for packaging, where flow production is used. Such combinations are particularly common in the food industry.

What factors of production will be used? Businesses are often faced with a wide choice between alternative production factors. For example, a builder planning to construct a new house must decide what building materials to buy, which tools to use, which sub-contractors to employ and whether to hire any extra labour. The builder will be faced with a choice in all of these cases. If he decides to hire a labourer, there may be hundreds or even thousands of people to choose from in the area.

How will the factors of production be combined? A third production decision concerns the way in which the available production factors should be combined. For example, should an assembly plant invest in a highly automated assembly operation, or employ a large semi-skilled labour force to undertake the work?

This unit focuses on the types of production a business might choose from.

Job production

Job production involves the production of a single product at a time. It is used when orders for products are small, such as 'one-offs'. Production is organised so that one 'job' is completed at a time. There is a wide variety of goods and services which are produced or provided using this method of production. Small-scale examples include the baking of a child's birthday cake, a dentist's treatment session or the construction of an extension to a house. On a large scale, examples could include the building of a ship, the construction of the Channel Tunnel or the manufacture of specialised machinery. Job production is found in both manufacturing and the service industries. Because the numbers of units produced is small, the production process tends to be labour intensive. The workforce is usually made up of skilled craftsmen or specialists and the possibility of using labour-saving machinery is limited. Many businesses adopt this method of production when they are 'starting up'. The advantages and disadvantages of job production are shown in Table 1.

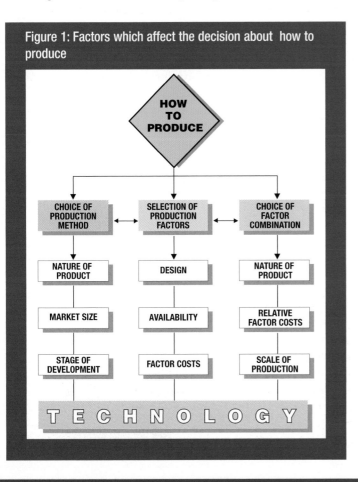

Figure 1: Factors which affect the decision about how to produce

Table 1: Advantages and disadvantages of job production

Advantages

- Firms can produce unique or 'one-off' orders according to customer needs. For example, a wedding dress may be designed and produced for the individual taste of a client. It is also possible to change the specifications of a job at the last minute, even if the work has actually begun.
- Workers are more likely to be motivated. The tasks employees carry out often require a variety of skills, knowledge and expertise. Their work will be more demanding and interesting. They will also see the end result of their efforts and be able to take pride in their work. Jobs may be carried out by a team of workers aiming to achieve the same objectives. This should help raise the level of job satisfaction.
- The organisation of job production is fairly simple. Because only one job is done at a time, co-ordination, communication, supervision and inspection can take place regularly. Also, it is easier to identify and deal with problems, such as a defective damp proof course in a house or a poorly cooked meal in a restaurant.

Disadvantages

- Labour costs will be high because production tends to be labour intensive. The workforce is likely to be skilled and more versatile. Such employees will be more expensive. The amount of time each employee spends on a particular job will also be long.
- Because there is a variety of work, subject to many specifications, the business would need a wide range of tools, machines and equipment. This can prove expensive. Also, it may not be possible to achieve economies of scale because only one 'job' is produced at a time.
- Lead times can be lengthy. When building a house, the business has to incur costs which cannot be recovered until the house is sold. Sometimes the sale of a house can take a long time.
- Selling costs may also be high. This is likely if the product is highly complex and technical. The sales team will need to be well qualified, able to cope with questions and deal with problems concerning sales and installation. Some firms employ agencies to help reduce their selling costs.
- Once the demand for a firm's product rises, job production may become costly. Firms may prefer to use a method more suited to producing larger quantities. This is not always the case. Even if demand is high, each customer may require a unique order. In addition, many firms believe that the 'personal touch' they can offer in job production is important. As a result, they may choose not to change to other production methods. Other production methods require some degree of product standardisation. This may result in more efficient production, but a loss of 'individuality'.

Table 2: Operations involved in the production of a batch of bread

1. Blend ingredients in a mixing container until a dough is formed.
2. Knead the dough for a period of time.
3. Leave the dough to rise for a period of time.
4. Divide the dough into suitable units (loaves) for baking.
5. Bake the loaves.
6. Allow loaves to cool.

Batch production

Batch production may be used when demand for a firm's product or service is regular rather than a 'one off'. An example might be a furniture factory, where a batch of armchairs is made to a particular design. Production is divided into a number of operations. A particular operation is carried out on all products in a batch. The batch then moves to the next operation. A baker uses batch production when baking bread. The operations in the baking process are broken down in Table 2.

These operations would be performed on every batch of bread. There is some standardisation because each loaf in the batch will be the same. However, it may be possible to vary each batch. The ingredients could be changed to produce brown bread or the style of baking tin could be changed for different shaped loaves.

A great number of products are produced using this method, particularly in manufacturing, such as the production of components and food processing. For example, in a canning plant, a firm may can several different batches of soup, each batch being a different recipe. Products can be produced in very large or very small batches, depending on the level of demand. Larger production runs tend to lower the **unit** or **average cost** of production. New technology is increasingly being introduced to make batch production more efficient. The advantages and disadvantages of batch production are shown in Table 3.

Flow production

Most people will have some idea of flow production from pictures of motor car factories. Production is organised so that different operations can be carried out, one after the other, in a continuous sequence. Vehicles move from one operation to the next, often on a conveyer belt. The main features of flow production are:

- the production of large quantities;
- a simplified or standardised product;
- a semi-skilled workforce, specialising in one operation only;
- large amounts of machinery and equipment;
- large stocks of raw materials and components.

Table 3: Advantages and disadvantges of batch production

Advantages

- Even though larger quantities are produced than in job production, there is still flexibility. Each batch can be changed to meet customers' wishes. It is particularly suitable for a wide range of similar products. The settings on machines can be changed according to specifications, such as different clothes sizes.
- Employees can concentrate on one operation rather than on the whole task. This reduces the need for costly, skilled employees.
- Less variety of machinery would be needed than in job production because the products are standardised. Also, it is possible to use more standardised machinery.
- It often results in stocks of partly finished goods which have to be stored. This means firms can respond more quickly to an urgent order by processing a batch quickly through the final stages of production.

Disadvantages

- Careful planning and co-ordination are needed, or machines and workers may be idle, waiting for a whole batch to finish its previous operation. There is often a need to clean and adjust machinery before the next batch can be produced. This can mean delays. In brewing, one day of the week is used to clean equipment before the next batch begins.
- Some machinery may have to be more complex to compensate for the lower skill levels required from the labour force. This may lead to higher costs.
- The workforce may be less motivated, since they have to repeat operations on every single unit in the batch. In addition, they are unlikely to be involved with production from start to finish.
- If batches are small then unit costs will remain relatively high.
- Money will be tied up in work-in-progress, since an order cannot be dispatched until the whole batch has been finished.

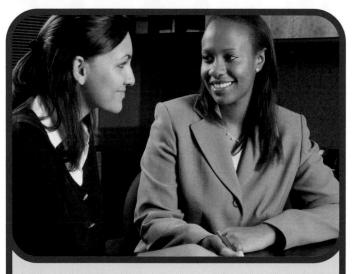

Question 1.

Samiksha Mirza is a chartered accountant. She runs a small business from an office in Kidderminster producing final accounts for sole traders, partnerships and small private limited companies. She has a client base of around 110 businesses and employs a secretary and a young trainee accountant. In addition to preparing accounts she offers other services such as:

- completing tax returns;
- taxation planning;
- advice on the financial management of businesses;
- advice on investment;
- auditing.

(a) Use this case as an example to explain what is meant by job production.

(b) Explain why job production might help to motivate Samiksha and her trainee.

Flow production is used in the manufacture of products as varied as newspapers, food and cement. It is sometimes called **mass production**, as it tends to be used for the production of large numbers of standard products, such as cars or breakfast cereals. Certain types of flow production are known as **continual flow production**, because products such as clothing material pass continually through a series of processes. **Repetitive flow production** is the manufacture of large numbers of the same product, such as plastic toy parts or metal cans.

The advantages and disadvantages of flow production are shown in Table 4. In the 1990s flow production processes were changed in an attempt to solve some of the problems. Japanese manufacturers setting up businesses in the UK introduced methods to improve efficiency. Just-in-time manufacturing, for example, helped to reduce the cost of holding stocks. Some vehicle manufacturers attempted to introduce an element of job production into flow processes by **customising** products for clients. For example, a range of different cars was produced on the same production line. Cars in the same model range differed in colour, engine size, trim and interior design.

Process production

PROCESS PRODUCTION is a form of flow production which is used in the oil or chemical industry. Materials pass through a plant where a series of processes are carried out in order to change the product. An example might be the refining of crude oil into petrol.

Flow production relies on the use of computers. Computers send instructions to machines, control production speeds and conditions, and monitor quality. They allow large numbers of products to be produced continuously to exact standards or control continuous production, which requires many processes.

Choice of production method

Table 4: Advantages and disadvantages of flow production

Advantages

- Unit costs are reduced as firms gain from economies of scale.
- In many industries the process is highly automated. Production is controlled by computers. Many of the operations are performed by robots and other types of machinery. Once the production line is set up and running, products can flow off the end non stop for lengthy periods of time. This can reduce the need for labour, as only machine supervisors are needed.
- The need to stockpile finished goods is reduced. The production line can respond to short-term changes in demand. For example, if demand falls the line can be shut down for a period of time. If it rises then the line can be opened.

Disadvantages

- The set--up costs are very high. An enormous investment in plant and equipment is needed. Firms must therefore be confident that demand for the product is sufficient over a period of time to make the investment pay.
- The product will be standardised. It is not possible to offer a wide product range and meet different customers' needs. However, modern machinery is becoming more flexible and is beginning to overcome this problem.
- For a number of reasons, worker motivation can be a serious problem. Most of the manual operations required on the production line will be repetitive and boring. Factories with production lines tend to be very noisy. Each worker will only be involved in a very small part of the job cycle. As a result of these problems worker morale may be low and labour turnover and absenteeism high.
- Breakdowns can prove costly. The whole production system is interdependent. If one part of the supply or production line fails the whole system may break down.

The method of production chosen might depend on a number of factors.

The nature of the product Many products require a specific method of production. For example, in the construction industry, projects such as bridges, roads, office blocks and sewers must be produced using job production. Cereal farming involves batch production. A plot of land undergoes several processes before it 'produces' a crop.

The size of the market Fast-moving consumer goods like soap, confectionery and canned drinks are normally produced using flow production because the market is so big. When the market is small, flow production techniques are not cost effective.

The stage of development a business has reached When firms are first set up, they often produce small levels of output and

employ job or batch production methods. As they grow and enjoy higher sales levels, they may switch to flow production.

Technology The current state of technology will affect all decisions concerning how to produce. As technology advances, new materials and machinery become available. Changes in technology often result in firms adopting new methods of production. For example, the development of computers and robotic welders has radically changed the way in which cars are manufactured. Also, car manufacturers are now able to produce different models on the same production line at the same time.

Question 2.

Uniform+ was established in 1997 and has become a leading supplier of workwear, leisurewear and promotional clothing to businesses and organisations across the UK. In 2006, the company moved to a purpose-built freehold head office and factory in Cannock. Uniform+ supplies over 12,000 garments a week to more than 5,500 customers. The company has an excellent reputation in the industry because of their:

- commitment to offering a wide choice of quality clothing at unbeatable prices;
- dedication to providing excellent customer service and value for money;
- fast turnaround and flexibilty to meet customers' needs;
- unique free logo and delivery service.

Like most companies in the clothes industry, Uniform+ uses batch production. The company can meet a wide range of different orders due the flexibility of its machinery and its multi-skilled workforce.

(a) Use the clothes industry as an example to explain what is meant by batch production.

(b) Why is batch production common in the clothes industry?

(c) How do you think Uniform+ has overcome some of the typical problems associated with batch production?

KEYTERMS

Batch production – a method which involves completing one operation at a time on all units before performing the next.

Flow production – very large scale production of a standardised product, where each operation on a unit is performed continuously, one after the other, usually on a production line.

Job production – a method of production which involves employing all factors to complete one unit of output at a time.

Process production – a form of flow production where materials pass through a plant where a series of processes are carried out in order to change the product.

Productive efficiency – production methods which minimise unit costs.

KNOWLEDGE

1. What are the three main decisions which have to be made regarding the method of production?
2. Under what circumstances might a business become more capital intensive?
3. State three types of products which may be manufactured using job production.
4. Describe the advantages and disadvantages of job production.
5. State three products that are generally manufactured using batch production.
6. Describe the advantages and disadvantages of batch production.
7. Describe four features of flow production.

Case Study: *Nacional*

Nacional is a major breakfast cereal manufacturer in Portugal and forms part of the grain milling Amorim-Lage Group. The popularity of breakfast cereals has grown in Portugal in recent years and one of Nacional's main production facilities was in need of a major update and expansion using new technology and new ideas. Early in 2004, Nacional carried out a major refit and expansion plan that was completed by mid-September. The investment in the new facility was estimated at 11.2 million euros.

Nacional's main product was cornflakes but since the expansion the facility has been able to manufacture a variety of extruded breakfast cereal products for marketing under its own brand names and also for supermarket own-brand labels. The adoption of extrusion techniques (drawing a dough mixture through a shape to produce a continuous strand with an identical cross section which can be cut into shapes such as stars or squares for example) in processing breakfast cereal at the Nacional plant has widened the production possibilities because a variety of grains can now be used. This has allowed the blending of different grains into unique cereal pieces. Extrusion has also made production more efficient by combining several processing steps into a single, continuous flow.

PV Baker has supplied and installed a complete processing plant for Nacional. It incorporates the entire production process, from compounding and mixing the recipe 'dough' through extrusion and cooking to drying and coating the final extruded product shapes. The new facility can make a variety of different products, including corn-balls, coco-balls, choco curls, golden squares, stars and rings, as well as co-extruded filled pillow shapes. All of these extruded shapes, except the pillows, will be coated with a honey, sugar or glucose based glaze.

Most of the products are cut into individual pieces by a die as they leave the extruder. A key design feature of the facility is the ability to change over rapidly between products in response to market demand, including those products involving different raw materials and syrup. For example, to create filled pillow products, which cannot be cut at the die, a mobile crimping unit is wheeled in and out of the line.

Source: adapted from www.foodprocessing-technology.com

(a) State four processes used in the production of breakfast cereals at Nacional. (4 marks)
(b) Explain how Nacional is using both batch production and flow production methods in its factory. (10 marks)
(c) When upgrading its production facilities, what role did technology play at Nacional? (6 marks)
(d) To what extent do you think the 11.2 million euro investment will benefit Nacional? (20 marks)

36 Quality

What is quality?

Consumers, faced with many goods or services at similar prices, are likely to consider QUALITY when making choices. Quality could be described as those features of a product or service that allow it to satisfy customers' wants. Take an example of a family buying a television. They may consider some of the following features:

- physical appearance – they may want a certain style;
- reliability and durability - will it last for 10 years?
- special features – does it have stereo sound?
- suitability – they may want a portable television;
- parts – are spare parts available?
- repairs – does the shop carry out maintenance?
- after sales service – how prompt is delivery?

They may also consider features which they perceive as important, such as:

- image – is the manufacturer's name widely recognised?
- reputation – what do other consumers think of the business or product?

The importance of quality has grown in recent years. Consumers are more aware. They get information through magazines such as *Which?* that contain reports on the quality of certain products. They also have more disposable income and higher expectations than ever before. Legislation and competition have also forced firms to improve the quality of their products.

Businesses, faced with competition, are also concerned about the quality of their:

- design – the ideas and plans for the product or service;
- production processes – the methods used to manufacture the goods or provide the services.

Poor designs may lead to problems with the materials and the functions of the finished good or service. It costs time and money to redesign poor products. Clients are unlikely to use businesses with poor designs again. Problems also occur with poor quality production processes. Faulty products are costly for a business. Machinery that breaks down or constantly needs to be repaired will also be expensive. Late delivery and ineffective productivity that results in poor quality can harm a business's reputation.

Traditional quality control

Traditionally, in manufacturing, production departments have been responsible for ensuring quality. Their objectives might have been to make sure that products:

- satisfied consumers' needs;
- worked under conditions they were likely to face;
- operated in the way they should;
- could be produced cost effectively;
- could be repaired easily;
- conformed to safety standards set down by legislation and independent bodies.

At Kellogg's, the cereal manufacturer, for example, samples of breakfast cereal have, in the past, been taken from the

Question 1.

Airbus S.A.S. is the aircraft manufacturing subsidiary of EADS N.V., a pan-European aerospace business. Based at Toulouse, France with significant operations in other European states, Airbus produces around half of the world's jet airliners. Airbus employs around 57,000 people at sixteen sites in four European countries. Airbus' customers expect quality in the aircraft they buy. Safety, reliability, comfort and maintenance costs are key areas where quality is crucial in an airline's judgment of an aircraft. To achieve the very highest standards in these and other aspects of an aircraft's performance the question of quality is addressed by Airbus at every stage, from design to final assembly and beyond. Repeated checks are made. Tests are applied. Airbus ensures every supplier of parts meets the strictest standards on quality. Defective work, parts and materials are rejected.

Delivering aircraft on time, on cost and on quality – getting it right first time – is the goal Airbus continually strives for. Airbus has a network of key employees who identify problems at various stages of design, production and assembly and recommend action to eradicate them, pre-empting possible costly delays at a later point. These employees also ensure continuous improvement in standards and efficiency by pinpointing ways in which people could work better or tools and materials could be improved. As it raises production to meet demand, Airbus knows setting even higher standards in quality is critical to maintaining its success.

Source: adapted from www.airbus.com.

(a) (i) What features do customers of Airbus consider important when buying aircraft?
(ii) Which of the features in (i) do you think is the most important?
(b) What measures does Airbus take to meet the high quality aspirations of customers?

production line every half hour and tested. The testing took place in a food review room twice a day and was undertaken by a small group of staff. Each sample, about 50 in total, was compared with a 'perfect' Kellogg's sample and given a grade between 1 and 10. 10 was perfect but between 9.8 and 7, although noticeable to the trained eye, was acceptable to the customer. Below 7 the consumer would notice the reduction in quality. The cereals were tested for appearance, texture, colour, taste etc. More sophisticated tests were carried out in a laboratory where the nutritional value of a sample, for example, was measured.

QUALITY CONTROL in UK organisations, in the past, often meant **quality controllers** or **quality inspectors** checking other people's work and the product itself after production had taken place. By today's standards this is not quality control, but a method of finding a poor quality product (or a problem) before it is sold to the consumer.

Quality assurance

Today businesses are less concerned about 'Has the job been done properly?' than 'Are we able to do the job properly?' In other words inspection is carried out during the production process. This means that problems and poor quality products can be prevented before final production.

Such a preventative approach has been used by Japanese businesses and is known as TOTAL QUALITY MANAGEMENT (TQM). It is now being adopted by many companies in the UK. It involves all employees in a business contributing to and being responsible for ensuring quality at all stages in the production process. QUALITY ASSURANCE is a commitment by a business to maintain quality throughout the organisation. The aim is to stop problems before they occur rather than finding them after they occur.

Quality assurance also takes into account customers' views when planning the production process. For example, customers may be consulted about their views through market research before a product is manufactured or a service provided. They may also be part of a consultation group involved at the design and manufacturing stage.

Total quality management

Errors are costly for business. It is estimated that about one-third of all the effort of British businesses is wasted in correcting errors. There are benefits if something is done right the first time. Total quality management (TQM) is a method designed to prevent errors, such as the creation of poor quality products, from happening. The business is organised so that the manufacturing process is investigated at every stage. It is argued that the success of Japanese companies is based on their superior organisation. Every department, activity and individual is organised to take into account quality at all times. What are the features of TQM?

Quality chains Great stress is placed on the operation of

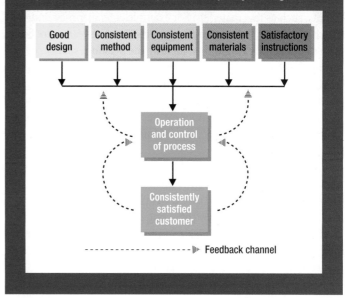

QUALITY CHAINS. In any business a series of suppliers and customers exists. For example, a secretary is a supplier to a manager, who is the customer. The secretarial duties must be carried out to the satisfaction of the manager. The chain also includes customers and suppliers outside the business. The chain remains intact if the supplier satisfies the customer. It is broken if a person or item of equipment does not satisfy the needs of the customer. Failure to meet the requirements in any part of the quality chain creates problems, such as delays in the next stage of production.

Company policy, accountability and empowerment There will only be improvements in quality if there is a company-wide quality policy. TQM must start from the top with the most senior executive and spread throughout the business to every employee. People must be totally committed and take a 'pride in the job'. This might be considered as an example of job enrichment. Lack of commitment, particularly at the top, causes problems. For example, if the managing director lacks commitment, employees lower down are unlikely to commit themselves. TQM stresses the role of the individual and aims to make everyone accountable for their own performance. For example, a machine operator may be accountable to a workshop supervisor for his work. They may also be empowered to make decisions.

Control Consumers' needs will only be satisfied if the business has control of the factors that affect a product's quality. These may be human, administrative or technical factors, shown in Figure 1. The process is only under control if materials, equipment and tasks are used in the same way every time. Take an example of a firm making biscuits. Only by cooking in the same way can the quality be consistent every time.

These methods can be documented and used to assess operations. Regular audits must be carried out by the firm to check quality. Information is then fed back from the customer to the 'operator' or producer, and from the operator to the supplier of inputs, such as raw materials. For example, a retailer may return a batch of vehicles to the manufacturer because the gears were faulty. The manufacturer might then identify the person responsible for fitting the gears. An investigation might reveal that the faulty gears were the responsibility of a component supplier. The supplier can then be contacted and the problem resolved. Quality audits and reviews may lead to suggestions for improvements - a different material, perhaps, or a new piece of equipment.

Monitoring the process TQM relies on monitoring the business process to find possible improvements. Methods have been developed to help achieve this. STATISTICAL PROCESS CONTROL (SPC) involves collecting data relating to the performance of a process. Data is presented in diagrams, charts and graphs. The information is then passed to all those concerned.

SPC can be used to reduce variability, which is the cause of most quality problems. Variations in products, delivery times, methods, materials, people's attitudes and staff performance often occur. For example, statistical data may show that worker attitudes may have led to variations in output late on Friday afternoon. Discussion might result in a change in the 'clocking on' and 'clocking off' times to solve the problem.

Teamwork TQM stresses that teamwork is the most effective way of solving problems. The main advantages are:
- a greater range of skills, knowledge and experience can be used to solve the problem;
- employee morale is often improved;
- problems across departments are better dealt with;
- a greater variety of problems can be tackled;
- team 'ideas' are more likely to be used than individual ones.

TQM strongly favours teamwork throughout the business. It builds trust and morale, improves communications and cooperation and develops interdependence. Many UK firms in the past have suffered due to lack of sharing of information and ideas. Such approaches have often led to division between sections of the workforce.

Consumer views Firms using TQM must be committed to their customers. They must be responsive to changes in people's needs and expectations. To do this, information must be gathered on a regular basis and there must be clear communication channels for customers to express their views. Consumers are often influential in setting quality standards. For example, holiday companies issue questionnaires to their customers on the way back from a package holiday. The information can be used to identify the strengths and weaknesses of their operations. Such information can be used to monitor and upgrade quality standards.

Zero defects Many business quality systems have a zero defect policy. This aims to ensure that every product that is manufactured is free from defects. A business that is able to guarantee zero defects in customers' orders is likely to gain a good reputation. This could lead to new clients and improved sales.

Quality circles TQM stresses the importance of teamwork in a business. Many businesses have introduced quality circles into their operations. Quality circles are small groups of staff, usually from the same work area, who meet on a regular and voluntary basis. They meet in the employer's time and attempt to solve problems and make suggestions about how to improve various aspects of the business. Issues such as pay and conditions are normally excluded. After discussions, the team will present its ideas and solutions to management. Teams are also involved in implementing and monitoring the effectiveness of solutions. In order for quality circles to be successful certain conditions must exist.
- A steering committee should be set up to oversee the whole quality circle programme.
- A senior manager should ideally chair the committee. Managers must show commitment to the principle of

---

Question 2.

Compsoft is a UK-based company which produces tailor-made data management software for high-growth businesses. One of Compsoft's first products was Delta, a market-leading DOS-based database which is still used by many organisations today. Compsoft also developed Equinox, a rapid application development tool and database environment. Equinox is used by SMEs, blue-chip companies and governmental bodies.

Compsoft is committed to quality assurance and has been awarded ISO 9001, the internationally recognised standard for the quality management of businesses. As a result Compsoft has adopted the BSI framework to monitor its business processes to ensure the quality of service provided to its customers. Some of the basic requirements of certification include:
- adapting a set of procedures that cover all key processes in the business;
- monitoring development processes to ensure they are producing quality products;
- keeping records;
- checking outgoing applications for defects, with appropriate corrective action where necessary;
- regularly reviewing individual processes and the quality system itself for effectiveness;
- facilitating continual improvement.

Regular monitoring ensures that these standards are upheld and that Compsoft remains worthy of its title as an accredited ISO 9001 provider.

Source: adapted from www.compsoft.co.uk.

(a) (i) What is quality assurance?
　　(ii) How does Compsoft ensure quality in its business?
(b) What role does the BSI play in Compsoft's quality assurance?
(c) What benefits might Compsoft enjoy as a result of ISO 9001 certification?

quality circles.

- At least one person on the committee should be accountable for the programme.
- Team leaders should be properly trained.

Using TQM TQM helps companies to:

- focus clearly on the needs of customers and relationships between suppliers and customers;
- achieve quality in all aspects of business, not just product or service quality;
- critically analyse all processes to remove waste and inefficiencies;
- find improvements and develop measures of performance;
- develop a team approach to problem solving;
- develop effective procedures for communication and acknowledgement of work;
- continually review the processes to develop a strategy of constant improvement.

There are, however, some problems.

- There will be training and development costs of the new system.
- TQM will only work if there is commitment from the entire business.
- There will be a great deal of bureaucracy and documents and regular audits will be needed. This may be a problem for small firms.
- Stress is placed on the process and not the product.

ISO standards

Businesses can work to quality assurance **codes of practice**. These show that a production process has been carried out to a certain standard and to the required specification. Once a business has been assessed and has achieved a certain standard, it is regularly checked by the awarding organisation to make sure standards are maintained. ISO 9000 is an international standard which businesses seek to achieve.

The **British Standards Institution** (BSI) is an independent organisation that attempts to set quality standards in industry. The BSI and other independent bodies, such as Lloyds, offer BS EN ISO 9000 registration. The title reflects the European (EN) and international (ISO) recognition for this series. BS EN ISO 9001 gives quality assurance in design, development, production, installation and servicing and is suitable for businesses which have a large element of design in their operations. BS EN ISO 9002 gives quality assurance in production, installation and servicing, for businesses which produce fairly standard products with little or no design. BS EN ISO 9003 gives quality assurance in final inspection and testing. This standard is suitable for small firms or where customers can check quality themselves through inspection.

Firms seeking certification have to show that their methods and procedures meet the recognised standards and comply with requirements. They are inspected on a regular basis to make sure that standards are being maintained. BS EN ISO 9000

certification can help a business to:

- examine and improve systems, methods and procedures to lower costs;
- motivate staff and encourage them to get things right first time;
- define key roles, responsibilities and authorities;
- ensure that orders are consistently delivered on time;
- highlight product or design problems and develop improvements;
- record and investigate all quality failure and customer complaints and make sure that they do not reoccur;
- give a clear signal to customers that it is taking measures to improve quality;
- produce a documented system for recording and satisfying the training needs of new and existing staff regarding quality.

Product standards

Businesses may include signs and symbols on their products which tell a customer about the product's standards. Certain bodies have also been set up to ensure the quality of goods and services.

British Standards Institution Any business can apply to the BSI for an inspection of its product. Those that achieve and maintain a standard can carry the BSI Kitemark. The Kitemark tells the customer that the product has been tested to destruction, to ensure that it meets with certain safety standards. Products that carry a Kitemark include some cricket helmets, kitchen units, child car safety seats, door locks, curtains, and sofa and duvet covers.

The BSI also issues a number of other product standards. These include ensuring:

- products conform to yachting standards;
- the tensile strength of yarns;
- performance levels for the amount of UV light through sunglasses;
- grades of carpet pile, according to quality and durability.

The British Electrotechnical Approvals Board (BEAB) Now part of Intertek, a global leader in testing, inspection and certification, this is a body which inspects domestic electrical equipment. Manufacturers of domestic electrical appliances will be keen for the BEAB to approve their products. Approval can serve as a recognition of quality that customers will recognise.

The Association of British Travel Agents (ABTA) The Association of British Travel Agents is a trade association which has drawn up a code of practice for its members. The code aims to improve the trading standards of activities related to the sale of holidays. Travel agents are allowed to register with ABTA if they agree to follow its code of practice.

The Wool Marketing Board This allows manufacturers to carry labels such as the Wool Mark if their garments are made entirely of pure new wool. Obtaining a trademark is a way for a firm to give quality assurance to customers. If customers know that the quality of a product is guaranteed, they are more likely to buy the product. Also, there is less need to inspect the product, and returns and re-ordering are reduced.

The British Toy and Hobby Association (BTHA) developed the Lion Mark as a symbol of toy safety to be displayed on toy packaging. Toy manufacturers that want to include the Lion Mark must take out a licence with the BTHA. The manufacturer must sign a strict code of practice which sets standards relating to toy safety and advertising, as well as counterfeiting and markings on toy guns. The Lion Mark was adapted by the BTHA and the British Association of Toy Retailers (BATR) for shops. If the symbol is displayed in a shop it indicates that the retailer has agreed to a strict code of practice. They agree only to offer safe toys for sale and to ensure staff are briefed on toy safety matters such as age warnings.

The Consumers Association This is a body which follows up complaints by people about faulty products or services. It also makes recommendations about products and services to customers. These take into account such things as quality, reliability and value for money. Often survey results appear in its *Which?* magazine.

The Institute of Quality Assurance (IQA) The Institute of Quality Assurance is a professional body in the UK whose purpose is the promotion and advancement of quality practices. The IQA has three main objectives.

- To seek the advancement of quality management and practices and help the exchange of related information and ideas.
- To promote the education, training, qualification and development of people involved in quality assurance and the management of quality.
- To provide a range of services to members and, where appropriate, to the community at large.

Some businesses support their products with WARRANTIES. If goods are warranted, it means that the manufacturer will undertake any necessary work arising from a defect in the product 'free of charge'. Warranties are popular with products such as cars and a wide range of electrical appliances.

A number of laws exist which protect consumers from poor trading practices. They have tended to focus on safety aspects and consumer exploitation. However, increasingly UK laws and EU regulations are taking into account product quality. Existing laws are enforced by local inspectors, called **Trading Standards Officers**.

Costs and benefits of ensuring quality

Firms will want to monitor the costs of quality control carefully. All businesses are likely to face costs when trying to maintain or

improve the quality of their products and services.

- The cost of designing and setting up a quality control system. This might include the time used to 'think through' a system and to train staff to use it.
- There might be a cost in terms of lost production. When a business introduces a major new system there may be some serious disruption while the new system is 'bedded-in'. This could lead to a loss of output and damage to customer relations if orders are not met.
- The cost of monitoring the system. This could be the salary of a supervisor or the cost of an electronic sensor.
- There will be costs if products do not come up to standard. Faulty goods may have to be scrapped or reworked. Product failures might also result in claims against a company, bad publicity and a possible loss of goodwill.
- The cost of improving the actual quality. This may be the cost of new machinery or of training staff in new working practices.
- If the whole quality system fails, there may be costs in setting it up again. Time may be needed to 'rethink' or adjust the system. Retraining might also be necessary.
- Quality initiatives will only be successful if the people involved in their implementation are properly trained. This can prove very costly. For example, if TQM is introduced the entire workforce will have to be trained. This may involve sending all staff on specialist training courses or outsourcing training to an expert in TQM.

It has been suggested that between 10-20 per cent of the revenue of a business is accounted for by quality related costs. This means that UK businesses could save billions of pounds by cutting such costs. The vast majority of these costs is spent on appraisal and failure, which add very little to the quality of the product. Eliminating failure will also help to reduce appraisal and failure costs.

Although quality control systems are costly, it is argued that their benefits outweigh the costs. The actual quality of the product should be improved, so customers are more likely to purchase the product. Business costs may be cut if faults in products are identified before the product reaches the market. The costs of failure once the product has reached the market are likely to be much higher than those incurred during manufacture.

Quality, USP and pricing flexibility

Some businesses use quality as a means of developing a unique selling point (USP). If a business can differentiate its product on grounds of quality and persuade the customer that its product is superior to its rivals, it may enjoy some benefits. One of the main benefits is the ability to charge a higher price. If consumers are convinced that a product is superior in quality to those of its rivals, they are often prepared to pay higher prices. This gives a business more flexibility in pricing. For example, Porsche, the performance car manufacturer, has a global reputation for high quality. Consequently it is able to charge premium prices for their range of sports cars.

KEYTERMS

Quality – features of a product that allow it to satisfy customers' needs. It may refer to some standard of excellence.

Quality assurance – a method of working for businesses that takes into account customers' wants when standardising quality. It often involves guaranteeing that quality standards are met.

Quality chains – created when employees form a series of links between customers and suppliers in business, both internally and externally.

Quality control – making sure that the quality of a product meets specified quality performance criteria.

Statistical process control – the collection of data about the performance of a particular process in a business.

Total quality management – a managerial approach which focuses on quality and aims to improve the effectiveness, flexibility, and competitiveness of a business.

Warranties – guarantees that faulty products will be repaired or replaced within a period of time.

KNOWLEDGE

1. What is meant by the quality of a product?
2. Explain the difference between actual and perceived quality.
3. Explain the difference between quality control and quality assurance.
4. State 5 implications of TQM for a business.
5. Why is teamwork so important in TQM?
6. How does ISO 9000 affect a business?
7. What is the role of the British Standards Institution?
8. Explain the advantage of manufacturing trademarks to a business.
9. What are the costs and benefits of ensuring quality?

Case Study: GNY Building Materials

GNY Building Materials is a multi-location ready mix concrete, sand and gravel supplier. It employs over 350 staff and is currently faced with the twin problems of escalating costs and ailing customer service. After an important board meeting it was decided to create a new business culture, a culture which valued quality, customer service and continuous improvement. A business consultant was commissioned to perform a TQM readiness assessment, organise a Quality Steering Committee, train the management and hourly employees in TQM and support the work of the departmentally based Quality Teams and the cross functional Corrective Action Teams.

When the consultant began work it was apparent that the company did not have a history of participative management and reacted slowly to opportunities. Initial interviews confirmed that management was viewed sceptically. Poor internal communication led to employees feeling fear and resentment. Also, the business faced increasingly aggressive competition. A major objective for implementing TQM was to eliminate the waste in delivery and improve the reliability of delivery. The chairman made it plain that the savings from improvements would fund the culture he needed to foster in order to implement TQM.

Implementing TQM

There was a number of steps involved in implementing TQM at the business.

STEP 1 Perform a TQM readiness assessment. Over a five day period all of the senior management team and several hourly employees were interviewed. This highlighted several areas for targeted customer service improvement and cost reduction. TQM training was developed and initial Corrective Action Teams (CATs) were formed.

STEP 2 Communicate the vision to every single employee in the company. The chairman told each employee his vision for the business.

STEP 3 Organise the steering committee and train the management

team. Training was further developed in the six TQM training sessions.

By incorporating their culture, credibility was improved. In addition, training improved the application of TQM ideas and broke down barriers to change. Four groups of twenty employees were then trained. The consultant trained in-house trainers to continue the training of employees. A second, but equally important, task continued parallel to the training. The Corrective Action Team (CAT) used the TQM process to improve the customer service levels and eliminate waste in trucking. It used each of the five critical areas in TQM to generate the needed changes in their trucking operations. These were considered to be the following.

- Customer Focus
- Waste Elimination
- Teamwork
- Continuous Improvement
- Problem Solving

Over three months the business generated cost reduction initiatives worth £600,000 and implemented over £300,000 of cost savings. This major victory by hourly and first line management demonstrated the effectiveness of TQM. GNY Building Materials realised a 25:1 payback on its investment in Total Quality Management. Their premier service reputation was restored and it became the preferred supplier to many contractors. According to the chairman, the company has become much more flexible and responsive. Improvements to the bottom line confirm this.

(a) What is a TQM readiness assessment? (4 marks)
(b) Why did GNY Building Materials introduce TQM? (6 marks)
(c) How important was training in the implementation of TQM at GNY Building Materials? (8 marks)
(d) Examine the likely costs incurred by GNY Building Materials when implementing TQM. (10 marks)
(e) Evaluate the benefits to GNY Building Materials of introducing TQM. (16 marks)

What is customer service?

CUSTOMER SERVICE is about meeting the needs of customers. Customer service can be defined as 'a series of activities designed to enhance the level of customer satisfaction – the feeling that a product or service has met the customer's expectations'. Customer service has become increasingly important in recent years due to market orientation and the belief held by businesses about the importance of customers. If businesses offer good customer service, they are more likely to see customers return. Customers may also recommend products to their friends and relatives if they have enjoyed good customer service. Some businesses aim to exceed customer expectations. This approach should go a long way to satisfying customers.

The nature of customer service can vary quite significantly depending on the type of business providing it. Some examples are given below.

- Being courteous, friendly and helpful to customers.
- Dealing with complaints and problems in a sensitive and practical manner.
- Providing an Internet tracking service so that customers can see how their orders are progressing.
- Providing information, and advice about products.
- Providing assistance such as helping a non-English speaker complete an application form for a sports club.
- Offering extra services, such as a hotel providing free champagne, chocolates, flowers and a bowl of fresh fruit to honeymooners.

Customer service and communication

Call centres Customer service can be provided over the telephone. Many financial institutions such as banks and insurance companies, travel companies and the providers of utilities, use CALL CENTRES to provide customer service. Call centres have large numbers of staff or **call centre agents** who deal with telephone calls from customers. Someone working at a call centre for a bank may deal with a query on a customer's bank statement, for example. People working at call centres generally sit in front of a computer and respond to customers' telephone calls all day. All the information they need to provide customer service, including customers' account details, can usually be accessed from the computer.

However, some customers do not like call centres and their criticisms generally follow a number of common themes, for example:

- operators working from a script – too impersonal;
- non-expert operators;
- incompetent or untrained operators incapable of processing customers' requests effectively;
- overseas locations, with language and accent problems;

Question 1.

Asda, the supermarket chain, provides a variety of customer services.

Instore Greeters Greeters are customer care specialists who are trained to help customers with all their enquiries. ASDA are proud of their warm and friendly Greeters who always give customers a genuine welcome as they walk into the store. They provide a range of help, from selecting the right shopping trolley to suit customers' shopping needs, helping wheelchair users and directing customers to the right aisle.

Trolley range Asda offers customers a wide range of trolleys ranging from smaller smart shoppers to larger 175 litre trolleys with child seats. Its fleet of trolleys also accommodates the elderly and disabled. It has low and high trolleys which attach to wheelchairs along with Senior Citizen trolleys to help less able customers to get around the store.

Electric Karts To help less able shoppers navigate stores Asda introduced Electric Mart Karts to all food stores. ASDA was the first major retailer to introduce them. The Mart Karts are easy to use and all customers are given a demonstration when joining the Asda 'Scooter Club'.

Refund policy If customers are not happy with any purchase of branded items they simply return the product and Asda will offer a full refund or a replacement product. A receipt is preferred but not essential.

Exchange policy When customers purchase an electrical item they can ask for their receipt to be placed into a free Guarantee Wallet. This means that their purchase is guaranteed for a full year. However, customers will need to keep their own receipt to cover the warranty.

Source: adapted from www.asda-corporate.com.

(a) Using examples from the case, explain what is meant by customer service.
(b) How might Asda benefit by training staff in customer service?

- automated queuing systems. This sometimes results in excessively long hold times;
- a lack of communication between different business departments

Online A growing number of businesses have their own websites and provide customer service online. For example, people can get information about products and services. They can also buy products online. One common customer service is to provide answers to a list of FAQ (frequently asked questions). Also, if a person wants further information from a business they can ask questions using email. Email is increasingly used as a means of responding to customers by businesses. In some cases this has replaced the work of call centres. Many businesses prefer to provide customer service in this way because it is cheaper than answering customers' telephone calls.

Methods of meeting customer expectations

Since the provision of customer service has become increasingly important, businesses have developed different ways of identifying customer expectations and meeting them.

Market research In order to meet customer expectations it is necessary to identify them. One obvious way is to carry out market research to find out exactly what customers expect. A wide range of market research techniques could be used. These include exit surveys, telephone surveys, customer satisfaction questionnaires, focus groups, in-depth interviews and online surveys. Online surveys have become very popular with businesses. They can be used to find out what customers thought about the quality of customer service when buying online or how useful customers found the website, for example.

Customer satisfaction surveys are widely used in leisure and tourism. For example, hotels often leave short questionnaires in their rooms for guests to complete before they leave. Tour operators often ask holidaymakers to complete customer satisfaction surveys on the plane during the journey home. Some businesses employ market research agencies to carry out in-depth customer satisfaction surveys. However, these can be very expensive.

Once information from market research has been gathered and analysed, it can be used to design customer service provision. Some businesses will aim to provide customer service which they hope will exceed customer expectations.

Training Businesses are more likely to meet customer needs if staff are trained to deliver good customer service. Staff who come into direct contact with customers might be trained in a variety of skills to help provide better customer service. Some examples are shown in Figure 1.

A business may use off-the-job or on-the-job training methods when improving staff skills in customer service. Large companies are likely to have their own training facilities and courses, some of which are likely to target customer services.

Figure 1: Training to provide effective customer service

Smaller businesses might rely more on experienced staff to teach new recruits 'good practice' while on the job. There is a number of businesses that provide training courses which focus on customer services. An example is shown in Figure 2. This gives details of an introductory course in customer training provided by Activia.

Training in customer service will help staff to do their job more effectively. Without proper training the quality of customer service is likely to be poorer. Training will also motivate staff. Without training they may become frustrated because they cannot do their jobs properly. Training is also likely to make staff more flexible. For example, staff from one

Figure 2: Introductory training course on customer services provided by Activia

This intensive one day training course teaches delegates the basics of customer service. They will learn how to develop and maintain a positive attitude, show extra attentiveness to customers, use customer-friendly language, and deal effectively with customer complaints and problems. Finally, delegates learn how to build rapport with customers, interpret non-verbal communication skills, provide quality customer service over the telephone and communicate effectively through email.

Source: www.activia.co.uk.

department might cover for an absent colleague in another if they have been widely trained. Training is often necessary to bring staff up to date with new technology or new legislation in customer services. For example, staff in a travel agency might be trained in a new computer-based booking system for clients.

Quality assurance, quality control and quality standards

Another way of meeting customer expectations is to adopt recognised quality standards in customer service. A business might also guarantee quality by taking into account customer needs and ensuring that quality is built into processes and systems used when providing customer service. This is called quality assurance. Some approaches to quality assurance and quality standards are outlined below.

Total quality management One of the main approaches to quality assurance used by businesses today is total quality management (TQM). This involves every single person in a business taking responsibility for quality, including those involved in customer service. TQM makes the customer the centre of attention. One of the advantages of using TQM is that the approach involves collecting data for monitoring purposes. Customer service data can be used to help maintain quality standards and also to improve them in the future. This is explained in the next section.

BS 8477:2007 The British Standard Institution (BSI), a body responsible for setting quality standards in industry, has recently published the first British Standard for customer service. It is the BS 8477:2007 Code of practice for customer service. It sets out essential, basic principles for establishing and maintaining effective customer service and provides recommendations for applying these principles. If businesses are granted certification in this standard, it will help to guarantee standards of customer service.

The Institute for Customer Service This organisation is the professional body for customer service. Their aim is to help members raise their customer service standards and individuals achieve professional recognition. In particular it:

- provides advice and guidance on world-class customer service issues;
- defines professional customer service standards;
- promotes a wide understanding of the nature of competent customer service and how individuals can acquire it;
- spreads authoritative customer service knowledge through breakthrough research papers;
- offers a range of quality products and services to help organisations and individuals improve customer service.

Businesses that become members of this organisation can use its services to help them maintain quality standards in customer service.

Charter mark Charter Mark is the government's national standard for customer service excellence. Charter Mark is a powerful, easy to use tool to help everyone in an organisation focus on and improve customer service. Achievement of the standard is recognised by awarding the right to display the prestigious Charter Mark logo. The Charter Mark is awarded for excellence in the provision of customer services by public sector or a voluntary organisation such as a hospital, a police force, a local authority, a prison, a primary school, a Jobcentre or a museum. To qualify for the Charter Mark organisations have to satisfy six criteria.

Monitoring and improving customer service

Many businesses monitor the quality of their customer service. They may do this by gathering data. The data can be analysed and the results used to make recommendations on how to improve the quality of customer service in the future. Businesses can use a number of methods to gather data.

Questionnaires Many businesses gather data using questionnaires. Customers might be asked to complete questionnaires in a follow-up procedure after a sale has been made. Corkills, the Volkswagen car dealer and service centre in Southport, uses a telephone questionnaire to gather information about customer service after customers have had their cars serviced. Questionnaires can be tailored to the needs of different businesses. Figure 3 shows a questionnaire used by Fred. Olsen Travel to gather information about the quality of its customer service.

Figure 3: Customer service survey used by Fred. Olsen Travel

Source: www.fredolsen.co.uk/travel/travelshops/question.htm

Question 2.

TSO (the stationery office) delivers managed print and publishing services to a variety of private and public sector clients. The company is committed to high quality customer service. It sets targets for performance which are outlined below.

- Answer 80% of our telephone calls in 10 seconds, 90% in 20 seconds and 95% in 30 seconds.
- Achieve an abandon call rate of no more than 2% of call volumes answered.
- Average time to answer a call of 6 seconds.
- Process standard written order requests sent by post within an average of 2 working days of receipt.
- Deliver a service that achieves a benchmarked satisfaction score of 83.1%.

- Achieve a fair outcome for customers when things go wrong and receive less than 1.4% of complaints received against overall despatches.

TSO also gathers data to monitor its performance. An extract from its results is shown in Table 1.

Source: adapted from www.tso.co.uk.

(a) How does TSO monitor performance in customer service?

(b) Comment briefly on TSO's performance in customer service provision in 2006.

(c) What are the main advantages of using quantitative data when monitoring customer performance?

Table 1: Performance standards for TSO customer service – an extract from 2006

													2006	
	Target	Jan	Feb	Mar	Apr	May	Jun	Jul	Aug	Sep	Oct	Nov	Dec
% of calls answered in 10 seconds	> 80.0	91.9	93.6	92.9	93	90.9	92.5	92.9	91.5	90.0	93.0	92.9	94.2
% of calls abandoned	< 2.0	0.7	0.6	0.6	0.7	1.1	0.7	0.6	1.0	1.1	1.0	1.29	2.2
Average time to answer (seconds)	6 max	6	6	6	6	7	7	6	8	10	7	7	7
Complaints - % of orders dispatched	< 1.25	1.2	1.3	1	1.3	0.79	1.08	1.18	1.28	1.12	1.4	1.14	1

Gathering performance data Businesses will especially benefit if they can produce quantitative data when monitoring customer service performance. Quantitative data is much easier and quicker to analyse than other types of data. For example, it is easier to make quick comparisons between different years using numeric performance indicators. Businesses that use quantitative data are likely to set performance targets. At the end of the year actual performance can be compared with the targets. Striving for targets will help to improve performance. An example of quantitative customer service performance data is shown in Table 1 in Question 2.

Recording telephone conversations One common way of monitoring the quality of customer service is to record telephone conversations between customers and staff providing customer service over the telephone. By analysing these recordings a business can identify areas for improvement. For example, a recording of a telephone conversation might reveal that a particular member of staff does not know enough about the products the employer is selling.

Complaints A common way of monitoring the quality of customer service is to keep an up to date record of all complaints from customers relating to customer service. By analysing the nature of complaints a business can take measures to improve the quality of its customer service in the future. Businesses generally take complaints quite seriously. If they fail to respond positively to customer complaints they are likely to lose customers in the future. 'Complaints can be used as business feedback to help drive decision making and customers should be able to complain through a variety of channels', says RightNow Technologies, a customer relations management software producer.

Monitoring and improving the quality of customer services are clearly important issues. Businesses can monitor the quality of customer service by gathering information using the methods described above. They must then take measures to improve the quality of customer service by acting on the results shown by an analysis of that data. This might involve retraining staff, modifying systems or introducing new ways of providing effective customer service.

The benefits of high levels of customer service

It has been argued that customer service is generally the critical factor in determining whether a customer buys and is retained. Consequently, the benefits of providing good quality customer service are huge. Some of the benefits of providing high levels of customer service are outlined below.

- Retaining customers through effective customer service enables easier growth. For example, healthier sales volumes and margins can be sustained and a business can expand as a result of word-of-mouth referrals.
- High levels of customer retention through effective customer service also improves staff morale and motivation. No-one enjoys working for a business where customers are not valued and customer service systems are either ineffective or non-existent. When customers are happy, staff are likely to be happier too. As a result they will be more productive.
- Improved staff morale and motivation resulting from reducing customer dissatisfaction also benefits staff retention and turnover, recruitment quality and costs, stress, grievance, discipline and counselling pressures.
- In some industries, where the product is fairly homogenous, the provision of customer service is one of the few ways in which the product can be differentiated. Consequently, providing good customer service is crucial.
- Reduced customer dissatisfaction will obviously reduce legal action from customers and claims that a business is breaking fair trading laws.
- Retaining customers also enables the business to focus more on proactive opportunities such as growth, innovation and development, rather than reactive tasks such as fire-fighting, crisis management and failure analysis.
- Having a culture of delighting and retaining customers improves the image of a business. A company's reputation in the media, and increasingly on the web in blogs and

KEY TERMS

Call centre – an office where large numbers of staff provide customer service over the telephone.
Customer service – a series of activities designed to enhance the level of customer satisfaction.

KNOWLEDGE

1. Give two examples of customer service a bank might provide.
2. How do call centres provide customer service?
3. State two criticisms of using call centres to provide customer service.
4. State two ways in which a business can meet customer expectations in relation to customer service.
5. What is the Charter Mark?
6. State four advantages of using the BS 8477: 2007.
7. State three ways in which a business might monitor the quality of customer service.
8. How can customer service be used to differentiate a product?

forums, for example, can be improved. The converse also applies. For example, one disgruntled customer and a reasonable network of web friends may cause a significant public relations headache.

So providing high levels of customer service will increase sales, assist growth, retain customers, improve staff motivation, reduce costs and improve the image of a business.

Case Study: ScottishPower

ScottishPower uses an intelligent web-based self-service system to enable faster, more accurate answers to customer queries. The system, from Transversal, the UK's leading provider of multi-channel eService solutions for customer-facing websites and contact centres, ensures customers receive rapid responses to their online account queries. 'We are committed to making it easy for our customers to benefit from the flexibility and cost savings of managing their accounts online,' said Nicola Morrison, online manager at ScottishPower. 'As part of our overall aim to be the industry's number one for customer service we needed to ensure that they had fast, accurate answers to their queries. Working with Transversal has not only helped underpin our online growth, but has given us an unparalleled insight into our customers' requirements through the ability to analyse the questions they are asking,' she said. By investigating the type and number of questions asked on its site, ScottishPower has been able to ensure that the right information is immediately available to its customers - without needing to invest in costly market research. For example, after seeing a growing number of queries on energy efficiency, this information was made more visible on the new site.

Increasing the number of its 5.2 million UK customers who manage their gas and electricity accounts online is part of ScottishPower's business strategy to become the UK's best integrated power provider. Some 95 per cent of customer questions are now answered automatically, improving customer service and encouraging consumers to adopt more online services such as meter reading and billing. ScottishPower introduced a new website in February 2007. Customers can enter meter readings online, view and pay bills, change services, update personal details and notify the company when changing address.

Source: adapted from www.e-consultancy.com.

(a) Describe some examples of customer service provided by ScottishPower. (6 marks)
(b) How has the provision of customer service probably changed for ScottishPower in recent years? (6 marks)
(c) How has Transversal helped to improve the quality of customer service at ScottishPower? (10 marks)
(d) How important do you think customer service is to ScottishPower? (10 marks)
(e) Evaluate the benefits to ScottishPower of providing high levels of customer service. (18 marks)

38 Working with suppliers

The role of suppliers in operations

Suppliers are important business stakeholders and will benefit from the success of a business. However, they can also contribute to that success. Operations managers need to find effective suppliers that provide good quality materials and services at competitive prices. Suppliers also need to be thoroughly reliable and offer some flexibility in their services. Having good suppliers, and maintaining effective relations with them, will help to improve the operational performance of a business

Controlling costs Businesses that use just-in-time (JIT) manufacturing techniques depend very heavily on their suppliers. JIT manufacturers need supplies delivered at regular intervals and at specific times. JIT manufacturers do not hold stocks of materials and components, so a break in supply leaves them vulnerable. If a supplier fails to deliver, or delivers the wrong order, the manufacturer may have to close down production for a time. This could be very expensive. Having good suppliers therefore reduces the costs of holding stock. It can also prevent costly delays.

Reliability and customer satisfaction For JIT manufacturers suppliers need to be 100 per cent reliable. Their role is critical. Many suppliers feeding JIT manufacturers have located their own operations very close to their customers. This helps to reduce the chances of a break in supply and fosters good relations. Even businesses that do not operate JIT will need reliable suppliers. For example, most large supermarkets receive daily deliveries of fresh fish. If these supplies did not arrive on time supermarkets might not be able to offer their customers the range of fish they have come to expect. This could result in lost sales and disgruntled customers.

The need for flexibility In some industries businesses need highly flexible suppliers. One reason for this is because some businesses are subject to sharply fluctuating demand. In the events and hospitality industry it is often very difficult to estimate demand. For example, a catering company providing meals at a cricket match might require additional supplies of food if the attendance was unusually high due to very good weather.

Purchasing

In many businesses it is the purchasing department that has responsibility for working with suppliers. Purchasing involves the buying of materials, components, fuel, tools, machinery, equipment, stationery and services by the business. It also includes adopting any method that allows the firm to obtain the

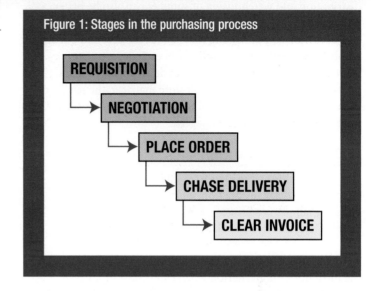

Figure 1: Stages in the purchasing process

REQUISITION → NEGOTIATION → PLACE ORDER → CHASE DELIVERY → CLEAR INVOICE

goods and services it needs, such as hiring.

The various stages in the purchasing process are shown in Figure 1. Purchasing usually begins when the purchasing department is notified of a particular need. For example, a firm's stores or a particular department may send a **requisition form** asking for more stationery. The purchasing department will then act on this. Most purchases are repeat purchases from regular suppliers. Orders are placed with the supplier at previously agreed prices and delivery is accepted under previously arranged terms. New products may need different materials and new suppliers. This will involve a period of search and negotiation, as the buyer tries to find the best deal. If there is a delay in delivery, it is the purchasing department's responsibility to find out why and speed up delivery. Once the goods have arrived the invoice is checked and then payment can be made.

In manufacturing the purchasing department works closely with the production and finance departments. Most purchasing is carried out on behalf of the production department. The finance department needs information about purchases to make payments and record the transactions.

The importance of purchasing is likely to vary according to the nature and size of the business. In many service industries purchasing is not very important. This is because materials are only a small fraction of the total cost of the final product. For example, hairdressing involves very little purchasing, as production involves a skill and uses few materials. However, a large manufacturer requires a large amount of materials, components etc. and so the firm will employ a purchasing department made up of specialists.

Centralised and decentralised purchasing

In some businesses, **centralised purchasing** is used. This is where the purchasing for the whole business is carried out by one department. The advantage of this method is that **economies of scale** can be gained as large-scale buyers enjoy lower rates and market power. Also, the same quality and standard of materials can be set throughout the business. The distribution and warehousing of supplies can also be better planned.

Decentralised purchasing may reduce the cost and burden of administration. Purchasing officers in each department may be more in touch with the needs of that department. In retailing, if purchasing is undertaken by each store manager, the needs of each store can be better catered for. The added responsibility might also motivate store managers.

Choosing effective suppliers

It is important for a business to evaluate suppliers. A poor supplier may delay production, which can be costly. When choosing suppliers a business is likely to use a number of **criteria** to evaluate their reliability.

Price For many businesses the price charged by suppliers will be the most important criterion when choosing a supplier. If businesses can lower the costs of raw materials, components and other services they will make more profit. Price will be particularly important if there is little difference in the quality of the material being purchased. For example, when finding an electricity supplier, only the price is likely to be considered.

Payment terms Payment terms can vary enormously. Payment terms usually refer to the length of the credit period and the method by which payment must be made. Businesses will tend to prefer long credit periods – 90 days or more perhaps. The method of payment is not likely to be a big issue today, although not many businesses will want to pay in cash unless there are significant discounts.

Quality Businesses will need good quality materials and services. They cannot produce good quality products themselves if they use poor quality materials. For example, a business that fits high quality kitchens cannot use poor quality tiles and kitchen units.

Capacity If a business is going to buy very large quantities from a supplier, it will want reassurance that the supplier has the capacity to meet demand. If there is a danger that the supplier may run out of capacity, supplies may be threatened which could disrupt production. A business may also consider the capacity of a supplier if it is likely that the business would be expanding in the near future.

Reliability Businesses want suppliers that deliver goods when they say they will. They also want the correct order first time. Suppliers that are late and prone to making mistakes in orders will be avoided.

Flexibility Many businesses prefer suppliers that can offer a flexible service. For example, can they change orders at the last

Question 1.

McPhersons Ltd is a chain of twenty butchers operating in Scotland and the North of England. Its head office is attached to the shop located in Leeds. All the purchasing is currently undertaken at head office and the meat is delivered in bulk to a warehouse in Leeds. The firm employs a driver to distribute orders to the varios shops twice a week. The board of directors is considering the decentralisation of the purchasing function, since the discounts from bulk buying are not particulary significant. If decentralisation takes place each shop manager will receive a £2,000 p.a. salary increase. The discounts lost from bulk buying are expected to total £20,000 p.a. Cold storage, handling and disitribution costs are expected to fall by £50,000 in total and administration costs will be £5,000 lower in total. It is expected that the quality of the meat will improve when purchasing is the responsibility of the shop managers.

(a) Advise the company whether or not decentralisation is a worthwhile change in operational policy, in purely financial terms.

(b) Explain the non-financial advantages and disadvantages to McPhersons of decentralising purchasing.

minute or can they deliver a day early? Flexible suppliers make operations management easier when planning production.

Vendor rating

The measurement of suppliers' performance is called VENDOR RATING. A business must choose criteria which could be used to measure the performance of a supplier.

A simple vendor rating system is shown in Table 1. The supplier is awarded a mark for performance based on five criteria. For example, the supplier has a good price record, scoring 18 out of a possible 20. Adding the scores gives a total vendor rating of 71/100. When deciding which supplier to choose, a firm is likely to pick the one with the highest rating. If a business feels that some criteria are more important than others, it may give them more value using a weighting system. One problem with this system is how to judge a supplier's performance against given criteria. It may be possible to use records. But sometimes evaluation may simply be based on the subjective opinion of a manager.

Table 1: A simple vendor rating system

Criteria	Maximum Score	Actual Score
Quality	20	17
Price	20	18
Delivery	20	10
Communication	20	12
Flexibility	20	14
Total	**100**	**71**

eSourcing

ESOURCING is the use of Internet technologies and electronic communications in the whole purchasing process. It is a systematic approach that can handle all stages in the purchasing process including identifying appropriate suppliers, tendering, negotiation and award and contract management. The various eSource tools available enable buyers and suppliers to connect and agree a contract quickly and efficiently in order to improve the company's competitiveness. eSourcing significantly reduces the length of time spent on the whole purchasing process. It also reduces the need for paper-based systems and labour-intensive processes. In general, eSourcing helps to improve operational efficiency and can benefit both buyers and suppliers. Buyers benefit from eSourcing for following reasons.

- Faster sourcing process and faster results – time reductions of up to 70%.
- Elimination of face-to-face meetings, travel time, and geographical barriers.
- More transparent, uniform and predictable pricing.
- Improved enforcement of corporate purchasing policies.
- Increased process transparency.
- Better supplier measurement.

Suppliers can also benefit from eSourcing for certain reasons.

- More efficient and objective sourcing process and more level playing field.
- Easier to respond – negotiations and travel are eliminated.
- Lower selling costs.
- Improved convenience for buyers, leading to more transactions.

KEYTERMS

eSourcing – using the Internet in the purchasing process.
Vendor rating – a method of measuring and evaluating the performance of suppliers.

Question 2.

Vi-Spring manufactures high quality beds. A feature of its large range is the ability to offer customers a wide variety of personalised options. It markets its well-known products around the world through a number of large and small retailers. Founded over 100 years ago, the company now employs 180 people and is located in Plymouth, Devon.

The company has recently adopted a just-in-time (JIT) approach to production. Vi-Spring now holds a very low stock of raw materials. Stocks required for production come in on a JIT basis from around two hundred suppliers, of which thirty are key sources. The majority - mainly those providing cotton ticking, padding and webbing - are in the North of England. Delivery of an order is on a next-day basis; other materials are on a longer lead time.

The company prefers to build close and reliable relationships with its suppliers, regarding them as key business partners. If a problem develops, rather than dropping a supplier Vi-Spring will work with it to overcome the issue concerned.

Source: adapted from http://datadialogs.com.

(a) Why is the reliability of suppliers so critical for Vi-Spring?
(b) Do you think Vi-Spring has good relations with its suppliers? Explain your answer.

KNOWLEDGE

1. Why is it important to develop effective relations with suppliers?
2. How important is the role played by suppliers for JIT manufacturers?
3. What are the different stages in the purchasing process?
4. What is the difference between centralised and decentralised purchasing?
5. State two benefits of centralised purchasing.
6. State four benefits of eSourcing to buyers.
7. State three benefits of eSourcing to suppliers.

Case Study: IXO Instruments Ltd

Based in Southampton, IXO Instruments Ltd is a privately owned company. It operates in the market for high-value, handheld test instruments. Its products are sold through a network of national catalogue houses, regional stocking distributors and international master distributors. The company has become one of the largest manufacturers and suppliers of test equipment. It has built an enviable reputation for providing innovative products offering unique and patented designs with features, functions and reliability at an affordable price. IXO is ISO 9001:2000 certified. Its products include portable meters for the measurement and testing of light, sound, temperature, humidity, airflow and water quality.

IXO has a supplier base of 120 but is always looking for new suppliers to keep costs down. The family who own the company set demanding financial targets, which often means that managers continually have to cut costs. At the moment a vendor rating system is used to find new suppliers. Recently a new supplier was found for a component in a new printer. The component is a circuit board and is called FFD 339. Table 2 shows some of the information that was used to find the new supplier.

Unfortunately, last year, the operations manager had to take early retirement due to ill health. A new manager was appointed and it was apparent that she wanted to make a number of operational changes. She was particularly concerned about the treatment of suppliers. She felt that IXO could not develop effective relations with suppliers if they continually looked for cheaper ones. To improve operational performance with regard to suppliers, she was extremely keen to make use of eSourcing in the organisation.

Table 2: Supplier information for FFD 339

Supplier name	Price	Quality	Reliability	Flexibility	Payment terms	Total
Reynolds Ltd	18	8	7	8	6	
AGT	12	8	9	9	5	
Adco	14	6	7	5	8	
Veelle	8	9	9	9	9	
Williams & Co	20	8	6	4	5	

NB All criteria are marked out of 10 except for price which is given more weight and marked out of 20.

(a) (i) How does IXO Instruments Ltd choose effective suppliers? (4 marks)

(ii) Which is the most important criterion for IXO when choosing suppliers? Explain your answer. (6 marks)

(b) Which of the suppliers shown in Table 2 would have been selected by IXO Instruments Ltd? Explain your answer. (8 marks)

(c) Analyse IXO's current relationship with suppliers. (8 marks)

(d) Evaluate the possible benefits to IXO Instruments Ltd if they adopt eSourcing. (14 marks)

39 Using technology in operations

The nature and impact of technology

One of the most significant factors affecting how businesses have operated in the twentieth century has been the impact of new TECHNOLOGY. It is easy to see its impact when we consider some of the changes that have taken place in business.

- New products, such as camcorders, compact discs, laptop computers and services such as direct purchasing from television.
- New production processes, such as robotic welding, and computer controlled cutting machines.
- New materials such as silicon chips for computer circuit boards and polystyrene for packaging.
- Changes in business operations and new skills. For example, as a result of automatic cash tills in banking, many staff have been retrained to sell financial services.

There are many ways in which technology can be defined. One approach is to say that it is 'a creative process which uses human, scientific and material resources to solve problems and generate better efficiency'. Some examples make this clear. A business that uses video conferencing to communicate with branches spread all over the country is using technology. So is a plant which uses lasers to detect faults in products as they move along the production line.

How does technological progress take place? It is usually by means of **invention** and **innovation**. Invention is the discovery of something new. Some examples include the laser beam developed in 1960 by Dr. Charles Townes and the micro-processor developed in 1971 by Marcian Hoff in the USA. Inventions are then developed into products. The laser beam has been used for cutting in industry, micro-surgery in hospitals and spectacular lighting shows in displays.

Inventions are sometimes made by creative people 'outside' business. For example, the ball point pen was invented by a sculptor, and the pneumatic tyre by a veterinary surgeon. Today, research is carried out by teams of people working for a business, university or the government. The rewards to inventors can be very high, if their inventions can be used commercially and patented.

In business, innovation is the commercial exploitation of an invention. An invention is not usually in a form that consumers will buy. The product must be developed to meet consumers' needs, so that it can be sold profitably by business. UK firms have, perhaps, been reluctant to do this in the past. For example, the first working computers were developed in the 1930s. Since then Japan and America have led the world in hardware production and computer research. Enormous investment is often required to innovate once a technical breakthrough has been achieved.

Type of technology in primary industry

Primary industry has been affected by the introduction of new technology in a number of ways. In agriculture the use of tractors, combine harvesters, lifting equipment, grain drying machines and automatic milking and feeding apparatus have helped to increase output, reduce time and waste, and improve conditions. Agrochemicals and pesticides have raised crop yields. Biological research has helped to develop plants and crops which are more resistant to disease and more attractive to consumers. Genetically modified foods are argued to have better resistance to disease. In extractive industries, such as mining, cutting, lifting and tunnelling machines have all led to increased output.

Question 1.

Barclays, Britain's third biggest bank, is planning to cut 1,100 jobs in its processing centre in Poole, Dorset, over the next three years. The redundancies are the result of automation in more of its systems. For instance, cheques which were previously processed by hand will now be handled by computers. The cutbacks will leave just 850 employees remaining. The bank will also shut its Barclays House operation in Poole and seek out smaller premises in the town or nearby Bournemouth.

Unite, the newly formed union which incorporates finance branch Amicus, expressed concerned about the 'large reduction of jobs in Poole'. Union official Steve Pantak said: 'Unite does, however, have robust agreements in place and the bank's plans are spread over the next three years, so we will be working with the bank to ensure the maximum number of redeployments and voluntary redundancies.

The new premises will be 100,000 sq ft compared with the 300,000 sq ft currently provided by Barclays House. The bank has had operations in Poole since 1976. The job reductions will affect a number of areas, including cheque processing as well as IT support and some human resources functions.

Source: adapted from *The Guardian*, 10.5.2007.

(a) Using this case as an example, explain what is meant by automation.
(b) What problem does this case highlight when introducing new technology?

There have also been improvements in safety equipment and mining conditions for workers. The extraction of oil now takes place on large oil rigs with computer controlled drilling equipment. This improves the speed and accuracy of production. In fishing, the introduction of refrigerated boats has helped to improve productivity. Forestry has benefited from cutting, lifting and haulage equipment.

One problem with the use of more efficient technology is that resources are used up more quickly. It may be possible to control this in the case of **renewable resources**, such as timber, by replanting and managed forestry. However, unless new forms of power can be developed, there are likely to be problems in future with extracting large amounts of the world's finite resources such as coal and oil. There have also been criticisms of genetically modified food and its possible effects on humans.

Type of technology in secondary industry

New technology has led to major changes in manufacturing. Many factories and production lines employ complex mechanical, electrical and electronic systems. Even smaller manufacturing businesses have benefited from the introduction of new equipment and processes. Examples of new technology can be found in a number of areas.

Robots Robots are increasingly used on assembly and production lines. They have some form of arm, which moves to instructions given by a computer. Repetitive tasks, such as installing components, can be carried out many times with great accuracy. Such tasks may lead to boredom, lack of motivation, tiredness and human error if undertaken by employees. Robots may also increase the flexibility of a business. For example, in 1998 small robots, each with its own set of paint cans, were installed in the paint shop of the Volkswagen-Audi car plant in Germany. The robot could be activated at a few minutes' notice when a customer wants a colour which is not included in the current program. Using the robot means that customer demand for less popular colours can be satisfied without having to clean out the pipes of the main painting apparatus, which would be costly.

Computer aided design COMPUTER AIDED DESIGN (CAD) is now used by businesses in the design process, before a product is manufactured. Examples of products designed using CAD include vehicle bodies, plastic containers to hold milk and oil, furniture and clothing. Designing on computer allows a business to produce accurate drawings, which can be viewed in 3D and altered cheaply and quickly for a client. Designs can be accurately measured and tested on computer for faults, such as unsuitable components or dimensions, which might have caused problems during manufacture.

Computer numerically controlled machines Products can be manufactured using COMPUTER NUMERICALLY CONTROLLED (CNC) machines. Instructions are given to the CNC machine by the operator. The machine then carries out its instructions, controlled by a computer. An example might be a CNC milling machine which is used to cut out a mould of a mouse in plastic. The computer controls the cutting to produce the shape of a mould. In the textile industry computer controlled sewing, cutting and printing machines are used. Some CNC machines make use of probes and **coordinate measuring machines** (CMMs). These are designed to make simple or complex measurements, check batches or components one at a time and inspect geometric or irregular shapes. CMMs are accurate to within a few microns. CNC machines can produce shapes and cut quickly and accurately. They can also carry out repetitive tasks without human error. The instructions can be changed easily to carry out different tasks. For example, JCB uses CNC machines to cut a wide range of patterns from metal plates for its mechanical diggers.

Computer aided manufacture In many factories computers are used to design products and the information is then fed into CNC machines. This automated operation is known as COMPUTER AIDED MANUFACTURE (CAM). For example, a manufacturer of telephones may design a new shape using a CAD software program on computer. The instructions may be taken from the CAD program and inputted into CNC machines. These machines will reproduce the shapes, guided by the information contained in the computer. Other examples of CAM include computer controlled manufacture of plastic bricks at Lego, computer controlled assembly lines at Sony and computer controlled temperatures, flow rates and ingredients for pizza production at McCain Foods. The computer controlled weaving system produced by Bonas stores designs on computer in one part of a factory and sends production information to looms in other parts of the factory. These then weave the designed fabric.

Computer integrated manufacture Some businesses have integrated the entire design and production process. Computers are used to guide and control the production of a good. Employees supervise the manufacturing part of the operation, checking that it is working effectively and repairing faults. This system is known as COMPUTER INTEGRATED MANUFACTURE (CIM). There is a number of stages in the operation. They are shown in Figure 1.

- Orders are received via email, fax or letter and inputted into the system. Costings are carried out on computer using spreadsheet programs. Customers are stored on databases. Accounts are kept on computer and regularly updated. Orders which are received are processed and invoiced at a later date.
- The design department uses CAD packages to design the product for a client, making changes on computer. The instructions to manufacture the design are produced and fed through to the production part of the system.
- Production is planned and scheduled. Parts and materials are ordered as required by the computer, which monitors

Figure 1: Computer integrated manufacture

stock and automatically reorders where necessary.
- The instructions for production are passed to CNC machines which manufacture the product. CMM machines monitor the quality of the work.
- Robots are used to transfer products from one CNC machine to another.
- Automatically guided vehicles (AGVs) take components to the machines.
- Finished products are taken to the stores or sent for dispatch.

Type of technology in tertiary industry

The supply of services has in the past been relatively more labour intensive than in the primary and secondary sectors. This is because supplying services often requires direct and personal contact with customers. However, today the use of technology in the tertiary industry is becoming more widespread in a number of areas.

Government and private services There is a range of services provided by government or private alternatives. New technology used in health care and dental care has improved services considerably. Developments in new vaccines and drugs have reduced suffering and cured diseases that not long ago may have led to deaths. Surgeons can carry out exact operations using lasers, viewing them on television screens with the use of fibre optics. Replacement teeth can be produced for patients which exactly fit jaw shapes from materials which will last for years. Government information can now be found easily on the Internet.

Financial services Businesses selling financial services match customers with appropriate financial products. For example, client information can be fed into a computer to identify the most suitable insurance policy or savings plan. The sale of financial products such as ISAs, pensions and insurance policies is increasingly carried out on the Internet. Some banks offer online banking services. Many financial organisations now have cash dispensers outside their premises. These can be used by customers who want to take out cash with a minimum of fuss or out of normal working hours. Some banks have cash dispensers inside, and customers can enter the bank in non-business hours using 'swipe cards' to open doors. This gives extra security to customers using the facilities.

Distribution The introduction of containers has made the handling of freight quick and easy. They can be hauled onto trailers and locked in position. This prevents movement during transport and possible damage and theft. At port or rail terminals, containers can be loaded safely and quickly onto trains or ships using cranes. Refrigerated containers allow perishable goods to be transported long distances without deteriorating.

Personal services Dating agencies use computers to match couples using personal information held on databases about clients' characteristics and preferences. Agencies also make use of video technology to record messages from clients. Online dating agencies allow people to register on the Internet.

Post and communication Technology has helped to improve the speed and efficiency of postal and packaging delivery. Many businesses have franking machines that weigh and record the required postage. Bar codes allow a free postal or business service to be provided by firms. A customer can return a leaflet or envelope without charge to a business. Machines at the post office will read the bar code and bill the business providing the service. Post offices make use of video and television to advertise their services.

Most business now make extensive use of email to communicate. Emails can also have attachments. These can be documents that have been scanned or saved as jpeg files. This means that the post does not have to be used, preventing delays in communication.

Hotels, restaurants and transport In the travel industry technology allows customers to travel without a ticket. They can book a flight over the telephone or the Internet using a credit card. The same card is then used to pick up a boarding pass from an airport machine or a check-in counter. Travellers to Australia can obtain an 'electronic visa'. Entry can be organised by giving passport details to a travel agent. These details are sent electronically to the appropriate port of entry. Booking for hotels or theatre tickets can also be made by credit card. Meals at restaurants can be paid for by a 'swipe or switch' card. The transaction is recorded by a machine and the money is automatically transferred from the current account of the customer.

Advertising In advertising, television makes increasing use of advances in filming technology and special effects to make adverts more sophisticated and entertaining. There is also a growing selection of advertising media. For example, advertisers have used electronic messaging on the 'touchlines' of sporting events and in city centres on the sides of buildings. The Internet provides worldwide advertising, but only to Internet users.

Retailing Retailing has benefited in many ways from new technology.

- The packaging of goods has changed greatly in recent years. New materials such as polystyrene and strong plastic wrap have improved the way in which goods are packaged. The materials have been lighter and stronger, have provided better protection, and have been easier to handle. Many firms have redesigned the packaging of goods to increase sales. In some cases new technology has helped. For example, Lucozade and other soft drinks have been packaged in flexible bags instead of cans and bottles.
- There has been a growth in home shopping. Computers and televisions have been linked together to enable shoppers to browse at home and then place orders by telephone or through a link. The Internet is a growing means of direct selling to customers at home.
- Payment has been made easier. Bar codes and hand-held recorders allow customers to register the prices of goods as they shop. This saves time and queues at the checkout. Goods can be paid for by credit or 'swipe cards', increasing security as the customer does not have to carry cash.
- Some supermarkets have unstaffed checkouts where customers can scan their own shopping and choose from a variety of payment methods.

Information and communication technology

INFORMATION AND COMMUNICATION TECHNOLOGY (ICT) is the recording and use of information by electronic means. Some of the uses of **information technology** (IT) have already been explained in the previous sections. However, there are some common uses of ICT which may apply to businesses operating in primary, secondary or tertiary industries.

Administration Many routine tasks can be carried out quickly

Question 2.

Coilcolor is one of the largest independent paint coating lines in the UK, specialising in organic coating of steel and aluminium coils. It offers a wide range of protective finishes and colours to suit its customer's requirements. The company has the ability to produce both extremely low and high volume quantities, a wide choice of colours and short lead times. Among their prestigious clients are B&Q, Ikea and Jaguar.

The original stock control and sales processing system was implemented in 1992. Since then Coilcolor's business model has undergone substantial changes. The original system, with its ageing technology base, no longer serviced the demands of this highly competitive industry. Consequently the company had to invest in an upgrade. A company called Computerisation developed two highly sophisticated, bespoke systems for Coilcolor – a Sales Order Processing System and a Stock Control System. The new systems efficiently manage Coilcolor's complex product portfolio. This consists of many product variables including stock code, material, colour etc.

The new systems were created to work alongside Sage MMS, a computerised accounts system. This has reduced administration time and costs by avoiding the need for multiple data entry. Coilcolor has achieved a sustainable competitive advantage through its quick turnaround times within the intensive manufacturing process. Improved administration has enhanced that advantage which was made possible by the implementation of Computerisation's systems. From a customer service aspect its new systems provide the company with the ability to monitor stock efficiently, satisfying customer demand with low minimum order quantities.

Source: adapted from www.computerisation.co.uk.

(a) Explain how Coilcolor makes use of computers in its operations.
(b) What benefits has Coilcolor enjoyed as a result of using computers?

by computer. These may include customer invoicing or billing. Standard letters or memos may be produced which can be easily changed if necessary. Large amounts of information about customers may be stored on databases.

Personnel Personnel files are now easily kept on databases. They can be regularly updated. Spreadsheets also allow calculations of salaries and deductions.

R&D Computer aided design can be used to research new materials or new product ideas. For example, tests may be carried out on the endurance of materials using a CAD simulation. Recording, monitoring, regulating, forecasting and analysing data are all tasks that can be carried out more easily.

Finance Many firms record all financial transactions on spreadsheets. Some allow instant production of financial information such as profit and loss accounts or income statements, cash flow forecasts, budgets and financial ratios. It is also possible to make checks on outstanding payments that are due from customers so that credit control will be effective.

Communications Developments in information and communications technology mean that information can be collected, stored and sent electronically in a fraction of a second. This saves money and makes sure information is passed correctly. Mobile telephones, faxes and email mean that people can work from a variety of locations. Information can be sent over great distances and at any time. The Internet provides wide ranging communication opportunities, including promotion, online buying and emailing.

Production information Information may be stored about the terms of suppliers. Production costs may be calculated on spreadsheets. The ordering of stocks or components may be carried out by computer. Purchasing may be undertaken using eSourcing, where the whole purchasing process is handled by online purchasing systems.

Stock control Technology is increasingly used to control stock. For example, retailers such as supermarket chains have a very sophisticated stock control system called EPOS (electronic point of sale). The system holds a record of every single stock item in the store. When a customer passes through the checkout every item purchased is subtracted automatically from the stock list. At any time a manager can enter the system to see how much of an item is left in stock. The system may even reorder stock automatically. Businesses may also have systems to reorder stocks online from suppliers, perhaps using intranets or extranets.

Information and sales Many businesses now have their own website on the Internet, providing company information. Some are using sites to provide information or to sell products to customers. A readers' survey by Marketing Technique about use of the Internet by businesses found 75 per cent of respondents worked for companies with their own site. Two-thirds of respondents used the Internet to monitor competitors' activities.

Benefits of new technology

There is a number of benefits to business of using new technology.

Reducing costs One of the main benefits of new technology to businesses is lower costs. If a task or activity is automated, people are replaced by machines which can operate more cheaply. For example, the cost to banks of dispensing cash has fallen considerably since ATMs were introduced.

Improving quality The quality of products is often improved when new technologies are introduced. This is because machines are usually more precise and consistent than humans. For example, robotic welders in car factories can maintain a consistent and high quality weld indefinitely once they have been programmed. This will help to improve the quality of the car.

Increased productivity More can be produced with less and, as a result, businesses may gain higher profits. In addition, fewer of the environment's resources may be used up.

Reducing waste Introducing new technology often results in time being saved and fewer materials being used. For example, technology has created printing machines which waste less paper when printing books or magazines. The ways in which resources are used have attracted a great deal of attention in recent years. As the world's population continues to grow it will be necessary to improve resource use even further.

Improving the working environment Statistics on accidents at work show that the working environment is safer as a result of new technology. Mining and manufacturing in particular have benefited. Modern equipment has made work easier and more tolerable. For example, fork lift trucks mean workers no longer need to load goods by hand. These improvements also help to remove workers' dissatisfaction.

Benefits to society Many new products have come onto the market in recent years. Personal stereo systems, video recorders, satellite and digital television, high performance cars and microwave ovens are some examples. New products mean wider consumer choice and possibly higher living standards. Other developments have helped to make our lives easier, such as ATMs, online shopping and mobile telephones.

Improvements in communications Faster means of transport (such as the jet aircraft), answerphones, email, computer network links and fax machines are all examples of inventions which have helped to improve the speed of communications.

Higher incomes If firms enjoy greater profits they can afford to pay higher dividends to shareholders and higher wages to employees. Also, if efficiency is improved then products may be sold at lower prices. As the country's income increases the government collects more tax revenue. This could be used to improve the quality of public services or alternatively to reduce the overall level of taxation or government borrowing.

Problems with new technology

The introduction of new technology can also cause problems for both business and society.

Cost Development, installation and maintenance can often prove costly. Also, businesses may have to lay off and retrain staff, leading to redundancy payments and retraining costs. If firms borrow to meet these costs, they will have to pay interest. Reorganisation may also be needed. Production may be changed from batch to flow production, job descriptions may be changed and in some cases a larger or smaller plant may be needed.

Labour relations In the past, trade unions have resisted the introduction of some new technology because of the threat to their members' jobs. The growth of union and business partnerships after the year 2000 may have made the introduction of new technology easier.

Job skills New technology creates jobs which require new, technical skills, but replace manual jobs. These new jobs cannot be done by the existing workforce unless it can be retrained. Often, this is not possible.

Breakdowns Automated production lines are interdependent. If one part of the line breaks down the whole process may stop. There may also be teething problems. Breakdowns often occur when technology is first installed. For example, it is argued that the Stock Exchange Automatic Quotation (SEAQ) share dealing system was partially to blame for the 1987 Stock Exchange crash. The system automatically triggered selling instructions, causing big falls in some share prices.

Motivation Some staff may dislike working only with machines. This may affect their motivation.

Management The management of technological change is considered very difficult. One reason is due to the rapid pace of the change. When new technology becomes available business managers have to decide whether or not to purchase it, or wait for the next important breakthrough. Deciding when to invest in new technology is very difficult. The management of the human resources leading up to the change, and during the change, requires great skill. People are often unhappy about change in their lives.

Unemployment and employment Much new technology is labour saving. Tasks once carried out by people will be done by machines. As a result people may become unemployed. For example, in automated production lines tasks such as assembly and quality checks are done by robots and CMMs. One or two employees may act as supervisors. On the other hand technology has to be designed, manufactured, installed, programmed, operated, serviced and replaced, which may create new jobs.

IT problems Computer software can become infected by viruses. A computer virus is a programme written to deliberately damage or destroy software and files. Such viruses are very damaging. It is possible for businesses to use software to check the existence of viruses. They can then be blocked from entering the computer system if included on emails, for example. If a virus has entered the system, it can be removed. Computer software has other problems which can affect a business. They may have to constantly buy the latest software to be compatible with clients or suppliers who use more modern versions. Modern machines may not run older software. New software may not be able to convert older programs.

Leisure time People have gained more leisure time as a result of new technology. They need to learn how to use this extra time in

KEY TERMS

Computer aided design – the use of computers when designing products.
Computer aided manufacture – the use of computers in the manufacture of products.
Computer numerically controlled machines – machines which have their operations controlled by a computer program.
Computer integrated manufacture – the use of computers to control the entire production process.
Information and communication technology – the recording and use of information by electronic means.
Technology – a creative process which uses human, scientific and material resources to solve problems and improve efficiency.

KNOWLEDGE

1. What is meant by technology?
2. What is the difference between invention and innovation?
3. State four areas of a business that might benefit from new technology.
4. How has new technology been used in marketing?
5. How might a business exporting products abroad make use of new technology?
6. How has information technology been incorporated in production?
7. How has business security used information technology?
8. Why was the Data Protection Act introduced?
9. In what ways has new technology benefited (a) business owners; (b) management?
10. Briefly explain problems that (a) workers and (b) management may face with the introduction of new technology.
11. How might business exploit the Internet?

a constructive way. Businesses are taking advantage of this. For example, it is argued that there is enough demand in the UK for many more golf courses.

An ageing population Medicine has benefited greatly from new technology. One effect of this is that the population of many countries is now 'ageing'. As a result the pressure has increased on those in work to support the aged. Demands on public funds will also increase and the government will have to find money for facilities which are needed for the elderly.

Data protection The rapid development in the use of IT has led to legislation about the collection, storage, processing and distribution of data. The **Data Protection Act, 1998** lays down a number of conditions with which users must comply. For example, personal data should be obtained and processed fairly and lawfully and can only be held for specified and lawful purposes. There is also some legislation regarding the use of the Internet. EU legislation prevents the downloading of copyright music and allows businesses to block downloading. For example. EU legislation in 2003 made it illegal to send junk email, known as spam, by businesses to individuals.

Case Study: Minco Manufacturing

Minco Manufacturing is an American company. It produces over 250,000 fuser rollers a month for more than 400 models of copiers, printers and facsimile machines at its state-of-the-art production plant in Colorado. Its products include sleeved, silicone and hard coated upper fuser rollers, and silicone coated lower pressure rollers.

As a result of adopting 16 new Stäubli robots in its production cells the company has improved product quality and reduced costs. The robots are used for a variety of tasks such as operating lathes. Robots keep labour costs down, allowing Minco to compete internationally. 'By using robots and reducing labour costs, we can compete with companies that make parts in China, for example.' said Brian Duff, manufacturing engineer. 'We are able to keep the work in the United States and still be competitive with the cheaper labour rates in Asian countries.'

'Once the robots have been programmed they just run. ... That frees up the operator to do inspections and move parts in and out of the cell, instead of having all these people loading lathes for 10 to 12 hours a shift,' Duff said. Stäubli robots are known for high-speed performance, and this speed also generated savings. Before the robots were installed, this process required an additional finish turning lathe. We had an operator manually feeding two lathes to work the ends and then feeding a third lathe to do the finish turn work. The finish turning machine was actually capable of twice the production that was possible by hand,' Duff explained. 'With three robotic cells currently running, we've saved three lathes that we can transfer into making another cell.'

They've also saved about 50 per cent more floor space. 'It allows us to design extremely compact work cells,' Duff said.

The quantity of fuser rollers produced and the level of quality needed, demanded repeatability as well as speed. 'Repeatability is key to the robot's performance in this application because of how we are locating the part into the draw tube. If we didn't place the part against the stop very accurately then we would have too much fluctuation and we could not control the quality of the roller,' Duff said. 'We need to meet a length accuracy of less than .005 of an inch, but we're not seeing even that much variation. We're seeing .002 or less.'

After the initial 16 robots are installed, Minco's plan is to integrate robots into other processes that could benefit from automation. Then the company will start replacing their older robots. 'We've talked to Stäubli about adding robots to load the initial paint station. It is very labour-intensive, because every roller we make gets painted. Rollers weigh up to eight pounds so it is exhausting work. We get a lot of operator fatigue and production begins to drop,' he said.

Minco Manufacturing is also considering installing robots to unload rollers off a conveyor after the coating has cured. 'This is very labour intensive, but also has to be done very carefully. At this stage the rollers cannot get nicked or scratched,' Duff said. Robots are also ideally suited for Minco's packaging process.

Source: adapted from www.roboticsonline.com.

(a) **Explain how robots are used in operations. (6 marks)**
(b) **Explain why the introduction of robots is an example of automation. (6 marks)**
(c) **How will workers benefit from the introduction of more robots? (6 marks)**
(d) **Discuss the benefits enjoyed by Minco Manufacturing as a result of employing more robots. (10 marks)**
(e) **Discuss the problems Minco Manufacturing could encounter when making more use of robots. (12 marks)**

What is marketing?

A **market** is any set of arrangements that allows buyers and sellers to exchange goods and services. It can be anything from a street market in a small town to a large market involving internationally traded goods. But what is meant by the term MARKETING?

Marketing is not just about selling products to customers. Before selling products, many businesses carry out a range of activities to find out consumer preferences, including market research and testing of products on consumers. Similarly, marketing and advertising are not the same. Advertising is just one of a number of promotion methods used by businesses. Other methods involve giving 'free' gifts and running competitions.

A widely accepted definition of marketing, from the Institute of Marketing, is that 'Marketing is the management process involved in identifying, anticipating and satisfying consumer requirements profitably.' Some others are shown in Table 1.

Table 1: Marketing definitions

Marketing is about supplying the right products, to the right customers, at the right price, in the right place, at the right time.
Anon

'The basic function of marketing is to attract and retain customers at a profit.'
P. Drucker, The Practice of Management (1993)

'Marketing is the process of planning and executing the conception, pricing, promotion and distribution of ideas, goods and services to create exchange and satisfy individual and organisational objectives.'
American Marketing Association (1985)

The purpose of 'Marketing is to establish, maintain and enhance long term customer relationships at a profit, so that the objectives of the parties involved are met. This is done by mutual exchange and fulfilment of promises.'
C. Gronroos, 'Marketing redefined', Management Decision, 1990.

Marketing effectively

Effective marketing will have certain features

- **A process.** It does not have a start and an end, but is ongoing all the time. Businesses must be prepared to respond to changes that take place. This is shown in Figure 1. For example, a business marketing office furniture would be unwise not to take into account consumers'

reactions. If the business sold modern designs, but sales were poor, it might consider designs for offices that had a traditional look.

- **A business philosophy.** It is not just a series of activities, such as advertising or selling. It is more a 'way of thinking' about how to satisfy consumers' needs. A business selling good quality products, cheaply, may be unsuccessful in its marketing if it has dirty, badly organised or poorly lit facilities. Retailers such as Ikea and Asda have large 'superstores' with restaurants and play areas for children. They could be said to cater for all their consumers' shopping needs.

- **Building relationships with customers.** Profitable businesses are often built upon good customer relations. This might involve dealing with customer complaints in a considered manner. Customers, as a result, are likely to develop a favourable view of the business and buy its products over a long period of time. RELATIONSHIP MARKETING is now used by some businesses, such as Tesco. This is an approach to marketing which stresses the importance of developing relationships with customers which last longer than the short-term.

The purposes of marketing

There is a number of reasons why businesses carry out marketing.

To satisfy consumers A product has a far greater chance of being a success if it satisfies consumers' needs. Businesses which make satisfying their customers a main concern are more likely to be effective at marketing. Marketing should affect all aspects of a business. A production department, for example, would not continue making a product that did not satisfy the needs of the

Figure 1: The marketing process

consumers at whom it was aimed.

To identifying consumer requirements Marketing should find out what consumer needs and requirements are and make sure that products meet them. Market research is often used by businesses for this purpose. Managers, however, also place stress on having a 'feel' for the market.

To anticipate consumer requirements Businesses have to understand what customers want in advance. In some cases this is easy. For example, supermarkets and butchers stock up with turkeys before Christmas. In other cases it is more difficult. What colours of clothes will be fashionable this year? A chain of stores with the wrong colours might find it difficult to sell its stock. Tastes and fashions in today's markets are changing faster than ever before. Marketing must anticipate and respond to these changes. Toy manufacturers, for example, try to be aware of the next 'craze'. In addition, rapid technological change has taken place in recent years and continues to do so. Firms constantly invent, design and launch new and advanced products onto the market. One example is the electronics industry which has introduced DVD players, digital camcorders, MP3 players and high definition televisions to the market in recent years.

To compete effectively The number of products competing for the consumer's attention is constantly increasing. Businesses today are finding it easier to change their products and enter new markets. Also, there has been increased competition from foreign products in UK markets. This means that businesses have to work even harder to be competitive. Effective marketing should help a business to achieve this.

To make a profit Most businesses today regard making a profit as their main aim. Businesses must make a profit in the long run to survive. Those that do not will cease to operate. Marketing that satisfies consumers' needs profitably is therefore essential. Even when profit is not the main objective, marketing has a vital role to play. Charities, such as Oxfam, and many public sector organisations such as colleges and hospitals, adapt and change the marketing of their services to satisfy their consumers' needs.

Consumer and business to business marketing

CONSUMER MARKETING is where a business is marketing to consumers. There are numerous examples of consumer marketing, including the marketing of the vast majority of products sold in retail outlets such as supermarkets, department stores and high street clothing stores.

BUSINESS TO BUSINESS MARKETING is where one business is engaged in marketing its products to another business. Examples of business to business marketing might include:

- an office furniture manufacturer marketing to business users;
- a car manufacturers providing company cars to a business;
- a local newspaper offering advertising space to local

Question 1.

Levens Farm is a fruit farm in Sussex. It allows customers to 'pick your own fruit'. But increasingly it is selling to retailers, encouraged by the news that Britain is fast becoming a nation of berry lovers.

Sales of British strawberries, blackberries and raspberries broke records in 2007 and many suppliers were struggling to keep up with demand. The soft fruits, which are credited with staving off cancer, saw sales of £204 million in the UK. 'It's because people are becoming more aware of the health benefits of eating fresh fruit, especially berries,' said Laurence Olins, the chairman of British Summer Fruits (BSF), which represents nearly all of Britain's soft fruit growers.

Strawberry sales accounted for £165 million, a 5 per cent sales increase from the previous year. In comparison, sales of blackberries shot up by 31 per cent to £4 million while raspberry sales were up 26 per cent to £35 million. Such is the demand that none of Britain's home-grown fruit is exported. And in July and August, when demand was at its highest, berries had to be imported from Europe.

Source: adapted in part from *The Independent*, 18.12.2006.

(a) Explain why Levens Farm is selling to (i) consumer markets and (ii) business to business markets.
(b) Explain how the information in the article might help Levens Farm to: (i) identify customer requirements, (ii) anticipate customer requirements; (ii) make a profit.

businesses;
- a software supplier providing software geared up to the needs of businesses.

Product and market orientation

Some businesses are said to be relatively product orientated or market orientated.

Product orientation Many businesses in the past, and some today, could be described as PRODUCT ORIENTATED. This means that the business focuses on the production process and the product itself. It puts most of its efforts into developing and making products which it believes consumers want and which will sell well.

In the past, businesses producing radios and televisions could be said to have been relatively product orientated. It was their novelty and the technical 'wonder' of the product that sold them. There were few companies to compete against each other, and there was a growing domestic market. There were also few overseas competitors. The product sold itself.

Some industries today are still said to be product orientated. The machine-tool industry, which produces machines used in the production of other goods, has to produce a final product which exactly matches a technical specification. However, because of increased competition, such firms are being forced to take consumers' needs into account. The technical specification to which a machine-tool business produces might be influenced by what customers want, for example.

Product orientated businesses thus place their emphasis on developing a technically sound product, producing that product and then selling it. Contact with the consumer comes largely at this final stage. There will always be a place for product orientation. A great deal of pure research, for example, with no regard to consumers' needs, still takes place in industry, as it does in the development of pharmaceuticals.

Market orientation A business that is MARKET ORIENTATED business is one which continually identifies, reviews and analyses consumers' needs. It is led by the market. A market orientated business is much more likely to be engaged in effective marketing if it is market orientated. Henry Ford was one of the first industrialists to adopt a market orientated approach. When the Ford motor company produced the Model T, it did not just design a car, produce it as cheaply as possible, and then try to sell it to the public. Instead, in advance of production, Ford identified the price at which he believed he could sell large numbers of Model Ts. His starting point was the market and the Model T became one of the first 'mass-market' products. This illustrates the market orientated approach – consumers are central to a firm's decision making. Sony is one of many modern businesses that has taken a market orientated approach. The

Sony Bravia High Definition television is an example of a product being developed in response to the wishes of consumers.

A more market orientated business may have several advantages over one which is more product orientated.
- It can respond more quickly to changes in the market because of its use of market information.
- It will be in a stronger position to meet the challenge of new competition entering the market.
- It will be more able to anticipate market changes.
- It will be more confident that the launch of a new product will be a success.

What effect will taking a market orientated approach have on a business? It must:
- consult the consumer continuously (market research);
- design the product according to the wishes of the consumer;
- produce the product in the quantities that consumers want to buy;
- distribute the product according to the buying habits and delivery requirements of the consumer;
- set the price of the product at a level that the consumer is prepared to pay.

The business must produce the right product at the right price and in the right place, and it must let the consumer know that it is available. This is known as the **marketing mix**.

The adoption of a market orientated approach will not always guarantee success. Many well-researched products have been failures. Coloroll was a business which started in the wallpaper market and expanded into home textiles and soft furnishings. Its attempt to enter the DIY burglar alarm market, however, was a failure. The company's reputation and design skills had little value in that section of the DIY market compared with other companies, whose reputations were based on home security or electronics. Whether a business places a greater emphasis on the product or on the market will depend on a number of factors.

The nature of the product Where a firm operates in an industry at the edge of new innovation, such as bio-technology, pharmaceuticals or electronics, it must innovate to survive. Although a firm may try to anticipate consumer demand, research is often 'pure' research, i.e. the researcher does not have a specific end product in mind.

Policy decisions A business will have certain objectives. Where these are set in terms of technical quality or safety, the emphasis is likely to be on production. Where objectives are in terms of market share or turnover, the emphasis is likely to be on marketing.

The views of those in control An accountant or a managing director may place emphasis on factors such as cash flow and profit forecasts, a production engineer may give technical quality control and research a high priority and a marketing person may be particularly concerned with market research and consumer relations.

Question 2.

Beverly Morgan started her home-based business, Kitz 4-U Inc. in Hamilton, Ontario, by selling first aid kits to fundraising organisations. She has also developed three other affordable 'Everything You Need In A Pinch' kits - the Bowling Kit, the Golf Kit, and the Travel Kit. The kits are also unique gifts and promotional items. Companies buy the kits to give away as a 'Thank You' to clients or as appreciation gifts to staff.

The challenges Beverly faced starting Kitz 4-U Inc. were those that every new business faces, including product development and defining the market. To produce the kits, she had to find the answers to questions such as, 'What will I put in each kit? What will the packaging look like? Where will I purchase the products I need? Who will do the graphic design? Who will make the packaging?'

To determine which products her potential customers would like to see in the kits, she carried out several market surveys, which she describes as 'very time consuming, but very important.' Once the product list was set, she had to find suppliers, which also took some searching. 'Some wouldn't sell to me, while others took a chance.'

Beverly prepared and rejected several designs before deciding on the final product. The graphic design for the packaging took the longest. Beverly almost went to print before she found the information she needed on packaging laws, which would have been an expensive lesson. Just in time, she discovered that everything was incorrect and the entire design had to be redone.

Source: adapted from http://sbinfocanada.about.com.

(a) Explain why Kitz 4-U Inc is likely to be selling to a niche market.
(b) Examine two problems that the business may have faced operating as a niche market.
(c) Discuss whether the business might grow to become a mass marketing organisation in future.

Figure 2: Product vs market orientation

More product orientated | More market orientated

Examples
Coal mining business
Wheat farmer
Water supply business

Examples
Clothing retailer
Soap powder manufacturer
Supermarket chain

The nature and size of the market If production costs are very high, then a company is likely to be market orientated. Only by being so can a company ensure it meets consumers' needs and avoid unsold goods and possible losses.

The degree of competition A company faced with a lack of competition may devote resources to research with little concern about a loss of market share. Businesses in competitive markets are likely to spend more on marketing for fear of losing their share of the market.

The distinction between product and market orientation could better seen as a spectrum, as in Figure 2. Most business are somewhere along the spectrum. For example, supermarkets may be more market orientated and a copper mining company more product orientated.

Asset-based or asset-led marketing

Both market and product orientated approaches have their limitations. Many businesses have failed because they have offered a high quality product, but have not met the needs of their customers. Perhaps the product was too expensive or the business failed to persuade enough retailers to stock it. Equally, market orientated businesses might fail because they put great effort into certain aspects of marketing, but fail to get the right product to the customer.

Another approach is ASSET-LED or ASSET-BASED MARKETING. A business which is asset-led is responsive to the needs of the market. But equally it takes into account its own strengths and weaknesses when producing a good or providing a service. Its strengths, for example, might include its product, production techniques, goodwill and branding, experience and knowledge.

A tobacco company, for example, might come up with the idea of offering life insurance to smokers. It could offer lower premiums (prices) to its customers than other insurance companies which group smokers and non-smokers together. It also might have a large customer database of users who could be contacted to advertise the insurance. However, selling insurance is a very different business from manufacturing and selling cigarettes. There are likely to be few **synergies**, or links, between the different businesses. The tobacco company has great expertise in the production of cigarettes, but little in selling insurance. Simply because market research shows there is a potentially profitable business opportunity does not mean

to say that a business should take it up.

Mass and niche marketing

In order to undertake effective marketing a business needs to consider whom it will be aiming its products at. One way of thinking about this is in terms of niche and mass marketing.

Mass marketing MASS MARKETING occurs when a business offers almost the same products to all consumers and promotes them in almost the same way. Examples of products that are generally mass marketed include Coca-Cola and Microsoft computer software. Mass marketing has a number of features and benefits. Products are usually sold to large number of consumers. They may also be marketed in many different countries, a process known as **global marketing**. This means that a business can manufacture large quantities and the average costs can be reduced as the business gains **economies of scale**. High sales and lower average costs can lead to high profits.

However, there can be problems. It is often expensive to set up production facilities to provide mass marketed products. Such products also face competition in parts of the market from producers who might be more effective in targeting market segments. So mass marketing does not necessarily guarantee profitable products.

Niche marketing NICHE MARKETING involves a business aiming or **targeting** a product at a particular, often small, segment of a market. It is the opposite of mass marketing, which

CRITIQUE

Supporters or marketing argue that it benefits both businesses and their consumers. Businesses that market effectively make profits. Customers who buy the products of these businesses have their requirements met. But some argue that businesses don't seek to meet consumer requirements as their first objective. Instead, they are more interested in profits. They point to the way that some businesses are alleged to 'harm' their customers. Examples might be businesses that make profits by selling foods that may possibly contribute to a poor diet or to obesity.

Critics of marketing would also question the extent to which businesses respond to consumer needs as opposed to creating them. Many would argue that businesses actively work to create the need to consume more, rather than just responding to what consumers want and need. They suggest that consumer needs in general would be better met if businesses encouraged them to spend less rather than more. So while marketing may make sense for individual businesses and their relationships with individual consumers, it does not necessarily work at a wider level. One consequence of this so-called pressure on consumers is that individuals spend beyond their means. This has led to many people taking on more debt than they can manage. Another consequence is more rapid use of the world's resources and the creation of higher levels of environmental damage.

Question 3.

Mark Boyd works as an electrical engineer and plays guitar in groups at weekends. His ambition has been to build and sell his own guitars. After years of testing he has designed a new style of pick-up for a guitar which will reduce noise. Together with his friend Tony, who currently makes hand made acoustic guitars, he wants to build hand made electric guitars which incorporate these new pick-ups. They have some interesting ideas for modern designs, but the guitars will be very labour intensive to build.

After researching the market, Mark and Tony produced the perceptual map shown in Figure 3. They have included mass manufactured guitars with traditional designs by Fender, modern designs such as Parker, and hand made designs by TCM Guitars.

Figure 3: A perceptual map for electric guitars produced by Mark and Tony

(a) How might Mark and Tony have collected the information to produce the perceptual map of electric guitars?
(b) Explain how the information in the perceptual map might help Mark and Tony when they are making marketing decisions about their new products.

involves products being aimed at whole markets rather than at particular parts of them. Why do firms attempt niche marketing?

- Small firms are often able to sell to niche markets which have been either overlooked or ignored by other firms. In this way, they are able to avoid competition in the short run at least.
- By targeting specific market segments, firms can focus on the needs of consumers in these segments. This can allow them to gain an advantage over firms targeting a wider market.

There is, however, a number of problems with niche marketing.

- Firms which manage successfully to exploit a niche market often attract competition. Niche markets, by their very nature, are small and are often unable to sustain two or more competing firms. Large businesses joining the market may benefit from economies of scale which small firms are unable to achieve.
- Many small firms involved in niche marketing have just one product aimed at one small market. This does not allow a business to spread its risks in the way that a business producing many goods might be able to.
- Because niche markets contain small numbers of consumers, they tend to be faced by bigger and more frequent swings in consumer spending than larger markets. This may mean a rapid decline in sales following an equally rapid growth in sales.

Perceptual maps

The positioning of a brand is influenced by customer perceptions rather than by those of businesses. For example, a business may feel its brand is a high quality, up-market product. But if customers see it as low quality and down-market, it is their views that will influence sales.

So, if a business wants to find out where its brand is positioned in the market, it might carry out market research. This will help it to understand how customers see the brand in relation to others in the market.

A business may also wish to launch a new brand. Having decided the target market, market research might show what characteristics the brand must have to succeed in that market. It could reveal the price that customers are prepared to pay. It could also suggest what sort of promotional support will be needed. For example, will a national television advertising campaign be used? Will promotion to retailers be a better strategy?

The results of market research can be displayed on PERCEPTUAL MAPS (sometimes also called MARKET MAPS or POSITIONING MAPS). Typically, the maps are drawn in two

Figure 4: A perceptual map for cars

dimensions, as in Figure 4. This allows two of the attributes of the brand to be shown visually. More maps need to be drawn if more than two attributes are shown.

Figure 4 shows a perceptual map for cars. Two characteristics are displayed - the price of a new car and its 'sportiness'. So Bentley cars might be highly priced, but considered traditional. Morgans might be less costly, but considered more sporty. Cateram produces cheaper sporty 'kit cars' which must be self-assembled.

Drawing maps can help a business make marketing decisions about new or existing brands. Market mapping reveals the extent to which brands are similar to or different from those of rivals. A business can then choose to emphasise those similarities or differences through promotion. Or it can change the characteristics if current sales are poor. It could, for example, change its price or its method of promotion. Perhaps the brand itself needs redesigning. Changing the characteristics will help **reposition** the brand in the market.

KEYTERMS

Asset-led or asset-based marketing – where a business combines its knowledge of the market with an understanding of its strengths and weaknesses to decide what products to bring to market.

Business to business marketing – where a business markets its products to other businesses.

Consumer marketing – where a business is marketing to consumers.

Marketing – the management process involved in identifying, anticipating and satisfying consumer requirements profitably.

Market orientation – an approach to business which places the requirements of consumers at the centre of the decision making process.

Mass marketing – the marketing of a product to all possible consumers in the same way.

Niche marketing – the marketing of products to a particular, small segment of the market.

Perceptual maps, positioning maps or market maps – typically a two dimensional diagram which shows two of the attributes or characteristics of a brand and those of rival brands in the market.

Product orientation – an approach to business which places the main focus of attention upon the production process and the product itself.

Relationship marketing – an approach to marketing which seeks to strengthen a business's relationships with its customers.

KNOWLEDGE

1. What is meant by the term marketing?
2. What are the features of effective marketing?
3. Distinguish between marketing and advertising.
4. Why is marketing described as a process?
5. Why might product orientation still be important today?
6. What are the main advantages of a market orientated approach?
7. Why might a market orientated approach still be unsuccessful?
8. What is the difference between mass and niche marketing?

Case Study:
House on the Hill Software

House on the Hill Software is a highly successful software business based in Marple near Manchester. The company was established by Iain and Trudy Broadhead in 1993 with the aim of helping businesses to manage their help desks through the use of specialised cost effective computer software. In the fast changing world of IT they provide customers with regular updates, which can be collected from the House on the Hill website and make every effort to adapt and amend their software in response to customer enhancement requests.

In the 14 years the business has been in existence House on the Hill Software has developed a large, diverse customer base spanning over 40 countries. Iain Broadhead explained the reasons for the success of the business as follows: 'Initially our software was developed based upon our own experience of working in the IT business, with sometimes only a partial understanding of the needs of our different customers groups. Gradually, however, we have come to understand what our customers want from our products. Accordingly we've been very careful to respond to these wishes. I think this has been central to our success. We've also never stood still and we are always looking for new ways of developing our products and meeting the evolving needs of our customers'.

One of the biggest selling items produced by House-on-the-Hill is a piece of software called SupportDesk. The driving force behind the continuing development of SupportDesk has been customer feedback based upon longstanding relationships with customers who appreciate the prompt and friendly support offered by the company.

The businesses House on the Hill supply products to are wide and varied and include manufacturing businesses, further education colleges, providers of adventure skills programmes and medical research institutes. House on the Hill maintains regular and close contact with its customers and has become aware of a number of key features it is looking for in SupportDesk. These include functionality (doing what it says it can do), value for money, allowing help desks to become more efficient, enabling help desks to provide quicker responses and being at the forefront of technology.

The business has discovered that one of the main ways in which it gains new business is through word of mouth recommendations from existing customers. 'Our customers are important to us and we pride ourselves on the individual care and attention that we provide. We have long-standing relationships with our customers' said Trudy Broadhead.

Source: www.houseonthehill.com and networkcomputing.co.uk.

(a) Identify whether House on the Hill is engaged in business to business or consumer marketing. Explain your answer. (3 marks)

(b) (i) Explain whether House on the Hill is selling to a niche or mass market. (3 marks) (ii) Explain TWO benefits of this approach to the business. (6 marks)

(c) Examine the factors that may have affected the change in approach to marketing at the business. (8 marks)

(d) Discuss whether the approach to marketing at House on the Hill is effective. (10 marks)

The markting mix

In order to market its products effectively a business must consider its MARKETING MIX. The marketing mix refers to those elements of a firm's marketing strategy which are designed to meet the needs of its customers. There are four parts to the marketing mix - product, price, promotion and place. These are often known as the four 'Ps', as illustrated in Figure 1. To meet consumers' needs and to create an effective marketing mix, businesses must produce the right product, at the right price, make it available at the right place, and let consumers know about it through promotion.

Product Businesses must make sure that their products are meeting the needs of their customers. This means paying close attention to a number of features of the product.
- How consumers will use the product. A furniture manufacturer, for example, would market different products for home use than it would for office use. Products created for the office would need to be sturdy, functional, able to withstand regular use and be long lasting. Products created for the home would need to stress features such as the quality of the fabric, the design and the level of comfort.
- The appearance of the product. This is likely to involve a consideration of such things as colour. Food manufacturers, for example, go to great lengths to ensure that their products have an appealing colour. In some cases this means adding artificial colourings to alter the appearance. There are many other factors to be taken into account during the product's design. These include shape, taste and size. Deodorant manufacturers and toilet cleaning fluid producers among others might also consider aroma.
- Financial factors. There is little point in a firm producing a product which meets the needs of consumers if it cannot be produced at the right cost. All things being equal, a good produced at high cost is likely to be sold for a high price. Unless consumers are convinced that a product is value for money, they are unlikely to purchase it. They might take into consideration factors such as the quality of the product or after-sales service.
- The product's life cycle. After a period of time the sales of all products rise and then later start to fall. A business must decide whether to allow the product to decline and cease its production or to try to revive it in some way.
- A product's UNIQUE SELLING POINT or PROPOSITION. This is the aspect or feature of the product that may differentiate it from its rivals. It may help a business to gain a competitive advantage over competitors.
- Market position. This is the view that consumers have of a product compared to that of its competitors. For example, a product might be seen as 'up-market' or alternatively 'low cost' by buyers.

Price The pricing policy that a business chooses is often a reflection of the market at which it is aiming. Prices will not always be set at the level which will maximise sales or short-run profits. For example, a business may charge a high price because it is aiming to sell to consumers who regard the product as exclusive rather than because production costs are high. However, factors such as production costs can also influence pricing.

Promotion There is a number of promotional methods a business can use including above the line promotions, such as TV advertising, and below the line promotions such as personal selling. A business will choose a promotion method it feels is likely to be most effective in the market in which it operates. For example, methods such as '10 per cent off your next purchase' are used with 'fast-moving consumer goods', such as canned food and packets of biscuits. National television advertising will only be used for products with a high sales turnover and a wide appeal.

Place This refers to the means by which the product will be distributed to the consumer. The product must get to the right place, at the right time. This means making decisions about the way in which the product will be physically distributed, i.e. by air, sea, rail or road. It also means taking into account how the product is sold. This may be by direct mail from the manufacturer or through retail outlets such as supermarkets.

When considering the marketing mix of services, the 4Ps are sometimes argued to be 7Ps. The importance of the following is also stressed.
- The people involved in providing the service.

Figure 1: Elements of the marketing mix

MARKETING MIX

PRODUCT	PRICE	PLACE	PROMOTION
Appearance Function Cost	Cost based Competitor based Consumer based	Retailers Wholesalers Distribution	Advertising Sales promotion Personal selling

- The process, i.e. the mechanisms, activities and procedures involved in delivering the services, such as delivery time of a meal.
- Physical evidence, such as the appearance of the environment in which the service is provided.

Choice of marketing mix

Each business must decide upon its own marketing mix. It is important that the right balance between price, product, promotion and place is achieved if this is to be as effective as possible. It could be argued that as businesses become more market orientated all elements are important. However, at times businesses may stress one or more elements of the mix. What is important for a business is that its marketing mix is integrated. This means that the different parts of the marketing mix must fit together well .

Take, for example, a business launching a new range of hand-made, luxury organic cheeses priced at over 50 per cent higher than rival cheeses, promoted in specialist food magazines, packaged by hand in high quality materials and with a taste, texture and smell positively commented upon by food experts. It would not make sense to distribute such cheeses through discount supermarkets, such as Aldi and Netto, or through discount cheese stalls at local street markets. Such a strategy would suggest a marked lack of integration between the product, price and promotion on the one hand and place on the other. Instead, if it is to be effective, each element of the marketing mix should support the other. In the example above it may mean distributing the cheeses through high quality specialist cheese shops and delicatessens. The marketing mix a business chooses will depend upon certain factors.

Finance available Some new products are launched onto the market with the backing of large businesses and with huge financial back-up. There is a huge range of choice as to the components of the marketing mix to be used to support these products. Other businesses with more restricted finances have far fewer options available to them.

Technological developments Technological developments have enabled businesses to adapt and develop their marketing mixes in ways that wouldn't previously have been possible. For example, the use of the Internet and mobile phone texts are relatively recent additions to the promotional techniques available to businesses. Information technology developments have allowed businesses to develop much more sophisticated pricing strategies, with prices rising and falling according to demand. This has been a particular feature of airline and rail travel businesses. In addition, the Internet has revolutionised the place many products are sold. Many consumer goods are now more likely to be purchased on the Internet than they are in shops.

The findings from market research As well as informing

Question 1.

Biome Lifestyle is an online shopping site (www.biomelifestyle.com) that offers eco-friendly and ethically-sourced products for the home. The emphasis of the business is upon products that are carefully chosen for how they look and for being made from recycled, sustainable, organic or fairly-traded materials. The business has grown rapidly since its launch in December 2005, but its founder Alexandra Bramham says it has not been easy. She spent the year before the official launch developing the idea and then had to wait for the public to cotton on. 'When we first started I was a bit naïve and thought people would flock to it. I quickly found that you have to develop ways of reaching the public,' she says.

One of those ways is a recently launched wedding list service for the eco-conscious couple. Another is online advertising. Although there are frustrations, Bramham insists she is enjoying trying to get the business off the ground. For the moment, she is keeping control of costs by outsourcing elements such as design and web development, but she has big plans. 'I want to be a one-stop shop for ethical products,' she says. The business' products are not always at low prices and include handmade recycled teddy bears for £32. There are also Eco Shopper Bags for £6 and recycled wrapping paper at £1.50 per sheet.

Source: adapted from the *Independent*, 5.7.2007 and www.biomelifestyle.com.

(a) Identify elements of the marketing mix from the article.
(b) Explain how these elements might help Biome Lifestyle to gain a competitive advantage over its rivals.

consumers about the nature of a product itself, market research can also help a business to decide on the make up of its marketing mix. Indeed, it is likely that an effective marketing mix will have been informed by market research. For example, market research may allow a business to find out about how consumers will respond to different prices and where a product should be made available.

The type of product it is selling For example, a business marketing highly technical products is likely to emphasise its products' qualities rather than giving a free good as a promotion. However, a business marketing a product very similar to that of its competitors may wish to emphasise a lower price or use some method of promotion.

The market it is selling to Businesses selling consumer goods aimed at the mass market are likely to emphasise the promotional and pricing aspects of their marketing mix. Firms selling machinery or industrial goods are likely to stress the product itself.

The degree of competition A business operating in a competitive market, with many close rivals, is likely to stress the importance of price in its marketing mix. In less competitive markets price might not be seen as being so important.

Question 2.

In 2003 Jenny Bodey set up the smallest of small businesses in a single shop. It was a wedding shop in Bootle, Liverpool, called The Bridal Lounge. By Christmas 2003 and January 2004 she had experienced record days of sales. Perhaps this was due to her choice of business. The profit margins on products in this market are very high. Dresses that are bought for £119 can be sold for £449 and still remain competitive. In the first year sales were predicted to be £56,000 but turned out to be nearer £80,000. She could now easily look at opening a second shop within a couple of years, although she needed to be careful because the area where her current shop is sited had very low overheads.

Jenny also has some advice for others looking to start up. She says budding entrepreneurs should not be too keen to offer discounts and promotions. 'I was giving people £100 of accessories with certain deals, but I've halved that. People don't expect a deal to be so generous. She also says 'I did quite a lot of advertising from regional based wedding magazines to wedding brochures and the local press. If I had a stall at a wedding fair I would take an advert in the brochure as everyone who visited my stall would take the brochure away with them.'

Source: adapted from *en*, February, 2004.

(a) Suggest reasons why the marketing mix of this business has been successful.

The marketing mix of competitors Businesses cannot afford to ignore the mix chosen by competitors. For example, confectionery manufacturers lay particular emphasis upon the availability of their products in a wide range of retail outlets. These include petrol stations, newsagents, off-licences and DIY stores. The emphasis here is on place. Any business wishing to compete in this market would, therefore, be unable to overlook the importance of place in its marketing mix.

The position of a business within an industry Businesses that are leaders within their industries tend to have a greater degree of freedom over the particular marketing mix which they choose. Such businesses include Nike and Coca-Cola. Other businesses are in less strong positions, but may operate in industries with strong market leaders. Where this occurs the relatively weaker businesses often choose to 'mimic' the marketing mix of the dominant business.

The marketing mix and small businesses

For many small businesses, particularly sole proprietors, sophisticated marketing strategies are beyond their means. As indicated above, financial factors restrict their choices in terms of creating an effective marketing mix. They often have so much work keeping their businesses ticking over on a day-to-day basis they do not get the chance to think strategically about their marketing.

Nevertheless, it is vital that even small businesses consider all aspects of their marketing mix. For example, a cake maker employing two staff would still need to think carefully about:

- the type of cakes, the **product**, that consumers would buy in the local area and how these migth be different from those of competitors;
- a **price** that would encourage local business to buy from a local business rather than a national distributor, but still allow the business to make a profit
- the type of **promotion** that would be most effective. Certain elements of the marketing mix may be more important for small business owners. For example, a survey by Barclays Bank found that 60 per cent of small businesses depend upon word of mouth to promote themselves;
- how to distribute to local shops and restaurants (**place**), for example, directly.

KNOWLEDGE

1. Identify the four main elements of an effective marketing mix.
2. What is a unique selling point?
3. What features of a business's product are important in the marketing mix?
4. Explain the difference between price and place in the marketing mix.
5. State five factors that influence a business's choice of marketing mix.
6. 'The size of a business is likely to affect its marketing mix.' Explain this statement.

KEYTERMS

Marketing mix – the elements of a business's marketing that are designed to meet the needs of its customers. The four elements are often called the 4 'Ps' – price, product, promotion and place.
Unique selling point or proposition – the aspect or feature of the product that differentiates it from its rivals.

Case Study: *A woman's own story*

Woman's Own has relaunched at the age of 75. The average age of its readers is 48. It is one of dozens of women's weeklies fighting for the over-35s in the UK national market. How has it survived? Forty seven per cent of the total magazine market in the UK is taken up with women's weeklies. They entertain readers with friendliness and real-life dramas. *Woman's Own* is a major brand, but not one that, up to now, has captured the 'excitement pushing-up circulation figures' elsewhere. All that, according to the title's publishers, IPC Connect, is about to change. The magazine, which was launched in 1932 with a cover showing three wraps of wool, relaunched in April, 2007 with a £2 million marketing budget that was to include TV and billboard advertising.

The new *Woman's Own* is the result of eight months of research into the sort of woman who buys the title and what she wants out of it. Its editor, Karen Livermore, and her team found a 'gap' between how the readers, typically women aged 35-plus, saw themselves (confident, outgoing, loves to gossip and shop) and how they saw other *Woman's Own* readers (settled, middle aged, mumsy, loves cooking and is a loyal friend and neighbour). This is the attitude gap Ms Livermore intends to tackle. But she has a battle on her hands, as these old-fashioned perceptions of the title are almost certainly shared by the wider marketplace. In fact, though more restrained than many rivals, *Woman's Own* has not been 'mumsy' and 'middle aged' for years. If it had, sales would have dropped even further than they have. Circulation has fallen in the past 10 years, from 808,311 in 1996 to 356,811 in December 2006. Despite this, it is still the 21st biggest-selling magazine on the UK news-stand.

In the late Eighties, two German companies, Bauer and Gruner and Jahr, launched their own titles into the UK market. *Best* and *Bella*, brought shorter, snappier stories and a new, 'value-for-money' feel. In 1990 Bauer launched *Take a Break*, and suddenly 'real-life stories were the undisputed currency of women's weeklies. *Woman's Own* responded by relaunching with its own strong true-life stories. Further competition came with the launch in 2002 of Emap's Closer, with its celebrity gossip and paparazzi pictures. When *Grazia* came along a few years later, calling itself a 'weekly glossy', yet another genre was born. For traditional titles to survive, reinvention has been the name of the game for the past 20 years. So what is so different about the relaunched *Woman's Own*?

'*Woman's Own* had lost connections with its readers. Their median age is 48 and that hasn't changed – what has changed is that women in their 40s are very different now. Yes, lots of our readers are housewives and they have homes to run, but they don't want to be reminded of it. Weekly readers can be an unforgiving lot. They are no one's fools – they are savvy and clued up. They're sick of tired old magazine speak – if they're on a diet, they don't want to be told to get off the bus one stop early for the exercise. Our challenge has been to launch the magazine as if it's launching for the first time in 2007. 'We have completely pulled it apart. We'd develop a section, try it out at two or three customer focus groups and then use the information to

redesign it and test a different version the following night,' says Ms Livermore.

Last week's issue definitely looked different, with bolder colours and cleaner, fresher lines. The cover is a glamorous shot of Sharon Osbourne. The content is not so different, but somehow the tone of the magazine is livelier, brighter and cheekier. The cover price has risen from 78p to 85p, the paper stock has been upgraded and there is a new, seven page section of news, views and celebrity gossip. Where magazines used to compete for reader loyalty, these days research shows that women are buying across the market, picking up several titles each week, a practice termed 'repertoire buying' by the marketing teams.

So is there room for the all-new *Woman's Own* in today's crowded market? The biggest hurdle is not so much producing a great magazine. It's getting across to the reader that *Woman's Own* is no longer about knitting a nice sweater and finding a good recipe for dinner.

Source: adapted from the *Independent* 22.4.2007.

(a) What is meant by the term marketing mix? (3 marks)
(b) How would you describe *Woman's Own's* unique selling point? (4 marks)
(c) Identify elements of *Woman's Own's* marketing mix using examples from the article. (6 marks)
(d) Using evidence from the article, explain the factors that may have influenced *Woman's Own's* marketing mix. (10 marks)
(e) Discuss whether IPC connect should place so much emphasis in its marketing mix upon the nature of *Woman's Own* as a product. (10 marks)

The product life cycle

Product is one part of the marketing mix. For marketing to be effective a business must be aware of its PRODUCT LIFE CYCLE. The product life cycle shows the different stages that a product passes through over time and the sales that can be expected at each stage. By considering product life cycles businesses can plan for the future. Most products pass through six stages – development, introduction, growth, maturity, saturation and decline. These are illustrated in Figure 1.

Figure 1: The product life cycle

Development During the development stage the product is being **researched** and **designed**. Suitable ideas must be investigated, developed and tested. If an idea is considered worth pursuing then a prototype or model of the product might be produced. A decision will then be made about whether or not to launch the product. A large number of new products never progress beyond this stage and will **fail**. This is because businesses are often reluctant to take risks associated with new products. During the development stage it is likely that the business will spend to develop the product and **costs** will be high. As there will be no sales at this stage, the business will initially be spending but receiving no revenue

Introduction At the start of this stage the product will be **launched**. As the product is new to the market. sales initially are often slow. Costs are incurred when the product is launched. It may be necessary to build a new production line or plant, and the firm will have to meet promotion and distribution costs. A business is also likely to spend on **promotion** to make consumers aware of the new product. Therefore, it is likely that the product will still not be profitable. **Prices** may be set high to cover promotion costs. But they may also be set low in order to break into the market. Few outlets may stock products at this stage. The length of this stage will vary according to the product. With brand new technical products, e.g. computers, the introduction stage can be quite long. It takes time for consumers to become confident that such products 'work'. At first the price of such products may be quite high. On the other hand, a

product can be an instant hit resulting in very rapid sales growth. Fashion products and some **fast moving consumer goods** may enjoy this type of start to their life.

Growth Once the product is established and consumers are aware of it, sales begin to grow rapidly, new customers buy the product and there are repeat purchases. Costs may fall as production increases. The product then becomes **profitable**. If it is a new product and there is a rapid growth in sales, **competitors** may launch their own versions. This can lead to a slowdown of the rise in sales. Businesses may need to consider their **prices and promotion**. For example, a high price charged initially may need to be lowered, or promotion may need to increase to encourage brand loyalty.

Maturity and saturation At some stage the growth in sales will level off. The product has become established with a stable market share at this point. Sales will have peaked and competitors will have entered the market to take advantage of profits. As more firms enter the market, it will become saturated. Some businesses will be forced out of the market, as there are too many firms competing for consumers. During the maturity and saturation stages of the product life cycle many businesses use extension strategies to extend the life of their products. These are discussed below.

Decline For the majority of products, sales will eventually decline. This is usually due to changing consumer tastes, new technology or the introduction of new products. The product will lose its appeal to customers. At some stage it will be withdrawn or sold to another business. It may still be possible to make a profit if a high price can be charged and little is spent on promotion or other costs.

Different product life cycles

Many products have a limited life span. Their product life cycles will look similar to that shown in Figure 1. For some products there is a very short period between introduction and decline. They are sometimes called **fads**. The slope of the product life cycle in the introduction and growth period will be very steep and the decline very sharp. Examples of such products include Micropets in 2003, Heelies in 2006 and Pokemon cards in 2005. Once consumers lose interest in a product and sales fall, a business may withdraw it from the market. It may be replaced with another new product. Sometimes poor selling products are withdrawn in case they damage the image of the company. However, businesses must take care not to withdraw a product too early. Over time, certain products have become popular again. For example, skateboards, which were popular in the 1980s regained popularity in the mid-1990s and the early 2000s.

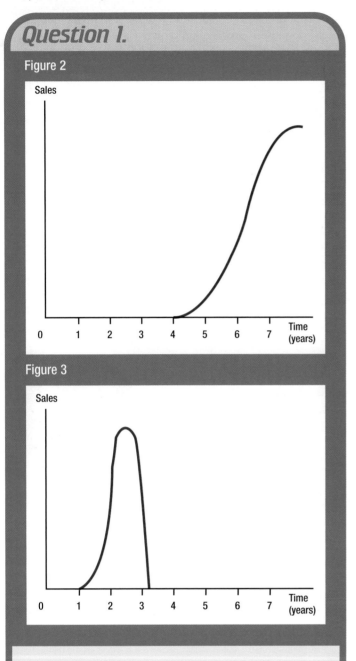

Figure 2

Figure 3

(a) Examine Figures 2 and 3. For each of these, name a product which you think might have a similar product life cycle.
(b) Why do some products have a very long life cycle (greater than 50 years)?
(c) Sketch the current product life cycle of three of the following products:
  (i) A compact disc or downloadable song by a leading performance artist/group (you will need to specify the name of the song and the performance artist);
  (ii) Walkers cheese and onion crisps;
  (iii) Coca-Cola;
  (iv) Hovis bread;
  (v) Rice Krispie bars;
  (vi) Golden Compass DVD;
  (vii) the Facebook website;
  (viii) a football strip of a Premier League team (you will need to specify the team).

Some businesses still enjoy profits from products which were launched many years ago. The Oxo cube was launched in 1910, Kellogg's Cornflakes were launched in 1906 and Theakston's Old Peculier, a strong ale, was launched in the eighteenth century. These products still sell well today in a form fairly similar to their original.

Because of the high cost of investment, car producers often set product life cycles of ten years for their models. For many products, life cycles are getting shorter, especially in areas like electronics. In the computer industry, some models and software have become obsolete within a very short period as new versions appear which are more technically advanced. For example, in 1995 Microsoft launched its operating software Windows 95. It was later replaced by Windows 98, Windows 2000 and Windows XP.

Extension strategies

It is clear from the product life cycle that the sales of products decline, although at different rates. Firms can attempt to extend the life of a product by using EXTENSION STRATEGIES. They may decide to use one or more of the following techniques.
- Finding new markets for existing products. Over the last 20 years there has been a boom in the sales of sports clothing. This has been largely due to the use of sports clothing as fashion wear.
- Developing a wider product range. Lucozade was originally sold as a product to those recovering from an illness. By extending the product range to include a 'Sports' version, a huge increase in sales has been achieved. Lego constantly develops new versions of a product that started out as a plastic set of building blocks.
- Gearing the product towards specific target markets. Mobile phone companies have packages geared to the needs of teenagers. Banks have accounts for young people.
- Changing the appearance, format or packaging. Coca-Cola is available in individual cans, in glass or plastic bottles, or in multipacks. Chocolate bars such as Toblerone are sold in standard sizes, in large bars or in mini sizes.
- Encouraging people to use the product more frequently. Manufacturers of what were previously known as 'breakfast cereals' have used promotional campaigns to encourage the use of their products at different times throughout the day.
- Changing the ingredients or components. Many microwaveable food products are available as 'weight watchers' or 'low fat' meals, as well as more traditional meals. Many cars are equipped with CD or MP3 players and air conditioning as standard.
- Updating designs. Car manufacturers regularly update models. Makers of computer gaming systems bring out new versions after a period of time.

The effect that an extension strategy can have on the product life cycle is shown in Figure 4. As the market becomes saturated and sales begin to fall, the decline in sales is delayed by the use of

Figure 4: Extensions strategies

an extension strategy. It would be sensible for a business to try to extend the life of a mature product before sales start to decline. Firms that can predict falling sales from market forecasts may attempt to use extension strategies before the decline takes place, i.e. in the maturity stage.

The product life cycle and capacity

Capacity utilisation is the extent to which a business uses the capacity that it has to produce a particular product. It is the relationship between what a business actually produces and what it is capable of producing. A business working at full capacity that is unable to produce any more of a product will be at maximum capacity utilisation. A business that can still produce more with its existing technology and machinery is likely to be working at less than full capacity.

The product life cycle is linked to capacity utilisation.

- At launch, sales of a product are likely to be limited. So a business will have spare capacity.
- When a product is at its growth stage a business will often be expanding its production and using up spare capacity to meet the rising demand for the product.
- When a product is in its maturity stage a business may be operating at full capacity. If sales continue to grow it must decide whether to invest to expand capacity.
- In the decline stage the capacity that a business has to produce a product will often be underutilised. This is because sales and therefore production may be cut back.

So during the development, growth and growth phases a business will have to make decisions over its capacity.

Creating new capacity A business may decide to build new capacity to deal with sales of a new product. New capacity could be created as sales grow. This would delay outflows of cash until they were needed. There would be less risk that the new capacity would be greater than sales. But, if sales were higher than

expected, the business might find it difficult to invest quickly enough to prevent shortages. Alternatively, new capacity could be created before sales take place. But this carries the risk that the investment would be wasted if sales did not grow in line with expectations. The cash to pay for the investment would flow out of the business earlier. Average costs would be higher too, because the cost of creating and running spare capacity at launch would have to be paid for. However, it would easier to deal with unexpectedly high sales than if investment took place when sales actually happened.

Utilising existing capacity There is less risk if a business uses existing capacity. If a business is operating at less than full capacity, it could use the spare capacity to launch a new product. This would help reduce cash outflow associated with new products. Or a business may be working at full capacity, but have products which are at the end of their life cycle. These could be taken out of production and replaced by the new lines.

A problem with this approach is that the average costs of

Question 2.

Rachel's is a manufacturer of organic dairy products. The business is very much a farm based enterprise. In 1952, Brynllys, a farm in Wales, began the process which made it into the first organic farm in the UK. Initially, its dairy production was confined to selling organic milk. But in 1982 it branched out into making and selling cream and butter, initially sold locally. 1984 saw the first commercial production of yoghurt. By 1987, Marigold, a leading London health food supplier, was an enthusiastic buyer and, in 1989, Rachel's yoghurts were on sale in Harrods.

In 1990, the owners of the business, the husband-and-wife team of Gareth and Rachel Rowlands, decided to expand. They borrowed the money, using their farm as collateral, to build a state-of-the-art dairy. It was capable of processing not just the 330,000 litres of organic milk a year from their farm, but 3 million litres – the entire organic output of Wales. Their decision to take this risk was helped by their first large contract to supply a supermarket chain, Sainsbury.

In 1999, they sold the business to Horizon Organic, the biggest wholly organic dairy supplier in the US. Horizon has introduced three new yoghurt flavours: low fat vanilla, whole-milk with maple syrup and Greek-style with honey. This month sees the debut of Rachel's organic fat-free yoghurt and a Welsh butter with bilingual packaging. However, Horizon promised not to alter Rachel's yoghurts in content or concept.

Source: adapted from *The Financial Times*, 24.11.2001.

(a) Discuss whether the introduction of (i) organic yoghurt in 1984 and (ii) organic fat-free yoghurt in 2001 were examples of a new product being brought to the market or an extension strategy for an existing product.
(b) Discuss the cash flow requirements of Rachel's yoghurts during and after the decision in 1990 to build a new state-of-the-art dairy.

production, excluding the cost of any investment, may be higher than if new capacity had been built. For example, it may cost 60p to produce an item on old machinery but only 40p if the latest equipment is used. The decision about whether to buy new equipment will depend upon the relationship between the cost of the new equipment and the saving on running costs. If a business only saves £10,000 a year on running costs by buying £100,000 of new equipment, then it probably won't buy. If it saves £90,000 on running costs for an investment of £100,000, it will probably purchase the new equipment.

As explained above, average costs of production may be higher at launch and during the growth phase if existing capacity to cope with high levels of sales is set aside for use at launch. But again, if sales exceed expectations, the business is more likely to cope if there is spare capacity.

The product life cycle and cash flow

Figure 5 shows the cash flow of a business over a product life cycle.

- Before product launch a business will spend to develop the product and yet no money is coming into the business from sales. So cash flow is likely to be negative.
- At launch, at point A, a product begins to sell. Cash flowing out of a business is still likely to be greater than cash flowing in, so cash flow will be negative. Sales have yet to take off and a business might be spending on promoting the product.
- In the growth period, eventually revenue from the product will be greater than spending (point B) and so cash flow becomes positive. This is because sales will be increasing and average costs may be falling as output increases.
- In the maturity stage cash flow will be at its highest. The product will be earning its greatest revenue.
- In the decline stage, sales will fall and so cash flow will decline.

Uses and problems of the product life cycle

Why might a business be interested in analysing the product life cycle of its existing products or anticipating the life cycle of new products?

- It will illustrate the broad trends in revenue that a product might earn for the business.
- It will identify points at which businesses may need to consider launching new products, as older ones are in decline.
- It will identify points at which extension strategies may need to be introduced.
- It may help a business to identify when and where spending is required, e.g. on research and development at the start, or on marketing at the introduction and when extension strategies are required.
- It may help to identify points at which a business should no longer sell a product.
- It will help a business to manage its product portfolio – its mix of products. This is discussed in the next section.
- It will give an indication of the profitability of a product at

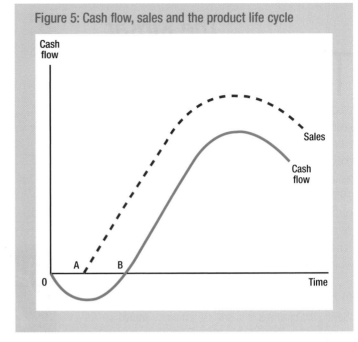

Figure 5: Cash flow, sales and the product life cycle

each stage in its cycle.
- It will allow a business to plan different styles of marketing that a product might need over its life cycle.

There may be problems, however, when using this model. It can be used to show changes over the life of a product. But it may not be effective in **predicting** the future sales of a product and how sales will change in future. In practice, every product is likely to have a slightly different product life cycle. Furthermore, it is important that the model does not **determine** decisions. For example, a product that is in the decline stage does not automatically have to be withdrawn. Sales may be falling due to a lack of promotion or poor distribution. The decline in sales may be more to do with management decisions than where the product is in its life cycle.

KEYTERMS

Extension strategies – methods used to extend the life of a product.
Product life cycle – shows the different stages in the life of a product and the sales that can be expected at each stage.

KNOWLEDGE

1. Briefly describe the various stages in the product life cycle.
2. Why might a product have a 'steep' life cycle?
3. Name three uses of the product life cycle.
4. How can a firm extend the life of its products?
5. State three ways in which the product life cycle is linked to capacity utilisation.
6. Name three links between the product life cycle and cash flow.

Case Study: *The KitKat*

The KitKat was launched as Rowntree's Chocolate Crisp in 1935 and renamed KitKat in 1937. The following year it was the company's most popular product. It first became a national favourite in the war years of the 1940s, when the government endorsed it as a healthy, cheap food. Ever since it has been the most popular chocolate bar in the UK. It was one of the main reasons behind the takeover of Rowntree by Nestlé in 1989. It maintained its supremacy even when faced with competition from Nestlé's own Smarties and Black Magic. According to the KitKat website, 47 bars are eaten every second in the UK and a year's production would stretch around the London Underground more than 350 times.

However, in 2003 sales fell by 5 per cent from nearly £123 million in 2002 to £116 million by the end of 2003. 'Saying the business is in crisis is extreme', argued a consumer brands analyst at the time, 'but maintaining its position in the UK confectionery market is going to be a challenge. It's a cut-throat market.' There was concern that saturation point had been reached.

Nestlé fought back by introducing a number of variants to the KitKat market as from 2004. These included an orange and mint flavour, a lemon and yoghurt flavour and a Halloween variant, Blood Orange. In addition, in 2005 a caramac KitKat was launched and the KitKat Dark has now established itself as a permanent addition to the KitKat range. Both the two and four finger versions of the KitKat have remained popular and they have been joined by the KitKat Chunky as mainstays of the KitKat product range.

There are many different variants upon the KitKat theme in those countries where the product remains popular. In Malaysia there is a hot weather version that is less likely to melt in the heat and in Japan a range of flavours, including green tea, passion fruit and lemon cheesecake, have been introduced. Japanese school children regard the KitKat as a lucky charm for exams and tests and take them into school on test days.

In England, health scares regarding childhood obesity have led to a school ban on vending machines selling crisps, chocolate and fizzy drinks as part of what has been termed the 'great KitKat clampdown'. These and other health moves have seen food manufacturers such as Nestle criticized for encouraging youngsters to eat what are seen as unhealthy foods. Health campaigners have also singled out the KitKat

chunky for particular criticism.

Source: adapted from *The Guardian* 10.9.2007, *The Independent*, 15.2.2004; www.nestle.co.uk and www.news.bbc.co.uk

(a) Using information from the article, draw and label the product life cycle for KitKat. (3 marks)
(b) Identify significant periods in the product life cycle of KitKat using examples from the article. (6 marks)
(c) Using information from the article, explain the product extension strategies used by Nestle in relation to the KitKat. (8 marks)
(d) Discuss how changes made in the future might affect the product life cycle of KitKat. (8 marks)

The nature of products

A PRODUCT is anything that can be exchanged and is able to satisfy customers' needs. It might be a tangible physical GOOD, such as a car or a packet of peas. Or it might be an intangible, non-physical SERVICE, such as a foreign holiday, a medical examination or defence.

A distinction can be made between PRODUCER (or INDUSTRIAL) PRODUCTS and CONSUMER PRODUCTS. Producer products are used to make other goods and services or in the operation of A business. For example, a coffee machine and a building are two producer products used by Starbucks to make a cup of coffee served to consumers. Producer products are sold by one business to another through business to business marketing. The cup of coffee is a consumer product because it is bought by individuals or households for personal use. A car bought from a dealer by an individual would be a consumer product bought in a consumer market. In contrast, a car bought by a business for use as a company car would be a producer product.

Consumers buy products because of the benefits given by these attributes. TANGIBLE BENEFITS are benefits which can be measured. For example, the benefit of a train journey might be that it gets you from London to Glasgow in four hours. The benefit of a washing machine might be that it will wash for five years without breaking down. INTANGIBLE BENEFITS are benefits which, though present, cannot be measured. Some products are bought because of the image they convey. For example, wearing a t-shirt in the colours of a national football team might have been considered fashionable during the World Cup of 2006. Other intangible benefits might be pleasure or peace of mind. Cadbury's advertisements stress the pleasure gained from eating a Cadbury's Flake. Insurance to cover funeral expenses is often sold to give peace of mind to the person who is going to die.

What are the characteristics of a 'good' product?

- It should be functional and fulfil the needs of customers. For example, food should taste good. A train service should be fast, frequent and reliable. A television set should give good quality pictures. A lawn mower should cut grass well.
- It should be aesthetically pleasing. Good design is not just about working properly. It is also about how a product looks to the customer. In some industries, such as clothing, cars and kitchen equipment, aesthetics and design have a great effect on how consumers spend their money.
- It should be affordable. Many people would like to take a journey into space, but at present it is too expensive for all but a few. On the other hand, a furniture company like Ikea has become extremely successful because it sells goods which are affordable to most. So the product should be

capable of being produced within the purchasing budgets of the target market.
- The product must conform to legal requirements. Toys, for example, should not contain lead paint. Food sold to people should be fit to eat.
- Ideally, products should be environmentally and socially friendly. Increasingly, products are being bought by consumers on the strength of their 'ethical' credentials. For example, people want paper made from recycled paper. They might also refuse to buy trainers made in factories with poor working conditions in low income countries.

Unique selling points of products

Successful products will have a **unique selling point** or **unique selling proposition** (USP). This is a characteristic of a product that makes it different from other products. The USP is often promoted by businesses to customers as being the 'best'. For example, cars may be advertised as being the safest, giving the smoothest ride or having the most space. Identifying and promoting the USP of a product can have a number of benefits.

- For consumers, it helps them to differentiate one product from others, which can make choices easier.
- For businesses, it helps differentiate its products from others. It will aim to show consumers that it is offering something that other products are not. This can increase sales and help to build up BRAND LOYALTY.

The product portfolio

Product life cycle analysis, outlined in the previous unit, shows businesses that sales of products eventually decline. A well organised business with one or more products will attempt to phase out old products and introduce new ones. This is known as managing the PRODUCT PORTFOLIO or PRODUCT MIX. The product portfolio will be made up of PRODUCT LINES. A product line is a group of products which are similar. For example, televisions are a product line including flat screen, HD widescreen and portable televisions. With a constant launch of new products, a business can make sure a 'vacuum' is not created as products reach the end of their life.

Figure 1 shows how a business can manage its product portfolio. Say that a business over a particular time period aims to launch three products. By organising their launch at regular intervals, there is never a gap in the market. As one product is declining, another is growing and further launches are planned. At point (i), as sales of product X are growing, product Y has just been launched. This means that at point (ii), when sales of product X have started to decline, sales of product Y are growing and product Z has just been launched.

This simple example shows a 'snapshot' of three products only. In practice, a business may have many products. It would hope that existing products remain in 'maturity' for a long period. The profit from these mature products would be used to 'subsidise' the launch of new products. New products would be costly at first, and would make no profit for the business.

Examples of businesses that have successfully managed their product portfolios are sweet manufacturers. Companies such as Nestlé produce a wide range of products, including KitKat, Milky Bar and Yorkie, and constantly look to launch new products.

Figure 1: Managing the product portfolio

Product portfolio analysis and the Boston Matrix

One problem for firms when planning their product portfolios is that it is very difficult in practice to tell what stage of the life cycle a product is at. Also, there is no standard lifetime for products. For example, young people's fashion clothing has life cycles which can be predicted with some certainty. Other poducts are less reliable. Who, for example, could have predicted the lengthy life cycles of products such as Heinz baked beans and the VW Beetle, or the short life cycle of products such as the Sinclair C5 – a sort of 'mini-car' introduced in the 1980s?

A useful technique for allowing firms to analyse their product portfolios is the Product Portfolio Matrix developed by the Boston Consulting Group. It is sometimes called the BOSTON MATRIX. This is shown in Figure 2. Products are categorized according to two criteria.

- **Market growth.** How fast is the market for the product growing? The market may be declining or it may be expanding. Sales of a product in a fast expanding market have a better chance of growing than a product in a stagnant or declining market.
- **Relative market share.** How strong is the product within its market? Is it a market leader that other products follow? Is it a product that is twelfth in terms of sales? To measure this the market share of a product is compared with the strongest rival product. For example, if Product X had a market share of 10 per cent and the market leader had 40

per cent then the relative market share of Product X is 0.25 (10 per cent ÷ 40 per cent). If Product Y is a market leader with 50 per cent market share and the next most important product had a market share of 25 per cent, the relative market share of product Y is 2.0 (50 per cent ÷ 25 per cent).

Using these criteria the products of a business can be placed into one of four categories on the Boston Matrix.

Stars A star is a product with a high market growth and a relatively high market share. Stars are valuable to businesses. The product will be in a strong position in its market as it has a high market share and the business can take advantage of a fast growing market. A star is already likely to be **profitable** as it has a relatively high market share. But a business will need to **invest** in the product to cope with a growing market and growing sales. This could mean investing in new production facilities or promotion to fend off competition. **Cash flow** may be nearly zero. This is because although profits will be high, bringing money in, spending will also be high, leading to outflows.

Cash cows A cash cow is a product with a relatively high market share. It is therefore well positioned in the market and likely to be **profitable**. But the market it is in will have weak growth. So there will be little chance of increasing sales and profits in future. There will be little need for **investment**. With slow growth in sales there should be little need for new premises for example. Cash cows have strong positive **cash flow**. Money coming into the business from profits will not be taken out via investment.

Problem children Problem children, also know as question marks or wildcats, are products with a relatively low market share in a fast growing market. This can be a problem for a business because it is unclear what should be done with these products. If a product is performing weakly it is unlikely to be **profitable**. But as it is in a fast growing market, there is potential to turn it into a star. **Cash flow** is likely to be zero or negative. Weak relative market share means that it will not be profitable. But **investment** will be needed to cope with expanding sales in a fast growing market.

Dogs These are products with a relatively low market share in a market with low growth. Dogs have poor prospects for future sales and **profits**. They may generate some **cash flow** because they will need little **investment** but may earn some profit. But if they make little or no profit, cash flow may be zero or even negative.

Businesses can make use of the Boston Matrix to manage their product portfolios.

Balancing product lines Businesses must ensure that their product portfolios do not contain too many items within each category. Naturally, they do not want lots of 'Dogs', but they should also avoid having too many 'Stars' and 'Problem children'. Products on the top of the Boston Matrix are in the early stages of the product life cycle and are in growing markets. But the cost of developing and promoting them will not yet have been recovered. This will drain resources. Balancing these with 'Cash cows' will mean that the revenue from the 'Cash cows' can be used to support products in a growing market. The development cost of 'Cash cows' is likely to have already been recovered and promotional costs should be low relative to sales. This does not mean though that a business would want lots of 'Cash cows' and few 'Problem children' and 'Stars'. This is because many of the 'Stars' and perhaps some 'Problem children' might become the 'Cash cows' of the future.

Taking appropriate decisions Products in different categories in the Matrix may require different approaches.
- Stars have great future potential. They are future cash cows. A business will need to **build** the brand of these products so that sales increase and competition is fought off successfully.
- Cash cows might be **milked** for cash, which can then be

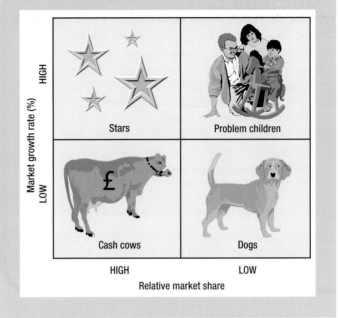

Figure 2: The Boston Matrix

Stars

Problem children

Cash cows

Dogs

Market growth rate (%) HIGH / LOW

Relative market share HIGH / LOW

used to develop other products. Or the business may decide to spend just enough on promotion and development to maintain sales and market share, known as **holding**.
- For problem children a business has choices. It can **build** the brand, hoping to turn it into a star, **harvest** the product by raising price and cutting promotion so that profits are increased, or **divest** itself of the product, withdrawing it or selling it because it is not making a profit.
- Dogs may be divested if they are not making a profit or in some cases harvested.

New product development

Planning the product portfolio requires the continual development and launch of new products. New products are needed to replace products coming to the end of their life cycles and to keep up with changes in the market. This is called **new product development**.

In some business sectors the need to plan ahead is very important. In the chemical industry, development work is done on products which might not reach the market for over ten years. In the motor industry many cars take over five years to develop. New products normally pass through five stages when they are being developed.

Generating ideas The first stage is when firms generate ideas. Ideas for new products come from a variety of sources.
- Identifying gaps in the market, perhaps through market research. An example of this has been the development of vegetarian microwave dishes by food producers. An important issue here for businesses is in identifying the unique selling point of a product.
- Scientific research. Pharmaceuticals businesses devote huge

Question 2.

The origins of the iPhone can be found in Steve Job's (the Apple Chief Executive) instruction to Apple engineers in 2003 to investigate touch screens. He believed that mobile phones were going to become important devices for portable information access and was determined to create a device that integrated a mobile phone, Internet access and an iPod. When it was launched in the UK in November, 2007 it was widely regarded as being far superior to anything else on the market with its multitouch technology and wide range of uses. Apple anticipate selling 10 million iPhones worldwide by 2008.

Source: adapted from adapted from *The Guardian*, 5.11.2007, www.wikipedia.org and www.apple.co.uk

(a) Explain TWO influences on the development of the iPhone.

(b) Discuss, using the Boston Matrix. whether the Iphone would be categorised as (i) a star or (ii) a problem child in future.

---

amounts to research and development expenditure. As a result they have developed products to tackle a range of ailments from heart disease through to cancer.
- Generating creative ideas through open discussions. Products such as the jet engine have come about as a result of this.
- Analysing other products. When developing new products many businesses will analyse products manufactured by competitors. They aim to include, adapt or improve upon the best features of these products in their own designs. Some businesses adapt their own successful products to make new products.

Analysis The second stage is the analysis of those ideas generated in the first stage. There are a number of questions a firm might ask. Most importantly, it must find out if the product is marketable – if enough consumers wish to buy it to allow the firm to make a profit. Businesses must also decide if the product fits in with the company's objectives, if it is legal and if the technology is available to produce it.

Development The third stage is the actual development of the product. This may involve technical development in the laboratory or the production of a prototype. Such work will be carried out by the research and development department. An important part of this process is the actual design of the product. Some preliminary testing may be carried out to find out whether or not the product actually meets consumers' needs.

Test marketing TEST MARKETING occurs when a new product is tested on a small, representative section of the total market. The test market area should share characteristics which are similar to those found in the market as a whole. The benefit of test marketing is the high degree of reliability of results

gained. It is carried out because of the high cost and risk of launching a product in a large, usually national, market. Test marketing can itself be costly, but not as expensive as a national launch which fails. One problem is that it allows competitors to see the new product and gives them the chance to take counter-action before a national launch.

Commercialisation and launch The final stage is the launch and commercialisation. Here any problems found during test marketing must be solved. The firm will then decide on the 'marketing package' it will use to give the product launch the greatest chance of success.

At each of the five stages, many ideas are rejected. This means that very few ideas generated in the first stage will actually end up as a product launched onto the market. In Figure 3, an example is shown where 40 ideas were put forward for a new product. In this company the majority of ideas do not get beyond the first stage. The pass rate at this stage is only 1 in 5, with 4 out of 5 ideas being rejected. After that, the number of ideas which survive from one stage to the next increases as the pass rate falls from 1 in 5 ideas to 1 in 2. At the end of the process, only 1 out of a total of 40 ideas has survived to be launched onto the market.

Influences on new product development

There is a wide range of influences on businesses developing new goods and services. These influences may encourage a business to go ahead with a new product or, alternatively, restrict the development of one or more new products.

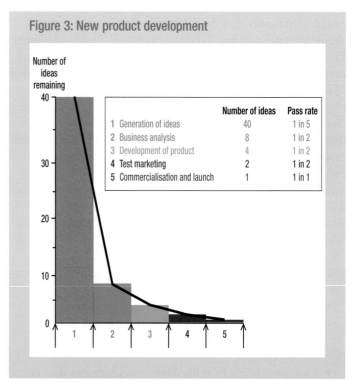

Figure 3: New product development

	Number of ideas	Pass rate
1 Generation of ideas	40	1 in 5
2 Business analysis	8	1 in 2
3 Development of product	4	1 in 2
4 Test marketing	2	1 in 2
5 Commercialisation and launch	1	1 in 1

Availability of finance and resources In highly competitive markets businesses find that their profit margins are squeezed. This means that financial and human resources are often not available to develop new products. An example of this is in the market for budget fashion clothing. Businesses in this market tend to copy products developed for designer labels. Other businesses may find that they have a number of mature products generating a healthy stream of income. Such businesses may invest this income in new product development, hoping to create the 'cash cows' of the future.

Technology The development of technology can affect the type of product or service provided. One hundred years ago computers did not exist. Today they are sold in a variety of ways to different businesses. Internet cafes and laptop computers are now standard products for a range of consumers. There are now many opportunities for new goods and services, such as the online retailing of music that are linked to these new technologies. Just ten years ago such opportunities for new products like these did not exist.

Cost Even when businesses have resources, the cost of developing new products may be prohibitive. The development of products in the electronics market can cost millions of pounds. As technological boundaries have been pushed forward, the cost of even modest new product development has risen sharply. Also, in many markets products have increasingly shorter life spans. This means that less time is available to recover development costs. Conversely, in those markets, such as the market for computer games consoles where technological developments are moving at a fast pace, there can be enormous rewards for successful new products. This creates a clear incentive for new products even when the costs are high.

Competitors' actions The behaviour of a business' competitors can strongly influence new product development. In some cases an innovatory competitor can act as a spur to other businesses in the same sector in their efforts to create new products. Some would argue, for example, that the new products produced by the Apple Corporation, such as the iPhone and iPod, have caused competitors to raise their game. Other businesses respond to innovatory competitors by copying, as far as possible within copyright and patent laws, their competitors' products.

Market constraints There is little point in a business developing a new product unless consumers are prepared to purchase it at a price which can cover development and production costs. Many so-called 'tremendous ideas' for new products have been abandoned. This is because firms believe they cannot find a profitable market for the product. In addition, consumers can be resistant to change. This is often because of the time and effort consumers need to spend in getting to know how new products 'work'. There is also evidence that consumers are resistant to new products which represent a radical departure from existing products. New versions of existing products are sometimes more popular with consumers than totally new ideas for this reason.

Entrepreneurial skills of managers and owners Some businesses are more likely to engage in new product development because of the skills and attitudes of their managers and owners. More entrepreneurial managers and owners of businesses are likely be more inclined to take risks rather than continue doing what they know best. Steve Job, for example, Chief Executive of the Apple Corporation, has been widely credited as being the driving force behind the revolutionary new products produced by Apple, including the iPod, iMac and iPhone.

Legal constraints Firms cannot develop whatever new products they wish. Legislation must be taken into account. For example, a pharmaceutical company wishing to develop a new product must be sure that it adheres to health legislation.

KNOWLEDGE

1. What is a product?
2. What is the difference between a consumer and a producer product?
3. Explain how a business can prevent a 'vacuum' in its product portfolio.
4. What is meant by a product line?
5. What is meant by the Boston Matrix?
6. How can the Boston Matrix help a business to manage its product portfolio?
7. What is meant by new product development?
8. State two ways in which a business can generate new product ideas.
9. State six factors that can influence the development of new products.

KEYTERMS

Brand loyalty – the extent to which customers of a brand repeat purchases of that brand rather than others.

Boston Matrix – a 2 x 2 matrix model which analyses a product portfolio according to the growth rate of the market and the relative market share of products within the market.

Consumer products – goods or services sold to individuals to households for personal consumption.

Goods – physical products.

Intangible benefits (of a product) – benefits that cannot be measured.

Producer or industrial products – goods or services that are sold by one business to other businesses.

Product line – a group of products which are very similar.

Product portfolio (product mix) – the particular portfolio of products which a firm is marketing.

Product – anything that can be exchanged and is able to satisfy customers' needs.

Services – non-physical products.

Tangible benefits (of a product) – benefits that can be measured.

Test marketing – testing out a product on a small section of a market prior to its full launch.

CRITIQUE

Critics of the Boston Matrix argue that the Matrix can cause businesses to focus too much upon pursuing increases in market share as opposed to, for example, attempting to consolidate market share or improve other aspects of the performance of a product. It is also suggested that the model fails to take account of the way in which products within a business can support one another. For example a business might sell a dog, but this might affect sales of other products it supports which could be stars or cash cows. Cash flow and profit can also be different for individual products. A dog may have strong cash flow and be profitable despite falling sales. A star might have negative cash flow if there is fierce competition.

Case Study: *Stubble trouble*

The Fusion Power Stealth is a razor with five pivoting blades and one at the back, a lubrication strip, a rubber guard to stretch the skin, a battery to make it vibrate and a microchip to control the level of vibration. It will also tell you when the battery's flat. It has a striking black and orange box to house the rubberised handle. Sports stars sell it to you, including David Beckham and Roger Federer. And it has a killer name.

It is, claims Gillette, the closest shave a man can get. They did, of course, say that about the last thing they came up with before Fusion Power Stealth - the one just called Fusion Power. Before that, it was just primitive old Fusion. And they said the same for the Mach3 Power, which came after Mach3 Turbo, which followed Mach3, and overtook Sensor Excel, Sensor, Atra Plus and Tracll Plus. The latter appeared in 1971 and seems positively primeval; it was smooth, it was safe, it meant you didn't leave the sink covered in blood and your face speckled with tissue paper. Nothing could better it, for a while at least.

The Fusion Power Stealth, which began appearing at chemists and supermarkets in September 2007, will probably only be 'the best' shaving system for a couple of years. After that, Gillette have other plans, which they are not keen to divulge as 'other people may be reading your story,' says Kevin Powell, Gillette's laboratory director, by which he means Wilkinson Sword. Gillette has 74 per cent of the total razor market in the UK, followed by Wilkinson Sword.

The razors aren't just thrown together by a marketing department in an attempt to sell us something we didn't know we needed. They are the result of years of called cutting-edge science and the endeavours of biologists, dermatologists, physicists, polymer scientists, biometricists and neurologists. There is a team concerned solely with how to make a razor vibrate just the right amount, and other people employed to optimise handle grip in a slippery bathroom environment. Only when these people have done their work (Fusion Power Stealth has taken four years to appear from the initial prototype), do the people who design the packaging and advertising slogans go to work.

Before the concept of the Fusion system went to Gillette's global HQ in Boston, it was tested on about 9,000 men throughout the world. When Fusion was tested against its predecessor Mach3, 30 per cent of men in the trials said they preferred their existing system. But the majority preferred it in 69 respects, including 'giving the closest shave without irritation'; 'blades shaving as close on the first stroke as the last'; 'the colour of the razor'; 'the texture of the handle'; and 'ease of rinsing'.

Source: adapted from *The Guardian*, 23.11.2007.

(a) Explain the unique selling points of the Fusion Power Stealth. (3 marks)

(b) Using information from the article, explain TWO influences on the development of the Fusion Power Stealth. (6 marks)

(c) Examine, using the Boston Matrix, the position in the market of the Fusion Power Stealth a couple of years after its launch and the decision about the product that Gillette may face. (8 marks)

(d) Discuss whether Gillette should have launched the Fusion Power Stealth when it had 74 per cent of the total razor market in the UK. (10 marks)

44 | Promotion

What is promotion?

PROMOTION is the attempt to draw attention to a product or business in order to gain new customers or to retain existing ones. There are many different forms of promotion. One way of distinguishing between these different forms is in terms of whether or not a business is promoting its products via independent media such as newspapers and TV. ABOVE-THE-LINE promotion is through independent media, such as television or newspapers. These allow a business to reach a wide audience easily. Most advertising is carried out 'above the line'. Some advertising, however, is carried out by methods over which a firm has direct control, such as direct mailing and branding. Such methods are known as BELOW-THE-LINE promotions.

The objectives of promotion

A business must be clear about exactly what it is trying to achieve through its promotion. The main aim of any promotion is to obtain and retain customers. However, there is a number of other objectives, some or all of which any successful campaign must fulfil.

- To make consumers aware or increase awareness of a product.
- To reach a target audience which might be geographically dispersed.
- To remind consumers about the product. This can encourage existing consumers to repurchase the product and may attract new consumers.
- To show a product is better than that of a competitor. This may encourage consumers to switch purchases from another product.
- To develop or improve the image of a business rather than a product. Much corporate advertising is carried out with this in mind, and is dealt with later in this unit.
- To reassure consumers after the product has been purchased. This builds up confidence in the product and may encourage more to be bought at a later date.
- To support an existing product. Such promotions may be used to remind consumers that a reliable and well thought of product is still available.

Businesses sometimes consider their promotion using **models**.

- AIDA is a method used to consider advertising. It suggests that effective advertising will raise Awareness (A) and encourage Interest (I), Desire (D) and Action (A), so that consumers buy the products.
- The DAGMAR (Defining Advertising Goals for Measured Advertising Results) model is also used to measure the effect of advertising. A business can measure how far the

group that is targeted has progressed along the scale:

Unawareness...Awareness...Comprehension...
Conviction...Action

- A similar model by Lavidge and Steiner suggests six stages – awareness, knowledge, liking, preference, conviction and purchase.

Above-the-line promotion

Above-the-line promotion is ADVERTISING. Advertising is often placed into different categories.

- INFORMATIVE ADVERTISING is designed to increase consumer awareness of a product. Examples include the classified advertisements in local newspapers, new share offers, grants available to small firms and entries in the *Yellow Pages*. New products may be launched with informative advertising campaigns to make consumers aware of their presence. It is argued that this type of advertising helps consumers to make a rational choice as to what to buy.
- PERSUASIVE ADVERTISING tries to convince consumers to purchase a product, often by stressing that it is more desirable than others. It is argued that this type of advertising distorts consumer buying, pushing them to buy products which they would otherwise not have bought. In reality, a great deal of advertising is persuasive to some extent.
- REASSURING ADVERTISING is aimed at existing customers. It tries to persuade them that their purchase was correct and that they should continue to buy the product. Banks and building societies often use this method to assure customers that their investments are safe.

There is a wide range of ADVERTISING MEDIA that firms can choose from in order to make consumers aware of their products including:

- commercial television, whether terrestrial such as ITV1 or Channel 4, or satellite such as BSkyB;
- commercial radio, which in the UK is local radio;
- national newspapers, such as *The Sun* or *The Times*;
- regional newspapers, such as the *London Evening Standard* or the *Birmingham Evening Post*;
- magazines, such as *Cosmopolitan* or *Loaded*;
- trade newspapers and journals, such as *The Grocer* or *Accountancy Age* which are read by workers or businesses in a particular industry, trade or profession;
- directories, including the telephone directories *Yellow Pages* and *Thomson Directory*;
- posters and transport, such as billboards by the side of the road or advertisements on the side of buses;
- the Internet.

The medium that is chosen will depend on a variety of factors including:

- **Cost** – most businesses could not afford television adverts, for example. Cost also has to be measured against effectiveness – how much extra new business will be generated by each £1 of advertising expenditure?
- **Media reach** – what media will best get to the audience the advertiser wishes to reach?
- **Delivery of the chosen message** – what media would best persuade consumers to change their brand of washing powder, for example, or give customers a telephone number to call if their washing machine broke down?
- **The marketing mix** – an advertising campaign may be part of a wider campaign using other elements of the marketing mix, such as below-the-line promotion or pricing. These other elements may help determine which media to use for advertising.
- **The law** – there are legal restrictions on the use of different media for advertising certain products, such as cigarettes.

Promotion below the line

Promotion below the line is any promotion that is not advertising. Above-the-line advertising in newspapers means that the promotion is seen by most of the readers, even though some will not be interested. With below-the-line promotions, firms aim their message at consumers who are either known to them or who have been chosen in advance, and who are interested. For example, businesses promoting through exhibitions, such as the Boat Show, can be certain that the majority of those attending will be interested in the products on show.

There may be problems that result from below-the-line promotions. As with advertising, they are expensive and their outcome can be difficult to predict. Also, they are often 'one-off' events, which have an impact for a limited period. Further, some types of promotion, such as direct mail and direct selling, are disliked by consumers.

Public relations PUBLIC RELATIONS is a attempt by a business to communicate with groups that form its 'public'. Such groups may include the government, shareholders, employees and customers. The aim is to increase sales by improving the image of the business and its products. This can be done directly by the business itself through a public relations activity or a television programme or a newspaper could be used. Because of the importance of maintaining good relations with the media, a business may appoint a **publicity manager**. As well as promoting favourable press stories, publicity managers must respond to criticisms and try to ensure that there are no unfavourable press notices.

Consumers appear to attach great importance to messages conveyed through public relations. For example, a new restaurant may promote a positive image of itself through promotional materials. Such communications may be taken 'with a pinch of salt' by consumers. However, a good write-up in

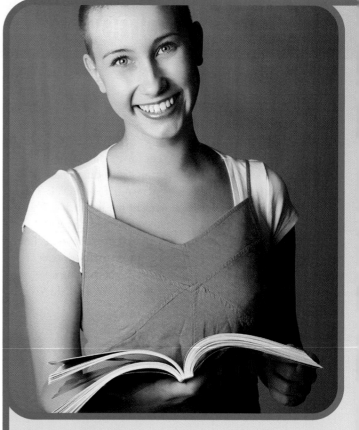

Question 1.

Anna Lever runs a shop which sells imported comics and graphic novels from the USA and Europe. She stocks well known comics by Marvel and DC, such as X-Men and Batman, and also a small line of European comics. Anna also sells comics by independent publishers in the UK. The market for comic sales in the UK tends to be a niche market, selling to specialist collectors, teenagers, students and children, and older people who Anna argues 'want to recapture their youth, by reading the stories they read when they were children and teenagers.'

There is a small number of chains selling comics in the UK, such as Forbidden Planet, but many other independent shops. The nearest competitor for Anna's shop is over 50 miles away. Anna often tries local mailing in the area. General mailing to all people tends to be a waste of time, so she must carefully target her audience. She also keeps clients regularly updated via emails. Most regular customers are happy to receive information about the latest issues although some newer customers have objected to this 'spam'.

Every month Anna makes the trip to the nearest city and puts up a stall in the comic mart on Sundays. She tends to see the same faces there all the time, and can build up contacts. There may also be people coming to 'have a look' on their day off and some have become regular clients. She has also occasionally taken a stand at the large fair held at the NEC in Birmingham a few times a year. She finds the trip is tiring, takes a lot of time out of her week and does not always pay for itself.

Source: adapted from company information.

(a) Why might it be important for Anna's business to use a trade fair as part of its promotional mix?

(b) Assess whether a trade fair might be more successful than direct mail advertising in promoting and selling comics.

a newspaper or restaurant guide is likely to be taken much more seriously by consumers. Businesses use a variety of methods to attract publicity.

- **Press conferences.** These might involve inviting journalists to a company presentation, where they are given information. The business may take the opportunity to launch a new or updated product. Sometimes, businesses provide free products for conference members to try out. Conferences may also be used for presentations to trade customers.
- **Press releases.** These are written accounts of events or activities which may be considered newsworthy. For example, new multi-million pound contracts gained by firms such as British Aerospace are announced on TV news bulletins. Such news stories usually originate from press releases issued by businesses.
- **Donations.** These can range from a small contribution to a college mini bus appeal to a large donation to Comic Relief's 'Red Nose Day' or the 'Children in Need' appeal . While some make payments anonymously, others take advantage of the opportunity for a good public relations event. The approach of a business to such an event is likely to be determined by its particular ethical stance.
- **Sponsorship.** This is popular in the sporting world. Examples have included the links between Coca-Cola and the Olympic Games, McDonald's and the World Cup, and Nike and Tiger Woods. Other types of sponsorship take place in the arts world with ballet, opera and theatre being sponsored by businesses.
- **Company visits.** Jaguar Cars and Warburtons Bakeries have allowed members of the public to visit their manufacturing and research plants as part of their public relations activities.

Branding A BRAND is a name, term, sign, symbol, design or any other feature that allows consumers to identify the goods and services of a business and to differentiate them from those of competitors. Some examples are shown in Table 1. A brand can be one product, a family or range of products or the actual business itself. So, for example, a Nestlé KitKat is an individual product produced by Nestlé. KitKat Chunky and KitKat Kubes are also part of the KitKat family. Nestlé is the name of the company which produces KitKats, other confectionery products,

---

Table 1: Examples of brands

- The use of the 'Mc' name by McDonald's in its products.
- The Nike 'swoosh' logo.
- The Apple on Apple computer and other products.
- The use of the colour orange in promotions by the Orange communications company or B&Q.
- The slogan 'Vorsprung Durch Technik' used for Audi cars.
- The 'tune' which accompanies references to the Intel Pentium Processor fitted into computers.

---

such as Milky Bar and Smarties, and foods such as breakfast cereals.

Brand names are the parts of the brand that can be spoken, such as the name of the product, ie Heinz Baked Beans or a Bratz doll. A **brand mark** is the design or symbol used in the brand, such as the apple used on Apple Macintosh computers. It is possible to protect the use of trademark by copyright. A company might use its **trade name** as a brand, such as Virgin, Disney or Starbucks. In some cases the company name might be as well known as its products or even more well known such as Sony or Ford.

There is a number of reasons why businesses use branding.

- **To create brand loyalty.** Consumers often have a high degree of **brand loyalty** to popular, well-established, brands. In many markets it can be difficult for firms to compete unless they have a strong brand identity.
- **To differentiate the product.** Especially in markets where products are fairly similar, it is important for a firm that its own products can be clearly distinguished from others. A clear brand identity can help to achieve this.
- **To gain flexibility when making pricing decisions.** The greater the loyalty of consumers to a particular brand, the more room for manoeuvre a firm will have in its pricing decisions. A survey by Business Marketing Services found that consumers were reluctant to switch from well-known brands in the hotel, car hire, computer and transatlantic flights markets. For example, in the car hire market pricing discounts of over 20 per cent were required to persuade consumers to switch from Hertz or Avis to one of the lesser known companies.
- **To help recognition.** A product with a strong brand identity is likely to be instantly recognised by most consumers. This may mean consumers trust the product and are therefore more willing to buy it. Some brand names are used to describe whole classes of products, such as Sellotape and Hoover. PESTER POWER can be important. Children often put pressure on parents to buy particular brands.
- **To develop a brand image.** It is argued that customers respond to brand images with which they identify. Some consumers respond to brands that allow them to pursue multiple goals. Volvo, for example, stresses that its cars not only protect but allow the user to escape to remote places. Consumers also react to brands that offer 'extreme consumption experiences' such as Häagen-Dazs ice cream or Starbucks coffee.

A brand must be **positioned** in the right place in the market for it to be successful. A business, for example, might sell a 'high quality' brand. It is more likely to be successful if the target market is people with high incomes looking for a superior product than those looking for a bargain. The marketing mix of the business is important to positioning the brand. So, for example, high quality jewellery is likely to be a product manufactured from high quality materials and design, sold for a premium price, promoted in a way that reflects the status of the product, sold in places that reflect the

Question 2.

How many copies of the *Sunday Times* can a delivery boy or girl carry? The answer is five. The reason for this is the polybags that now accompany newspapers. For newspapers delivering news is not enough. Added value is required in the form of supplements, additional sections and gifts. During 2006 the *Daily Mail* added 37,000 new customers. This was largely ascribed to a drive to increase homesales deliveries but was also linked to the free gift of two major DVDs per month. In the same year the *Sun* experienced a 0.6 per cent rise in readers partly linked, it is thought, to a 20p price cut in the South of England. The *Daily Mirror*, by contrast, suffered a 4.7 per cent drop in readers over the same period despite its free collection of 13 classic Ladybird books. The *Daily Star Sunday* leaped by 12 per cent as it music CD series continued, while the *People* plummeted by 12 per cent despite offering free cross channel ferry tickets.

Source: adapted from *The Independent*, 12.11.2007.

(a)   Identify the diferent promotional methods described in the article.

(b)   Explain whether the methods are above-the-line or below-the-line methdos of promotion.

(c)   Discuss whether a local newspaper should use this type of promotional method.

product's features, such as high quality jewellery stores.

Large retail chains may offer OWN BRANDS for sale. These are products that are manufactured by suppliers but sold under the name of the retailer. They are an attempt by the retailer to use the brand name of the company to sell products. They are often lower in price than BRAND LEADERS, although the retailer will try to match the quality of the leading brand. Retailers may gain from this as:

• it helps them to be competitive against other retailers;
• own brands can have higher profit margins than leading brands.

Merchandising MERCHANDISING is an attempt to influence consumers at the POINT OF SALE. The point of sale is anywhere that a consumer buys a product. It may be, for example, a supermarket, a department store, a bank or a petrol station. Consumers are intended to buy based on 'what they see' rather than from a sales assistant. The aim of merchandising is to encourage sales of a product and therefore to speed up the rate at which stocks are turned over. There is a number of different features of merchandising.

• **Display material.** A good display should attract attention, enhance certain aspects of a product and encourage the 'right frame of mind' to make a purchase. Department stores lay great stress on window displays. Banks make sure that the services which they offer, such as insurance and loan facilities, are well displayed in their branches.

• **The layout of products at the point of sale.** Many retail outlets, such as supermarkets, design the layout of their stores very carefully. Their aim is to encourage consumers to follow particular routes around a store. Retail outlets often place popular items at the back or sides of a store. Consumers, on their way to these, are encouraged to walk past other items which they might buy. Another tactic is to

---

Table 2: Sales promotions

• **Coupons and loyalty cards** involve either providing money off or refunds on specific purchases or allowing savings to be made over time for being a loyal customer. The Nectar card which includes Sainsbury's and PC World is now used by hundreds of retailers in this way.

• **Competitions**. Prizes are sometimes offered for competitions. To enter, consumers must first buy the product. Tabloid newspapers often use this type of promotion. They try to attract customers through large cash prizes in their 'bingo' competitions.

• **Product endorsements** are widely used by a range of manufacturers, where well-known personalities are paid to use products. For example, sports products companies will sign up teams and successful sports personalities to promote their products. The competition between sports companies has often been reflected by the teams they supply – Real Madrid has worn Adidas while Manchester United and Barcelona have worn Nike.

• **Product placing** involves a firm paying for product brands to be placed on the sets of films and TV programmes. Car manufacturers are often eager to see their vehicles driven by Hollywood stars in popular movies.

• **Free offers**. A free 'gift' may be given with the product. An example of might be music magazines, which regularly offer readers free CDs of featured artists.

• **Special credit terms** have been increasingly used by firms. They include offers such as interest free credit and 'buy now pay later' schemes.

place related products next to each other, so consumers buy both.

- **Stocks.** A firm must make sure that stock levels are maintained and shelves are quickly restocked. Shelf space is usually allocated according to the amount of a product which a business expects to sell. For example, a super-market will give more space to products on special offer.
- **Appropriate lighting and the creation of desirable 'smells'.** Generally lighting is kept soft where browsing is encouraged and bright where there is a need to suggest cleanliness as, for example, at a cosmetics counter. Smells are used to encourage the right atmosphere. Bread smells are often wafted into supermarkets and food retailers.

Sales promotions SALES PROMOTIONS are the incentives offered to consumers to encourage them to buy goods and services. They are used to give a short-term 'boost' to the sales of a product. This is different to building up brand recognition and loyalty, which may be a longer-term aim. There is a variety of sales promotions that a business can use, as shown in Table 2. Why have these methods become popular?

- Sales promotions can be used as a method to break into a new market or introduce a new product into an existing market. They can also be used as a means of extending the product life cycle of an existing product.
- They encourage consumers to sample a good or service which they might not have bought otherwise. Once the initial good has been purchased it is likely that further goods will be bought. Many magazines offer free gifts ranging from CD ROMS to make-up in their first issues hoping that their consumers will continue to buy.
- Customers feel 'rewarded' for their custom. They may, as a result, develop a loyalty to a particular product or business.
- Customers identify products or businesses with things that they like or are attracted to. A customer is therefore more likely to purchase a product.
- Sales promotions provide businesses with feedback on the impact of their marketing expenditure, for example, through the number of coupons returned or the amount spent on loyalty cards.

Sales promotions are not without problems. The free flight offer of Hoover in 1992 is one example. It offered two free flights to the US with the purchase of products worth over £200. The company misjudged the number of people taking advantage of the offer. This meant extreme pressure on the company to produce the goods consumers were demanding. Also many consumers did not receive the holidays on dates or at times they wished. By 1993 there were so many complaints that Maytag, Hoover's US parent company, had to intervene to make sure flights or compensation were provided. It was estimated that the cost of dealing with these problems was £21.1 million.

Direct selling Direct selling or personal selling occurs when a company's sales team promotes a product through personal contact. This can be done over the telephone, by setting up

Question 3.

A firm from Walsall in the West Midlands has won an order to provide electrical wiring for the world-beating Subaru rally cars raced by drivers such as Richard Burns. Teepee Electrical Systems said that the wiring had been subjected to extensive testing to ensure it met the standards of reliability and performance needed for rally cars. Teepee Electrical Systems sells electrical wiring to other businesses. It is involved with a range of industries, from railway rolling stock, to conveyor belt systems at airports and even the submarine controls in a James Bond film. Kevin Jones, managing director of the company, put the success of the company down to the skills its workers bring to the business. 'A wiring loom is a wiring loom, but our people add engineering skills from widely diverse fields.'

Source: www.teepee-electrical.co.uk and www.expressandstar.com.

(a) In what ways might branding benefit Teepee Electrical Systems.
(b) Suggest why Teepee might find it difficult to establish a strong brand in this market.

meetings, in retail outlets, or by 'knocking on doors'. In general, the more highly priced, technically complex or individual the product, the greater the need for personal selling. Most firms supplying industrial markets rely upon personal selling in the form of sales representatives. The main reason for using personal selling rather than other methods is that individuals can be given personal attention. Most forms of promotion tend to deliver a 'standard message' to a 'typical' consumer. With personal selling the individual consumer's needs can be dealt with and the product shaped to meet these needs. There are other reasons for using direct or personal selling.

- Creating awareness of and interest in a product.
- Explaining the functions and technical aspects of a product.

- Obtaining orders and, in some cases, making deliveries.
- Encouraging product trials and test marketing.
- Providing rapid and detailed feedback from the consumer to the producer via the sales representative.

A disadvantage with personal selling is that it can be expensive. The cost of maintaining a team of sales representatives can be very high. Another problem is the dislike of 'callers' by consumers. There are also legal and ethical issues about the way products are sold that need to be considered.

Direct mailing Direct mailing involves sending information about a product or product range through the post. The consumer can usually buy the product by placing an order by post or telephone. Although sometimes unpopular with the public, direct mail is a fast growing area of promotion. It has proved very effective for firms trying to reach a target audience. Some companies use direct e-mailing, where consumers or businesses receive product information through their email inbox. Systems, however, exist for unwanted emails to be blocked as this method of selling has proved unpopular for some people. Direct mail is one means of **direct marketing**, which is often seen as part of a firm's distribution network.

Packaging A product's packaging is important in its overall marketing. This is because consumers often link the quality and design of a product's packaging with the quality of the product itself. Unsuitable packaging may affect sales. What factors should firms consider when deciding upon how to package their product?

- **Weight and shape.** These can affect the cost of distributing a product. For example, bulky packaging may mean high distribution costs.
- **Protection.** Products must not be damaged in transit or in storage. They must also be protected against light, dust and heat.
- **Convenience.** The packaging must be easy to handle by the consumer and distributors.
- **Design.** The design of the packaging should be eye-catching and help the consumer to distinguish it from others. It should also fit in with the overall marketing of the product and project the brand image. Colour is likely to be important here.
- **Information.** It is likely that the package will contain information required by the consumer. For technical products, the packaging will need to include information about how the product should be used. For food products, there are legal requirements about the information that must be on the package, such as details of the ingredients contained.
- **Environmental factors.** Manufacturers are facing increasing pressure to cut down on the amount and type of packaging placed around products. Consumers and pressure groups stress the wastefulness of this and its impact upon the environment. The response of some manufacturers to this pressure has been to use recyclable materials.

Exhibitions and trade fairs Exhibitions and trade fairs are used by firms to promote their products. They are visited by both industrial and ordinary consumers. Examples of better known fairs and exhibitions include the Motor Show, the Boat Show, the Ideal Homes Exhibition and BETT (the British educational technology exhibition). Why do businesses find them useful?

- They give the chance to show how a product actually works. This is important in the case of bulky or complex technical products. Business to business marketing, including the promoting of industrial and agricultural machinery is often done through trade fairs.
- Consumer reaction to a product can be tested before it is released onto the market.
- Some trade fairs and exhibitions are held overseas. They can form a part of a firm's international marketing strategy.
- A fair or exhibition may attract press coverage. New products may be launched to take advantage of this. The Motor Show is widely used for this purpose.
- They allow customers to discuss a product with members of the management team. It is not unusual for the managing directors of a business to attend a trade fair. For industrial consumers, in particular, this can be a valuable point of contact.
- Technical and sales staff are available to answer questions and discuss the product.

The promotional mix

Businesses usually use a range of different types of the promotional methods described above at any one time. This range is the PROMOTIONAL MIX employed by the business. For example, a business launching a new product might advertise it on television, but also send press releases to newspapers and magazines that it thinks might cover the story. There is a number of influences on the promotional mix that a business decides to employ.

The type of product Some products are better suited to some promotional methods than others. For example, trade fairs and exhibitions are strongly suited to business to business marketing and, in particular, for the promoting of business specific products such as machinery, equipment and software. On the other hand fast moving consumer goods are often better suited to different forms of advertising so that their qualities can be communicated to a wide audience.

The type of market This includes it size, geography, socio-economic characteristics and whether it is a consumer or business to business market. For example, a small business such as a small decorating business might rely upon an occasional advertisement in a local newspaper or a listing in the *Yellow Pages*. This is partly because such a business restricts its operations to a small locality and so promotional methods designed to reach a regional or national market would not be appropriate.

Cost Many small businesses find that they are restricted by considerations of cost when deciding upon use of promotional methods. Many forms of advertising, such as in national newspapers or on television or radio may not be affordable to such businesses. This means that their choice of promotional method will be strictly limited by considerations of cost.

The promotional mix of competitors If competitors are spending a great deal on advertising, for example, a competitor may feel the need to match this. Many small businesses restrict their promotions to word of mouth and personal selling, but the use of other methods by a competitor may cause a business to reconsider this strategy.

The stage of a product in its life cycle The promotional needs of a product at its launch may be very different from those used in its decline stage. Many business, both small and large, make use of public relations when first launching a product on to the market.

Legal and social constraints There is a variety of legislation that affects promotion, particularly advertising, which may influence the choice of media by a business.

- There are laws which affect the nature of advertisements. For example, the **Trade Descriptions Act 1968** states that products must correspond to claims made for them on advertisements.
- The **Advertising Standards Authority (ASA)** is the main independent body in the UK which regulates and controls advertising. It ensures that business correspond with the **British Code of Advertising, Sales promotion and Direct Marketing**, the CAP code. If the ASA finds that an advertisement breaches the code it will ask the business to withdraw the advertisement, to which they usually comply. Although it has no legal powers to force the business to withdraw the advertisement it can put pressure on it by publishing its findings or ask the media to refuse the carry the advertisement. It can also refer the advertisement to the Office of Fair Trading.
- Certain **pressure groups** seek to influence advertising. FOREST, for example, campaigns for the right of people to

smoke. ASH, on the other hand, seeks to make public the health risks of smoking.

- People may resent certain types of promotion. Email campaigns are often resented by people with computers.

Above-the-line promotion – promotion in the form of advertising.

Advertising – a form of communication between a business and its customers where the business uses visual, oral or pictorial images in the media to encourage the purchase of products.

Advertising media – the various means by which advertisements can be communicated to the public.

Informative advertising – advertising which primarily seeks to provide consumers with information about a product.

Below-the-line promotion – promotion that is not media advertising.

Brand – a name, term, sign, symbol, design or any other feature that allows consumers to identify the goods and services and differentiate them from those of competitors.

Brand leader – a brand with the high sales or sometimes the brand with the highest sales in the market.

Merchandising – a promotion specifically at the point of sale of a product.

Persuasive advertising – advertising which seeks to influence and persuade consumers to buy a product.

Own brand – a product sold under the brand name of a retailer but manufactured by a supplier of the retailer.

Pester power – the ability of children to persuade parents to buy products.

Promotion – an attempt to retain and obtain customers by drawing attention to a firm or its products.

Promotional mix – the mixture of promotional techniques used by a business to promote its products.

Point of sale – any point where a consumer buys a product.

Public relations – an organisation's attempts to communicate with interested parties.

Reassuring advertising – a method used to assure consumers about their purchases and encourage them to make repeat purchases.

Sales promotions – methods of promoting a product in the short term to give a boost to sales.

KNOWLEDGE

1. What is above the line promotion?
2. What choices of advertising media do firms have?
3. What is below the line promotion?
4. What is direct mailing?
5. Why do businesses promote their products at trade fairs and exhibitions?
6. Identify four different types of sales promotions.

7. Identify five features that a brand might have.
8. Where is merchandising likely to take place?
9. Which aspects of their merchandising should businesses pay attention to?
10. What is the main advantage of personal selling?
11. What is public relations?
12. Identify five factors that might influence the promotional mix.

CRITIQUE

Critics of marketing question the extent to which businesses respond to consumer needs as opposed to creating them. Promotion is a major part of this. Many would argue that promotions actively seek to create the need to consume more, rather than just responding to what consumers want and need. They suggest that consumer needs in general would be better met if businesses encouraged them to spend less rather than more. So whilst promoting their products strongly may make sense for individual businesses and their relationships with individual consumers it does not necessarily work at a wider level. One consequence of this so-called pressure on consumers is individuals spending beyond their means. This has led to many people taking on more debt than they can manage. Another consequence is more rapid use of the world's resources and the creation of higher levels of environmental damage.

Case Study: *Advertising*

Retailers signalled a big push for Christmas sales in 2007 with the launch of TV advertising campaigns. Leading the way was Marks & Spencer, which signed up A-list movie star Antonio Banderas to front adverts that recreate memorable moments from classic Hollywood films. But competing for screen space will be retailers who traditionally do not use TV advertising such as John Lewis and Next. Many retail chiefs have forecast trade is going to be tough this Christmas and they are pouring cash into advertising to persuade shoppers to part with their cash. Last year's M&S Christmas campaign had a James Bond theme and starred Dame Shirley Bassey. Banderas – who starred in the Mask of Zorro - will appear with M&S's usual roster of models: Twiggy, Erin O'Connor, Laura Bailey, Lizzie Jagger and Noemie Lenoir. M&S's advertising, masterminded by marketing director Steve Sharp, has been credited with helping to rebuild the reputation of the retailer.

Next week also sees the launch of a John Lewis advertising campaign. It is spending more than £6 million to promote the 27-strong chain of department stores – three times last' year's advertising spend - and will be using TV adverts for only the second time in its history. The move is the brainchild of the company's new marketing director, Gill Barr, who joined the company in January and was made a member of the board in June. The television advertisement, which is set to 'Morning Serenade', the theme from Prokofiev's ballet Romeo and Juliet, is deliberately understated to contrast with other retailers' celebrity focused Christmas ads. It shows a diverse group of people carefully arranging John Lewis products in such a way that the combined shadow casts the outline of the person for whom the gifts are intended. The image will also be used for billboards and press and in cinema and online advertising. The spend – up from £1.75 million last year – signifies a departure for the department store chain which has traditionally invested little on advertising, believing the brand has grown essentially through word of mouth and that it was not necessary to 'boast about it'.

Ms Barr, a former business development director at Woolworths, said that when she joined the company there wasn't a tradition of advertising, but there was 'an ambition to be more articulate about the brand and to talk to customers more'. She added: 'This campaign is directional for the John Lewis brand. "The creative execution is stylish, intriguing and intelligent. The media plan is more comprehensive than ever before, reinforcing the core idea with three different shadows in press and outdoor. The TV advertisement will also run in cinemas.'

Next recently unveiled its first national television advertising campaign for more than a decade. It is pouring £20 million into advertising this year – double last year's marketing budget. Chief executive Simon Wolfson said recently that he was 'acutely aware that the full effect of recent interest rates has not yet filtered through to our customers' and despite the advertising push forecasts a dip in sales of up to 3.5 per cent, compared to last year, over the current six months. She added that the ad intended to use the extent of the company's range, which includes 350,000 products, to inspire customers with their Christmas shopping. The television ad, which will run from next Tuesday, differs widely from the glitzy ads of Marks & Spencer, which star Shirley Bassey, Twiggy and Myleene Klass, and Next, which launched its first major television ad campaign in September. Next is spending £18 million more than usual on advertising this year, including £2 million more on its Christmas window displays.

Source: adapted from *The Guardian*, 3.11.2007 and the *Independent*, 2.11.2007.

(a) Identify the different promotional methods used in the case study. (6 marks)

(b) Explain, using examples, how the methods of promotion might be made:
(i) persuasive; (ii) informative; (iii) reassuring;
for customers of the businesses. (6 marks)

(c) Examine the factors which might affect the choice of promotional method for each business. (10 marks)

(d) In the light of the information in the article, evaluate the potential promotional methods available to a small independent fashion clothing business. (12 marks)

Influences on pricing

The pricing strategies used by a business may be influenced by a number of factors.

Objectives The pricing strategy chosen by a business is likely to reflect the extent to which it wants to maximise profits or sales. A business seeking to maximise short-term profits may use more aggressive and perhaps risky pricing strategies.

The marketing mix The price chosen by a business must complement the marketing mix. This means that the price must fit in with the nature of the product itself and the way in which it is being promoted and distributed to consumers. For example, a low quality product being sold in retail outlets at the bottom end of the market is likely to be sold at a fairly low price.

Costs A business which cannot generate enough revenue over time to cover its costs will not survive. In the long run, a business must charge a price which earns enough revenue to cover its total cost of production at any level of output. This means that businesses must take account of all of their costs when setting price. In the short run a business may not expect to cover the fixed costs of its factory or machinery. Providing its price is high enough to generate revenue that covers its variable costs, the firm will stay in business. Revenue below this will cause the business to cease production. As a result businesses may have greater flexibility in the short term when making pricing decisions.

Competition Competition can affect pricing decisions For a market trader, the price of her goods is largely determined by prices on nearby stalls selling similar goods. Such a trader will have little room for manoeuvre compared to a business which faces less competition. A monopolist that dominates the market may be able to charge higher prices.

Demand The higher price set the lower the quantity sold. The effect that a higher prices has on sales is dealt with in the unit titled 'Elasticity of demand'.

Consumer perceptions Businesses must pay attention to what consumers think a product is worth. A product priced above what consumers consider its value to be may generate low sales because of doubts about its value for money. A product priced too low may also generate low sales. This is because consumers often suspect that such products have something wrong with them or that they are of inferior quality. In some cases businesses actually encourage consumers to think of their products as expensive to encourage high income earners to buy them.

Market segment Businesses that produce a range of products are likely to have some aimed at particular market segments. This is true, for example, of all major car manufacturers. They are, therefore, likely to charge different prices for each segment. However, the price which they charge to one segment of the market will affect the prices charged to other segments. A product competing in the top end of the market will need to have a different price from one aimed at the middle or bottom end of the market.

Laws and regulations The price of a number of products is affected by government. Taxes can raise the price above the level that might have been set by manufacturers. Products affected greatly by taxation include cigarettes, alcoholic drinks and petrol. There is also a number of products which are offered to consumers below the price that producers would normally charge. Such products are subsidised by the government. Maximum prices can also be set. For example, the price of products such as water and gas in the UK are determined by regulatory bodies.

Question 1.

The price of each product in a market will be influenced by a variety of factors. For some products, the ability of a business to set its price is limited. For others, there will be more scope for a business to set the price it wants to charge.

(a) What factors may have influenced the prices of the products in the photographs?

Question 2.

A range of prices being offered by various retailers for a Fuji S9600 FinePix Digital Camera is shown in Table 1.

Table 1: Prices of Fuji S9600 FinePix Digital Camera in December 2007

Cameras2u.com	£205.20
Amazon.co.uk	£206.00
Littlewoods Direct	£339.00
Argos	£249.99
Jessops.com	£279.99
Computerwebstore.com	£234.37

(a) Describe the pricing tactic that might be being used by Argos.
(b) Compare the pricing strategies of Cameras2u.com with Jessops.com.

Pricing strategies

A strategy is a set of plans designed to meet objectives. PRICING STRATEGY is part of the marketing strategy of the business. Other strategies such as product and distribution strategy also make up a marketing strategy. Marketing strategy is then part of the corporate strategy of the business. Other strategies include production and financial strategy.

Pricing strategy is therefore a set of plans about pricing which help a business to achieve its marketing and corporate objectives. For example, a corporate objective might be to double in size over the next five years. A marketing objective to achieve this might be to take the products of the business 'up-market'. The pricing strategy developed from this could be to increase the average price of the products made by the business.

- Some pricing strategies can be used for: **new products**, such as market skimming or penetration pricing.
- Some strategies are more suitable for **existing products**, such as price.

Price skimming or creaming

If a business realises that its product has a **unique selling point** it may be in a position to charge a high price for a limited time in order to take advantage of the newness of the product. This is known a PRICE or MARKET SKIMMING or CREAMING skimming. New generation mobile phones with fast Internet connections, email facilities and music facilities are priced much higher than 'traditional' phones as mobile phone companies skim this new market. The aim is to gain as much profit as possible for a new product while it remains unique in the market. It usually means selling a product to the most profitable segment of the market before it is sold to a wider market at a lower price.

There are two reasons why businesses adopt skimming. They may try to maximise revenue before competitors come into the market with a similar product. Often new techniques or designs mean that entirely new products, or new versions of a product can be offered. Examples include new fashions in clothes, new children's toys and new inventions. When first launched, a basic digital watch could cost as much as £50 or £60. Now they often sell for as little as a few pounds. Price skimming can also be used to generate revenue in a short period of time so that further investment in the product can be made. Companies in the electronics and pharmaceutical industries often use skimming for this reason.

Penetration pricing

A business may set its price deliberately low in order to gain a footing in the market. This could also be used when a business is launching an existing product into a new market, for example. This is known as PENETRATION PRICING. It involves pricing a product at a low level so that retailers and consumers are encouraged to purchase the product in large quantities.

There are two main reasons why businesses use penetration pricing.

- Consumers are encouraged to develop the habit of buying the product, so that when prices eventually begin to rise they will continue to purchase it.
- Retailers and wholesalers are likely to purchase large quantities of the product. This should mean that they will not buy from other suppliers until they have sold most of their stock. Businesses can thus gain a significant slice of the market.

Penetration pricing, because of its high cost, is often used by large businesses operating in mass markets, such as those selling biscuits, sweets, washing powder and canned drinks. It is also a policy used by new businesses or established businesses in other areas to break into a new market. It is not a policy that is suitable for products with short life cycles. There is usually not enough time to recover the cost of lost revenue from the initially low price.

Price leaders

In some markets, often controlled by a small number of large companies, or just one large business there is an accepted PRICE LEADER or PRICE MAKER. They will decide first to increase or lower prices, knowing that other companies will soon follow. It occurs when one dominant business establishes a position of price leadership within a market. Other firms will follow suit when the price leader changes its prices. This type of policy can be seen when a petrol company changes the price of a gallon of petrol or when banks and building societies change interest rates.

Price takers

In very competitive markets a business might decide to follow closely another firm's price increases or reductions. The business is a PRICE TAKER or PRICE FOLLOWER. This is an example of COMPETITION-BASED PRICING or GOING RATE PRICING, where a business takes into account competitor's prices. The retail market for 'white goods' such as fridges and freezers is an example. It also occurs in markets where businesses are reluctant to set off a price war by lowering their prices and are concerned about a fall off in revenue if prices are raised. Price taking is an example of pricing based upon competition. Where businesses are price takers they may be frustrated by their inability to control prices more closely. A strategy often used in such circumstances is to establish a strong brand identity and to differentiate it from others on the market. An oil company's decision to upgrade all of its service stations is an example of an attempt to achieve this. A strong brand identity and unique product features allow firms much greater scope for choosing their own price levels.

Destroying competition or capturing the market

The aim of **destroyer pricing** is to eliminate opposition. It involves cutting prices, sometimes greatly, for a period of time long enough for your rivals to go out of business. It could be argued that the offering of low price airline tickets by Ryanair and easyJet in the 1990s was designed to drive out competition from the national European airline carriers and force some of them out of business. Some responded by setting up their own low-price carriers and cutting prices. Others, like Sabena and SwissAir, did go out of business.

Price discrimination

Price discrimination occurs when a firm offers the same product at different prices when consumers can be kept separate. An example is BT's policy of charging different prices to business and residential users at different times of the day and the weekend. This allows BT to take into account the differences in cost which exists at peak and off-peak times. So, for example, calls may be charged at a higher rate on Monday to Friday, 8am-6pm, than at weekends.

This price discrimination is **time based**. The price you pay for a phone call is based upon the time of day or the day of the week when you use the service. Other businesses which use this policy are rail companies (cheaper off-peak travel), and holiday firms which charge higher prices for their product during school holidays. Price discrimination can also be **market based**. This involves offering different market segments the same product at different prices. An example of this is students being given discounts on coach and bus travel. Price discrimination is an example of MARKET-ORIENTATED PRICING, where a business takes into account conditions in the market when setting prices.

Customer value pricing

This is pricing according to what the consumer is wiling to pay. It involves charging the price that consumers are prepared to pay. Products which have prestige names attached to them, such as Rolex, may be able to command a higher price because of the status of these names. Products for one-off events, such as music festivals or sports finals, may be given a high price because they are unique. Businesses sometimes use PRESTIGE or PREMIUM PRICING. This is where a high price is charged for luxury, up-market products to reassure customers about their quality and that they are buying 'the best'.

Cost-based pricing

All businesses are influenced by their costs when determining prices with costs acting as a 'bottom line' when choosing a price. But some use COST-BASED PRICING as their strategy for price setting. Businesses using cost-based pricing are those where the influence of cost is more important than other factors such as market conditions or competitors' pricing. Many small businesses such as the local garage repair business or domestic repair services like electricians and plumbers are likely to take a cost-based approach.

Cost-plus pricing. This involves setting a price by calculating the average cost of producing goods and adding a MARK-UP for profit. If a business produces 10,000 goods costing £50,000, the average cost would be £5.00. A mark-up of 20 per cent would mean goods would cost an extra £1.00 and the price would be £6.00 per product. Retailers often use this method of pricing. Say that a department store buys a colour TV from wholesalers for £200 and its mark-up to allow for a profit is 100 per cent. The retail price to consumers will be £400. The attractiveness of cost-plus pricing is that it is a quick and simple way of setting a selling price. It also ensures that sales revenue will cover total costs and generate profit. A criticism, however, is that a fixed mark-up does not allow a business to take market needs into account when setting prices. In addition, no attempt is made to allocate indirect costs to particular products. This means they do not reflect the resources being allocated by the business to that particular product or product range. Cost-plus pricing is shown in Figure 1.

Figure 1: Cost-plus pricing

Mark-up
Fixed cost
Variable cost

=

Price

Contribution (or marginal) pricing The costs of a business can be divided into two types. **Variable costs** are costs which change as output changes. For example, leather is a variable cost for a shoe manufacturer. The more shoes that are made, the more leather is used. **Fixed costs** are costs which stay the same whatever the level of output. For example, the shoe manufacturer may rent a factory. The rent is a fixed cost because it has to be paid whether a million pairs of shoes are made or zero.

Say that the variable costs for an order of 5,000 pairs of shoes were £40,000. If the order were priced over £40,000, it would cover its variable costs of production and make a **contribution** towards the fixed costs and profit of the business. Contribution is defined as:

Contribution = revenue - variable costs

So, if the order were priced at £50,000, it would make a £10,000 contribution. If it were priced at £65,000, it would make a £25,000 contribution.

CONTRIBUTION PRICING can be used to decide whether to accept a lower price. This is shown in Figure 2. The usual price of shoes might be £20. If fixed costs were £8 per pair, costs would be £18 (variable costs of £10 + fixed costs of £8). Profit may be £2 per pair. Should the business accept a lower price for an order?

This pricing method would suggest that it could accept any price as long as it was at least £10, the variable cost of production. At a price of £12, for example, each pair makes a loss of £6 (£12 price - £18 costs). But it still makes a contribution of £2 per pair (£12 price - £10 variable cost). If it doesn't take the order, the business will be worse off. There will be no £2 contribution per pair of shoes.

In the long run, businesses have to cover all their costs and make a profit to survive. So the total contribution on sales has to be greater than fixed costs. But in the short run, the contribution method of pricing suggests that businesses might accept orders where the price fails to cover total costs, so long as the contribution is positive.

There are certain advantages of using contribution pricing.
- It encourages flexibility when pricing. Variable costs represent the minimum acceptable price. After that, the business can try to maximise the amount of contribution it can earn from any single sale.
- Products in high demand can be sold at high prices. Where there is intense competition, or the product is not popular with customers, the price can be lower.
- It may lead to one-off orders being accepted at a lower price.
- It may be used to break into new markets. Products can be sold at lower prices to attract initial customers (known as **entry pricing**).
- It may encourage the use of **excess capacity** at times of the year when there is low demand. This is often the case in the printing or airline industries.

Figure 2: Contribution costing

Usual price — Profit / Fixed cost / Variable cost

Lower price — Contribution / Variable cost

The main disadvantage is that those in charge of sales can focus too much on sales and not on selling at a profit. If all businesses in an industry adopt contribution pricing, this may lead to widespread selling below full cost. Businesses compete with each other for sales and the business with the lowest price can often increase market share. This puts a downward pressure on prices.

Pricing tactics

Once a company has decided upon its overall pricing strategy, it can also use price as a tactical promotional tool. PRICING TACTICS usually involve temporary, changes in prices to attract customers to specific products for a period. These pricing tactics may include the following.

Loss leaders LOSS LEADERS are products priced at very low levels in order to attract customers. The price of a loss leader is set lower than the average total cost of producing the product. The company selling the product makes a 'loss' on each product sold. Businesses use this pricing technique because they expect the losses made on the loss leader to be more than compensated for by extra profits on other products. It is often used by larger supermarkets which sell everyday products such as baked beans, bananas and corn flakes for very low prices. They aim to attract more customers into their stores, drawn in by the low prices. The 'captive' customers will then buy more highly priced and profitable items. Baked beans, bread and whisky have all been used by food and drink retailers as loss leaders in recent years.

Psychological pricing Many businesses seek to take account of the psychological effect of their prices upon consumers. This is known as psychological pricing. A common example is the use of prices just a little lower than a round figure, such as £199.99 rather than £200, or £29.99 rather than £30 for a period of time. Businesses using these slightly lower prices believe that they will influence the consumers' decision as to whether or not to purchase. Such slightly lower prices also suggest that consumers will be looking for value for money. For this reason, the producers of high status products such as prestige cars or designer clothing tend to avoid such prices. Instead, they often choose prices which psychologically match their consumers expectations of higher quality. So, for example, a price of £100 may be charged for a designer shirt rather than £99.99.

Special promotional offers These include offers such as buy one, get one free. Waterstone's, for example, has offered three paperback books for the price of two and Morrisons two pizzas for £5.

Discounts on normal prices In many industries businesses have fixed prices for products. For example sometimes there are manufacturers **recommended prices** or **list prices**. A discount might be offered on this price. This might be for a period of time, such as just before Christmas, for regular customers, such as special offers for loyalty card holders, or for people who buy larger quantities, for example schools getting discounts on supplies of pens, paper and stationery.

Introductory offers This is where the price a customer pays for the first purchase is lower than for subsequent purchases. For example, Broadband has been offered by service providers at £7.50 per month for the first three months and then £15.50 per month after three months.

Sales Sales are typically used to sell stocks of goods which have proved difficult to sell. For example, shops have sales in January for stock which has not sold in the peak selling season of September to Christmas. In some cases, businesses will run a sale on all their stock, whether it has been selling slowly or not. This attracts customers who are seeking a bargain.

KEY TERMS

Competition-based pricing – where a business takes into account competitors' pricing when setting its price.
Cost-based pricing – methods of pricing products which are based upon costs.
Contribution pricing - when a business sets its price to cover all of its variable costs, but only a contribution is made to its fixed costs and profit.
Going rate pricing – where price is set equal to the price of similar products in the market.
Loss leaders – products with prices set deliberately below average total cost to attract customers who will then buy other, more profitable, products.
Mark-up – that part of a price which seeks to provide a business with profit as opposed to covering its costs. It is used in cost-plus pricing.
Market-orientated pricing – where a business takes into account conditions in the market when setting prices.
Penetration pricing - when a business sets a low price in an attempt to enter a new market.
Prestige or premium pricing – where high prices are charged to reinforce the quality and luxury image of a product.
Price leader or price maker – a business that sets prices that other businesses follow.
Price or market skimming or creaming – where a product has a unique selling point may have a high price for a limited time in order to take advantage of the newness of the product.
Price taker or price follower – a business that is unable to choose the price it sets and follows the market price.
Pricing strategies – the pricing policies or methods of pricing adopted by businesses.
Pricing tactics – ways of using price as a promotional tool usually over a short period of time.
Tender – a bid to secure a contract for work.

KNOWLEDGE

1. State five pricing strategies a business might use.
2. Identify four different pricing tactics that a business might use.
3. What is price skimming?
4. Why might a firm use penetration pricing?
5. What is the difference between cost-plus pricing and contribution pricing?
6. Explain the difference between a price leader and a price taker.
7. What types of business might use pricet skimming as a pricing strategy?
8. Why might a business sell a product as a loss leader?
9. What is meant by psychological pricing?

Case Study: *Finding a deal that will float our boat*

With the summer travel season approaching, another ferry service is being introduced across the English Channel, raising the prospect of a price war on the more expensive western routes into France. LD Lines, which will run from Newhaven to Le Havre from May, is offering summer return prices from £142 for a family plus car. This route into Normandy costs less than a third of peak season prices into the Brittany ports further west along the coast.

It might only be a narrow strip of water, but there are huge variations in the cost of taking a car across – with some routes seven times more expensive for a crossing on the same day. Long criticised for their complex charging structures, ferries have become much more like airlines – with websites showing a much more transparent range of port-to-port prices. And after years in the doldrums, ferries have been making a modest revival, boosted by the soaring number of French holiday homes bought by Britons and by a disenchantment with the overcrowding and stress of airports in summer. While ferries might be a more relaxing way to travel, they can also be extremely expensive.

The great divide in this cross-channel market is between the west and the east. On the 'eastern' route, there are the short ferry crossings from Dover and the tunnel crossing at Folkestone into north-eastern France and the Pas de Calais. And on the 'western Channel' routes there are longer crossings to St Malo and Cherbourg.

These are two different holiday markets – one about high-volume, price-sensitive shuttling of passengers; the other a more leisurely, more expensive trip, with restaurants and cinemas.

On the highly competitive Dover route, passenger numbers are rising. Last year, 13.7 million people travelled through the port to Calais, Boulogne and Dunkirk. And the arrival of operators such as Speedferries and Norfolk Line has brought the budget airline pricing model, with one-way crossings for a car plus five passengers from £15.

A car with two adults and two children could travel off peak on the P&O Dover-Calais ferry route for £85 return. And depending on how flexible you could be about crossing times, there are still Eurotunnel summer fares for £98.

But on the western Channel routes it's been a different story, with Brittany Ferries dominating after competitors such as P&O pulled out. And the strategy has been to go upmarket rather than compete with the budget airlines. In terms of prices, the off-peak fare for a return trip from Portsmouth to St Malo, for two adults and two children, can be £300. And for some overnight sailings, accommodation is an additional, compulsory part of the booking. If you were travelling from the west country on the Plymouth to Roscoff route, a summer return could cost £689, if a cabin was included.

Spokesperson Steve Tuckwell says that rather than only focusing on price, passengers are ready to pay a premium for 'floating hotel' services. And although the budget airlines have 'eaten into our business' for short break trips, he says for longer summer holidays people prefer to take their cars on the ferry.

Source: adapted from *The Guardian*, 17.3.2007.

Source adapted from www.drive-alive.co.uk

(a) Using examples from the article, explain what is meant by:
 (i) price discrimination. (3 marks)
 (ii) cost-plus pricing. (3 marks)
(b) Explain the pricing strategy used by Brittany Ferries on its 'western' routes. (6 marks)
(c) Explain, using examples, why prices are higher on the 'western routes' than on the 'eastern' routes across the channel. (8 marks)
(d) Discuss how budget airlines might respond to the strategies used by their ferry competitors. (10 marks)

46 | Elasticity of demand

Demand

DEMAND for a product is the quantity bought over a given time period. For example, demand for cars in the UK in 2006 was 2.4 million vehicles. The quantity bought of a product is affected by a number of factors. These include:

- price – the lower the price, the higher tends to be the quantity demanded; the higher the price, the less tends to be bought;
- the income of customers – for most goods, the higher the income of customers, the more will be bought and vice versa. However, there are some goods, called **inferior goods**, where customers buy less of the good as their incomes rise;
- the price of other goods – for example, if one chocolate bar goes up in price by 10 per cent, demand for other chocolate bars is likely to increase if their price remains constant;
- advertising – successful advertising can increase demand for a product;
- seasonal factors – many goods, from ice creams and beer to toys and foreign holidays are affected by the time of year and the weather. For example, hot summer weather increases demand for ice creams and beer. The run up to Christmas is the peak selling time for toys and clothing.

Price elasticity of demand

Demand theory suggests that quantity demanded varies with price. The higher the price, the lower the quantity demand and vice versa. But it doesn't say by **how much** the quantity demanded will fall or rise if there is a change in price. This varies from product to product. The relationship between the effect of a change in price on quantity demanded is known as PRICE ELASTICITY OF DEMAND.

If there is a **large** percentage change in quantity demanded when price changes by a small percentage, there is said to be ELASTIC DEMAND. The word 'elastic' is used to give an idea that there would be a large response. Think of an elastic band. When you pull it, can you easily double its length? Then it is 'elastic'. But if it is thick, it may be difficult to change its length. It is 'inelastic'. This is also the case with price elasticity. If a large percentage change in price brings about only a **small** percentage change in quantity demanded, there is said to be INELASTIC DEMAND.

Take the example of a Mars Bar made by Mars Corporation. If it puts up the price by 10 per cent, and there is a fall in quantity demanded of 30 per cent, then the demand for Mars Bars is elastic. The percentage change in quantity demanded of Mars Bars is much bigger than the percentage change in price which caused it. But if quantity demanded fell only 5 per cent

when prices went up by 10 per cent, then there would be inelastic demand. The percentage change in quantity demanded is smaller than the percentage change in price.

It is important to realise that price elasticity compares **percentage** changes in quantity and price. Percentages allow the relative changes to be measured and compared.

The formula for price elasticity of demand

The exact value of price elasticity of demand can be calculated by using the formula:

$$\text{Price elasticity of demand} = \frac{\text{\% change in quantity demanded}}{\text{\% change in price}}$$

For example, say that the price of Mars Bars increases by 10 per cent.

- If the quantity demanded falls by 20 per cent as a result of the 10 per cent price rise, then price elasticity of demand is:

$$\frac{-20 \text{ per cent}}{+10 \text{ per cent}} = -2$$

- If the quantity demanded rises by 5 per cent as a result of the 10 per cent price fall, then price elasticity of demand is:

$$\frac{+5 \text{ per cent}}{-10 \text{ per cent}} = -0.5$$

Price elasticity of demand is always negative. This is because a rise (+) in price is always followed by a fall (-) in quantity demanded and vice versa. A plus divided into a minus is a minus. Because it is always minus, the sign is normally left out when talking about price elasticity of demand.

Elastic and inelastic demand

It is possible to give a more precise definition of elastic and inelastic demand using the formula for price elasticity.

Price elastic demand Demand is **price elastic** when it is **greater than 1**. This means that the percentage change in quantity demanded (on the top of the formula) is greater than the percentage change in price (on the bottom of the formula). A 12 per cent rise in quantity demanded resulting from a 10 per cent fall in price would give a price elasticity of +12 per cent ÷ -10 per cent or -1.2. This would be an example of elastic demand.

Price inelastic demand Demand is **price inelastic** when it is **less than 1**. This means that the percentage change in quantity demanded (on the top of the formula) is less than the

Question 1.

A stationery shop selling fibre tipped pens has estimated the following demand schedule for its products.

Table 1: Demand for fibre tipped pens

Price (£)	Quantity demanded
2	800
3	600
4	500
5	400
6	350
7	300
8	260
9	225
10	200

(a) Calculate the change in total revenue for fibre tipped pens of:
   (i) an increase in price from £2 to £3;
   (ii) an increase in price from £7 to £10;
   (iii) a decrease in price from £5 to £3.
(b) Explain why the business might be reluctant to raise prices above £7 per pen.

percentage change in price (on the bottom of the formula). An 8 per cent fall in quantity demanded resulting from a 10 per cent rise in price would give a price elasticity of -8 per cent ÷ +10 per cent or -0.8. This would be an example of inelastic demand.

Estimating price elasticity

There is no easy way to find out the exact price elasticity of demand for a particular product. The business environment is constantly changing. So when the price of a product changes, it is likely that other factors will change too. For example, competing businesses may all change their prices at roughly the same time.

One way of estimating the price elasticity of demand is to assume that all these other factors remain the same. Then a business could consider the impact of its price changes on demand in recent years. If it has changed price four times in four years, it could estimate the impact this has had on quantity demanded each time and calculate a price elasticity figure for each price change. These four figures might be averaged to provide an approximate price elasticity.

Alternatively, a business could use market research. It could ask customers how much they would buy of a product at different prices. Price elasticity of demand for the sample could then be calculated. A problem is that what respondents actually do can be different from what they say they will do in a survey.

A business could consider the behaviour of its customers. For example, the price elasticity of demand for the gas that British

Gas sells to households might be inelastic. A 10 per cent rise in price is likely to have little effect on quantity demanded. This is because households tend not to turn off their central heating when the price of gas rises. Most customers, also, won't switch to another gas company.

In contrast, a small clothing manufacturer might face elastic demand. All its work could come from larger companies that only want limited quantities of dresses or trousers. There are many UK businesses doing this sort of work and others in countries like India or China. So if it quotes a slightly higher price for a contract it is unlikely to get the order. In this industry, businesses find it difficult to raise their prices without losing many customers.

Price elasticity and sales revenue

Price elasticity of demand is important when developing a **pricing strategy**. This is because the price of a product affects **sales revenue**. Sales revenue is the amount a business receives from the sale of its products. It is calculated by multiplying the price of the product by the quantity sold. For example, a business selling 1 million products at £10 each would have sales revenue of £10 million (£1 million x £10).

Sales revenue is affected by the price at which a product is sold and price elasticity of demand. Assume that the product sold at £10 has a price elasticity of 2.

* This means that a 10 per cent increase in price would lead to a fall in quantity demanded (and therefore sales) of 20 per cent. Sales revenue would then fall from £10 million (1 million x £10) to £8.8 million (800 000 x £11).
* If, on the other hand, price was lowered by 10 per cent, quantity demanded (and therefore sales) would rise by 20 per cent. Sales revenue would then rise from £10 million (1 million x £10) to £10.8 million (1.2 million x £9).

This is an example of a more general rule. If demand is price elastic, then putting up price will lead to a fall in sales revenue. The increase in price will be more than offset by a decrease in sales. Conversely, lowering price when demand is price elastic will lead to a rise in sales revenue. The fall in price will be more than offset by an increase in sales.

Equally, the opposite relationship applies if price is inelastic. A rise in price will lead to a rise in sales revenue whilst a fall in price will lead to a fall in sales revenue. For example, if price elasticity of demand is 0.7, then a 10 per cent rise in price leads to a 7 per cent fall in sales. This leads to an approximate 3 per cent rise in sales revenue. This relationship between price elasticity and sales revenue is shown in Table 2.

Changing the price can therefore affect sales revenue. But the

Table 2: Effect on sales revenue of a change in price

	Elastic demand	Inelastic demand
Price increase	Revenue down	Revenue up
Price decrease	Revenue up	Revenue down

exact effect, and whether it leads to an increase or decrease, depends on the price elasticity of demand.

Price elasticity and profit

Price elasticity also has an effect on **profit**. Profit is calculated as sales revenue minus costs. Costs are likely to change with sales. The more that is produced, the higher the costs.

If demand is price inelastic, a rise in price will lead to lower sales but increased sales revenue as explained earlier. But the lower sales will mean lower costs. So profits will increase, not just from higher sales revenue but also from lower costs.

If demand is price elastic, an increase in sales revenue can be achieved by lowering price and raising sales. But higher sales also mean higher costs. In this situation, higher profits will only occur if the increase in sales revenue is greater than the increase in costs.

Factors affecting price elasticity of demand

The value of price elasticity of demand for a product is mainly determined by the ease with which customers can switch to other similar SUBSTITUTE PRODUCTS. A number of factors is likely to determine this.

Time Price elasticity of demand tends to fall the longer the time period. This is mainly because consumers and businesses are more likely to turn to substitutes in the long term. For example, fuel oil is highly price inelastic in the short term. If the price of petrol goes up 20 per cent in a week, the fall in quantity demanded is likely to be only a few per cent. This is because car owners have to use their cars to get to work or to go shopping. But over a ten year period, car owners will tend to buy more fuel-efficient cars. Businesses with boilers using fuel oil may replace these with gas boilers. Homeowners with oil-fired central heating systems might install more insulation in their houses to cut running costs or change to gas boilers. As a result, demand for oil in the long run is likely to be price elastic.

Competition for the same product Some businesses face highly price elastic demand for their products. This is because they are in very competitive markets, where their product is either identical (i.e. are perfect substitutes) or little different from those produced by other businesses. Farmers, for example, when selling wheat or potatoes are in this position. If they push their prices above the market price, they won't be able to sell their crop. Customers will simply buy elsewhere at the lower market price.

Branding Some products are **branded**. The stronger the branding, the less substitutes are acceptable to customers. For example, many buyers of Kellogg's corn flakes do not see own label brands, such as Tesco or Asda cornflakes, as good substitutes for Kelloggs. They will often pay 50 per cent more to buy Kelloggs rather than another brand. Successful branding therefore reduces the price elasticity of demand for the product.

Product types vs the product of an individual business Most

products are made and sold by a number of different businesses. Petrol, for example, is processed and sold by companies such as Shell, Esso and Total. The major supermarkets also sell petrol which they have bought from independent refiners. The demand for petrol is price inelastic in the short term. But the demand for Shell petrol or Esso petrol is price elastic. This is because petrol has no real substitutes in the short term. But Esso petrol is a very good substitute for Shell petrol. In general, a product category like petrol, carpets or haircuts has a much lower price elasticity of demand than products within that category made by individual businesses.

However strong the branding and however little the competition that an individual product faces, it is still likely that a business will sell at a price where demand is price elastic. To understand why, consider a product which has inelastic demand. As explained above, raising the price of the product would increase sales revenue. It would also reduce sales and costs of production would fall. So profits would rise. A profit maximising firm should therefore continue raising price until demand is price elastic.

If demand is price elastic, raising price leads to a fall in sales revenue, but also a fall in costs because less is sold. At the profit maximising point, any further increase in price would see the fall in sales revenue being greater than the fall in costs.

This would suggest that even strongly branded goods, such as Coca-Cola or McDonald's meals, have a price elasticity of demand greater than one at the price at which they are sold. It also suggests that luxury brands, such as Chanel or Gucci, also have elastic demand at their current price.

Problems of measuring price elasticity of demand

There may be problems for small businesses in calculating the price elasticity of demand for their products.

Collecting data A business wanting to know about the price elasticity of its products would need to collect data on demand changes in relation to price for its own products to know the price elasticity of demand for these products. This would mean that they would need to experiment with price changes and to

Question 2.

Kaldor Ltd manufactures reproduction juke boxes which play CDs. Jukeboxes that play old 45 records can cost around £1,000 or a great deal more. Large jukeboxes in pubs can cost thousands of pounds as well. But Kaldor had seen other 'reproduction' jukeboxes that did not cost as much and were far smaller. It decided to manufacture smaller jukeboxes that stand on a table. They sold for £200 and hold three CDs at a time. The jukeboxes have been selling well and so the business raised the price to £240. As a result sales fell from 800 to 600 per month. Kaldor is now questioning the decision to raise the price.

(a) Discuss whether or not the decision to raise the price was a good choice by the business.

monitor consumer reaction. For many small businesses, especially those with a very small number of customers this would be impractical. The dangers of experimenting in this way could lead to a loss of business that would be difficult to recover. Small businesses also often do not have the time or resources to research such matters.

Predicting human behaviour Human behaviour is notoriously difficult to predict and the way that people respond on one day of the week, for example, may be different to how they will respond on others. In addition, consumers do not always act as they say they will. For this reason small businesses attempting to research their price elasticity of demand by observing and talking to their customers may not always find it easy to collect reliable data.

Interpreting data When seeking to research their price elasticity of demand it is not always easy for small business to make sense of the data they collect. Take, for example, a small business selling ice cream from one retail outlet. Were this business to trial a new higher price for its ice creams on one particular day it might find that sales actually rose. They might conclude from this that their ice cream is relatively price inelastic. However, on this same day there could have been because several large coachloads of pensioners swelling the total number of potential consumers and especially high temperatures also inflating demand. In this case it would be difficult for the business to isolate the effect of the price change.

For these reasons many small business estimate their price elasticity of demand rather than calculate it based upon actual research. They will do so based upon their observations of how their customers behave, information from similar businesses and actual sales levels.

KEY TERMS

Demand – the quantity of a product bought over a given time period.
Price elasticity of demand – the responsiveness of quantity demanded to changes in price. It is measured as percentage change in quantity demanded ÷ percentage change in price.
Price elastic demand – when price elasticity is greater than 1, which means that the percentage change in quantity demanded is greater than the percentage change in price which caused it.
Price inelastic demand – when price elasticity is less than 1, which means that the percentage change in quantity demanded is less than the percentage change in price which caused it.
Substitute product – a product which has similar characteristics to another good. For example, gas is a substitute for oil as a fuel in heating systems. Shell petrol is a good substitute for BP Amoco petrol for use as a fuel in cars.

KNOWLEDGE

1. Explain, without using the formula, what is meant by 'price elasticity of demand'.
2. 'The demand for journeys taken on the London Underground is price inelastic.' Explain what this means.
3. (a) What is the formula for price elasticity of demand?
   (b) How does it differ from the formula for income elasticity of demand?
4. How can a business estimate the price elasticity of demand for one of its products?
5. Explain why a rise in price would lead to higher revenues if demand for the product were price inelastic.
6. Explain the link between price elasticity of demand and profit.
7. Explain why strongly branded goods such as Coca-Cola or Chanel perfumes are likely to be price elastic at the price at which they are currently sold.

Case Study: *Taxi pricing*

Bill Finch is a London taxicab driver. Towards the end of 1999, all the talk amongst taxicab drivers was about the new Millennium - whether they were going to drive or be out partying on New Year's Eve. In November 1999, the government, which sets London taxicab fares, announced that London taxis would be able to charge double rate for journeys taken between 8 pm on December 31 and 6 am on January 1st. Those taking journeys long enough to cost more than an ordinary fare of £25 would have to pay a flat rate £25 supplement. This compared to the usual New Year supplement of £3 per journey.

Bill decided he would drive on the Millennium eve, expecting that demand would be highly price inelastic. But he was disappointed with his takings. Many party goers had decided to stay at home because restaurants, pubs and clubs as well as taxis were charging double or more on the night. There was a general feeling amongst the public that they were going to be ripped off if they went out. Where journeys were

necessary, many took a private car and agreed in advance which of the party goers would be the non-drinking driver. Bill Finch found that he carried 30 per cent fewer passengers than he typically did on a normal Saturday night in the winter months. None of his journeys on the Millennium eve exceeded the £25 limit.

(a) Explain what is meant in the passage by 'demand would be highly price inelastic'. (3 marks)
(b) Explain (i) why it was expected that demand for taxi cab rides would rise on Millennium eve; (4 marks)
    (ii) how this might have affected the ability of travellers to get a taxi cab ride on that night if fairs had NOT risen from their normal levels. (6 marks)
(c) Using the concepts of price elasticity of demand, revenue and profit, discuss whether Bill made the right decision to drive on Millennium eve. (11 marks)

47 Place

Place and the marketing mix

Place is one of the 4Ps of the marketing mix. It is no less important than the other Ps of product, price and promotion. However good the product, if it isn't available to customers to buy at the right place and at the right time, it won't sell.

The right place Products need to be available to customers in the place where they want to buy. For example, 75 per cent of all groceries in the UK are now bought from large supermarket chains. So if a grocery product is not available in a supermarket, its sales will be severely restricted. Equally, a car manufacturer might insist that parts are delivered to its plant by the component manufacturer. Unless the business agrees to deliver, it won't get the order.

The right time Products need to be available to customers at the time they want to buy. For example, often at Christmas there is a toy which becomes popular. Supplies may run out in shops. The manufacturer of the toy knows that unless it can increase supply to meet demand before 25th December, the sales it could have made will be lost. Equally, if there is a strike at the printers of a daily newspaper and a day's production is lost, those sales will never be recovered. Nobody will want to buy yesterday's newspaper today.

Coca-Cola has become the world's largest soft drinks distributor by making sure that its drinks are available to consumers not just in the right place, but also at a time when consumers want to buy. Coca-Cola vending machines, for example, are part of this strategy.

Distribution channels in consumer markets

The DISTRIBUTION CHANNEL for a product in a **consumer market** is the route it takes from manufacturer to the consumer. Figure 1 shows some common channels of distribution. They can be distinguished by the number and type of intermediary involved. A MARKETING INTERMEDIARY is a business or individual which acts as a link between the producer and customer.

Manufacturers to consumers DIRECT MARKETING involves a business selling its product straight to consumers. A manufacturer might advertise its products directly for sale to the public through advertisements in magazines. It might also operate a mail order catalogue or offer online ordering through a website on the Internet. It might even sell via its own sales representatives. Some manufacturers have factory shops where consumers can buy products. **Services** are also usually distributed straight to the customer, for example solicitors or accountants.

Manufacturers to consumers via retailers A RETAILER is a service business which sells goods to consumers. Retailers are typically called **shops**. But there are many other names for retailers, such as department stores, supermarkets and hypermarkets, superstores and convenience stores. Jewellers, butchers, grocers and hardware stores are also examples of shops.

Retailers provide certain services. First, they BREAK-BULK. They buy large quantities from suppliers and sell in smaller quantities to consumers. For example, a supermarket chain might buy 1 million packets of butter from a food manufacturer, but sell butter to consumers in single packets. Breaking-bulk is a service both to manufacturers and consumers. Most manufacturers don't want to sell in small quantities to consumers. Equally, consumers don't want to buy large quantities from manufacturers.

Figure 1: Examples of channels of distribution

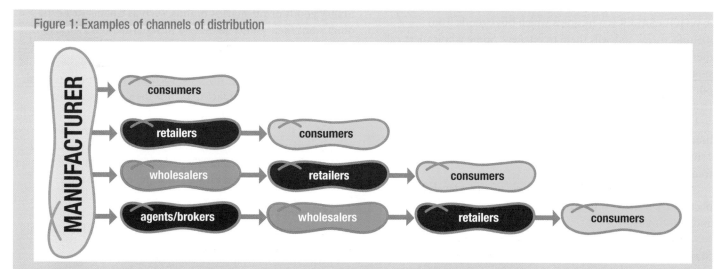

Question 1.

KFM Ltd manufactures interactive whiteboard software. Interactive whiteboards are used in education to support teaching and in business for conferences and presentations. KFM started as a small operation selling direct to customers from an industrial estate in Milton Keynes. It would place adverts in specialist magazines and often tailor products to the specific needs of customers.

Recently the business has expanded and now wants to sell more standardised products in greater quantities. KFM has been approached by a retail chain which wants to stock its product range in stores under the 'business and education' section. The retailer feels that the growing market in interactive whiteboards means that more customers will be looking for this type of software. KFM has also been looking to expand in the USA. It is interested in adapting its products for the US market. However, it is aware that legislation might affect its product specification and also that it lacks knowledge about the US market. It has considered a number of alternatives – using an agent to find a retail chain to stock the products, selling to a warehouse business or licensing the product to a US manufacturer.

(a) Examine the factors that might affect KFM's channel of distribution:
  (i) as a small operation; (ii) as it expands in the UK;
  (iii) as it expands abroad.
(b) Which channel of distribution would you advise KFM to use? Explain your answer.

Retailers also sell goods in locations which are convenient to consumers. A yoghurt manufacturer may have a plant in Wales, for example. But consumers in London don't want to travel to Wales every time they want to buy a yoghurt.

Retailers also provide other services which add value to the good being sold. These may include home delivery, repair services, extra guarantees and gift wrapping.

Manufacturers selling to customers via retailers is a **one level channel** because there is a single intermediary between manufacturers and consumers.

Manufacturers to consumers via wholesalers and retailers
A WHOLESALER is a business which buys goods from manufacturers and sells them to retailers. Some wholesalers call themselves a **cash-and-carry** because their customers, usually small shops, visit the premises and take away what they have purchased. In most cases, though, wholesalers deliver to retailing customers.

Like retailers, wholesalers provide two main services. They break-bulk and they are located or deliver to a location which is convenient to the retailer. They may also offer services such as trade credit.

The use of wholesalers is an example of a **two level channel** because there are two intermediaries between manufacturers and consumers.

Manufacturer to consumers via agents and/or wholesalers and retailers A manufacturer may use an intermediary called an

AGENT or BROKER. They bring buyers and sellers together. Agents are often used when selling into a foreign country. They often have better knowledge of the laws, needs of consumers and trading conditions in that country.

The choice of distribution channel

Which distribution channel is used depends upon a variety of factors.

Cost The longer the supply chain, the greater may be the cost to the final consumer. This is because each intermediary has its own costs to cover and wants to make a profit. Large supermarket chains often reduce these costs by cutting out the wholesaler and buying directly from the manufacturer.

However, in some cases short supply chains can be more costly than long supply chains. For example, a small upmarket food manufacturer may find that supermarkets will not stock its goods. To survive, it might have to supply directly to the customer, by mail order or the Internet. But the cost of a catalogue, an Internet site and delivery may be far more than the cost of supplying through a retailer. Some businesses employ sales representatives to sell directly. These can also be very costly.

Distribution Manufacturers may find it difficult to reach large numbers of consumers without an intermediary. This might be because the manufacturer lacks resources. It may not be able to afford to run a sales team, for instance. Equally, a manufacturer such as Heinz or Kellogg's may want to sell to every household in the country. The only way it can achieve this might be to use the large network of retailers, including supermarket chains.

Another factor may be knowledge of the market. A UK company that wants to sell a small quantity of goods to Australia may know nothing about this market. By using an agent to sell the goods, it will gain the agent's expertise.

Control Some manufacturers want to control the distribution channels they use carefully. For example, manufacturers of luxury goods or up-market brands, such as Chanel or Levis, don't want their goods being sold in supermarkets. This is because the place of sale can give important messages to consumers about the product. Expensive perfumes or jeans sold in Tesco or Asda detract from the exclusive image of the brand, according to their manufacturers. It is then going to be more difficult to sell these luxury goods at a high price and high profit margin.

Safety may be another issue. Some products require careful installation or maintenance. The manufacturer may find it easier to control safety aspects if it sells directly to the customer.

Legal factors The law may affect how a product is distributed. For example, drugs which need a doctor's prescription can only be sold through licensed chemists.

Distribution channels in business to business markets

The distribution channel for a good in a **business to business market** is the route it takes from the manufacturer to another business. As in consumer markets, there can be none, one or more intermediaries. For example, some businesses sell directly to others using their own 'sales reps'. Small tradespeople and businesses in the building industry, such as plumbers or carpenters, often buy from builders' merchants or building wholesalers. These intermediaries distribute products for the building industry. Agents might also be used by a producer dealing with a manufacturer in a foreign country.

Services are often distributed straight from one business to another, for example cleaning services, or through an agent, such as secretarial help.

The number of intermediaries depends upon a variety of factors, including cost and ease of distribution.

Distribution targets and objectives

A business that wants to be successful is likely to have clear **marketing objectives**. These are the goals that the business wants to achieve through its marketing, such as increasing sales.

When choosing which distribution channels it will use, a business will set DISTRIBUTION TARGETS. These are plans which might include, for example, the quantity to be sold over a future time period and to whom products will be sold. They will take into account marketing objectives. For example, a toy manufacturer that has the objective of increasing sales may set a target of selling 5,000 extra toys a month. It might decide that

Question 2.

Sales of CDs slumped by 8 per cent in the UK in the first half of 2007 but strong growth in legally downloaded music helped offset some of the decline. The collapse in CD and DVD sales on the UK high street has come into focus after music chain Fopp closed its 81 outlets last week. Retailers such as HMV and Virgin have come under intense pressure from low-cost online competitors as well as illegal downloading of music. However, the overall decline in CD sales was not quite as dramatic as the music retailers' woes suggest. The latest data from the BPI, the UK music industry trade body, showed that 60 million albums were sold in the first half of the year, down from 65 million in the same period in 2006. Nearly 97 per cent of those albums were sold as CDs.

Geoff Taylor, the BPI chief executive, said: 'CDs remain very attractive to consumers because of the flexibility and outstanding value for money they offer, and for this reason they represent the overwhelming majority of sales. Consumers vote with their pay packets and 58 million CD album sales in just six months is a very significant number indeed.'

The UK market for CDs is holding up better than other markets such as the US, helped by strong sales of UK artists such as Amy Winehouse and the Kaiser Chiefs. The BPI said that UK music fans buy more CDs per capita than anywhere else in the world, with the UK market accounting for more than 150 million sales for four years running.

The BPI also said the UK was 'ahead of the curve' in terms of legally downloaded music, with digital album sales partially offsetting the decline in physical sales. It said that 2.1 million albums were downloaded in the first half, with more than 100,000 sales a week achieved during June. Digital sales have also breathed life into the flagging singles market, helping to drive a 23 per cent increase in single sales in the first half of the year.

Source: adapted from *The Independent*, 11.7.2007.

(a) Identify the channels of distribution for music referred to in the article.
(b) Analyse the possible responses of a small UK based record shop/CD retailing business to the information in the article.

KEYTERMS

Agent or broker – an intermediary which arranges contracts for the sale of products between a supplier and a customer.

Break-bulk – dividing a larger quantity of goods ordered from a supplier and selling them in smaller quantities to customers. A key function of retailers and wholesalers is to break-bulk.

Direct marketing – selling by manufacturers direct to consumers without passing through retailers or wholesalers.

Distribution channel – the path taken by a product as it goes from manufacturer to the ultimate customer.

Distribution targets – goals set by a business for future sales of goods, for instance, through particular channels of distribution.

Marketing intermediary – a business or individual which acts as a link between the producer and customer.

Retailer – a type of business which buys goods from manufacturers and wholesalers and sells them, typically in smaller quantities and in a place convenient to the buyer, to customers.

Wholesaler – a type of business which buys goods from manufacturers and sells them in smaller quantities to retailers.

the best way to do this is to sell in bulk to wholesalers. Or a new computer magazine may want to target computer users. It may decide to sell directly over the Internet for a charge, allowing buyers to download and print out the magazine.

KNOWLEDGE

1. Explain why it is important for businesses to have goods available for sale (a) at the right price and (b) at the right time.
2. What is the difference between a zero level channel of distribution and a two level channel of distribution?
3. Explain why a mail order catalogue is an example of direct marketing.
4. What is the difference between a retailer and a wholesaler?
5. What services do retailers provide to consumers?
6. What services do wholesalers provide to retailers?
7. What factors determine which channel of distribution is used by a manufacturer?
8. What channels of distribution might there be in producer markets?
9. Why are distribution targets important for achieving marketing objectives?

Case Study: *Sunny side of the street*

Kamil Soud is the proprietor of Matrix Mobiles a business selling mobile phones through their website cheaphonesonline.co.uk. 'With e-retailing you are always fighting to provide the lowest price, so I thought it might be good to get a shop' explains Soud.

'I could tell from the traffic on my website what type of people bought from us', Soud said and he had considered setting up in Brighton, but had some strong reservations, 'Brighton was just not right for that client group. There are a lot of lifestyle businesses which are set up there which really never make enough money to survive, so there is a high turnover of businesses, but they drive the cost of shops up,' he explained.

Not only is "location, location, location" the retailing mantra - but renting a shop on the wrong side of the street can be the difference between healthy profits and commercial disaster. This is where the big multiples have the edge. They spend thousands of pounds analysing local retailing environments before deciding where to locate. In particular, they use software that enables them to compare their knowledge of their existing customers with the demographic profile of a new investment area.

Until recently, it has been very difficult - and very expensive - for a new, small independent trader to match this expertise. Consequently, a large proportion of independent retailers close in their first year of trading. And the mistake of many, perhaps most, is that good ideas are ruined by opening in the wrong place.

To help him with his decision about where to open a shop Soud employed the services of a business called Cartogen. They did an analysis of the areas where he had thought about opening a shop. As any business advisor will say, saving a firm from making a bad decision is just as important as helping one make a good choice. And retailers that understand much more about their potential locations are likely to make much better commercial decisions.

Cartogen gives clients a clear indication of the mix of customer types within a catchment area, their behaviour and purchasing habits. Demographic data such as age, ethnicity, family structure, employment status and housing type in any location is held on the database, along with behavioural information indicating the local population's lifestyle and spending habits. The database also provides information on potential competitors.

The service is offered across commercial retailing sectors - including bars, cafés, restaurants, health clubs and salons. "It works for all sectors, especially for customer profiling information," says Kennedy. But what makes the service particularly attractive is its affordability - a basic survey costs just £95, rising to £450 or £750 for more comprehensive information. Cartogen is keeping its charges low in the hope that initial surveys will lead to continuing retail consultancy services.

In the end Matrix Mobiles decided not to open a shop in Brighton after receiving advice from Cartogen. Paul Jukes is managing director of Vivid Design & Print, one of Cartogen's first customers. "It's great," he says. "I moved into my premises two years ago." But he remained concerned about the quality of his local market analysis, which he admits was "amateurish". "Cartogen checked all the area for me to check that my research was correct," explains Jukes. As a result, Jukes is able to commit more strongly to his existing marketing strategy, knowing that he chose the correct location for his business.

Source: adapted from The *Independent* 3.7.2007.

(a) Identify the distribution channels:
  (i) currently used by Matrix Mobiles; (3 marks)
  (ii) under consideration by Matrix Mobiles. (3 marks)
(b) Explain TWO reasons why finding the most suitable method of distribution is so important for Matrix Mobiles (6 marks)
(c) Examine the factors influencing Matrix Mobile's decision to open a shop. (8 marks)
(d) Discuss whether Matrix Mobile should open its own shop. (10 marks)

48 | Marketing and competitiveness

Markets and competition

There are many different markets in the UK. Markets might be divided by geographical boundaries, for example:

- local markets, such as the market for housing in South London;
- regional markets, such as the market for entertainment in the North West of England;
- national markets, such as the market for national newspapers in the UK;
- international markets, such as foreign exchange markets.

On the other hand they could be markets differentiated by use such as:

- highly specialised markets, such as the market for water polo playing equipment;
- non-specialised markets, such as the market for carrots.

Assessing the level of COMPETITION faced by business in a market may not always be straightforward. For example, two businesses operating on a local bus route may seem to have little competition but each other. However, they may actually face competition from other forms of transport, such as taxis, cars and trains

The degree of competition in a market will affect the **marketing mix** of a business. It will influence the:

- **prices** charged by the business;
- nature of the **products** offered by the business for sale;
- **promotion** used by the business to make consumers aware of the product and influence their spending;
- **places** where the products are for sale.

Determinants of competitiveness

Not all markets are the same. Different markets have different features and characteristics. The features and characteristics of markets are known as MARKET STRUCTURES. It is these market structures that largely determine how competitive a market is.

The number and relative size of businesses in the market In some markets, such as farming, a large number of businesses compete with each other. None of these businesses is particularly large compared to other businesses in the market. So the market share of any single business is small.

In other markets, a few businesses dominate the market, even though there might be a large number of other small firms. For example, in the UK washing powder and liquid detergent market, two businesses (Unilever and Procter & Gamble) have over 80 per cent of the market between them.

In some markets, there is only one business, a monopolist. For example, on most railway routes in the UK, there is only one train company operating a service.

The extent of barriers to entry In some markets, it is easy for a new business to set up. Many people each year set up small shops selling everything from groceries to clothes to toys. This is because the BARRIERS TO ENTRY are low. It doesn't cost much to open a shop. The amount of knowledge of the industry required is fairly little. In most cases, there are no special licences or other legal obstacles in the way. In certain markets, barriers to entry are high. In the rail transport industry or mobile telephone industry, the government gives licences to a limited number of businesses to operate. In the drug industry, newer drugs are protected by patent. This prevents other businesses from copying them.

In other markets, the costs of starting up a business are large. Car manufacturing, aeroplane production or oil refining are examples. In the perfume industry, the main companies devote a large proportion of their costs to marketing. Any new entrant then has to be able to afford to spend millions of pounds launching its new product.

Where barriers to entry are high, competition tends to be lower. One consequence of this is that businesses often compete on issues other than price. This means that they tend to emphasise the non-price elements of the marketing mix, such as promotion and place.

Potato supplier | Bank | Small cafe | Water supplier

Question 1.

(a) Explain the factors that may influence competition for the businesses in the photographs above.

Question 2.

It isn't difficult to set up in the grocery industry. A few tens of thousands of pounds will give you a grocery store on a little parade of shops giving personal service to the local inhabitants. But don't expect to survive or make a large profit because the grocery industry today is dominated by just a few supermarket chains.

Supermarket chains are valued in the billions of pounds. They do change hands from time to time. Asda, for example, was bought by the US giant Wal-mart in the late 1990s. Safeway was the subject of a fierce takeover battle in 2003 and was eventually bought by Morrisons. Somerfield made a huge mistake when it took over the KwikSave chain in the mid-1990s. However, it would be almost impossible now for a new chain to set up from scratch because it is so difficult to acquire sites for large new supermarket stores.

There is no rocket science involved in running a supermarket. Success is about making a few key decisions. What mix of goods are you going to sell? How are your stores going to present the goods for sale? How much are you going to charge and how much will you make in profit on each item? How are you going to organize your supply chain? What price will you offer your suppliers? Different supermarkets offer different mixes. Asda, for example, combines groceries with other goods such as clothes. Its market share has increased in recent years due both to this and to its low price policy.

(a) What is the relative size of businesses in the grocery industry?
(b) What barriers to entry exist?
(c) How do supermarkets differ in what they offer?
(d) To what extent is knowledge about how to run a supermarket chain available to all grocery store and supermarket owners?
(e) If Tesco increases its sales, what could be the impact on Asda?

The extent to which products can be differentiated In some markets, products are homogeneous. This means that they are the same whichever business produces them. Typically, there are standards to which products conform. So nine carat gold is the same quality whatever business produces it. Homogeneous products are often found in raw materials markets and in basic manufacturing, such as steel. Where products are homogenous competition tends to be largely based upon price with this element of the marketing mix emphasised.

In other markets, products differ according to which business makes them. A McDonald's meal is different from a Burger King meal. Ford cars differ from Volkswagen cars. Heineken lager is different from Budweiser lager. Individual products or product ranges can then be branded. The stronger the perceived difference, the stronger the brand. Where product differentiation is strong the non-price elements of the marketing mix such as promotion tend to be emphasised by businesses.

The knowledge that buyers and sellers possess In some markets, buyers and sellers have access to all the information they need to make rational decisions. Buyers, for instance, would be able to find out the best price in the market. Sellers would have open access to the most efficient methods of production. This is known as having perfect knowledge. Where knowledge is perfect, price is strongly emphasised in the marketing mix.

In other markets, knowledge is not available to all. One business might not be able to find out how much a rival business is charging for its products. A consumer might not know which of 20 cars will be most environmentally friendly. If there is imperfect information in the market, this can give a competitive advantage to some businesses over others. Where knowledge is imperfect businesses will tend to place a great deal of importance upon non-price elements of the marketing mix such as the product and promotion.

Degree of interrelationship In some markets, the actions of one business have no effect on another business. Businesses are independent of one another. In farming, the decision by one farmer to plant a field with carrots has no impact on a nearby farm in terms of the price it will receive or how much it produces.

In other markets, such as car production, increased sales by one business will mean reduced sales by another business if the size of the market remains the same. Businesses are then interdependent.

Legal factors Competition between businesses is generally seen as being in the best interests of customers. They can shop around between businesses offering the same or similar products for the best deal. This means that businesses have to offer what the customer wants or face closing down through lack of customers.

In contrast, monopoly is usually argued to be bad for customers. They are forced to buy from one supplier whatever the quality of the product and whatever the prices. The monopolist has enormous power over customers and acts to maximise the benefits to itself.

Monopolies, therefore, tend to be controlled by governments. In the USA, they are illegal. In the UK and the rest of the European Union they are **regulated**. A monopolist exists where there is only one firm in a market. However, firms in a market can act as if they were a monopoly by COLLUDING. This means they get together, usually to fix prices and output in a market. They then have formed a CARTEL. For example, a group of firms making vitamins may fix a high price between themselves at which they will sell vitamins to customers. Then they have to restrict output between themselves to sustain those high prices.

The degree of competition and the marketing mix

Markets may be classified into a number of different types according to their mix of characteristics. The market conditions in which a business operates and the degree of competition it faces will affect its market mix.

Perfect competition PERFECT COMPETITION is a situation where there is a large number of small businesses, producing almost exactly the same product. Consumers are aware of what is being offered by all businesses. There are no barriers to prevent businesses setting up. Businesses are **price-takers**. They have no influence over the price they charge. If a firm charged a higher price than others, customers would know exactly where to go to buy an alternative. An example of this type of competition is found in agricultural markets. There are often many small farmers, each with a relatively small market share, producing almost identical products.

Businesses operating under these conditions have little or no scope to determine their prices. Therefore, they may have to consider other elements of the marketing mix, such as promotion methods or how distribution channels can be used. For example, some farms have attempted to sell directly to customers through farm shops, but others through national supermarket chains. Some farms have promoted themselves as free range or organic producers.

Monopolistic competition MONOPOLISTIC COMPETITION is a situation where there is a large number of relatively small businesses in competition with each other and there are few entry barriers. Each business has a product that is differentiated from others through **branding**. But the brand identity of products is weak. A business will face competition from a wide range of other businesses in the market with similar, but differentiated, products. Businesses operating under these conditions are not price-takers. But they will only have a limited degree of control over the price they charge. Examples of this type of competition in the UK might include legal service providers and certain types of clothing retailing.

Given limited scope for price changes, businesses operating under monopolistic competition may stress other elements of their marketing mix, such as product, place and promotion. So a business might use promotional techniques that help to compete against other businesses. For example, a financial services advisor might promote its services aimed at business investors. A clothing retailer may stock clothes aimed at a particular market, such as young people, older people or taller men and women.

Oligopoly When there are many firms, but only a few dominate the market, OLIGOPOLY is said to exist. Examples include the markets for petrol, beer, detergents, paint and sweets. The majority of businesses in the UK operate under this type of competition.

Under oligopoly, each firm will have a differentiated product, often with a strong brand identity. Several brands may be competing in the same market. Brand loyalty amongst customers is encouraged by advertising and promotion. Firms in such markets are often said to compete in the form of non-price competition. Prices are often stable for long periods, disturbed only by short price wars.

Although brand loyalty does allow some price control, businesses often follow the price of the market leaders. This means that they tend to be interdependent.

Barriers to entry exist. If it was easy for new firms to enter the industry, they would set up and take the market share of the few large producers. Examples of barriers to entry might be:

- legal restrictions, such as patents which prevent other businesses copying products for a period of time;
- high start-up costs, such as the cost of manufacturing;
- the promotion or advertising required, for example, in the tobacco or soap powder industries;
- arrangements between businesses, for example in the 1990s newsagents could not stock ice creams by other producers in certain manufacturers' freezers (known as freezer exclusivity);
- collusion between businesses in cartels, which act together to prevent new entrants.

Businesses operating under oligopoly emphasise promotion in order to maintain their brand. They promote heavily in order to develop and maintain brand loyalty. However, pricing may also be an important feature of the marketing mix. A strong brand may enable a business to charge a relatively high price for a product if, for example, it has a market leading brand. Customers loyal to the brand will continue to buy the product rather than switching to another.

Monopoly MONOPOLY occurs when one business has total control over a market and is the only seller of the product. This

Question 3.

In January 2004 TelePassport Telecommunications, the first private telephone operator in Cyprus, pledged to reduce call rates by 15 per cent after gaining approval from the Telecommunications Regulator. Previously the only telephone company had been CyTA, a government controlled company.

TelePassport's president, Socratis Hasikos, said 'Statistics show that in 1998 CyTA made a profit of £50 million which increased to £62 million in 1999 and in 2001 reached £91 million. According to CyTA they expected to reap a profit of £107 million from the period 1998-2002, yet they earned a profit of £218 million. How can this be possible if they are not over-charging their customers? Now, they must present their costs and expenses to the Telecommunications Regulator, who has given them 15 days to do so.' He believed that CyTA delayed presenting its expenses because 'they have been paying out too much money and need to earn it back by charging more, or they have simply been ripping off customers'.

It was suggested that the entry of Cyprus into the EU would open the door to healthy competition for CyTA. Hasikos argues 'Our aim is not to attack CyTA, but to offer customers a better service at cheaper rates. Competition need not be negative, but could push CyTA into also lowering their prices.'

Source: adapted from www.xak.com.

(a) Identify and explain the type of competition before the entry of TelePassport Telecommunications into the market in Cyprus.
(b) Examine how (i) businesses and (ii) consumers are likely to be affected by the change in competition that is taking place in Cyprus.

pure monopoly should not be confused with a **legal monopoly**, which occurs in the UK when a firm controls 25 per cent or more of a market.

Monopolists are likely to erect barriers to prevent others from entering their market. They will also exert a strong influence on the price which they charge for their product. However, because monopolists are the only supplier of a product, it does not mean that they can charge whatever they want. If they raise the price demand will fall to some extent. Because of the influence monopolists have on their price, they are often called **price-makers**.

In the past, in the UK, certain businesses have come close to exerting pure monopoly power. For example, British Gas used to enjoy a monopoly position in the gas market. It was the sole supplier of piped gas in the UK. On the other hand, it could be argued that British Gas was operating in the energy market and therefore faced competition from electricity and oil companies. One of the main reasons why one gas company no longer exerts control over the market for gas is that the government introduced **legislation** to increase competition in markets where monopolies previously existed.

Today, the markets for water, power, rail and communications are regulated by **regulatory bodies** such as Ofcom (communications), Ofgem (gas and electricity) and Ofwat (water). Former state monopolies have been PRIVATISED. Limits are placed on their price increases. So telecommunications businesses offer an ever-expanding range of services and water and power companies promote to home-owners to attract their custom. In the absence of regulation monopolies may stress pricing as part of their marketing mix. Being the only provider of a product, they may seek to set a price that will maximise sales revenue. So the only supplier of a boat repair service in a harbour area, which has a **local monopoly**, may be able to regularly increase prices and not lose customers as there is no alternative service.

Methods of improving competitiveness

The market structure a business is operating within does determine to a large extent the competition that a business faces. However, businesses also adopt a range of strategies intended to increase their own competitiveness. The intention of such strategies is that they can compete more effectively within this given market structure. What businesses generally seek is to gain a **competitive advantage** over competitors.

Methods of improving competitiveness may be **marketing methods**. This will involve adapting and developing the marketing mix. The marketing mix is fundamental to a business' ability to compete effectively within a given market. By amending and developing its marketing mix a business can become more competitive. For example, a business marketing a fast-moving consumer good in an oligopolistic market might develop a new national advertising campaign that captures the imagination of consumers. This would enable the business to boost sales in the short term and, if other aspects of the marketing mix were developed to support this campaign, it might form the basis for a

medium- and/or long-term increase in sales.

However, the methods used may be **non-marketing** methods.

Reducing costs Businesses use a range of strategies to reduce costs, including the setting of new budgets, changes in management processes and procedures, renegotiating contracts with suppliers, reducing staffing and employing a range of measures to improve efficiency and productivity.

Improving quality For manufacturing businesses this means producing a product that consumers recognise as being of higher quality. For service providers it means improving consumer perceptions of the quality of service that they receive. For businesses other than those operating under perfect competition improving quality enables a business to increase its competitiveness in a given market.

Staff training Staff training is a key component in a business' efforts to manage their competitiveness. A well trained and efficient staff responsive to the needs and wishes of customers can enhance competitiveness considerably. This is true in all

KEY TERMS

Barriers to entry – factors which make it difficult or impossible for businesses to enter a market and compete with existing producers.

Cartel – a group of businesses (or countries) which join together to agree on pricing and output in a market in an attempt to gain higher profits at the expense of customers.

Collusion – in business, where several businesses (or countries) make agreements among themselves which benefit them at the expense of either rival businesses or customers.

Competition – rivalry between businesses offering products in the same market; competition may take forms such as price competition, distinctive product offerings, advertising and distribution.

Market structures – the characteristics of a market, such as the size of the barriers to entry to the market, the number of businesses in the market or whether they produce identical products, which determine the behaviour of businesses within the market.

Monopolistic competition – a market structure where there is a large number of small businesses producing differentiated, branded products, where barriers to entry are low and businesses are price-setters.

Monopoly – a market structure where there is a single business in the market and there are barriers to entry.

Oligopoly – a market structure where a few large businesses dominate the market producing differentiated, branded, products, where barriers to entry are typically high and where businesses are price-setters.

Perfect competition – a market structure where there is a large number of small businesses producing identical products, where barriers to entry are low and where businesses are price-takers.

Privatisation – the sale of government-owned assets to the private sector.

business sectors but it is especially the case in those service industries, such as personal services like hairdressing, where

responding effectively to customers on a daily basis is at the heart of the business' activities.

KNOWLEDGE

1. How do businesses compete with each other?
2. Explain three possible barriers to entry into a market.
3. Explain two ways in which businesses can engage in unfair competition.

4. In what ways might the marketing mix of a business operating under perfect competition and a business operating under oligopoly differ?
5. State three non-monetary methods of improving competitiveness.

Case Study: **UK sandwich sales**

Are British workers losing their taste for the traditional sandwich as their favourite midday snack? New research suggests that this may be so. Office or manual workers are more likely to have a ready-chilled curry in their lunchbox, rather than a cheese sandwich. Almost three-quarters told researchers for Geest, an own-label manufacturer of convenience foods for supermarkets, that they were fed up with sandwiches and about half said they looked forward to something hot to give them a boost. Some 30 per cent of the 919 employees questioned said they bought ready-chilled supermarket soups or meals to take to work and heat up in a microwave, taking a bite out the sandwich market. The survey also found that 17 per cent thought lunch was the 'highlight' of their working day. But a quarter described colleagues with plastic lunch boxes as 'very sad'.

The market for sandwiches in the UK is shared between a range of operators of varying size. These range from the supermarkets such as Tescos and Sainsbury's and large specialist bakers such as Greggs through to small independent bakers' shops and specialist sandwich shops found mainly in town and city centres. Important arrivals on the UK sandwich market in recent years have included sandwich chains such as Pret a Manger which is largely focused in big cities such as London and Manchester.

Bakers' shops have seen their share of the sandwich market slip in the past year with competition from sandwich and snack bars and supermarkets increasing, according to a new report from market research company Key Note. The report says bakers' shops (a category that includes the Greggs chain) are still the dominant player in UK sandwich sales but their market share in terms of the value of sandwich sales value fell from 28.6 per cent in 2005/06 to 26.4 per cent over the year to May 2007. At the same time, supermarkets have increased value sales up from 12.2 per cent to 13.4 per cent over the same period. Sandwich chains had a 9.8 per cent value share of the market, with Subway the dominant player with a 7.2 per cent share of sandwich sales by value, up 4.2 per cent.

Figures on total sandwich sales don't entirely correspond with the research conducted for Geest. Total sandwich sales were £3.73 billion in the year ending May 2007, up from £3.61 billion the year before, although the 2.46 billion packs sold in 2007 was less than the 2.54 billion the previous year. The report also says that 51 per cent of sandwiches sold

are wedges, 17 per cent rolls and baps, 13 per cent baguettes and 5 per cent sub rolls. Other sandwich carriers, such as pittas and wraps, accounted for 10 per cent of volumes.

Retailers say there are no signs of customers turning their backs on the humble British sandwich. Marks & Spencer, which claims to be the leading retailer in this sector, says it is 'an extremely buoyant market'. Its most popular sandwiches include chicken salad, prawn and mayonnaise and chicken tikka. However, the retailer says it has noticed an upturn in sales of foods which can be heated up, such as stuffed naans. M&S is also expanding its range of lunch foods and as recently as six weeks ago launched a line of sushi in response to customer demand.

Upmarket sandwich chain Pret a Manger also denies the threat of the ready meal to its sandwich business, saying people always turn to hot food in winter. The company adds that it is planning to increase its total number of shops in England to 200 from its present 74 over the next two years.

Source adapted from www.bbcnews.co.uk and www.bakeryinfo.co.uk.

(a) Explain what is meant by the terms (i) competition (3 marks) and (ii) dominant player. (3 marks)
(b) How would you classify the UK sandwich market? Justify your answer. (6 marks)
(c) Examine TWO factors that might influence the competitiveness in the Uk sandwich market. (6 marks)
(d) Explain how a small retailer might improve its competitiveness in the sandwich market. (8 marks)
(e) Discuss whether a small business could grow to dominate over 50 per cent of sales in the UK sandwich market. (10 marks)

Objectives

An OBJECTIVE or GOAL of a business is an outcome which allows a business to achieve its aims. Businesses can have a wide variety of objectives such as:

- to increase pre-tax profits by 10 per cent over the next 12 months;
- to increase sales in the USA by 5 per cent over the next 6 months;
- to recruit an extra 10 highly motivated staff in the marketing department over the next 3 months;
- to cut carbon emissions in European operations by 5 per cent over the next 24 months;
- to switch to sourcing 100 per cent organic food over the next 3 years.

Objectives should be practical outcomes from the operation of a business. One way of summarising this is to use SMART criteria. This says that objectives should be:

S specific - they must set out clearly what a business is attempting to achieve;

M measurable - they must be capable of being measured so that it can judged whether or not they have been achieved;

A agreed - everyone responsible for achieving an objective must have agreed with the objective and understood what it meant;

R realistic - the objective must be achievable given the resources available and the market conditions;

T time specific - the objective must specify over what period of time it is to be achieved.

Corporate objectives

CORPORATE OBJECTIVES are the objectives set by the most senior management and directors for the company as a whole. For example, multinational companies like BP, Wal-Mart (which owns Asda in the UK), Toyota or Vodafone have corporate objectives which cover the performance of the whole of their operations. Corporate objectives will differ from industry to industry. But they might include objectives such as the following:

- for profit before tax to grow by 15 per cent over the next three years;
- for sales revenue to grow by 30 per cent over the next five years;
- to increase market share by 5 per cent over the next two years;
- for dividends paid to shareholders to increase by 6 per cent per year over the next four years;
- for operating costs to fall by 3 per cent over the next 24 months;
- for carbon emissions from company operations to fall by 15 per cent over the next 5 years.

Corporate objectives for UK and US companies tend to be financial objectives. This is because corporate objectives are aimed at satisfying the needs of the owners of the company, the shareholders. Financial objectives are also easier to quantify at a corporate level than other possible objectives. For example, it is more difficult to quantity something like 'increase the motivation of staff' or 'increase consumer satisfaction with our products' when there are 30,000 staff and 20 million customers worldwide than 'increase profit before tax by 2 per cent' or 'increase sales by 3 per cent'.

Functional objectives

Medium to large sized companies are organised on a functional basis. They are organised into **departments**. Each department specialises in performing a particular type of task. There are many ways in which companies can be organised by function but by far the most common is to divide them into marketing, finance, operations and human resources. Depending upon the industry and company, these departments will be given different names. In some companies, there may be additional departments like a legal department where a particular function is very important. In some companies, responsibility for one of these functions may be split between two different departments. Marketing and sales, for example, may be split. In addition, large companies are likely to be split into a number of subsidiary companies, each of which, for example, will have its own marketing department or finance department. So a large company may have 20 different finance departments, 19 in subsidiary companies and one finance department at head office.

FUNCTIONAL OBJECTIVES (sometimes also called DEPARTMENTAL OBJECTIVES) are the objectives of each department. For example, the objectives of the marketing department might be to:

- increase sales by 3 per cent each quarter;
- stem the fall in sales in Asian market to 2 per cent per year;
- increase the ratio of visits to the online ordering website to sales placed from 1 in every 10 to 1 in every 8 on the company website;
- increase the sales placed with sales representatives from £50,000 per quarter to £52,000 per quarter;
- increase market share in the Eastern European market from 5 per cent to 6 per cent over the next three years.

Functional and corporate objectives

In the best run of companies, functional objectives will be completely tied to corporate objectives. In poorly run companies, functional objectives will lead to outcomes which have little to do with corporate objectives.

For example, a company might set itself the corporate objective of increasing operating profit by 4 per cent per year over the next 36 months. The company has no subsidiary companies and it is organised into four departments: marketing, finance, operations and human resources. Profit is the difference between revenues and costs. So marketing might be given the functional objective of increasing sales revenues by 2 per cent per year. The operations and human resources department might be given the functional objective of reducing staffing costs by 1 per cent per year through increased efficiency. Operations might also be given the functional objective of reducing the use of raw materials by 1 per cent per year whilst producing 2 per cent more output per year. If these functional objectives are achieved, then this will add up to the corporate objective of increasing operating profit by 4 per cent per year.

Functional objectives and functional strategies

Objectives are not usually reached by chance. Businesses have to PLAN how they will achieve their objectives. Long-term planning to achieve objectives is known as STRATEGY. Corporate strategy is long-term planning to achieve corporate objectives. FUNCTIONAL (or DEPARTMENTAL) STRATEGY is long-term planning at a departmental level to achieve functional (or departmental) objectives.

For example, the operations department may be given a functional objective of cutting costs per unit produced by 4 per cent over the next three years. It then has to plan how to achieve this objective. It decides that this can be achieved by sourcing raw materials more cheaply saving 2 per cent in costs, increasing labour efficiency by 5 per cent, saving 1 per cent in costs after

the annual pay rise has been taken into account, and reducing wastage saving a further 1 per cent. These plans together with the objectives form the departmental strategy for the coming 36 months.

Exactly what 'long term' means varies from situation to situation. It could mean 12 months or ten years. Given the quick changing nature of the business environment, businesses are most unlikely to plan for the next ten years except in industries where there is a very long lead time in investment. For example, an oil company will have strategies for oil exploration and development which cover perhaps the next ten years. But this is the exception rather than the norm. Typically, long term might mean between 3 and 5 years.

Question 1.

A national brewery has set out its corporate objectives for the next three years. It faces a difficult market with very strong competition from other brewers. Its mass market brands have declined in sales over the past five years, although its specialist brews have increased. Overall, however, sales have been falling at over 2 per cent per year. Over the next two years, the company has set itself the objective of maintaining the value of sales and its market share for all beers. Profits are to rise by 3 per cent per annum.

Andy Snow is in charge of marketing. His job is now to draw up a set of objectives for his department given the corporate strategies. He knows that he needs to focus on issues such as sales volumes, prices, market segments and costs. He must be realistic about his objectives given the difficult trading conditions of the past few years.

(a) Suggest FOUR objectives for the marketing department of the company over the next two years and analyse how each might contribute to the achievement of the corporate objectives.

KEY TERMS

Corporate objectives – the objectives of a medium to large sized business as a whole.

Functional (or departmental) objectives – the objectives of a department within a business.

Functional (or departmental) strategy – strategy of a department within a business.

Objective or goal – a target of or outcome for a business which allows it to achieve its aims.

Planning – the process of deciding how a business will run and operate in future in areas such as production, marketing and finance and, deciding what resources will be needed and how they be used.

SMART – acronym for the attributes of a good objective – specific, measurable, agreed, realistic and time specific.

Strategy – a set of long-term plans drawn up to achieve a given set of objectives.

KNOWLEDGE

1. Explain the difference between a functional objective and a corporate objective.
2. Why should objectives be SMART?
3. Why might corporate objectives mainly be expressed as financial objectives?
4. Explain the relationship between a functional objective and functional strategy.

Case Study:
Sainsbury's

In 2001, Sir Peter Davis, chief executive of Sainsbury's had told shareholders that his 'business transformation' programme would deliver a saving of £600 million every year by the end of the programme in 2004. In October 2004, a new chief executive, Justin King, said the programme had failed. He wrote off £260 million against ineffective supply chain equipment and ineffective IT systems. Worse than that, the failure had lost loyal customers and those still shopping at Sainsbury's were spending less.

At the heart of the problems were four brand new automated warehouses designed to handle all the products being delivered to the Sainsbury's chain in the UK. They should have delivered cost savings through economies of scale in distribution. Instead, they led to a breakdown in communication between the individual stores and the suppliers. IT systems should have matched what was being sold in a store with deliveries from the automated warehouses. What actually happened was that stores were failing to get deliveries on time. The result was 'stockouts': empty shelves in the stores where there should have been products for sale. If it isn't on the shelves, the customer can't buy it and so sales fall. Equally, some Sainsbury's customers got so frustrated by continual stockouts that they abandoned Sainsbury's altogether and did their regular shop at another supermarket.

But there was another problem. Stock was in the system but not in the right place. So, for example, fresh fruit and vegetables which should have been on display for sale in a supermarket was languishing in one of the warehouses undelivered. The result was a considerable increase in wastage. Instead of being bought by customers, it was being thrown away. When Justin King took over as chief executive in 2004, he quickly

appointed Lawrence Christensen, the former operations manager at Safeway, to sort out the supply chain problem. Lawrence Christensen put in place a number of solutions which haven't completely solved the problem but, where fully implemented, have resulted in a fall in stockouts of 75 per cent. He went back to Witron and Siemens, the two groups behind the equipment IT systems, to try to make improvements. He put in extra labour to manually sort products where needed. He is also implementing a 'step change' programme across all Sainsbury's stores to put clear systems in place around deliveries, stock auditing and making sure the inventory was correct.

Sainsbury's supply problems were symptomatic of much wider problems. In the 1990s, it lost market leadership to Tesco. By 2008, Tesco had one third of the grocery market, twice the market share of Sainsbury's. The company has to address the fact that it isn't the cheapest supermarket at which to shop, customers don't seem to value the differences between it and its competitors and yet it aims to be a distinctive mass market grocery retailer. It cannot afford to make mistakes at the functional level if it is to stand any chance of closing the gap between itself and Tesco.

Source: adapted from the *Financial Times*.

(a) 'The 'business transformation' programme was a functional level strategy which went badly wrong.' To what extent do you agree with this view? (15 marks)

(b) A functional objective of the 'business transformation' programme was to deliver savings of £600 million per year. Evaluate the extent to which the failure of the programme might have affected Sainsbury's ability to achieve its corporate objectives. (15 marks)

50 | Understanding financial objectives

What are financial objectives?

When a business first starts trading it may simply want to survive. A financial objective in the first year might be to break-even. However, once a business is established its financial objectives are likely to change.

FINANCIAL OBJECTIVES are the goals or targets a business sets itself for its financial performance. Financial targets are likely to be more challenging. Shareholders, for example, will want to see a return on their investment. Financial institutions, such as pension funds and insurance companies that have invested in public limited companies, will often expect these companies to achieve particular financial objectives. If companies fail to meet investors' expectations, they may withdraw their support by selling shares.

Larger businesses are likely to employ a team of accountants to help set financial targets. They are also likely to develop systems to monitor the financial performance of the business. Some of the financial objectives of an established business may relate to:

* cash flow targets;
* cost minimisation;
* return on capital employed;
* shareholders' returns.

Cash flow targets

The cash flow of a business is the money flowing into and out of the business. Monitoring cash flow in a business is a crucial activity. Financial managers must ensure that the business has enough cash when it is needed. If a business runs out of cash it is likely to collapse.

Cash flow forecasts will be produced to help plan the future cash position of the business. One of the advantages of setting cash flow targets is that the business is less likely to run out of cash. Different cash flow targets can be set.

* Targets might relate to the need for cash at particular times of the trading year. For example, a business might plan to undertake some heavy capital expenditure in September. To avoid borrowing, a cash flow target might be set so that enough cash is generated by the business to pay for the capital expenditure.
* Businesses can set monthly cash flow targets. This might be part of their budgeting procedure. They may aim to have a particular amount of cash at the end of each month.
* Figure 1 shows an example of a large business that sets annual cash flow targets.

Cost minimisation

Most businesses will make an effort to reduce costs. If costs are lower then profits will be higher. A business might choose from a wide range of measures to reduce costs. Some examples include:

* reducing waste by recycling;

Figure 1: Cash flow target set by Telenor

Norwegian telecom group Telenor ASA aims to increase cash flow from its Nordic mobile and fixed-line operations to more than 10 billion crowns ($1.66 billion) a year in the medium term. Chief Executive Jon Fredrik Baksaas confirmed to Reuters that the group's main revenue, profitability and capital expenditure targets for 2007 remain unchanged. 'We are putting up a target to manage the cash flow situation really well in the Nordic region,' Baksaas said. In 2006, Telenor's operations had a cash flow of around 9.6 billion crowns. Baksaas said the Nordic cash-flow target 'might be a tough one, but the base is as good as it can be'. He said Telenor had made the basic investments needed to achieve the cash flow target.

Source: adapted from http://asia.news.yahoo.com

Question 1.

Cygnus Business Media publishes 80 business-to-business media products including trade magazines, directories and cards, and produces 50 trade shows within 15 major markets. In 2007 the company announced a number of cost cutting measures. Cygnus said it was going to cut all employee salaries by 7.5 per cent, put all hourly workers on a 37-hour workweek, and cut the basic pay of senior managers by a significant but unspecified amount starting October 1 and continuing through the end of the year.

The dramatic cost cutting comes in response to greater-than-expected revenue shortfalls. 'Recently we have begun to experience the decline in print revenue that has been affecting our industry for the last several years,' Davis and O'Brien, the company's chief executives said in a memo. 'This decline has accelerated and is significantly larger than we projected during our business reviews, held less than three months ago. Because print represents more than 70 percent of the company's revenue, the growth from other areas is not enough to cover our growing deficit.'

Source: adapted from www.foliomag.com

(a) How does Cygnus Business Media plan to cut costs?
(b) Why has Cygnus Business Media decided to cut costs?
(c) Explain a possible disadvantage of this objective.

Figure 2: Cost minimisation at British Airways

British Airways (BA) is planning to upgrade its ba.com website and increase the use of self-service check-in as part of a £200m investment aimed at slashing the airline's costs by £450 million. The two-year programme to drive down costs and improve customer service is the first business plan of new BA CEO Willie Walsh since he took over in October last year. BA is aiming to make cost savings of £225m in the financial year 2006/07 and a further £225m in the following financial year.

The £200 million investment covers upgrading ba.com, a new Club World seat and on-demand films in all cabins. Last year a third of BA customers booked their seats directly with the airline and most of those booked on ba.com. The new business plan aims to raise that to half by 2008. Further savings will come from new processes introduced ahead of the Heathrow Terminal 5 opening and greater use of BA's self-service check-in system.

Source: adapted from http://management.silicon.com 10.3.2006.

- reducing staffing levels through automation;
- adopting lean production techniques;
- closing down unprofitable activities;
- finding cheaper suppliers;
- reorganisation;
- outsourcing activities.

When setting financial objectives a business may set costs minimisation targets. For example, a business might aim to cut costs by £50 million per year for the next three years by reorganising its international activities. An example of cost minimisation at British Airways is outlined in Figure 2.

Some organisations might use **cost minimisation analysis**. This involves working out the costs of undertaking a particular activity in different ways. This approach is used in the NHS. For example, it is used to compare the cost of caring for patients at home and to that of caring for them in a hospital. Cost minimisation analysis found a mean cost to the NHS and social services of caring for a patient in the home was £2,516. In contrast, the cost of caring for the same patient in a hospital would be £3,292. This means that for every £10,000 spent, routine hospital care could be provided for three patients, while early discharge to care in the hospital at home scheme could be provided for four patients.

Return on capital employed

The return on capital employed (ROCE) is the amount of profit a business generates in relation to the amount of money invested in that business. Most companies are likely to set ROCE objectives. The ROCE is likely to be of particular interest to the owners of the business. This is because they are the ones that have probably invested the most. To calculate the ROCE:

$$\text{ROCE} = \frac{\text{Profit}}{\text{Capital employed}} \times 100$$

This can be used to make comparisons over time or between different companies.

Shareholders' returns

Financial objectives can be influenced by the shareholders in a company. Shareholders are the owners of a company. Consequently some financial objectives are linked to the returns made by shareholders. There is a number of these and some examples are outlined below.

- **Dividend per share** The DIVIDEND PER SHARE is the amount of money a shareholder is paid for every share owned. For example, if a shareholder owns 10,000 shares in a company and a dividend per share of 3p is paid by the company, the shareholder will receive a £300 (10,000 x 3p) dividend payment. An objective for a company might be to increase the dividend per share every year. However, the dividend per share does not provide an accurate measure of the returns to shareholders. This is because the dividend per share must be compared with the price of the share. This involves calculating the dividend yield.
- **Dividend yield** The DIVIDEND YIELD is the dividend per share expressed as a percentage of the share price. In the example above, if the share price is 90p the dividend yield will be:

$$\text{Dividend yield} = \frac{\text{Dividend per share}}{\text{Share price}} \times 100$$

$$= \frac{3p}{90p} \times 100 = 3.3 \text{ per cent}$$

A company might set targets for the dividend yield. For example, the company in this example might aim to generate a dividend yield of over 3 per cent, in which case the objective has been met.

- **Total shareholder return (TSR)** Many public limited companies aim to increase TOTAL SHAREHOLDER RETURN (TSR). This is a measure of financial performance which combines both share price increases and the dividend paid. PLCs have to publish this

Question 2.

ITtop.com is an IT services provider. It designs and builds data management systems. The company's board of directors has set an annual ROCE target of 15 per cent. Table 1 shows the capital employed and profit for ITtop.com over the last four years.

Table 1: ROCE at ITtop.com

	2004	2005	2006	2007
Capital employed	£35m	£35m	£37m	£39m
Profit	£4.48m	£4.86m	£5.883m	£6.708m
ROCE				

(a) Calculate the ROCE for the four years.
(b) Account for the changes in ROCE over the time period.
(c) Explain whether the directors will be happy with the values calculated in (a).

information in their annual report and accounts. Figure 4 shows the TSR for Bovis Homes, the construction company, over a five year period. After a slow rise in 2003, the TSR has risen throughout the time period. The graph also shows movements in the FTSE Mid-250 Index. This is an index of share prices for the top 250 companies after the top 100. This is used to make an immediate comparison. In this case Bovis Homes has outperformed the index almost entirely over the time period.

Internal influences on financial objectives

The financial objectives set by a business are affected by a number of factors. Some of these are internal, from within the business.

Stakeholders The financial objectives set by a business are likely to be influenced by the stakeholders. It is likely that the strongest stakeholder group will have the most influence over the objectives. For example, if the shareholders are the dominant group it is likely that shareholders objectives will be set, such as increasing dividend yield.

Capacity There is usually a limit to the amount a business can produce. Consequently this might act as a constraint on financial objectives. For example, if a business is running at full capacity it may not be possible to generate increasing amounts of cash.

Corporate strategy Financial objectives are likely to be linked to the corporate strategy of a business. For example, if a company is pursuing rapid growth through acquisitions, it may mean that dividends are held stable for a period of time. The company may need to retain more profit to fund the acquisitions.

Departmental influence Many large businesses are organised into departments or divisions. In these circumstances particular departments might influence financial objectives. For example, if a company has a strong sales department, it may mean that the company pursues sales growth at the expense of profit margins.

Ethical stance Some companies want to be seen as 'good corporate citizens'. This means they might devote more resources to minimising their effect on the environment or

Figure 4: TSR for Bovis Homes 2002-06

Total Shareholder Return (TSR) (1 January 2002 = 100)

- FTSE Mid-250 Index
- Bovis Homes Group PLC

Source: adapted from Bovis Homes, *Annual Report and Accounts*, 2006.

going further to meet the needs of the local community, for example. Consequently financial objectives may be less of a priority.

External influences on financial objectives

Financial objectives are likely to be affected by factors outside the control of a business. These are called external factors.

Economic climate If the economy is stable and growing at a sustainable rate a business is likely to have more choice when setting financial objectives. However, if the economic climate is poor a business may have less control. For example, if the economy goes into recession, businesses selling non-essential goods and services may have to set more modest financial objectives.

Competition The activities of rival businesses can have an impact on financial objectives. For example, if a rival starts a price war, financial objectives are likely to be less optimistic.

Consumer tastes Changes in market conditions brought about by a shift in consumer tastes can affect the financial objectives set by a business. For example, increasing numbers of consumers are using gaming sites on the Internet. Consequently, companies that offer these services may be setting quite high financial objectives as they take advantage of the boom.

Political factors A change in government, for example, to one spending more on road building may encourage a business that provides materials to revise its targets for inflow of cash.

Legislation Quite a lot of government legislation is aimed at businesses. Generally, more legislation means extra costs which may dampen profits. Consequently financial objectives will be less optimistic.

World events Rising global oil prices may force companies that are heavily reliant on oil as raw material to downgrade financial objectives.

Pressure groups Pressure groups such as Greenpeace, for example, may persuade companies to focus more on environmental objectives.

Population trends The aging population might mean some businesses will benefit from greater demand. Therefore, a company selling retirement apartments might upgrade financial objectives.

KEYTERMS

Dividend per share – the amount of money received by a shareholder for every share owned.

Dividend yield – the amount received by a shareholder as a percentage of the current share price.

Financial objectives – the goals or targets a business sets itself for its financial performance.

Total shareholder's return (TSR) – a financial return which takes into account both the increase in the share price and the dividend paid.

KNOWLEDGE

1. How are financial objectives likely to change as a business becomes more established?
2. Why might businesses set cash flow targets?
3. What is meant by cost minimisation analysis?
4. How is dividend per share calculated?
5. What is the difference between dividends per share and dividend yield?
6. What is meant by shareholders total return (STR)?
7. State two (i) internal and (ii) external factors that might influence the financial objectives set by a business.

Case Study: Case Alarm Systems

Gloucester-based Case Alarm Systems (CAS) designs and installs a wide range of wireless electrical security systems. During recent years the demand for security systems using new technology has grown. CAS has provided help for designers, installers, and users in the application of the new technology available from British manufacturers. CAS is an authorised distributor for a number of high technology companies producing equipment that requires specially trained engineers to ensure that systems are selected and applied properly. CAS also offers an after sales service to ensure that systems are maintained to a very high standard.

The financial performance of CAS has improved significantly in recent years. In 2006 CAS won a huge contract with a local authority to fit security systems in all of the authority's schools. As a result of winning this contract financial objectives have been upgraded. Table 2 shows the return on capital employed (ROCE) for CAS between 2002 and 2007.

Early in 2007 CAS ran into some problems. The contract with the local authority was using a lot of the company's resources. CAS found that it was having to turn down other work because it did not have the capacity to undertake further installations. It could not recruit enough of the highly skilled engineers it needed. Neither could CAS devote enough time and resources to train its own. To add to the company's troubles

serious floods in the summer of 2007 caused faults in many of the systems that had already been installed. This resulted in more work and a greater strain on the company's resources. Much of the flood work carried out did not generate any revenue because CAS were liable for faults under their warranties. These problems were set to have an impact on the company's financial performance and future financial objectives.

Table 2: ROCE for CAS – actual and targets

	2002	2003	2004	2005	2006	2007
ROCE Target	15.0%	15.0%	17%	18.0%	22%	25%
Actual ROCE	15.2%	16.4%	18%	18.6%	23%	N/A

(a) What is meant by the return on capital employed? (4 marks)

(b) To what extent has CAS achieved its financial objectives between 2002 and 2006? (6 marks)

(c) CAS shareholders have suggested recently that financial objectives should meet their needs more effectively. How might CAS achieve this? (12 marks)

(d) To what extent have internal and external influences affected the financial objectives set by CAS? (18 marks)

Using financial data to measure and assess performance

Many of the performance indicators used by businesses are financial in nature. This means they are measured in **money** terms. In order to compile a range of performance indicators such as sales revenue, profit, return on capital employed, working capital and dividend payments, it is necessary to gather appropriate financial data. One way in which businesses gather such data is to prepare financial statements and **accounts**. Financial statements such as **balance sheets** and **profit and loss accounts** or **income statements** are important examples. ACCOUNTING is 'the process of identifying, measuring and communicating information to permit informed judgments and decisions by users of the information' according to the American Accounting Association.

Balance sheets

What does a BALANCE SHEET show? It is like a photograph of the financial position of a business at a particular point in time. The balance sheet contains information about the assets of a business, its **liabilities** and its **capital**.

- ASSETS are the resources that a business owns and uses. Assets are usually divided into current assets and fixed assets. Current assets are used up in production, such as stocks of raw materials. They can also be money owed to a business by debtors. Fixed assets, such as machinery, are used again and again over a period of time.
- LIABILITIES are the debts of the business, ie what it owes to other businesses, individuals and institutions. Liabilities

are a source of funds for a business. They might be short term, such as an overdraft, or long term, such as a mortgage or a long-term bank loan.

- CAPITAL is the money introduced by the owners of the business, for example when they buy shares. It is another source of funds and can be used to purchase assets.

In all balance sheets the value of assets (what a business uses or owns) will equal the value of liabilities and capital (what the business owes). Why? Any increase in total assets must be funded by an equal increase in capital or liabilities. A business wanting to buy extra machinery (an asset) may need to obtain a bank loan (a liability), for example. Alternatively, a reduction in credit from suppliers (a liability) may mean a reduction in stocks that can be bought (an asset). So:

$$\text{Assets} = \text{capital} + \text{liabilities}$$

This is shown in Figure 1. The diagram shows the types of asset and liability that might appear on the balance sheet of a private limited company. There are differences in the assets and liabilities shown in the balance sheets of sole traders and limited companies. This is explained later in this unit.

Presenting the balance sheet

Table 1 on the next page shows the balance sheet of Breakout Ltd. It is a business that owns a small chain of nightclubs. It is presented here in a vertical format. The balance sheet is a record of the company's assets, liabilities and capital.

One advantage of presenting the balance sheet in this format is that it is easy to see the amount of **working capital** (current assets - current liabilities) that a business has. This is important because the working capital shows whether a business is able to pay its day-to-day bills. The net assets (total assets - current liabilities - long-term liabilities) of a business are also clearly shown.

The balance sheets of public limited companies

In 2005 all publicly traded EU companies were required to present their balance sheets in a slightly new format. This change, along with others in the preparation and presentation of accounts, was introduced to bring Britain and other EU countries into line with international accounting standards. Table 3 shows the balance sheet for Bridgeford Holdings, an engineering company. It is presented according to the new international standards and reflects the type of transactions of a public limited company.

Non-current assets The term NON-CURRENT ASSETS replaces the term fixed assets. Non-current assets are any assets

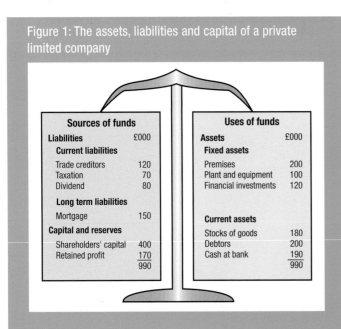

Figure 1: The assets, liabilities and capital of a private limited company

Sources of funds	£000	Uses of funds	£000
Liabilities		**Assets**	
Current liabilities		**Fixed assets**	
Trade creditors	120	Premises	200
Taxation	70	Plant and equipment	100
Dividend	80	Financial investments	120
Long term liabilities			
Mortgage	150	**Current assets**	
Capital and reserves		Stocks of goods	180
Shareholders' capital	400	Debtors	200
Retained profit	170	Cash at bank	190
	990		990

Table 1: Balance sheet of Breakout Ltd

BREAKOUT LTD
Balance sheet as at 31 August 2008

	£000	£000
Fixed assets		
Premises	1,200	
Fixtures and fittings	1,100	
Equipment	700	
		3,000
Current assets		
Stocks	800	
Debtors	500	
Cash at bank	400	
	1,700	
Current liabilities		
(Creditors amounts falling		
due within one year)		
Trade creditors	200	
Dividends	200	
Other liabilities	300	
	700	
Net current assets		
(working capital)		1,000
Total assets less		
current liabilities		
		4,000
Creditors: amounts		
falling due after one year		
Bank loan	200	
Mortgage	1,100	
		1,300
Net assets		**2,700**
Capital and reserves		
Ordinary share capital		
(2,000,000 shares at £1)	2,000	
Retained profit	700	
		2,700

FIXED ASSETS are assets with a lifespan of more than one year. They might include the buildings, musical and lighting equipment, drinks equipment behind the bar, tables and seating.

CURRENT ASSETS are assets that are likely to be changed into cash within one year. For Breakout they might include:
- *stocks* of goods such as cigarettes and drink – in a manufacturing business this would include stocks or raw materials, semi-finished goods and finished goods;
- customers or businesses that owe money to Breakout Ltd – the *debtors* of the business;
- *cash* 'in hand' at the business or deposited in the bank.

Current assets are liquid assets. The liquidity of an asset is how easily it can be changed into cash.

CURRENT LIABILITIES are debts that have to be repaid within 12 months. They are sometimes called Creditors: amounts falling due within one year. In this case they might include:
- money owed to suppliers of drinks or food, telephone companies or suppliers of electricity that have provided goods or services to Breakout Ltd – these are the *trade creditors* of the business;
- *dividends* – payments to shareholders out of profit which has been announced but is yet to be paid. Other current liabilities might be:
- *taxation* – this may be corporation tax or employees' income tax owed to the tax authorities;
- *overdrafts* – monies borrowed from banks which are repayable within 12 months;
- *short-term loans* – typically loans from banks or similar financial institutions which must be repaid within 12 months;
- *leases* – any lease agreements, on machinery or property for example, are classified as a current liability.

The value of **NET CURRENT ASSETS** or *working capital* can be found by:
Current assets – current liabilities
Calculating working capital is important for a business. The working capital a firm has indicates whether or not it can afford to pay its day-to-day bills.

The value of *total assets less current liabilities* can be found by:
(Fixed assets + current assets) – current liabilities

LONG-TERM LIABILITIES Creditors: amounts due after one year are the LONG-TERM LIABILITIES of the business. These are the debts that a business owes that do not need to be paid for at least 12 months. They might include:
- a *loan* from a bank or other financial institution;
- a *mortgage* – a loan taken out to purchase buildings;
- a long-term *lease* or *hire purchase* agreement, such as a five year contract to lease or buy machinery, although Breakout Ltd does not have this.

The value of **NET ASSETS** can be found by:
(Total assets less current liabilities) – long-term liabilities

CAPITAL AND RESERVES The capital and reserves figure is equal to the value of net assets. The total of capital and reserves is sometimes called capital employed or shareholders' funds. Capital and reserves are a liability for a business – money that it owes. They include:
- share capital – the amount of money put into the business by investors buying shares. It is the value of shares when first sold, not the current market value;
- retained profit – the amount of profit that the business has made in previous years. It is money which is owed to the owners. However, it has been retained in the business to buy equipment or to help cash flow rather than distributing it as a dividend.

Question 1.

The Maltings is a care home for the elderly based in Colchester. It accommodates up to 22 elderly people and has a waiting list for places due to its good reputation in the area. The care home is run by a family and the business operates as a private limited company. A balance sheet for the company is shown in Table 2 (some information is excluded).

Table 2: Balance sheet for The Maltings as at 31.12.08

The Maltings
Balance sheet as at 31.12.08

Fixed assets	
Property	1,200,000
Fixtures & fittings	21,000
Equipment	16,000
	1,237,000
Current assets	
Stocks	2,300
Debtors	6,400
Cash at bank	31,000
	39,700
Current liabilities	
Trade creditors	4,500
Other liabilities	12,900
Dividends proposed	5,400
	22,800
Net current assets	********
Total assets less current liabilities	1,253,900
Long-term liabilities	
Mortgage	500,000
Other liabilities	22,000
	522,000
Net assets	********
Capital and reserves	
Share capital	500,000
Other reserves	45,100
Retained profit	********
	731,900

(a) Suggest two examples of: (i) fixtures and fittings; (ii) trade creditors; that the business might have.

(b) Complete the balance sheet above by calculating:
(i) Net current assets; (ii) Net assets;
(iii) Retained profit.

(c) Why is the value of net current assets an important figure in the balance sheet?

which are not expected to be sold within 12 months. A number of entries are likely to be found in this section of the balance sheet.

- Goodwill is likely to be shown as a separate item. This is the amount the business is worth above the value of net assets. Goodwill exists if a company has built up a good reputation and its customers are likely to return. Goodwill is an **intangible asset**. This is a non-physical asset of a business.
- Other intangible assets may appear in some plc balance sheets. Examples include brand names, copyrights, trademarks and patents. There is no entry for this on the Bridgeford balance sheet.
- Property, plant and equipment are the **tangible assets** which the business owns. In this case it might be a factory and machines used in engineering by Bridgeford. Tangible assets are the physical assets of a business.
- Investments are the financial assets owned by the company. An example might be shares held in other companies. If investments are listed under non-current assets it means that they are not expected to be sold for at least 12 months. If investments are likely to be sold within 12 months they should be listed under current assets.
- Deferred tax assets relate to the prepayment of tax. Deferred tax assets can be created if a company is likely to offset losses against tax in future years. Details of this will be explained in the **notes to the accounts**.

Current assets Most current assets in a plc balance sheet are the same as those found in other types of balance sheet. However, some different terminology is used.

- Inventories refers to stocks of raw materials and components, stocks of finished goods and work-in-progress.
- Trade and other receivables are trade debtors, prepayments and any other amounts owed to the business that are likely to be repaid within 12 months.
- Cash at bank and in hand is the same as in other types of balance sheet.

Current liabilities Again, most current liabilities in a plc balance sheet are the same as those in other balance sheets but have different names.

- Borrowings is a new term that relates to any short-term loans or bank overdrafts taken out by the business.
- Trade and other payables refer to trade creditors and other amounts owed by the business to suppliers of goods, services and utilities, for example.
- Current tax liabilities refers to corporation tax, employees' income tax and any other tax owed by the business that must be repaid within 12 months.

Non-current liabilities The long-term liabilities of a plc are called NON-CURRENT LIABILITIES. Any amount of money

Table 3: Balance sheet for Bridgeford Holdings – a plc

Bridgeford Holdings
Balance sheet as at 31.12.08

	2008 £m	2007 £m
Non-current assets		
Goodwill	12.4	10.8
Property, plant & equipment	15.7	14.5
Investments	3.8	3.4
Deferred tax assets	2.1	2.3
	34.0	31.0
Current assets		
Inventories	5.6	4.9
Trade and other receivables	8.6	7.8
Cash at bank	2.4	2.7
	16.6	15.4
Total assets	50.6	46.4
Current liabilities		
Borrowings	2.1	2.2
Trade and other payables	6.7	6.9
Current tax liabilities	1.9	1.8
	10.7	10.9
Net current assets	5.9	4.5
Total assets less current liabilities	39.9	35.5
Non-current liabilities		
Other loans and borrowings	5.8	6.2
Retirement benefit obligations	10.1	9.6
Provisions	2.9	3.1
	18.8	18.9
Net assets	21.1	16.6
Equity		
Called up share capital	6.2	5.0
Share premium account	5.6	4.8
Other reserves	4.1	3.2
Retained earnings	5.2	3.6
Total equity	21.1	16.6

Table 4: Balance sheet for Joanna Cullen as at 31.5.2008

Joanna Cullen
Balance sheet as at 31 May 2008

2007 £		2008 £	£
	Fixed assets		
10,000	Car		8,000
7,900	Fixtures and fittings		7,000
17,900			15,000
	Current assets		
30,000	Stocks	35,000	
4,000	Debtors and prepayments	5,000	
3,000	Bank account	4,000	
1,000	Cash in hand	1,000	
38,000		45,000	
	(less) **Current liabilities**		
20,000	Creditors and accrued charges	25,000	
18,000	Working capital		20,000
35,900	**NET ASSETS**		35,000
	(FINANCED BY)		
30,000	**Opening capital**		35,900
–	Capital introduced		4,500
48,100	*(add)* Net profit		59,600
78,100			100,000
42,200	*(less)* Drawings		65,000
35,900			35,000

warranties. Repairing some machinery sold to a customer might be an example. If these provisions are short term they will appear under current liabilities.

owed for more than one year will appear in this section of the plc balance sheet.

- **Other loans and borrowings** refers to money owed by the company that does not have to be repaid for at least 12 months. Examples would be long-term bank loans and mortgages.
- **Retirement pension obligations.** Plcs must now show any money owed to past employees in the form of pension obligations.
- **Provisions.** Provisions have to be made if a company is likely to incur expenditure in the future. Such expenditure might arise as a result of agreements in contracts or

Equity The bottom section of the plc balance sheet shows the amounts of money owed to the shareholders. Most of the entries are the same or similar to those found in the capital and reserves of a private limited company balance sheet.

- **Share capital** is the amount of money paid by shareholders for their shares when they were originally issued. It does not represent the current value of those shares on the stock market. Share capital is not usually repaid to the shareholders in the lifetime of a company.
- **Share premium account** shows the difference between the value of new shares issued by the company and their nominal value. For example, the nominal value of a share may have been £1. The company may decide to issue

Question 2.

Melanie Cooper is a sole trader and runs a gift shop in Brighton. She sells gifts, souvenirs and novelty products to day-trippers and other visitors to the seaside town. Melanie has been successful in recent years and her balance sheet for 2008 is presented in Table 5.

Table 5: Balance sheet for Melanie Cooper as at 31.7.08

Melanie Cooper Balance sheet as at 31.7.08	2008 £	2007 £
Fixed assets		
Fixtures & Fittings	8,000	9,000
Equipment	3,000	3,500
Vehicle	4,000	5,000
	15,000	17,500
Current assets		
Stock	18,600	16,500
Debtors and prepayments	2,900	3,500
Cash in hand & at bank	12,900	10,100
	34,400	30,100
Current liabilities		
Trade creditors	9,800	9,500
Other current liabilities	6,300	5,600
	16,100	15,100
Working capital	18,300	15,000
Net assets	33,300	32,500
Financed by:		
Opening capital	32,500	26,400
Net profit	29,600	32,100
	62,100	58,500
Less drawings	28,800	26,000
Closing capital	**33,300**	**32,500**

(a) Explain why the value of fixed assets has fallen over the two years.
(b) How is the opening capital calculated in 2008?
(c) Why do you think drawings has increased over the two years?
(d) What is the value of Melanie's business?

be worth £160,000. This £160,000 would be included in the tangible assets figure. However only £100,000 would appear under capital and reserves as this was the original amount spent. Capital and reserves have to be revalued by £60,000 so that assets still equal liabilities plus capital and reserves. There is no revaluation reserve for Bridgeford.

* Other reserves refer to any amounts owing to the shareholders not covered by the other entries under equity.
* Retained earnings is the same as retained profit. It is the amount of profit retained by the business to be used in the future, for example to fund investment projects.

Company law requires both **private and public limited** companies to show both this year's and last year's figures in published accounts. This allows comparisons to be made.

Sole trader balance sheets

Earlier it was mentioned that sole trader balance sheets will be different to those of limited companies. Take the example of Joanna Cullen, a sole trader running a retail outlet that sells computers. Her balance sheet is shown in Table 4. There is a number of differences between a sole trader and a limited company balance sheet.

* The sole trader has a capital account rather than a 'capital and reserves' section. Sole traders are set up with the personal capital introduced into the business by the owner. Joanna Cullen introduced a further £4,500 into the business during 2007, according to the balance sheet in Table 4.
* It is likely that a sole trader will need to withdraw money from the business for personal reasons during the year. This is subtracted from the capital account and is shown as DRAWINGS in the balance sheet. The balance on the capital account is the amount owed to the owner. This is equal to the assets of the company.
* A limited company has many sources of capital and reserves. However, all companies will show shareholders' funds (often listed as capital and reserves), which will not be in a sole trader's balance sheet.
* The shareholders of a limited company are paid a dividend. This appears in the figure for current liabilities. As sole traders do not have shareholders no such figure will be included in their accounts.

Assessing performance and potential

Balance sheets can be used to evaluate the performance and potential of a business.

* In general, it provides a summary and valuation of all business assets, capital and liabilities.
* The balance sheet can be used to analyse the asset structure of a business. It can show how the money raised by the business has been spent on different types of asset. The balance sheet for Breakout in Table 1 shows that £3 million was spent on fixed assets in 2007. Current assets, however, accounted for only £1.7 million.

2 million new shares. If the company sold them for £3, each new share is now worth £2 more than the nominal price. In total this would be £4 million (£2 x 2 million). This £4 million would be entered on the share premium account in the balance sheet.

* Revaluation reserve sometimes appears under capital and reserves to balance an increase in the value of fixed assets. A business may buy a building for £100,000. Later it may

- The balance sheet can also be used to analyse the capital structure of a business. A business can raise funds from many different sources, such as shareholders' capital, retained profit and long-term and short-term sources.
- Looking at the value of working capital can indicate whether a firm is able to pay its everyday expenses or is likely to have problems. The value of working capital is the difference between current assets and current liabilities. It shows the money left over after all current liabilities have been paid that can be used to settle the day to day debts of the business. In the balance sheet for Breakout the value of working capital was £1 million.
- A balance sheet may provide a guide to a firm's value. Generally, the value of the business is represented by the value of all assets less any money owed to outside agents such as banks or suppliers. The value of Breakout in 2007 was £2.7 million.

However, there are limitations to using balance sheets to assess performance.

- The value of many assets listed in the balance sheet may not reflect the amount of money the business would receive if it were sold. For example, fixed assets are listed at cost less an allowance for depreciation. However, the depreciation allowance is estimated by accountants. If estimates are inaccurate, the value of assets will also be inaccurate.
- Many balance sheets do not include intangible assets. Assets such as goodwill, brand names and the skills of the workforce may be excluded because they are difficult to value or could change suddenly. If such assets are excluded, the value of the business may be understated.
- A balance sheet is a static statement. Many of the values for assets, capital and liabilities listed in the statement are only valid for the day the balance sheet was published. After another day's trading, many of the figures will have

changed. This can restrict its usefulness.
- It could be argued that a balance sheet lacks detail. Many of the figures are totals and are not broken down.

KEYTERMS

Accounting – the process of identifying, measuring and communicating information to permit informed judgments and decisions by users of the information.

Assets – resources used or owned by the business in production.

Balance sheet – a summary at a point in time of business assets, liabilities and capital.

Capital – a source of funds provided by the owners of the business used to buy assets.

Current assets – assets likely to be changed into cash within a year.

Current liabilities – debts that have to be repaid within a year.

Drawings – money withdrawn by a sole trader from the business for personal use.

Fixed assets – assets with a lifespan of more than one year.

Liabilities – the debts of the business which provide a source of funds.

Long term liabilities – debts that are payable after 12 months.

Net assets – the value of total assets minus current liabilities minus long-term liabilities. The value is equal to capital and reserves on the balance sheet.

Net current assets – current assets minus current liabilities. Also known as working capital.

Non-current assets – the long-term assets of a plc which are not expected to be sold within 12 months/a year.

Non-current liabilities – the long-term liabilities of a plc – any amount of money owed for more than 12 months/a year.

KNOWLEDGE

1. What is a balance sheet?
2. Why is a balance sheet a static business document?
3. Why must the value of assets on a balance sheet be equal to the value of liabilities plus capital?
4. What is the difference between fixed and current assets?
5. State three examples of the fixed assets that a business might have.
6. State three examples of the current assets that a business might have.
7. What is the difference between tangible and intangible fixed assets?
8. What is the difference between current and long-term liabilities?
9. State three current liabilities that a business might have.
10. Why is revaluation of assets sometimes included under capital and reserves?
11. How does depreciation affect the balance sheet?
12. Suggest three uses of balance sheets for a business.
13. Suggest three limitations of balance sheets.

Case Study: *Winters Timber Ltd*

Winters Timber Ltd is a timber merchant. The business originally started out as timber merchants, supplying to manufacturers. However, the company realised that it could expand by making its own timber products. A major area of the business is the manufacture of fencing panels, pallets and landscape products. This is now a major part of the business and 90 per cent of the stock in this area is made on site. Winters Timber has recently installed a panelmaster system for the manufacture of fence panels. One of the reasons why the business is successful is because it holds a wide range of stock. Table 6 shows a balance sheet for Winters Timber.

Table 6: Winters Timber balance sheet as at 31 December 2008

WINTERS TIMBER LTD
BALANCE SHEET AS AT 31.12.08

	2008 £000s	2007 £000s
Fixed assets		
Equipment and machinery	1,200	1,400
Vehicles	340	310
	1,540	1,710
Current assets		
Stock	230	160
Debtors	65	80
Cash at bank	180	100
	475	340
Creditors: amounts falling due in one year		
Trade creditors	120	105
Accruals	20	25
Taxation	100	80
	240	210
Net current assets	235	130
Creditors: amounts falling due after one year		
Mortgage	(500)	(500)
Net assets	1,275	1,340
Capital and reserves		
Share capital	200	200
Other reserves	115	540
Retained profit	960	600
	1,275	1,340

(a) Why does a business like Winters Timber produce a balance sheet? (4 marks)

(b) Using examples from this case, explain what is meant by fixed assets. (4 marks)

(c) Explain why: (i) retained profit; (ii) vehicles; has increased in the balance sheet over the two years. (8 marks)

(d) How would you describe the financial situation of Winters Timber Ltd? (8 marks)

(e) Evaluate the usefulness of this balance sheet to the shareholders of Winters Timber Ltd. (16 marks)

The nature of profit

Profit is the driving force in most businesses. There are few, if any, which attach no importance to making profit, the exceptions perhaps being charities. Even state run industries, whose major objective has been to provide a comprehensive service, have pursued profits in recent years.

Profit has a number of functions. The prospect of making profit motivates people to set up in business. Without profit there would be little incentive for individuals to commit their time and personal resources to business activity. Economists often refer to **normal profit**. This is the minimum reward an entrepreneur must receive in order to maintain interest in the business. If the business does not earn this amount of profit the owner will pull out and pursue other opportunities.

Profit also helps resource allocation in market economies. Businesses that make profits are able to purchase more raw materials and labour in order to expand production. Investors are attracted to those businesses that are likely to give the greatest financial reward. Economists call this abnormal profit - the amount by which total profit is greater than normal profit.

The amount of profit that a business makes is a measure of how well it is performing. Those firms that supply quality products which are efficiently produced and sold at prices which are attractive to consumers will tend to be more profitable. However, there are other factors which affect the performance of a business, such as the competition a business faces. From an accountant's point of view, profit is the amount of money left over in a particular trading period when all business expenses have been met. Profit can then be:

- retained;
- used to pay tax;
- distributed to the owners of the company.

If expenses exceed sales revenue in a trading period then there will be a loss. It is the accountant's definition of profit which we will be referring to in this unit.

Measuring profit

At the end of the trading year most owners like to see how well their company has performed. One initial indication of performance is the amount of profit (or loss) that the business has made during that year. Figure 1 illustrates how profit (and loss) is measured. It is the difference between turnover and business costs.

Businesses measure their profit by compiling a PROFIT AND LOSS ACCOUNT or an INCOME STATEMENT. These provide a summary of a company's profit or loss during any one given period of time, such as a month, three months, or one year. Before January 2005 all businesses produced profit and loss accounts. After, public limited companies were required to adopt

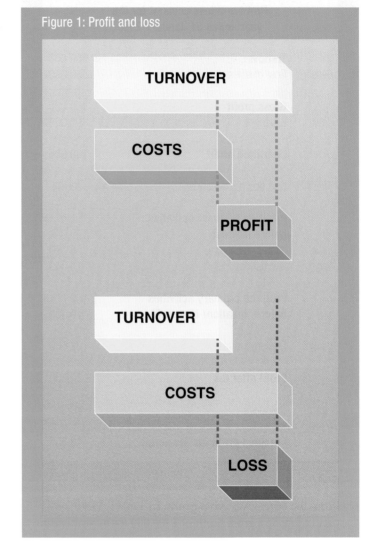

Figure 1: Profit and loss

international accounting standards (IAS) and produce an income statement. This has a slightly different format to a traditional profit and loss account. Other types of businesses continue to use profit and loss accounts.

Profit and loss account

A profit and loss account for the year ending 31 January 2008 is shown in Table 1. It shows the business transactions for Virginian Carpets Ltd, a carpet wholesaler which specialises in Moroccan carpets. It is divided into three sections: the TRADING ACCOUNT; the PROFIT AND LOSS ACCOUNT; the PROFIT AND LOSS APPROPRIATION ACCOUNT.

The trading account

The trading account shows the revenue earned from selling products (the turnover) and the cost of those sales. Subtracting

VIRGINIAN CARPETS LTD
Profit and loss account for the
year ended 31 January 2008

		£
	Turnover	900,000
(less)	Cost of sales	500,000
	Gross profit	400,000
(less)	Expenses	300,000
	Operating profit	100,000
(plus)	Non-operating income	20,000
	Profit on ordinary activities before interest	120,000
(plus)	Interest receivable	5,000
(less)	Interest payable	15,000
	Profit on ordinary activities before taxation/ Net profit	110,000
(less)	Corporation tax	27,500
	Profit after tax	82,500
(less)	Dividends	40,000
	Retained profit for the period	42,500

Table 2: Cost of sales adjusted for stock

Opening stock 1.2.07	80,000
Purchases during the year	600,000
	680,000
less Closing stock 31.1.08	180,000
Cost of sales	500,000

- Errors often occur on invoices - documents which tell the purchaser how much is owed for the goods that are purchased. If there is an error which overstates the value of a sale, an adjustment must be made to turnover. Businesses usually send a credit note to cover the exact amount that the purchaser has been 'overcharged'.
- Sometimes a customer who has bought goods on credit is unable to pay for them. The turnover figure is usually left unchanged. However, businesses do record the value of an unpaid sale as a business expense in the profit and loss account as a bad debt.

The second figure listed in the trading account is the **cost of sales**. This refers to all costs of production. It will include direct costs such as raw materials, the wages of labour and other indirect costs or **overheads** associated with production (known as production overheads) such as fuel and rent.

It is often necessary to adjust the cost of raw materials for changes in stock. The cost of sales for Virginian Carpets Ltd in Table 1 is £500,000. This is mainly the cost of buying carpets for resale from Morocco. However, it is likely that during the trading year some of the carpets sold were bought in previous trading years and held in stock. Also, some of the carpets bought during the trading year will remain unsold and so the cost of sales must be adjusted.

In Table 2, at the beginning of the trading year, Virginian Carpets had £80,000 worth of carpets in stock. During the trading year £600,000 worth of new carpets were imported from Morocco. At the very end of the trading year the stock of carpets unsold was valued at £180,000. Therefore the cost of sales was £500,000. Only purchases of goods for resale are included in 'cost of sales' figures. Expenditure, such as stationery, that is not for resale is not included.

The gross profit of £400,000 in Table 1 is found by subtracting the cost of sales from the turnover.

The profit and loss account

The **profit and loss account** is an extension of the trading account. In practice, there is no indication of where the trading account ends and the profit and loss account begins. However, once a business has calculated its **gross profit** it can then calculate how much profit (or loss) it has made by adding any extra income it has earned and subtracting its expenses and tax.

one from the other gives **gross profit**. In Table 1, Virginian Carpets Ltd made a gross profit of £400,000 in the year ending 31.1.08.

The **turnover** or **sales revenue** figure shows the income from selling goods or services. For the year ending 31.1.08, Virginian Carpets Ltd had sales revenue of £900,000. According to the **realisation concept** a sale is made only when goods are delivered to customers. This is important because profit must be **included** in the same trading period as sales. Goods which have been manufactured but not sold to customers are **excluded** and goods which have been sold and payment not received are **included**. The final turnover figure may have to be adjusted for a number of reasons.

- Businesses must exclude indirect taxes such as VAT from the turnover figure. VAT is added to the sale price of goods. It is paid by consumers to businesses, which then hand it over to the government. Including VAT would overstate a firm's turnover.
- Sales of goods which are returned because they are faulty or unwanted must be removed from the turnover figure. Turnover will be overstated if their value were included.

Question 1.

Berry Ltd is a stockist of metals. The company is based in Telford and supplies a wide range of customers such as engineers and metal fabricators in the local area. Some of its stock items include metal tubes, angle iron, plate and sheet metal, galvanised, corrugated and cladding metal sheet, perforated metals, square and rod metals and stair treads.

Table 3: Trading account for Berry Ltd, year ending 31.12.08

Berry Ltd
Trading account for year ending 31.12.08

	£	£
Turnover		780,400
Cost of sales		
Purchases	489,300	
Plus opening stock	******	
	554,600	
Less closing stock	71,300	
		483,300
Gross profit		
		******

(a) What is the purpose of a trading account?
(b) Complete the trading account in Table 3 by calculating opening stock and gross profit.
(c) Explain why Berry's turnover will be exclusive of VAT.

Table 4: Operating (administrative) expenses for Virginian Carpets Ltd

	£	£
Expenses		
Wages and salaries (admin.)	110,000	
Rent and rates	40,000	
Heating and lighting	30,000	
Advertising	15,000	
Motor expenses	24,000	
Telephone	8,000	
Printing and stationery	13,000	
Insurance	9,000	
Accountancy fees	4,000	
Provision for bad debts	12,000	
Depreciation	35,000	
		300,000

In Table 1 the **profit after tax** earned by Virginian Carpets Ltd for the year ended 31 January 2008 was £82,500.

The first item to be subtracted from the gross profit figure is **expenses**. Expenses are those overheads or indirect costs that are not involved in production of goods and services. They include advertising and promotion, wages of the administration staff and depreciation. Table 4 gives a breakdown of the expenses incurred by Virginian Carpets Ltd during the trading year. They reflect the type of costs associated with companies. The breakdown of these figures is normally shown in the notes to the accounts or a separate Trading and Profit and Loss Account.

Subtracting expenses from gross profit gives a figure for OPERATING PROFIT. Operating profit is often regarded by businesses as the key indicator of trading performance. It is generally defined as the profit made by a company as a result of its ordinary trading activities.

The company will then add any non-operating income to its operating profit. Non-operating income is income which is not earned from the direct trading of the company. This could include dividends from shares held in other companies or rent from property that is let out.

The next stage is to add or subtract interest. Interest is received by a business from deposits in financial institutions and is paid out on borrowings. If any interest is receivable it is added. If any

interest is paid out it is subtracted. This is sometimes shown as one figure. It is called **net interest receivable** if interest received is more than interest payable. However, for Virginian Carpets (Table 1) the figure would be **net interest payable** of £10,000 as £5,000 has been received but £15,000 is payable.

When this final adjustment has been made the resulting figure is the **profit on ordinary activities before tax** (sometimes known as **net profit**) of £110,000. In the notes to the accounts there are often further details of expenses incurred during the year. For example, by law, the notes must show the directors' rewards, ie salaries, the auditor's fee, depreciation of fixed assets, donations and the number of employees receiving payments.

The final entry in the profit and loss account is the profit after taxation, £82,500. All limited companies have to pay corporation tax on profits over a certain amount to the government. The amount paid by Virginian Carpets Ltd is £27,500.

The profit and loss appropriation account

The final section in the profit and loss account is the **appropriation account**. This shows how the company profit or loss is distributed. Any profit made by a company is distributed in a number of ways. In Table 1, the profit of Virginian Carpets Ltd is distributed as follows:

- £27,500 is paid to the HR Revenue and Customs for corporation tax;
- £40,000 is paid to shareholders in the form of a dividend;
- £42,500 is retained by the business for the year (2008) for internal use in future periods. The business is also likely to have profit from previous years. If, for example, it had £127,500 retained profit from previous periods then it would have £127,500 plus £42,500 or £170,000 profit to **carry forward** to future years.

Most companies retain a proportion of profit for investment

or as a precaution. The amount paid out in dividends is determined by the board of directors and approved by the shareholders at the Annual General Meeting. Although the business is not legally obliged to pay dividends, shareholders may be dissatisfied if they are not paid.

Sole trader accounts

Table 5 shows the trading and profit and loss account for Joanna Cullen, a retailer selling computers. The differences and similarities between the profit and loss account of a sole trader and a limited company can be illustrated from Table 5. The profit and loss account of a sole trader normally shows how the year's purchases are adjusted for stock by including opening and closing stocks. In addition, a more detailed list of expenses is included. This allows a comparison with the previous year. A

profit and loss appropriation account is not included since there is only one owner and all profit is transferred to the capital account in the balance sheet.

The presentation of a sole trader profit and loss account can vary quite significantly. Variations occur due to the nature of the business and preferences in the style of presentation.

Table 5: The profit and loss account for Joanna Cullen, a sole trader

JOANNA CULLEN
Trading and profit and loss account for the year ended 31.5.08

2007 £		£	2008 £
130,000	**Turnover**		150,000
25,000	Opening stock	30,000	
65,000	Purchases	70,000	
90,000		100,000	
30,000	*less* Closing stock at selling price	35,000	
60,000			65,000
70,000	**Gross profit**		85,000
	less:		
1,000	Casual labour	2,000	
2,500	Motor expenses	3,000	
800	Telephone	1,000	
2,500	Printing, stationery & advertising	3,000	
1,300	Electricity	1,500	
8,000	Rent and rates	9,000	
400	Insurance	500	
2,500	Bank interest & charges	2,500	
2,000	Depreciation – car	2,000	
900	Depreciation – fixtures & fittings	900	
21,900			
			25,400
48,100	**Net profit**		59,600

Table 6: The Frozen Food Centre

Profit and loss account year ending 31.12.08

	2008 £	2007 £
Turnover	785,600	529,700
Opening stock	37,300	36,900
Purchases	498,400	369,100
	535,700	406,000
Less closing stock	38,100	37,300
Cost of Sales	497,600	368,700
Gross profit	288,000	161,000
Less:		
Wages	45,300	44,100
Motor expenses	10,600	15,900
Telephone	900	800
Electricity	2,300	2,100
Rent & rates	12,000	12,000
Advertising	10,800	400
Insurance	2,300	2,100
Accountancy fees	1,600	1,500
Depreciation	6,500	6,500
	92,300	85,400
Net profit	195,700	75,600

(a) Explain how the profit and loss account distinguishes between gross profit and net profit.

(b) Explain one main difference between the sole trader account shown in Table 6 and that of a private limited company.

(c) Explain the change in turnover between 2007 and 2008.

(d) Comment on the performance of the Frozen Food Centre over the two years.

Public limited company accounts

Public limited companies have similar accounts to those of private limited companies, such as Virginian Carpets. They must also publish their accounts by law. In 2005, plcs were required to replace the profit and loss account with an **income statement**. The income statement records all revenues for a business during this given period. It also shows the operating expenses for the business. It is very similar to the profit and loss account of a private limited company. Table 7 shows the income statement for J Sainsbury plc. The following points should be noted.

- Plcs must show separately profit from continuing operations (businesses they currently own) and discontinued operations (businesses that were sold during the year). In this case J Sainsbury does not have any discontinued operations.
- The term 'revenue' is used instead of turnover or sales.
- The terms 'finance income' and 'finance costs' are used instead of interest received and interest paid.
- The income statement does not show dividends or retained profit. It just shows the profit attributable to the equity holders of the parent company (the shareholders of Sainsbury) and minority interests (shareholder groups with a very small interest).

- Plc accounts show the **earnings per share** (EPS) at the bottom of the income statement. This is calculated by dividing the profit after tax by the total number of issued shares. The earnings per share gives an indication of a company's performance. The higher it is the better. The EPS is always shown for the basic shareholding and the fully diluted shareholding (the diluted shareholding includes shares which may be purchased as a result of share option schemes the company has).
- From time to time business may make a 'one-off' transaction. An example of an **exceptional item** might be a very large bad debt which is deducted as normal in the profit and loss account, but disclosed separately in the notes. In recent years some of the commercial banks have had to make such entries after incurring bad debts from Third World countries. An example of an **extraordinary item** might be the cost of management restructuring. Generally they arise from events outside the normal business activities and are not expected to occur again. The expenditure would normally be listed in the profit and loss account, below the line showing profit after tax.
- Limited companies often produce consolidated accounts. This happens when a business group is made up of several different companies or divisions. Each company is likely to retain a separate legal identity and produce its own accounts. However, the group is also obliged to produce accounts for the whole organisation. These consolidated accounts are produced by adding together the results of all the individual companies.

Assessing performance and potential

Profit and loss accounts and income statements can be used to evaluate the performance and potential of a business.

Overall profit Business owners are keen to see how much profit they have made at the end of the trading year. The size of the profit may be a guide to the performance of the business. A comparison is also possible because a profit and loss account will show the previous year's figures. It is possible to calculate the gross profit margin and net profit margin from the profit and loss account.

Controlling costs A profit and loss account can be used by managers to see how well a business has controlled its overheads. If the gross profit is far larger than the net profit, this would suggest that the company's overheads are quite high. However, if there is little difference between the two this could suggest that a business has controlled its overheads.

Measuring growth A business can use the profit and loss account to help measure its growth. A guide to a business's growth may be the value of turnover compared with the previous year's. If the turnover is significantly larger than the previous year's, this could suggest that the business has grown.

Table 7: Income statement for J Sainsbury plc

J Sainsbury plc Group Income Statement
For the 52 weeks to 24th March 2007

	2007 £m	2006 £m
Continuing operations		
Revenue	17,151	16,061
Cost of sales	(15,979)	(14,994)
Gross profit	1,172	1,067
Administrative expenses	(669)	(839)
Other income	17	1
Operating profit	520	229
Finance income	64	30
Finance costs	(107)	(155)
Profit before taxation	477	104
Tax	(153)	(46)
Profit for the financial year	324	58
Attributable to:		
Equity holders of the parent	325	64
Minority interests	(1)	(6)
	324	58
Earnings per share	Pence	Pence
Basic	19.2	3.8
Diluted	18.9	3.8

Source: adapted from J Sainsbury, Annual Report and Accounts, 2007.

Question 3.

Ultra Electronics is a defence and aerospace company specialising in the design, manufacture and support of electronic and electro-mechanical systems, sub-systems, products and services for aircraft, ships, submarines armoured vehicles, surveillance and communication systems, airports and transport systems. Table 8 shows the company's income statement for 2006.

Table 8: Income statement for Ultra Electronics 2006

Ultra Electronics
Income statement for year ending 31.12.06

	2006 £000	2005 £000
Continuing operations		
Revenue	377,040	342,410
Cost of sales	(274,466)	(250,160)
Gross profit	102,574	92,250
Other operating income	1,505	4,805
Distribution costs	(810)	(825)
Administrative expenses	(48,569)	(48,393)
Other operating expenses	(753)	-
Operating profit	53,947	47,837
Investment revenue	4,939	553
Finance cost	(3,874)	(7,688)
Profit before tax	55,012	40,702
Tax	(15,404)	(11,292)
Profit attributable to equity holders of the parent company	39,608	29,410
Earnings per share (pence)		
Basic	58.8	43.9
Diluted	58.3	43.5

Source: adapted from Ultra Electronics, Annual Report and Accounts, 2006.

(a) Give two possible examples of administrative expenses for Ultra Electronics
(b) What is meant by the term 'finance cost' in the income statement above?
(c) What is meant by 'continuing operations' in the above statement?
(d) Comment briefly on the performance of Ultra Electronics over the two years.

Benefits to shareholders The earnings per share is also shown on the profit and loss account for limited companies. This shows shareholders in a limited company how much each share has earned over the year. However, this is not necessarily the amount of money which they will receive from the company. This is the dividends per share.

Benefits to other stakeholders Other stakeholders may also use the profit and loss account. For example, workers may use it to argue for improvements in their pay and conditions of service. Banks are likely to ask to see the profit and loss account if a business wishes to borrow money. Suppliers may check the profit and loss account of a business to decide whether or not to give trade credit. Potential investors in the business may use the profit and loss account as one indication of whether the business is likely to do well in the future. The tax authorities use the profit and loss account to calculate some taxes on businesses. All businesses, including sole traders who are self-employed, have to keep records of financial transactions. Finally, the media may publish stories about businesses using accounts as a source of information.

However, there are certain limitations when using profit and loss accounts and income statements to assessing performance.

Other financial data The profit and loss account only gives data about revenue, costs, profit and how the profit is used. Much more financial data is needed to assess accurately the performance of a business. For example, the cash flow position of the business is a vital indicator of performance. So too is the size of the borrowings of the business.

Other business data The profit and loss account gives data about the finances of a business. But it does not say anything about the environmental or social impact of the business and only indirectly gives information about new product development or efficiency of production. Financial data is only one source of data for evaluating the overall performance of a business.

Past, present and future The profit and loss account is a record of the past performance of a business. So it can be used as one piece of evidence to evaluate the performance of the business in the past. But it is not necessarily a good indication of present or future performance. Much can happen within six months or a year to a business. The economy might go into recession. There might be a sudden fall in demand for the products of a business. A new competitor might enter the market and be highly successful. A business whose profit and loss accounts show a period of ten years of successful growth in revenues and profits might suddenly see a fall in turnover and a slump into loss in the eleventh year.

Trends The profit and loss account for a single year is of limited value when judging performance. It gives an indication of the profitability of the business. But one year's figures would not indicate whether the business is growing or declining, or whether the profit is unusually high or low. The more periods of data available, the more reliable any evaluation can be.

The level of detail in the account The more detail in the profit and loss account, the more information available to be analysed.

Companies tend to give the minimum information required by law. So anyone looking at published accounts will not necessarily pick up important trends or features within the accounts. Far more background information will, however, be available to managers within the company if they are using profit and loss figures to assess performance. Sole traders and partnerships should have full access to all the detail behind the final profit and loss account drawn up.

'Window dressing' the accounts For sole traders and partnerships, profit and loss accounts are typically prepared for the tax authorities. There may be a temptation to minimise profit, for example by not putting some revenue 'through the books' or exaggerating costs. This will then reduce the amount of tax that has to be paid. Companies too may manipulate their accounts to present a better picture than is actually the case.

Special characteristics of individual accounts Profit and loss accounts can have special features which need to be noted in evaluating performance. Occasionally a business will change its tax year. Accounts might for a single period be presented for 9 months or 15 months, say, instead of the usual 12 months. An increase in profit would be expected if the accounts covered 15 months rather than 12 months. Exceptional and extraordinary items should also be carefully studied. Some businesses are constantly taking over and closing down businesses. Every year they may record extraordinary items in their account as a result. This makes it very difficult to judge performance over time from the profit and loss account. Equally, the costs and revenue sources of these businesses are constantly changing. It becomes very difficult to judge from the profit and loss account whether the operations of the business are being well managed because so much of the profit is coming from new parts of the business.

The importance of profit utilisation and profit quality

When making decisions using financial data one of the key financial indicators used is profit. Most businesses pursue profit and generally businesses will choose the course of action that is likely to generate the most profit. However, it will be necessary to consider PROFIT QUALITY. It is possible for a business to earn a high level of profit due to exceptional or extraordinary circumstances. For example, in a particular year a large proportion of the profit made by a company may be the result of selling part of its business for a much higher than expected price. In this year the profit quality would be considered low. It is important to analyse the profit of a business over a period of time – at least five years, say. High quality profit is profit that can be sustained by the normal trading activities of a business over a period of time.

It is also necessary to consider PROFIT UTILISATION. The profit after tax made by a business may be **utilised** in two ways. Most businesses return some of the profit to the owners. In the case of limited companies the shareholders are likely to be paid dividends from the profit. Clearly, if the owners of the business do not receive a fairly regular 'financial payback', they are likely to withdraw their interest. In the case of plcs this may involve investors selling their shares. If this happens on a large enough scale the share price will fall and the company could become the target of a takeover. This might mean that the directors could be replaced.

Any profit remaining after owners have been compensated is retained by the business. This may be used for investment purposes – to expand operations, for example. Alternatively it may be placed in reserve to be used when the business has an urgent need for such funds. It might even be used to pay dividends in a year when profits are low.

How much profit should be retained? In plcs it is the job of directors to find the 'right balance' between dividends and retained profit. Using retained profit to fund investment in the business is a very cheap source of finance. However, shareholders may be more interested in the shortterm gains from holding shares. Directors will have to use their judgment when deciding how much profit to retain and how much to give back to shareholders.

KEYTERMS

Operating profit – the profit made by a business as a result of its ordinary trading activities.

Profit and loss account or income statement – a financial document showing a company's revenue/income and costs/expenditure over a particular time period, usually one year.

Profit and loss account – shows net profit after tax by subtracting business expenses and taxation from operating profit.

Profit and loss appropriation account – shows how the profit after tax is distributed between shareholders and the business.

Profit quality – occurs when profits are sustained over a period of time; there is low profit quality if profit in one time period is mainly due to some one-off factor which is not sustainable.

Profit utlisation – the way in which profit made by a business is distributed.

Trading account – shows operating profit by subtracting the cost of sales from turnover.

KNOWLEDGE

1. What is meant by profit from an accountant's point of view?
2. What is likely to happen to a business if normal profit is not made?
3. Distinguish between gross and operating profit.
4. What adjustments might need to be made to turnover during the year?
5. Why is it necessary to adjust purchases for changes in stock levels?
6. What is meant by non-operating income?
7. How might a limited company appropriate its profits?
8. How are earnings per share calculated?
9. What is the difference between an extraordinary item and an exceptional item?
10. How might the profit and loss account of a sole trader be different from that of a limited company?
11. How might the profit and loss account be used by a business?
12. How might a business calculate its: (a) gross profit ratio; (b) net profit ratio?

Case Study: *Elgood Construction plc*

Table 9: Income statement for Elgood Construction plc

Elgood Construction plc
Income statement for the year ending 31.12.08

Continuing operations	2008 £m	2007 £m
Revenue	*******	1,980
Cost of sales	920	810
Gross profit	1,380	1,170
Distribution expenses	600	500
Admin expenses	230	250
Operating profit	550	420
Finance costs	30	********
Profit on ordinary activities before tax	520	390
Taxation	******	80
Profit attributable to equity holders	420	310
Earnings per share		
Basic	23.6p	18.9p
Diluted	22.1p	17.7p

Elgood Construction plc is a large construction company. Located in South Wales, it is a well-established business, which offers a wide range of construction services and undertakes large construction projects for the Welsh government and other high profile customers. The company has been trading for over 25 years and takes pride in the provision of a reliable, professional service and has a reputation for quality workmanship. The company is also a member of the Guild of Master Craftsmen. Throughout the life of the company it has never spent money on advertising or promotion. According to Arthur Elgood, the company chairman, 'We rely on client recommendations to build our business, so you can bet we are never happy with our services until you are'. The income statement for Elgood Construction plc is shown in Table 9.

(a) Complete the income statement by calculating (i) revenue in 2008; (ii) finance costs in 2007; (iii) taxation in 2008. (6 marks)
(b) Explain what is meant by (i) earnings per share; (ii) cost of sales; shown in the account. (6 marks)
(c) Who might be interested in Elgood's income statement? (8 marks)
(d) Analyse the performance of the company over the two years. (10 marks)
(e) Discuss the drawbacks to Elgood Construction plc of using the income statement to analyse the performance. (20 marks)

53 | Working capital

What is working capital?

WORKING CAPITAL, sometimes called circulating capital, is the amount of money needed to pay for the day-to-day trading of a business. A business needs working capital to pay expenses such as wages, electricity and gas charges, and to buy components to make products. The working capital of a business is the amount left over after all current debts have been paid. It is:

- the relatively liquid assets of a business that can easily be turned into cash (cash itself, stocks, the money owing from debtors who have bought goods or services); *minus*
- the money owed by a business which needs to be paid in the short term (to the bank, to creditors who have supplied goods or services, to government in the form of tax or shareholders' dividends payable within the year).

In the balance sheet of a company working capital is calculated by subtracting current liabilities from current assets:

Working capital = current assets - current liabilities

The amount of working capital a business has is an important issue. It can reflect how well a business is performing. For example, a business that is struggling and threatened with closure is likely to have low levels of working capital. Consequently, if a balance sheet shows a low level of working capital, this should act as a signal that the business may be in trouble.

The working capital cycle

Managing working capital in a business is crucial. In many types of business, particularly manufacturing, delays or **time lags** exist between different stages of business activity. For example, there is a lag between buying materials and components and changing them into finished goods ready for sale. Similarly, there may be a delay between finishing the goods and the goods being sold to a customer. The WORKING CAPITAL CYCLE, shown in Figure 1, helps to illustrate the intervals between payments made by a business and the receipt of cash. The cycle shows the movement of cash and other liquid resources into and out of a business.

Time lags can occur at a number of stages in the working capital cycle.

Lag 1 Businesses usually purchase resources such as raw materials, components, fuel and other services from suppliers on credit. This means that a business can obtain resources without having to pay for them immediately. There might be a lag of up to 90 days before payment to suppliers has to be made. The length of the lag depends on suppliers' conditions. When a business is first set up, trade credit may not be granted until that business has proved to be creditworthy.

Lag 2 The next lag may occur as resources are turned into products using fixed assets, such as equipment. Work-in-progress (partially finished goods) is created and other costs are incurred, such as wages. The production process can take a long time depending on the nature of business activity. For example, for a cereal farmer this time lag could be about nine months. This would be the time it takes for corn seeds to be planted, grow into plants and eventually ripen so that the corn can be harvested. Alternatively, a furniture manufacturer might take about four to six weeks to make two armchairs and a settee for a customer.

Lag 3 Even when production is complete, a time lag can exist. Businesses may store their finished goods before they are sold to customers. This can be expensive. There may be warehousing costs and opportunity costs. However, storage enables a business to cope with unexpected increases in demand and allows continuous production. In recent years many businesses have adopted just-in-time manufacturing methods. Goods are only produced to order. This minimises stock holdings and reduces this time lag. When goods are distributed to customers further costs result, such as transport and handling costs.

Lag 4 A fourth time lag occurs when goods have finally been sold to customers. It is common business practice to allow customers to pay their bills over 30-90 days. However, depending on the nature of the business activity, this time lag can vary. For example, in many areas of retailing, goods are sold for cash only and this time lag is eliminated. Once cash has been

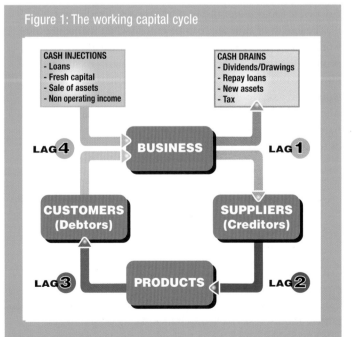

Figure 1: The working capital cycle

CASH INJECTIONS
- Loans
- Fresh capital
- Sale of assets
- Non operating income

CASH DRAINS
- Dividends/Drawings
- Repay loans
- New assets
- Tax

LAG 4   BUSINESS   LAG 1

CUSTOMERS (Debtors)   SUPPLIERS (Creditors)

LAG 3   PRODUCTS   LAG 2

Question 1.

Williams & Son

Williams & Son is a small property development company in Bradford. It buys plots of land or derelict properties and then builds houses or small apartment blocks. The business aims to complete one or two developments each year. Williams & Son incurs legal costs and pays architects fees before any building can begin. Most of the materials used by Williams & Son are bought on 60 days' credit from local builder's suppliers. Sometimes the new properties are not sold until after they have been completed. The business employs two other workers.

Tina's Taxi Service

Tina McKenna leases two minibuses and operates an airport taxi service in Gloucester and Cheltenham. She employs two drivers and also drives herself. The 24 hour service is successful, but competition is tightening in the area. Drivers are paid 25 per cent of their fares and get to keep their tips. They are paid weekly. All journeys are booked through Tina and drivers are instructed to accept only cash when collecting fares. In addition to the drivers' wages the main variable cost is diesel. Tina has an account with a local garage and is given 30 days' credit.

(a) Analyse the differences in the working capital cycles of the two businesses above.

collected from customers much of it is used to keep the process going, for example buying more materials and paying wages.

Figure 1 also shows that a business can enjoy injections of cash from sources other than the sale of products. Loans, the sale of assets and new capital are common examples. However, at the same time there will be cash drains from the business. Cash will leak from the cycle to pay dividends or drawings, to pay tax, to repay loans and to purchase new fixed assets.

The length of time lags can be crucial when managing the working capital cycle. Business managers must attempt to prolong the first time lag by delaying payments to suppliers. However, this requires careful judgment because a business would not want to damage relations with valuable suppliers. Also, if payments are delayed for too long this could cause hardship for suppliers and eventually contribute to their downfall. Managers would ideally want to reduce:

- production time;
- the storage time of finished goods before they are dispatched to customers, by reducing stock holdings or encouraging just-in-time manufacturing, for example;
- the time it takes for customers to settle their bills, by monitoring and checking late payments or offering discount for early settlement, for example.

Different working capital needs

Different businesses have different working capital needs.
- **Size of business.** Sales typically generate a need for stocks,

trade credit and cash. Hence the larger the business, the larger the amount of working capital there is likely to be. Equally, expanding businesses are likely to need growing amounts of working capital.
- **Stock levels.** Businesses in different industries have different needs for stocks. A window cleaning business is unlikely to carry much stock. A retailer is likely to carry considerable amounts of stock. Businesses which are able to adopt just-in-time techniques will carry lower stocks than other businesses. The more stocks a business needs, the higher will be its working capital, all other things being equal.
- **Debtors and creditors.** The time between buying stock financed by trade credit and selling finished products can influence levels of working capital. For example, a builder may need high levels of working capital because the time between starting a project and receiving payment from the client may be long.

At the other extreme, large supermarket chains can often operate with negative working capital (i.e. the current assets are less than their current liabilities). This happens because they buy in stock from suppliers and do not pay them for at least 30 days. The stock though is sold quickly on supermarket shelves, often within days of delivery from suppliers. Customers pay cash. So large supermarket chains can operate safely owing suppliers large amounts, but having very few debtors. The result is negative working capital.

Few businesses are fortunate enough to be able to operate with negative working capital. The textbook rule is that the typical business needs around twice the amount of current assets as current liabilities to operate safely. This means that its current ratio is between 1.5:1 and 2:1. This is how we can measure whether the business is performing effectively with regard to working capital.

The importance of keeping adequate levels of working capital

Businesses need to keep adequate levels of working capital. If they keep too little (ie current assets are too low and current liabilities are too high) they will start to encounter trading problems.

- If a business does not carry enough stocks of raw materials, it could find that production is halted when items run out of stock. If it does not carry enough finished stock, it might be unable to fulfil orders on time.
- If there is not enough cash in the business, it might not be able to pay its bills on time.
- If it has borrowed too much through trade credit, so it owes too much to creditors, it might be unable to pay invoices when they are due.

On the other hand, a business does not want too much working capital (ie current assets are too high and current liabilities are too low).

- Stocks are costly to keep. The more stock, the higher the

Question 2.

F&H Welding Products is a Black Country business which specialises in high-value high-specification welding contracts. The company has recently been through difficult times but has emerged stronger and financially more prudent.

The company had always tended to live from hand to mouth financially. There never seemed to be enough cash to pay the bills. Each month, the company would have to put off paying some bills that were due, or would be putting pressure on its bank to increase its overdraft facility. Two years ago, the company took on four large contracts, all of which were completed at roughly the same time. The company offered its customers 45 days credit but was buying from suppliers which were only offering 30 days credit. None of the customers for the four large contractors paid their invoices on time. After 60 days the company was on the verge of going into liquidation because it had exhausted all its sources of cash.

Frank Smith, the managing director, then went to see the four customers personally. He explained his dire situation. Two of the customers paid within 48 hours, enough to stave off the crisis. The other two said they would pay immediately, but in fact took another 30 days to pay.

The crisis had been made worse because the company had ordered extra stock in the belief that there would be an increase in new orders. In fact, orders fell 20 per cent over six months due to fierce competition from overseas suppliers.

Having sought advice, Frank Smith changed the way the company operated. He changed all customer contracts to give only 30 days free credit. He also offered a 5 per cent discount on the invoice for paying on time, which was paid for mainly by raising prices. He refused to accept orders from customers who were persistent late payers. He also reduced his stock levels and moved to ordering from suppliers who were prepared to deliver at short notice. Although the number of orders fell by one third, turnover only fell 15 per cent and profits were hardly down at all.

(a) 'F&H Welding Products suffered from poor credit control and overstocking.' Explain this statement.

(b) Examine how the company overcame these problems.

(c) 'F&H Welding Products simply didn't have enough working capital.' Discuss whether or not this was the case.

cost of physically storing and handling it. The stock will need to be insured while it may be liable to shrinkage (a business term for theft, usually by employees). Stock is also financially expensive because money tied up in stock could be used to reduce borrowing and so save interest for the business.

- Too much cash is also a problem because the cash is unlikely to be earning very high rates of interest. It could be used, perhaps, to pay back debts or to invest in higher interest long-term investments.

- If the number of debtors is high, the company could be allowing its customers too long to pay their invoices. If customers are taking 45 days on average to pay their bills when they only have 30 days credit given, the business would be losing the interest that could be earned on 15 days of credit. They also might have to spend scarce time chasing up late payments. In the UK, according to a 2004 survey by Intrum Justitia, invoices in the UK were on average paid 18 days late. Forty-seven per cent of all invoices are paid late, with 89 per cent of businesses saying that they suffered from late payments. Small businesses are more likely to suffer from late payment of invoices than large companies. The cost to British businesses of late payment was an estimated £20 billion, although many businesses benefit from themselves paying late.

Reasons for working capital problems

Many businesses find themselves in difficulties over working capital for a variety of reasons.

Poor control of debtors Too many businesses fail to control their debtors effectively. Partly this is because they fail to collect debts on time. Partly, it is because they give credit to businesses which fail, leaving the debt unpaid. For a small business, a bad debt, one which will not be paid, can be devastating. If large enough, it can lead to the business itself failing. Credit control systems can help avoid these problems. When a new customer approaches a business wanting trade credit, it should run a credit check on the customer. This could involve getting a bank reference from the customer, checking at Companies House to get the latest accounts of the customer or getting a credit rating agency report. A credit rating agency is a business which specialises in investigating and reporting on the creditworthiness of businesses. The business then has to decide whether to trade with the potential customer and if so set a maximum amount of **trade credit** that will be extended to it at any one time. Once a customer has received trade credit, the business should chase any overdue payments. This may involve a mixture of telephone calls or emails requesting payment, warning letters and in the last resort taking the customer to court. Customers who are too overdue with payments should be refused any new credit.

Overstocking and understocking Many businesses carry too much stock. Overstocking may arise because the business is being run inefficiently. Managers or owners have failed to realise the business could run with less stock, or they have failed to put in place systems which would minimise stock levels. A less common problem is understocking, where businesses carry too little stock. This leads to production problems. For instance, if a shop runs out of a line which is selling well, then it will lose sales.

Overtrading A common problem faced by small growing businesses is overtrading. This is when a business has insufficient working capital for its level of turnover. For example, a business might accept orders but then run up against trade credit limits set by its suppliers. It therefore can't order enough stock to complete the orders. It could turn to its bankers to get a higher overdraft limit, but its bankers may refuse because of the risk of failure of the business. The great danger in this situation is that one of the creditors of the business could take legal action to recover debts outstanding. Then the business may be forced to close even though its order book is profitable.

Overborrowing Businesses can borrow too much in the short term. For example, they can take too much trade credit. This might push them up against trade credit limits, risking a refusal to supply on extra orders. If the business fails to pay on time because it does not have the cash to pay, this can lose the business discounts for paying on time. Borrowing on overdraft from the bank also carries risks. If the business experiences trading difficulties, its bank may demand repayment of the overdraft afraid that the overdraft will not be repaid in the future. Being constantly at overdraft limits also doesn't allow for the unexpected. A small extra bill then could force the business to close because it does not have the cash to pay it.

Downturns in demand When the economy goes into recession, the number of business failures increases. Often this is because of problems with working capital. In a recession, orders and sales fall. Businesses often fail to react quickly enough. They allow stocks of finished goods to increase, causing overstocking. They then experience cash flow problems as they have to pay invoices from suppliers but don't have enough cash from sales of their own goods or services. In a recession, debtors also become more of a problem. If all businesses are experiencing difficulties, they will often try to solve short-term cash problems by delaying paying their bills. Recessions may also be associated with higher interest rates, as was the case in 1990-92. This increases the cost of running overdrafts and causes further cash flow problems.

Seasonal demand Businesses which face seasonal demand have to be careful that they have enough working capital at times of both peak demand and off-peak demand. A toy shop, for instance, may not have enough stock in the run up to Christmas, losing potential sales. On the other hand, it may have too little cash to pay for invoices in August when sales are likely to be very low.

Solving working capital problems

Businesses experience problems with working capital either because they have the wrong amount of working capital or because there is an imbalance between the different constituents of working capital. What tactics and strategies might a business use to try to deal with such working capital problems?

Too little or too much working capital in total What if the business does not have enough working capital to operate efficiently? There is a number of solutions to this.
- Raise more long-term finance. This could be long term loans, a share issue or putting new retained profit into working capital assets for example.
- A business unable to do this may choose to reduce its size to cope. By turning away orders and reducing sales, for example, it will need less stock and will reduce its debtors. In many cases, not enough working capital causes cash flow problems. Typically, a business with this sort of problem is continually short not just of cash but also of stocks and credit with suppliers.
- In some cases, management may manipulate working capital so that there is enough cash in the business. However, cash may be generated by running down stocks to crisis levels, or by increasing overdraft borrowings.

Sometimes businesses have too much working capital. They then need to identify which elements of working capital it would be best to reduce. The cash raised could then be used, for example, to pay off long-term debts, increase investment in the business or to pay a higher dividend to the owners.

An imbalance in the constituents of working capital Sometimes businesses have enough working capital in total, but it is badly allocated. For example, a business may not have enough cash to pay its weekly bills. But it may be holding more stock than it needs to operate efficiently. Reducing stock levels could increase the amount of cash in the business and so resolve the problem.

Similarly, a liquidity problem might occur at the same time as a business has an excessive amount of debtors. Chasing up debtors and getting more to pay on time through better credit control will inject cash into the business.

Improving cash flow may not be the problem though. It could be that a business has too much cash but too little stock. Management might be too cautious and hold excessive amounts of cash leading to production problems as stock levels are too low. Equally, management may turn away orders to avoid having to give trade credit to customers when it has more than enough cash to finance an expansion of sales.

Working capital and cash flow

It might be assumed that working capital problems are the same as cash flow problems. Although cash flow and working capital are interlinked, and many working capital problems are cash flow problems as well, they are not the same.

For example, one way of dealing with a cash flow problem is to increase borrowing through an overdraft facility or a short-term bank loan repayable within one year. Borrowing more in the short term will lead to an increase in cash, a current asset. So it could solve a cash flow problem. But it will not increase working capital. This is because such borrowing also increases current liabilities. The money borrowed is, in theory, repayable within 12 months. Another way in which a business can solve a cash flow problem is to run down its stocks. Not reordering stock means that less cash is leaving the business. But improving cash flow in this way leaves the amount of working capital exactly the same. On the balance sheet, all that happens immediately is that the value of stocks falls whilse the value of cash rises. Equally, a common short-term way of dealing with a cash flow problem is for a business to delay paying its bills. This increases the amount of cash in the business. But it also increases the amount of creditors. There is no change in overall working capital.

However, a business with persistent cash flow problems is likely to have a shortage of working capital. The most likely solution to both problems is to increase the equity in the business or to borrow more in the long term.

Working capital and profit

Loss making businesses are likely to have working capital problems. But so do some profitable businesses. Working capital and profit are not the same. For example, a business might be offered a contract which would be highly profitable. However, it may be unable to take it because it does not have enough working capital. Payment for the contract might only arrive in four months' time, one month after completion. In the meantime, stocks need to be paid for, wages of extra workers will be owed and other costs will be incurred. If the firm's

suppliers will not extend any more credit and if the firm's bank will not extend its overdraft, the finance for these expenses will not be available.

In general, businesses which are unprofitable run into working capital problems. Losses drain cash away from the business. This ultimately leads to both cash flow problems and therefore inadequate levels of working capital. However, a business may get around this by raising long-term finance. An unprofitable business can survive if long-term finance is being used to top up its working capital.

KEYTERMS

Working capital – the funds left over to meet day-to-day expenses after current debts have been paid. It is calculated by current assets minus current liabilities.
Working capital cycle – the flow of liquid resources into and out of a business.

KNOWLEDGE

1. How is the value of working capital calculated?
2. At what point does a business have sufficient working capital to avoid a problem?
3. State four time lags that exist in the working capital cycle.
4. State two ways in which time lags can be reduced.
5. State three examples of cash drains from the working capital cycle.
6. Why can some businesses operate with negative working capital?
7. Can a business have too much working capital? Explain.
8. Explain the link between working capital and profit.

Case Study: *LED Ltd and Hopes Ltd*

LED Ltd

LED Ltd is a family company and manufactures gears for conveyer belt systems. Some examples of their products are shown below.

- **Worm gears** – gears which offer protection against corrosion.
- **Bevel gears** – used to redirect the shaft from a horizontal gas turbine engine to the vertical rotor.
- **Ring gears** – gears which increase or decrease motion.
- **Helical gears** – gears which allow motors to be installed at right angles to the axis of equipment.
- **Bevel helical gears** – used as a storage and retrieval unit.

LED Ltd operates in a fairly stable market and uses just-in-time (JIT) manufacturing techniques. It holds very little stocks of raw materials, components, work-in-progress or finished goods. Most of LED's sales are on 90 day trade credit. In 2007 the company increased its turnover to £3,640,000 and made a profit of £221,000.

Hopes Ltd

Hopes Ltd is a large independent DIY store located in Edinburgh. Its product range is fairly typical for a DIY store and includes paint, wall coverings, tiles, bathroom units, kitchen units, kitchen appliances, tools, building materials, fittings, flooring, garden tools and furniture and heating and plumbing materials. It has managed to maintain its independence and compete with some of the larger DIY stores such as B&Q by offering exceptional levels of customer service. For example, Hopes will deliver orders for customers free of charge. The company also offers trade credit to a selection of regular customers (although most sales are still for cash). Hopes buys its stock from a wide range of manufacturers and wholesalers and on average enjoys 45 days trade credit.

In 2008, Hopes Ltd took out a short-term loan to pay for the construction of a large greenhouse adjacent to the store. This allowed the company to grow and stock a wider range of plants and similar products.

Table 1: Financial information for LED Ltd and Hopes Ltd, 2008

	LED Ltd (£)	Hopes Ltd (£)
Turnover	3,640,000	3,786,000
Profit before tax	221,000	289,000
Current assets		
Stocks	10,000	460,000
Debtors	385,000	112,000
Cash at bank and in hand	343,000	123,000
	738,000	695,000
Current liabilities		
Short term bank loan	0	200,000
Trade creditors	369,000	387,000
Dividend proposed	50,000	60,000
Corporation tax	45,000	53,000
Other creditors	22,000	45,000
	486,000	745,000

(a) Explain what is meant by working capital. (4 marks)
(b) Describe the cash injection into Hopes' working capital cycle in 2008. (4 marks)
(c) Explain two possible reasons why Hopes Ltd has a much higher figure for stocks than LED Ltd. (8 marks)
(d) What difficulties might LED Ltd encounter operating with such a low level of stocks? (6 marks)
(e) Calculate the working capital for LED Ltd and Hopes Ltd. (6 marks)
(f) Account for the differences in working capital between the two companies. (12 marks)

54 | Business assets and depreciation

Assets

Assets are the **resources** used by business. A company will use the funds it earns to purchase assets which add value to a company. Most assets are physical in nature and are used in production. However, there are some, such as goodwill, which do not fall into this category, although they still add value. They are called intangible assets because they are non-physical. One of the functions of a **balance sheet** is to provide a summary of all business assets and their values. Assets are usually valued at their original cost, less a deduction for depreciation. This is to take into account that they wear out over a period of time and are worth less.

Fixed assets

Resources with a lifespan of more than one year are called **fixed assets**. Fixed assets, such as machinery, can be used again and again until they wear out. Some fixed assets like land and property do not depreciate, although they have to be maintained. In the balance sheet, fixed assets are divided into **tangible**, **intangible** and **financial assets**. Each of these are dealt with in detail in the following sections.

Tangible assets

TANGIBLE ASSETS are physical assets that can be touched. The most long term or the least **liquid** of these assets (the most difficult to turn into cash) appear at the top of the list of fixed assets on the balance sheet. For a farmer or a small manufacturing company these are likely to be the most important and largest fixed assets, if owned.

Land and property can either be **freehold** or **leasehold**. Freehold property is owned outright by the business. It is valued on the balance sheet at its original cost, less depreciation. In the past, inflation has resulted in soaring property prices. Accountants have advised many companies to revalue their land and property so that the accounts reflect more accurately a 'true and fair view' of the company. When assets are revalued in this way on the assets side of the balance sheet, an equivalent entry must be made on the liabilities side in reserves to balance the accounts. This is called a revaluation.

Leasehold land and property is rented from an owner and is a company asset. Any capital amount paid for the lease appears separately as 'leasehold property'. This amount is **written off** over the period of the lease. This means the value of the lease is reduced by an amount each year as it depreciates.

Fixed assets which are not land or property are referred to as plant, machinery and equipment. Again, they are valued at cost less depreciation. Large companies often have vast amounts of these assets. The balance sheet will, in this case, not list separate assets, but give only a total.

Intangible assets

Some fixed assets are not tangible, but are still valuable, income-generating resources. These are INTANGIBLE ASSETS.

Goodwill Over many years of trading companies build up goodwill. They may have gained a good reputation, which means that customers will use their services or purchase their products. If the company is to be sold in the future, some value needs to be placed on this goodwill and included in the purchase price. From an accountant's point of view, goodwill is equal to the amount by which the purchase price of a business exceeds the **net assets** (total assets - total liabilities).

Take the example of Amanda Storey, a young, newly qualified accountant, who decides to set up in business. She considers renting an office, advertising her services in the local press and distributing business cards. However, she is approached by Geoff Horrocks, an accountant who is considering retirement. Clearly it would pay Amanda to buy Geoff's list of established clients. The agreed price would represent goodwill.

Before 2005, the value of purchased goodwill was shown on the balance sheet and then depreciated (or amortised) over its expected useful economic life. Since the introduction of international accounting standards in 2005, plcs are expected to show intangible assets on the balance sheet and write them off over a much longer period. Many companies choose a period of 20 years.

Patents, copyrights and trade marks If a company or an individual invents and develops a unique product, a patent can be obtained from the patent office. This is a licence which prevents other firms from copying the product. Patents have been granted in the past for products as diverse as catseyes in 1935 and Polaroid cameras in 1946.

Copyright prevents the reuse of published works, such as books, plays, films and music without the author's consent. Michael Jackson allegedly paid £48 million for a back catalogue of 250 Beatles' songs, out-bidding former Beatle Paul McCartney. Substantial fees are paid to copyright owners of music used in TV advertisements. Occasionally, certain magazines will allow a part of their publication to be used free of charge. Trademarks generally signify a manufacturer's name. The right to sell another company's products may have to be registered if they carry a trade mark and a fee may be charged.

Research and development Normally research and development (R&D) costs are classified as revenue expenditure. However, if a project is expected to earn a substantial income in the future, its costs may be recorded as capital expenditure and included as an intangible asset in the balance sheet. The costs are written off over the period when income is generated.

Brand names Many companies enjoy successful brand names. Recently, some of these companies have debated the inclusion of these intangible assets in the balance sheet because they generate income for a lengthy period of time in some cases. This means that the amount a successful brand name is estimated to be worth should be included as an intangible asset on the balance sheet, so that the true value of a company's assets is made clear.

When an intangible asset is written off it is described as **amortisation** rather than depreciation.

Financial assets

These are often called **investments** in the balance sheet. They usually refer to shares held in other companies. If the shareholding in a particular company is more than 50 per cent then that company is classified as a **subsidiary**. If the holding is between 20 per cent and 50 per cent then the company is described as an **associated company**. Finally, any holdings of less than 20 per cent are called trade investments.

There is a number of motives for holding shares in other companies. These are shown in Figure 1. Some companies hold shares to earn income. Holding companies such as Kingfisher, for example, specialise in buying and controlling other companies. In some cases, businesses are bought, broken up, and parts sold at a profit. This activity has been described as **asset stripping**.

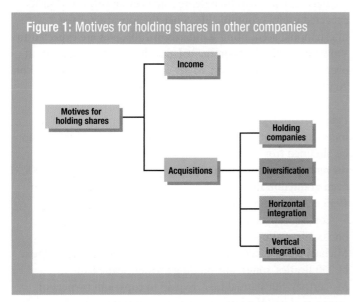

Figure 1: Motives for holding shares in other companies

Another motive for holding shares is to diversify in order to reduce risk. Companies also buy firms in the same line of business to exploit economies of scale, ie horizontal integration. They may also seek to buy out their suppliers or distribution networks, ie vertical integration.

Finally, other financial investments might include government bonds or deposits of foreign currency. All financial assets are listed at cost in the balance sheet.

Current assets

Short-term assets which can be changed into cash within one year are called **current assets**. There is a number of common current assets.

Stocks Most businesses hold stocks of finished goods. Stocks are classed as current assets because the business would hope to sell them within 12 months. The quantity of stocks held by a company will depend on the nature of the company.

Work-in-progress is also classified as stock. It represents partly finished goods, e.g. half-built properties. We also include stocks of raw materials and components in **current assets**. The business would expect to change them into finished goods which would then be sold, hopefully within a year.

Debtors In some lines of business, when a sale is made, it is common to receive payment at a later date. Any amounts owing by these customers at the end of the financial year are listed as **debtors** in the balance sheet. In order to speed up the payment of bills some firms offer cash discounts. In addition, debt factors offer a debt collecting service.

Related to debtors is another current asset – **prepayments**. A prepayment is a sum, such as insurance, rent or uniform business rate, which is paid in advance. At the end of the financial year any service which has been paid for but not fully consumed is listed in the balance sheet as a prepayment.

Cash at bank Most businesses deposit their takings in a bank. From the bank account various business expenses are paid for. If the bank balance is positive at the end of the trading year the amount will be shown as a current asset in the balance sheet.

Cash in hand Many businesses have cash on their premises. This is often called **petty cash**. Cash is used to pay for small or unexpected transactions, e.g. the purchase of toilet paper.

Together, cash at bank and cash in hand represent the firm's most **liquid resources**. Businesses need to hold just the right amount of cash. Too much cash means business opportunities are being wasted as the money could be invested in other assets. Too little cash may prevent the business from making urgent purchases.

Investments Some investments held by businesses may be short term. They may include shares in other companies, bonds or deposit accounts. If it is possible to convert these investments into cash within 12 months they are listed as investments under current assets.

Liquidity

Liquidity refers to the speed or ease with which assets can be converted into cash without suffering any capital loss. For example, a house is an illiquid asset. It could be sold for cash for, say, £100, but the owner would be likely to lose money. In the balance sheet the least liquid assets (fixed assets) are listed at the top and the most liquid (current assets) are placed at the bottom.

Question 1.

Corbridge Engineering Limited was established in 1981 as a sub-contract supplier of pressed components and metal pressings to customers' own specifications. It manufactures bespoke presswork and metal pressings, using ferrous and non-ferrous metals in sheet coil or tube form. Corbridge also offers a range of ancillary processes such as sub-assemblies, spot welding, surface finishing, thread rolling and tube sawing.

During 2006 the company began to experience cash flow problems. The directors felt that too much money was tied up in stock and many customers were taking too long to pay. At the beginning of 2007 some measures were taken to improve cash flow by addressing the stock and debtor problems. Table 1 shows the current assets for Corbridge Engineering Ltd for 2006 and 2007.

Table 1: Current assets for Corbridge Engineering Ltd

	2007 £	2006 £
Current assets		
Stocks of raw materials	134,000	135,600
Work-in-progress	321,900	342,600
Stocks of finished goods	238,900	243,100
Debtors	289,600	438,000
Prepayments	34,000	36,400
Cash in hand and at bank	187,600	2,900
	1,206,000	**1,198,600**

(a) Explain what is meant by current assets.
(b) To what extent has Corbridge Engineering Ltd improved its cash flow over the two years?

Fixed assets like land and buildings tend to be very illiquid. It can sometimes take a long time to sell such assets. Possibly the most illiquid of all assets is a highly specialised item of machinery, ie a machine which has been especially made for a company. This type of capital good will prove very difficult to sell since demand will be limited. Some fixed assets may be much easier to sell and are therefore more liquid. Vehicles, non-specialised machinery like a cement mixer or a JCB, and standard tools and equipment, which have a variety of uses, are all examples.

The least liquid of the current assets is stock. Stocks of finished goods are expected to be sold, but business fortunes change and sales can never be guaranteed. The liquidity of raw material stocks can vary. Non-specialised materials like coal will be more liquid than specialised components since they are easier to sell. Debtors are more liquid than stocks because goods have been sold and the business is legally entitled to payment. However, money has not yet been received so it cannot be spent. In addition, there are times when firms cannot pay and so the debt has to be written off (known as bad debts).

Cash at the bank and cash in hand are obviously the most liquid assets of all.

Asset structure

The ASSET STRUCTURE of a business refers to the amount of capital employed in each category of asset. Asset structures will vary according to the nature of the industry in which a business is competing. Manufacturing companies will tend to have a large amount of capital tied up in plant, machinery and equipment. Construction firms will have a significant amount of work-in-progress. Businesses which face seasonal demand may hold large stocks of finished goods at particular times of the year. In the retail trade, public houses and restaurants will have very few debtors, or even none.

A profit maximising company will want to purchase those assets which yield the greatest return. Fixed assets are the productive assets of a business, so firms will want to invest as much of their capital as possible in these. However, some capital must be kept in current assets to fund day to day expenditure. It is not possible to conduct business activity without current assets. Some firms may exist with very little capital employed in fixed assets. Retailers often have a large proportion of current assets if they rent premises (stock in particular).

Valuing assets

One of the problems in financial accounting is how to place a value on assets. Accountants value assets at **historical cost**, ie the cost of the asset when it is first purchased. There are reasons why assets should be valued in this way. Business transactions are entered into records as they occur. For example, if a firm buys a vehicle for £15,000 and pays cash, two entries will be made in the records. Also, accountants would argue that historical cost can be checked. It is based on actual costs and is better than methods which involve estimates. Other methods of valuation, such as those which take into account inflation, are also used. As yet, though, a suitable replacement has not been found.

One problem with historical cost accounting is how to put a value on fixed assets like property. In recent years there have been times when the values of land and buildings have risen sharply – as much as 30 or 40 per cent in one year. Unless the accounts are amended, they will not reflect the true value of the business. It is common now to revalue assets such as property every few years. Inflation distorts the value of assets and any other value which is measured in money terms.

Depreciation

Fixed assets are used again and again over a long period of time. For example, a milling machine might be used for many years to produce metal components. A motor business would expect automated production lines to run for many years. During their operation fixed assets are consumed and their value is 'used up'. This measure of consumption or any other reduction in the useful economic life of a fixed asset is known as DEPRECIATION. Figure 3 shows the possible causes of depreciation.

Question 2.

FRD Ltd is a small haulage company owned by Mandy Armstrong and her partner John Entwhistle. The business has a small office in Lincoln and provides haulage services to farmers in the county. FRD Ltd owns two Scania trucks and three specialist trailers to cope with a variety of agricultural loads. It also employs one other driver.

Allens is an electrical goods cash and carry based in Stoke-on-Trent. The store employs three staff and stocks a very wide range of electrical goods such HD TVs, sound systems, computers and white goods. Figure 2 shows the asset structure of the two businesses.

Figure 2: The asset structure of FRD Ltd and Allens

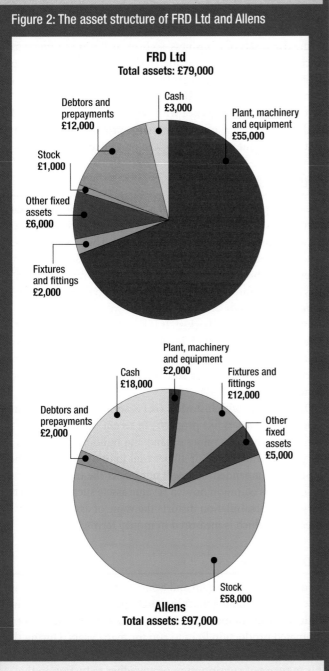

FRD Ltd
Total assets: £79,000

Cash £3,000
Debtors and prepayments £12,000
Plant, machinery and equipment £55,000
Stock £1,000
Other fixed assets £6,000
Fixtures and fittings £2,000

Plant, machinery and equipment £2,000
Cash £18,000
Fixtures and fittings £12,000
Debtors and prepayments £2,000
Other fixed assets £5,000
Stock £58,000

Allens
Total assets: £97,000

(a) Account for the differences in the asset structures of FRD Ltd and Allens.
(b) Which of the two businesses would have the largest annual depreciation charge? Explain your answer.

- Machinery, tools and equipment all suffer wear and tear when they are used. They deteriorate, which can sometimes affect their operation or effectiveness. Eventually they will have to be replaced.
- Changing technology can often make assets OBSOLETE. Although a machine may still work, it may not be used because a new machine is more efficient.
- Capital goods which are hardly used or poorly maintained may depreciate quickly. The life of machinery can be prolonged if it is 'looked after'.
- The passing of time can also lead to depreciation. For example, if an asset is leased, the 'buyer' can use the asset for a period of time. As the expiry date gets close, the lease becomes worth less and less.

Figure 3: Possible causes of depreciation

Wear and tear

Passing of time

CAUSES OF DEPRECIATION

Obsolescence

Lack of maintenance

Depreciation and the accounts

Each year accountants must work out how much depreciation to allow for each fixed asset. This can then be used in the balance sheet and the profit and loss account. The **balance sheet** will show the NET BOOK VALUE of assets. This is their original value minus depreciation. So if a piece of machinery is bought for £10,000 and depreciates by £2,000 in the first year, its net book value in the first year would be:

£10,000 - £2,000 = £8,000.

The net book value falls each year as more depreciation is deducted. So in the second year the net book value would be:

£8,000 - £2,000 = £6,000

This simple method of calculating depreciation is called the **straight line method** as the same value for depreciation is used each year. Another method, the **reducing balance method**, involves depreciating fixed assets by a fixed percentage each year.

Depreciation is shown in **profit and loss accounts** or **income statements** under expenses. This indicates that part of the original value is 'used up' each year (known as revenue expenditure). Eventually the entire value of the asset will appear as expenses, when the asset depreciates fully. This process of reducing the original value by the amount of depreciation is known as writing off.

Intangible assets are also depreciated or **amortised**, as explained earlier in this unit. For example, a business may 'write off' the value of its goodwill over a 20 year period.

The importance of depreciation

There are good reasons why a business should allow for depreciation each year in its accounts.

Accurate accounts If it does not, the accounts will be inaccurate. If the original value of assets was placed on the balance sheet this would overstate the value. The value of assets falls each year as they depreciate. If the value of assets on a balance sheet is inaccurate, then any financial analysis based on the balance sheet will be flawed. For example, ratio analysis would be ineffective.

Valuing the business The value of a business is represented by the net assets on a balance sheet. Clearly, if assets have not been depreciated then the value of the business would be overstated.

Matching benefits with costs Fixed assets generate profit for many years. It seems logical to write off the value of the asset over this whole period, rather than when it is first bought. This matches the benefit from the asset more closely with its cost.

Provision A sensible firm will know that assets must be replaced in future and allow for this. Even though depreciation appears as an expense on the profit and loss account, it is actually a PROVISION. Expenses involve paying out money. In the case of depreciation, no money is paid out. A business simply recognises that assets have to be replaced and 'provides' for this by placing a value in the accounts.

KEYTERMS

Asset structure – the proportion of capital employed in each type of asset.
Depreciation – the measure of wearing out, consumption or other reduction in the useful life of a fixed asset.
Intangible assets – non-physical business assets.
Net book value – the historical cost of an asset less depreciation accumulated every year.
Obsolete – an asset that is no longer any use to a business.
Provision (in relation to depreciation) – an allowance made in the accounts for depreciation.
Tangible assets – assets which are physical in nature.

KNOWLEDGE

1. What is the difference between tangible and intangible assets?
2. How is it possible to calculate the value of goodwill?
3. Distinguish between a subsidiary, an associated company and a trade investment.
4. What is meant by asset stripping?
5. What is the difference between debtors and prepayments?
6. What is the difference between a liquid and an illiquid asset?
7. Why is a specialised machine an illiquid asset?
8. What is the main determinant of a firm's asset structure?
9. State four causes of depreciation.
10. Why is depreciation a provision?

Case Study: **Domino's Pizza**

omino's Pizza Group Limited is a wholly owned subsidiary of Domino's Pizza UK and Irl plc and holds the master franchise licence to own, operate and franchise Domino's pizza stores in England, Scotland, Wales and Ireland. Domino's Pizza Inc. founded in the United States in 1960, is recognised as world leader in the delivery of freshly-made, home-delivered high quality pizza. The first UK store opened in 1985 and Domino's now has 451 stores operating in the UK and Ireland.

2006 was a record breaking year for Domino's Pizza. Store sales, store count and e-commerce all reached record levels. Store sales rose 19.7 per cent to £240.1 million, 46 new stores were opened and e-commerce sales were up 43.8 per cent to £20.1 million.

One of the reasons for Domino's continued success is its commitment to reducing 'out-the-door' time. This is the time it takes for a pizza order to leave the store after receiving an order. Domino's displays the 'real-time' average speed of the pizza making and baking process in their stores. By using this approach it has been able to improve the number of orders leaving the store in under 15 minutes by 34 per cent. The 'real-time' screens show the national average as well as the individual store. This has introduced a competitive spirit in the organisation which has helped to improve efficiency. Table 2 shows some information on fixed assets and depreciation for Domino's Pizza.

Table 2: Fixed assets and depreciation for Domino's Pizza 2006

	Freehold land and buildings	Leasehold improvements	Equipment	Total
Cost:	£000	£000	£000	£000
At 1 January 2006	8,245	1,315	9,655	19,215
Additions	38	311	1,945	2,294
Disposals		(206)	(317)	(523)
At 31 December 2006	**8,283**	**1,420**	**11,283**	**20,986**
Depreciation:				
At 1 January 2006	648	116	4,858	5,622
Provided during the year	124	170	1,377	1,671
Disposals		(5)	(82)	(87)
At 31 December 2006	**772**	**281**	**6,153**	**7,206**
Net book value:				
At 31 December 2006	**7,511**	**1,139**	**5,130**	**13,780**

Source: adapted from Domino's Pizza, *Annual Report and Accounts*.

(a) What is meant by the term 'wholly owned subsidiary' in the case. (4 marks)

(b) Using examples from this case, explain what is meant by tangible assets. (4 marks)

(c) What might account for the additions to equipment of £1,945,000 in 2006? (4 marks)

(d) Explain how the net book value of fixed assets (£13,780,000) is calculated. (6 marks)

(e) (i) Why do businesses provide for depreciation? (6 marks)

(ii) What might cause Domino's fixed assets to depreciate? (6 marks)

(f) In 2006, Domino's had £773,000 of goodwill shown in the balance sheet. Explain what is likely to happen to the net book value of Domino's goodwill in the future. (10 marks)

55 Financial data and performance

Using financial data for comparisons

When evaluating the performance of a business it is necessary to make comparisons. Comparisons will help a business to gauge more effectively how well it has performed. Three types of comparisons are common:

- interfirm comparisons;
- comparisons over time;
- interfirm comparisons over time.

Interfirm comparisons

A business can get a good idea of how it has performed by comparing its results with those of another company in the same industry. For example, Sainsbury might want to compare its results with those of Tesco or Morrisons. These businesses are all supermarket chains. Therefore a comparison would be meaningful. It is important to compare 'like with like' when making interfirm comparisons. Comparing the net profit margin of a supermarket with that of a chemical engineering company is not likely to be appropriate. This is because the two businesses have many different features.

Interfirm comparisons might highlight particular strengths or weaknesses. For example, a bus company with a turnover of £12.4 million might think its £2.1 million profit is satisfactory. Another bus company might have made a £2 million profit on a turnover of just £7.5 million. Assuming the two firms are similar and operate in similar circumstances, the relative profit of the first business is not as good.

Table 1: Revenue and net profit of two construction companies, 2006

	Bellway £000	George Wimpey* £000
Revenue	1,240,193	3,147,400
Net profit	155,742	256,000
Net profit margin	12.60%	8.10%

* Before exceptional items.

Table 1 shows financial information of two construction companies Bellway and George Wimpey. Bellway homes are designed, built and marketed by local teams operating from regional offices managed and staffed by local people. George Wimpey also builds homes and has been trading for around 125 years. Table 1 shows revenue, net profit and net profit margin for 2006 for both companies. The Bellway figures are for the year ending 31.7.2006 while the George Wimpey figures are for the year ending 31.12.2006.

George Wimpey has generated the most turnover and profit.

For example, George Wimpey's net profit is 64 per cent larger than Bellways. However, it could be argued that Bellway is the better performer. This is because the net profit margin is higher for Bellway. This means that Bellway has generated more profit per pound of turnover. But it must be noted that the two companies have different year ends so the figures may not be 100 per cent comparable.

Comparisons over time

Looking at performance indicators for a single year is not always helpful. This is because one year's trading figures may not reflect what has been going on over a longer time period. Most accounts show figures for the current year and the previous year. This is helpful but only up to a point, even two years' figures could disguise the long-term trend. A more thorough evaluation of a company's performance can be undertaken by looking at many years' figures. This is called TREND ANALYSIS. Trend analysis involves looking at data over a long period of time and spotting patterns in data. Most public limited companies publish key performance data for five years in their annual report and accounts.

Table 2: Revenue and net profit of Punch Taverns

					(£ million)
	2006	2005	2004	2003	2002
Revenue	1,546.10	770.1	637.6	429	391.8
Profit after tax	194.8	167.2	121.5	97.6	67.9
Net profit margin	7.90%	21.70%	19.10%	22.50%	17.30%

Table 2 shows financial information of Punch Taverns. It operates over 8,400 pubs and has grown rapidly in recent years through a series of acquisitions. For example, in 2006 the company bought Spirit Group, a 1,830 pub estate, for £2.7 billion. Table 2 shows revenue, profit after tax and the net profit margin for a five year period.

The data show clearly that the company has grown spectacularly over five years. Turnover has increased from £391.8 million in 2002 to £1,546.1 million in 2006. This is a very strong trend. Profit has also increased impressively between 2002 and 2006 – from £67.9 million to £194.8 million. The net profit margin has fluctuated and is at its lowest in 2006. This might be due to the large acquisition made in this year. There may have been some high costs associated with this – financing perhaps. Trend analysis shows that Punch Taverns is a rapidly growing and profitable company.

Interfirm comparisons over time

Using a combination of the two methods above we can make interfirm comparisons over time. This means that more meaningful comparisons can be made between businesses in the same industry. It also means that trends in a particular industry might be identified. Enfield Publishing and Durrant Press are both medium-sized publishers. They have similar financial circumstances and compete in the same markets. Table 3 below shows the capital employed and net profit margins of the two companies.

Table 3: Financial data, Enfield Publishing Ltd and Durrant Press Ltd

	2006	2005	2004	2003	2002
Enfield Publishing Ltd					
Return on capital employed	11.50%	12.60%	14.10%	15.10%	15.90%
Net profit margin	9.20%	8.90%	9.90%	10.50%	11.20%
Durrant Press Ltd					
Return on capital employed	12.30%	13.20%	12.50%	13.90%	14.10%
Net profit margin	10.50%	11.10%	11.90%	12.60%	13.00%

The financial data shown suggest that Durrant Press Ltd is the best performing company. Its return on capital employed is higher than Enfield's for the whole time period. The same pattern is evident with the net profit margin. Durrant Press has higher margins in every year. It is also clear from the data that over the time period the performance of both companies has worsened. For example, the ROCE for Enfield has fallen from 15.9 per cent to 11.5 per cent. Similarly, the ROCE for Durrant has fallen (although not so sharply) from 14.1 per cent to 12.3 per cent. The net profit margins also show a decline. This suggests that the industry has suffered over the time period. Perhaps it has become more competitive.

Using data for decision making

One of the reasons for producing accounts and compiling other forms of financial data is to help make business decisions. When choosing between different courses of action a business will want to gather as much relevant information as possible. Having relevant and accurate information is likely to help businesses make more informed decisions. It is also helpful to have a range of quantitative information because it is easier to analyse. Financial data falls into this category. Financial data is likely to be used to help make the strategic decisions outlined below.

Acquisitions Many companies grow through acquisitions. However, before a company takes over another business it needs to look very closely at the financial circumstances of that business. A wide range of financial data will be analysed before a bid can be made. The size of the bid is likely to depend on the results of this financial analysis. In some cases a company might employ a specialist to carry out this work, such as a merchant bank.

Investment All businesses have to invest from time to time. Making an investment decision is fraught with uncertainty. Businesses are likely to use quantitative appraisal methods when choosing between different investment projects. Financial data will have to be gathered in order to carry out such detailed appraisals.

Strategy A business will use financial data when deciding its corporate strategy. For example, if a business is considering a venture into overseas markets for the first time, it will have to evaluate the impact such a venture would have on the financial position of the business.

Product portfolio Developing and launching new products is a highly risky activity. In order to minimise the risk businesses will consider carefully the impact such a move would have on the financial standing of the business. A wide range of financial data might be analysed when making such a decision. If a new product fails, the effect on the performance of the company could be severe and far reaching.

When making strategic decisions like the ones outlined above, a wide range of financial information and performance indicators might be considered. Examples might include profit, earnings, return on capital employed, sales revenue, sales volumes, costs, working capital and debt. Much of this information can be extracted from the financial statements produced by a business – the profit and loss account or income statement and balance sheet for example.

Assessing strengths and weaknesses of financial data in judging performance

The importance of using financial data to assess the performance of a business is clear. Performance indicators such as the net profit margin and return on capital employed can go along way to show how effectively a business is performing. Such indicators have clarity and can be used to make direct comparisons. These are key strengths when using financial data to judge performance.

However, financial data can be imperfect. For example, accounts can be 'window dressed' to distort the true financial circumstances of a business, much financial data is historic and is of limited use when looking into the future and inflation can distort financial values. It must also be remembered that qualitative data can be of use when judging performance. Using questionnaires to assess the views of other stakeholders such as employees, customers and environmentalists, can also help to judge performance. These issues and many others are discussed in more detail in the units on the balance sheet, profit and loss account and limitations to ratios.

KEYTERMS

Trend analysis – looking for patterns in data over a period of time.

KNOWLEDGE

1. Why might businesses compare their performance with rivals?
2. State two problems of using one year's figures to assess the performance of a business.
3. Briefly explain the value of trend analysis to a business.
4. State two ways in which financial data might be used to make decisions in business.
5. State two problems a business should be aware of when using financial data to judge performance.

Case study *Sainsbury's and Tesco*

Sainsbury's and Tesco are two of the major supermarket chains in the UK. Tesco has operations overseas but about 80 per cent of its revenue is generated in the UK. Tesco employs about 250,000 people in the UK in 1,779 stores. Tesco has four store formats. In order of size starting with the smallest these are Express, Metro, Superstore and Extra. Much of Tesco's growth in recent years has come from the development of the smaller stores. Growth has also come from extending the product range into more and more non-food items.

Sainsbury is the smaller of the two groups but is still a leading UK food retailer with interests in financial services. It consists of Sainsbury's Supermarkets, Sainsbury's Local, Bells Stores, Jacksons Stores and JB Beaumont, Sainsbury's Online and Sainsbury's Bank. It employs 148,000 people and operates 788 stores. In addition to its grocery stores Sainsbu a joint venture with HBOS. It offers financial services such as savings, loa and credit cards. Table 4 shows some financial data for the two superma

Table 4: Financial data for Sainsbury and Tesco

	2003	2004	2005	2006	(£000) 2007
Sainsbury					
Revenue	18,144	18,239	16,573	17,317	18,518
Profit	695	675	254	267	380
Profit margin					
Tesco					
Revenue	26,004	30,814	33,974	39,454	42,641
Profit	1,401	1,708	2,029	2,277	2,545
Profit margin					

Source: adapted from Sainsbury and Tesco, *Annual Report and Accounts*, 2007.

(a) Calculate the profit margins for Tesco and Sainsbury's. (10 marks)
(b) What type of comparison can be made using the financial data in Table 4? (4 marks)
(c) (i) Explain why trend analysis allows a more meaningful comparison between two businesses. (4 marks)
(ii) Compare the financial data for the two supermarkets and explain which has performed the best over the five year period. (10 marks)
(d) Explain how the two supermarkets might use financial data to help make decisions? (12 marks)

The investigation process

Financial data is used by a range of stakeholders to assess the performance of a business and help make decisions. Different stakeholders are interested for different reasons. For example, shareholders may want information to assess the rewards for holding shares. Managers may try to gauge performance. This unit explains how the information in the **final accounts** can be interpreted. It is possible to base investigation on some of these figures alone. Also, information can be obtained by combining some of these figures and carrying out a RATIO ANALYSIS. The chairperson's report, the directors' report and the notes to the accounts provide extra material as well.

The investigation process is shown in Figure 1. There is a number of steps involved.

Figure 1: Steps in the investigation process

IDENTIFY

COMPILATION & PRESENTATION

INTERPRET

COMPARE

Identification Figures that are relevant must be identified from the final amounts. Suitable data must be used. For example, an accountant might need information on current assets and current liabilities, rather than total assets and total liabilities, in order to assess the solvency of the business.

Presentation Once the correct figures have been chosen they can be compiled and presented into a useful form, such as percentages.

Interpretation To interpret ratios an understanding of their significance is needed. Ratios can be used to find out the firm's financial position, assess performance, analyse capital structure and help shareholders when deciding whether to invest.

Comparison Ratios may be used by businesses to compare figures in the accounts which are related in some way. A ratio be one number expressed as a percentage of another or simply one

number divided by another. For an accounting ratio to be useful the two figures must be connected, eg profit is arguably related to the amount of capital a firm uses. These comparisons might include interfirm comparisons, comparisons over time and interfirm comparisons over time. There may be other bodies or institutions which might use ratios. The media produce reports about businesses which they publish. They might use a range of ratios when reporting on particular businesses. In some newspapers the dividend yield and price/earnings ratio are actually published every day for a range of public limited companies. The Inland Revenue might also use ratio analysis when investigating the performance of a business. Some businesses collect business data and sell it to other users. For example, an agency might write a financial report on a business and part of it might consist of comments about particular ratios.

Tables 1-3 show the profit and loss account and balance sheet for Hudsons Ltd, and some additional information from the notes to the accounts. Hudsons Ltd, a large private limited company, sells electrical goods such as TVs, videos, DVD players, music systems and computers from its 130 stores. The figures shown in the accounts will be used in this unit to illustrate how ratios can be calculated and interpreted.

Table 1: Profit and loss account, Hudsons Ltd

Hudsons Ltd Profit and Loss Account Y/E 31.7.08		
	2008 £000	2007 £000
Turnover	70,000	63,000
Cost of sales	55,000	50,000
Gross profit	15,000	13,000
Operating expenses	9,500	9,000
Operating profit	5,500	4,000
Income from investments	100	80
Profit on ordinary activities before tax and interest	5,600	4,080
Net interest paid	1,100	600
Profit on ordinary activities before tax (net profit)	4,500	3,480
Taxation	1,100	680
Profit on ordinary activities after tax	3,400	2,800
Dividends	900	700
Retained profit	2,500	2,100

Table 2: Additional information, Hudsons Ltd

	2008	2007
Number of ordinary shares	40,000,000	40,000,000
Share price 31st July	135p	94p

Table 3: Balance sheet, Hudsons Ltd

Hudsons Ltd Balance Sheet
As At 31.7.08

	2008 £000	2007 £000
Fixed assets		
Tangible assets	21,000	19,800
Investments	500	400
	21,500	20,200
Current assets		
Stocks	8,500	7,100
Debtors	500	400
Cash at bank and in hand	3,000	2,100
	12,000	9,600
Creditors:		
amounts falling due within one year (current liabilities)	8,100	7,000
Net current assets (working capital)	3,900	2,600
Total assets less current liabilities	25,400	22,800
Creditors:		
amounts falling due after one year (long term liabilities)	(8,000)	(6,500)
Net assets	17,400	16,300
Capital and reserves		
Called up share capital	2,000	2,000
Other reserves	1,400	2,800
Profit and loss account	14,000	11,500
Shareholders' funds	17,400	16,300

Liquidity ratios

LIQUIDITY RATIOS illustrate the solvency of a business - whether it is in a position to repay its debts. They focus on short-term assets and liabilities. Creditors are likely to be interested in liquidity ratios to assess whether they will receive money that they are owed. Money lenders and suppliers, for example, will be interested in how easily a business can repay its debts. Potential investors might also have an interest in liquidity ratios for the same reason. In addition, managers might use them to aid financial control, ie to ensure that they have enough liquid resources to meet debts.

A business must make sure that it has enough liquid assets to pay any immediate bills that arise. Liquid assets include cash and assets that can be quickly switched into cash such as stocks, debtors and short-term investments. Two widely used ratios to monitor liquid assets are the current ratio and the acid test ratio.

Current ratio The CURRENT RATIO focuses on current assets and current liabilities. It is also known as the working capital ratio and is calculated using the formula:

$$\text{Current ratio} = \frac{\text{Current assets}}{\text{Current liabilities}}$$

For Hudsons, current assets were £12,000,000 in 2008 and current liabilities were £8,100,000. Both of these figures are shown in the balance sheet.

$$\text{For 2008} \quad \text{Current ratio} = \frac{£12,000,000}{£8,100,000} = 1.48 \text{ or } 1.48{:}1$$

$$\text{For 2007} \quad \text{Current ratio} = \frac{£9,600,000}{£7,000,000} = 1.37 \text{ or } 1.37{:}1$$

It is suggested that a business will have sufficient liquid resources if the current ratio is between 1.5:1 and 2:1. If the ratio is below 1.5 it might be argued that a business does not have enough working capital. This might mean that a business is overborrowing or overtrading. Operating above a ratio of 2:1 may suggest that too much money is tied up unproductively. Money tied up in stocks does not earn any return.

The current ratio for Hudsons has hardly changed over the two years, rising slightly from 1.37:1 to 1.48:1. As with other ratios, judgement on what is satisfactory depends to a large extent on comparisons within the industry. For example, retailers often have very low current ratios, perhaps 1:1 or below. This is because they hold fast-selling stocks and generate cash from sales. Since Hudsons is a retailer, it might be well satisfied with a current ratio of 1.48:1 in 2008.

Hudsons may be able to improve its current ratio by increasing its current assets relative to current liabilities, or reducing its current liabilities relative to its current assets. For example, current assets might be improved by better stock or credit control. Current liabilities might be reduced by reducing short-term creditors.

Acid test ratio The ACID TEST RATIO or QUICK RATIO is a more severe test of liquidity. This is because stocks are not treated as liquid resources. Stocks are not guaranteed to be sold and they may become obsolete or deteriorate. They are therefore excluded from current assets when calculating the ratio.

$$\text{Acid test ratio} = \frac{\text{Current assets} - \text{stocks}}{\text{Current liabilities}}$$

The information required to calculate the acid test ratio are found in Hudsons' balance sheet.

For 2008
$$\text{Acid test ratio} = \frac{£12,000,000 - £8,500,000}{£8,100,000} = 0.43 \text{ or } 0.43: 1$$

For 2007
$$\text{Acid test ratio} = \frac{£9,600,000 - £7,100,000}{£7,000,000} = 0.36 \text{ or } 0.36: 1$$

If a business has an acid test ratio of less than 1:1 it means that its current assets less stocks do not cover its current liabilities. This could indicate a potential problem. However, as with the current ratio, there is considerable variation between the typical acid test ratios of businesses in different industries. Again, retailers with their strong cash flows, may operate comfortably with acid test ratios of less than 1. Since Hudsons is a retailer and its stock is likely to be sold quite quickly, an acid test ratio of 0.43:1 may be acceptable to the business. The

Question 1.

HR Owen operates a number of vehicle franchises in the prestige and specialist car market for both sales and aftersales, predominantly in the London area. For example, it sells Bentleys, Rolls Royce's, Maseratis, Ferraris and Lamborghinis. Bpi (British Polythene Industries) manufacture over 300,000 tonnes of polythene products in a year for a variety of applications. Table 5 shows current assets and current liabilities for the two companies.

Table 5: Current assets and current liabilities for HR Owen and Bpi

| | HR Owen | | Bpi | |
	2008 £000	2007 £000	2008 £000	2007 £000
Stocks	42,481	81,559	59,500	55,300
Other current assets	20,074	49,615	60,500	64,100
Total current assets	62,555	131,174	120,000	119,400
Current liabilities	53,757	136,531	68,300	75,500

Source: adapted from HR Owen and Bpi, *Annual Report and Accounts*.

(a) Calculate the: (i) current ratios; (ii) acid test ratios for both companies in 2008 and 2007.
(b) (i) Which is the more liquid of the two companies?
    (ii) Suggest and explain one reason for your answer in (i).

methods of improving the current ratio can all be used here, although changing stock levels are not an option as stocks are excluded from the calculation.

Profitability ratios

PROFITABILITY or PERFORMANCE RATIOS help to show how well a business is doing. They tend to focus on profit, capital employed and turnover. Stakeholders such as owners, managers, employees and potential investors are all likely to be interested in the profitability and performance of a business. Competitors might also use these ratios to make comparisons of performance. The profit figure alone is not a useful performance indicator. It is necessary to look at the value of profit in relation to the value of turnover or the amount of money that has been invested in the business.

Return on capital employed (ROCE) One of the most important ratios which is used to measure the profitability of a business is the RETURN ON CAPITAL EMPLOYED (ROCE). This is sometimes referred to as the primary ratio. It compares the profit, ie return, made by the business with the amount of money invested, ie its capital. The advantage of this ratio is that it relates profit to the size of the business. When calculating ROCE, it is standard practice to define profit as net profit (or operating profit) before tax and interest. This is sometimes described as earnings before interest and tax (EBIT). Tax is ignored because it is determined by the government and is therefore outside the control of the company. Interest is excluded because it does not relate to the business's ordinary trading activities. ROCE can be calculated using the formula:

$$\text{ROCE} = \frac{\text{Profit before tax and interest}}{\text{Long-term capital employed}} \times 100$$

For Hudsons the profit before tax and interest in 2008 was £5,600,000. Long-term capital employed was £25,400,000. Long-term capital employed is shareholders' funds plus any long-term loans, i.e. £17,400,000 + £8,000,000.

$$\text{For 2008 ROCE} = \frac{£5,600,000}{£25,400,000} \times 100 = 22.0\%$$

$$\text{For 2007 ROCE} = \frac{£4,080,000}{£22,800,000} \times 100 = 17.9\%$$

The return on capital employed will vary between industries, however, the higher the ratio, the better. Over the two years Hudsons has seen its ROCE increase from 17.9 per cent to 22.0 per cent. To decide whether Hudsons has performed well, this would have to be compared with another business in the same industry. An investor might also compare the ROCE with the possible return if the capital was invested elsewhere. For example, if £25,400,000 was placed in a bank account in 2008 it might have earned a 5 per cent return. So the 22 per cent ROCE in 2008 seems impressive. However, an investor in the company will also want to be rewarded for the risk involved. The £25,400,000 invested by shareholders in Hudsons is at risk if the business fails. So, for the investment to be worthwhile, the ROCE must be far greater than the return that could be earned in a 'safe' investment. Increasing profit with the existing capital employed will improve the ROCE ratio for a business.

Gross profit margin The gross profit margin is also known as the mark-up. This shows the gross profit made on sales turnover. It is calculated using the formula:

$$\text{Gross profit margin} = \frac{\text{Gross profit}}{\text{Turnover}} \times 100$$

For Hudsons in 2008 gross profit was £15,000,000 and turnover was £70,000,000.

$$\text{For 2008 Gross profit margin} = \frac{£15,000,000}{£70,000,000} \times 100 = 21.4\%$$

$$\text{For 2007 Gross profit margin} = \frac{£13,000,000}{£63,000,000} \times 100 = 20.6\%$$

Higher gross margins are usually preferable to lower ones. It may be possible to increase the gross profit margin by raising turnover relative to cost of sales, for example by increasing price. Or cost of sales could be reduced relative to turnover. However, the gross profit margin required will tend to be different for different industries. As a rule, the quicker the turnover of stock, the lower the gross margin that is needed. So, for example, a supermarket with a fast stock turnover is likely to have a lower gross margin than a car retailer with a much slower stock turnover. Some supermarkets are therefore very successful with relatively low gross profit margins because of the regular and fast turnover of stock. The gross margin for Hudsons has improved slightly over the two years. Interfirm comparisons would help to confirm whether this was a satisfactory performance.

Net profit margin The net profit margin helps to measure how well a business controls its overheads and cost of sales. If the difference between the gross margin and the net margin is small, this suggests that overheads are low. This is because net profit equals gross profit less overheads. The net profit margin can be calculated by:

$$\text{Net profit margin} = \frac{\text{Net profit before tax and interest}}{\text{Turnover}} \times 100$$

Question 2.

Grantham Paints is an established producer of paint and other coverings. An important aspect of its manufacturing strategy is to use modern materials and technology that minimise environmental impact. It favours waterborne finishes that are low in volatile organic compounds. In 2006 the company began to experience cash-flow problems. In order to resolve the problem it devoted more resources to debt collection and renegotiated the terms of payment with some key suppliers. Table 4 shows some financial information for Grantham Paints plc.

Table 4: Financial information for Grantham Paints plc

	2008 £000	2007 £000
Revenue	102,876	98,433
Cost of sales	58,981	56,670
Value of stock	3,889	3,467
Debtors	11,870	15,600
Creditors	14,300	11,800

(a) Calculate for 2008 and 2007 the (i) debt collection period; (ii) creditor days period.

(b) To what extent do you think Grantham's measure to improve cash flow may have worked?

(c) (i) Calculate the stock turnover for Grantham Paints and comment on the change over the two years.
(ii) How might the company raise stock turnover to help improve cash flow?

For Hudsons in 2008 net profit before tax and interest was £5,600,000 and turnover was £70,000,000.

$$\text{For 2007 Net profit margin} = \frac{£5,600,000}{£70,000,000} \times 100 = 8.0\%$$

$$\text{For 2007 Net profit margin} = \frac{£4,080,000}{£63,000,000} \times 100 = 6.5\%$$

Again, higher margins are usually better than lower ones. The net profit margin for Hudsons has improved over the two years. This suggests that the business was able to restrict overhead spending as a proportion of turnover more effectively in 2008 than in 2007.

Financial efficiency ratios

FINANCIAL EFFICIENCY, ACTIVITY or ASSET UTILISATION RATIOS are used to measure how effectively a business employs its resources. Such ratios are likely to be used internally by managers. This is because they focus on how well a business uses its resources. For example, the performance of the credit control department could be assessed by looking at how quickly debts are collected.

Asset turnover The ASSET TURNOVER ratio measures the productivity of assets. It looks at how much turnover is generated by the assets employed in the business. The formula is:

$$\text{Asset turnover} = \frac{\text{Turnover}}{\text{Net assets}}$$

The turnover for Hudsons in 2007 was £70,000,000 and the net assets were £17,400,000.

$$\text{For 2008 Asset turnover} = \frac{£70,000,000}{£17,400,000} = 4.02$$

$$\text{For 2007 Asset turnover} = \frac{£63,000,000}{£16,300,000} = 3.87$$

The ratio shows that, in 2008, for every £1 invested in net assets by Hudsons, £4.02 of turnover was generated. Over the two years the asset turnover improved by a few pence. The asset turnover varies in different industries. In retailing, where turnover is high and the value of fixed assets is relatively low, like Hudsons, the asset turnover can be 3 or more. In contrast, in manufacturing, where there is often heavier investment in fixed assets, the ratio is generally lower. For example, it can be 1 or less. Increasing turnover using the same assets, so that assets work more effectively, is a method of improving the ratio.

Stock turnover The STOCK TURNOVER ratio measures how quickly a business uses or sells its stock. It is generally considered desirable to sell, or 'shift', stock as quickly as possible. One approach to stock turnover is to calculate how many times during the year a business sells its stock. The formula is:

$$\text{Stock turnover} = \frac{\text{Cost of sales}}{\text{Stocks}}$$

The cost of sales for Hudsons in 2008 was £55,000,000. The value of closing stocks as shown in the balance sheet was £8,500,000.

$$\text{For 2008 Stock turnover} = \frac{£55,000,000}{£8,500,000} = 6.5 \text{ times}$$

$$\text{For 2007 Stock turnover} = \frac{£50,000,000}{£7,100,000} = 7.0 \text{ times}$$

Another approach to stock turnover is to calculate the number of days it takes to sell the stock. This is found by:

$$\text{Stock turnover} = \frac{\text{Stocks}}{\text{Cost of sales}} \times 365$$

$$\text{For 2008 Stock turnover} = \frac{£8,500,000}{£55,000,000} \times 365 = 56 \text{ days}$$

$$\text{For 2007 Stock turnover} = \frac{£7,100,000}{£50,000,000} \times 365 = 52 \text{ days}$$

High stock turnovers are preferred (or lower figures in days). A higher stock turnover means that profit on the sale of stock is earned more quickly. Thus, businesses with high stock turnovers can operate on lower profit margins. A declining stock turnover ratio might indicate:
- higher stock levels;
- a large amount of slow moving or obsolete stock ;
- a wider range of products being stocked;
- a lack of control over purchasing.

So improvements to purchasing methods or better control of stock levels, for example, should improve the stock turnover ratio of a business.

Stock turnover differs considerably between different industries. Supermarkets often have a relatively quick stock turnover of around 14 to 28 days. This means that they sell the value of their average stock every two to four weeks. Manufacturers generally have much slower stock turnover because of the time spent processing raw materials. However, in recent years, many manufacturers have adopted just-in-time production techniques. This involves ordering stocks only when they are required in the production process and, therefore, stock levels tend to be lower. As a result stock turnover is faster. Businesses which supply services, such as banks, travel agents and transport operators, are not likely to hold very much stock. Therefore this ratio is not likely to be used by service industry analysts.

Over the two years, Hudsons' stock turnover has worsened very slightly. However, to determine whether a stock turnover of 56 days is good, comparisons with other electrical goods retailers would have to be made.

Creditor days (creditors' payment period) This ratio measures how quickly a business pays its debts to its suppliers and other short-term creditors. The CREDITOR DAYS or CREDITOR PAYMENT PERIOD is the average number of days it takes to pay debts. It can be calculated using the formula below.

$$\text{Creditor days} = \frac{\text{Creditors}}{\text{Cost of sales}} \times 365$$

According to the accounts for Hudsons Ltd, the amount owed to short-term creditors in 2008 was £8,100,000. The cost of sales for 2007 was £55,000,000.

For 2008 Creditor days = $\dfrac{£8,100,000}{£55,000,000}$ x 356 = 54 days

For 2007 Creditor days = $\dfrac{£7,000,000}{£50,000,000}$ x 365 = 51 days

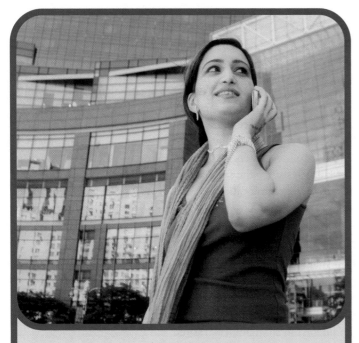

Question 3.

Najia Khan works for a merchant bank. In 2008 she received a £50,000 performance-related bonus. She already has a large share portfolio and decided to invest the bonus in a mining company. The prices of natural resources such as oil, minerals and metals had been climbing rapidly in recent years but she felt there was further to go. Najia identified three companies which she felt might be suitable for investment. Some financial information for the three companies is shown in Table 6.

Table 6: Financial information for three mining companies

	Alum Resources	GTR plc	Aztec Mining
Dividends paid	£27.6m	£12.8m	£143.2m
Number of shares	400m	30m	600m
Share price	300p	1334p	1327p

(a) Calculate the: (i) dividend per share; (ii) dividend yield; for the three mining companies.
(b) Which company should Najia invest in? Explain your answer.
(c) Do you think there is sufficient information in the case upon which to make such a decision? Explain your answer.

For Hudsons, the creditors' payment period has increased slightly from 51 to 54 days. This is to their advantage because they have been able to delay paying bills for slightly longer. However, Hudsons would have to be careful not to damage relations with suppliers by delaying the payment of bills for too long.

Ideally, businesses would want to operate in a situation where the creditors payment period is higher than the debt collection period. This would improve cash flow because it would be receiving cash from customers before having to pay it to suppliers. In this case Hudsons is in a very favourable position. Its creditors' payment period is far higher than its debt collection period in both years. To improve the ratio, the creditors' payment period can be increased by negotiating a longer trade credit period with suppliers.

Debtor days (debt collection period) This ratio measures the efficiency of a business's credit control system. The DEBTOR DAYS or DEBT COLLECTION PERIOD is the average number of days it takes to collect debts from customers. It can be calculated using the formula:

$$\text{Debt collection period} = \frac{\text{Debtors}}{\text{Turnover}} \times 365$$

According to the balance sheet the value of debtors for Hudsons in 2008 was £500,000. Turnover was £70,000,000.

For 2008 Debt collection period = $\dfrac{£500,000}{£70,000,000}$ x 365 = 2.6 days

For 2007 Debt collection period = $\dfrac{£400,000}{£63,000,000}$ x 365 = 2.3 days

Businesses often vary the amount of time they give customers to pay for products they have bought on credit. They keep a list of **aged debtors**, showing how much is owed and over what period. Credit periods may be 30, 60, 90 or even 120 days. Businesses prefer a short debt collection period because their cash flow will be improved. Retailers will have a very low debt collection period, perhaps just a few days. This is because most of their sales are for cash. This appears to be the case for Hudsons. Although the debt collection period has risen from 2.3 days to 2.6 days over the two years, there is unlikely to be a problem. Hudsons' sales will be for cash and the debtors value on the balance sheet is likely to be for prepayments not customer debts. Improving turnover relative to debtors will improve the ratio. However, businesses often try to improve this ratio by reducing debtors relative to turnover using credit control.

Gearing ratios

GEARING RATIOS show the long-term financial position of the

business. They can be used to show the relationship between loans, on which interest is paid, and shareholders' funds, on which dividends might be paid. Creditors are likely to be concerned about a firm's gearing. Loans, for example, have interest charges which must be paid. Dividends do not have to be paid to ordinary shareholders. As a business becomes more highly geared (loans are high relative to share capital) it is considered more risky by creditors. The owners of a business might prefer to raise extra funds by borrowing rather than from shareholders, so they retain control of the business. Gearing ratios can also show the relationship between fixed interest bearing debt and the long-term capital of a business.

Gearing ratios can be used to analyse the capital structure of a business. They compare the amount of capital raised from ordinary shareholders with that raised in loans and, in some cases, from preference shareholders and debentures. This is important because the interest on loans and dividends for preference shareholders are fixed commitments, whereas the dividends for ordinary shareholders are not. Gearing ratios can assess whether or not a business is burdened by its loans. This is because highly geared companies must still pay their interest even when trading becomes difficult.

There are several different versions of the gearing ratio. One widely used relates the total long-term loans and other fixed cost capital to long-term capital employed. The formula is:

$$\text{Gearing ratio} = \frac{\text{Fixed cost capital}}{\text{Long-term capital}} \times 100$$

Fixed cost capital includes long-term loans from banks, certain preference shares and debentures. Long-term capital includes shareholders' funds, any reserves and long-term loans. For Hudsons in 2007 the fixed cost or interest/dividend bearing debt, according to the balance sheet, is loans of £8,000,000 (creditors: amounts falling due after one year). The value of shareholders' funds, including reserves, was £17,400,000.

$$\text{For 2008 Gearing ratio} = \frac{£8,000,000}{£17,400,000 + £8,000,000} \times 100 = 31.5\%$$

$$\text{For 2007 Gearing ratio} = \frac{£6,500,000}{£16,300,000 + £6,500,000} \times 100 = 28.5\%$$

If the gearing ratio is less than 50 per cent the company is said to be low geared. This means that the majority of the capital is provided by the owners. If the ratio is greater than 50 per cent the company is high geared. This means that a much higher proportion of total capital is borrowed. With a gearing ratio of around 30 per cent in both years, Hudsons is low geared. Although gearing rose slightly over the two years, the increase is not significant.

Another version of the gearing ratio looks at the relationship between borrowing and equity. In this context borrowing is

defined as long-term loans. For Hudsons in 2007 it was the creditors: amounts falling due after one year of £8,000,000. Equity is defined as ordinary share capital plus reserves which for Hudsons in 2008 was £17,400,000. The ratio is calculated using the formula:

$$\text{Gearing ratio} = \frac{\text{Borrowing}}{\text{Equity}} \times 100$$

$$\text{For 2008 Gearing ratio} = \frac{£8,000,000}{£17,400,000} \times 100 = 46.0\%$$

When this definition of gearing is used, a ratio that is greater than 100 per cent means that debt is greater than equity. In most industries, this would be regarded as high geared and could prove to be an unacceptable risk for potential lenders. This is because, if there was a downturn in trading, a company might struggle to meet interest payments. However, this is not the case for Hudsons since the ratio is below 100 per cent. A business can improve its gearing ratio by reducing its long-term borrowing relative to its capital.

Shareholders' ratios

The owners of limited companies will take an interest in ratios which help measure the return on their shareholding. Such ratios focus on factors such as the earnings and dividends from shares in relation to their price. Potential investors will also show an interest in shareholders' ratios.

SHAREHOLDERS' RATIOS provide information to help investors to make decisions about buying or selling shares. They are often used to analyse the performance of public limited companies. However, they can also be helpful to the owners of private limited companies.

Dividend per share The dividend per share is the ratio that shows how much money ordinary shareholders receive per share.

$$\text{Dividend per share} = \frac{\text{Dividend (ordinary shares)}}{\text{Number of shares}}$$

For Hudsons the dividend paid to shareholders in 2008 was £900,000. This is shown in the profit and loss account. The number of shares issued by Hudsons in 2008 is shown as additional information and was 40,000,000.

$$\text{For 2008 Dividend per share} = \frac{£900,000}{40,000,000} = 2.25\text{p per share}$$

$$\text{For 2007 Dividend per share} = \frac{£700,000}{40,000,000} = 1.75\text{p per share}$$

The dividend per share paid to Hudsons' shareholders increased from 1.75p to 2.25p over the two years. This is quite a significant improvement. However, to determine whether or not this is satisfactory the dividend per share must be compared with the share price. This involves calculating the dividend yield.

Dividend yield The dividend yield is the dividend per share expressed as a percentage of the current share price.

$$\text{Dividend yield} = \frac{\text{Dividend per share}}{\text{Share price}} \times 100$$

For Hudsons the share price is shown in Table 2. On 31.7.07 it was 135p. The dividend per share was calculated above and was 2.25p in 2008.

$$\text{For 2008 Dividend yield} = \frac{2.25p}{135p} \times 100 = 1.7\%$$

$$\text{For 2007 Dividend yield} = \frac{1.75p}{94p} \times 100 = 1.9\%$$

Over the two years the dividend yield has fallen for Hudsons, even though the dividend per share rose significantly. The reason for this is that the share price also rose sharply. Whether a dividend yield of 1.7 per cent is adequate depends on expectations and what might be earned in other companies and other forms of investment. However, it must be remembered that dividends are not the only return on shares. Investors may make a capital gain if the shares are sold for a higher price than they were bought.

KEY TERMS

Acid test ratio – similar to the current ratio but excludes stocks from current assets. Sometimes called the quick ratio.

Asset turnover – a measure of the productivity of assets.

Creditor days or credit payment period – the average number of days it takes to pay short-term debts.

Current ratio – assesses the firm's liquidity by dividing current liabilities into current assets.

Debtor days or debt collection period – the number of days it takes to collect the average debt.

Dividend yield – the amount received by the shareholder as a percentage of the share price.

Financial efficiency, activity or asset utilisation ratios – measure how effectively a business employs its resources.

Gearing ratios – explore the capital structure of a business by comparing the proportions of capital raised by debt and equity.

Liquidity ratios – illustrate the solvency of a business.

Profitability or performance ratios – illustrate the relative profitability of a business.

Ratio analysis – a numerical approach to investigating accounts by comparing two related figures.

Return on capital employed – the profit of a business as a percentage of the total amount of money used to generate it.

Shareholders' ratios – provide information to help investors to make decisions about buying or selling shares.

Stock turnover – the number of times in a trading year a firm sells the value of its stocks.

KNOWLEDGE

1. Briefly describe the steps involved in the investigation process when analysing a set of accounts.
2. What is the difference between profitability and financial efficiency ratios?
3. What is the difference between liquidity ratios and gearing ratios?
4. A business has a current ratio of 6.8:1. Comment on this.
5. How do gross and net profit margins differ?
6. What do stock turnover and debt collection period measure?
7. Explain why it is preferable for a business to have a high creditor days ratio.
8. Describe the difference between the current ratio and the acid test ratio.
9. What is meant by a high geared company?
10. How is the dividend yield calculated?

Case Study: *easyJet*

easyJet is a popular low cost airline. It is based in London Luton Airport and provides cheap 'no-frills' flights to a wide range of European destinations. Since the company was launched by Sir Stelios Haji-Ioannou in 1995 it has grown from strength to strength. Some of the key business highlights for 2006 were as follows:

- Record profit before tax of £129 million, up 56 per cent from £83 million in 2005.
- Passenger numbers rose by 11.5 per cent to 33 million.
- Passenger revenues increased by 5.9 per cent or £2.13 per seat, driven by strong summer trading.
- Ancillary revenues improved significantly in all areas, rising by 34 per cent or £0.86 per seat.
- Unit costs excluding fuel fell by 1.5 per cent or £0.42 per seat from £28.78 to £28.36.
- Unit fuel costs increased by 33 per cent or £2.48 per seat.
- 58 new routes and 11 new destinations were launched, expanding the network to 262 routes and 74 airports in 21 countries.
- The fleet grew to 122 aircraft with an average age of 2.2 years, making it one of the most modern and environmentally friendly fleets in Europe.
- The balance sheet remains strong with cash of £861 million and gearing at 31 per cent.

Table 7 shows some financial information for easyJet extracted from the income statement and balance sheet in 2006.

Table 7: Financial information for easyJet – 2006

	2006 £m	2005 £m
Revenue	1,619.70	1,341.40
Profit (EBIT)	117.8	66.2
Capital employed*	1,614.60	1,215.30
Net assets	982.9	863.4
Current assets	1,087.20	890.9
Current liabilities	509	414.5

* Long-term capital employed (equity + non-current liabilities)
Source: adapted from easyJet, *Annual Report and Accounts*, 2006.

(a) Explain how ratio analysis can be used to interpret accounts. (4 marks)
(b) According to the key business highlights, gearing for easyJet was 31 per cent in 2006. Explain what this means. (6 marks)
(c) For 2005 and 2006, calculate: (i) net profit margin; (ii) ROCE; (iii) current ratio; (iv) asset turnover; for easyJet. (16 marks)
(d) To what extent do the results in (c) support the view that easyJet has 'grown from strength to strength'? (14 marks)

The value of ratio analysis

Ratio analysis is used by people such as business owners, managers, financial analysts and the media to help evaluate the performance of businesses. It is a tried and trusted approach to financial analysis and has a number of distinct advantages.

Simplicity Ratios are easy to calculate. They are generally one number divided by another, using figures that can be taken directly from the accounts (or notes to the accounts). Most ratios have a consistent formula and only a few (such as gearing) are subject to variation in definition by different users. This simplicity makes ratios easy to understand. For example, a net profit margin of 7 per cent is easily recognisable as being better than one of 4 per cent.

Speed Ratio analysis can be carried out very quickly. Once the necessary information has been gathered from annual reports the financial situation of a company can be analysed very quickly indeed. Most companies make their annual reports available on the Internet and other important information, such as share prices, can also be accessed instantly online.

Comparisons Ratios are ideal for making comparisons between companies, especially those in the same industry that operate under the same environmental conditions. They may be companies of a different size and shape but ratio analysis can be used to look at them in the same light. Interfirm comparisons, comparisons over time and interfirm comparisons over time can all be made using ratio analysis. A business might also use ratios to make internal comparisons. For example, it could compare the net profit margins for different products or the ROCE in different divisions.

Decision making Ratio analysis may be of use to decision makers in businesses. This is because ratio analysis can help to identify strengths and weaknesses in the organisation. For example, if a business discovers that its gross profit margins are very high but net margins are very low, the manager may decide to undertake a cost minimisation strategy.

Limitations to ratio analysis

Unfortunately ratio analysis is not without its problems, consequently it must be used with caution. Some of the key limitations are outlined below.

The basis for comparison A great deal of care must be taken when making comparisons using ratios. It is very important to compare 'like with like'.

- **Comparisons over time** Care must be taken when comparing ratios from the same company over time. Many companies remain broadly in the same industrial sector over time. But others can diversify and change very rapidly. Equally, some companies remain the same size over time. Others grow rapidly or shrink quickly. Such factors can affect the way in which ratios can be used as a measure of performance. The measures of performance of a small company which starts off in the defence sector and grows rapidly to become a leading telecommunications equipment manufacturer will change over time. The value of a particular ratio that is appropriate for the company will therefore change. This must be taken into account when comparing ratios.

- **Interfirm comparisons** Caution must also be used when comparing ratios between companies at a point in time. Comparing the ratios of two companies which make broadly the same products is likely to say something about their relative performance. But comparing the ratios of a supermarket chain with a cement manufacturer is unlikely to be helpful in most cases. The two companies, for example, will have different working capital needs, different profit margins and different asset turnover ratios. Even companies operating in the same industry can have 'subtle' differences. An example is shown in Figure 1.

Figure 1: Comparing 'like with like'

Tesco and Sainsbury are supermarket chains. However, Tesco is selling more and more non-food products such as electrical goods, clothing and kitchen equipment. This makes a direct comparison less meaningful. For example, the profit margins on non-food items might be much higher than those on groceries.

- **Other differences** Even when companies are well matched in their activities and operating circumstances, there may be other differences between them which must be observed. For example, two similar companies may use different accounting techniques. They may use different methods to calculate depreciation or employ different stock valuation methods. If the same accounting conventions have not been used comparisons may be misleading. Companies can also have different year-ends. For example, two companies publishing their accounts for 2008 could be presenting financial information in two quite different time periods. This would happen if one company ended its financial year on 31 December and the other on 31 July. In this case only six months of the year would be truly comparable.

Limitations of the balance sheet Because the balance sheet is a 'snapshot' of the business at the end of the financial year, it might not be representative of the business's circumstances through the whole of the year. If, for example, a business experiences its peak trading activity in the summer, and it has its year-end at a time when trade is slow, in the New Year, figures for stock and debtors will be unrepresentative.

Qualitative information is ignored Ratios only use quantitative information. However, some important qualitative factors may affect the performance of a business. Such factors may be ignored by ratio analysis. For example, in the service industry the quality of customer service may be an important performance indicator. Ratio analysis cannot easily embrace such information.

The quality of final accounts Ratios are based on financial accounts such as the balance sheet, profit and loss accounts and income statements. Consequently ratio analysis is only useful if the accounts are accurate. One factor that can affect the quality of accounting information is the change in monetary values caused by inflation. Rising prices can distort comparisons made between different time periods. For example, in times of high inflation, asset values and revenue might rise rapidly in monetary terms. However, when the figures are adjusted for inflation, there might be no increase in **real terms**. There is also the possibility that the accounts have been **window dressed**. This is discussed next.

Window dressing

Accounts must represent a 'true and fair record' of the financial affairs of a business. Legislation and financial reporting standards place limits on the different ways in which a business can present accounts. These limits are designed to prevent fraud and misrepresentation in the compilation and presentation of accounts. However, businesses can manipulate their accounts legally to present different financial pictures. This is known as WINDOW DRESSING. Businesses may want to window dress

their accounts for a variety of reasons.

- Managers of companies might want to put as good a financial picture forward as possible for shareholders and potential shareholders. Good financial results will attract praise and perhaps rewards. They might also prevent criticism from shareholders and the financial press.
- If a business wants to raise new capital from investors, then it will want its financial accounts to look as good as possible.
- Where a business has experienced severe difficulties during the accounting period, it may decide to take action which will make the financial position look even worse now but which will improve figures in the future.
- Making the financial picture look worse is often a way of lowering the amount of tax that is paid.
- If the owners of a business want to sell it, the better the financial position shown on the accounts, the higher the price they are likely to get. Equally, a company which wants to avoid being taken over can discourage predators by showing flattering accounts because these accounts would make the cost of buying the company higher.

There is a number of ways of window dressing accounts explained in this unit.

Manipulating sales Increasing the level of revenue recorded on the profit and loss account or income statement will increase profit in that accounting period. This can be done in a number of ways. Some businesses, for example, are able to choose when they record a sale onto the profit and loss account. For example, a software company can choose under UK accountancy practice either to record a software licence deal when a contract has been signed or when the revenue has been received. Choosing to record a deal today will boost profits at the expense of profits in future accounting periods.

Another practice relates to stocks. At the financial year end, a business may make a special effort to dispatch all outstanding orders. This can boost sales in that accounting period and so flatter the profit and loss account figures. It also reduces stocks of finished goods. This can flatter the balance sheet figures, for example, by increasing the stock turnover ratio.

Costs and depreciation Profits on the profit and loss account or income statement can be increased if costs are reduced. One way of reducing costs is to reduce the cost of depreciation. Depreciation of assets like buildings, vehicles or machinery takes place over a number of years. Take a building initially valued at £1 million. If the business depreciates the building over 10 years using the straight-line method, then each year the cost of depreciation will be £100,000 (£1 million ÷ 10). This is a cost on the profit and loss account. What if the business were to depreciate the building over 25 years instead? Then the annual depreciation charge would be £40,000 (£1 million ÷ 25 years). For the first ten years, profits on the profit and loss account would then be £60,000 (£100,000 - £40 000) a year higher with depreciation over 25 years compared to a depreciation over a ten

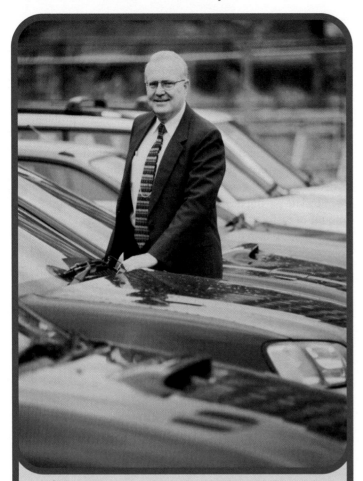

Question 1.

Pennell's plc is a medium sized car dealership in East Anglia. This year has been very disappointing for sales. Despite record sales nationally, Pennell's sales have actually declined. Senior management were worried about the impact this would have on the share price and on shareholder reaction. They therefore agreed on a strategy to boost sales in the all important last financial month of the year to 30 April.

All car sales staff were offered twice the bonus they normally received for selling cars during April so long as the customer took delivery of the car and paid for it in full by the last day of the financial year. As the end of the month approached, sales staff were having to be very persuasive to get some customers who had chosen a car and placed a deposit on it to take delivery of the car on the 30 April rather than in early May.

At the same time, employees were told to cut all unnecessary expenses. There had been a ban in place since mid-February on replacing existing staff who left. Stocks of parts were also run down as far as possible. All this led to some operating difficulties. Waiting times for a service lengthened from around 3 days to 4 days, while some customers found that their repairs took a day longer because parts, normally kept on site, had to be ordered specially from suppliers.

(a) Explain how the managers at Pennell's manipulated (a) sales and (b) costs to window dress the profits of the company at its year end.

(b) Discuss what impact this window dressing might have had on revenues, costs and profits for the next financial year.

year period. However, for years 11-25, profits would be £40 000 lower. This is because if it has been depreciated over ten years, there is no cost for years 11-25. But if it has been depreciated over 25 years, £40 000 a year is still being accounted for as a cost on the profit and loss account.

Depreciation also has an effect on the balance sheet. In the above example, depreciating the building over 25 years rather than 10 years means that profit on the profit and loss account would be higher in the first ten years because the annual depreciation charge, an expense, would be lower. In later years profit will be lower. On the balance sheet, the reverse is true. Fixed assets will tend to be higher if the asset is depreciated over 25 years rather than 10 years. For example, if the £1 million building is depreciated over 25 years, then it has a fixed asset value of £600 000 at end of year 10 (£1 million x 15 ÷ 25). But if it is depreciated over 10 years, it has £0 value at the end of year 10.

A business can also 'write off' its R&D (research and development) costs. Accounting standards allow R&D costs to be written off immediately. Or they can be 'capitalised', treated as an intangible asset and then amortised (i.e. depreciated) over a number of years. What if development costs are depreciated immediately instead of over a number of years? This will reduce profits this year on the profit and loss account but increase them in future years. For example, assume that a company has spent £10 million on R&D this year. It could write these off immediately, increasing costs on the profit and loss account by £10 million and so reducing profit by £10 million. Or it could capitalise the R&D and depreciate it over, say, 10 years. Then each year, including the first year, there would be a cost on the profit and loss account of £1 million (£10 million ÷ 10 years) reducing profit each year by £1 million.

A business must be consistent in the method of depreciation it uses. Businesses don't frequently change their method of depreciation. Indeed, accounting standards only allow a business to change methods if there are 'justifiable reasons'. However, businesses occasionally do change their method of depreciation, for instance by lengthening the period of depreciation or changing the way in which R&D is amortised. This can provide a boost to profits over a number of years and is helpful to a company which is perhaps experiencing low profits and is being criticised by shareholders.

Extraordinary items Businesses are allowed to classify some costs as **extraordinary items**. These are 'one-off' costs such as the costs associated with shutting down a factory or writing off the goodwill from the acquisition of a company. Writing off assets in this way might seem to put a business in a bad light with investors or shareholders. But some companies choose deliberately to write off assets in an accounting period when the business has done badly anyway. Getting all the 'bad news' out at once is better than having continued poor performance over a number of years.

For example, take a business which made some disastrous acquisitions in the past. The companies it bought have performed very poorly. It also paid more for the companies taken over than the value of their tangible assets. Hence, there is now, say, a £100 million entry on the balance sheet as goodwill, an intangible asset. This year, the company is due to announce a £50 million loss. So its directors decide to get all the bad news out at once by writing off the £100 million in goodwill. The loss this year then becomes £150 million. But in future years, reported profits will be higher because there will be no depreciation on the goodwill.

Writing off assets like this also improves future rates of return on capital. In the example, the company now has higher future profits from writing off the £100 million. But in future it will also have £100 million less in assets. Since the rate of return on capital is profit divided by assets, the rate of return will inevitably increase.

Bad debts A business may choose to write off some of its bad debts. This has exactly the same effect as writing off fixed assets. In the short term, profit is reduced by the value of the bad debts. But future profit figures are likely to be improved. This is because most of those bad debts would have had to be written off anyway. A few of the debts may, however, suddenly be paid. This would then be counted as part of revenue boosting profit.

Changing asset values A business can increase the value of tangible fixed assets such as land and buildings, where this is justified by property valuations. Unlike equipment, land and property can increase in value over time, rather than depreciate. A business choosing to revalue its property on the balance sheet would boost the value of its assets, possibly making the balance sheet look stronger. Note that a company which chooses to do this must make an equal and opposite adjustment under capital on the balance sheet under the revaluation reserve.

Boosting liquidity A business may be able to boost liquidity on its balance sheet. Some businesses have too little liquidity, giving rise to cash flow problems as well as working capital problems. One way to boost liquidity is to use sale and leaseback with property. By selling property to a property company and arranging for that property to be leased back to it, a business can release cash tied up in a fixed asset. In the first year, the cash benefit to the business is the value of the property sale minus the lease payment. Sale and leaseback therefore is a way of increasing liquid assets through the sale of fixed assets. If the cash generated from a sale and leaseback scheme is used to pay off long-term loans, the business will also be able to reduce its gearing. Gearing is loans ÷ equity expressed as a percentage. If equity was £20 million and loans £30 million, then gearing

would be high at 150 per cent (100% x £30 million ÷ £20 million). If a sale and leaseback deal generated £8 million, loans could be reduced to £22 million (£30 million - £8 million) and gearing would fall to 110 per cent (100% x £22 million ÷ £20 million).

Current assets and liabilities Some businesses have problems with aspects of their current assets and liabilities. The year end can be a time when the business makes a special effort to improve its performance. For example, a business can improve its debtors' data by making a special effort to collect in money owed by late paying debtors. This is likely to increase the amount of cash in the business or reduce short-term borrowings on overdraft. It also improves debtors' ratios. It can attempt to improve its creditors' position by repaying as much as possible, for example by repaying early. It could also get discounts for doing this, which might help show its accounts in a better light. As explained above, a business could try to hide a problem of excessive stock levels by not ordering new stock towards the year end and by making a special effort to dispatch finished stock to customers.

KEYTERMS

Window dressing – the legal manipulation of accounts by a business to present a financial picture which is to its benefit.

KNOWLEDGE

1. Explain three advantages of using ratio analysis.
2. When making comparisons with ratios it is important to compare 'like with like'. Explain what this means.
3. Why does ratio analysis ignore qualitative information?
4. Explain why a company may want to window dress its accounts.
5. How can a company manipulate (a) its sales and (b) its costs to flatter its recorded profits on the profit and loss account?
6. How might (a) extraordinary items and (b) exceptional items be used to window dress accounts?
7. How might bad debts be manipulated to window dress accounts?
8. How might liquidity be boosted on the accounts?
9. How might a company manipulate its current assets and liabilities to window dress its accounts?

Case Study: *CNV Plastics*

CNV Plastics is a large private limited company based in Leeds. It is an engineering business which designs and produces pvc piping, tanks, scrubbers and hoods. In 2008 the business began to struggle financially. It was undercapitalised and needed to raise £10 million to boost working capital and provide funding for product development. A bank loan was being considered by the directors. Unfortunately the 2007 accounts did not look good. Some of the ratios used to analyse the company's performance suggested that most banks would be reluctant to lend money to the company. However, at an emergency board meeting the financial director suggested that the performance of the company could be enhanced by 'window dressing' the accounts. The managing director was dubious about this. However, the finance director reassured all board members that 'window dressing' was legal and could be used to show the company in a better light. She suggested two actions.

- The method used to calculate depreciation could be changed. This would increase profit in 2008 by £2 million from £6 million to £8 million.
- Selling its factory and leasing it back. This would boost liquidity by injecting some cash into the company. The financial director also explained that this would also help to boost working capital.

The board of directors eventually agreed with the finance director and the suggested actions were taken. Table 1 shows some financial ratios for CNV Plastics after the accounts had been window dressed in 2008.

Table 1: Financial ratios for CNV Plastics

	2008	2007
Net profit margin	5.40%	2.40%
ROCE	4.60%	1.90%
Current ratio	1.6	1.1
Gearing	42%	41%

(a) What would be the value to CNV of using ratio analysis? (8 marks)

(b) What is meant by 'window dressing' the accounts? (4 marks)

(c) What might be the danger of 'window dressing' to CNV Plastics? (6 marks)

(d) (i) Explain the effect on the net profit margin and the ROCE of changing the method used to calculate depreciation. (8 marks)

(ii) Explain the effect on the current ratio and gearing ratio of selling the factory and leasing it back. (8 marks)

(e) What might be the long-term effects on CNV Plastics of selling the factory and leasing it back? (8 marks)

What are financial strategies?

Most businesses have financial objectives such as increasing the return on capital employed, generating cash flow or increasing shareholder value. In order to meet these objectives a business is likely to employ FINANCIAL STRATEGIES. A financial strategy is a detailed action plan designed to achieve a specific financial objective. For example, in order to increase the return on capital employed a business might try to bring down its costs. It might do this by introducing **cost centres** to make individual parts of the business more accountable. Examples of financial strategies include:

* raising finance;
* implementing cost or profit centres;
* cost minimisation;
* allocating capital expenditure.

Financial strategies may also be linked to other functions such as production, research and development and marketing. For example, there may be a need for a company to spend more on research and development to keep up with competition. If the company decides to go ahead with such an investment there will be financial implications. For example, there may be a need to raise more long-term finance.

Raising finance

The need for finance is a vital issue for businesses. There are few businesses that can self-finance all of their activities. Businesses need money to set up and get established, but the need for finance continues indefinitely. Raising finance is often a **strategic** issue. This is because it affects many aspects of the business and can have an impact over the long-term. Some of the key financing issues are outlined below.

Flotation Many businesses decide to 'go public' as a means of raising finance. This means changing the legal structure of the business from a private limited company to a public limited company. Such a move will have a huge impact on the organisation. There will be new owners of the company, legal issues to deal with and the prospect of a change in culture. However, operating as a plc means that much more finance can be raised and the profile of the business will be raised. In 2007, for example, CVS, the veterinary practice group which operates 128 small practices, floated on AIM. It raised £92.7 million after placing 45.2 million shares at 205p each. Much of this was to be used to acquire other businesses, to help the company grow.

Financial restructuring Sometimes established companies have to restructure their finances. This often means raising new finance and changing the emphasis of funding methods. The need for financial restructuring often arises when a company gets into difficulties. For example, a company might be

pressured into handing over some of its equity in exchange for debt. An example of a company restructuring its finances is outlined in Figure 1.

The problems of being under capitalised Some businesses are UNDER CAPITALISED. This means that the owners have not provided enough funds to support its activities. In order for the business to survive and flourish such companies have to find new funding. Businesses must employ appropriate financial strategies to avoid being under capitalised.

* The current owners might provide more capital. If the shareholders in a company can inject more capital they will retain ownership and enjoy all the future profits made by the company. An approach might be to use a **rights issue**. This involves selling more shares to existing shareholders at a discount. However, the current owners may be unable or unwilling to do so. Consequently this option may have limited scope.

Figure 1: Financial restructuring at Biofuels Corporation

A slump in the price of crop-based diesel and technical difficulties with its processing plant forced a fledgling biofuels company into a drastic financial restructuring. Shares slumped 40% to 7.25p as the board of Biofuels Corporation agreed to a deal under which it will hand over 94% of the company to Barclays Bank in return for retiring £40m of the company's £100m debts.

Shareholders were called to an extraordinary general meeting where they were asked to vote on the decision to dilute their equity to a tiny stake. They were warned that the company faces insolvency if the restructuring is not agreed. 'The board has undertaken a thorough review of the group's options, including seeking purchasers of the company, but the board has concluded that, given the existing financial structure, neither a trade sale nor an equity fundraising is possible,' said chairman Mike Buzzacott. Biofuels blamed their problems on US government incentives which have boosted production in America and forced down the global price of biodiesel since last September.

Source: adapted from *The Guardian* 26.6.2007.

- A business can raise more capital by inviting new owners to join and make a contribution. A limited company may decide to issue more shares. Another option is to 'go public' as explained above. Alternatively, a business might seek specialist investors such as business angels or venture capitalists.
- A business can take out more long-term funding. This might involve taking out a 25 year mortgage for example. One advantage of this is that such funding might be cheaper. Taking out longer-term funding gives the business more time to repay the amount borrowed and reduces uncertainty as the business is trying to develop.

Implementing cost and profit centres

One way in which a business might achieve its financial objectives is to implement cost or profit centres. This will help to control costs and improve accountability.

Cost centres A COST CENTRE is an individual part of the business where costs are incurred and can be recorded easily. For example, Canning Insurance has four types of insurance which it offers customers – Car Insurance, House Insurance, Holiday Insurance and Life Assurance. Each of these operates as a cost centre. The total costs incurred by the business during 2008 were £5.6 million. The costs incurred by each cost centre were:

- Car Insurance £1.2 million;
- House Insurance £2.0 million;
- Holiday Insurance £0.9 million;
- Life Assurance £1.5 million.

Canning Insurance might conclude from this information that the Holiday Insurance has the best control over its costs. However, other factors will have to be taken into account, such as the size of each department.

How can a business be divided into cost centres? There is a number of ways and the method chosen by a business will depend on its circumstances.

- **By product.** Canning Insurance, in the example above, uses this method. It means that costs are measured for each of the products of a business. So each product is a cost centre.
- **By department.** Many businesses are divided into departments such as marketing, production, accounts and human resources. Each department can be treated as a cost centre.
- **By geographical location.** A business which has operations all over the country or world might use this method. For example, a supermarket chain with stores all over the UK may treat each one as a cost centre.
- **By employee.** In some businesses it is appropriate to measure the costs incurred by individual members of staff. For example, a salesperson could be treated as a cost centre and examples of costs might be wages, National Insurance contributions, motor expenses, overnight accommodation expenses and entertaining expenses.

- **By machine.** It is possible to use a machine, such as a vehicle, as a cost centre by recording all its costs. These might be leasing charges and payments for fuel, motor tax, insurance and maintenance.

Profit centres A PROFIT CENTRE is very similar to a cost centre. The difference is that in addition to recording costs at each centre, revenues are also recorded. This allows a business to calculate how much profit each centre makes. The use of profit centres makes it much easier to compare the performance of each different part of the business. For example, a supermarket chain can identify the most profitable stores in the country by comparing the profit each centre makes. Profit centres can only be used effectively if an activity generates revenue. For example, since a research and development department does not generate any revenue directly, it is unlikely to be used as a profit centre. A business can be divided into profit centres in the same way as it would be into cost centres, provided the centre generates revenue.

Advantages of using cost and profit centres

There are certain advantages to a business of using cost and profit centres.

Improving accountability Although it is important to measure the performance of the whole business, it is also helpful to monitor the progress of different products, regions or departments, for example. Cost and profit centres can be used to hold individual parts of the business accountable. Without cost and profit centres an inefficient department might not be identified and held accountable for its poor performance.

Helping decision making To make decisions about different parts of the business managers need financial information about those different parts. Cost and profit centres help provide this information. For example, if managers are trying to decide which product to discontinue, to make way for a new product, it can use information gathered from profit centres. Managers are likely to stop supplying the least profitable product.

Improving motivation The performance of cost and profit centres is likely to depend on the quality of work done by the people employed in them. It is possible to motivate staff in centres by offering them incentives to achieve goals or targets. For example, a clothes chain might give bonus payments to staff working in stores if they achieve monthly profit targets. This should help to motivate them to produce their best work. It is also

Question 2.

Frank O'Connell runs a small independent chain of bakeries in Northern Ireland. He is concerned about the problems the company is having with the bank and overdraft facility. The account is constantly in excess of its limit and so cheques are being returned. After a discussion with his bank manager it became apparent that the financial position of the business was unclear and the property valuation was not up to date. After a closer analysis of the situation, and a property revaluation, the entire finance was restructured onto a loan with an agreement that the interest rate would be reviewed after 12 months. The existing commercial mortgage and overdraft facility were converted to a new mortgage over a longer term. This released cash back into the business and reduced the monthly repayments. As this was a restructure of the business finance, an agreement was reached that the interest rate would be reviewed if the trading was better. If the bank account remained in credit then the interest rate would be reduced.

(a) Using this case as an example, explain what is meant by financial restructuring.
(b) When is a company likely to use restructuring as a financial strategy?

common to delegate control of cost and profit centres to middle managers. Managers may be better motivated if they are offered promotion, for example, when targets are met.

Tracing problems If part of the business is suffering it may be possible to trace a specific problem if cost or profit centres are used. For example, if one of the stores in a supermarket chain is suffering from a high labour turnover, its recruitment and training costs will be high. Labour productivity may also be lower. This will restrict the performance of the store and will show up as higher costs if it were operating as a cost centre. This may not come to light so easily if the costs of the entire business were recorded together.

Problems of cost and profit centres

Dividing a business into cost and profit centres might also lead to problems.

Conflict If a business is divided into individual parts, conflict between those parts may arise. Staff are likely to be more interested in the performance of their own centre than the performance of the whole business. This might lead to competition for resources and a reluctance to share valuable information. The performance of the whole business might suffer as a result.

Cost allocation Not all costs are incurred directly by a particular cost centre. Some costs are incurred by the business as a whole. For example, a chain store might spend £2 million on a national advertising campaign. How should this cost be allocated between cost or profit centres? One way might be to divide the cost equally between all the stores. But this might not be fair because a very large store may get more benefit from the campaign than a smaller store. This suggests that the larger store should bear more of the campaign's cost. In practice, the allocation of such costs between centres is difficult. When costs are not allocated fairly the performance of a particular centre can be distorted.

Factors outside the business It is common for the performance of a business to be affected by external factors such as the state of the economy, competition, the weather or pressure groups. However, it is possible that the performance of each individual cost or profit centre is not affected to the same extent. For example, a UK fast-food chain might experience intense competition in the south-west, therefore the performance of centres operating in that region will be hit. This might have a demotivating effect on staff in those centres.

Wasting resources Operating cost or profit centres may result in the business as a whole wasting money. If all centres are responsible for performing the same tasks there may be some duplication of resources. For example, it may be more cost effective if the purchasing of resources for each department in a business is done centrally. Resources may also be wasted gathering financial information from each centre. It is possible that the costs of operating cost or profit centres may not be outweighed by the benefits.

Staff pressure Some of the staff given the responsibility of running a cost or profit centre may not have the skills to do so. This might create pressure and demotivate staff. This is more likely to happen if responsibility is delegated too far down the hierarchical structure.

Cost minimisation

Many financial objectives can be aided by minimising business costs. For example, if costs are reduced, profits will be higher and shareholder value will increase. Many businesses are likely to use cost minimisation as part of their financial strategy. Some examples of approaches that might be used to reduce costs are outlined below.

Outsourcing A business may decide to outsource a particular activity because another business can do the job at a lower cost. For example, a business may use a recruitment agency to recruit staff. Not only will costs be lower but the contractor is likely to do a better job because they are specialists.

Waste reduction and recycling Many firms are looking for ways of reducing waste in their organisations. For example, they may opt for lean production techniques that are designed specifically to reduce all types of waste. An increasing number of businesses are looking to cut costs by recycling their waste. For example, businesses might call on the services of a company like Computacenter. It offers to develop more effective environmental policies for the acquisition, operation, reuse and disposal of IT equipment. Responding to increasing electricity costs and pressures to improve the corporate environmental footprint, their service will introduce significant cost savings while reducing carbon emissions and landfill usage. It is based on a series of practical steps, starting with an energy efficiency audit of a company's current IT usage.

Sourcing new suppliers Businesses often review the performance of their suppliers. Suppliers that have grown expensive may be replaced or contracts with them renegotiated. Increasingly businesses are using eSourcing to reduce the cost of buying raw materials and components. eSourcing involves using the Internet and electronic communications in the whole purchasing process. eSourcing enables buyers and suppliers to connect and contract quickly and efficiently in order to improve the company's competitiveness.

Introducing technology A business may reduce costs by automating certain processes. For example, the introduction of robotic welders in factories has cut costs significantly. New technology is often more efficient and cost effective than labour.

Downsizing Firms may minimise costs by reducing their capacity. This might involve laying off workers or closing down unprofitable divisions in the organisation. This should result in a leaner, more competitive operation made up of profitable businesses with 'no dead horses to flog'.

There are many other ways in which a business might attempt to minimise costs. The approach chosen will depend on the circumstances of the business and what their specific aims are. For example, a business with dated machinery may opt for the introduction of new technology. However, a company with an ailing division may choose to downsize by closing the unprofitable operation.

Allocating capital expenditure

Most businesses will have to undertake capital expenditure to meet financial and other objectives. Capital expenditure is spending on assets that last more than one year. It includes spending on assets such as machinery, equipment, factories or offices. For example, a supermarket chain that wants to increase shareholder value by growing will need to invest in new stores. When allocating capital expenditure a business has to consider a number of issues.

Current needs The pattern of capital expenditure for a business will often centre on the current needs of the business. The amount of money a business has for capital expenditure is often restricted and there may be multiple demands on the limited amount of money available. Consequently a business has to look at the current needs of a business and favour those which are more urgent. For example, if a business needs to urgently upgrade its IT systems it is not likely to allocate money to a speculative product development project. Financial strategies clearly have to address the company's immediate needs.

Return on investment Inevitably, when faced with a choice between alternative investment projects a business will prefer to invest in the project with the greatest return. However, calculating the return on investment projects is notoriously problematic. This is because it is so difficult to estimate future revenues and costs. However, there is a number of different quantitative investment appraisal techniques that can be used to select the most profitable project once future costs and revenues have been estimated. These are outlined in the next unit.

Risk Investment in capital expenditure is fraught with risk. This is because the return on an investment project is not certain. It is possible for an investment project to yield a negative return and even endanger the survival of a business. For example, Leeds United football club went into liquidation twice in 2006 and 2007 after its heavy investment in new players failed to bring success on the football field.

Some businesses are likely to take a lot less risk than others when allocating capital expenditure. This may be because their management team is risk averse. However, others may be prepared to take more risks. This is because the rewards for taking risk can often be very high. For example, launching a new product is often very risky. However, if it is successful the business is likely to enjoy a lengthy stream of profits. The amount of risk involved in a particular financial strategy will depend on the managements' attitude to risk.

External factors The allocation of capital expenditure may be influenced by external factors. One very important one is competition. A business may select a particular investment project because a rival's action has forced its hand. For example, television companies often invest in certain new programmes because rival television companies have launched a new and successful series. Failure to bring out a version of the programme may result in lower viewing figures and lower advertising revenue. The economic climate is also likely to affect capital expenditure. For example, during a recession a business is likely to have a more defensive financial strategy and cut back on all but necessary capital expenditure.

The range of external factors that might affect the allocation of capital expenditure in financial strategies is wide. Other examples include interest rates, exchange rates, social and political factors, changes in consumer tastes, the availability of new technology and the availability of investment funds in capital markets.

Assessing the value of strategies

Managers will select financial strategies that they think will achieve the financial and functional objectives of the business. The financial strategies chosen will depend on the circumstances of the business, the pressure from key stakeholders and the nature of the business. Different companies will have different financial strategies. However, the financial objectives of companies quoted on the stock exchange are not likely to differ very much. Most shareholders want to see an increase in shareholder value (higher dividends and higher share prices). Each company has to decide how they can best deliver this and most opt for growth. Some examples of different financial strategies are outlined below. Many are linked strongly to corporate strategies.

- The financial strategies of many pharmaceutical companies involve heavy investment in research and development. They rely on the revenue from new drugs to generate profits in the future. They protect revenue streams by patenting new drugs and treatments

- For many businesses financial strategies are based on growth through acquisitions. Investment is channelled into the purchase of new businesses which they hope to integrate effectively and push for more economies of scale.

- Some businesses restructure their activities to meet financial objectives. They may decide to focus more on core activities for example. This might involve demerging some non-core activities. Cost minimisation strategies are likely to play an important role here.

- Companies that have limited financial resources may opt for a strategy of organic growth. This might be funded from retained earnings and less so from external sources of funds.

KEYTERMS

Cost centre – an individual part of a business where costs can be identified and recorded easily.
Financial strategies – actions taken by a business to achieve its financial objectives.
Profit centre – an individual part of the business where costs and revenue can be identified and recorded easily.
Undercapitalised – where the owners have not put enough money into a business to support all of its activities.

KNOWLEDGE

1. Why do businesses need a financial strategy?
2. What is the main purpose of a flotation?
3. When might a business need to be financially restructured?
4. Explain how it is possible to use a product as a cost centre.
5. State three other ways of choosing a cost centre.
6. Explain the difference between a cost centre and a profit centre.
7. State three ways a business may reduce costs.
8. How might the current needs of a business affect the allocation of capital expenditure?
9. Why is capital expenditure so risky?
10. Why might businesses have different financial strategies?

Case Study: *Ambercom plc*

Ambercom plc is a multinational manufacturer of fertilisers and pesticides. It operates five divisions with plants in the following locations.

- **UK** – based in Basingstoke, employs 340 staff and supplies the entire UK market.
- **US** – based in Conneticut, employs 250 staff and supplies the North American and Canadian markets.
- **India** – based in Dehli, employs 450 staff and supplies many Asian countries such as India, Pakistan, Bangladesh, Thailand and increasingly, China.
- **Germany** – based in Dortmund, employs 320 staff and supplies the European market.
- **Australia** – based in Brisbane, employs 130 staff and supplies the Australasian market.

Ambercom plc operates profit centres. This helps to monitor the performance of each division. In June 2007, the directors organised a board meeting to agree on a medium-term financial strategy for the organisation. The strategy has three elements which are outlined below.

- Close down the Australian operation. Unfortunately there has been a growing resistance to the use of fertilisers and pesticides in Australia. The number of customers in the region has fallen by 40 per cent in the last three years and there is no reason to believe that the decline is about to halt. The remaining customers in the region will be served by the Indian plant.
- Invest £100 million in a new research and development centre. The main purpose of the centre will be to develop more environmentally friendly fertilisers and pesticides.
- Raise £150 million through a rights issue. The money will be used to fund the new research and development centre and help pay for the closure of the Australian division.

Ambercom plc mission statement

Building value for our shareholders is our goal. We achieve this through sustained, controlled growth – driven by a focus on providing the very best products and solutions for the worlds' food producers. We are committed to the needs of all stakeholders and believe that the development of financial strength will help meet these needs.

Table 1 shows some financial information for Ambercom plc relating to the five profit centres.

Table 1: Ambercom's profit centres 2007

						(£ million)
	UK	**US**	**Germany**	**India**	**Australia**	**Total**
Revenue	245.9	211.8	265.9	198.7	103.8	1,026.1
Cost of sales	101.1	95.1	112.6	67.4	67.9	444.1
Gross profit	144.8	115.7	153.3	131.3	35.9	582.0
Admin costs	87.2	54.3	91.1	54.1	32.5	319.2
Distribution costs	34.9	29.8	41.4	21.0	18.9	146.0
Total overheads	122.1	84.1	132.5	75.1	51.4	465.2
Profit before tax	**22.7**	**31.6**	**20.8**	**56.0**	**-15.5**	**115.6**

(a) What do you think the main financial objective is for Ambercom plc? (4 marks)

(b) Why is Ambercom plc closing down the Australian division when the company is committed to pursuing growth? (6 marks)

(c) Explain two advantages to Ambercom plc of operating profit centres. (8 marks)

(d) (i) What is meant by a rights issue? (4 marks)
(ii) What is the purpose of the rights issue in this case? (4 marks)

(e) To what extent do you think the financial strategy outlined in this case will help to achieve Ambercom's financial objective? (10 marks)

(f) Evaluate the factors that the directors may have considered before committing the company to a £100 million investment in a new research and development centre. (14 marks)

The nature of investment

Investment refers to the purchase of capital goods. Capital goods are used in the production of other goods, directly or indirectly. For example, a building contractor who buys a cement mixer, some scaffolding, a lorry and five shovels has invested. These goods will be used directly in production. If the contractor buys a computer, a filing cabinet and a photocopier for the firm's office, this is indirect investment. Although these items will not be used in production the business would not run as efficiently without them.

Investment might also refer to expenditure by a business which is likely to yield a return in the future. For example, a business might spend £20 million on research and development into a new product or invest £10 million in a promotion campaign. In each case, money is being spent on projects now in the hope that a greater amount of money will be generated in the future as a result of that expenditure.

Types of investment

Investment can be placed into various categories.

- **Capital goods.** This includes the purchase of a whole variety of mechanical and technical equipment. Vans, lathes, computers, robots, tools, vehicles and information technology are examples.
- **Construction.** This includes spending on new buildings that are bought or constructed by the firm. Factories, shops, warehouses, workshops and offices are examples.
- **Stocks.** This is a less obvious item of investment, since it does not fit neatly into the earlier definition. However, because stocks of finished goods and work-in-progress will earn income in the future when they are sold, they are classed as investment.
- **Public sector investment.** Central and local government fund about 25 per cent of all investment in the economy. Examples of public sector investment include the building of schools, motorways, hospitals and expenditure on goods like buses, dustcarts and equipment for the civil service. The factors which influence the level of public sector investment are often very different from those which affect private sector investment. This is dealt with later in this unit.

Reasons why businesses invest

One of the main reasons why businesses invest is because they have to. Most businesses use plant, machinery, equipment, vehicles, tools and other capital goods. Without capital goods most businesses could not operate. Consequently a lot of investment may take place when a business is setting up. However, even when a business is established investment will

continue. Eventually some of the capital goods bought by a business will wear out or become obsolete. These will have to be replaced. This type of investment is called **autonomous** investment.

Most businesses will also carry out **induced** investment which is new investment. Such investment is usually undertaken to help achieve the **functional objectives** of the business. Some examples are given below.

- If the business wants to increase its market share a big investment in a national marketing campaign might be planned.
- Some businesses are committed to lengthy research and development programmes. For example, Oxford Biomedica invested £19.523 million in research and development in 2006. Such investment in research and development is very common in pharmaceutical companies like Oxford Biomedica.
- Some businesses invest in new technology to minimise costs or improve quality, for example. Investment in automation will help to reduce labour costs and improve consistency in production, for example.
- It is common for business to invest in new capacity to help the business grow organically. For example, in 2007, Royal Dutch Shell and a Saudi Arabian partner pledged to invest $7 billion in doubling the size of their refinery in Texas.
- Many business commit investment funds to the acquisition of other businesses. This helps the company to grow faster. For example, in 2006, Ultra Electronics, a defence and aerospace company, invested £7.8 million buying Polyflex Aerospace Ltd and Winfrith Safety Systems.

Investment criteria

Figure 1 shows the factors which might affect private sector investment decisions.

Motives To begin with, firms must have a reason to invest.

- All firms have to replace worn out equipment.
- To be competitive on costs, price and quality, firms may have to invest or risk losing customers to their rivals. Much investment is related to the company's functional objectives.
- The availability of new technology may persuade firms to invest. When technology becomes available, firms are often keen to use it if they can afford to.
- Firms may wish to grow, to be more profitable or to increase their market influence. Growth involves investment in more plant, equipment and other productive assets.

Return If firms have a reason to invest, they must then decide

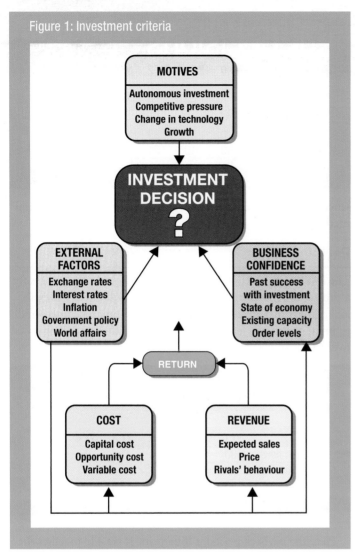

Figure 1: Investment criteria

External factors External influences can be direct or indirect. For example, high interest rates may directly affect the cost of investment. If money is borrowed the business will pay back more. This can indirectly affect confidence. Inflation could affect costs, revenue and confidence.

The factors affecting public sector investment

What factors influence investment by central government and local authorities?

- Investment in new schools, roads and hospitals, for example, will be influenced by national and local needs. As the demands of the population grow, more of these facilities will be needed.
- Political factors may also influence the quantity and type of investment. In recent years, the government has invested heavily in education and the NHS.
- The availability of government funds and the opportunity cost of investment spending. If revenue from taxes is falling, there may be fewer investment funds. If the opportunity costs of investment projects are high, then they may be cancelled. The state of the economy will be important. For example, falling unemployment in the late 1990s and early 21st century reduced government spending on unemployment benefit. This perhaps meant that extra funds were available for spending on health or education.

Assessing the risks and uncertainties of investment decisions

The decision to invest by business is the most difficult it has to make because of the risk involved. There is often a number of alternative choices. A firm buying a new fleet of cars for its sales staff has to decide which model of car will suit the company best of all. There may also be a considerable choice of projects. For example, a firm may need to choose whether investment in a new packaging machine which increases efficiency would be more profitable than a new computer system.

If all cost and revenue data upon which a decision would be based was accurate, there would not be a problem. However, revenue information in particular comes from predictions. It may be based on forecasts of future demand and conditions in the economy. Even costs, which are perhaps easier to predict, can vary.

Most investment decisions are uncertain because they are long-term decisions, where resources are committed for a period of time. Investment projects have failed both in the private sector and the public sector. For example, in the private sector, independent TV production company, the Television Corporation, had to write off £13 million on Californian subsidiary Pacifica in 2003. The company was still reeling from a failed bid to set up a Formula One version of power boating. The company had already written off £2.6 million, including £400,000 in the previous year. In the public sector, the government spent a lot of money on equipment which was used in the development of the Concorde aircraft. This also proved to

whether it is worthwhile. One influence on this is the return on the investment. The return on an investment project can be found by subtracting the cost of the project from the expected revenue. There are three major costs. Capital costs might be the cost of a new factory. Opportunity costs are the foregone alternatives the investment funds might have been used for, e.g. higher dividends to shareholders. Direct variable costs include the running costs of the project, e.g. labour or fuel costs.

Calculating the expected revenue is not easy. Expected sales are hard to predict with accuracy because many factors affect them. Market research can only predict sales to some extent. Sales can also be influenced by the price set by the business in the future and by rivals' behaviour. Both of these factors are unpredictable.

Business confidence Entrepreneurs and managers will be either optimistic or pessimistic about the future of their businesses. Confidence may be influenced by a range of factors. These include whether or not previous investment has been a success, the state of the economy, the existing level of capacity and future order levels. A pessimistic business person may be less likely to invest than an optimistic one.

be commercially unsuccessful. Concorde services were stopped in 2004.

Investment is also said to be risky because it is often funded with borrowed money. This means that the return on any investment project must also cover the cost of borrowing. Also, if the investment project fails the company may be left with a heavy debt burden and possibly without the means to repay it. The Channel Tunnel project experienced such problems in the late 1990s. Around £5 billion was owed to several hundred banks following the construction of the tunnel link. Although the company was covering its operating costs, it has ceased interest payments to the banks. It was suggested that it unlikely ever to be able to repay the original £5 billion borrowed. This was still the case in 2007.

Investment appraisal and net cash flows

INVESTMENT APPRAISAL describes how a private sector business might objectively evaluate an investment project to determine whether or not it is likely to be profitable. It also allows businesses to make comparisons between different investment projects. There is a number of quantitative methods that a business might use when evaluating projects. However, they all involve comparing the **capital cost** of the project with the **net cash flow**.

- The capital cost is the amount of money spent when setting up a new venture.
- The net cash flow is the amount of money the business expects to receive each year over the life of the investment project, less the estimated running costs.

Consider a haulage company that invests in a new lorry. Table 1 shows the capital cost, the estimated revenue, the estimated running costs and the net cash flow each year over the life of the lorry. The lorry is expected to last for five years. The capital cost is the £80,000 paid to the vehicle supplier. The lorry is purchased in year 0, i.e. 'now'. The net cash flow by the end of year 1 is £19,000. This is found by subtracting the estimated running costs, such as fuel, drivers' wages and insurance, from the estimated revenue generated by the lorry from carrying goods (£56,000 - £37,000). In this example the business would compare the capital cost of £80,000 with the total net cash flow of £87,000 (£19,000 + £21,000 + £22,000 + £15,000 + £10,000),

Table 1: Capital cost and net cash flow from an investment

						£000
	Yr 0	Yr 1	Yr 2	Yr 3	Yr 4	Yr 5
Capital cost	80	0	0	0	0	0
Estimated revenue	0	56	60	62	58	55
Estimated running costs	0	37	39	40	43	45
Net cash flow	-80	19	21	22	15	10

when evaluating the investment. It may use one of the appraisal methods discussed in this unit.

Payback period

The PAYBACK PERIOD refers to the amount of time it takes for a project to recover or pay back the initial outlay. For example, an engineer may invest £500,000 in new cutting machinery and estimate that it will lead to a net cash flow (after operating costs) over the next five years, as in Table 2.

Table 2: Expected net cash flow from some new cutting machinery

						£000
	Yr 0	Yr 1	Yr 2	Yr 3	Yr 4	Yr 5
Net cash flow	(500)	100	125	125	150	150
Cumulative net cash flow	(500)	(400)	(275)	(150)	0	150

Here the payback period is four years. If we add together the net cash flows from the project in the first four years it amounts to £500,000 (i.e. 100 + 125 + 125 + 150).

The payback period can also be found by calculating the **cumulative net cash flow**. This is the cash flow each year taking into account revenue and operating costs (net cash flow) and the initial cost of the machine. When the machine is first bought, in year 0, there is negative cash flow of minus £500,000, the cost of the machine. Next year the revenue minus operating costs are £100,000. So the cumulative net cash flow is -£500,000 +

Table 3: Expected net cash flow from three investment projects

	Yr 0	Yr 1	Yr 2	Yr 3	Yr 4	Yr 5	Yr 6	Total net cash flow	Payback period
A Net cash flow	(70)	10	10	20	20	30	40	60	4 yrs 4 mths
A Cumulative cash flow	(70)	(60)	(50)	(30)	(10)	20	60		
B Net cash flow	(70)	20	20	20	20	20	20	50	3 yrs 6 mths
B Cumulative cash flow	(70)	(50)	(30)	(10)	10	30	50		
C Net cash flow	(70)	30	30	20	10	10	10	40	2 yrs 6 mths
C Cumulative cash flow	(70)	(40)	(10)	10	20	30	40		

Table 4: Advantages and disadvantages of payback method

Advantages

- This method is useful when technology changes rapidly, such as in the agriculture industry. New farm machinery is designed and introduced into the market regularly. It is important to recover the cost of investment before a new machine is designed.
- It is simple to use.
- Firms might adopt this method if they have cash-flow problems. This is because the project chosen will 'payback' the investment more quickly than others.

Disadvantages

- Cash earned after the 'payback' is not taken into account in the decision to invest.
- The method ignores the profitability of the project, since the criterion used is the speed of repayment.

£100,000 = -£400,000. In year 4 it is zero, so all costs have been covered.

When using this method to choose between projects, the project with the shortest payback will be chosen. Assume a business is appraising three investment projects, all of which cost £70,000. The net cash flow expected from each project is shown in Table 3.

In this example project C would be chosen because it has

the shortest payback time, i.e. two years and six months. How is this calculated? In years 1 and 2 the net cash flow is £30,000 + £30,000 = £60,000. To pay for an investment of £70,000 the remaining £10,000 (£70,000 - £60,000) comes from year 3's net cash flow. This is £20,000, which is more. So the number of months in year 3 it takes to pay the £10,000 can be calculated as:

$$\frac{\text{Amount required}}{\text{Net cash flow in year}} \times 12 = \frac{£10,000}{£20,000} \times 12 = 6 \text{ months}$$

Project A's payback is four years four months and project B's is three years and six months. Note that total cash flow is not taken into account in this method. In fact project C has the lowest total return over the six years. The advantages and disadvantages of the payback method of appraisal are shown in Table 4.

Average/accounting rate of return

The AVERAGE RATE OF RETURN or ACCOUNTING RATE OF RETURN (ARR) method measures the net return each year as a percentage of the capital cost of the investment.

$$\text{Average rate of return (\%)} = \frac{\text{Net return (profit) per annum}}{\text{Capital outlay (cost)}} \times 100$$

For example, the capital cost and expected net cash flow from three investment projects are shown in Table 6.

A business would first calculate the profit from each project by subtracting the total net cash flow of the project from its capital cost, ie £70,000 - £50,000 = £20,000 for project X. The next step is to calculate the profit per annum by dividing the profit by the number of years the project runs for, ie £20,000 ÷ 5

Question 1.

Delrose Associates is a full service digital marketing agency. The company offers a blend of consultancy and creativity, resulting in fully managed, highly successful online marketing campaigns. Delrose has clients in a variety of sectors including consumer, corporate, commercial, retail and not-for-profit. Their main work is developing targeted campaigns to drive quality traffic to websites using highly cost-effective methods.

In 2007 the managing director of the company recognised the need for a new computer system. She carried out some research into three new systems and put together the financial information shown in Table 5.

(a) Explain what is meant by 'expected net cash flow'.

(b) Calculate the payback period for each system and state which system Delrose Associates should select.

(c) Explain one reason why Delrose used the payback method of investment appraisal in this case.

Table 5: Capital costs and expected net cash flows from three new computer systems

| | | | | | | | | £000 |
Computer system	Capital cost	2007	2008	2009	2010	2011	2012	Total
System A	24,000	6,000	6,000	6,000	6,000	6,000	6,000	36,000
System B	37,000	8,000	8,000	9,000	9,000	6,000	6,000	46,000
System C	12,000	4,000	4,000	4,000	2,000	1,000	1,000	16,000

= £4,000 for X. Finally, the ARR is calculated by using the above formula, i.e.

$$\text{ARR (Project X)} = \frac{£4,000}{£50,000} \times 100$$

$$= 8\%$$

The results for all three projects are shown in Table 7. Project Y would be chosen because it gives a higher ARR (10 per cent) than the other two. Table 8 outlines the advantages and disadvantages of the ARR method.

Table 6: The capital cost and net cash flow from three investment projects

	Project X	Project Y	Project Z
Capital cost	£50,000	£40,000	£90,000
Return Yr 1	£10,000	£10,000	£20,000
Yr 2	£10,000	£10,000	£20,000
Yr 3	£15,000	£10,000	£30,000
Yr 4	£15,000	£15,000	£30,000
Yr 5	£20,000	£15,000	£30,000
Total net cash flows	£70,000	£60,000	£130,000

Table 7: The ARR calculated for three investment projects

	Project X	Project Y	Project Z
Capital cost	£50,000	£40,000	£90,000
Total net profit (ncf - capital cost)	£20,000	£20,000	£40,000
Net profit p.a. (profit ÷ 5)	£4,000	£4,000	£8,000
ARR	8%	10%	8.9%

Table 8: Advantages and disadvantages of the ARR method

Advantages
The advantage of this method is that it shows clearly the profitability of an investment project. Not only does it allow a range of projects to be compared, the overall rate of return can be compared to other uses for investment funds. In the example in Table 7, if a company can gain 12 per cent by placing its funds in a bank account, it might choose to postpone the investment project until interest rates fall. It is also easier to identify the opportunity cost of investment.

Disadvantages
The method does not take into account the effects of time on the value of money. The above example assumes that, for project X, £10,000 of income for the firm in two years' time is the same as £10,000 in one year's time. Some allowance must be made for the time span over which the income from an investment project is received for it to be most useful.

Question 2.

Hastings Group focuses on the development, production, installation and support of electrical, electronic, and mechanical components for aircraft, helicopters, missiles and targeting systems. The company has a leading position in the field of aircraft and helicopter services, customisation and modification. Hastings' employees are engineers and skilled workers. In 2007 the directors identified three investment projects that would benefit the company:

- R & D project;
- Marketing campaign;
- Some new CNC machinery.

The capital cost and expected cash flows for the investment projects are shown in Table 9.

(a) (i) Calculate the average rate of return for each project.
(ii) Explain which project should be selected.

(b) Explain the advantages to Hastings Group of using this method of appraisal.

Table 9: Capital cost and expected cash flows for three investment projects

							£000	
Investment project	Capital cost	2008	2009	2010	2011	2012	2013	Total
R & D	9,600	0	0	2,500	4,600	5,000	5,500	17,600
Marketing campaign	9,000	5,000	4,000	3,000	2,000	1,000	1,000	16,000
New CNC machinery	7,800	2,000	2,000	2,000	2,000	2,000	2,000	12,000

Table 10: Value of £100 invested over five years at 10 per cent per annum compound interest

Year	1	2	3	4	5
Value of £100	£110	£121	£133	£146	£161

Table 11: Discount table

			Rate of discount		
Year	5%	10%	15%	20%	25%
0	1.00	1.00	1.00	1.00	1.00
1	0.95	0.91	0.87	0.83	0.80
2	0.91	0.83	0.76	0.69	0.64
3	0.86	0.75	0.66	0.58	0.51
4	0.82	0.68	0.57	0.48	0.41
5	0.78	0.62	0.50	0.40	0.33
6	0.75	0.56	0.43	0.33	0.26
7	0.71	0.51	0.38	0.28	0.21
8	0.68	0.47	0.33	0.23	0.17
9	0.64	0.42	0.28	0.19	0.13
10	0.61	0.39	0.25	0.16	0.10

Discounted cash flow (DCF)/net present value (NPV)

Present value and DCF When making an investment decision a business might take into account what cash flow or profit earned in future is worth now. Look at Table 10. This shows that £100 invested today at a compound interest rate of 10 per cent would be worth £161 in five years' time.

- In one year's time, the investment would be worth £110. Of this, £10 would be the interest and £100 would be the initial investment.
- In two years' time, it would be worth £121. With compound interest, the interest is based not on the initial investment but on the investment at the end of the first year. So interest is 10 per cent of £110, making £11. Then this has to be added to the £110 value at the end of the first year to make a total of £121 for the second year.

This carries on until the value after five years is £161.

If £100 today is worth £161 in five years' time, it must be true that £161 in five years' time is worth just £100 today. This is an example of an important insight of DISCOUNTED CASH-FLOW techniques. Money in the future is worth less than the same amount now (the PRESENT VALUE). This is because money available today could be invested and it could earn interest.

Note that this is a completely different idea to the fact that money in the future can also become devalued due to the effects of inflation. Inflation does indeed affect future values of money. So there are two effects on the value of future money. Discounted cash-flow techniques just deal with one of these, the effect of interest rates.

Discount tables can be used to show by how much a future value must be multiplied to calculate its present value. Table 11 shows a discount table with five different rates of interest. If an investment project were predicted to give a net cash flow of £10,000 in three years' time, and the discount rate were 10 per cent, then reading off the table, the £10,000 would need to be multiplied by 0.75. To arrive at its present value the calculation would be:

£10,000 x 0.75 = £7,500

So £10,000 received in five years' time at a discount rate/interest rate of 5 per cent is worth £7,500 today. Cash flow or profit of £15,000 from an investment project received in five years' time, a discount/interest rate of 20 per cent, would be £15,000 x 0.40 or £6,000.

The discount table shown in Table 11 also shows two features of discounting.

- The higher the rate of discount, the less the present value of cash flow in future. This is the reverse of saying that the higher the rate of interest, the greater will be the value of an investment in the future.
- The further into the future the cash flow or earnings from an investment project, the less is their present value. So £1,000 earned in five years' time is worth less than £1,000 earned in one year's time. Again this is simply the opposite way of saying that £1,000 invested today at a fixed rate of interest will be worth more in five years' time than in one year's time.

Calculating NPV The NET PRESENT VALUE method makes use of discounted cash flow. It calculates the rate of return on an investment project taking into account the effects of interest rates and time. Using discount tables, it is possible to calculate the net present value of an investment project.

Table 12 shows three investment projects. The initial cost of each investment project is £50,000, shown in the Year 0 row. In years 1 to 10, each produces a stream of net cash flow. When added up, these come to far more than the initial £50,000. So it might appear that each investment project is profitable. However, if the net cash flow is discounted using a discount rate of 20 per cent, the picture is very different.

- Project A. The sum of the present values in years 1-10 for Project A is just £41,700. The net cash flow each year is constant at £10,000. But the present value of each of those £10,000 falls the further away it is received. By year 10, the present value of £10,000 discounted at 20 per cent is just £1,600. The net present value can be calculated simply by totalling the present value figures in years 0–10, including subtracting the initial cost. Or it can be calculated using the formula:

Net present value = present values - initial cost = £41,700 - £50,000 = - £8,300.

So project A is unprofitable according to discounted cash-

Table 12: Net present value of three investment projects discounted at 20 per cent

| Year | Project A | | Project B | | Project C | | Discount table Rate of discount at 20% |
	Net cash flow £	Present value £	Net cash flow £	Present Value £	Net cash flow £	Present Value £	
0	(50,000)	(50,000)	(50,000)	(50,000)	(50,000)	(50,000)	1.00
1	10,000	8,300	5,000	4,150	20,000	16,600	0.83
2	10,000	6,900	8,000	5,520	16,000	11,040	0.69
3	10,000	5,800	10,000	5,800	14,000	8,120	0.58
4	10,000	4,800	12,000	5,760	12,000	5,760	0.48
5	10,000	4,000	12,000	4,800	12,000	4,800	0.40
6	10,000	3,300	12,000	4,000	12,000	4,000	0.33
7	10,000	2,800	12,000	3,360	12,000	3,360	0.28
8	10,000	2,300	14,000	3,220	10,000	2,300	0.23
9	10,000	1,900	16,000	3,040	8,000	1,520	0.19
10	10,000	1,600	20,000	3,200	5,000	800	0.16
Total net cash flow before discounting	50,000		71,000		71,000		
Present values years 1–10		41,700		42,850		58,300	
Net present value (NPV)		(8,300)		(7,150)		+8,300	

flow techniques.

- Project B. The total net cash flow before discounting is higher than for Project A, £71,000 compared to £50,000. But once discounted, there is little difference in the sum of the present values. This is because net cash flow in Project B is weighted towards later years. The net present value of this project is £42,850 - £50,000 = - £7,150. Again, Project B is unprofitable according to discounted cash flow techniques.
- Project C. The total net cash flow before discounting is the same as with Project B. Indeed, the pattern of net cash flow is an exact reverse of those of Project B. Here, the higher net cash flow figures are concentrated at the start and fall off towards the end. This means that the total present value is much higher than with Project B. The net present value of Project C is £58,300 - £50,000 = £8,300. This is the discounted profit that the business will make on this project.

The net present value method would suggest that a business should go ahead with any investment projects that have a positive net present value. If a business has to make a choice between investment projects for whatever reason, it should go for those with the highest net present value. So in this case it would choose Project C.

Qualitative factors influencing investment decisions

In addition to the factors which might influence investment decisions already outlined in this unit, a number of other qualitative factors might be considered. These are non-financial considerations.

Table 13: Advantages and disadvantages of net present value method

Advantages
- The net present value method, unlike the payback method and the average rate of return, correctly accounts for the value of future earnings by calculating present values.
- The discount rate used can be changed as risk and conditions in financial markets change. For example, in the 1990s, the cost of bank borrowing for many businesses fell from over 15 per cent to 7–8 per cent. Investment projects therefore did not need to make such a high rate of return to be profitable and so the rate of discount could be lowered.

Disadvantages
- Calculating discounted cash flow is the most complex of the three methods. It certainly can't be done 'on the back of an envelope' as can the other two methods. As such, it is rarely used by small businesses.
- The rate of discount used is critical in determining what is and is not profitable. The higher the discount rate, the fewer investment projects are likely to be profitable.

Human relations Some investment projects can have a huge impact on the staff in an organisation. For example, investment in plant automation might lead to mass redundancies. A business might decide to postpone plans to automate their plant if it thought the damage to human relations in the organisation would be too severe.

Ethical considerations Along with many other business decisions, managers are taking more of an ethical stance when choosing courses of action. For example, a chemicals producer might decide to build a new plant in a location which does not minimise financial costs but does reduce environmental damage. Such a decision might help to enhance the image of a company. Companies are increasingly keen to be seen as 'good corporate citizens'.

Corporate strategy Many businesses have long-term corporate objectives which are laid down in their corporate strategy. Such long term objectives might influence short-term investment decisions. For example, a business operating a chain of theme pubs might be considering some repairs to a fire-damaged pub. Repairs might be postponed because the pub in question was due for complete refurbishment in the next financial year.

Risk The financial position in which a business finds itself is one factor in assessing the risk of an investment project. Others include the state of the economy and the markets into which a business sells. Investment projects which have long payback periods are also riskier than ones with shorter payback periods.

Government legislation Investment may have to take place for a business to conform to government laws and regulations. So, for example, a business may have to install anti-pollution equipment to bring down its emission levels even though this investment project could make a loss for the business. Or it may have to adapt its premises to conform to various disability regulations without seeing any return on this investment.

Availability of funding A large number of investment projects fail to get started because businesses are unable to raise the necessary money to fund the project. A significant proportion of these will be small businesses which have difficulty in persuading investors and lenders to provide funding.

Question 3.

Gethings is a garment manufacturer in London. It is considering making an investment in one of two machines, A and B. The projected net cash flows for each machine are shown in Table 14.

Table 14: Expected net cash flow from two investment projects

							£000
Year	0	1	2	3	4	5	6
	Initial cost						
Machine A							
Net cash flow	(600)	100	150	200	300	200	100
Discounted cash flow							
Machine B							
Net cash flow	(600)	200	300	200	150	100	100
Discounted cash flow							

(a) Calculate the discounted cash flow for each machine and each year using a discount rate of 15 per cent from the discount table, Table 11.
(b) Calculate the net present value for each machine.
(c) Explain why Gethings might buy Machine B if it uses the net present value method of decision making.

Business confidence Entrepreneurs, managers and businesses tend to have different attitudes and cultures from each other. One aspect of this is confidence or optimism. Some decision makers tend to be very cautious, seeing all the problems that might arise if things go wrong. Others are confident and optimistic. They see the future as much better and brighter than the average. This has a crucial impact on investment. The cautious, unconfident entrepreneur or manager may delay or abandon possible investment projects. In the same circumstances with the same investment projects, confident and optimistic managers will tend to go ahead and authorise the expenditure. So the deeply held attitudes of decision makers have an important influence on investment decision making.

KEYTERMS

Average rate of return or accounting rate of return (ARR) – a method of investment appraisal which measures the net return per annum as a percentage of the initial spending.

Discounted cash flow (DCF) – a method of investment appraisal which takes interest rates into account by calculating the present value of future income.

Investment appraisal – the evaluation of an investment project to determine whether or not it is likely to be worthwhile.

Net present value (NPV) – the present value of future income from an investment project, less the cost.

Present value – the value today of a sum of money available in the future.

Payback period – the amount of time it takes to recover the cost of an investment project.

KNOWLEDGE

1. What is meant by the term investment?
2. Explain the difference between autonomous and induced investment.
3. State the 4 types of investment.
4. Why is the investment decision risky?
5. State the factors that might influence (a) private sector and (b) public investment?
6. What is the function of investment appraisal in business?
7. Explain briefly how a business would appraise investment using the payback period.
8. What are the advantages and disadvantages of the payback method?
9. What does the average or accounting rate of return method of investment appraisal aim to measure?
10. Why is the discounted cash flow/NPV method of appraisal used in business?
11. Suggest how environmental considerations may affect an investment decision.

Case Study: *Chambers plc*

In 2006, Chambers plc, an ailing cylinder manufacturer, was bought by a management team for £4 million. The company employs 169 staff and operates from a factory in Tipton, West Midlands. It designs and manufactures custom high-quality, heavy-duty hydraulic cylinders for the mobile, off-highway, specialty vehicle and heavy hydraulic machinery markets.

The new management team believe they can transform the company into a profit-making concern. Last year the company lost £560,000 on sales of £13,256,000. The team believe that in the past the people running the company were not prepared to take risk. Consequently they have failed to invest in new technology and working methods and fallen behind their competitors.

Dave Williams, the new managing director, has already earmarked £5 million for investment. Initially four investment projects were identified but two were eliminated at a preliminary stage using the payback method of appraisal. The two remaining projects are now being appraised. One of these projects involves automating about 60 per cent of the production process. The other involves introducing total quality management (TQM) right across the organisation. The capital cost of the two projects and the expected cash flows are shown in Table 15. The present value of £1 receivable at the end of five years at 5 per cent is shown in Table 16.

The new owners of the company are very optimistic about the future direction of the company. However, the workforce does not share their enthusiasm. Most of them are worried about the proposed investment plans. The age profile of the workforce is very high. Many of the workforce joined the company when they left school and undertook apprenticeships. More than 50 per cent of the workers have never worked anywhere else

and are over 55. If Chambers select the automation project about 50 staff are certain to lose their jobs. Also, an employee representative said, 'The introduction of TQM will create pressure and stress for many of the lads here'… 'Some of them just aren't up to it.'

Table 15: Capital cost and expected cash flows for Chambers investment projects

Investment project	Cost	2007	2008	2009	2010	2011	(£m) Total
Automation	5.0	2.3	2.6	2.8	3.3	3.2	14.2
Introduce TQM	4.4	2.1	2.1	2.3	2.4	2.5	11.4

Table 16: The present value of £1 receivable at the end of 5 years at 5 per cent

After	0 yr	1 yr	2 yrs	3 yrs	4 yrs	5 yrs
Present value of £1	£1.00	£0.95	£0.90	£0.86	£0.82	£0.78

(a) Explain what is meant by investment appraisal. (4 marks)

(b) Suggest why the previous management team were 'not prepared to take risk'. (6 marks)

(c) (i) Calculate the average rate of return of each investment project. (6 marks)

(ii) Calculate the net present value of each project. (8 marks)

(d) Explain which of the two investment projects Chambers plc should select. (2 marks)

(e) To what extent will qualitative factors have an influence on the investment decision in this case? (14 marks)

Marketing objectives

When businesses construct their marketing strategies they will usually engage in a number of different activities. These include:
- analysing the markets in which they operate;
- setting marketing objectives;
- selecting marketing tactics and strategies;
- developing and implementing marketing plans.

This unit focuses upon MARKETING OBJECTIVES. These are the **goals** that a business is trying to achieve through its marketing. Marketing objectives are often more effective if they have a target and a time limit. For example, a marketing objective might be to increase market share by 10 per cent in the next three years. Business marketing objectives commonly focus upon the following areas.

Growth and profitability A business might want to increase sales, revenue, profit through marketing. It might be able to increase its revenue by selling more products. Or it might be able to charge a higher price. Both should lead to higher profits. So might launching new products. Businesses aiming to grow often attempt to create a competitive advantage over their rivals Marketing can help a business to do this. Examples of businesses that have grown rapidly as a result of marketing include the low-cost flight companies EasyJet and Ryanair.

Gaining and maintaining sales and market share A business may attempt to prevent losses and declining sales, and maintain market share, through its marketing. There are reasons why a business might do this.
- When a new product is launched. New products often require marketing and promotion to break into the market and for sales to take off.
- To develop over the long term. Some products have very long life cycles such as the Mini motor car and Heinz Beans. They have sold continuously over many years as a result of marketing extension strategies designed to maintain sales. Extension strategies are often used in the mature stage of the product life cycle to prevent a decline in sales.

Product differentiation It is possible to differentiate products from those of competitors by changing the marketing mix, such as charging a lower or higher price, changing the packaging, design and ingredients of the product, advertising and other forms of promotion, or selling the product in different types of retailer. Examples might be the change in the name and advertising of the sweets Opal Fruits to Starburst or the setting up of a website by BA to sell flights through the Internet.

Product introduction The marketing objective of a business might be to launch new products onto the market. Market research could have indicated that this product would be successful. Some businesses introduce products regularly, such as new versions of computer software and games. Car producers regularly introduce newer versions of cars to replace older models. For example, the Ford Mondeo replaced the Sierra and the Ford Focus replaced the Escort.

Product innovation Some products are genuinely new and innovative. It might be that new technology has created a new product or research has found a new medicine, for example.

Consumer knowledge Consumers need to know what products are available from businesses. Without awareness they may not buy products. Raising the awareness of products, for example

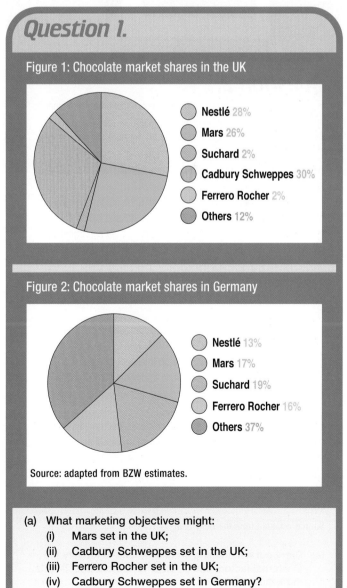

Question 1.

Figure 1: Chocolate market shares in the UK

- Nestlé 28%
- Mars 26%
- Suchard 2%
- Cadbury Schweppes 30%
- Ferrero Rocher 2%
- Others 12%

Figure 2: Chocolate market shares in Germany

- Nestlé 13%
- Mars 17%
- Suchard 19%
- Ferrero Rocher 16%
- Others 37%

Source: adapted from BZW estimates.

(a) What marketing objectives might:
(i)   Mars set in the UK;
(ii)   Cadbury Schweppes set in the UK;
(iii) Ferrero Rocher set in the UK;
(iv)   Cadbury Schweppes set in Germany?

through a variety of promotion measures, can therefore be an important objective.

Consumer satisfaction Consumers also need to be happy about the products they buy. Businesses which have satisfied consumers are more likely to gain brand loyalty.

There is a relationship between the different marketing objectives. For example, in the early 1990s Adidas found its market share under threat in the European sports shoe market. This was a partly as a result of a successful promotional campaign by Nike. Adidas attempted to regain market share by

Question 2.

In 2004 Kodak announced it would cease production of traditional 35 mm cameras in the US and Europe at the end of the year. Sales in America fell below 8 million in 2003, a 20 per cent fall since 2002. The decision was based largely on the runaway success of digital cameras. Sales of film for traditional cameras had fallen by £2 billion in two years.

Kodak was betting its future on digital photography, printing and health imaging. The President of Kodak's digital and film imaging systems said 'We will focus our film investments on opportunities that provide faster and attractive returns'. But Kodak did not intend to halt production of traditional cameras totally. There were plans to expand manufacturing in Asia, Latin America and Eastern Europe where demand was still growing. It would also continue to produce disposable 35 mm cameras.

Kodak also announced plans to cease production of its Advanced Photo System cameras, launched in 1996, which gave wide-shot capability. Demand had failed to live up to expectations.

Digital cameras are now outselling traditional cameras. Previously they had been more expensive, produced poorer quality pictures and needed large amounts of battery power. However, the quality of digital cameras sold for less than £200 has now improved greatly. Statistics show that only 14 per cent of pictures taken on digital cameras are printed. The rest are downloaded, emailed or deleted.

Supporters of traditional cameras argue that their photographs are still superior to those of digital cameras, particularly in the depth of colour.

Source: adapted from the *Daily Mail*, 14.1.2004.

(a) Carry out a marketing audit of Kodak to identify the
     (i) internal factors and (ii) external factors affecting its
     marketing objectives.

its own marketing campaign, with the objective of differentiating its product. It promoted its trainers as having 'street credibility'. After the year 2000, Adidas launched a number of product ranges with a 'retro' 1970s look in an attempt to increase sales and win market share.

There is also a relationship between the marketing objectives of a business and its MARKETING TACTICS. Marketing tactics are short-term, small-scale methods a business might use to achieve its marketing objectives. For example, a furniture business with the objective of increasing sales revenue after Christmas might have a 30 day offer where customers can choose a free chair with any three seater sofa they buy.

It is argued that the marketing objectives a business sets should be SMART in the same way as the overall objectives of the business They should be specific, stating exactly what is trying to be achieved, able to be measured to decide if they have been achieved, which usually involves setting targets, agreed by everyone involved, realistic and able to be achieved within the constraints of the business and time specific, stating exactly when they should be achieved.

Internal influences on marketing objectives

There is a number of influences that affect the marketing objectives set by a business. Some may be internal factors, from within the business itself.

Corporate aims and objectives A company's marketing objectives will be influenced by the corporate aims and objectives of the business. For example, the aim of a DVD and video rental chain might be to become the most well known name in the UK. Its objective might be to increase sales turnover by 20 per cent over two years to achieve this. So its marketing objectives could be to spend an extra £1 million on promotion to teenagers in magazines and product 'tie-ins' to make them more aware of the service.

Finance The availability of finance will influence what it is that a business aims to achieve. It may be difficult to launch new products, for example, if a business lacks funds. Similarly, a business with limited finances and access to only small pools of additional finance may find that some marketing objectives are beyond its realisable ambitions.

Operational and organisational issues The operation and organisation of a business may influence its marketing. A business which does not, for example, have a specialised marketing department might have a different marketing strategy from to one which does. A business operating in many countries might market differently from one in a local or national market.

Human resources To some extent the nature of a business's marketing objectives will reflect the human resources of that business. For example, a new business staffed by recent graduates may well opt for marketing methods different to a

Figure 3: PESTLE factors

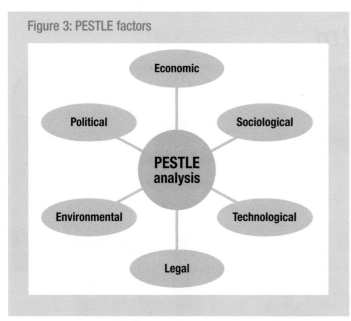

more established business with a wider range of employees.

External influences on marketing objectives

Factors outside the business can also influence its marketing objectives.

Competitors' actions The actions of competitor businesses may well affect the marketing objectives of a business. Take the example of a large and dominant business operating in a market where it is seeking to gain market share. In such conditions a less dominant business may seek to defend and maintain its market share.

Technological change Businesses operating in markets characterised by fast-changing technologies are likely to set themselves ambitious marketing objectives possibly with large increases in sales volume. This is because such markets are often relatively open with new businesses able to gain large slices of market share quickly. Many web-based networking businesses such as Facebook have been able to realise ambitious marketing objectives in this way. By way of contrast businesses operating in relatively slow-changing markets with few technological changes are more likely to set modest marketing objectives reflecting their belief that future circumstances may be likely to resemble in many ways those already experienced.

Market factors One of the main market factors influencing a business' marketing objectives is the degree of competition faced by a business. In a mature market with little or no room for new entrants, businesses are likely to set modest marketing objectives given that they are constrained by the intensity of competition and the relatively few opportunities to grow significantly. The global market for cars, for example, is saturated with many producers competing. This means that car businesses cannot expect to see the kind of growth experienced by Google when they entered a new market, for Internet searches, with few competitors.

External factors influencing marketing objectives also include a range of factors shown in Figure 3 known as PESTLE factors.

- **Political factors.** This may include political pressure from bodies that can exert political pressure, such as government agencies, or at local level, such as town councils.
- **Economic factors.** Increases in consumer spending, falls in interest rates and low inflation can all improve the chances of a business increasing its sales and profit. An increase in the number of new businesses may reduce the market share of a company that is dominant.
- **Social factors.** Changes in tastes can affect spending by consumers. Fashionable products can often increase sales rapidly.
- **Technological factors.** New products may be created as technology develops. The Internet has also helped to increase consumer awareness of products.
- **Legal factors.** This can include legislation from government. For example laws might restrict the type of advertising used for a product in an attempt to differentiate it from those of rivals. It would also include
- **Environmental factors.** These can often influence the type of product that a business produces, such as the development of businesses selling managed wood as an alternative to other wood or plastic products.

These factors are often found by carrying out a MARKETING AUDIT. This is an analysis of the internal organisation and procedures of the business and the external factors which affect its marketing decisions. It will also help to identify the strengths, weaknesses, opportunities and threats faced by the business, called SWOT analysis.

KEYTERMS

Marketing audit – an analysis of the internal organisation and procedures of the business and the external factors which affect its marketing decisions.
Marketing objectives – goals that a business attempts to achieve through its marketing.
Marketing tactics – short-term, small-scale methods a business can use to achieve its marketing objectives.

KNOWLEDGE

1. Identify five marketing objectives.
2. Explain the difference between an internal and external marketing audit.
3. State four internal factors influencing a business' marketing objectives.
4. Name three external factors affecting a business' marketing objectives.
5. What are the PESTLE factors?

Case Study: *Recovery Kitchens Ltd*

Recovery Kitchens Ltd is owned and run by Elle Jeffers and Arturo Vasques. The business manufactures kitchens using recycled and reclaimed wood. It sells mainly to two types of customer – those who are concerned about the environment and want to see wood recycled rather than destroyed, and those who want a genuinely 'old'-looking and aged kitchen to fit in with the style of their house. The business operates from a workshop in the North West of England which has enough space for its current needs but little room for expansion.

The kitchens do not come cheap. There is a tremendous amount of work involved in reclaiming old wood and making it suitable for production. Sources of wood have to be found. The wood has to be sanded, prepared and recut. Sometimes wood that has been bought turns out not to be suitable.

The business has been operating for about three years and now has a strong loyalty from customers who want this type of product. They tell their friends, who also buy kitchens. And sales have started to pick up in other areas of the country, particularly East Anglia, where the style of kitchen suits a great deal of older housing which is relatively cheaper than nearer to London.

Recovery Kitchens Ltd has been thinking of making some changes. It is concerned about its long-term position. It is facing competition from some local businesses that offer cheaper pine products which can look very similar to reclaimed wood kitchens or more expensive 'Shaker-type' kitchens which have a simple style and traditional feel. And it feels that it can take the idea of the environmental image of the business further by making kitchens from managed wood. This is wood where the supplier guarantees to replant trees for all those cut down. Recovery Kitchens Ltd can then use this in its promotion to further enhance its green image and offer something a little different to customers wanting kitchens for older properties. It is also considering whether it should reduce its price a little. It has asked local people for their views on the prices charged by some kitchen manufacturers and their knowledge of the company name. The business is concerned about whether it will have the finance to buy the managed wood. It might have to borrow, and interest rates look set to rise.

Source: adapted from independent research.

(a) What are the target markets of the business? (4 marks)
(b) Based upon the information in the article explain TWO marketing objectives of Recovery Kitchens Ltd. (6 marks)
(c) Explain the internal and external factors that might affect the marketing objectives of the business. (12 marks)
(d) Discuss the possible objectives of the business in moving to managed wood kitchens. (12 marks)

Market analysis

Faced with competition in most markets, it is vital for businesses to analyse these markets and how they market their products within them. Effective analysis of the markets and marketing can help businesses to be successful. They can improve the quality of their decision making. Market analysis is a study of the conditions in the market. The research can be used to predict current and future trends or identify relationships between factors within the market.

Businesses may analyse markets for certain reasons.

Gathering evidence for devising new marketing strategies
Market analysis techniques enable businesses to improve the quality of information they hold about market. This can be important when devising their marketing strategies. For example, a business that is planning to launch an existing product in a new market abroad would want to know how customers would react to this. A business that is deciding to lower its prices or increase its spending on Internet promotion would want to know whether customers would buy more as a result of the change in price or change in promotion strategy.

Identifying significant patterns in sales By carefully analysing sales data businesses are able to identify patterns in sales that can be critical in terms of understanding their past performance and in making predictions for the future. For example, if a business predicted that sales of particular products were likely to fall in future, it might decide to launch new products to compensate. Alternatively, it might decide that it could be faced with a difficult trading period and make changes in its costs and credit control to ensure that the business was not too badly affected.

Information technology and market analysis

The widespread availability of information technology to businesses has increased the capacity of even small businesses to analyse the markets within which they work. This is for two main reasons.

- Businesses are now more readily able to analyse their own market data for themselves. The vast majority of businesses now have access to personal computers and software that are capable of undertaking complex tasks with raw data.
- Information technology has led to a huge growth in the quantity of readily available market data analysing trends in a variety of markets. Such information is often held by specialist market research and analysis organisations that will make it available to businesses for a fee.

The use of IT for market analysis can have many benefits for businesses.

- They can manage large amounts of data. This gives a better chance of making more accurate predictions or illustrating relationships between variables.
- Extensive calculations can be carried out accurately. Human error can be minimised, although the input of incorrect data is always a possibility. Again this might help prediction to be accurate.
- Information can be manipulated and illustrated in a variety of ways, allowing trends to be shown clearly.
- Data manipulation can be carried out quickly, which might help a business to find out about possible changes before they take place. This can be especially important if a decision needs to be made before other factors change or if changes take place that could affect a decision after it is taken. For example, the launch of a new product 6 months before a major change in the market takes place could be a disaster. Accurate market analysis could prevent this problem.

Test marketing and market research

One way in which a business might analyse whether a product is successful is to use **test marketing** methods. This is when a business sells a new product to a limited group of customers to assess their reaction. If the response is favourable, the product can then be sold to the whole market. If not, it may be withdrawn. It can be very costly to sell a new product to the whole market. New products often need heavy promotion. Large numbers of goods may need to be made prior to launch to satisfy potential demand. If the product fails, the business will have wasted its spending on promotion and be left with unsold stock. The cost of failure in a test market is much smaller. Test marketing in the UK tends to take place in a small geographical area, like the North East.

Market research Market research, including test marketing, may help in constructing a sales forecast. For example, there may be no past data from which to extrapolate trends for a new product. Test marketing of a new product, focus groups or shopping surveys should all give some indication of future sales.

Market research may also be able to spot new trends in the market, which cannot be picked up by looking at past data. A product, for example, may be about to become 'fashionable' and desirable. Others may be about to go out of fashion. In the 1980s and 1990s, Doc Martin shoes enjoyed cult status amongst some young buyers, but sales fell sharply in the 2000s because they became less fashionable. Denim jeans became unfashionable in the 1990s as young people did not want to look like their parents. New designs using denim after the year 2004 made denim clothing popular again.

Using market research has the advantage that extra information not available from within the business can be used to forecast sales. However, market research is not always reliable, particularly if the methodology used is inadequate. If test marketing is used, this will give competitors a chance to see the new product and react to it. For example, **viral** or **buzz marketing** techniques, where a well known 'face' in an area is seen with a product such as a car, is used to develop excitement amongst consumers. Competitors may rush forward 'me too' products which are almost identical to the product being test marketed. They may also increase promotion of similar products in the test market area to reduce the sales of the product being test marketed.

Hunches and guesses Small businesses often don't have access to sophisticated past data or market research. Equally, when the market is changing very fast, using past data and market research may be unreliable when forecasting future sales. So sales forecasts can often be based upon hunches and guesses. Hunches and guesses could be argued to be an unscientific way of producing a forecast. Even when some such forecasts are accurate, this could be simply due to chance and the laws of probability. However, it can also be argued that some individuals have a very good instinctive feel for the market in which they operate. Using their past knowledge, some individuals may be far better at spotting trends than others.

Extrapolation from trends

Total spending in the UK has been rising over the past 50 years. This is a TREND. The trend rate of growth of real spending (spending after inflation has been taken into account) is approximately 2¼ per cent. But the rate of spending on individual items is not changing at the same rate over time. Spending on foreign holidays, for example, has been rising at a much faster rate than the average growth in spending. Spending on jam in real terms has been falling.

Businesses need to have an understanding of trends to make decisions. A food manufacturer, for example, may know that sales of frozen ready meals have been growing at an average of 8 per cent per year over the past five years. On the other hand, sales of jam may have been declining at 1 per cent per year. These trends are likely to affect decisions about investment in new facilities or machines, how to allocate the marketing budget, or in what areas to recruit new workers.

What will happen in the future can be forecast by looking at past trends. This technique is known as EXTRAPOLATION. For example, if sales have been growing on average at 5 per cent per annum over the past ten years, then a business might forecast that sales next year are likely to grow by 5 per cent as well.

Forecasting

How might a business predict future values of a variable such as sales? Consider Table 1. This shows sales volumes for a company manufacturing sofas over time. A business can calculate a trend using a technique known as a four quarter centred moving average. The trend smooths out fluctuations in actual figures, making it easier to observe the pattern which is taking place. In Table 1 the trend in sales has been calculated over three years. It shows that there has been a trend for a rise in sales over the period. The trend is also shown on Figure 1, which is a graph

Table 1: Sales, 2006-08, sales quantities

Year	Quarter	Sales	4 period moving average	Centred 4 period moving average	Seasonal variation
2006	1	600			
	2	100			
			450		
	3	300		400	-100
			350		
	4	800		400	+400
			450		
2007	1	200		500	-300
			550		
	2	500		600	-100
			650		
	3	700		650	+50
			650		
	4	1,200		650	+550
			650		
2008	1	200		700	-500
			750		
	2	500		800	-300
			850		
	3	1,100			
	4	1,600			

drawn from the information. The calculation of moving averages is explained in the unit titled 'Analysing business data'.

A business can use the trend line to predict future sales. It is possible to draw a LINE OF BEST FIT through the trend line, as in Figure 1. This is a straight line that fits the figures in the trend 'best'. It is possible to draw a line of best fit in two ways.

- The line can be drawn by eye. This means drawing a straight line through the points which appears to represent

Figure 1: Trend line and line of best fit showing sales forecasts for 2009

Question 1.

Wildmans is a manufacturer of dyes for the textile industry. Table 2 shows how its sales have changed between 2006 and 2008.

Table 2: Wildmans' sales, 2006-2008

	£ million		
	2006	2007	2008
Q1	5.3	5.5	5.6
Q2	5.3	5.5	5.7
Q3	5.2	5.3	5.3
Q4	5.9	6.1	6.3

(a) Draw up a table with the time quarters and the sales figures from Table 2. Calculate a three quarter moving average for sales from the figures.

(b) Draw up another table with the time quarters and the sales figures from Table 2. Calculate (i) a four quarter moving average and (ii) a centred four quarter moving average.

(c) Draw the axes for a graph. On the horizontal axis, put quarters 1-4 for the five years 2006-2009. On the vertical axis, start the axis at £5.0 million and extend it to £6.5 million. On the graph, plot (i) the sales figures as shown in Table 2 and (ii) the centred four quarter moving average of sales figures you have calculated in 2(ii).

(d) (i) From the four quarter moving average, estimate a line of best fit, drawing this on your graph. (ii) Extend the line of best fit to the fourth quarter of 2009. What is your estimate of the value of sales in that quarter from the line of best fit?

(e) Analyse what factors might cause the actual level of fourth quarter 2009 sales to be above or below your estimate.

the general trend that is taking place.
● The line can be drawn using a mathematical technique known as the sum of least squares.

Once the line of best fit has been drawn, it can be extended to forecast sales in a future period. So, for example, in Figure 1 the line has been extended so that the extrapolated figure for sales in the first quarter of 2005 is 958 and for the second quarter it is predicted to be 1015. These predictions take into account the trend for rising sales in the past. Whether these predictions are totally accurate will depend on a number of factors, discussed in the next section.

Problems with using trend forecasts

Using trend forecasts can be problematical for a number of reasons.

The future is not necessarily the same as the past Simply because there has been a clear trend in the past does not mean to say that the trend will continue in the future. For example, international airline companies have suffered large drops in demand over the past 20 years whenever there has been a terrorist incident involving airlines. US travellers are particularly sensitive to perceived terrorist activity. New technology can suddenly make an old technology redundant. So manufacturers of the old technology can face a sudden fall in demand. When CDs took off in the 1980s, there was a sharp fall in demand for cassette tapes. So sudden random shocks can play havoc with a business forecast.

Cyclical variations Capitalist economies tend to experience **business cycles**. These are fairly regular ups and downs in the level of business activity in the whole economy. In a boom, sales tend to be high. In a recession, with increased unemployment, sales can become stagnant or fall. Businesses must take account of where the economy is in the business cycle when forecasting. If the economy this year is at the bottom of the business cycle, sales next year might be higher as the economy recovers. Even if a business takes into account the current position of the economy in the business cycle, its forecasting can still be inaccurate. No two business cycles are the same. The economy might come out of a recession faster or slower than it has done on average in the past. Cyclical variations are subject to randomness, which makes forecasting more difficult.

Seasonal variations Businesses must also take account of seasonal variations when forecasting. For example, ice cream manufacturers sell more in the summer than in the winter. Clothes retailers tend to sell more in the run up to Christmas than at other times of the year. As with the trade cycle, businesses need to know about past seasonal fluctuations to extrapolate future trends. Even then, seasonal variations can be subject to randomness. A spell of very hot weather in August will send ice cream sales soaring. On the other hand, there will be a sharp reduction in the number of customers visiting clothes shops as shopping becomes a less desirable activity than sunbathing or going to the pub.

The prediction from Figure 1 can be used to show the effect of seasonal variations. It was predicted from the trend that sales in the second quarter of 2005 would be 1015. However, the trend is a smoothed out version of actual figures, which have seasonal variations depending on which quarter is considered. Table 1 shows the seasonal variations in actual sales figures from the trend. The average seasonal variation in the two second quarters shown in 2007 and 2008 is:

$$\frac{(-100) \text{ and } (-300)}{2} = -200$$

So a more accurate prediction for the second quarter might be 815. This is the predicted figure of 1015 but takes into account the average second quarter variation of -200.

Extrapolation of future trends from past trends can therefore be a complex process by the time that cyclical and seasonal trends are taken into account. Even then, random occurrences or sudden changes in the market can make actual outcomes different from forecasts.

Figure 2: A weak but positive correlation

Figure 3: A strong negative correlation

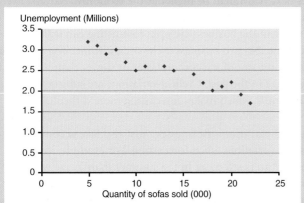

Figure 4: Little or no correlation

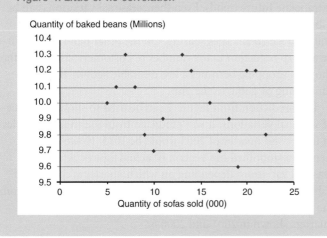

The reliability of forecasts

Forecasts are likely to be more reliable when:

- the forecast is for a short period of time in the future, such as six months, rather than a long time, such as five years;
- they are revised frequently to take account of new data and other information;
- the market is slow changing;
- there is plenty of backdata from which to produce a forecast;
- market research data, including test marketing data, is available;

- those preparing the forecast have a good understanding of how to use data to produce a forecast;
- those preparing the forecast have a good 'feel' for the market and can adjust the forecast to take account of their hunches and guesses about the future.

No forecaster is accurate all the time. Even in slow moving markets, sales can change by a few per cent for no apparent reason. One way to take this into account is to produce a forecast range. Forecasters might, for example, prepare three sets of figures – an optimistic forecast, a pessimistic forecast and a central forecast. The two outlying forecasts would have low probabilities of occurring but would indicate a best and worst case scenario. The central forecast would be the forecast which had the highest probability of occurring. Supplying these forecasts to other departments, such as production, would give them an indication of the possible variations they might have to face. They could then prepare their own plans for these eventualities. In a very sophisticated forecast there would be a whole range of possible outcomes, each with a probability attached to its occurring.

Even though forecasts are rarely 100 per cent accurate, they do provide an indication of likely future trends. As such, they are important tools for any planning or budgeting.

Correlation

A CORRELATION exists between two or more variables when a change in one variable results in a change in the other variables. For example, sales of sofas are likely to be related to marketing expenditure by the sofa manufacturer, consumer confidence and levels of unemployment. The greater the level of marketing expenditure and the level of consumer confidence, and the lower the level of unemployment, the greater might be the sales of sofas.

Figures 2-4 show a SCATTER GRAPH or DIAGRAM where each item of data is shown by a point or a cross. The whole series of data, when plotted, tends to be scattered across the graph. Each point on Figure 2 shows the quarterly spending on marketing by the company and its sales in that quarter for the past three years. Sixteen points (4 years x 4 quarters in each year) are therefore shown.

Positive correlation In Figure 2 there is a **positive correlation** between sales of sofas and marketing expenditure. As more is spent on marketing, more sofas are bought. However, the correlation in Figure 2 is not particularly **strong** because the points are not close to the line of best fit. Mathematically, the degree of correlation can be measured between -1 and +1. There is a positive correlation when it is between 0 and 1. The nearer the correlation is to the value of 1, the stronger the correlation between the two variables.

Negative correlation Figure 3 shows a situation where there is a **negative correlation** between the two variables. In this case, it is the level of unemployment in the economy and sales of sofas. When unemployment rises, those made unemployed have less income to spend and hence fewer sofas are bought. Rising

Question 2.

Table 3 shows the sales, marketing expenditure and average price per unit sold for Wildmans.

Table 3: Wildmans, sales, marketing expenditure and average price per unit sold, 2002-2004

		Sales £million	Marketing expenditure £million	Average price per unit sold (pence)
2002	Q1	5.3	0.10	80.2
	Q2	5.3	0.10	80.0
	Q3	5.2	0.10	79.3
	Q4	5.9	0.30	77.5
2003	Q1	5.5	0.13	79.1
	Q2	5.5	0.14	78.3
	Q3	5.3	0.15	78.6
	Q4	6.1	0.40	77.1
2004	Q1	5.6	0.17	77.6
	Q2	5.7	0.18	77.2
	Q3	5.3	0.19	78.1
	Q4	6.3	0.50	77.0

(a) Draw a graph with marketing expenditure on the vertical axis (from 0 to £0.6 million) and sales on the horizontal axis (starting at £5.0 million and going to £6.5 million). Plot each quarter's sales against marketing expenditure to produce a scatter diagram.

(b) Draw a second graph with price on the vertical axis (starting at 76p and going to 82p) and sales on the horizontal axis (starting at £5.0 million and going to £6.5 million). Plot each quarter's sales against price to produce a scatter diagram.

(c) What sort of correlation is there between (i) sales and marketing expenditure and (ii) sales and price?

(d) Discuss whether the correlation shown in the data is of significance for Wildmans' marketing strategy.

unemployment also makes some of those in work fearful of losing their jobs too. They then tend to reduce their borrowing and sofas are often bought through loans. Here there is a strong negative correlation between unemployment and sales. The points on the scatter graph are close to the line of best fit. The stronger the negative correlation, the closer to the value of -1 is the correlation.

No correlation If there is no correlation between two variables, the points on the scatter diagram will be randomly distributed. Figure 4 shows the relationship between sales of sofas and sales of baked beans. There is very little or no correlation between the two.

The significance of correlation

Correlation is important for a business. It needs to know what impact, if any, a change in one variable will have on another variable. For example, a rise in interest rates in the economy is likely to lead to a fall in the sale of sofas because borrowing will become more expensive. On the other hand, a rise in interest rates is likely to have no impact on the sale of baked beans. In general, interest rate changes are important for furniture manufacturers but not for food manufacturers.

When targeting particular markets, businesses need to estimate the correlation between marketing expenditure and sales. In the market for soap powders, it has been suggested that the two largest manufacturers in the world, Unilever and Procter & Gamble, can spend up to one quarter of the price of a packet of soap powder on marketing. They believe there is a strong correlation between expenditure on marketing and sales. On the other hand, a local painter and decorator may spend nothing on marketing. Experience may have shown that advertising in, say, the local newspaper doesn't bring in extra work.

Simply because two variables are correlated does not mean that a change in one variable **causes** the other to change. If a manufacturer significantly increases its advertising spending this quarter and sales rise at the same time, then common sense would suggest that the rise in sales is likely to be due to the rise in advertising. But what if, at the same time, interest rates had significantly fallen? It then becomes difficult to know whether the rise in sales was due to the rise in advertising spending or the fall in interest rates or some combination of the two. It could be that the advertising campaign was actually a failure and had no effect on sales. The rise in sales may have been due entirely to the reduced cost of borrowing. So although there was a positive correlation between advertising and sales, in fact increased advertising did not cause the rise in sales.

There are also examples of **nonsense correlations**. Studies have shown that there may be a high correlation coefficient between two variables, but in practice little chance of any real relationship. For example, it has been shown that a strong negative correlation of -0.98 exists between the birth rate in the UK and the production of pig iron in the USA between 1875 and 1920.

It is therefore important for businesses to understand what other variables may have changed at the same time. In a fast-moving economy, there may be many changes which have an impact on a variable such as sales.

KNOWLEDGE

1. State two reasons why a business might analyse it markets.
2. State three benefits of using IT in market analysis.
3. Why might a business want to know the trends in sales for a product it makes?
4. 'A business can extrapolate future trends by looking at past trends.' Explain what this means.
5. How might a line of best fit be drawn on a scatter diagram?
6. Explain briefly why trend forecasts may prove to be wrong.
7. What is the difference between a positive correlation and a negative correlation?
8. Why might two variables be correlated and yet one variable not be the cause of the other variable?

KEYTERMS

Correlation – a measurement of the extent to which there is a relationship between two variables.
Extrapolation – a technique to forecast future variables, such as sales, through analysing past trends.
Line of best fit – a straight line which best represents the general trend taking place from a series of data.
Scatter graph or diagram – a graph on which is plotted a series of points, each point showing the value of the two variables on each axis. If there is a correlation between the two variables, it will be possible to draw a trend line on the graph and to extrapolate future values of the two variables.
Trend – the direction of movement of a variable such as sales or costs.

Case Study: *Propoil*

Propoil is a small oil production and exploration company. It operates globally, but 60 per cent of its production comes from oil fields in Latin America.

Production varies from quarter to quarter, as can be seen from Table 4. With existing oil fields, technical problems can force a well to cease production for a time. Equally, some of Propoil's wells are relatively old and the amount of oil that can be pumped out of these wells declines over time. New wells, however, are also coming onstream.

Oil exploration is much riskier than oil production. There is no guarantee that any exploratory well drilled will yield oil. Over the past couple of years, oil businesses had increasing difficulty in finding new sources of oil. Some argue that all the large oil fields around the world have now been discovered. New fields will be smaller and more expensive to develop per barrel of oil recovered. The directors at Propoil have recently discussed whether to stop exploration altogether. If exploration were stopped, the company would, in the short term, be more profitable. An alternative approach would be effectively to outsource exploration by buying up oil fields that other companies had discovered. Figure 5 shows the amount of money spent by Propoil on exploring new fields and the number of commercially viable fields that it

has found as a result. Most of the exploratory wells sunk by Propoil prove to be uncommercial.

(a) (i) Calculate a centred four quarter moving average for Propoil's oil production shown in Table 4. (6 marks)
   (ii) Plot this centred four quarter moving average on a graph. (2 marks)
   (iii) Using your graph, estimate production in the first quarter of 2006 and the first quarter of 2007. (2 marks)
   (iv) Discuss whether your estimates are likely to prove accurate for production in the first quarters of 2006 and 2007. (10 marks)

(b) (i) To what extent is there a correlation shown in Figure 5 between the amount of money spent by Propoil on exploration and the number of commercially viable wells found? (6 marks)
   (ii) Discuss whether the company should continue exploring for oil. (14 marks)

Figure 5: Oil exploration costs and number of commercial oil wells found

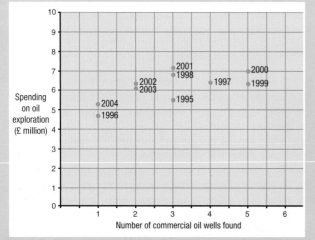

Table 4: Propoil: oil production and crude oil prices

		Oil production, millions of barrels	Brent crude oil, $ per barrel, start of each quarter
2001	Q1	18.3	23.18
	Q2	18.5	23.85
	Q3	18.6	25.96
	Q4	18.8	21.08
2001	Q1	19.4	19.90
	Q2	19.1	26.87
	Q3	19.3	25.53
	Q4	19.7	29.35
2003	Q1	19.4	30.64
	Q2	19.8	27.21
	Q3	19.9	27.93
	Q4	19.5	28.23
2004	Q1	20.3	30.15
	Q2	20.4	32.19
	Q3	20.1	33.64
	Q4	20.8	47.29

62 | Marketing budgets

Marketing budgeting

A budget is a plan of operations for a future accounting period. A MARKETING BUDGET is therefore a plan of operations for a future accounting period which relates to the marketing department. As with all budgets, the marketing budget is:

- **quantifiable**, i.e. expressed in numerical terms;
- linked to the **objectives** of the business;
- a **plan** showing what the business wants to achieve and is different from a forecast.

For example, a **sales budget** sets sales targets over a period of time. Table 1 shows part of a sales budget for two different medicine products, Lynix and Polix, within a company's product range. Sales targets are set for each month over a six month period. They are expressed in terms of the physical number of products sold, the average sale price, the value of total sales and the market share for each product. Sales budgets can also break down targets in a variety of other ways. For example, it might be broken down by area or region, by distribution channel, or type of customer.

Other parts of the marketing budget are concerned with expenditure. These set out how the marketing department plans to spend resources allocated to them over a time period. For example, the marketing department has to plan how much to spend on above-the-line and below-the-line promotion. This is not just spending on advertising but also, for example, on market research, direct sales promotion or the sales force.

Methods of setting budgets

There is a variety of methods which a business might use to set its marketing budgets.

Historical budgeting HISTORICAL BUDGETING (sometimes called INCREMENTAL BUDGETING) is where the budget in the next time period is based on the outcome of the previous time period. For example, if sales were £220,000 this year, the budget might allow for a 5 per cent increase in sales to £231,000. Historical budgeting tends to rely upon looking at past trends and projecting them forward. This can have its problems because past trends are not always accurate predictors of future events. For example, changing inflation rates, changes in competition or a boom in the economy can alter the value of sales.

Affordable budgeting Businesses have many costs, including raw material costs and labour costs. The AFFORDABLE BUDGETING method bases planned marketing expenditure on what is left over after all these other more essential costs have been paid. The impact of affordable budgeting can be seen when an economy moves from boom to recession. Marketing expenditure is then often badly hit. This is because businesses typically cut their marketing spending before they cut costs such as staffing.

The advantage of affordable budgeting is that businesses only spend on marketing what they can afford. The disadvantage is that there is no attempt to match marketing spending with its effects on sales and profits. In a downturn in the economy, for example, it might make more sense to increase marketing to stabilise sales or minimise their fall. Increased marketing in a recession might also allow a business to gain market share at the expense of businesses which have cut their marketing budgets. Instead, the affordable budgeting method would see a typical business cutting its marketing spending.

Sales-based budgeting SALES-BASED or SALES-RELATED budgeting is a method used for marketing expenditure budgets. Marketing expenditure on individual products, product ranges or sales areas in the budget is based on sales achieved. For example, a product which sold £1 million would have ten times the amount of marketing expenditure allocated to it than a product which only sold £100,000.

The **percentage of past sales method** uses past sales to determine the marketing expenditure budget. In contrast, the **percentage of future sales method** uses the figures for future sales. Sometimes, businesses use the **advertising: sales ratio** as a method for planning advertising expenditure. The advertising: sales ratio is the proportion of sales which is spent on advertising. If the advertising: sales ratio were 10 per cent, for

Table 1: A six month sales budget for two products of a pharmaceuticals company

	January	February	March	April	May	June
Lynix						
Number of sales (000s)	75	73	72	75	77	79
Average price	1.21	1.24	1.24	1.25	1.26	1.26
Sales value (£000)	90.75	90.52	89.28	93.75	97.02	99.54
Market share (%)	9.6	9.6	9.7	9.7	9.8	9.8
Polix						
Number of sales (000s)	167	162	160	167	170	174
Average price	0.46	0.48	0.48	0.49	0.5	0.5
Sales value (£000)	76.82	77.76	76.80	81.83	85	87
Market share (%)	15.8	15.8	15.9	16.1	16.2	16.2

Question 1.

Look at the six month sales budget in Table 1.

(a) Explain whether the data in Table 1 represents actual sales, forecast sales or target sales.

(b) Discuss which product, Lynix or Polix, has been set the more ambitious sales target over the six month period.

example, then for every £10 of sales, there would be £1 spent on advertising.

Sales-related budgeting methods are simple to understand and implement. They also allocate scarce marketing resources towards more successful products. However, it is a crude way of planning marketing spending. For example, more sales might be generated by spending an extra pound of advertising on a product with 50,000 sales per week than one with 500,000 sales per week. Advertising a highly successful product may have little impact on sales. Advertising a product with far fewer or declining sales may generate a large number of extra sales. Also, marketing expenditure is not just about gaining extra sales. It is about gaining extra profitable sales. Spending money on promoting high profit margin niche products may be far more profitable than expenditure on the promotion of low profit margin mass market products.

Competitor budgeting COMPETITOR BUDGETING (also known as COMPETITOR-BASED or PARITY BUDGETING) allocates marketing expenditure according to what rival businesses are spending on competing products. For example, a soap powder manufacturer may spend £10 million a year on advertising because a rival soap powder manufacturer is spending this amount.

Competitor budgeting has the advantage that it takes into account market forces. Marketing expenditure clearly has an impact on sales and profits of the average product. It is also simple to understand as a method. However, like sales-related budgeting, it is not necessarily true that matching rivals' spending is the optimal way to allocate scarce marketing resources. If a rival spends 20 per cent more on advertising a particular product, it may be better for the business not to match this even if sales decline. Instead, there may be more profitable ways of allocating spending where the decline in sales is more than matched by increases in sales and profits on other

products. Also, businesses may find it difficult to identify exactly how much rivals spend. Finally, the planned spending may not help the business to achieve its objectives set out in the marketing plan.

Objective and task budgeting OBJECTIVE AND TASK BUDGETING allocates marketing expenditure according to the objectives of the business and the tasks that must be carried out to meet those objectives. For example, if an objective is to increase sales of a product by 20 per cent over three years, then extra marketing resources will probably have to be allocated to that product in the budget. A mature product may need little marketing support if sales growth is not an objective. In contrast, a new product may need heavy marketing to get it past its launch stage successfully. At its most sophisticated, a marketing department may have to justify its spending by calculating its rate of return. Then it can be compared with other possible spending such as investment in training of workers, or investment in new machinery. When marketing departments refer to 'investment in marketing', they are implying that such comparisons can be made.

Objective and task budgeting most clearly ties marketing spending in with objectives and the tasks needed to ensure that those objectives are met. As such, it is often seen as the most effective way to plan a budget. However, it requires a sophisticated approach to marketing where no simple rules apply. There is also no guarantee of success. Products launched at considerable marketing expense may fail. Mature products with little marketing expenditure back-up may suddenly go into the decline phase of the product life cycle because a rival business launches a better competing product.

Setting the budget

In practice, the marketing budget in a medium to large sized business is likely to be set by the marketing manager or director together with the managing director. It is the managing director, perhaps with the board of directors, who will determine the overall size of the budget and possibly set the targets for sales and profits. The marketing director will determine how spending is allocated between different products and different types of marketing. In a large marketing department, parts of setting the budget may be delegated further down the chain of command to budget holders. A **budget holder** is an employee responsible for a particular budget area.

How much involvement middle managers will have in preparing the budget will vary from business to business. In a centralised organisation, it is more likely that budgets will be drawn up by those higher up the organisation. In a more decentralised organisation, aspects of preparing the budget may be pushed down the hierarchy. In a centralised organisation, senior management may wish to keep a tight control on decision making, using their expertise to draw up budgets which will further the objectives of the business. In a more decentralised organisation, employees may be more motivated

Question 2.

TPG is a magazine publisher with a wide range of titles in the UK, France and the USA. One of its most successful magazines is Got Ya!, part of the 'lads mags' segment of the market. Sales of Got Ya! in established markets has been declining for the past five years, part of the overall trend for all lads mags magazines. TPG has been unwilling to increase the marketing budget for Got Ya! in recent years because it feels that an increased marketing spend would have little impact on sales. The problems with the magazine relate to the decline in the market, the strong product offering of competing magazines and the inability to find a new angle on the product format. Its research also shows that there has been little if any increase in marketing spend by competing magazines.

However, the Chinese market has recently been liberalised, with Western publishers able to sell titles to a potential 1.3 billion customers. TPG has decided to launch a Chinese version of Got Ya!. It aims to have initial sales of 250,000 magazines per month rising to 500,000 within three years. It expects the magazine to break even within 6 months and thereafter to have a net profit margin of 20 per cent. It has allocated an extra £800,000 to the marketing budget for Got Ya! for the six month period after the launch. It will then review the budget and decide whether further spending is required for the magazine to achieve its sales and profit goals.

Source: adapted from the Financial Times, 13.5.2004.

(a) Using a diagram, explain where Got Ya! is in its product life cycle (i) in the UK and (ii) in China.
(b) Discuss what methods of setting marketing budgets are being used by TPG.

marketing budgets.

As with any other type of budgeting, marketing budgetary control tends to become more common the larger the size of the business. Without proper marketing budgetary control, it would impossible to run a large business because there would be no effective control of expenditure. Equally, planning for growth would not be present. So budgetary control is an important tool of management for medium to large businesses.

KEY TERMS

Affordable budgeting – a budgeting method where planned marketing expenditure is based on what is left over after all other more essential costs have been paid.
Competitor budgeting (or competitor-based budgeting or parity budgeting) – a budgeting method where marketing expenditure is allocated according to what rival businesses are spending on competing products.
Historical budgeting (or incremental budgeting) – where the budget in the next time period is based on the outcome of the previous time period.
Marketing budget – a plan of operations for a future accounting period which relates to the marketing department.
Objective and task budgeting – where the budget is set according to the objectives of the business and the tasks that must be carried out to meet those objectives.
Sales-based budgeting (or sales-related budgeting) – where the size of the marketing budget is determined by the level of sales achieved and where the allocation of the marketing budget between different products, product ranges or sales areas is based on their relative sales.

if they have been part of the decision making process. On the other hand, they may deliberately choose undemanding targets, or inflate their expenditure budgets. If planned sales, for example, are targeted to grow by 1 per cent in the budget when sales have been growing at 5 per cent per annum over the last five years, then the marketing department is likely to achieve its 1 per cent target easily. They can then get the credit for achieving their target even though it was far too low in the first place. Equally, departments have a tendency to inflate their planned costs. It then becomes much easier to stay within budget. It also allows departments to spend on their favourite projects even if it is unlikely that this will benefit sales or profits.

The usefulness of budgeting

There is a number of advantages and disadvantages to a business of budgetary control. They are explained in the unit titled 'Using budgets'. Exactly the same arguments for budgets in general apply to marketing budgets. Variances can also be calculated for

KNOWLEDGE

1. What might be contained within a marketing budget?
2. What is the difference between a budget set using the historical budgeting method and one set using the affordable budgeting method?
3. What is the difference between a budget set using the sales-based budgeting method and one set using the competitor budgeting method?
4. How might a business set a marketing budget using the objective and task method?
5. Who might be involved in setting a marketing budget in a large company?
6. What are the advantages and disadvantages of involving middle managers in the marketing budget setting process?
7. Explain the advantages and disadvantages to a business of marketing budgetary control.

Case Study: *Haffner plc*

Haffner plc is an international cosmetics company. It has four main ranges described in more detail in Figure 1. To fix the marketing budgets for its products, it uses the percentage of past sales method. Since 2000, it has allocated 20 per cent of last year's sales to the marketing budget for the current year. Sales and marketing budgets are shown in Table 2.

Table 2: Annual sales and marketing budgets for Haffner's four main product ranges, £ million

	Emme		Gee		Vee		Cee	
	Sales	Marketing budget	Sales	Marketing budget	Sales	Marketing budget	Sales	Marketing budget
2005	10.6	1.98	23.4	4.74	50.2	10.18	36.8	7.24
2006	10.8	2.12	23.2	4.68	49.2	10.04	37.8	7.36
2007	12.6	2.16	21.8	4.64	47.8	9.84	40.2	7.56
2008	16.6	2.52	20.4	4.36	46.2	9.56	44.6	8.04

(£ million shown in top right corner)

Figure 1: Main product ranges

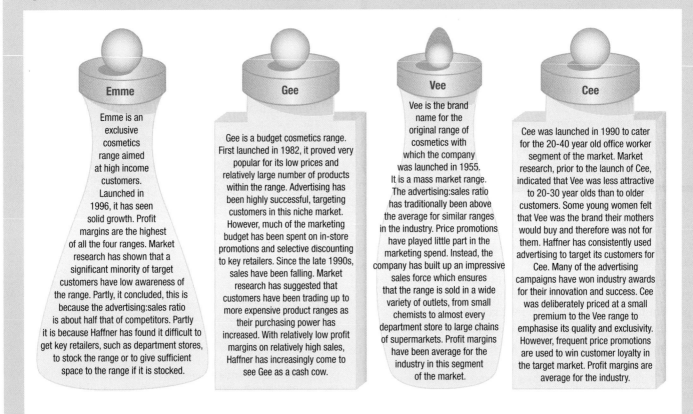

Emme

Emme is an exclusive cosmetics range aimed at high income customers. Launched in 1996, it has seen solid growth. Profit margins are the highest of all the four ranges. Market research has shown that a significant minority of target customers have low awareness of the range. Partly, it concluded, this is because the advertising:sales ratio is about half that of competitors. Partly it is because Haffner has found it difficult to get key retailers, such as department stores, to stock the range or to give sufficient space to the range if it is stocked.

Gee

Gee is a budget cosmetics range. First launched in 1982, it proved very popular for its low prices and relatively large number of products within the range. Advertising has been highly successful, targeting customers in this niche market. However, much of the marketing budget has been spent on in-store promotions and selective discounting to key retailers. Since the late 1990s, sales have been falling. Market research has suggested that customers have been trading up to more expensive product ranges as their purchasing power has increased. With relatively low profit margins on relatively high sales, Haffner has increasingly come to see Gee as a cash cow.

Vee

Vee is the brand name for the original range of cosmetics with which the company was launched in 1955. It is a mass market range. The advertising:sales ratio has traditionally been above the average for similar ranges in the industry. Price promotions have played little part in the marketing spend. Instead, the company has built up an impressive sales force which ensures that the range is sold in a wide variety of outlets, from small chemists to almost every department store to large chains of supermarkets. Profit margins have been average for the industry in this segment of the market.

Cee

Cee was launched in 1990 to cater for the 20-40 year old office worker segment of the market. Market research, prior to the launch of Cee, indicated that Vee was less attractive to 20-30 year olds than to older customers. Some young women felt that Vee was the brand their mothers would buy and therefore was not for them. Haffner has consistently used advertising to target its customers for Cee. Many of the advertising campaigns have won industry awards for their innovation and success. Cee was deliberately priced at a small premium to the Vee range to emphasise its quality and exclusivity. However, frequent price promotions are used to win customer loyalty in the target market. Profit margins are average for the industry.

(a) Showing all your workings, and assuming that the method of setting budgets remains the same, calculate
   (i) the total marketing budget for Haffner in 2008;
   (ii) total sales for Haffner in 2008;
   (iii) sales of Cee in 2004;
   (iv) the marketing budget for Vee in 2009. (8 marks)

(b) Discuss how marketing budgets might have been different if Haffner had used a percentage of forecast sales method to determine marketing budgets over the period 2004-2009. (12 marks)

(c) To what extent could Haffner increase its overall profitability if it used a different method of setting budgets than the percentage of past sales method? (20 marks)

Marketing strategy

A MARKETING STRATEGY is a set of plans about marketing which are designed to fulfil the objectives of a business. A marketing strategy might, for example, set out plans about product development, pricing and promotion to achieve marketing objectives, such as breaking into new markets or increasing sales of existing products.

A marketing strategy is a set of plans about the future. A successful marketing strategy must have plans which are achievable and realistic. Marketing plans in practice may simply be the 'wish lists' of the marketing department, which have little chance of success. For example, at the moment it may be unrealistic for Waitrose to have as its marketing strategy 'the growth of the business so that it becomes the number 1 supermarket chain in the UK within two to three years'. It is so far behind the current number 1, Tesco, that within three years it highly unlikely that it would achieve this. But a realistic strategy could be to 'increase market share at the expense of small independent grocery retailers'.

Marketing strategy will differ from one business to another. Partly this is because there are many different markets and industries in which they operate. But even businesses in the same market adopt different marketing strategies. For example, the marketing strategy of Aldi and Netto in the grocery market is to offer goods at lower prices than larger rivals, such as Sainsbury or Tesco. The marketing strategy of Sainsbury and Tesco places more importance on their product ranges and the quality of their products.

Another reason why marketing strategy differs is because no two businesses have identical resources. Jaguar cars, for example, has expertise in developing, producing and marketing luxury cars. Vauxhall in the UK may have more expertise in the family car market. So their marketing strategies are likely to be different.

Developing a marketing strategy

There are many ways in which a marketing strategy can be developed.

For a small, established business, a marketing strategy could be simply to continue as before. Only if circumstances change might a business change its marketing strategy. This is an example of a rational marketing strategy, if the objective is to continue making the same level of profit. Developing a marketing strategy requires time and resources. It also involves predicting how a market will develop, which could be wrong. Formal planning, therefore, would be costly and could be of little value.

Similarly, in businesses where there are charismatic leaders, planning may be pointless. The leader may be constantly making

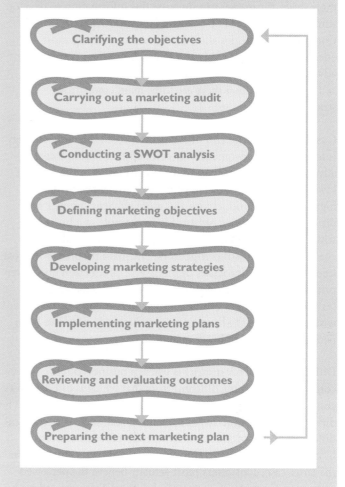

Figure 1: The stages of preparing a marketing strategy

- Clarifying the objectives
- Carrying out a marketing audit
- Conducting a SWOT analysis
- Defining marketing objectives
- Developing marketing strategies
- Implementing marketing plans
- Reviewing and evaluating outcomes
- Preparing the next marketing plan

decisions as events change. These decisions might have little to do with a prepared strategy.

However, many larger businesses use a method of preparing marketing strategies which is logical and rational. The main stages of this method are shown in Figure 1.

Competitive marketing strategies

Many businesses are finding that the markets in which they operate are increasingly competitive. Two factors might explain this. First, the increasing internationalisation of trade means that many markets that were dominated by domestic business are now open to foreign competition. Businesses operating within the EU experienced increases in competition after the creation of the single European market. Second, government attempts throughout the world to release market forces have led to many markets being privatised and liberalised. This has often led to greater competition. China, in the 2000s, opened up its economy so that foreign business can operate in the country.

These changes have led businesses to pay careful attention to their competitors when creating marketing strategies. Businesses often carry out competitor analysis. Competitor analysis allows a business to develop a knowledge and understanding of its competitors' behaviour before deciding on a suitable strategy. This provides businesses with a variety of information about their rivals. Businesses can then use this information to develop suitable COMPETITIVE MARKETING STRATEGIES. Competitive strategies allow businesses to compete most effectively with their rivals and to maximise their competitive advantage.

It is suggested that there are three main competitive strategies.

Cost leadership The aim of following a cost leadership strategy is to gain a cost advantage over competitors. This **low cost** advantage can then be passed on to consumers in the form of lower prices. Businesses can gain a cost advantage by having higher levels of productivity and more efficient supplier and distribution networks. Amstrad is an example of a business which has pursued this strategy. It provides electrical goods cheaper than those of competitors. The main problem with cost leadership is that it focuses upon costs of production and lower prices rather than the needs of customers. This may create certain problems. For example, consumers might not always wish to purchase the lowest price product as it may have been perceived as being of lower quality.

Differentiation This strategy is where a business offers consumers something different from that which is offered by its competitors, in order to gain a competitive 'edge' over them. The difference can be in terms of something real, such as a technical difference in the product itself, or perceived, such as a strong brand identity developed through a promotional campaign. In the latter case, consumers must actually believe the perceived difference. Guinness, for example, has been differentiated both in terms of its smooth consistency and taste, and through marketing campaigns which promote it as an 'intelligent' drink.

Focus Businesses adopting focus strategies concentrate upon particular market segments rather than the market as a whole. They attempt to meet effectively the needs of a clearly defined group of consumers. By following this strategy, a business seeks to gain a competitive advantage over other businesses which spread their efforts over a wider range of consumers. For example, there is a small but thriving market for hand made, made-to-measure suits.

Market positioning

Another set of competitive marketing strategies is based upon the 'position' which a business wishes to occupy in relation to other businesses operating in the same market.

Market leader strategies In many markets there is one business which is generally recognised as the market leader. Market

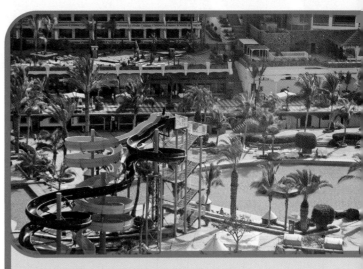

Question 1.

Travel giants, such as Thomas Cook and JMC, slashed their prices of Spanish holidays by an average £150 in 2004. This was almost unheard of. But it was in response to the growing impact made by cut price airlines. It was seen as a deliberate attempt to win back custom from the low cost airlines.

It was the first time that the major companies felt that they had to cut the cost of ordinary family holidays to popular destinations. Two adults travelling to Majorca with Thomas Cook would save £120. Five adults going to Gran Canaria with JMC would save £210. Cosmos introduced a 'two kids free' deal to seven family resorts.

Bookings for holidays in popular resorts such as Spain had been sluggish. However, resorts outside the eurozone, such as in the eastern Mediterranean, were doing well.

Source: adapted from *The Daily Mail*, 26.1.2004.

(a) **Analyse the competitive strategies and market positions of the businesses in the travel industry using examples from the data.**

leaders tend to have the largest share of a particular market. Market leaders may also be businesses which lead the market in terms of price changes and promotional spending. An example of a market leader might be Microsoft in the software market. There is a number of strategies which market leaders can adopt to improve or maintain their market leadership.

- Expanding the total market. As holders of the largest market share, market leaders stand most to gain by expanding the market. Expanding the market can be achieved by attracting new product users, promoting new uses for the product or encouraging greater product usage. For example, breakfast cereal manufacturers have tried to get consumers to eat cereal at different times of the day.

- Expanding market share. Market leaders may use the range of elements in the marketing mix to expand their current market share at the expense of competitors'. For example, Microsoft increased its share of the computer software market by establishing its product as the standard PC operating system.

- Defending current market share. The aim here is to prevent competitors from increasing their market share at the expense of the market leader. Most market leaders take the view that defending market share can best be achieved by continually improving the way in which they meet consumer needs. Often this is achieved with the use of complex and sophisticated marketing strategies. For example, some commentators have seen the development by Nestlé of a range of brands in the instant coffee market not only as an example of meeting new needs, but also as a sophisticated form of defence. The development of the Alta Rica, Cap Colombie and Blend 37 brands can be seen as a defence of Nescafé and Gold Blend against competitors seeking to damage Nestlé's share of this market by gaining a foothold in smaller segments.

Market challenger strategies MARKET CHALLENGERS are those businesses with a substantial share of the market. However, they hold second, third or lower positions in the market in relation to the market leader. Not all businesses with lower market shares than the leader are market challengers. To be defined as market challengers businesses must be in a strong enough position to challenge the leader and be willing to adopt strategies to win more market share. There are three main types of strategy that market challengers can adopt.

- Direct attacks on the market leader. Here the market challenger must be prepared to directly compete in terms of the market leaders' strengths and also to match its marketing mix. To do this the market challenger must be able to match the resources of the market leader and to respond to retaliatory actions by the market leader. Such retaliatory actions often take the form of price cutting and aggressive promotion and distribution campaigns.
- Indirect attacks on the market leader. Because of the problems involved in mounting a direct attack upon a market leader, many market followers choose to adopt less confrontational strategies. One of the most common is to identify areas in which the market leader is less strong and to develop products designed to address these weaknesses. For example, businesses have attempted to compete with the crisp manufacturer Walkers by offering exotic snack foods, such as popadums and Chinese rice crackers.
- Attacking firms other than the market leader. This allows a business to increase its market share by attacking relatively weaker businesses. For example, many of the larger brewing businesses have increased their market share in this way in the UK by taking over smaller breweries.

Market follower strategies Many businesses occupying lower positions in a market do not wish to challenge the market leader. Challenges to a market leader often lead to retaliatory action and cause expensive battles, which often hurt challengers more than they do leaders. For this reason many businesses choose to follow the strategies of market leaders. There are three main types of MARKET FOLLOWERS.

- Those who imitate market leaders. Own brand products in supermarkets fall into this category, as do canned drinks such as Virgin Cola. In more extreme cases imitation may lead to cloning. This occurs when one business seeks to copy the market leaders' products without originating anything itself.
- Innovative businesses. Such businesses lack the resources to challenge market leaders. They tend to willingly follow moves made by market leaders so that they do not change the structure of the market.
- Businesses not capable of challenging market leaders which are content to satisfice. It is not unusual to find such businesses in the take-away food market. These businesses have little competitive advantage. They tend to be vulnerable to changes in the market and may fail as a consequence.

Market niche strategies Market niches are very small segments of the market. They are sometimes described as segments within segments. The majority of businesses which operate in niche markets tend to be small and medium sized. However, some larger businesses have divisions specialising in market niches. Niches can be based upon geographical location, specific product differentiation, customer group or product type. Examples of businesses adopting market niche strategies include Tie Rack, Reuters and TVR, the sports car manufacturer.

Marketing strategies for growth

Many businesses operate in or intend to move into markets where business growth is both desirable and possible. Businesses operating in such markets will tend to emphasise growth in their corporate and marketing objectives. Growth may be in the form of increased sales revenue or turnover, greater profits, increased capital or more land and employees. There is a range of marketing strategies that growth orientated businesses can adopt. Growth orientated marketing strategies are not suited to all businesses, however. In shrinking markets, for example, a business may wish to maintain previous sales levels or just survive rather than aim for growth.

The ANSOFF MATRIX is a useful tool for businesses aiming for growth. The Ansoff Matrix shown in Figure 2 illustrates both existing and new products within existing and new markets.

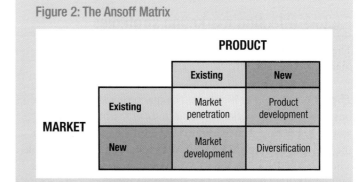

Figure 2: The Ansoff Matrix

Four possible marketing strategies to achieve growth are revealed by the Matrix.

Market penetration As suggested by the Ansoff Matrix, the purpose of market penetration is to achieve growth in existing markets with existing products. There is a number of ways in which businesses can achieve this.

- Increasing the brand loyalty of customers so that they use substitute brands less frequently. Well known brands such as Kellogg's Corn Flakes make use of this strategy.
- Encouraging consumers to use the product more regularly. An example might be encouraging people to drink canned drinks at breakfast.
- Encouraging consumers to use more of the product. An example might be a crisp manufacturer producing maxi sized crisp packets rather than standard sized crisp packets.

Product development This is concerned with marketing new or modified products in existing markets. The development of the Ford Focus, intended to act as a replacement for the Ford Escort, is an example of product development. Confectionery manufacturers, such as Cadbury and Nestlé, regularly use this strategy in order to stimulate sales growth.

Market development This involves the marketing of existing products in new markets. For example, the Halifax has extended its banking activities to the Spanish market and Harvey Nichols, a retail outlet previously limited to London, has opened branches in Leeds and Manchester.

Diversification This occurs when new products are developed for new markets. Diversification allows a business to move away from reliance upon existing markets and products. This allows a business to spread risk and increase safety. If one product faces difficulties or fails, a successful product in another market may prevent the business overall facing problems. However, diversification will take a business outside its area of expertise. This might mean that its performance in new markets is relatively poor compared to more experienced operators. The move by Mercedes Benz into the market for small, high volume cars and the move by Virgin into financial services and the air passenger business are perhaps examples of this marketing strategy.

Factors affecting marketing strategies

There is a number of factors that may influence a business's marketing strategy.

The objectives of the business The marketing strategy that a business uses must reflect the objectives of the business as a whole. Marketing strategies must therefore be consistent with the wider corporate objectives of the organisation. For example, a business which is aiming to reduce the number of countries into which it operates should not develop international marketing strategies which go against this wider, corporate

strategy. However, marketing strategies are not always secondary to corporate objectives. In some businesses, marketing information and strategies often have a strong influence upon corporate objectives and strategies. A growing market for ethical customers, for example, may persuade the business to deal only with those businesses that conform to certain ethical principles.

The strategies of competitor businesses As shall be seen later in this unit, many businesses take account of the strategies of their competitors when setting their own marketing strategies. For example, if a competitor promotes all of its company products on the Internet successfully, other businesses may follow.

The structure of the market Marketing strategies will be influenced by the level of competition and the degree of change within different markets. In less competitive markets, with relatively little change, for example, businesses may find that their strategies require only minor adjustments from one period to another. In more competitive and dynamic markets businesses may find that marketing strategies require far reaching changes on an annual basis. For example, a manufacturer of active wear clothing aimed at 16-24 year olds may need to constantly monitor changes in tastes.

The attitudes of key decision makers within businesses Marketing strategies are likely to be influenced by the attitudes of decision makers towards matters such as the desirability of risk and change. Such attitudes are influenced by the environment within which a business operates, but also by the views of managers and directors and the culture of the business itself. For example, new managers aiming to alter the 'direction' of a business may decide to change the entire distribution network to mail order and sell off its retail outlets, because this has worked successfully in other businesses.

The size of the business Larger businesses are likely to be strongly influenced by one or more of the above factors when making decisions about their marketing strategies. Smaller and medium-sized businesses, however, often find strategic decision making more challenging. This is because the owners and managers of such businesses are often so immersed in the operational side of their work that they take few opportunities to adopt a strategic outlook. As a result, marketing strategy may be influenced by 'intuition' and responses to daily pressures.

The strengths of the business Asset-based or asset-led marketing is where a business develops those products that make the best use of its 'core competences'. These are the major strengths of the firm. It produces goods or services that make the best use of its resources. Many businesses see brand loyalty or goodwill as a major **intangible asset**.

The marketing strategy adopted by such businesses will therefore attempt to develop products that can be associated with the brand names of its successful products. Many food manufacturers have followed this marketing strategy in recent years. Examples have included ice cream Mars Bars and Kit Kat Chunky. One of the most successful companies in the world, the Walt Disney Company, has perhaps followed this strategy into a number of areas. The launch by Ikea of a new range of furniture or a construction company moving into house renovation might be other examples. Examples in the service industry might include travel companies buying cottages to let for holidays or buying ships to sell cruise holidays.

International marketing strategy

Many businesses view the world as having 'shrunk' over the last 30 or so years due to, among other things, rapid changes in international transport and telecommunications. One effect of this is that a business now needs to consider the threat from

Question 2.

In 2004 Levi went back to the drawing board with its classic Levi 501 jeans. They were recut in a bid to attract a new generation of wearers. Too many young people were put off by 'middle aged men' such as Top Gear presenter Jeremy Clarkson, who continued to wear jeans. The company planned to spend £10 million on the new jeans aimed at the under 25s rather than over 40s. The jeans would retail at £50 a pair and would resemble the original denim work trousers designed and marketed by Levi Strauss in 1873. A TV campaign would support the launch. The company suggested that the 501s on general sale in the UK were very eighties and nineties and had begun to look dated. Levi had faced competition from a wide variety of jeans manufacturers. These included own brand jeans from shops such as Gap and 'designer' jeans from Firetrap, Armani and Ted Baker, as well as traditional jeans manufacturers such as Wrangler.

In the USA everybody's heard of Levi jeans, but not enough people are buying them. Instant brand recognition is not enough. It had some success in wooing women, particularly with its new low waist jeans for young women. People know that Levis made good quality jeans, but want more than a box fit. Research has shown that its image perception is improving, but it needs to react more quickly to fast changing trends in the fashion scene.

Source: adapted from *The Daily Mail*, and www.mercurynews.com.

(a) Identify the factors that may have contributed to the changes in marketing strategy by Levis.
(b) To what extent do you think that Levis might make use of its assets in its new strategy?

foreign competition and the opportunities which might be gained from marketing internationally. For many firms international marketing is no longer an option. It is necessary if a business is to survive in a competitive business environment. For British firms this was the case after trade barriers between European Union nations were lifted in 1992 and intensified with the expansion of the EU in 2004. The increase in the size and number of multinationals has also contributed to the increase in international trading. The globalisation of business activity has also affected business marketing strategy as it becomes increasingly common even for small businesses to engage in international trading.

There can be many rewards for a business entering an overseas market.

- **Profits.** By selling in overseas markets, a business might have the potential to increase its profits through an increase in sales. Overseas markets may be more lucrative than domestic ones. Manufacturing and distribution costs may be lower abroad. The product might also sell at a higher price on foreign markets than in the home market.
- **Spreading the risk.** If a business only produces in one country then it may face problems caused by downturns in demand due to recession. The more countries a firm operates in, the less vulnerable it is to changes in the business climate of any single country.
- **Unfavourable trading conditions in the domestic market.** Businesses often find that the market for a product is saturated or in decline. One option for a firm is to try and breathe new life into the product by introducing it into an overseas market. This is an example of an extension strategy. British American Tobacco industries, for example, have started to sell in developing countries as domestic market sales have declined.
- **Legal differences.** Legal restrictions on the sale of products vary from one country to another. For example, developing countries have fewer restrictions on which drugs can be offered for sale. Some pharmaceutical companies (in what many regard as unethical practice) have sold drugs banned on health grounds in the UK to these nations.

Why the overseas market is different

There can be many rewards for a business entering an overseas market.

One problem that it will face, however, is that market conditions will be different to those in the domestic market. This makes selling abroad very risky. What are the differences that are likely to affect the success of foreign sales?

Political differences A firm must take into account the political stability of the country in which it plans to sell. Political instability can make trading almost impossible. Also, a change of government can bring about a change in attitude towards foreign companies. A firm thinking of investing a large sum in its operations abroad will need to weigh up the political situation carefully. A number of businesses, for example, were affected by the change in government in Hong Kong in 1997 as ownership of the area was transferred from the UK to China.

Cultural differences One difference which often causes problems for British businesses is that English is not the main or even the second language in many countries. In Eastern Europe for example, German and Russian may be more widely spoken than English.

Other cultural differences may influence the way a product is marketed. For example, a product name suitable in one country may have a totally different meaning in another – the French lemonade Pssschit would require a new name were it to be sold in the UK. Colours have different meanings throughout the world. In the Far East, white rather than black is associated with mourning. In India fashion models of the sort used to promote products in the West are considered too thin. In some countries, what may be regarded as a 'bribe' in the UK is common business practice. Payments to government or industry officials may be required to get things done, from electricity connection to securing contracts.

Differences in legislation Such differences can affect the way in which a business produces and markets its products.

- **Product labelling.** US laws are far more stringent than UK laws about the amount of information which should be included on food labels.
- **Product safety.** Some countries have very strict legislation governing safety standards on childrens' toys. Others are less strict.
- **Environmental impact.** All cars sold in California, for example, must be fitted with a catalytic convertor.
- **Advertising.** Cigarette advertising on television is outlawed within EU countries.

Economic and social differences Some of the economic factors which businesses must consider include levels of income, levels of sales and corporation tax, how income is distributed, the use of tariffs or other import barriers and the level and growth of population. For example, many foreign businesses took advantage of investment opportunities in China in 2004 after the country 'opened up' its economy and its trading arrangements.

Social factors which firms may need to consider include literacy levels, the role of women, religious attitudes, readiness to accept new ideas, and the habits and attitudes of social groups.

Differences in business practice The usual amount of time it takes to receive payment may vary in different countries. Other differences include accounting techniques, company ownership (most British companies are relatively independent whereas those in other EU nations are often controlled by families or banks) and distribution (in many EU countries greater use is made of rail transport than in the UK).

Adapting products to fit in with local, national and regional needs can be costly. It is cheaper to have one product with one brand name and a promotional package which fits all markets. Businesses must attempt to cater for national consumer tastes, whilst trying to gain economies of scale from operating in international markets.

KEY TERMS

Ansoff Matrix – a model which identifies growth strategies for businesses based on an analysis of their products and their markets.

Competitive marketing strategies – marketing strategies directly based upon particular approaches to dealing with competitors.

Market challengers – businesses which are in a position to threaten the market leader.

Market follower – a business which mimics or copies the strategies of the dominant businesses or businesses in the market.

Marketing strategy – a set of plans designed to achieve the marketing objectives of a business.

KNOWLEDGE

1. What is meant by a strategic marketing decision?
2. Outliine the stages in developing a marketing strategy.
3. State the three aspects of competitor analysis.
4. Explain the difference between a cost leadership and a differentiation strategy.
5. Suggest three ways in which a market leader might protect its market position.
6. Suggest three ways in which a market challenger might improve its market position.
7. What four methods of growth strategy are suggested by the Ansoff Matrix?
8. How might a business gain greater penetration in an existing market with an existing product?
9. State two reasons why a business might engage in international marketing.
10. Identify three problems that a business might face when entering an overseas market.

Case Study: *Marketing coffee in India*

Café culture has taken a firm grip on India's cities, and coffee shops spring up almost daily. Technopak, a consultancy specialising in Indian consumer businesses, argues that 40 per cent-a-year growth is 'conservative'. Not surprisingly foreign chains have begun to scent the profits. Costa Coffee was the pioneer, launching its first coffee shop in Delhi two years ago. John Derkach, UK managing director, says: "The growth in the young Indian middle classes is driving massive growth in the coffee shop market at the moment."

Costa now has 32 outlets in Delhi and is close to opening its second in Mumbai. It plans to have 300 outlets in India within five years, half as many as it has in the UK. But its UK rival Caffè Nero is also planning an entry. Last year it held talks with Dubai's Landmark Group on a franchise agreement, but Landmark wanted a partner with international experience. This September it was back for a second try, holding discussions with a new potential partner.

Another UK brand, Caffè Ritazza, part of travel food services group SSP, has an outlet in Mumbai airport and wants to set up shop across Indian airports and rail stations as they are updated and overhauled.

America's Starbucks, meanwhile, is struggling. Its entry, planned for this autumn, was postponed in July after the Indian government rejected its application for a second time.

Other countries' chains are also getting in on the act. Italy's Lavazza took the most decisive step in March, buying out Barista, India's second-largest chain. Landmark will choose one of two US chains as a partner by mid-December and Gloria Jean's Coffees is expected to arrive by the end of the year.

But no foreign entrant comes close to matching the growth rate of Cafe Coffee Day, India's largest chain, which is backed by Asia's largest coffee-growing business. It is churning out 20 new cafés a month and plans to grow from 480 today to 750 by the end of 2008, and to hit 1,400 in five years. Mr Derkach thinks the chains are thriving in India because they are meeting a previously untapped need: 'Despite India's reputation as a tea-drinking nation, there is no real heritage of tea shops as places for people to sit. Coffee shops are filling a complete gap in the market.'

Simrin Sablok, head of marketing at Cafe Coffee Day, agrees, adding that the parental tight reins on Indian teens makes cafes their only option. 'In India, there's really no place for the youth to hang out, and a cafe is a place where there's no alcohol served, so the parents are happy.'

Mr Singhal is convinced the Indian market is so huge that it can easily accommodate the 10 or more international chains looking to take the plunge. 'While the premium locations have been taken up, India is expanding in every direction. If I was them, I'd feel there's no urgency or hurry.'

Source: adapted from the *Independent on Sunday*, 2.12.2007.

(a) Use the Ansoff Matrix to analyse Costa Coffee's marketing strategy in India. (10 marks)

(b) Examine the factors that may have influenced the strategy chosen by Starbucks. (12 marks)

(c) Discuss whether the strategies used by Starbucks in its efforts to enter the Indian coffee market are likely to be successful. (20 marks)

64 | Marketing plans

Components of a marketing plan

A MARKETING PLAN is a set of proposed marketing actions to be undertaken over a period of time which, if carried out, should enable the business to achieve its marketing objectives. The marketing plan is likely to contain the following, which have been outlined in the previous units.

- **Marketing objectives.** An objective could be to increase market share by 5 per cent over the next year. To accompany this a set of actions may be detailed, such as 'extend local advertising to the North West region' or 'ensure product is competitively priced'. In addition, responsibilities may be allocated between departments, sections and individuals.
- **A marketing budget.** A budget will be set which details how the marketing department will spend its funds.
- **Sales forecasts.** For example, based upon the forecasting techniques employed a business may forecast that sales will increase by 20 per cent over a two year period.
- Marketing strategies. Many of these will centre around the marketing mix. Price, product, promotion and place will be at the core of the actions detailed in the marketing plan.

In a large business, the marketing plan is likely to be developed in outline as part of the overall strategic or corporate plan. A small group of senior marketing managers are likely to be responsible for drawing up the plan. Once this has been agreed, detailed plans will be made within the marketing department. Managers at all levels may be involved in drawing up these more detailed plans.

In a small business, the owner/manager may have drawn up a written marketing plan. This is usually necessary if the business approaches a bank for extra loans or a larger overdraft facility. The marketing plan would be a part of the overall business plan. Often, though, the marketing plan is not written down. The entrepreneur has the plan in his or her head. Equally, the owner may have no marketing plan but may simply react to events as they arise. Using 'hunches' for decision making can be effective if the entrepreneur has a good intuitive understanding of the business environment.

Targets within the marketing plan

Targets should be set within the marketing plan. These should be measurable and understood by those operating the plan. These targets can then form part of the evaluation of the marketing plan. A business could use a number of different criteria.

Sales Sales targets can be set in many forms. For example, sales targets might be set by value (i.e. total sales x average selling price) or by volume (i.e. the number of sales made). Sales targets could be given for different areas of a country or different countries or continents. A multinational company might have sales targets for North America, Europe, Asia and the rest of the world for example. Sales targets are also likely to be set by product. For example, one product might have a sales growth target of 10 per cent per annum, while another might have one of 2 per cent.

Market share Market share can be an important target indicator of competitiveness. A business which aims to increase market share in its marketing plan is attempting to become more competitive relative to other businesses over time. A business which aims to limit loss of market share is likely to take into account that other businesses are going to become more competitive. As with sales targets, market share targets can be split down into market share by product and by region.

Marketing spending and market profitability analysis One criticism of marketing spending is that it is impossible to work out whether it has had an effect on sales, sales revenues and profits. For example, a business might spend £1 million on an advertising campaign and sales values might rise by 2 per cent. It could be that the £1 million spending caused the 2 per cent sales rise. But if at the same time the overall economy had grown by 3 per cent, it could be that the rise in sales was simply due to greater customer spending power. Or the 2 per cent rise in sales values could have been caused by new products entering the product range.

Market profitability analysis is concerned with the relationship between profits and costs. In the context of marketing planning, profitability analysis is calculated by subtracting the marketing costs of a product from the revenue gained from the product:

MARKETING PROFIT = sales revenue of a product (quantity sold x price) - marketing costs marketing research, advertising, distribution, promotion etc.)

Thus a product with high revenue and relatively low marketing costs will be highly profitable. In contrast, a product with low sales revenue and relatively high marketing costs will be less profitable.

The main benefit of calculating marketing profitability is that it can highlight some of the most and least profitable markets. Take the example of a business seeking to increase sales of a particular product by moving into two new markets, A and B. In market A, an increase in sales of 10 per cent can be achieved with additional marketing costs of 5 per cent. In market B, an increase in sales of 45 per cent can be achieved with additional marketing costs of 5 per cent. This business may wish to focus

Question 1.

According to the 2001 census, ethnic minorities make up 9 per cent of England's population. Consumers with an ethnic minority background are typically younger and more likely to own a business than other people. They also tend to live in large urban centres, such as London or the West Midlands conurbation, creating opportunities for cost-effective local marketing. Yet British businesses are only beginning to think seriously about the needs of ethnic minority consumers.

One business area which is taking its ethnic minority customers seriously is financial institutions such as banks and building societies. Banks and building societies with branches in the West Midlands conurbation serve large numbers of customers from ethnic minority backgrounds. Some have developed policies of providing help to such customers. For example, some produce leaflets about saving and mortgage products in a number of different languages including Punjabi. Some also employ people from ethnic minorities who are able to talk to customers in their own language. This means, for example, that a Punjabi speaker can arrange a mortgage by talking to a customer adviser who will conduct the interview in Punjabi.

The financial institutions involved have benefited from this approach. Many ethnic groups have a close-knit character that makes word of mouth a powerful force to be reckoned with. Alexandria Hough, a customer services adviser at the Smethwick branch of the West Bromwich Building Society, says 'recommendation is hugely important. A lot of mortgages we sell to Sikh customers come about through parents telling their children about us.'

Source: adapted from the *Financial Times*, 28.3.2003.

(a) The decision to market to ethnic minorities will have been contained in the marketing plan of a building society. Explain three possible features that might be contained in this marketing plan.

(b) Suggest how a building society in the West Midlands could evaluate the part of its marketing plan relating to ethnic minorities.

upon the more profitable market B.

The problem with calculating marketing profitability is that it is often difficult to calculate the marketing costs of particular products. For example, many promotional activities, such as trade fairs and corporate advertising, cannot be easily apportioned to individual products in businesses with a range of products.

Satisfaction surveys Many businesses undertake analysis of their customer satisfaction surveys. These are detailed surveys designed to identify the reactions of customers to their products. They use this data to assess the extent to which marketing plans are leading to increases or decreases in customer satisfaction.

Number of enquiries generated Many businesses pay very careful attention to the numbers of enquiries generated in particular aspects of their business. For example, financial service businesses monitor and evaluate the enquiries generated by direct mailshots as a means of evaluating the success of such promotions.

It is possible to produce clear data in some areas. For example, a bank which sends out half a million direct mail letters offering loans can measure the proportion of customers who respond. In turn, the proportion of customers finally given a loan can be calculated. So the cost per loan given or the cost per £1 loaned as a result of the direct mailing can be calculated. Equally, a business which is advertising on the Internet can measure the number of 'clicks' on an advert which take a potential customer from the advert to a website. Or the number of 'hits' on a website can be measured and the proportion which leads to a sale on the Internet can be calculated.

But the number of areas where there is such a clear link between marketing spending and sales is limited. Some businesses attempt to get around this problem by using sophisticated mathematical techniques which use correlation techniques to strip out the effect of changes in other variables. Targets for the effect on sales and profits of marketing spending can then be set. However, most businesses would not set such targets in their marketing plan because of the difficulty of getting accurate and reliable data.

Evaluating a marketing plan

A marketing plan should be evaluated at different stages.

At the start While it is being written, managers need to consider whether:
- it meets the objectives set in the marketing strategy and fits in with the corporate strategy of the business;
- the actions described in the marketing plan and their outcomes are realistic;
- the marketing department will be given a sufficiently large budget to carry out its plan.

In operation While the plan is operational, it should be monitored. A number of factors might lead to the plan failing.
- The external environment might become much harsher. For example, it may be difficult to increase sales in a recession.

- Other parts of the overall corporate plan might fail. For example, if the production department planned to increase output by 6 per cent a year, but only managed 2 per cent, then a planned 6 per cent increase in sales is unlikely to come about.
- There might be unforeseen cuts in the marketing budget.
- The original plan may have been too optimistic about the relation between changes to the marketing budget and changes in sales. For example, an expensive advertising campaign may not lead to the increase in sales hoped for. Equally, the marketing plan may have been too pessimistic. For example, the external environment may prove far more favourable than anticipated or an advertising campaign may work far more successfully than predicted.

When a marketing plan clearly is not on target while it is operational, managers should adjust the plan to take account of the new realities facing them. If they don't, they risk the plan becoming useless for operational purposes, as the predictions of the plan become more and more out of line with what is actually happening.

At the end The marketing plan should also be evaluated at the end of the plan. This evaluation should help those drawing up the next plan to see what has been successful and what has gone wrong with the existing plan. They can then build these insights into the new plan.

Co-ordinating the marketing plan with the other business functions

Marketing plans should not be written in isolation from the plans of other departments. In a large business, co-ordination is essential if plans are not to conflict with each other. For example, the marketing department might plan to set up an Internet site and require extra staff to run and develop the operation over the next three years. But the human resources department could be planning to reduce overall staff numbers in the business to achieve greater efficiency. These two plans may conflict. Therefore it is important that both departments agree on a plan which has the same effects.

Co-ordination in a large business is often difficult to achieve. Different departments have different and often conflicting agendas. It may need strong and charismatic leadership from the top of the organisation to get a whole business moving in the same direction. Planning can help achieve this unity of direction, but it is unlikely to be a business solution for problems of poor co-ordination.

Internal influences on marketing plans

There is a number of possible factors that may influence a marketing plan. These include both **internal** and **external** factors. Internal factors are those factors within the business that affect its marketing plans.

The marketing mix Of great importance will be an examination

of the effectiveness of the marketing mix. This will include an analysis of each element of the marketing mix. For example, projections regarding the life span and future profitability of each of the firm's products may be carried out. It should also include an analysis of how well the elements of the marketing mix fit together, for example, the extent to which distribution channels are compatible with the promotions may be considered.

Finance Firms can set themselves ambitious marketing goals. However, unless finance is available to fund plans, such goals are unlikely to be achieved. Consequently, the availability of finance can act as an important constraint upon a business' capacity to realise its marketing plan. For example, the so-called 'credit crunch' experienced by many businesses in 2007-08 meant that for some businesses, most particularly those operating in the property market, the necessary finance to realise marketing plans was not available.

Operational issues There is a number of operational issues internal to a business that can impact upon marketing plans. Two important operational issues in this respect include a business' production processes and the people it employs. Any marketing plan must take into account whether the firm can produce the product. There is little point in planning to increase market share unless enough of the product can be produced to achieve this. A firm cannot plan to launch a new product if it cannot manufacture it. Similarly, a huge range of people will be involved in devising and implementing marketing plans. The objectives of these people will determine the targets set in the plan. Also, the skills and abilities of those people working for a firm will determine whether targets can be met.

External influences on marketing plans

There is also a range of external factors that can influence marketing plans. These are factors outside the business that affect its marketing plans. A major factor can be **competitor's actions**. The behaviour of rival businesses can be an important influence upon a business' marketing plan. For example, the entry into a market of an aggressive new competitor might mean that an existing business within that same market scales down its forecasts for sales growth. On the other hand a rival business exiting a market as a result, for example, of bankruptcy, might open up new opportunities for an existing business.

It is possible to analyse external influences using the PESTLE ANALYSIS. This includes the political, economic, social, technological and environmental factors which affect a business's performance.

- **Political.** This can include the effect of pressure groups or other political organisations. For example, ASH is a pressure group which aims to 'eliminate the harm caused by tobacco'. It might provides information on its website about the effects of smoking and lobbies government to introduce legislation to limit the effects of smoking.

- **Economic.** A wide range of economic factors may affect a business's marketing plans. A buoyant economy, for example, may lead to increased demand for products, higher incomes and the possibility of price increases. Growing unemployment may lead to a fall in future levels of demand. Marketing plans should also take into account the pricing, promotion, distribution and product policies of rival businesses.
- **Social.** Changes in society can have consequences for marketing planning. The decline of the so-called nuclear family and the changing role of women may influence how a business promotes its product. The ageing of the population may influence the types of products which are developed and the channels of distribution used to deliver products to customers.
- **Technological.** Changes in technology can affect marketing plans in a variety of ways. It may make it possible for businesses to manufacture products that were previously thought to be too costly. It may also lead to greater obsolescence and shorter product life cycles. New technological developments, such as interactive television and the Internet, may change the promotional methods that a business uses.
- **Legal factors.** There is an increasing amount of legislation and regulation that may affect the marketing plans of a business. It can vary from controls on the ingredients of products to restrictions on price changes of public utilities, such as water and gas. Much of the legislation affecting the UK comes from the European Union.
- **Environmental factors.** Environmental factors are playing an increasing role in the operation of businesses. Legislation on pollution and emissions might influence production. The expectations of consumers about packaging and ingredients might affect marketing. Pressure groups can affect decisions. Taking into account the effects of operations on the environment can increase business costs, but may also increase sales.

Marketing audits and SWOT analysis

Examining the external and the internal and external factors that affect the marketing of a business is part of a marketing audit as explained in the unit 'Understanding marketing objectives'. The marketing audit should identify the internal strengths (S) and weaknesses (W) of the business. It should also identify the external opportunities (O) and threats (T). SWOT ANALYSIS outlines these factors. Table 1 gives an example of a SWOT analysis for a soft drinks manufacturer.

The advantages of marketing planning

There are advantages to a business of planning its marketing effectively.

- The process of drawing up a marketing plan forces a business to think about how it will act in the future. It can therefore be proactive in its marketing and not just

Table 1: SWOT analysis of a soft drinks manufacturer

STRENGTHS (the strong points of the business)
- Current products are market leaders in some countries in terms of sales and market share.
- Brand loyalty to products and to the corporate identity.
- Effective promotion.
- Flexibility in production methods.
- Excellent distribution network.
- Constant R&D leading to new ideas.

WEAKNESSES (the problems it has at present)
- Age of the life cycle of certain products.
- Restricted product range could cause problems if sales suddenly fall.

OPPORTUNITIES (that may arise in future)
- Expansion into newer markets such as sports drinks, low calorie drinks and drinks with new flavours.
- Expansion into new geographical areas such as Eastern Europe.
- Development of a global brand and possible global marketing.
- Possible growing demand for soft beverages.
- Legislation on drink driving may encourage growth of soft drink sales.

THREATS (that may arise and should be avoided/prevented if possible)
- Growing competition from supermarket own brands.
- Increasing competition from competitors bringing out new products.
- Competition from producers of alcoholic beverages and non-alcoholic beers and lagers.
- Legislation on ingredients could force changes in production.

reactive. The larger the business, the more likely it is that successful marketing will only come about through careful planning.

- Because a wide range of employees should be involved in drawing up the marketing plan in a large company, there is more chance that workers will be committed to ensuring that the goals of the company are achieved. It is a way of motivating and informing staff.

- A thorough planning process will mean that the marketing plan is co-ordinated with other plans in the business. Therefore all departments will be pulling in the same direction.

- Marketing plans are drawn up in the light of the objectives of a business. There is therefore more chance that these objectives will be achieved than if there were no plans.

The problems of marketing planning

However, marketing planning can also have certain problems.

- Scarce resources, for examples in terms of management and employee time, are used up in creating a marketing plan. Those resources could have been used elsewhere. There is therefore an opportunity cost in drawing up a marketing plan.

- Too many marketing plans are poorly drawn up. They may fail to take account of the objectives of the business. They may be created by a few individuals who see them as 'paper-pushing' exercises. The marketing plan may be filed away and never used. Those creating the plan may include actions which the business could never do, or may be far too cautious in their approach. The marketing plan may not be co-ordinated with other plans in the business.

Question 2.

Paul Rossington had just been appointed Marketing Manager of SBC plc, a firm which had forty years' experience of supplying a range of instrumentation and components to the aircraft industry. Paul had decided that his first act would be to involve a range of managers in drawing up a marketing plan. To this end, he called a meeting requesting the presence of all senior managers within the firm. At the meeting, he began with a short presentation outlining the advantages to SBC plc of marketing planning. He then invited comments from all those assembled. The sales manager chipped in with the first comment; 'It's about time we started advertising more heavily in trade journals and stopped turning out products with the wrong specifications'. The production manager came next; 'I don't know why you dragged me up here to this meeting. You concentrate on the marketing and I'll get on with the production side. So long as you keep me informed of developments we'll be happy down in production.'

Paul was beginning to feel uncomfortable, but it wasn't until the senior accountant's remark that he really felt worried about having accepted this new post. 'I suggest you go away and write this plan and then call another meeting when you're in a position to discuss it with us', she had said.

(a) What advantages of marketing planning would you have advised Paul to mention in his brief presentation?

(b) From the comments made at the meeting, explain any problems which you think SBC plc will have with marketing planning.

KEY TERMS

Marketing planning – the process by which marketing activities are identified and decided upon.

Marketing plan – a set of proposed marketing actions to be undertaken over a period of time which, if carried out, should enable the business to achieve its marketing objectives.

PESTLE analysis – an analysis of the external political, economic, social, technological, legal and environmental factors affecting a business.

SWOT analysis – analysis of the internal strengths and weaknesses of a business and its external opportunities and threats.

KNOWLEDGE

1. State four aspects of the marketing plan.
2. In a large company, who might be involved in writing a marketing plan?
3. What targets might be set within a marketing plan?
4. State three internal and three external factors that may affect a marketing plan.
5. State three benefits of marketing planning.
6. State three problems of marketing planning.

Case Study: *The XBox, 2001-2007*

Xbox launch, 2001

Microsoft launched its XBox video game console in 2001. It spent $500 million on the launch of the new product, including spending on marketing, advertising and support to retailers and software makers.

Prior to the launch, the senior vice president of the company's games division said 'We have to build demand for this to be successful.' The new product, which would include DVD drive and Internet access, was part of the plans of the business to move beyond the PC market. Microsoft also planned to tap into the market for devices that combine television and the Internet, and to offer online gaming. Microsoft was developing 30 video games inhouse and approving many games from other software developers. It was suggested that the XBox would have three times the performance of Sony's PlayStation 2 (PS2). By the time the XBox was released, Sony's PS2 and Sega's Dreamcast would already have been on the market for a year.

Sources: adapted from www.instat.com., news.com., asia.cnet.com,and www.forbes.com., xcox.the maingroup.com, www.ciol.com, abcnews.go.com., *The Independent* 23.11.2007.

(a) Using examples from the information, outline the benefits of marketing planning for businesses in the game consoles market. (6 marks).

(b) Examine the external and internal factors affecting businesses in the game consoles market. (12 marks)

(c) Carry out a SWOT analysis of X-Box's position in the market. (12 marks)

(d) Evaluate the success of marketing planning by Microsoft for X-Box. (20 marks)

2002-2004 One down, three to go. In February 2002 Sega announced that it would cease production of the Sega Dreamcast games console and quit the hardware business. Instead it decided to produce games for other games consoles. The three left remaining were Sony's PS2, Microsoft's XBox and Nintendo's GameCube. In 2002 there were 30 million PS2 consoles worldwide (as well as 90 million old PS1 consoles). Contrast that to the 4 million XBoxes worldwide.

The Internet gaming market is growing. It was estimated at the time that it would be a $20 billion industry by 2005. In 2002 Sony's PS2 and Microsoft's XBox were planned to be linked to the Internet for interactive gaming. However, unlike the XBox, the PS2 would require additional equipment to be bought. Previously people could play games through their PCs on the Internet. But now they could take advantage of the stunning graphics of games consoles.

2002-2003 Between August 2002-03 Microsoft's XBox was the only gaming console to show positive market share growth in the US. It was suggested that sales increased 6 per cent in the US, giving it a 27 per cent market share. In comparison sales of Sony's PS2 fell to 36 per cent and Nintendo's GameCube fell to 22 per cent. In May 2003 the price of the XBox was cut in the US from $199 to $179 in response to a similar cut in the price of Sony's PS2. XBox sales have been fuelled by the success of its almost 400 software games, including Star Wars games. XBox Live, Microsoft's online gaming service, had over half a million subscribers.

In October 2003 Nintendo reduced the price of its GameCube to $99 in the US. Within 35 days it was suggested that it had doubled its market share in the US from 19 to 37 per cent as a result, becoming a strong second in the market.

2004 In 2004 Sony announced that it had shipped over 50 million consoles since the launch of PS2 in 2000. This compared to nine million sales worldwide of Microsoft's XBox. This gave XBox 15 per cent of the global market, a long way from Sony's estimated 70 per cent global market share. The majority of XBoxes are in the US (6 million), with 2.2 million in Europe. Microsoft admits it is weak in Asia, where it has struggled to make an impact in Japan in particular.

Analysts suggested that Microsoft loses $100 on every XBox it sells. Yet the company has strong relationships with retailers and is pinning many of its hopes on the broadband market. It is particularly concentrating its marketing on areas of the world where broadband penetration is high, such as South Korea. This gives great possibilities when XBox Live is launched in these countries.

2007 The balance of power in the games console market has tipped towards Nintendo and away from Microsoft and Sony after the phenomenal success of the Wii gaming console helped the Kyoto-based company almost triple its profits in the first half of the year.

The reversal of fortunes within the games console sector has been stunning and highly unexpected given Nintendo's Wii was tipped to struggle to compete with its competitors. Sony – which had achieved unparalleled success with the first two incarnations of its PlayStation machine – and Microsoft were widely expected to dominate the market for next-generation consoles with state-of-the-art machines.

Nintendo stuck to its guns and despite concerns that the Wii would be another also-ran compared with the top-end Play-Station 3 and Xbox 360, the console has sold like wildfire and proved the doubters wrong. It has outsold the PS3 three-to-one in the Japanese market and five-to-one in the US and has taken the PS2's mantle as the fastest selling console in history in the UK after shifting 1 million machines in just eight months. The Wii has reinvigorated the video games sector by appealing to consumers outside the 'hard-core' gaming market, particularly female gamers and families. While titles such as the ultra-violent Grand Theft Auto: San Andreas and Resident Evil sold well to traditional fans who lust after eye-boggling graphics and more complex adventures, Nintendo recognised that there was a vast untapped market of people who wanted more simple and fun games. The Wii's motion-sensor-based controllers revolutionised the market by allowing consumers to physically play simple games, such as tennis and ten-pin bowling, on the screen. The games are far more basic than the likes of Halo 3 that boast the best graphics, but that has not deterred consumers from outside the traditional video games audience.

David Yarnton, managing director of Nintendo UK, said the decision to target non-traditional gamers with the Wii has led to household penetration of consoles rising for the first time in 25 years.

What are operational objectives?

Operations management involves organising and controlling the process by which inputs such as labour, materials and machinery are transformed into products, or by which services are provided to customers. The management of this process is likely to be more effective if a business can identify clear operational objectives. By setting clear objectives the business can more easily design operational strategies which will help to achieve these objectives. For example, a business may aim to reduce costs by 10 per cent. A cost cutting strategy involving automation might be used to achieve this target. Operational objectives might involve setting targets in relation to the following.

- Quality.
- Cost.
- Volume.
- Innovation.
- Efficiency.
- The environment.

The operational objectives set by a business are likely to be influenced by a range of internal and external factors, such as the financial resources available and competition.

Quality targets

Increasing the quality of products will help to raise sales and develop a good reputation for a business. Also, due to intense competition and an increasing demand for high quality products, businesses are under pressure to continually raise quality. Setting quality targets will help businesses to raise quality. Examples of quality targets might include the following.

- **Reducing complaints.** Many businesses record the number of complaints they get. If a business is able to reduce the number of complaints, this is likely to be a result of an improvement in quality. Therefore targets might be designed to reduce the number of complaints. For example, a utilities provider might reduce complaints about the time it takes to answer the telephone by employing more staff to deal with calls from customers.
- **BS EN ISO 9000.** One way of imposing strict quality targets is to gain certification with BS EN ISO 9000. Businesses seeking and gaining certification are inspected at regular intervals to ensure that quality standards are being maintained or improved. Inspectors may impose targets for improvement every time they visit.
- **Aspire to be the 'best'.** Some businesses aim to improve quality by aspiring to be the 'best' in the industry. This is obviously quite a challenging target. However, it may be achieved through **best practice benchmarking**.

There are many strategies which businesses can use to improve quality in their organisations. Some examples include total quality management, quality assurance, best practice benchmarking and the use of quality circles. All of these can be used to reach quality targets.

Cost targets

Keeping costs down will benefit most stakeholders in a business. Lower costs will increase profit and reduce waste. Cost targets

Question 1.

Euro Disney operates a Disneyland resort in Paris and 2006 was the 15th Anniversary of the resort. During the year it generated a revenue of 1,087.7 million Euros and enjoyed some operational improvements. These are shown in the graphs in Figure 1. Euro Disney is also committed to innovation and during 2006 introduced some new attractions, new parades and new characters. For example, in the Disneyland Park the Buzz Lightyear Laser Blast and The Little Book of Big Dreams was opened. In the Walt Disney Studios three new attractions were opened. These were Crush's Coaster, Cars Race Rally and The Twilight Zone Tower of Terror.

Figure 1: Operational data for Euro Disney, 2006

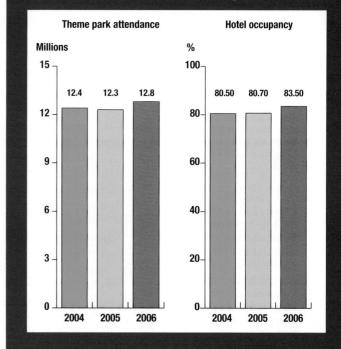

Source: adapted from Euro Disney, *Annual Review*, 2006

(a) Using Figure 1, explain two operational objectives that may have been set by Euro Disney in recent years.
(b) (i) What evidence is there to support the view that Euro Disney is committed to innovation?
(ii) How might Euro Disney set innovation objectives?

might be set for:
- the whole organisation;
- individual departments;
- specific processes;
- particular resources;
- certain products.

The more specific the target the more likely it will be achieved.

A number of approaches can be used to cut costs. These may include outsourcing, using cheaper labour, introducing new technology, finding cheaper suppliers, more rigorous budgetary control, retrenchment and lean production. The approach used by a business will depend on its circumstances. For example, a business which faces rising input costs may find new suppliers. They may use eSourcing to do this. On the other hand, a business may decide to cut costs right across the organisation by introducing lean production methods.

Volume targets

Businesses are often keen to increase volumes. This means they aim to produce more. By increasing output, better use is made of resources. Volume targets are common in a wide range of business situations. For example, during a working day or week or month:
- factories will aim to increase production to create more output;
- call centres will aim to answer more calls;
- airlines will aim to carry more passengers;
- farmers will aim to increase yields per acre of land;
- hotels will try to fill more rooms;
- sales teams will aim to sell more units.

Volume targets are quite easy to set, which is probably why they are common. However, such targets have to be realistic otherwise staff will become demotivated. They will also have to take into account the capacity of operations. Volume targets are often achieved by providing staff with incentives. For example, a sales team may be paid commission on every unit it sells. Factory workers may get a bonus if the whole factory achieves a weekly production target.

Innovation targets

One of the ways in which a business stays ahead of its competitors is to be innovative. This is likely to involve improving existing products and developing new ones. However, innovation is also about finding new ways of 'doing things' such as developing new processes, systems or services. Innovation may also be used to solve problems. For example, to help solve the problems caused by computer viruses 'firewalls' were developed.

Setting targets for innovation may be quite difficult in practice. This is due to the uncertain nature of research and (R&D) development and innovation. However, many businesses do aim to speed up product development. They may set time limits for the development of new products, for example. To

speed up innovation a business may use CAD, **simultaneous engineering** or **lean design**. To encourage more innovation a business might invest more in R&D, introduce **kaizen**, or at a more simple level, use staff suggestion schemes.

Efficiency

If businesses can improve their efficiency better use will be made of resources. This should help to reduce costs and increase profit. It may also mean a business can operate with fewer resources. Some aspects of efficiency can be measured quite precisely. For example, it is possible to calculate labour productivity. Wherever it is possible to quantify efficiency in this way, targets are likely to be set. Some examples of efficiency

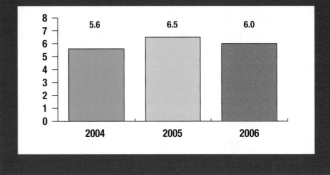

Question 2.

BG Group is a leading business in the global energy industry. It aims to understand, build and supply natural gas markets around the world. It operates in four key business sectors.
- Exploration and Production.
- Liquefied Natural Gas.
- Transmission and Distribution.
- Power.

BG's growth brings opportunities for environmental improvement with it, but also brings challenges in managing the environmental impact. A major benefit from BG Group's core business is that the substitution of gas for coal or oil can be a net benefit in terms of reduced greenhouse gas (GHG) emissions and improved air quality. On the other hand, as the business grows so, potentially, does the 'environmental footprint'. BG Group's aim is to reduce the carbon footprint growth to a minimum. BG Group's Business Principles define the values by which the Group conducts its business, not by behaving only in an environmentally responsible manner, but also by recognising that BG Group has a positive role to play in environmental protection.

Figure 2: Greenhouse gas emissions from BG Group-operated facilities (million tonnes carbon dioxide equivalent)

	2004	2005	2006
	5.6	6.5	6.0

Source: adapted from BG Group, *Annual Report and Accounts*, 2006

(a) What environmental target has BG set?
(b) To what extent do you think BG is reaching its environmental target?
(c) Explain one important external influence on BG's operational objectives in relation to this case.

targets are outlined briefly below.

- **Capacity utilisation.** This can be calculated easily by comparing current use with actual use. For example, a hotel might try to increase capital utilisation by setting targets for room occupancy. Capital utilisation is measured as a percentage, so it is easy to see whether targets have been met.
- **Labour productivity.** Labour productivity can be measured where it is possible to identify clear units of output. It is calculated by dividing the output over a certain time period by the number of workers employed. For example, if a car factory employs 2,500 people and produces 10,000 cars in a year, labour productivity is 4 (10,000 ÷ 2,500). Targets for labour productivity are easy to set.
- **Capital productivity.** Capital productivity can also be measured. This involves dividing output by the capital employed. A business may set targets for the productivity of particular machines like a press or a CNC machine.
- **Other operational performance indicators.** Businesses often have their own efficiency targets which are unique to their organisation. For example, easyJet measures cost, revenue and profit per seat from its airline operations. In 2006, profit per seat was £3.22. A mail order company might measure how long it takes to process and deliver a customer order.

There are many ways in which a business might improve efficiency. For example, to improve labour productivity a business might provide financial incentives for staff to work harder. Capital productivity might be improved by better maintenance of machinery. Capital utilisation might be improved by selling off unused assets such as machinery or property.

The environment

Businesses are under increasing pressure to improve their environmental performance. In addition, many companies want to become good corporate citizens and take into account the needs of a wider range of stakeholders. One way in which they achieve this is to measure their environmental performance. Many businesses go further and try to meet targets. Some of these targets might be related to the environmental indicators below.

- The amount of waste sent to landfill sites.
- The amount of fuel used up in production.
- The amount of recycled materials used in the business.
- The emissions from a factory chimney.
- The amount of rural land used up by new developments.
- The amount of dirty water discharged into the waterway systems.

The type of environmental targets set by a business will obviously depend on the nature of the business. For example, an airline might try to cut down on night flights to reduce noise pollution near to the airport. A chemical processing plant may try to cut emissions. Businesses can meet targets by investing in recycling systems, adopting leaner production methods and training staff to be more 'thrifty', for example.

Internal influences on operational objectives

The operational targets set by a business will depend on a range of factors. Some of these are internal, which means they come from within the business. Some key internal influences are outlined below.

Nature of the product The type of product that a business produces will have a significant influence on the operational objectives. For example, some businesses are involved in activities where the potential threat to the environment is significant. So companies in the oil and chemical industries, for example, are likely to attach a great deal of importance to environmental targets. The operational targets set by manufacturers and retailers are likely to be very different. For example, efficiency targets in retailing are likely to be linked to sales per square metre. In manufacturing targets are more likely to be linked to labour or capital productivity. In the transport industry operational targets might centre around the reliability and punctuality of services, passenger loads and cost per passenger.

The availability of resources Sometimes a business will want to set targets to improve its performance but may not have enough money. For example, a business might want to reduce emissions but cannot afford the specialist equipment needed to achieve the improvement. Many businesses want to be innovative but the cost and risk associated with research and development acts as a constraint. A business may want to improve quality by introducing total quality management but is discouraged by the huge cost of staff training. Clearly the availability of financial resources is a key influence on the selection of operational objectives. Businesses with more resources are likely to set more ambitious targets.

Internal stakeholders The operational objectives set by a business are likely to be influenced by the people who have an interest in the success of the business. Since different stakeholders may have slightly different needs, the objectives set by a business are likely be shaped by the stakeholder groups that exert the most pressure on decision makers. For example, shareholders are likely to be more interested in targets relating to costs and efficiency. This is because achieving such targets will probably increase profits. On the other hand employees may resist efficiency targets because it might mean they have to work harder. There may also be some departmental or divisional competition inside the business. As a result the department or division with the most power will have the most influence on objectives. For example, if the finance department is influential, operational objectives might focus on costs. Budgetary targets might pressurise other departments to reduce costs.

External influences on operational objectives

Some of the influences on operational objectives will come from outside the business. These are external influences. Some examples are outlined below.

Competitors' performance Businesses are often put under pressure by their rivals. Most industries are highly competitive and businesses have to set objectives which reflect the pattern of development and activity in the industry. For example, if rivals are focusing on quality and setting ambitious quality targets, a business will be under pressure to do the same. In the 1980s and 1990s many British manufacturers aimed to improve their efficiency by adopting lean production and other Japanese production techniques. Firms that failed to adopt these new methods were often left behind. At the moment the performance of Chinese and Indian producers is putting pressure on western producers to reduce their costs.

Demand for the product One important external influence on businesses when setting operational objectives is the volume of demand. If a business is facing steadily rising demand, as the airline industry is at the moment, there will be pressure to meet this demand. Consequently businesses will have to set targets which help to raise volume. In the airline industry this is being achieved by building capacity (buying new aircraft for example) and offering new routes. The pattern of demand can also influence objectives. For example, in the food industry there is a growing demand for 'healthy' food products. Consequently, businesses are having to set new quality targets.

External stakeholders Even though external stakeholders exist outside the business, they can still influence operational objectives. One important external stakeholder group is customers. They would probably prefer a business to set targets relating to quality and innovation. This is because they will benefit from improved and new products and services. Another external group, environmentalists, would obviously prefer a business to focus on environmental targets.

KNOWLEDGE

1. Why do businesses set operational objectives?
2. How might quality operational objectives be set?
3. What is meant by a volume target?
4. State two ways in which a business might meet efficiency targets.
5. State two ways in which volume targets can be achieved.
6. What external factors might influence the operational objectives of a supermarket chain?
7. How might the resources available influence operational objectives?

Case Study: Haifa Oils

Haifa Oils is an oil refining business based in the Mediterranean. Using its state-of-the-art industrial facilities, it is capable of refining 9 million tons of crude oil per year, and has a maximum crude oil refining capacity of 180,000 barrels per day. It produces a variety of products used in industrial operations and agriculture and for transport and private consumption. Over 75% of the company's output is used for local consumption, while the balance is exported, mainly to countries in the Mediterranean area.

In June 2008 an important meeting was held between the board of directors and the operations manager. The following issues relating to operational objectives were discussed.

- The institutional shareholders (external shareholders) were unhappy with the financial performance of the company. The net profit margin fell from 6.7 per cent in 2007 to 5.9 per cent in 2008. The directors have agreed that the best way to restore profit margins is to cut costs. As a result the board would like the production manager to find ways of cutting general production costs over the next three years by 4 per cent per year.

- The current capacity utilisation is 85 per cent. The directors want to increase this to 95 per cent by 2011. If this target is achieved the production manager will receive a bonus payment of £50,000.

- The Nelson Complexity Index is a measure of the secondary conversion capacity of a petroleum refinery relative to the primary distillation capacity. The higher the value of the index, the higher the value of its products, which will include more lighter, higher-value, products. If this index can be raised to 8.0 it will be possible to increase sales. Some large potential customers have agreed in principle to buy products from Haifa Oils if the quality of products can be raised to the 8.0 level. However, the production manager pointed out that this would require some investment in new plant and the board should consider carefully whether the resources are available to meet the cost.

(a) Using this case as an example, explain what is meant by operational objectives. (4 marks)

(b) (i) Calculate the number of barrels per day Haifa Oils will be producing if it raises capacity utilisation to 95 per cent. (4 marks)

(ii) Which stakeholders are likely to benefit the most if capacity utilisation can be increased to 95 per cent by 2011? (4 marks)

(c) What measures might the production manager take to meet the cost targets? (8 marks)

(d) Examine two internal influences on operational objectives in this case. (8 marks)

(e) To what extent have external factors influenced the operational objectives set by Haifa Oils? (12 marks)

66 Scale and resource mix

Scale of a business

The term SCALE in business means size. When managers and owners talk about increasing the scale of operations they mean that the business should be bigger. Large-scale businesses use more resources and produce more output. They also have higher turnover, enjoy lower unit costs and generally make larger profits. Consequently there are some strong motives for increasing the scale of operations. Unilever, which produces foods, beverages, cleaning agents and personal care products, is a large-scale operator. It is a multi-national company, employs over 180,000 people and enjoyed a turnover of over $50 billion and a profit of over $5 billion in 2006.

Scale and productive efficiency

One objective of production managers is to achieve **productive efficiency**. This occurs when the average cost per unit of output is at its lowest. So if a business produced bolts at 6p per 1,000 when it could produce them at 4p per 1,000, then it would be productively inefficient. It would only be productively efficient if average costs were 4p per 1,000.

There are many reasons why businesses can be productively inefficient. For example, from a production viewpoint, they might:

- not be paying the cheapest price for the materials they buy in;
- be employing more workers than is necessary;
- be using outdated technology;
- hold too much stock;
- have badly organised or inappropriate production methods.

Inefficiency can also be caused by failing to manage human resources effectively. For example, workers might:

- be demotivated and not be working as hard as they could;
- not have received sufficient training;
- apply for a job, but fail to get it despite being the best candidate because of poor recruitment procedures;
- suffer from weak leadership and be less productive;
- be in a poorly organised business where the organisational structure is a barrier rather than a help to efficient working;
- be underemployed and have too little to do because of over recruitment due to poor workforce planning;
- be unable to do their jobs fully because poor workforce planning has led to under-recruitment of staff.

Productive efficiency and economies of scale

The size of a business has a major impact on average costs of production. Typically, there is a range of output over which average costs fall as output rises. Over this range, larger businesses have a competitive advantage over smaller businesses. They enjoy ECONOMIES OF SCALE. In the long run, a business can build another factory or purchase more machinery. This can cause the average cost of production to fall.

In Figure 1 a firm is currently producing in a small plant and its short-run costs are $SRAC_1$. When it produces an output equal to Q_1 its average cost will be AC_1. If it raises production to Q_2, average costs will rise to AC_2. This is the result of the **law of diminishing returns**.

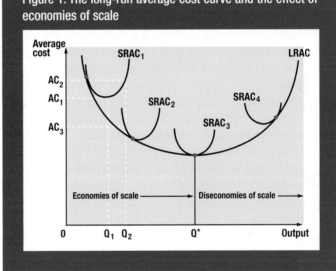

Figure 1: The long-run average cost curve and the effect of economies of scale

If the firm expands the scale of its operations (which it can do in the long run) the same level of output can be produced more efficiently. With a bigger plant, represented by $SRAC_2$, Q_2 can be produced at an average cost of just AC_3. Long run average costs fall due to economies of scale and will continue to do so until the firm has built a plant which minimises long run average costs. In the diagram this occurs when a plant shown by SRAC3 is built. This is sometimes called the MINIMUM EFFICIENT SCALE of plant. When output reaches Q^* in this plant, long run average costs cannot be reduced any further through expansion. The business is said to be **productively efficient** at this point.

At any output level higher or lower than Q^*, the business is productively inefficient because average costs could be lower. For example, if the firm continues to grow it will experience rising average costs due to DISECONOMIES OF SCALE, as in $SRAC_4$ in Figure 1. This is dealt with later in the unit.

Internal economies of scale

What are the different economies of scale a firm can gain? INTERNAL ECONOMIES OF SCALE are the benefits of growth that arise within the firm. They occur for a number of reasons.

Purchasing and marketing economies Large firms are likely to get better rates when buying raw materials and components in bulk. In addition, the administration costs involved do not rise in proportion to the size of the order. The cost of processing an order for 10,000 tonnes of coal does not treble when 30,000 tonnes are ordered.

A number of marketing economies exist. A large company may find it cost effective to acquire its own fleet of vans and lorries, for example. The cost to the sales force of selling 30 product lines is not double that of selling 15 lines. Again, the administration costs of selling do not rise in proportion to the size of the sale.

Technical economies Technical economies arise because larger plants are often more efficient. The capital costs and the running costs of plants do not rise in proportion to their size. For example, the capital cost of a double decker bus will not be twice that of a single decker bus. This is because the main cost (engine and chassis) does not double when the capacity of the bus doubles. Increased size may mean a doubling of output but not cost. The average cost will therefore fall. This is sometimes called the **principle of increased dimensions**. In addition, the cost of the crew and fuel will not increase in proportion to its size.

Another technical economy is that of **indivisibility**. Many firms need a particular item of equipment or machinery, but fail to make full use of it. A small business may pay £400 for a laptop computer. The cost will be the same whether it is used twice a week by a part time clerical worker or every day. As the business expands, more use will be made of it and so the **average cost** of the machine will fall.

As the scale of operations expands the firm may switch to mass production techniques. Flow production, which involves breaking down the production process into a very large number of small operations, allows greater use of highly specialised machinery. This results in large improvements in efficiency as labour is replaced by capital.

Businesses often employ a variety of machines which have different capacities. A slow machine may increase production time. As the firm expands and produces more output, it can employ more of the slower machines in order to match the capacity of the faster machines. This is called the **law of multiples**. It involves firms finding a balanced team of machines so that when they operate together they are all running at full capacity.

Specialisation and managerial economies As the firm grows it can afford to employ specialist managers. In a small business one general manager may be responsible for finance, marketing, production and personnel. The manager may find her role demanding. If a business employs specialists in these fields, efficiency may improve and average costs fall. If specialists were employed in a small firm they would be an indivisibility.

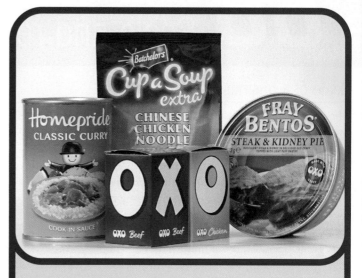

Question 1.

Premier Foods, the owner of Branston Pickle, bought the Campbell Soup Company for £450 million ($830 million) in 2006. Premier Foods said the purchase would give it control over well-known brands including Oxo, Batchelors, Homepride and Fray Bentos in the UK and Ireland. After the purchase, Premier Foods said it planned to continue its strategy of acquisitions. The purchase of these brands should help Premier Foods to further exploit economies of scale. 'The Campbell's UK business fits Premier like a glove,' said Robert Schofield, chief executive of Premier foods. 'This acquisition will bring an excellent portfolio of powerful and iconic brands which we intend to drive forward with increased resource and innovation,' he added. The cost of the transaction was met in large by issuing new shares to existing shareholders.

Source: adapted from http://news.bbc.co.uk.

(a) Explain why Premier Foods may be able to exploit (i) marketing economies and (ii) purchasing economies as a result of the acquisition.
(b) Discuss whether the business would be able to exploit further economies of scale in future.

Financial economies Large firms have advantages when they try to raise finance. They will have a wider variety of sources from which to choose. For example, sole traders cannot sell more shares to raise extra funds but large public limited companies can. Very large firms will often find it easier to persuade institutions to lend them money since they will have large assets to offer as security. Finally, large firms borrowing very large amounts of money can often gain better interest rates. In the past the government has recognised the problems facing small firms. A number of schemes have been designed to help small firms raise funds.

Risk bearing economies As a firm grows it may well diversify to reduce risk. For example, breweries have diversified into the provision of food and other forms of entertainment in their public houses. Large businesses can also reduce risk by carrying out research and development. The development of new products can help firms gain a competitive edge over smaller rivals.

External economies of scale

EXTERNAL ECONOMIES OF SCALE are the reductions in cost which any business in an industry might enjoy as the industry grows. External economies are more likely to arise if the industry is concentrated in a particular region.

Labour The concentration of firms may lead to the build up of a labour force equipped with the skills required by the industry. Training costs may be reduced if workers have gained skills at another firm in the same industry. Local schools and colleges, or even local government, may offer training courses which are aimed at the needs of the local industry.

Ancillary and commercial services An established industry, particularly if it is growing, tends to attract smaller firms trying to serve its needs. A wide range of commercial and support services can be offered. Specialist banking, insurance, marketing, waste disposal, maintenance, cleaning, components and distribution services are just some examples.

Co-operation Firms in the same industry are more likely to co-operate if they are concentrated in the same region. They might join forces to fund a research and development centre for the industry. An industry journal might be published, so that information can be shared.

Disintegration Disintegration occurs when production is broken up so that more specialisation can take place. When an industry is concentrated in an area firms might specialise in the production of one component and then transport it to a main assembly car plant. In the West Midlands a few large car assembly plants exist, while there are many supporting firms.

Diseconomies of scale

If a business expands, the scale of its operations beyond the minimum efficient scale, diseconomies of scale may result. This is where average costs rise as output rise. There is variety of sources of diseconomies of scale. As shown in Figure 1, long-run average costs start to rise once the output if a business passes Q^* on the diagram.

Internal diseconomies of scale Most internal diseconomies are caused by the problem of managing large businesses.

- Communication becomes more complicated and co-ordination more difficult because a large firm is divided into departments.
- The control and **co-ordination** of large businesses is also demanding. Thousands of employees, billions of pounds and dozens of plants all mean added responsibility and more supervision.

- Motivation may suffer as individual workers become a minor part of the total workforce. This can cause poor relations between management and the workforce.
- Technical diseconomies also arise. In the chemical industry, construction problems often mean that two smaller plants are more cost effective than one very large one. Also, if a business employs one huge plant and a breakdown occurs, production will stop. With two smaller plants, production can continue even if one breaks down.

External diseconomies of scale These may occur from overcrowding in industrial areas. The price of land, labour, services and materials might rise as firms compete for a limited amount. Congestion might lead to inefficiency, as travelling workers and deliveries are delayed.

Factors influencing the scale of operation

The scale of operation differs widely from industry to industry. In industries like leather making and furniture manufacture, economies of scale tend to be relatively small. In car assembly or the chemicals industry, they tend to be large. The reasons why they differ are related to the sources of economies of scale.

Technical economies In some industries, there are considerable technical economies. In car manufacturing, for instance, plants need to be a certain size to reach the lowest average cost scale of production. In leather manufacturing, however, even quite small businesses can be highly efficient because the machinery required is relatively little and relatively cheap.

Specialisation In car manufacturing, the organisation of production is complex and there are considerable opportunities to exploit specialisation of labour and capital. In leather manufacturing, the organisation of production is relatively simple with far fewer opportunities to gain the benefits of specialisation.

Purchasing economies Car manufacturers buy billions of pounds of components each year. So there is scope for a large business like Ford to negotiate large discounts compared with a small manufacturer like Morgan cars. In leather manufacturing, the market is much smaller. So no business would ever approach the size of orders that are common in car manufacturing. Hence the difference in purchasing power between small and large firms in the industry is greatly reduced.

Marketing economies In marketing, Ford markets models which sell in their millions around the world. The cost of marketing per car is therefore likely to be far less than, say, for Morgan Motor Company which sells only a few hundred per year. In leather manufacture, it is difficult to mass market any product because leather goods tend to be produced in small quantities to individual designs which are constantly changing. So larger manufacturers are unlikely to have much lower marketing costs per unit sold than small manufacturers.

Because of these factors, leather manufacturers tend not to be large. On the other hand car manufacturers are among the larger companies in the world.

Choosing the optimal mix of resources

A business has to choose an appropriate combination of materials, tools, equipment, machinery and labour before production can begin. The more complex the product, the more difficult this will be. There is often a variety of materials and equipment to choose from. For example, a small manufacturer of jeans has to consider which type of cloth, cotton, stud, zip, sewing machine and labour to use. What influences the factors of production a business chooses?

- The actual design itself may specify which materials to use. For example, a new savoury snack will be made to a strict list of ingredients.
- There may be limited amounts of labour, capital or materials. A company recruiting people with specialist skills may find that supply 'runs out'. It may then have to recruit unskilled workers and train them.
- Businesses will aim to use the cheapest factors, assuming that there is no difference in quality. If there is a difference in quality then the firm must decide which factor most suits its needs and budget. For example, when a company buys a new computer there is a wide range of models to choose from, at a range of different prices. It will have to select a model which suits its needs, and also one which it can afford.

Capital and labour intensity

One of the most important production decisions which operations managers have to make is what combination of capital and labour to use. LABOUR INTENSIVE PRODUCTION techniques involve using a larger proportion of labour than capital. CAPITAL INTENSIVE PRODUCTION techniques involve employing more machinery relative to labour. For example, chemical production is capital intensive, with only a relatively small workforce to oversee the process. The postal service is labour intensive, with a considerable amount of sorting and delivery done by hand.

The optimal resource mix between labour and capital depends on a number of factors.

- The nature of the product. Everyday products with high demand, like newspapers, are mass produced in huge plants using large quantities of machinery. However, in modern economies like the UK an increasing number of the products supplied by businesses are services. Generally, the provision of services is labour intensive.
- The relative prices of the two factors. If labour costs are rising then it may be worth the company employing more capital instead. In countries like China and India where labour is relative cheap, labour intensive production methods are preferred. However, in most developed economies like the UK, labour is more expensive and a

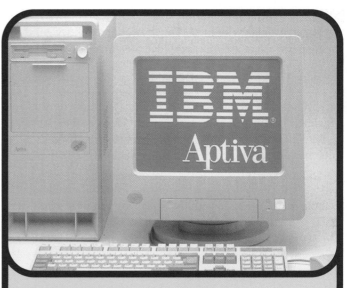

Question 2.

In the 1970s, it was argued that large companies could be very profitable if structures were crystal clear and rational. Through these means, human error or deviance could be minimised. But in the 1990s, a variety of studies were conducted which showed that around 1,000 employees in one location is about the maximum size for any company if it is to retain the advantages of economies of scale and minimise the human diseconomies arising from adding more people.

Take the case of IBM, the world's first large computer company. In the 1970s and 1980s, IBM came to symbolise the success of big business. It had pioneered the manufacture of large mainframe computers. But by 1993, it was in trouble, losing £5.6 billion in that year alone. It had failed to move with the times. Part of the business was saying that the future lay with cheap small personal computers. Part of the business was making a profit from computer software. Those at the top failed to listen and persisted in thinking that the future lay with expensive mainframes.

A new chief executive, Lou Gerstner, was appointed. He reduced IBM's workforce by 50 per cent. The company was refocused on providing e-business services and solutions, research and design and semiconductor architecture. Very importantly, the company was segmented into small operational units. IBM employees were remotivated to develop services, discover solutions and be innovative.

Source: adapted from *The Financial Times*, 4.1.2002.

(a) Explain what is meant by 'diseconomies of scale' and, using the example of IBM, explain why they occur.

great deal of manufacturing is capital intensive.
- The size of the firm. As a firm grows and the scale of production increases, it tends to employ more capital relative to labour. For example, in the UK, Morgan cars, a small sports car manufacturer, uses a labour intensive approach to production. In contrast, Honda, which has a huge car factory in Derby, uses capital intensive production.

Table 1: The effect on output as more workers are employed, given a fixed amount of capital

								(Units)
Capital	40	40	40	40	40	40	40	40
No. of workers	1	2	3	4	5	6	7	8
Total output	4	10	18	30	45	52	55	56

Table 2: The benefits and drawbacks of capital and labour intensive strategies

Capital intensive strategies

Benefits
- Generally more cost effective if large quantities are produced.
- Machinery is often more precise and consistent.
- Machinery can operate 24/7.
- Machinery is easier to manage than people.

Drawbacks
- Huge set up costs.
- Huge delays and costs if machinery breaks down.
- Can be inflexible – much machinery is highly specialised.
- Often poses a threat to the workforce and could reduce moral.

Labour intensive strategies

Benefits
- Generally more flexible than capital – can be retrained for example.
- Cheaper for small-scale production.
- Cheaper for large-scale production in countries like China and India.
- People are creative and can therefore solve problems and make improvements.

Drawbacks
- People are more difficult to manage than machines. They have feelings and react.
- People can be unreliable. They may go sick or leave suddenly.
- People cannot work without breaks and holidays.
- People sometimes need to be motivated to improve performance.

The law of diminishing returns

Combining different amounts of labour and capital can affect the productivity of these factors in the short run. As more units of labour are added to a fixed amount of capital, the output of the extra workers will rise at first and then fall. This is shown in Table 1, where the amount of capital is fixed at 40 units. For example, when the second worker is hired the total amount produced (total output) rises by 6 units (10-4). When the third worker is employed, output rises by 8 units (18-10), i.e. a higher amount.

The amount added by each extra worker (the marginal output) continues to rise until the sixth worker is employed. Then output rises by a smaller amount (7 units = 52-45). This is called the law of diminishing returns. Output rises at first because workers are able to specialise in particular tasks, which improves the productivity of extra workers. However, there reaches a point where workers are not able to specialise any more and the productivity of the extra worker begins to fall.

The benefits and drawbacks of capital and labour intensive strategies

Whether a business chooses a capital or labour intensive approach to production, there will be some benefits and drawbacks. These are summarised in Table 2.

KEY TERMS

Capital intensive production – production methods which employ a large amount of machinery relative to labour.
Diseconomies of scale – rising long-run average costs as a firm expands beyond its minimum efficient scale.
Economies of scale – the reductions in cost gained by firms as they grow.
External economies of scale – the cost reductions available to all firms as the industry grows.
Internal economies of scale – the cost reductions enjoyed by a single firm as it grows.
Labour intensive production – production methods which rely on a large workforce relative to the amount of machinery.
Minimum efficient scale (MES) – the output which minimises long-run average costs.
Scale (of a business) – the size of the business.

KNOWLEDGE

1. What is meant by productive efficiency?
2. What are the main sources of internal economies of scale?
3. What are the main sources of external economies of scale?
4. Explain the principle of increased dimensions.
5. Why do diseconomies of scale arise?
6. Explain why the oil extraction industry is dominated by large businesses while hairdressing is dominated by small businesses.
7. State two reasons why a business may use a labour intensive approach to production.
8. State two benefits and two drawbacks of capital intensive production strategies.

Case Study: Timmings plc

Timmings plc manufactures and distributes, through a worldwide network of dealers and distributors, a full line of skid steer and mini skid steer loaders as well as attachments, mobile screening plants and six models of mini excavators. In addition to its industrial and construction products. Timmings has recently added a complete line of potato harvesting and handling equipment. The company employs 210 people and turned over £987 million in 2007. Timmings now operates from a large production facility in Birmingham.

Timmings began as a small engineering company in 1978. It repaired agricultural implements for farmers in Hereford and Worcestershire. The business was successful and eventually began making its own agricultural implements after recognising some basic flaws in the machinery it was so often asked to repair. The company grew and by 1996 it had a work force of 240. Between 1978 and 1996 it outgrew its premises in Worcester three times. During this time the company extended its product line and gained a national reputation for high quality agricultural and construction equipment.

In 1996 Timmings moved to a spacious new factory on an industrial estate in Birmingham. The move was the result of receiving a large contract to make and supply potato harvesting equipment. The company expanded by taking on more and more staff. However, in 2001 it began to experience problems recruiting high quality engineers. It was also at this time that the company was sold by the original owners to a large US engineering company. The US parent retained the name of the company and invested very heavily in capital equipment. Around £180 million was spent on CNC machines and robots. Two categories of robot were purchased by Timmings.

- Processing operations robots. These generally perform a specific task such as spot welding or spray painting. These robots are outfitted with a specialised tool to perform the programmed task.
- Assembly line robots. These usually perform a single task in the assembly line process, such as fitting a component. Inspection robots are widely used to examine a finished part or product for defects or irregularities, for example, utilising any number of tools, such as lenses and scanners.

The switch to capital intensive production was met with mixed feelings. For example, all manufacturing robots perform monotonous or repetitive and often dangerous work involving heavy machinery, industrial pollutants, poisonous chemicals or other hazardous materials. However, on the down side some staff may lose their jobs, robots can be expensive to introduce and products may have to become standardised. In the case of Timmings, around 30 staff were laid off.

(a) Using this case as an example, explain what is meant by 'increasing the scale of operations'. (4 marks)

(b) When Timmings began to grow it became more productively efficient. Explain what this means.(6 marks)

(c) Why do you think Timmings plc switched to capital intensive production? (6 marks)

(d) Describe two technical economies of scale that Timmings plc is likely to exploit. (8 marks)

(e) To what extent do you think the benefits of switching to capital intensive strategies outweigh the drawbacks for Timmings? (16 marks)

67 | Innovation, research and development

Innovation, research and development

Businesses must be able to develop new products, materials, systems and processes and improve existing ones in order to grow and to survive. Today, the pace of technological change, coupled with the rising wants and spending power of consumers, has forced firms to respond by investing in research and development (R&D).

- RESEARCH is the investigation and discovery of new ideas in order to solve a problem or create an opportunity. Methods used to generate new ideas include laboratory research, product evaluation of a business' own and its competitors' products and discussion groups designed to think up new ideas.
- DEVELOPMENT involves changing ideas into products, materials, systems or processes. Quite often a business will identify a number of possible ideas which have scope for development. The first stage is to select the idea which shows the most promise. One of the problems with development is the time scale involved. Some projects take many years to complete and success cannot be guaranteed.
- INNOVATION in business is the commercial exploitation of an invention. It involves committing resources and bringing a new idea to the market. Innovations are intended to make someone better off, and the succession of many innovations grows the whole economy over a period of time.

The purpose of innovation, research and development

Certain purposes of innovation and R&D may be identified.

Solving problems Some R&D is designed to solve problems. For example, in the pharmaceuticals industry most R&D is aimed at developing new drugs and medicines to cure diseases, save or prolong life and reduce human suffering.

Improving quality It is possible to improve the quality of existing products through R&D. In the motor industry a lot of R&D is aimed at improving the safety of cars by improving braking systems for example. Or enhancing the performance of cars by developing new technology, such as the turbo charger. Improving quality is also a means of extending the life cycle of products.

Developing new products One of the main reasons why businesses invest in R&D is to extend their product range or replace products that have come

to the end of their life cycle. For example, the development of laptop computers helped to increase the range of products offered by the computer industry. In the electronics industry MP3 players have replaced CDs. The development of new products can help a business discover new markets.

Reducing costs The purpose of some R&D is to find cheaper ways of doing things. A great deal of innovation has focused on the machinery used by businesses. New technology in production and other areas of business has helped to lower costs. For example, the development of robots has reduced labour costs in factories.

Developing new materials Some R&D is designed to develop new materials. Synthetic materials have helped to reduce the use of natural resources. New materials often have features and characteristics which make them better than natural ones. They might be more durable, heat resistant or malleable, cheaper or lighter. DuPont, for example, created Tactel, a lightweight fabric with great strength. Two years after its invention it had captured 50 per cent of the skiwear market. In addition, the development of new materials often results in the creation of new products.

Reducing environmental damage An increasing amount of R&D has been directed at measures to help reduce the damage done to the environment. For example, some businesses are trying to find new ways of reducing energy consumption, cutting toxic emissions and recycling materials.

The cost of innovation, research and development

R&D is often a highly expensive business activity. For example, in the pharmaceuticals industry it can cost up to a £1 billion to

Table 1: The amount of money spent on R&D by the UK's top 10 firms

Rank	Company	R&D (£bn)	Growth	Sector
1	GlaxoSmithKline	3.14	10%	Pharmaceuticals
2	Astra Zeneca	1.97	-11%	Pharmaceuticals
3	BAE Systems	1.45	31%	Aerospace
4	BT	0.73	39%	Telecommunications
5	Ford*	0.69	-10%	Automotive
6	Unilever	0.65	-8%	Food products
7	Rolls Royce	0.35	25%	Aerospace
8	Pfizer*	0.35	-41%	Pharmaceuticals
9	Airbus*	0.34	-1%	Aerospace
10	Royal Dutch Shell	0.34	6%	Oil and gas

* Foreign-owned UK company.
Source: adapted from www.innovation.gov.uk.

bring a single new product to the market. About 45 per cent of all R&D in the UK is in the pharmaceuticals and aerospace industries. Table 1 shows the amount of money spent on R&D by the top 10 UK firms.

The amount of money allocated to R&D by different businesses varies greatly and may depend on a number of factors.

- It is common for businesses to vary their investments according to the funds available in any year. If profits fall for a period of time, R&D spending might fall. Also, a business might be criticised by shareholders if too much profit is allocated to R&D at the expense of dividends.
- Certain industries, such as pharmaceuticals, chemicals, motor cars, computers and defence, tend to have high levels of spending on R&D. This is due to the nature of the industry. For example, new drugs are constantly needed to prevent or cure new or existing illnesses.
- Larger public limited companies tend to be more committed to R&D. They are better able to meet the cost and bear the risk involved than smaller businesses. All the companies listed in Table 1 are plcs.
- Some businesses are committed to high levels of R&D spending because it is part of their corporate objectives and culture. This is certainly the case in pharmaceuticals and aerospace.
- In some industries businesses are forced to invest in R&D to compete. Failure to keep pace with the investment of rivals may mean that a business struggles to survive in the market.
- Businesses are more likely to invest in R&D when the economy is booming. During a recession R&D funding might be cut or frozen.

The benefits of innovation, research and development

Those businesses that do spend on R&D may enjoy a number of benefits.

Competitive edge R&D leads to the development of new products. Firms which are able to develop new products ahead of their rivals will enjoy a competitive advantage in the market. If they can obtain a patent, they will be able to sell the product without competition from other businesses for a period of time. During this time they may be able to raise prices and make **higher profits**. Examples of businesses benefiting from new products include Dyson, the bagless vacuum cleaner manufacturer, and Microsoft, the creators of the world's main operating system for computers.

Improved working environment In some industries, such as mechanical and electrical engineering, research projects are designed to develop new types of machines. Computer controlled machines, for example, have been introduced into many component and textile manufacturers and assembly plants. New technology is capable of cutting costs and raising

Question 1.

Wolfson is a global leader in the supply of high performance mixed-signal chips for the digital consumer market. Its products can be found at the heart of consumer electronic applications in the home, in the office and on the move. Wolfson's headquarters are in Edinburgh, where it employs some of the most experienced and innovative designers and engineers in the industry. Over the past few years Wolfson has established an enviable reputation for its audio brand. Many of the world's leading electronics manufacturers are customers, with their chips providing the audio in products such as MP3 players, personal media players, mobile phones, digital cameras, games consoles, flat screen TVs and hi-fi systems. The company has developed a broad range of products and continues to invest heavily in research and development to expand its product portfolio. Wolfson targets growing consumer markets, where added functionality and increased performance are essential to meet customers' expectations. It believes the digital revolution is still in its early stages of development and further advances in technology will allow ever more complex and sophisticated consumer products to be created, providing new opportunities for the company. In 2006 Wolfson spent $29.3 million on research and development. Its turnover was $204.1 million. In 2005 its net profit was $29.0 million.

Source: adapted from Wolfson, *Annual Report and Accounts*, 2006.

(a) Using this case as an example, explain what is meant by innovation and research and development.

(b) How important do you think innovation and R&D is to Wolfson?

(c) What do you think is the main purpose of R&D and innovation to Wolfson?

productivity. In addition, new machinery is often safer, cleaner and more ERGONOMICALLY designed. This helps to make the working environment better for employees.

Image It is often argued that expenditure on R&D helps to enhance a firm's image. Consumers may be impressed by businesses which are committed to R&D. This is because consumers themselves appreciate the benefits of R&D and often recognise that such expenditure is risky. Also, breakthroughs in R&D can be highly prestigious. For example, a pharmaceuticals company developing an effective vaccination to combat Aids would receive a huge amount of positive publicity and recognition.

Motivation Investment in R&D creates opportunities for creativity and invention. Many employment positions in the R&D department will help staff to satisfy their higher order needs, such as self-esteem and self-actualisation. A successful R&D department might also generate a mood of optimism and anticipation in the organisation. This is likely to have a positive effect on the motivation of staff.

Consumer benefits Consumers enjoy an increasing variety of goods and services as new products come onto the market. They are likely to pay lower prices for products because new technology lowers costs. They may also enjoy better quality products resulting from higher grade materials and more effective production methods. New medicines and drugs will improve health.

Risk and innovation

Allocating resources to R&D is extremely risky. Expenditure on R&D does not guarantee new products. Quite often money spent on R&D is wasted. For example, in the pharmaceuticals industry, many of the drugs invented do not reach the market. Trials may be carried out to see whether the drugs have the intended effect and if they have any serious side effects. If drugs fail the trial process they cannot be marketed.

Setting a budget for R&D expenditure is also fraught with uncertainty. R&D departments often spend more than they are allocated. Businesses may have to raise funds externally to finance R&D projects. In recent years a number of pharmaceutical companies have had to use rights issues, to raise extra finance to fund research in medicines and drugs. There are several reasons why setting an R&D budget might be difficult.

- The cost of a scientific research project may be difficult to estimate accurately. This is because researchers will not know when a breakthrough is going to occur. Some research, for example into cancer and aids cures, has been ongoing for many years.
- During an R&D project, there may be unforeseen spending. For example, a business might have to unexpectedly recruit staff with specialist knowledge and experience to further the programme.
- Some R&D programmes run for many years. Therefore their costs tend to rise with inflation. There is a tendency to underestimate inflation and businesses then have to obtain further funding to meet rising costs.

It may be possible to reduce risks by taking out a PATENT. A patent aims to protect the inventor of a new product or manufacturing process. It allows a business to design, produce and sell a new invention and attempts to prevent competitors from copying it. New inventions are protected for 15 years. The developer must make details of the invention available to the Patent Office.

Obtaining a patent can be a lengthy process. To qualify for a patent the invention must be brand new. Checks are then made to ensure it is authentic. The patent is published 18 months after its application and signed and sealed some time after this. The developer must pay annual fees to the Patent Office, which become more expensive after the first four years. This is to encourage production of the new idea. Both the inventor and the consumer can benefit from patents. Some benefits to businesses of patents are:

- a higher level of sales;
- reduced competition;
- legal protection that encourages continued research;
- higher profits, which can be ploughed back into further research and development;

- the benefits to the industry of having the technical information as a result of the patent;
- high risk research and development is encouraged.

Consumers also benefit. New products mean more variety and perhaps a better standard of living. New, more efficient, productive techniques mean lower costs and lower prices.

There is a number of criticisms of the patent system. The granting of sole production and distribution rights to one firm creates a legal monopoly. If this monopoly power is abused then consumers may be exploited.

Implications of innovation strategies

Innovative companies that are committed to high levels of R&D are likely to have differences in the way they operate. The culture of the organisation might be quite different. For example, in companies that emphasise creativity and innovation there is often an informal culture. There may also be more trust and less supervision. If a company pursues innovative strategies there are likely to be implications for other functional areas of the business. The possible implications for finance, marketing and human resources are outlined briefly below.

Finance Innovative companies are likely to have different financial priorities. Inevitably they will spend much larger

---

Question 2.

In 2006, Rolls-Royce invested a total of £747 million in research and development, of which £395 million was funded from Group resources. Some of the money invested in R&D is being used to address the environmental challenge. During 2006 Rolls Royce launched a new £95 million technology demonstrator programme, the Environmentally Friendly Engine (EFE), which will deliver further improvements in turbine efficiency and combustion emissions. EFE involves a range of industrial and university partners and will validate technologies for pull-through from 2008 into all of their gas turbine products.

Rolls-Royce is a lead partner in the development of the European 'Clean Sky' Joint Technology Initiative. Alongside its industrial partners, it hopes to gain European Commission approval to launch this seven-year programme in mid 2007. In combining this programme with the EFE programme, Rolls Royce will continue with its progress towards achieving the Advisory Council for Aeronautics Research in Europe (ACARE) goals for environmental improvements by 2020. Also, during 2006 Rolls Royce filed a record 330 patent applications.

Source: adapted from www.rolls-royce.com.

(a) Rolls Royce spent a total of £747 million on R&D in 2006. Outline two factors that might influence the amount a business spends on R&D.

(b) Discuss whether some of the R&D expenditure carried out by Rolls Royce was designed to reduce environmental damage.

(c) During 2006 Rolls Royce filed a record 330 patent applications. Explain the purpose of a patent.

amounts on R&D. This may have implications for fund raising. For example, many investors may not be prepared to risk their money in companies that rely heavily on innovation and R&D. This is because they know that R&D can often result in failure. Consequently such companies may struggle to attract funding. They often have to rely more on share capital than on loans when raising money.

Another issue for the finance department is cash flow. R&D has a habit of draining the cash resources of a business. The finance department must monitor cash flow carefully. On the one hand ensuring that the R&D department has enough cash to be effective, but on the other making sure that all of the company's cash does not disappear into a 'black hole'.

Marketing Innovative companies have to work very closely with the marketing department. One of the main sources of new ideas is from customers. Businesses must be responsive to the needs of consumers and R&D projects must address these needs. The marketing department must gather up to date and reliable information from the market and communicate it effectively to R&D centres. Innovative companies will be far more successful if their new products meet the needs of consumers.

When a new product is developed, it may take a time to get accepted in the market. For example, consumers may not believe that a new technical product really works. The marketing department will have to use all their skill to launch the new product successfully. However, once established, innovative products will get good distribution. Large retailers are likely to prefer innovative new products when allocating shelf space to manufacturers.

Human resources Innovative companies may have a more relaxed approach to working. This is to accommodate the needs of their creative people. Working practices may be more flexible and less regimented. Innovative companies may also have to recruit different types of people. They may require a lot of graduates for example. An increasing number of research companies are 'spin-offs' from university departments. For example, privately owned Molecular Profiles was founded in 1997, as a spin-off company from the School of Pharmacy at the University of Nottingham UK. The company specialises in advanced solid state analysis.

Workers in innovative companies are more likely to be involved in the introduction of new methods and working practices. For example, innovative companies may adopt a kaizen (continuous improvement) approach to business, where it is the responsibility of everyone to look for improvements. This view is supported by the management guru Tom Peters. He believes that innovation is the responsibility of everyone in the organisation. In this way, the organisation can harness the creative power of an even wider range of specialists. Also, innovation often comes when people from different backgrounds work in teams. An innovative business must be prepared to adopt such working practices with its employees.

KEYTERMS

Development – the changing of new ideas into commercial propositions.
Ergonomics – the study of people in their working environment and the adaptation of machines and conditions to improve efficiency.
Innovation – the commercial exploitation of an invention.
Patent – a licence which prevents the copying of an idea.
Research – an investigation involving the process of enquiry and discovery used to generate new business ideas.

KNOWLEDGE

1. What is the difference between R&D and innovation?
2. State four purposes of innovation.
3. Why is R&D risky?
4. State four benefits of R&D to a large clothes chain.
5. State three benefits of R&D to businesses.
6. State two industries where R&D expenditure tends to be high.
7. What might be the implications of innovative strategies for human resources?

Case Study:
Video games market

By 2011, the worldwide gaming market will be worth $48.9 billion at an annual growth rate of 9.1% from 2006. Key growth engines will include online and wireless games, new-generation consoles, as well as the expanding in-game advertising business. The overall gaming audience continues to expand and become somewhat more female and older than in the past thanks to casual games and games becoming an 'important part of culture'.

Nintendo, which has outsold Sony and Microsoft in the videogame console market, recently became the leader in game revenue, toppling Sony, said iSuppli, a market research agency. Worldwide revenue from Nintendo DS and Wii gaming software amounted to $1.2 billion in the quarter, up more than 31% from the $943.6 million Nintendo enjoyed in the second quarter. In comparison, Sony generated $1 billion in gaming software revenue for its PlayStation 3, PlayStation 2 and PSP players, while Microsoft posted revenue of $317.8 million for Xbox and Xbox 360. In the second quarter, software sales for Sony and Microsoft were $1 billion and $271.9 million, respectively.

Nintendo is expected to maintain its lead, as it ships about 200 additional titles by the end of the year, bringing the number of games to more than 350, many from outside publishers, iSuppli analyst David Carnevale said. In addition, game sales could get a further boost from the expected introduction of a new flagship title for the Wii, called Wii Fit. The game encourages players to engage in full-body exercises using Wii Balance Boards, performing activities including yoga, push-ups, aerobics, and stretching.

Nintendo has achieved mass-market appeal through easy to use games, and the Wii's motion-sensing control that allows players to get more physically involved in games, which could involve swinging a virtual tennis racket or golf club. In contrast, Sony's PlayStation 3 and Microsoft's Xbox 360 are aimed at more serious gamers with cutting-

edge titles, such as the popular Halo 3 for the Xbox 360. Microsoft reported recently that sales of Xbox 360 jumped 100% in its fiscal first quarter ended September 30, thanks to the debut of Halo 3. Microsoft hopes the trend will continue through the holiday shopping season.

Halo 3 has, to date, broken a number of gaming industry records, including the record for first day sales. The title pulled in $170 million on its September 25 launch. Sales of PlayStation 3 software, however, have been suffering due to the console's high price and a lack of compelling titles. The problems have affected third-party game publishers, such as leading game maker Electronic Arts, iSuppli said. EA is losing revenue due to meagre PlayStation 3 sales and the company is rooting for price cuts and improvements to the console in order to encourage software sales. Sony recently cut the price of the PlayStation 3 but, because the company was slow to drop prices and produce compelling games, third-party publishers are flocking to other platforms, the research firm said.

Source: adapted from www.blog.futurelab.net.

(a) (i) Comment on the size and growth potential of the global video games market. (4 marks)
(ii) How has Nintendo become the market leader? (4 marks)
(iii) Why is PlayStation 3 struggling in the market? (4 marks)

(b) What are the purposes of R&D and innovation in the video games market? (8 marks)

(c) In 2007, Sony cut its R&D expenditure on games by nearly 10 per cent to 97.9 billion yen. Explain why R&D in the video games industry is risky. (8 marks)

(d) How might CAD be useful in the video games market? (8 marks)

(e) To what extent are innovations and creativity the keys to success in the video games market? (14 marks)

Figure 1: Global video game market – projected growth

68 | Location strategies

The effects of expansion on location

If a business is successful the owners will probably want to expand operations. There are motives for growth, such as dominating the market, economies of scale and greater financial security. One of the issues that businesses need to address when growing is location. Most fast growing businesses are likely to outgrow their premises. This means they have to either expand at their current location or relocate to premises which can accommodate a larger scale of operations. Some businesses will have the scope to stay where they are and add to capacity. For example:

- a restaurant may be able to use an upstairs floor to double the number of covers;
- a shop may be able to acquire the premises next door and double capacity. Indeed, there are examples where a shop has acquired many of its neighbours over a period of time;
- a factory may be able to build an extension or occupy adjacent units;
- an office might increase capacity by occupying more floors in an office block.

However, there is likely to come a time for many expanding businesses where relocation is the only option. This might be because there is limited space in the current location, the current premises are unsuitable or expansion requires multiple locations such as a retail chain would. When this happens a business has to make another location decision.

Methods of making location decisions

The decision about where to relocate a business, or a new part of the business, will depend on the costs and benefits of particular sites. Businesses are likely to look at a number of sites, compare the costs and benefits and then make a decision. A decision might be made using a quantitative approach. For example, a business might use investment appraisal techniques when deciding where to locate. However, qualitative factors must not be overlooked.

Quantitative methods

Table 1 shows two possible sites for a business which is considering relocating its premises. It gives the initial cost of the move and then the cost savings to be made in each year compared with the existing site. Three investment appraisal methods can be used to show which, if any, site should be chosen. It is assumed that at the end of five years, the business will be relocating again. So no cost savings will be taken into account after the end of five years.

Payback method With the payback method, the business calculates how long it will take to recoup the initial investment.

In location A, the initial cost is £12 million and with annual savings (the equivalent of increased cash flows) of £3 million, the investment will be recouped in 4 years. With location B, the initial cost is higher at £15 million, but the cost savings are £5 million per year. The result is that the investment will be recouped in 3 years. So on the payback method, location B is the preferred location.

Average rate of return (ARR) With the average annual rate of return method, the net return is divided by the initial investment and expressed as a percentage. With location A, there will be a total cost saving (i.e. increased cash flow) over 5 years of £15 million. With an initial cost of £12 million, this gives a return of £3 million (£15 million - £12 million). So the ARR is [(£3 million ÷ £15 million) ÷ 5 years] x 100 per cent, which is 4 per cent. With location B, the cost saving is £25 million over five years with an initial cost of £15 million. So the ARR is [(£10 million ÷ £25 million) ÷ 5 years] x 100 per cent, which is 8 per cent. On the average rate of return method, location B is also the preferred location.

Discounted cash flow With discounted cash flow, the value of future cash flows must be discounted back to the present. The important point about discounted cash flow is that, just as money invested today will grow in value because of compound interest, so the reverse is true: the value of cash available in the future is worth less today. In Table 2, the cost savings (or net cash flows) have been discounted back assuming a discount rate of 15 per cent. The net present value of the cost savings falls the further into the future it occurs. When it is totalled up, the net present value of the cost savings at location A don't cover the initial investment needed. So moving to location A is unprofitable at this rate of discount. On the other hand, moving to location B shows a positive net cash flow. The cost savings outweigh the initial cost of the investment by £1.9 million. So this would suggest that the company should move to location B.

Table 1: Initial costs and cost savings of two new locations

	£ million Location A	Location B
Initial cost	12	15
Annual cost savings/increased cash flow		
Year 1	3	5
Year 2	3	5
Year 3	3	5
Year 4	3	5
Year 5	3	5

Table 2: Initial cost and cost savings of two new locations discounted at 15 per cent

	Location A £ millions	Location B £ millions	Discount table 15%	£ million Location A £ millions	£ million Location B £ millions
Initial cost	12	15	1.00	12.0	15.0
Annual cost savings/ increased cash flow					
Year 1	3	5	0.87	2.6	4.4
Year 2	3	5	0.76	2.3	3.8
Year 3	3	5	0.66	2.0	3.3
Year 4	3	5	0.57	1.7	2.9
Year 5	3	5	0.50	1.5	2.5
Total cost savings	15	25		10.1	16.9
Net cash flow	3	10		-1.9	1.9

Whatever the rate of discount used, location B would always be preferred over location A. However, if the rate of discount were much higher than 15 per cent, the discounted cash flow technique would suggest that even location B would give overall negative cash flows and therefore moving would not be profitable.

Qualitative factors

Qualitative factors are factors which cannot be measured using numbers. Qualitative factors are important when making location decisions partly because quantitative methods, such as investment appraisal techniques, cannot capture all the information needed to make a location decision. Qualitative factors are also important because quantitative methods can never give an accurate answer since they are based on assumptions about the future. Forecast revenues one, three or ten years from now, for example, are unlikely to match the actual revenues achieved. The further away in time the forecast, the less likely it is to be accurate. This doesn't mean to say that quantitative techniques are not important. But they must be placed alongside qualitative factors in decision making and their limitations recognised.

There is a variety of qualitative factors which a business might take into consideration when making a location decision.

Laws and regulations Any location decision will have legal and regulatory aspects. In many cases, laws and regulations will determine what type of business can occupy what type of premises in what areas. Getting planning permission will be necessary if a business is building new premises. If two sites are being compared in different countries, the legal frameworks may be very different. For example, one country may have much looser regulation of pollution than another country. Health and safety regulations may differ too.

Social, environmental and ethical considerations Many businesses, particularly larger ones, may take social, environmental and ethical considerations into account. For example, a manufacturer may be reluctant to move away from a local area because it has a long history of involvement with the area, is a major employer and moving away would severely damage the local community. Another business may decide against a particular location because the environmental impact of moving to that location would be too negative. A third business may deliberately choose a location in a high unemployment area as a positive ethical choice to create jobs. Businesses tend to make these choices for two reasons. Some businesses are set up with social, environmental and ethical goals which override the profit motive. Other businesses exploit their social, environmental and ethical decisions to promote themselves to their customers. Equally, businesses may want to avoid negative public relations (PR) which arise when they are accused of acting in an anti-social or unethical way.

Quality of life Evidence suggests that the interests of those making a location decision are very important. Small businesses, for example, tend to be located where their owner managers live. Small to medium sized businesses, when considering relocating, will typically relocate within a few miles of the present location. Owner managers don't want to move house or locality even if cheaper premises could be found just 50 miles away. Large companies will consider whether the managers who have to be sent to a location to run a plant or factory will enjoy the posting. Quality of housing, local schools and the environment are important considerations. So too are factors such as risk to employees. A multinational may choose to locate in China rather than, say, parts of South America or Africa for these reasons.

Political stability In the UK, political stability is taken for granted in most areas. But when large companies make decisions about where to locate around the world, political stability is a key factor. Foreign investment in certain countries may be lower than it would be if there were more political stability in these countries. At worst, political instability can lead to new governments which seize foreign owned assets or suddenly impose high taxes.

Quality of the workforce The quality of the local workforce is important. A business is unlikely to locate to a place where it is unable to recruit the right quality of local labour. China, for

Question 1.

Edney's is a manufacturer of frozen food products. It needs to move because it has outgrown its current premises. It is considering two sites, A and B. Site A has the lowest initial cost at £4.5 million but the move will cause more disruption to production initially than at Site B. In the longer term, however, the financial benefits of Site A are greater than at Site B.

The managing director has asked you to do some calculations on the two sites and make a recommendation about which site should be chosen. He has asked you to consider only any costs and cash flows over a seven year period.

Table 3: Initial costs and net cash flow of two sites, A and B

	Location A £millions	Location B £millions	Discount table Rate of discount at 20%
Initial cost	4.5	6.0	1.00
Net cash flow			
Year 1	1.0	2.0	0.83
Year 2	1.5	2.5	0.69
Year 3	2.0	2.5	0.58
Year 4	2.5	2.5	0.48
Year 5	3.0	2.0	0.40
Year 6	3.0	2.0	0.33
Year 7	3.0	2.0	0.28

(a) For both sites, calculate (a) the payback time;
(b) the average rate of return (ARR); (c) the net present value assuming a rate of discount of 20 per cent.

(b) Explain which site you would recommend the company should choose.

that they have found the **optimal location**. The optimal location is the best possible site for the business. It is the site where costs are minimised and benefits maximised. An optimal location will generate a number of benefits for a business. Some examples are outlined briefly below.

- The best access to markets. Customers will find the location convenient. Consequently businesses will find it easier to attract customers.
- Lowest site costs such as rent, business rates, maintenance and servicing costs.
- Easy access for staff. This is important because travelling to work is becoming increasingly difficult and stressful.
- Good working environment. This will help to improve the quality of life and improve the morale of all those who work there.
- Competitive advantage. If a business occupies the best possible site, it may be at the expense of a competitor. Consequently it will have the advantage over that competitor. Recently, supermarkets have bought up certain plots of land so that rivals cannot use the land to develop a store and compete against them.

Multi-site locations

Some large businesses operate from more than one site. This is quite normal and usually arises for a number of reasons.

- In retailing it is not practical to serve a national market from one giant store. For example, Next, the fashion clothes retailer, could not expect people to travel from all over the country to a centrally located store in, say, Birmingham. The alternative is to operate a chain of stores, each of which serves a local market such as a town or part of a city. This is very common in retailing and there are numerous examples of chain stores – River Island, M&S, Sainsbury, Asda, W H Smiths, Boots, to name but a few. Other types of businesses and franchises such as pub chains, car hire companies, hotel chains, restaurant chains and banks also have multiple outlets for the same reason.
- Large multi-national businesses have operations all over the world. This allows them to serve international markets and exploit local business conditions. For example, Kellogg's operates about 20 factories in countries such as the US (Battle Creek), England, Malaysia, Italy, Germany, Thailand and Australia for this reason.
- Some businesses have different types of operations in a number of different locations. For example, a large manufacturing company might have an assembly plant in one location, components manufacturers in a number of other locations, a head office in London and several warehouses around the country.
- Diversified businesses may have operations all over the place. Companies that grow through acquisition inevitably end up with businesses in multiple locations. For example, Ultra Electronics, a defence and aerospace company, has a large number of businesses operating in three main

example, has attracted a considerable amount of inward investment because it has a relatively well educated labour forceprepared to work for low wages. In the UK, London and the South East continue to attract new companies because, despite relatively high wages, there is a large pool of highly educated workers from which to draw.

Infrastructure Infrastructure, such as roads, railways, airports, hospitals and schools, can play an important part in location decisions. The quality of the infrastructure in a particular location will have an impact on costs and will therefore be part of any quantitative calculation. However, for a multinational company, having a local airport which takes international flights might be an important consideration. For a national company, being near the motorway network might influence a location decision. For a company located in London, which has many workers commuting in every day, nearness to a railway station or a tube station might influence a location decision.

The benefits of optimal location

If businesses make good decisions about location they may find

Table 4: Advantages and disadvantages of multi-site locations

Advantages

- The main advantage of operating with multiple sites is that a business can cover a wider market. Each site can serve a local market and together multiple sites can serve a national market. Retailers and other chains will enjoy high levels of recognition if they can operate outlets all over the country.

- Operating chains allow each outlet to cater for the needs of a local market. It is possible that the needs of a local market in Penrith are slightly different to the needs of a local market in Brighton. Each local outlet can adapt and meet local needs.

- Manufacturers and other businesses can exploit the advantages that local towns and regions have to offer. For example, a large automotive company may have an assembly plant in the West Midlands where there is a ready supply of trained and experienced labour (the West Midlands has a history of car manufacturing). On the other hand its head office may be in London where it can entertain important visitors, such as customers and potential investors, in one of the most exciting cities in the world.

- Having different sites can allow specialisation to flourish. A company like Ultra Electronics, described above, operates a large number of factories and other business activities across multiple sites. Each site is likely to specialise in a particular product. For example, one of its businesses, Pneumatic Systems, provides leading edge technology in the design development and manufacture of high pressure pneumatic components for the control of gases for critical applications in the aerospace and defence industries. Working as a single specialised operation, Pneumatic Systems will be able to focus more easily and not be distracted by other activities.

Disadvantages

- One of the main disadvantages of multi-site operations is that it may be more difficult to exploit economies of scale. For example, it may be difficult to exploit managerial economies because each site will require its own managers. Also, there may be some duplication of resources. For example, every restaurant in a chain will need an electronic cash register. It is unlikely that such a resource will be fully utilised and therefore money is wasted.

- It may become difficult for senior managers to keep a tight control on every single site. This might result in some sites underperforming because there is an inadequate level of control, supervision and accountability. This could lead to diseconomies of scale if a business has too many different sites.

- Communication is likely to be more difficult. For example, because of geographical distances, senior managers are less able to have face-to-face meetings with workers much lower down the hierarchical structure. There may also be language barriers if sites are spread across the globe.

- It may be difficult to foster a positive and successful organisational culture when a business operates from multiple sites. What could happen is that each site develops its own unique culture. This might be a problem when bringing together people from different sites for meetings and cross-site ventures, for example.

- It may be more difficult to standardise systems, procedures and other activities if there are lots of different sites. This could be confusing for customers and also for employees if they have to move around different sites.

divisions. The company produces a wide range of electronic, electro-mechanical systems and sub-systems, products and services. It provides these for aircraft, ships, submarines, armoured vehicles, surveillance and communication systems, airports and transport systems. Most of its operations are based in the UK and the US. During 2006 Ultra bought Polyflex Aerospace based in Cheltenham and Winfrith Safety Systems based in Dorset. As Ultra increases the number of its acquisitions, it will have a growing number of sites around the world. The advantages and disadvantages of multi-site location are shown in Table 4.

International location

Multinational companies operate in a number of different locations across the world. International location decisions can be more complex than those made within a country. There is a number of reasons why businesses choose to locate overseas.

Avoiding trade barriers Countries put up trade barriers, such as tariffs (taxes on imports) and quotas (physical limits on the quantity of a product that can be imported). They do this to protect their own national businesses from foreign competition. One way a multinational business can get round such trade barriers is to locate within the country. For example, Japanese car producers set up car plants in both Europe and the USA in the 1980s and 1990s, partly to get around trade barriers put up by EU countries and the US to keep Japanese producers of cars out of their markets.

Financial incentives Businesses may be attracted to a particular country or area if cash or other financial incentives are offered for locating there. Some of the regional aid available in parts of Europe may have influenced the location of Asian multinationals in the 1990s. In some cases governments offer cash, sometimes called 'sweeteners', to businesses if they locate in their country.

Cost of labour Many manufacturing multinational companies have located plants in cheap labour countries such as India or China. Cheap labour then gives them a competitive advantage. However, jobs may be retained in high labour cost countries where high quality labour is needed. Education, training and the skills of the workforce in countries like the UK are vitally important for keeping facilities such as headquarters or research departments in high labour cost countries.

Proximity to markets or suppliers Transport costs can be much greater over larger distances. So multinational companies may have to locate near their markets or their suppliers to remain competitive. A car component manufacturer, for example, may have to set up a factory in the Far East to be near a customer, a car manufacturer. It is not always true, though, that transport costs are significant in international location decisions. If a product is high value, transport costs may be only a small fraction of the final price charged. Equally, transport costs vary according to modes of transport. Sometimes, it can cost less to send an item thousands of miles across the globe by ship than it does to take it from the ship and transport it by lorry for the final 50 miles.

Exchange rate fluctuations Exchange rate fluctuations can be important determinants of location decisions. Businesses trading internationally can experience sudden large movements in exchange rates. Sometimes these movements are beneficial to a business but sometimes they have a negative impact. For example, a UK business may import components from Germany. If the exchange rate of the pound falls sharply against the euro, then the UK business is likely to face a larger bill for imports. One way of getting around this risk is for a company to balance its costs and revenues in a single currency through location decisions. For example, a UK company may export $20 million of goods from UK factories to customers in the USA and import €15 million of goods from a factory it owns in France to the UK. This exposes it to risks of changes in the value of the pound against both the euro and the US dollar. One way around this problem would be to close the factory in France and relocate it to the USA. Then there would be roughly equal and opposite transactions in US dollars, which would considerably reduce the company's exchange rate risks.

Political stability As already mentioned above, political stability is an important qualitative factor in determining decision making. Some countries have very little inward investment by foreign companies because of chronic political instability. Equally, some countries are currently boycotted by western companies because of the nature of their political regimes. To locate in these countries, which may have a poor record on human rights, could attract consumer boycotts or shareholder disapproval.

Language barriers Language can be an important factor in location decisions. One reason why the UK is favoured as a location by US companies is because the UK and the US share a common language. Much of the foreign investment over the past ten years in China has been by companies owned by Chinese people living outside of China. Locating new facilities in China allows them the advantage of low cost labour and they share a common language.

Question 2.

In early 2007, Burberry, the prestigious clothing and accessories company, closed one of its factories in Treorchy, South Wales. It moved production to China, where costs are significantly lower as a result of workers being paid extremely low wages. Profits for the company are likely to soar as the cost of producing one of the famous polo shirts will fall from £11 to about £4.

The closure attracted a huge amount of negative publicity. One of the reasons was the size of the original redundancy offer made to the 300 workers in South Wales. It was a meagre £1000 each; not even enough to buy this year's hottest Burberry accessory the Beaton handbag, priced at a lucrative £1095! It was also reported that the company could lose its royal warrants as the row intensified over the closure. Chris Bryant, Labour MP for Rhondda, allegedly wrote to the Lord Chancellor to demand that MPs have a say in which firms get the warrant. This is currently determined by the Queen and the Prince of Wales. Bryant also called for a Constitutional Affairs Select Committee investigation into the same issue.

Source: adapted from www.burberry.com.

(a) Explain the main reason why Burberry is shifting some production from South Wales to China.
(b) What are the drawbacks of moving production to China?
(c) Burberry operates from multiple sites. Explain one advantage of this.

KNOWLEDGE

1. Why do expanding firms have to consider relocation?
2. Why might quantitative methods help a business to make a more informed decision when choosing a site for location?
3. How can the ARR be used to make a location decision?
4. State four qualitative factors that might affect the location decision.
5. What is meant by the optimal location?
6. State two reasons why a business might operate from multiple sites.
7. State two advantages of operating from multiple sites.
8. State two disadvantages of operating from multiple sites.
9. Explain why governments might offer 'sweeteners' to businesses to locate in their country.
10. Explain why a bank might set up a call centre in India.

Case Study: Debenhams

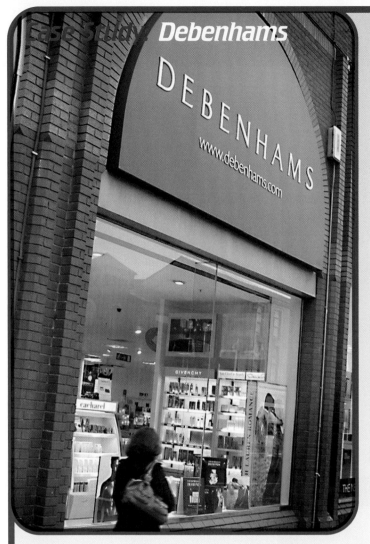

Debenhams is a leading multi-category retailer in UK, with a unique mix of own brands, international brands and concessions. Its main product categories are women's, men's and children's clothing and accessories, products for the home, health and beauty, lingerie and food services. The original 'Debenham & Freebody' store was based at Number 33 Wigmore Street, London. This site is still used by the company and houses its communications departments, including their Press Office.

The modern Debenhams group grew from the acquisition of department stores in towns and cities throughout the UK. The first of such purchases, Marshall & Snelgrove in Oxford Street, London was acquired in 1919. Later purchases included stores such as Harvey Nichols in London's Knightsbridge and Browns of Chester. Most stores retained their former identities until a unified corporate image was rolled out across the stores.

Debenhams was listed on the London Stock Exchange in 1928 and continued to expand. In 1985 the company was acquired by the Burton group. At this point the company owned 65 stores. Debenhams demerged in 1998 and was once again listed as a separate company.

In 1997, Belinda Earl, who had previously worked for the company, returned to become its Chief Executive. She and Spencer Hawken introduced 'Designers at Debenhams' which brought a variety of well known fashion talents to the stores at affordable prices, shaking off the dated perception of the company. The company expanded rapidly throughout the 1990s and now has a total of 140 stores in the UK and Ireland, with new stores recently opened at the MetroCentre in Gateshead and Hemel Hempstead, Hertfordshire.

The store has been trialling a compact version called 'Desire by Debenhams' which is mainly aimed at the female market with clothing ranges by 'Designers at Debenhams' and cosmetics. Aside from department stores, Debenhams operates a number of other divisions, including 'Debenhams Finance' (offering home, car and travel insurance and bureau de change services) and 'Debenhams Mobile' (offering mobile phones). In 2006 Debenhams bought 9 of the 11 Roches Stores department stores in Ireland and operate them as Debenhams.

Finally, Debenhams also has an international operation. It has 36 international franchises in 16 different countries. For example, it has stores in Dubai, Turkey, Bahrain, Qatar, Sharjah, Indonesia and Kuwait.

Source: adapted from Wikipedia and www.debenhams.com.

(a) How has expansion affected the location of Debenhams? (6 marks)

(b) (i) What might be the optimal location for a Debenhams store? (6 marks)
(ii) What might be the benefits of an optimal location for Debenhams? (10 marks)

(c) Analyse the difficulties Debenhams may encounter in operating multiple sites. (12 marks)

(d) Evaluate the advantages and disadvantages to Debenhams of having international locations. (16 marks)

The effective management of time

In business there is a well known saying that 'time is money'. One interpretation is that if tasks are completed more quickly, a business will benefit financially. For example, if a business completes an order in five weeks instead of six weeks there will be some real benefits. Once the order is completed resources are available for other tasks, the customer will get the order more quickly and the business can ask for payment earlier. Completing tasks more quickly will improve efficiency and profitability. Therefore it is not surprising that in recent years businesses have adopted methods such as **lean production** to make better use of time. One established method used to improve the management of time and other resources is **critical path analysis**.

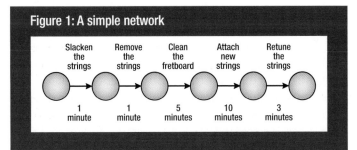

Figure 1: A simple network

Slacken the strings	Remove the strings	Clean the fretboard	Attach new strings	Retune the strings
1 minute	1 minute	5 minutes	10 minutes	3 minutes

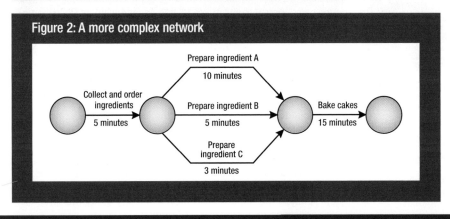

Figure 2: A more complex network

Prepare ingredient A — 10 minutes

Collect and order ingredients — 5 minutes

Prepare ingredient B — 5 minutes

Bake cakes — 15 minutes

Prepare ingredient C — 3 minutes

Networks

Many of the operations carried out by businesses are made up of a number of tasks. The operation is only complete when all of the tasks have taken place. For example, the tasks involved in changing a set of strings on a guitar for an instrument repairer might include:

- slackening the strings;
- removing the strings;
- cleaning the fretboard;
- attaching new strings;
- retuning the strings.

These tasks must be carried out in order for the operation to take place. Each task will take a certain amount of time. The operation is shown in Figure 1 on a NETWORK DIAGRAM. The operation takes 20 minutes to carry out (1 minute + 1 minute +5 minutes + 10 minutes + 3 minutes).

Some operations are less simple, with many tasks involved. Figure 2 shows a network diagram for an operation carried out by a cake manufacturer to make cakes for a wedding reception. In this operation some of the tasks can be carried out at the same time. So, for example, some of the ingredients can be prepared at the same time. Ingredient A takes 10 minutes to prepare, which is longer than any of the other ingredients. So the whole operation must take 30 minutes (5 minutes + 10 minutes + 15 minutes). This assumes tasks A, B and C can be carried out at the same time.

Network analysis

Businesses often have to complete large projects, which involve a series of complicated tasks or activities which must be carried out in a certain order. The use of networks helps a business to manage these projects effectively.

Question 1.

An airline company is considering improvements to its turnaround time for planes from the moment a plane arrives at the airport terminal to the time it leaves. Figure 3 shows a network diagram for the turnaround.

(a) What is the minimum amount of time it takes for the turnaround of the aeroplane?

(b) If the company could cut the time it takes to clean a plane from 20 minutes to 14 minutes, would that affect the time change?

Figure 3: Turnaround time for a passenger aircraft

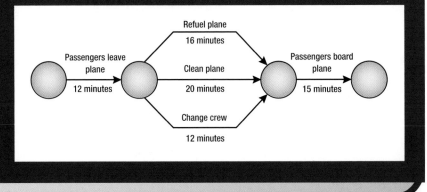

Refuel plane — 16 minutes

Passengers leave plane — 12 minutes

Clean plane — 20 minutes

Change crew — 12 minutes

Passengers board plane — 15 minutes

Figure 4: Network for a cottage renovation

It is vital that a business knows the minimum length of time a project will take to complete. It is also important to know whether a delay in completing individual tasks in an operation will delay the whole project or not. This is known as NETWORK ANALYSIS. It is also called CRITICAL PATH ANALYSIS as it allows a business to find the sequence or 'path' of tasks which are critical to the project and which, if delayed, will cause delays in the entire operation. In practice, businesses may use computers to manage large projects, such as the construction of a road system or hospital, or the manufacture of a large urgent overseas order for new machinery.

Before any project starts, it is important that networks are planned. This involves identifying the tasks that are to take place, how long each will take and the order in which they will take place. This information may be based on previous experience of projects or from research carried out by the business.

Figure 4 shows a network for a construction company which is renovating a cottage. There are certain features to note about the network.

- Arrows and lines show the task or activities to be carried out to complete the project. For example, Task B involves removing and replacing brickwork and flooring in the cottage.
- Some tasks can be carried out together, at the same time. For example, Tasks B and C can take place together but only after Task A has been completed.
- Arrows and lines cannot cross.
- Each task takes a certain amount of time. For example, the business plans to take four days to complete Task B, removing and replacing the brickwork and flooring in the cottage.
- Tasks must be completed in a certain order. Certain tasks are dependent on others being completed. For example, Task D, fitting new windows, and Task E, rewiring, cannot begin until Task B, removing and replacing brickwork and flooring, has taken place.

- Circles on the diagram, called NODES, show the start and finish of a task or activity. For example, Task A, preparing and organising materials, starts at Node 1 and ends at Node 2.
- There is always a node at the start and end of the project.
- Nodes contain information about the timing involved in the project.

Calculating the earliest start times

The first stage in determining the critical path in the network is to calculate the earliest time at which each of the tasks or activities can start, called the EARLIEST START TIME (EST). These are shown in the top right of the nodes. Figure 5 shows the earliest start times for all tasks in the renovation of the cottage.

Node 1 Task A can begin immediately. So 0 is placed in the EST in Node 1.

Node 2 Task A takes 1 day to complete. Tasks B and C, which can be carried out at the same time, can only begin after Task A is completed. So they can only begin after 1 day. This is placed in the EST in Node 2.

Node 3 Task B takes 4 days to complete. Together with the 1 day to complete Task A, this means that Tasks D and E can't start until after 5 days (4 days + 1 day). This is placed in the EST in Node 3.

Node 4 Task C takes 8 days to complete. Together with the 1 day to complete Task A, this means that Task F can't start until after 9 days (8 days + 1 day). This is placed in the EST in Node 4.

Node 5 What will be the earliest start time for Task G which begins at Node 5?

- Tasks A, B and D take 7 days to complete (1 day + 4 days + 2 days);
- Tasks A, C and F take 17 days to complete (1 day + 8 days + 8 days);
- Tasks A, B and E take 19 days to complete (1 day + 4 days + 14 days).

Task G can only begin when all preceding tasks are

Figure 5: Network showing the earliest start times for the cottage renovation

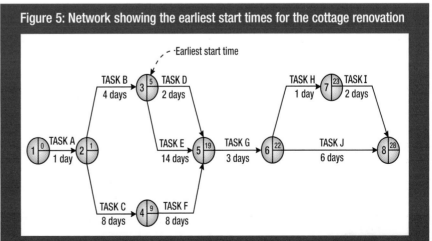

Question 2.

An advertising agency is working on a campaign for a large client for the launch of a new product. It has constructed a network showing the earliest start times for the different phases of the campaign.

(a) Copy out the network in Figure 6 and fill in the earliest start times marked by '?'.

(b) What is the minimum amount of time the campaign will take to complete?

(c) In the one month taken to plan the campaign at the start, the advertising agency revises its estimate of the time taken to plan the newspaper and magazine campaign to 10 months. How will this affect (a) the earliest starting times and (b) the overall time taken to complete the campaign?

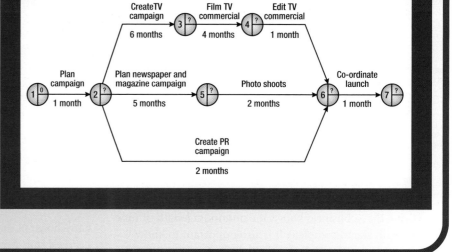

Figure 6: Network for an advertising campaign

completed. It is dependent on earlier tasks. The longest time to complete these tasks is 19 days. So the EST in Node 5 is 19 days and Task G can't start until after 19 days. This highlights an important rule when calculating earliest start times. Always choose the longest amount of time when placing the ESTs in nodes.

Node 8 Another example of this can be found when calculating the final node, Node 8. Tasks up to Node 6 have taken 22 days to complete. So Tasks H and J can only begin after 22 days. The time taken to complete Task J is 6 days. This is longer than the time taken to complete Tasks H and I, which is 3 days (2 days + 1 day). So the EST placed in Node 8 is 22 days + 6 days = 28 days.

As Node 8 is the final node, then 28 days is the time taken to complete the entire project.

Calculating the latest finish times

The next step involves calculating the latest times that each task can finish without causing the project to be delayed. The LATEST FINISH TIMES (LFTs) of the project to renovate a cottage are shown in Figure 7. They appear at the bottom right of the nodes.

Calculating the latest finish times begins at the final node,

Node 8. It has already been calculated that the project will take 28 days. This is placed in the LFT of Node 8. To calculate the LFTs of earlier nodes, use the formula:

LFT at Node - time taken to complete previous task

So the LFT at Node 7, for Task H, is 28 days - 2 days = 26 days.

To calculate the LFT for Task G, to be placed in Node 6, again use the tasks which take the longest amount of time. Task J takes 6 days and Tasks H and I only 3 days (2 days + 1 day). So the LFT at Node 6 is 28 - 6 days = 22 days.

Identifying the critical path

It is now possible to identify the CRITICAL PATH through the network. This shows the tasks which, if delayed, will lead to a delay in the project. The critical path on any network is where the earliest start times and the latest finish times in the nodes are the same. But it must also be the route through the nodes which takes the longest time.

Figure 8 shows the critical path and the tasks which can't be delayed if the renovation of the cottage is to be completed on time. These are tasks A, B, E, G and J. The critical path can be indicated by a broken line or crossed lines, or by some other method, such as highlighting the line in colour, by pen or on computer. Other tasks in the network do not lie on the critical path.

Calculating the float

A business can use the information in the network to calculate the float time in the project. This is the amount of time by which a task can be delayed without causing the project to be delayed. For example, Task I takes 2 days to complete. However, as it does not lie on the

Figure 7: Network showing latest finishing times for the cottage renovation

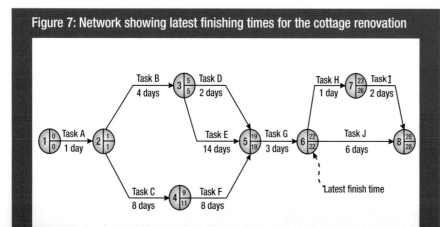

Figure 8: Critical path for the cottage renovation

Free float The FREE FLOAT is the amount of time by which a task can be delayed without affecting the following task. It can be calculated by:

$$\frac{\text{EST start of}}{\text{next task}} - \frac{\text{EST start of}}{\text{this task}} - \text{duration}$$

So for Task C it would be:

$$9 - 1 - 8 = 0 \text{ days}$$

critical path, it is possible that some delay can take place in this task without delaying the whole project. A delay of 1 day, for instance, would not lead to the project taking longer than 28 days.

How much delay can there be in tasks which do not lie on the critical path?

Total float The TOTAL FLOAT is the amount of time by which a task can be delayed without affecting the project. It can be calculated as:

$$\text{LFT of activity} - \text{EST of activity} - \text{duration}$$

So for Task B in Figure 8, for example, it would be:

$$5 \text{ days} - 1 \text{ day} - 4 \text{ days} = 0 \text{ days}$$

Activities which lie on the critical path will always have a zero total float value.

For Task C, which does not lie on the critical path, the total float is:

$$11 \text{ days} - 1 \text{ day} - 8 \text{ days} = 2 \text{ days}$$

Table 1 shows the total float for all tasks.

Assessing the value of critical path analysis

Critical path analysis can have a number of benefits for a business.

Efficiency Producing a network can help a business to operate efficiently. For example, a network shows those tasks which can be carried out at the same time. This can help save manufacturing time and the use of resources. Highlighting exactly which delays are crucial to the timing of the project can help a business to meet deadlines. Inability to meet a deadline can be costly for a business. Orders may be lost if goods are not manufactured on time. In the construction industry, clients sometimes have penalty clauses on contracts. These are costs payable by a building company which does not meet its deadlines. Identifying tasks which can be delayed, without affecting the whole project, can help project management. For example, if Task A takes 3 days and Task B takes 4, then a business knows that a delay in Task A will not delay the project. However, it might be able to reduce the length of time that Task B takes to 3 days. This may reduce the length of time the entire project will take. Sometimes building firms earn bonuses for coming in 'on time' or beating deadlines.

Decision making It can aid decision making in the organisation. The use of business models such as network analysis is argued to be a more scientific and objective method of making decisions. It is suggested that estimating the length of time a project will take, based on past information and an analysis of the tasks involved, should lead to deadlines being met more effectively, as the implications of delays can be assessed, identified and prevented.

Time based management Some businesses operate time based management systems. These are techniques to minimise the length of time in business processes. Identifying tasks which have to be done in order, tasks which can be done together and tasks which may delay the whole project will all help to ensure that the least time

Table 1: Float

| | | | | | | | | (days) |
Task/activity	LFT	EST	Duration	Total float	EST next	EST this	Duration	Free float
A	1	0	1	0	1	0	1	0
B	5	1	4	0	5	1	4	0
C	11	1	8	2	9	1	8	0
D	19	5	2	12	19	5	2	12
E	19	5	14	0	19	5	14	0
F	19	9	8	2	19	9	8	2
G	22	19	3	0	22	19	3	0
H	26	22	1	3	23	22	1	0
I	28	23	2	3	28	23	2	3
J	28	22	6	0	28	22	6	0

Question 3.

Hurford's is a specialist zinc galvanising business, coating steel components with zinc to prevent them from rusting. A network for one of its processes is shown in Figure 9.

(a) Copy out Figure 9 and fill in the earliest start times for each job on your diagram.
(b) Fill in the latest finishing times on the diagram.
(c) Show the critical path on the diagram.

Figure 9: Network for a zinc galvanising business

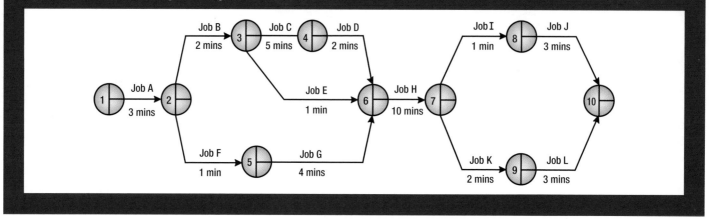

is taken to complete an operation.

Working capital control Identifying when resources will be required in projects can help a business to manage its working capital cycle. Networks allow a business to identify exactly when materials and equipment will be used in a project. They can be purchased when required, rather than holding costly stocks. This is especially important if a business operates a just-in-time system of stock control. If a business has to borrow to purchase materials then charges or interest costs may be reduced if materials are only bought when required. If delays are identified and taken into account then resources can be allocated to other operations until they are needed.

Although critical path analysis is clearly of value, a business must not assume that simply because it produces a network its project will be completed without delay. Information used to estimate times in the network may be incorrect. For example, management might have estimated times based on past performance. But a new project may have special requirements which could take longer. Also, changes sometimes take place when projects are carried out. For example, construction companies may need contingency plans to deal with unforeseen events such as the weather. These would need to be taken into account when producing the network. Large projects may require detailed and extensive networks, calculated on computer.

KNOWLEDGE

1. Why is network analysis also known as 'critical path analysis'.
2. What is shown by a node on a network diagram?
3. Explain the difference between (a) the earliest start time and the latest finishing time; (b) the total float and the free float.
4. Why can network analysis help improve the efficiency of a business?
5. What are the implications of network analysis for working capital control?

KEYTERMS

Earliest start time – how soon a task in a project can begin. It is influenced by the length of time taken by tasks which must be completed before it can begin.
Critical path – the tasks involved in a project which, if delayed, could delay the project.
Critical path analysis/network analysis – a method of calculating the minimum time required to complete a project, identifying delays which could be critical to its completion.
Free float – the time by which a task can be delayed without affecting the following task.

Latest finish times – the latest times that tasks in a project can finish.
Network diagram – a chart showing the order of the tasks involved in completing a project, containing information about the times taken to complete the tasks.
Nodes – positions in a network diagram which indicate the start and finish times of a task.
Total float – the time by which a task can be delayed without affecting the project.

Case Study: *Newport Holdings*

Newport Holdings manufactures electronic components for domestic appliances. The company has received some large orders recently after a successful sales drive. However, to increase capacity and improve productivity it must replace the entire assembly line with up-to-date technology. The directors are keen to go ahead with the investment, but are worried about the disruption that will be caused. During the construction of the new assembly line production will be zero. The company can hold up to 30 days of stocks so the new line must be up and running within one month. If the new line isn't ready, Newport Holdings will lose approximately £200,000 per day. This will be unacceptable to the directors.

Table 2: The tasks, task order and task times required to construct the new assembly line

Task	Description	Order/dependency	Duration
A	Dismantle old line	Must be done first	3 days
B	Retrain staff	Must follow A	15 days
C	Position lifting gear	Must follow A	2 days
D	Remove roof panels	Must follow A	2 days
E	Lower in new plant	Must follow D	2 days
F	Replace roof panels	Must follow C and E	3 days
G	Install new plant	Must follow F	11 days
H	Test run	Must follow B and G	3 days
I	Safety checks	Must follow H	2 days

Figure 10: Network diagram for the installation of new technology at Newport Holdings

(a) State two objectives of critical path analysis. (4 marks)

(b) For the activities required to install the new technology, calculate the (i) earliest start times (ESTs) and (ii) the latest finish times (LFTs). (12 marks)

(c) Identify the critical path on the network diagram. (4 marks)

(d) Will the construction be completed in time? Explain your answer. (4 marks)

(e) How will the construction time be affected if task B is delayed by 4 days? (6 marks)

(f) Evaluate the advantages and disadvantages to Newport Holdings of using critical path analysis. (10 marks)

70 Lean production

What is lean production?

LEAN PRODUCTION is an approach to production developed in Japan. Toyota, the Japanese car manufacturer, was the first company to adopt this approach. Its aim is to reduce the quantity of resources used up in production. Lean producers use less of everything, including factory space, materials, stocks, suppliers, labour, capital and time. As a result, lean production raises productivity and reduces costs. The number of defective products is reduced, lead times are cut and reliability improves. Lean producers are also able to design new products more quickly and can offer customers a wider range of products to choose from. Lean production involves using a range of practices designed to reduce waste and to improve productivity and quality.

Kaizen (continuous improvement)

KAIZEN is perhaps the most important concept in Japanese management. It means continuous improvement. Every aspect of life, including social life, working life and home life, is constantly improved. Everyone in the business is involved. Kaizen is said to be an 'umbrella concept'. A wide range of different production techniques and working practices must be carried out for it to be effective. Figure 1 shows examples of the techniques, principles and practices. They should result in ongoing improvements. This approach argues that a day should not pass without some kind of improvement being made

somewhere in the business.

There is a number of features of Kaizen which affect a business.

Continuous improvement Kaizen has been the main difference between the Japanese and the Western approaches to management in the past. The attempts of Western businesses to improve efficiency and quality have tended to be 'one-offs'. In Figure 2 the solid line illustrates the Western approach. Productivity remains the same for long periods of time, then suddenly rises. The increase is followed by another period of stability, before another rise. Increases in productivity may result from new working practices or new technology. The dotted line shows the Japanese approach. Improvements are continuous. They result from changes in production techniques which are introduced gradually.

Eliminating waste The elimination of waste (called muda in Japan) in business practices is an important part of Kaizen. Waste is any activity which raises costs without adding value to a product. Examples may be:

- time wasted while staff wait around before starting tasks, such as waiting for materials to arrive;
- time wasted when workers move unnecessarily in the workplace, such as walking to a central point in the factory to get tools;
- the irregular use of a machine, such as a machine which is only used once a month for a special order;
- excessive demands upon machines or workers, such as staff working overtime seven days a week which causes them to be tired and work poorly.

Firms that adopt the Kaizen approach train and reward

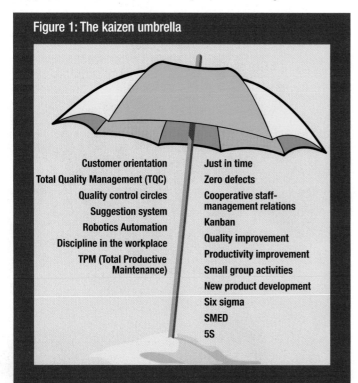

Figure 1: The kaizen umbrella

Customer orientation
Total Quality Management (TQC)
Quality control circles
Suggestion system
Robotics Automation
Discipline in the workplace
TPM (Total Productive Maintenance)

Just in time
Zero defects
Cooperative staff-management relations
Kanban
Quality improvement
Productivity improvement
Small group activities
New product development
Six sigma
SMED
5S

Figure 2: The Western and Japanese approaches to improvement

Output per worker (productivity)

Continuous improvements

One-off improvements

Time

workers to continually search for waste and to suggest how it might be eliminated.

Implementing continuous improvement It is often difficult for workers in a business to look for continuous improvement all the time. Japanese businesses tried to solve this problem by introducing the PDCA (Plan, Do, Check, Action) cycle. It is a series of activities that lead to improvement.

- Plan. Businesses must identify where improvement is needed. Data must be gathered and used to develop a plan which will result in improvement.
- Do. Once the plan has been finalised it must be carried out. The plan is likely to be implemented by workers, on the production line perhaps.
- Check. The next stage in the cycle is to check whether or not there has been an improvement. This task may be carried out by inspectors.
- Action. If the plan has been successful, it must be introduced in all parts of the business.

Just-in-time manufacturing

JUST-IN-TIME (JIT) MANUFACTURING is an important part of lean production and the kaizen approach. It was developed in the Japanese shipbuilding industry in the 1950s and 1960s. The industry recognised that a great deal of money was tied up in stocks. Traditionally, one month's supply of steel was held by a shipyard. However, as the industry became more competitive, shipbuilders insisted that steel suppliers deliver orders 'just-in-time', i.e. a few hours or less before the steel was needed. This reduced the need for high levels of working capital and improved the financial performance of the business. JIT was extended to every stage of production. For example, raw materials were delivered JIT to be made into parts, parts were delivered JIT to be made into goods and goods were produced and delivered JIT to be sold.

JIT was introduced in other Japanese industries, such as the car industry, and then spread to other parts of the world, such as the USA and Europe. JCB has used JIT in its Rochester plant. When JCB excavators are manufactured, every machine on the production line has already been sold. Supplies of components, such as engines from Perkins, and raw materials, such as steel plate, arrive on the day they are needed. JIT manufacturing requires high levels of organisational skills and reliable suppliers.

Table 1 shows the advantages and disadvantages of JIT manufacturing.

The 'Kanban' system

KANBAN is a Japanese term which means signboards or cards. The Kanban system is a method used to control the transfer of materials between different stages of production. The kanban might be a solid plastic marker or coloured ping-pong ball. They might be used to:

- inform employees in the previous stage of production that a particular part must be taken from stocks and sent to a

specific destination (conveyance kanbans);
- tell employees involved in a particular operation that they can begin production and add their output to stock (production kanbans);
- instruct external suppliers to send parts to a destination (vendor kanbans).

Kanbans are used to trigger the movement or production of resources. Used properly, they will be the only means of authorising movement. Kanbans are an important part of JIT manufacturing as they prevent the build-up of stock or parts in a factory.

Time-based management

TIME-BASED MANAGEMENT involves reducing the amount of time businesses take to carry out certain tasks, such as launching new products or cutting lead times in production. Time-based management is a feature of lean production because it involves eliminating a type of waste, i.e. time. Time in business is a valuable resource. Productivity can be improved if tasks are carried out more quickly. Time-based management has a number of effects on a business.

Table 1: Advantages and disadvantages of JIT manufacturing

Advantages

- It improves cash flow since money is not tied up in stocks.
- The system reduces waste, obsolete and damaged stock.
- More factory space is made available for productive use.
- The costs of stockholding are reduced significantly.
- Links with and the control of suppliers are improved.
- The supplier base is reduced significantly.
- More scope for integration within the factory's computer system.
- The motivation of workers is improved. They are given more responsibility and encouraged to work in teams.

Disadvantages

- A lot of faith is placed in the reliability and flexibility of suppliers.
- Increased ordering and administration costs.
- Advantages of bulk buying may be lost.
- Vulnerable to a break in supply and machinery breakdowns.
- Difficult to cope with sharp increases in demand.
- Possible loss of reputation if customers are let down by late deliveries.

Question 1.

New Balance Athletic Shoes (UK) Ltd is a US owned company producing a range of high performance athletic shoes. The business has been manufacturing in the UK since 1982 and moved to its current site in Flimby, near Workington, in 1991. New Balance had developed a five year strategic business plan to increase turnover from £70 million to £250 million. In order to achieve this, the manufacturing plant would have to triple the output of the one million pairs of shoes produced in 2005. Land was acquired adjacent to the current site to build another factory unit and the management team was looking for new ways to increase capacity and productivity.

The company employed a consultant to run a series of team workshops with process workers to introduce the basic principles of lean manufacturing. These teams were then challenged to analyse their current process, which led to the development of a new cellular layout requiring 35 per cent less space and only four operatives instead of five. The total work content was balanced between the four operatives to create product flow around the cell. Once the cell footprint had been agreed, a new future state 'ideal' factory layout was developed to convert freed up space into additional cells. The switch to lean production generated a number of benefits for the company.

- Output increased from 10 to 14 pairs of shoes per person per hour.
- Cell teams reduced from five to four people.
- Thirty five per cent reduction in space taken up by manufacturing cell.
- New cells created.
- £1.5 million positive cost variance compared to 2005 manufacturing costs.
- £1.5 million cost avoidance, as there was no longer any requirement to build an additional factory.

Source: adapted from www.mas.dti.gov.uk.

(a) Using this case as an example, explain what is meant by cell production.
(b) Explain why cell production lends itself well to teamworking.
(c) How did the introduction of cell production benefit New Balance Athletic Shoes Ltd?

Focus on customer needs Customers are given a wide range of products to choose from, i.e. different models with different specifications. The same model car can be produced according to different specifications, such as different colours, engine sizes and trims. Manufacturers can achieve this by reducing the length of production runs. Shorter production runs will also allow a firm to cut customer lead times, so customers are not kept waiting.

Use other lean production methods Examples include:
- just-in-time manufacturing;
- simultaneous engineering
- Single Minute Exchange of Dies (SMED);
- flexible manufacturing.

These methods prevent delays on production lines, reduce stock levels and improve scheduling. This means employees are not waiting around for work to arrive.

Machines must be versatile They must be able to produce a variety of products and be adjusted to a range of settings. Settings must be changed quickly and easily to deal with shorter production runs.

Speed up the design process They do this by carrying out a number of design tasks simultaneously. The traditional approach to design is to carry out one task after another. However, time can be saved if design tasks can be completed at the same time. This is called SIMULTANEOUS ENGINEERING. It is a project management approach, not a method of production. Such an approach needs co-ordination and communication between each design team. This approach to speeding up the design process has been called LEAN DESIGN.

Mass producers argue that economies of scale will only be achieved and costs cut if products are standardised and production runs are long. Producing a variety of different models will lead to shorter production runs and higher average costs. Time-based management challenges this view. It may be possible to produce smaller quantities, because costs can be reduced by time savings.

There may be certain advantages for a business using a time-based management system.
- Customers will benefit. A wider range of products will be available and there will be faster delivery times. This might result in higher sales levels for the firm.
- Lean design will result in shorter lead times. This means that resources will be used more effectively and product development will be faster. This will give the business a competitive edge in the market.
- Other lean production techniques will increase efficiency, the quality of products will be improved and waste will be minimised.
- The time spent on a range of production tasks is reduced. This helps to improve productivity and reduce unit costs. As a result manufacturers may offer their products at lower prices or enjoy higher profit margins.

However, it could be argued that some costs might rise as a result of using time-based management. The versatile machinery which this method requires may be more expensive. Staff may also need to be trained in a wider range of skills and tasks to cope with the flexibility in production. Shorter production runs may result in the loss of some economies of scale.

Flexible manufacturing One of the reasons why flow production techniques tend to lead to lower average costs than batch production or job production is because time is not lost changing tools or other equipment to make a new product. For example, a chocolate manufacturer could easily lose a day or two days' production when changing from production of one chocolate bar to another using batch production techniques. Machines have to be completely cleaned to prevent contamination and tooling within the machines has to be changed.

FLEXIBLE MANUFACTURING aims to reduce or even

eliminate changeover time from one product to another so that it becomes as cheap to produce 10 units of one item, 8 of another, and 12 of a third as it is to produce 30 units of the same item. On a car production line, the ideal is for every car produced to be unique. It might be the same model with different specifications. Or it might be two or more models being made at the same time. Flexible manufacturing is achieved by using equipment which can be changed from one use to another use very quickly and ideally instantaneously. It also means that workers must be flexible too, having the skills to deal with different products. Flexible manufacturing requires the back-up of other lean production techniques. For example, on a vehicle production line, if there are 14 different sets of doors fitted during a shift, each a different colour, then there must be just-in-time production techniques used to deliver those doors to that work station at the right time. Otherwise flexible manufacturing would require huge levels of stocks. Similarly, every worker must be responsible for the quality of work done.

Just-in-time production Just-in-time (JIT) manufacturing can be seen as another example of time-based management. JIT cuts the amount of time that stocks are held by a business. In a car manufacturing company, for example, car seats may have been held on average 10 days at the factory in the 1970s before being assembled inside a car. Today, the average stock time held may be three hours because seats are being delivered three times a day to the car plant.

Empowerment

Empowerment involves giving employees the power to make decisions in a business. The aim of empowerment is to give employees more control over their own work conditions. Workers in the past have tended to follow the instructions of managers. They were rarely required to think, make decisions, solve problems or work creatively. There was often conflict between management and workers, and little co-operation and team-spirit.

In recent years many businesses have learned that efficiency will improve if workers are given the opportunity to involve themselves in decision making. Workers will be better motivated and the business may gain from the creativity of its workers. Workers may also be more flexible and adaptable. For example, a worker may speak directly to a customer about changes in an order. For empowerment to be successful, managers must have faith in their workforce. They must also trust them and work in partnership without conflict.

Empowerment is not without difficulties. Some workers may not be able to make their own decisions and training may be required to teach them such skills. Managers may resent giving up authority. Some staff may even abuse their power to make decisions.

Teamworking

A growing number of businesses are introducing teamworking into their organisations. This involves dividing the workforce into fairly small groups. Each team will focus on a particular area of production and team members will have the same common aims. Teamworking probably works best in businesses that do not have a hierarchical structure and which have an organisational culture which supports group work. Effective teamworking requires co-operation between workers and management, training for staff and decision making responsibility for workers.

Both the business and its employees might benefit from teamwork. Workers should develop relationships with colleagues and a 'team spirit' which may improve motivation and productivity. Flexibility might improve. For example, team

---

Question 2.

Jenx Ltd is one of the UK's longest established companies designing innovative, therapeutic and development products for children with spinal problems. The company was founded in 1982 and is still run by a Paediatric Physiotherapist and her husband. The company sells its products to over twenty countries worldwide and is committed to a continuous process of review and improvement to offer children the best products available.

After attending a lean training workshop in 2005, Mr Jenkins learned about lean production and the importance of developing an improvement plan. He could see where this could potentially help his business to improve, develop and grow. The key objective from the outset was to involve employees in an improvement programme that allowed them to learn how to make and sustain their own improvements. A team was formed in the machine shop and they were taught the fundamentals of lean manufacturing. This set the foundations for implementing a 5S improvement programme in the machine shop. It was felt that this would help to create a better working environment, improve productivity and provide the best way forward for a programme of change.

As a result of the 15 day 5S Improvement Project, the company has achieved the following.

- Noticeable change in employee commitment and contribution to business improvement.
- Gross value added has increased by £60,000, and productivity by 15 per cent, as a result of the creation of manufacturing cells.
- Distance travelled to manufacture products has reduced from 80 metres to 5 metres (93 per cent).
- Manufacturing finishing cells have been developed and lead times have reduced (60 per cent).
- Stock and WIP (work in progress) has reduced.
- Investment in a new extraction system and sawing equipment has been made.
- Work flow and space utilisation has improved by 20 per cent

Source: adapted from www.mas.dti.gov.uk.

(a) Which lean production method may have been used to reduce stock and WIP?
(b) What is meant by 5S?
(c) How did the implementation of 5S help Jenx Ltd?

members might be more willing to cover for an absent colleague. Teams might plan their own work schedules, share out tasks, choose their methods of work and solve their own problems. This should lead to quicker decision making and the generation of more ideas. It is also suggested that communication and labour relations may improve as a result of teamworking. However, there may be conflict between team members and managers may resent the responsibility delegated to teams. Teamwork also results to some extent in a loss of specialisation among workers, which is often found in flow or mass production techniques.

Cellular manufacturing

Flow production involves mass producing a standard product on a production line. The product undergoes a series of operations in sequence on a continuous basis until a finished product rolls off the 'end of the line'.

CELLULAR MANUFACTURING or CELL PRODUCTION adopts a different approach and involves dividing the workplace into 'cells'. Each cell occupies an area on the factory floor and focuses on the production of a 'product family'. A 'product family' is a group of products which requires a sequence of similar operations. For example, the metal body part of a machine might require the operations cut, punch, fold, spot weld, dispatch. This could all be carried out in one cell. Inside a cell, machines are grouped together and a team of workers sees the production of a good from start to finish.

Take the example of a furniture manufacturer making parts for a kitchen range in a cell. The raw material, such as wood, would be brought into the cell. Tasks such as turning on a lathe or shaping by routing would be carried out at workstations. The part would then be assembled and passed on to stock. The cell may also be responsible for tasks such as designing, schedule planning, maintenance and problem solving, as well as the manufacturing tasks which are shared by the team.

The advantages of cellular manufacturing include:
- floor space is released because cells use less space than a linear production line;
- product flexibility is improved;
- lead times are cut;
- movement of resources and handling time is reduced;
- there is less work-in-progress;
- teamworking is encouraged;
- there may be a safer working environment and more efficient maintenance.

Benchmarking

BEST PRACTICE BENCHMARKING (BPB) is a technique used by some businesses to help them discover the 'best' methods of production available and then adopt them. BPB involves:
- finding out what makes the difference, in the customer's eyes, between an ordinary supplier and an excellent supplier;
- setting standards for business operations based on the best

practice that can be found;
- finding out how these best companies meet those standards;
- applying both competitors' standards and their own to meet the new standards and, if possible, to exceed them.

Figure 3 illustrates the five main steps in BPB. The first step is to **identify** exactly what the company intends to benchmark. Benchmarks that are important for customer satisfaction might include consistency of product, correct invoices, shorter delivery times, shorter lead times and improved after-sales service. For example, Motorola, the communications company, has benchmarked the yield and product characteristics of a range of its activities including its assembly, warehousing and purchasing performance.

The second step involves **choosing a company** to set the benchmark against. This may be done by asking customers who they feel is the best in the field. Business analysts, journalists, stockbrokers or industrialists may also be used. Rank Xerox and Centreparc, the leisure group, have used other parts of their own organisations which have developed a reputation for excellence.

In the third step, information can be **gathered** from a number of sources, such as magazines, newspapers, trade association reports, specialist databases, customers and suppliers. Companies in the same industry often share information. An example may be businesses supplying local markets, such as garden centres. The benefits of this are that the worst performers can get advice from the best and perhaps visit their premises.

The **analysis** of information is best done with quantitative techniques. For example, a firm might compare numerical data relating to delivery times.

The final stage involves **using** the information. Once

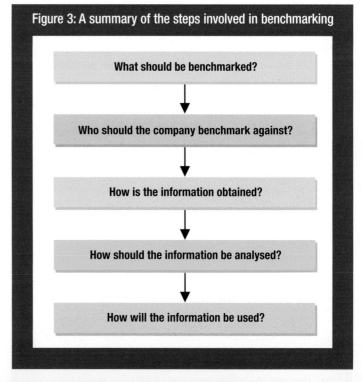

Figure 3: A summary of the steps involved in benchmarking

What should be benchmarked?

↓

Who should the company benchmark against?

↓

How is the information obtained?

↓

How should the information be analysed?

↓

How will the information be used?

standards have been found and set, they must be communicated throughout the business. Improvements must be funded, introduced and monitored. Once a company becomes the best in the field others will begin to benchmark against them. This means the company must continue to benchmark its own process.

Six Sigma

Six Sigma is a Japanese method developed by Motorola. It takes its name from the Greek letter 'sigma' used in statistics to indicate standard deviation. It is a statistical approach designed to eliminate defects in processes. A process must not produce more than 3.4 defects per million. A Six Sigma defect is defined as anything that fails to match customer specifications. Six Sigma involves collecting data on performance in processes and then evaluating it. Businesses can reduce variations in performance by using one of two Six Sigma approaches. DMAIC (define, measure, analyse, improve, control) is an improvement system for existing processes that result in too many defects. DMADV (define, measure, analyse, design, verify) is an improvement system used to develop new processes.

Single Minute Exchange of Dies (SMED)

Many manufacturers are under pressure to offer a wider variety of products. This has resulted in companies having to reduce the size of the batches they produce. So it is important to reduce changeover or set-up time. Bottling industries can spend more than 20 per cent of production time on changeovers, for example. Single Minute Exchange of Dies (SMED) is an approach to reduce output and quality losses due to changeovers. It was developed in Japan by Shigeo Shingo and has allowed companies to reduce changeover times from hours to minutes. He developed a method to analyse the changeover process, enabling workers to find out for themselves why the changeover took so long, and how this time could be reduced. There are four key steps in SMED.

- Suppress useless operations and convert IS operations (those which must be done while the machine is stopped) into ES operations (those which can be done when the machine is running).
- Simplify fittings and tightenings.
- Work together.
- Suppress adjustments and trials.

SMED has often resulted in workers approaching changeovers with a 'pit-stop mentality'.

5S (Sort, Set, Shine, Standardise and Sustain)

5S is a Japanese approach to housekeeping in the factory. It is a method of organising, cleaning, developing and sustaining a productive work environment. What does 5S stand for?

- **Sort.** This is about getting rid of the clutter in the factory. Only items such as necessary work tools should be in the factory environment. All other items, such as excess

inventory, should be removed.
- **Set in order.** The work area should be organised so that it is easy to find what is needed.
- **Shine.** This is to do with keeping the work area clean. Make it 'shine'.
- **Standardise.** Once the most effective cleaning and sorting methods have been established, they should be used as standards for the whole factory.
- **Sustain.** Mechanisms should be implemented to ensure that the standards achieved are recognised by everyone and used in the future.

This approach has helped businesses to improve efficiency because the work environment is less cluttered and more organised.

KEYTERMS

Best practice benchmarking – imitating the standards of an established leader in quality and attempting to better them.

Cellular manufacturing or cell production – involves producing a 'family of products' in a small self-contained unit (a cell) within a factory.

Flexible manufacturing – a system designed to allow a number of products and product variants to be produced using the same resources over a short space of time.

Just-in-time manufacturing – a production technique which is highly responsive to customer orders and uses very little stock holding.

Kanban – a card which acts as a signal to move or provide resources in a factory.

Kaizen – a Japanese term which means continuous improvement.

Lean design – keeping the resources and time used in the design process to a minimum.

Lean production – an approach to operations management aimed at reducing the quantity of resources used up in production.

Simultaneous engineering – an approach to project management where some, or all of the tasks involved in a project, are carried out at the same time.

Time-based-management – involves setting strict time limits in which tasks must be completed.

KNOWLEDGE

1. What are the aims of lean production?
2. What is meant by the Kaizen umbrella?
3. Explain the purpose of the PDCA cycle.
4. Describe four advantages of JIT manufacturing.
5. What is the purpose of the Kanban system?
6. Describe the three principles of time-based manufacturing.
7. What are the advantages of time-based manufacturing?
8. Give two advantages and two disadvantages of empowerment.
9. Why is teamworking a growing trend in businesses?
10. Describe how cellular manufacturing works.

Case Study: FTL Company Ltd

Family-owned FTL Company Ltd manufactures stainless steel hose assemblies in various types and sizes for a number of industry sectors. The utilities market is the largest share of the business; supported by automotive tuners for power assisted steering applications, payphone handsets, stainless steel metallic hoses and associated pipework. The management team at FTL operates with continuous improvement in mind, and have always encouraged employee involvement in the development of new processes. The company has so far achieved ISO9001:2000 quality standard and is currently working towards BS EN ISO14001.

The company has implemented kaizen principles to reduce costs and improve output. FTL had been successful in winning new contracts which required an increase in production of 50 per cent to support the continued company growth. The company also had an underlying need to reduce waste and improve productivity to respond to competitive pressures and offset recent energy cost increases. FTL therefore decided to bring all of its production in house – a vital step for the company if it was to continue to grow and remain competitive, fighting off competition from India, Turkey and China.

To begin the programme of work, a presentation was delivered to the entire workforce explaining, in simple terms, the need for change. The principles of 'lean' were introduced along with the need for 'total employee involvement'. A kaizen project team was formed comprising operators from the multi-spindle auto-production area, engineers and supervisors. The team was invited to discuss the current method of manufacturing for turned parts and to identify any areas of concern. The major problem area they highlighted was in set-up and changeover times. As a result SMED training was given to the team leading to a full analysis of the process using video footage. Opportunities for improvement were identified, which resulted in a reduction from 27 minutes per shift to 9.5 minutes per shift in set up for turning and grinding.

The team then explored potential improvements in the machine tooling layout and the tooling technology that was being used. A number of improvements were made which extended tool change frequencies further and reduced cycle times from 12 seconds per part to 10 seconds per part. A quality plan was also developed and introduced to ensure that defects were checked for as they happened. The operators were fully trained to carry out the checks independently, giving them greater control of their working environment.

The kaizen team was trained to monitor the machines' ongoing performance and react to any output. Their training also covered how to deliver these results via a Power Point Presentation to management on a monthly basis.

As a result of a 10 day manufacturing efficiency project, FTL has achieved the following.

- 30 new jobs created.
- 65 per cent reduction in set-up times using SMED analysis.
- An additional £72,000 in Gross Value Added.
- 60 per cent increase in people productivity.
- Kaizen activities highlighted a 75 per cent reduction in rework.
- Customer demand is being satisfied from 100 per cent in-house production.
- No loss of customers to low cost labour economies of China, Turkey and India despite increasing competition.
- A quality plan introduced which checks for defects as they happen.
- A self managed Kaizen team has been established to monitor and improve production.
- Staff morale has improved as the multifunctional team has driven improvement - all ideas have been listened to and actions deployed as a team.

Source: adapted from www.mas.dti.gov.uk.

(a) (i) What prompted FTL Ltd to introduce kaizen principles? (4 marks)
    (ii) Explain what is meant by kaizen. (6 marks)
(b) Explain the purpose of introducing SMED at FTL. (8 marks)
(c) How important was training when introducing kaizen principles at FTL? (8 marks)
(d) What evidence is there in the case to suggest that FTL is committed to quality? (8 marks)
(e) To what extent has FTL benefited from the introduction of lean production? (16 marks)

71 Understanding human resource objectives and strategies

Personnel management vs human resource management

Personnel management is the process of administering the workforce of a business. Personnel management historically arose in the first half of the twentieth century out of two distinct and separate needs.

One was the need to provide labour administration for businesses which were tending to grow larger over time. In a small business of ten workers, the owner or 'boss' might have handled the weekly payment of wages for example. The owner would almost certainly have been responsible for hiring and firing staff. But in a business of 100 or 1,000 people, it became more efficient to hire specialist staff to deal with these functions. Hence there was a growth in personnel departments in larger firms.

The second was the need to look after the welfare of staff. In the nineteenth and early twentieth centuries, there were a few pioneers such as George Cadbury, Joseph Rowntree and William Hesketh Lever who recognised that, as the owners of large and successful businesses, they had a social responsibility to care for the welfare of their workers. The First World War saw a large influx of women into the workforce and it was felt particularly important that their needs should be looked after.

Personnel departments came to be responsible for a wide range of issues concerning staff, from administering payrolls, to selection of new staff and dismissal of existing staff, training and development and staff discipline.

However, many in personnel management felt that their function within the business organisation was considered to be of secondary importance. Personnel management was a 'client department' for the more important functions such as sales, production or finance. Very few companies had the head of personnel on the board of directors. Yet the head of sales and the head of finance might expect to sit on the board.

In the 1980s and 1990s, it was strongly argued that personnel management was just as important as the sales or production function within a business. To signify this importance, business increasingly referred to 'human resource management' (HRM). It can be argued that human resource management differs from personnel management in a number of ways.

- Human resource management sees its function as part of strategic management. Strategy is a set of plans to achieve the goals set by a business. HRM claims that the way human resources are managed will have a crucial impact on whether a business achieves its goals. The business must therefore plan how to use its human resources if it is to be a successful enterprise.
- Human resource management claims that human resources are as important, if not more important, than the physical or financial resources of a business. In service sector businesses in particular, the quality and effectiveness of human resources can be what gives a business its competitive edge. HRM is about ensuring that the workforce is highly committed, is of high quality and is flexible. For example, the payroll function of the personnel department is not just about organising the efficient payment of salaries to workers. It is also about motivating workers. They expect to receive an efficient and friendly service. When there are problems, such as not receiving the correct amount of overtime pay or a promised bonus, workers can become demotivated. The best solution is that mistakes are not made. But if they are made, then they should be rectified quickly and efficiently and in a friendly manner. The motivation of workers can actually be increased if they see their problems being resolved quickly and fairly.
- HRM sees the management of human resources in an integrated way. So the payroll function is not just about paying workers, but is also about motivation. Recruitment is not just about getting a new worker to fill a post, it is also about identifying training needs and ensuring flexibility. Conforming with new legislation is not just about keeping to the letter of the law, it is about changing practices and policies so that the business can run efficiently and be seen to be a good employer.

Integrating plans

Human resource management stresses that the plans of the HRM department must be integrated into the strategic or corporate plan for the business. Therefore, its plans must help the business achieve its overall objectives. Its plans must also be co-ordinated with the plans of other departments such as sales and production.

For example, if the sales department plans to increase sales by 10 per cent, this is likely to have implications for both the production department and the finance department. Increased sales are likely to require increased levels of staffing. This must therefore be taken into account in the **workforce** or **human resource plan**. Equally, increased production may be achievable through staff training and development. A better trained workforce may be a more productive workforce. Therefore, training needs must appear in the workforce plan. The plans of the finance department also need to be taken into account. Increased sales should lead to higher revenue but increasing staff levels or increased training will also lead to higher costs. If the plans of the different departments are integrated, the finance department plan is likely to show increased profit from the higher sales. Higher profits are likely to be one of the goals of the business.

Human resource objectives

HUMAN RESOURCE OBJECTIVES are the goals that a business intends to achieve from its human resources. A business may have a number of human resource objectives.

Matching the workforce to the needs of the business This involves getting the right number of people, with the right skills,

Question 1.

Glenmorangie is best known as a producer of Scottish Whisky. In 2004 the business was sold by the Macdonald family which owned 52 per cent of shares and had been involved in the business since 1893 to LVMH (Loius Vuitton Moet Hennessy). It has just under 400 staff in three main distilleries in Tain, Elgin and the Isle of Islay, with a main site at Broxburn outside Edinburgh, where most staff are based. The change in ownership would need to be effectively handled. Communication was essential with staff.

Glenmorangie has a 'consultation and involvement' culture with staff. This involves communicating information to staff as early as possible on any changes and receiving feedback. It also includes training and development for all staff. Staff are directly involved in these training and development initiatives. The business recognises the importance of its staff as a key resource and asset of the business and values their input. The stress is very much on human resource management. But this was not always the case. Staff surveys showed that managers in the past were often too task orientated - taking a more traditional view of employees.

A survey of staff in 2001 identified a need for more people recognition at the business. Staff wanted managers to be less task centred and more people centred. This would support the culture of the business and motivate staff. The business identified its promotion strategy as perhaps leading to this problem. It often promoted people who were 'good at their job' but not necessarily good managers. The surveys helped to highlight this difficulty. Glenmorangie initiated a management development programme based on the employee feedback. Training was in the form of 'Champions' - people with a reputation in a particular area of the business. Glenmorangie argues that, without effective training, staff could not reach their true potential.

Source: adapted from *People Management*, 24.2.2005.

(a) Using Glenmorangie as an example, explain the differences between a personnel approach and a human resource management approach.
(b) Analyse why taking a human resource management approach rather than a personnel management approach could have been more effective in the situation that Glenmorangie faced.

in the correct part of the business at the right time to meet the strategic objectives of the business. For example, construction business may be expanding into a new area of buildings and anticipate extra demand for its services. In this case it might set an objective of employing extra staff to cope with the increased number of clients. But it would also need to set objectives about the type of staff it would need. If it was expanding into more modern designs it might need builders who were skilled at working with large glass constructions. If it was expanding abroad it might need to employ workers in another country.

Minimising labour costs This involves ensuring that labour costs are kept to an acceptable minimum, but without compromising the quality of staff within the business. For example, a manufacturer of electrical components facing a difficult trading period as a result of competition from Internet sales and abroad may set the strategic objective of staying in business for the next three months. It may be forced to reduce its workforce to keep costs down. However, it must be careful that it retains the knowledge of key staff about areas that are expanding and developing in the industry.

Making effective use of the workforce A business may set objectives to ensure that it makes the best use of its employees. One area in which it might set such an objective is in developing the skills of its staff. Training and developing staff so that they reach their full potential can allow the business to maximise returns. For example, a hotel might aim to have all staff qualified with an appropriate vocational course. This could help it to meet customers' needs better, encouraging customer loyalty and return bookings. A business may also set objectives in understanding the needs of employees and what motivates them to commit and achieve in business. For example, it might set targets for the motivation at work of employees in staff surveys. It might aim for 90 per cent of staff to say that they were satisfied that their views were taken into account by the business.

Maintaining good employee/employer relations This could involve developing business organisational structures, procedures, communication systems and employee representation that feel equitable to employees and to which employees can commit. A large plc, for example, may set targets for the number of days lost through disputes or absences from work. A business may also set objectives such as establishing a works council by a particular date or improving communication between management and the workforce.

Hard and soft human resource management

Human resource management today is implemented in different ways in different businesses. In some, HRM is seen as a strategic function. In others, it is seen still as very much of secondary importance to functions such as sales and finance.

John Storey (1989) in *New Perspectives on Human Resource*

Management argues that there is no accepted definition of 'human resources management'. The term is used in different ways in different contexts. For example, he puts forward a distinction between 'hard' and 'soft' versions of HRM.

Hard HRM HARD HRM sees human resources in the same way that it sees physical resources such as machines, or financial resources. Hard HRM is quantitative. It is associated with **workforce planning**. Businesses must calculate how many workers they need and of what type. They can then forecast how many workers they must recruit in the future from knowledge of their existing workforce and how it will change, for example, through staff turnover. Workers are then numbers to be manipulated in the production process. Their wages are costs to be minimised. Their work is output to be maximised. Training is for the benefit of the business. Workers who don't need training do not receive training because training is a cost. If it is cheaper to employ temporary workers or outsource work, then this should be the strategy pursued. Low pay, poor working conditions or work tasks which give little job satisfaction only become an issue if they affect the productivity of workers.

Hard HRM is therefore a control mechanism by management of their subordinates. Some businesses which adopt a hard HRM philosophy might superficially seem to be good employers. They might pay high wages or stress how important is the contribution of employers to the business. Working conditions might be excellent and work tasks might be designed to give high levels of job satisfaction. But all of this might be simply a structure to generate high levels of profit through maximising the output of highly efficient staff. Here, hard HRM remains a control mechanism which has been dressed up to look like 'soft' HRM.

Soft HRM SOFT HRM sees workers as stakeholders within the business. Their goals are part of the goals of the whole business. Soft HRM emphasises the importance of motivating staff and developing their skills. A work environment where staff are well paid, there is job security and high levels of job satisfaction is one where workers are likely to be highly committed. Giving staff high levels of control over their work environment will also increase job satisfaction and motivation. Soft HRM would discourage practices such as the deskilling of jobs, or the fragmentation of work tasks which demotivated workers.

Hard and soft HRM could be compared to the different approaches of the scientific management school and the human relations school of motivation. Equally, hard HRM could be seen as reflecting a Theory X approach to motivation, whilst soft HRM reflects a Theory Y approach.

In practice, businesses tend to use both hard and soft HRM approaches. Most businesses need to make a profit to survive in the long term. Therefore they have to pay attention to the costs of the workforce and to their productivity. Equally, management in most businesses recognise that they have responsibilities to their workforce even when fulfilling these responsibilities leads

to higher short-term costs.

Human resource strategy – leadership styles

Hard and soft HRM may be linked to leadership styles.

Authoritarian leadership Hard HRM tends to be associated with authoritarian styles of leadership. Authoritarian leaders tend to be TASK ORIENTATED. This means that they are focused on completing a particular task within limits such as time and cost. They achieve this by structuring the work of their subordinates. Task orientation can be motivating for subordinates. If a job is going well, subordinates can feel that they are part of a high achieving team. Structure and order can provide a sense of security for workers which is important in motivational needs.

Democratic leadership Soft HRM tends to be associated with democratic styles of leadership. Democratic leaders tend to be PEOPLE ORIENTATED. They understand that there is a task to be completed. But democratic leaders are as concerned with the needs of subordinates. They listen to subordinates and take their advice. They support subordinates when problems arise with their work or outside of the workplace. By building an atmosphere of trust and respect, where subordinates are encouraged to take initiative, democratic leaders succeed in motivating workers. In all of this, effective communication is essential. A democratic leader who cannot communicate effectively is likely to fail.

Human resource strategy – creating a competitive advantage

Those who advocate an HRM approach argue that it can give a business a competitive advantage. P Boxall, in an article in the *Human Resource Management Journal*, 1996, argues that this competitive advantage comes from two sources.

Human capital advantage HUMAN CAPITAL is the sum of all the education, training, experience and innate skills of a worker or group of workers. Just as individuals with high levels of savings will be able to earn high amounts of interest, so individuals with high levels of human capital will be able to gain high levels of earnings. Businesses offer higher earnings to workers with higher levels of human capital because such workers are more productive. The managing director of a company is paid more than a cleaner because the managing director's much higher level of human capital contributes more to the profit of the company than the cleaner.

The human capital of a worker can be increased through education and training. It can also be increased through giving a worker wider experience. Hence, workers in their thirties tend to have higher levels of human capital than workers in their early twenties starting out their career.

A business can gain a competitive advantage by building up a level of human capital within its workforce which is greater than in its rivals. Using an HRM approach, this is done through managing the HUMAN RESOURCE CYCLE.

- Workers need to be **selected** for their ability to contribute to the strategic goals of the business. Selection is not just about filling vacant posts with workers. It is about questioning whether the post should exist at all, what might the post holder contribute to the business, what qualities and skills should the selectors be looking for, and if no suitable candidates present themselves, what is the most appropriate course of action at that point.
- Workers need to undergo regular **appraisal**. The appraisal should take place in relation to the goals of the business. The appraisal system should therefore be constructed in such a way as to ask how has the individual contributed towards achieving those goals.
- **Rewards** should be given to workers who contribute towards the business achieving its goals.
- Staff **development** should be linked to the needs of the business. What training and experience should an individual receive to better enable them to achieve the goals of the business? With a limited training budget, what is the optimal way to spend that budget in order to secure the firm's objectives?

The human resource cycle of selection, appraisal, rewards and development (also known as the Michigan model) affects the **performance** of employees. The better the selection, the appraisal system, the reward system and staff development, the higher is likely to be the level of human capital in the business. This is what will then give the business its HUMAN CAPITAL ADVANTAGE.

Human process advantage The success of a football team is greater than the sum of the individual human capital of each of its players. It is about how they play as a team and not just about how they play as individual players. It is also about the network of support from everyone else at a football club. The processes of a business may be as important, if not more important, than the human capital of a business. The processes include:

- the way in which different departments within a business co-operate to achieve the goals of the business;
- the quality of the communication processes, both formal and informal, which determine how knowledge,

information and commands are passed through the organisation;
- the relationships between superiors and subordinates and the extent to which both superiors and subordinates are able to use their talents and skills to further the goals of the business;
- the underlying ethos of the business, and whether or not it motivates workers to achieve the goals of the business;
- the way in which a business learns over time, its **organisational learning**, to improve the way in which it conducts business, from R&D to production to marketing to HRM and finance.

HUMAN PROCESS ADVANTAGE is the competitive advantage a business gains over its rivals through the learned interaction of individual workers, which creates a business culture that is independent of any single worker.

Total competitive advantage is the sum of both human capital advantage and human process advantage. Businesses which gain a competitive advantage through human resource management policies will be more likely to survive and earn high profits than their rivals in the market. To retain that competitive advantage, human resources must be an integral part of the overall strategy of a business. This is the argument that human resource professionals use to justify why human resource management is so important to a business.

Human resource strategy – using remuneration

REMUNERATION policy is seen in a different way from a Human Resource Management (HRM) perspective. HRM is the process of administering the workforce of a business to achieve its objectives. Remuneration policy is an important part of HRM. Effective remuneration policy, from an HRM perspective, must contribute towards achieving the goals of the business. This is done through ensuring that workers are motivated and are able to employ their skills and talents to the full. From an HRM perspective, the workforce should be highly flexible and adaptable. Team working and ongoing training are likely to be features of a business adopting a HRM approach. Payment systems which contribute towards achieving this will therefore help contribute towards achieving the goals of the business.

There is a number of key features of a payment system influenced by an HRM perspective.

Pay flexibility Instead of rigid structures, the payment system allows for considerable variation in pay for employees doing the same job. This flexibility allows managers to reward and motivate employees who are performing well. Employee goals, set through an appraisal system, are aligned with the goals of the business. Hence, high performing employees are helping the business to achieve its goals. Flexible pay structures include individual pay bargaining. Where there is collective bargaining, this should be done at local level, with small groups. National or even regional pay agreements should be discouraged.

Job flexibility Jobs are not rigid and do not have fixed job

Figure 1: The human resource cycle: the Michigan model of human resource management

descriptions. Jobs are not boxes on a hierarchy which limit the ability of an employee to contribute to the business. Rather, jobs are flexible, allowing employees to grow into roles and to grow those roles. Their pay is then set according to the contribution they have made to the business and not according to some set amount given on a rigid pay scale. Pay systems then become people centred rather than job centred.

Training The development of the individual through experience and training should be linked to the payment system. It might be appropriate to link pay increases with completion of training or gaining qualifications. Part of the pay package might be an allowance for the individual worker to spend on the training which they feel is appropriate for their career needs.

Team working The reward system should encourage team working and team performance where appropriate. For example, the reward system might give bonuses to teams of workers who achieve the objectives they have been set. Or bonuses might be given to teams which have shown flexibility and the ability to adapt.

Decision making Decisions about pay and other rewards should not be decided solely by the HR (or personnel) department. Some responsibility should be devolved to line managers. They are often best placed to operate reward systems tailored to the needs of individual subordinates. For example, a worker might

receive a basic pay package which was offered by the HR department when the worker was first appointed to the job. But responsibility for giving bonuses or other rewards might be passed down the line to managers. These managers would have money included in their budgets for this purpose.

Employee needs The reward given to the employee is matched to their needs. For example, many large businesses now operate flexible fringe benefit packages where an employee is given a notional amount of money and can 'buy' fringe benefits from a car, to extra holiday entitlement to private health care insurance and even simply to higher pay. By giving more control to employees of their total remuneration package, workers are able to satisfy more of their needs. This leads to increased commitment to the business and therefore higher motivation. However, the reward given to employees is not just financial. The reward system must take into account the non-financial needs and aspirations of individual employees. So some employees might be motivated by being offered extra training which will help them in their chosen career path. Others may be motivated by the ability to work very flexible hours over the year. Parents who are the main carers of their children might feel high levels of commitment to an employer who allows them to work around the needs of those children.

Recruitment and retention Payment systems should take account of recruitment and retention. In some parts of the

---

Question 2.

Gerham-Nevis is a motor repair company in the North East area. It has three workshops. Each workshop employs three mechanics and two administration staff. All mechanics work a 38 hour week. At times, there is overtime work which is paid at a higher hourly rate. The two administration staff are paid at a lower rate. There is no system of progression or promotion at the business, although the manager's post at the head office in Newcastle has been filled by an experienced worker from the business each time it has become vacant. A new employee has been hired as a mechanic to take his or her place.

Last year, one of the workers at the Gateshead workshop was given a verbal warning for arriving late in the morning. He became angry and said that mechanics at other garages locally were paid more. Two weeks later, he gave in his notice saying that he had got a better paid job at a garage half a mile away. His post was vacant for three months because, despite advertising it every week in the local newspaper, the company didn't get any suitable applicants. In the end, the company had to take on a trainee. With only two qualified mechanics now at the workshop, productivity fell. Output has still not recovered as the trainee is still learning the trade.

Six months ago, management at Gerham-Nevis decided it needed to differentiate its product more. It took the strategic decision to move into the market for respraying vehicles. For example, some motorists choose to respray their car or motorcycle completely. Gerham-Nevis would also offer a service respraying individual or business vans and trucks with unique designs. Some of the mechanics, however, are opposed to the business moving into this area. They feel that they do not have the

necessary skills and are concerned about the extra hours they may be forced to work. Two workers at the Newcastle workshop, in particular, have young children and have to travel to work.

One of the tasks in the office is to collate and deal with all accounts. The owners of the business would like to convert the entire system of invoicing and accounting to a computerised system using a software programme called Sage Line 50. They feel that one of the administration staff could take over this role, although some of them are part time with young children.

(a) Examine the reasons why remuneration at the business may need to change.
(b) Recommend and justify changes that the business could make to its remuneration.

business, it might be highly desirable to have stable teams of workers employed over time. The payment system may then give high rewards to these workers relative to the market rate. High relative rewards will discourage workers from leaving to find better jobs with another employer. In other parts of the business, it might be healthy to have a regular turnover of staff to bring in new ideas and fresh enthusiasm. Paying the 'going' market rate for the job would then be an appropriate strategy.

Appraisal Many remuneration systems now incorporate appraisal into the process of determining pay through performance related pay. Appraisal is where the performance of

an individual worker is reviewed against a set of criteria. Businesses use appraisal to assess the performance of an individual worker over a period of time and to feedback that assessment to the individual. Typically, goals are set for future performance and this may be linked to training needs. Assessment may also be used to discuss career development within the business. Appraisal is not always linked to pay and bonuses. However, for many workers, pay rises or bonuses are conditional upon what takes place within the appraisal process. Fundamentally, using appraisal and performance related pay is an attempt to align the goals of the individual with the goals of the business.

The concepts of 'hard' and 'soft' HRM can be applied to remuneration policy. Where there is a hard approach, payment methods should be linked directly to performance and the contribution of the worker to output and profit. Rewards for success should be clear and transparent to the workforce. Where there is a soft approach, payment methods should be related to the goals of workers as well as those of the business.

For example, with a hard approach to HRM, workers who were taken sick would receive exactly their entitlement under policies laid down by the business. With a soft approach, local managers would be able to 'bend the rules' where they thought

KEYTERMS

Hard HRM – a human resource management perspective which sees human resources as no different from other resources available to the business, such as financial or physical resources. Their costs, requirements and contribution and can be quantified and businesses can manipulate these to achieve their aims and objectives.

Human capital – the sum of all the education, training, experience and innate skills of a worker or group of workers; the higher the level of human capital of workers, the higher on average will be the rewards they will be able to earn by hiring themselves out to employers.

Human capital advantage – the competitive advantage that a business gains by having a workforce with a higher level of human capital than its rivals. This advantage can be gained through the human capital cycle of selection, appraisal, rewards and development leading to improved performance of workers.

Human process advantage – the competitive advantage a business gains over its rivals through the learned interaction of individual workers which creates a business culture which is independent of any single worker.

Human resource cycle – the process through which human resources are recruited, selected, rewarded and appraised by a business.

Human resource objectives – the goals that a business intends to achieve from its human resources. A business may have a number of human resource objectives.

Payment systems – structures which set out how employees would be rewarded for their work.

People orientated leadership – where a leader focuses on the needs of subordinates and gives them some autonomy to decide how best a task should be completed. People-orientated leaders tend to be democratic.

Remuneration – the total reward given to employees for the work they do; it includes financial rewards such as a wage or salary, as well as non-financial rewards such as fringe benefits.

Soft HRM – a human resource management perspective which prioritises the needs and development of employees in order to motivate them and make them committed to achieving the goals of a business.

Task orientated leadership – where a leader focuses on completing tasks rather than on the needs of the individual workers who will help complete the task. Task-orientated leaders tends to be autocratic.

KNOWLEDGE

1. List three differences between personnel and human resource management.
2. State four objectives a business could have for its human resources.
3. What is the difference between the hard and soft sides of human resource management?
4. What is the relationship between hard and soft human resource management and Theory X and Theory Y?
5. What is the relationship between hard and soft human resource management and leadership styles?
6. Why must human resource management take into account the plans of other functions of the business?
7. What are the steps in the human resources cycle?
8. How can the human resources cycle affect human capital advantage?
9. Explain the difference between human capital advantage and human process advantage.
10. List five features of a traditional payment system.
11. What is meant by flexibility in a payment system?
12. List three ways in which rewards can take into account employees' needs.
13. How can payments be structured to improve recruitment and retention?
14. What is the relationship between appraisal and rewards?
15. Briefly explain the relationship between:
    (i) the hard side of human resource management and remuneration;
    (ii) the soft side of human resource management and remuneration.

this was appropriate. Equally, where a parent had to take a day off work to look after a sick child, the hard approach would be to count it as unpaid leave, or as a day's holiday entitlement. A soft approach might be either to ignore it and for colleagues to cover, or allow the worker to make up the missed hours at another time.

Where a soft approach was associated with democratic leadership, payment systems would reward those who contributed to effective decision making and were good team players. For example, bonus payments for all team members might be linked to their performance as a team. Where a hard approach is associated with autocratic leadership, the leaders of teams alone might receive the bonuses if they motivated their team members sufficiently for the team to achieve its targets.

Case Study: *Metro*

Newspaper groups are not noted for their training initiatives. There is often too much pressure to meet deadlines. People issues tend to have low priority. But *Metro*, the so-called 'saviour of bored communities', is bucking the trend. Launched in 1999 it reached a 1 million circulation in September 2004. *Metro* was considered to be a classic start-up, explained Steve Auckland, its managing director. 'It was terribly autocratic and people were not the most important aspect of it all' he said. *Metro* prides itself on its different approach to readers. It gives straight talking news and features that fit perfectly into a 20 minute commute to work. Now it wants to take the same approach to human resource management.

Metro's parent company is Allied Newspapers. It persuaded the company to employ a dedicated HR professional. Laura Ashworth was employed in 2003 to look after recruitment, retention and development of the paper's 180 staff. Not all people at the paper were in favour. Some wondered why there should be spending on increased skills when people were leaving to go elsewhere. After her appointment however, attrition rates of staff leaving fell from 25 per cent to 16 per cent.

Auckland argues that although people leave, it is important to allow them to develop whilst they are at the paper. They then take the good name of the business elsewhere with them. An induction process gives employees in London a three day course and £100 to have a night out of their choice, for example. The aim is to get people to understand the audience – young ABC1 professionals with high incomes - by experiencing their activities. Most newspapers work on the basis that, when you get a job with a national paper, you already have been fully trained. In contrast, *Metro* is committed to giving training to all its employees. More than 80 per cent of staff have had training now, up from 34 per cent in 2003. An internal booklet was developed showing courses that staff could take. They could pick one course relevant to their career and one to their future ambitions.

The business is now moving to the next stage. Managers are being trained in how to conduct appraisal. Members of teams also discuss how their needs can be met by courses in one to one discussions with Laura Ashworth. Commercial staff who have reached the top of their grade are also being taken into account. They can arrange special projects, such as a thank you for commercial clients who place large advertising campaigns. Projects that are successful are incorporated into the job of the person involved.

Staff surveys conducted at *Metro* in 2004 showed that 75 per cent of employees understand the goals of the business, compared to 55 per cent in 2003. Seventy two per cent agree that developing people is now one of the key goals of the business. For every £1 spent on training, the business calculates that there is a 1 per cent improvement in skills. Other surveys have shown that a break is occurring with the 'old school' mentality. Workers , for example, have in the past worked to the stop watch. Now they often stay later than required, just because they want to.

Source: adapted from *People Management*, 13.1.2005.

(a) (i) **Explain the type of approach to human resources taken by many publishing companies. (8 marks)**
(ii) **Identify the approach taken by Metro and analyse the potential benefits of this different approach. (12 marks)**

(b) **To what extent should a new small publishing company follow the current approach of Metro to its human resources? (20 marks)**

Components of a workforce plan

WORKFORCE PLANNING is the process of determining the labour needs of the business now and in the future, including the number of workers and their skills, and ways of achieving labour targets. It has several aspects.

How many? The business must plan how many workers it needs. A food business that is planning to expand, for example, might require an extra 34 workers next year. When deciding how many staff are needed, the business must take into account whether workers are full or part time and how many hours they will be expected to work.

What skills? The types of workers and their skills must be decided upon. Of the 34 workers, there could be a need for 1 office worker, 15 production workers with no previous qualifications or skills, 2 supervisors with previous experience in the catering trade, and so on.

When needed? The business must decide when new workers will be needed. Is a worker needed immediately or will a vacancy arise in 12 months' time?

Where needed? In larger businesses, there may be many sites where employees are based. So the workforce plan must specify where the employee will be needed.

Achieving targets The human resource plan should identify what changes to staffing will be needed and indicate how this might be achieved. Staffing might need to increase. This can be done in a number of ways.

- Existing staff might have to be **trained** to increase their skills to cope with new demands in their existing jobs.
- Staff might have to be REDEPLOYED (i.e. change their jobs) within the organisation. This is also likely to mean that staff will need to be trained, perhaps to learn different skills.
- New staff may have to be **recruited** from outside the business.

Alternatively, the number of staff required may need to fall. A business may need to **rationalise**.

- This might be achieved through NATURAL WASTAGE. This is where staff who leave because of retirement, to look after children or to get a better job in another business are not replaced.
- A VOLUNTARY REDUNDANCY scheme may be offered to workers. This is where staff are invited to resign from their jobs. Businesses often offer inducements, such as generous redundancy payments, to persuade workers to take voluntary redundancy.

- Those nearing retirement age might be offered an early retirement package. They will be able to draw their pensions now rather than at the age of retirement.
- As a last resort, the business may be forced to make COMPULSORY REDUNDANCIES. This is where selected employees are told they will lose their jobs. A business is legally able to make workers REDUNDANT if their job 'no longer exists' and they do not intend to appoint another worker to do that job.

Assessing and anticipating demand

Businesses use a wide variety of information to calculate their existing and future demand for labour. The starting point is likely to be existing employment patterns. A business knows what it can produce with a given amount of labour. For example, McDonald's knows from previous experience how many staff are needed to run an outlet. A construction company might know how many workers it needs to build a new housing estate. A taxi firm will know how many drivers it needs on a Saturday night. Then, human resource managers can build in a variety of **internal factors** which may influence current or future demand for workers by the business.

Staff turnover STAFF or LABOUR TURNOVER is the proportion of staff leaving a business over a period of time. Staff leave for a variety of reasons. Some may retire and some leave their jobs to look after their children. Others leave because they want a different job. Labour turnover is measured by the formula:

$$\frac{\text{Number of staff leaving over a period of time}}{\text{Average number of staff in post during the period}} \times 100\%$$

Labour turnover varies enormously between different types of job, between industries and between businesses. McDonald's, for example, has a staff turnover of around 100 per cent per quarter in the UK. This means that on average staff only stay three months in their job. Staff turnover for most jobs is much lower than this. Human resource managers have to take staff turnover into account when planning for the future. Businesses with high staff turnover must recruit more frequently than those with low staff turnover. If staff turnover is concentrated amongjust a few jobs in the business, then recruitment will focus on those jobs.

Sales A change in the level of sales for a business is likely to lead to different staffing needs. A business that forecasts a drop in sales of 20 per cent over the next 12 months is likely to need fewer employees. An expanding business is likely to need more.

Question 1.

Penny Dunseith is director of personnel at Pickerell's, a nationwide chain of retailers selling a wide range of goods, including perfumes. Every year she has to present a report to the board of directors outlining the work of the personnel department over the previous 12 months and the personnel issues likely to face it over the next 12 months. In an appendix to the report is a detailed statistical breakdown of staffing requirements. Part of a table from this report is shown in Table 1.

In 2003, she reported that turnover of management the previous year had been 22 per cent, which was roughly what it had been over the previous five years. Turnover of full-time staff below manager level in stores was 38 per cent, whilst for part-time staff excluding weekend staff it was only 52 per cent. Turnover of part time weekend only staff was 125 per cent.

Part-time weekend only staff were mainly 16-25 year old students looking for a little extra money to supplement their pocket money or student grants. In London, there was also a significant minority of young people, mainly from the EU, who had come to the capital to acquire language skills and see the sights. They would often take a weekend job immediately on arrival to start earning some cash and then quickly leave to work more hours.

Ordinary part-time staff who worked during the week as well as weekends were typically again either students, young people from overseas or young females with at least one small child. Full-time staff

below manager level were on average five years older than part-time staff. For many, the job was simply one of a succession of jobs, where the worker was constantly looking for a job at the same level offering better pay or working conditions, or nearer to their home. For some, though, it was a stepping stone into management. Penny wanted to devote more resources to training this category of worker, both to reduce staff turnover and to make it easier to recruit at store management level.

(a) Assuming that labour turnover rates and overall staffing levels remained the same in 2008 as in 2007, calculate to the nearest whole number the number of staff that need to be recruited in 2008 in the following categories:
  (i) full-time staff below manager level;
  (ii) weekday part-time store staff;
  (iii) weekend only part-time store staff.

(b) How would your answer to 1 (a) differ if, through the provision of extra training in 2008, the labour turnover of full-time staff below manager level fell by 20 per cent?

(c) Suggest why posts filled by students aged 16-25 are likely to have a higher labour turnover than posts filled by young women aged 21-30.

Table 1: Average number of employees, 2007

	Number of posts
Full-time store staff below managerial level	6,258
Weekday part-time store staff	4,780
Weekend only part-time store staff	3,524

In larger businesses, the type of sales that are expanding and contracting will affect staffing levels. If US sales are falling but UK sales are rising for a fast food chain, then the number of US employees is likely to fall but in the UK numbers will rise. Within a management consultancy firm, expanding contracts for IT consultancy will require more IT experts, while falling contracts for financial consultancy will require fewer accountants.

Functional and strategic decisions Decisions made by one part of a business may affect recruitment. For example, if the marketing department changes its methods of promotion then it may need to employ people with experience in direct marketing or Internet sales. Strategic decisions can also affect recruitment. A decision to diversify into a new product area will mean production and marketing staff with skills currently not in the business may be needed.

In addition to internal influences, there will also be **external influences** from outside the business.

Competition Competition between businesses will affect staffing. In manufacturing today, there is fierce competition between firms in the supply of household goods. Some manufacturers have ceased production in the UK as a result. Others have been forced to become more efficient, producing more output with fewer resources and so bringing down prices. Fewer staff have often been needed. Remaining staff often have to have higher levels of skill and to be flexible.

Technology Changes in technology will probably change the skills needs of a business. In general, improved technology requires more skilled workers to use it. Office technology today requires many white collar workers to be computer literate and able to use software programs. Improved technology is also likely to be labour saving. Fewer workers are needed to produce the same amount of output.

Changing production techniques There can be considerable differences in productivity (output per worker) between businesses. Changing how employees work with existing resources, such as machinery, can considerably improve productivity. Teamworking, for example, can improve productivity. Improved productivity will mean that fewer workers are needed to produce the same amount of output. Equally, they often need greater skills, changing the composition of the workforce.

Legislation There are legal influences on demand. Businesses that only want younger staff may be prevented from doing so by age discrimination legislation.

Assessing and anticipating supply

Understanding how the demand for labour will change over time is only one side of workforce planning. The supply of labour must also be taken into account. Human resource managers must first understand the skills and talents of existing staff. This might be done by conducting a SKILLS AUDIT, a survey of the skills of the workforce. They must also decide whether or not existing employees are likely to remain in their posts or not. They must carry out projections on staff training needs and whether staff can be recruited from within the business or from outside.

Whether a business can meet its future workforce requirements from its existing employees, its **internal supply**, will depend on a number of factors.

Promotion A business may decide to promote employees from inside the organisation. Some businesses encourage internal promotion. The advantage of promoting existing workers is that they already know about the business's practices and culture. They may also be able to adapt more easily to a new job than an outsider. Some workers may also have been 'filling in' temporarily and have experience of the job. Promoting internally would leave a vacancy further down the hierarchy which would need to be filled. This would add costs and time to filling the vacancy.

Staff development and training A business is more likely to be able to find a suitable employee from inside the organisation if it has training and development programmes. Training may provide the skills needed to allow an employee to move to a new position. For example, many larger businesses have graduate training programmes which train employees with degrees for management positions. Businesses that have development programmes which identify how workers can improve, appraise workers' abilities and view the development of employees as important, are more likely to employ an internal candidate. If a business needs to reduce its workforce in a particular department, it may consider retraining its employees and redeploying them to another part of the organisation.

Staff loss and retirement A workforce supply plan should also take into account staff loss and rates of retirement. High rates of labour turnover, as explained earlier, create vacancies. However, they may also lead to large numbers of skilled workers leaving a business which can affect the number of suitable internal candidates for a job. If large numbers of employees are retiring, this may lead to problems when trying to fill senior management posts which require experienced employees. A business may make use of retirement as a means of reducing the workforce if necessary. People can sometimes be encouraged to take 'early retirement', if they are given a financial incentive.

Flexibility A business may be able to change its workforce practices and conditions in order to meet its labour supply requirements. For example, a business may change the number of hours that people work in a period. Employees may be asked to work 1,950 hours in a year rather than 37.5 hours a week. This means that a business can have employees in work for longer than 37.5 hours when they are needed at peak times. If a business wants to add extra responsibility to the role of workers, it may encourage teamwork or the multiskilling of workers. It may also decide to make new jobs part time or to create jobs that can be shared by two people in order to increase the flexibility of the business.

Legal factors If a business finds that its demand for workers is likely to fall in future it may decide to make workers redundant. There are legal conditions which affect how and when workers can be made redundant. They may also be entitled to redundancy or severance payments.

Certain **external factors** will influence the supply of these workers. A business may plan to employ workers from outside the organisation. There are local and national factors that have to be taken into account by a business when planning its external employee requirements.

The availability and price of housing in an area Some employees may not be able to afford housing in a highly priced area such as London, for example. The availability of new housing on a nearby estate may encourage young families with children to move to an area.

The ease and availability of public transport Working at a factory in a remote area may prove difficult for an employee without a car. Areas with efficient rail or bus links may prove popular for some workers. Possible restrictions or charges on cars in city areas may influence external employee supply in future.

Competition The closing or opening of other businesses in an area may either help or hinder external supply of labour. If businesses close, there may be more skilled labour from which to choose. New businesses may reduce the availability of skilled workers. However, they are also likely to train workers, so that it may be possible to 'headhunt' required employees more easily.

Unemployment High rates of unemployment in an area lead to a large supply of workers who are available for work. This increases choice for a business looking to recruit from outside

Question 2.

Seasonal workers employed by Asda at Christmas 2003 would have benefits and job security equivalent to those of full-time colleagues. The new 'seasonal squad' would have the same status as permanent staff, but with a contract to work an annual, rather than weekly, number of hours. The new recruits would be allowed to work for as little as ten weeks of the year. The contracts would cover Christmas, Easter and the school summer holidays. Positions included greeters, porters, checkout operatives and warehouse workers. 'We recognise that people are looking for flexibility across the working year, not just the working week' said Caroline Massingham, Asda retail people director. 'If you're one of the many people that want to balance long periods of leave with a fulfilling job, the options are limited,' she also added.

Asda hoped that more over 50s would be encouraged to join its 22,357 workers in this age group. The supermarket's flexible working package includes one week's leave for new grandparents and up to two years for a career break. It said that since recruiting older workers, it has seen absence levels drop, customer service improve and labour turnover fall.

Source: adapted from *The Guardian*.

BT confirmed plans to open two new call centres in India in 2003 that would create more than 2,000 jobs. The centres would be in Delhi and Bangalore. The cost of opening call centres in India is up to 30 per cent cheaper than in the UK. The two new call centres, which will cost around £3 million to set up, will deal with operations such as telephoning people in the UK to remind them to pay their bills. Last summer, HSBC's Indian call centre employees were praised by the company for being more efficient, polite and enthusiastic than their British counterparts.

Research by recruitment business Adecco suggested British companies will create up to 100,000 call centre jobs in India by 2008. This would slash their wage costs and take advantage of a pool of skilled workers, many of them graduates. Once a call centre is set up, the wage bill makes up two-thirds of its operation costs. Indian call centre workers earn about £1,200 a year, less than a tenth of the £12,000 starting salary of an employee in Britain. But there can be problems. Businesses can have difficulties keeping a grip on everyday operations in a centre so far away from their base and there may be quality control issues.

Source: adapted from *The Guardian*.

(a) Explain why these situations are examples of planning employee supply from outside the organisation.

(b) Examine the factors that might affect the recruitment of workers from outside the organisation in these situations.

the organisation. High rates of national unemployment may make workers more willing to travel.

Availability of skills Specialist skills may be found in particular areas. For example, the area around Stafford, known as the Potteries, traditionally had skilled pottery workers. Some workers made unemployed in shipyard areas such as Tyneside were able to transfer their skills to other related industries when shipyards closed.

The availability of flexible workers Many businesses are taking advantage of the use of teleworkers. These are people who are employed to work at home and make use of technology, such as the fax and computer, to communicate with the business. They work from home which reduces business costs. Some workers are 'employed' by the business, but are not guaranteed work. They are brought in only when required, such as when demand is high. An example might be a delivery firm asking drivers to be 'on call' in case of busy periods. The availability of these workers increases the flexibility of businesses.

Government training and subsidies Government funded training and employment schemes subsidise businesses for taking on young workers for a period of time. This reduces their cost to a business and allows a 'trial run' of a possible employee.

Population and demographic trends Changes in the structure of the population can affect external recruitment. In the UK there is a growing number of older workers who are available for work. The increase in the number of women joining or returning to the workforce is also likely to affect the supply plans from outside the organisation.

Government legislation There are restrictions on the nature and type of advertisements that can be used when recruiting from outside the business. There are also laws which protect the pay and conditions of workers when they are employed.

Costs The earnings of workers from outside the business might affect recruitment. Hiring workers on lower wages can reduce costs. The cost of setting up factories or offices to employ workers must also be taken into account and businesses must assess the relative costs of employees in different areas and with different skills.

Issues in implementing workforce plans

Businesses need to be aware of a number of issues developing and then implementing workforce plans.

Employee/employer relations The ways in which a business meets the targets of its workforce plan can affect employer/employee relations. Internal recruitment can prevent demotivation as staff will see that the business is attempting to reward staff within the business. In addition, training staff to acquire new skills can also reinvigorate staff with new challenges. Staff development and training can also help a business promote employees into more responsible positions. Flexible working conditions can assist employees to develop the work-life balance appropriate to their needs. However, internal recruitment may not suit the needs of employers. Further, if a business fails to employ adequately qualified staff, this can lead to tension and potential difficulties for existing staff who find their workload increased or they are covering for the mistakes of others.

Costs Internal promotion can often be more cost effective and than recruiting a new employee from outside. There are still likely to be interview costs, but relocation costs and the costs involved with a new employee settling in may be prevented. However, when recruiting internally, there may be additional costs associated with training and development and the business may need to weigh up the cost-benefit analysis of different forms of supplying its employees' needs.

Corporate image Businesses are ever more conscious of how their corporate plans are interpreted by the public and what type of image they may generate. This can affect the extent to which the public may want to purchase goods/services from the business and also influence the extent to which potential external candidates may wish to apply for vacancies at the business. Workforce plans must be carefully prepared so that they do not present the business in a poor light. This may be the case if the business is trying to downsize for example.

The value of using workforce plans

Workforce plans are important for all businesses, whether they are expanding or reducing their workforce. They help a business to set out its employee requirements to prevent unforeseen difficulties. For example, a business that is diversifying is unlikely to be successful unless it has planned to recruit staff needed for the areas into which it will move. Plans are also needed so that future budgets can be prepared.

However, workforce plans are only as effective as the quality of information on which they are based and how appropriate the plans are to current and/or future business development. For example, changes in the business environment may require a change in business strategy that may mean a need to redeploy staff to other departments/functions. In addition, increased competition in the market may make a business more vulnerable to the poaching of key staff. If a business is uncertain about the future or its future requirements, this can have an impact on the value of the workforce plans developed.

KNOWLEDGE

1. What are the different components of a workforce plan?
2. What internal influences might affect the potential demand for employees in a business?
3. What external influences might affect the potential demand for employees in a business?
4. What internal influences might affect the potential supply of employees to a business?
5. What external influences might affect the potential supply of employees to a business?
6. Explain how a workforce plan might improve employer/employee relations.

Case Study: *Stewart and Mathers*

Stewart and Mathers is a solicitor, with offices in Lancashire and London. Its head office is situated in Skelmersdale, a 'new town' created to rehouse the overspill of people moving out of Liverpool in the 1960s as inner city housing was knocked down. Skelmersdale is situated next to the M58 and is a half an hour's drive from the cities of Manchester and Liverpool. The planners decided that:

- high private car usage must be catered for, while still encouraging public transport;
- pedestrians and traffic should be separated in the town centre and residential areas;
- industry should be concentrated in separate, but easily accessible, areas;
- open spaces should be provided, but the housing should be designed to foster a close community atmosphere;
- there must be no urban sprawl, and a clear boundary between town and country;
- the town must try and attract a balanced population structure;
- housing in Skelmersdale was to be high density, but without high rise flats;
- residential areas were to be close to the town centre where most facilities were concentrated.

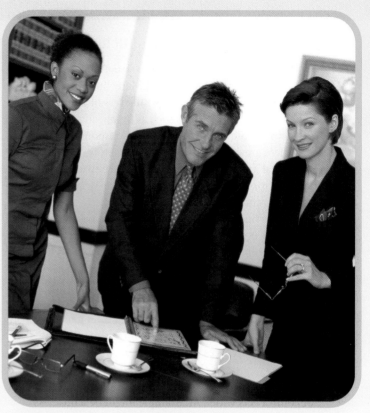

After the year 2004 the business saw a steady growth in its sales of services. Table 2 shows figures relating to the workforce over the period 2004-2008. Stewart and Mathers realised that more cases were being taken out against individuals and companies for accidents which led to personal injury. This mirrored the situation in the USA. Large sums were often paid to employees injured at work, to people who had been hurt in 'road rage' attacks and for complaints against the State for injuries as a result of badly maintained roads or pavements. Most of the decisions in the business were taken by the three partners, two of whom had previous experience of working in other countries. There were ten people in the business who were 'fee earners'.

The organisation decided that it wanted to expand rapidly to take advantage of growing business in this area. It encouraged its administrative staff lower in the hierarchy to train in law qualifications or take the Institute of Law examination. This would allow them to progress to become solicitor's assistants. It advertised widely in the local area to fill vacancies and 'headhunted' graduates of the ILEX (Institute of Legal Secretaries) courses at local colleges who had been trained in basic law skills. It would also be able to take advantage of the government's New Deal by employing young workers for a small number of posts.

However, some of its senior management positions needed to be filled quickly and so the business advertised in national magazines and quality newspapers. If necessary it was prepared to subsidise managers for a short time if they were prepared to move to the area immediately. This might mean that they had to leave property unsold in a different part of the country or leave family and work away from home for a period.

Table 2

	Sales revenue (£m)	Total employees	Employees leaving
2004	1.1	70	3
2005	1.2	72	4
2006	1.4	75	5
2007	1.6	80	5
2008	2.0	100	6

(a) What factors could have affected the promotion of internal employees within the business to higher posts? (6 marks)

(b) Explain how the business may have forecast the increased need for employees after the year 2004. (10 marks)

(c) (i) Calculate the labour turnover of the business over the period 2004-2008. (4 marks)

    (ii) Examine the possible effects of changes in labour turnover on the business. (10 marks)

(d) To what extent might the business be able to recruit workers from outside the organisation for:

    (i) jobs at the base of the hierarchy;

    (ii) managerial jobs? (10 marks)

Influences on organisational structures

The unit titled 'Improving organisation structures' explained the organisational structure of a business. Many businesses have traditional, hierarchical structures, with layers of management and employees. They face issues such as organising the span of control, chain of command, authority and responsibility. However, there are other organisational structures, including entrepreneurial and matrix and independence structures. A number of factors can influence the particular structure that a business might choose.

- **Size.** As a business grows, it is likely to move away from an entrepreneurial structure towards one where authority is passed to other employees. A large firm will also tend to have a longer chain of command, with more levels in the hierarchy.
- **Views of the owners or leadership styles.** If owners wish to retain control in the business, they will want a narrow span of control. Owners or managers who wish to motivate or encourage employees may delegate decision making.
- **Business objectives.** If the business decides to expand rapidly, perhaps by merger, it is likely to find that its span of control gets wider. An example might be a business setting up an operation in a foreign country or deciding to sell into a foreign market.
- **External factors.** Changes in external factors can often influence business organisation. In periods of recession or rising costs, a business may be forced to reduce its chain of command to cut costs. Similarly, in a period of economic growth, a firm may employ extra managers as specialists to gain economies of scale.
- **Changes in technology.** The introduction of new technology can change the structure of a business. For example, a new system of production may remove the need for quality controllers, or an information technology system could reduce the role of administration.
- **The informal structure.** If the informal structure does not complement and support the formal structure, this may lead to problems.
- **Corporate culture.** The norms of behaviour in a business might influence its organisational structure. For example, a business that has developed with a team based approach to decision making, a casual dress code and a management that are very approachable might find it difficult to change suddenly to a structure with layers of hierarchy and formal decision making processes. Charles Handy in *Understanding Organisations* (1976) identified four cultures. The **power** culture is a structure with one powerful decision maker. The **role** culture is a structure where everyone in the hierarchy has a clear role. The **task** culture is a structure based on a team approach. The **person** culture is a structure with an emphasis on individuals.

Question 1.

Laura — WESLEY HAINS — Mitchell
Kieran — WESLEY HAINS — Ella

Wesley Hains runs a card design business in Cardiff. He employs four staff – Laura, Mitchell, Kieran and Ella. Laura manages the office in Cardiff dealing with telephone and email enquiries, visitors, administration and a small amount of marketing. Mitchell, Kieran and Ella are card designers and all work from home in various parts of the country. Mitchell lives and works in a small croft in Glen Cona in North West Scotland. The designers are all linked by computer to the main Cardiff office. This ensures good communications. For example, design briefs are sent direct by Wesley using email and design copy is transmitted direct to Wesley's terminal when designs are completed. Some specialisation takes place amongst the designers. Mitchell designs birthday cards, Kieran designs postcards and Ella works on specialist projects. Wesley is occupied with customers, ensuring that design briefs are satisfied by his designers and looking for new business. He spends three days a week out of the office.

(a) In September, Wesley secured a contract with an American card manufacturer. Wesley had to recruit four more designers as a result. He decided to employ a full-time salesperson to sell designs in the US. He also bought a small printing business in Newport to print and supply cards as well as designing them. Explain why Wesley might decide to change the organisational structure of his business.

Adapting organisational structures

The organisational structure of a business may have to change in order to better fit the type of business and the products and services it provides. This is often the case if there are internal changes within the business or changes in external influences. Modern OPEN SYSTEMS THINKING suggests that the design of the organisation must meet the needs of the situation, such as changing lifestyles or customer tastes. A closed system makes little allowance for such changes and often traditional pyramid or hierarchical business structures are rigid with clear boundaries, responsibilities for the way the business works. Open systems thinking favours greater experimentation and innovation in response to changing circumstances. In particular, it sees greater opportunities for employee engagement. This unit considers how a business can adapt its structure to become more competitive.

Centralisation and decentralisation

CENTRALISATION and DECENTRALISATION refer to the extent to which authority is delegated in a business. If there was complete centralisation, subordinates would have no authority at all. Complete decentralisation would mean subordinates

Question 2.

In 2003 The Future Network plc, the international specialist magazine publisher, announced the final stages of the restructuring of its UK business, which began in February 2001. Under the reorganisation plan, Future divided its UK business into three operating divisions – games, computing and entertainment. This was to be accompanied by a reduction in fixed operating costs in the UK by approximately £4 million, through cuts in staffing levels and property overheads.

The changes to the business involved reductions in centralised support services, and in Internet and magazine teams and rationalisation of the company's property portfolio. There was also to be an important change in the way the UK business was managed, by devolving operational responsibility to the individual divisions as profit centres.

Colin Morrison, Chief Operating Officer of The Future Network, said 'This plan is important because of the substantial reduction in our fixed operating costs against a broadly unchanged magazine portfolio. But much more than that, this restructuring and decentralisation plan simplifies our business, and will improve our focus, agility and control. We will now be more streamlined and much better placed to take advantage of our market-leading positions in the important UK market'.

Source: adapted from www.thefuturenetwork.plc.uk.

(a) Describe the organisational changes at The Future Network plc.
(b) Examine the possible benefits and disadvantages for the business of these changes.

Table 1: Advantages of centralisation and decentralisation

Advantages of centralisation
- Senior management has more control of the business, e.g. budgets.
- Procedures, such as ordering and purchasing, can be standardised throughout the organisation, leading to economies of scale and lower costs.
- Senior managers can make decisions from the point of view of the business as a whole. Subordinates would tend to make decisions from the point of view of their department or section. This allows senior managers to maintain a balance between departments or sections. For example, if a company has only a limited amount of funds available to spend over the next few years, centralised management would be able to share the funds out between production, marketing, research and development, and fixed asset purchases in different departments etc.
- Senior managers should be more experienced and skilful in making decisions. In theory, centralised decisions by senior people should be of better quality than decentralised decisions made by others less experienced.
- In times of crisis, a business may need strong leadership by a central group of senior managers.
- Communication may improve if there are fewer decision makers.

Advantages of decentralisation
- It empowers and motivates workers.
- It reduces the stress and burdens of senior management. It also frees time for managers to concentrate on more important tasks.
- It provides subordinates with greater job satisfaction by giving them more say in decision making, which affects their work, as explained by McGregor's Theory Y.
- Subordinates may have a better knowledge of 'local' conditions affecting their area of work. This should allow them to make more informed, well-judged choices. For example, salespeople may have more detailed knowledge of their customers and be able to advise them on purchases.
- Delegation should allow greater flexibility and a quicker response to changes. If problems do not have to be referred to senior managers, decision making will be quicker. Since decisions are quicker, they are easier to change in the light of unforeseen circumstances which may arise.
- By allowing delegated authority, management at middle and junior levels are groomed to take over higher positions. They are given the experience of decision making when carrying out delegated tasks. Delegation is therefore important for management development.

would have all the authority to take decisions. Some delegation may always be necessary in all firms because of the limits to the amount of work senior managers can carry out. Tasks that might be delegated include staff selection, quality control, customer relations and purchasing and stock control. Even if authority is delegated to a subordinate, it is usual for the manager to retain responsibility.

In pyramid structures subordinates often have little authority, with most decisions being taken at the top of the organisation. Open systems thinking would suggest that this form of organisation may not suit the various markets that a growing and competitive business could face. Individuals close to comsumers might be better placed to make decisions. Hence regional, divisional, or in some cases for multinational companies' national, operations may become a 'business unit' with its own cost and profit centre. However, it would still remain accountable to the head office. The advantages of centralisation and decentralisation shown in Table 1.

Delayering

DELAYERING also involves a business reducing its staff. The cuts are directed at particular levels of a business, such as managerial posts. Many traditional organisational charts are hierarchical, with many layers of management. Delayering involves removing some of these layers. This gives a flatter structure. In the late 1980s, the average number of layers in a typical organisational structure was seven, although some were as high as 14. By the early 2000s this was reduced to less than five. The main advantage of delayering is the savings made from laying off expensive managers. It may also lead to better communication and a better motivated staff if they are **empowered** and allowed to make their own decisions.

However, remaining managers may become demoralised after delayering. Also staff may become overburdened as they have to do more work. Fewer layers may also mean less chance of promotion.

Flexible workforces

In the 1950s and 1960s, the UK economy was relatively stable and slow changing. Workers tended to have full-time permanent jobs. However, in the 1970s and 1980s, economic conditions worsened. Primary and secondary industry saw enormous change. Many businesses in these sectors became uncompetitive against foreign firms and closed. There was a rapid shift of output and employment towards the tertiary sector. There was a considerable increase in participation of women in the labour force. Part-time work became far more common.

It was against this backdrop that, in 1985, John Atkinson and the Institute of Manpower Studies put forward the concept of a flexible firm. This was a business which had a 'core' and a 'periphery'.

- The core was made up of workers who organised the essential tasks necessary for the firm's survival. They would tend to be skilled, full-time workers on permanent contracts. Because of their job security, their relatively high

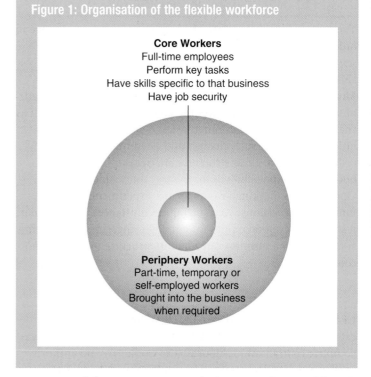

Figure 1: Organisation of the flexible workforce

Core Workers
Full-time employees
Perform key tasks
Have skills specific to that business
Have job security

Periphery Workers
Part-time, temporary or
self-employed workers
Brought into the business
when required

pay and their importance to the business, they would tend to be highly motivated.

- The periphery was made up of a variety of workers not central to running the business. They could be employed according to how much demand there was for the firm's products. They could include temporary workers ('temps') on short-term contracts and part-time workers whose hours can easily be increased or decreased. They would also include workers whose jobs had been OUTSOURCED to other businesses. This would include self-employed workers who were paid by the business for doing specific jobs. They might also include **teleworkers** or **home workers**, working from home and operating mainly via computer and email link. It is sometimes argued that peripheral workers are motivated mainly by the pay they receive. Their loyalty to the business employing them is not as great as core workers, since they have insecure jobs and never know whether they will still be in work in 12 months' time.

The advantages and disadvantages of flexible working for businesses

There is a number of advantages of a FLEXIBLE WORKFORCE for a business.

- A flexible workforce allows a business to expand and contract quickly in response to changes in demand for its products. In contrast, a workforce made up of permanent staff is difficult to slim down quickly because of the cost and because of the time it takes to fulfil legal requirements. Businesses may also be reluctant to take on new permanent staff in case demand falls again and they are left with too many staff.

- Some specialist jobs need to be done but it would be wasteful to employ a permanent worker to do them. For example, most small businesses employ accountants to manage their accounts. It is far cheaper to do this than to employ an accountant within the business because the amount of work needed is relatively small.

- In some cases, temporary staff or subcontractors are cheaper to employ than permanent staff. For example, a business may not offer certain benefits to certain staff, although it must be careful not to infringe legislation. If the temporary staff are treated as self-employed or subcontractors, the business may also be able to save on National Insurance contributions. It isn't always cheaper to employ temporary staff and in some cases it may be more expensive because temporary staff or their agencies are able to bid their pay upwards. But temporary staff can be laid off almost immediately they are not needed with little cost, which is not the case for permanent staff.

- Employers are responsible for training their permanent workers. By outsourcing work or employing temporary workers, businesses may be able to pass that cost onto subcontractors or whoever has paid for the training of a temporary worker.

- Employing workers who can job share or work flexible hours may allow a business to operate more efficiently. For example, a business may be able to employ an employee in the day and another in the evening to respond to clients' needs over a longer period. A restaurant may be able to react to increased orders by asking staff to work longer hours at certain times of the week than others.

However, using peripheral workers has its disadvantages.

- Peripheral workers may have less loyalty to the business where they work temporarily. They may be motivated mainly by financial gain.

- Some businesses have found that their outsourced work has been of poor quality, damaging their reputation with customers. The peripheral workers move on and don't have to take responsibility for the poor work. But the business may have lost customers as a result.

- Communication can be a problem. Peripheral workers are not necessarily available when the business would like to communicate with them, although IT and the mobile phone has to some extent solved this problem.

- Employing peripheral workers can be a costly process. For example, a business may put a piece of work out to tender to a subcontractor. It might get the lowest price as a result, but the efficiency gains from putting it out to tender rather than hiring core permanent staff to do the job might be more than outweighed by the costs of the tender process itself.

- Temporary staff can be excellent, well qualified and highly motivated. But equally, some temporary staff are simply workers who have found it difficult to hold down a permanent job. When employing temporary staff, there is no guarantee that they will perform their job as well as would have a permanent member of staff.

- Too many peripheral workers employed alongside core workers can cause demotivation amongst the core workers. Core workers may want to be part of a stable team to form relationships and fulfil some of their higher order needs. Constant turnover of peripheral workers may lead to core workers feeling disorientated.

The impact of flexible working on workers

There are many ways in which workers are affected by flexible work practices. Such practices can affect temporary, part-time or subcontracted employees. However, they might also affect full-time, permanent employees at times.

- For those on temporary contracts and the self-employed, flexible working brings greater insecurity. Temporary workers can lose their jobs at short notice. The self-employed can lose contracts or business overnight. But even workers on permanent contracts face greater uncertainty. They can find themselves being made redundant and their jobs outsourced to a contracting firm. Equally, they can find their pay fringe benefits, such as pensions, and conditions of work worsen to make them 'more competitive' against flexible workers. Insecurity makes most individuals less happy and content and is therefore generally undesirable.

- A more flexible labour force is one where workers can expect their earnings to go down as well as up. It is one where there might be periods of no income coming into the household. It is also one where the individual worker can't expect employers to provide them with a pension. The individual worker therefore must plan to cope with this by saving more and investing in their own personal pension scheme.

- Flexible workers must be prepared to adapt and retrain to a changing job market. A self-employed photographer who finds she can't make a living out of photography may have to find another line of work to survive. Permanent workers are, to some extent, cushioned from this because their employer may pay for retraining and reassign them to other jobs within the business. A flexible market highlights the need for **lifelong learning** on behalf of workers.

- Flexible workers must be prepared to move quickly from job to job. They must also be prepared to become PORTFOLIO WORKERS. These are workers who don't have a single full-time job but a mix of part-time jobs. A worker might have a cleaning job in the morning and work behind a bar in the evening. Or an individual may do consultancy work for rten days a month, and be a part time non-executive director for one company for six days a month and for another company for four days a month.

Flexible working in the UK

The UK government has increasingly encouraged the growth of flexible working in the last 20 years. Legislation has been

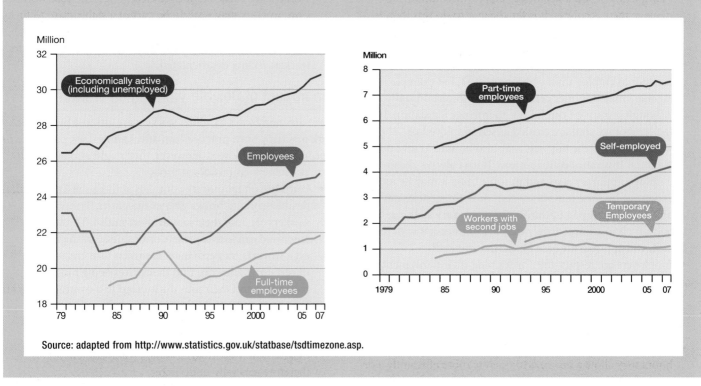

Figure 2: Economically active, employees and full-time employees, UK, millions

Figure 3: Self-employed, part-time employees, workers with second jobs and temporary employees, UK, millions

Source: adapted from http://www.statistics.gov.uk/statbase/tsdtimezone.asp.

introduced to encourage flexible work time, for example. However, it could be argued that it has had limited success as shown in Figures 2 and 3.

- The number of self-employed workers in 2007 was 4.2 million, only slightly higher than in 1990. The growth in self-employment came in the 1980s when it rose from 1.8 million in 1979 to 3.5 million in 1989.
- The number of part-time employees has grown significantly, mainly due to the increased number of women in the workforce. Even so, by 2007, part-time workers represented only one quarter of those economically active.
- The number of portfolio workers (workers with second jobs) has also grown. But in 2007 there were still only 1.1 million such workers, just 3 per cent of those economically active.
- The number of temporary workers has also grown, but in 2004 there were only 1.5 million such workers, just 5 per cent of those economically active.

Most workers today are still on permanent full-time contracts and this is likely to remain so for the foreseeable future. Whilst some industries, such as construction, might have fairly flexible workforces, others such as manufacturing are likely to remain with more traditional work practices.

Flexible working and the Employment Act, 2002

The term 'flexible working' can be used in a different way to the one described above. In the **Employment Act, 2002**, the government gave employees the right to request more flexible working patterns from their employer. Flexible working is then seen as ways in which the employer can give employees choices about when they work. Areas covered by flexible working then include:

- the ability of workers to choose when they start their day and when they finish;
- giving choices about which days of the week an employee works;
- options to move from full-time to part-time working and back again;
- maternity and paternity rights;
- opportunities to take periods of time out for an extended holiday or to look after a child;
- opportunities to job share.

The government argues that flexible working improves productivity. By giving workers greater control over their **work-life balance**, it motivates them to work harder. Labour turnover is also reduced because workers don't have to leave their jobs if their circumstances change and they have to alter their working hours. Reduced labour turnover saves the business the cost of recruiting and training new workers. It also helps retain staff who have received expensive training.

However, many smaller businesses argue that they don't have enough staff to make flexible working practical. If there are only three staff in a business, it may be impossible for one of them suddenly to start working different hours from the other staff. Equally, some aspects, such as better maternity and paternity rights, simply add to the costs of the business.

Question 3.

Colin Traynor, the owner and then manager of Castle Gate Hotel, decided ten years ago to slim his workforce to a minimum and buy in services wherever possible. Twenty two of his fifty permanent staff lost their jobs as work was outsourced. His hotel has a seasonal trade. In July and August, the hotel is fully booked. During the rest of the year, occupancy can fall to as low as 50 per cent despite the hotel being popular with business people and being used as a conference centre. He quickly moved to a model where he employed enough permanent staff to run the hotel at its minimum occupancy levels in the winter and then hired casual labour to cope with the rest of the year. Jobs like laundry, which used to be done in house, were subcontracted to a local firm. Two of the workers in the accounts team lost their jobs and were re-employed by the day as and when they were needed. The marketing of the hotel was contracted out to a local business.

This year, Colin retired and management of the hotel passed to his daughter, Emma. For a long time, she had felt that the quality of service provided by the hotel to its customers was not good enough. Casual staff employed for the peak of the season often showed a lack of knowledge and a lack of commitment. Too much of her time was spent recruiting casual staff. Permanent staff were resentful of casual staff because they were always 'sorting out the mess' created by casual staff. Absenteeism amongst permanent staff was high. Emma was also unhappy with the marketing contract. It was very expensive and she questioned whether the marketing was very effective.

(a) **Assess the possible advantages and disadvantages to Castle Gate Hotel of flexible working.**

Knowledge management

Many businesses today see KNOWLEDGE MANAGEMENT as important to their operation. It involves:
- identifying the knowledge of a business, such as the knowledge of employees;
- assessing how the knowledge can be used and planning how to use it effectively;
- ensuring that knowledge is shared by all people in the organisation.

The management of knowledge can have a number of benefits for a business. The speed at which a business gains knowledge and puts it to good use is one way in which it can gain an advantage over its rivals. For example, Sky was the first company to launch digital television in the UK. It could be argued that this will give it an advantage in future as many customers will have 'signed up' and be unwilling to change to another supplier.

It may also prevent a duplication of services. For example, ICL found that several of its businesses were bidding for the same project at the same time without each knowing about the others' activities. It also found 23 different uncoordinated information services for employees, often providing the same information. Knowledge management could have prevented this waste of resources.

Sometimes people leave a business and take years of knowledge and experience with them. It often exists 'in the head' of the employee, who has found the best way to carry out a task or the most suitable skills to use. Making sure that this knowledge is collected and passed on may prevent problems for new employees to the job. It will also reduce time and costs for the business.

KNOWLEDGE

1. What is open systems thinking?
2. Identify three advantages of (i) centralisation and (ii) decentralisation.
3. How can delayering affect the workforce?
4. What is the difference between the core and the periphery in a flexible firm?
5. What might be the advantages of outsourcing work to a business?
6. What could be the disadvantages to a business of using peripheral workers?
7. What are (a) the advantages and (b) the disadvantages to being a portfolio worker?
8. Why might small businesses suffer from flexible working rights given by the 2002 Employment Act?
9. Suggest three advantages of knowledge management.

KEYTERMS

Centralisation – a type of business organisation where major decisions are made at the centre or core of the organisation and then passed down the chain of command.

Decentralisation – a type of business organisation where decision making is pushed down the chain of command and away from the centre of the organisation.

Delayering – removing layers of management from the hierarchy of an organisation.

Flexible workforce – a workforce that can respond, in quantity and type, to changes in demand a business may face.

Knowledge management – the collection, retention and distribution of vital knowledge that exists within a business.

Open systems thinking – the view that the design of the organisation must meet the needs of the situation.

Outsourced – work which is organised to be carried out workers who are not employees of the business, such as homeworkers or teleworkers.

Portfolio worker – a worker who has a variety of part-time jobs at any one time rather than a single full time job.

Case Study: *The growth of teleworking*

Teleworking is becoming popular for both employers and employees. The Labour Force Survey (LFS) and other market research estimates suggest that the number of teleworkers in the UK is around 2.2-2.4 million. This is about 7.4-8.6 per cent of the UK working population. The LFS defines teleworkers as 'people who do some paid or unpaid work in their own home who could not do so without using both a telephone and a computer'. This includes:

- people who work in their own home (teleworker homeworkers);
- teleworkers who work elsewhere but use home as a base;
- occasional teleworkers who spend at least one day a week working in their own home or using home as a base.

Lloyds TSB has recognised the benefits of teleworkers. A spokesperson stated 'Under the company's new Work Options scheme, employees can ask to work a variety of ways – job sharing, variable hours, teleworking, reduced hours and term-time working.' These provide staff with a means to 'balance home and work life effectively in a win-win initiative which aims to meet the aims of the business and individuals'. The initiative has been introduced not only to allow staff to work differently but to enable the business to retain skilled workers and attract new employees. The option was not just available to women, men or carers with children, but all staff, whether for study, sport or other commitments.

Source: adapted from www.royaldeaf.org,uk.

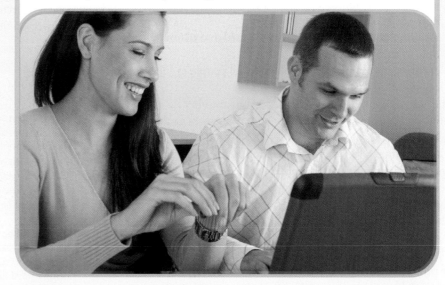

Footballfangs.com is a London based business that offers football kits, fashion clothing and fancy dress outfits for dogs. The business was set up by Tracey Davis and is run by her and her friend from home. They do not employ other full-time or part-time staff. The products are sold online via a website. The business also sells wholesale football shirts for dogs to Premiership and League clubs. All products are imported and sold globally. The website is updated every day and designed and managed in-house.

The business hopes to expand in future. It aims to be the market leader in the UK and Europe and take a sizeable chunk of the US market. It has thought about the possibility of using teleworkers in future to increase sales.

Source: adapted from www.the-bag-lady.co.uk.

Internet service provider, Eclipse Internet, is calling for greater business understanding of the benefits of teleworking. It suggests that the uptake of teleworkers has been slow, rising from one million to three million over a decade since 1997. The major benefit of teleworking is that it allows businesses to cut costs whilst increasing staff productivity and work-life balance. The average cost of a work station in a UK office is £6,422. This rises to £14,778 in London's West End. Providing broadband, a PC/laptop and a phone to an employee's home is an attractive alternative.

Better working styles can lead to better, more productive, workers. On average, 20 per cent of workers spend over an hour a day commuting. Also, according to the Labour Force Survey, more than seven per cent of people spend over two hours a day commuting. With rising petrol, rail and congestion charge costs, cutting commuting time looks more attractive to businesses and employees.

Source: adapted from www.the-bag-lady.co.uk.

Table 2: Teleworkers: employees and self-employed, part-time and full time

Teleworker homeworkers

	All	Men	Per cent Women
Employees	44	43	45
Self-employed	56	57	55
Full-time	52	74	34
Part-time	47	26	66

Home-based teleworkers

	All	Men	Women
Employees	41	40	46
Self-employed	59	60	54
Full-time	81	88	57
Part-time	19	12	43

Occasional teleworkers

	All	Men	Women
Employees	84	82	88
Self-employed	16	18	12
Full-time	90	96	78
Part-time	10	4	22

Source: adapted from *Labour Force Survey*.

Table 3: Teleworkers by occupations

Teleworker homeworkers

	All	Men	Per cent Women
Managers & senior officials	22	28	16
Professional	19	30	10
Associate professional & technical	27	31	23
Administrative & secretarial	24	5	40
Skilled trades	3	*	*
Sales and customer service	*	*	*
Other	5	*	7

Home-based teleworkers

	All	Men	Women
Managers & senior officials	21	22	20
Professional	20	19	24
Associate professional & technical	24	21	34
Administrative & secretarial	3	*	9
Skilled trades	23	29	*
Sales and customer service	3	2	5
Other	6	6	6

Occasional teleworkers

	All	Men	Women
Managers & senior officials	37	42	28
Professional	33	31	35
Associate professional & technical	17	15	20
Administrative & secretarial	5	*	11
Skilled trades	5	7	*
Sales and customer service	*	*	*
Other	3	3	*

Source: adapted from *Labour Force Survey*.

(a) Examine the benefits to Lloyds TSB of using teleworkers. (8 marks)
(b) Analyse why teleworking is more popular with certain types of occupation. (12 marks)
(c) Discuss whether Footballfangs.com should employ teleworkers in its business in future. (20 marks)

74 Managing communication

What is communication?

COMMUNICATION is about sending and receiving information. Employees, managers and departments communicate with each other every day in business. For example, in a sole trader organisation, the owner may inform the workers verbally that an order for goods has to be sent out in the next two days. In a company, the personnel manager might send a 'memo' to all departments informing them about training courses that are available.

Good communication is vital for the efficient running of a business. A company exporting goods abroad is likely to have major problems if it fails to give the exact time of departure to its despatch department. Similarly, problems will also arise if instructions are not clear and goods are delivered to the wrong address.

Effective communication will only happen if information is sent, received and then understood. Some examples of information and methods of communicating in business might be:

- information on how to fill out expenses claims forms in a memo sent from the accounts department;
- verbal comments made by a manager to an employee informing them that continued lateness is likely to result in disciplinary action by the company;
- employment details given to a new employee on a written contract of employment;
- information on sales figures sent from the sales manager to the chief executive by email or saved as a spreadsheet on computer disk;
- face-to-face negotiations between management and employee representatives over possible rewards for agreeing to changes in work practice;
- a group meeting taking place to discuss how quality could

be improved in a work section;
- an order for 20 books faxed to a publisher from a bookshop;
- an advertisement for a salesperson placed on a company website on the Internet.

The communication process

Communication within business can take many forms. There are, however, some common features of all communications that take place in the workplace. Figure 1 shows an example.

Who sends and receives information? Information must be sent by a **sender** and received and understood by the **receiver**, the person or group to whom the information is sent. Communication can take place between managers and employees, as well as between representative bodies, such as trade unions. Information is also passed to people and organisations outside the company. For example, company newspapers not only inform employees about the firm, but present a picture to the outside world of its operations.

What message is being communicated? For communication to be effective the correct message must be sent and received. Messages can be sent for a number of reasons.

- To provide information about the company. Management might inform the workforce about production levels achieved during the previous year. Some information is required by law, for example, the business has to tell employees about their conditions of employment.
- To give instructions, for example, to instruct market research to be carried out.
- To persuade people to change attitudes or behaviour, for example, to warn an employee who is consistently late of the likely action.

Figure 1: An example of information passing through the communication process

Sender	Message	Channel	Medium	Receiver
MANAGERS	DECISION TO REDUCE SHIFT WORKING	VIA UNION REPRESENTATIVE IN THE BUSINESS (formal and internal)	A WRITTEN STATEMENT WITH EXPLANATION	SHOP-FLOOR EMPLOYEES IN FACTORY

Feedback
REACTION OF SHOP FLOOR WORKERS TO DECISION
eg POSSIBLE PROTEST LETTERS OR ACTION

Figure 2: Vertical and lateral communication

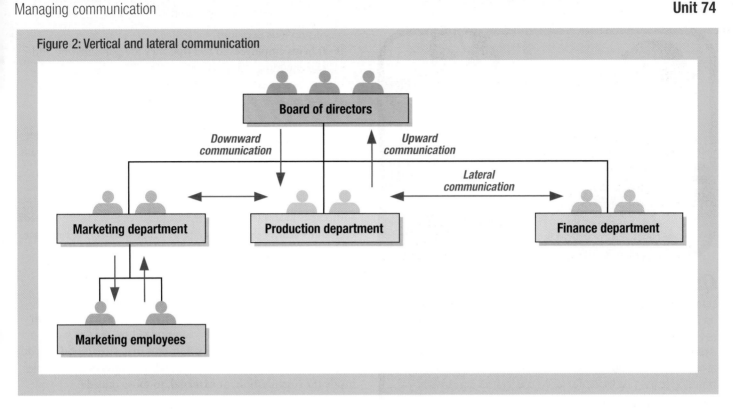

What channel is being used? Communication can be along different routes or CHANNELS OF COMMUNICATION in the organisation. Sometimes this can be between a manager and a subordinate (vertical) or between two departments (horizontal). As well as this formal type of communication, information is often passed informally between departments and employees. Communication can also be to other people within the organisation (internal) or to those outside the organisation (external).

What medium is being used? Information can be communicated in a variety of ways or through different COMMUNICATION MEDIA. These vary from written methods, such as annual reports, to oral methods such as discussions, to the use of information and communication (ICT) technology, such as a fax machine, email or the Internet.

What feedback is given? Communication is not complete until the message is received and the receiver confirms that it is understood through feedback of some sort, for example written or verbal confirmation.

Formal and informal communication

Within a business there are both formal and informal channels of communication.

Formal communication Formal channels of communication are recognised and approved by employers and employee representatives. Examples of formal channels would be a personnel department giving 'notice' to an employee about redundancy, meetings between managers and trade union representatives or team meeting held each week.

Informal communication Informal communication is through non-approved channels. This can both help and hinder formal communications. Information that is communicated through the grapevine may become distorted. This might, in extreme situations, cause industrial relations disputes. However, the grapevine can be acknowledged by management and actively approved of. Some firms issue a 'leak' along the grapevine to see what reaction it might provoke, making changes based on the reaction of employees to proposals, before issuing final instructions. **Rumours**, such as of a launch of a new product by a competitor, can be useful to a business.

Research has shown that effective communication requires both formal and informal channels. Formal statements can then be supported by informal explanations. A business might inform employees that it is introducing new machinery and then management may discuss this with employees and their representatives to find the best way to do it.

Vertical and lateral communication

Information can be communicated vertically (downwards or) upwards and laterally. These different channels of communication are shown in Figure 2.

Vertical communication VERTICAL COMMUNICATION can be downwards or upwards. Downwards communication has, in the past, been used to tell employees about decisions that have already been made. It may be important as it:
- allows decisions by managers to be carried out by employees;

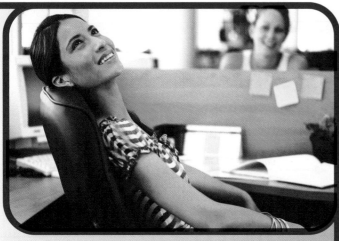

Question 1.

Leila likes her work routine. She gets up at 6.00 each day and is in her open plan office by 7.30. The first thing she does is make a cup of coffee and have a chat with Elle, another early bird into the office. Then she replies to any emails which came in overnight. By 8 o'clock, she is looking at her diary and reminding herself of her priorities for the day. The office is now filling up and Leila knows that for the next hour, colleagues will be dropping by her desk to say good morning, get clarification about the day's work or chat about problems. Her secretary comes in at 8.30 and she always briefs her on the day ahead. When she is not talking, she is reading briefings and memos which don't require too much concentration. 9.00 to 11.00 is Leila's time to write reports for clients based on site visits. Then it is time for a coffee and chat by the coffee machine. Often there are internal meetings in the late morning. The afternoon is typically spent on site visits to external clients. Depending on when the visit finishes, she might go home or pop back to the office to deal with emails and begin writing up the report on her visit.

(a) Explain the meaning of the following using examples from the passage to illustrate your answer.
  (i) Internal and external communication.
  (ii) Messages, senders, receivers and feedback.
  (iii) Channels of communication.
  (iv) Medium of communication.
  (v) Formal and informal communication.
  (vi) Vertical and lateral communication.

- ensures that action is consistent and co-ordinated;
- reduces costs because fewer mistakes should be made;
- should lead to greater effectiveness and profitability as a result of the above.

There is evidence, however, that the flow of information upwards can also help in decision making.

- It helps managers to understand employees' views and concerns.
- It helps managers to keep more in touch with employees' attitudes and values.
- It can alert managers to potential problems.
- It can provide managers with the information that they need for decision making and gives feedback on the effects

of previous decisions.
- It helps employees to feel that they are participating and can encourage motivation.
- It provides feedback on the effectiveness of downwards communication and how it can be improved.

Lateral communication LATERAL COMMUNICATION takes place when people at the same level within an organisation pass information. An example might be a member of the finance department telling the marketing department about funds available for a sales promotion. One problem that firms sometimes face is that departments may become hostile towards each other if they don't understand the problems that each face. The marketing department may want these funds, but this might adversely affect the firm's cash flow.

It is also possible to make the distinction between **line communication** and **staff communication**. Line communication has authority behind it. Staff communication does not. An example of staff communication may be where a manager attempts to persuade a worker that it is a 'good idea' to do something. Communication can also be **internal**, to people inside the organisation, or **external**, to those outside.

The importance of communication

Communication is a vital factor affecting motivation and vice versa. Theories of motivation suggest different ways in which this occurs.

The scientific management school Frederick Taylor's scientific management theory suggests that subordinates must be given clear instructions about how best to complete tasks. It is the role of those in authority to work out what is the optimum way to complete any given task. In scientific management theory, pay is the main motivation of workers. Frederick Taylor suggested that directly linking pay to output achieved through piece rates was, in many cases, the best way to motivate workers to achieve maximum output. Although piece rates for manual workers have fallen out of fashion, bonuses, commissions and stock options for white collar workers including senior management are common in UK businesses today. Individual pay rises are also often linked to achieving targets set for a 12 month period through performance related pay.

Communicating the goals which workers have to achieve to gain bonuses is a vital part of the process of motivation. If workers are unclear what they have to achieve to gain high remuneration, they will become demotivated when they are judged to have failed to reach their targets. Equally, if managers have set unrealistic goals, or insist on staff working in an inefficient way, workers are likely to become demotivated.

Elton Mayo and the human relations school Elton Mayo, in his pioneering studies at the Hawthorne plant in the USA, showed that workers were more motivated if managers took an interest in them. Interest was expressed not just through formal

Northern Lights plc

Victoria Tomlinson runs Northern Lights, a Yorkshire-based public relations and research company. She has found the perfect people to do her telephone research: the mums waiting at the gates of her daughter's school. Many of these women are highly qualified. Before leaving full-time employment to look after children, several held high-powered jobs. The senior executives they interview on behalf of Northern Lights are happy to talk to them. The women do more than fill in the boxes. If the interviewing goes off on interesting tangents, they follow these up, and ask the relevant questions. The interviews over, they come back with suggestions on how the questionnaires could be improved.

JetBlue

JetBlue is a relatively young low-cost US airline. Like most airlines, it has a customer service centre where customers can ring up and book or change flights. But unlike most airlines, its customer service centre is not a physical call centre where all the operators work in one building. Instead, the 900 customer service staff work from home in Salt Lake City. The airline estimates that 70 per cent of them are stay-at-home mothers. The company provides the computer and telephone equipment they need to deal with customers. How do the staff cope during non-school hours? This is where employing mothers becomes more complicated. JetBlue employees have to be prepared to work any shift. The company does, however, encourage them to trade their hours over the company intranet. JetBlue also demands that employees ensure their workspace is quiet: no yelling or piano practice in the background. To get around the problem that working from home can be isolating, JetBlue makes sure everyone visits the office once a month.

Xansa

Xansa is a UK computer services group. Founded in 1962, the company initially specialised in computer programming done by female computer programmers working from home. Today, only 2 per cent of Xansa's 6 500 employees work from home. Valerie Huges D'Aeth, human resources director, insists that the company is still very flexible about working arrangements. However, not all jobs lend themselves to flexible working. For example, clients often insist today that computer programmers work on their premises because of security worries. Another problem is managers who do not believe people are working unless they can see them. About two-thirds of Xansa's employees came to the company through acquisitions. It sometimes takes time to persuade their managers to measure them by what they produce rather than by how much time they spend at work.

Source: adapted from the *Financial Times*, 22.9.2004.

Question 2.

(a) Explain how the workers in the three companies described in the data communicate effectively (i) with each other and (ii) with customers.

(b) Discuss whether motivation at companies like JetBlue, Northern Lights and Xansa would be improved if workers were forced to work in an office environment rather than from home.

channels. Communication through informal channels was also important to improve morale amongst workers.

Maslow and the hierarchy of needs Maslow suggested that workers had a hierarchy of needs, from physiological needs to self-actualisation needs. Fulfilment of the higher order needs requires effective communication in the workplace. For example, workers have social needs for love and belonging. Through formal channels of communication, workers can be organised into working groups, such as cells or teams, where group members have to co-operate and communicate for the group to function effectively. Through informal channels, such as chatting over a coffee or working out at the company gym, workers can feel that they belong to a working group with shared values and shared goals. Workers also have self-esteem needs according to Maslow. So the business needs to communicate to workers that they are doing a good job. This can be done through simple verbal messages, such as just saying 'thank you', to more complex formal appraisal systems. Finally, some workers will be able to satisfy their need for self-actualisation at work. Part of fulfilling this need will be having the opportunity to communicate effectively with others.

Herzberg's two factor model In Herzberg's two factor model, achievement, recognition and responsibility are all motivators. A necessary part of each of these is communication. For example, a worker may get promotion, but this in itself will not be a motivator unless the worker feels that this is a recognition of achievement. That recognition comes through effective communication by the business. Equally, communication can be an important part of factors which lead to dissatisfaction. For example, good communication is vital if supervision is to be effective. Management must communicate to their workers that their jobs are safe.

Effective communication is central to many modern innovations in working in business.

Team working When working in teams, workers must communicate effectively to achieve the tasks set. Failure to communicate will result in inefficiency and poor quality work. Equally, team working encourages effective communication. By working as part of a group, workers are encouraged to communicate more than if they were working in isolation. Communication then becomes motivating because team members want the group as a whole to achieve its goals.

Kaizen groups Kaizen groups are teams of workers set up to consider ways of changing work practices to bring about improvements in efficiency and quality. Workers in Kaizen groups have to communicate their ideas to others. Promising ideas then need to be explored and developed. Membership of Kaizen groups is often motivating for individual workers. They feel that they are contributing something important to the group and that their skills and talents are being recognised. Communication between group members is therefore

Question 3.

Juan Parente moved from Madrid to Leeds 10 years ago, first to work in the kitchens of a Spanish restaurant and then to open his own restaurant. A year ago, he employed Jason Belfield as an assistant chef. Initially, everything went well but, three months ago, Jason began being late for work once or twice a week. Juan took Jason aside and gave him a severe reprimand, but Jason found it difficult to understand everything Juan was saying because he spoke English with a Spanish accent and included Spanish words in sentences. As time went on, Juan became more angry with Jason's timekeeping and informed him that he may be faced with disciplinary action. Matters came to a head when Jason arrived an hour late on a day when the restaurant was fully booked for the evening and another member of the kitchen staff was off sick. For Juan, the reputation of the restaurant was at stake.

Jason began to dislike working at the restaurant. Three months ago, Jason's mother had fallen seriously ill and he had found it difficult juggling work with hospital appointments and caring for her. He had confided in Emily, another assistant chef, but she did not tell Juan about Jason's problem. The day the restaurant was fully booked Juan was incensed by Jason's lateness, but Jason could only think of his mother lying ill at home. At that moment in time, he didn't care about the restaurant and its reputation.

(a) Explain what barriers to communication existed between Juan and Jason.
(b) Discuss how these barriers to communication could have been overcome for the benefit of both Juan and Jason.

motivating both for individual workers and the group as a whole. This motivation can then spill over into the everyday activities of the workers in the group.

Single status In a single status organisation, every worker is offered the same conditions of work. One of the aims of creating a single status organisation is to foster effective communication between different workers at different levels and different places in the organisation. So shop floor workers should be able to communicate directly with the managing director, or a sales administrator with someone in accounts. Creating the conditions for improved communication between workers should then be motivating for staff. Instead of having a traditional 'them and us' attitude between workers at different grades or in different departments, workers should be encouraged to see every worker as one of 'us'.

Removing barriers to communication

Effective communication will take place if the message is received and understood by the receiver. There is a number of factors that might prevent this from happening. Solutions to some of these problems may simply be using tactics to change how the communication takes place. However, in other cases company-wide strategies may be needed.

Form of the message If the message is unclear or unexpected the receiver is unlikely to understand it or remember it. The rate at which we forget is considerable. We have probably forgotten half of what we hear within a few hours of hearing it, and no more than 10 per cent will remain after two or three days. To ensure a message is communicated effectively the sender must make sure it:

- does not contain too much information;
- is not poorly written;
- is not presented too quickly;
- is not presented in a way that the receiver does not expect;
- conveys the information that he actually wants to communicate;
- is written in a way that the receiver will understand.

Jargon A word or phrase which has a technical or specialised meaning is known as jargon. The terms understood by a certain group of people may be meaningless to those who don't have this knowledge. One example of this was in Schools of Motoring, where for many years drivers were given the instruction 'clutch in' or 'clutch out', which nearly always confused the trainee. Later the instruction was changed to 'clutch down' and 'clutch up'. Technical information about a product which is not understood by the marketing department may result in misleading advertising and poor sales. Being careful that the communication is written appropriately for the receiver may help to prevent this, for example through editing or rewriting.

The skills of the sender and receiver The ability of the sender to explain a message and the receiver to understand it are important in communication. If an order must be sent out by a certain date, but the sender simply asks for it to be sent as early as possible, communication would not have been effective. If the receiver does not understand what stocks to take the order from, incorrect goods may be sent. Solving such a problem may simply mean checking that both sender and receiver the message and that it is carefully explained. However, if either lacks the skills required then training may be required.

Choice of communication channel or medium Sometimes the channel or medium chosen to send the message may not communicate the information effectively. An example of this might be where a manager attempts to pass a message to an employee, but would have been more successful if the message had gone through a representative. Another example is that safety campaigns are sometimes unsuccessful because slogans and posters are used to persuade individual employees about the importance of safe working practices rather than changes being discussed.

Incorrect target for the message Businesses sometimes send the wrong information to the wrong person. This can result in costly delays and errors and perhaps a poor image in the eyes of the public.

Stereotypes, perceptions and attitudes How employees perceive other people can affect how they interpret the message that is sent. Employees are more likely to have confidence in people they trust, because of past experience of their reliability. On the other hand, if an employee has learned to distrust someone, then what she says will be either ignored or treated with caution. The way employees view things can be affected by being part of a group.

People can also have beliefs about others. This may result in stereotyping of some people. It is possible that, if one person stereotypes another, this may affect how they interpret a message. So, for example, if a manager takes the view that younger people are less knowledgable than older people, this may affect the manager's judgment on a younger employee's opinions.

Training workers to behave objectively when dealing with colleagues can prevent such problems. However, preconceptions might be difficult to remove unless everyone in the business is committed to this approach and it is supported and led by management.

Layers in the hierarchy The length of chain of command or distance can affect communication. If information is passed down by word of mouth through a number of receivers, it is possible for the message to be distorted. This may result in the wrong emphasis or wrong information being received by the individual or group at the end of the communication chain. Industrial relations problems in business have sometimes been a result of a long chain of command. A long chain of command may also prevent effective feedback. Some businesses have delayered their organisations. Removing a layer of the hierarchy could help to ensure that the message is communicated more quickly and becomes less distorted.

Breakdown of the channel This could be due to technical problems. For example, a business may rely on its management information system on the computerised network. If this breaks down, businesses might have problems dealing with enquiries. Banks, for example, are unable to tell customers what their balances are if computer terminals are not working.

Different countries, languages and cultures A business may have a problem sending a message from one country to another because of time differences. This is particularly a difficulty if an urgent decision is needed. Languages may also be different. The use of ICT, as explained later, may help to prevent this problem to some extent. There could be problems if communication about technical details needed to be explained. The solution may be to ensure communications are multilingual.

Individual cultural traits can also sometimes affect communication. A study of North and South American business people found that they each had different 'conversation distances'. In meetings, problems developed as South American business people came towards people they were talking to, while North Americans retreated. This is often problem for

multinational organisations, where operations in different countries behave in different ways. Establishing a common corporate culture and training workers in a shared corporate culture which everyone understands may help to prevent this difficulty.

Intermediaries When there are intermediaries, messages can become distorted, as in a game of 'Chinese whispers'. The more complex the message, the more likely it is to be altered as it passes through a chain of communication. For example, the managing director of a company telling the board of directors that there 'may be redundancies in the future' could easily leak out and become, after many tellings, that there 'will be large scale redundancies now'.

Too many meetings In large businesses, there tends to be far more meetings per employee than in small businesses. Meetings are essential for effective communication. However, they can be unproductive. Some employees will be invited to a meeting although they will have little interest or understanding of the issues to be discussed. Meetings tend to go on far too long, with some employees talking too much and not concentrating on the issues in hand. Meetings may also involve unproductive travel. For example, a meeting of seven employees from different sites in the UK may take place at head office. Those involved may spend a whole day in travelling to and from a meeting which lasts perhaps only four hours. Those attending meetings will also need to be paid travel expenses, further adding to costs.

There are several possible solutions to these problems. Businesses can adopt policies which limit the number and length of meetings and the number of employees taking part. Equally, it is becoming increasingly easy to arrange telephone or video conferences to link up employees in different parts of the country or the world or simply a large site. Some businesses are able to hold meetings online through their company intranets sites or using email.

Lack of common sense of purpose When workers lack a common sense of purpose, they can often misinterpret messages. For example, an administrator in the accounts department may receive a message from the finance director that late payment of invoices must be chased up more vigourously. The administrator may know that the business is experiencing cash flow problems and therefore needs to increase its inflow of cash quickly. At the same time, the marketing director is trying to expand sales to existing customers. In the event, the measures taken are too tough. Long standing large customers are threatened with being taken to court if they don't pay now, while other late paying customers are refused further trade credit. Although invoices are now paid more promptly, the company loses customers and the marketing director is furious. The administrator has misunderstood the message given because she failed to reconcile the goals of the marketing director with those of the finance director.

Equally, different stakeholders often have different aims and objectives, which can lead to problems. For example, local residents fighting against the siting of a waste disposal factory in an area might interpret figures on pollution caused by the factory differently to the owners of the factory. The owners might argue that the figures for pollution are acceptable, whereas local residents might not.

Over-reliance on written communication In a small business, it is easy for workers to talk to each other face to face on a day-to-day basis. In a large company, with perhaps thousands of employees and a number of different site locations, face-to-face contact becomes more difficult. Hence, workers rely much more heavily on written communication, including email. Written communication, however, has its limitations. Messages can be misinterpreted because, unlike face-to-face communication, feedback is often slow and the signals that come from body language are missing. In large businesses, there can be an over-reliance on written communication.

Use of information and communication technology Although new technologies can help communication, there are problems both with the amount of information sent and the use of **information and communication technology** (ICT).

- **Information overload.** Large amounts of information can be sent instantly by such media as fax, email and the Internet. This may result in information overload. Individuals and organisations may not be able to fully process all of the information that is sent. As a result, effective communication may not take place.
- **Introduction.** Electronic media can sometimes create problems when they are first introduced. Staff need training, which is time consuming. Mistakes can be made if information is not stored, as there may be no written record. There may also need to be a change in working methods and employees may work at a slower pace as they get used to the new methods and equipment.
- **Misuse of new technology.** There is evidence to suggest that employees spend more time using the Internet and email facilities than is necessary. 'Browsing' the Internet and constantly checking email for new messages can waste time. Employees may also use the technology for non-business messages.
- **Confidentiality.** Electronic media often send messages that can be seen be people other than the intended receiver. This can be a problem if the sender wants the message to remain confidential.
- **Viruses.** Computer viruses can damage information kept on computers, although it is possible to protect information by using software.

Preventing technical problems which result in communication breakdowns may simply require regular updates of machinery and software or effective maintenance. But training may also be needed to ensure that employees know how to use communication media effectively. As communication technology changes rapidly, training needs regularly updating.

KEY TERMS

Communication – the sending and receiving of messages between two or more individuals, groups or organisations.
Channel of communication – the route by which a message is communicated from sender to receiver.
Communication media – the written, oral or technological methods used to communicate a message.
Lateral communication – when there is communication between employees and departments at a similar level in the organisational hierarchy.
Vertical communication – when there is communication up and down the hierarchy.

KNOWLEDGE

1. Why is good communication important for a business?
2. Why might a business want feedback in the communication process?
3. Explain the difference between:
   (a) formal and informal communication;
   (b) lateral and vertical communication;
   (c) internal and external communication;
   (d) the channel of communication and the medium of communication
4. How might upward communication be useful to a business?
5. How does effective communication motivate workers according to (a) Maslow and (b) Herzberg?
6. How might (a) working in a team and (b) single status organisations improve communication?
7. Explain why the following might be a barrier to communication within a business:
   (a) a subordinate who does not trust the judgment of his boss;
   (b) a long chain of command;
   (c) a place of work in the UK where for half the workers English is not their first language;
   (d) management deciding that quality is the main priority in production whilst production workers are mainly motivated by their pay.
8. Explain why a large business might face more communication problems than a small business because of the following:
   (a) the amount of information available;
   (b) the length of the chain of command;
   (c) the increased percentage of written rather than oral communication;
   (d) use of ICT;
   (e) meetings;
   (f) cultural and linguistic differences.

Case Study:

Hovers Travel is one of the South's largest independent travel agents. Formed in 1965, it has today a sales turnover of £98 million with pre-tax profits of £1 million. It runs a chain of travel agent outlets in the South of England in towns like Bournemouth, Bath and Worthing. One quarter of its sales come from selling cruise holidays. Much of the rest is a mix of package holidays from major companies and its own package holidays.

Its main market has traditionally been older, high disposable income customers. Over the past 20 years as the population has aged, the more affluent pensioner market has become increasingly dominant in its sales and hence the very high proportion of cruise holidays sold to destinations in Europe and further afield. However, like all travel agents, the arrival of the Internet and low cost airlines has had a serious impact on turnover and profit. Five years ago, sales turnover was £110 million and pre-tax profits £7 million. The Internet has eroded sales to younger customers who have chosen to go online to book a package holiday directly or to put together their own package of flights plus hotels. Low cost airlines have encouraged customers to book directly over the Internet, eroding the market for airline ticket sales through travel agents.

Hovers Travel has been fortunate in that it has never attempted to be the lowest price agent in the market. Instead, it has concentrated on quality of service. This has been much appreciated by its most loyal customers who are prepared to pay more for a service where the needs of the customer are always put first. It has also been lucky in that its core group of customers are the least likely to own a computer and have Internet access. But over the next 20 years, this will rapidly change. The over 60s will increasingly have access to the Internet, either through their computer or through their television, and will be comfortable using it.

Within the family owned company, there are increasing divisions about how best to communicate with customers. Margaret Hovers, 68, the wife of the founder of the company, and owner of 49 per cent of the shares, is very much in charge. She believes that the downturn in sales is temporary. Her sales strategy is to open more travel agent outlets across the company and accept that some existing customers will migrate to the Internet. Richard Hovers, her son and the Sales Director, wants to compete more aggressively on the Internet. He owns 25.5 per cent of the shares. The company has had a website for the past three years which currently accounts for 5 per cent of bookings. By cutting prices, he believes the company could increase Internet sales substantially even if it means sacrificing profit margins. Jane Hovers, Margaret's daughter, owns the remaining 25.5 per cent of the shares of the company, is on the Board of Directors, but doesn't play an active role in the company. She has seen the value of the company slide as sales have fallen. She wants to sell the company as soon as possible.

The three shareholders are barely on speaking terms with each other. They communicate via memos, letters, emails and intermediaries. The Finance Director, Patrick Dagnall, a non-family employee, is the person through whom communication tends to flow. He is constantly trying to reconcile the different points of view. The problem is that a stalemate has developed where no strategic decisions are being taken or implemented. Only one Board of Directors' meeting has taken place annually in each of the past four years and only business needed to conform with the Companies Act is transacted.

The profound disagreements at the top have filtered down the hierarchy of the company. Those working in the travel agents outlets don't encourage their customers to visit the company's website. The few working on the website see themselves as the future of the company and have kept references to the physical outlets to a minimum on the website. Richard Hovers would like to see a delayering of the organisation. He believes strongly that shifting to a more web-based operation would allow many middle managers to be cut, lowering costs. Margaret Hovers, on the other hand, believes that middle managers are vital to providing a high quality service. Many of the middle managers have worked for the company for at least ten years and Margaret has got to know them well as she works at head office and travels around the outlets.

(a) Evaluate how barriers to communication between Hovers Travel and its customers could be reduced and discuss whether this would benefit the company in the long term. (20 marks)

(b) (i) Explain what barriers to communication exist within the company. (8 marks)
(ii) Discuss whether barriers to communication would be lowered internally to the company if Margaret Hovers were to retire. (12 marks)

Employers and employees

EMPLOYERS are businesses or other organisations, such as government, which hire workers to work for them. An employee is a worker hired to work for a business or other organisation. Both employers and employees may feel that it is important for workers' views to be heard and taken into account in the workplace. Workers may be more motivated and employers may benefit as a result, for example. Workers therefore need effective EMPLOYEE REPRESENTATION at work. They need groups or forums both within and outside the organisation to speak with authority on their behalf.

INDUSTRIAL DEMOCRACY is where employees are given the right to elect representatives who will be directly involved in the internal decision making of the business. There is a variety of ways in which employees can be represented in an organisation.

Trade unions

These are perhaps the best known of the representative bodies. TRADE UNIONS are organisations of workers who join together to further their own interests. Trade unions have existed in the UK for over 200 years. Early unions were made up of workers with similar skills and interests, for example the General Union of Operative Spinners set up in 1829. Over time, their **objectives** or goals have remained broadly the same, although the importance of any single objective may differ from union to union. Their main objectives are to:

- secure high wages and maximise other financial and non-financial benefits for their members;
- prevent the loss of their members' jobs;
- gain safe working conditions;
- see that their members are entitled to welfare benefits if they fall ill, become unemployed or retire;
- provide a range of other services which might increase the welfare of their members;
- fight for causes, such as improved public services or nuclear disarmament or the election of a political party which their members support.

The functions of trade unions

Trade unions have a number of functions. These functions allow unions to achieve their objectives.

- They negotiate with employers on behalf of their members in the workplace. This is known as **collective bargaining**. Negotiations include everything from pay rates to conditions of service, redundancies and health and safety.
- They represent individual members in cases such as discrimination and dismissal. This may involve negotiating with the employer. If this fails, the union may pay to have the member represented at an **employment tribunal** or a

Question 1.

Eurotunnel is the operator of the high speed shuttle service which links the UK to France. It has a 99 year lease to operate the Channel Tunnel link, running freight trains and maintaining the infrastructure. It employs 3,400 people, of which about 1,400 are based in the UK on British contracts. To harmonise the workforce, management set up a company council in 1992.

Until June 2000 the company only recognised the council for consultation. But after the Employment Relations Act, 1999, it signed a recognition agreement with the T&G (Transport and General Workers Union) and a single partnership deal to cover all non-managerial employees and a joint management-union negotiating forum. The company suggested that the threat of industrial action and having to negotiate with many different unions swayed its decision, and the fact that the costs involved of action and negotiations would affect a company already £6.5 billion in debt. There were now two negotiating bodies - the council, representing all employees, and the TU forum, representing union members with sole negotiating rights over pay and conditions.

Two surveys were carried out, one just before recognition and the other 18 months after. Certain results were found.

- About 35 per cent of employees said they were union members in the second survey, but only 12 per cent in the first.
- Over 50 per cent of employees said there was an active union presence in the second survey compared to 6 per cent in the first.
- In the first survey there had been strong support for unions in all sections at Eurotunnel. Most said that unions would improve their pay and benefits (over 70 per cent), work conditions (75 per cent), health and safety, and grievances. In the second survey fewer than a third agreed that the T&G had been effective in representing employee interests and only 10 per cent said that the union had improved pay and benefits.
- Most employees wanted the council to be retained. But this was not a vote to replace the TU forum, as employees agreed the council had largely been ineffective as well.

Source: adapted from People Management.

(a) (i) Explain how the role of trade unions changed at Eurotunnel.
(ii) Examine the reasons for these changes.
(b) Discuss to what extent employee representation was affected as a result of the changes at Eurotunnel.

court of law.

• They provide members with a range of benefits. These vary enormously from union to union, but they tend to include free legal representation and access to cheap insurance and credit cards.

• They act as a **pressure group** to influence the behaviour of businesses in general, as well as to affect government and the law. Since the beginning of the twentieth century, major trade unions have sponsored Labour MPs and the trade union movement still plays an important role within the Labour Party.

• Trade unions are also responsible, along with management, for INDUSTRIAL RELATIONS. They communicate their members' wishes to employers and try to negotiate the most favourable conditions. However, successful industrial relations means that each party must take into account the wishes of the other when bargaining. It may not be in members' interests for a union to push for a longer work break if this reduces the efficiency of the business, perhaps resulting in job losses in future. However, it may not be in employers' interests to reduce breaks, even if this cuts costs, if it results in worker dissatisfaction.

The organisation of trade unions

In 2008, there were 174 trade unions in the UK. They vary enormously in size and in the way they are organised. However, they can grouped into different **types** of union.

Craft or skill unions These unions represent workers who have a particular craft or skill. For example, musicians can join the Musicians Union, journalists can join the National Union of Journalists and bakers can join the Bakers, Food and Allied Workers Union. Craft unions are the oldest type of union in the UK.

Industrial unions These unions represent workers in a single industry. They don't necessarily represent all the workers in the industry, but they don't accept members from outside of that industry. Examples are the National Union of Mineworkers, the Firebrigades' Union and the National Union of Teachers.

General unions General unions represent workers from different industries and different types of workers. General unions, traditionally, recruited from unskilled workers. However, over the past 20 years there has been a trend for unions to merge to create general unions which represent both skilled and unskilled workers, and blue-collar and white-collar workers. An example in 2007 was the creation of Unite. With its two million members, Unite would be the main trade union in the manufacturing, transport, finance, food and agriculture and printing industries.

White-collar unions These unions represent white-collar workers. Until the 1950s and 1960s, most union members were blue-collar workers. Hence, white-collar unions were seen as a

separate type of union. Today, most union members are white-collar workers. It can be argued that all white-collar unions, such as Unison or the National Union of Teachers, can be placed into one of the three types of Craft, Industrial and General Union.

The organisation of a trade union varies. However, in a typical trade union there will be both voluntary and full-time trade union workers. **Shop stewards** or **trade union representatives** are ordinary workers elected within a place of work by members. This group of workers is sometimes called a **branch** of the union. The role of shop stewards is to represent workers' interests to management on issues such as pay, redundancies and working conditions. They also represent the interests of their members at local, regional or national meetings of the union. Shop stewards are typically unpaid volunteers who work for the union in their own time.

Full-time officials are paid officials of the union who work full time for the union. They will be based in offices of the union. They specialise in a particular type of union work, such as recruitment, training or legal advice. The most important full-time official will be the leader of the union, whose title varies from union to union, but is often called the **General Secretary** of the union. The General Secretary is elected by a postal ballot of all members.

Changing industrial relations and the effects on business

Industrial relations have changed over the last 40-50 years. This has been caused by changes in the power and role of trade unions, legislation and views on human resources management. These changes have affected businesses in a variety of ways.

Membership and union density Trade union membership has been in decline since the late 1970s as shown in Figure 1. Trade

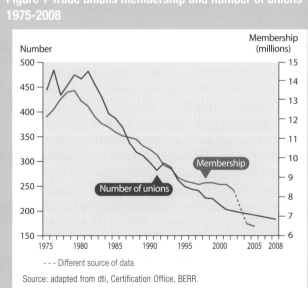

Figure 1 Trade unions membership and number of unions 1975-2008

Source: adapted from dti, Certification Office, BERR.

unions have traditionally been strong in primary and secondary industries and public sector services. Also, membership in the past tended to be dominated by male workers. But changes in the make-up of the workforce have altered the pattern of trade union membership. There has been a significant reduction in employment in primary and secondary industries, which has contributed to a decline in overall membership of unions in the UK. Partly this has been due to growing competition from foreign companies and the trend towards globalisation. The largest growth in the workforce has come from private sector service industries where trade unions have traditionally been weak. Moreover, there has been a shift in employment between males and females. In the past there were far more male than female trade union members partly because primary and secondary industries were male dominated. Jobs created in the last 20 years have been predominantly in the service sector and have been often taken by female workers.

Trends in union membership can be seen in the changes in UNION DENSITY, the proportion of any workforce that belongs to a trade union, in the UK. The formula for calculating union density is:

$$\text{Union density} = \frac{\text{number of union members}}{\text{number of workers in the workforce}} \times 100\%$$

Figure 2 shows that trade union density has fallen consistently. It fell from 32 per cent at the end of 1997 to around 27 per cent in 2006. This was because over the period the number of union members fell, but the number of workers in the workforce rose. In contrast, union density amongst female workers was greater in 2006 than in 1997. It has been suggested that the fall in union membership and union density have contributed to a reduction in the power of trade unions. Figure 3 shows that trade union density for both men and women is far greater in the public sector than in the private sector. This might suggest that unions could have greater influence on employers in the public sector.

Legislation Another important factor in changing the power of trade unions and the nature of industrial relations has been legislative changes. In the 1980s, the Conservative government passed a number of trade union 'reform' laws which effectively curbed the power of trade unions. As a result, workers saw unions as less powerful and less relevant to them. Employers, on the other hand, were encouraged to refuse to **recognise** unions in their workplace (i.e. refuse to acknowledge that unions could negotiate on behalf of their members through collective bargaining). Trade unions as a result found it more difficult to recruit members and to represent them in the workplace.

However, in the late 1990s and the early twenty-first century changes in legislation may have led to unions regaining some of their ability to influence business. For example, the **Employment Relations Act, 1999** allowed employees to vote for trade union recognition. Employers could be compelled to

recognise unions for collective bargaining under certain conditions. Applications for union recognition are made to the **Central Arbitration Committee (CAC)**. This is an independent body designed to provide guidance on union recognition and make judgments about recognition if disputes occur between employees and employers. This Act led businesses to increasingly recognise unions in the early twenty-first century.

Human resource management Human resource management philosophy in the last two decades has emphasised the need for individual pay bargaining and flexible workforces. Traditional union goals of nationwide pay agreements with workers getting the same rate of pay whatever their performance were seen as outdated. Moreover, the 'them and us' philosophy, associated

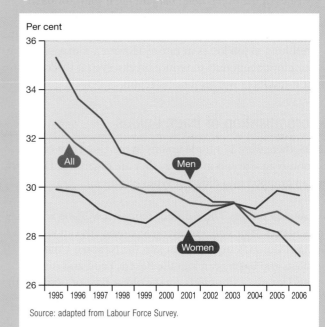

Figure 2 Trade union density, 1995-2006

Source: adapted from Labour Force Survey.

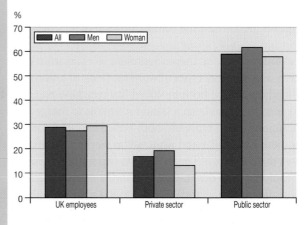

Figure 3 Trade union density by sector, 2006

Source: adapted from Labour Force Survey.

with traditional trade unionism, was seen as contrary to a human resource management perspective, which suggested that the goals of workers should be aligned with the goals of the business. Existing employers were therefore encouraged by this to abandon or limit collective bargaining agreements. New businesses may have not recognised trade unions. The number of workers covered by collective bargaining agreements fell from 71 per cent to below 35 per cent in the 25 years before 2006. All this meant that trade unions may have found it more difficult to recruit members in private sector industry.

The overall result is that trade unions are active and recognised in a smaller percentage of businesses than they were 30 years ago. In some businesses, workers are unrepresented and are subject to individual bargaining procedures. Where trade unions are recognised, there has been a significant change in industrial relations.

- Industrial action is rarer. Confrontational approaches to problems are less common. Trade unions in particular recognise that it is in their interests to reach negotiated settlements. There is a much greater realism on the part of trade unions that their actions can make businesses less competitive, putting their members' jobs at risk. Equally, more businesses have recognised that by working with rather than against trade unions, they can improve industrial relations. Trade unions can play a useful role in channelling workers' demands and in reducing the number of negotiating partners for the business. They can also exercise some discipline over their members, helping them to see what is reasonable and unreasonable.
- Some businesses have formalised their relationships with unions by signing a **partnership agreement**. Such agreements lay out medium to long-term plans for industrial relations. They vary from business to business. But they typically cover pay, conditions of work, employment and training. For example, a business may agree that there will be no compulsory redundancies in return for trade unions agreeing to changes in working practices. Or a more flexible working year for workers might be agreed in the context of a three year pay deal.
- In a few high profile cases, some businesses and unions have signed a SINGLE UNION AGREEMENT. A business agrees to recognise only one trade union for collective bargaining purposes. In return, that trade union agrees to a range of conditions about how it will operate. For example, it might sign a NO STRIKE AGREEMENT where it agrees never to bring its members out on strike. Or it might agree to **flexible working practices**. Single union agreements are controversial amongst trade unions. Other trade unions will be excluded from representing workers in that business. If every business concluded single union agreements, there would be major winners and losers amongst trade unions for members. What is more, many trade unionists see single union agreements as a 'sell out' to management. They argue that workers' interests are damaged because a union, to get a single union agreement, has to agree to unfavourable terms with the employer. In practice, single union agreements and no strike agreements have not given businesses a clear competitive advantage. For this reason, they remain the exception rather than the norm in British industry.

The number of unions The number of trade unions in the UK has fallen greatly since the 1970s. In 1975 there were 446. This had fallen to 213 in 2002. In 2008 there were 174 listed by the Certification Officer. This has been almost entirely due to merger activity. As union membership has shrunk and total subscriptions have fallen, trade unions have found it more difficult financially to cope. By combining, they have been able to spread their overhead costs more and so survive financially. Equally, it can be argued that larger trade unions are able to give a better service to their members than very small trade unions. They are able to employ specialist staff and campaign more effectively than smaller unions. It can also be argued that very small unions do not have the industrial strength to be as effective in collective bargaining as larger unions.

Works councils

Works councils are bodies which consist of selected managers and elected representatives of workers. The council meets to discuss issues such as conditions of work, health and safety, training, investment, redundancies and site closures. They have access to information about strategic planning, the finances of the business and company performance. Works councils have often existed in European countries such as in France and Germany. Some were set up in the UK in the 1990s. Under the EU Information and Consultation Directive, however,

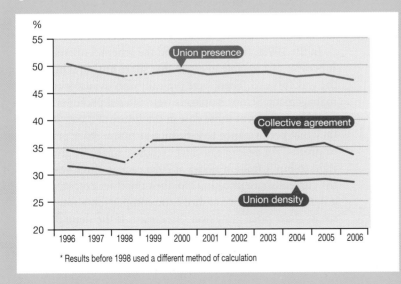

Figure 4 Union collective agreements, coverage and presence

* Results before 1998 used a different method of calculation

EUROPEAN WORKS COUNCILS (EWCs) were to be introduced into the UK from 2000. Any business with at least 1,000 employees and at least 150 employees located in two or more EU countries has to have a European Works Council. This will therefore include UK multinationals.

Exactly what impact EWCs will have in the UK may take time to assess. In Europe, works councils have traditionally been important. This is because workers are seen as significant stakeholders alongside shareholders. In the UK, workers have traditionally not been seen as significant stakeholders in the business. They have certainly been seen as less important than shareholders. So it could be argued that, in the UK, European Works Councils will do little to enhance industrial democracy in business.

On the other hand, there is evidence that, where EWCs have been introduced in the UK, they provide benefits for business, such as employee motivation and the development of a positive corporate culture. Proposals for reform in future may encourage greater training and involvement for employee members. EU legislation may also continue to promote greater industrial democracy through EWCs.

Staff associations

Staff associations represent workers, but tend to perform only some of those functions carried out by trade unions. These might include consultation and bargaining with management. Their members are often made up of workers in a particular business. Examples of staff associations are the Retail Book, Stationery and Allied Trades Employees Association (RBA) or the Balfour Beatty Group Staff Association. In some cases staff associations develop into trade unions. Some associations are affiliated to the TUC, such as the Gallaher Sales Staff Association.

Professional associations

Professional associations perform similar functions to trade unions and sometimes become TUC members. They represent 'professional' occupations. Examples include the British Dental Association, the Prison Officers Association and the Professional Footballers' Association. Some associations, such as the British Medical Association (BMA), represent their members in collective bargaining with employers. They are also responsible for the setting and maintaining of standards. For example, the BMA insists on certain qualifications before admitting employees to its membership. For this reason professional associations tend to be associated with 'white-collar' workers and higher paid groups of employees.

Worker directors

Worker directors are sometimes found in the UK, but are more common in countries such as Germany. One or more directors of the company are elected from the workforce. They are on the Board of Directors to represent the interests of workers as stakeholders in the company. They don't necessarily increase employee participation in practice. Sometimes the worker directors are 'captured' by the rest of the Board and act as if they were representing the interests of shareholders rather than the employees. In other situations, the rest of the Board of Directors find ways of minimising the influence of the worker directors. They might starve the worker directors of information about what is going on in the company. They might simply outvote them on any key issue where the interests of workers and shareholders don't coincide. Ordinary workers are then likely to see worker directors as of marginal importance in helping them to influence what is happening in the company.

Workers' co-operatives

In a workers' co-operative, the business is owned by some or all of the employees of the business. The workers elect some of their number to the Board of the company. Important decisions are also taken at regular, often monthly, meetings of all the worker-owners. In the UK, workers' co-operatives have tended to be rare.

Employee shareholders

Employee shareholders are workers in a business who own shares issued by the business. In the 1970s and 1980s, some argued that conflict between workers and management and the 'them and us' attitude which was common in British manufacturing industry could be resolved if workers were also owners of their business. Workers would then see that going on strike, demanding high wage increases or sharply improved working conditions was against their interests as owners. The higher the cost of employing labour, the less profit the business would make. This would reduce dividends and the share price, hurting those workers who were also shareholders. A number of large companies created schemes where employees could buy shares in the company for which they worked. It has been argued that too few workers took advantage of these schemes to make any significant impact on employee participation or motivation. Moreover, workers that did buy shares often bought too few for them to significantly affect business decisions.

In the 1990s, the argument and the schemes offered changed. It became fashionable to argue that **share option schemes** were the way forward. These were typically only available to senior management. Senior managers were offered packages where they could buy shares at some date in the future at a very low price if they met performance targets, such as future share prices, sales or profits. For example, a chief executive might be given the right to buy 1 million shares at 200p each in three years' time. If the current share price is 220p, then the chief executive will have a significant incentive to direct the company in a way which will see its share price grow over three years. If the share price in three years' time were 300p, this is good for shareholders who have seen a 36 per cent increase in their share price. The reward to the chief executive is to be able to buy the shares in three

Question 2.

Suma is a multimillion pound company, supplying 2,500 customers across the UK and abroad. It has 100 employees and is the largest independent wholesaler in the health food and wholefood trade in the UK. Founded in the 1970s as a workers co-operative, it is owned by its member workers. They run the business in a democratic way.

The 'boss' of the firm is the General Meeting of members. This takes place six times a year. The General Meeting agrees strategies, business plans and major policy decisions. Any member can make proposals to the General Meeting and if passed they are mandatory on all workers. The General Meeting elects six of its number to the Management Committee which meets weekly to implement the Business Plan and other GM decisions. The Management Committee in turn appoints company officers: Personnel, Operations, Finance and Function Area co-ordinators.

The Management Committee monitors the implementation of the Business Plan by the Function Areas. Weekly Business Information covering finances, quality of services and labour productivity indicators are reported to the Management Committee by company officers. The Management Committee then issues Action Points when what is actually happening on the ground differs from what is laid out in the Business Plan.

Working at Suma is quite unlike other businesses. Workers must be more self-motivated and take more initiative. Suma departmental co-ordinators do not have an overseer role in the normal sense. Workers support each other to fulfil daily tasks and get home on time. Working as an effective member of a co-operative, not just doing the daily tasks but taking part in the management of the business, is a new skill which all new members have to learn, whether they have been shop floor or management previously. The business can only succeed when all members share this responsibility.

All Suma workers are paid the same daily wage plus allowances and overtime or time off in lieu. It is a good wage for manual warehouse workers and the extra reflects the collective management element of the jobs. In return for the better than average wages, Suma expects much more commitment from its employees. When the need arises, when customer orders are waiting, employees are expected to

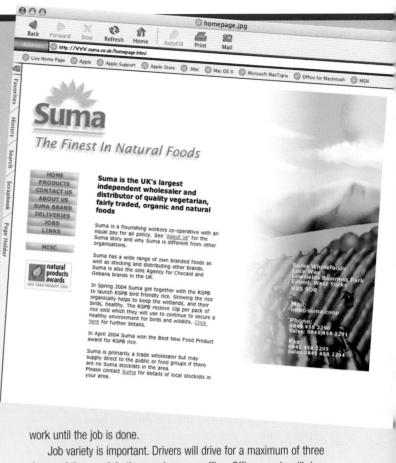

work until the job is done.

Job variety is important. Drivers will drive for a maximum of three days and then work in the warehouse or office. Office people will do manual work for at least one day a week. Most members will have done a far wider range of jobs and taken on greater responsibilities within Suma than equivalent workers in other businesses. Suma encourages members to take up training and courses to bring in new skills.

Source: adapted from About Us, Suma, www.suma.co.uk.

(a) **Explain why employee representation can be said to exist at Suma.**

(b) **Discuss the possible advantages and disadvantages to Suma of employee representation.**

---

years' time at 200p and sell them immediately for 300p, making 100p profit each on 1 million shares, i.e. a profit of £1 million.

Share option schemes are a form of payment by results. They are based on F W Taylor's view that money is the key way to motivate workers. They have also been justified on the grounds that, when there is a vacancy, the best senior workers will not be attracted to the company if it doesn't offer generous share option schemes. However, they have been controversial in recent years. This is because schemes have benefited senior employees even when the performance of the company has been poor. Senior executives who have been sacked for poor performance have sometimes been able to exercise their share options on leaving, giving them large sums of money. It can also be argued that share option schemes are a way for senior employees to gain at the expense of other shareholders. If senior employees would have worked just as hard anyway, offering them extra in the

form of share options merely reduces the amount available to shareholders. Further, it could be argued that share ownership may only be really motivating in smaller companies. Buying a relatively small number of shares could mean that employees own a reasonable proportion of the business and can affect its decision making.

The advantages and disadvantages of employee representation

Advantages Employee representation can have certain advantages for employees. There may also be advantages for employers.

- Representation can lead to workers achieving higher rewards or better work conditions, for example, if a strong union of employee association supports their claims for higher wages.

- If workers feel their views are being represented to employers, and employers are paying attention to them, they may feel more valued. This in turn leads to greater motivation for employees. Employers may benefit from higher output as a result It can also lead to benefits such as lower absenteeism and lower turnover of staff.

- Representation can lead to a greater use of the ideas of the workforce. Employee representation can increase the ability of employees to contribute effectively to the business. It encourages a greater interchange of information and ideas within a business. With more information and ideas, it may be easier to make the correct decision on any issue. For example, employees may be able to assess changes in the workplace more easily than employers who are not directly involve dint he day to day operation of certain aspects of the business.

- Employers may be more sympathetic to the needs of employees. This may help when making decisions. For example, it may put them in a better position to decide if changes are going to cause disruption or unrest.

- It can help a business to develop a common culture and allow a business to achieve its objectives.

Disadvantages Employee participation can also have its disadvantages for both employees and employers.

- The decision making process can be slowed down. If employee's views are constantly being taken into account, it may take several times as long to come up with a decision compared to employers simply making a decision that best suits their needs. This is particularly important at times of crisis when decisions have to be made quickly or even instantly.

- it can be expensive and time consuming. There may be constant meetings with employee representatives. Employees may need to be given time off for union training or meetings, which can delay production.

- It may lead to conflict. Employees represented by a strong organisation at work are likely to have more influence than individual workers. Employers' objectives and those of employees may differ. This could lead to industrial action.

- Some employees will pursue their own interests at the expense of the interests of the business when given the opportunity. Employee respresentation can give them more opportunity to do this.

- Employee representation may encourage workers to believe they have more power than they actually have. This may lead to demotivation when they feel that their advice is not being acted upon.

KEYTERMS

Employee – a worker hired to work for a business or other organisation.

Employers – businesses or other organisations which hire workers to work for them.

Employee representation – the 'standing in' for employees and speaking with authority on their behalf.

European Works Councils – bodies which consist of selected managers and elected representatives of workers which meet to discuss issues such as conditions of work, health and safety, training, investment, redundancies and site closures; under the EU Information and Consultation Directive, any business with at least 1 000 employees and at least 150 employees located in two or more EU countries has to have a European Works Council.

Industrial democracy – where workers are given the right to elect representatives who will be directly involved in the internal decision making of a business, including the highest levels of the business.

No strike agreement – an agreement between unions and an employer that industrial disputes will not lead to any form of strike action by employees.

Single union agreement – an agreement between an employer and a trade union that only that trade union will be recognised for collective bargaining purposes; it effectively means that other trade unions cannot organise in that business and the business only has to negotiate with one union.

Trade unions – organisation of workers which exist to promote the interests of their members.

Industrial relations – the relationship between employers and employees, particularly groups of workers represented by a union.

Union density – the percentage of any given workforce that belongs to a trade union.

KNOWLEDGE

1. What is the difference between an employee and an employer?
2. State three objectives of trade unions.
3. State three functions of trade unions.
4. Explain two ways in which changes in union density have affected employee presentation.
5. How did the Industrial Relations Act, 1999 affect employee representation?
6. What is the difference between an ordinary company and a worker co-operative?
7. What is a worker director?
8. How might a European works council benefit employees?
9. Why might employee shareholding benefit employees in a small company?
10. State three advantages of employee representation.
11. State three disadvantages of employee representation.

Case Study: *Ryanair*

Ryanair is a fast-growing Irish airline company. It has based its success on offering low fares for a basic service. Costs compared to a traditional airline are low per passenger mile travelled and food, for example, is not offered for free on any flight.

The company has had a difficult relationship with trade unions. Its policy is not to recognise trade unions. Instead, it prefers to bargain with individual employees, or use the Employee Representative Committees it has established to communicate with workers. It has gained a reputation for dealing aggressively with trade unions that attempt either to gain recognition or influence the activities of the company. It has also been argued that individual employees who attempt to organise collectively are dealt with in a punitive manner.

For example, in January 2005, The Irish Airline Pilots Union (IALPA) argued successfully before the Labour Court in Ireland that Ryanair pilots should be given a copy of their Terms and Conditions of Employment. This ruling also meant that a complaint of victimisation in the workplace could be heard by an Irish Rights Commissioner. The complaints centred around training for flying new aircraft. Pilots had been informed by Ryanair that if they joined a trade union over the next five years they would have to commit to paying a bond of €15 000 (£10 000) for training to fly the new aircraft which is being introduced into the Ryanair fleet. If they did not undertake the training, the pilots were told they faced redundancy when the older aircraft were phased out. Others reported threats including no pay increases, no promotions, cancellation of staff travel and increased restrictions on taking holidays.

'Ryan be fair', a website critical of Ryanair employment practices, also claimed in 2004 that Ryanair was recruiting in Eastern Europe to cut wages. It said that an 'English language school' had been established in Poland where participants paid €1,900 (£1 200) for a place on a course. Some of the participants were then offered a three year employment contract with a firm called 'Crewlink', which in turn leased out the workers to Ryanair. They received two-thirds of the pay of normal European Ryanair cabin crew staff.

Ryanair claims that its average wages per employee are higher than comparable unionised airlines. In September 2004, for example, it claimed that its staff earned an average of €50,582 a year, compared to the heavily unionised Scandinavian airline SAS which paid €50,425. Trade unions pointed out that Ryanair tends to contract out a number of services which use a high proportion of low-paid workers compared to normal airlines. Not directly employing the same proportion of relatively lowly-paid ground staff would automatically boost the average wage at Ryanair.

Ryanair also claims that its employment practices have benefited customers through lower prices. Speaking about a dispute with Siptu, an Irish trade union representing baggage handlers at Dublin Airport, Michael O'Leary, Chief Executive of Ryanair, said 'Siptu is the union that was quite happy to have £200 airfares and a monopoly (of airline flights) in and out of Ireland'. Driving down costs is central to the Ryanair strategy of competing against other low-cost airlines. The 21 per cent increase in productivity achieved by staff in 2003 compared to the 3 per cent pay increase they received was one part of this relentless drive to cut costs.

Sources: adapted from www.ryan-be-fair.org, Airwise News, 6.9.2004.

(a) Analyse two possible objectives of trade unions dealing with Ryanair. (8 marks)

(b) To what extent should trade unions involved with Ryanair consider the interests of passengers? (12 marks)

(b) Discuss whether Ryanair's anti-union stance is beneficial to the stakeholders of the company. (20 marks)

Employer-employee relations

Employers and employees are in a relationship together. Employers hire workers because they need their time, skills and talents to produce goods and services. Employees take on jobs for a variety of motives including pay, fringe benefits and job satisfaction. Employers and employees therefore have different needs from the relationship that exists between them. EMPLOYER-EMPLOYEE RELATIONS is the way in which employers and employees interact on key issues such as pay, conditions of work, output and productivity.

The different needs of employers and employees means that sometimes they are in **conflict** with each other. Conflict between these two groups may result from a number of factors.

- Rates of pay. Employers could attempt to keep wage costs down to remain competitive, whereas unions could try to maximise employees' rewards.
- The introduction of machinery. For example, a business may want to introduce machinery which requires workers to learn new production techniques. Employees, however, may feel that this extra responsibility is an unwanted burden.
- Flexible working. Businesses often require a more flexible workforce. A printing works might decide to operate a 24 hour shift, for example, to cope with extra work. Employees may be unwilling to work at night.
- Work conditions. Workers may feel that better canteen facilities are needed, but employers could see this as an unnecessary increase in costs.

The aim of industrial relations procedures is to make sure that each party finds an acceptable solution to any conflict that may exist. Successful industrial relations should prevent the need for industrial action by employers' or employees' groups.

Industrial action

Today, most conflict within the workplace is usually resolved through negotiation. However, during an INDUSTRIAL DISPUTE, both workers and management can resort to INDUSTRIAL ACTION. This is direct action aimed at putting pressure on the other side to give in to their demands. There is a variety of forms of industrial action that employees can take.

Strikes Strikes are when workers withdraw their labour and don't go to work. Strikes can be costly to employees because they lose pay when they are on strike. For employers, the damage is the lost output and the disruption to work.

Prolonged, **all-out strikes**, when all workers go out on strike for an indefinite period, are rare. Strikes tend to be **selective strikes**, where employees aim to cause maximum disruption at minimum cost to themselves. For example, there might be a one-day strike. In an industry like the rail industry, this can cause severe disruption. Or a particular group of key workers might be brought out on strike which brings all work to a halt. **Picketing** often takes place during a strike. Workers on strike will stand or picket outside their place of work in the hope of persuading other workers to not cross the picket line and therefore not to work. Equally pickets hope to discourage customers and suppliers from going into the premises to deliver supplies.

Strikes can also be **official** or **unofficial**. Official strikes are where a union officially supports its members in accordance with union rules during a dispute after a ballot for action has been carried out and agreed by union members. Unofficial strikes have no union backing or support. They have, in the past, been called by shop stewards in particular factories, often in response to a particular incident. Such strikes are likely to be short term, local, unpredictable and disruptive for a business.

There is no single reason that explains the trend in stoppages in the UK. A study of strikes in Britain over an extensive time period was carried out by researchers for the government. They discovered that:

- strikes appear to be over major issues;
- strikes are concentrated in a very small proportion of plants – often the larger ones in certain industries and in certain areas of the country;
- industries and regions that have large factories, on average, tend to experience relatively high numbers of strikes. These strikes occur fairly often.

Overtime ban This is when workers refuse to work more than the basic working hours laid down in their contract of work. Overtime bans are particularly effective in industries where overtime is routine, or at times of the year when orders are abnormally high. For example, unions in the airline industry often choose the summer or bank holiday weekends to organise overtime bans or selective strikes in pursuit of a claim.

Go slow or work to rule A **go-slow** is when workers deliberately reduce their work rate to reduce output. A **work to rule** has the same effect. Working in exact conformity to the rules and procedures laid down by employers can reduce productivity because rules and procedures may not have been updated. Both of these actions can affect the profitability of the employer.

Sit-ins and work-ins A SIT-IN or WORK-IN involves a mass occupation of premises by workers. A work-in is where employees continue production with the aim of demonstrating that the factory is a viable concern. It is sometimes used when there is a threat of closure. In a sit-in, production does not continue. The aim is to protest against management decisions and, in the case of factory closure, prevent the transfer of machinery to other factories. A **redundancy sit-in** or work-in is a protest against the closure of a plant or company. A **collective bargaining sit-in** may be used instead of other forms of industrial action such as working to rule, overtime bans and all out strikes, to give employees a position of strength in negotiations.

Sit-ins and work-ins mean the illegal occupation of premises by workers. They also allow workers to gain control over the factory. Why are these tactics used? First, they offer some degree of control over the factory or plant being occupied, which is obviously important in redundancy situations where the removal of plant and machinery to other locations is being threatened. Also by working-in or sitting-in, employees are better able to maintain their group solidarity.

Employers too can take their own forms of industrial action.

Lock-out This occurs when employers don't allow their workers into work and don't pay them either. By stopping pay, employers hope to put pressure on employees to concede to employers' demands.

Withdrawal of overtime or benefits Employers may threaten to withdraw overtime. Alternatively, they may threaten to or actually withdraw benefits given to workers which are not part of their contract of employment, such as non-guaranteed overtime payments or membership of clubs.

Redundancy and dismissal An employer may make employees taking industrial action redundant or may dismiss workers. Employees who feel that they are unfairly dismissed may take their case to an employment tribunal.

Hiring workers If unions take action to withdraw their labour, employers sometimes recruit outside workers or contractors to do their jobs. It has also been suggested that some employers hire 'union busters' to intimidate workers to stop unions winning strike ballots.

Problems of industrial action

There are certain problems which result from industrial action, both for employers and employees.

Employers' problems
- Industrial action can lead to lost production for the business. A go-slow or work to rule may reduce output. Strike action could mean that orders are unfulfilled and revenue and profits could fall.
- If industrial action results in production being stopped, then machinery and other resources will be lying idle. A business will have many fixed costs which have to be covered, even if production is not taking place. If output ceases, revenue will not be earned to pay for these costs.

- Industrial action may lead to poor future relationships in a business. Sometimes grievances can carry on after a dispute. This could result in poor motivation and communication.
- Industrial disputes divert managers' attention away from planning. If a business is concerned with solving a dispute that exists now, it may neglect plans for the future.
- Loss of output and delays in production or deliveries caused by action can harm the firm's reputation. This may lead to lost business in future.

Employees' problems
- A work to rule, go-slow or strike can lead to a reduction or a loss of earnings.

Question 1.

In January 2005, firefighters at Glasgow Airport went on indefinite strike and began picketing the airport. The dispute centred around plans by their employer, the British Airports Authority (BAA), to change the way in which fire safety was organised. Up to this point, the 59 firefighters at the airport were responsible both for fire safety on the runways and land of the airport, but also for the airport terminal building. To deal with the airport building, the firefighters had a fire engine crewed by four people fully equipped for firefighting and rescue duties. BAA proposed to transfer responsibility for the terminal building to Strathclyde Fire Service, the fire service provided by the local authority. Staffing levels at the terminal would be reduced to a two person fire safety team which would not be equipped with protective clothing or equipment to carry out any firefighting duties.

The Transport and General Workers' Union (T&G) said the changes would put airport staff and passengers at risk. The response times to any incident in the terminal would increase from two minutes to fourteen minutes.

BAA stated that safety would not be compromised by the changes. It suggested that the main concern of the firefighters was not safety but a loss of 'traditionally high levels' of expensive overtime that would result from the changes. It also said that the fire engine at the centre of the dispute was brought in as an extra precaution during refurbishment in the 1990s when parts of the airport were effectively a building site.

A month after the strike began, the 59 firefighters accepted a compromise solution. The new arrangements would go ahead but eight specialist officers would be recruited to improve fire safety at the terminal. The firefighters would also receive a one-off payment of £1 500 for accepting the changes.

Source: adapted from BBC News World Edition 29.1.2005 and 27.2.2005; Socialist Worker Online, 5.2.2005.

(a) Suggest what the Glasgow firefighters hoped to achieve by going out on strike.
(b) To what extent did the firefighters achieve their possible objectives when the dispute was resolved?

Prolonged industrial action may, in some cases, lead to the closure of the business. Employees would then be made redundant.

- Action is likely to place stress on the workforce. It can also cause friction between levels of the hierarchy. For example, managers on the other 'side' in a dispute are unlikely to find their employees motivated.
- If action is unsuccessful, the employees' position may be weaker in future. Members may also leave a union if they feel that it is unable to support their interests.
- Public support may suffer if the action affects people's everyday lives.
- Strike action must conform to current legislation or unions may be liable for damages and employees may be disciplined or dismissed.

Benefits of industrial action

Industrial action is often used as a 'final' measure by unions and employers because of the disruption it causes. There are, however, some benefits for both groups.

- It 'clears the air'. Employers and employees may have grievances. Industrial action can bring these out into the open and, once the dispute is solved, this could improve the 'atmosphere' in the business.
- Introducing new rules. How groups operate in businesses is influenced by rules, such as rates of pay or what is meant by unfair dismissal. Conflict is often about disagreement over these rules. When industrial action has been resolved, this often leads to new rules which each group agrees upon.
- Changing management goals. Management often change their goals and the ways they are achieved after industrial action. For example, a business may have attempted to introduce new working practices without consulting unions, which led to industrial action. In future it may consult with unions before changing work practices.
- Understanding the position of each group. Industrial action often makes the position of employers and employees very clear. It allows each group to hear the grievances of the other, consider them and decide to what extent they agree.

Collective bargaining

In many places of work, employees choose to join trade unions or other representative organisations, such as a professional association. These organisations negotiate on behalf of their members with employers. This is known as COLLECTIVE BARGAINING. It is collective because employees join together to represent themselves when dealing with their employers.

Collective bargaining can take place at many levels. In a large business or organisation, bargaining can take place:

- covering one type of worker across all places of work in the country, so, for example, the National Health Service might set the pay rates of all nurses or doctors in England and Wales;
- region by region, so London workers of a business might negotiate separately from those in Scotland;
- plant by plant, where a 'plant' is any place of work, so a factory or office in the South East might have separate pay negotiations to another factory or office in Wales owned by the same business;
- by type of worker, so office workers might negotiate a completely separate agreement to factory workers in a manufacturing company and negotiations can take place at national, regional or local level.

Collective bargaining can also take place between trade unions and a number of different businesses typically in the same industry. So, in the engineering industry there might be a minimum level of pay negotiated between the representatives of engineering employers and the trade unions of engineering workers.

Collective bargaining leads to COLLECTIVE AGREEMENTS. These are agreements signed by all parties involved in the collective bargaining on both the employers' and employees' sides. There are two types of collective agreement.

- **Substantive agreements** cover issues such as pay and conditions of work.
- **Procedural agreements** cover how bargaining should take

Table 1 Advantages and disadvantages of collective bargaining

Advantages

Employees Trade unions argue that collective bargaining gives workers the power to gain the pay and employment rights which they deserve. Economic theory suggests that collective bargaining gives workers some monopoly power in the workplace. In many cases, this forces employers to pay higher wages and give better working conditions to employees than they would do if there was individual bargaining. When collective bargaining takes place, national rates are often agreed with employers. Once an agreement is reached, all members of the trade union will be paid the agreed rate.

Employers Collective bargaining can reduce the cost of bargaining with employees. Instead of having to negotiate with workers on an individual basis, a business can negotiate a settlement for all workers which will be accepted by these workers.

Disadvantages

Employees Many businesses which don't have collective bargaining agreements with their workers simply impose pay settlements on them without consultation. No individual bargaining takes place and therefore there are no costs attached to individual bargaining.

Employers Collective bargaining may encourage militancy amongst workers because as a group they feel they have more power.

place on issues such as pay, recruitment, dismissal, redundancy and promotion.

Collective bargaining differs from JOINT CONSULTATION. Collective bargaining is about making decisions. Joint consultation is about informing either management or workers about issues and discussing possible courses of action. In a small business, consultation is likely to be an informal chat about what is going on and how things may change in the future between the boss and individual workers. In a large business, there may be regular consultative meetings between management and workers. Under EU law, consultation must take place in certain circumstances. Under the Social Chapter of the Treaty of Maastricht, which the UK signed into law in 1998, multinational companies within the EU must have **European works councils**. These must be consulted on issues such as redundancies or restructuring of work. Under the **Employment Relations Act, 1999**, businesses with union recognition must invite unions to meetings to consult on training policies.

There was a shift away from collective bargaining in the 1980s and early 1990s. Partly this was due to legislation which removed power from trade unions and encouraged employers to adopt individual bargaining procedures. Partly it was caused by a major shift of employment from primary and manufacturing industry, which was heavily unionised, to private sector service industry where trade unions were poorly represented. In 1984, 71 per cent of workers were covered by collective agreements. By 1996, this was down to 36 per cent, approximately the same as in 2004.

Individual bargaining

INDIVIDUAL BARGAINING occurs when employees negotiate on their own with their employee without the support of a trade union or other association. This bargaining may cover pay, conditions of work or performance levels. Many businesses in the UK in the early twenty-first century did not engage in collective bargaining with trade unions and many employees did not belong to a trade union. So individual bargaining tended to be more common than collective bargaining. This was especially true in private sector businesses since a much larger percentage of workers in the public sector belonged to trade unions than in the private sector.

Individual bargaining in practice differs widely from business to business.

- In small businesses, there is unlikely to be any formal bargaining process. In many small businesses, employees will simply accept the pay and conditions set down by the owner manager. In others, there will be informal negotiations from time to time.
- In medium to large sized businesses, there are likely to be more formal processes for bargaining. There might, for example, be annual pay reviews. There might be a clearly defined pay structure where each job is put into a particular category. Within this, however, there might be a range of pay for each job. Individuals might have to negotiate to get higher in the range, or to be promoted. In

---

Question 2.

According to the GMB trade union, Asda the supermarket chain has withdrawn a 10 per cent pay offer to more than 700 workers at a goods distribution centre in the north-east of England. Asda said it had put forward a package of changes to workers' terms and conditions covering areas such as overtime, holiday and premium rates, with savings being used to increase basic pay. The changes would also have seen a move away from collective bargaining to settle pay negotiations to individual bargaining. However, when balloted, the workforce had rejected the package.

Asda has two depots in Washington, Tyne and Wear, one which it has always owned and the one at the centre of the dispute, which it bought several years ago. The two depots have different terms and conditions and the dispute is understood to have arisen from efforts to put both on a similar footing.

Labour relations are a sensitive area for Asda. Its US parent, Wal-Mart, has a reputation of being staunchly anti-union. Earlier this week, Wal-Mart said it was closing a store in Canada just six months after workers there won the right to join a union.

Source: adapted from *The Guardian*, 12.2.2005.

(a) Explain what it would have meant for the workers at the Asda depot in Tyne and Wear to have moved from collective bargaining to individual bargaining.

(b) What might be the advantages and disadvantages to (a) Asda and (b) the depot workers to have changed to an individual bargaining system?

Table 2 Advantages and disadvantages of individual bargaining

Advantages

Individual bargaining in theory allows an employer to pay workers exactly the amount that is needed to motivate and retain them. Wages costs are kept to a minimum whilst wages are used to maximise motivation and productivity. This might work well with high paid white-collar workers, where it is cost effective to negotiate a salary level each year.

Disadvantages

In most businesses where there is no collective bargaining, most workers tend to be put on a grade or level and paid the same as workers on the same grade. There might be bonuses linked to performance reviews. But it can be argued that these often fail to motivate workers in the way intended. Individual bargaining, where different workers are paid different rates for the job, can demotivate workers who are paid worse. Although their employer might argue that they don't perform as well, these workers may see the system as 'unfair'. According to Maslow's theory, this threatens both their safety needs and their esteem needs.

many large businesses, some employees will be on performance related pay (PRP) schemes. With PRP, there is typically an annual review of performance where individual employees have to show that their performance during the year justifies a particular level of pay or the award of a bonus.

- Individual one-to-one bargaining is more likely to take place the more senior or more highly paid the employee. Individual bargaining will certainly take place between the Chief Executive Officer (CEO) of a large company and the board directors responsible for pay. The workers who clean the CEO's office at the end of the day will simply be told what the rate of pay is for the job. If the cleaners don't like the pay and conditions, then their only option is to find another job.

Conciliation and arbitration

Direct negotiations between workers and management result in a resolution of industrial issues in almost all cases. In a few cases, however, negotiations break down. Both sides refuse to move from their positions. Two ways of then resolving the dispute are CONCILIATION and ARBITRATION.

Conciliation Conciliation occurs when both sides to a dispute agree to invite an independent third party to help them resolve the conflict. The conciliator's role is not to make any judgment about who is right or wrong. The conciliator is there to find ways of getting both sides to talk to each other and explore new ways of resolving the dispute.

Arbitration With arbitration, both sides agree to the appointing of an arbitrator. The arbitrator will listen to both sides and then make a judgment about how the dispute should be resolved. In most cases, the arbitration ruling is non-binding (i.e. it is not legally binding) but it is rarely ignored. There is a strong moral pressure to accept the arbitration ruling even if it goes against you. In a few cases, both parties agree to binding arbitration where the ruling is legally binding.

Conciliation and arbitration services are offered by a number of organisations. However, in 1974, the government set up the Advisory, Conciliation and Arbitration Service (ACAS) specifically to offer such services. In addition, ACAS today offers a variety of other services.

- It gives advice to employers and employers' associations and to trade unions on a wide range of personnel issues such as the application of legislation, payment systems and contracts of employment.
- It sometimes conducts enquiries into personnel issues such as handling redundancies or the flexible use of labour. These enquiries help inform ACAS of good and bad practice and help it to write advisory booklets on key issues.
- It issues codes of practice on industrial relations which outline good practice in this area.

- A growing workload for ACAS has been the investigation of individual cases of unfair dismissal and unfair discrimination. Today, it investigates around 100 000 such cases per year.
- It attempts to conciliate in cases before they reach a hearing at an employment tribunal. The **Employment Rights (Dispute Resolution) Act, 1998** set up an arbitration scheme for alternative dispute resolution (ADR). It aims to find solutions to disputes which do not involve court action. It has been relatively successful in this. For example, in 2003 only around 20 per cent of cases went further than this arbitration stage.

The role of ACAS

Sometimes parties fail to reach agreements after consultation and negotiation. In these situations the Advisory, Conciliation and Arbitration Service (ACAS) can be of great value to both sides.

During the period of industrial action in the 1970s, groups of employers and employees called for the setting up of a conciliation and arbitration service, independent of government control and of civil service influence. The result was ACAS, which took up its formal duties in September 1974. ACAS is a public body funded by tax, with around 730 staff employed in 11 regional centres and a head office in London. It has a chair, a chief executive and a council made up of 11 other members, ranging from union members to academics. Its main role is to prevent and resolve problems in the workplace. It provides a wide range of services to employers and employees in business.

Resolving industrial disputes ACAS has conciliation and arbitration duties. It can intervene in industrial disputes at the request of either management or unions. Its role is to try and encourage a settlement that all parties may agree to, using procedures that both parties accept. Alternatively it can act as an abitrator.

Advisory work ACAS carries out advisory work with employers, trade unions and employers' associations. This can be short visits to answer specific questions or long-term, in-depth, projects and surveys. The questions ACAS deal with are wide ranging and can include issues such as contracts of employment, industrial relations legislation, payment systems and personnel policies.

Codes of practice ACAS issues codes of practice. These contain practical guidance on how to improve industrial relations between employers and employees.

Enquiries ACAS has carried out enquiries into the flexible use of labour, appraisal systems, labour turnover, employee involvement, handling redundancy and the use of quality circles. Much of this research is published by ACAS as advisory booklets. Employers use them to help improve industrial

Question 3.

In January 2005, WM Morrison, the supermarket group, was pressed into rewriting a recognition agreement with the Transport & General Workers Union (T&G). The issue started in January 2004 when 87 per cent of the 1 600 T&G members working at two distribution centres at Wakefield and Northwich rejected a pay offer. Under the terms of the existing agreement, Morrisons had the right to refer any dispute to binding arbitration, where both sides were bound to accept the results of arbitration. Morrisons duly referred this dispute to arbitration. The arbiter confirmed the offer that Morrisons had originally made, much to the disappointment of the T&G.

The T&G responded by attempting to renegotiate the recognition agreement to remove the binding arbitration clause. Morrisons refused. Then the company invited other trade unions to 'bid' for T&G members. This meant asking other trade unions to enter negotiations with Morrisons with a view to changing the union to which existing T&G members belonged. Not surprisingly, the T&G were outraged by such action and in June 2004 conducted a ballot of the 1 600 members for strike action. Over 90 per cent of members supported full strike action.

With the strike ballot result in their pocket, the T&G returned to the negotiating table with Morrisons. In November 2004, the company agreed to remove the binding arbitration clause. It also offered substantial pay increases to the workers. Some drivers received as much as a 15 per cent pay increase taking their pay to £8.33 an hour.

The T&G said that it was very pleased with the outcome. It would

now target the 400 non T&G workers at the two sites and hopefully persuade them to join the union. The aim was to get 100 per cent membership of the T&G in the workforce.

Source: adapted from Timesonline, 12.1. 2005, Personnel Today, 12.1.2005, T&G News, January/February 2005.

(a) **Suggest why binding arbitration was unpopular with T&G members at the two Morrisons distribution depots.**

(b) **What might have been the advantages to Morrisons of getting another trade union to 'take over' T&G members at the two sites?**

(c) **Discuss whether binding arbitration would always have acted against the interests of the union members at Morrisons.**

---

relations and personnel management practices.

Individual cases ACAS investigates individual cases of unfair discrimination and unfair dismissal.

Tribunals Employment tribunals hear a wide range of employment disputes, including unfair dismissal and discrimination. ACAS operates independently from the tribunals. Its role is to offer conciliation on disputes, with the aim of settling the matter without a tribunal hearing. This is known as alternative dispute resolution (ADR). The **Employment Rights (Dispute Resolution) Act, 1998** set up an ACAS arbitration scheme designed to find other methods than the courts for solving disputes.

ACAS has developed its services to meet the needs of a changing industrial relations climate. While the bulk of its work continues to be conciliation, mediation and arbitration, it has steadily developed advisory and training services. ACAS has also become more involved in helping business to improve personnel and management practices. These include:
- effective recruitment and selection of employees;
- setting up and operating equal opportunities policies;
- improving communications and joint consultation;
- developing the skills of managers to help them introduce changes in work organisation.

The role of the Central Arbitration Committee

The **Employment Relations Act, 1998** set out a process for unions to be recognised automatically or where a majority of workers voted for it. The Central Arbitration Committee (CAC) is a permanent independent body responsible for union recognition. It has a number of functions.
- It judges applications relating to the statutory recognition and derecognition of trade unions when recognition or derecognition cannot be agreed voluntarily.
- It helps to determine disputes between trade unions and

KNOWLEDGE

1. What factors may lead to conflict between employers and employees?
2. What types of industrial action can employees take to further their interests in industrial disputes?
3. Why is collective bargaining important to employees?
4. What are the benefits of collective bargaining for (i) employees and (ii) employers?
5. What is the difference between collective bargaining and individual bargaining?
6. Explain the difference between arbitration and conciliation.
7. State five services provided by ACAS.
8. What is the main role of the Central Arbitration Committee?

employers over the disclosure of information for collective bargaining.
- It handles claims and complaints regarding the establishment and operation of European works councils in Great Britain.
- It provides voluntary arbitration in industrial disputes.

In the case of union recognition, the CAC would first encourage parties to settle the matter themselves. If this failed, it could award recognition or the union could hold a ballot. The CAC has the power to instruct the employer to co-operate with the ballot or risk a fine.

KEYTERMS

ACAS – a body which mediates where conflict exists in business.

Arbitration – where both sides in a dispute agree to an independent party making a judgment about how a dispute should be resolved. In some cases this judgment can be legally binding.

CAC – the government body responsible for union recognition.

Collective agreement – an agreement reached through the process of collective bargaining.

Collective bargaining – a method of determining conditions of work and terms of employment through negotiations between employers and employee representatives.

representatives before a decision is taken.

Conciliation – where both sides in a dispute agree to an independent party helping to find a solution.

Employer-employee relations - the way in which employers and employees interact on key issues such as pay, conditions of work, output and productivity.

Individual bargaining – when an individual worker negotiates over pay and other conditions of work with his or her employer without the help of a collective group such as a trade union.

Industrial action – direct action, such as strikes or lock-outs, taken by employees or employers in the course of an industrial dispute to put pressure on the other side to agree to their demands.

Industrial dispute – a disagreement between employees and their employer over an issue such as pay or redundancy which has not been resolved through negotiation or other means.

Joint consultation – informing management or workers about issues and discussing possible actions.

Sit-in/Work-in – the illegal occupation of premises by workers, which allows workers to gain control of the factory.

Case Study: *Proposed industrial action at British Airways*

In January 2007 British Airways (BA) called for talks at Acas, the conciliation service, in an effort to avoid strike action by its cabin staff. A spokesperson for the Transport and General Workers Union (T&G), which represented about 11,000 of BA's 14,000 crew at the time, said the call for intervention was 'premature' and the union wanted 'to get the issues resolved directly in bilateral talks'. The T&G announced that cabin crew would carry out three 72-hour strikes, from Monday to Wednesday in the following three weeks. BA cabin crew had voted overwhelmingly in favour of strike action over a series of issues, including the airline's management of sickness absence, differential pay scales and the reduction of pensions' benefits.

In a move described by the T&G as 'provocative', BA released information in a letter sent by David Lebrecht, BA's head of employee relations and chief negotiator, to Jack Dromey, T&G deputy general secretary. It claimed that meeting the union's demands would add £37 million to its annual costs. It would also raise the earnings of the best paid cabin crew by 18 per cent to more than £30,000 a year.

BA said that a new sickness management policy, accepted in a deal with cabin crew in October 2005, had cut sickness absence by cabin staff from 22 to 12 days per employee. In the letter Mr Lebrecht said that the union was trying to remove certain conditions from the absence policy including 'colds, blocked ears, diarrhoea and vomiting,

visible injuries, conjunctivitis, cold sores, loss of voice, one-off life events and operations.'

Amicus, which represented engineering employees and cabin crew at BA, announced that it would recommend planned reforms of BA's main pension scheme. Brian Boyd, Amicus national officer, said that 'under the current circumstances' the union had negotiated 'the best possible benefits package'. Amicus intended to hold a ballot of its 6,200 members.

In spite of appearing to reach a common position to recommend the pensions deal earlier in the month, BA's four unions were split over the issue. Amicus and Balpa, the pilots union, recommended the deal in ballots. The GMB, which represents check-in staff, was calling for a ballot for strike action. The T&G, with more than 20,000 members, abstained in the decision to recommend the pensions deal. The T&G's position was made difficult by the cabin crew dispute, with crew unhappy about the planned increase in the retirement age from 55 to 65.

Source: adapted from *The Financial Times*, 21.1. 2007.

(a) Examine the reasons why employees and employers at British Airways might want to avoid strike action. (10 marks)

(b) Evaluate whether the resolution to the dispute might be achieved more effectively through the involvement of Acas or through bilateral talks. (20 marks)

Stakeholder perspectives

Businesses vary from very simple organisations where there is only one person working in the business to very complex organisations spanning five continents and with hundreds of thousands of employees. Businesses also operate in an **external environment**. They have to deal with customers, suppliers and governments for example.

STAKEHOLDERS in a business are any individual or group which is affected by the business and so has an interest in its activities. The main stakeholders in a business, shown in Figure 1, are likely to be the owners (the shareholders, in the case of a company), managers and directors in a company, the employees, the customers, the suppliers and local communities politically represented by local government. Large businesses may impact on national communities represented by central government, and international communities represented by a variety of organisations such as the United Nations. Environmental issues also point to other animals and plants possibly being stakeholders as well as future generations of human beings. **Stakeholder perspectives** (i.e. how each of these groups of stakeholders might view a business) will now be considered in turn.

The owners of a business The owners of a business are stakeholders because they have put up the capital which runs the business. Their reward is the gain they make from owning the business. In a company, this is a mix of their share of the profits made and the capital gain from any increase in the value of shares (the **shareholder value**). With a sole trader and partnership, it is a mix of the drawings from the business (part wage, part profit) together with any increase in value of business assets, such as shop or factory premises. If owners were unable to get any reward for investing in the business, no one would bother to invest. So owners are vital to the workings of a market economy. Without owners, the whole capitalist economic system in the western world would collapse.

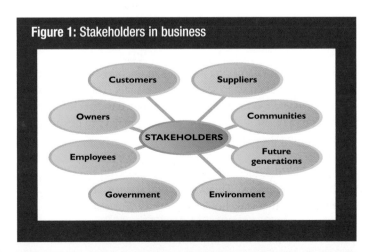

Figure 1: Stakeholders in business

Customers · Suppliers · Owners · Communities · **STAKEHOLDERS** · Employees · Future generations · Government · Environment

Directors and senior managers In a small business, the owner or owners are likely to run the business on a day-to-day business. But the larger the business, the more likely it is that owners will appoint managers to do this. In a company, there will be a board of directors, some of whom will be the senior managers in the company (called **executive directors**) and others who will have nothing to do with the day-to-day running of the business (called **non-executive directors**). The board of directors will be responsible for corporate strategy. The executive directors, the senior managers of the company, are stakeholders because how the business performs has a direct impact on them. If it performs poorly, they could be made redundant. If it performs well, they might be rewarded with higher salaries, promotion or bonuses.

Workers Employees from middle management downwards have a stake in the business for which they work. For example, the business pays them a wage on which they have to live. It might also give them a variety of **fringe benefits** such as pensions. Job security is important because workers have bills to pay in the future such as a mortgage. Jobs can give workers satisfaction and a sense of self worth. The success of the business is important to employees. If the business is performing poorly, they may lose their jobs. A successful business in one where there are likely to be more opportunities for promotion and for gaining pay rises.

Customers Customers are important stakeholders in the business. On the one hand, businesses need customers to survive. Without customers there would be no sales and no revenues coming into the business. The business then could not buy the factors of production needed to make goods and services. On the other hand, customers need businesses because they want to buy goods and services. Businesses provide them with the food they eat, the houses they live in and the services such as entertainment which they enjoy.

Suppliers Suppliers are stakeholders in a business because they depend upon that business for sales. Equally, the business is dependent on its suppliers. If it can't get supplies, it will be forced to cease production. As with customers, there is a mutual dependence between a business and its suppliers.

Local, national and international communities Local, national and international communities can be stakeholders in a business in a variety of ways.
- The economic prosperity of a community is dependent upon particular businesses. For example, businesses provide jobs in the local community, which in turn support other businesses such as shops where wages are spent. In some communities, a single business may provide a large proportion of the jobs. The prosperity of the local

community can then become totally dependent upon one employer. This can be true of nations too. In Africa, for example, some small countries are highly dependent on single mining companies or oil companies.

- A few businesses play important roles in their communities by supporting local charities or getting involved with schools and colleges. In the past in the UK, and in some countries today, businesses have also built and owned the housing in which their workers live. The Rowntrees in York or the Cadbury's in Birmingham were examples.
- Some businesses, such as McDonald's or The Body Shop, have a very high media profile and, arguably, have had an important influence upon the way we live. McDonald's outside of the USA has been accused of being the face of American capitalism. In France, it has been accused of destroying traditional cuisine by encouraging people to eat fast food. The Body Shop, by its ethical stance, has arguably encouraged other businesses to be more ethical.

The environment and future generations In recent years, there has been a growing awareness that environmental issues are important to stakeholding. The stakeholders are sometimes human beings who are affected by the impact that a business has on the environment today. For example, a business might be responsible for noise or visual pollution. Some would argue that animals and plants are also in some sense stakeholders because business activity has an impact on them. Equally, future generations are stakeholders of todays' businesses. For example, building a nuclear power plant today means, almost certainly, that future generations will be left clearing up the nuclear waste created. Taking a barrel of oil from the ground today means that it will not be available to people 200 years from now. Sending a lorry to deliver goods 100 miles away probably contributes to global warming, a problem that will be faced mainly by people living 50 to 100 years from now.

The conflicting objectives of stakeholders

Different stakeholders in a business have different objectives. They want different things from the business.

Owners When owners play no part in the running of the business, their objective is usually to maximise their returns. Typically, this occurs when the business is a medium to large sized company owned by shareholders. Shareholder returns come from being able to sell their shares for a higher price than they paid for them and from receiving dividends, a share of the company profits.

Directors and managers Directors and managers of large companies have a mixture of motives. On the one hand, they have been appointed to look after the interests of shareholders. Their job is, therefore, to maximise returns for shareholders. On the other hand, maximising returns to shareholders may not coincide with maximising their own returns. Top management work partly to maximise their own pay and remuneration package. So there can be a conflict of interest between senior management and owners. This problem is often referred to as one which comes from the 'divorce of ownership from control'.

Workers Ordinary workers from middle management down have little interest in the objectives of the owners of the company. They come to work for a variety of motives including pay and job satisfaction. When it comes to agreeing the annual pay rise, their objective is to have to the highest rise possible. But this could lead to lower profits. Improved working conditions could lead to higher costs again damaging profits. On the other hand, it is not in the workers' interests to see the business fail. There are many examples where too high labour costs have led to the closure of a business or a business operation. So workers have to be careful about pushing their claims too far.

Customers Customers want the best prices with the highest quality at these prices. They want good service. This may conflict with other stakeholders' interests. For example, spending more on research and development to create new products might lower the amount payable in dividends to

Question 1.

EADS, the European manufacturer of aeroplanes and maker of Airbus, in partnership with the US company Northrop Grumman, has won a $35 billion contract to supply refuelling tankers for the US airforce. The deal is for 179 aircraft together with service and support. What's more, the group is now in a strong position to capture a large share of the remaining 400 aircraft tankers the US airforce needs to replace, a contract which could ultimately be worth $100 billion.

A number of groups will benefit from the order. EADS plants in France, Spain and Germany will supply some of the parts. The wings for all the planes will be manufactured at the EADS plant at Broughton in Wales, which already employs 6,000 people. A number of British companies will also supply parts. For example, Cobham plc will produce equipment to transfer fuel between planes, a contract that will be worth $1 billion in sales over the life of the programme.

To secure the deal, EADS and Northrop Grumman had to locate 60 per cent of the work by value in the United States. One of the main beneficiaries will be the city of Mobile in Alabama where the aircraft will be assembled. More than 1,000 jobs will be created.

The loser has been the US aircraft manufacturer, Boeing, which was the main rival to EADS. Not only has it lost sales and profits, but it will have to restructure some of its operations. The assembly line at its plant in Everett, Washington, is now likely to close by about 2012 because there will no longer be any work for it to do. Around 600 production workers and other support staff will lose their jobs, almost more will probably be offered jobs elsewhere in Boeing. But the area has lost out on 2,000 jobs that would have been created had Boeing won the order. A further 4,000 jobs elsewhere in the USA have also been lost due to Boeing's failure to win.

Source: adapted from *The Financial Times*, 3.3.2008, 4.3.2008.

(a) List the possible stakeholders in EADS and Boeing.
(b) Explain how the different stakeholders in EADS and Boeing have gained and lost because EADS won the contract to build refuelling tankers.

shareholders today. Improving quality might lead to higher costs and lower profits, adversely affecting shareholders. Sunday opening for banks or shops might be unpopular with workers but be very popular with customers.

Suppliers Suppliers want to charge high prices to the business so as to maximise their profits. On the other hand, the business wants to minimise the price it pays to suppliers, also to maximise profit. A whole range of other issues such as quality, delivery times and service may also lead to conflicting objectives between suppliers and the business.

The community and government The communities in which a business operates have a variety of objectives with regard to businesses. On the one hand, they tend to welcome the jobs, taxes and prosperity which businesses can bring to an area. On the other hand, they don't like the environmental damage that businesses can cause. These objectives can conflict with those of the business. For example, a business might want to put up a building as cheaply as possible in order to minimise cost. But the local authority may insist on a variety of 'improvements' which increase the cost of the build. Businesses in general tend to lobby against the introduction of new regulations by government because they tend to raise costs.

Environmental groups Environmental groups tend to see

business as a necessary evil. Clearly businesses have to exist to provide human beings with goods and services. But every business damages the environment in some way simply by using energy or by occupying buildings which stand on land which was once populated by animals and plants. Businesses tend to want to see fewer environmental regulations and more spending on infrastructure like roads and airports. Environmental groups tend to lobby against business expansion.

Costs and benefits to businesses of adopting a stakeholder approach

In the UK, adopting a 'stakeholder approach' means giving less importance to the interests of owners and more importance to other stakeholders than the typical business. The costs and benefits to businesses of adopting such an approach tend to be measured in terms of their impact on profits, sales, revenues and accounting costs. The advantages include the following.

- Having good employment policies will tend to attract better applicants for posts and help motivate and retain existing staff. Improved motivation and retention should lead to increased profits.
- Effective customer care policies should lead to higher sales and hence higher profits.
- Working well with suppliers should enable the purchaser to get value for money. It should be much easier to sort out problems of late deliveries or defective work with suppliers with whom there is a good relationship.
- Putting something into the community, such as giving to local charities, taking on workers or backing training projects should give the business good public relations. This might help sell products or attract good applicants for jobs.
- Being environmentally friendly could lead to lower overall costs. For example, recycling heat in a boiler might cost money for new equipment but quickly save money because of the lower fuel inputs needed. Being seen as environmentally friendly may help sales of products and thus increase profit.
- For some high profile companies such as Shell or BP, becoming more socially responsible deflects the criticisms of pressure groups. As companies such as Monsanto (over GM crops) or Nike (over poor conditions of work in factories making Nike trainers in the Third World) have

Question 2.

Northumbrian Water Group (NWG) is a local water company in the North East and South East of England. It provides water and sewerage services, supplying clean water to businesses and to homes and treating their sewage waste.

On its website in 2008, it stated that 'NWG is a business with significant resources - notably employees, water and land. We believe it has a responsibility to use those resources for the benefit not only of customers and shareholders, but also for the wider community.'

'Our recognised stakeholders include customers, employees, investors, suppliers, Government and the wider local community. NWG tries to balance social, environmental and economic priorities to ensure that, whilst maintaining economic stability, the environment is protected and society is enhanced. Stakeholders expect a secure supply of water - a basic necessity for health - and they expect us to protect or enhance the environment when we return waste to that environment. Stakeholders also expect NWG to

- behave fairly and responsibly
- use resources wisely
- improve quality of life
- contribute to economic development.

Source: adapted from www.nwg.co.uk.

(a) Compare the possible objectives of customers, investors and 'the wider community' in NWG.

(b) Do you think that stakeholders apart from shareholders should have more influence over the running of a water company like NWG than an engineering company which manufactures parts for the automobile industry?

KNOWLEDGE

1. List the major stakeholders in a typical business.
2. Explain two ways in which the interests of the owners of a large business might conflict with the interests of its workers.
3. Explain two ways in which the interests of the senior management of a large business might conflict with the interests of environmental groups.
4. Why might the owners of a large business benefit rather than suffer by (a) giving their workers a large pay rise and (b) spending £1 million on environmental projects?
5. How might (a) workers and (b) the owners of a large business exert pressure to influence decision making within the business?

found, bad publicity can affect sales. In the mid -1990s, Shell faced a consumer boycott of its petrol filling stations over its plans to dispose of a North Sea oil platform by sinking it in the middle of the Atlantic ocean. Spending money on becoming more socially responsible is a way of reducing the risks to sales and profits that would come from bad PR.

The main disadvantage of the stakeholder approach is that, in practice, it tends to add to costs and thus lower profits for most businesses. If this weren't the case, every employer would increase the benefits given to workers, or give money to local charities or devote resources to pursuing environmentally friendly policies. Only some businesses benefit from a 'stakeholder approach'.

KEYTERMS

Stakeholder – an individual or group which is affected by a business and so has an interest in its activities.

Case Study: The Body Shop

On its website in 2008, The Body Shop stated: 'The Body Shop International plc is a global manufacturer and retailer of naturally inspired ethically produced beauty and cosmetics products. Founded in the UK in 1976 by Dame Anita Roddick, we now have over 2,100 stores in 55 countries,with a range of over 1,200 products, all animal cruelty free, and many with fairly traded natural ingredients.'

High Street beauty products retailer Body Shop has been taken over by French cosmetics giant L'Oreal in a deal worth £625 million. L'Oreal makes a wide range of cosmetics, including Ambre Solaire sun cream and Lancome lipsticks. Body Shop – with its ethically-sourced products – was one of the icons of the High Street in the 1980s. Its fortunes have been hit in recent years as rivals started making similar products. Body Shop will be operated as a stand-alone company by L'Oreal rather than being fully integrated into the L'Oreal business.

The sale has attracted criticism because L'Oreal is 26 per cent owned by the Swiss multinational Nestlé, which has long been embroiled in controversy about the sale of baby milk in Third World countries.

Source: adapted news.bbc.co.uk 17.3.2006; www.independent.co.uk 10.4.2006.

(a) Evaluate whether the objectives of the different stakeholders in The Body Shop must inevitably conflict with each. (40 marks)

(b) Assess the costs and benefits to The Body Shop of adopting a stakeholder approach to business. (40 marks)

In its 2007 Values Report, The Body Shop stated that: 'We are committed to running a commercially successful, sustainable business, and using resources responsibly withy due regard for the needs of future generations. We do not believe that there is any conflict between commercial success and social or environmental responsibility. The greater our economic performance the more credible example we can set for other businesses, the wider ethical choice we can offer to consumers and the stronger our voice for the causes we champion.'

In its 2007 Values Report, The Body Shop stated that its stakeholders were:

Figure 1: The Body Shop: stakeholders

- customers: 'We know from our customer surveys and focus groups that 80 per cent of our customers shop with us because of our Values';
- employees and consultants: 'The Body Shop International plc directly employs 10, 034 people but there is a total of 31, 000 people globally working in our stores, in offices and warehouse operations and as The Body Shop At Home™ consultants.
- NGOs (non-governmental organisations): NGOs are mainly charities such as Greenpeace, WWF (World Wildlife Fund), Friends of the Earth and local groups in countries in which The Body Shop operates;
- franchisees: 'Our franchisees are responsible for the largest part of our business and their contribution to building our brand and Values is significant';
- suppliers: 'Our engagement with suppliers takes a range of different forms. We visit each of our Community Trade suppliers at least every two years, and assess our product suppliers annually. .... For example, we have been in close contact with our packaging suppliers to increase the use of recyclate, and work with other suppliers to use new natural ingredients or find alternatives to chemicals of concern.'
- Other companies and multi-stakeholder networks: 'We want to share what we have learned with other companies, as well as understand how others have made progress. We are therefore a part of a number of formal networks which include progressive companies, both within and outside our sector.'

Soruce: adapted from www.thebodyshopinternational.com.

78 | Corporate aims and objectives

Business aims

All businesses have AIMS. An aim is what the business intends to do in the long term – its purpose. Ultimately it is what the business is striving to achieve. Different businesses have different aims. A business might also have more than one aim. What might be the aims of a business?

Profit It could be argued that the main aim of businesses is to make a profit. Some businesses try to PROFIT MAXIMISE. This comes about when the difference between the **revenues** and **costs** is greatest over a period of time. Profit maximisation is most likely to benefit the owners of the business. For a sole trader, the profit is usually equivalent to the wage drawn from the business. The bigger the profit, the more money can be taken. In a company, the level of dividend paid is likely to depend on the profit made. In a public limited company, quoted share prices too are affected by profits. Companies which the stock market thinks will be highly profitable in the future have high share values. Companies which have poor profit forecasts tend to have low share values. Existing shareholders want the price of their shares to be as high as possible.

Shareholder value In the 1980s and 1990s, it became fashionable for large companies to argue that their aim was to maximise SHAREHOLDER VALUE. Shareholder value can be interpreted in different ways. Shareholders make a return from their shares partly through the dividend they receive and partly through increases in value of shares on a stock exchange. Increasing dividends and increasing share price may go together for a growing company. However, companies can pay out too much in dividends in the short-term to please their shareholders at the expense of the long-term success of the business. Profits,

instead of being paid out as dividends, can be retained by the company and used for investment. If there is too little investment by the company, it can see sales and profits stagnate and even fall. High dividend payouts can, therefore, **destroy shareholder value** in the longer term. Maximising shareholder value is in the interests of the shareholders. It may even be in the interests of managers too if it secures their jobs.

Survival For some businesses, survival is the main aim. This is particularly true for small businesses just starting up and for larger businesses which have got into financial difficulties. Unless a business survives, it cannot generate benefits for its stakeholders, such as profits for its owners or jobs for employees.

Sales revenue An alternative objective for a business might be SALES REVENUE MAXIMISATION. Earning the highest level possible of revenue over a period of time might lead to high levels of profit, so benefiting the owners of the business. But the owners of a business are not its only stakeholders. In medium to large sized businesses, managers are stakeholders too. They control the day-to-day running of the business. They may have more influence on how the business is run than its owners. Maximising revenue might be more in the interests of managers than maximising profit. The larger the business, the higher the salaries of top managers and their fringe benefits are likely to be. A growing business can be an exciting environment in which to work. There is plenty of opportunity for managers to gain promotion and exercise power over how money is spent, recruitment of staff and new products. The opposite is true in a business which is reducing in size. Job cuts, for instance, are demoralising for all workers. The tendency for managers to pursue revenue maximisation rather than profit maximisation is one of the main reasons why many companies link the remuneration (the total pay package) of top managers with profits. It is common today, for instance, for top managers to be given share options. In small businesses, where the owners are the managers, this conflict of interest between them does not arise.

Growth Another aim of a business might be to grow. Revenue is just one measure of the **size** of a business. A business might aim to be the 'number one company in the market', i.e. have the largest market share. There are other measures of growth, such as capital value, and the number of employees it has. If the owners control a business, they might be prepared to sacrifice short-term profits for long-term growth which leads to higher profits in the long term. Maximising growth could

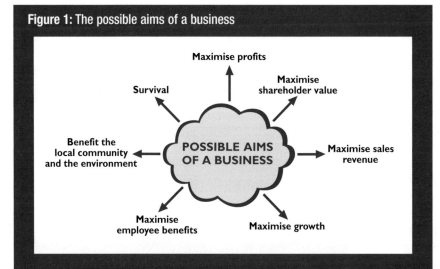

Figure 1: The possible aims of a business

POSSIBLE AIMS OF A BUSINESS

- Maximise profits
- Maximise shareholder value
- Survival
- Benefit the local community and the environment
- Maximise sales revenue
- Maximise employee benefits
- Maximise growth

be in their best interests. If managers are in control, growth may become the main business objective because it suits their objectives more than profit maximisation. As already explained, the pay of top managers and their power tends to be linked with business size.

Customer welfare Many businesses state that one of their aims is to benefit their customers. This might be in the form of providing 'best value', or innovative products, or high quality service. Without customers, businesses could not survive. So some argue that customer satisfaction must be an aim of any business.

Employee benefits Employees are stakeholders in a business too. The success of the business is vitally dependent upon the skills and motivation of staff. So it could be argued that the aim of any business must be to benefit employees. The existence of **trade unions** in the workplace can also put pressure on a business to make employee benefits one of its aims.

Benefiting the local community and the environment A few businesses, like The Body Shop, have been set up explicitly with the aim of benefiting the local communities in which they operate and respecting the environment. Equally, some large companies, such as Tesco or BP, have stated aims with regard to community and environmental issues.

What is the main aim of the business?

The main aim of small businesses, such as sole traders or partnerships, is usually to maximise profits. Owners want to maximise the return on their work in a business. There are many exceptions though. For example, doctors working in partnership may make the needs of their patients an important priority.

For companies, though, the situation is more complex. In the UK and the USA, it has been traditional for the needs of shareholders to be most important. So it can be argued that UK and US companies are usually profit maximisers or maximisers of shareholder value. This is true even though there is a **divorce of ownership and control**, where the owners are a different group of people from those who run the company.

In continental Europe and Japan, however, workers, customers and the local community are seen as being much more important stakeholders than in the UK or the USA. So a European or Japanese business may have several aims.

It can also be argued that this is true even in the UK and the USA. According to BEHAVIOURAL THEORIES OF THE FIRM, shareholders, managers, workers, customers, local communities and pressure groups, such as environmental activists, share power within a business. The business aims to reconcile the often **conflicting aims** of each group of stakeholders. For example, it PROFIT SATISFICES, making enough profit to keep shareholders happy, but this is not the maximum level of profit it could make. Instead, it spends more than it otherwise would on environmental projects, or servicing the local community.

Perhaps it pays better wages to staff than it needs to recruit and motivate them. Senior managers and directors, who have some control over their own pay, are able to negotiate larger remuneration packages than might otherwise be the case.

Over time, the balance of power between stakeholders can change and, therefore, so can the aims of a business. For example, it could be argued that over the past 40 years in the UK the power of employees has gone down as trade union power

Question 1.

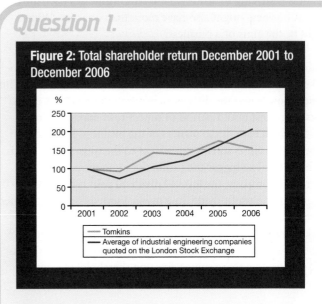

Figure 2: Total shareholder return December 2001 to December 2006

Tomkins is a global engineering and manufacturing group. We manufacture a variety of products for the industrial, automotive and building products markets across North America, Asia and the rest of the world.

Our strategy is focused on the creation of shareholder value by achieving long-term sustainable growth in the economic value of Tomkins. We are targeting growth in revenue and profit through a combination of new product innovation and operational excellence, geographic expansion and strategic bolt-on acquisitions.

(a) Suggest what are the aims of Tomkins as a company.
(b) To what extent has Tomkins achieved its aims between 2003 and 2006?

Table 1: Tomkins-sales, profit, dividends share price per share

	2003	2004	2005	2006
Sales, £ million	2,790	2,721	2,948	3,125
Profit before tax, £ million	193	254	263	245
Dividend per share, pence	12	12.6	13.23	13.89
Ordinary share price, pence	269	254.25	299.75	245.75

Source: adapted from Tomkins, *Annual Report and Accounts*, 2006.

has decreased. This could be one of the main reasons why the share of profits in the income of the whole UK economy has risen sharply whilst that of earnings has fallen. On the other hand, the power of environmentalists has increased. Forty years ago, few companies acknowledged that the environment was of any importance in their decision making.

Some economists have suggested that, in a company, there are in fact only two sets of stakeholders with sufficient power to influence the running of the business. According to the MANAGERIAL THEORY OF THE FIRM, shareholders and managers share power. Managers have to make enough profit to keep shareholders happy, otherwise they risk losing their bonuses and jobs. But managers have enough day-to-day control to be able to reward themselves more than is strictly necessary.

Objectives

The objectives of a business are its goals outcomes or targets which allow it to achieve its aims. Objectives should be practical outcomes from the operation of a business. One way of summarising this is to use SMART criteria. This says that objectives should be:

- **specific (S)** - they must set out clearly what a business is attempting to achieve;
- **measurable (M)** - they must be capable of being measured so that it can judged whether or not they have been achieved;
- **agreed (A)** - everyone responsible for achieving an objective must have agreed with the objective and understood what it meant;
- **realistic (R)** - the objective must be achievable given the resources available and the market conditions;
- **time-specific (T)** - the objective must specify over what period of time it is to be achieved.

So a business must choose suitable objectives to help it achieve its aims. There could be many ways in which this could be done.

- The aim of a business might be to make a profit. An objective to achieve this could be to increase sales or cut costs by 20 per cent over the next two years.
- The aim might be to become more environmentally friendly. An objective to achieve this could be to double spending on community projects next year.
- The aim of the business might be to be the number one producer in three years. An objective to achieve this could be to be innovative and change the whole product range within the next three years.

It is important to understand that the same measure could be either an aim or an objective (but not both at the same time). Take, for example, profit maximisation. This is traditionally seen as an aim of a business. But it could be an objective if the aim of the business is to maximise shareholder value. Note that maximising profit is not a SMART objective because it is not measurable. Another example would be market share. Becoming

the number one company in a market could be the aim of a business. Equally, it could be an objective if the aim of the business were to maximise profits. This is because becoming the market leader could enable the business to charge higher prices to customers than if it were second or third in the market. Becoming 'the number one' in a market is a SMART objective because it is measurable.

Mission statements, aims and objectives

Larger businesses often have a MISSION STATEMENT. This is a statement, written by the business, of its purpose and its values. It is meant both to state the aims of the business and to provide a vision for its stakeholders.

For example, MSB International PLC is a UK based company which provides other businesses with services in the field of human resources. Amongst other services, it helps businesses recruit temporary and permanent staff. Its mission is: 'To provide human capital solutions that enable our clients to achieve their business goals. Expand our organisation globally both organically and through acquisition, whilst enhancing and broadening the services. We are committed to rewarding shareholders and employees through sustained growth in profitability.'

Mission statements often illustrate the problem of distinguishing between aims and objectives. For example, in the MSB International mission statement, the stated aim is to expand the organisation. It then goes on to say how this will be achieved - through organic growth and acquisition. It is likely that organic growth and acquisition are in fact objectives. They are the means through which the aim of expansion of the organisation will be achieved. However, it could also be argued that expansion of the organisation is not an end in itself, but is there to increase the rewards to shareholders, another stated aim. Also, is the business equally committed to 'rewarding shareholders' and 'rewarding employees'? Some might argue that rewarding employees is an objective, not an aim, but it is a way of motivating workers to generate high profits for shareholders.

Often, writers use the terms 'aims', 'objectives' and 'goals' as if they were the same, to overcome this problem of distinguishing between what is an aim and what is an objective.

It could also be argued that those in business blur the distinction between aims and objectives. Managers and directors might themselves find it difficult to distinguish between the two. They might also be unwilling to reveal their actual aims. For example, large multinational corporations tend to state, that their aim is to benefit shareholders, customers, workers and the environment. But if their actual aim was simply to benefit shareholders, they would be unlikely to admit to this publicly in a mission statement. This is because they could attract a great deal of adverse publicity for being 'uncaring', 'greedy', 'capitalist' organisations. In practice, they do have to reward their employees sufficiently to motivate them. They have to be at least environmentally friendly enough to avoid risking prosecution under the law. So, employment and environmental issues must form part of their objectives. But they are not necessarily part of the aims of the company. Mission statements, and what companies say about their aims, should therefore be examined critically and not taken at face value.

KEY TERMS

Aim – the intention or purpose of a business; what a business is ultimately striving to achieve.

Behavioural theories of the firm – theories which suggest that businesses have multiple aims set by their main stakeholders.

Managerial theories of the firm – theories which suggest that businesses are controlled by managers who run them for their own benefit subject to the need to make enough profit to satisfy shareholders (profit satisficing).

Mission statement – a statement, written by the business, of its purpose and its values; it is meant both to state the aims of the business and to provide a vision for its stakeholders.

Profit maximisation – earning the highest profit possible over a period of time.

Profit satisficing – making enough profit to satisfy the needs of shareholders whilst pursuing at least one other aim such as rewarding managers and directors.

Sales revenue maximisation – earning the highest possible revenue over a period of time.

Shareholder value – the value of a company to its owners over a period of time as measured by a combination of the size of its dividend payments and the rise in its share price.

KNOWLEDGE

1. What is the difference between maximising profit, maximising sales revenue and maximising shareholder value?
2. Under what circumstances is survival likely to be the main aim of a business?
3. Why might a business aim to (a) maximise employee benefits and (b) maximise customer welfare?
4. Why might the aim of a small business be different from the aim of a large company?
5. What is the difference between managerial theories of the firm and behavioural theories?
6. What is the difference between an aim and an objective for a business?
7. Why should objectives be SMART?
8. What is the purpose of a mission statement?

Case Study: Sports Direct International plc

Sports Direct International plc is run by Mike Ashley, now a billionaire having floated a minority stake company on the London stock exchange. The deal valued the company at £2.2 billion, not bad for someone who left school at 16 and began trading from one shop in Maidenhead, Berkshire.

However, City investors have very quickly fallen out of love with the company. The share price of the company had halved within five months of flotation. Investors have complained that they cannot get sensible financial information from the company. The company is also being run in a highly irregular manner for a publicly quoted company. The non-executive chairman of the company, David Richardson, resigned recently in frustration at the way Michael Ashley regularly flouted corporate-governance guidelines.

Sports Direct is successful partly because it sources its stock cheaply, direct from the Far East. It uses those costs to slash the prices of big brands such as Adidas or Nike, making itself one of the most price competitive sports retailers in the country. Mike Ashley has also bought up a number of famous sports brands from sports equipment manufacturers such as as Lonsdale, Slazenger and Karrimor to rival sports retailers such as Gilesports and Lillywhites.

Before flotation, sales and profits rose together. By April 2007, sales were an annual £2 billion with profits before tax of nearly £200 million. However, within months of flotation, the company was issuing a profit warning as England failed to qualify for the World Cup, killing sales of England football shirts and other replica kit.

Michael Ashley was unrepentant, accusing the City of short-termism. 'I am building a long-term business', he said. 'I can't spend all my time worrying if the share price goes up and down. It may drop to 80p, but over three years I am betting it will be nearer 800p. I have built the company over 25 years and I am planning the next 25 years. But all anyone wants to talk to me about is what happened in June' (the time of the World Cup). He went on to say: 'The current share price is pathetic. I can't think of many safer long-term investments at this price. What annoys me the most is that some people are saying they didn't get what they bargained for (when buying shares). In my opinion they got exactly what it said on the tin.'

By his own admission, Michael Ashley is consumed by a 'ferocious' desire to succeed. He believes that one day Sports Direct could be a £4 billion company. His vision for the future is clear. Sports Direct will need to expand into mainland Europe, take 100 per cent ownership of more brands and acquire large strategic stakes in others.

Source: adapted from *The Sunday Times* 29.7.2007; en.wikipedia.org

(a) Evaluate whether Michael Ashley and City shareholders might have different aims for the company. (40 marks)
(b) Do you think that Michael Ashley would have any short-term objectives for Sports Direct?

Corporate strategy

CORPORATE STRATEGY deals with how to achieve the main objectives of the whole business. It is concerned with plans and policies which allocate resources in a way which will allow the business to achieve its corporate objectives. It is also concerned with two key issues.

- Whether or not the size of the business will give it the resources to achieve the objectives set.
- What range of activities the business needs to undertake to achieve its goals.

For many businesses, concentrating on a single industry or market is the appropriate corporate strategy. By doing this, they can exploit their knowledge of the industry and develop their competitive strategies. A business pursuing such a strategy then has to decide on its optimal size. Could it create value by growing in size or perhaps downsizing?

However, a business may be able to create value for its owners by moving into other markets. It may grow **vertically**, moving into markets which either it sells into or buys from. It may grow **horizontally**, expanding into its existing market. Or it may become a **conglomerate**, moving into unrelated markets. Equally, it may grow **organically** from within. Or it may grow by **taking over** or **merging** with other businesses. A key issue in growth is whether it will create **synergies**. Will the sum of the parts be greater than the individual parts working as completely separate businesses?

Equally, a large business should consider whether it can create value by **divesting** itself of businesses. Parts of the business may be underperforming. This may be because it is in a low profit industry. Or perhaps it is a relatively small part of the whole business and insufficient management time is being devoted to its running. Equally, since the 1990s, there has been a growing

Question 1.

Littlewoods was once one of the UK's largest private limited companies. It owned a football pools company (a form of gambling) and was a major retailer through its home shopping catalogue and a chain of high street stores. The arrival of the National Lottery in 1994 took away much of the market for football pools and, in 2000, Littlewoods sold its pools business for £161 million. The Littlewoods home shopping catalogue and high store stores had also been struggling against fierce competition and was barely profitable at best. In 2002, the rest of the company was sold for £750 million to the Barclay brothers, entrepreneurs who had a track record of turning around ailing companies. In 2003, the Barclay brothers bought the home shopping and catalogues business of GUS plc. This was made up of a number of catalogue brands, including Additions Direct, Great Universal, Marshall Ward, Choice and Kays.

Following a strategic review, the 120 branch high street chain of Littlewoods stores was sold by the Barclay brothers to Associated British Foods for £409 million. Associated British Foods converted some of these into branches of Primark, a clothing subsidiary which it owned. The rest were sold to other retailers. Littlewoods, the retail chain, disappeared from Britain's high streets in 2006.

The Littlewoods catalogue operation was merged with the rest of the company's catalogue brands to form Littlewoods Shop Direct Group with sales of over £2 billion per year. More than £200 million has been spent rationalising and re-organising the portfolio of catalogues, head offices, warehouse operations and call centres. The Littlewoods catalogue itself was relaunched in 2007. Traditionally, the Littlewoods catalogue had a reputation for selling mainly to the lower D and E socio-economic groups. Today, the catalogue has gone up-market. Brands such as Bench, Miss Sixty, Replay and Diesel are now stocked. Trinny and Susannah, famous fashion experts from their TV show, have been recruited to feature in an advertising campaign. Very importantly, large

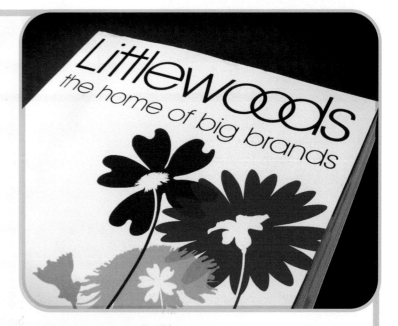

amounts have been invested in developing an online store which is fun and friendly. Today, Littlewoods Shop Direct Group is the UK's fourth largest Internet retailer behind Amazon, Tesco and Argos. It has targets to double Internet sales over the next three years.

Source: adapted from *The Sunday Times*, 8.4.2007; en.wikipedia.org

(a) Corporate strategy is concerned with the size of the business and the markets in which it operates. Explain why (i) selling off the Littlewoods high street chain and (ii) creating Littlewoods Shop Direct Group were examples of corporate strategy.

(b) Evaluate whether the corporate strategy for Littlewoods Shop Direct Group is likely to be successful.

Question 2.

Burberry is a luxury goods brand. It has its roots in the manufacture and sale of trench coats designed with the characteristic Burberry checks. Today it has expanded beyond outerwear to handbags, accessories and other apparel. In 2006-2007, it conducted a major strategic review. Out of this came five strategic themes, to:

- grow and leverage its franchise operations;
- intensify the development of non-apparel (i.e. non-clothes) sales and products;
- accelerate growth from its chain of retail shops;
- invest in under-penetrated areas;
- pursue excellence in its operations.

As part of continued investment in 'under-penetrated areas', the company continues to expand in North America. In 2007-2008, it planned to open another ten new stores in the USA bringing its total to 50. Stacey Cartwright, finance director, said: 'There are still further opportunities beyond that in the US and if you look at our peers they have between 70 and 100 stores there. We would be targeting those sorts of numbers.' The US market is attractive for a number of reasons, not least because it is home to an increasing number of consumers who favour luxury goods and accessories. Some also believe that the Burberry brand is more highly rates overseas than in the UK.

2007 also saw a strategic milestone for the company. For the first time, revenues from its own chain of retail stores exceeded the value of sales of Burberry merchandise through other retail channels.

Source: adapted from Burberry Group plc, *Annual Report and Accounts, 2007*; *The Financial Times*, 25.5.2007.

(a) Explain the link between Burberry opening another ten stores in the USA and its strategic direction.

(b) Evaluate whether expanding further in the USA by opening its own stores might help Burberry to achieve its strategic objectives of raising sales and profits.

trend for businesses to **outsource** functions. The argument is that a business needs to concentrate on its CORE CAPABILITIES (or CORE COMPETENCES): what it is best at doing. For example, a business which specialises in manufacturing canned food does not necessarily have an expertise in logistics (getting raw materials to the business and then transporting finished products to customers). It might be more cost-effective to outsource logistics to a specialist logistics company.

Fifty years ago, it became fashionable for large businesses to be conglomerates. A conglomerate is a business which produces a range of products in widely differing markets. A steel producer which also owns a fast food change would be an example. Today, it is more fashionable for businesses to focus on a narrow range of markets in which senior management have an expertise. A water company should, therefore, concentrate on providing water management services. A train operator should concentrate on providing train services. A key feature of corporate strategy is deciding which part of the business should be retained and which should be sold off or closed down.

Strategic direction and strategic gaps

Corporate and business strategies are corporate and business plans which show how a business can achieve its objectives in the medium to long term. The strategic plan may be to do what the business currently doing, only more effectively. So the business may see itself making the same products in the same places and selling into the same markets in three to five years' time. Alternatively, the strategic plan may be to move the business in a new direction. For example, a UK manufacturer may have a plan which says that the value of products sourced (i.e. made) in the UK should fall from 60 per cent to 25 per cent as production is shifted off shore to low wage economies, such as Eastern Europe or the Far East. Or the plan may be to move into adjacent higher profit margin markets. A fixed line telephone company, for example, may plan to acquire a mobile telephone company in the medium term. So the STRATEGIC DIRECTION of a business is the path which a business plans to follow to achieve its goals.

Once the strategic direction has been established, a detailed set of plans will be produced. These will enable lower and middle management to make the correct decisions to ensure the success of the plan. The period of time for which detailed plans can be made is called the PLANNING HORIZON. This might be from one to three years for a business in a stable market environment.

Sometimes, though, a STRATEGIC GAP may emerge between what a business wants to achieve and its objectives. For example, a company may have as one of its objectives that it will achieve a 20 per cent growth in sales each year. A new strategic plan is worked out and senior managers find that, given the existing strategic direction of the company, it is most unlikely that this objective will be realised over the next three to five years. Senior management, therefore, either has to produce a different strategy to **close the strategic gap**, or it has to modify its objectives. A new strategy might be to expand sales overseas. Or it might be to enter new product markets. Or sales might be increased by spending more on R&D to develop new products in existing markets.

Corporate strategy in relation to other types of strategy

The term 'strategy' is used widely in business. There are many different types of strategy. How do some of these relate to corporate strategy?

Corporate strategy v business unit strategy and departmental strategy Corporate strategy relates to objectives and plans for the whole company or corporation. It is a term used in connection with medium to large companies. Large companies are often split up into divisions. Some choose to do this geographically with, for example, a North American division, a European division and a division which covers the rest of the world. Others choose to do this by product, for example with a building materials division and an engineering division. Each division (or business unit) will have its own DIVISIONAL or BUSINESS UNIT STRATEGY. Divisions themselves may contain a number of subsidiary companies each of which will have their own strategies. Then, within companies, there will be **functional** (or **departmental**) strategies for each department. In theory, divisional strategies are developed to meet the objectives of corporate strategies. Functional strategies are developed to meet the objectives of business unit strategies.

Corporate versus business strategies Corporate strategies differ from **business** (or **generic**) strategies. Business strategies are concerned with how a business can gain a competitive advantage in the market place. They deal with issues such as product differentiation, cost advantages and market niches. Effective business strategies are ways in which corporate strategies can be achieved.

Global strategies and corporate strategies GLOBAL or INTERNATIONAL STRATEGIES are needed by any company which sells products to overseas customers or has production facilities in more than one country. Global strategy can refer to the part of corporate strategy which deals with international issues. Or it could refer to business strategies and how the company can gain a competitive advantage in global markets.

Corporate strategy vs tactics Corporate strategy sets out the long-term objectives of the company and plans for how they will be achieved. Tactics are short-term strategies to achieve limited objectives. For example, a corporate (or strategic) objective might be to grow the North American market by 50 per cent over the next five years and the plan to achieve this objective might be to grow the company organically. One year into the strategy, a company in the North American market may come up for sale. A tactic might be to take it over to help achieve the corporate objective.

KEYTERMS

Business unit (or divisional) strategy – strategy of a division or a subsidiary company owned by a parent company.
Core capabilities (or competences) – the most important strengths of a business, which should be central to decision making when corporate strategy is devised.
Corporate strategy – the plans and policies developed to meet a company's objectives. It is concerned with what range of activities the business needs to undertake in order to achieve its goals. It is also concerned with whether the size of the business organisation makes it capable of achieving the objectives set.
Global or international strategy – strategy of a business relating to sales or production internationally.
Planning horizon – the period of time for which detailed plans have been made which will allow a business to achieve its strategic objectives. This may vary from business to business from a few months to a few years, in part depending upon the pace of change in the markets into which a business sells.
Strategic direction – the path which a business plans to follow to achieve its goals.
Strategic gap – the difference between where a business predicts it will be in the medium to long term and where it wants to be as shown by the objectives it has set itself.

KNOWLEDGE

1. Explain the possible connection between corporate strategy and downsizing.
2. Why is a long decision to move into a new market an example of corporate strategy?
3. What is the link between corporate strategy and the planning horizon?
4. 'The company intends to close its strategic gap by increasing its marketing spending.' Explain what this means.
5. Explain the difference between corporate strategy and (a) functional strategy; (b) competitive strategy.

Case Study: Glenaden Shirts

There is almost nothing left today of what was once one of Britain's major industries. But Glenaden Shirts, based in Derry in Northern Ireland, has survived the closure of most of the UK's textile industry. However, survival was a close thing. In 2000, the owner of the Derry factory, Coats Viyella, moved to close it and it was only saved by a management buy-out led by Andrew Lowden, now managing director. Last year, a controlling stake in the company was bought by Amicus Capital, a private equity company, which installed Terry McCartney as Chairman.

Glenaden Shirts has gone from strength to strength since 2000. According to Terry McCartney, 'They're becoming a supplier of branded consumer goods rather than an old-fashioned textile company.' Their location in Northern Ireland puts them at a cost disadvantage to competitors elsewhere in the world. Wages of staff, for example, are many times what would be paid to staff if they were in China or India. However, the company has transformed a cost disadvantage into a marketing advantage. Unlike competitors, it can put a 'Made in Britain' label on its products. 'There are a growing number of consumers who value the Made in Britain label. Its a sort of snobbery I suppose,' says Andrew Lowden. The Made in Britain label particularly helps the 45 per cent of sales overseas. In markets such as the USA and Japan, the label carries considerable cachet. 'A Wall Street banker doesn't want to find what he thought was a British-made shirt was, in fact, made in Taiwan,' says Terry McCartney. In the UK, the company has moved away from supplying mainly City gents in London to marketing its products through a network of independent retailers in cities and towns outside London for professionals who want a tidy work shirt or a fashion piece for a special occasion.

Glenaden makes 300,000 high quality shirts a year. It has two parts to its business. There is a sub-contracting arm which supplies Thomas Pink, the UK's largest upmarket shirt retailer, and other Jermyn Street retailers. There is also an operation which makes shirts for sale under the Thread & Bone label owned by Glenaden. The company took a further step towards achieving its goal this week by buying Coles, an old Jermyn Street brand that had closed its London shops and had become an Internet-based mail-order business. Coles, it believes, will fit neatly into this portfolio.

Source: adapted from *The Financial Times*, 20.1.2007.

Note: Jermyn Street is a street in central London famous for shirtmakers. Just as Saville Row is associated with fine cut suits and tailoring, so Jermyn Street is associated with the production and sale of up-market finest quality shirts.

(a) 'They're becoming a supplier of branded consumer goods rather than an old-fashioned textile company.' Define 'corporate strategy' and suggest what might be the corporate strategy of Glenaden. (40 marks)
(b) Evaluate the success of Glenaden's corporate strategy. (40 marks)

Economic growth

For the past 50 years, the UK economy has grown at an average rate of 2.5 per cent. This is the long-run trend rate of growth of the UK economy. ECONOMIC GROWTH is measured by changes in the size of NATIONAL INCOME. This is the value of total income in the economy. It is also equal to the value of total spending and total production or output. There is a number of different ways of calculating national income. The method most often used by economists and the media is GROSS DOMESTIC PRODUCT or GDP.

Economic growth means that more is produced. In turn, this means that households and individuals can, on average, consume more goods and services. The standard of living enjoyed by the typical family today is far higher than it was 25 or 50 years ago as Figure 1 shows.

The business cycle

GDP does not rise at a steady rate each year. There are fluctuations and in some years the level of GDP may even fall. These fluctuations tend to occur on a regular basis and follow the same broad pattern. This is known as the BUSINESS CYCLE or TRADE CYCLE or ECONOMIC CYCLE. There are four phases to the business cycle, shown in Figure 2.

Boom In a BOOM, the economy is doing well.
- Output is high and the economy is growing strongly.
- Consumer spending is high. Also consumers are willing to borrow to finance their purchases.

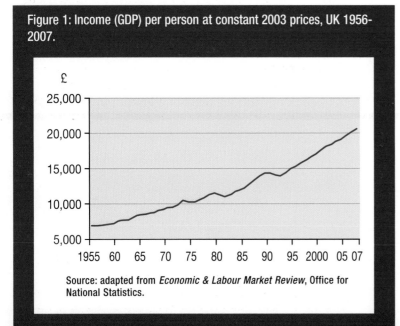

Figure 1: Income (GDP) per person at constant 2003 prices, UK 1956-2007.

Source: adapted from *Economic & Labour Market Review*, Office for National Statistics.

- House prices are likely to be growing, helped by high mortgage lending by banks and building societies.
- Unemployment is low and businesses may find it hard to recruit new workers.
- Wages are likely to be rising at a fast rate, as businesses compete to employ a limited pool of workers.
- Strong growth in demand for goods and services, combined with above average increases in wages, might increase inflation rates. Inflation is the rise in the general level of prices in the economy.
- With many domestic businesses working at full capacity, they could find it difficult to provide all the products that customers want to buy. So demand for imports might grow at a faster than average rate.
- There might be bottlenecks in certain sectors of the economy. This is where customers want to buy products, but they aren't available in sufficient quantities from domestic producers or importers. Delivery times might be longer. In some industries, waiting lists may develop.
- Businesses, encouraged by strong demand, will tend to increase their investment spending to increase their capacity.
- Record numbers of new businesses will be created, attracted by the possibility of earning high profits.

Downturn In a DOWNTURN or ECONOMIC SLOWDOWN or DOWNSWING, the rate of growth of the economy begins to fall.

- Lower growth in demand will cause unemployment to rise, which in turn will lead to even lower demand growth.
- Wage increases will start to slow and businesses will find it more difficult to push through price increases. So the rate of inflation will start to fall. Some sectors of the economy might be more affected than others.
- Many businesses will see a fall off in growth of sales and some will see an absolute fall.
- Profit growth will falter and could become negative.
- The rate of growth of imports will fall as the the rate of growth in overall spending by UK customers slows.

Recession or depression The bottom of the business cycle has a number of different names. If economic growth becomes negative, i.e. GDP falls, then it tends to be called a DEPRESSION or SLUMP. The last major prolonged depression in the UK economy occurred during the 1930s. However, there were short depressions in 1974-75, 1980-82 and 1990-92.

When GDP is still growing, but at a very low rate at the bottom of the cycle, the media use both the terms

Figure 2: The actual rate of growth measured by changes in GDP fluctuate from year to year round the long run trend rate of growth for the economy. These fluctuations are known as the business cycle. In the business cycle, recessions can either be very mild or deep.

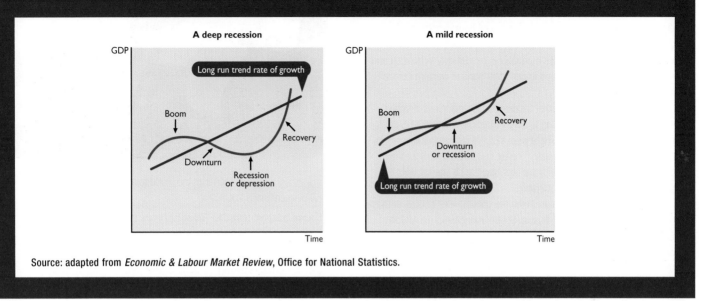

Source: adapted from *Economic & Labour Market Review*, Office for National Statistics.

Question 1.

The largest speculatively built office block outside London has opened to lettings in Birmingham. Owned by the private equity firm, Carlyle Group, Colmore Plaza is around 300,000 square feet.

The Birmingham economy has boomed over the last 15 years. It has, for the most part, recovered from the loss of much of its manufacturing industry in the 1970s, 1980s and 1990s. Today, the Birmingham economy is mainly service based. But up until now, Birmingham has had a shortage of modern office space. Offices built in the 1960s and 1970s are often scruffy and lacking in space for cabling. 'Historically there has been a dearth of decent office space in Birmingham', said Philippa Pickavance, a partner at property consultants Drivers Jonas. 'This year and in spring 2009 around 700,000 square feet of space will come onstream. But this is space we need.' Ms Pickavance calculates that 662,000 square feet were let last year in Birmingham, a 12 per cent increase on 2006.

However, the economy could be going into a recession. In turn, this could impact on the ability of Colmore Plaza to attract tenants. So far, one floor of the £150 million building has been rented to Davis Langdon, a project manager. This leaves another 11 floors to rent at target prices of over £30 per square foot. Carlyle Group must be hoping that any dip in growth of the Birmingham economy will be small and short lived.

Source: adapted from *The Financial Times*, 11.3.2008.

(a) Explain the links between economic growth and the building of office space.
(b) Evaluate whether Carlyle Group will have to lower its rents in 2008 and 2009 to attract tenants for its Colmore Plazza building.

downturn and RECESSION. So the word recession can be used both to describe a period of very low growth or a period when GDP is actually falling.

At the bottom of the business cycle:
- unemployment is relatively high and inflation relatively low;
- low increases in demand or, at worst, falls in demand will lead to workers being laid off;
- it will be difficult for businesses to increase their prices without losing sales;
- investment by businesses will be low and there will spare capacity in the economy.

Recovery In a RECOVERY or UPSWING, the economy begins to pick up again, and:
- the rate of growth of GDP starts to increase or moves from being negative to positive;
- unemployment begins to fall as businesses take on more workers to cope with the rise in economic activity;
- inflation might start to increase as the rate of growth of demand increases;
- businesses will begin to increase their investment spending as business confidence increases.

The impact of the business cycle on business

Changes in the level of economic activity affect all businesses. But some are affected more than others.

Output The major impact of the business cycle is on output and sales. In a boom, output and sales will be growing. In a recession, growth will be sluggish at best. At worst, output and sales fall. Some businesses will be more affected than others. Businesses that make or sell consumer necessities, such as food,

Question 2.

JCB warned of a 'flat' year ahead because of weakening demand in the US and parts of Europe. John Patterson, the chief executive of Britain's biggest maker of construction equipment, said he was cautious about 2008. There were increasing signs that the slowdown in the economy would affect demand for JCB's productions, used widely in housing and road construction in the US and in important parts of western Europe including the UK.

In the US, the overall market for construction machines slumped 13 per cent in 2007, according to John Patterson, and JCB's US sales fell by almost that amount. There were signs of similar weaknesses in countries such as Spain and Italy. The UK had held up fairly well in 2007, but 'there is a question mark over how the UK market will perform this year' said Mr Patterson.

However, the company highlighted the opportunities outside of these markets, particularly in India, Russia, South America and the Middle East. 'The growth in these places is likely to offset what could be a downturn elsewhere', commented Mr Patterson. He singled out India as the country were JCB had made the most headway recently. In 2007, India, where JCB has three plants, accounted for sales of 17,000 JCB

machines, almost a quarter of the world total. This was an increase of 60 per cent since 2006.

Source: adapted from *The Financial Times*, 12.3.2008.

(a) Explain, using a diagram and examples from the data, what is meant by a 'slowdown in the economy'.
(b) Evaluate strategies JCB could use to deal with a slowdown in its western European and US markets.

---

gas or petrol will not be too affected. People will continue to buy these products. Businesses which make luxury products or products whose purchase can be delayed, such as restaurant meals or cars, will suffer more.

Profit In a boom, it is easier for even inefficient businesses to make a profit. Markets are buoyant and there is often little pressure to lower prices.

In a recession, inefficient businesses or those making products that are not necessities can often make losses.

Business start-ups, expansion and closures In a boom, with sales and profits relatively easy to make, there is likely to be a high number of business starts-ups. Existing businesses might expand.

In a recession, businesses are forced to close down or abandon investment and expansion plans. Many businesses will contract in size, closing unprofitable areas. In a prolonged recession, there will be far more businesses closing down than starting up.

Employment In a boom, businesses will tend to take on workers to cope with expanding demand. However, recruitment may be difficult because unemployment is low and there are fewer workers looking for jobs. There will also be pressure on businesses to raise wages to stop staff leaving for better paid jobs.

In a recession, businesses will tend to reduce their workforces. Staff leaving may not be replaced, a process known as **natural wastage**. There may also be a need for compulsory redundancies.

Stocks and investment In a boom, stock levels and investment will be high, as explained above.

In a recession, both will fall, typically at a faster rate than the fall in demand.

Strategic responses to economic growth

Over time, the UK economy is growing in size at an average rate of 2.5 per cent. This presents businesses with considerable opportunities. On average, their sales and profits should be increasing by 2.5 per cent a year after inflation has been taken into account. Unfortunately, the situation facing businesses is far more complex. Over time, the pattern and structure of the economy is also changing.

- Rising incomes lead to demand for some products rising by far more than the average whilst for others they can lead to a fall in demand. For example, sales of jam have been falling for the past thirty years. With more income to spend, consumers prefer to buy other foods. On the other hand, demand for computer equipment has risen by far more than the average over the past 20 years.
- The structure of the economy is changing. Most of the UK's manufacturing industry has disappeared over the past 50 years because goods can be produced more cheaply overseas. New products and new production processes have also transformed what is produced and how it is produced.

Companies have a variety of possible strategies they can use in these circumstances.

- They can move from slow growing markets to fast growing markets in the hope of raising sales. For example, they can buy companies in fast growing markets and sell those parts of their existing business that are in slow growing markets. Or they can expand their own operations into fast growing markets and cut back on investment in those parts of the business which are in slow growing areas.

- Companies can stay in a slow growing market but hope that their competitors will leave it. Or they can take over some of their competitors. Either way, they can increase both sales and market share. It could also give them greater control of the market and allow them to raise prices and profit margins. So the strategy is for the company to grow at a fast rate whilst the market as a whole is growing slowly.
- Where companies are coming under pressure from cheap foreign competition, they need to reduce their own costs. One way is to increase sourcing of services, components and finished goods from overseas. A UK company then retains high value added processes in the UK.

Over time, companies find it difficult to make the changes needed to cope with profound, long-term changes in the economy as a whole. Most of the top 100 companies quoted on the London Stock Exchange today, for example, will have ceased to exist in 50 years time. They will have shrunk in size, been taken over, been split up or maybe even have disappeared completely.

Strategic responses to the business cycle

When fluctuations in the level of economic growth are very small, most businesses are unlikely to need to make any strategic response. This is because small changes in economic growth don't have much impact on sales for most businesses.

However, if the economy were to go into a severe recession, then many businesses would have to act decisively in order to survive. Sharp downturns in sales should be met by cuts in output and stocks. The business may need to make workers redundant. Companies may have to close down factories, offices and other facilities. Budgets, such as those for marketing and research, may have to be cut because of cash flow problems.

Some businesses, like grocery supermarkets, may feel relatively little impact of a recession because they sell necessities which consumers will continue to buy when their incomes fall. Other businesses, like house builders or furniture manufacturers, may see very sharp falls in orders. This is because consumers will make sharp reductions in purchases of what they see as luxuries like moving house or buying new furniture. Businesses which rely on consumers to buy their goods on credit could also be badly affected because in a recession consumers will be reluctant to take on new debt.

Recessions can be a business opportunity as well as a threat.

- Companies that have the cash may be able to buy up assets at a cheap price. Share prices of other companies are likely to be low. So it might be a good time to expand through acquisitions.
- Businesses which maintain their marketing spending through a recession may be able to gain a competitive

advantage over rivals who have been forced to cut their marketing spending.
- Maintaining spending on research and development and on staff training can also give a competitive advantage over rivals which have been forced to cut their spending.
- Some businesses may collapse and exit the market. This is an opportunity for another business to step in and gain the customers that have been abandoned.

KEY TERMS

Boom – the peak of the business cycle, when the economy is growing fast and unemployment is low but when there could be problems with rising inflation.

Business cycle or trade cycle or economic cycle – regular fluctuations in the level of output of the economy, going from boom through recession and depression to recovery.

Destocking – when a business reduces the levels of stock held.

Downturn or downswing or economic slowdown – when the rate of economic growth begins to fall and unemployment begins to rise.

Economic growth – the change in the productive potential of the economy; it is usually measured by changes in national income and in particular GDP.

Gross Domestic Product (GDP) – the commonest way in which national income is measured.

National income – the value of total income in the economy; it is also equal to the value of total spending and total production or output.

Recession or depression or slump – the bottom of the business cycle when economic growth is negative and there is high unemployment. Recession may also be used to describe a period of very slow economic growth.

Recovery or upswing – when the rate of economic growth begins to increase following a recession or depression and unemployment begins to fall.

KNOWLEDGE

1. What is the link between GDP and economic growth?
2. What are the differences between (a) a boom and a depression, (b) a recession and a recovery?
3. What impact might the business cycle have on (a) sales and (b) business start-ups?
4. A company is in a slow growing sector the economy. What might be its strategic response?
5. A company is faced with intense price competition from overseas competitors despite strong growth in the economy as a whole. What should be its strategic response?
6. Explain how a business manufacturing furniture might respond if the economy went into a deep recession and sales of furniture nationally fell by 20 per cent.

Case Study: UK housing

The slide in house prices is gathering momentum, according to Hometrack, the housing data company. Its survey suggests that values have fallen 0.3 per cent since last month, the third consecutive monthly fall and the largest in almost two years. Richard Donnell, direct of research at Hometrack, said: 'The second half of the year has seen a major reversal in confidence on the back of higher interest rates and concerns over the outlook for the financial markets.'

The downturn in the economy is affecting businesses. For example, Taylor Wood, one of Britain's biggest housebuilders, apparently took the decision to freeze all land purchases in mid-October and has completed only on deals agreed before then.

Source: adapted from business.times.online.co.uk 24.12.2007.

Hup Housebuilding plc is a UK regional housebuilding company operating mainly in the North of England. Over the past seven years, it has experienced a boom in sales. It expanded from approximately 1,000 completions of new properties in 2000 to 3,000 completions in 2006. The start of 2007 looked highly promising but conditions in the economy deteriorated suddenly and by the end of the year, the company was experiencing difficulties in selling newly completed properties. Whilst Hup Housebuilding completed almost 3,000 properties in 2007, it had 300 properties left unsold at the end of the year.

Its competitors were in a similar position. They were offering a wide variety of 'deals' to customers to entice them to buy. But they were also cutting back on starting new projects. For the first time in many years, applications for jobs with Hup Housebuilding had gone up. Hup Housebuilding also noticed that land prices were easing.

The Bank of England governor, Mervyn King, admitted yesterday that the economy might grind to a halt this year. When asked whether a recession was possible this year, he said the Bank's predictions were 'not inconsistent; with two quarters of falling GDP, the technical definition of a recession. He also warned that house prices could fall.

Source: adapted from www.guardian.co.uk 14.2.2008.

(a) Evaluate the strategies that Hup Housebuilding could use to cope with a possible recession in the economy in 2008.
    (40 marks)
(b) Discuss whether a downturn in the housing market could be more of an opportunity than a threat for Hup Housebuilding.
    (40 marks)

Interest and interest rates

If a business or an individual borrows money, they usually have to pay **interest** on the loan. Equally, if they put their savings into a bank or building society, they expect to receive interest.

The INTEREST RATE is the price of borrowing or saving money. For example, if a small business borrows £10,000 from a bank for one year, and the interest rate is 7 per cent, it has to pay £700 in interest. Equally, if a business has £1 million in the bank for a year which it uses as working capital, and the rate of interest the bank offers is 3 per cent, it will earn £30,000 in interest.

Different interest rates

A business might be able to borrow money on overdraft at 6 per cent. If it took out a five year loan, the interest rate might be 7 per cent. A consumer buying a house might be offered a mortgage rate of 8 per cent. The interest rate on a credit card might be 15 per cent.

These are just four of the thousands of interest rates in an economy. Each interest rate is set within a market for money. In each market, there is a **demand** for money. This comes from those who want to borrow money. There is also a **supply** of money from those who want to lend money. The forces of demand and supply will fix the price of money in that market, which is the interest rate.

Many money markets are influenced by the rate of interest set by the central bank of a country. In the UK, the central bank is the Bank of England. It has the power to fix the rate of interest charged and offered by the major banks in the UK on short-term loans and savings. Banks such as Barclays or HSBC will change their BASE RATE when the Bank of England declares a change in interest rates. The base rate of a bank is the rate around which all its other interest rates are structured. For short-term savings with the bank, it will offer interest rates below the base rate. For borrowing, it charges above the base rate. The profit it makes out of borrowing and lending has to come from the difference between the lower rate of interest it gives to savers and the higher rate of interest it charges to borrowers.

Base rates are linked to other rates of interest in the economy. When base rates fall, so do long-term rates of interest. The rate of interest on other types of borrowing, such as borrowing through a credit card, also tends to fall. But there is no direct link between these other interest rates and the base rates set by the Bank of England. So short-term interest rates can change and long-term interest rates can remain unaffected. Sometimes, long-term interest rates can be rising when short-term interest rates are falling. It depends on market conditions.

Effect on business overheads

Changes in interest rates are likely to affect the overheads of a

Question 1.

Dalton's is an industrial manufacturer of canning products. It currently has an overdraft of £1.2 million and loans of £4.3 million. Of these loans:

- £1.3 million are variable rate loans, with interest at 2 per cent above base rate;
- £1 million is at a fixed rate of 8 per cent;
- the remaining £2 million is at a fixed rate of 9 per cent.

(a) Explain why interest on borrowings is an overhead cost for Dalton's.

(b) Base rates in the economy fall from 6 per cent to 5 per cent. As a result the overdraft rates for Dalton's falls from 7 per cent to 6 per cent. Calculating the change in interest payments, explain how this will affect the company's overhead costs.

business. Interest charges are part of overhead costs. If interest rates rise, businesses are likely to have to pay higher interest payments on their borrowing. For example, a business might borrow £10,000 on overdraft. The annual payments on this would rise from £600 to £700 if the rate of interest rose from 6 to 7 per cent a year.

Not all borrowing is at variable rates of interest. Variable rates mean that banks or other lenders are free to change the rate of interest on any money borrowed. Many loans to businesses are at fixed rates of interest. This is where the bank cannot change the rate of interest over the agreed term (the time over which the loan will be paid off) of the loan. A rise in interest rates in the economy won't affect the overheads of a business with only fixed term loans. But, if a business wanted to take out new loans, it would have to pay the higher rates of interest the bank or other lender was now charging. So overhead costs would rise.

Question 2.

Bill Lockington was devastated when his business went up in flames. He made a range of tyres, manufactured from existing worn out tyres. His 'retreads' had proved popular with customers because of their high quality and low prices compared with brand new tyres. Due to the high cost of insurance, he was uninsured at the time of the accident and it looked as though ten years' hard work had come to an abrupt end.

However, having got over the psychological shock of seeing £250,000 worth of equipment and stock destroyed overnight, he decided that it was possible to rebuild the business. Two important things had not disappeared. First, he still had a list of customers who wanted to buy his tyres. Second, he had the knowledge and a skilled workforce to produce quality retreads. Low interest rates were vital to success too. He could not have afforded to borrow the money to restart the business if he could not have borrowed at 7 per cent from his bank. The retread business was also highly dependent on buoyant consumer confidence. Low interest rates encouraged customers to buy vehicles and motorcycles and so create the demand for retreads in the longer term.

Even so, he had to make economies. Before the fire, he had built up stocks worth £100,000 of used tyres. Such large levels of stock were unnecessary for the efficient running of the business. His new business started with just £20,000 worth of stock.

(a) Explain carefully how low interest rates affected Bill Lockington's business.
(b) Suggest why he only bought £20,000 worth of stock to restart the business when previously he had held £100,000 worth of stock.
(c) Discuss whether Bill Lockington could have recovered from the fire if interest rates had been high at the time.

Effect on investment decisions

Changes in the rate of interest affect the amount that businesses invest, for example in new buildings, plant and machinery. There are four main reasons for this.

The cost of loans Investment projects are often financed through loans. A rise in interest rates increases the cost of borrowing money. So projects financed this way will find that the total costs have risen, reducing profitability. This might be enough to persuade some businesses to shelve their investment plans. Total investment in the economy will then fall.

Attractiveness of saving Businesses have the alternative of putting their funds into savings schemes rather than investing in machinery or buildings, for example. A rise in interest rates makes putting money into financial assets relatively more attractive. For example, if interest rates rise from 5 to 8 per cent, a business might decide to shelve an investment project and save the funds instead.

Paying off existing loans A rise in interest rates will increase the cost of existing variable rate borrowing. A business could choose to pay off existing loans rather than increase its investment. This will reduce its costs. It also reduces the risk associated with borrowing.

A fall in demand A rise in interest rates is likely to reduce total

spending in the economy, as explained below. This might affect the profitability of many investment projects. For example, a business might forecast that an investment project would be profitable with 20,000 sales a year. But if sales were projected to be only 15,000 a year because of a downturn in demand, then the investment project could be unprofitable and might not go ahead.

Effect on demand

The level of interest rates affects aggregate demand (i.e. total demand) for goods and services in the economy. A rise in interest rates will tend to push down aggregate demand. A fall in interest rates will tend to increase demand.

Businesses are directly affected by changes in demand. When demand falls, their sales go down because less is being bought. If demand rises, businesses receive more orders and more sales.

There are many different ways in which changes in interest rates lead to changes in the sales of businesses.

Domestic consumption Consumers will be hit by a rise in interest rates. The cost of loans will rise. This will deter consumers from buying goods bought on credit, such as cars, furniture and electrical equipment. These goods are known as CONSUMER DURABLES because they are 'used up' over a long period.

In the UK, people who have a mortgage (a loan to buy a house) are also likely to see their monthly repayments rise because most mortgages are variable rate loans. Existing mortgage holders will then have less to spend on other goods and services. Some potential new home buyers will be put off because they can't afford the repayments, directly hitting the new housing market. If unemployment begins to rise because of less spending, consumer confidence will fall. This will make consumers even less willing to take out loans and spend.

Domestic investment As explained above, businesses are likely to cut back plans for new investment if interest rates rise. Investment goods, like new buildings or machines, are made by businesses. So these businesses will see a fall in their demand.

Stocks Businesses keep stocks of raw materials and finished goods. Stocks cost money to keep, because a fall in stock levels could be used to finance a fall in borrowing and interest payments. So a rise in interest rates will increase the cost of keeping stock. This will encourage businesses to destock, i.e. reduce their stock levels. This will be especially true if the rise in interest rates has hit demand in the economy. With fewer sales, less needs to be produced. So less stock needs to be kept. But cutting stock reduces orders for businesses further up the chain of production. For example, a retailer cutting stocks affects demand from its suppliers. Destocking due to higher interest rates will therefore cause a fall in demand throughout much of industry.

Exports and imports A rise in interest rates tends to lead to a rise in the value of one currency against others. A rise in the pound, for example, will make it harder for UK businesses to export profitably. At the same time, foreign firms will find it easier to gain sales in the UK domestic market because they will be able to reduce their prices. The result is likely to be a fall in exports and a loss of sales to importers in the domestic market. Both will reduce demand and hit UK businesses.

Variable impact on businesses

Changes in interest rates affect different businesses in different ways. Businesses that are most likely to be affected are those which:

- have high levels of borrowing at variable rates of interest;
- sell consumer goods, typically bought on credit;
- are directly linked to the housing market, such as house builders;
- produce investment goods for other businesses;
- depend on exports or are in markets where competition from imports is particularly strong.

A rise in interest rates might have little impact on some of these. For example, a rise in interest rates might not deter consumers from taking out loans because their confidence is

high. Or the rise might have little impact on the value of the pound and so not affect exports and imports. The impact depends very much on what else is happening in the economy.

There are also many businesses that are unlikely to see much change in their demand even if other businesses are suffering. For example, consumers tend not to cut back on their spending on food even when times are hard. So supermarkets are often unaffected by changes in interest rates. A hairdressers or a village post office are unlikely to be much affected either.

Strategy and interest rates

Different businesses should have different strategic reactions to changes in interest rates.

- If interest rate changes are relatively small, then there is little need for businesses to change their strategies at all. When interest rates are low, a movement of 1 or 2 per cent in interest rates is unlikely to have much impact.
- Highly indebted businesses are particularly at risk from interest rate rises. Sharp rises in interest rates over a short period of time can push such businesses towards insolvency. They need to reduce their debt burden as quickly as possible. In the short term, this may mean selling assets, if necessary at the expense of future sales and profits. Some businesses may be able to refinance debt. It could be that shopping around banks or other financial institutions will give a lower rate of interest on borrowings. Alternatively, a company may be able to raise share capital and convert some its debt into equity.
- Significant falls in interest rates should stimulate investment by businesses. With the cost of borrowing significantly cheaper, investment projects, which in the past would have been unprofitable, now become profitable. Extra investment might make a business more competitive and allow it to expand sales or market share with the objective of increasing profit and shareholder value. Conversely, a significant rise in interest rates will increase the cost of borrowing, making investment less profitable. So a business is likely to reduce its investment.
- If rises in interest rates are large enough to cause a sharp downturn in the economy, then businesses exposed to markets most affected by the downturn will need to react. A supermarket chain will not see much impact on sales from a downturn and so need take little action. A furniture manufacturer, on the other hand, could see a large drop in sales. It needs to take immediate action to reduce production levels. It should cut stocks and, if necessary, cut the number of workers it employs. The longer the recession, the deeper it will need to cut.

KEYTERMS

Base rate – the rate of interest around which a bank structures its other interest rates. A rise in the base rate will result in a rise in most saving and borrowing rates and vice versa.

Consumer durables – consumer goods such as televisions, furniture and cars which are used over a long period of time. They are often bought on credit.

Interest rate – the price of borrowing or saving money. There are many different interest rates charged in an economy because there are many different markets for borrowed funds.

KNOWLEDGE

1. A business has borrowed £100,000 on overdraft. Bank base rates rise. How is this likely to affect the amount of interest the business pays?
2. What is the difference between variable and fixed rates of interest for a business that has borrowed money?
3. Explain briefly why the investment plans of a business may change if there is a fall in the rate of interest.
4. (a) How might consumers react to a fall in the rate of interest and (b) why might this benefit businesses?
5. Why might businesses destock if interest rates rise?
6. Why might a fall in interest rates lead to a change in export orders?

Case Study: *Fastenings*

n 1991 bank base rates had been at the crippling level of 14-15 per cent for nearly two years. The economy was in the midst of a deep, prolonged recession which had begun in 1989. Al Farrall had run his fastening business for 23 years, but he had never known conditions like this.

He manufactured fastenings mainly for the car and furniture industries. Bolts, castor pegs, nuts and pins were the staple products. Like many businesses, he had expanded in the mid-1980s. Furniture sales were booming in the climate of relatively low interest rates. The housing market was also booming, which encouraged home owners to buy new furniture as they moved house.

At the same time, car production picked up, first for the domestic market and then later for export. But, in 1989, the bottom dropped out of this market. Bank base rates had gone from a low of 7.5 per cent in mid-1987 to 14 per cent by mid-1989. Car production fell back and furniture sales slumped. He not only lost sales volumes, but found himself having to offer ridiculously low priced contracts to win orders.

By early 1991, Al's business was facing closure. He had already been forced to cut the workforce from 20 in 1989 to 12 in 1991, helping to swell the ranks of the UK unemployed which had risen from 1.5 million to 3 million over the period. While his workforce shrank, his borrowing just kept growing. With the benefit of hindsight, he knew that he had made a huge mistake to borrow £150 000 to buy new equipment in 1988. A third of his equipment now lay idle because of lack of orders. His borrowings stood at an unsustainable £200,000 given that the business had made a loss of £25 000 in 1990 and was on track to make a loss of £30,000 in 1991. The business desperately needed a cut in interest rates and a return to growth in the economy.

(a) To what extent were Al Farrall's business problems caused by overborrowing in the late 1980s? (40 marks)

(b) Bank base rates fell from 14 per cent in February 1991 to 6 per cent in February 1993. Discuss whether this change could have helped Al's business to survive. (40 marks)

82 | Exchange rates

The exchange rate of a currency

An EXCHANGE RATE is the price of one currency against another. For instance, the exchange rate of the pound might be €1 = £0.58 or £1 = US$1.60. At these exchange rates, a business wanting to buy €1 million through its bank would have to pay £580,000 (€1 million x 0.58) plus a commission.

Currencies can change in value. If the exchange rate changed to € = £0.60, the business would now have to pay £600,000 (€ million x 0.60) plus commission.

- A rise in the value of the pound against other currencies means that the pound will buy more foreign currency. For example, if the value of the pound changed from £1 = €1.60 to £1 = €1.75, this would a rise in the value of the pound. Each pound is now worth €0.15 more than before. A rise in the pound is sometimes called an APPRECIATION of the currency.
- A DEPRECIATION or **fall** in the value of the pound would mean that the pound would buy less foreign currency than before. A change from £1 = $1.50 to £1 = $1.30 would be an example. The pound buys $0.20 less than before.

Sometimes, the value of a currency is said to be high. This means that it can buy more foreign currency compared to the recent historical average. For example, the recent historical average value of the pound against the euro might be £1 = €1.40. If the actual value of the pound today were £1 = €1.60, the value of the pound would be high. On the other hand, it would be low if it were well below the £1 = €1.40 level. So, for example, it would be low if the exchange rate were £1 = €1.20.

Exports and exchange rate changes

Businesses can be directly or indirectly affected by changes in the exchange rate. Those most affected are likely to be EXPORTING (selling goods and services to foreign governments, businesses and individuals) or IMPORTING (buying goods and services from abroad).

Take a UK company that EXPORTS marmalade abroad. The price of a pot of marmalade is 50p. If the value of the pound is £1 = €1.60, a company abroad buying a pot of marmalade will pay €0.80 for it (1.60 x 0.50p). What if the value of the pound now appreciates (i.e. rises) to £1 = €1.80? How might the UK business react?

Keep the price in pounds the same The UK company could keep the price in pounds the same. So at 50p per pot, it would now cost the foreign company €0.90 (1.80 x 0.50p). This rise in price from €0.80 to €0.90 would affect demand (i.e. the quantity bought). It is likely that the quantity demanded would

fall. The UK company would see a fall in sales abroad. By how much depends on how price sensitive was demand. If it was highly price sensitive (i.e. price elasticity of demand is high), the percentage fall in sales would be high. If demand was fairly insensitive (i.e. price elasticity of demand is low), then there would be little effect on sales.

Keep the foreign currency price the same The UK company could keep the foreign currency price the same, i.e. keep the price of the pot of marmalade at €0.80. If it did, the price it would receive in pounds would fall to around 44p (€0.80 ÷ the exchange rate = €0.80 ÷ €1.80). By adopting this pricing

Question 2.

Rugol & Flynn's is a company which manufactures household goods. The managing director, George Rugol, is an outspoken critic of Britain's failure to join the European Monetary Union. Over the years, he has seen large fluctuations in the value of the pound against European currencies and against the US dollar. Within a matter of weeks, the pound can go up or down against key trading currencies by 5 per cent or more. This is highly disruptive to his business since his company exports mainly to Europe but also to the USA.

George Rugol is very careful to ensure that all export contracts are hedged – that is, the company buys or sells foreign currency in advance so that it knows how much it will receive in pounds on any given order. But this takes both time and money to arrange with its bankers. The company wouldn't have to do this for sales in Europe if the UK used the same currency, the euro, as its main trading partners.

Equally, the business imports raw materials. The exact price to be paid is uncertain because of day-to-day exchange rate fluctuations. Again, the company hedges all contracts but this adds to the costs of the contract.

George Rugol wants it to be as risk free to sell his products to Germany or France as it is to London or Scotland. This means that Britain must adopt the euro.

(a) Rugol and Flynn's signs a contract to export goods to France in one month's time for 50,000 euros. A week later, the value of the pound rises by 5 per cent against the euro. Explain whether the company would gain or lose out as a result?

(b) Explain whether the UK joining the euro would help Rugol and Flynn's with its exports to the USA.

strategy, demand for marmalade should remain unchanged. But profits from marmalade sales would fall. It might even be the case that at 44p the business would make a loss on the sale.

So for an exporting business, a **rise** in the value of the pound is likely to result in either a fall in export sales, a fall in profits on those sales, or both. Which of these occurs depends on the pricing policy the exporting company adopts following the appreciation of the currency.

The reverse is true if the value of the pound **falls**. Exporting companies can choose to let the foreign currency prices of their goods fall. This should lead to a rise in export sales. Or they can improve their profit margins by raising the price in pounds to a level where the foreign currency price is unchanged. Or they can do a combination of the two, seeing some increase in sales and some increase in profits.

Imports and exchange rate changes

Businesses that IMPORT goods are affected by exchange rate changes too. For example, the marmalade manufacturer might import oranges from Spain. What happens if the value of the pound changes?

A rise in the value of the pound If the price of the pound goes up against the euro, it means that the company can now buy more euros for £1. So the price of imports should fall. For example, assume that it can buy 10 kilos of oranges for €1.60. At an exchange rate of £1 = €1.60, 10 kilos cost £1. But if the exchange rate of the pound now appreciates to £1 = €1.80, the cost of 10 kilos of oranges, still priced at €1.60, falls to around 89p (€1.60 ÷ €1.80).

A fall in the value of the pound The opposite occurs if the value of the pound falls. For example, the pound might depreciate from £1 = €1.60 to £1 = €1.40. Before, 10 kilos of oranges cost €1.60 or £1. After, 10 kilos of oranges still cost €1.60. But the price in pounds is around £1.14 (€1.60 ÷ €1.40). A fall in the value of the pound leads to higher import prices.

As with exports, foreign companies could adjust their own prices to compensate for the change in the exchange rate.

So, if the value of the pound **rises**, import prices in pounds will fall and foreign firms will become more competitive in the UK market. Instead of selling more exports to the UK, however, foreign firms could choose instead to raise prices in their currency. If they raised them so that the price in pounds remained the same, they wouldn't sell any more products to the UK. But they would increase their profit on each sale.

If the value of the pound **falls**, import prices in pounds will go up and foreign businesses will find it more difficult to sell into the UK market. By cutting prices in their own currency, foreign firms can bring the price in pounds back to what it was before. They, however, suffer lower profits as a result.

Direct and indirect effects of exchange rate changes on a business

Businesses can be affected directly and indirectly by changes in the exchange rate.

Directly Businesses might be affected by changes in the exchange rate directly because they sell abroad or buy imports. Many of these businesses are both exporters and importers. For them, exchange rate changes can have complicated effects.

- A UK business that buys roughly the same amount of imports as it exports can be unaffected by an exchange rate change. If the pound falls in value, the extra cost of imports can be offset by rises in the UK price of its exports.
- A UK business that has high levels of exports, but imports little, is likely to benefit from a **depreciation** of the pound. It can either allow foreign currency prices to fall and so become more competitive overseas, or it can increase its prices in pounds and so increase profit margins.
- A UK business that has high levels of exports, but imports little is likely to suffer from an **appreciation** of the pound. Either it will have to put up foreign currency prices and become less competitive or it will have to absorb the exchange rate rise by lowering its prices in pounds, resulting in lower profit margins.

Indirectly UK businesses can also suffer indirectly from exchange rate changes. This is because of the effect of a change in the value of the pound on inflation.

A **depreciation** in the value of the pound will mean that the price of imported goods and services is likely to rise. UK businesses that import these products could pass on some of the rise in price to customers, many of whom will be other businesses. So a business that doesn't import anything may still pay higher prices for supplies because of a fall in the exchange rate.

Similarly, an **appreciation** of the pound can lead to importing businesses passing on the saving made on imports to their customers in the form of lower prices.

Exchange rates and the rate of interest

Changes in interest rates can lead to changes in exchange rates. A fall in interest rates, for example, is likely to lead to a fall in the exchange rate. Lower interest rates discourage saving and investment in a country. So if UK interest rates fall, fewer pounds will be bought to invest in the UK. A rise in interest rates is likely to raise the exchange rate.

How might lower interest rates and exchange rates affect a business? Lower interest rates can **benefit** UK businesses:
- borrowing money in the UK, as they pay back less;
- selling to the UK market, because lower interest rates will encourage UK consumers to borrow and spend more;
- selling exports. They can either sell more, since prices will be cheaper to foreigners, or increase their prices and profit margins.

A fall in interest rates is likely to **harm** UK businesses because:
- inflation in the UK may increase as a result of higher import prices;
- UK businesses that import materials from abroad may be affected by a fall in the exchange rate which causes import prices to rise.

The opposite is true if interest rates rise.

Strategy and exchange rates

Many businesses find that exchange rate changes can have a major effect on their finances. They have to develop strategies to cope with exchange rate changes.

Balancing exports and imports A business could try to balance the value of exports and products that are imported. Some car manufacturers operating in the UK have adopted this strategy. If the value of the pound rises, the manufacturer lowers its export prices in pounds to leave the foreign currency price the same. But the lower revenues it earns in pounds are matched by the lower prices it has to pay for imported products. The net result is that profit is unaffected.

Similarly, if the value of the pound falls, import prices will rise for the business. But it can offset this by raising the price of its exports in pounds, which leaves the foreign currency price to its customers the same.

Becoming more competitive Changes in the value of the pound can affect two main groups of businesses. If the value of the pound rises:
- exporters will find that the foreign currency price of their goods will rise if they maintain existing prices in pounds. This will damage export sales;
- imports are likely to fall in price. This will harm sales of UK businesses that make products competing against imports.

A fall in the value of the pound will help both UK exporters and those UK businesses in competition with imports.

Both exporters and UK businesses that compete against imported products can attempt to become more COMPETITIVE. They can do this in two ways.

First, they can try to reduce their costs so they can reduce their prices to customers. If the value of the pound rises by 10 per cent, for example, UK exporters need to cut their prices in pounds by 10 per cent to maintain the same price in foreign currency. Greater price competitiveness can be achieved by more efficient methods of production. The business might be able to get better prices on the products it buys in from suppliers. The workforce may need to be reduced in numbers, with the remaining workers working more efficiently than before. In a few cases, businesses have been forced to cut the wages of workers to achieve cost savings.

Second, they can become more competitive by adding value to the products they sell. Their products might be more reliable or better designed than those available from overseas competitors. Or the UK business might promise faster delivery times.

Marketing changes One response to a rise in the value of the pound for an exporter would be to pull out of the export market. If the business judged that it simply couldn't compete at the new higher exchange rate, then it should concentrate on the domestic market. The opposite strategic response might come from a UK business which suffers competition from abroad. A rise in the value of the pound will make imports cheaper and so give foreign companies a competitive advantage. To compensate for lower UK sales, the UK business may decide that it must expand into foreign markets and so it will start to export products.

Similarly, if the value of the pound fell, this would make UK products more competitive abroad. This could be a marketing opportunity for existing exporters to expand their markets. It could also be an opportunity for a UK firm which hadn't exported before to seek out new markets abroad.

Joining the euro

At present, the UK is not part of the eurozone. Most of the rest of the European Union has had a singe currency, the euro, since 2001. What would be the implications for British businesses if Britain joined the eurozone and replaced the pound with the euro?

Over 50 per cent of all UK exports and imports go to and come from other European Union countries. Joining the euro would mean that the price of those exports and imports would be fixed for UK businesses. There would be no more appreciation or depreciation of the UK currency against other European currencies. Selling to France or Italy would be the same as selling to Northumberland, London or Northern Ireland. As a result, businesses trading with other euro countries wouldn't have to pay commission to banks to change pounds into foreign currencies. It would also remove the uncertainty

caused by changing exchange rates. What will be the exchange rate when payment is made on the import or export contract?

However, UK businesses would still face these risks when selling or buying outside the eurozone. Just as the pound can fluctuate against the US dollar or the Japanese Yen, so does the euro.

KNOWLEDGE

1. What is the difference between an appreciating pound and a depreciating pound?
2. (a) An exporter charges £20 for a product sold to the USA. What would be the price in US$ if the exchange rate were (i) £1 = $1.60; (ii) £1 = $1.85; (iii) £1 = $1.35? (b) At what exchange rate would the exporter be most competitive?
3. The value of the pound changes from £1 = $1.70 to £1 = $1.40. How might a UK exporter to the USA change its prices as a result and what would be the effect on sales?
4. Why might a rise in the value of the pound force UK exporters to become more competitive?
5. How might exchange rate changes affect marketing?

KEYTERMS

Appreciation of a currency – a rise in the value of a currency.
Competitiveness – the extent to which a business or a geographical area such as a country, can compete successfully against rivals.
Depreciation of a currency – a fall in the value of a currency.
Exchange rate – the price of one currency in terms of another currency.
Exports – goods or services produced domestically and sold to foreigners.
Exporting – selling goods and services produced domestically to foreigners.
Imports – goods or services produced outside the country and purchased from foreigners.
Importing – buying goods and services produced outside a country from foreigners.

Case Study: Hot dogs

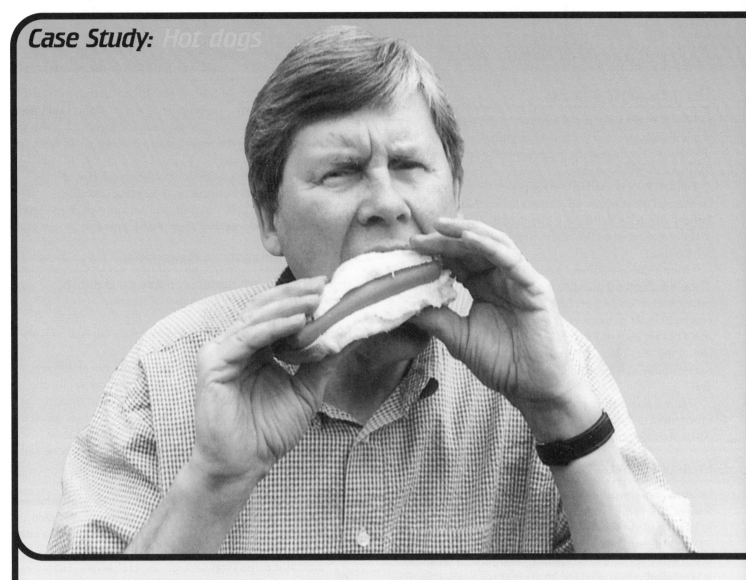

Joseph Wolff is a major importer of hot dogs to the UK. He founded his business 20 years ago and imports mainly from Germany and Denmark. Over the years, he has had to cope with large changes in the value of the pound against both the German deutschmark, the old German currency, and the Danish krona. Today, he is no better off. The German deutschmark has been replaced by the euro. But the Danish krona still exists because Denmark, like the UK, refused to adopt the euro as its currency in 2002 when the euro was launched.

The hot dog business is fiercely competitive. When the pound depreciates in value, Wolff is unable immediately to put up prices to his UK customers. He simply has to see his profit margins reduced. On the other hand, his short-term profit margins improve when the pound appreciates in value against the euro and the krona. Over a longer period of time, he make small price adjustments, but he has to be careful not to put up his prices too much or else he would lose orders from customers.

Over the years, Wolff has tried to reduce exchange rate risks by seeing if he could buy hot dogs from UK sausage manufacturers. The quality of the UK product has been disappointing though. UK manufacturers seem to have little idea of how to make a truly great hot dog.

(a) Discuss the possible impact of changes in the value of the pound on Wolff's hot dog business. (40 marks)
(b) Consider whether Wolff would be better off setting up his own hot dog manufacturing business in the UK. (40 marks)

The meaning of inflation

INFLATION is a general **rise** in prices in the economy. A 5 per cent inflation rate over the past 12 months, for example, means that the average increase in prices across the economy during the past year was 5 per cent.

DEFLATION is a **fall** in average prices. Deflation means that, on average, the products are cheaper to buy than before. Note, however, the term 'deflation' is also used to describe a recession in the economy, when the inflation rate is falling but inflation is still positive.

Figure 1 shows inflation since 1959 for the UK economy. There have been considerable fluctuations in the yearly rise in prices, from a low of 0 per cent in 1959 to a high of 24.1 per cent in 1975. At its worst in 1975, a basket of products which cost £1 at the start of the year had risen in price to £1.24 at the end of the year. Today, the Bank of England is given the responsibility of keeping inflation at around 2.5 per cent per year.

Figure 2 shows price changes for Japan since 1990. It experienced deflation in a number of years during the 1990s and 2000s. Average prices were falling in Japan.

Inflation, deflation and businesses

Inflation is not necessarily a problem. If prices are rising by a few per cent each year, and the inflation rate is fairly constant, inflation is likely to have little impact on businesses.

The situation is different if inflation is high. At 5 per cent and over, businesses have to be managed to cope with inflation. When inflation gets over, say, 20 per cent per annum, there are serious consequences for businesses. This is particularly true if inflation is fluctuating. For example, if yearly inflation goes from 5 per cent to 25 per cent to 150 per cent and then back down to 10 per cent in a four year period, then a business could easily be forced to close.

Equally, even quite low levels of deflation can have a significant impact on business. So there is considerable difference between 2 per cent inflation per year, which has little or no effect on business, and 2 per cent deflation.

Effects of inflation on businesses

High and particularly fluctuating inflation is likely to be damaging to business for a number of reasons.

Increased costs High or fluctuating inflation imposes a variety of costs on businesses.

- With suppliers' prices rising all the time, but at different rates, time must be spent researching the market for the best deals. Equally, more time has to be spent tracking the prices of competitors to decide when and by how much to increase your own prices. These costs are called **shoe leather costs,** because before the age of the telephone and the Internet, businesses would have to send their employees round on foot to gather this information.
- Raising prices costs money. Customers have to be informed of the new prices. Brochures might have to be reprinted and sent out. Websites might have to be updated. The sales force has to be made familiar with new prices. These costs are called **menu costs** because, for a restaurant, increasing prices means that it has to reprint its menus.

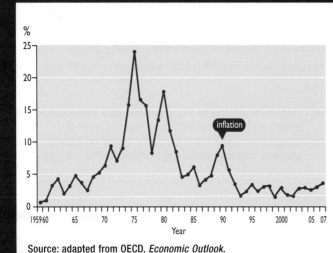

Figure 1: Inflation in the UK

Source: adapted from OECD, *Economic Outlook*.

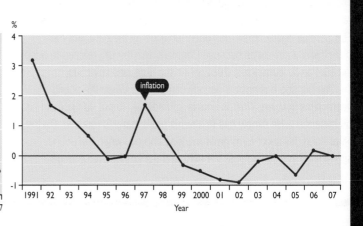

Figure 2: Inflation in Japan

Source: adapted from OECD, *Economic Outlook*.

- Management is likely to have to spend more time dealing with workers' pay claims. Instead of being able to sign a two or three year deal, annual pay negotiations are likely to be the norm. If there is **hyperinflation**, where inflation is running into 100 per cent per annum or over, pay negotiations may have to take place each month. There is also a much larger risk of strikes because workers and managers will probably have different views of future inflation rates. Workers will be worried that any deal they make will leave them worse off after inflation. So they might be more willing to take industrial action to get high pay settlements.

Uncertainty With high and fluctuating inflation, businesses don't know what prices will be in three or six months' time, let alone in one or five years. But decisions have to be made now which will affect the business in the long term. For example, businesses need to invest to survive. But how much should they invest? The price of a new machine, a shop or a new computer system will probably be higher in six months than today. But are they worth buying if interest rates are at very high levels? What if the new machine is bought, financed by very high cost borrowing and there is a **recession**, where demand for goods and services falls?

Another problem with uncertainty is linked to entering long-term contracts. A customer might approach a business wanting to buy products on a regular monthly basis for the next two years. How can the supplier put a price on this contract if it doesn't know what the inflation rate will be over the next 24 months?

Borrowing and lending Borrowing and lending becomes an opportunity and a problem for businesses. On the one hand, the real value of debts incurred in the past can become quickly eroded by inflation. If inflation is 100 per cent per annum, the real value of money borrowed a year ago is halved in one year. Inflation initially benefits borrowers and harms lenders.

But in an inflationary environment, interest rates rise to match inflation. If inflation is 100 per cent, interest rates might be 110 per cent. If there is prolonged inflation, interest rates are likely to become INDEX LINKED – linked to the index of prices. So interest might be charged at the rate of inflation plus 5 per cent or plus 10 per cent.

Consumer reactions Consumers react to inflation as well as businesses. Prolonged inflation tends to lead to more saving. Inflation unsettles consumers. They become less willing to borrow money, not knowing what will happen in the future. The value of savings tends to fall as inflation erodes their real value. So people react by saving more to make up savings to their previous real value. Increased saving means less spending and so businesses will sell less.

If inflation is very high, consumers will adopt different spending patterns which may affect businesses. For example, if there is hyperinflation, prices will be changing by the day. Consumers will then tend to spend wages or interest as soon as they receive them. On 'pay day' there can be huge activity in shops. Supermarkets have to be geared up to selling most of the weekly or monthly turnover in just a few hours. Suppliers of fresh produce to supermarkets have to be geared to delivering most of their goods on one day a week.

Question 1.

Zeenat is a small garment manufacturer in Nottingham, with 15 employees. It makes up clothes for a variety of buyers, including a couple of high street chains. The past four years have been very difficult for the company. Prices paid have been falling consistently as retailers have increasingly sourced clothes from the Far East. Last month, for example, official statistics were published showing that the price of clothes on the high street had fallen by 1.8 per cent the previous month.

It had all been different when the company was started up ten years previously. Then, prices could be increased each year to cover increased costs such as wage increases or raw material price rises. Today, costs were still going up but prices were falling. Take, for example, the minimum wage which the company has to pay its remaining workers. This had increased by 4 per cent last year and would be going up another 3.5 per cent next year.

(a) Why are falling prices a problem for a company such as Zeenat?
(b) Discuss whether high inflation would pose worse problems for Zeenat than mild deflation would..

International competitiveness High inflation poses problems for businesses that buy or sell abroad.

If the inflation rate in the UK is 10 per cent, but is only 2 per cent in France, then UK **exporters** will become uncompetitive against French businesses. For example, if a UK product is priced at 58 pence, it would be sold at €1 in France (assuming the exchange rate is €1= £0.58). Now assume there is inflation in the UK and the manufacturer has to put its prices up by 10 per cent to 63.8p or €1.10. In contrast, competitors in France only experience 2 per cent inflation and put their prices up to €1.02. The UK exporter has therefore lost price competitiveness and will find it harder to sell into the French market.

UK businesses facing competition from French firms will also suffer because French imports to the UK will be relatively cheaper. UK companies might have to put up their prices by 10 per cent because of cost-push pressures in the UK economy when French competitors are only putting up their prices by 2 per cent. UK companies will therefore lose market share in their home market.

Effects of deflation on businesses

Deflation, a general fall in overall prices, can also lead to problems for businesses.

A stagnant economy Deflation tends to be associated with an economy which is not growing in size. It might even be shrinking. This is because falls in price are often associated with falling levels of demand. Consumers are reluctant to spend money. Businesses don't want to increase their investment because their output is stagnant. Demand for exports may also be stagnant, perhaps because of a recession in the world economy. In a stagnant economy, problems could be made worse by rising unemployment. This also tends to reduce the willingness of consumers to spend and borrow. Faced with deflation, businesses will find it difficult to expand their own production. Many could face falling demand for their products if they are selling into markets which are in decline because of changes in spending patterns.

Reducing costs Deflation means that businesses are being forced to cut their prices. When deflation initially occurs, businesses may choose to pay for the price cuts by simply cutting their profits or accepting a loss for the year. But if deflation is prolonged, businesses have to cut their costs to survive. Cost cutting year on year is very difficult. It may be possible to achieve lower costs through more efficient production methods. An alternative is to cut the wages of workers. This is likely to lead to demotivation and threats of industrial action. It is perhaps more difficult to manage a business that continually has to cut its prices than it is to manage one where prices can be slowly pushed upwards.

In recent years, some industries, particularly in the manufacturing sector, have seen the prices of their products fall when prices in the economy as a whole have been rising. They have been suffering from deflation when there has been mild inflation in the whole economy. The cause has been intense price competition, particularly from the Far East and countries like China. They have been forced either substantially to increase their productivity, or to move upmarket where price competition is less intense.

Strategy and inflation

If inflation is low, businesses are unlikely to need to have strategies to cope with changing prices. It is only when inflation rates rise considerably that businesses may need to adapt their strategies. The main strategic responses of businesses to high inflation should be to push up their own prices while at the same time attempting to minimise the rises in their own costs.

Pushing up prices Moderate to high general inflation in an economy is likely to mean that a business is facing increases in its own costs. Suppliers will be pushing up their prices while workers will be demanding higher wages. Businesses can respond strategically to these cost pressures by putting up their own prices and so maintaining their profit margins. Putting up prices will be much easier if competitors are also putting up their prices. Equally, if a business is selling a popular differentiated product, this will reduce the ability of customers to buy elsewhere when prices are raised. However, there is always a danger when putting up prices that sales will fall and market share will be lost.

Reducing costs An alternative strategy to inflationary pressures is to cut costs. For example, a business may buy labour saving equipment in order to cut the cost of labour. It may seek out alternative suppliers willing to charge lower prices. It may look at all its production processes and make changes to increase efficiency in production. Cost cutting is likely to most successful as a strategy when inflation is relatively low. When inflation is relatively high, the best a business might hope to achieve is to have lower cost inflation than its competitors.

KEYTERMS

Deflation – strictly defined, it is a fall in the general price level within an economy. It is often used, however, to describe a situation when the rate of economic growth is falling or is negative and when inflation is falling.
Index linked – in the context of inflation, adjusting the value of economic variables such as wages or the rate of interest in line with a measure of inflation such as the Retail Price Index.
Inflation – a general rise in prices.

KNOWLEDGE

1. What is the difference between inflation and deflation?
2. Explain the problems that a business might face if:
   (a) there is very high inflation of 25 per cent per year;
   (b) there is high inflation and it does not know whether inflation will rise or fall next year;
   (c) it has financial reserves of £2 million deposited with its bank and there is high inflation;

   (d) it is a major exporter and inflation is much lower in other countries;
   (e) prices in the economy are, on average, falling.
3. What strategies might a business use if inflation is high?

Case Study: McGinnel's

McGinnel's is a small independent oil supply company in the south west of England. It buys oil on the open market from refineries and sells to businesses and home owners with oil fired central heating systems. Its green and white liveried tankers are a familiar sight in its local market.

The single largest cost for the company tends to be the oil it buys. The price of crude oil over the years has fluctuated enormously. The result has been that the cost base of the business has also fluctuated significantly.

Another major cost facing the company has been the wage costs of employees, together with related costs such as National Insurance contributions, pension contributions and training. These costs have tended to rise at roughly the same rate as average inflation in the UK. Although tanker drivers' pay has risen faster than the rate of inflation, this has been, to some extent, offset by rises in productivity. Through improved working practices and the introduction of new technology, fewer staff have been needed to deliver the same amount of oil.

Other costs include running a small fleet of tanker trucks for delivery of oil to customers and the overhead costs of the central office and plant for storing oil. Over time, these costs have risen at a little over the average rate of inflation for the economy.

The price that the company charges its customers is very much affected by the price charged by its competitors, the oil majors such as BP Amoco or Texaco. McGinnel's has survived the competition over the years by giving very slightly better prices to customers than the oil majors. Sometimes this pricing policy has caused financial problems because McGinnel's has had to pay higher prices for its oil supplies, but has been unable to pass on the higher cost because the oil majors have left their prices constant. Equally, McGinnel's has sometimes had a profit windfall when oil prices have dropped but the oil majors have been slow to respond with falls in the price of oil to customers. Over time, though, the oil majors have adjusted their prices in line with changes in the price of crude oil.

More importantly, perhaps, for sales, McGinnel's has offered customers excellent service. It has been prepared, for example, to offer same day delivery to customers who suddenly find they have run out of oil. By being a highly efficient, value for money 'local' company, McGinnel's has built up a very loyal customer base.

(a) **To what extent is McGinnel's affected by inflation in the wider economy? (40 marks)**
(b) **Discuss whether McGinnel's should change its pricing policy to one where its prices change immediately the price of its oil supplies change. (40 marks)**

Unemployment and underemployment

There are always unemployed workers in a market economy. However, the level of UNEMPLOYMENT can vary as Figure 1 shows. Official statistics on unemployment tend to measure those who do not have a job, but who are actively looking for work.

There are many more, however, who would take on a job if it were available, but are not actively seeking work. The largest group of these **underemployed** people is women who remain at home to look after children. Another large group is the over-50s. Many have taken early retirement because they were made redundant from an existing job. However, they would re-enter the workforce if there were a suitable job available.

Effects of unemployment on businesses

Changes in the unemployment levels in a local area, region or country can have major effects on businesses.

Output Rises in unemployment are likely to affect output and sales of businesses. For example, a small town may have a factory that employs 10 per cent of its workers. If that factory closes, shops in the town will almost certainly see a downturn in trade because unemployed workers will spend less. Suppliers to the factory, perhaps in the local area, will also see a fall in sales.

Low unemployment, on the other hand, is associated with rising output as employed workers spend their wages and other firms invest.

Redundancies and recruitment A fall in output because of rising unemployment could lead to businesses making some of their workers redundant. Redundancies have many effects on businesses. It can be costly if redundancy pay is given. It takes management time to organise. It leads to demotivation amongst staff. On the other hand, if a business is able to recruit in a high unemployment period, it could have a large number of applicants from which to choose. High unemployment can also help put downward pressure on pay and reduce the willingness of workers to take industrial action to support a pay claim.

Low unemployment, on the other hand, is associated with recruitment of workers in tight labour markets. So businesses may have relatively few workers applying for a job. There is also upward pressure on wages because the demand for labour is high and the supply relatively low.

Capacity If unemployment is rising and a business is suffering falling orders as a result, it is likely to suffer from excess capacity. Machines will be idle and office and factory space will be underutilised. This can raise average costs because fixed costs won't change, but less will be produced. Eventually, businesses will be forced to cut their excess capacity by closing sites, not replacing equipment and moving to smaller premises.

On the other hand, falling unemployment leading to higher output is likely to increase capacity utilisation and reduce average costs. Eventually, businesses will increase their capacity, which will fuel demand in the economy further.

Government spending and taxes In a downturn, with rising unemployment, government spending will increase. This is because there will be a rise in social welfare payments to the unemployed. The government is unlikely to raise taxes at this point for fear of reducing spending in the economy even further.

However, if unemployment starts to fall, the government may begin to raise taxes to reduce its borrowing. Higher taxes may be targeted at households, which will slow down the pace of recovery. Taxes could also be targeted at businesses. For example, corporation tax, a tax on company profits, might be raised. This would hit profits.

Sectoral and regional effects Some businesses would be more affected than others by rising unemployment. If the rising unemployment was structural, then businesses in certain industries or certain regions would be affected. For example, the decline of heavy industry in the UK between 1950 and 1990 hit regions such as Scotland, Wales,

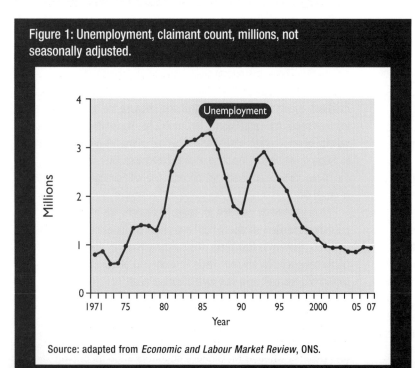

Figure 1: Unemployment, claimant count, millions, not seasonally adjusted.

Source: adapted from *Economic and Labour Market Review*, ONS.

Question 1.

Last year was a watershed year for Gill's, the US fast food chain. For the first time, it made a loss. Outside of the USA, the company is still expanding profitably. But in its core US market, it has experienced significant difficulties. Competition has been intense and US consumers have begun to desert Gill's for fast food chains offering healthier alternatives.

Problems for Gill's have been made worse by a downturn in the US economy which has seen rising unemployment. The result has been that fast food chains have suffered from a lack of lunchtime foot traffic. The company claims that it is fairly recession proof because 'when people are cutting back we tend to be one of the last things to be eliminated because our product is not very expensive'. However, to offset rising unemployment and increased competition, the company recently introduced a $1 menu.

A sign that not everything was well with Gill's was the announcement this year that it would be closing 175 outlets, many in the US where there were simply too few customers due to fierce local competition. Some analysts believe that a more savage cut in capacity in the USA, particularly where Gill's outlets were very close to each other, would boost profits.

(a) Explain why rising unemployment could lead to problems for Gill's.
(b) Discuss whether closing outlets in the USA in a recession would be a sensible strategy for Gill's to adopt.

Northern Ireland and Northern England very hard. Many service industries in these regions were then affected by the knock-on decline in demand from workers who became unemployed.

If the rising unemployment was caused by a recession in the economy, then industries which provide essential goods and services would suffer far less than industries providing luxury goods. For example, in the UK recession of 1990-92, supermarket chains were relatively unaffected as households maintained spending on food. However, the car industry was badly affected because many households and businesses delayed buying new cars and made do with their existing vehicles.

Social issues Long-term unemployment tends to create areas of poverty where the unemployed tend to live. Vandalism, crime and other types of antisocial behaviour can result in those areas. This will affect any business located there. For example, business premises may be broken into, equipment stolen, or vandals may set fire to the premises. New businesses thinking of setting up in such areas might be deterred, whilst existing businesses may relocate or shut down, making the problems of unemployment worse.

Strategy and unemployment

If there are small changes in unemployment, then businesses need not change their existing strategies. If there is a large rise in unemployment, this is likely to be associated with a recession and falling demand in the economy as a whole. Different businesses will then be affected in different ways. Businesses which produce essentials like food may see little change in demand for their products. However, businesses making products which see a sharp fall in demand should cut their production too. This could mean making workers redundant and closing factories, outlets and offices. Businesses which fail to make the necessary cuts could themselves become casualties of the recession. Rising unemployment, however, could be an opportunity to pick up workers who are better skilled and motivated.

Large falls in unemployment are likely to be good for most businesses. Demand is likely to be increasing at an above – average rate. Sales will be rising. Businesses should use the opportunity to expand. However, they may have increasing problems recruiting the right sort of workers.

KEY TERMS

Unemployment – when those actively seeking work are unable to obtain a job.

KNOWLEDGE

1. Explain the difference between (a) frictional unemployment and seasonal unemployment; (b) cyclical unemployment and structural unemployment.
2. Explain why 300 workers being made redundant in a small town could affect services industries in the local area.
3. Why might rising unemployment lead to overcapacity in industry?
4. Why might a business be deterred from setting up in an area of high unemployment?

1807 - 1848

Case Study: UK textile industry

The UK textile industry employs around 300, 000 workers, more than the farming, car manufacturing or chemicals industries. When a car production plant like Dagenham in Essex or Longbridge in Birmingham faces closure, it is national news. But the 41, 000 job losses in the textiles industry last year passed almost unnoticed by the media. One difference between textiles and these other industries is that the textile job losses being experienced are almost all amongst low paid women. In the car production, farming and chemicals industries, the workforce is often made up of better paid male workers.

Maggie Rowley provides an example of the story. She worked as a machinist for Coates Viyella, a major supplier to Marks & Spencer, for 20 years. She was one of 450 women made redundant 18 months ago when M&S moved its manufacturing base for the trousers on which she worked to Morocco. Her factory was one of two in Rossington, an old mining village outside Doncaster. On the one road into the village is the pit where her brothers, all miners, were once employed; one still is, the rest work on chicken farms.

Maggie Rowley was lucky enough to get another textiles job after the factory closed, but it was two bus rides away and only paid at the national minimum wage rate. She was quickly made redundant from that job too and now she works in a lighting components factory. Commenting on her job loss at Coates Viyella, she said that it was caused because 'there was no investment, no training, no planning. Now we're losing a whole industry and it's devastating.'

There are significant centres of textile production around the country with a quarter of the industry based in the East Midlands. In Maggie Rowley's home area, 1,000 textile jobs have gone, plus more jobs lost in Doncaster itself. Closures can hit an area hard. Often, textile plants close in areas where there is already high unemployment, particularly male unemployment. Women working in textiles may well be the only wage earner in their household. They often don't have cars and find it difficult to travel far to get a job.

(a) Discuss the possible effects of textile closures on manufacturing and service businesses in the Doncaster area. (40 marks)

(b) 'There was no investment, no training, no planning.' To what extent can a UK business avoid closing down plants and making workers redundant by investment, training and planning? (40 marks)

Globalisation and emerging markets

Over the past 50 years, the rate of growth of exports and imports has been faster than the rate of growth of output. The UK, along with almost all other countries in the world, is becoming ever more integrated with the world economy. This is the process of GLOBALISATION. Globalisation means, for example that:

- most of the clothes we buy are made abroad;
- the Chinese buy financial and legal services from the City of London;
- letters from a British hospital might be typed in India before being emailed back to the UK and printed out to be sent to patients.

It also has implications for the movement of labour. Increasing numbers of workers are leaving their country of origin to find work in richer countries. For example, an estimated 600,000 workers from Eastern Europe arrived to work in the UK following the accession of countries like Poland to the European Union. Equally, there are an estimated 2 million Britons living abroad. Some have gone to work. Others have retired, for example to Spain and France.

Globalisation has also led to increasing movements of capital across national boundaries. Each year, US and EU companies are buying up British companies. Equally, British companies are buying up US and other EU companies and expanding abroad. British companies are building factories in China. Japanese companies are building factories in the UK.

Most of the movement of goods, labour and capital is between the rich, developed countries of the world. But the fastest growing economies are in poorer developing countries. China, with a population of 1.1 billion has been doubling its output every seven years for the past 30 years. India, with a projected population of 1.4 billion by 2050, is moving towards achieving the same level of economic growth. These EMERGING MARKETS have already had a profound impact on the UK businesses. The UK textile industry, once one of the largest employers in the country, has been almost wiped out by foreign competition. In contrast, China represents one of the UK's fastest growing markets for a wide range of goods and services.

A growing number of companies worldwide are MULTINATIONAL COMPANIES. These are companies which have production facilities in more than one country. Multinational companies can have important competitive advantages. Their size can lead to economies of scale of production which cuts their average costs. A number of multinational companies have to be large to accumulate the knowledge required to operate in their industry. Large oil companies and car manufacturing companies are examples. Some multinational companies, such as McDonalds or Coca-Cola, also gain a competitive advantage from knowledge in

marketing a product.

So, how do businesses survive in the global market place? How do they remain INTERNATIONALLY COMPETITIVE?

Production

For a business to be internationally competitive in the long run, it must make sure that its production is efficient. A business will be **productively efficient** when it is producing at lowest cost. In markets for commodity products, such as wheat, computer assembly or call centres, price is one of the most important factors in determining sales so costs have to be kept as low as possible. How can a business improve productive efficiency?

Minimising inputs Part of productive efficiency is technical efficiency, using the least inputs to achieve a given level of output. Some of the ways of minimising inputs are to:

- ensure that employees are working to their full potential all the time. The scientific management school would encourage the use of piece rates for example. Another approach might be to invest in training;
- minimising wastage of materials, for example by designing products in such a way that the least materials are used;
- using just-in-time production techniques to minimise stock;
- use machinery and other equipment which will increase the productivity of workers.

Location or sourcing To remain internationally competitive, manufacturing businesses in rich industrialised countries have increasingly relocated production facilities in cheap labour Third World countries. Alternatively they have changed the sourcing of their supplies to Third World suppliers. China, for example, is becoming an increasingly important source of products for Western markets.

Investment To remain internationally competitive, a business may have to invest in the latest equipment. This may allow it to reduce costs or produce higher quality items.

In certain cases a business may be competitive without being productively efficient.

- Not all businesses compete on price. In a niche market for example, quality or delivery times may be more important. There is less competitive pressure on businesses in niche markets to be productively efficient. However, producing at lowest cost will help maximise profit and shareholder value, which might be part of the objectives of the business.
- In markets where customers are prepared to pay higher prices, costs can be higher too, allowing products to be produced to higher specifications.
- Ethical and marketing issues may affect production. Certain businesses have been attacked in the press and by

Question 1.

Goodyear in Wolverhampton was once a major employer in the city. In 1998, it still employed 2,200 workers and the site contained the UK national headquarters offices of the company. By 2004, only 550 workers remained and the UK national headquarters had been moved to Birmingham.

Workers at the site blame the 1998 acquisition by Goodyear of a stake in the Sava Tires in Slovenia in Eastern Europe: Goodyear purchased the rest of the company in 2004. The world's biggest tyre company said at the time that the move was 'to further strengthen its position in the rapidly expanding central and Eastern European market, as well as consolidating its low-cost sourcing capabilities'. Following the acquisition, Goodyear invested more than £55 million in modernisation at Sava Tires. The international company also has another three plants in Eastern Europe and the Middle East: in Debica, Poland; Izmit in Turkey; and Adapazari, also in Turkey. The four plants between them produced around 40 per cent of the 84 million tyres last year. Workers in Eastern Europe are paid a fraction of the wages in the UK. Although wages will eventually catch up, there will be many years to come in which the wage gap will remain substantial.

The security of the remaining 550 jobs at Goodyear Wolverhampton was questionable. All that was left was retread work, storage and the mixing and calendering of tyre ingredients for 'export' to other Goodyear Dunlop factories in the UK. In 2006, another 40 jobs were lost when Goodyear's plant at Wearside in the North East of England was shut due

to competition from Eastern European producers. In 2007, however, the now 350 people still employed at the plant received a boost when a new multi-million pound machine, the size of a four storey building, was installed. Gerard Coyne, from the Transport and General Workers' Union, said the investment would give some security for the future.

Source: adapted from the *Express & Star*, 8 April 2004; news.bbc.co.uk 5.4.2006 and 15.3.2007.

(a) Explain why moving production from Wolverhampton to Eastern Europe might improve Goodyear's productive efficiency.

(b) Discuss what might persuade Goodyear to retain remaining production at Wolverhampton.

pressure groups for using 'sweatshop' factories or child labour in the Third World to manufacture their products. The benefits of buying from cheap Third World suppliers may be outweighed if customers boycott the company in protest. In contrast, businesses such as the Co-op and The Body Shop make a point of sourcing their products from fair trade or ethical businesses around the world to appeal to customers who value this ethical stance.

Labour

Workers are important to the international competitiveness of a business. Increasingly, low skilled manufacturing jobs are being lost in rich industrialised countries to poorer Third World economies. This is because:

- there are abundant supplies of cheap labour;
- workers are prepared to work for a fraction of the wage demanded in rich industrialised countries;
- other employment costs, such as taxes on labour and fringe benefits, are often lower;
- workers are often prepared to work in conditions which would be unacceptable to European or US workers. Indeed, some Third World factories might be closed down if they had to conform to EU health and safety regulations.

Not surprisingly, some multinational companies are closing down factories in rich industrialised countries and opening up new factories in cheap labour economies. Equally, many businesses are switching their purchases of supplies from factories

or premises in rich countries to those located in poor countries. The trend has mostly affected manufacturing. However, increasingly services are being affected too. For example, some UK companies are switching their call centres from the UK to Third World countries. When a UK customer rings up about their bank account or to enquire about a travel booking, the call may be answered by a worker in a call centre in India.

To remain internationally competitive, though, businesses in rich industrial countries tend to locate high value added work in their own countries. This is because the workforce is more highly skilled than in the Third World. Tasks such as research and development or complex manufacturing have tended to remain in the rich countries of the world. There are also many service jobs which have to be done locally. A computer manufacturing company might be able to assemble components in Thailand, but its UK sales force needs to be in the UK to make personal contact with customers.

With increasing globalisation, businesses have a greater choice about where to source products and locate their premises. Those which will remain internationally competitive are those which maximise the division of labour to their own advantage.

Marketing

Successful marketing is vital for businesses which aim to remain internationally competitive. International marketing is no different to other types of marketing. It centres around the '4Ps' of the marketing mix – product, price, promotion and place.

Product Some multinational companies produce homogeneous goods. Copper, wheat, cotton and steel, whilst having many different grades and types, are the same whether they are produced in the UK, the USA or South Africa. Commodity producers can differentiate their products by entering niche markets. On the whole, however, product is not a unique selling point for such businesses.

For most businesses, their products are different from their competitors. Sony, British Aerospace, Cadbury Schweppes and Intel all attempt to differentiate their products and establish strong brands. There are two approaches to product branding in the international market place. One is to sell an identical product into all markets. For example, the Coca-Cola formulation is the same whether the product is sold in the UK or Nigeria. At the other end of the spectrum, a business may adapt its products to individual markets. McDonald's, for example, sells different menus and different products in India compared to France or the USA.

Producing one product worldwide may make sense from a technical viewpoint. A Rolls Royce aeroplane engine needs to work in exactly the same way whether it is fitted to a US aeroplane or a Saudi Arabian plane. It may also help strengthen the brand image. For Coca-Cola, a worldwide identical product enables it to market its drink as a universal drink. It also gives economies of scale in areas such as product development and marketing. Choosing a strategy of selling different products into different markets is likely to increase unit costs. However, it is then possible to appeal to a wider range of customers. McDonald's, for example, has to adapt its products for local markets if only to get around religious objections to the eating of meat in various countries. But it also puts ingredients into its products in countries like India and Indonesia to cater for local tastes. Understanding local markets is likely to require market research, adding to costs.

Price Producers of homogeneous goods have to accept the international market price for their output. Many businesses, however, have some market power to set their own prices. There is a variety of pricing strategies a business could adopt.
- A business may use a competition-based strategy. It could set prices which reflect those of competitors, for example.
- A business may use the market-orientated pricing policy of price discrimination. This is where the same product would be sold at different prices in different countries or

Question 2.

Martin Winterkorn, the chief executive of the German car manufacturer, speaking at VW's annual press conference, said that the days of building one car for the whole world were 'dead and buried'. For 20 years, the dream of the world's major car manufacturers had been to build a car which could be sold into all national car markets. The car manufacturer to achieve this would, so the thinking went, be able to gain a competitive edge over its rivals because it would be able to get costs down due to economies of scale in production. Selling 30 million vehicles a year of one model would have lower costs per unit than selling 6 million vehicles but in five different models each.

Martin Winterkorn announced that Volkswagen would be introducing 20 new models in the next years, including vans and pick-ups. The plan was to sell 8 million cars a year by 2010, up from 6.2 million in 2007. With Toyota now the world's largest car manufacturing company by sales volume, he said he hoped to beat Toyota in sales and profitability, customer satisfaction and quality. 'In the coming years, we will make the VW group the world's most international carmaker.' It could only happen if customers were offered vehicles appropriate to their needs, which included affordability. 'Our customers in China or India expect us, as a global player, to offer entirely different solutions than we do in the US or Western Europe' he said.

VW's desire to beat Toyota is made more difficult by its extremely weak position in the key US market. It is weighing whether to construct a new factory there to build a mid-sized saloon. A decision on this matter would be made in the summer, executives said.

Source: adapted from *The Financial Times*, 14.3.2008.

(a) Explain why a customer in India or China might have to be offered an 'entirely different solution' in terms of model of car than a customer in the UK or the USA.

(b) Volkswagen wants to overtake Toyota as the world's largest car manufacturer. Evaluate ways in which it could gain a competitive advantage over Toyota.

groups of countries. Audio and the visual media, books, CDs and DVDs tend to be sold at lower prices in North America compared to Europe, for example. Publishing and media companies exploit the fact that European consumers tend to be less price sensitive than North American consumers. Price discrimination allows a business to maximise its profit in the different markets into which it sells round the world.

- In some industries, cost-plus pricing is used. In defence contracts, for example, a business may win an order where the price is equal to the cost of production plus an agreed mark-up.

Promotion Promotion strategies vary from business to business. Some businesses tend to use the same promotional strategies in whichever country or region they operate. This may extend, for example, to using the same advertising slightly adapted for linguistic differences between target customers. A television commercial for a car being used across Europe would be an illustration. Or a chocolate bar may have the same name whether it is sold in the UK, the USA or Malaysia. Other businesses use different promotional strategies in different countries to reflect different cultures and different ways of doing business.

Which strategy is best depends upon a variety of factors. A business which sells only in Europe, for example, is far more likely to be successful in having one promotional approach than a business which is selling across all continents. Goods which are not culturally specific are far less likely to need targeted marketing.

Place International marketing is dependent upon 'place' in the marketing mix. If a company doesn't have a presence in Australia or China, for example, it is unlikely to sell into those countries. For some companies, like Coca-Cola, having the product available to customers where they want it and when they want it, is vital to their marketing strategies.

Different businesses will need different distribution channels for their products. Most businesses have their own sales teams or trade outlets in the markets into which they sell. A few use agents to seek sales opportunities.

External factors

Not all factors which determine whether a business is internationally competitive are within the control of the business. There is a number of external factors which can affect competitiveness.

Exchange rates Exchange rate movements can affect the competitiveness of individual operations in individual countries. Between 1998 and 2002, when the value of the pound was very high, some UK companies and UK based foreign firms suffered. A rise in the value of pound sterling of 20 per cent, for example, will mean that a UK-based exporter could be forced to raise its prices by up to 20 per cent in foreign currency terms. This would severely affect its international competitiveness.

The business cycle and economic growth When demand is growing in an economy, such as in a boom in the business cycle or when there is economic growth, it is relatively easy for a business to expand. Often higher sales can lead to economies of scale. Lower costs can then either be used to push down prices and so increase sales further, or increase profit margins. However, if the economy suffers low or negative economic growth for a long time, like Japan in the 1990s, or there is a prolonged depression as occurred in the UK in the early 1990s, businesses are likely to experience spare capacity. This is likely to push up their average costs. In turn, this will make them less internationally competitive compared to businesses in other countries which are not experiencing these difficulties.

Taxes and government grants Governments can tax businesses in a variety of ways. Taxes on profits (corporation tax in the UK) or the employment of labour (Employers' National Insurance contributions in the UK) can have a significant impact on international competitiveness. In the 1980s and 1990s, both the UK and the Republic of Ireland pursued policies of having low taxes on businesses. This helped make factories and businesses in these countries more internationally competitive. In contrast, it is often argued that Germany has become less internationally competitive over the past 20 years because of high taxes on businesses.

Equally, sometimes governments or the EU give grants to businesses to set up factories or plants. In the UK, grants have been given to companies such as Nissan and Lucky Gold (LG) to set up factories in depressed regions of the UK. Such grants should make the difference about whether the factory will be internationally competitive or not.

Trade restrictions International competitiveness is sometimes affected by trade restrictions. For example, a US company might have to pay tariffs to sell goods manufactured in the USA to an EU customer. One way of getting around trade restrictions is to set up a production base in the country or trading bloc which is imposing the restrictions. So, major Japanese motor manufacturing companies now have car plants in the EU to get around import problems.

Education, training and wage rates The long-run competitiveness of a country is crucially dependent upon the education and training of the labour force. Education and training make a workforce more productive. So the average UK worker can create more output in money terms than the average Indian or Chinese worker. However, workers in the UK are on average paid much more than the average worker in India or China. Whether a UK business can remain competitive against Indian or Chinese businesses depends therefore upon the relationship between the output and value added of workers to the wages they are paid. Over time, many jobs and businesses are being lost from rich industrialised countries like the UK to Third World countries as wages become too high in the UK and levels of education and training improve in the Third World. Textile companies in the UK, for example, have become less competitive over the past 50 years, forcing most of them to close down. There is little that an individual business can do faced with such large long-term changes to remain competitive.

Strategic issues

Businesses have to decide whether competing in international markets will help them achieve their strategic objectives. If so, they then have to decide which markets they will sell into and where they will locate their production facilities. Their decision will be partly based on costs and partly on potential sales. External constraints such as exchange rates and taxes will influence their decision making too.

Operating internationally is likely to increase the risks faced by a business in its activities. Equally, it will considerably increase marketing opportunities. For already large companies, selling globally is the only way they can expand because their domestic markets are too small. However, it opens them up to the competition of other large international companies. Strategic decision making becomes even more important at this level.

KEY TERMS

Emerging markets – economies, such as China, India or Russia, which have previously had relatively low output per capita but which have markets open to trade and are now expanding, in many cases more rapidly than rich developed countries like the UK or the USA.

Globalisation – the process of ever-increasing specialisation, trade and interdependence between different parts of the world economy, which creates world markets for products, labour and capital.

International competitiveness – the extent to which a business can sell products to customers in its home market or in a number of different countries.

Multinational company – a business which has production facilities in at least two countries, usually selling products into both domestic and export markets.

KNOWLEDGE

1. Explain the link between globalisation and emerging markets.
2. Why is it important for a business which is internationally competitive to be productively efficient?
3. Why may a business be a high cost supplier and yet still be internationally competitive?
4. Why are labour costs important in international competitiveness?
5. What impact does marketing have on international competitiveness?
6. Explain how the following might affect the international competitiveness of a UK business:
   (a) a rise in the exchange rate of the pound against all other currencies;
   (b) a depression in the US economy;
   (c) a rise in taxes on profits in the UK;
   (d) a rise in UK wage rates.

Case Study: Louis Vuitton and Chanel

Louis Vuitton and Chanel will this week be competing for the limelight as both open stores in Hong Kong. Louis Vuitton and Chanel are luxury fashion houses, selling very expensive luxury goods to the very rich. Louis Vuitton is re-opening a store that it has over-hauled and expanded. The outlet will be its second-largest worldwide, after its flagship Champs Elysees store in Paris. Louis Vuitton's event will close on Friday night with a party for 2,500 guests held in a golden tent.

Asia is a fast growing market for the luxury fashion market. With a population of 1 billion, and a growth rate which is seeing incomes double every seven years on average, it only needs the smallest fraction of this population to want to shop at a luxury fashion house for it to be a highly lucrative market. The luxury fashion houses are moving from having outlets in 'first tier' cities like Beijing and Shanghai, to 'second tier' cities, large provincial cities which still have a rich elite.

Growth, however, brings its own challenges. Simply taking what works in Paris or London to an Asian city is not necessarily going to be successful. The brand needs to adapt to local culture whilst at the same time retaining its distinctive image. Thibault Villet, President of Coach, the US maker of handbags and other accessories, for example says: 'We are clearly a New York brand and so need to communicate an image in accordance with our DNA. But the right way for us to go local is when we do events, where we certainly want to be working with the local celebrities.'

Another challenge for Asia's fashion development is a shortage of skills. Customers expect sales staff to be knowledgeable, friendly and yet deferential. Inexperienced sales staff can drive customers away. There are likely to be fewer repeat customers and fewer introductions by word of mouth.

A key question is whether image-conscious fashion houses will join the outsourcing bandwagon by shifting production to Asia. Last year, Louis Vuitton made its first manufacturing move outside of Europe by establishing a shoe production venture in Pondicherry, India. About 100 people are employed in its workshop there but the company has no plans to go further. After all, part of the brand image of a luxury Paris or Milan fashion house is that its goods are made by highly skilled craftsmen in France or Italy. No one will pay hundreds of pounds for a handbag if they think it has been made in a sweatshop in Thailand. So the fashion houses have to be ultra-cautious about what functions they outsource to low cost locations.

Source: adapted from *The Financial Times*.

(a) Evaluate the opportunities and threats to European and US luxury goods businesses in emerging markets. (40 marks)
(b) Evaluate the strategies a French luxury fashion house might adopt if the value of the Euro rose against Asian currencies at a time when Asian economies went into a sharp recession.

The role of government in the economy

Governments play a number of roles in an economy which affect business.

- Government creates the legal and regulatory framework which govern the way in which businesses and individuals relate to each other. In the UK, for example, government gives rights of ownership to private property. This is fundamental to businesses. Without this right, they would not be able to protect their property, from land and buildings, to stocks of goods to intellectual property such as patents and copyright. UK law also regulates contracts. All businesses buy and sell. Without an effective law of contract, this process would become uncertain and discourage businesses from operating. The impact of the law on business is discussed in more detail in the unit titled 'Business and the law'.
- Government provides goods and services from health and education to roads and the police.
- The government uses taxes and spending to influence the way individuals and businesses behave. For example, it taxes cigarettes to discourage individuals from smoking. It subsidises training of workers to encourage individuals to become more skilled.
- It uses its powers of spending and tax to influence the amount of demand in the economy. This can help prevent the economy from suffering a recession or experiencing rising inflation. Some of the same effects can also be had through its power to control the rate of interest.

Government provision of goods and services

In the UK, government (i.e. the public sector) accounts for between 40 and 45 per cent of all the goods and services produced in the economy. In addition, it redistributes income through a variety of welfare benefits. Some of the main areas of government spending, shown in Figure 1, are:

- social protection or welfare benefits such as the State old age pension and Child Benefit;
- health which is mainly spending on the National Health Service;
- education including primary and secondary schools as well as universities;
- transport including roads and subsidies for rail transport.

Businesses benefit directly from the provision of goods and services by government. For example, the workers they employ have mainly been educated in the British education system. Roads allow their goods to be transported between business premises. Spending on the police and the judiciary ensure that property rights are respected.

Some of what is provided by government is produced by state owned enterprises and organisations. For example, education in schools is provided mainly by local authorities. But a significant proportion of public sector goods and services are produced by the private sector. For example, new roads are built by private construction companies under contract from government. Tanks and military aircraft are purchased by government from private sector companies. Social services departments purchase residential care for the elderly from private businesses. Supplying products to the public sector is a major sales opportunity for many businesses.

Changing what is bought and how it is produced

In most circumstances, the prime purpose of taxes is to raise revenues that will pay for government spending. But sometimes, taxes are used deliberately to change the behaviour of businesses and consumers. For example:

- taxes on alcohol and tobacco are used to discourage consumption of these drugs;
- taxes on cars and petrol are used to encourage the purchase of 'green' cars and discourage the purchase of cars with high emissions and heavy fuel use; they are are also used to reduce the level of traffic to reduce congestion on roads;

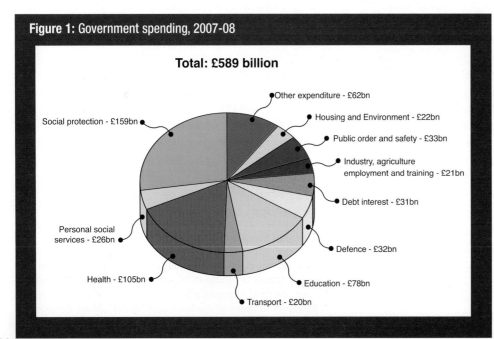

Figure 1: Government spending, 2007-08

Total: £589 billion

- Other expenditure - £62bn
- Housing and Environment - £22bn
- Public order and safety - £33bn
- Industry, agriculture employment and training - £21bn
- Debt interest - £31bn
- Defence - £32bn
- Education - £78bn
- Transport - £20bn
- Health - £105bn
- Personal social services - £26bn
- Social protection - £159bn

- pollution and environment taxes such as the Landfill Tax are used to encourage businesses to adopt more environmentally friendly practices;
- tax allowances on investment encourage businesses to invest.

Governments also sometimes use **subsidies** to alter behaviour. A subsidy is a grant given to lower the price of a good. For example, governments may subsidise businesses to train workers by paying part of the costs of training. Governments may subsidise some elements of the costs of a business start-up to encourage more people to set up their own business. Governments may also provide subsidies to businesses that set up in a high unemployment area to encourage job creation.

Fiscal policy

FISCAL POLICY is the government use of its spending, taxes and its borrowing to influence economic activity. Fiscal policy can be used to influence the behaviour of individuals and businesses as described above. However, it can also be used to influence the economy as a whole.

When governments increase their spending more than they increase taxes, total spending in the economy rises. For example, if the government increases spending by £20 billion but taxes only rise by £5 billion, then there is an increase in spending by the government sector of £15 billion. The exact impact of this on the economy is complex. However, this net increase in spending will give a boost in the short term to total demand (or **aggregate demand**). The economy will expand. Hence this is called **expansionary fiscal policy**.

Expansionary fiscal policy should be used by government when the economy is going into a **recession**. This is when unemployment is rising and spending is slowing down or even falling. Businesses should therefore benefit from expansionary fiscal policy. This explains why, when trading conditions are difficult, business groups such as the CBI call for the government to adopt expansionary fiscal policies by either increasing its spending or cutting taxes.

Restrictive fiscal policy is the opposite of expansionary fiscal policy. It occurs when the government raises taxes more than any increase in its spending. It reduces demand from government in the economy. It should be used by the government when the economy is overheating at the top of a boom and there is too much spending. Too much spending

Question 1.

Zaphrom is a UK company which manufactures pharmaceutical products. It currently provides 70 cars to its employees, from the Chief Executive to senior managers to sales staff. In his 2008 budget, the Chancellor announced major changes to the tax payable on cars. The tax on cars which emit high levels of CO2 (carbon dioxide) would increase substantially. From April 2009, companies would only be allowed to write off 10 per cent of the value of a car emitting more than 160 gm of CO2 per kilometre compared to 25 per cent as at present. This would substantially increase the cost to the company of owning cars. In addition, from 2010, road tax (the cost of the tax disk on cars) would increase substantially for the first year of

a car's life. For example, on the Chief Executive's Land Rover, it would increase from the current £500 to £950. On the Finance Director's Jaguar, it would increase from the current £400 to £750. Given that the company buys cars from new and then sells them after two or three years, this would lead to a significant rise in the cost of the company car fleet.

The HR director, who is responsible for making decisions about the company car fleet, wants to see the car fleet become greener so as to minimise the effects of the Chancellor's budget. Inevitably, some staff will be told that they will no longer be supplied with the model of car they have grown to like. She is going to 'sell' the changes in terms of the company's contribution to reducing greenhouse gas emissions, helping to solve the global warming problem and 'doing our bit' to save the planet. This will go down well with some staff. But she hasn't yet decided how to tell the Chief Executive that he can no longer have his Land Rover. She wonders how he would take it if she suggested he might like to trade it in for a Vauxhall Astra.

Source: adapted from *The Financial Times*, 14.3.2008.

(a) Explain how the Chancellor can use taxes to alter the behaviour of companies on green issues.
(b) The HR Director has chosen to change the composition of the company car fleet. (i) What would have been the impact on the company if she had decided to make no change? (b) The change could have both a positive and a negative impact on the motivation of staff. Evaluate whether the net impact is likely to be positive.
(c) Evaluate whether the Chief Executive would seriously consider making the switch from a Land Rover to a Vauxhall Astra.

Question 2.

The US economy is threatening to slide into a recession. Faltering spending led to fierce lobbying by business groups for the government to give a fiscal boost to the economy. Earlier this month, their lobbying was rewarded when Congress approved a $152 billion package of tax cuts. Tax payers will receive a one-off rebate sometime between May and the end of the summer. Cheques for up to $600 (£300) will be sent to individuals earning up to $75,000 (£37,500) and $1,200 for married couples who earn up to $150,000 (£75,000). Families with children will gain an additional $300 (£150) per child.

The National Retail Federation, representing US retailers, estimates that 40 per cent of the rebates will be spent, with the rest either used to pay off debts or saved. Not every retailer, though, will be a winner from the rebates. Past experience shows that consumers increase their basic spending but don't increase their discretionary spending when given tax rebates in a recession. So consumers will purchase lower-margin food and small basic household items like a new kettle. But they won't go out and buy luxuries like a new $2,000

high definition television. They might buy ice cream from Wal-Mart but they will think twice about going out to a restaurant. Wal-Mart, the largest supermarket chain in the USA, whose core customer is the average to below average income earner, could benefit. Starbucks, the coffee chain, which has already reported fewer customers visiting its outlets, might see little benefit.

Source: adapted from the *Financial Times*, 19.2.2008.

(a) Explain why Wal-Mart could be a beneficiary from the tax rebates but Starbucks and furniture retailers might see little benefit.

(b) A chain of US electrical retailers sells kitchen equipment like fridges, cookers and electric kettles, entertainment equipment such as televisions, games consoles and DVD players, and a range of computers and printers. In February 2008, it was having to make some decisions about its stock levels for the next 9 months. Discuss much stock it should buy and what sort of stock it should hold compared to the nine months to December 2007.

leads to inflation and is unsustainable in the long term.

Using fiscal policy to smooth out booms and recessions in the business cycle benefits business in the long term. It creates a more predictable economic climate which allows businesses to plan with greater certainty. It reduces risk and encourages investment.

Monetary policy

MONETARY POLICY is policy which uses interest rates to influence the economy. Control of interest rates has been given by the UK government to the Bank of England. Each month, the Bank of England has to decide whether to raise interest rates, leave them at the same level or reduce them.

The Bank of England uses interest rates to control inflation in the economy. Rises in interest rates reduce total spending by households and businesses. This reduces total demand for goods and services and moderates the rate of inflation. Falls in interest rates tend to come when the Bank of England believes the rate of inflation will fall below its target level, currently 2 per cent per annum. Falls in interest rates will boost spending by households and businesses.

High levels of inflation in general harm business and business activity. Controlling inflation is therefore important for businesses. Changing the rate of interest also helps smooth out the business cycle.

How businesses might respond to changes in interest rates is covered in more detail in the unit titled 'Interest rates'.

Supply-side policies

Fiscal policy and monetary policy is used to affect aggregate demand. By adjusting its total spending, level of taxes or interest rates, the government can increase or reduce the amount of total spending in the economy. This can then have a short-term impact on economic variables such as inflation, unemployment, and the business cycle.

However, a key long-term aim of the government is to increase the productive capacity of the economy. Growth in capacity is often called the 'underlying rate of economic growth' to distinguish it from growth in GDP. Policies to increase the productive capacity of the economy are called SUPPLY-SIDE POLICIES. This is to distinguish them from fiscal and monetary policies which affect aggregate demand. There are three main ways in which supply-side policies can increase the productive capacity of the economy.

Increasing investment The government can use policies to promote investment by businesses. For example, it can give tax relief on money used to buy investment goods. Or it can give grants to pay for investment. It can also invest itself. Building new roads and bridges or reclaiming derelict land are examples of infrastructure spending which will benefit business.

Improving the quality of the labour force A workforce which is better educated and trained and has more experience will be more productive than one which is less well trained. So the average UK worker might be able to produce more in money terms than the average Indian or Thai worker. Through better education and promoting training, the government can therefore increase long-term economic growth.

Making sure that both capital and labour are fully utilised Businesses can invest in new machines but if those machines stand idle, they won't be productive. Similarly, if workers are out of work or their skills are underutilised, then the economy will not grow as fast as it could. So a key role of government is to ensure that resources are being used productively. Policies which encourage employment, such as the New Deal or increased vocational training, help to achieve this. So do macroeconomic policies which smooth out the business cycle. Sound financial policies which result in low inflation will encourage investment. So too will a legal system which allows businesses to own property, sign enforceable contracts and trade goods without too much fear of crime. Countries that do not have a sound legal and financial framework often fail to grow as fast as they could as a result.

There are other examples of supply-side policies used by government in an effort to increase the efficient use of resources in the economy. For example, there are regular attempts by government to simplify 'red tape', the rules and regulations ranging from tax returns to health and safety inspections to labour laws. Red tape imposes considerable costs on businesses, particularly small businesses. There are also regular changes to amount of tax paid by businesses or workers to encourage them to work more efficiently.

KEY TERMS

Fiscal policy – the government use of its spending, taxes and its borrowing to influence economic activity.
Monetary policy – government policy which uses monetary variables such as the rate of interest to influence the economy.
Supply-side policies – government policies aimed at increasing the productive capacity of the economy.

KNOWLEDGE

1. Why are property rights important for businesses?
2. How do businesses benefit from government spending?
3. Explain the difference between a tax and a subsidy.
4. How might expansionary fiscal policy benefit businesses?
5. What might be the impact on businesses of a fall in the Bank of England's interest rate?
6. How might supply-side policies benefit businesses?

Case Study: Micro-brewing

Steve Haynes sold his bar when the government announced that a ban on smoking in public places would be introduced. Only a fraction of the sales came from food and he could see that the ban would have a significant impact on his takings. He decided to move into micro-brewing, producing speciality ales sold both to bars and pubs, but also to retailers. Since the smoking ban came into force, his sales to retailers have increased 10 per cent, vindicating his hunch that drinkers would consume more at home.

However, he is angry about the higher-than-inflation increases in tax on beer in the Chancellor's last budget. The Chancellor justified the tax increase by arguing that binge drinking was now too serious a problem and that something had to be done about it. Raising the tax on alcohol would discourage young people from excessive drinking. However, Steve argues that young people don't binge drink on the traditional types of beer that he brews. So why should his beers be taxed more highly?

The last budget also saw slightly higher income taxes on low to medium income earners, the typical customer for his beers. With the economy slowing and consumer debt at record levels, Steve has shelved plans for expansion for the time being. But he is hopeful that extra marketing and greater awareness of his products amongst retailers could at least compensate for the negative trends in the economy.

The Bank of England has cut interest rates by a whole 1 per cent over the past months to counter growing recessionary pressures. This has helped reduce Steve's overheads because he took out a £100,000 variable rate loan to finance the purchase of the micro-brewery. The cost of hops, however, has increased considerably in line with the large increases seen in the price of many agricultural commodities.

(a) Evaluate the impact of the changes in government policy described in the passage on Steve Hayne's micro-brewery business. (40 marks)
(b) Would Steve Hayne's micro-brewery business have higher sales and higher profits if the government cut every tax and every type of government spending by 20 per cent? Justify your answer.

Politics and trade

Governments ultimately control the ability of domestic businesses to trade with the rest of the world. In the past, some governments have banned all trade. Most governments have used foreign trade as a source of tax revenue. They have also protected their own industries by putting barriers such as taxes in the way of international trade. Over the past 60 years, there has been a move towards greater FREE TRADE where there are no restrictions on the movement and purchase of goods and services across national boundaries. For the UK, its membership of the European Union has led to a substantial fall in trade barriers. However, the UK has also, through international treaties, reduced its trade barriers with the rest of the world. This unit explores what has happened in more detail and its implications for UK businesses.

The European Union

The UK has been a member of the EUROPEAN UNION (EU) since 1973. Around 60 per cent of UK exports and imports of goods are to and from the EU. So the EU is by far the largest trading partner for the UK.

The UK has been a reluctant partner within the EU. It refused to join when the EU was established in 1956. It has tended to resist changes which would deepen both economic and political integration. For example, the UK refused to join the Single Currency. British businesses are divided about the benefits of the EU. To understand why, it is necessary to know about the history of the EU, its institutions and the costs and benefits for businesses of being within the EU.

1956 The Treaty of Rome In 1956, six European countries, France, Germany, Italy, Belgium, the Netherlands and Luxembourg , signed the Treaty of Rome. This established a Common Market between the countries. There are two aspects to a common market. First, there is a CUSTOMS UNION. This exists when a group of countries remove all barriers to trade of goods and services between themselves but erect a common tariff barrier to products coming in from outside the customs union area. Second, barriers to the mobility of labour and financial capital are removed.

1986 The Single European Act In practice, whilst barriers to trade such as tariffs and quotas had been removed between member countries, there remained many other barriers to trade. For example, individual governments still regularly only gave contracts to domestic suppliers. Banks couldn't operate freely across the whole EU. So in 1986, member countries agreed to deepen economic links by removing these barriers to create a SINGLE EUROPEAN MARKET by December 31st

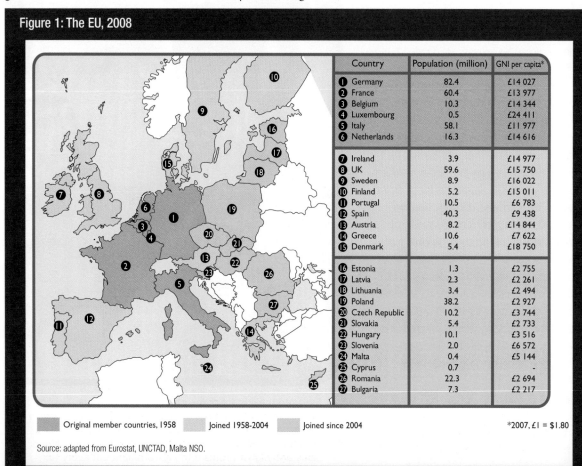

Figure 1: The EU, 2008

	Country	Population (million)	GNI per capita*
❶	Germany	82.4	£14 027
❷	France	60.4	£13 977
❸	Belgium	10.3	£14 344
❹	Luxembourg	0.5	£24 411
❺	Italy	58.1	£11 977
❻	Netherlands	16.3	£14 616
❼	Ireland	3.9	£14 977
❽	UK	59.6	£15 750
❾	Sweden	8.9	£16 022
❿	Finland	5.2	£15 011
⓫	Portugal	10.5	£6 783
⓬	Spain	40.3	£9 438
⓭	Austria	8.2	£14 844
⓮	Greece	10.6	£7 622
⓯	Denmark	5.4	£18 750
⓰	Estonia	1.3	£2 755
⓱	Latvia	2.3	£2 261
⓲	Lithuania	3.4	£2 494
⓳	Poland	38.2	£2 927
⓴	Czech Republic	10.2	£3 744
㉑	Slovakia	5.4	£2 733
㉒	Hungary	10.1	£3 516
㉓	Slovenia	2.0	£6 572
㉔	Malta	0.4	£5 144
㉕	Cyprus	0.7	-
㉖	Romania	22.3	£2 694
㉗	Bulgaria	7.3	£2 217

Original member countries, 1958   Joined 1958-2004   Joined since 2004

*2007, £1 = $1.80

Source: adapted from Eurostat, UNCTAD, Malta NSO.

1992. This would greatly increase MARKET ACCESS for businesses in one country to another country.

1991 The Maastricht Treaty This treaty gave greater powers to the EU to create common policies in the areas of social affairs, industrial affairs, education, defence and health. For example, EU legislation states that workers should not work more than 48 hours per week. The Maastricht Treaty also set the EU the goal of creating a monetary union, abolishing individual currencies and creating one currency for the whole union.

2002 The launch of the euro On 1st January 2002, most EU countries replaced their currencies with the euro. This eliminated a major barrier to trade. The UK decided not to participate in the single currency at the time. UK companies therefore still faced exchange rate risks and the cost of exchanging pounds for euros when trading with the rest of Europe. The group of countries which have adopted the single currency is often called the EUROZONE.

Enlargement since 1973 Between 1956 and 1972, the European Union was made up of just the original six founder countries. Since then, over 20 countries have joined, starting with the UK, Ireland and Denmark in 1973. In 2004, seven countries from Eastern Europe joined, followed by a further two in 2007. More

countries wish to join including some of the states of the former Yugoslavia and, more controversially, Turkey.

European institutions

There are four main institutions which govern the EU.

The European Commission The European Commission (EC) is located in Brussels. It is responsible for proposing policy and legislation to the European Council of Ministers. Once accepted, it is then responsible for implementing that policy and legislation. The EC is headed by the President of the European Commission who is responsible for acting in the interests of the EU. Commissioners are appointed to represent each member country.

The Council of Ministers The Council of Ministers is made up of ministers from each member country who meet on a regular basis. Twice a year, heads of government from each country also meet at the European Council. The Council of Ministers is the decision making body of the EU. It approves or rejects proposals from the European Commission about new regulations and directives.

The European Parliament The European Parliament is based in Strasbourg. Voters in EU countries elected MEPs, Members of the European Parliament, to sit in the parliament. Its role is to

---

Question 1.

In April 2005, a preliminary judgment from the European Court of Justice gave victory to Marks & Spencer (M&S) in a battle over taxes. M&S had wanted to offset the losses it had made in France, Germany and Belgium against profits made in the UK. This would have reduced the amount of corporation tax the company would have paid in the UK by around £30 million. The UK Inland Revenue had declared that the company could not do this. Only losses made in the UK could be offset against profits made in the UK by the company.

The preliminary ruling from the European Court of Justice agreed with M&S that the Inland Revenue's policy breached a core European treaty principle: that member states cannot hinder an EU national in one country from establishing a business in another. The preliminary ruling stated that a group relief scheme that does not allow a parent company to deduct the losses of its foreign subsidiaries under any circumstances is incompatible with European law. The ruling rejected the Inland Revenue argument that a national government cannot offer a tax advantage to a subsidiary based in a foreign country where it has no power of taxation.

However, the ruling does seem to prevent 'double dipping': where a company reclaims tax on the same losses in two countries. The ruling says that where a government allows subsidiaries of foreign companies to claim tax relief on losses made, then those tax benefits must be claimed in that country.

What made the Marks & Spencer case special was that the

company pulled out of continental Europe in the early 2000s because it was making losses on these operations. So it had no prospect of future profits against which it could offset these losses in Belgium, France and Germany.

Source: adapted from the *Financial Times*, 8.4. 2005.

(a) Explain why Marks & Spencer was able to appeal against a UK tax ruling.

(b) Both the Treaty of Rome and the Single European Act mean that 'member states cannot hinder an EU national in one country from establishing a business in another'. How could membership of the EU both (a) benefit and (b) harm the interests of a UK company like Marks & Spencer?

comment on proposals put forward by the European Commission to the Council of Ministers. It does not have the power to make laws as in national parliaments. Its major power, which it has used once, is that it can dismiss the President of the European Commission and European Commissioners.

The European Court of Justice The European Court of Justice is the final court of law within the European Union. Its decisions are binding. Individual citizens and businesses can appeal to the European Court of Justice against decisions made in local or national courts. The European Court of Justice bases its decisions on EU law.

EU laws are called **directives**. In some cases, these have to be agreed by all member countries through the Council of Ministers. In other cases, they can be passed if a majority of countries agree. Directives become EU law by being made law in each individual national parliament. The European Commission then has the power to issue **regulations** based on these directives. Directives tend to be broad and general in nature. Regulations are specific and detailed.

The impact of the EU on UK businesses

The EU provides UK businesses with export opportunities. The low barriers to trade which exist within the EU make it easier on the whole for a UK company to export into the EU than to, say, the USA or Japan.

However, the EU is also a threat for some UK businesses. Just as the EU makes it easier for UK exports to sell into Europe, so it is easier for other EU businesses to sell into the UK. When products are traded, the EU increases the potential competition in the domestic market.

To survive in a competitive EU market, UK businesses which face increased imports or have the opportunity to increase exports must therefore develop a pan-European strategy. A strategy is a set of plans which when implemented will achieve the objectives of the business. Strategies should be realistic and therefore they should take account of the current trading position of the business and, its strengths and weaknesses in areas such as products, marketing and human resources. They also need to reflect the ability of the business to change. For example, plans must not be so ambitious that they cannot be financed.

Pan-European strategies can include a number of different ways of dealing with the opportunities and threats that come from larger markets and increased competition.

Operations management The production operations of a business may be affected by Britain's membership of the EU.

- The Single Market means that businesses can source supplies relatively easily across the EU. Transport costs and the need for fast deliveries may make foreign supplies uncompetitive. However, in many cases, businesses can reduce their costs by taking advantage of the large market.
- A more radical measure to reduce costs is to relocate. Some

Question 2.

BWD Entertainment is a UK based media company. Originally a magazine company, it has diversified into radio and trade newspapers and also runs a book publishing business. In the 1990s, it acquired stakes in magazine publishing companies in Spain, the Netherlands and Italy and owns radio companies in both Germany and France.

The directors of the company have recently completed a strategic review and have decided that the new entrants to the EU in Eastern Europe should be targeted for acquisitions. Their economies are likely to grow at a faster rate than the EU average over the next 10-20 years and this should give plenty of scope for increasing sales over time.

They are particularly looking at the largest new entrant country, Poland, with a population of 38.2 million. One strategy would be to buy an established Polish magazine company and use its editorial expertise and distribution system to push a number of new magazines based on ones which have proved popular in the UK, Spain and Italy. A different strategy would be to buy a Polish magazine company which already had strong market share. By giving new finance, BWD would allow the existing Polish management greater opportunities to launch new magazines aimed at the local market. A third possible strategy would be to set up a company from scratch, recruiting editors and other workers from established Polish magazine companies, but also putting in staff from existing BWD operations in other European countries. This would probably be the highest risk strategy.

(a) Explain why there might be greater scope for marketing magazines in Poland than in, say, the UK or Italy over the next ten years.

(b) By considering the possible advantages and disadvantages of each of the three strategic options, discuss which is likely to be the most successful for BWD. In your answer, identify what other information would be needed to make an informed choice.

foreign companies from the USA and Japan, for example, have closed factories in the UK and relocated them in lower wage EU countries. Some UK companies have closed their factories and relocated in the EU to take advantage of transport links. This allows them to gain economies of scale in production. Conversely, businesses in other EU countries have developed plants in the UK.

- Some businesses have to set up near to their customers. Service businesses like Tesco, the supermarket chain have established outlets in some EU countries. Equally, just-in-time delivery systems may force UK manufacturers to set up near their customers to retain orders.

Marketing A pan-European strategy will be centred around the 4Ps of the marketing mix.

- The EU gives UK businesses the opportunity to sell into a much larger market than just the UK. To take advantage of this, a business may have to increase its product range. For example, national preferences may have to be recognised. Different standards and specifications may have to be adhered to. Competition though may force a business to slim down its product range. By concentrating on fewer products, perhaps become a niche player in the market, a business can specialise and so gain a competitive advantage. Businesses also have to make strategic decisions on names and packaging. Should the same product be sold under the same brand name across the EU? Should common packaging be used whether the product is sold in the UK, Italy or Poland?

- Increased competition within the EU may force a business to lower its prices. Increased size to achieve economies of scale may be one way of achieving this. Many businesses price differentiate in different national markets. Charging different prices allows them to maximise profits. Alternatively, some businesses may charge the same prices across the EU, reducing marketing costs.

- Businesses face the same decisions about promotion. Should they have different promotional campaigns in each country or region of the EU or should they adopt a common approach across the EU? Adopting a common approach gives economies of scale in marketing. However, national markets may differ depending upon what product is being sold.

- The importance of place varies from product to product. Service industries, such as retailing or hotels, depend on location for their success. A component manufacturer, on the other hand, may find that it can be located anywhere in the EU so long as its products can be transported safely within a given time to its customers. With more and more trade occurring between EU member countries, businesses have to make sure that their logistics systems can meet the demands placed on them by customers.

Human resources Operating across the EU may have human resource implications. Whilst English is commonly understood throughout the EU, it may be easier to sell into markets outside the UK if some staff have foreign language skills. If a UK business has operations abroad, it will need to understand the labour law in each country in which it operates. Some middle and senior management workers may expect as part of their work to spend time abroad. This may benefit the business because it helps in creating a single culture within the organisation. However, human resource departments need to develop policies about how such workers are to be treated in the case of issues such as housing, salaries or company cars.

Finance Selling into foreign countries within the EU has major implications for finance departments. Will foreign customers be given trade credit and if so on what terms? How can the creditworthiness of a customer in, say, Poland or Italy be

checked? Will the price of exports be quoted in euros or pounds sterling? If it is in euros, how will the business cope if the value of the euro changes significantly between the time a contract is signed or an order placed and the time the payment is received? If the business has sites abroad, profitability could be significantly affected in pounds sterling by significant movements of the exchange rate. What strategy does it have to cope with this? Does the business with sites abroad have sufficient knowledge of local accounting and tax regimes? What is the strategy for a UK multinational raising finance abroad?

The external environment The external environment may differ in the EU than in the domestic UK market. For example, interest rates may differ between the UK, the eurozone and EU countries not in the eurozone such as Denmark, and Bulgaria. The exchange rate of the pound fluctuates against the euro. Some countries may be in a recession, whilst the UK market is in boom. Pressure groups may have different concerns from country to country. A business must therefore adopt strategies to deal with the risks and opportunities that a fast-changing external environment can present.

Overall, evidence suggests that being a member of the EU favours those with two distinct strategies. Some businesses remain successful because they are small and can target niche markets. However, the opportunities offered by larger markets pushes other businesses to increase in size. By becoming larger, they can gain economies of scale and thus become more competitive. In a wide variety of industries, from steel to pharmaceuticals to chemicals and cars, the past 20 years have seen the creation of European multinationals through the takeover or merger of national companies.

A few companies have set up JOINT VENTURES. This is where a company in the UK, joins with a company in Poland, for example, to set up a jointly owned subsidiary. In this subsidiary company, the two companies work together supplying their own expertise. The UK company might want to expand in Poland and so the Polish company supplies knowledge about the country, its business environment and potential customers. The UK company might provide technology, brands or finance capabilities. The UK company may also transfer some of its production from the UK to Poland to take advantage of cheap labour, exporting the goods back into its UK markets for sale.

The World Trade Organisation and free trade

Between 50 and 60 per cent of the UK's trade in goods is conducted with other countries in the European Union. So Europe is by far the UK's largest trading partner. However, the rest of the UK's trade is conducted with countries in the Americas, Africa and Asia. Trade with the rest of the world is governed by a complex set of rules, set out in international treaties which the UK has signed.

Over the past 60 years, world trade has grown faster than world income. The world is becoming ever more integrated. One of the reasons for this has been the political decisions made by governments to move towards FREE TRADE and bring down barriers to trade. There are many barriers to trade but two of these are tariffs and quotas.

- A TARIFF is a tax on imports. It is sometimes called a customs duty. The higher the taxes on imports, the more expensive imports become. Hence, high tariffs restrict the volume of trade.
- A QUOTA is a limit on the physical number of goods that can be imported over a period of time. For example, a quota might be 1 million passenger cars over a year. Quotas are set to limit the volume of imports.

There are always businesses in an economy which would like to see increases in barriers to trade. Measures like tariffs and quotas reduce competition in the market. It makes it easier for businesses which suffer competition from abroad to survive and make a profit. But PROTECTIONISM, the view that barriers to trade should be high, in the long term tends to lead to lower output and living standards. This occurs for two main reasons.

- Customers, whether businesses or consumers, have to pay higher prices for goods and services because they cannot buy them at world prices.
- Reduced competition reduces the incentive for businesses to innovate and change. Instead of competing with those businesses in the world which are most efficient and have the best products, they only have to compete with the best businesses in their own country.

The UK is limited in the political decisions it can make about protectionism because it is a member of the European Union. However, all members of the European Union are members of the World Trade Organisation (WTO). The WTO is an organisation which encourages its members to negotiate deals which will reduce trade barriers worldwide. It also provides a court where countries can bring complaints against other countries they think have broken the rules of international trade treaties. When a judgement goes against a country, it has to comply and change its behaviour.

Over the past 60 years, the UK has benefited from the international trade agreements negotiated with the help of the WTO and its predecessors. Prices of goods have fallen and competition has forced British industry to innovate and invest. However, some industries and businesses have suffered badly as a result. The UK textile industry, for example, has almost been wiped out because of foreign competition.

Global strategies

To compete in the world economy, UK businesses which are exposed to trade should have a GLOBAL or INTERNATIONAL STRATEGY. A business has four main strategic choices in its global strategy.

- It can export the same products or a service format that have been highly successful in its domestic market. For example, A UK chocolate manufacturer could export a new chocolate bar launched in the UK to Hungary or Thailand. A UK furniture retailer could set up identical stores in France and Germany. The advantage of this strategy is that

the product or service has already proved successful in one market and the cost of introducing it into a new overseas market will be less than if the product were adapted. It allows for greater economies of scale to be achieved. Coca-Cola is an example of how successful this strategy can be. However, the main disadvantage is that what is successful in one country may not appeal to customers in another country.

- A second strategy is to take a successful product in one market and adapt it for overseas markets. For example, McDonald's sells different food in India from France from the USA. The advantage is that there should be more chance that the product will prove attractive to local customers. The main disadvantage, apart from the risk that the product in practice doesn't appeal, is that economies of scale will be lost. Producing a number of slightly different products, each for a different market, is likely to be more costly per unit than a single mass produced product.
- A third strategy is to concentrate on minimising production costs by locating wherever in the world it is least costly to produce. Manufacturing industries in the rich industrialised countries of the world have been migrating to a small number of Third World countries, including China and South Korea, over the past 20 years. They have relocated low skill jobs to countries where

KEYTERMS

Customs union – a union of countries which establish free trade amongst themselves and put up a common tariff to imports from outside the union.

Eurozone – the group of countries which have adopted the single European currency, the euro.

European Union – a customs union whose aim is economic integration with a single market and which also has political and defence objectives.

Free trade – the import and export of goods and services with no barriers to trade such as tariffs or quotas.

Global or international strategy – the range of activities across the world a business needs to undertake in order to achieve its goals.

Joint venture – when two companies create a jointly owned subsidiary company to produce an agreed range of products.

Market access – the extent to which a business can enter a market and buy from or sell into the market.

Protectionism – government policies aimed at limiting the import of products into a country.

Quotas – limits on the physical quantity of products that can be imported into a country.

Single European market – the market for goods and services produced within the European Union, a market which is free of trade barriers and and restrictions to trade.

Tariff – taxes, also called customs duties, on goods imported into a country.

workers are paid a fraction of the wages paid to similar workers.

- A fourth strategy is to combine both customising products to local markets with locating where costs are lowest. This is the most difficult strategy to implement because it requires the business to pay attention both to product and

to costs.

These strategies assume trade between countries is broadly free. Where businesses come up against protectionist barriers, they have to modify their strategies. This limits their freedom both to sell goods and services but also where to source products and where to locate their operations.

KNOWLEDGE

1. Explain briefly the terms of (a) the Treaty of Rome; (b) the Single European Act; (c) the Maastricht Treaty.
2. Compare the roles of the European Commission, the Council of Ministers, the European Parliament and the European Court of Justice in the EU.
3. A British company manufacturing gardening equipment is coming under intense pressure from two Polish companies which are taking away its export sales and taking market share away in its UK home market. Briefly outline how the UK

company could respond in the areas of (a) operations management; (b) marketing; (c) human resources.
4. What is the difference between a tariff and a quota?
5. How might the decision of the UK government to sign an international treaty reducing tariffs on manufactured goods affect UK businesses?
6. Explain two ways in which restrictions on trade by the UK government might affect the global strategy of a UK business.

Case Study: Western supermarket chains to enter the Indian market

The Indian retail market is currently estimated to be worth £180bn per year. But with India's economy growing fast, retail sales could double over the next ten years.

At present, retailing is highly fragmented. 98 per cent of all sales go through around 12 million small family owned shops and stalls. About 40 million people are employed in the retail industry, nearly 4 per cent of India's estimated 1.1 billion population.

But that is all about to change with the entry of large supermarket chains into the market.

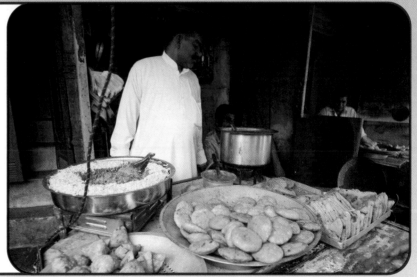

Om Prakesh is one of India's 12 million shopkeepers. With premises in New Delhi, the nation's capital, he is already feeling competitive pressure from a handful of privately owned supermarkets that have opened in the local area. For example, where once he sold 12 jars of jam a week, now he only sells two.

His store is a jumble of items from food, brooms,

disposable cups and school exercise books to unappetising samosas made by his wife. The items for sale are stacked on dusty, crooked shelves. The new supermarkets are bright and air-conditioned and sell a much wider variety of products.

Om Prakesh understands the danger he faces. 'Wal-Mart will buy in bulk and offer lower prices and big discounts. I can't compete because I have to buy a bit of everything.'

The world's largest supermarket chains want to grab a slice of the Indian market. This is not surprising given that an estimated 17 per cent of the world's population lives in India. But under present Indian laws, non-Indian companies can only enter the market in partnership with an Indian company. They are also banned from food retailing.

In 2007, Wal-Mart, the world's largest supermarket company and owner of Asda in the UK, signed a deal with the Indian company Bharti to operate wholesale cash-and-carry stores. The venture will be 50-50 owned by the two companies. The first store is to open by the end of 2008 and 15 are planned by 2015. Bharti, which owns a string of businesses in different sectors of the economy, plans to open a chain of retail stores, Bharti Retail, which will buy its produce from the wholesale operation.

The deal is seen as a way for Wal-Mart to get into the Indian market ahead of its other Western competitors. Companies like Tesco and Carrefour have been in negotiations with a number of parties to sign a similar deal but has so far failed to bring any negotiations to a successful conclusion.

Reliance Industries, India's biggest private company, has become the first company to implement a plan to create a nationwide grocery chain. It has plans to open stores in 784 cities and large towns and 6 000 smaller towns under the 'Reliance Fresh' brand. Included in this are 100 stores to cover the nation's capital New Delhi.

However, in September 2007, it was forced to put on hold its plans in a number of Indian states following protests and riots. In the state of Uttar Pradesh, India's most populous state, government officials shut ten Reliance Fresh stores in the face of protests. Reliance itself closed down stores in the western state of Orissa and the capita, New Delhi, after they were attacked by mobs. The government of communist controlled West Bengal was sitting on Reliance's application to open 145 stores, an investment of £500 million for the state which has a recent history of being innovate and business friendly.

A Reliance official said the losers would be consumers who face higher prices and workers who would lose job opportunities. 'There are states like Gujarat, Maharashtra and Andhra Pradesh that are moving ahead and will benefit,' he said. 'The others will miss out.'

However, the stakes are high for the millions who depend on small retailing businesses for their livelihoods. They know the arrival of supermarket chains will destroy most of their businesses. Dharmendra Kumar, of India FDI Watch which campaigns against changes in the retail sector, said that the jobs of '40 million hawkers, farmers and small shops are at stake. Big supermarkets want monopolies. Small retailers cannot compete. They'll simply get squeezed out. That is what happened in Britain.' Direct action, such as demonstrations and destruction of property, by those whose livelihoods will be destroyed, is likely to be a continued feature of the Indian move towards Western style retailing.

Source: adapted from news.bbc.co.uk 21.5.2007, 6.8.2007; www.bharti.com; www.independent.co.uk 28.11.2006; www.telegraph.co.uk 12.3.2007; www.guardian.co.uk 27.9.2007.

(a) Evaluate the difficulties to a company like Tesco or Wal-Mart of entering the Indian retail market. (40 marks)

(b) Discuss whether expansion in India should be an essential part of Tesco's or Wal-Mart's global strategy. (40 marks)

The law

Businesses must operate within the law. So the law acts as a **constraint** on their activity. Businesses face two main types of law.

- CRIMINAL LAW is enforced by government. Under criminal law, individuals or businesses can be **prosecuted**. If found guilty of having broken the law, they can be fined or imprisoned.
- CIVIL LAW allows an individual or business to **sue** another individual, business or the government to gain compensation.

For example, a business may sell food which is unfit for human consumption. It can then be prosecuted by government and fined. But it could also be sued by a consumer who has fallen ill as a result of eating the food.

Existing and new laws come from a number of sources. Local authorities have some powers to make laws. In Scotland, Wales and Northern Ireland, regional assemblies have law making powers. Parliament in Westminster passes laws which apply across the country. Finally, the UK is subject to EU law which applies across the European Union.

Health and safety legislation

There has been health and safety legislation on the statute books in the UK since the 19th century. However, the main Act of Parliament which governs health and safety today is the Health and Safety at Work Act 1974. Under the Act, government departments can issue further **regulations** as and when needed to cover new situations.

The Act states that employers have a duty to 'ensure, so far as is reasonably practicable, the health, safety and welfare at work' of all staff. It also states that employers must protect the safety of the public from the activities of employees. For example, in a supermarket, employees must not carry such heavy loads that they are likely to suffer back injuries. Equally, if a bottle of milk is spilt in the shopping area, staff must mop it up as quickly as possible to prevent customers from slipping over and injuring themselves.

The Act is enforced by the Health and Safety Executive. This is a government body which has the power to issue new codes of practice to govern safety issues as they arise. It also has a team of inspectors responsible for inspecting premises. Inspectors can order changes to be made or, if the situation is serious enough, an immediate closure of the premises until faults are rectified. Sometimes, businesses are taken to court for gross infringements of Health and Safety legislation, typically when a worker has been injured or killed. Courts have the power to fine businesses for infringements.

Businesses are affected in different ways by health and safety legislation. Businesses where there is little risk of industrial injury find it easy to comply at little cost to themselves. However, where there is a strong likelihood of injury, such as in mining or construction, complying with health and safety legislation can be extremely costly and time consuming. Large businesses tend to take health and safety issues seriously, partly because they have the resources to do so and partly because they do not wish to suffer adverse publicity if there is a bad accident. Small businesses, particularly in construction and farming, have a poor safety record. They are often unclear about the law and find it too costly to comply with anyway. In construction, there are major problems because many workers are self-employed and move from site to site picking up work. Pay is usually more important to them than health and safety.

Some businesses claim that they are internationally uncompetitive because of having to comply with health and safety laws in the UK. Businesses in, say, the Far East have lower costs because they do not provide as safe a work environment as required in the UK. However, working in a safe environment should motivate staff. For example, according to Maslow's theory, safety is a fundamental need of human beings.

Employment law

Laws relating to employment can be divided into two categories. One group of laws, **collective labour law**, deals with trade unions and industrial relations. In UK law, workers have a right to join a trade union. If sufficient workers in a place of work vote in favour, the employer must also recognise the trade union. This gives the trade union bargaining rights with the employer on behalf of its members. Workers can take industrial action, such as go on strike, in pursuit of their claims. However, the law regulates how a strike can be called and conducted.

Another group of laws, **individual labour law**, deals with the rights and obligations of individual employees. Individual labour law tends to be dealt with through **employment tribunals** rather than courts of law. Industrial tribunals were originally set up so that individual workers could represent themselves and, at little cost to themselves, pursue a claim against an employer. In practice, industrial tribunal cases tend to be dealt with by lawyers. Workers taking cases to the industrial tribunal are often represented by lawyers working for their trade union.

A number of different Acts of Parliament give workers the right to receive a **contract of employment** when they start work. This states conditions of work, such as how long an employee has to work for per week or month or year. The rates of pay must also be stated. Workers are protected from unfair **dismissal**. If an employer wants to dismiss or make a worker redundant, then the law lays down procedures for this. Workers are entitled to maternity and paternity leave. Employers cannot ask workers to work more than 48 hours a week except in

Question 1.

Sixteen years ago, Vince Regan set up Sports Tours International. The Manchester company, employing 16 people, organises sports teams' trips abroad, for training or for matches. He has the same problems as most managers in keeping up with the government's enthusiasm for employment legislation.

To cope with the flood of new and existing regulations, Regan pays an employment law firm to act as a helpline and to keep him abreast of the changes. It may seem an extravagance, but he knows it is worth it. Last year, a female member of staff felt that she was being sexually discriminated against because it was always the men who were given work abroad. The first Regan heard about her grievance was in a letter from a lawyer. 'We have a small but happy team, so the letter came as a real shock', he says. 'The fact is that we needed to send experienced athletes on these trips. They happened to be men.' But Regan did not make the mistake of underestimating the threat. He immediately sought expert advice on how he should respond. 'I followed instructions on replying to the letter, explaining my position and organising meetings with the employee', says Regan. 'I'm glad I did. Left alone, I would have done things differently and could have faced a large fine.'

Plenty of managers might not have been as careful, but experts say they need to be. The number of employment tribunal cases brought against bosses has more than trebled since 1990, with 128,000 cases being filed last year. The maximum award limit has risen from £12,000 to £50,000 over that time. At the same time, government red tape has multiplied, placing a heavy burden on small businesses.

Adapted from *The Sunday Times*.

(a) What Act of Parliament deals with sexual discrimination in the workplace? (i) What was the grievance brought against Sports Tours International by the female employee?

(a) What were the costs to Sports Tours International of dealing with grievance? (i) Suggest what might have been the potential cost to Sports Tours International if the company had not followed proper legal procedures.

(c) Explain the cost to businesses of having to comply with 'government red tape' in the field of employment.

'exempt professions'.

There are major pieces of legislation which also promote workers' rights.

- The Equal Pay Act 1970 states that workers are entitled to the same pay rates and conditions as other workers in a place of employment doing the same or 'broadly similar' work. It is the main act used to ensure that women are paid the same as men.
- The Sex Discrimination Act 1975 makes it unlawful to discriminate on grounds of gender or marital status. For example, employers can't reject a job applicant simply because they are a woman or they are married.
- The Race Relations Act 1976 makes it illegal for employers to discriminate on grounds of colour, race, nationality or ethnic origin.
- The Disability Discrimination Act 1995 makes it illegal for an employer with 20 or more employees to discriminate against a worker with a disability.
- The Minimum Wage Act 1998 established a national minimum wage for workers.
- The Employment Equality (Age) Regulations 2006 make it illegal to discriminate on grounds of age. Similar regulations exist for religion and beliefs and sexual orientation.

Labour law is an area where small to medium sized businesses feel particularly vulnerable. The volume of legislation is large and, without expert legal help, small employers can infringe the law particularly when it comes to issues such as dismissals and contracts of employment.

Large businesses have human resource departments which specialise in dealing with these issues. But all sizes of businesses complain about the cost of implementing legislation. '**Red tape**', the jargon word for a large amount of complicated rules and regulations imposed by government, can harm competitiveness and profitability. Businesses engaging in foreign trade often claim that red tape has made them uncompetitive against cheap labour Third World country producers.

Consumer protection

Consumers have long been protected by the law from businesses attempting to exploit them. Weights and measures legislation which prevented traders from giving underweight amounts existed in the Middle Ages. Today, consumers have rights under both criminal law and civil law.

In criminal law, a variety of different acts make it illegal for a business to:

- sell underweight or undervolume products; for example, a pub can't serve less than a pint of beer when one pint has been paid for;
- sell goods or services which have been misleading descriptions; a 100 per cent cotton shirt for example can't be 50 per cent cotton and 50 per cent nylon;
- products must be safe; for example, food must be fit for human consumption, and paint on toys cannot contain lead.

Consumer law is mainly policed by local authority **Trading Standards Departments**. Trading Standards officials inspect premises on a regular basis, particularly food premises. They will also investigate dangerous products. When necessary, they will take businesses to court where they can be fined for infringing the law.

However, for consumers to win compensation against injury or faulty products, they must use **civil law**. Consumers can sue a business if the goods or services it sells are not of merchantable

Question 2.

Vanessa Charles had a bad day on April 23rd. It was her son's birthday. She had bought him a motorised cycle from a large high street chain of stores. When he tried it out, though, the motor wouldn't work. She rang the store worried that she might not have carried out all the instructions properly to get it working. It suggested checking the connections in the motor. When she undid the screws and pulled off the plate, the motor was covered in dirt and had obviously been used already.

At least there was the party to look forward to. In the afternoon, she cooked all the foods that children like, including some mini sausages from the local butcher. Some of the children fell ill after the party, all of them having eaten the sausages. All the children who didn't eat the sausages had no problems.

When she took the cycle back to the store, they were extremely apologetic, and offered her a replacement cycle and 10 per cent of the price back as a 'goodwill gesture'.

(a) What rights in law did Vanessa Charles have concerning (a) the faulty cycle and (b) the sausages?
(b) Discuss the costs and benefits to large chains of retailers of offering 'goodwill gestures' to complaining customers.

quality, fit for the purpose for which they were sold or as described by the business. So a shirt sold with a hole in it is not of merchantable quality. Envelopes which do not stick down are unlikely to be fit for the purpose they were sold. A case of six bottles of wine where there are only five does not meet the description given by the seller for the product.

Consumer protection legislation has increased costs to businesses. However, this varies from product to product. Businesses involved in food sales have probably seen the highest increase in costs because they have had to change work practices and often buy expensive equipment to conform to the law. Consumer legislation, though, is unlikely to affect the competitiveness of individual businesses since all businesses have to conform to these laws. This is true of imported goods as well. Toys manufactured in China or Thailand for sale to the UK market have to conform to the same safety standards as toys made in London. The cost of improved standards can also be passed on to the consumer.

Some businesses have made it a unique selling point (USP) to give consumers more rights than they have in law. Many clothing chains, for example, allow consumers to bring back goods they decide they do not like and give full refunds. Electronics goods manufacturers might give one year's warranty on a good.

The environment

In recent years, businesses have seen increasing regulation of

their activities in relation to the environment. This, together with the impact of environmental regulation on business, is discussed in detail in the unit titled 'The Social and physical environment'.

Competition law

Competition in the market is generally considered to be beneficial to customers. Competing firms have to offer good value products if they are to survive. Good value might be in terms of the quality of the product or in terms of lowest price for a given quality of product. However, competition may be limited for two reasons.

- **Monopolies** may exist. In economic theory, a monopoly is the sole business in a market. In practice, there are very few monopolies. Railtrack, which owns all the rail infrastructure in the UK would be one example. But there are many businesses which have very high **market shares**. In UK law, a monopoly is said to exist if a single business has more than 25 per cent of the market. Monopolies can be created by the **merger** of two or more businesses. Therefore mergers must be of concern to any government which wants to promote competition.
- Businesses in a market may **collude**. This means that they get together to fix prices, sales or any other factor which will benefit their profits. The measures that they take are called ANTI-COMPETITIVE PRACTICES because they restrict trade. An example of an anti-competitive practice

would be a supplier forcing retailers to sell only at a price which has been set by the supplier. The supplier can then charge high prices to retailers knowing that the customers will be forced to pay the high price. This in turn allows the supplier to charge a high price to the retailers and so enjoy high profits. Another example would be a group of bus companies getting together to fix tenders for contracts. They share out the contracts between them, deciding in advance which firm will win which contract. The lowest bidder on each contract has in fact put in a high price to make high profits. The other bus companies simply put in an even higher price to allow the one bus company to win the contract. The result is that customers have to pay high prices.

In general, UK and EU law forbids businesses to collude unless government permits them to do so in the public interest. Monopolies are not illegal unless the monopolist acts in a way which harms customers. Equally, mergers which create monopolies are not illegal unless customer interests are likely to be harmed.

Sixty years ago, monopolies and restrictive practices were both legal and common in the UK. In one sense, this benefited many existing businesses because they were able to make higher profits than if there was competition in the market. However, businesses which were outside cartels, or small businesses in a market with a dominant supplier suffered as a result. Competition law is designed to give all businesses a 'level playing field' in their market. It allows new businesses to be created and challenge existing businesses in the market. Ultimately, the

purpose of competition law is to prevent customers from being harmed. However, all businesses are customers of other businesses, so they benefit as well as consumers. Competition law is not there to prevent businesses making a profit. The UK government and the EU recognises that profits are the essential incentive for businesses to produce goods and services. The business community can therefore be argued to be a major beneficiary of competition law.

KEY TERMS

Anti-competitive practices – measures taken by firms in a market to limit competition with the goal of raising their profits.

KNOWLEDGE

1. Explain the difference between civil and criminal law.
2. A worker is injured at work. Why might this affect her employer?
3. To what extent does health and safety legislation benefit businesses?
4. Summarise the main provisions of the law relating to (a) employment and (b) consumer protection in the UK.
5. To what extent does (a) employment law and (b) consumer protection legislation benefit businesses?
6. Outline the law relating to competition.
7. To what extent does competition law benefit businesses?

Case Study: Redundancy

Peter Tildersley runs a software company in London which specialises in contract work for City financial firms. In 2008, with the stock market having crashed to its lowest levels since the early 2000s, City institutions were shedding staff and cutting back on investment. Tildersley's company felt the backwash of this downturn and sales fell by a third over just six months.

He felt that the downturn could be prolonged and knew that the company was making a substantial loss at current sales levels. The only option was to slim down his staff, his major cost. He calculated that he would need to make 15 staff redundant. It was at this point that things began to go wrong. Not understanding the law, he called in the staff he had chosen to go, one by one, and told them they were going to lose their jobs. Nine of them had worked for the company for more than two years and therefore would be entitled to redundancy pay. Three of those chosen he found 'difficult' as employees. Two of them were in jobs which no one else on the staff could do and Peter knew he would have to spend money on training other staff to take on the jobs. One of the members of staff, told in the morning that he would be made redundant, was part of a small team seeing a new client in the afternoon, hoping to win a major contract. He was so demoralised that the presentation to the client was a disaster and the company failed to

win the contract. Two of the staff subsequently took the business to an industrial tribunal for unfair dismissal. The staff that remained were angry about what had happened and Peter lost three of his key workers within two months as they could get other jobs.

Peter Tildersley consulted a lawyer about the cases brought against the business. The lawyer explained that he would lose the two cases because he hadn't followed the law. He was legally obliged to consult with his employees before making anyone redundant. It could be that some staff would have gone voluntarily or some would have been prepared to work reduced hours. Only after consultation could he issue redundancy notices. He also was not entitled to dismiss workers because he found them 'difficult'. If the redundancies were about a fall in demand, then legally he had to be able to show that those workers made redundant no longer had work to do. The lawyer pointed out that he should have foreseen the other problems he encountered and taken steps to avoid them.

(a) Discuss whether Peter Tildersley should have made 15 staff redundant. (40 marks)

(b) To what extent did the problems he encounter over the dismissals arise from having to comply with government 'red tape'? (40 marks)

The social environment

The social environment is changing rapidly and this has a major impact on businesses. The social environment is changing in a number of different ways. For example, three important social changes impacting on business are the ageing population, immigration and the position of women in society.

The ageing population The UK's population is ageing. There is forecast to be some small increases in the population of 0-60 years over the next 20 years but the big increases will be in the 60-100 year olds. As Figure 1 shows, this is not an isolated phenomenon. It is occurring throughout Western Europe and the United States. This poses both opportunities and threats for UK businesses. On the one hand, there will a considerable increase in demand for services bought by pensioners. In particular, there will be a need for a large increase in care services for those who are no longer able to look after themselves in their own homes. Demand for residential and nursing care homes, for example, will rise. However, some businesses will find the shift in demographics difficult. Many aged 60-80 are fit and active and still see themselves as relatively young. Up till now, however, many businesses have ignored this growing market. They have not adjusted their marketing to a group of consumers who are more discerning in what they buy than, say, the average 20 year old. They could lose market share to companies which have addressed the issue of the 'grey pound'.

Immigration In recent years, there has been a large net influx of immigrants to the UK, many from Eastern Europe. They have been attracted to the UK by much higher wages than they could earn in their own home countries. However, for many immigrants, this 'higher wage' is the UK Minimum Wage, a relatively low wage for UK businesses. So this is an opportunity for UK businesses to employ workers at low wages, giving them a cost advantage. It is also an opportunity for UK businesses to recruit skilled workers in short supply in the UK labour market. The construction industry, for example, could not operate at anywhere near its current output levels without employing immigrant labour. For businesses selling products, immigration provides an opportunity to sell to the immigrant community. For example, the large supermarket chains often have ranges of goods in local stores aimed at the particular ethnic groups found in their area.

Women Over the past thirty years, there has been a transformation in the position of women in society. Attitudes have fundamentally changed and businesses need to recognise this. In the workplace, women by law must have equal opportunities to men. In practice, this means that women should be found at every level of the organisation of a business. With women of all ages now having the same, if not better educational qualifications than men, there should be a strong incentive for businesses to recruit and train women for all types of position in the organisation. Women are also now powerful consumers for all types of products. Fifty years ago, it may have been assumed that women bought the soap powder and the bread, whilst men bought the car and lawn mower. Businesses will fail to make crucial sales if they maintain these stereotypical images of how spending decisions are made.

The UK is a fast changing society. There are many other aspects of social change apart from the three analysed above. For example, educational standards are rising in the UK which has implications both the workforce and for what consumers buy. There is a changing attitude to 'Britishness'. Some businesses can sell products based on nostalgia for the past whilst other businesses can emphasise the internationalness and universality of their products. Distinct groups have emerged which can be targeted for marketing. For example, as explained above, there is the 'grey pound', spending by old people. But there is also the 'pink pound', or spending by children or the Bangladeshi community. Attitudes towards the environment have also been changing. This will be analysed in the rest of this unit.

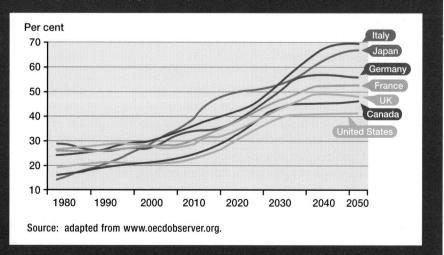

Figure 1: Elderly dependency: population aged 65 and over as a percentage of the working-age population (aged 20-64), G7 countries

Source: adapted from www.oecdobserver.org.

Question 1.

The population of over-65s in the UK is forecast to grow from 9.7 million today to 17 million in 30 years time. Britain's housing stock will have to adjust to allow the growing number of the elderly to live safely in their own homes. This is the thinking behind the 16 new government standards for all new homes which will become enforceable by 2013. New homes will have to be 'age-friendly' with features such as downstairs washrooms and wider doorways.

Builders have warned, however, that the plans would saddle them with additional costs at a time when the housing market was going into recession. 'Putting requirements on builders at a time like this could have a big impact on affordability', said the Home Builders Federation. Evidence of a weakening housing market can be seen in the dramatic fall-off in the number of new housing starts. Figures shows builders began work on 9,135 private homes in January 2008 compared to 14,998 in the same period last year.

This suggests that the governments' target for 3 million new homes by 2020 is looking every more optimistic. The age-friendly regulations are not the only new regulations in the pipe-line. By 2016, all new homes will have to be carbon-neutral.

Source: adapted from *The Financial Times*, 26.2.2008.

(a) The growing number of elderly people in the population is both an opportunity and a threat for building companies. Explain why and evaluate the extent to which the opportunities exceed the threats.

(b) To what extent would a house building company be affected at the same time by a recession in the housing market in 2008 and the new age-friendly building regulations?

The environmental problem

Society faces major environmental challenges today.

- The world's non-renewable natural resources are being depleted at a rapid rate. Oil, coal, natural gas, iron ore and copper are just some examples. There is only a finite amount of these resources. By using up huge quantities today, society is depriving future generations of their use. Businesses, motivated by profit, play a key part of this depletion.

- Renewable resources are being squandered too. Rainforests in South America and Asia are being cut down faster than they can be grown again. Farming land in many areas of the world is being degraded to the point where some of it becomes unusable. Thousands of species of plants and animals are becoming extinct each year, resources which are important for bio-diversity. Fisheries are being fished to the point of extinction.

- Pollution of the planet by business activity continues especially in Third World countries. Businesses are responsible for noise pollution, water pollution and air pollution on a local basis.

- Global warming, caused by excessive emissions from industrial activity of greenhouse gases, could have enormous consequences for life on this planet. Rising sea levels and shifts in temperature zones could force the relocation of large numbers of peoples and businesses at considerable cost.

- Depletion of the ozone layer, again because of industrial emissions, raises the possibility that harmful rays from the sun could increase skin cancer levels.

Business and external costs

Businesses do not always pay for the pollution they create. When this happens, the business is said to create an EXTERNAL COST or EXTERNALITY. The external cost is the difference between what the business pays, its PRIVATE COSTS, and the full cost to society of the production, the SOCIAL COSTS. External costs are therefore the difference between social and private costs.

External costs = social costs - private costs

For example, a business may recycle tyres. Its private costs include the wages of its staff, purchases of old tyres from suppliers, the transport costs of taking the tyres once recycled to customers and the energy used by the plant. However, the plant may also emit air pollution which at times can create nasty smells within a quarter of a mile radius from its plant. The people who live in that area may suffer as a result. The business is unlikely to give compensation to the local residents for this pollution. The external cost is then the value that the local inhabitants place on their loss of clean air. So the social cost is the private costs of the business plus the external cost of the air pollution.

When businesses create externalities, they are not paying the full cost to society of production. This then creates a situation of **market failure**. When markets work properly, the value that society places on a product, which is shown by the price that is paid for it, is equal to the cost to society of making the product, shown by the private costs to the business. If there are substantial externalities, the cost to society is much larger than the benefit gained by customers. The costs (the social cost) of production is much greater than the price paid by customers. This leads to overproduction of the good or service. If the price paid by the customer is low, reflecting only the private costs of production, the customer will buy more than if it is high and reflects all the costs of production, the social cost.

Legislation and business

Over the past 60 years, there has been increased pressure for government to intervene and reduce pollution levels in the UK. EU legislation has played an increasingly important role in policy. The UK has also signed international treaties such as the Kyoto Protocol to reduce emissions. Businesses are affected by legislation in a number of ways.

Physical controls Many businesses are subject to physical controls on pollution. For example, there are limits and bans on what can be discharged into rivers and into the air.

Taxes Some activities are now regulated by taxes. One example is the Landfill Tax which businesses have to pay to dispose of their rubbish at landfill sites. By raising the cost of disposing of rubbish, businesses are encouraged to recycle and create less waste.

Pollution permits A few industries, including electricity generation, are controlled by pollution permits such as carbon emission permits. Firms are given or sold permits which allow them to emit so much, for example, carbon, into the atmosphere. They can then trade these amongst themselves. Firms which have too many permits can sell them to firms which have too few. The number of pollution permits issued corresponds with government targets about overall emission levels.

The business response to environmental issues

Environmental issues offer both threats and opportunities to businesses. Businesses which stand to gain the most from growing environmental regulation are those selling pro-environmental and anti-pollution products. These businesses range from engineering companies selling equipment designed to reduce emissions, to service companies which advise other businesses on how they can comply with regulations, to businesses selling environmentally friendly products, such as managed wood.

Those which stand to lose the most are companies which are high polluters and who face competition from other businesses which don't face similar problems. For example, a specialist chemicals company may cease trading because there are many good substitutes to its products which have only a fraction of the environmental impact in production. Or a heavily regulated UK company may face competition from a Third World producer whose government places little restriction on its activity.

Question 2.

Marks & Spencer, the UK high street retailer, has caught the mood of the moment by announcing yesterday that it would charge for carrier bags in its grocery departments from November. Bags will now cost 5p each. The Daily Mail and the Women's Institute immediately gave their support to the move. Both Gordon Brown, the Prime Minister, and David Cameron, the leader of the oppositions, have said they would like to see retailers abandon giving away single use plastic bags.

Groundwork, an environmental charity which has been working with M&S, and which will receive all the revenues from the sale of M&S grocery plastic bags, said: 'Not only will this scheme reduce the amount of food carrier bags sent to landfill sites but it will also help improve the quality of life in towns and cities across the country.'

Adam Jones, UK sales director of Papier-Mettler, the company which supplies M&S with plastic bags, commented there was 'never a dull moment' in the world of plastic bags.

However, there is some controversy about the environmental impact of banning plastic bags. If it leads to far more paper bags being used, then paper bags are far more energy-intensive to produce that thin plastic bags.

The announcement by M&S led to other retailers giving reminders about their own initiatives. Aldi, the supermarket chain, already charges for bags. Tesco said its bags were degradable. Sainsbury said it was concentrating on encouraging recycling.

Charging for plastic bags, based on experience from the UK and other countries, is likely to lead to a drop of at least 90 per cent in the number of bags used. Cynics have noted eliminating the use of plastic bags will add to company profits.

Source: adapted from *The Financial Times*, 29.2.2008.

(a) Why might the move by M&S to charge for grocery plastic bags be an example of effective marketing for the company?

(b) Evaluate whether it would benefit both businesses and the environment if the government banned the giving away of free plastic bags by retailers such as supermarket chains, clothes retailers, DIY stores and music shops.

Marketing Environmental issues can be a highly effective marketing tool for some businesses. Companies such as the Co-operative Bank and The Body Shop have made a particular point of pursuing environmentally friendly policies. Many businesses on their packaging or in their advertising claim to be environmentally friendly in some way. However, some businesses have found that environmental issues pose a marketing threat. Oil companies, for example, are accused by environment pressure groups such as Greenpeace or Friends of the Earth of harming the environment. In the 1990s, when Shell planned to dispose of a disused oil platform by sinking it in the middle of the Atlantic, environmental pressure groups organised a consumer boycott of Shell petrol stations in Germany. This anti-marketing pressure was successful enough to influence the business to abandon its plans. Perrier was one of the leading brands of bottled water in Europe in the 1990s and in the UK was the top brand by sales. However, a contamination scare affected the image of the brand. Such examples show that businesses must take quick and positive action when an environmental issue suddenly arises. It also shows that some businesses have to work constantly to improve their environmental image.

Finance In some cases, responding to environmental concerns or new laws and regulations can have a positive financial impact on a business. Energy saving measures, for example, can lead to a business having lower costs than before because of previous inefficiencies. In most cases, though, taking environmental action is likely to lead to higher costs. If all businesses in the industry also face these higher costs, prices are likely to rise to reflect the higher costs. Profits would then be largely unaffected. But if higher costs fall more heavily on one business than another, then some will gain a competitive advantage and others lose it. This in turn will have different impacts on profitability. Installing expensive new equipment will also have a negative impact on cash flow. In the nuclear power industry and the car industry, businesses must also make investment decisions knowing that there will be heavy costs at the end of a product's life. In the case of the nuclear power industry, this is in terms of decommissioning plant. For motor manufacturers, they have to take back old cars for recycling. This will affect the outcomes of appraisal methods like the payback method and discounted cash flow.

Operations management Pollution controls and other environmental measures could have an impact on how a product is made. This could range from changes in the type of materials used, to production methods to storage and after-sales service. For example, asbestos was widely used in industry years ago but its use today is severely restricted. Industries such as electricity generation and chemicals have had to introduce much cleaner production methods to reduce emissions. The landfill tax encourages businesses to reduce the amount of waste they produce.

Human resources Environmental concerns and policies have human resource implications. Staff will need to be recruited and trained to deal with ever increasing government regulations concerning the environment. Some businesses may choose to outsource the guidance they need. Larger businesses are likely to put environmental policies in place. This could include an environmental audit where key measures relating to the impact of the business on the environment are audited each year and the results are made public. Implementing policies means that staff throughout the organisation are aware of the policies and what they must do to comply with the policies. As with any policy, unless there are good procedures and training in place to ensure compliance, staff will tend to interpret the policies as they see fit. Effective communication up and down the hierarchy is therefore essential. The very small minority of businesses which make environmental concerns an important business objective can use this as a way of motivating staff. Over time, it will tend to attract employees who are interested in this aspect of business. However, a tension between meeting financial targets such as profits targets and meeting environmental targets is likely to arise. For a business to survive, it must at least break even. In this sense, financial targets tend to be more important than environmental targets. This tension between targets could demotivate staff who want to see environmental targets as the most important for the business.

KEYTERMS

External cost or externality – the difference between the private cost to an individual or business of a product or activity and its full cost to society, its social cost. So external cost equals social cost minus private cost.
Private cost – the cost to an individual or business of a product or activity. For business, this is likely to be roughly equivalent to the accounting cost.

Social cost – the cost to society of a product or activity. this includes the private cost born by the individual or business together with the external cost which is borne by those other than the initial producer.

KNOWLEDGE

1. Explain the opportunities and threats to businesses posed by (a) an ageing population; (b) a population with significant immigration; (c) a society where women have more spending and earning power.
2. Explain the difference between private and social costs.
3. Explain briefly how businesses might be affected by pollution controls imposed by governments.

4. How might a business respond to environmental issues from the viewpoint of (a) marketing; (b) finance; (c) operations management; (d) human resources.

Case Study: Supermarket recycling disappoints

The big food retailers are letting both their customers and the environment down according to a report published by the Local Government Association. The study saw a range of common food items being bought from eight retailers: Asda, Lidl, Marks & Spencer, Morrisons, Sainsbury's, Tesco, a local high street and a large market. The content and the packaging of the items were weighed. The packaging was then analysed as to whether or not it could be recycled. Lidl came out as having the heaviest packaging at 799.5g per basket. M&S came out worst for recycling. 40 per cent of its packaging couldn't be recycled.

Friends of the Earth said the results of the survey were very disappointing. 'Despite constant green claims, supermarkets continue to act as a hindrance, not a help, when it comes to green consumer action. Packaging urgently needs to be minimised and made from materials that are easy to reuse, recycle or compost'.

Marks & Spencer's head of corporate social responsibility Mike Barry said: 'We've set ourselves clear and demanding targets to reduce our packaging and only use materials that can be easily recycled or composted. Whilst we've made good progress over the last 12 months, we know there's still much more yet to do in both areas.' The retailer added that councils needed to be more consistent about what was recyclable, pointing out that some councils allowed cardboard to be put in recycling boxes, whilst others did not.

The Local Government Association said: 'People are working to increase their recycling rates, but their efforts are being hamstrung by needlessly overpackaged products. Many supermarkets are taking action to cut back on excessive packaging, but there is an urgent need to do more. Councils and taxpayers are facing fines of up to £3 billion if we do not dramatically reduce the waste thrown into landfill.'

Table 1: % of packaging that is recyclable

Ranking	Retailer	%
1	Local market	79
2	Local retailers	79
3	Asda	70
4	Sainsbury's	70
5	Morrisons	68
6	Tesco	62
7	Lidl	61
8	M&S	60

Source: adapted from www.timesonline.co.uk; www.telegraph.co.uk; www.brandrepublic.com 23.10.2007.

(a) Evaluate whether it is in the commercial interests of supermarket chains to reduce the packaging on their products and make the packaging recyclable. (40 marks)

Ethics

ETHICS is about morality and doing 'what is right' and not 'what is wrong'. All businesses have to make many ethical decisions. Some are affected by the law. For example, it is illegal for businesses to dump waste by the roadside or send their drivers out on the road in unroadworthy vehicles. However, many ethical decisions have to be made without the help of the law. For example, should an employer allow a worker to take a day off work to look after a sick child and still be paid? Should a company stop buying goods from a factory in the Far East where it knows that work conditions are poor and wages are very low?

Making ethical decisions can be complicated because of differences of opinion. Some argue that it is wrong for businesses to manufacture toy guns to sell to children. Others suggest that they do no real harm. Muslim restaurant owners might face a dilemma about whether to sell alcoholic drink because the Koran forbids the drinking of alcohol. Other restaurant owners might not face such an ethical dilemma. Despite these differences, in many situations most people often take the same ethical stance. For example, most would agree that a company should not use employees' money in a pension fund to bail it out if it is making a loss.

Ethical issues

All businesses have to make ethical decisions. Should a self-employed plumber charge a senior citizen extra when a job takes longer than estimated? Should a finance manager delay payments if the business has cash flow difficulties?

Over the past 20 years, a number of issues have arisen for large firms which require decisions based on ethics.

The environment In countries like the UK or the USA, the law prevents businesses from polluting or destroying the environment. However, businesses must decide whether to adopt even more stringent measures to protect the environment. For example, should a business recycle materials, especially if this will lower profits? Multinational businesses often face lower environmental standards in Third World countries. Should they lower their own environmental standards in the Third World to take advantage of this?

Animal rights Some companies, such as pharmaceutical companies or cosmetics manufacturers, might use animals to test products. Animal rights groups argue this is unethical. Other companies, particularly food manufacturers or oil groups, can destroy habitats and endanger animals. Wildlife conservation groups argue against farming which destroys forests or oil installations, which can pollute the environment leading to the destruction of animal life.

Workers in the Third World A number of companies have been criticised for exploiting workers in Third World countries. Companies manufacture in the Third World because it reduces their costs. However, there is an ethical question about the extent to which low costs should be at the expense of low paid workers.

Corruption In some industries, such as defence, bribes might be used to persuade customers to sign contracts. It has been suggested that this takes place in the Third World, where civil servants or government ministers want money from any deal to buy arms. The ethical question is whether it is right to use bribes even if a business knows that its competitors do.

New technologies Some industries are at the cutting edge of science and technology. Most new products developed, such as

Question 1.

Huntingdon Life Sciences (HLS) is a company which carries out scientific experiments on animals for commercial clients. Since the 1990s, it has been embroiled in a long running dispute with animal rights activists, led by SHAC (Stop Huntingdon Animal Cruelty) which want to close the company down. The long-term term aim of the animal rights activists is for all animal experimentation to be banned. Once Huntingdon Life Sciences has been closed, they will turn their attention to other companies engaged in animal experimentation in pursuit of that aim.

What has been unusual about the dispute is its length and ferocity. The company's main laboratory in Huntingdon is picketed every week. Workers and managers have been subject to threatening telephone calls. The managing director has been attacked with baseball bats at his home. Failing to close down the company, the protesters turned to shareholders and financial companies dealing with Huntingdon. Shareholders were picketed outside their homes. Stockbrokers and bankers were subject to a campaign of abuse. The result was that most shareholders sold their shares in the company, and the banks and stockbrokers in the UK refused to deal any more with Huntingdon. Today, the company's banking facilities are provided by the Bank of England. The campaign has spread to the USA where customers and financial institutions dealing with the company have been targeted. SHAC continues to organise demonstrations against any company which supplies HLS both in the UK and the USA as well as continental countries such as Sweden and France. The purpose of these demonstrations is to 'shame' the company into ceasing to have any commercial contact with HLS.

(a) Discuss whether Huntingdon Life Sciences can ever be an 'ethical' company.
(b) Evaluate whether customers, such as pharmaceutical companies developing new drugs, should continue to use Huntingdon Life Sciences.

DVD players or a new chocolate bar, do not cause problems. But since the 1950s, nuclear power generation has been an issue. In the 1990s, GM crops hit the headlines. In the future, many biological processes, such as cloning, could arouse strong ethical reactions.

Product availability If a poor family cannot afford an expensive car, most would not see this as an ethical issue. But if an Aids sufferer in South Africa cannot afford drugs for treatment because pharmaceutical businesses charge such a high price, many would argue that it is an ethical issue. The direction of research is also important. Companies might research new drugs for complaints suffered by only a few in the industrialised world. Or they might research illnesses such as malaria which kill millions each year in the Third World. The choice that businesses make is an ethical issue.

Trading issues Some countries have been condemned internationally for the policies pursued by their governments. They may even have had sanctions or trade embargoes placed upon them. Companies must decide whether to trade with or invest in these countries.

Question 2.

Tate & Lyle is to adopt the Fairtrade label for all its retail sugar (packets of sugar sold to consumers) in the UK. It said the change would expand the UK Fairtrade sugar sector, currently only a few million pounds a year, by £80 million by the end of 2009. This will add another household name to the rapidly growing UK market for Fairtrade-branded products following announcements in recent years from companies such as Marks and Spencer.

Harriet Lamb, executive director of the Fairtrade Foundation, said: 'In terms of size and scale, this is the biggest ever Fairtrade switch by a UK company and it's tremendous this iconic brand is backing Fairtrade.'

Fairtrade certification is given when a product meets agreed environmental, labour and developmental standards. Usually, Fairtrade agreements for commodities like bananas or coffee guarantee farmers in developing countries a minimum price above market levels. However, in this case, the deal will involve Tate & Lyle paying sugar-growers a 'social premium' that can be used for community projects such as schools and health clinics. The premium is initially likely to be about £2 million a year, paid to Tate & Lyle's suppliers in Belize in central America. It will affect Belize Sugar Industries, the country's sole sugar processor, and about 6,000 small-holder sugar can growers.

The impact on Tate & Lyle is difficult to quantity. The agreement does not cover the company's much large operation selling industrial sugar to other companies. Nor has Tate & Lyle said what proportion of total cost for retail sugar is accounted for by the cost of the sugar imported from Belize.

(a) **Assess the possible advantages and disadvantages to Tate & Lyle of adopting Fairtrade.**

Codes of practice

In recent years, some large businesses have adopted ETHICAL CODES OF PRACTICE. These lay down how employees in the business should respond in situations where ethical issues arise. Ethical codes will differ from one business and one industry to another. However, they may contain statements about:
- environmental responsibility;
- dealing with customers and suppliers in a fair and honest manner;
- competing fairly and not engaging in practices such as collusion or destroyer pricing;
- the workforce and responding fairly to their needs.

Ethics and profitability

As with social responsibility, there might be a conflict between business ethics and profitability. Acting ethically when not required to do so by the law can have a negative impact on profit in two ways.
- It can raise costs. For example, paying higher wages than is necessary to Third World workers increases costs. Having to find other ways than animal experiments to test a new drug might add to costs. Adopting an ethical code of practice can raise costs. Staff have to be made aware of it and trained to implement it. It takes management time to prepare a code of practice.
- It can reduce revenues. A business might lose a contract if it refuses to give a bribe. Selling medicines to the Third World at low prices might increase sales, but total revenue is likely to be lower. Refusing to develop GM crops might mean a competitor getting into the market first and becoming the market leader. Acting ethically might even mean the destruction of the company. For example, a cigarette manufacturer which took full account of the costs it causes to customers would probably decide to cease trading.

However, adopting an ethical stance can produce benefits.
- Some companies have used their ethical stance for marketing purposes. In the UK, for example, the Co-operative Bank and The Body Shop have both increased sales by having a strong ethical stance and drawing in customers which are attracted by this. But adopting an ethical stance is no guarantee of success. Since the mid-1990s, The Body Shop has had disappointing sales growth. An ethical stance which may catch the mood of today's customers may not interest them ten years later.
- For most companies which have taken ethics seriously, it is the equivalent of an insurance policy. They don't want to be caught out behaving unethically and face serious penalties for breaking the law or see sales fall as customers protest against this behaviour. In 2002, two major companies paid the price for unethical behaviour. Enron, a large US energy trading company, collapsed. It was found to have manipulated its accounts to inflate its profits. Senior management had acted unethically by hiding this

from shareholders and government. This also led to the collapse of one of the world's top five accounting firms, Arthur Anderson. It had audited Enron's accounts and was accused of hiding the irregularities. As a result, it began to lose its major customers and decided to close down.

Ethics has become a serious issue for large companies. Customers and society have become less tolerant of businesses which behave in a way they see as unethical. However, most companies tend to follow trends and adopt ethical policies which will prevent them from coming to harm in the marketplace or by law. A few have adopted an aggressive ethical stance which sometimes has led to them gaining more customers. Often, small to medium sized businesses do not have management time or resources to draw up an ethical code of practice. Their ethical stance and behaviour is influenced by the society in which they operate.

KEY TERMS

Ethics – ideas about what is morally correct or not.
Ethical code of practice - a statement about how employees in a business should behave in particular circumstances where ethical issues arise.

KNOWLEDGE

1. Give two examples of ethical decisions an oil production company might have to make.
2. Explain which types of companies might be particularly affected by ethical issues relating to:
   (a) the environment; (b) animal rights issues; (c) Third World labour; (d) bribery; (e) new technologies; (f) access to products; (g) trading with politically unacceptable countries.
3. What might be contained in an ethical code of practice?
4. To what extent can businesses increase profits by becoming more ethical?

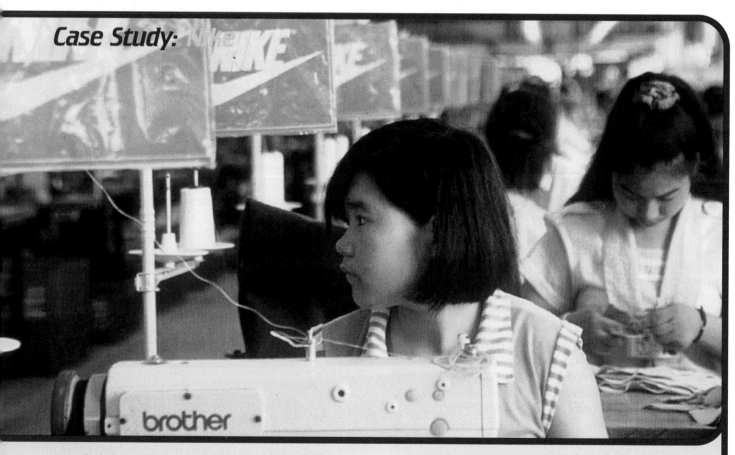

Case Study: Nike

Nike is the world's number one trainer brand. It doesn't manufacturer anything though. It designs shoes and markets them. Production is subcontracted to hundreds of factories round the world. In 2008, around 800,000 workers, 80 per cent of them women aged between 18 and 24 and living in Third World countries, made Nike footwear and apparel.

So how did such a successful company come to face a protracted negative ethical campaign? It started in 1992 when Jeff Ballinger, a US based activist working in Indonesia, published a damning report about conditions in the country's factories, detailing labour abuses, unsanitary conditions and forced overtime. Nike, as a high profile US company, became a symbol for the activists wanting to change the system. Student groups in the US lobbied for independent monitoring of factories of companies selling goods on US campuses, threatening

Nike's share of a $2.4bn business in college wear. Activist groups such as Global Exchange bombarded the media with anti-Nike stories.

Nike's initial response was stumbling but it soon gathered pace. In 1992, the company implemented a code of conduct that dealt explicitly with labour rights. There followed a series of initiatives: Ernst & Young, the international firm of auditors, began monitoring labour conditions in 1994; Nike joined President Bill Clinton's Fair labour Campaign in 1996. The company asked Andrew Young, a prominent black American who had been Ambassador to the United Nations, to review factories in Vietnam, China and Indonesia. The company also set out to improve the lives of workers. It launched lending programmes for workers, adult education and better factory monitoring. By 2007, it was committing itself by 2011 to 'improving working conditions in our contract factories through a holistic, integrated business approach to our supply chain'. In particular, it would eliminate excessive overtime in contract factories; implement management training on workers' rights, women's rights and freedom of association and collective bargaining in contract factories; and work with other companies on compliance issues in 30 per cent of their supply chain. Nike is also one of the few companies which publicly disclose the exact location of their contract factories worldwide.

Despite all these initiatives, Nike continues to receive criticism. In 2000, for example, a BBC documentary accused Nike of using child labour in Cambodia. The company as a result reviewed all 3,800 workers records and interviewed those it suspected were under age. But it couldn't verify that all the workers were adult. As a result, it pulled out of production in Cambodia in an attempt at damage limitation. Oxfam Community Aid Abroad, the Australian-based organisation that closely monitors Nike, alleges that 'workers producing for companies like Nike, FILA, adidas, Puma, New Balance and Asics commonly face low wages, long hours, verbal abuse, dangerous working conditions, denial of trade union rights and high levels of sexual harassment'.

Nike itself admits that it is not perfect. In its first 'corporate responsibility report', published in October 2001, it said that making Nike trainers was 'tedious, hard and doesn't offer a wonderful future'. It knew far too little about what happened in the factories it uses. Finally it admitted that its monitoring system did not work well enough. By the time it published its 2005-06 Corporate Responsibility Report, Nike was being much more assertive about its ability to create a supply chain where contract factories could be made to comply with Nike imposed rules about the use of labour.

Nike knows that it will now continue to be targeted by activists unless it uses factories with Western style conditions of work, if not pay. To do that would almost certainly turn a highly profitable company into one making huge losses, unable to compete against other companies continuing to use cheap Third World labour. It also knows that almost all large clothing manufacturers, or giant retailers such as Wal-Mart (which owns Asda), routinely buy from Third World 'sweatshop' factories where conditions of work are just as poor, if not poorer, than Nike factories. However, perhaps more so than other businesses, it is addressing issues in a realistic way and attempting to put itself ahead of competitors in the corporate social responsibility stakes.

Source: with information from *The Financial Times* 21.12.2000, 7.3.2002 and 18.6.2002; www.wikipedia.org; www.oxfam.org.au; www.nikebiz.com

(a) Discuss whether, from an ethical standpoint, Nike should source its products mainly from low cost locations in the Third World rather than from factories in the USA. (40 marks)

(b) Evaluate the costs and benefits to Nike of working with other companies to monitor conditions in its supply chain. (40 marks)

Social responsibility and business ethics

Businesses act in the interests of their owners. But social custom, the law and the market force them also to acknowledge responsibilities to their other **stakeholders**, such as their workers, their customers and suppliers and the communities in which they operate. Equally, businesses have to act within an ethical framework. If nothing else, businesses should operate within the law.

However, there is a considerable difference between businesses in the way in which they operate in these areas. Businesses like the Co-operative Bank or The Body Shop make a point of acting in a socially responsible and ethical way. Other businesses like arms manufacturers, by the very nature of the products they make, can be accused of being socially irresponsible.

For many businesses, there is a direct trade-off between the interests of different stakeholders. The opportunity cost for a business which spends £1 million a year supporting charity projects in the local area could be £1 million which is not paid in dividends to shareholders, or £1 million which is not paid to employees in higher wages. The best case scenario for a business is when acting in a socially responsible and ethical way brings benefits to all stakeholders. For example, a doughnut manufacturer may have a policy of sponsoring children's sporting activities. If sales rise as a result, the owners and employees can benefit through higher dividends and more jobs. The local community also benefits from the sponsorship of its young people. Even then, there could be disadvantages. The sponsorship may encourage customers to eat more doughnuts, which could be argued to be unhealthy. The sugar used in the product might have been produced by child labour. There will also be those who will accuse the company of sponsoring children's sporting activities as a mere PR (public relations) exercise.

Many businesses do not have a carefully thought out attitude to social responsibility and ethics. However, large companies are increasingly being forced by the law and by pressure groups to develop policies in these areas. For example, some companies have published social and environmental audits (see below). Others have developed ethical codes of practice.

For some businesses, attitudes to social and ethical responsibility form part of the wider culture of the business. If there is a strong culture of caring towards all the stakeholders, there is more likely to be a strong social and ethical culture. In businesses where the emphasis is mainly on financial targets, social and ethical issues may play little part in decision making.

In some companies, there could also be a clash of cultures between different layers of the organisation, or different parts of the company. Newly appointed senior executives, for example, may put social and ethical policies in place. But these may not filter down the organisation hierarchy. Or head office in London may follow a strong ethical stance but a subsidiary of the company in another country may conceal from head office poor work conditions and the use of labour on very low wages in its factories in order to boost profits.

Changing business culture is often difficult, whether it is aimed at increasing profitability, cutting costs or adopting more ethical codes of conduct. In an autocratic organisation, change is only encouraged if it comes from above. Change may then encounter resistance as it passes down the management hierarchy. Ultimately it may be frustrated because of the unwillingness to change of those at the bottom of the hierarchy. With more democratic leadership, there will be an increased emphasis on consultation, delegation and empowerment. But this too can frustrate change. If social responsibility and ethics are not seen as high priority by all within the organisation, it becomes very difficult for a few, even if they are at the top of the hierarchy, to get their message across. Delegating responsibility and empowering workers is only successful if those workers share the same goals as the business. Getting everyone to share those goals can take a long time.

Corporate social responsibility (CSR)

Some large businesses have responded to concerns about CORPORATE SOCIAL RESPONSIBILITY, their responsibility not just to their shareholders but to all stakeholders, by auditing relevant activities. These audits may then be made available to the public in a Corporate Responsibility Report, in the same way that the financial accounts of the company are published. Auditing involves inspecting evidence against established standards. Auditors can then say that the evidence presented by the business is 'true and fair'.

In accounting, standards for accounting audits are set by accounting bodies such as the Accounting Standards Board. In contrast, social and environmental auditing is voluntary and there is no body which draws up rules about how audits should take place. At present, companies are free to choose what standards they should be measured against and who the auditors will be. Indeed, the vast majority of businesses do not undertake any social or environmental accounting.

Businesses which do compile social and environmental audits use a wide range of measures, which differs from business to business. An oil company, for example, may measure the number of oil spills for which it is responsible. This would not be appropriate for a drinks company which might use other indicators such as levels of air pollution created by its breweries and distilleries. Social and environmental audits might include some of the following.

Employment indicators How well does the business treat its staff? This might include indicators about pensions, healthcare benefits, trade union representation, training and education, number of accidents involving staff, payment of minimum wages, equal

Question 1.

Lucent Technologies was a US manufacturer of telecommunications equipment. It was created by a demerger with AT&T, a large US telecommunications company, in 1996. In 2006, Lucent merged with Alcatel, the French telecommunications equipment company.

Whilst still an independent company, Lucent was pursuing a strategy of selling into the Chinese telecommunications market. As part of its marketing effort, it invited Chinese officials to the USA. The US Department of Justice in an investigation found that the company spent more than $10 million (£5 million) on about 315 trips for 1,000 Chinese government officials and telecoms executives. The problem was that they 'spent little or no time' touring Lucent's production facilities. Instead, they enjoyed sightseeing in Hawaii, Las Vegas, the Grand Canyon, Niagara Falls, Disneyland and Universal Studios. Despite paying for travel, hotels and meals, Lucent also gave some Chinese officials a daily cash allowance of $500 to $1,000. As for relatives or associates of the invited Chinese officials, these were offered 'educational opportunities' both in the USA and back in China. The total cost of these 'educational opportunities' to Lucent was over $100,000.

Lucent was last December was fined $2.5 million by the US Department of Justice under the Foreign Corrupt Practices Act for attempting to bribe Chinese officials to place orders with the company.

Source: adapted from *The Financial Times*, 6.3.2008.

(a) Explain why Lucent was fined $2.5 million.
(b) Discuss whether European and US businesses should be allowed by their governments to use bribery to win contracts in emerging markets such as China and India.

products sold by the business? For example, were there customer health and safety issues? Was after-sales service adequate? Was advertising true and fair? Did the company manage its information on customers and suppliers in such a way as to preserve their privacy?

The environment These indicators can form a separate **environmental audit**. Some businesses may only compile an environmental audit and not include any of the other social indicators described above. Indicators might include the amount of energy or other raw materials such as water or pesticides used by the business. How much waste or effluent was produced? What were levels of greenhouse gas or ozone-depleting emissions? What percentage of materials used were recycled? What was the company's impact on bio-diversity? What impact did it have on protected and sensitive areas? How many times was it fined during the period for failure to comply with environmental regulations and what was the total level of fines?

Some of these measures are **financial**, i.e. they are measured in money terms. Many, however, are **non-financial**. For this reason, it is difficult to get a quick and easy overall measure of how well a business is doing from its social and environmental audit. In contrast, with a financial audit like a set of financial accounts, it is possible, for example, to look at the profit and loss account and say that the business has performed better or worse in terms of revenues, costs and profit. The data from social audits are therefore more difficult to assess and compare from year to year than from financial accounts.

Exposing social costs or just PR?

Social and environmental auditing can be controversial. Those in favour argue that businesses should be encouraged to conduct social and environmental audits for a number of reasons.

- It helps both businesses and their stakeholders to understand the **social costs** of their activities and not just the private costs shown in their financial statements.
- It is a way for management of a business to manage the business in a more socially responsible way and identify issues of **market failure**.
- It allows the stakeholders of a business to evaluate its success using wider criteria than simply financial measures.
- It might be used to plan more effectively for the future. For example, a business might be able to identify new markets, different sources of supply, and different production methods which might suit the needs of its stakeholders, including customers.
- It might prevent some stakeholders, such as pressure groups, from distorting facts to suit their own agendas.

Many pressure groups, however, argue that social and environmental auditing is inadequate. Businesses have the freedom to choose on what they report. It can also be difficult for auditors to verify the statistics produced by the company. In the case of illegal trading, for example, it is in the interests of both the employees and those they are trading with to keep illegal deals

opportunities and the level of women in higher management or director positions.

Human rights indicators How well does the company perform on human rights issues? For example, does it encourage its workers to join trade unions and give those trade unions negotiating rights with the company? Does it have works councils? Does it or its suppliers use child labour? Does the company operate in, buy supplies from or sell products to countries which have poor human rights records? Does it discriminate on grounds of race, gender or age when recruiting or promoting staff?

The communities in which the business operates What impact does the business have on the life of the communities in which it operates? For example, how much does it give to charities? How much is spent on local schools, hospitals and housing?

Business integrity and ethics How ethical is the business in its activities? For example, have there been any cases of trading which breaks legislation involving the company? Did the company make political contributions and to whom? Was the company involved in cases associated with unfair competition?

Product responsibility What was the social impact of the away from the eyes of auditors. Investigative journalism also uncovers instances of issues such as use of child labour and poor working conditions in Third World factories which have not been reported in the official social audit. So **social and environmental** audits may be misleading.

Pressure groups would like to see tough uniform standards for social and environmental audits with which all businesses would have to comply. Then it would be possible to compare the performance of one business with another. It would also force businesses to account for externalities which at present they prefer to ignore or, at worst, conceal from their stakeholders.

Current social auditing, pressure groups would argue, is little more than a PR (public relations) exercise. To make themselves look socially and environmentally aware, companies publish social and environment audits. They can use this when talking to the press, to their shareholders and to pressure groups to say that they understand the issues and are taking tough action to combat externalities.

Voluntary social auditing might also be an obstacle to the introduction by government of tougher laws and regulations on social and environmental issues. Companies could argue that their social audits show that they are responsible organisations which have the best interests of the community amongst their goals. Introducing laws and regulations would mean more red tape and higher costs to business without necessarily improving current practice. On the other hand they may be more concerned with

maximising shareholder value. Social auditing is therefore an obstacle to what might really be needed – tough laws and regulations to control anti-social businesses.

KEYTERMS

Corporate social responsibility – the responsibility that a business has towards all stakeholders and not just to owners or shareholders.

KNOWLEDGE

1. To whom might a business have social responsibilities?
2. To what extent do all businesses have a strong social and ethical culture?
3. What might be the conflict between implementing ethical decisions and delegation?
4. What is an audit?
5. Why are recognisable and accepted standards important in auditing?
6. What measures might be used when conducting a social and environmental audit?
7. What are the arguments (a) in favour of and (b) against conducting social and environmental audits?

Case Study: BAT

British American Tobacco is one of the world's largest cigarette manufacturers. In its *Social Report 2005* it said: 'Our vision is to achieve leadership of the global tobacco industry through strategies focussed on growth, productivity and responsibility supported by a winning organisation. By growth we do not mean 'selling smoking', but growth in our share of the global market, growth in profit, and continuing growth in shareholder value. By productivity, we mean using resources smartly, enabling additional money to be generated for reinvestment to strengthen our competitive position and performance. We believe that because our products pose risks to health, it is all the more important that our business is managed

responsibly and we see responsibility as fundamental to building long-term shareholder value. Through dialogue with our stakeholders and by listening and responding, we are working to pursue our commercial objectives in ways consistent with changing expectations of a modern tobacco business. Our Business Principles are Mutual Benefit, Responsible Product Stewardship and Good Corporate Conduct. In our Social Report, we aim to demonstrate how we are working to live by them.'

Source: adapted from British American Tobacco, *Social Report* 2005.

Table 1: British American Tobacco: key statistics 2003, 2006

	2003	2006
Gross turnover (including duty, excise and other taxes)	£25 622 million	£25 189 million
Operating profit	£2 781 million	£2 622 million
Profit after tax	£788 million	£2048 million
Worldwide excise and tax contribution	£14 360 million	£16 143 million
Group environmental, health and safety expenditure	£34.8 million	£23.6 million
Group charitable and community donations	£12.7 million	£17.6 million
Employees (including associate companies)	86 941	97 431
Factories	87 in 66 countries	52 in 44 countries

Source: adapted from British American Tobacco, Social Report 2003/4; *Social reporting 2006: Progress and review.*

Can the maker of a lethal product be socially responsible? Martin Broughton, the outgoing chairman of British American Tobacco, says of corporate social responsibility (CSR) that: 'To say it's not important for controversial industries to operate responsibly is a very strange way of looking at life. I think because the product is controversial and dangerous, it is more important that the industry is in responsible hands than in what you might call a 'normal' industry.'

BAT's claims of responsibility, however, face an obvious credibility gap. A survey of MPs and non-governmental organisations has just named it the worst of Britain's top 50 companies for corporate social responsibility. 'It would seem that no matter what tobacco companies try to do on the subject of CSR, it's the nature of the product that is the key issue and the two are incompatible', says BPRI, the WPP group consultancy that carried out the survey.

Source: adapted from *The Financial Times*, 28.9.2004

Table 4: Diversity and opportunity: composition of management (including the board of directors), male and female ratios

		Management trainees	Level 1 (junior management)	Level 2 (middle management)	Level 3 (senior management)	Level 4 (senior management)
2003	Male	0.61	0.73	0.78	0.87	0.94
	Female	0.39	0.27	0.22	0.13	0.06
	Male to female ratio	1.6:1	2.7:1	3.6:1	6.7:1	15.7:1
2006	Male	0.54	0.69	0.75	0.84	0.93
	Female	0.46	0.31	0.26	0.16	0.07
	Male to female ratio	1.2:1	2.3:1	2.9:1	5.1:1	13.3:1

Source: adapted from British American Tobacco, Social Report 2003/4; *Social reporting 2006: Progress and review.*

British American Tobacco (BAT) supports community and charitable projects. On its website in 2008, it said that: 'We recognise the role of business as corporate citizens and our companies have long supported local community and charitable projects. We approach corporate social investment (CSI) as an end in itself, rather than as a way to promote ourselves, and our companies have always been closely identified with the communities where they operate.'

It went on to say that 'Our global CSI expenditure in 2006 .... was £17.6 million ... of which £3 million was spent in the UK.'

BAT encourages its companies to focus their CSI activities around the three themes of sustainable agriculture, civic life and employment. For example, 'Sustainable agriculture covers CSI contributions to the social, economic and environmental sustainability of agriculture. It includes activities such as efforts to improve bio-diversity and access to water, afforestation, programmes to prevent child labour, grants for agricultural research or training to help farmers grow non-tobacco crops.'

Table 3: Total amount of waste generated by BAT by type and destination. (Destination = method by which waste is treated, including composting, reuse, recycling, recovery, incineration or landfilling.)

	2002	2006	
	Metric tonnes	Metric tonnes	% change
Non-hazardous waste			
Sent to landfills	50,701	23,449	-53.8
Recycle	98,909	108,290	9.5
Incinerated	1,456	611	-58.0
Other	4,345	529	-87.8
Total	15,5411	13,2879	-14.5
Hazardous waste			
Sent to approved landfills	110	411	273.6
Recycled	362	816	125.4
Incinerated	263	279	6.1
Other	176	56	-68.2
Total	911	1,562	71.5
Hazardous and non-hazardous waste, total	156,322	134,441	-14.0
Per million cigarettes equivalent produced	0.153	0.127	-5.9

Source: adapted from British American Tobacco, Social Report 2003/4; *Social reporting 2006: Progress and review.*

(a) Using BAT and its corporate social responsibility reporting as an example, discuss the extent to which 'the maker of a lethal product (can) be socially responsible' (Box 2). (40 marks)

Technological change

The use of **technology** is one of a number of characteristics which separate human beings from most other animals. Over time, humans have developed a range of technologies, such as the wheel, water power, steam power, electricity and telephony. The latest technology to transform society has been the microchip. This has given rise to computers and information and communication technology. The next major wave of technologies is likely to centre around biotechnology.

It has been argued that technological change is **exponential**. This means that the rate of change accelerates over time. Two thousand years ago, the rate of technological change hardly altered at all over a person's lifetime. One hundred years ago, there was significant change for many people in industrialised countries over their lifetime. Today, major changes take place almost every decade.

Business opportunities

Technological change provides businesses with two main opportunities.

New products In some industries, developing new products is vital to the competitiveness of a business. For example, vehicle, domestic appliance and electronic goods manufacturers all survive by constantly bringing out new and improved products. The **product life cycle** varies from industry to industry. In the car industry, models may be changed every five years, although there will be minor modifications made each year. With a new product like a DVD player, the product life cycle may be less than one year. In these industries, failure to bring out new products based on the latest technology is likely to lead to falling

Question 1.

Ever since General Motors installed the first industrial robot in its Trenton, New Jersey, plant in 1962, the car industry has been in the vanguard of robotics. Robots do not demand pay rises, do not join trade unions and are happy to do dirty, smelly, dangerous jobs. They are also pinpoint accurate time after time, an essential ability if your job is to weld together hundreds of thousands of cars a year. Yet car factory automation seems to have reached its peak for two different reasons.

First, car makers have come to realise that robots are expensive compared to workers. Not only is their initial purchase cost high, but they are costly to maintain. Breakdowns are costly too. 'We had to realise in the car industry that a high degree of automation in the factory will give you reliability problems and then you will have downtimes – and downtimes cost you money', said Noirbert Reithofer, director of production at BMW.

Second, robots have proved too inflexible in final assembly where the variety of options on any individual car explodes. Robots are well suited to making standard movements using standard components. But the complexity of options in final assembly is too great. Even in one of the few areas of final assembly that have been colonised by robots - attaching windscreens - some new factories are reverting to human beings. At the new Honda plant in Swindon, the experience gained with the glazing robot in the old factory gave the company the expertise to fit windscreens manually.

Third, with flexible manufacturing systems, car manufacturers want to be able to switch production from one model to the next relatively quickly. Robots can be too inflexible for this. 'There has been a rebalancing', according to Steve Young, automotive vice-

president at consultants AT Kearney. 'There is a better understanding of the real cost of automation from real experience.' In particular, he says, it costs a lot more to reprogram the machine for a new vehicle than was expected – as much as buying the robot in the first place.

Source: adapted from *The Financial Times*.

(a) Explain the link between automation and robots.
(b) What are the main advantages to car manufacturers of using robots?
(c) Why have some car manufacturers begun to use less technology in their plants and relied more on human workers?

sales and the survival of the business may be threatened.

However, in other industries, new technology has little if any impact on the product. Heinz Baked Beans, for example, are sold with the marketing message that they haven't changed over time. Today's baked beans are the same as the 'original'. New technologies can also be fiercely resisted by customers. Foods containing GM (genetically modified) crops have had to be withdrawn from supermarket shelves in the UK because some consumers didn't want to buy the products.

So the introduction of technologically improved products is vital in some industries. At the other other end of the scale, some businesses are successful because the product is the same as before, unaffected by technological change.

Product processes Even though Heinz Baked Beans have not changed over time, the technology used in their production is likely to have changed. Much of manufacturing industry has been transformed over the past thirty years, partly due to the introduction of microchip technology. This has resulted in further AUTOMATION of processes where workers have been replaced by machines.

For example, **computer numerical controlled (CNC)** lathes and milling machines are now standard in UK manufacturing. In design, **computer aided design (CAD)** packages are commonplace. These are programs which allow a design to be completed on a computer rather than on paper. The package is also able to do the numerical calculations necessary for the job. **computer aided manufacturing (CAM) (or CAD/CAM engineering)** links CAD packages with CNC machines. The CNC machines can be programmed from the CAD package. Computers are also used in other departments of manufacturing companies. Accounts are likely to be produced using an accounting program and financial information stored on computer or disks. Deliveries can be tracked online with some delivery companies.

Service industries too have been transformed. Even a traditional restaurant, for example, is likely to use a till which is controlled by a microchip. People might pay for a meal using a swipe card. In the kitchen, cookers, refrigerators and utensils will have changed from thirty years ago. In many service industries, there has been a revolution in the way in which the service is delivered. Computerisation has swept away the keeping of manual records. Email communication is becoming more common than written letters. The Internet allows advertising and sales to be made directly to customers via computer link.

Using technology to change the way in which work is done has several benefits. One is that production becomes more efficient, reducing costs. Another is that the quality of production can be improved. Email allows a faster response time to a query. The use of robots lets car manufacturers achieve zero defects in production. Improved technology can be used to improve the health and safety of workers. By automating dangerous processes, workers can be protected from harm.

Impact of changes in technology

New technology can present businesses with considerable opportunities. But it can also pose a major threat. There is a variety of ways in which this occurs.

Implementing technological change Buying a new computer system, installing a new CNC machine or developing a new product with the latest technology will not necessarily be successful in improving productivity or sales. The introduction of new technology is often a high risk process. Many new products fail. It may prove impossible to integrate the new machine into the existing production process. Computerisation may not save a worker time compared to a pen and paper system.

The introduction of new technology might also affect business organisation. Improvements in communication might mean changes in work practices, such as a reduction in face-to-face meetings. It might also allow a business, for example, to set up in another country and keep in regular contact to better meet the needs of a foreign market.

Managing technological change requires skill and often a certain amount of luck on the part of a business.

Competition and survival It is often expensive to install new technology in production processes. Designing new products containing new technology is also costly. Many businesses don't make enough profit or generate the cash flow to be able to afford this investment. However, they risk being left behind in the market if they don't invest. In the UK, manufacturing companies which have consistently failed to invest have become less and less cost competitive. Many businesses have been forced to close due to competition from cheap labour producers in the Far East. In a competitive market place, the businesses that survive are those which invest enough and manage the new technology successfully.

The workforce New technology will have an impact on the workers in a business. Introducing new technology in production is likely to require **training** of workers. This may be on-the-job training or off-the-job training. Not all workers will necessarily be able to cope with the changes. Some workers, for example, may not have the basic skills needed. Others may be reluctant to change to new ways of working. Management may then have to consider redeployment of some staff. Redundancy may also be a possibility. If the new technology is labour saving, and sales are not increasing, then redundancies may be inevitable.

Change can affect **motivation**. Some workers may be highly motivated by working with new products or new processes. Other workers may find it threatening and demotivating. They may be afraid that they will lose their job or their position in the hierarchy. They may worry about having to work with a new group of people or under a different manager. If the workplace is unionised, these fears may lead to trade unions objecting to the changes and attempting to stop, delay or alter them. Management, therefore, need to handle change with great care.

Business culture Technology has radically transformed business culture: the values, attitudes, beliefs, meanings and norms that are shared by people and groups within an organisation. One fundamental shift has been the transfer of workers from doing heavy manual labour in manufacturing to much lighter work in the service sector. The business culture of a coal mine or a factory is very different from an office, a shop, a care home or a hospital. However, technology has influenced business culture even when the same products are being made. For example, the culture on a car production line is different today than it was 50 years ago. Then, workers were typically unskilled, performing repetitive tasks for which they took little responsibility. Today, far more production is now automated, particularly hazardous and dangerous procedures. Production line workers are given responsibility for quality assurance. They may work in teams. Instead of the technology encouraging a spirit of alienation among workers, it has enabled workers to develop more positive attitudes to work.

KEYTERMS

Automation – the process of the replacement of workers by machines in production.

KNOWLEDGE

1. Give three examples of technological change that has occurred over the past three hundred years.
2. What does it mean to say that the rate of technological change is 'exponential'?
3. How can technological change lead to (a) changes in products and (b) changes in production processes?
4. Why might introducing new technology into a workplace be disruptive to production?
5. What are the human resource implications of introducing new technology?

Case Study: Kesslers International

esslers International is one of Europe's biggest makers of display stands for retailers. This is a fast-changing category of product, where success depends on translating design into manufacturing as smoothly as possible. At the company's factory in east London, a piece of metal can be cut into a complex shape on the shop floor using digital instructions generated 20 minutes earlier by a designer sitting at a computer terminal on the other side of a partition. 'We spend half our time working on creative design and the other half turning a concept into a working product without losing the aesthetic appeal', says George Kessler, one of two brothers who run the family-owned company.

Each year the company makes up to 1,000 types of display, selling from just a few pounds to £1,500 each, in production runs that are rarely above a few thousand. The displays use about 70,000 types of component. These are made on a variety of machines, including robot welders, vacuum forming machines, laser cutters, injection moulding systems, silk screen printers and powder coating equipment. About 80 per cent of what it makes will not be repeated the next year because of fashion changes.

The main contacts of customers among Kesslers' 300 employees are with its 30 or so designers and product developers. These people use computer-aided draughting systems to turn ideas into product

specifications, normally in a matter of weeks after receiving an order. The close link between the design and manufacturing teams means the company can make late changes to orders on behalf of customers, even a few days before the order is delivered. The customers like the flexibility, for which Kesslers charges extra.

Maintaining such a close link between manufacturing and design requires heavy investment. The company spends up to £500,000 a year on capital equipment and puts another £80,000 a year into training. It is putting its employees through special training courses organised by Cardiff University's lean enterprise implementation group to tutor them in the latest thinking in fields such as just-in-time manufacturing and ways to minimise waste. 'There is absolutely no point in investing in machinery if you don't put substantial sums into improving the capabilities of your employees', says George Kessler.

Source: adapted from *The Financial Times*.

(a) Discuss whether technological change in new products or in business processes is more important for Kesslers. (40 marks)

(b) Evaluate the problems that Kesslers might face in using new technologies in production. (40 marks)

Markets and competition

Markets have a number of characteristics.
- A market exists in any place where buyers and sellers meet to exchange goods and services.
- The place may be a physical one, such as a street market, or a supermarket. Equally, many transactions today take place by post, fax, over the phone or on the Internet.
- Markets can be local, national or international.
- Some markets, such as that for cricket bats, are small. In some, such as the car market, sales are so large that they dwarf the output of many countries in the world today.

Almost every business has to compete in the market place. COMPETITION can take a variety of forms depending upon the particular market in which a business operates. One simple way of characterising competition is the 4Ps of marketing. All other things being equal:
- the lower the **price** charged, the more sales there will be;
- businesses which sell superior **products** to their rivals will sell more;
- **promotion** can help increase sales;
- getting products to customers at the right **place** and at the right time will stimulate sales.

Classifying markets: an economics approach

Markets can be classified into a number of different types according to their mix of characteristics.

Perfect competition In perfect competition, there are a large number of small businesses, none of which has any significant market share. They are independent of one another because the actions of one business have no effect on other businesses. In a perfectly competitive market, businesses produce homogeneous (or generic i.e. identical) products so there is no product branding by individual businesses. **Barriers to entry** to the market are low. This means that it is easy for a new business to set up in the market. This allows freedom of entry to new businesses.

The main example of a perfectly competitive market is agriculture. It is called 'perfect' competition because it is at one extreme of the spectrum of competition.

Perfectly competitive businesses, such as farms, have little or no control over the price at which they sell. They are **price-takers**. A farmer taking cattle to market has to accept whatever price is set at the auction. A farmer selling potatoes from a farm shop has to price them at roughly the same price as in local shops. Other commodity industries, like coal, copper or iron ore, tend also to be perfectly competitive. So too do industries such as steelmaking, paper manufacture or ship-building where firms find it difficult to differentiate their products from their competitors.

Monopolistic competition In monopolistic competition, there are many small businesses competing in the market. However, there is a very weak branding of products. As with perfect competition, barriers to entry are low and so new businesses can set up easily. Branding means that businesses can choose the price they set: they are **price-setters**. However, their influence over price is weak because the power to brand is weak. An example of monopolistic competition is the sportswear retail market. There are a few large sportswear chains of shops such as RSB. Equally, there are thousands of independent sportswear retailers. Each shop has a brand image and can choose where it wants to position itself in the market in terms of price, products sold, promotion and location. These will all affect how much each sells. For instance, on price, the higher the price charged, all other things being equal, the lower will be the volume of sales.

Oligopoly In oligopoly, a few businesses dominate the market. For example, there might be 2,000 businesses in the market, but if three of them have 80 per cent of the market between them, then the market would be oligopolistic. Because a few firms dominate the market, the actions of one business affects other businesses. For example, if the market share of one business grows from 25 per cent to 28 per cent, other businesses must have lost market share.

Often oligopolies exist because there are high barriers to entry. In car manufacturing, one barrier to entry is cost: when a car assembly plant can cost billions of pounds and a new model £500 million to develop, it is not surprising that there are relatively few businesses in the market. Another major barrier to entry may be the existence of strong brands, often supported by high levels of marketing expenditure.

Branding is a key characteristic of oligopolistic markets. Brands don't just deter competition. They also allow businesses to charge premium prices and sometimes to earn high profits. So oligopolistic businesses are **price-setters**. Branding, though, most favours the top brand in the market. Being number two or number three in terms of market share tends to make it difficult to charge premium prices and earn high profits.

Monopoly With monopoly, there is just one business in the market. Examples of monopoly include rail companies which have the exclusive right to provide a service along a rail route, or water companies which have the exclusive right to provide water to houses in a particular area. Monopolies exist because there are barriers to entry to the market. National monopolies in the UK today tend to be ones where the government has legally restricted competition to the market. However, there can be local monopolies for other reasons. For example, in rural areas, there may only be one large supermarket which effectively has a monopoly on supermarket grocery sales. Or a bus operator may provide the only service along a route even though other bus operators may be legally entitled to run a rival service. In both these cases, the market is not large enough to allow two businesses to offer a service and make a profit.

Monopolies may be able to exploit their market by charging high prices and earning high profits. For this reason, governments either make monopolies illegal, or monitor their activities to prevent them from exploiting the market. In the UK, a number of industries, such as water, rail and telecommunications, are regulated and maximum prices set down.

Changes in competitive structure

Classifying markets into perfect competition, monopolistic competition, oligopoly and monopoly helps to understand the impact on business of changes in the competitive structure of a market.

New competitors New competitors in a market will have a different impact depending on the number of firms in an industry. If a farm switches to growing wheat, this will have no impact on other wheat farmers. Supply from one farm is too small to affect market price. This is why local farmers often co-operate rather than act as rivals. But a new business entering a local newspaper market, or a local bus market could provoke a fierce response from an existing firm. If a local newspaper is a monopolist with 100 per cent of the market, then a new rival could take away a significant share of its market and at worst even force to it close. In oligopolistic or monopoly markets, where a few businesses or just one business dominate the market, existing firms will react strongly to destroy new entrants. For example, they might engage in **predatory pricing**, lowering their prices to such an extent that the new entrant can't make a profit. Or they might increase their marketing spending to limit the sales of the new entrant. They might use the law to prevent the new entrant from operating effectively. Tying up a new competitor in a law suit for a year, even if it comes to

nothing, can lead to mounting costs for the new competitor which force it to leave the market.

Creating a dominant business The fewer the number of large firms in an industry, the more market power each remaining firm is likely to have. So two oligopolistic firms each with 50 per cent of the market are likely to have more market power than four firms with 25 per cent of the market each. Market power enables firms to charge higher prices and enjoy higher profit margins. There is a strong tendency, therefore, in oligopolistic industries for firms to merge. An alternative is for firms to **collude**. Collusion occurs when two or more firms agree, typically, to fix prices and sales between themselves. They have then formed a **cartel**. The most powerful cartels are ones which create an effective monopoly in the market. Cartels today are particularly found in markets where firms find it difficult to differentiate their products from each other. Bus services, cement manufacture and vitamins are all examples of industries where cartels have been found in recent years. Cartels and collusion are illegal in the UK and the EU. This is because they push up prices for customers without giving any benefits to them. The beneficiaries are the firms themselves who can enjoy higher profits.

The process of creative destruction Where the industry or market is effectively a monopoly, and barriers to entry are higher, the only way for the monopoly to be broken might be through the process of **creative destruction**. This is when a new entrant enters the market with a revolutionary new product which in itself creates a new monopoly. In the market for pharmaceutical drugs, for example, the goal of all large pharmaceutical companies is to discover a new 'blockbuster' drug. This is a drug which is far superior to anything else on the market. It can be patented and so rival companies cannot copy it. Then it can be sold at very high prices, earning large profits for its makers. The profits of large pharmaceutical companies are crucially dependent on just a handful of drugs they manufacture.

Question 1.

British manufacturers are combating threats from low-cost producer countries by moving into fields where price competition is less important, according to a survey published today. More companies are competing 'on the basis of customer service and quality and less on price' according to the report. Since 1990, manufacturing has slipped from 21 per cent to 14 per cent of the UK economic output, partly as a result of competition from lower-cost nations. Only 40 per cent of companies surveyed said they suffered from low-cost competition in export markets, compared to 50 per cent three years ago. Over the same period, the proportion moving into 'niche' markets, defined as product areas aimed at specialist needs in which global competition is relatively low, increased from 45 per cent to 55 per cent.

An example of a company that has shifted its strategies to compete in areas other than price is JCB, the earthmoving equipment supplier. In the past decade, the company has launched a range of

specialist products such as military trucks and telescopic handlers that can pick up loads in restricted spaces. These sorts of machines are made by few other businesses around the world, which means JCB has relative freedom to set prices backed on manufacturing costs and desired profits.

Source: adapted from *The Financial Times*, 3.3.2008.

(a) 'UK manufacturing companies have been moving from competitive markets to oligopolistic markets'. Explain, using the data, what this means.
(b) What might be the advantages to UK businesses of moving from competitive markets to oligopolistic markets?
(c) How might a company like JCB become the dominant business in its market?

Porter's 5 forces analysis

Another way of looking at the competitive environment is to consider a model put forward by Michael Porter in his book, *Competitive advantage: creating and sustaining superior performance (1985)*. In the book, he outlines five forces or factors which determine the profitability of an industry. He argues that the ultimate aim of competitive strategy is to cope with and ideally change those rules in favour of the business. Where the collective strength of those five forces is favourable, a business will be able to earn above average rates of return on capital. Where they are unfavourable, a business will be locked into low returns or wildly fluctuating returns. The five forces, shown in Figure 1, are as follows.

The bargaining power of suppliers Suppliers, like any business, want to maximise the profit they make from their customers. The more power a supplier has over its customers, the higher the prices it can charge and the more it can reallocate profit from the customer to itself. Limiting the power of its supplier, therefore, will improve the competitive position of a business. It has a variety of strategies it can adopt to achieve this. It can grow vertically (backward vertical integration), either acquiring a supplier or setting up its own business by growing organically upwards. It can seek out new suppliers to create more competition amongst suppliers. It might be able to engage in technical research to find substitutes for a particular input to broaden the supply base. It may also minimise the information provided to suppliers in order to prevent the supplier realising its power over the customer.

Bargaining power of buyers Just as suppliers want to charge maximum pricers to customers, so buyers want to obtain supplies for the lowest price. If buyers or customers have considerable market power, they will be able to beat down prices offered by suppliers. For example, the major car manufacturers have succeeded in forcing down the price of components from component suppliers because of their enormous buying power and the relatively few number of major car manufacturers in the world. One way a business can improve its competitive position viz-a-viz buyers is to extend into the buyers' market through forward vertical integration. A car manufacturer might set up its own component manufacturing division, for example. It could encourage other businesses to set up in its customers' market to reduce the power of existing customers. It could also try to make it expensive for customers to switch to another supplier. For example, one way in which games console manufacturers keep up the price of computer games for their machines on which they receive a royalty is by making them technically incompatible with other machines.

Threat of new entrants If businesses can easily come into an industry and leave it again if profits are low, it becomes difficult for existing businesses in the industry to charge high prices and make high profits. Existing businesses are constantly under threat that if their profits rise too much, this will attract new suppliers into the market who will undercut their prices. Businesses can counter this by erecting **barriers to entry** to the industry. For example, a business may apply for patents and copyright to protect its intellectual property and prevent other businesses using it. It can attempt to create strong brands which will attract customer loyalty and make customers less price sensitive. Large amounts of advertising can be a deterrent because it represents a large cost to a new entrant which might have to match the spending to grow some market share. Large sunk costs, costs which have to paid at the start but are difficult to recoup if the business leaves the industry, can deter new entrants.

Substitutes The more substitutes there are for a particular product, the fiercer the competitive pressure on a business making the product. Equally, a business making a product with few or no substitutes is likely to be able to charge high prices and make high profits. A business can reduce the number of potential substitutes through research and development and then patenting the substitutes itself. Sometimes, a business will buy the patent for a new invention from a third party and do nothing with it simply to prevent the product coming

Figure 1: The five competitive forces that determine industry profitability

Potential entrants

Threat of new entrants

Suppliers → Bargaining power of suppliers → Industry competitors / Rivalry among existing firms ← Bargaining power of buyers ← Buyers

Threat of substitute products or services

Substitutes

Question 2.

Fudges was founded in 1926 as a bread bakery. By 1988, however, the bakery was in trouble. Bread consumption was in decline and the outlook for the business was bleak. The two brothers who now owned the firm decided that only a fundamental change could save the business. They switched out of bread making and began to sell products that could be transported long distances with a good shelf life. Given their West Country heritage, cheddar wafers seemed a good product to sell along with other biscuits and high quality cakes.

The switch was so successful that the business needed more space for production. In 1998, the business moved to larger premises, buying out the Dorset Village Bakery in Stalbridge. However, the premises were larger than they needed. It decided to use the space they didn't need and the equipment that came with the Bakery to return to bread making. The decision proved disastrous. The bread making side of the business 'haemorrhaged cash'. Bread making was once again abandoned and the company went back to concentrating on its branded biscuit and cake ranges.

All of its 80 lines of wafers, crackers and seasonal offerings are sourced and marketed to reinforce the high-quality, Dorset country brand. The company works closely with suppliers and customers. For example, it has linked with companies like Unilever and Tate & Lyle to produce products featuring Marmite, Colman's mustard and golden syrup. It has just retooled a cutter to change the shape of the Marmite biscuits to look like the iconic tub container in which Marmite is sold. 'A bigger company would not have been able to do that because the volume would not have been large enough', said Mr Fudge, one of the owners.

The competitive advantage of being able to respond quickly with new products is reinforced by Mr Fudge's interest in innovative processes in the bakery, which is full of industrial ovens, long conveyor belts and bespoke machines. However, this sits alongside traditional handbaking techniques. With a staff of 160, all the mixes are weighed and mixed by hand, as is much of the decorating, dipping in chocolate, packing and marzipan ball-rolling. The company did consider moving some production to China. But this would compromise the brand's image of being a Dorset country local product.

Source: adapted from *The Financial Times*, 20.2.2008.

(a) Explain what business strategies Fudges has used to give itself a competitive advantage.
(b) Evaluate whether Fudges could ever gain a competitive advantage in bread making.

to market. Businesses can also use marketing tactics to stop the spread of substitute products. A local newspaper, for example, might use predatory pricing if a new competitor comes into its market to drive it out again.

Rivalry among existing firms The degree of rivalry among existing firms in an industry will also determine prices and profits for any single firm. If rivalry is fierce, businesses can reduce that rivalry by forming cartels or engaging in a broad range of anti-competitive practices. In UK and EU law, this is illegal but it is not uncommon. Businesses can also reduce competition by buying up their rivals (horizontal integration). Again, competition law may intervene to prevent this happening but most horizontal mergers are allowed to proceed. In industries where there are relatively few businesses, often businesses don't compete on price. This allows them to maintain high profitability. Instead they tend to compete by bringing out new products and through advertising, thus creating strong brands. As a result their costs are higher than they might otherwise be, but they can also charge higher prices than in a more competitive market creating high profits.

Business strategies

BUSINESS or GENERIC STRATEGIES (sometimes also called business level strategies) are strategies which can be used by a business to give a COMPETITIVE ADVANTAGE over business rivals.

There are many different ways of analysing business strategies. However, Michael Porter in the 1985 book argues that there are three ways in which a business can achieve superior performance to competitors. These strategies are summarised in Figure 1.

Cost leadership One way is for the business to become the cost leader in the market. This means being the lowest cost producer for a given quality of product. For example, Wal-Mart in the USA and its subsidiary Asda in the UK have gained market share over time by offering lower prices to customers than competing hypermarket chains. Low cost in itself will not guarantee success. It has to be accompanied by the level of quality of product which a customer expects. So Asda in the UK may have been more successful than its rivals because it has offered a wide range of products, including wellknown branded products, at very low prices. Sainsbury's on the other hand may be regarded as a higher cost, higher price competitor but offering better quality products.

Differentiation A second way is for the business to differentiate its product from rivals. Differentiation is about making a product within a product range different from competitors. It is about giving a product a unique selling point. Differentiation is in itself not sufficient to give a competitive advantage. It has to be a differentiated product which customers want to buy. So Heinz or Coca-Cola have been successful because they have products made to unique formulations which customers prefer over other formulations.

Focus A third way is for the business to focus on a particular sector of the market, i.e. to select a market **niche**. There are two forms of focus. **Cost focus** occurs when a business drives down its costs in the market segment to undercut the prices of competitors. **Differentiation focus** occurs when a business sells a unique and differentiated product within the market segment. In many cases, a business adopting a focus strategy will see its main competitors as larger businesses serving the much broader mass market. Because they serve the mass market, they are not always very competitive in individual niche markets. This gives businesses targeting niche markets an opportunity to become more competitive than much larger rivals. However, a focus strategy does not necessarily guarantee success. There may be other highly competitive niche businesses in that market already. Equally, a business may find it difficult either to cut costs compared to mass market businesses or to produce a differentiated product which customers value.

Cost leadership can be developed in the broad market. Wal-Mart has developed its cost strategy in the broad market of retailing. Differentiation too can be developed in the broad market. Coca-Cola has developed its differentiation strategy in the broad market of soft drinks. A business may also seek a competitive advantage in a narrow market. This competitive advantage can be either a cost advantage or a differentiation advantage. For example, BMW has developed a differentiated product in the narrow market for luxury cars.

There are many other ways of considering competitive advantage. Business strategies, for example, can centre around:
- product design and development;
- pricing;
- promotion;
- place in the marketing mix;
- economies of scale;
- quality of production;
- delivery times including just-in-time production;
- the skill and motivation of the workforce;
- a low cost labour force;
- the flexibility of workers;
- an ethical stance for the business.

Figure 2: Business or generic strategies

	COMPETITIVE ADVANTAGE	
	Lower cost	Differentiation
Broad Target	1. Cost leadership	2. Differentiation
Narrow Target	3A. Cost focus	3B. Differentiation focus

COMPETITIVE SCOPE

KEYTERMS

Barriers to entry – factors which make it difficult or impossible for businesses to enter a market and compete with existing producers.

Business or generic strategy – strategies which can be used by a business to give a competitive advantage over business rivals, including pursuing cost leadership, product differentiation or focusing on a market segment.

Competition – rivalry between businesses offering products in the same market; competition may take forms such as price competition, distinctive product offerings, advertising and distribution.

Competitive advantage – an advantage which a business has that enables it to perform better than its rivals in the market.

KNOWLEDGE

1. What is the link between competition and the 4Ps?
2. What is the difference between (a) a perfectly competitive market and a monopoly; (b) an oligopolistic market and one with monopolistic competition?
3. Why might a business engage in predatory pricing?
4. What are (a) the benefits and (b) the costs of collusion to a business?

5. What is the process of creative destruction?
6. Explain the benefits a business may obtain if it has market power over the businesses from which it buys.
7. How might the degree of rivalry between firms in an industry affect prices and profits?
8. Explain the difference between competitive advantage and competitive scope.

Case Study: The Nano

In January, talk at North America's biggest automobile show of the year in Detroit was dominated not by any of the new models on display at the show but by a chunky, oblong, little hatchback which just been unveiled half way round the world in India. The car was The Nano, produced by the Indian car manufacturer Tata Motors. It was to go on sale at $2 500 ex tax. Tata Motors was proclaiming it as the car which the emerging middle classes in India could afford to buy. On the day of its launch, Tata's website for the car had 4 million hits; such was the interest in the car.

Low cost cars have already been developed by other car manufacturers, but none has come anywhere near the price of The Nano. Bosch, the German automobile and industrial group, estimated low-cost vehicles prices at less than $7,000 could reach a 13 per cent share of the world market, or about 10 million vehicles, in 2010. The Indian market alone is potentially huge given its current population of 900 million people. It is generating hundreds of thousands of first-time car buyers every year. What's more, there is a culture of frugality in India. Indian suppliers are used to cutting costs, whilst Indian consumers are happy to buy low cost cars.

The Nano doesn't pass EU safety standards and so it couldn't be sold in the UK in the version unveiled in India.

Source: adapted from *The Financial Times*, 4.3.2008.

China is confounding the pundits. Car manufacturers, both Chinese and non-Chinese, had expected the fast-growing demand for cars in China to be weighted towards the small car market. With relatively low incomes and growing congestion in China's cities, the small car seemed to be the obvious choice for the Chinese customer. However, whilst the overall car market has continued to expand at a dramatic rate, demand for small cars is growing far less. Sales of micro and subcompact cars were almost flat last year whilst sales of small-engined vehicles fell by more than 20 per cent.

Chinese consumers appear to be more concerned than car-buyers in other emerging markets about the social status implied by their vehicles. Research by Volkswagen last year found that the average Chinese first-time buyer spent twice his or her annual salary on the vehicle. This has benefited multinational companies like Volkswagen, the market leader, which offers a range of more expensive cars. It has disadvantaged the new generation of Chinese motor manufacturing companies, many of which had hoped to enter the market by selling cheaper, small vehicles to cost-conscious consumers. However, Chinese companies are renowned for copying the successful practices of rivals, especially Western companies. The trend to buy more expensive cars has only given companies like Volkswagen a breathing space. They need to remain at the forefront of innovation and development to provide the Chinese consumer with a car which they aspire to purchase.

Source: adapted from *The Financial Times*, 4.3.2008.

(a) Evaluate how the launch of The Nano has changed the competitive environment for multinational car manufacturers like Volkswagen and Ford. (40 marks)
(b) Discuss how a multinational car company like Volkswagen or Ford should respond to Tata Motor's launch of its Nana car. Use Michael Porter's analysis of business strategies to help you answer this question. (40 marks)

Internal causes of change

Organisations operate in a changing environment. This change creates both opportunities and threats which businesses have to manage successfully if they are to survive. Internal causes of change can come about by the changing size of a business. Some businesses are growing in size as their sales and profits increase. Some businesses are less successful and are forced to RETRENCH as their sales and profits fall. Poor business performance is often a catalyst for change. The business may change hands with new owners coming in to revitalise the business. Or the business may replace its existing senior management team with new leadership. New leaders sometimes can turn a business around. Sometimes, they too fail and the business continues to decline. At worst, the business will fail and be broken up. In this unit, we will consider the causes of internal change and how businesses may respond to them.

Organic growth

Most businesses which grow in size do so through INTERNAL GROWTH (also called ORGANIC GROWTH). This is where sales and profits rise due to factors such as creased investment, new product development or better marketing. Internal growth may not necessarily be at a constant rate. External factors such as the state of the economy or the ability to gain finance may lead to differences in growth rate from year to year. More importantly, internal growth is often linked to the growth of the industry or industries in which a business operates. For example, some Internet companies like Google have seen spectacular growth rates because the market itself has grown so fast. Food manufacturing companies, in contrast, have been struggling to grow internally over the past twenty years because spending on food overall is not rising at a very low rate.

Takeovers and mergers

Sometimes a business will grow in size through EXTERNAL GROWTH. This can be a TAKEOVER or ACQUISITION where one business buys another business. Or it can be through a MERGER where two (or more) businesses join together to become one business.

Takeovers and mergers can take place in any size business with any legal organisation. For example, a sole trader who owns two chemist shops may buy up, and therefore takeover, a third chemist shop from its owner. Two partnerships may merge to become one partnership.

However, takeovers and mergers tend to be associated more with limited companies. In a takeover, one company must acquire at least 51 per cent of the shares of the company which is being taken over. They buy these shares from existing shareholders. There are a variety of takeover rules for public limited companies in the UK. For example, the same offer must be made to all shareholders: the takeover company cannot offer a higher price to some shareholders and a lower price to others. The takeover company only has a limited amount of time to make its offer. Some takeovers are **contested** or are **hostile**. This means that the board of directors of the company recommends to its shareholders that they should not accept the bid. Most takeovers, however, are **agreed takeovers**. The board of directors recommends to its shareholders that they should sell. Often a company will make a takeover offer which the board of directors rejects because the price is too low. The takeover company then raises its bid which the board of directors of the company being targeted may accept or reject.

In a merger, the boards of directors both agree to the merger having negotiated the terms of the merger. These terms include how many shares in the new company each existing shareholder will get. It also typically includes who will become the new chairman and chief executive of the company, and who will become its directors. Cost cutting plans may also be announced. For example, if each company has a headquarters, then it may be announced which headquarters will be closed and which will become the new headquarters.

Occasionally, a business will DEMERGE. This is when the business splits into two or more independent businesses.

Types of integration

Integration takes place when one business takes over or merges with another business. There are three main types of integration.

Horizontal integration HORIZONTAL INTEGRATION occurs when two businesses making similar products join together. For example, one car manufacturer buying another car manufacturer would be horizontal integration. So too would a supermarket chain buying another supermarket chain, or an aerospace company buying another aerospace company.

Vertical integration VERTICAL INTEGRATION occurs when a business integrates with either a supplier (backward vertical integration) or a customer (forward vertical integration). It is vertical because the integration takes place between two businesses at different points on the chain of production for a product. For example, a car manufacturer buying a car component company would be an example of backward vertical integration. A catering company buying a chain of fast food outlets would be an example of forward vertical integration.

Conglomerate integration CONGLOMERATE INTEGRATION takes place when two businesses making unrelated products join together. For example, a cigarette manufacturer buying an insurance company would be a conglomerate takeover. A steel manufacturer merging with a health care company would be a conglomerate merger.

Reasons for integration

There are a variety of reasons why a business may takeover or merge with another business. Some relate to the SYNERGIES to be gained from combining two organisations, including cutting average costs and increasing sales and profits. Others relate to the potential for asset stripping, the reduction of risk through diversification or the potential for gains by management.

Cost savings The most frequently cited reason is cost savings. Cost savings can take place in a number of ways. The larger business will be able to cut duplicate expenditure. For example, a business would not need two headquarters. Marketing budgets could be merged to produce cost savings. A larger business should also be able to exploit other types of **economy of scale**. By being larger, for example, it should be able to buy in greater bulk, forcing down the prices of its suppliers, or borrow on better terms than a smaller business.

Greater control of markets A takeover or merger may allow a business to gain greater control of its markets. For example, it may give it control of important brands needed to strengthen its product range. Forward vertical integration may allow a supplier to buy out an important customer and so secure orders. There is always a danger that a proposed merger or takeover may be blocked by competition authorities. In the UK, mergers may be referred to the Competition Commission (CC) by the Office of Fair Trading (OFT), for example under the Enterprise Act, 2002. The Competition Commission must then determine if the merger has or might result in a lessening of competition. It may then take action which it feels is reasonable and practical to counteract any adverse effects of the merger.

Undervalued assets The management of one business may see that another business is undervalued. For example, one company may be able to buy another company for £2 million. It then sells off key assets of the company taken over for £3 million and is still left with assets it values at £1 million. In the past, some companies have specialised in this sort of **asset stripping**. Their main profits have come from buying other companies and selling off their most valuable assets rather than the sale of products from the existing operations. Alternatively, the company being taken over or merged may have significantly underperformed. New management may be able to reduce costs and raise sales with little extra investment. By turning round a poorly performing business, the value of the business will increase substantially.

Diversification A business may wish to diversify. This means expanding into new product markets. Diversification may allow a business in static or declining markets to move into growth

markets. Or the business may wish to reduce the risks it faces from being in a particular market. For example, a steel manufacturer which sees large swings in demand and prices according to the business cycle may wish to enter a market which is less volatile. Diversification and the creation of conglomerate companies was fashionable in the 1960s and 1970s. By the 1990s, many conglomerates were breaking themselves up. Partly this was because it was argued that conglomerates had no synergies between the different parts of the business. If a steel manufacturer owned an electricity generation business, there was nothing of benefit that the steel manufacturer would contribute to the electricity generation business and vice versa. More importantly, it was argued that the most senior management of a business could not be experts in running both a steel manufacturer and an electricity generation company. Parts of the business would inevitably suffer from poor management. Hence conglomerates were particularly likely to suffer from managerial diseconomies of scale. Less profitable or low growth parts of the business could also be starved of investment as scarce finance was channelled into more profitable or high growth parts. If the less profitable business was an independent business, it might make higher profits because of more specialised management or more investment. Finally, many conglomerate companies had a relatively low share price. The highest growth highest profit parts of the business were undervalued because they were lumped in with low growth low profit businesses. It was argued that shareholder value would increase if the conglomerate were split up into separate companies.

Rewards to management Studies made of public limited company takeovers and mergers suggest that most destroy shareholder value. For example, the share price of the new company tends to perform worse compared to the average for companies in the industry than the share price of the two separate companies before. Cost savings promised before the takeover or merger often fail to emerge in full after integration. Sales don't increase as much as was predicted or actually decline. It may prove difficult to create one corporate culture from two companies which might have had very different ways of working. Motivation of staff in one company may decline if less generous pay and conditions in the other company is imposed upon them. The computer systems of the two companies may be incompatible and it may be necessary to completely replace them at considerable cost to the new company. So why are there so many takeovers and mergers if they clearly don't benefit shareholders? The answer probably lies in the divorce of ownership from control. In public limited companies, it is the senior management and not the owners, the shareholders, who initially suggest the takeover or merger. Senior management is likely to gain from the merger or takeover. The new senior management of the merged company is likely to be paid more than before because senior managers are running a larger company. In the case of friendly mergers, senior personnel who lose their jobs may receive generous pensions if they are in their

50s and 60s. Or they may get a generous redundancy package which more than covers them in the time taken to get another job. The only management losers are likely to be the management team of a company taken over in a hostile bid. They can expect to lose their jobs within minimum compensation. So there is an incentive for senior management to look for mergers or to agree to friendly mergers.

Reasons for demergers and sales

Sometimes businesses choose to sell off assets. They might put up subsidiary companies or whole divisions for sale. Very occasionally, they will even break themselves into two or more separate parts and give existing shareholders shares in the new parts. Demergers occur for a number of reasons. Some of them have already been discussed in explaining why conglomerates have fallen out of fashion (see above).

- Some parts of the business may be performing relatively poorly. Selling them could then improve the performance of the company.
- A company may have a great deal of debt. One way of reducing this is by selling off parts of the company.

- Some companies specialise in starting up new companies or investing in poorly performing companies and then, when they have become successful, selling them.
- Demergers allow management to concentrate on running a smaller more focused business. This business will perform better than it would have done as part of the former larger business. This implies that the previous large business was suffering from diseconomies of scale.
- For public limited companies, if it splits itself into two companies, the combined share price of two separate companies may be above that of the old single company. Hence it increases shareholder value.

New owners or new leaders

If a firm is taken over, it is usual for the senior management of the company to lose their jobs. Partly this is because their roles will be absorbed within the roles of the management of the company which has bought it. A single company doesn't need two finance directors for example. Partly it is because the management of the purchasing company will probably wish to make significant changes and the existing senior management could be an obstacle to effecting these changes. Partly it is also on cost grounds: takeovers are supposed to lead to cost cuts which feed through to higher profits.

However, new leadership for a business more usually comes about without any takeovers or mergers. An existing Managing Director (MD) or Chief Executive Officer (CEO) may move to a better job or retire. Or the CEO may be pushed out of the job by the board of directors because of the poor performance of the company. When new leaders for businesses are appointed, it often triggers major changes at the senior management of a company. The new CEO replaces some senior managers. Other senior managers choose to move to another job.

When the existing business is successful, the same corporate strategies may continue to be used by the new leader. When the existing business has not been performing well, the new CEO will be expected to devise new corporate strategies to turn the performance of the company round.

Management buy-outs and venture capitalists

In recent years, management buy-outs and takeovers of companies by venture capitalists have often been in the news. A MANAGEMENT BUY-OUT occurs when the management of a company buys the company from its current owners. Managers rarely have enough financial capital to buy the business outright. Instead, they put together a financial package which includes their own investment in the new company, loans from banks and, crucially, equity investment from a venture capital company.

Venture capitalist companies specialise in buying shares in medium sized companies which they think have significant growth potential. Their aim is to support the company for perhaps five years and then float the company on a stock exchange, selling their stake in the company hopefully for a large

---

Question 1.

Virgin Media is carrying out a review of its TV channels that could lead to a sale of some or all of the division. Virgin Media is a cable television company which also runs a number of digital television channels including Trouble, Bravo and Living. Virgin Media is part of Richard Branson's Virgin Group empire. The move appears to mark an about-turn for Virgin which only 15 months ago was trying to buy ITV. An outright sale of Virgin Media could raise £800 million.

The most likely course of action is that it will try to sell the jewel in its crown, the half-share in UKTV, which it owns in partnership with BBC Worldwide. UKTV owns channels such as UKTV Gold and UKTV History. On the other hand, Virgin is though to be keen to retain and add to its portfolio of shopping channels.

Source: adapted from *The Sunday Times*, 2.3.2008.

(a) 'Virgin Media buying ITV would have been an example of a horizontal merger.' Explain what this means.
(b) Suggest why Virgin Media might want to sell some TV channels but at the same time buy other TV channels.

Question 2.

Stephen Nelson has resigned as Chief Executive of BAA (British Airports Authority), the company which runs a number of UK airports including Heathrow, Gatwick and Stansted. He was recruited from the supermarket chain J Sainsbury in 2005 and appointed as BAA's retail director, in charge of managing shopping concessions at airports. Fairly quickly, BAA was bought by the Spanish company Grupo Ferrovial for £10.1 billion. Some of the senior executives at BAA subsequently left and Stephen Nelson found himself being appointed Chief Executive. Almost immediately, he was embroiled in controversy about the poor level of service being offered at BAA airports and Heathrow in particular. Lengthy delays of flights, high levels of lost luggage, cramped and chaotic waiting areas, and interminable waits to get through airport security were just some of the problems that passengers encountered. A contrast was made between the shiny, glitzy, spacious shopping facilities at the airports with broken chairs, dingy toilets and long queues in the passenger areas. BAA tried to counter the criticism by pointing out that its airports were often working at full capacity, unlike most other European airports. Also pressures at Heathrow would lighten once a new terminal building was opened in 2008. However, as Kevin Done, newspaper analyst put it, 'Mr Nelson was perhaps always a questionable choice for the job of turning round BAA's reputation for running successful shopping centres and poorly performing airports.'

Stephen Nelson's successor will be Colin Matthews. Until last autumn, he was Chief Executive of Severn Trent, one of the UK's largest water companies. He has been director of technical operations at British Airways, BAA's biggest customer and worked at Hays, the business services group. This experience should prove invaluable in steering BAA through difficult times ahead.

Source: adapted from *The Financial Times*, 28.2.2008.

(a) Explain, using BAA as an example, why leadership is important in a company in the process of change.

(b) To what extent do you agree with the statement that 'Mr Nelson was perhaps always a questionable choice for the job of turning round BAA's reputation for running successful shopping centres and poorly performing airports.'

---

profit. Or the company may be sold to a larger company in a takeover. Management buy-outs account for a small percentage of the monies that venture capitalist companies invest each year.

Opportunities for management buy-outs or venture capital acquisitions may arise because:

- a large company wishes to sell off a subsidiary which is either performing poorly or which does not sell products which are part of a newly defined 'core' for the business;
- an individual or family wish to sell the business, perhaps because they want to retire;
- a company has gone into receivership and the receivers are looking for someone to buy the company and continue to operate it.

In addition, venture capitalists buy into medium sized growing companies which finance to expand.

Management buy-outs have tended to be successful. There are a variety of reasons for this.

- Becoming the owners of the company means that management become highly focussed on making a success of the new company. Venture capitalist backers, who will almost inevitably have at least one seat on the Board of Directors, will also be very focussed on success. The primary objective is likely to be maximising profit to ensure short-term survival.
- Management is uniquely placed to know the strengths and weaknesses of the company. Before the buy-out, they were often unable to formulate their own strategy as to how the business should be run. Implementation of a new strategy after the buy-out often leads to the turn round of the company.
- The previous owners may have starved the company of cash. This limited the ability of management to invest, to promote their products more widely and to train staff. By spending more in key areas, buy-out management are able to raise revenues and increase profits.

- If the company had been bought from the receivers, it would almost certainly have come without very much debt. Equally, if it was bought from a larger company, the larger company might have sold it relatively debt free. Previously, payment of debt might have been a serious financial problem for the company. If it was an independent company, it would have been the ultimate reason why it might have gone into receivership. A lack of debt would give the new management a much greater chance to make a profit.

- Management buy-outs are often associated with a downsizing of the business. The buy-out will create the conditions in which the new management is faced with taking difficult decisions. If they don't make them, they face losing their investment. So, for example, the new management may make significant cuts in the workforce or close down factories. This helps reduce costs and so improve the company's profit position.

- If the buy-out company had been part of a larger company, some management time would have been spent liaising with headquarters. Decision making might have been slow because of the constant need to refer them back to headquarters to gain approval. The more centralised the organisation, the more this could have been an obstacle to the success of the company. The new management buy-out becomes free to make its own decisions quickly. This may help it to improve the efficiency of decision making.

Other acquisitions made by venture capital companies can be more risky. With a management buy-out, at least the existing management know the company and have a strong incentive to make it successful. However, venture capitalist companies earn a profit by making very large returns on a minority of their investments and some return on the majority whilst on the rest they make a loss.

Management buy-outs and venture capital companies are sometimes criticised because investors in the new company can make millions of pounds profit within a relatively short space of time by turning round the company and then selling it. In the process, many workers might have lost their jobs. Those remaining workers will have received no financial gain from the turn round of the company even though they might feel they were the ones who worked hard to ensure its success.

Such criticisms, however, are really a criticism of the capitalist market system. Investors can make large profits. Equally, they can lose their whole stake in the business in which they invest. Workers in businesses which make continued losses will lose their jobs. A management buy-out or a purchase of the company by a venture capitalist may at least save some of them. Most workers receive a flat rate of pay which is not linked to the success or otherwise of their employer. Their earnings are likely to be far more stable than the earnings of investors because profits and share prices tend to go down as well as up over a period of time.

KEYTERMS

Conglomerate integration – when two businesses making unrelated products integrate into one business.
Demerger – when a business splits into two or more independent businesses.
External growth – when the size of the business increases through the takeover of another business or a merger with another business.
Horizontal integration – when two or more businesses making similar products integrate.
Internal growth – when the size of a business increases, for example by sales and profits growing through increased investment, new product development or better marketing.
Management buy-out – when the management of a company buys it from its current owners.
Merger – when two (or more) businesses join together to become one business.
Retrenchment – in terms of business growth, when a business is shrinking in size typically because its sales and profits are falling.
Synergy – when two or more activities or businesses put together create a greater amount than the sum of the individual parts.
Takeover or acquisition – when one business buys another business.
Vertical integration – when one business integrates either with a supplier (backward vertical integration) or a customer (forward vertical integration).

KNOWLEDGE

1. Explain the difference between (a) internal and external growth and (b) takeover and merger.
2. Explain, giving examples, the difference between horizontal, vertical and conglomerate integration.
3. What synergies might be created by a merger between two companies?
4. Why might a company wish to diversify?
5. What is the possible link between mergers and the divorce of ownership from control?
6. What impact might new leadership have on corporate strategy?
7. Why might managers buy their company from its owners?

Case Study: Rentokil

For a time, Rentokil was one of the most admired companies in the UK. In the late 1980s and for much of the 1990s, earnings per share grew by 20 per cent per year. Sir Clive Thompson, its chairman at the time, became known at 'Mr 20 Per Cent'. Today, the company has fallen from grace.

The name Rentokil came from a company started in 1925 as a pest control business. Rentokil was acquired in 1957 by another pest control group, British Ratin, but the new combined company was branded under the Rentokil name. Between 1957 and 1995, the company grew both organically and by acquisition. Its pest control business continued to see rises in sales. But it diversified into a range of business services including office cleaning, indoor tropical plant care, office machinery maintenance, washroom services, security services and parcel deliveries. In 1996, it took over BET for £2.1 billion. BET was a major competitor in some of Rentokil's markets. Putting the two companies together created both cost and marketing synergies. However, the corporate strategy began to fall apart in 1998 when the company was forced to announce that in

would not achieve its 20 per cent growth target. In 2000, it announced that it future its profit growth target would only be 8 to 15 per cent per annum. But it struggled to achieve this and in 2004, Sir Clive Thompson was sacked by the board of directors from his position as non-executive chairman.

He was replaced by Brian McGowan and Doug Flynn became Chief Executive. They set about cutting the number of markets in which the company operated, with the sale of the manned guarding, electronic security and conferencing businesses. At the same time, they expanded existing businesses, buying a US pest control business and a clutch of companies in Asia and the Pacific. Their biggest acquisition was Target for £210 million in December 2006.

What followed has been described by one analyst as 'a catastrophic and monumental screw-up'. Target was a parcels delivery company which was combined with Rentokil's existing parcels delivery service called City Link. There had already been problems managing change at City Link. The company had been run as a franchise operation but in 2005 it was decided to buy out the franchisees. Then the company was doubled in size by the acquisition of Target. The integration of the two companies was a disaster. The business had lost customers as service quality levels fell. The result was falling revenues and a slip into the red on profits at City Link.

The bulk of Rentokil's revenues now come from its textiles and washrooms services division and building management. However, it remains big in parcels and pest control. The company is still making a profit and it argues that, apart from its parcels business, the company is in good shape. However, the company has made too many promises of a recovery over the past ten years for such claims to have credibility. Poor strategy and poor execution could see

Rentokil being broken up further with parcels and pest control being sold off.

Source: adapted from *The Financial Times* 29.2.2008; en.wikipedia.org.

(a) 'Rentokil's strategy of growing by acquisition has been highly successful over the years.' To what extent do you agree with this comment? (40 marks)

(b) Evaluate under what circumstances Rentokil's shareholders would be better off if the parcels and pest control operations were demerged from the rest of the business. (40 marks)

Purpose of corporate plans

Planning is important at every stage of the life of a business and at every level. For example, a small business starting up is far more likely to survive if it has drawn up a business plan than if it hasn't. A department of a large company is more likely to achieve its objectives if it has drawn up a functional or departmental plan. Similarly, a large business is far more likely to achieve its goals if it has drawn up a **corporate plan**.

Corporate plans have a variety of purposes.

- Corporate plans help businesses to define their objectives. In theory, objectives are set before the plan is devised. In practice, objectives may have to be modified if the plan shows that there is little chance of the objectives being met. For example, an objective may be to increase sales in the Far East by 20 per cent per year. But research undertaken whilst drawing up the plan may show that this would lead to the company increasing its market share in the Far East from 10 per cent to 30 per cent which, given the response of competitors, would be almost impossible to achieve. So this sales objective may have to be modified.
- Corporate plans identify the path over time that needs to be taken to achieve corporate objectives. It maps out corporate strategy. For example, a company objective may be to increase sales in the North American market by 50 per cent within 4 years. The plan may state that the company will have to make an acquisition of an existing company within 2 years to increase its sales by 30 per cent. The other 20 per cent will come from organic, internal growth of the business including the company which has been taken over.
- Corporate plans should identify risks and probabilities. The business environment is constantly changing. Favourable opportunities arise unexpectedly which the company should take advantage of. Equally, the company may be knocked off course by unexpected adverse events. The corporate plan should allow for these eventualities where it is possible to identify the probability of risk and opportunity. The unit called 'Contingency planning' discusses planning for future crises. Corporate planning, however, cannot effectively deal with opportunities and risks that cannot be identified or quantified. Planning therefore has its limitations.

Developing a corporate plan

There are many ways of developing a corporate plan but one standard model is to develop a strategy systematically as follows.

1 Clarify objectives.
2 Gain information about the business and its external environment by carrying out an audit.

3 Summarise and analyse the results of the audit by carrying out a SWOT analysis.
4 Make plans to achieve the objectives set.
5 Implement the plans.
6 Review and evaluate outcomes.
7 Prepare the next plan.

Each of these stages, shown in Figure 1, will now be considered in detail.

Clarifying the objectives of the business

The first stage of developing a strategy is to identify objectives. Unless objectives are clear, it will be impossible to devise plans to achieve them. There are different types of objective which can be identified for planning purposes.

Strategic objectives STRATEGIC OBJECTIVES are the main objectives of a business. They are the objectives which will help the business achieve its **aims**. They will almost certainly be LONG-TERM OBJECTIVES. This is because it is most unlikely that the aims of a business can be achieved in, say, the next 6 or 12 months. Long-term objectives tend to be objectives for the next 3-5 years.

Tactical objectives TACTICAL OBJECTIVES are SHORT TERM OBJECTIVES. They are objectives which will help

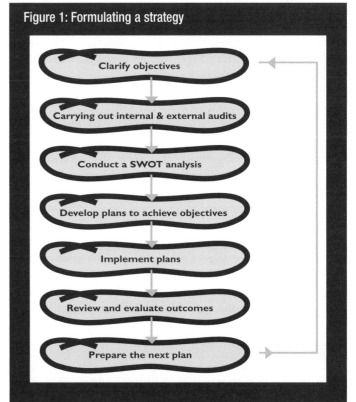

Figure 1: Formulating a strategy

- Clarify objectives
- Carrying out internal & external audits
- Conduct a SWOT analysis
- Develop plans to achieve objectives
- Implement plans
- Review and evaluate outcomes
- Prepare the next plan

Question 1.

Sixcor is a UK private limited company which manufactures food equipment for sale to businesses in the food processing and food retailing sectors. Last year was a difficult year for the company. Sales were down 5 per cent whilst profits fell from £3.5 million the previous year to £0.1 million. Part of the problem was the strength of the pound. Overseas orders were lost to competitors on price. Those orders which Sixcor did gain were at such low prices that they were barely profitable. In the UK market, Sixcor suffered because of the movement of the economy into a mild recession.

However, problems within the company didn't help the situation. During the year, the company moved to a larger site so that production could be expanded. But there was considerable disruption during the move. An estimated four weeks' production was lost as a result. There were continued difficulties recruiting sufficient skilled production workers and as a consequence some orders were sent out late. The marketing department reported that the failure to deliver some goods on time made it more difficult to get repeat orders, whilst the finance department warned that the situation adversely affected cash flow.

The company continued to roll out new products in response to changing customer needs and to advances in technology. Competitors too, though, were bringing out innovative products, making the trading environment difficult. There was considerable debate at board level about whether the expenditure on research

and development for new products was too great or too little. Any increase in spending would hit profits in the short term, but could enhance profits in the long term if it gave the company a competitive advantage.

(a) (a) From the information given list (i) SIX issues which would be included in an internal audit of the business and (ii) SIX issues which would be included in an external audit. (b) would any issues be included in a PESTLE analysis?

(b) Which problems facing the company last year were short-term problems and therefore unlikely to affect performance in the long term?

(c) Evaluate the most important problems facing the business in the long term.

achieve the strategic objectives set by the business. For example, a strategic objective might be to increase sales by 10 per cent per year over the next five years. A tactical objective to help achieve this could be to increase spending on promotion by 5 per cent over the next year. Increased spending on promotion would be a TACTIC employed by the business.

Operational objectives OPERATIONAL OBJECTIVES are very short-term objectives which are typically small scale and cover the day-to-day running of the business. They are set to achieve tactical and strategic objectives. For example, the marketing department might set itself the operational objective of finalising an advertising campaign within the next seven days. The production department may set itself the objective of getting an important order out on time in 21 days' time.

Strategic planning is therefore concerned with setting out how the strategic objectives of the business can be achieved over the long term. An annual plan for the business will be more concerned with short-term objectives. It will set out the tactics to be used to achieve this year's part of the strategic plan.

Auditing the business and its external environment

The next stage in developing a strategy is to audit the business and its external environment.

The internal audit An INTERNAL AUDIT is an analysis of the business itself and how it operates. It attempts to identify strengths and weaknesses of its operations. It would cover areas such as:

- products and their cost, quality and development;
- finance including profit, assets and cash flow;
- production, including capacity, quality, efficiency and stock management;
- internal organisation including divisional and departmental structures;
- human resources including skills, training and recruitment.

In a large business, the internal audit might be conducted by outside **management consultants**, brought into the business to conduct an independent analysis.

The external audit An EXTERNAL AUDIT is an analysis of the environment in which the business operates and over which it has little or no control. It can be split into three parts: the market, competition and the political, economic, social and technological environment.

The audit should analyse the **market** or markets in which the business operates. For example, it should analyse:

- the size and growth of the market;
- the characteristics of the customers in the market;

- the products on offer;
- the pricing structure;
- how products are distributed;
- how products are promoted;
- industry practices, such as whether there is a **trade association** or government regulation.

The audit should also analyse the **competition** in the market. The nature of the competitive environment will be important in setting strategy. For example it should analyse:

- the structure of the industry including the number and size of competitors, their production capacity and marketing methods, the likelihood of new entrants to the market or businesses leaving the industry;
- finance including profits of competitors, their investment programmes, costs, revenues, cash flow and assets.

Third, the external audit should use PESTLE ANALYSIS. This is analysis of the political (P), economic (E), social (S), technological (T), legal(L) and environmental (E) issues relevant to the business. It is also sometimes called PEST-G analysis (Political, Economic, Social, Technological and Green factors).

- Politics, government, taxes and the law affect the business. For example, the tax environment will affect the price of goods (through VAT), investment (through corporation tax) and the number of workers employed (through National Insurance contributions and pension legislation).
- The economic environment is very important to the business. Whether the economy is likely to be in boom or recession could have an important impact on sales. Levels of unemployment will affect both customer demand and ability to recruit workers. Inflation will impact on pricing policy. Barriers to international trade will affect exports.
- The social and cultural environment covers areas such as education, demographics (i.e. population), migration, religion, roles of men and women and changing consumer tastes. For example, more and more women going out to work has increased the market size for ready made meals and takeaway food. Increased educational attainment over the past 40 years has increased the skills of the workforce.
- Changes in technology can have a radical impact on businesses. Manufacturing is continuing to be transformed by automated machinery. Computers have eliminated large numbers of jobs in banking and insurance. Quality has been considerably improved through applications of information technology.
- Legilsation can affect businesses. For example, customers and suppliers will have certain rights in law which need to be taken account of when trading. Trade union legislation

Question 2.

Phipps is a company which specialises in producing colour pigments. These are used to colour everything from cans, wrappers, cartons, plastic products, textiles to magazines. It is a global company with customers and plants across the world. Its fastest growing market is in the Far East where it has plants in China and Thailand. But it faces intense competition at the bottom end of its market from Far Eastern producers who have even lower costs of production than Phipps.

Economists are predicting a major slowdown in the world economy over the next 12 months led by a recession in the United States. The Japanese market remains weak following a decade of weak or no economic growth. The combination of weakness in demand in the United States and Japan threatens to make any recession in the Far East severe and deep.

Three weeks ago, Graham Downy, the managing director (MD) of the company for the past ten years, left to take up an appointment with a larger rival company. This has left a major gap in the senior management team. Graham was considered to be an excellent MD and had overseen substantial growth in the company. It could take months to find a suitable replacement.

An audit of two plants in the United States found that management there had allowed a substantial stock of pigment to build up. The management has since been replaced, but decisions about what to do with the excess stock have yet to be taken.

A new pigment suitable for metal coatings is about to be launched. It has superior colour retention qualities, but is more expensive to produce than traditional pigments for metal coatings. A debate about pricing policy is taking place within the company.

(a) What is meant by SWOT analysis?
(b) Use SWOT analysis to discuss the future of Phipps.

will affect employment. Controls on advertising will affect promotion.

- The impact of environmental changes have been felt by some businesses more than others. Extraction companies, such as oil companies or copper mining companies, have been forced to change the way in which they work because of pressure from environmental groups and governments. Businesses need to be seen to be green if only to create a positive public relations image with both their workers and with consumers.

SWOT analysis

The internal and external audits should yield a large amount of information about the business and its external environment. However, this information needs to be summarised. There are many ways of doing this, but one useful way is to complete a SWOT ANALYSIS.

SWOT analysis involves looking at the internal strengths and weaknesses of a business and its external opportunities and threats.

Strengths These are positive aspects of the business arising from the **internal audit**. For example, it might have a loyal customer base, its products may be seen as amongst the best in the market or it might make large profits.

Weaknesses These are the negative aspects of the business arising from the **internal audit**. For example, fault rates in production may be high, recent promotional campaigns may have failed or staff training may be poor.

Opportunities The **external audit** should show up what opportunities are available to the business. For example, there may be an opportunity to expand into a new market with existing products. Or the weakness of a competitor may enable the business to gain market share. Or technological developments may permit the development of new products.

Threats The **external audit** should also show up what threats face the business. For example, falling numbers of customers in the 16-25 age group may threaten the sales of the business. The government may be about to increase the minimum wage, which would push up the wage bill and overall costs for the business. The business may be liable to come under attack from environmental pressure groups because of its poor record on environmental issues.

SWOT analysis is often carried out in brainstorming sessions before being written up. It can be a powerful way of summarising and building upon the results of internal and external audits.

Developing strategies

The next stage is to develop strategies. The business has identified its objectives. It has carried out an audit and analysed

its internal strengths and weaknesses, as well as the opportunities and threats posed by the external environment. So it can now plan how to use its strengths and overcome its weaknesses and seize the opportunities presented, whilst countering threats, to achieve its objectives.

Planning can take place at a variety of levels. There could be a 3-5 year plan for a business, prepared by senior management and designed to meet its corporate objectives. This will have far less detail in it than a departmental plan for the next 12 months by the production department designed to meet short-term tactical objectives.

Implementing plans

Plans need to be implemented on a day-to-day basis. The plan should inform workers about the actions they take and the decisions they make. For example, if the plan is to take a product upmarket, then managers should work on improving quality and making sure that the supply channels for the product reflect this. If the plan is to increase profit margins by cutting costs, then a cost reduction plan should be implemented.

Reviewing and evaluating outcomes

Having implemented a strategy, it is important for it to be reviewed. Did it achieve the objectives set? If not, what was achieved? What lessons can be learnt from the failures encountered?

The value of corporate plans

Corporate planning is an essential tool for large companies. It helps them map out a path which will allow them to achieve their objectives and their aims. However, there are many reasons why corporate plans often prove to be a failure.

Unrealistic objectives The objectives may have been unrealistic. There is often a tendency for managers to set objectives which are too ambitious. When set, they impress shareholders or more senior managers. But they prove to be unattainable.

Conflicting objectives The objectives may have been poorly thought out and may conflict. This can often be a problem when different layers of an organisation set objectives. The objectives of the marketing department, for example, may conflict with those of the production department. The overall aim of the business might be to increase profit. The marketing department sets itself the objective of moving its product range upmarket, selling fewer goods but at a high price and profit margin. The production department, on the other hand, sets itself the objective of increasing production to exploit economies of scale, reducing cost per unit and so increasing the potential for profit.

Poor planning Plans to achieve objectives may be badly thought out. For example, the production department may plan to increase production by 20 per cent but fail to build sufficient spending on new equipment into its plan to achieve this.

Poor execution of the plan Even if objectives and plans have been carefully and realistically thought through, workers may not implement them. It could be that the workers lack the skills and training to do so. It could also be that workers are not motivated to implement the plan. Many workers see planning and objective setting as a distraction from the 'real work' of making a sale or getting an order out to a customer. So they do what they think is best, rather than following the plan. The plan may also conflict with the interests of individual workers. For example, a plan may call for a 10 per cent reduction in staff in the production department. But the production manager in charge may resist the job losses to defend his or her staff. Or the production manager may think that making workers redundant will be far more time consuming and less pleasant than getting senior management to change their decision.

Corporate culture Many businesses find it difficult to make planned changes because of the **business** (or **corporate**) **culture** they face. This is a set of ways of doing things and unwritten rules which dominate how the business is run in practice. If the new plan conflicts with the culture of the business, frequently the plan fails. This is one reason why many large businesses stress the importance of a **change culture** in their organisation. Unless staff are prepared to change, there is often little chance of planning being effective because plans often call for change.

Uncontrollable variables Even if a strategy is well executed within a business, events outside the control of the business can knock the strategy off course. For example, the economy may go into **recession**. This can have a severe effect on sales and profitability. New technology may make existing products obsolete far quicker than expected. Or severe weather conditions may affect production or demand in unexpected ways.

Corporate plans are all too frequently poorly drawn up or knocked off course by events. Also, in some companies where there is a very strong, successful and entrepreneurial leader, corporate plans don't have much impact on the strategic direction of the company. Such leaders make strategic decisions as opportunities and threats arise, rather than sticking to any plan. So it could be argued that there is little value in drawing up a corporate plan.

However, many corporate plans do provide a successful map for a business to follow. By carefully drawing up the plan and evaluating alternative courses of action, the business has identified a possible successful strategy. Without a plan, outcomes are likely to be much worse. Decisions will be made which have not been carefully analysed and evaluated. Moreover, relatively few companies have leaders who are able to make sound strategic decisions without a planning framework.

So, corporate planning often fails to deliver the anticipated outcomes. But without corporate planning, the outcomes are likely to be even worse for the company.

KEY TERMS

External audit – an audit of the external environment in which a business finds itself, such as the market within which it operates or government restrictions on its operations.
Internal audit – an analysis of the business itself and how it operates.
Long-term objective – objective of a business over the next 3-5 years.
Operational objectives – Small scale, short-term objectives to be achieved on a day-to-day basis.
Short-term objectives – objectives of a business which are likely to be achieved within the next 12 months.
Strategic objectives – the main objectives of a business designed to achieve its aims.
SWOT analysis – analysis of the internal strengths and weaknesses of a business and the opportunities and threats presented by its external environment.
Tactical objectives – short-term objectives which help a business to achieve its strategic objectives.
Tactics – short term, specific ways in which the short term objectives of the business can be achieved.

KNOWLEDGE

1. Briefly explain the purpose of a business plan.
2. Explain the difference between strategic objectives, tactical objectives and operational objectives.
3. What is strategic planning?
4. Explain the difference between an external audit and an internal audit.
5. What is PESTLE analysis?
6. Explain the role of external and internal audits in SWOT analysis.
7. Briefly outline the reasons why a corporate plan may fail.

Case Study: Premier Foods

The company

Premier Foods was a subsidiary of the food company Hillsdown Holdings. It made a range of traditional British food brands including Typhoo Tea. In 1999, it was sold off to a private equity company, Hicks, Muse Tate and Furst. Under the leadership of Robert Schofield, the new company expanded in 2002, buying a number of brands from Nestlé including Branston, Crosse & Blackwell, Sarson's and Sun Pat. In 2003, it bought Ambrosia custard and rice pudding from Unilever. In 2004, the company was floated on the London Stock Exchange and became Premier Foods plc. Within the next three years, the company bought Bird's custard, Angel Delight, Quorn, Cauldron, Oxo, Batchelor's, Homebridge and Fray Bentos.

In November 2006, Premier Foods raised its game substantially by buying the food company RHM for £1.2 billion, taking on £800 million of RHM debt, making the total cost £2 billion. RHM owned a variety of brands but most importantly was the UK's leading maker of bread with brands such as Mother's Pride and Hovis. The stock market liked the deal and at its height valued the company at £2.8 billion. However, since then, problems have emerged and today the stock market valuation of the company is a mere £777 million. What went wrong?

The corporate plan

Premier Foods under Robert Schofield wanted to 'drive value for all our stakeholders' (Annual Report 2006). The corporate plan was to use 'its scale to drive the business, managing costs and driving brands through marketing and innovation' (Annual Report 2006). Increasing the scale of the business through acquisitions would allow economies of scale to be achieved. When acquisitions were made, in the short term, costs could be reduced through closing manufacturing plants where production could be rationalised with other existing plants. For example, following the acquisition of RHM, the company announced the closure of six plants with 1,000 workers. In the longer term, scale would give cost advantages through factors such as greater buying power and lower marketing costs per unit sold. The company estimates that eventually its annual operating costs will be £113 million lower compared to the cost of Premier Foods and RHM operating separately. Premier Foods also uses its expertise in marketing and product innovation to grow sales of its brands organically. So the corporate plan is more brands, more sales per brand and lower average costs. Unfortunately, the plan has been knocked off course.

Wheat prices

One problem has been the doubling of the price of wheat, the most important ingredient in bread. Last summer within a few months the price of wheat doubled from around £100 a tonne to £200 a tonne. On a typical loaf of bread, this increased costs by 7.5p. When retailers then add another 7.5p in profit margin, the price of a loaf of bread goes up by 15p in the shops. Premier Foods has been in a dilemma. Should it try to absorb as much of the extra cost as possible to minimise the price increase to the consumer, but suffer reduced profits as a result? Or should it pass all the increase on in higher prices and risk seeing sales and market share fall?

The competition

When Premier Foods bought RHM in November 2006, RHM had an estimated 19 per cent of the UK market for bread. Within a year, this had fallen to an estimated 16 per cent. In a static market for bread, this means that bread sales at RHM are falling. The most important reason for RHM's loss of market share has been the steady growth of Warburtons, a privately owned company. Five years ago it had less than 15 per cent of the market. Today, it is nearly 23 per cent. It has grown by providing a higher quality bread than its main rivals which it sells at a slightly higher price. Consumers seem to be prepared to pay the higher price for the perceived quality.

Debt problems

In the background to the problems in its core bread operations is the financial position of the company. Premier Food has net debts of nearly £2 billion, built up as the company made its acquisitions. City investors are worried that profits at the company will fall, putting at jeopardy its ability to finance its debt. There is some expectation that Premier Foods may sell off some non-core assets like a French company it owns making part-baked products. But it is unlikely to pay a final dividend this year and there are fears that it will be forced to raise new equity through a rights issue. This would then justify the large fall in the share price in the company seen over the past 12 months.

Source: adapted from *The Sunday Times*, 2.3.2008; Premier Foods, *Annual Report and Accounts*, 2006; en.wikipedia.org

(a) Using SWOT analysis, evaluate the position in which Premier Foods found itself in March 2008. (40 marks)

(b) Evaluate the strategies that Premier Foods could use to improve its position. (40 marks)

96 | Contingency planning

Crises

Every business faces crises in its day-to-day operations. A CRISIS is usually an unforeseen event which threatens the business in some way. Crises in a business occur for a variety of reasons.

Production Production crises are common in business. On a day-to-day basis, machinery and vehicles may break down, causing production delays. Over a short period a company might receive unexpectedly large orders, causing it to run out of stock of raw materials. More rarely, a fire might destroy premises or flooding might bring work to a halt for several days. In winter, construction businesses, for example, may lose time because of abnormal weather conditions. Snow may also prevent workers getting into work.

Finance Many businesses experience financial crises. A common financial problem is a cash flow crisis. This is when a business does not have enough cash to pay its bills. However, some businesses face a financial crisis because of unforeseen events, such as the sudden loss of a major customer. Another problem that can arise is that a firm's bankers may suddenly decide to withdraw an overdraft facility or recall a large loan, which could force the business into receivership.

Human resources Human resource problems are as common as production and finance problems for businesses. A crisis may take place simply by a worker not turning up for work. In a restaurant, for example, if there are just two cooks in the kitchen and one fails to turn up on a business night, the kitchen might be in crisis. Equally, a sudden walkout by staff over an industrial relations issue can cause chaos within the business. Other events which can cause problems include key workers suddenly leaving for a better job elsewhere, a flu virus sweeping through a workforce leaving many unable to come into work, or the sacking of a popular manager.

Product quality Most businesses at some time experience a problem with the product they make or with the quality of supplies coming into the business. In a bakery, a whole batch of bread might have to be thrown away because it was overcooked. In the car industry, a car model might have to be recalled because a fault is found. Production might come to a sudden stop because supplies of a key component are found to be faulty and unusable.

Public relations Some large businesses have faced public relations crises. A newspaper, for example, may run a story about how a company is sourcing materials from Third World producers which use cheap labour. A television company may broadcast a programme about poor work conditions in one of the company's factories. These stories can have an immediate effect on sales, with some customers boycotting the company.

Environmental issues Some businesses face considerable environmental challenges. Nuclear power, the chemicals industry or any form of mining may suffer crises because of environmental issues. For example, a crisis might occur because of the breakdown of safety equipment, a sudden spillage of waste into a river or a fire which releases toxic chemicals into the atmosphere.

Corporate crises Some crises threaten the business as a whole. For example, a company may suddenly face a takeover bid. Major shareholders may decide to sell their shares, threatening to destabilise the share price.

Contingency planning

Most businesses recognise that crises will arise in the future. However, it could be argued that relatively few have effective plans in place to deal with unforeseen eventualities. Those that do have plans tend to be larger businesses or well planned SMEs. Planning now, about how to do deal with a crisis in the future, is

Question 1.

In February 1997, Aisin Seiki, a brake manufacturer in Japan making parts for Toyota, was completely destroyed by fire. The impact on Toyota was devastating. The brake manufacturer was the sole supplier of brakes to Toyota plants in Japan and Toyota used a just-in-time delivery system for the brakes. Within hours, Toyota plants were running out brake parts and overall, 18 of Toyota's Japanese plants were shut down for almost two weeks. Estimated sales losses were 70,000 vehicles worth $325 million.

The fire didn't just affect Toyota. Hundreds of Toyota's other suppliers were forced to shut down because they could no longer supply Toyota's assembly lines whilst they were out of action.

Toyota resolved the problem in the short term by working with other brake manufacturers that usually supplied Toyota's rivals, Nissan and Honda. These brake manufacturers agreed to supply Toyota with brake parts at a competitive price. In the long term, Toyota has diversified its component purchases to ensure that no single plant can bring Toyota's production to a standstill again.

Source: adapted from www.converium.com.

(a) Explain, using the example of Toyota, why just-in-time manufacturing can lead to a crisis which shuts down a factory.
(b) Discuss whether manufacturers should hold large stocks of components and raw materials to avoid the problem experienced by Toyota.

Question 2.

Jocelyn Milne is the office manager at Reid Architecture, a small business employing 100 staff with an Office in Oxford Circus, London. Chatting with staff from some of the businesses nearby, she was shocked to learn that they were working in an area that was a possible terrorist target. A few months ago, she was asked by the firm's professional-indemnity insurers what contingency plans had been put in place should disaster strike. She discovered that nothing had been organised.

As a result, Mark Taylor, a director at the company, began formulating an action plan. 'When we discussed this at board level, everyone had seen what had happened since September 11 and realised how real problems could be. But we didn't quite realise how complex it was to formulate a disaster plan.' On September 11 2001, terrorists flew two planes into the World Trade Centre in New York destroying the building. Taylor had to develop a brief that identified the company's key workers and set out what to do if staff could not get into the building, how to make sure that all important information stored on the computers was saved or retrieved, and how to maintain internal and external lines of communication. He planned for a variety of scenarios, ranging from being evacuated for a day to a week or permanently.

Source: adapted from *The Sunday Times*, 29.6.2003.

(a) Explain why Reid Architecture needed a contingency plan to deal with a situation such as its location being a terrorist target.

(b) Suggest why the measures in the contingency plan drawn up by Reid Architecture, such as making sure all computer data was retrievable, was important to an architectural practice.

called CONTINGENCY PLANNING.

The first step in contingency planning is to identify the possible crises that could affect the business. The second step is to think about possible ways of dealing with each crisis. Then the best solution can be identified and plans drawn up showing how the business will respond. In some cases, it may be desirable to carry out practice exercises to familiarise staff with how the crisis will be dealt with. For example, a business may identify fire on the premises as a possible risk which would threaten the lives of employees. Escape routes would then be planned and employees notified of what to do in the event of a fire. There may follow regular fire practices, where staff practise evacuating the building.

Contingency planning is a cost for a business. Management time has to be spent on this activity. Most potential crises are either too trivial or too unlikely to be worth considering. So contingency planning has to be limited to:

- situations where contingency planning is required by law, such as under the Health and Safety Act;
- crises with a relatively high probability of occurring, such as an incident which could potentially generate negative public relations;
- crises with a relatively low probability of occurring, but which if they did occur would have a very high cost for the business.

For example, a particular crisis which could cost a business £5 million might have a 20 per cent probability of occurring in any 12 month period. The cost to the company if the crisis occurred over the next 12 months is mathematically £1 million (£5 million x 20 per cent). If the cost of contingency planning for the event is £5,000, then there is a clear advantage to the business of carrying out contingency planning. Equally, if a particular crisis would cost a business £100 million and there is a probability of 0.1 per cent of the event happening, then the potential cost is £100,000 (£100 million x 0.1) If the cost of carrying out contingency planning for this event is £5,000, then there is still an advantage to the business of doing this despite the low probability of the event. On the other hand, if the cost of a crisis were to be £5 million, but there is a 0.01 per cent chance of the event happening over the next 12 months, then the potential lost is only £500 (£5 million x 0.01 per cent). If the cost of formulating a contingency plan for this event is £5,000, it may not be worth carrying out.

Contingency planning and crisis management

Contingency planning and CRISIS MANAGEMENT will involve a number of different areas of the business.

Finance A crisis may have financial implications. For example, if a fire destroys a factory, output will be lost and so revenue will fall. Then there will be costs of rebuilding. The cost of replacing machinery of buildings due to fire and flooding, and the interruption to a business's activity, can be insured against. However, a loss of profit caused as a result of a downturn in the market, the failure of a product due to poor design or industrial action cannot be insured against. A business may also hold contingency funds. These are reserves of cash held back to deal with the financial implications of a crisis. Equally, a business may arrange for an overdraft or loan facility with its bankers to be drawn up in a crisis.

All these methods lead to extra costs for the business. Insurance premiums have to be paid, holding cash means that it cannot be used productively elsewhere in the business and banks charge fees for arranging overdrafts and loan facilities even if no money is borrowed.

Production Potentially, there are many different crises which involve production. A simple problem is machinery breaking down. A business may plan to transfer production to another machine, or it may have a 24 hour 365 day a year call out contract with a machine repair business. A more serious crisis would occur if a large company used just-in-time production techniques and its sole supplier of a key component suffered a fire which stopped all production. The company's contingency plan may identify an alternative source of supply. Or it may have drawn up plans with the supplier to organise a resumption of production within 48 hours by using rented equipment and new rented premises.

Human resource management If a crisis is to be successfully resolved, it must be clear who is responsible for dealing with the crisis. A contingency plan must therefore include the names of who will take charge in the crisis and what roles they will fulfil. Chains of command and channels of communication should be clearly set out. For example, a holiday company may run coach tours in Germany. There is a risk that a coach may suffer a crash, with casualties amongst the passengers. A contingency plan for such a risk may give responsibility for dealing with the problems resulting from the crash to a senior manager. Underneath the senior manager may be another manager responsible for setting up a crisis call centre where relatives can ring to get information. The plan may state that call operatives have the authority to offer relatives affected a free flight to Germany. A more senior employee may have the authority to give out immediate hardship grants of £1,000 to families affected. Meanwhile, it may be planned that a small team will fly out to Germany to deal with victims in hospitals and to deal with the dead. The team would also be responsible for looking after the relatives as they arrive in Germany. An individual may be made responsible for dealing with the press, issuing press releases and giving interviews.

Equally important in a crisis is the motivation of staff. In practice, employees tend to react positively in a crisis. If there is a fire or flood, for example, staff will typically work long hours to deal with the aftermath. However, the contingency plan should consider how employees will be rewarded for their positive response in a crisis. If a fire completely destroys a factory, and it takes three weeks to start up again in new premises, will the staff be paid for those three weeks even though they stay at home not working? Should staff be given a bonus for dealing with a crisis? If temporary staff need to be taken on to deal with a crisis, what in the contingency plan deals with possible friction between existing employees and the new staff leading to poor morale?

Marketing Marketing may pose considerable problems in a crisis. The contingency plan must deal with these marketing challenges. For example, if there is a fire which disrupts production, how will the business look after its customers? The contingency plan may say that supplies should be bought from rival producers and delivered to customers. Or customers may be contacted individually to explain the problems and given a timetable for when supplies will be resumed. Compensation may be offered to customers for the disruption caused by a temporary loss of supply. If the crisis is caused by a fault with a product, the contingency plan may state that all existing supplies will be recalled with the company paying for the recall. Compensation may be offered to customers who have already bought faulty products.

The contingency plan may outline how public relations will be handled in the event of a crisis. An individual may be nominated to deal with the press. The amount of information to be given out may be decided in advance in the contingency plan.

Success and failure

When faced with a serious crisis, such as the destruction of premises, a small business which does not have contingency plans may be forced to cease trading. Even large companies without plans can be forced out of business by a single catastrophe. When a foreign exchange trader working for Barings Bank lost $1 billion, the bank was forced to put itself up for sale to survive. Lesser crises are still likely to harm a business. Fires, floods and faulty products all tend to lead to one-off costs to a business which are not offset by gains elsewhere. Without contingency planning, these costs are likely to be higher than if there is planning in place.

Occasionally, however, crises can have an overall positive impact on a business. An airline, for example, which looks after its customers when it has to suspend flights may gain positive public relations. A devastating fire may be an opportunity to

KEYTERMS

Contingency planning – the creation of plans of how particular crises which might affect a business will be dealt with should they arise.
Crisis – usually an unforeseen event which threatens the business in some way, such as a sudden drop in sales, a fire which destroys premises or the discovery of a fault in a product.
Crisis management – dealing effectively with an unforeseen or unplanned event.

KNOWLEDGE

1. What type of crises might a small engineering company face?
2. Explain how a contingency plan might be drawn up.
3. Should every contingency be considered by a business in contingency planning?
4. How might a business react to a crisis in (a) finance; (b) production; (c) human resources; (d) marketing?
5. Why do contingency plans need to be reviewed regularly?

rebuild to allow more efficient production.

Contingency planning does not guarantee that a business will survive a crisis. For example, a business may have planned for a range of crises, except for the one that actually occurs. Or the plans may have been drawn up too long ago to reflect the current situation in which the business finds itself. The planning itself may have been faulty. When tested, solutions may prove inadequate.

Because of the changing business environment, contingency plans need to be reviewed on a regular basis. Current assumptions about potential crises must be constantly questioned and methods to deal with them constantly updated.

Case Study: *Maya Lim*

Table 1: Profit and loss account of Maya Lim

Profit and loss account for year ended 31.5.2008	
	£
Turnover	83,890
Cost of sales	41,498
Gross profit	42,392
Expenses	37,720
Net profit	4,672

Maya Lim found her life turned upside down when a leak, followed by an explosion, effectively destroyed her premises which were part of a shopping centre. Maya was ill-prepared for such a disaster. She, along with all the other people in the shopping centre at the time, were safely evacuated so at least there was no loss of life and few injuries. However, her business was one of a number of firms that never recovered.

Part of the problem was that her business had not been doing particularly well financially. Table 1 shows the profit and loss account for her last year of full trading. She had an agreed overdraft limit of £8,000 with her bank and on the day of the explosion, she was overdrawn on her bank account by £7,854. She had also £10,450 of outstanding trade credit, much of it already overdue to her suppliers from the run up to the previous Christmas which had seen very disappointing sales.

In the aftermath of the explosion, Maya, along with other retailers in the centre were unable to visit the premises for a number of days. She didn't know what she was going to find, but it was worse than she imagined. Her entire stock was so damaged that none of it was saleable and fixtures and fittings were not worth salvaging. The small office at the back of the outlet where she kept most of her business records was particularly badly affected. Some of the records were completely destroyed, whilst others were only useable with difficulty.

Maya spent days worrying about what she would find. Seeing the premises in such a condition worried her considerably. She knew she had to decide what to do about her business, but she found she couldn't face up to the difficult decisions that lay ahead. The management of the shopping centre let her know that it would have to be completely rebuilt and so premises would not be available certainly in the short term and possibly for more than a year. So she would have to look for new premises. Then she would have to buy in new stock. But she had no cash. The insurance payout for the damage would take months to come. It would only cover the cost of the stock and fixtures and fittings anyway. She had no insurance for loss of earnings while she couldn't trade. She couldn't see how her bank would increase her overdraft limit. Nor could she see any supplier giving her more trade credit given her existing debts.

By the time her unit in the centre had been repaired, Maya had got a management job paying £30,000 a year and she was no longer interested in taking back the premises.

(a) Explain the nature of the crisis that faced Maya Lim from the perspective of finance, marketing, production and human resources. (40 marks)

(b) Discuss whether any amount of contingency planning would have saved Maya's business in the aftermath of the crisis. (40 marks)

97 | Management

What is management?

Managers are an important group involved in business activity. It may be difficult to define exactly what is meant by 'management'. However, many agree that managers are responsible for 'getting things done' – usually through other people. The term manager may refer to a number of different people within a business. Some job titles include the word manager, such as personnel manager. Other job holders may also be managers, even though their titles do not say it. It could be argued that managers:

- act on behalf of the owners – in a company, senior management are accountable to the shareholders;
- set objectives for the organisation, for example, they may decide that a long term objective is to have a greater market share than all of the company's competitors;
- make sure that a business achieves its objectives, by managing others;
- ensure that corporate values (the values of the organisation) are maintained in dealings with other businesses, customers, employees and the general public.

The functions of management

Henri Fayol, the French management theorist, listed a number of functions or elements of management in his book *General and Industrial Administration* (1916).

Planning This involves setting objectives and also the strategies, policies, programmes and procedures for achieving them. Planning might be done by line managers who will be responsible for performance. However, advice on planning may also come from staff management who might have expertise in that area, even if they have no line authority. For example, a production manager may carry out workforce planning in the production department, but use the skills of the personnel manager in planning recruitment for vacancies that may arise.

Organising Managers set tasks which need to be performed if the business is to achieve its objectives. Jobs need to be organised within sections or departments and authority needs to be delegated so that jobs are carried out. For example, the goal of a manufacturing company may be to produce quality goods that will be delivered to customers on time. The tasks, such as manufacturing, packaging, administration, etc. that are part of producing and distributing the goods, need to be organised to achieve this goal.

Commanding This involves giving instructions to subordinates to carry out tasks. The manager has the authority to make decisions and the responsibility to see that tasks are carried out.

Co-ordinating This is the bringing together of the activities of people within the business. Individuals and groups will have their own goals, which may be different to those of the business and each other. Management must make sure that there is a common approach, so that the company's goals are achieved.

Controlling Managers measure and correct the activities of individuals and groups, to make sure that their performance fits in with plans.

Managerial roles

Henry Mintzberg in the 1980s suggested that, as well as carrying out certain functions, the manager also fulfils certain roles in a firm. He identified three types of role which a manager must play.

Interpersonal roles These arise from the manager's formal authority. Managers have a figurehead role. For example, a large part of a chief executive's time is spent representing the company at dinners, conferences etc. They also have a leader role. This involves hiring, firing and training staff, motivating employees etc. Thirdly, they have a liaison role. Some managers spend up to half their time meeting with other managers. They do this because they need to know what is happening in other departments. Senior managers spend a great deal of time with people outside the business. Mintzberg says that these contacts build up an informal information system, and are a means of extending influence both within and outside the business.

Information roles Managers act as channels of information from one department to another. They are in a position to do this because of their contacts.

Decision making roles The manager's formal authority and access to information means that no-one else is in a better position to take decisions about a department's work.

Through extensive research and observation of what managers actually do, Mintzberg drew certain conclusions about the work of managers.

- The idea that a manager is a 'systematic' planner is a myth. Planning is often carried out on a day-to-day basis, in between more urgent tasks.
- Another myth is that a manager has no regular or routine duties, as these have been delegated to others. Mintzberg found that managers perform a number of routine duties, particularly 'ceremonial' tasks.
- Mintzberg's research showed that managers prefer verbal communication rather than a formal system of communication. Information passed by word of mouth in an informal way is likely to be more up to date and easier to grasp.

Management by objectives (MBO)

In 1955, Peter Drucker, a US business adviser and writer, published a book called *The Practice of Management*. In the book, he suggested that managers had five functions:

➤ setting objectives;
➤ organising work;

➤ motivating employees and communicating information to them;
➤ job measurement – checking that tasks have been performed and objectives met;
➤ developing people, including organising training.

Setting objectives Drucker argued that businesses could run into problems if managers and employees worked towards different objectives. For example, the marketing department might want to launch a new product. This could raise revenues, but would also increase costs. In contrast, the finance department might frustrate those plans by not agreeing to any increase in spending for the next six months. So Drucker put forward the idea that a business could be run and controlled through:

• the setting out of objectives;
• making plans to realise those objectives;
• carrying out those plans;
• monitoring whether objectives have been reached.

This is MANAGEMENT BY OBJECTIVES (MBO). It is a scientific approach to management, where the same principles can be applied to different businesses and different situations. MBO requires managers to use the skills identified by Drucker as essential to their role as managers.

Planning and MBO In a large organisation, the system to implement MBO is likely to be complex. This is because there is a large number of employees who must be involved at different levels in the hierarchy of the business. In a large organisation, objectives or goals for the whole business (corporate objectives) are set by senior managers and the directors of the company. Those objectives are derived from their aims (sometimes written out in the mission statement of the business). Senior management then has to plan how to achieve those objectives.

The next stage is to involve the next layer of management in the hierarchy. A corporate objective might be to increase sales by 30 per cent over the next three years. Senior management of a subsidiary company of the business would then be asked how they could contribute to realising that goal. Following discussions and analysis, they could agree on their objective. They might, for example, agree to an objective of increasing sales by 10 per cent. Planning is then required to map out how the 10 per cent increase will be achieved.

This might then be taken down to managers of individual departments within the subsidiary company. What objectives would those departments have to help achieve the 10 per cent increase in sales? Ultimately, it can be taken down to the level of individual workers. Through systems of performance appraisal, individual workers can be set goals, say for the next year. Achieving these goals will form a small part of the way in which the objectives of the whole business will be achieved.

Participation and MBO The MBO process should encourage participation and negotiation. Orders should not simply be

Question 1.

Alison Broomes had a typical morning as personnel manager for a company employing 750 people.

8.00	In her office dealing with her emails.
8.10	Interrupted by the production manager asking whether she had any luck in getting applications for the toolsetter's job.
8.30	Secretary arrives and they go through her diary appointments for the day.
8.40	Meeting with accounts manager to discuss the wording of an advert and job description for an accounts executive. Interrupted by mobile phone call from managing director's personal secretary confirming 3.45 meeting.
9.20	Back into the office to deal with the mail. Delegate tasks arising from the mail to her 2 assistants and 1 secretary in their open plan office.
9.40	Meeting with trade union representative to discuss disciplining of a worker for persistent lateness.
9.50	Review file for interviews taking place the following day. Interrupted by phone call from managing director's personal secretary to ask if the meeting could be moved to 4.00 p.m.
10.10	Checks progress on two job vacancies with one of her assistants.
10.30	Monthly meeting with head of marketing to discuss current personnel issues in her department.
11.30	Attendance at small ceremony where 15 employees are given their CIEH Basic Health and Safety awards.
11.50	Back in the office reading over letters and documents that are to be sent out by her secretary which require her signature.
12.10	Discussion with one of her assistants about a pay issue that has cropped up.
12.25	Accesses emails and replies to them.
12.40	Calls assistant head of production about application for training course from two of his workers.
12.55	Working lunch with her two assistants in the office.

(a) Explain what functions of management Alison Broomes has fulfilled during her morning according to (i) Fayol's theory of management and (ii) Mintzberg's theory.

Table 1: Advantages of MBO

- Managers and workers in the organisation will know their objectives. So the business can work to a single purpose.
- Objectives and plans can be co-ordinated throughout the organisation. So one part of an organisation should not be working in a way which will frustrate the objectives of another part of the organisation.
- Clarity of purpose, negotiation and payment systems should lead to workers and managers being better motivated.
- MBO allows senior managers to control the organisation. The MBO system allows them to steer the business in the direction in which they have agreed to go.

passed down the chain of command. Instead, objectives and how to achieve them should be the subjects of discussion and negotiation. There are two main reasons for this.

- Those lower down the chain of command often have a better understanding of what is possible than those further up the chain. Their knowledge and experience should be used rather than ignored. So they should be fully involved in objective setting, planning and execution.
- Participation is likely to increase motivation. Managers and workers are likely to be committed to achieving goals which they have helped to set.

Compensation and MBO Compensation of individual workers or groups of workers can be linked into the achievement of objectives. Bonuses can be paid to managers and workers who meet targets. Bonus systems should be designed to reward those who achieve. They should therefore motivate managers and workers. Reward-based compensation systems also force businesses to be clear about whether they have achieved their objectives. Information about what has been achieved must be collected to decide whether or not bonuses are to be paid. They force everyone to concentrate their attention on what is to be achieved and what has been achieved.

Advantages and problems of MBO

Table 1 shows the benefits of a MBO approach. However, there may be some problems. Some large organisations have attempted to adopt MBO, although perhaps not as a complete management system. Others have not, for a number of reasons.

Time and resources Properly implemented, the system requires a considerable amount of time and resources to be allocated to it. Involving managers at all levels of an organisation is costly. It can be argued that these costs outweigh the benefits to be gained from implementation.

Obstruction MBO assumes that managers and workers can be moulded into employees who will understand objectives and carry out plans which will fulfil those objectives. But each

manager and worker is different. Some are highly motivated and are good at seeing objectives and implementing them. Others might have less positive attitudes towards work. They might have little interest in seeing the business achieve its objectives. Equally, many workers and managers find it difficult to understand large-scale objectives and plans. In their view, getting on with familiar routine tasks is all that is important. Meetings to them are mostly a waste of time and the outcomes are usually best ignored. There are also employees who find it difficult to work in ways which are fixed by others. They are not necessarily good team members because they do things in the way which suits them. But they can be highly valuable to an organisation, particularly where individuality and creativity are needed. So, many managers and workers conform to the type of working required by the MBO system. This reduces its effectiveness.

Creativity Some argue that MBO fails to recognise the importance of creativity and spontaneity in a successful business. MBO is a system of control to ensure that managers

Question 2.

Kaplin Price is a manufacturer of scaffolding and safety equipment. It is increasingly facing stiff competition from abroad, but is not certain how best to react to this. Should it expand rapidly? Or should it rationalise to some extent? What would happen if it differentiated its products in some way from those of its competitors? Unless it makes a decision soon, it might find that its costs have escalated and it may be forced to shut down.

It has also experienced difficulties with its internal organisation. Last year it attempted to launch a new range of products with the intention of expanding its market share. It was not clear exactly what share it wanted to achieve, just that it wanted sales to grow. It set in place an incentive system for its sales representatives. Those that reached a certain target of sales would receive a bonus. However, it did not explain to the reps exactly what the target would be. This meant that they lacked motivation and whether they should be paid the bonus or not was decided by managers with a 'gut feeling' about individuals if there had been improved sales from the whole team.

(a) Using examples, examine ways in which adopting an MBO approach might solve the difficulties faced by Kaplin Price.

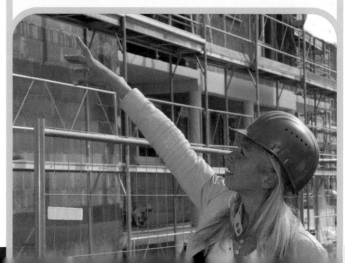

carry out the objectives and plans of senior management. But success in many businesses comes about because workers react as individuals to individual situations. MBO stifles that initiative and makes it more difficult for managers to react to an unpredictable environment.

A changing environment MBO assumes that the environment in which a business finds itself is likely to be fairly predictable. But in practice, the business environment can be volatile. Objectives set one month can be unrealistic the next. War, recession, collapsing markets or new competitors can completely change what is possible. So, too much planning can be a waste of resources. Even worse, it can paralyse a business when circumstances change. Managers can carry on working to old objectives and plans when these have become redundant.

In practice, all medium to large businesses have formal or informal strategies (plans to meet objectives) and systems to implement those strategies. These systems include elements of MBO. But most accept that management by objectives is not the only way to run a successful business.

Being a manager

Charles Handy, an Irish author specialising in organisational behaviour and management, has outlined what is likely to be involved in 'being a manager'.

The manager as a general practitioner Handy made an analogy between managing and staying 'healthy'. If there are 'health problems' in business, the manager needs to identify the symptoms. These could include low productivity, high labour turnover or industrial relations problems. Once the symptoms have been identified, the manager needs to find the cause of the trouble and develop a strategy for 'better health'. Strategies for health might include changing people, through hiring and firing, reassignments, training, pay increases or counselling. A manager might also restructure work through job redesign, job enrichment and a redefinition of roles. Systems can also be improved. These can include communication systems, reward systems, information and reporting systems, budgets and other decision making systems, e.g. stock control.

Managerial dilemmas Handy argued that managers face dilemmas. One of the reasons sometimes given for why managers are paid more than workers is because of the dilemmas they face.

- **The dilemma of cultures** When managers are promoted or move to other parts of the business, they have to behave in ways which are suitable for the new position. For example, at the senior management level, managers may deal more with long term strategy and delegate lower level tasks to middle management more often. If a promoted manager maintains a 'culture' that she is used to, which may mean taking responsibility for all tasks, she may not be effective in her new position.
- **The trust-control dilemma** Managers may want to control

the work for which they are responsible. However, they may have to delegate work to subordinates, trusting them to do the work properly. The greater the trust a manager has in subordinates, the less control she retains for herself. Retaining control could mean a lack of trust.
- **The commando leader's dilemma** In many firms, junior managers often want to work in project teams, with a clear task or objective. This can mean working 'outside' the normal bureaucratic structure of a larger organisation. Unfortunately, there can be too many project groups (or 'commando groups') for the good of the business. The manager must decide how many project groups she should create to satisfy the needs of her subordinates and how much bureaucratic structure to retain.

The manager as a person Management has developed into a profession and managers expect to be rewarded for their professional skills. Managers must, therefore, continue to develop these skills and sell them to the highest bidder.

Theory X and Theory Y

In 1960 Douglas McGregor published *The Human Side of Enterprise*. It was an attempt to apply the implications of Maslow and the work of Taylor and Mayo on motivation to business. In the book, he gives different reasons why people work. He coined the terms Theory X and Theory Y to describe these differences. Table 3 shows the main ideas behind the two theories.

- **Theory X** THEORY X assumes that people are lazy. If this is accepted, then the only way to get people to work is by using strict control. This control can take one of two forms. One method is to use coercion – the threat of punishment if rules are broken or targets not achieved. This is often known as the 'stick' approach. The problem with threats is that they are only effective if the person being threatened believes that they will be carried out. Modern employment laws and company-wide agreements,

Table 2: Theory X and Theory Y	
Theory X	**Theory Y**
• Workers are motivated by money	• Workers have many different needs which motivate them
• Workers are lazy and dislike work	• Workers can enjoy work
• Workers are selfish, ignore the needs of organisations, avoid responsibility and lack ambition	• If motivated, workers can organise themselves and take responsibility
• Workers need to be controlled and directed by management	• Management should create a situation where workers can show creativity and apply their job knowledge

Question 3.

In 2007 BP's new chief executive, Tony Hayward, vowed to fix the problems at the company after announcing a slide in second quarter profits. He said there would be a revamp of BP's structure and promising to rein in operating subsidiaries in favour of a more centralised management style. Previously BP's head office issued financial targets, but left divisional heads with a high degree of operational independence. Mr Hayward is thought to admire the greater 'command and control' style of industry leader Exxon Mobil.'We are not moving to a completely functional operation,' he said, 'but there will be much stronger boundaries and standards within which to operate.'

Promising the end of 'duplication' around the group, Mr Hayward detailed cost cuts, including the redeployment of 25 per cent of head office staff into the field. Hayward has already indicated that the management style and approach that he wants to filter down to the grass roots will be less about politics and cult of personality and more focus used on profits and operations. Hayward has written of BP's failure to 'listen enough to what the bottom of the organisation is saying'. The word 'collegiate' crops up a lot in conversations with BP personnel about the management approach that Hayward aims to cultivate.

Source: adapted from the *Telegraph*, 2007.

(a) What are the potential dilemmas of a manager's role at BP?
(b) To what extent does Mr Hayward subscribe to a Theory X or Theory Y approach to management?

earlier in this unit.

• **Theory Y** THEORY Y, on the other hand, assumes that most people are motivated by those things at the top of Maslow's hierarchy. In other words, people are responsible, committed and enjoy having control over work. Most people, given the opportunity, will get involved in work, and contribute towards the solution of a problem that may arise. This theory is similar in some ways to the **human relations school**.

Business managers tend to say that their own assumptions are closer to Theory Y than to Theory X. But tests on management training courses tend to show that their attitudes are closer to Theory X than they might like to admit. In addition, many managers suggest that, while they themselves are like Theory Y, workers are closer to Theory X. This theory has been used by managers to organise employees in business.

In practice, it could be argued that most firms behave according to Theory X, especially where shopfloor workers are concerned. The emphasis is on the use of money and control to encourage workers to behave in the 'correct way'. The same organisations might behave according to the assumptions of Theory Y when dealing with management. A representative of a banker's union wrote in *The Independent on Sunday*, 'The lower down the ladder you are, the less control you have over your work environment. Managers can do as they please, stretch their legs whenever they want. Clerical workers, if they are working in a data-processing centre, for example doing entries for cheques or credit cards, are disciplined if they don't complete a given number of key strokes in an hour or a day. Half the time they don't know what they are doing. They don't see any end product. More and more work has been downgraded.'

have made this difficult for managers. For this reason, a 'carrot' approach may be more suitable. People have to be persuaded to carry out tasks by means of promises or rewards. In many ways this theory is similar to Taylor's **scientific management** view of people at work as shown

Case Study: MBO in banking

Management by objectives was the driving management philosophy of a particular bank. For example, each month bank branches would be given a new target. One month it would be the number of new savings accounts opened. Another month it would the number of loans sold. Another month it would the number of student accounts opened. Quite what was the plan of head office was unclear, but bonuses for the staff at the branches depended on hitting those targets month after month.

The branch manager at one of the Bournemouth branches, Patricia McGuire, regularly went on 'away' days. At these conferences, the objectives that head office were setting its managers were explained. Patricia was expected to communicate those objectives to her staff – to help get them to see the big picture of how they fitted into the big plan. But many branch managers found it difficult to be motivated by these training sessions. Often, the targets were completely unattainable. Take the target in September for signing up students. Her branch was in Bournemouth, capital city of England for senior citizens. She would be lucky to sign up one student, let alone the target of 50.

At Patricia McGuire's annual performance appraisal, her line manager didn't seem unduly worried that her branch had missed its target for 9 out of the previous 12 months. She concentrated on other aspects of Patricia's work and recommended that she be given her individual bonus for the year. During the interview Patricia expressed her frustration that she had no control over what targets were set for her branch staff. The line manager said that the system was not

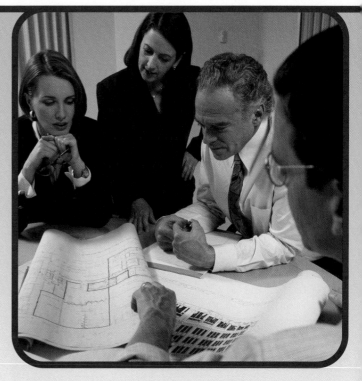

designed to incorporate feedback from staff further down the line. Head office decided what it wanted and that was what went out to the branches.

(a) **Discuss whether the management by objectives approach of the bank was effective. (40 marks)**

Leadership and management

Management has a number of functions. For example, managers, according to the management theorist Henri Fayol, should predict what will happen in the future, plan to achieve their objectives, organise resources, exercise command over staff lower down the hierarchy, co-ordinate day-to-day tasks and monitor how well objectives are being achieved. Peter Drucker, writing 40 years later, added motivating and communicating with staff and giving them training opportunities to this list.

Some writers make no distinction between management and leadership in an organisation. Managers are leaders because of the roles they play. Others, however, suggest that leaders are not necessarily the same as managers. Leaders may perform the same functions as managers. But in addition, they may do some or all of the following.

- Leaders can be **visionaries**, understanding where an organisation is at today and seeing the direction in which an organisation has to change to survive and flourish.
- Leaders tend to be good at carrying through the **process of change**. Because they understand the starting point and the end point, they can chart a route from one to the other. Where others may see only chaos and think the organisation is taking the wrong road, the leader has the ability to see through the details and small setbacks which are a part of any change.
- Leaders are often excellent at **motivating** those around them, allowing them to perform at their best. They are particularly good at motivating others to change both themselves and the organisation.

It could be argued that, in large businesses, leaders devise **strategies** whilst managers are responsible for implementing them. However, sometimes leaders do get involved in implementation because they appreciate that it is just as important to implement change as it is to devise strategies. In small businesses, leaders often have the skills to both devise and carry out a strategy.

The characteristics of leaders

One approach to finding out what makes good leaders is to identify the **qualities**, **characteristics** or **traits** that they should have. A number of characteristics have been suggested.

- Effective leaders have a positive self-image, backed up with a genuine ability and realistic aspirations. This is shown in the confidence they have. An example in UK industry might be Richard Branson, in his various pioneering business activities. Leaders also appreciate their own strengths and weaknesses. It is argued that many managers fail to lead because they often get bogged down in short-term activity.

- Leaders need to be able to get to the 'core' of a problem and have the vision and commitment to suggest radical solutions. Sir John Harvey-Jones took ICI to £1 billion profit by stirring up what had become a 'sleeping giant'. Many awkward questions were raised about the validity of the way things were done, and the changes led to new and more profitable business on a worldwide scale for the firm.
- Studies of leaders in business suggest that they are experts in particular fields and well read in everything else. They tend to be 'out of the ordinary', intelligent, and articulate. Examples might be Anita Roddick, the founder of Body Shop or Bill Gates, the founder of Microsoft.
- Leaders are often creative and innovative. They tend to seek new ideas to problems, make sure that important things are done and try to improve standards.
- Leaders often have the ability to sense change and can respond to it. This is dealt with later in this unit.

Leadership styles

Another approach is to examine different styles of leadership. There is a number of styles that managers might adopt in the work setting.

Autocratic An AUTOCRATIC leadership style is one where the manager sets objectives, allocates tasks, and insists on obedience. Therefore the group become dependent on him or her. The result of this style is that members of the group are often dissatisfied with the leader. This results in little cohesion, the need for high levels of supervision, and poor levels of motivation amongst employees.

Autocratic leadership may be needed in certain circumstances. For example, in the armed forces there may be a need to move troops quickly and for orders to be obeyed instantly.

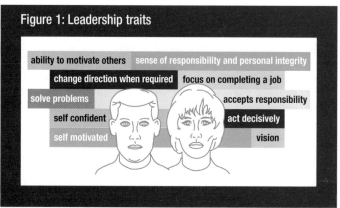

Figure 1: Leadership traits

ability to motivate others | sense of responsibility and personal integrity
change direction when required | focus on completing a job
solve problems | accepts responsibility
self confident | act decisively
self motivated | vision

Question 1.

Britain's bosses are becoming more dictatorial in style, causing increased absenteeism among staff and lower productivity, the Chartered Management Institute warned. After surveying more than 1,500 managers, it found most organisations were suffering from overbearing and dogmatic leadership, in spite of overwhelming evidence that the authoritarian approach is ineffective.

Managers were asked to describe the organisation in which they worked. They could choose three characteristics from a list of ten, ranging from 'authoritative', 'risk averse' and 'secretive' to 'accessible', 'empowering' and 'trusting'. The institute said: 'The most widely experienced leadership styles in UK organisations are bureaucratic (40 per cent), reactive (37 per cent) and authoritarian (30 per cent).' Over the same period, the proportion of managers saying they worked in empowering organisations fell from 37 per cent to 25 per cent. The institute said staff in organisations with a dictatorial style were less likely to enjoy their work and more likely to have high rates of sickness absence.

In authoritarian companies, 44 per cent of managers said they got job satisfaction, compared with 71 per cent in other organisations. In innovative and trusting companies, 10 per cent of managers said absence was increasing, compared with 45 per cent in organisations where the culture was suspicious. The most successful businesses had empowering leadership styles. By contrast, 56 per cent of declining companies were stifled by bureaucracy and 26 per cent had a secretive environment.

The institute said organisations should have learned long ago that the authoritarian style was ineffective. 'If not from the management schools, they should have picked up the message from sitcoms such as Blackadder and the Office,' a spokesman said. But whenever organisations failed to meet their targets, it appeared that senior managers responded by creating secretive and bureaucratic environments. This might be due to a shortage of managers with the right mix of skills.

An organisation in difficulty faced more pressure to deliver good results with fewer management resources. Jo Causon, the institute's marketing director, said: 'The effect of management styles on performance can be marked. It has a direct bearing on the levels of health, motivation and commitment linking employers and staff. Of course, improving the sense of wellbeing, determination and productivity is no easy task, but it is one that cannot be ignored.'

The report said: 'It is disappointing that bureaucratic, reactive and authoritarian styles prevail in the UK, when entrepreneurial, accessible and empowering styles are associated with far higher levels of motivation, health and productivity.'

Source: adapted from *The Guardian*, 12.12. 2007.

(a) Identify the different leadership styles in the article.
(b) Examine the relationship between these styles and motivation in business.
(c) Discuss an appropriate leadership style for a business in difficulty facing more pressure to deliver good results with fewer management resources.

Democratic A DEMOCRATIC leadership style encourages participation in decision making. Democratic leadership styles can be persuasive or consultative.

- **Persuasive.** This is where a leader has already made a decision, but takes the time to persuade others that it is a good idea. For example, the owner of a business may decide to employ outside staff for certain jobs and persuade existing staff that this may ease their work load.
- **Consultative.** This is where a leader consults others about their views before making a decision. The decision will take into account these views. For example, the views of the marketing department about whether to launch a new range of products may be considered.

Democratic leadership styles need good communication skills. The leaders must be able to explain ideas clearly to employees and understand any feedback they receive. It may mean, however, that decisions take a long time to be reached as lengthy consultation can take place.

It has been suggested that a democratic style of leadership can be more effective in business for a number of reasons.

- There has been increased public participation in social and political life. Democratic management reflects this trend.
- Increasing income and educational standards means that people now expect greater freedom and a better quality of working life.
- Research suggests that this style is generally more effective. Managers are able to 'tap into' the ideas of people with knowledge and experience. This can lead to better decisions being made.
- People involved in the decision making process are likely to be more committed and motivated, to accept decisions reached with their help, to trust managers who make the decisions and to volunteer new and creative ideas.

Paternalistic PATERNALISTIC leaders are similar to autocratic leaders. They make all the decisions and expect subordinates to obey these decisions. However, whereas an autocratic leader may be uninterested in the well-being of subordinates, a paternalistic leader places a great deal of importance on their welfare. In the past there have been a number of paternalistic leaders, such as Joseph Rowntree and George Cadbury. Examples of their concern for employees included the building of new houses which they could rent at low rates. As with autocratic leaders, paternalistic leaders do not give subordinates control over decision making.

Laissez- faire A LAISSEZ-FAIRE type of leadership style allows employees to carry out activities freely within broad limits. The result is a relaxed atmosphere, but one where there are few guidelines and directions. This can sometimes result in poor productivity and lack of motivation as employees have little incentive to work hard.

Team-based leadership

The growth of flatter and matrix style structures, empowerment, job redesign and team working has affected the type of leadership that managers might use in a business. Managers are more likely today to organise and co-ordinate the workings of a variety of employees at different levels, in different functions and with different skills. In a sense they have become team-based leaders.

Traditional approaches to leadership and management that are linked to authority, status and power are likely to be of limited use to team based leaders. Team leaders are less likely to be individuals who give orders and have a clear understanding of exactly how a task is to be done than people who:

- have the the ability to bring together the right blend of workers to allow business problems to be solved and action implemented;
- can motivate staff in the team to problem solve and accomplish a task;
- know and understand corporate objectives;
- know what resources are available to implement actions in order to achieve objectives;
- evaluate a team and decide if the task has been carried out.

Team-based leadership often happens in businesses where the idea and use of a hierarchy is less relevant. This may happen, for example, in a SINGLE STATUS organisation where every worker is treated the same. They have the same facilities, same dress codes and same terms and conditions of employment. Every worker is made to feel as if they are an important part of the organisation.

Factors affecting leadership styles and approaches

The type of leadership style adopted by managers will depend on various factors. These factors may be **internal** factors, within the business, or **external** factors, from outside the organisation.

The task A certain task may be the result of an emergency, which might need immediate response from a person in authority. For example, if there is an emergency brought on by external factors such as a power failure leading to production ceasing, the speed of decision needed and the action taken may require an authoritarian or autocratic style of leadership.

The tradition of the organisation A business may have developed its own internal culture which is the result of the interactions of all employees at different levels. This can result in one type of leadership style, because of a pattern of behaviour that has developed in the organisation.

The type of labour force A more highly skilled workforce might be most productive when their opinions are sought. Democratic leadership styles may be more appropriate in this case. Certain types of profession in the labour force, for example, may be more used to making their own decisions and require a more democratic style of leadership.

The group size Democratic leadership styles can lead to confusion the greater the size of the group.

The leader's personality The personality of one manager may be different from that of another manager and certain leadership styles might suit one but not the other. For example, an aggressive, competitive personality may be more suited to an authoritarian leadership style.

Group personality Some people prefer to be directed rather than contribute, either because of lack of interest or previous experience, or because they believe that the manager is paid to take decisions and shoulder responsibility. If this is the case, then an autocratic leadership style is more likely to lead to effective decision making.

Situation A model of leadership by Ken Blanchard and Paul Hersey suggests that a SITUATIONAL LEADER adopts the most appropriate leadership style for the situation being faced. A leader will have **task behaviour** or **relationship behaviour**. Task behaviour reflects the extent to which the leader has to organise what a subordinate should do. Relationship behaviour reflects how much support is needed and how close personal contact is.

Question 2.

In 2007 a national leadership scheme for the Fire and Rescue Service was launched. The programme aimed at 17,000 managers over four years, would be delivered through training centres, online resources and coaching and mentoring. Des Pritchard, HR director of the Chief Fire Officers' Association, said that the programme would move the service's leadership from a 'transactional' based model to a 'transformational and empowered' one. He said: 'Today's world is much more complex and there are greater demands on leaders. We hope the programme will help them to be more resilient.'

Sue Hopgood, director of organisational development at the Fire Service College, said various reviews had identified that leadership in the service "needed to be developed to be more attund to the twenty-first century". Leaders will be expected to demonstrate core behaviours relating to respect, integrity and trust, service to the public and working with colleagues. Hopgood said the model was unique because "it makes it very clear that the operational domain they work in is as important as their political and leadership domains".

The programme is also part of the Fire and Rescue Service's new diversity strategy. 'Transformational leaders are more likely to bring on board a more diverse workforce. They think differently about recruitment and selection,' Hopgood said.

She admitted that the service 'continues to be a predominantly white male organisation', having just over 2 per cent women and just under 3 per cent BME staff out of a 56,000 strong workforce. Only one out of the 46 fire and rescue services across England currently has a female chief executive. But she is positive that the scheme will help to address the balance. 'Leadership and diversity run alongside each other,' she said.

Source: adapted from *People Management*, 13.12.2007.

(a) Examine the factors that may have influenced the need for a leadership scheme at the Fire and Rescue Service.

Together these will decide which of the following leadership styles will be used.

- **Delegating leadership** is where a leader allows subordinates to solve a problem. For this type of leadership style to work, subordinates need to be mature and require little support at work.
- **Participating or supporting leadership** is where a leader and subordinates work on a problem together, supporting each other. In this situation subordinates are slightly less mature than when a leader delegates and so need more support.
- **Selling or coaching leadership** is where a leader persuades others of the benefits of an idea. Workers are likely to be only moderately mature and require a great deal of support.
- **Telling or directing leadership** is where a leader tells others what to do. Workers are fairly immature. They are told exactly what to do and little contact or support is needed.

The role of leadership in managing change

Leadership is vital in periods of change for businesses. For example, one of the key leadership issues facing growing businesses is how to deal with international markets and globalisation. Leaders may face challenges such as:

- international recruitment to overcome domestic staff shortages;
- cross-border mergers, acquisitions and joint ventures;
- the opening of new markets in Eastern Europe, South East Asia and China;
- European social policy directives, affecting business in member countries;
- developments in information and communications technology.

Earlier it was explained that leaders often have the ability to sense change and respond to it effectively. For example, an effective leader may be able to:

- predict a decline of sales in an important product due to changes in the market or the likelihood of a new production technique being available in the future;
- anticipate possible solutions to changes that may affect a business;
- have a clear vision of the main objectives of a business during periods of change and be able to guide the business to achieve these;
- organise and motivate employees to accept challenges;
- ensure stability and minimise or prevent disruption

There are various stages that leaders work through when managing change.

Preparing for change This involves laying the foundation or groundwork for any changes that may occur in the future. It includes building organisations that are better able to deal with change.

Early stages of implementing change Leaders also play an important role during change implementation. During this period the organisation is often at its most unstable. There may be confusion, fear, reduced productivity and lack of clarity about direction among staff. Employees may want to retain old ways and be unable to look to the future. During this period, leaders may need to:

- acknowledge the feelings and confusion of employees;
- work with employees to create a new vision of the altered workplace;
- help employees to understand the direction of the future.

Focusing only on feelings may not be enough. Leaders often need to initiate the movement into the new practices or situations. However, focusing only on the new vision may result in the perception that the leader is out of touch with the needs of employees. A key part of leadership is knowing when to focus on the difficulties that employees are experiencing, and when to focus on building and moving into the future.

CRITIQUE

The media often suggests that 'heroic' leaders are vital to making a successful business. Such leaders make things happen. They are heroes because they alone have the vision, personality and capability to bring things about in the business, either by themselves or through others. Although not denying that leaders have special qualities, it could be argued that focusing too much on leadership can create problems. For example, this approach may lead to the conclusion that a business without a heroic leader may not be able to function properly. Or it might suggest that the heroic leader is the most important thing to organisational effectiveness. It also perhaps devalues the role and importance of other employees.

There is evidence to suggest that effective businesses are those which are more concerned with the creativity of their products and organisational structures that enable those products to be produced and sold than those that rely heavily on leadership. It could be argued that the ability to teamwork, delegate and manage others effectively is more important in the daily workings of creative organisations than the attributes of heroic leadership, such as vision, command and personality.

Mainstream approaches to leadership also take consensus in organisations for granted, i.e. that employees are generally happy to be at work and that leadership is about providing them with the direction to get the most out of them. Where there is conflict, this is often seen as being related to problems with an individual or about resistance to change. The possibility that there might be underlying conflicts associated with inequalities of wealth, status or power between leaders and subordinates is not considered. Critics argue that although businesses may appear to be consensual, this is because leaders occupy positions in the hierarchy that enable them to suppress conflict or because subordinates have an understanding that compliance or consent is in their own 'best' interests. In other words, the absence of conflict is a consequence of dependence - subordinates depend on managers for terms and conditions, including retaining their jobs, promotion, future employment and references.

Later stages of implementing change Over time employees become less emotional, more stable and more open to new directions and ways of doing things. This can be a good time for leaders to introduce positive new changes, such as changing unwieldy procedures. Leaders during this stage need to offer hope that the business is working towards being better, by solving problems and improving the quality of work life. While the new vision of the business may have begun when people were struggling with change, this is the time for leaders to make sure that employees 'buy into it', and understand their roles in the changed business.

KNOWLEDGE

1. Explain the possible differences between a manager and a leader.
2. What are the characteristics or traits of leaders?
3. Explain the difference between autocratic and paternalistic leadership styles.
4. Explain the difference between democratic and laissez-faire leadership styles.
5. What are the implications for leadership of
(a) teamworking; (b) single status structures?

KEYTERMS

Autocratic leadership – a leadership style where the leader makes all decisions independently.
Democratic leadership – a leadership style where the leader encourages others to participate in decision making.
Laissez-faire leadership – a leadership style where employees are encouraged to make their own decisions, within limits.
Paternalistic leadership – a leadership style where the leader makes decisions, but takes into account the welfare of employees.
Single status organisation – a business where all employees have equal conditions.
Situational leadership – where a leader adopts a style that suits the situation being faced as a result of the competence and commitment of subordinates.

Case Study:

Martin Guntac owns a small chain of four car dealerships in the Yorkshire area. Part of the business is selling cars, both new and second hand. The other half provides servicing and repairs for customers. When he first started the business 30 years ago, he had two employees doing repair work from a run down garage in the back streets of Leeds. Today, he has over 100 employees spread across four premium sites. Each site has a manager, with a head of sales and a head of servicing and repairs underneath them.

Martin relies heavily on the four experienced site managers. They have day-to-day operational control of the business. He monitors their work and keeps a careful check on the performance of each site. Performance is checked both against previous periods and site to site. Martin is capable of making hard decisions. For example, five years ago he sacked one site manager who had been in the post for just 18 months when his site consistently underperformed compared with the other sites in the group.

This was a difficult decision, though, for Martin. He sees himself as a 'people person', and believes strongly in teamworking. Employees are encouraged to develop their own capabilities with a heavy emphasis on staff training and empowerment. Workers are encouraged to make decisions for themselves. Occasionally mistakes are made mainly because of a lack of guidance, but Martin believes firmly that this is an inevitable part of taking responsibility. A staff survey last year showed that over 90 per cent of staff felt 'motivated' at work.

Each week, he has a three hour meeting with the four site managers, his 'board of directors' as he likes to call them. Everything

to do with the running of the business is discussed at these meetings. Martin expects his site managers to be frank and there can be major differences of opinion about how to develop the business. Ultimately, he has to make the key decisions but he always consults with others to hear what they have to say.

(a) Discuss the most important factors to have influenced the choice of leadership style by Martin. (40 marks)
(b) Discuss whether the leadership style adopted by Martin is the most suitable for the business. (40 marks)

Organisational culture

Every place of work has a slightly different atmosphere. Some are busy, some are friendly, some are disorganised and some are shabby. This reflects the ORGANISATIONAL CULTURE (sometimes also called ORGANISATION CULTURE or CORPORATE CULTURE or BUSINESS CULTURE) of a business. Organisational culture is the values, attitudes, beliefs, meanings and norms that are shared by people and groups within an organisation.

Edgar Schein, a US writer, suggested in 1985 (*Organisational culture and leadership*) that organisational culture existed at three levels within a business. These three levels are shown in Figure 1.

Surface manifestations These are examples of organisation culture which can easily be seen by a wide range of stakeholders. They include:

- artifacts, such as furniture, clothes or tools – wearing a uniform would be an example;
- ceremonials, such as award giving ceremonies or the singing of the company song at the start of work;
- courses, such as induction courses, or ongoing training courses for workers used to instil organisational culture;
- heroes of the business, living or dead, such as Bill Gates, Richard Branson or Walt Disney, whose way of working provides a role model within the business;
- language used in a business specific way, such as Asda referring to its workers as 'colleagues' or McDonald's calling its workers 'crew members';
- mottoes, which are short statements which never change, expressing the values of an organisation such as John Lewis's motto 'Never knowingly undersold';
- slogans, which are short statements that can change over time, such as British Airways 'the worlds favourite airline';
- stories, which tell of some important event which exemplifies the values of the business;
- myths, which are frequently told stories within a business about itself but there is not necessarily any evidence that these stories are literally true;
- norms, which are the ways in which most workers behave, such as not worrying if you turn up for work late, always being prepared to cover for workers who are off sick, or thinking it is acceptable to use the company's telephone to make personal calls;
- physical layout of premises, such as open plan offices, 'hot desking', or allocating the size of an office according to a manager's place in the hierarchy;
- rituals, which are regular events that reinforce the culture of an organisation, such as always supporting Red Nose Day (we are a caring organisation), having a weekly 'dress down day' (we are a relaxed organisation), or holding an annual Christmas party (we are a sociable organisation);
- symbols, which are signs that represent the business, such as McDonald's 'Golden Arches', or the apple logo of Apple computers.

Surface manifestations are a constant reminder to stakeholders of the culture of an organisation. They are visible and frequently used to create and reinforce that culture. However, they are not the culture itself.

Organisational values Organisational values are located below the surface manifestations of organisational culture. They are consciously thought out and expressed in words and policies. The values expressed in a mission statement would be an example. Often these are the values which have come from the top of an organisation. Perhaps they have come from the original founder of the business. Or perhaps they have come from the current senior management which has attempted to impose a culture on the business. Organisational values might reflect the actual culture of a business. But, equally, they might not. Workers at the bottom of the hierarchy might have very different values from the ones that senior management want them to possess.

Basic assumptions Basic assumptions are the organisation's culture. They represent the totality of individuals' beliefs and how they then behave. They are 'invisible' and below the surface and therefore often difficult to see, understand and change.

In practice, there may be discrepancies between the three levels. For example, a company might organise regular social events for employees (a surface manifestation). It might say in documents that it is a 'friendly and caring employer' (its organisational values). Yet, throughout the organisation there might be a culture of competitiveness which tends to make

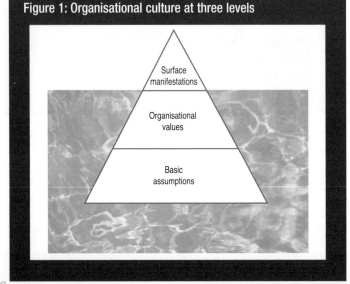

Figure 1: Organisational culture at three levels

- Surface manifestations
- Organisational values
- Basic assumptions

people 'look out for themselves' and makes everyone distrustful of everyone else. In this situation, the actual organisational culture is different from the surface manifestation and the organisational values. In contrast, another organisation might call its employees 'partners' (the surface manifestation). Its mission statement may say that it is committed to 'rewarding employees as well as shareholders' (its organisational values). It may then, year after year, pay employees above the average for the industry and give regular annual bonuses based upon how much profit the business has made during the year (the organisational culture). Here the underlying organisational culture fits with the stated values and the surface manifestation. There is a culture of rewarding employees because they are stakeholders.

Types of organisational culture

There are many ways of classifying organisational culture (i.e. grouping the organisational cultures of different businesses into categories and then describing the general characteristics of those cultures). One attempt to classify organisational culture was made by Charles Handy in *Understanding Organisations* (1981). He argued that there were four main types of organisational culture.

Power culture A power culture is one where there is a central source of power which is responsible for decision making. There are few rules and procedures within the business and these are overridden by the individuals who hold power when it suits them. There is a competitive atmosphere amongst employees. Amongst other things, they compete to gain power because this allows them to achieve their own objectives. This creates a political atmosphere within the business. Relatively young, small to medium sized businesses, where a single owner founded the firm and is still very much in control, could typically have power cultures.

Role culture In a role culture, decisions are made through well established rules and procedures. Power is associated with a role, such as marketing director or supervisor, rather than with individuals. In contrast to a power culture, power lies with the roles that individuals play rather than with the individuals themselves. Role cultures could be described as bureaucratic cultures. The Civil Service could be an example of a role culture.

Task culture In a task culture, power is given to those who can accomplish tasks. Power therefore lies with those with expertise rather than with a particular role, as in a role culture. In a task culture, teamworking is common, with teams made up of the experts needed to get a job done. Teams are created and then dissolved as the work changes. Adaptability and dynamism is important in this culture. Examples of task culture could be businesses which operate cellular manufacturing of components, teamworking in the manufacture of cars, scientific or medical project research operations or exploration of raw materials.

Question 1.

Dodgeville, Wisconsin USA, is home to the corporate headquarters of Lands' End, the mail order clothing company selling everything from shirts to swimwear. Founded in 1963, it came to the UK in the 1990s setting up in Oakham in Rutland. Just in case you were wondering about why there is an apostrophe at the end of 'Lands', when the first letterhead was produced, the printers put the apostrophe in the wrong place and the company couldn't afford to change it. The story says something about the genuineness of the company and its ability to own up to making mistakes.

Mindy Meads is president and chief executive officer. She is your typical corporate American executive, perfectly pleasant yet unable to see outside the tunnel vision of the company's culture. Asked to describe Lands' End, she replies 'If you were to sum up what Lands' End is for the apparel, it is very high quality, with the fabric we use, some of the workmanship that we put into the product.' Summing up the company ethos, she says: 'We have a very unique culture in our company; so customer driven. Everybody is working together to one goal: to get what the customer wants.'

To illustrate this, she talks about the customer, on the eve of her wedding, ringing and asking a Lands' End saleswoman to give her a 5 a.m. wake-up call. She was happy to oblige. Then there was a rogue batch of turtleneck sweaters. Lands' End voluntarily sent out 800,000 replacements to customers who had already bought the defective product. 'That was quite a bit of money', Mindy Meads conceded, insisting that the goodwill it engendered with customers made it worthwhile. She also talks about Lands'

End's stain resistant trousers, perfect for coping with hazardous spills. As the brochure puts it: 'The moment a rogue splash of coffee lands, you'll be thankful for the Teflon technology that causes liquids to simply bead up and roll off.'

On the Lands' End website, you can find 'The Lands' End Principles of Doing Business'. Included in the eight principles are phrases like 'we do everything we can to make our products better', 'we price our products fairly and honestly', 'we accept any return for any reason, at any time', 'we believe that what is best for our customer is best for all of us' and 'we encourage our customers to shop for our products in whatever way they find most convenient'.

Source: adapted from *The Times*, 6.3.2004.

(a) What (a) surface manifestations and (b) organisational values are described in the passage of Lands' End's organisational culture?

(b) If the surface manifestations and organisational values permeate the whole organisational culture, what sort of beliefs would you expect Lands' End's workers to have and how would you expect them to behave?

Question 2.

In 2005, there was a large explosion at the BP oil refinery in Texas City, Texas. Fifteen people were killed and 180 more were injured. A number of enquiries were launched, including one by the US Congress, the equivalent of the UK Parliament and one by BP itself.

Part of the blame for the accident was put by the BP enquiry on the company's global management culture. There was a lack of clear lines of responsibility within BP's refining business. BP managers routinely ignored standard procedures. Guidance from corporate headquarters was too often interpreted as orders and managers had a 'lack of respect for audit findings' that were too often not sent to the appropriate people. Within the refining group, the corporate culture suffered from a 'lack of corporate memory' and 'broken' performance management systems at the highest levels. 'Incompetent' workers were allowed to remain in their posts and 'mavericks' who ignored standard procedures were tolerated, it added.

The congressional investigation suggested, however, that BP managers may have deliberately underspent on maintenance in an effort to meet corporate cost cutting goals. This followed deep cost cutting ordered by BP headquarters after it had acquired the refinery in a merger.

Source: adapted from news.bbc.co.uk, 1.11.2006.

(a) BP puts safety above profit. Explain, however, why organisational culture might have led to the Texas disaster.
(b) Evaluate how BP's organisational culture needs to change to prevent a repetition of the Texas accident.
(c) What might be the obstacles to changing BP's organisational culture?

Person culture A person culture is one where there is a number of individuals in the business who have expertise but who don't necessarily work together particularly closely. The purpose of the organisation is to support those individuals. Examples of person cultures could be firms of accountants, lawyers, doctors or architects.

Changing organisational culture

Some writers, such as Tom Peters and Robert Waterman in *In Search of Excellence* (1982) have claimed that organisational culture can give a business a competitive advantage. Companies such as Microsoft, McDonald's or Virgin have been successful because they had an appropriate organisational culture for their industry. When the organisational culture is not right, then the organisation is likely to suffer from a competitive disadvantage.

For example, in the 1970s and 1980s, Japanese motor manufacturers gained a competitive advantage over their US and European rivals through the introduction of lean manufacturing techniques. Part of this was an attention to quality. Poor quality work became unacceptable within the Japanese car industry. The business used the slogan 'zero defects'. The values were expressed in the work procedures of car plants. But underlying all this was

an understanding amongst workers that quality standards had to be met all the time. Quality was put above maximising output. In contrast, US and European manufacturers at the time paid lip service to quality but on the factory floor, poor quality workmanship was a daily fact of life. In the 1990s, US and European car manufacturers copied Japanese lean production techniques simply to survive. Part of that was completely changing the attitudes of workers to quality. Through training and changing the way in which employees worked, quality has improved enormously.

Changing business culture can, however, be difficult. The CULTURE GAP, the difference between the current culture and the culture that is desired by certain stakeholders such as senior management, can be very large. There is a variety of obstacles which need to be overcome if culture is to change.

Workers' and managers' views Both management and workers can be resistant to change. Many will have worked within the business for a long time. They will be used to certain ways of working. Change can threaten this. Change may also threaten their jobs or pay. One way of dealing with such problems is to work with managers and workers to change their attitudes and beliefs. Careful and sensitive implementation of change over a period of time can lead to a change in culture. For example, training can be used to explain why change is needed and how it is to be implemented. Equally, where there are performance-related pay systems, increases in pay or bonuses can be linked to changes in work methods and work attitudes. A more radical method is to make managers and workers redundant who resist change. Or they might be redeployed to jobs where they cannot influence the changes taking place. In extreme cases, businesses have been known to close a whole site and move the work elsewhere. In the UK motor industry, for example, some car plants have been told that unless they make the changes to lean production techniques, they would be closed. Sacking workers is more likely to take place where there is some urgency to change the culture. For example, if managers at a factory are told that they must raise productivity by 40 per cent over the next twelve months or risk closure, this can lead to very rapid change.

Technology and the physical environment Culture can often be maintained and promoted by the physical environment in which the business operates. An office building made up of small rooms will not promote open communication between staff. A production line where workers are stationed in isolation along the line, performing repetitive tasks, is unlikely to promote responsibility and quality assurance. Changing culture often means changing the physical environment in which workers operate. Building a new facility and hiring mostly new workers presents a real opportunity to completely change organisational culture. Few businesses, however, can do this. Instead, they have to make a large number of small changes, such as buying new equipment or moving the office furniture around, to create a change in culture. The inability to make a completely new start means that changes in culture can take a long time. It also explains why some new businesses can be so successful at winning market share from older more established businesses.

The external environment Sometimes it is the external environment which is the obstacle to changing organisational culture. For example, health and safety legislation or employment law might limit the ability of businesses to encourage a new culture within the business. A lack of competition in the market might reinforce a culture of complacency and no change. There were significant changes in those industries that were privatised and opened up to competition in the UK in the 1980s and 1990s. National and regional cultures can also have an important impact on organisational cultures. It can be argued that French companies have different organisational cultures to Japanese or US companies. Trying to make a business more entrepreneurial, for example, might be easier in the USA with its strong focus on individualism than in a country with a strong focus on collectivism.

KEYTERMS

Culture gap – the difference between the current culture and the culture that is desired by certain stakeholders such as senior management.
Organisational or organisation or corporate or business culture – the values, attitudes, beliefs, meanings and norms that are shared by people and groups within an organisation.

KNOWLEDGE

1. Explain the difference between surface manifestations, organisational values and basic assumptions of corporate culture.
2. Explain the differences between a power culture, a role culture, a task culture and a person culture.
3. How can organisational culture give businesses a competitive advantage?
4. How can a culture gap hold back a business?

Case Study:

Brian Strode was appointed Chief Executive of Radigan's two years ago. Radigan's is a medium-sized engineering company with 750 employees. Once, the company was much larger, with at its peak some 5,000 employees spread over three sites. Today, the company is based on one site reflecting the need to concentrate resources to gain competitive advantage.

When Brian Strode came into the company, he could see that it faced massive problems. Previous management had underinvested in every part of the business. Equipment was old, products were not at the cutting edge in the field and training of staff was non-existent. It was not surprising that Radigan's was struggling to maintain sales.

When talking to workers and managers about change, most seemed to think that the attitudes of other staff could not be changed. They put forward a variety of reasons why change was almost impossible. Some pointed to the main trade union representing shop floor workers as a major obstacle. They said it would resist any changes in the conditions of service of employees. Others said that staff were too set in their ways to change. They had always done the job like this and it would be impossible to get them to do it a different way. Half the workforce, including most of the managers, were over the age of 45 and there were only two employees under the age of 25. Another problem often cited was the strong division of workers into separate informal groups with distinct identities. Typically, there would be around 10-15 people in a group who took their breaks together, socialised informally together at work and formed friendship patterns outside the workplace. Each group built up a 'them and us' mentality. Each thought it was doing the hardest work in the company whilst other groups were contributing little or nothing to the organisation. Workers on the shop floor saw managers as 'pen pushers' who knew nothing about the 'real' work of the company that they were doing in making products. Managers saw shop floor workers as lazy and inflexible, always ready to find an excuse why something couldn't be done. Overall, most workers were highly cynical about the contribution that other workers made to the company. Equally, most workers and many managers had little idea of the competitive pressures that the company was now facing, particularly from Far Eastern imports.

Looking through the paperwork, Brian Strode could find little that was written down that could inspire change. The company had no mission statement. There was nothing coherent about a vision for the future. Most of what was there seemed to be about reacting to events rather than shaping them. He was surprised that there didn't seem to be much that even supported the very conservative nature of the company.

Looking round the site, Brian observed that everything was very boxed in. The very walls of the factory and offices seemed to emphasis the small group mentality of the workforce. Office staff, for example, were all working in small cramped offices, mostly on their own. Amongst the office staff, there were a lot of posters and stickers on walls or mugs with little work slogans like 'I'm the boss', 'Overworked and underpaid', 'The buck doesn't stop here - keep going' and "Hard work never killed anyone, but why chance it?'. By 5.30 each evening, the place was deserted. Shop floor workers, office staff and most managers worked to the clock. The minute they were due to leave, they were out like a shot.

Brian set about trying to change the culture of the business. It had to be more responsive to the needs of customers. Costs had to be reduced to maintain sales. Quality needed to be considerably improved. To achieve this, he wanted to see a more flexible and far better trained workforce, probably working in teams and whose goals were aligned to those of the company.

(a) Discuss whether 'working to the clock' was the most important part of the company's culture which Brian Strode needed to change. (40 marks)

(b) Evaluate whether creating a task culture within the organisation could lead to the company achieving its long-term goals. (40 marks)

Types of decision

All businesses have to make decisions. The type of decision will vary depending on its nature and the effect on the business.

Routine, low level decisions These have to be made on a day-to-day or week-to-week basis. Examples include which workers will work which shift or what stationery will be ordered for the next month by an office. Routine decisions will be made by all levels of workers within a business.

Operational decisions These are likely to be non-routine low level decisions. Examples include whether to call out a maintenance engineer immediately to fix a broken machine or wait until the regular weekly visit from the engineer, or whether to increase staffing on a particular production line to cope with higher than expected orders. Like routine decisions, operational decisions are likely to be made by all levels of workers within a business. However, the more hierarchical and centralised the organisation, the more likely it is that operational decisions will be made at a more senior level, and the less likely it is that workers at the bottom of the chain of command will have scope to make such decisions.

Tactical decisions These are medium-term decisions made by middle or senior management. They address specific issues and problems. For example, a business may have to decide whether to produce a new colour for its range of dishwashers or whether to increase spending on promotion for its dishwasher range.

Strategic decisions These are long-term decisions about the direction of the whole business. They are made by senior management and directors. For example, should the business turn away from its traditional UK suppliers to buy from cheaper suppliers in the Third World? Should the business diversify away from its current core range of products?

The higher the level of DECISION MAKING, the greater the impact on the business if the wrong decision is taken. Strategic decisions are far riskier to the long term survival of the business than operational decisions. For example, Marconi's strategic decision in the 1990s to sell most of its traditional manufacturing subsidiaries and concentrate on the manufacture of IT and telecommunications equipment almost bankrupted

Karen Hooton owns and runs an engineering company employing 150 people. Over the past 12 months, she has been hard hit by a doubling in the price of steel, a crucial raw material for the company. What's more, she has often been unable to buy steel because it is in short supply. The steel crisis has been caused by a significant increase in demand for steel by Chinese industry. The steel crisis couldn't have come at a worse time for the company. Two years ago, Karen made the decision to

expand capacity by moving into larger premises, taking on more workers and investing £900,000 in new equipment. The business is now being forced to run at less than full capacity.

On a day to day basis, the steel shortage is having a considerable impact on how the business is run. Yesterday, for example, Karen had to decide which order to make up because she didn't have enough stocks of the right sort of steel for the two orders she had in hand. That meant that one customer would be receiving its order late. The weekly rostering of staff is also having to be adjusted on a day-to-day basis. Karen hopes to be able to get supplies of steel for the second order tomorrow. Staff will then be taken off other jobs to make the order. Her workers don't like having their rosters changed at the last minute and sometimes this can cause bad feeling.

In the short term, Karen is trying to push up her prices to cover the extra cost of the steel. But she is having difficulty passing on the higher costs. Customers are threatening to take their business elsewhere and Karen knows that her competitors are sometimes winning orders because they aren't putting up their prices. These are difficult times for Karen Hooton and she expects her profits this year to fall substantially.

(a) By using examples from the passage, explain what is meant by (i) routine decisions; (ii) operational decisions; (iii) tactical decisions; (d) strategic decisions.

(b) Discuss what sort of information Karen Hooton would have collected before making her decision to invest £900,000 in new equipment.

(c) The business in 'now running at less than full capacity'. Discuss whether this was the result of poor decision making by Karen Hooton.

the company when the new technology bubble burst at the end of that decade. Microsoft's strategic decision to bundle its Explorer Internet browser with its Windows operating system has helped Windows maintain a 90 per cent share of the computer operating system market and has generated large profits. Virgin has made strategic decisions to move into air and rail transport and financial markets which are unrelated to its previous operations in music and the media. This has helped the organisation to grow and helped to establish a well known corporate brand.

In contrast, an operational decision which led to too many paper clips being ordered for a company in the month of March is unlikely to have much impact on its performance in the long term.

Information management

Successful decision making relies upon good information. Poor information or a lack of information is likely to lead to poor decision making. For example, launching a product into a market without any information about whether there is a need for the product is highly risky. Putting a price on a product without any understanding of how much it costs to make could lead to losses. Firing a worker without knowing the requirements of employment law could lead to a business being taken to an industrial tribunal. Managing the flow of information into the business is therefore crucial to the success of a business.

Businesses have a variety of sources of information which include the following.

- Financial information comes from the day-to-day accounts of the business. Cash flowing into and out of the business can be analysed. Accounting software packages available to even the smallest business will calculate a range of financial indicators such as profit margins and stock turnover levels. Large companies will have finance directors part of whose job is to organise the collecting of relevant information.
- Marketing information partly comes from within the business. Data about sales, prices and changes in volumes following marketing campaigns is all available. Marketing information is also available outside of the business. For example, market research may give relevant information for decision making.
- Production information comes from within the production department, such as production times, stock levels, costs and employment levels. Outside the business, information is available from suppliers, equipment manufacturers and trade journals. Techniques such as benchmarking rely upon information from outside the business.

Management approaches to decision making

Decisions are made in a variety of different ways. In smaller businesses, all types of decision are often made quickly and informally. Owners and managers have a good understanding of

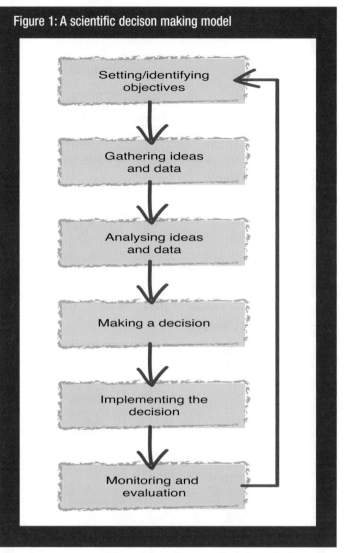

Figure 1: A scientific decison making model

- Setting/identifying objectives
- Gathering ideas and data
- Analysing ideas and data
- Making a decision
- Implementing the decision
- Monitoring and evaluation

what they want to achieve. They then use their knowledge and experience to make decisions. Decision making is often INTUITIVE. Even in large companies, where there is a strong entrepreneurial culture, intuition can play a large role in decision making at the highest level. However, complex decisions will be based on a significant amount of data having been gathered, processed and synthesised. Information management is vital even when decision making seems to be intuitive and informal.

However, the more complex the decision, the more data is likely to be available. There then needs to be more complex ways to analyse and interpret this data. This is reason why SCIENTIFIC DECISION MAKING methods are used by business. Figure 1 shows such a model. It is based upon six stages.

Setting or identifying objectives First, decision makers have to understand what they are aiming to achieve. Objectives might already have been set, such as to purchase the best machine for less than £100,000, or to launch a new product which will gain at least 2 per cent of the market. Or decision makers might have to set their own specific objectives in the context of wider

Figure 2: Examples of models used in decision making

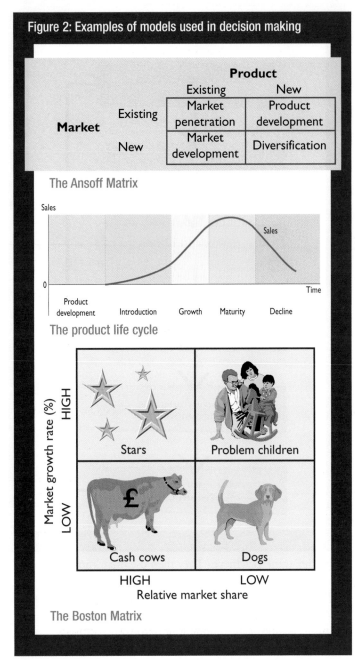

		Product	
		Existing	New
Market	Existing	Market penetration	Product development
	New	Market development	Diversification

The Ansoff Matrix

The product life cycle

The Boston Matrix

objectives. For example, a business might have an objective of increasing profit by 10 per cent per year. The manager of a particular factory within the company might then decide that the objective of the factory will be to cut its costs by 10 per cent a year.

Gathering ideas and data Decision making should be based on evidence. So decision makers need to gather ideas and data relating to the decision. This can be quite a chaotic process spread over a period of time. It will become apparent that some data is impossible to obtain. Some initial ideas might prove to be a dead end, whilst others, generated late in the whole process, might prove to be the most valuable.

Analysing ideas and data Ideas and data need to be brought together and analysed. Several possible courses of action may

emerge with advantages and disadvantages for each one. SWOT analysis or PEST-G analysis might be used at this stage. Some outcomes may be quantifiable (i.e. measurable in numbers) in terms such as output, raw material inputs or cash. Other outcomes may prove unquantifiable, such as consumer satisfaction or staff morale.

Making a decision The culmination of thought and research will be the decision making itself. There is a variety of ways in which this can be done. It might be an individual person who makes the final decision. It could be a committee which recommends a decision to a higher committee such as the board of directors of a company. A provisional decision might be made and then that is put out to consultation before a final decision is made. A decision might be postponed if it is not vital to make the decision immediately.

Implementing the decision The decision then needs to be implemented. This can take place immediately or might be a long-term decision where a course of action takes years to implement.

Monitoring and evaluation Once the decision has been made, the outcome of the decision should be monitored and evaluated. Some decisions can be reversed quickly if the outcome is unsatisfactory. For example, a shop may decide to stock a new line of frozen ready meals. If sales are not satisfactory within the first month, it can quickly and easily cease to stock the line. Other decisions are likely to be irreversible. For example, the decision to build the Channel Tunnel proved to be a commercial disaster for Eurotunnel, the company which now owns and runs it.

A business may also choose to use models such as the Ansoff Matrix, the product life cycle model or the Boston Matrix shown in Figure 2. The advantage of using these models is that they provide a way of seeing a problem from a particular perspective. Any model is an abstraction from reality. It is never 100 per cent realistic because if it were it would be as complex to use as real life. However, models such as the Ansoff Matrix can be a powerful tool in focusing on a particular issue because they simplify issues and are easily understood.

Another decision making model is a DECISION TREE. This shows different alternatives, placing a value on each of these alternatives. An example of a decision tree is shown in Figure 3. A business has two alternatives: either invest in new machinary or not invest in new machinery. If the business makes the investment, what will be the profit or loss depending on how much the new machinery is used? If there is high utilisation of the machinary, the profit will be £5 million. But even if there is low utilisation, the profit will be £1 million. The alternative, which is not to make the investment, has worse outcomes. Decision trees used in practice are likely to be more complex. For example, probabilities of outcomes occurring can be estimated and then used to calculate values for particular decisions.

Figure 3: A decision tree showing the alternative to investing in new machinery

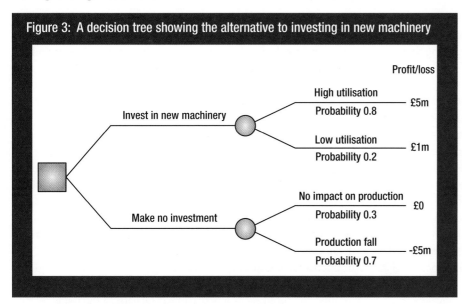

Profit/loss

Invest in new machinery

High utilisation
Probability 0.8 — £5m

Low utilisation
Probability 0.2 — £1m

Make no investment

No impact on production
Probability 0.3 — £0

Production fall
Probability 0.7 — -£5m

Decision trees illustrate both the advantages and disadvantages of using scientific methods of decision making compared with more intuitive methods. On the one hand, quantitative decision making gives numbers and facts as outcomes. So, when a business has to decide whether or not to buy a new machine, a decision tree can show the potential profits and losses and how these would change depending upon particular assumptions. On the other hand, the 'facts' that come out of scientific decision making models are only as accurate as the data that is put into the model and the validity of the model. It is often difficult to provide perfectly reliable data to make the calculations. Estimates of sales, for example, in 12 months' time are most unlikely to be correct. Equally, models may not take into account external variables which make their assumptions invalid.

Scientific decision making methods and models are therefore likely to be used alongside more intuitive, qualitative decision making methods. It should also be remembered that, in business, luck and chance play an important part in determining success. However good the decision making model, events can knock a business off course.

Influences on corporate decision making

It is easy to assume that decision making at the top of a large company is rational and scientific. In practice, decision making is influenced by many factors. One is the relative influence of the different stakeholders in a business. Decision making in a large business is a highly complex process where different stakeholders may be able to exert considerable power to pursue their own objectives.

Senior management Senior management have power over the day-to-day running of the business. In one sense, they have the most influence on the direction of the business. In recent years, there has been growing controversy about the pay of senior management and directors of large companies. Their pay and bonuses have been increasing much faster on average than the pay of workers. Directors and senior managers tend to argue that market forces are pushing up their earnings. They deserve

Question 2.

major financial outlay for the company. As part of its decision making process, the finance director has drawn up a decision tree showing the expected values of the two alternatives, to invest or not to invest. He has estimated probabilities as well as factoring in the initial cost. The finance director has used this quantitative model in the context of a much wider report which also takes into account qualitative factors.

Decision tree analysis shows clearly that the investment should go ahead. The expected value of making the investment is 30 per cent higher than not making it. Qualitative factors would also point toward making the investment. To survive competition from low cost producers in the Far East, Beville Tools has to retain an edge in terms of quality of product and speed of delivery. The investment will help it lower its own costs whilst improving quality and speed of production. The main argument against the investment is whether demand from motor manufacturers will continue to be strong. A recession in the economy with a downturn in car sales could make all the financial calculations a nonsense and make the investment unprofitable.

Beville Tools is a specialist toolmaker serving top brand customers in the automotive industry. It is considering whether to buy an £800,000 compression moulding machine. The investment would represent a

(a) Using examples from the passage, explain the difference between quantitative and qualitative decision making methods.
(b) To what extent should Beville Tools rely on quantitative decision making methods in its decision as to whether it will buy the compression moulding machine?

large remuneration packages because of their contribution to the success of a business. Others argue that directors and senior managers control what they earn. So its not surprising that their pay is rising faster than those of workers.

Owners When owners or shareholders do not control the day-to-day running of the business, they can lose control of it. There is a danger that the business is then run in the interests of the directors and senior managers who do control the day-to-day running of the business. In the UK, shareholders have a variety of ways of influencing the people they appoint to run the company on their behalf. One is simply to sell their shares. For a public limited company, a constant stream of selling will lower the share price. This will make the company more vulnerable to being bought out by another company through a takeover bid. If this happens, typically most of the senior management will be forced to leave. Senior managers also know that bad publicity and criticism at Annual General Meetings make their jobs vulnerable. Too much bad publicity and criticism tends to see the Chief Executive resign. In public limited companies, the appointment of non-executive directors is also meant to control the power of the executive directors or senior managers. They are appointed, like executive directors, at the Annual General Meeting to serve the interests of the shareholders. However, it is often argued that shareholders have too little power in the UK and managers too much power. The threat of takeover or public censure is unlikely. Non-executive directors are too often uncritical of senior management.

Employees Employees can exert pressure on a business in two main ways. One is by resigning and leaving the business. A business with high staff turnover compared to its competitors is likely to see its costs rise and efficiency reduced. Many businesses therefore recognise they have to take the interests of their workers into account when making decisions. A second way in which workers can exert pressure is through pressure from their representatives such as trade unions. Bargaining backed up the threat of industrial action can help promote the interests of workers. Only a minority of workers are represented by trade unions today. Not surprisingly, many businesses prefer their workers not to be unionised.

Customers Customers have real power over a business because they can refuse to buy its products. However, large businesses attempt to counteract this power by using marketing. Advertising, for example, is the deliberate use by a business to alter favourably the perceptions of customers towards its products. Some businesses don't need to worry too much about customers because they are monopolists. When one firm supplies all the market, customers have no alternative but to buy its products. This power is why governments tend to regulate monopolies.

Suppliers Suppliers might seem to have no power over a business. After all, suppliers need customers. However,

suppliers can refuse to supply to a business. If the supplier doesn't like the terms of a contract, for example, it can walk away from a deal. A number of companies refuse to supply the large UK supermarket chains like Tesco. Some do so because the supermarket chains want suppliers to sell at too low a price. Others refuse because they don't want to see their upmarket brands sold in a supermarket.

The community and government The community mainly exercises its control over businesses through laws and regulations. Organisations representing businesses like the CBI tend to lobby against further laws and regulations which restrict the ability of businesses to act as they wish. The law is therefore a very powerful way in which the community as a whole influences how businesses behave. However, communities sometimes can influence businesses through campaigns. The best way to do this is often through the media. A group of local residents might oppose the building of a new runway by getting the issue constantly aired in newspapers, on radio and on television. But staging demonstrations might be another tactic used.

Environmental groups Very few businesses will be directly affected by groups such as environmental pressure groups. Very large companies, however, can expect to be lobbied directly and indirectly. Oil companies, for example, are constantly being challenged by environmental groups concerned about their activities. Because of the potential bad publicity, businesses have to take their considerations into account when making decisions.

Another way of considering the influence on corporate decision-making is to look at the constraints under which a business operates. Figure 4 shows some of these constraints and influences.

- Resources are one influence. A local petrol station business has fewer resources than a major oil company. This restricts the activities of the local petrol station. In recent years, many large companies have focused their activities on their **core businesses** or **competences**. These are businesses or activities where they are most successful and where they have a proven expertise. Having better resources than competing businesses is key to earning higher sales and profits.
- The legal environment is a major influence on corporate decision making. Businesses have to stay within the law or risk prosecution and being sued. At worst, companies in the past have gone out of business because of the after-effects of their having broken the law.
- Businesses have to stay within the law but they have no obligation to act ethically. Nevertheless, many businesses feel constrained to act in an ethical manner. Some exploit their ethical positions for marketing or motivational purposes. Others act ethically despite the fact that it gives them no advantage.
- The social environment influences decision making. Some changes can easily be measured such as changes in the

structure of the population. Others are less quantifiable. The changing role of women in society over the past 50 years has had a significant impact on business decision-making but the changes are more difficult to measure.

- The economic environment influences what decisions are made. For example, different decisions might be made depending on whether the economy is in a boom or in a recession, or whether the business operates in a market with few competitors or a market with many competitors.

- Sometimes the political environment will intrude on business decision-making. Some large companies, such as those supplying water, electricity or rail services, are particularly vulnerable to political influence. For example, water, electricity or gas companies can come under political criticism for poor service levels, too high prices or too large profits. These companies therefore need to take account of political concerns about their activities.

The quality of decisions

If the right decisions are made the business will benefit. The quality of decisions depends on a number of factors.

Training If people are trained, their performance is likely to be better. The people making important decisions in a business should receive training. Courses are offered by business schools and other educational institutions which concentrate on decision making.

Quantity and quality information Decision making will be improved if there is access to information. For example, if a firm is thinking of a price increase, the more information it has on the reactions of customers, the more likely it is to decide whether this is the right course of action. Information technology in business has helped decision makers a great deal. They are able to store more information, retrieve it instantly and change it into a form which is more useful to them.

Inadequate and inaccurate information can lead to the wrong decision being made and may cause serious problems. For example, when an insurance company is setting premiums for motor insurance, if the estimate of the cost of repairing cars is too low then premiums will be set too low. It is also argued that the use of quantitative information helps to improve the quality of the decision.

Ability to use decision making techniques The ability to use decision making techniques will help accurate decisions to be made. For example, one technique used to evaluate the likely returns from choosing a particular course of action is the use of decision trees.

Risk Some decisions involve considerable risk, such as the launching of a new product. It is argued that UK managers are too cautious in their approach to decision making. This is because they prefer to choose courses of action which carry the

Figure 4: Influences on corporate decision making

lowest risk, and avoid taking riskier courses of action which might result in higher profits.

Human element Most decisions are made by people. Different people are likely to make different decisions. How do people differ?

- The level of experience might be different. More experienced decision makers will often, but not always, make much more accurate decisions.

- The attitude to risk may differ. Cautious decision makers will choose different courses of action to 'risk takers'.

- People have different capabilities. Those who are skilled at decision making will enjoy better results than those whose judgements are poor.

- Self-interest may affect the course of action chosen. For example, management and trade unions are likely to reach different conclusions when setting wage levels for the workforce.

- People often have different perceptions. This may influence the decisions they make. For example, two people on an interview panel for a new recruit may have different views of an interviewee's performance.

KEYTERMS

Decision making – choosing between alternative courses of action

Decision tree – a method of decision making where alternative courses of action are stated, their costs and benefits calculated and probability attached to outcomes so that the optimal decision can be taken.

Intuitive decision-making – where decisions are made based on gut reactions, feelings or intuition rather than using formal models or procedures.

Scientific decision making – choosing between alternative courses of action based upon models, procedures and information.

KNOWLEDGE

1. Compare routine decision making with strategic decision making.
2. Why is information management important for decision making?
3. What financial information does a business have which can help it in its decision making?
4. What is the difference between intuitive decision making and scientific decision making?
5. 'Decision trees assess different possible outcomes from a variety of alternatives.' Explain this statement.
6. 'Ultimately it is customers which have the most important influence on how a business is run.' Explain in what ways this might be correct.
7. Explain how (a) attitudes to risk and (b) the training of senior management can affect corporate strategic decision making.

Case Study: Brent Spar

The Brent Spar shot to public attention in 1995. It was an oil storage and tanker loading buoy in the North Sea, 147 metres high and 29 metres in diameter, displacing 66,000 tonnes of water. Owned by Shell UK, it had ceased to be of economic use following the completion of an oil pipeline from the Brent oil field to an oil terminal in the Shetlands in 1991.

Shell management, after weighing up the options, decided that the Brent Spar needed to be removed and disposed of in a location where it would be no danger to shipping. It was decided to tow it out to the North Atlantic and sink it in British territorial waters to the west of Scotland. Shell conducted an extensive survey of the environmental impact of a sinking of the platform on its chosen site. It concluded that whilst there would be some environmental impact, it would be small and short term. It received approval from the British government for the disposal plan in December 1994.

The environmental group, Greenpeace, had long campaigned against the dumping of waste in ocean waters. When they found out about the plans in February 1995, they immediately made objections. They were concerned about the environmental impact and were worried that this disposal would set a precedent. The Brent Spar was just one of many North Sea oil structures which would eventually have to be removed. If the Brent Spar was sunk at at sea, this would give the green light for other installations to be disposed of in the same way. They accused Shell of adopting the cheapest solution to disposal.

In April 1995, Greenpeace activists occupied the Brent Spar. They conducted tests on the amount of oil and other contaminants left in the installation and claimed that there were 5,500 tonnes of oil present. Shell said that there was only 50 tonnes. From this point, Greenpeace mounted a highly successful media campaign against Shell, arguing that the Brent Spar should be dismantled on land, a much higher cost solution for Shell.

Over the following months, the Brent Spar was continually in the headlines. Shell evicted the protesters from the Brent Spar in late May and had towed the platform to its disposal position by 11 June. In the meantime, however, the German government had issued a formal objection to the British government about the dumping plan. A consumer boycott of Shell petrol was gathering pace in Germany and Shell staff received threats. Sales of petrol at Shell service stations were falling in Northern Europe. Not surprisingly, the share price of Shell began to drop.

On June 20, despite continued and active support from the British government for the original solution, Shell announced that it was abandoning plans for sinking the platform. It said: 'Shell's position as a major European enterprise has become untenable. The Spar had gained a symbolic significance out of all proportion to its environmental impact. In consequence, Shell companies were faced with increasingly intense public criticism, mostly in Continental northern Europe. Many politicians and ministers were openly hostile and several called for consumer boycotts. There was violence against Shell service stations, accompanied by threats to Shell staff.'

Eventually, the Brent Spar was broken up and part of it was used to build a quay extension at the Norwegian port of Mekjarvik. The eventual cost to Shell of the disposal was £43 million. On top of that, Shell had lost sales and profits due to the boycott. Shell also suffered damage to its reputation. However, Greenpeace also suffered criticism. The amount of oil and other contaminants on the Brent Spar were roughly in line with Shell's initial estimates. Greenpeace's initial estimates were gross overestimated. There remains controversy about whether the overall environmental damage caused was greater from the final disposal on land than it would have been had the Brent Spar been disposed of at sea.

Source: adapted from en.wikipedia.org; news.bbc.co.uk.

(a) Evaluate the relative power of stakeholders in Shell during the Brent Spar incident. (40 marks)

(b) To what extent would a more intuitive approach to decision making have helped Shell management avoid what actually happened in 1995? (40 marks)

What causes change in business?

Businesses today have to operate in rapidly changing markets and conditions. They can no longer rely on a constant stream of customers, the same production process or the same product over a long period of time. They must constantly be aware of, and be prepared to respond to, changes in a number of areas.

Developments in technology The introduction of new technology can affect a business in many ways. There have, for example, been rapid changes in communications technology, production techniques and electronic components in recent years.

Market changes Businesses must respond to changes in the markets in which they sell. There may be competition from new businesses. This has been the case in the energy supply market. Former public sector owned gas and electricity suppliers were privatised and markets opened up to competition. New markets have opened up, such as the mobile phone market for companies such as BT. Competition may also come from new businesses entering a market, such as the offering of financial services by supermarkets. Other factors such as the Single European Market, globalisation, the opening up of markets in eastern Europe and China, the introduction of the euro and the expansion of the EU in 2004 were all likely to change how businesses operate.

Consumer tastes Businesses must also be prepared for changes in the tastes of consumers. Examples might be the purchase of environmentally friendly products, the desire for greater knowledge about products or the need for more efficient methods of shopping, such as purchasing via the Internet.

Legislation Government legislation can force changes in business activity. Taxation of pollution would affect the production methods of many firms. Safety standards, such as EU regulations for VDU users, are also likely to affect how employees operate. Government aid or subsidies may affect the possible location of a business. Legislation on the number of hours employees can work may change work practices.

Changes in the workforce Population changes will affect the age and make-up of the workforce. The ageing of the population in the UK in the early part of the twenty first century was likely to result in changing recruitment policies for businesses. A falling population is also likely to change how a business plans its human resources.

Changes in the economy It is argued that economies go through periods of boom and slump, recession and recovery. This is known as the business cycle. Income, spending, saving, investment and economic variables such as unemployment and inflation are all likely to be different at different stages in the cycle.

The effects of change

The changes illustrated in the last section can have a number of effects on business.

- Product life cycles could become shorter. This means that businesses must constantly be looking to develop new and profitable products or services.
- The role of market research is likely to increase. A business must not be 'surprised' by sudden changes in the market. Research and forecasting techniques should help a firm to predict more accurately the situation in future.
- Research and development will be essential in industries where rapid change is taking place. As well as anticipating market changes, a business must be prepared to respond to the needs of the market with new products, which can compete with those of competitors.
- Retraining of managers and 'shop floor' workers might be necessary. This may be to learn skills associated with new technology or to develop skills to meet changing consumer tastes. Examples may be the education of office staff in communications technology, such as e-mail or videoconferencing or the learning of foreign languages by UK business people wishing to enter foreign markets.
- Businesses must take account of changes in their human resource planning. This could mean employing a more flexible workforce that could be changed quickly to meet the needs of the business, for example employing part time workers, or the use of job sharing. It might also mean employing workers in low cost countries, such as in call centres abroad.
- A business must develop a culture and organisation which is prepared to respond to change.
- Businesses must be aware of competitors' actions and be prepared to react to them. Businesses now benchmark their activities against those of rivals or other companies. Business must also be able to respond to new and emerging markets. These might be new markets abroad or markets for new products within a country.
- Quality is likely to become more important as consumer awareness develops and competition increases. Firms must consider the quality of their products and also their after sales service and customer relations. For example, many businesses have tried to achieve the international BS EN IS0 9000 quality standard.
- Changes in equipment. Rapid change often makes equipment redundant. Businesses may find problems from the inability to read computer disks because software has

been updated to the need for new systems to cope with just-in-time requests. These changes could involve a large amount of spending if businesses do not wish to become outdated.

- Changes in production methods. Rapid changes can sometimes lead to increasing costs. Some businesses have reacted by outsourcing their production to low cost countries. Others have changed the technology they use to reduce costs.

Why manage change?

The management of change in business has grown in importance in recent years. Under pressure from competitors, higher costs and economic conditions, many firms in the UK developed company-wide change programmes.

There are some examples of firms that have made only minor changes to their business operations and remained successful. The Morgan Car Company still retains many of the original production methods and design features that have been part of its operation since the 1930s. It argues that it is exactly these 'original' features that attract consumers. However, most businesses that refuse to change will eventually go out of business.

Resistance to change

Businesses are likely to face some resistance to change from parts of the workforce for a number of reasons.

- Workers and certain levels of management sometimes fear the unknown. They feel safe with work practices, conditions and relationships that they have been used to

for a period of time.
- Employees and managers may fear that they will be unable to carry out new tasks, may become unemployed or may face a fall in earnings.
- Individual workers might be concerned that they will no longer work with 'friends', or may be moved to a job which they dislike.

If change is to be carried out effectively, the business must make certain that these fears are taken into account. Only if employees feel they can cope with change, will the business be operating to its potential.

Owners of businesses may also be resistant to change for similar reasons. They might fear operating in unknown markets and conditions. They might not want the cost of any changes. They may also fear that they might not be able to adjust to new situations and be forced out of business.

Resistance may also be found in the **culture** of the organisation. Custom and practice are embedded in systems which reflect the norms, values and beliefs of the organisation. While this may give stability, it presents problems of rigidity when a business needs to change.

Customers and **suppliers** too may resist change. They may be unwilling to change their own practices when the business they are dealing with changes. For example, a company may reorganise its sales force and decide that it will no longer visit clients which give it less than £5 000 worth of orders per year. Instead, it will develop a website and telesales operation to deal with small customers. Inevitably, it will lose some customers which are not prepared to place orders in this way.

In order to deal with resistance to change, many theorists have suggested the need for a multi-step approach. Psychologist

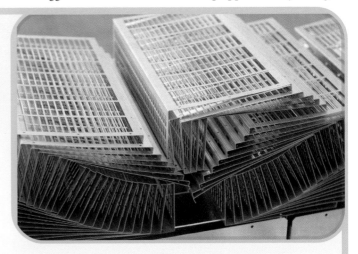

Question 1.

Eversholt Ltd manufactures metal sheets used in the production of a wide range of products. It has recently found that it has been producing increasing amounts of waste metal in its manufacturing processes. As a result charges at landfill sites have risen considerably over the last two years.

Jemma and Niall Kilburn, two of the directors, have come back from a fact finding mission to other countries to see how to make use of recycled waste. In the USA they found a number of businesses which, with the right machinery, were able to move into associated production areas. There was a strong and growing interest in recycled products in the US. Consumers were often prepared to pay a little more knowing their money was helping to preserve the environment. This had led to a growth in a number of new businesses manufacturing recycled metal products.

Jemma and Niall drew up a business plan and presented it to the other directors. They felt that some of them would require a great deal of convincing before the business could make such a great change in direction. The reorganisation also had some wide ranging implications. The recycling machinery would require a large initial investment and would need to have the latest

specification to conform to operating standards. Some of the workers at the business would need to be retrained to operate the machines. It was also likely that if the business took off, the operation would need to expand, with everything that would involve.

(a) Identify the factors which might have led to change at the business.
(b) Examine the implications for the business of any change in its operations.

Kurt Lewin emphasised a three step process.
- Introducing an innovation with information aimed to satisfy a need.
- Overcoming resistance by group discussion and decision making.
- Establishing a new practice.

Removing resistance to change

There are certain ways in which resistance to change might be prevented and barriers to change removed.

- There should be clear objectives given to everyone involved in the change. Individual departments or work sections or workers may disagree with the objectives. But it is far worse from a motivational viewpoint for them not to understand why the changes are taking place.
- People who are affected by change might be involved in discussions about the changes that are taking place. This will give them the feeling that they are involved in shaping change and have a stake in its outcome.
- The business should attempt to prevent misinformation and rumours. It may be possible to organise formal meetings where employees are informed about decisions taking place.
- There must be sufficient resources allocated to achieving the change. For example, if an engineering company sets itself the objective of increasing labour productivity (output per worker) by 30 per cent within 12 months but is not prepared to spend any extra on capital investment, it might not be possible to achieve the change. Equally, change often necessitates training of staff. If workers are expected to perform new tasks and new roles, but are given no training, then the level of actual change achieved may be disappointing.
- Following company procedures backed up by the requirements of the law often reduces resistance to change. If workers can see that everyone is being treated equally and that their legal rights are being preserved at all times, they will feel more reassured and less willing to attack the changes being proposed.
- PROJECT CHAMPIONS are usually associated with successful change management. A project champion is someone with power and influence within the organisation that is supporting the change. Project champions are different to project managers, the individuals responsible for managing the change on a day to day basis. Change is often difficult to achieve. Unless there is someone with power and influence to support the project, plans for change can be shelved or fail to be implemented. Project champions maintain motivation for those involved in the project, provide help and advice, secure resources to implement change and push the change agenda with more senior colleagues.
- PROJECT GROUPS are groups of individuals charged with implementing a particular one-off task. The task might be to research a market or consider the impact of

new legislation on a business for example. Sometimes, project groups are appointed to implement and manage change. The advantage of creating a project group to implement change is that it makes a group of people responsible for the task. Some project groups include representatives of the main stakeholders in the change. This helps to give the group an insight into the main issues involved in the change. It also creates lines of communication with the stakeholders in the change. By being more involved and better informed, stakeholders are more likely to accept and embrace change.
- The business should try to ensure that its organisational culture fits in with its new operations and organisation. This is discussed in the next section.

Developing an organisational culture for change

An **organisational culture** includes the beliefs, norms and values of a business. It is a generally held view about how people should behave, the nature of working relationships and attitudes. Many companies, especially Japanese firms such as Honda, Toyota and Sony, place great emphasis on all employees understanding the company's 'culture'.

It has been suggested that a business which creates a culture of change is likely to manage it far more effectively. Management at the top must have a clear idea of how they expect the business to change. Structures, methods of training, management styles etc. must then alter to reflect this. Finally a culture must be established where all employed are aware of the new relationship and methods of working.

One model that was widely used to implement change in the 1990s was total quality management (TQM). A feature of TQM is that everyone in the business is responsible for maintaining and improving quality, including the quality of the product, production methods and the supply to the customer. TQM's motto is 'getting it right the first time' and this is applied to external customers and what are known as 'internal customers' - the people employees work with. This approach helps develop a culture where all employees, managers etc. are trying to achieve the same goal, which should motivate, develop teamwork and improve communication, accountability and rewards.

There are those, however, who suggest that organisational culture is not something that can be easily manipulated. They argue that culture depends on human interaction and is continuously being recreated. Hence, to believe that a senior management team can unilaterally change an existing culture according to some blueprint is mistaken. Organisational culture, according to this view does change, but often slowly and in unpredictable ways. There is also a danger of thinking of organisational culture as a single over-arching idea to which all members of the business subscribe. Organisations, however, may have sub-cultures linked to particular groups. There may be conflict between these subcultures. In addition, even if new culture is established, there is no evidence that simply having a new culture improves performance.

Different approaches to managing change

Research by John Storey has suggested that the way businesses manage change can be classified into four different approaches.

A total imposed package One approach to managing change is for people at the 'top' of the business to plan out major restructuring programmes without consultation with workers or worker representatives. The main advantage of this method is that a company can have a 'vision' of where it is going. It can compare where it is 'now' with where it was 'then'. It is possible, using this approach, to prepare departmental action plans, set timetables and measure how far change has been achieved. The business can also make changes without having to take into account the wishes of other groups. The disadvantage of planning change from the top is that middle managers, supervisors and employees may not feel involved.

Imposed piecemeal initiatives A different approach is to have unplanned or piecemeal initiatives designed to bring about change. Initiatives might be introduced by employers to solve particular problems or only at times when they are needed in the business. Examples of initiatives that might take place are:

- the introduction of team meetings or quality circles;
- improvements in technology or channels of communication;
- improvements in incentive payments or rewards;
- improvements in the flexibility of work practices;
- changes in the workforce, such as teleworkers or subcontracting;
- the introduction of performance appraisal.

A problem with piecemeal initiatives is that they sometimes have different objectives. One might be trying to improve management leadership. The other might to trying to encourage greater participation. Another difficulty is that piecemeal initiatives tend to be short lived. In difficult times businesses may decide to drop costly changes.

Negotiated piecemeal initiatives Productivity agreements are often used to help change take place. Unions agree to changes in work practices, usually in exchange for extra payments or improved conditions for workers. These negotiated changes tend to be ad-hoc, without any coordinated policy by the business.

Negotiated total packages This is where a 'total package' for change is put together. It is negotiated by employers and union representatives. It may be in the form of a 'national deal', which involves changes in work practices for all employees in every plant or office in exchange for increased rewards or improved conditions. In practice this method of managing change was rarely used in Britain before the 1990s. However, the changing roles of trade unions and the likelihood of partnerships between business and unions after the year 2000 may have seen this type of negotiation taking place more often.

Evaluating the management of change

Managers will have a clear idea of the improvements to performance that they want from change in business. They may want productivity gains as a result of the use of multi-skilled teams or improved response times to customer demands due to new communication technologies. These are sometimes referred to as **performance indicators**. Performance indicators can be used to evaluate the management of change. Any evaluation strategy will have quantitative and qualitative methods of analysing changes in working practices.

- A rise in output from 10,000 to 15,000 as a result of change or an improvement in average delivery time from two days to 24 hours would be measurable, quantitative improvements.
- Employees' responses to a questionnaire, stating that change had improved their motivation, could be a qualitative method of evaluating the management of change.

KEYTERMS

Project champion – an individual who believes in the objectives of a project, seeks support for it from management and other stakeholders and helps to remove barriers which prevent the project from succeeding.

Project group – a number of individual members of an organisation who have been given responsibility for a one-off task, such as preparing a report or implementing an IT software change.

KNOWLEDGE

1. State five factors that may cause change in a business.
2. How might change affect:
   (a) market research
   (b) research and development;
   in a business?
3. Why is it important for businesses to manage change?
4. How might (a) workers and (b) the culture of the organisation prove resistant to change?
5. How might a project champion help the process of change?
6. What is meant by 'developing an organisational culture for change'?
7. Briefly explain four approaches to change.

Case Study: A successful merger

When Lowke's bought Feraday's, many at Feraday's feared the worst. The company had performed poorly over the past few years and there had been persistent rumours that it would be sold off and broken up. Senior management at Lowke's, however, saw Feraday's as an opportunity to revitalise what had once been one of the best companies in the food processing sector.

From the first, all talk of 'takeover', 'asset stripping' and 'downsizing' was banned. Instead, management was encouraged to talk about 'creating a world class company', 'moving forward', 'expanding the business' and 'taking what is best in our partnership'. There was no immediate move to make anyone redundant, despite the obvious overlap of roles, particularly at senior management levels. Instead, it was made clear to everyone that the new company would take shape after a period of 24 months of intense reflection on how best to create a successful business. The board of directors set the company the goal of raising its sales by 5 per cent within those two years and by 25 per cent within five years. Operating profits were to rise by 5 per cent within two years but by 40 per cent within five years. The strategy to achieve these objectives was left to senior management to devise. However, the Board made it clear that it expected the strategy to evolve from consultation at every level of the new company.

Not everyone was prepared to engage meaningfully in the consultation. Some could not see beyond their own life goals and were simply not interested in the future success of the business. It was impossible to shift them from the 'I've worked here for 20 years, so the company owes me my job with no changes' type attitude. But most could see that change was needed and were prepared to think about how best to achieve that change.

Managers and workers from both companies looked at how each was operating. Sometimes it was clear that one company was performing a task or function more efficiently than the other. This then became the catalyst for change as the whole company standardised on best practice. Where there was overlap and cost savings could be achieved through rationalisation, all workers were consulted and interviewed before any decisions about their personal future was taken. Some didn't want to move forward with the company but were very satisfied with early retirement packages. Others were helped to find jobs and even promotion with other employers. Yet others were offered different jobs within the company. It might be in a different location. Or it might be a different job for which they were offered

training to fulfill.

Because there was fairly intense contact between workers within the two companies over the 24 months, it soon became apparent to workers at Feraday's that there was no favouritism being given to either business methods or individual workers at Lowke's. This helped build up a climate of trust which made it easier to secure changes at Feraday's.

Lowke's was a large private limited company whose Board of Directors were committed to long-term growth. They were aware that profits could have been higher in the short term if they had wielded an axe to Feraday's very quickly. The solutions that came out of the consultations were not necessarily very different to what senior managers at Lowke's would have come up with anyway. However, the Board of Directors wanted to preserve as much talent as possible within the new company. It also wanted to avoid the demotivation of staff that often took place after a takeover. The Board was equally aware that takeovers by other companies in the industry had led to problems with both suppliers and customers. For example, the needs of customers could easily be lost by an organisation undergoing radical change. Its model of change, it hoped, would create an organisation which would continue to evolve successfully in future years.

(a) Evaluate the costs and benefits to Lowke's of adopting a fairly lengthy, consultative model of change. (40 marks)
(b) Discuss whether the model of change adopted by Lowke's could be implemented by a public limited company. (40 marks)

Presenting data

Businesses gather a variety of data. Some data are used **internally**, within the business. Some are available to people outside the business, such as customers, suppliers or the government. Data can be presented in a variety of ways.

In words Data can be presented in written form. For example, a report might state that 'first quarter sales in 2008 were £1.2 million, falling to £1.1 million in the second quarter and £0.8 million in the third quarter, whilst rising to £1.5 million in the fourth quarter'. A QUARTER here is a period of three months. If too much data is presented in a report it can be difficult to read and understand. It can also be difficult to tell at a glance what is happening. For these reasons, data is often presented in a table or chart.

Tables Table 1 shows the data from a report in the form of a table. When presenting a table, it is important to number the table clearly if it is to be referred to elsewhere. It must also be given a title, which explains what the table shows. If the data refer to a period of time, this should be shown clearly in the title or on the table. Units of measurement must also be included, usually as a label for the table. In Table 1, the unit of measurement is '£ million'. Tables have the advantage over graphs that exact figures can be read. For example, in the fourth quarter, sales were exactly £1.5 million. This is more difficult to read off the line graph or bar graph in Figures 1 and 2. When there is a great deal of data, though, it can often be difficult to identify trends or see relationships between different variables in a table.

Line graphs Line graphs show the relationship between two variables. Figure 1 is a graph showing the data in Table 1. The two variables are time and quarterly sales. On a line graph, time is usually shown on the horizontal axis. The number of times something occurs, the FREQUENCY, and the value or amount, such as sales, are usually shown on the vertical axis. Line graphs are good for showing trends which can be seen at a glance. On the other hand, values of variables can be difficult to read accurately from the scale on the vertical axes. There can also be problems constructing or reading line graphs where there are several lines showing more than two variables, with very different values. For example, it would be difficult to construct a readable line graph with 2008 quarterly sales figures for 10 companies with sales

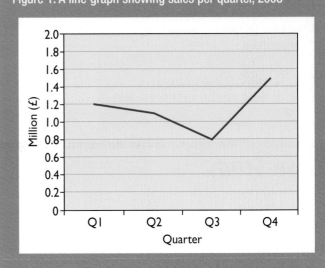

Figure 1: A line graph showing sales per quarter, 2008

ranging from £30,000 to £250 million. A table would be far more effective at showing this information.

Bar charts A BAR CHART shows information in the form of bars. Table 1 has been converted into two types of bar chart in Figure 2. The first is a vertical bar chart, the most often used of the two. As with line graphs, time is usually placed on the horizontal axis. The second is a horizontal bar chart. Here time

Table 1: Sales per quarter, 2008

	£ million
Quarter	**Sales**
Q1	1.2
Q2	1.1
Q3	0.8
Q4	1.5

Question 1.

John Menzies plc is a company which specialises in logistics - transporting products from one place to another for other businesses. Table 2 shows the value of its profit between 2002 and 2006.

(a) Describe in words the change in profit of the company.
(b) Construct a line graph showing profit between 2002 and 2006.
(c) Construct a bar chart showing the information in Table 2.

Table 2: John Menzies plc, profit before taxation 2002-2006

	2002	2003	2004	2005	2006
£ million	17.7	-0.10	37.6	36.7	35.6

Source: adapted from Menzies Group, *Annual Report 2006*.

Figure 2: A bar chart showing sales per quarter, 2008

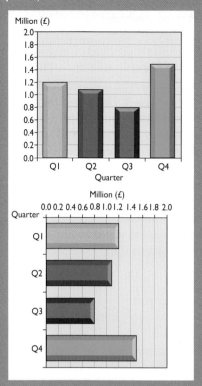

Table 3: Sales per quarter, 2007 and 2008

Quarter	£ million 2007	£ million 2008
Q1	1.5	1.2
Q2	1.3	1.1
Q3	0.9	0.8
Q4	1.7	1.5

Figure 3: A component bar chart showing sales per quarter, 2007 and 2008

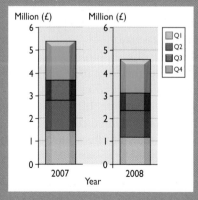

Table 4: Sales dispatched by cost of order, third quarter 2008

Cost of sales order, £	Number of orders
0-1,000	30
1,001-3,000	80
3,001-6,000	60
6,001-10,000	20

is shown on the vertical axis. A horizontal bar chart is simply a vertical bar chart turned clockwise through 90 degrees.

A **component bar chart** allows more complex data to be presented clearly on a bar chart. Table 3 shows the 2008 value of sales for the business in Table1. But it also adds the 2007 figures. Figure 3 shows two bars, one for total sales in 2007 and the other for 2008. But each bar is broken up according to the sales for each quarter. These quarterly sales when added together make up the total yearly sales.

An advantage of using a bar chart is that it can be easier to read values from a bar chart than a line graph, but less so than from a table. As with a line graph, it is often easier to see trends from a bar chart than from a table. However, the more data displayed on a bar graph, the more difficult it is to read.

Histograms A HISTOGRAM looks similar to a bar chart. However, in a vertical bar chart the value of a variable (its frequency) is shown by the **height** of the bar. In a histogram, it is shown by the **area** of the bar.

Table 4 shows the number of orders dispatched in the third quarter of 2008 by the cost of the order. For example, there were 30 orders sent out costing between £0 and £1,000 and 20 orders costing £6,001-£10,000. If the data were drawn as a vertical bar chart, as in Figure 4, there would be four bars of equal width with values (i.e. frequencies) of 40, 80, 60 and 20. On the horizontal axis, the bars would be labelled '£0-£1,000, £1,001-£3,000, £3,001-6,000 and £6,001-10,000'.

If the data in Table 4 is drawn as a histogram, as in Figure 5, the unequal ranges of the cost of deliveries are now taken into account. The horizontal axis is divided up into equal **ranges**. From the data in Table 4, an easy division would be to mark every £1,000. Then the bars are drawn.

- There are 30 orders in the first £1,000 range. This is shown by a bar with a height of 30 orders.
- There are 80 orders in the range £1,001 to £3,000. This is made up of two £1,000 ranges, whose average value is 40 orders (80 ÷ 2). So the height of the bar is 40 orders and its horizontal length is two £1,000 ranges (i.e. from £1, 001 to £3,000). The area of the bar is 2 x 40 orders, i.e the 80 orders shown in Table 3.
- There are three £1,000 ranges between £3,001 and £6,000. So, with a total of 60 orders over this range, the height of the bar will be 20 orders (60 orders ÷ 3).
- With four £1,000 ranges between £6,001 and £10,000, the height of the last bar will be 5 orders (20 orders ÷ 4).

Looking at a histogram compared to a bar chart, the visual difference is that the bars are of different horizontal length. Note too that there is never any gap between the bars. The bars form a continuous area. This is because the histogram records **continuous data** - data which covers a complete range of values.

Figure 4: A bar chart showing sales dispatched by cost of order, third quarter 2002

Figure 5: A histogram showing sales dispatched by cost of order, third quarter 2002

Figure 6: A pie chart showing market share, 3rd quarter, 2008

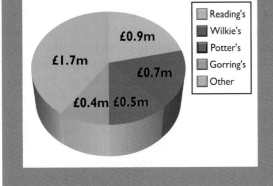

Legend:
- Reading's
- Wilkie's
- Potter's
- Gorring's
- Other

£0.9m £1.7m £0.7m £0.4m £0.5m

Table 5: Sales of four largest companies and all other businesses, 3rd quarter 2008

	£ million Sales
Reading's	0.9
Wilkie's	0.7
Potter's	0.5
Gorring's	0.4
Other	1.7
Total	4.2

Sometimes, a **frequency curve** is added to a histogram. This is a line which connects the horizontal mid points of the vertical value of each histogram bar. This is shown in Figure 5. The area bounded by the frequency curve and the horizontal and vertical axes is called a **frequency polygon**.

Pie charts A pie chart represents data as segments of a circle. The pie chart in Figure 6 is drawn from the data in Table 5. This shows the value of sales for the four largest companies in a market, and sales for all other businesses in the market. The pie chart has five **segments**, representing the value of sales for each company together with the 'all other businesses' component. The number of degrees of each segment is calculated by finding the proportion of total sales for each company and multiplying it by 360°. As a formula:

$$\frac{\text{Value of the part}}{\text{Total}} \times 360°$$

For example, the segment representing sales for Reading's would be equal to:

$$\frac{£0.9m}{£4.2m} \times 360° = 77°$$

Pie charts are useful for getting an idea of the relative values of the various parts of a total. However, unless clearly labelled with the absolute quantities of the parts, it can be difficult to read an accurate value off the chart. Pie charts are unsuitable for displaying complex data with many components. They are also not particularly suited for showing changes over time.

Mean, medium and mode

Frequently, businesses want to calculate an average. There are three types of average commonly measured.

The mean The arithmetic MEAN is perhaps the most often used average measure. Say that a business had sales over the last five years of £0.9 million, £1.2 million, £1.7 million, £1.7 million and £1.5 million. The mean is calculated by adding together the value of sales and dividing by the number of values. So the mean is:

$$\frac{£0.9m + £1.2m + £1.7m + £1.7m + £1.5m}{5} = £1.4m$$

The median The MEDIAN is the 'middle value'. It is found by placing values in rank order, from the least to the most. Placing sales values in rank order would be:

£0.9m, £1.2m, £1.5m, £1.7m, £1.7m

The middle value or median is the third number of the

Question 2.

Table 6 shows the number of customers visiting a supermarket chain in four age ranges.

(a) Draw a histogram showing the number of customers in each age range. Note that there will be four blocks. Put age on the horizontal axis and frequency of customers on the vertical axis.

(b) On your histogram, draw a frequency curve.

(c) Explain in words where the frequency polygon is located on your diagram.

(d) Draw and label a pie chart to show the data in Table 6. Note that each segment of your pie chart will represent the number of customers in a particular age range.

Table 6: Number of customers visiting a supermarket chain

Age range of customers	Number of customers (millions)
10-19	0.6
20-39	1.4
40-69	2.4
70-79	0.3
Total	4.7

sequence of five numbers which is £1.5 million.

If there had been six numbers, the median would have been found by taking the mean of the third and fourth values, the middle two values. Assume that sales in the sixth year were £0.8 million. Then the rank order would be:

£0.8m, £0.9m, £1.2m, £1.5m, £1.7m, £1.7m

The middle two values are £1.2 million and £1.5 million. So the median would be:

$$\frac{£1.2 \text{ million} + £1.5 \text{ million}}{2} = £1.35 \text{ million}$$

The mode The MODE is the most frequently occurring number. In the sales figures only one number occurs more than once. This is 1.7. So 1.7 is the mode.

These three methods of calculating an average are useful in different circumstances. The mean uses all the data available. However, one untypical value can lead to a distorted picture. For example, assume that sales in one of the five years was not £1.7 million but £12 million due to a one-off special order. The mean for the five years would then be £3.46 million (£0.9m + £1.2m + £1.7m + £12m + £1.5m ÷ 5) and not £1.4 million. This is over twice as high as the values in the other four years. One advantage of the median and the mode is that a £12 million order would not influence the average because it would be an extreme figure. On the other hand, if there is relatively little data, the mode can produce unhelpful results. For example, can it really be said that the two years when sales were £1.7 million were typical simply because the mode is £1.7 million?

Moving averages

Sometimes, data can be subject to fluctuations. For example, most clothes retailers are faced with large changes in sales over the year. In the run-up to Christmas, sales peak and may be four times greater than those in August. It can be difficult to spot a trend from such figures. One way around this is to calculate a MOVING AVERAGE. This smooths out fluctuations, allowing a trend to become clearer.

Table 7 shows quarterly sales figures for a business over three years. There are great fluctuations in sales between quarters. So it is not immediately obvious whether the business is performing better at the end of the period than at the beginning. Calculating a moving average should help make the trend clearer.

Moving averages can be calculated using any period of time. In Tables 7 and 8, they are calculated for three quarters or four quarters. The longer the period chosen, the more fluctuations from period to period will tend to be smoothed out.

A three period moving average Look at Table 7. Using a period of three quarters for averaging, the moving average for Q2 in 2006 is £3.3 million. This is calculated by adding together sales in the two quarters either side of Q2, i.e. Q1 and Q3, to Q2 itself and dividing the total by 3:

$$\frac{£5m + £3m + £2m}{3} = £3.3m$$

Table 7: A 3 period moving average: quarterly sales figures for a clothing retailer

Year	Quarter	Actual sales	£ million 3 period moving average
2006	Q1	5	
	Q2	3	3.3
	Q3	2	4.3
	Q4	8	5.3
2007	Q1	6	5.7
	Q2	3	3.7
	Q3	2	4.0
	Q4	7	4.3
2008	Q1	4	4.3
	Q2	2	2.7
	Q3	2	3.7
	Q4	7	

Table 8: A 4 period moving average: quarterly sales figures for a clothing retailer

Year	Quarter	Actual sales	4 period moving average	£million Centered 4 period moving average
2006	Q1	5		
	Q2	3		
			4.5	
	Q3	2		4.625
			4.75	
	Q4	8		4.75
			4.75	
2007	Q1	6		4.75
			4.75	
	Q2	3		4.625
			4.5	
	Q3	2		4.25
			4.0	
	Q4	7		3.875
			3.75	
2008	Q1	4		3.75
			3.75	
	Q2	2		3.75
			3.75	
	Q3	2		
	Q4	7		

Similarly for Q3, the moving average is:

$$\frac{£3m + £2m + £8m}{3} = £4.3m$$

No moving average can be calculated for the Q1 2006 because there are no sales figures for Q4 2005. Similarly, the moving average for Q4 2006 cannot be calculated because there is no figure for Q1 2007.

Odd number moving averages are easier to calculate. This is because there is a **mid-point** in the series. The mid-point of a seven period moving average, for example, would be the fourth period, as there are three periods either side.

A four period moving average Even number moving averages are more complex. No single period provides a mid-point around which an average can be calculated. For example, the mid-point of Q1, Q2, Q3 and Q4 of 2006 in Table 8 lies **in-between** Q2 and Q3. Calculating a four period moving average for this in-between point would be:

$$\frac{£5m + £3m + £2m + £8m}{4} = £4.5m$$

Calculating a four period moving average for the mid-point of Q2, Q3, Q4 of 2006 and Q1 of 2007 would be:

$$\frac{£3m + £2m + £8m + £6m}{4} = £4.75m$$

To resolve this problem, a process called CENTRING is used. This allows an average to be plotted against a central figure. Look at Table 8. How can a four period moving average for Q3 2006 be calculated? One method is to take an average of the two figures above. This gives a centred average of:

$$\frac{£4.5m + £4.75m}{2} = £4.625$$

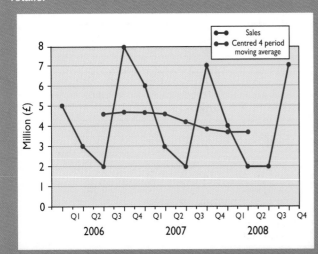

Figure 7: Moving averages: quarterly sales figures for a clothing retailer

Eco-Gaveda is a business which specialises in selling eco-friendly products by mail order. New customers are sent a catalogue with their first order. Table 9 shows the number of catalogues sent.

Table 9: Numbers of catalogues sent to customers

Year	Quarter	Actual catalogues
2006	Q1	500
	Q2	300
	Q3	100
	Q4	10,400
2007	Q1	540
	Q2	340
	Q3	170
	Q4	11,100
2008	Q1	580
	Q2	350
	Q3	210
	Q4	11,200

(a) Calculate (i) a three period moving average; (ii) a four period moving average; (iii) a centred four period moving average from the data in Table 9.
(b) Plot (i) the actual number of catalogues; (ii) the three period moving average data; (iii) the centred four period moving average data onto a graph.
(c) Discuss what the data indicate about the sales of Eco-Gaveda.

Mathematically, it is often quicker to add together the eight numbers which form the four period moving averages and divide by 8 rather than calculating the two averages and dividing by 2. For example, to calculate the centred average of Q3 in 2006:

$$\frac{(5+3+2+8) + (3+2+8+6)}{8} = 4.625$$

To calculate the centred average for Q4 of 2006 would be:

$$\frac{(3+2+8+6) + (2+8+6+3)}{8} = 4.75$$

It is possible to plot the data from Table 8 on a graph, as shown in Figure 7. Looking at Figure 7, a clearer trend picture can be seen from the centred 4 period moving average than from the sales data. Trading conditions deteriorated in 2007, but may have stabilised towards the end of 2008.

Index numbers

Table 10 shows sales figures for two companies over a five year

Table 10 Heart's and Tyler's, value of sales, £ million, 2004-2008

	£ million	
	Heart's	**Tyler's**
2004	742.3	487.4
2005	769.6	521.5
2006	801.5	560.5
2007	802.6	587.8
2008	826.5	599.0

Table 11 Heart's and Tyler's, index of the value of sales, 2004-2008, 2004 = 100

	2004 = 100	
	Heart's	**Tyler's**
2004	100.0	100.0
2005	103.7	107.0
2006	108.0	115.0
2007	108.1	120.6
2008	111.3	122.9

£769.6 million in 2005. If £742.3 million is 'called' 100, then the index value of £769.6 million is 103.7. This is calculated as:

$$\frac{\text{2005 value}}{\text{2006 value}} \times 100$$

i.e. 769.6 ÷ 742.3 x 100 = 103.7. The same process is used to calculate the index numbers for sales in 2006-2008, shown in Table 11.

One advantage of using index numbers is clear from Table 11. It is much easier to see at a glance how Heart's has performed. Instead of the large numbers used before, it can be seen that over the five period sales rose by 11.3 per cent. It is also possible to compare the performance of Tyler's with Heart's. The 1998 value of sales for Tyler's is also 'called' 100, since 1998 is the BASE PERIOD. This is the year around which all other values are compared. In relative terms, Tyler's has outperformed Heart's. Its sales over the five year period increased by 22.9 per cent, compared to 11.3 per cent for Heart's.

The disadvantage of using index numbers is that they do not give absolute values. For example, just using the data in Table 11, it is not possible to say how much in £ million were the sales of

period. It is not obvious which company has performed better. One way to make comparisons easier is to present the data in INDEX NUMBER form. This converts one value into the number 100. The rest of the values are then changed so that their proportions remain the same. For example, Heart's sales in 2004 were £742.3 million. They increased to

Heart's in 2008. Nor is it possible to say which of the two companies had the largest sales turnover.

Index numbers can be used to simplify the presentation of a single set of data, as in Tables 10 and 11. They are also used when the results of complex averages are presented. Indexes often mentioned in the news are the **Retail Price Index (RPI)** and the **Consumer Price Index (CPI)**. The RPI is an average of the prices of a typical basket of goods and services bought in the UK by the average household. It is calculated monthly from thousands of different prices which are averaged out using a complex formula based on the relative amounts spent on different items. Rather than saying that the average household spent £1,263.98 last month on this typical basket of goods, the value is converted into index number form. This makes it much easier to see the relative **change** in prices from month to month and year to year. This relative change in prices is called the **rate of inflation**. It is easier to see that the rate of inflation was approximately 2 per cent when the index of prices rose from 106 to 108 than if the price of the average basket went up from £1,263.98 to £1,289.26.

KNOWLEDGE

1. What is the difference between a line graph and a bar chart?
2. What is a component bar chart?
3. What is the difference between a bar chart and a histogram?
4. Total sales for a company are £300 million. Of this, £200 million comes from the UK and £100 million from the USA. If you were drawing a pie chart to show this, how many degrees would you measure to draw the segment for (a) UK sales and (b) US sales?
5. Using an example, explain the difference between the mean, the median and the mode of a set of sales figures.
6. Using an example, explain the difference between the way that a three period moving average would be calculated and the way a four period moving average would be calculated.
7. Sales for company A increased by 10 per cent between 2008 and 2009. Over the same period company B saw its sales increase by 20 per cent. Using 2008 as the base year, explain how this data could be expressed in index number form.

Question 4.

Severn Trent Water and Bristol Water are two UK water companies. Table 12 shows the value of sales turnover of the two companies between 2003 and 2007.

(a) (i) Convert the sales turnover figures for Severn Trent Water into index number form using 2003 as the base year. (ii) Do the same for Bristol Water.

(b) Compare the sales performance of the two companies between 2003 and 2007.

Table 12: Sales turnover: Severn Trent Water and Bristol Water

	£ million	
	Severn Trent Water	**Bristol Water**
2003	1,852	70.0
2004	2,015	70.6
2005	1,252	70.6
2006	1,455	81.9
2007	1,480	86.3

Source: adapted from Severn Trent Water, Bristol Water, *Annual Report and Accounts*.

KEYTERMS

Bar chart – a graphical presentation of data where the value of a variable (its frequency) is shown by the height of a block on a vertical bar chart, or the length of a block on a horizontal bar chart.

Base period – the period, such as a year or a month, with which all other values in a series are compared.

Centring – a method used in the calculation of a moving average where an average can be calculated for a particular period rather than in between periods. It is used where there is an even number of periods, such as two periods or four periods, to be averaged.

Frequency – the total number of times a variable occurs; on a graph or vertical bar chart, it would be shown as a value on the vertical axis.

Histogram – a graphical presentation of data where the value

of a variable (its frequency) is shown by an area on the chart rather than, as with a vertical bar chart, the height of a block.

Index number – an indicator showing the relative value of one number to another from a base of 100.

Mean – often called the average, it is a method of representing a set of numbers by adding up the value of the numbers and dividing by the quantity of numbers.

Median – the middle value of a set of numbers when the data is put in rank order.

Mode – the value which occurs most frequently in a set of data.

Moving average – a method of smoothing out fluctuations in data by calculating an average for several periods around a single period and recording it as the average for that period.

Quarter – a period of a quarter of a year, i.e. three months.

Case Study: Littway

Littway plc

Littway is a UK based company which specialises in creating and producing high quality freshly prepared foods. It sells its 1,500 different products to retailers who in turn sell them on to consumers. Freshly prepared food is a fast growing segment of the UK market. Last year, it grew by 10 per cent compared to just 2 per cent for all food.

Although the freshly prepared foods sector continues to grow strongly, it still represents only 9 per cent of total food purchases by value. Less than one-third of consumers buy freshly prepared foods in any month, and for most product categories it is less than 10 per cent of consumers. In addition, the average purchase is two items per month or less. These statistics suggest that there is considerable scope for further growth.

Table 13: Real[1] household spending, UK 1971-2007, index numbers

	Food	1971=100 All household spending
1971	100	100
1981	105	121
1991	117	167
2001	137	227
2007	153	267

1 i.e. after inflation has been taken out of the figures.
Source: adapted from *Economic & Labour Market Review*, Office for National Statistics.

Table 14: UK market for freshly prepared food

	Total UK market £m	% UK market growth year on year
Sectors into which Littway sells products		
Ready meals	954	15
Prepared salads	289	2
Prepared leaf	249	22
Pizza (incl. in-store delicatessen)	259	5
Prepared vegetables	125	38
Fresh pasta	96	9
Chilled breads	70	7
Fresh sauce	71	9
Fresh soup	75	1
Dips	65	3
Stir fry	55	12
Prepared fruit	57	18
Other major fresh prepared food sectors into which Littway does not sell		
Yoghurt/Fromage frais	742	0
Sandwiches (multiple retailers & stores)	525	11
Hot eating pastry products	428	2
Dairy desserts	355	16
Chilled cake	247	16
Cold eating pastry products	215	4
Quiche and flan	162	12
Hot eating desserts	89	30
Party food	63	9

(a) Explain what is meant by an 'index number' (Table 13). (3 marks)

(b) Using Table 14, calculate (i) the mean growth rate of those UK markets in which Littway is active; (ii) the mean growth rate of those UK markets into which does not sell; (iii) the name and size of the median sector of the freshly prepared food market; (iv) the name and size of the mode of the sectors of the freshly prepared food market. (8 marks)

(c) Examine and compare the growth rate of total UK household spending with that of the UK food sector, freshly prepared food, and the sectors within it. (8 marks)

(d) Comment on whether Littway is pursuing a strategy which will optimise its growth and profit. (12 marks)

103 | Study skills

Studying and assessment

Study skills are the skills that a student needs to plan, organise and carry out their work effectively. They also help a student to answer questions and carry out tasks which are designed to test their abilities. This unit and the next are set out like a manual. They provide guidance and examples to help students when working in term time or when taking examinations. Examples are shown in italics. The units could be used:

- at the start of the course to get ideas on the best way to study;
- constantly throughout the course when studying;
- before examinations during revision preparation.

Action planning

Studying is more effective if there is a plan or strategy. An action plan can be formally written out, but it does not have to be. For any piece of work, it is important for a student to plan:

- how long it will take, bearing in mind any deadline;
- where the student will work;
- when the student will work;
- in what order tasks will be carried out;
- factors likely to affect the work, such as unforeseen occurrences.

A plan can be made for an individual piece of work, work over a term, coursework or project work, revision or an entire scheme

Title and nature of work	What needs to be done? What is the focus? How will it be judged?
Start and finish date	What is the deadline? How long will it take?
Collecting information	Where from? How can it be obtained? What help is needed? How long will it take? How will it be used?
Carrying out the work	Where? When? How long? Who with? What order? Continuous or broken down? Help needed? What factors might affect the work? Possible changes?
Review	Did the plan work? Was the outcome successful? How could it have been done better? Was everything covered?

of work. It is important for a student to develop a **routine** of work that is effective. It is also important for students to be **committed** to complete the plan. The table below shows a possible action plan that may be used for study, work or revision.

Time management

An important part of the action plan is planning how long to study or work. Certain factors must be considered when deciding how much time to take when studying.

When to start and when to finish There is a deadline for most pieces of work. This is the date by which they have to be completed. It is important to start early enough and to leave enough time to finish the work. Some people work faster than others. This will affect the time they allocate.

How long the work will take Some pieces of work will take longer than others. Short answer questions will perhaps take less time than an essay. A piece of coursework or project work may take months. So will revision. Some people work more quickly than others, which may reduce the time taken.

How long to work The length of time spent on work can affect its quality.

- Spending a greater amount of time preparing and planning may improve a piece of work.
- The time spent writing may also improve work.
- Working for too long can be tiring and work may suffer. Sometimes it is better to take a short break.
- Some work, such as coursework and revision, cannot be done all at once and must be broken up.
- It is useful to try to break up revision, by learning as you go along. There is likely to be too much to learn in one session at the end. Spreading the work also allows practice.

When to study This will depend on the time available. Some people have a free choice of time. They could work in free time in the day, at lunchtime, in the evening or at weekends. People with part-time jobs or with great commitments may find it more difficult. They may have to work when they can. Sometimes there may be free time which could be usefully used, such as travelling to school or college on a bus or train. Students should also consider that it may not be useful to work:

- late at night because they are tired;
- after strenuous exercise because it may be difficult to concentrate;
- when they are doing lots of other things.

Where to study

It is important to consider where to work. Some students will work better in certain environments than others. Should you work at home or in a different place such as school, a library or another person's house? Issues to consider might be:

- the availability of materials. A library will have books you can use. It may also have a facility to find book titles, newspapers and magazines, perhaps on CD Rom, and access to the Internet. If you keep all your materials at home, it may be better to work there;
- ease of access. Working at home allows easy access to drinks and food. Some people may also want to take a break to watch television or do something else;
- comfortable or not? Working in a familiar environment, such as home, can make work easier. Other people prefer to work in a more 'academic' atmosphere;
- alone or in a group? Some people prefer to work alone. Others like to work with someone else, even if they are doing their own work. Sometimes group activities demand that people work together;
- silent or not? Some people prefer to work in silence as they concentrate better. Working in a library would allow this. Others prefer things to be happening around them.

Other learning considerations

There are other factors that students may want to take into consideration when working.

- Some people prefer to sit on a hard chair. Some prefer to be more comfortable and sit on a soft or relaxing chair.
- Some people like to listen to music whilst they are working. Others prefer silence.
- Some people prefer bright lighting so that everything is clear. Others work better in dimmed lighting.
- Some people prefer to carry out several tasks or activities at once. Others prefer to do one task and then move on to another.
- Some people prefer to eat or chew while they are working as it helps them to concentrate. Others don't.
- Some people learn better by moving around from time to time and some by standing up.

Learning and memory strategies

Different people learn in different ways. Some people learn and remember more easily when they hear something. Others prefer to see it written down and to read it. Some prefer a diagram or picture. Each of these styles of learning may be useful in different circumstances. If a student finds learning something difficult in one way, he or she might try another.

Written methods In many cases students will have to read information and take notes. This is often the most common form of learning on a course at advanced level.

A possible technique used to read information is to:

- choose a section of written material that you will read and quickly scan through it to get the overall idea;
- read the material more slowly;

- put the written material aside and recite the key ideas or points that you have read;
- check that you have covered the main points;
- if you have missed anything, re-read the information.

Often in work or for revision students have to condense large amounts of information into shorter note form. This makes it easier to remember. Steps to note taking may involve the following:

- reading the information and making sure that you understand it first;
- dividing up the information into topic headings and subheadings;
- making suitable notes that are clear and easy to read, and are in a logical order;
- underlining or highlighting important words or key phrases that will trigger memory of the point;
- using page references to the written material;
- leaving space for additions;
- creating an index for your notes, either using a card system or a computer package and updating the order.

Once you have a set of notes you can use the reading technique above to make sure you understand them or for revision.

Example – Business failure

In January 2008, Martha Williams walked out of her farm office for the last time. Her market garden business had ceased trading that day – it had run out of cash. In four weeks' time the assets would be auctioned off and the proceeds used to pay creditors. Heath Farm Food Supplies had become another victim of the 'credit crunch'. Martha needed to borrow around £40,000 to keep the business running until the spring when produce such as lettuces, spinach, watercress, rocket and other salad leaves would be ready to sell and generate much needed cash. Unfortunately, Martha could not find a single bank, or any other financial institution, that would lend her the money.

It all started to go wrong for Martha in early 2007. Against the advice of her accountant, Martha decided to purchase some new harvesting equipment rather than lease it. Martha believed that the long-term cost of leasing was far too high and would eat savagely into profits. However, the £45,000 cost of the equipment left the business very short of working capital. Martha argued that a good harvest would pay for it and the loan of £30,000 was easily affordable at current interest rates.

Unfortunately, during March and April a very dry spell of weather had an adverse affect on yields. In a six week period not a single drop of rain fell. This reduced yields by 40 per cent and put back the beginning of the harvest by five weeks. As a result Martha had to extend the bank overdraft by about £10,000. At about the same time interest rates started to rise. The Monetary Policy Committee increased rates three times in 2007. This raised costs for Heath Farm Food Supplies and the business was beginning to struggle. Martha realised that a problem existed and took some appropriate action. She decreased drawings, laid off a member of staff, cancelled all but essential spending and chased up a few long standing debts. This helped for a while but later in the year things got very tight. 'The problem is the yields' said Martha. 'They were 40 per cent down in the spring and since then they haven't recovered enough'.

In January 2008, the business received another very serious setback. One of its main customers, a local supermarket chain, had gone into receivership. The supermarket owed Heath Farm £24,000. This had been due in December 2007 and Martha had been waiting tentatively for the cheque to arrive. She knew that the customer had been struggling and in some ways was half expecting the news. However, it wasn't the end of the world. Provided some long-term funding could be raised Heath Farm Food Supplies would soon begin to flourish, Martha thought. However, she hadn't counted on the 2008 'credit crunch'.

Notes – Business failure (Heath Farm Food Supplies)

- *Heath Farm Food Supplies closes down in 2008 due to the 'credit crunch' – it couldn't raise £40,000 to boost cash flow.*
- *Early 2007, £45,000 equipment purchased with £30,000 loan – tight working capital.*
- *Poor weather reduces yields – bank overdraft extended to £10,000.*
- *Interest rates rise – business starts to struggle and action is taken to help improve cash flow.*
- *January 2008 - bad debt of £24,000 – can't raise cash – business collapses.*

Oral methods It is sometimes easier to remember or understand something if you hear it. When you meet people do you remember their name? If so you may have a strong oral memory. Strategies for learning might include:

- answering questions asked by another person;
- making oral notes onto a tape recorder and playing them back regularly;

- constantly repeating phrases or key words, perhaps in an order;
- make up a **mnemonic**, rhyme or phrase which can be repeated. For example, PESTLE analysis considers the Political, Economic, Sociological, Technological, Legal and Environmental factors that can affect a business.

Pictorial/visual When you meet people do you remember their face? If so you may have a strong visual memory. Visual material can provide an instant 'picture' of information. Sometimes it is easier to see relationships by means of visual representation. Visual information may make use of some of the note taking techniques explained above. It may also make use of photographs. Examples of visual presentation include the following.

(a) Mind maps. *Promotion methods.*
(b) Family trees. *The sources of funds.*
(c) Flow diagrams. *The stages in the design process.*
(d) Horizontal family trees. *Herzberg's two-factor theory.*
(e) Block diagrams. *Calculating profit and loss.*
(f) Method of loci. This involves taking a room you know and imagining certain key words in parts of the room. *Types of integration.*

Learning by doing You may think that you know something or know how to do it. But you might only find out if you test yourself by doing something. It may be possible to test yourself by using:

- classroom or homework activities you have already completed earlier in the course;
- activities in textbooks or workbooks;
- applying ideas in a project or a piece of coursework;
- past examination questions;
- your own activities.

(a) Mind maps

(b) Family trees

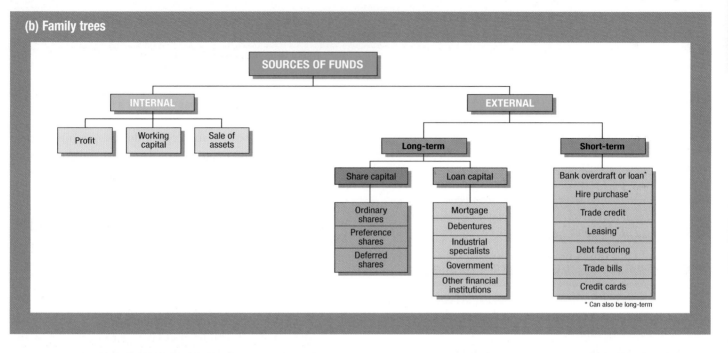

(c) Flow diagrams

(d) Horizontal family trees

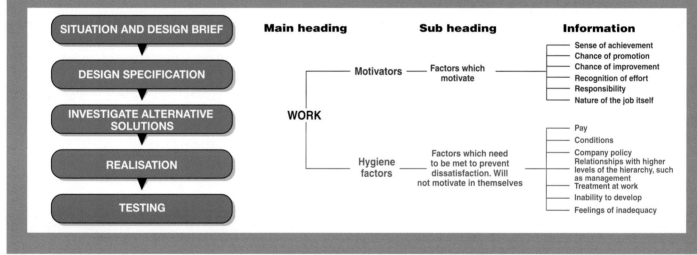

(e) Block diagrams

(f) Method of loci

Assessment criteria/objectives

It is possible to use a range of criteria when assessing the performance of students. This means that examiners or assessors want students to demonstrate a range of different skills. In order to be successful students must:

- understand the skills required by examiners or assessors;
- recognise the skill that is being assessed in a particular question;
- demonstrate all of the skills assessed by the examiner;
- practice skills before the examination.

The criteria used by examiners may fall into the following categories.

Knowledge Students have to demonstrate that they:

- understand business theories and concepts;
- recognise and understand business terms;
- interpret information given in a business context.

Students can recognise questions which test knowledge by looking at the command words in the question. Such words are explained in the next section. An example of a question assessing knowledge might be: *What is meant by best practice benchmarking?*

Application and understanding This assessment criterion requires students to apply theories and concepts in both familiar and unfamiliar situations. This might involve:

- using a business formula in appropriate circumstances, for example, calculating the current ratio for a business;
- using a theory to explain why a business has chosen a particular course of action, for example, using McGregor's Theory Y to explain why a business has introduced quality circles;
- using a business theory to suggest a suitable course of action for a business, for example, suggesting that a chainstore uses loyalty cards to increase repeat sales.

Questions requiring application can again be recognised by looking at the command word. An example of a question requiring application might be: *Explain why the business has cut its research and development budget.*

Analysis Students have to demonstrate that they can break down information and understand the implications of what they have been presented with. Students will encounter both qualitative and quantitative information and will need to:

- identify causes and effects and interrelationships, for example, recognise from a graph that sales are falling and could be a result of new competition in the market;
- break down information to identify specific causes or problems, for example, realise that a business is suffering from inefficiency because according to the information

staff motivation has fallen, equipment is worn and working practices are outdated;
- use appropriate techniques to analyse data, for example, use ratio analysis to assess the solvency of a business;
- use appropriate theories, business cases/practices to investigate the question, for example, use elasticity theory to show that raising price may be ineffective.

Questions requiring analysis can be recognised by looking at the command word. An example of a question requiring analysis might be: *Examine the factors which have influenced the firm's decision to close its Cardiff factory.*

Evaluation Evaluation involves making a judgment. Evaluation questions are often used to award the highest grades in examinations. Students might be expected to:

- show judgment in weighing up the relative importance of different points or sides of an argument, in order to reach a conclusion;
- comment on the reliability of information or evidence;
- distinguish between fact and opinion;
- distinguish between relevant and irrelevant information;
- draw conclusions from the evidence presented;
- show judgment on the wider issues and implications.

Questions requiring evaluation can be identified by looking at the command word. For example, *To what extent has the decision to delayer the business been successful?*

When evaluating it is often possible for a student to draw a number of different conclusions. Examiners may be less concerned with the particular conclusion drawn. Very often in business studies there is no 'right' answer. They are more interested in whether students have actually made a judgment and also the quality of their argument in support of the judgment.

Synthesis Opportunities to demonstrate this particular skill may be limited. Synthesis is required in long written answers such as essays, project work or report writing. It involves bringing together a wide range of information in a clear and meaningful way. In particular, students must:

- develop points and themes in a way which builds on previous material and ends with a rounded conclusion;
- produce an argument in a logical sequence;
- provide a clear summarised argument which draws on all the individual elements.

Examiners will tend to look for evidence of synthesis in essays and report writing questions. The sections below on essay writing and report writing will explain how students can demonstrate synthesis.

Quality of language Codes of Practice may require the

assessment of candidates' quality of language wherever they are required to write in continuous prose. In these circumstances students are required to:

- avoid errors in grammar, punctuation and spelling;
- provide well structured arguments which are consistently relevant;
- write in sentences and paragraphs which follow on from one another smoothly and logically;
- express complex ideas clearly and fluently.

Command, directive or key words

When presented with a task or question as part of internally assessed work or externally assessed examinations:

- how do you know what the question is asking?
- how do you know what the assessor or examiner wants you to do?

In many forms of assessment certain **command, directive or key words** in a question will tell the student what is expected of them. Sometimes two or more words appear together in a question. They must all be taken into account when giving the answer.

Information and knowledge Certain command words are designed to find out what a student knows about the subject.

- Define - to state the exact meaning of a term or a phrase. *Define what is meant by marketing research.*
- Describe - to give an account or a portrayal of something. *Describe the hierarchy and span of control of the business.*
- Give - to write down or say something. Sometimes followed by 'an example' or 'an account of'. *Give an example of a private limited company.* May also be followed by 'reasons for' which may involve greater analysis.
- How - to present an account of something. *How has the business raised funds to buy new machinery?*
- Identify - to pick from a variety of information. *Identify three reasons for the merger.*
- Illustrate - to show clearly, often with the use of an example. *Illustrate the main methods used to promote the product.*
- Outline - to give a short description of the main aspects or features. *Outline the view of workers by management.*
- State - to write down or say something. Sometimes followed by what that 'something' should be. *State three features of an effective leader.*
- Summarise - to provide a brief account covering the main points. *Summarise the approach to quality at the business.*
- What - to clarify something. *What is meant by a stakeholder?*
- Which - to select from certain options or to indicate a choice. *Which location did the business find most suitable?*

Application and explanation Certain command words are designed to allow the student to apply knowledge to a given situation, to work out why something has happened and to give

reasons for something that has happened.

- Account for - to give reasons for. *Account for the growth in part time workers over the period.*
- Analyse - to examine the importance of certain things in detail, show relationships and make criticisms if applicable. *Analyse the approach to lean production of the organisation.*
- Apply - to bring knowledge to bear on a situation. Note that sometimes the word does not appear in the question. For example, 'Using examples from the article, explain how the business might promote its product' requires an application of knowledge to a particular situation. *Apply the Boston Matrix to the product mix of the company.*
- Calculate - to work out mathematically, usually numerically, but sometimes from a graph for example. *Calculate the return on net assets for the business.*
- Compare and contrast - to show the similarities and differences between two or more things. *Compare and contrast the approaches to recruitment of the two companies.*
- Distinguish - to show the differences between two or more things. *Distinguish between job and batch production.*
- Examine - to investigate closely to find out the 'truth' of the situation as if carrying out an inquiry. *Examine the factors that may have led to cash flow problems.*
- Explain - to make clear a concept, idea or viewpoint. It may involve giving an illustration of the meaning or examples. Note that it is sometimes followed by the word 'why' (see below). *Explain the pricing strategies used by the business.*
- Explore - to investigate or examine in detail, as explained above. *Explore the ways in which a business is affected by changes in interest rates.*
- Investigate - to carry out a detailed examination. *Investigate the factors that may have led the business to go into liquidation.*
- Suggest or give reasons for - to explain why, giving a justification. *Suggest reasons why the business chose to reduce its workforce.*
- Why - to present reasons for something. *Explain why labour turnover has increased.*

Evaluation Certain command words are designed to allow students to make a judgment or to evaluate a judgment that has taken place.

- Assess - an invitation to measure or place a value on the importance of something. *Assess whether the change to just-in-time manufacturing is likely to be successful.*
- Comment on - to give an opinion about the extent to which something has occurred. *Comment on the environmental policy of the organisation.*
- Criticise or critically analyse - to pass judgment on a debatable area. *Critically analyse the growing globalisation of business.*
- Determine - to settle, decide, or find out the nature of. *Determine the most suitable new location for the business.*
- Do you think - to comment on or give an opinion on the

basis of evidence. *Do you think the decision of the business to expand was a suitable strategy in the circumstances?*

- Discuss - to consider a contentious statement or to review an area which might have two or more views. *Discuss whether the business should have introduced group decision making.*
- Evaluate - to make an appraisal of something and to find out how important it is. *Evaluate the strategy used by the business over the period.*
- To what extent (does/do) - to make a judgment or to measure. *To what extent has the change in corporate culture been successful?*

Structured questions

The main features of structured questions are as follows.
- They contain several parts.
- The parts normally follow a sequence or pattern.
- Some of the parts may be linked in some way.
- They are generally accompanied by some data to provide students with a stimulus.
- The whole question may require students to demonstrate all skills covered by the assessment criteria, but only one part may be testing a particular skill.
- The parts of the question generally get more demanding as students work through it.
- Different parts may be assessed by different levels of response.
  Structured questions are broken down into 'parts'.

First part The first part of the structured question is usually the easiest. This may help students to 'settle' into a question and perhaps give them some confidence. The first part of a structured question:
- is usually designed to test knowledge of a business concept or business term;
- may require a student to perform a simple skill, e.g. a calculation;
- may require a student to give a straightforward explanation or definition;
- usually requires students to provide a basic level response.
- would carry only a few marks.

Examples
(a) Explain the term 'working capital'.
(a) Distinguish between job analysis and job evaluation.

Middle part The middle part of structured questions may vary. There is no set pattern and this gives examiners and assessors some flexibility when setting structured questions. However, the middle part of structured questions:
- may contain two or more parts;
- usually test knowledge, application, analysis and sometimes evaluation;

- may require students to perform simple or more difficult calculations;
- may require a mixture of straightforward explanation and more complex analysis;
- may carry more marks than the first part.

Examples
(b)(i) Calculate the gross profit margin and the net profit margin for the business.
  (ii) Comment on your findings in (i).
(b)(i) Explain the meaning of the term price inelastic.
  (ii) To what extent is the concept of price elasticity helpful to a business?
(c) Analyse the possible reasons why increasing numbers of companies are introducing flexible working practices.
(c) Examine the possible implications of the data for:
  (i) employees;
  (ii) a large manufacturer planning to export for the first time.

Final part This part of the question is usually the most demanding part. The final part of the structured question:
- will nearly always require a higher level response;
- will usually test knowledge, application, analysis and evaluation;
- will usually carry a higher mark allocation;
- may not be broken down into smaller parts.

Examples
(d) Assess the view that business advertising practices should be more heavily regulated.
(d) Evaluate the non-financial factors which might influence the firm's decision to relocate its operations.
(d) Discuss the factors that have influenced the business to change its marketing strategy.

Data response questions

Data response or case study questions are used to test student skills in unfamiliar circumstances. The key features of data response questions include:
- the provision of qualitative or quantitative data, or both, to provide a stimulus for students;
- hypothetical or real case study data;
- the use of structured questions;
- opportunities for students to demonstrate knowledge, application, analysis and evaluation.

Hints
- Always read the data at least twice.
- Use a felt pen to highlight important words, sentences or key numerical information.
- Read the structured questions very carefully, perhaps highlighting command words and other key terms.
- Some of your answers must be related to the data

provided.
- Some of your answers must use ideas, concepts and theories not mentioned in the data.
- Answer the parts of the question in order.
- Allocate your time according to the number of marks offered for each part.
- Show all your working out when performing calculations.
- Always attempt all parts of the questions.
- Do not use bullet points when writing your answers.

Answering the first part The information below contains data from a case study question. The data is just a small extract from the question.

The directors are recommending a final dividend of 18p, making a full year dividend of 27p, an increase of 8 per cent over the previous year. The Directors will consider further limited reductions of dividend cover in the medium-term, allowing real dividend growth to be maintained.

(a) Explain the term 'dividend cover'

- To begin with it is helpful to highlight the key words in the question and the key words in the data as shown above. This might help students to focus.
- To pick up all marks in this case it would be necessary to use a couple of sentences to explain the term and then give the formula which is used to calculate the dividend cover.
- The explanation needs to be crisp, clear and uncomplicated. Students need to demonstrate in their answer that they understand the term. The formula can be added at the end.
- A student could give a numerical illustration here. *For example, if a business made a total dividend payment of £300 million and net profit for the year was £500 million, dividend cover would be given by:*

$$\frac{Net\ profit}{Dividends} = \frac{£500m}{£300m} = 1.67\ times$$

Answering the middle part The data below is from another case study.

One of the things troubling Renton's is the accumulation of stock. Both stocks of raw materials and stocks of finished goods have been building up over recent years. The build up of finished goods is linked to poor sales performance. However, there seems no real reason why stocks of raw materials should have grown. The suggestion made by the production manager to introduce just-in-time methods may be worth considering.

Renton's current assets and current liabilities 2005 - 2008

	2005	2006	2007	2008 (£)
Raw materials	21,000	22,900	26,600	34,200
Finished goods	31,300	36,800	42,300	49,600
Other current assets	42,300	41,200	44,900	43,800
Current liabilities	109,900	113,500	119,400	138,600

(b) (i) Use ratio analysis to show how the build up of stocks is causing liquidity problems for Renton's.
   (ii) Analyse the advantages and disadvantages to Renton's of introducing just-in-time methods.

- Again the first step is to highlight the key words in the question as shown above.
- The question cannot be answered without reference to the data. The first part of the question requires students to analyse the data using a quantitative technique (ratio analysis)
- Students need to calculate the current ratio and/or the acid test ratio to comment on Renton's liquidity position.
- To earn all the marks in this question the student would need to perform the calculations correctly, interpret the results appropriately and draw a meaningful conclusion.
- In this case both the current ratios and the acid test ratios are below the 'ideal' range of 1.5:2 and 1:1 respectively. The acid test ratio is particularly low. This suggests that Renton's has liquidity problems.

The second part of this question requires more analysis.
- Again, begin by highlighting the key words in the question and data as above.
- Before writing the answer it is helpful to jot down a few key points for analysis, such as two advantages and two disadvantages of JIT. Advantages could be less money tied up in stock, more space for other activities or less waste stock. Disadvantages might be vulnerability to a break in supply, loss of flexibility in production or increased ordering and administration costs. These points are not likely to be in the case material. Students will have to bring in outside knowledge. There is nothing to be gained from identifying lots of advantages and disadvantages. The quality of application and analysis will generate marks for this question.
- Marks will be awarded for knowledge, application and analysis. Evaluation marks might also be awarded at this stage.

Answering the final part It is important that students leave enough time to answer this part properly as it usually carries high marks. The data below contains an extract from another case study.

It has been suggested that the economy will grow at a slower rate next year – around 2 per cent. Currently interest rates are historically higher than they have been in the recent past, for example in 2002-03. However, they are predicted to come down in future. The use of credit cards to finance spending is likely to continue and the amount spent using this method of payment may fall due to the higher interest rates.

UK interest rates

(d) To what extent do external factors, such as those mentioned in the case, influence the performance of a business?

- Students will need to introduce a lot of their own material into their answers.
- Before writing, students should jot down a plan. A plan for this question might appear as follows.
  1. *Explain how external factors, e.g. interest rates, affect businesses.*
  2. *Identify two other factors which might affect businesses, e.g. consumer confidence, borrowing.*
  3. *Analyse the two factors.*
  4. *Evaluate, for example, by saying that external factors have a great influence because they are beyond the control of businesses. However, a good business will include their effect in its forecasting.*
- If the above plan is executed effectively the student will demonstrate all the skills required.
- Students should remember that it is not necessary to identify and list lots of factors. Listing is a low order skill and more marks are awarded for application, analysis and evaluation.

Decision making and problem solving case studies (unseen)

These are often in the form of extended case studies. They can be demanding and require a slightly different approach to answering than shorter data response questions.

- The case material tends to be hypothetical but is usually based on a real life situation.
- The case material tends to focus on a single business.
- The volume of material given is much greater.
- There tends to be some financial information in the case material.
- The case often emphasises analysis and evaluation skills.
- Many of the case questions require an integrated approach when answering. This means that students will need to embrace the full range of the specification in their answers. A single answer may need to address issues such as marketing, production, human resources, finance and external factors all at the same time.
- Questions set usually require students to make decisions or solve problems. For example, a question may require students to suggest a suitable future strategy for a business.
- One question will often require students to use a quantitative technique when answering.
- Examiners often want students to be critical.

Hints
- Skim read the case material to get a feel for the business, its people, its circumstances and its objectives (see section below on things to think about).
- Read again thoroughly, highlighting key information.
- Look at the numerical information and analyse it briefly, without performing any calculations.
- Make brief notes on the key objectives and key themes.
- Read the questions, highlighting command words and other key terms.
- Identify some business theories you might consider discussing in your answers. Questions will probably not request specific theories. The onus is on students to introduce relevant theories.
- Re-read the hints on answering data response questions above.

Issues to think about when planning answers
- People. Business is about people and your answers need to reflect this. Consider the age, family circumstances, the attitudes and personal interests of the people involved in the case material. What motivates them? What is their background? What are their objectives? What are their strengths and weaknesses? These are some of the people issues which students need to consider when shaping their answers.
- Situation. It is important to think about the context in which the business is set. Examples of issues to consider include the type of business organisation (Ltd, plc or sole trader), the prevailing culture, the type of industry, the nature of competition, the size, its financial position, its age, history and potential. It is often helpful to liken the case material to a business which actually exists in a similar context. However, this may not always be possible.

- Objectives. Answers to questions are bound to be linked to what the business is trying to achieve in its given context. A business may be trying to survive following a recession, it may be trying to break into new markets, it may be trying to raise finance for a big investment project, it may be trying to change its culture or take over another business. It is often useful to consider, and distinguish between, short-term and long-term objectives.
- Theories. Students should introduce business theories into their answers. There may be little or no guidance as to what theories are required. Students need to be on the lookout for opportunities to introduce some business theory into every answer they write. For example, if a business is considering a price change, price elasticity theory could be introduced. If a business is merging with another, economies of scale may be discussed. If a business is downsizing the effect on staff might be discussed, in which case motivational theories such as Herzberg or Maslow might be applied.
- Be critical. Be prepared to challenge statements or claims made in a case study if relevant and applicable. Students with an enquiring and critical approach will be rewarded.

Example 1

Most of the structured questions in decision making/problem solving case studies usually require lengthy answers with analysis and evaluation. Therefore it is important to plan before writing an answer. Below is an extract from part of an extended case study. The case study is about Henshaws Ltd, a components manufacturer for the computer industry. It has faced difficulties in recent years due to escalating costs. It is considering ways of improving efficiency and reducing costs.

One option currently being considered by Henshaws Ltd is to outsource its marketing activities. The directors of the company have not been impressed with the performance of this department. Their expenditure has consistently exceeded their budget and they seem to get new business and then lose it. In addition, communications between the department and others in the organisation have not been good. Two of the four company directors have long claimed that the company's strength is in manufacturing high quality components, although the other two directors argue that the company must avoid clinging to 'past glories' and move forward with the times. A number of marketing agencies have given presentations to the board of directors and a decision about whether to outsource marketing is imminent.

(b) Assess the likely advantages and disadvantages to Henshaws Ltd of outsourcing its marketing function.

- To answer this question it is necessary to identify and analyse two or three advantages, identify and analyse two or three disadvantages and then evaluate by making a judgment about whether Henshaws should outsource marketing or not.
- Although the question does not specifically ask for a judgment examiners are probably expecting one. This is because the mark allocation may be quite high.
- A plan should be drafted which might look like this:

Adv.   1. Costs fall.
              2. More focus on manufacturing.
              3. More effective marketing by specialists.
Disadv.   1. Redundancies.
              2. Loss of control of a vital function.
              3. Long-term marketing costs might rise.
Eval.   Yes - outsource because current marketing is expensive, ineffective and is causing problems. Henshaws will then be more focused and able to exploit its strengths.

- In the answer it is necessary to analyse the above advantages and disadvantages in detail explaining their relevance.
- In the evaluation some students may suggest that Henshaws should not outsource its marketing function. This does not matter. Examiners just want students to make a judgment and support it with a coherent and plausible argument. Remember that these case studies are decision making case studies and therefore a decision must be made!

Example 2

Some quantitative analysis is usually required in extended case studies. It may be quite complex and students often make the mistake of spending too long on this section. The data below contains an extract from an extended case study about a business which is considering a new investment. Arpan Shrinath & Co manufactures training shoes and Arpan is deciding which investment project to go ahead with.

Project 1. *Arpan has considered buying a large delivery van and undertaking his own distribution. At the moment he pays a local company to distribute training shoes to his customers. This has proved expensive and often ineffective.*

Project 2. *A new moulding machine has just been launched on the market by a German machine manufacturer. It is computer numerically controlled and would help to improve the quality of Arpan's products. It would also be more productive than his existing machine.*

		Expected returns						
	Cost	Year 1	Year 2	Year 3	Year 4	Year 5	Year 6	Total
Project 1	£15,000	£4,000	£4,000	£4,000	£4,000	£4,000	£4,000	£24,000
Project 2	£40,000	£12,000	£10,000	£10,000	£9,000	£9,000	£9,000	£59,000
Project 3	£30,000	£7,000	£7,000	£7,000	£7,000	£7,000	£7,000	£42,000

Project 3. *Arpan is becoming increasingly concerned that his office staff are working in conditions which are too cramped. Staff frequently complain and he is aware of inefficiencies due to a lack of space. He is considering the construction of a purpose built annex to the factory where office staff can work more effectively.*

The table on the previous page shows the costs and expected returns for each of these projects over a 6 year period.

(c) *Calculate the (i)payback; (ii)average rate of return for the three investment projects and decide which project is the most attractive. Take into account your results from the calculations and any other information you feel is appropriate.*

- This question requires knowledge and understanding of investment appraisal techniques. Provided students have revised the quantitative techniques required they just need to apply the appropriate formulae.
- It is often helpful to produce calculations (or the results of calculations) in tables. One way in which the answers to the above question might be presented is:

	Project 1	Project 2	Project 3
Cost	£15,000	£40,000	£30,000
Total return	£24,000	£59,000	£42,000
Total profit	£9,000	£19,000	£12,000
Profit p.a.	£1,500	£3,167	£2,000
ARR	10%	7.9%	6.6%
Payback	3.75 years	3.88 years	4.29 years

- According to the calculations above project 1 appears the most attractive. It has the highest ARR and also the shortest payback period.
- There is likely to be other information in the case which will influence the decision here. For example, if customers are complaining about the quality of products, Arpan might decide to buy the new machine to improve quality, even though the projected financial returns are slightly lower.
- This question is likely to offer a high mark allocation. The calculations alone would not generate all the marks. Students must bring in other information from the case, use their own ideas and also evaluate.
- Some thought must be given to the setting out of numerical answers. Good presentation is important. Avoid deletions and sprawling calculations. Space answers generously and underline final answers.

Example 3
The final question in an extended case study often requires

students to suggest a strategy or give an overall view. The question might also carry higher marks. A possible question might be:

(d) *Taking the whole case into account, do you consider that the board of directors should discontinue production at the Newport factory?*

- Again, planning is very important here. A lengthy answer is required with relevant points being identified, thorough analysis and evaluation. Students need to bring together a range of relevant points and make a decision.
- Timing is also crucial. Students must ensure that they leave sufficient time to plan and write the answer to this final, and important, question properly.
- Students may use some of the material generated in other answers in the case. But obviously repetition must be avoided.
- Again, it probably does not matter in this question whether students suggest that production is discontinued or not. Examiners want to see a well structured, logical argument with a meaningful conclusion drawn.
- Remember to consider the people, the situation, the objectives and to introduce theories.

Pre-seen case studies

A pre-seen case study is a method of assessment which involves giving students case study material before the day of the examination. This allows students to prepare more thoroughly for the examination by analysing the information and forming ideas in advance.

- Case study material may be issued a number of weeks before the day of the examination.
- The structured questions relating to the case study will not be known until the day of the examination.
- Additional information regarding the case may also be supplied within the question structure.
- The nature of the material provided in the case is likely to be the same as any other case study, but perhaps in more detail. Students should read the previous sections on data response and decision making questions.

Hints
- The general approach to pre-seen case studies is little different from those which are not pre-seen. The only important difference is that students have a great deal of time to study the data. Again, the hints in previous sections on answering data questions should be read.
- There is much more time to read the material so more time can be spent highlighting key words and terms. Students could also note theories, issues or themes which are relevant.
- Any words, terms or theories which are unfamiliar or forgotten can be looked up in the text book. For example, if the case contains an extract from a balance sheet, it

might be helpful to consult the balance sheet unit to reinforce understanding of balance sheet terms and structure.

- It is helpful to try and predict possible questions which the examiner might set. This will allow students to prepare answers.
- Try to identify trends, patterns and links in the data and account for them.
- Get help from friends and parents.
- When answering the questions in the examination it is very important to answer the ones set. Students should not try to reproduce their own 'model answers'.

Essay writing

An essay is an assessment method used to find out how students can respond in depth to an open question. It involves writing in continuous prose and provides an opportunity to explain something in detail.

- The quality of grammar, vocabulary, sentence construction and spelling is particularly important.
- A strong emphasis is usually placed on analysis, evaluation and synthesis.
- Essay questions may be integrated and synoptic. This means that students must consider the full range of the specification areas when writing answers. Essays based on one section of a specification or syllabus, such as marketing, may draw on all areas within it.
- The length will vary depending on the time allocated.
- They require a great deal of thought and planning before writing begins.
- The use of real world examples to illustrate points is essential.
- The use of diagrams, such as the Boston Matrix, is encouraged.
- There is rarely a 'right' answer. It is possible for two students to put forward opposing arguments and for both to be awarded high marks. It is the quality of the argument which is important, not the nature of it.

Planning

- Read the question very carefully.
- Highlight the command words and other key words to help provide focus.
- Planning could be in two stages. Stage one might involve a two or three minute session where students jot down an explosion of points and issues they think might be relevant.
- Stage two would then involve sorting points into an appropriate order and planning out a structure which will accommodate an argument.

Introduction

- It is common to begin with a short introduction where key terms are defined and the question is put into context.

Some general information may also be given. An introduction should be no more than a third of a side long, for example.

The main body

- When writing the main body of an answer it is important to follow the plan and write in detail, ensuring that evidence of analysis and evaluation is provided.
- It is vital to answer the question. It is better to write one side of relevant material than five sides of 'waffle'.
- Never use bullet points in essays.
- Never use subheadings in essays.
- Never write lists in essays. Extra marks are not awarded for identifying a large number of relevant points.
- Remember to include real world examples where appropriate.
- It is inadvisable to switch emphasis during the essay. It is best to stick to the plan.
- Diagrams, graphs and other illustrative material may be used but make sure they are clearly labelled and explained in the text.

Conclusion

- It is important to write a conclusion. It may be a statement which answers the question 'in a nutshell', drawing on the points analysed in the main body.
- Conclusions should not repeat material used elsewhere.
- The best conclusions are those which demonstrate evaluation and synthesis.
- Students are often required to make a judgment or give an opinion. Do not 'sit on the fence'.

Example

It has been argued that the productivity of UK businesses falls well behind that of its overseas rivals. Suggest possible reasons why this might be the case and examine the measures which might be taken by UK businesses to improve productivity?

- Essay questions can carry a relatively high number of marks.
- The words highlighted in the title are productivity, UK businesses, overseas rivals, suggest possible reasons, examine, measures and improve productivity.
- The following ideas may be suggested for the essay.

  Define productivity, labour, capital, Rover productivity poor, Nissan good, lack of investment, lack of funds, lack of R&D, dividends too high, too short-termist. Standardisation, re-engineering, kaizen, JIT, outsourcing, virtual companies, TQM, benchmarking, work study, culture, trade unions, weak management, quality circles, technology, training, labour flexibility, delayering, downsizing.

- The ideas generated may not be in any particular order.

The focus in the above responses appears to be on production and ways of improving efficiency.

- Another two or three minutes spent planning might deliver the following essay structure.

Introduction

▶ *Define productivity - output in relation to inputs.*

▶ *An example of evidence which might support the statement is the low productivity of Rover compared with, say, Japanese car makers.*

▶ *Suggest that there is a number of approaches to improving productivity, some specific and some strategic.*

Main body

▶ *Analyse three possible reasons why productivity is lower in UK.*

▶ *Low investment, therefore inadequate and dated technology.*

▶ *Lack of R&D because the City wants higher dividends NOW.*

▶ *Trade unions may have resisted changes which might improve productivity.*

▶ *Explain that measures designed to improve efficiency might be specific or strategic.*

▶ *Analyse three specific measures - JIT, benchmarking and new technology.*

▶ *Analyse three strategic measures - kaizen, re-engineering and TQM.*

Conclusion

▶ *Argue that the statement is probably right for the reasons given. Evaluate by saying that one particular reason may be more important, e.g. lack of investment.*

▶ *Argue that the methods employed to improve efficiency depend on the individual firms and their needs.*

▶ *Evaluate by suggesting that particular methods may be more suitable, if, for example, a business has dated machinery new technology may have a very significant impact on productivity.*

▶ *Argue that all measures will require co-operation of staff if they are to be successful.*

- When the essay is finished it is important to read through it and check for errors such as spelling, grammar and punctuation. However, avoid frantic crossing out at the last minute because this tends to have a negative effect on presentation.

Index

Index

Index

Index

Index

Index